THIRD EDITION

for AQA 'A'

Psychology A2

The Complete Companion
Student Book

Mike Cardwell · Cara Flanagan

OXFORD
UNIVERSITY PRESS

OXFORD
UNIVERSITY PRESS

Great Clarendon Street, Oxford OX2 6DP

Oxford University Press is a department of the University of Oxford.
It furthers the University's objective of excellence in research, scholarship,
and education by publishing worldwide in

Oxford New York

Auckland Cape Town Dar es Salaam Hong Kong Karachi
Kuala Lumpur Madrid Melbourne Mexico City Nairobi
New Delhi Shanghai Taipei Toronto

With offices in

Argentina Austria Brazil Chile Czech Republic France Greece
Guatemala Hungary Italy Japan Poland Portugal Singapore
South Korea Switzerland Thailand Turkey Ukraine Vietnam

© Oxford University Press 2012

The moral rights of the author have been asserted

Database right Oxford University Press (maker)

First published 2012

British Library Cataloguing in Publication Data

Data available

ISBN 978 019 912984 3

10 9 8 7 6 5 4

Printed in Singapore by KHL Printing Co Pte Ltd

Paper used in the production of this book is a natural, recyclable product made
from wood grown in sustainable forests. The manufacturing process conforms to the
environmental regulations of the country of origin.

Acknowledgements

Project development: Rick Jackman (Jackman Publishing Solutions Ltd)

Editorial management & layout: GreenGate Publishing Services, Tonbridge, Kent

Design: Patricia Briggs

Cover design & photography: Chris Cardwell

Cover typography: Patricia Briggs

Picture credits

Dedication

To Alex and Jon (MC)
To Geraldine, my mum (CF)

Acknowledgements

The authors would like to thank the hardworking and
enthusiastic team behind the production of this book. First
and foremost, our long-standing publisher, Rick Jackman,
who is unfailing in his enthusiasm, support, admiration
and advice – we simply couldn't do it without him. Louise
Wilson (editor) and Patricia Briggs (designer) deserve
an enormous thank you for the tremendous amount of
work that went into producing the second edition of this
book. For the third edition we are grateful for the steady
hand of Carrie Baker and others at GreenGate. It has been
a painstaking task. Also thank you to everyone at OUP,
most especially Sarah Flynn and Claire Beatt, for all of their
support and enthusiasm.

About our cover dog

Ellie is an eight-year-old Irish Setter who lives with her
owner Sally in a village north of Bristol. Ellie has the gentlest
nature and enthusiasm in abundance, but is not well
known for her brains. Suggest a walk and she runs around
with gay abandon, failing to appreciate that standing still
long enough to clip on a lead will speed up the whole
process. If asked to leave the room it is enough for her
to put her head out, believing that if she cannot see you
then you cannot see her. She is, however, the perfect
companion, full of unconditional love.

Mike Cardwell   Cara Flanagan   Ellie

CONTENTS

46
total

HOW TO USE THIS BOOK

The contents of this book are designed to follow the AQA A A2 specification as closely as possible. The book is divided into 16 chapters matching the topics in the specification.

- There are eight chapters for Unit 3 of the A2 examination, *Topics in Psychology*. You will study a minim0um of three of these.
- There are eight chapters for Unit 4 of the A2 examination, *Psychopathology, Psychology in Action, Research Methods*. You select a minimum of one chapter from *Psychopathology* and a minimum of one chapter from *Psychology in Action*. Finally, you must study the chapter on *Research Methods*.

In the top left of each spread there is an **introduction** to the topic. This explains what the topic is about and may identify some key issues or links to previous topics.

Each chapter begins with a list of the topics covered.

The full details of the specification to be covered by each chapter are presented on the chapter's opening page.

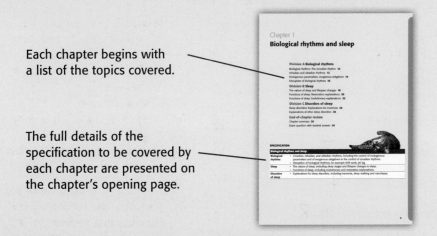

The **main text** for the spread is in the middle of the page.

On the left-hand side of each spread we give a description (AO1) of the topic area.

On the right-hand side there is evaluation (AO2). In your exam answers you will need to present a mixture of these skills so we thought it was helpful to separate them clearly in this way.

The content of each chapter consists of six to nine double-page spreads. All the features on these spreads are illustrated on the two sample spreads on the right.

Each chapter ends with some useful features in the end-of-chapter review consisting of:

We constantly post information about new research that we think might interest students on our blog – see www.oxfordschoolblogs.co.uk/psychcompanion/blog

There is also a discussion forum there if you have any queries or comments.

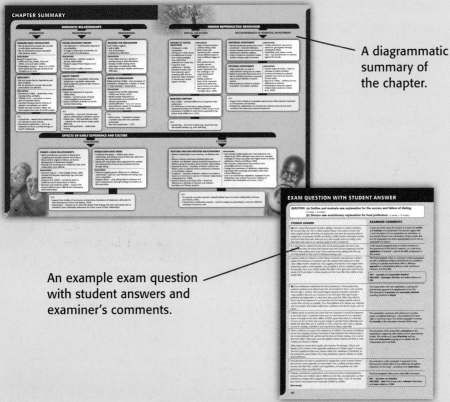

A diagrammatic summary of the chapter.

An example exam question with student answers and examiner's comments.

WWW We have also included the occasional **website**, but as sites come and go, don't be disappointed if some links turn out to be non-existent.

Sometimes there is a helpful **comment** to enhance understanding.

Around the edge of each spread we have highlighted some points of special importance.

In the *blue boxes* we have dealt in greater depth with some special **evaluation points**, for example looking at descriptions of key research studies or at individual differences.

Some *blue boxes* include information about research methods. For example, we might discuss the validity of the research described on the spread. You can use these as points of evaluation as long as you make the criticism explicitly relevant to the theory or study you are criticising.

In the *beige boxes* we have provided further descriptive material that focuses on a particular aspect of the topic or provides some background information.

Green boxes contain information on **issues, debates and approaches (IDA)**. This includes topics such as real-world applications, ethical issues, gender and cultural bias, determinism, reductionism, the biological or evolutionary approach and so on (see page 8 for more information about IDA).

In the chapters for Unit 4 (chapters 9–16) there are no IDA boxes because it is not explicitly credited in that exam.

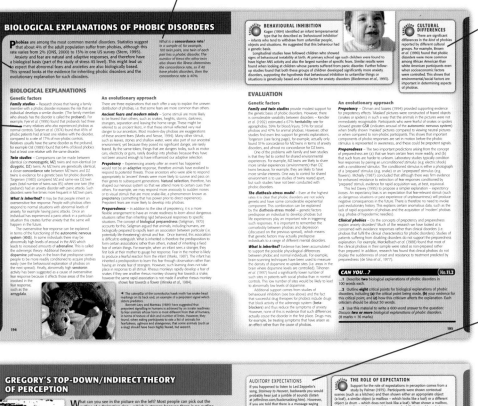

We have provided **exam tips** embedded in the text, but occasionally we have thought of a special one.

We have tried to find a balance between making material interesting and informative, but at the same time comprehensive yet concise and useful for your exam.

You will not be required to reproduce the amount of detail on these spreads, so we have included these **CAN YOU...?** boxes to give you an indication of what you might expect to find in examination questions for each topic, and to ensure that you at least have that minimal level of understanding that will enable you to perform well in the exam.

THE A2 EXAMINATION

A2 EXAM QUESTIONS

All exam questions are worth a total of 24 marks, except for 'Psychological Research and Scientific Method' – this question is worth 35 marks. The 24 marks are separated into 8 marks of description (AO1) and 16 marks of evaluation (AO2).

In each question part you need to know how many AO1 marks are available and how many AO2 marks are available. This is indicated by the use of injunctions (see right) and by the marks at the end of the question.

Example: *Outline and evaluate* **one** *theory of the formation of relationships. (8 marks + 16 marks)*

We know that AO1 and AO2 are required because the injunctions (outline and evaluate) tell us and because there are two marks – 8 marks for AO1 and 16 marks for AO2.

Example: *(a) Outline and evaluate* **one** *theory of the formation of relationships. (4 marks + 8 marks)*
(b) Outline and evaluate …

Sometimes questions are parted, so one part might add up to less than 24 marks.

Example: *Outline* **one** *theory of the formation of relationships. (4 marks)*

The question above is all AO1 because it starts with the injunction 'Outline' and only one skill is required (only one mark given).

Example: *Evaluate* **one** *theory of the formation of relationships. (8 marks)*

The question above is all AO2 because it starts with the injunction 'Evaluate' and only one skill is required (only one mark given).

Injunctions

AO1: outline, describe, identify, explain

AO2: evaluate, consider, assess, explain (note that 'explain' is used for and AO2 AO1, AO2 OR AO1 + AO2)

AO1 + AO2: discuss

Unit 4 Section B

On this section of the exam the questions are always parted, and at least one of the questions may be an 'apply your knowledge' question (a bit like the ones you had in your AS exam).

Example: *Tom's mother has said he is not allowed to play video games any more.*
Outline **two** *arguments that Tom could present to his mother so she might change her mind. (6 marks)*

Example: *Design a campaign to reduce smoking addiction. The campaign should be based on the theory of planned behaviour. (8 marks)*

In such questions the marks are all AO2 because you have to apply your knowledge to a novel situation (see mark scheme on the facing page).

Numbers are specified where appropriate

Exam questions usually specify 'how many' – '*Discuss* **two** *theories of the formation of relationships*' rather than '*Discuss theories the formation of relationships*'. This gives you clear guidance about the number of theories to include to attract the full range of marks.

Sometimes you might be asked '*Discuss* **two or more** *theories of the formation of relationships*' in which case you can achieve maximum marks if you only cover two theories but you may also do more, if you wish. Beware, however, the temptation to spread yourself too thinly, in which case your answers start to lose detail (and marks).

To find out more about what the exam questions look like, use our book the Psychology A2: The Exam Companion. This contains lots of practice questions with guidance about how to answer them and advice on how they are marked.

You can also download past papers from the AQA website – but remember that the specification changed from 2012.

HOW EXAMS ARE MARKED

On the facing page we have talked about AO1 and AO2. These are assessment objectives. In the exam your ability to describe and evaluate psychological knowledge is assessed with the two assessment objectives – AO1 for description and AO2 for evaluation.

There is also AO3 (evaluation is actually referred to as AO2/AO3). Assessment objective 3 concerns your understanding of 'how science works' (although this is not marked separately, but as part of the overall AO2 mark).

Make your answers fit the mark allocations

The mark allocations are shown on the right.

AO1

Knowledge and understanding – Make sure you do understand the theories and studies. Don't just hope it will sound OK.

Detail – This is not necessarily about writing lots, it is about ensuring that what you write contains specific information.

Range of material refers to how many things are covered in your answer. This might be the number of studies or number of different aspects of a theory.

Depth and breadth – If you try to provide too much breadth (e.g. lots of studies) you won't have time for depth (detail). Less is more – write about *less* studies but provide *more* detail.

Organisation and structure – Use lots of paragraphs. In each paragraph, make your point and provide a detailed explanation of that point.

AO2

Analysis and understanding – The analysis bit is your attempt to work out what features of the topic can be criticised/ discussed.

Focus – You won't receive credit for information that isn't directly relevant to the question, in fact you will lose marks for an answer lacking focus.

Elaboration – One line criticisms receive little credit. You must identify, provide evidence, justify and link back to the point your are criticising (a **four-point rule**).

Line of argument – Your answer should read a bit like a story so that each paragraph makes sense coming after the previous one.

Issues, debates and approaches (IDA) are discussed on the next page.

Quality of written communication assesses the fluency of your writing and the extent to which you have used psychological terms effectively as well as your grammar, punctuation and spelling.

AO3

Calling evaluation 'AO2/AO3' is a bit misleading because there are no criteria in the mark allocation tables that mention 'how science works' (AO3). Therefore you can still receive full marks without any mention of methodological issues.

However, if you do make any AO3 criticisms (e.g. of methodology used) these could demonstrate the skill of analysis and would be credited. Such criticisms must be contextualised to gain any credit.

AQA A specification changes from 2012

From January 2012 there were some changes to the specification. This means that past exam papers contain some questions that would no longer be set.

The contents of this book match the new specification.

However – remember that exams do evolve and there are often changes to the rules. Use our blog to keep you up to date: www.oxfordschoolblogs.co.yk/psychcompanion/blog/

AO1 mark allocation

Mark	Knowledge and understanding	Range of relevant material	Breadth and depth	Organisation and structure
8–7	Accurate and well-detailed	Good range	Substantial evidence of depth and breadth	Coherent
6–5	Generally accurate and well-detailed	Range	Evidence	Reasonably coherent
4–3	Basic, relatively superficial	Restricted		Basic
2–1	Rudimentary and may be muddled and/ or inaccurate	Very brief or largely irrelevant		Lacking
0	No creditworthy material			

AO2 mark allocation

The IDA criterion is not used on Unit 4.

Mark	Analysis and understanding	Focus	Elaboration	Line of argument	Issues, debates, approaches	Quality of written communication
16–13	Sound	Well-focused	Coherent	Clear	Used effectively	Fluent, effective use of terms
12–9	Reasonable	Generally focused	Reasonable	Evident	Reasonably effective	Clear, appropriate
8–5	Basic, superficial	Sometimes focued	Some evidence		Superficial reference	Lacks clarity, limited use of terms
4–1	Rudimentary, limited understanding	Weak, muddled and incomplete	Not effective	May be mainly irrelevant	Absent or muddled/ inaccurate	Often unconnected assertions, errors
0	No creditworthy material					

AO2 mark allocation for 'apply your knowledge' questions

Mark	Analysis and understanding	Application of knowledge	Elaboration	Quality of written communication
8–7	Sound	Effective	Coherent	Fluent, effective use of terms
6–5	Reasonable	Reasonably effective	Some elaboration	Clear, approriate
4–3	Basic, superficial	Basic		Lacks clarity, limited use of terms
2–1	Rudimentary, limited understanding	Weak, muddled and mainly irrelevant		Often unconnected assertions, errors
0	No creditworthy material			

Number of words

In 30 minutes (the time you have for each question on Unit 3) you can write about 600 words. This means that you should aim to write about 25 words for every mark.

In Unit 4 you have a bit more time but the questions are parted which means you need the extra thinking time.

ISSUES, DEBATES AND APPROACHES

In the Unit 3 exam the mark scheme requires evidence of IDA in order for you to achieve high marks. There are several common questions that students ask, which we have answered on this page.

What are issues, debates and approaches?

IDA are the threads that run across all of psychology. Being able to discuss these in your essays demonstrates a good grasp of what psychology is about.

IDA includes:

- **Ethical issues** – Explain why a study has raised ethical issues, which probably means it cannot be replicated and the findings cannot be verified.
- **Gender**, **cultural** or **historical bias** – A bias is not the same as a difference. The issue is, for example, that a study might be conducted using a questionnaire that is biased towards Americans (the questions might not be as clear for someone from a different culture). This means it is likely that Americans participants are portrayed more positively and so the study is culturally biased.
- **Real-world applications** – The value of any research is enhanced if it can be used to explain a real-world phenomena. If such applications are successful this confirms the validity of the research.
- **Determinism** is the view that an individual's behaviour is shaped or controlled by factors other than the individual's will. Such factors can be internal (e.g. hormones) or external (e.g. environmental conditioning). Determinism is sometimes seen as good (e.g. science aims to discover cause and effect) and sometimes as bad (e.g. removes moral responsibility).
- **Reductionism** involves breaking complex phenomena into more simple components or down to a simpler level of explanation (e.g. nerves and hormones). This again can be seen as good (e.g. part of the process of science) or bad (e.g. it may oversimplify a complex process such as understanding the experience of mental disorder).
- **Nature–nurture** – The debate about whether genetic or environmental factors best explain behaviour.
- **Any of the approaches** (cognitive, social, biological, evolutionary and so on).

On each of the Unit 3 spreads in this book we have presented at least one IDA point. You may wish to develop some IDA points of your own.

What happens if there are no IDA points in my essay answer?

You can still receive a good mark. The mark allocation works by deciding on the band that best describes your answer. If one criterion is weak, it will pull your mark towards the bottom of the band but it doesn't mean you get no marks.

It is best to focus on providing good evaluation and add IDA if you can.

How many should I include?

A good essay will include *one or two* IDA points. That is the maximum you should cover. The mistake that students make is to present a number of IDA points but fail to elaborate any of them. This would be described as 'superficial', placing you in the 'basic band' (see mark allocation on previous page).

What makes an IDA point 'effective'?

In order to move into the top bands for your IDA content, the points must be effective. This means they must be specifically related to the content, i.e. **contextualised**.

Just saying *'One issue is determinism'* is a superficial point.

You must then add more. For example, you could say *'This explanation suggests that excessive dopamine activity has caused a person to develop schizophrenia'*.

And further add *'as high levels of dopamine may be a consequence of schizophrenia rather than the determining factor'*.

Quality rather than quantity

And finally, consider 'so what?', *'The problem with a determinist explanation of schizophrenia is that it leads to the assumption that antipsychotics will be the most effective treatment, whereas this may not be an appropriate therapy'*.

Effectiveness is gained through the *quality* of your *discussion*.

The way to check whether you have achieved this is to imagine moving the IDA point you have written and drop it into another essay (called the **drop in**) – does it still seem appropriate? If so, then you have failed to contextualise it and will get almost NO credit for a generic point.

What about Unit 4?

IDA is not required in Unit 4. This means that an essay with no IDA can receive full marks.

However, any IDA points (that are effective) would be credited as good evaluation.

Chapter 1
Biological rhythms and sleep

SPECIFICATION

Biological rhythms and sleep	
Biological rhythms	• Circadian, infradian, and ultradian rhythms, including the control of endogenous pacemakers and of exogenous zeitgebers in the control of circadian rhythms. • Disruption of biological rhythms, for example shift work, jet lag.
Sleep	• The nature of sleep, including sleep stages and lifespan changes in sleep. • Functions of sleep, including evolutionary and restoration explanations.
Disorders of sleep	• Explanations for sleep disorders, including insomnia, sleep walking and narcolepsy.

Biological rhythms are cyclical changes in the way biological systems behave. The most obvious rhythm is the sleep-wake cycle – people and many animals go to sleep when it is dark and wake up when it is light. There are other many other rhythms, such as the opening and closing of flowers with daylight or the seasonal patterns of activity in hibernating animals. What controls these rhythms?

- Internal biological 'clocks', called **endogenous pacemakers**.
- External cues from the environment, called **exogenous zeitgebers**. These include sunlight, food, noise, or social interaction.

'Endogenous' means 'inside', whereas 'exogenous' means 'outside'.

The word 'zeitgeber' is from the German meaning 'time-giver'.

RESEARCH SUPPORT FOR A FREE-RUNNING RHYTHM

Evaluation

Evidence for free-running circadian rhythms comes most memorably from a series of studies conducted by the French cave explorer, Michel Siffre, a specialist in the study of the human internal clock. On several occasions he has spent long periods of time living underground in order to study his own biological rhythms. While underground he had no external cues to guide his rhythms – no daylight, no clocks, no radio. He simply woke, ate and slept when he felt like it. The only thing influencing his behaviour was his internal 'clock' or 'free-running' rhythm. Before Siffre's study little was known about internal (endogenous) biological rhythms.

After his first underground stay of 61 days in the southern Alps in 1962, he resurfaced on 17 September believing the date was 20 August. On the second occasion he spent six months in a Texan cave (Siffre, 1975). His natural circadian rhythm settled down to just over 24 hours but sometimes this would change dramatically to as much as 48 hours. On his final underground stay in 1999, he was interested in the effects of ageing on biological rhythms (by this time he was 60 years old). He found that his internal clock ticked more slowly compared to when he was a young man. He also found that his sleep patterns had changed (see page 18).

His case study was supported by other studies. For example, Aschoff and Wever (1976) placed participants in an underground WWII bunker in the absence of any environmental and social time cues. They found that most participants displayed circadian rhythms between 24 and 25 hours in length, although some rhythms were as long as 29 hours. This shows that the cycle operates in the absence of external cues and that the natural free-running cycle is about 24–25 hours.

RESEARCH SUPPORT FOR THE IMPORTANCE OF EXTERNAL CUES

Evaluation

Siffre's research and the study by Aschoff and Wever (see above) show that circadian rhythms persist despite isolation from natural light, which demonstrates the existence of an endogenous 'clock'. However, this research also shows that external cues are important because the clock was not perfectly accurate; it sometimes was unusually long.

Folkard *et al.* (1985) conducted an experiment to see if external cues could be used to override the internal clock. A group of 12 people lived in a cave for three weeks, isolated from natural light and other time cues. These volunteers agreed to go to bed when the clock indicated 11.45 pm and to get up when it indicated 7.45 am. Initially the clock ran normally, but gradually they quickened the clock until it was indicating the passing of 24 hours when actually only 22 hours had passed. At the beginning the volunteers' circadian cycle matched the clock but as it quickened their rhythm ceased to match the clock and continued to follow a 24-hour cycle rather than the 22-hour cycle imposed by the experiment (except for one participant who did adapt to the 22-hour cycle). Overall, this suggests that the circadian rhythm can only be guided to a limited extent by external cues.

An interesting feature of these experiments is that, as soon as the experiments were over, the participants took only a few days to resynchronise their cycles to the available external time cues (such as clocks and daylight) showing the influence of such external cues.

CIRCADIAN RHYTHMS

Circadian rhythms are those rhythms that last about 24 hours; the word circadian comes from the Latin 'circa' (about) plus 'dies' (a day). The two best-known circadian rhythms are the sleep-wake cycle and the body temperature cycle.

The sleep-wake cycle

You might think that the reason you go to sleep and wake up at fairly regular times is because of changes in daylight. You feel sleepy when it gets dark and are roused by sunlight streaming through your curtains in the morning. Or perhaps your sleep-wake cycle is governed by knowing what time of day it is. These are all external cues and they are important in guiding the circadian sleep-wake cycle. However, there is also an internal (**endogenous**) 'clock'. This internal circadian clock is free running, i.e. it works without any external cues, setting a cycle of about 24–25 hours. Under normal circumstances the internal clock does not work alone. There are external cues, most importantly daylight, and these help adjust the internal clock to the environment in which you live. These studies show that circadian rhythms persist despite isolation from natural light, which demonstrates the existence of an endogenous 'clock'. However, this research also shows that external cues are important because the clock was not perfectly accurate: it varied from day to day.

Core body temperature

Core body temperature is one of the best indicators of the circadian rhythm. It is lowest at about 4.30 am (about 36°C) and highest at around 6.00 pm (about 38°C). There is a slight trough just after lunch which is not just due to the effects of having had lunch – the dip occurs even when people have not eaten. In many countries the practice of having an afternoon siesta is related to this dip in body temperature. The temperature dip is a bi-daily rhythm, which is an example of the **ultradian rhythms** we will look at on the next spread.

Hormones

Hormone production also follows a circadian rhythm. **Cortisol** is at its lowest around midnight and peaks around 6.00 am. Cortisol is a hormone produced when we are stressed but is also related to making us alert when we wake up, and can explain why, if we awaken at 4.00 am, it is hard to think clearly. It is because cortisol levels are not sufficiently high for alertness. **Melatonin** (which induces sleepiness) and **growth hormone** are two other hormones that have a clear circadian rhythm, both peaking at around midnight.

WWW Try some activities at faculty.washington.edu/chudler/clock.html, or a Daily Rhythm Test at www.bbc.co.uk/science/humanbody/sleep/crt/

EVALUATION

The sleep-wake cycle

Research methodology – Early research studies suffered from an important flaw when estimating the 'free-running' cycle of the human circadian rhythm. In all studies, participants were isolated from variables that might affect their circadian rhythms, such as clocks, radios and daylight. However, they were not isolated from artificial light because it was thought that dim light, in contrast to daylight, would not affect the circadian rhythm. Recent research suggests that this may not be true; for example, Czeisler *et al.* (1999) altered participants' circadian rhythms down to 22 hours and up to 28 hours just using dim lighting.

Individual differences – There are two important types of individual difference. One is the cycle length; research has found that circadian cycles in different people can vary from 13 to 65 hours (Czeisler *et al.*, 1999). The other type of individual difference relates to cycle onset – individuals appear to be innately different in terms of when their circadian rhythms reach their peak. For example, Duffy *et al.* (2000) found that morning people prefer to rise early and go to bed early (about 6.00 am and 10.00 pm), whereas evening people prefer to wake and go to bed later (10.00 am and 1.00 am).

Core body temperature

Effects of core body temperature changes – The circadian variation in core body temperature has been used to explain changes in cognitive abilities, a real-world application. For example, Folkard *et al.* (1977) read stories to 12- and 13-year-old children at either 9.00 am or 3.00 pm. After one week, the afternoon group (higher core body temperature) showed both superior recall and comprehension, retaining about 8% more meaningful material. This suggests that long-term recall is best when body temperature is highest. Gupta (1991) found that performance on IQ tests was best at 7.00 pm as compared with 9.00 am or 2.00 pm, a factor which might be an important consideration when taking examinations.

Cause or correlation? – There is evidence that temperature changes do actually cause the changes in cognitive performance. Giesbrecht *et al.* (1993) lowered body temperature (by placing participants in cold water) and found that cognitive performance was worse on some tasks.

However, other research has found that the link is spurious. For example, Hord and Thompson (1983) tested cognitive performance in a field rather than lab situation and didn't find any correlation between core temperature and cognitive performance. It may be that higher core body temperature leads to increased physiological arousal and this leads to improved cognitive performance (Wright *et al.*, 2002).

IDA A BIOLOGICAL AND DETERMINIST APPROACH

The explanations offered for circadian rhythms suggest that sleep-wake patterns are fixed (determined) by internal mechanisms. The power of these biologically determined rhythms is illustrated by the case of a young man who was blind, which meant that light did not reset his circadian rhythm. He was exposed to various external cues, such as clocks, yet found these had little effect on his internally set circadian rhythms. This made it very difficult for him to function in a world tuned into cues, such as clocks and daylight (Miles *et al.*, 1977).

However, this determinist view may be somewhat misleading. It is clear that the internal mechanism is very powerful but there is some flexibility in the system. For example, we can decide to go to bed two hours later than normal and wake up at the same time the next day, without too much difficulty. In the study by Folkard *et al.* (see facing page) one person did manage to keep to a 22-hour rhythm, which shows that other factors can override the internal clock.

IDA REAL-WORLD APPLICATION

Chronotherapeutics (also called chronopharmacology) is the study of how timing (chronos) affects drug treatments (therapy). Since the circadian rhythm affects digestion, heart rate, hormone secretions and other functions, this should be taken into account when taking drugs. For example, medications that act on certain hormones may have no effect if taken when target hormone levels are low, but are fully effective if taken when levels are high. Another example is taking aspirin to treat heart attacks (which normally occur in the early morning). This is most effective at around 11.00 pm which allows the aspirin to peak in the blood stream (this takes 2–4 hours). A further application of this research is when deciding on the best time to study. You are most alert in the morning and early evening, so those are the best times to work.

CAN YOU…? No.1.1

…**1** Write a description of circadian rhythms (a) in about 200 words and (b) in about 100 words.

…**2** Identify **eight** criticisms related to research into circadian rhythms, including **at least one** IDA topic. Each criticism should be about 50 words. Remember that criticisms can be positive as well as negative.

…**3** Use this material to write a 600-word answer to the question: *Describe and evaluate research on circadian rhythms.* (8 marks + 16 marks)

VALIDITY

The study by Michel Siffre might be described as a case study – it is the study of one individual and therefore has unique features. His body's behaviour may not be typical of all people and, in addition, living in a cave may have particular effects due to, for example, the fact that it is cold. However, subsequent studies above ground have confirmed the findings of research in cave environments.

Siffre's study was also an experiment – he controlled key variables (exogenous zeitgebers) to observe the effects on the sleep-wake cycle. The experimental approach is important because it allows us to demonstrate causal relationships.

INFRADIAN AND ULTRADIAN RHYTHMS

The circadian rhythm isn't the only biological rhythm – there are two other important rhythms. The ultradian rhythm spans less than a day, one example is the bi-daily temperature rhythm described on the previous spread. The infradian rhythm has a period of more than one day but less than one year, such as the menstrual cycle in women.

ULTRADIAN RHYTHMS

Sleep stages

In humans, daily cycles of wakefulness and sleep follow a circadian rhythm. However, within the sleep portion of this cycle another type of rhythm, an example of an ultradian rhythm, exists. These are the five stages of sleep (outlined below). The first four stages are called **NREM sleep** (non-rapid eye movements) and the fifth stage is **REM sleep** (rapid eye movement), so called because of the accompanying movements of the eye beneath the closed eyelids. One sleep cycle goes through all five stages and lasts about 90 minutes.

Stages 1 and 2 are light sleep, characterised by a change in the electrical activity of the brain. The awake brain produces a typical pattern called a *beta wave* (see diagram below). As you become more relaxed, your brain waves become slower and more regular, and have a greater amplitude. This is called an *alpha wave*. As you go to sleep, the waves slow down further i.e. have a greater wave frequency. This is called a *theta wave*, which is accompanied by bursts of activity – increased wave frequency (*sleep spindles*) and increased wave amplitude (*K complexes*). Stages 3 and 4 are characterised by even slower *delta waves*. These stages are called **slow wave sleep (SWS)**. In this stage it is very hard to wake someone up, although a person is not unconscious and will be aroused by, for example, their baby crying. In deep sleep (SWS) most of the body's physiological 'repair work' is undertaken and important biochemical processes take place, such as the production of **growth hormones**. In REM sleep there is fast, desynchronised EEG activity resembling the awake brain.

These cycles continue throughout the night with the SWS period getting shorter and REM periods getting slightly longer as the night progresses (see drawing below). Each sleep cycle is about 60 minutes in early infancy, increasing to 90 minutes during adolescence.

Basic rest-activity cycle

The 90-minute sleep cycle is itself located within a 24-hour circadian cycle, so it would make sense to find that this 90-minute 'clock' was also ticking throughout the day. It is called the **basic rest-activity cycle (BRAC)**. Friedman and Fisher (1967) observed eating and drinking behaviour in a group of psychiatric patients over periods of six hours. They detected a clear 90-minute cycle in eating and drinking behaviour.

NREM sleep	
Stages 1 and 2	Relaxed state, easily woken. Alpha and theta waves, heart rate slows, temperature drops.
Stages 3 and 4 SWS	Delta waves, metabolic rate slowest, growth hormone produced.
REM sleep	
REM	Called 'paradoxical sleep' because brain and eyes active but body paralysed.

▲ The 90-minute ultradian sleep rhythm – descending the 'sleep staircase'.

▶ The illustration shows EEG (electroencephalograph) recordings of characteristic brain waves. As a person goes to sleep their brain waves increase in amplitude (the height of the wave) and the wave frequency also increases (the distance between the crest of one wave and the next).

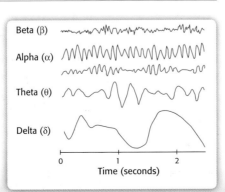

INFRADIAN RHYTHMS

Monthly cycles

The most obvious infradian rhythm is the human female menstrual cycle driven by fluctuating hormone levels. The function of the menstrual cycle is to regulate ovulation. The **pituitary gland** releases hormones (FSH – *follicle stimulating hormone*, and LH – *luteinising hormone*) which stimulate a follicle in one ovary to ripen an egg and also triggers the release of the female hormone **oestrogen**. Once the egg has ripened, the ruptured follicle starts to secrete **progesterone** which causes the lining of the womb to prepare for a pregnancy by increasing its blood supply. About two weeks after ovulation, if there is no pregnancy, progesterone is reduced and this causes the lining of the womb to be shed.

Less well known are the monthly rhythms affecting males. In one study 21 male participants had their body temperature and alertness levels measured over periods varying from 49 to 102 days. The study found some evidence in males for a periodic variation of both body temperature and subjective ratings of morning alertness, with a cycle length of approximately 20 days (Empson, 1977).

Seasonal affective disorder (SAD)

Infradian rhythms don't have to be monthly, they can also apply to behaviours that occur once a year. Some people suffer from a depressive condition called **seasonal affective disorder (SAD)**. They become depressed during the winter months and recover during the summer. We may all experience some lowering of mood when there is more darkness than daylight but SAD sufferers experience severe symptoms.

What causes this depression? Research studies have shown that the hormones **melatonin** and **serotonin** are secreted when it is dark (by the **pineal gland**); more darkness means more melatonin, and more melatonin means less serotonin (because melatonin is produced from serotonin). Low levels of serotonin are associated with depression (see page 180).

▼ An illustration of the changing ultradian rhythm of sleep during the night.

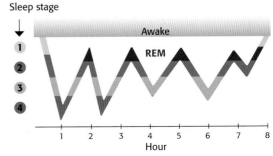

The study of biological rhythms is an important topic of study and is even given a name – 'chronobiology'. There are academic journals (e.g. Frontiers in Sleep and chronobiology) and professional organisations (e.g. The American Association for Medical Chronobiology and Chronotherapeutics).

IDA **A DETERMINIST APPROACH**

On this spread we have described two psychological disorders which arise from infradian rhythms – PMS and SAD. PMS has been used as a legal defence – for example, in one case a Ms English drove her car into her married lover after an argument, killing him. She was charged with murder but ultimately placed on probation because it was argued in court that her actions were related to severe PMS (Johnson, 1987). Dr Katharina Dalton, a GP and pioneer researcher into PMS, has often acted as an expert witness and argued that severe PMS was akin to a mental disorder and therefore individuals should not be held responsible for their actions. This suggests that biological rhythms may be beyond our control.

On the other hand, there is evidence that we can 'will' our biological rhythms to change. One study found that people who were told to wake up at earlier times of the night than usual had higher levels of the stress hormone **ACTH** (which contributes to the waking-up process) than normal at the designated time and they woke up earlier (Born et al., 1999).

EVALUATION

Sleep stages

One issue with studies on REM sleep is the assumption that it is dreaming sleep. Dement and Kleitman (1957) were the first to demonstrate this link. They woke participants up at the times when their brain waves were characteristic of REM sleep and found that participants were highly likely to report dreaming. However, they also found that dreams were recorded outside REM sleep and that sleepers, when awoken in REM sleep, were not always dreaming. The importance of the REM/dream link is that it potentially provides a way to identify when someone is dreaming and therefore might provide theorists with a way to explain dreaming – for example Hobson and McCarley (1977) proposed that dreams are just a psychological read-out of the random electrical signals typical of REM sleep. However, such theories of dreaming are based on the erroneous assumption that REM activity = dreaming.

Basic rest-activity cycle

The basic rest-activity cycle shows that sleep stages are part of a continuum – a 90-minute cycle that occurs throughout the day within the circadian rhythm. The importance of this 90-minute rhythm is probably as a form of timing to ensure that the biological processes in the body work in unison, in the way that a conductor keeps an orchestra in time.

Menstruation

Exogenous cues – The menstrual cycle is normally governed by an endogenous system – the release of hormones under the control of the pituitary gland. However, it can be controlled by exogenous cues. Research has shown that when several women live together and do not take oral contraceptives, they tend to menstruate at the same time every month. In one study, daily samples of sweat were collected from one group of women and rubbed on to the upper lip of women in a second group. The groups were kept separate yet their menstrual cycles became synchronised with their individual odour donor (Russell et al., 1980). This suggests that the synchronisation of menstrual cycles can be affected by **pheromones** – chemicals which are released in, for example, sweat. Pheromones act like hormones but have an effect on the bodies of people close by rather than the body of the person producing them.

Consequences of the menstrual cycle – Premenstrual syndrome (PMS) is a disorder that affects many women during the week before menstruation begins. Symptoms can include depression, mood swings and aggression. The importance of research on the menstrual cycle is that it shows that PMS is physiological rather than psychological. For many years, PMS was dismissed as being a psychological problem (it's in your head), but we now know that it is a physiological problem (with psychological symptoms) caused mainly by hormonal changes related to infradian rhythms. Dalton (1964) found that PMS was also associated with an increase in accidents, suicides and crime (see above).

Seasonal affective disorder

SAD has been explained in terms of being a natural outcome of infradian rhythms, but alternatively it could be the consequence of a disrupted *circadian* rhythm. In the UK, as the seasons change from summer to winter, the circadian rhythms may be thrown out of phase. People continue to get up at about the same time but often go to bed earlier because it is darker earlier. This means that the biological system gets the impression that time is shifting and the result is similar to jet lag, which is discussed later in this chapter.

IDA **REAL-WORLD APPLICATION**

The understanding of the role of darkness in SAD has led to effective therapies, most notably the use of **phototherapy**, as illustrated below. This uses very strong lights in the evening and/or early morning to change levels of melatonin and serotonin. The lights are between 6,000 and 10,000 Lux which is equivalent to full daylight; a 60-watt light bulb produces about 1000 Lux.

SAD sufferers have reported that daily use of such boxes is enough to relieve them of their feelings of lethargy, depression and other related symptoms. However, there is some question about whether this may be due to a **placebo** effect (a belief that the therapy will work). One study found that a placebo condition (fake negative-ion generator) was less effective, but 32% of participants did improve with the placebo alone (Eastman et al., 1998).

CAN YOU…? No.1.2

…1 Write a description, in about 100 words, of ultradian rhythms.

…2 Identify **four** criticisms related to research into ultradian rhythms, including **at least one** IDA topic. Each criticism should be about 50 words.

…3 Write a description of infradian rhythms in about 100 words.

…4 Identify **four** criticisms related to research into infradian rhythms, including **at least one** IDA topic. Each criticism should be about 50 words.

…5 Use this material to write a 600-word answer to the question: *Describe and evaluate research on ultradian and infradian rhythms.* (8 marks + 16 marks)

The previous two spreads looked at different kinds of biological rhythms. Such rhythms have evolved for two reasons. First the world we live in has cyclic changes – day and night, summer and winter, and so on. Animals and plants need to be attuned to these changes and therefore they need to have internally-managed rhythms (endogenous pacemakers) that are similar to the likely cyclic changes in the environment. However, these rhythms also need to be fine-tuned by external cues (exogenous zeitgebers) in order to remain in time with the external world which fluctuates in its rhythms (e.g. shorter days in winter).

The second reason is that biological organisms are complex systems where lots of different chemical processes are going on. To co-ordinate these processes you need something like the conductor of an orchestra to keep everything in time. This is another reason for having an internal clock (endogenous pacemaker).

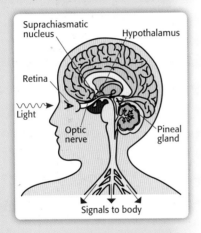

► Diagram of the brain showing the position of the suprachiasmatic nucleus and pineal gland.

Suprachiasmatic nucleus
Hypothalamus
Retina
Light
Optic nerve
Pineal gland
Signals to body

ENDOGENOUS PACEMAKERS

The suprachiasmatic nucleus

In mammals, the main endogenous pacemaker is a tiny cluster of nerve cells called the **suprachiasmatic nucleus (SCN)**, which lies in the **hypothalamus**. It is located just above the place where the optic nerves from each eye cross over (called the optic chiasm – thus 'supra', which means 'above' the chiasm). The SCN obtains information about light from the eye via the optic nerve. This happens even when our eyes are shut, because light penetrates the eyelids. If our endogenous clock is running slow (e.g. the sun rises earlier than the day before), morning light automatically shifts the clock ahead, putting the rhythm in step with the world outside.

In fact each SCN is actually a pair of structures, one in each hemisphere of the brain, and each of these is divided into a ventral and dorsal SCN. The ventral SCN is relatively quickly reset by external cues, whereas the dorsal SCN is much less affected by light and therefore more resistant to being reset (Albus *et al.*, 2005).

The pineal gland and melatonin

The SCN sends signals to the **pineal gland**, directing it to increase production of the hormone **melatonin** at night. Melatonin induces sleep by inhibiting the brain mechanisms that promote wakefulness. In birds and reptiles the pineal gland lies just beneath the bone of the skull and is directly regulated by light; light inhibits the production of melatonin. In fact many lizards have a 'third eye' near the pineal gland which actually protrudes through a small opening in the skull and receives information about light.

EXOGENOUS ZEITGEBERS

The process of resetting the biological clock with exogenous zeitgebers is known as **entrainment**. The opposite of entrainment is 'free-running' – where the biological clock operates in the absence of any exogenous cues.

Light

Light is the dominant zeitgeber in humans. As we have seen, light can reset the body's main pacemaker, the SCN. It can also reset the other oscillators located throughout the body because the protein CRY (cryptochrome), which is part of the protein clock (see left), is light-sensitive. This may explain why Campbell and Murphy (1998) found that if you shine light on the back of participants' knees this shifted their circadian rhythms.

Social cues

Until fairly recently, biologists thought that social cues were the main zeitgebers for human circadian rhythms. We eat meals at socially determined mealtimes, and go to bed and wake up at times designated as appropriate for our age, and so on. Our daily rhythms appeared to be entrained by social convention, not internal biology. Today we know that light is the dominant zeitgeber, but in fact it is also now understood that all parts of the body produce their own oscillating rhythms and some of these are not primarily reset by light. For example, the zeitgeber for cells in the liver and heart is likely to be mealtimes because these cells are reset by eating (Davidson, 2006).

Temperature

In cold-blooded animals variation in external temperature affects the setting of the circadian rhythms – cold temperature signals a time for reduced activity and warm temperature is the time for activity (sleep-wake). In warm-blooded animals, such as humans, recent evidence suggests that the daily changes in body temperature (described above) are governed by their own circadian clock and these temperature changes entrain other circadian rhythms (Buhr *et al.*, 2010).

THE TICKING OF THE BIOLOGICAL CLOCK

The basis of the circadian rhythm lies in interactions between certain proteins, creating the 'tick' of the biological clock; it is an ingenious negative feedback loop. Darlington *et al.* (1998) first identified such proteins in the fruit fly, *drospholia*.

- In the morning, two proteins, CLOCK and CYCLE (CLK-CYC) bind together.
- Once joined, CLK-CYC produce two other proteins, PERIOD and TIME (PER-TIM).
- PER-TIM has the effect of rendering the CLK-CYC proteins inactive, so that, as PER-TIM increases, CLK-CYC decreases and therefore PER-TIM starts to decrease too (negative feedback).

This loop takes about 24 hours and, hey presto, you have the biological clock! The actual proteins vary from animal to animal. In humans the main pairs are CLOCK-BMAL1 and PER-CRY (BMAL1 and CRY are also proteins).

This protein mechanism is present in the SCN (the central oscillator), and is also present in cells throughout the body (peripheral oscillators). The presence of peripheral oscillators explains why there are different rhythms for different functions, such as hormone secretion, urine production, blood circulation and so on.

EVALUATION

Research evidence

Evidence for the role of endogenous and exogenous factors is apparent in many of the studies reviewed on the previous two spreads, and can be useful evaluation on this topic.

The role of the SCN has been demonstrated in animal studies. Morgan (1995) bred 'mutant' hamsters so they had circadian rhythms of 20 hours instead of 24 hours, and then transplanted their SCNs into normal hamsters. The normal hamster then displayed the mutant rhythms.

Separate rhythms – Under normal conditions the central oscillator (the SCN) coordinates all other body rhythms, but in certain circumstances the body's separate oscillators will desynchronise. For example, a young woman, Kate Aldcroft, spent time in a cave. After 25 days her temperature rhythm was a 24-hour one, yet her sleep rhythm was on a 30-hour cycle (Folkard, 1996). Such desynchronisation leads to symptoms similar to **jet lag** – which is essentially a state of desynchronised biological rhythms (see next spread).

The power of artificial lighting

Light is the dominant zeitgeber, but the question is whether any lighting level will act as a zeitgeber. In the early studies of biological rhythms (e.g. Siffre and Aschoff and Wever), participants were exposed to artificial lighting but it was assumed this would not be bright enough to entrain rhythms. On the other hand Campbell and Murphy (see left) shifted circadian rhythms just by shining a light on the back of someone's knees. Recent research has shown that, in general, artificial lighting does have an effect. For example, Boivin *et al.* (1996) found that circadian rhythms can be entrained by ordinary dim lighting, although bright lighting was more effective (this study is described on the next spread).

If dim lighting does reset the biological clock, then the fact that we live in an artificially lit world may have some negative consequences. For example, Stevens (2006) suggests that exposure to artificial lighting disrupts circadian rhythms and thus disrupts melatonin production and this might ultimately explain why women in industrialised (and well-lit) societies are more likely to develop breast cancer.

When the biological system fails

The downside of a biologically-determined system is that, when it fails, it may cause a multitude of problems. One example of this is when there are mutations in the genes which contribute to the ticking of the biological clock. Familial advanced sleep-phase syndrome (FASPS) has been linked to an inherited defect in one of the PER genes (Chicurel, 2001). This syndrome typically causes sleep onset at around 7.00 pm, and spontaneous awakening at around 2.00 am in affected family members who therefore have great difficulty leading a normal life. There are many other sleep phase disorders; in fact some research suggests that brain changes during adolescence lead to a form of **delayed sleep phase syndrome** which would explain why some adolescents have rather unusual sleep patterns (see page 18).

The blended system

It sounds as if we are talking about two systems – one endogenous and the other exogenous – but such neat divisions do not really exist. Apart from total isolation experiments, the running of the biological clock is a combined endogenous-exogenous exercise.

CAN YOU...? No.1.3

...1 Write a description, in about 200 words, of endogenous pacemakers, including research evidence.

...2 Write a description, in about 200 words, of exogenous zeitgebers, including research evidence.

...3 Identify **eight** criticisms related to the methods used in researching endogenous pacemakers and/or exogenous zeitgebers, including **at least one** IDA topic. Each criticism should be about 50 words. Ensure that any synoptic points are fully contextualised.

...4 Present **two** comments about the advantages and/or disadvantages of circadian rhythms.

...5 Use this material to write a 600-word answer to the question: *Discuss the role of endogenous pacemakers and exogenous zeitgebers in circadian rhythms.* (8 marks + 16 marks)

DISRUPTION OF BIOLOGICAL RHYTHMS

Biological rhythms are driven by endogenous pacemakers (oscillators). As we have seen, some of these oscillators are easily reset by exogenous zeitgebers (such as daylight, mealtimes and so on) whereas other oscillators are more resistant. The result is desynchronisation. The two most common examples of the disruption of biological rhythms and the resultant desynchronisation are shift work and aeroplane travel – resulting in **shift lag** and **jet lag**.

When you have a temperature it makes you feel quite ill. This may be another example of the disruption of biological rhythms, because raised body temperature entrains some oscillators causing desynchronisation (Herzog, 2003).

PHASE ADVANCE AND PHASE DELAY

The notion of phase advance and phase delay applies to all circadian disruptions, including both shift work and jet lag as well as simply staying up late and/or getting up early. In terms of jet lag, most travellers report less difficulty in adjusting when they are flying west (e.g. London to New York) than when they are flying east (e.g. New York to London). The diagram below illustrates what happens.

We all know that it is easier to stay up later than usual rather than to get up earlier than normal – if you have to get up early you feel slightly out of sorts and have difficulty concentrating. Why should phase delay (east to west travel or staying up late) be easier than phase advance? It is probably because phase delay means, on the first morning, you get up when your body is already quite awake – a bit like having a lie-in. On the other hand, with phase advance, you have to get up when you are in a circadian trough.

East to West Phase delay; easier (like going to bed later than usual)

New York
Arrive 6 hours later
London time = 10pm
Minus 5 hours time difference
New York time = 5pm

London
Leave 4pm

West to East Phase advance; more difficult (like having to get up earlier than usual)

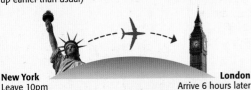

New York
Leave 10pm

London
Arrive 6 hours later
New York time = 4am next day
Plus 5 hours time difference
London time = 9am

EXAMPLES OF DISRUPTION

Shift work and shift lag

Night workers are required to be alert at night and so must sleep during the day, which is the reverse of our natural rhythms and out of line with most of the available cues from zeitgebers.

Decreased alterness – Nightworkers often experience a circadian 'trough' of decreased alertness during their shifts (Boivin *et al.*, 1996). This occurs between midnight, when **cortisol** levels are lowest, and 4.00 am, when core body temperature is at its lowest.

Sleep deprivation – Workers who have to sleep by day often experience sleep problems because when they finish work it is daytime and there are other interruptions (e.g. noises outside) and daylight reduces sleep quality. Daytime sleep is typically between one and two hours shorter than a nocturnal sleep period; REM in particular is affected (Tilley and Wilkinson, 1982). Poor quality daytime sleep then makes it even more difficult for shift workers to stay awake through the night, especially when they hit the circadian trough.

Effects on health – There is a significant relationship between shift work and organ disease. For example, Knutsson *et al.* (1986) found that individuals who worked shifts for more than 15 years were three times more likely to develop heart disease than non-shift workers. Martino *et al.* (2008) linked shift work to a range of organ diseases, including kidney disease. This may be due to the direct effects of desynchronisation or indirect effects, such as sleep disruption.

Jet travel and jet lag

The term 'jet lag' is generally used to refer to the physiological effects of disrupted circadian rhythms – even those that do not arise from jet travel. Our biological rhythms are not equipped to cope with sudden and large changes; it is estimated that the dorsal portion of the SCN takes several cycles to fully resynchronise to abrupt large changes in environmental time – a process we experience as jet lag. Winter *et al.* (2008) calculated that this is equivalent to one day to adjust to each hour of time change. Symptoms of jet lag include loss of appetite, nausea, fatigue, disorientation, insomnia and mild depression.

Performance decrement – A popular way to demonstrate the debilitating effects of jet lag has been to study American major league baseball teams who have to travel from coast to coast to play league games. The west coast of America is three hours behind the east coast so, when east coast teams have to play on the west coast, they experience their clocks going backwards – a phase delay; west coast teams experience phase advance when they play teams on the east coast. In one such study Recht *et al.* (1995) analysed US baseball results over a three-year period. Teams that travelled east to west won (on average) 44% of their games; whereas, when travelling from west to east, the percentage of games won dropped to just 37%.

Evaluation INDIVIDUAL DIFFERENCES

The effects of circadian disruption vary considerably between individuals. It is possible that those people whose circadian rhythms change least are the ones who cope best overall. Reinberg *et al.* (1984) found that people who gave up shift work because they couldn't cope tended to have rhythms that changed a lot while on shift while the 'happy shift workers' had unchanging rhythms.

▶ The *Exxon Valdez* oil tanker ran aground at 12.04 am in 1989, dumping more than 10 million gallons of oil into Prince William Sound, Alaska, and killing thousands of marine animals and sea birds. It was by no means the only major accident to occur in the middle of the night – the Chernobyl nuclear power station disaster began at 1.23 am, and Three-Mile Island nuclear power station accident at 4.00 am. Most lorry accidents occur between 4.00 am and 7.00 am. Moore-Ede (1993) estimated the cost of shift worker fatigue in the US to be $77 billion annually as a result of both major accidents and ongoing medical expenses due to shift work-related illnesses.

EVALUATION

Our society cannot function without night working (and hence shift lag) and jet travel (and hence jet lag) so we need to understand the consequences in order to find ways to deal with such disruptions of biological rhythms, both to protect individuals and to protect all of us from associated accidents (see above).

Other factors

Shift work effects are not just due to the disruption of biological rhythms. They may be due to the lack of sleep associated with having to go to bed at unusual times. There are other factors too. One is that shift workers experience social disruption as well as disruption to their biological rhythms. It is difficult to meet friends and spend time with family when working on shift; divorce rates may be as high as 60% among all-night shift workers (Solomon, 1993).

Jet lag may also be affected by factors other than the disruption of biological rhythms. An individual may sleep badly the night before travelling because of worry. Travel itself is tiring, and many holidays involve long hours getting to the airport before flying. Drinking alcohol or coffee, constant noise, low-oxygen cabin air and annoying passengers can be cumulative factors.

Reducing the harmful effects

Rotating shifts – Research indicates that more problems occur when people have to do rotating shifts, where shifts alternate every few days (Gold *et al.*, 1992). Non-fluctuating shifts (where an individual always works nights) are less disruptive because the individual can get used to one sleep-wake pattern – although days off are likely to mean temporary changes in sleeping patterns which will disrupt the biological rhythms.

Forward-rotating shifts follow the logical order of the day (phase delay) and may be easier on the body and less damaging to worker health, according to a review of research by Bambra *et al.* (2008). An example of such a shift pattern would be a shift in the morning for one week, then an afternoon shift the next week and finally a night shift for the third week. Bambra also concluded that rotating workers through shift changes more quickly (such as every three to four days, as opposed to every seven days) is better for health and work-life balance.

Artificial lighting is moderately effective in re-setting the rhythm, as found in the study by Boivin *et al.* (see top right). This study also found that dim lighting actually had the opposite effect (i.e. it didn't re-set the rhythnm)! Gronfier *et al.* (2007) were able to entrain circadian rhythms to longer than 24 hours just by using bright light pulses – modulated light exposure (MLE).

Melatonin has been put forward as a 'miracle' cure for shift lag and jet lag. This makes sense, because it is the natural hormone that induces sleep. Herxheimer and Petrie (2001) reviewed 10 studies and found that where melatonin was taken near to bed-time, it was remarkably effective. However, if taken at the wrong time of day it may actually delay adaptation.

Social customs can help to entrain biological rhythms. For example, when travelling, it helps to eat at the right time and go to sleep when the clock says it is time to go to sleep. Recent research suggests that a period of fasting followed by eating on the new time schedule should help entrain biological rhythms (Fuller *et al.*, 2008), possibly because some of our body clocks are reset by food intake.

RESETTING BIOLOGICAL CLOCKS

Boivin *et al.* (1996) investigated the power of artificial light in resetting our biological clocks. Thirty-one male subjects were divided into four groups and put on an inverted sleep-wake cycle for three days (kept awake at night and allowed to sleep during the day). Each 'day' when they woke they were exposed to five hours of very dim light, followed by one of four conditions: Group 1 was exposed to very bright light (10,000 lux), group 2 to bright light (1,260 lux), group 3 had ordinary room light (180 lux) and group 4 remained in dim light. Core body temperature was used to assess each person's current circadian rhythm.

After three days, members of group 1 (very bright light) had advanced five hours earlier; group 2 (bright light) had advanced by three hours; group 3 had advanced by one hour; and group 4 had drifted one hour *later* in their circadian rhythms. This shows that even room lighting can have an effect on the circadian rhythm and very bright light has a significant effect.

CAN YOU...? No.1.4

...**1** Write a description, in about 100 words, about how shift work can affect biological rhythms.

...**2** Write a description, in about 100 words, about how jet lag (i.e. jet travel) can affect biological rhythms.

...**3** Identify **eight** criticisms related to the evidence that shift work and/or jet lag disrupt biological rhythms, including **at least one** IDA topic. Each criticism should be about 50 words.

...**4** Use this material to write a 600-word answer to the question: *Discuss the disruption of biological rhythms.* (8 marks + 16 marks)

LAB EXPERIMENTS

The strength of lab experiments, such as the one by Boivin *et al.* (top right), is that extraneous variables can be carefully controlled to isolate causal variables. However, there is a question over whether the same 'laws' will apply in everyday life. It is therefore important to conduct field experiments as well to confirm the findings. Boivin and James (2002) used intermittent bright lights in a field study of nurses which confirmed the effectiveness of bright lighting to promote circadian adaptation.

REAL-WORLD APPLICATION

The importance of research on shift work and jet lag lies in the applications it has to our everyday lives, for example the use of artificial lighting to entrain and reset circadian rhythms. Being able to do this may help avoid disasters, such as the Exxon Valdez (see top of the page).

What is sleep?

- Sleep usually involves being very still. However, dolphins and other marine mammals are not still, they must come up to the surface regularly to breathe and, to do this, they sleep one hemisphere (half of the brain) at a time.
- Sleepers are usually quite unresponsive, although they are not unconscious. Most animals are woken by significant noises. For example, most parents will wake if they hear their baby crying.
- Animals usually sleep in a quiet, private, secure place and they usually do it lying down in the dark, although it is even possible to sleep on a busy underground train sitting up. Cows sleep standing up (except during REM sleep) and cats snooze in the sun.
- The time spent sleeping varies widely. The two-toed sloth sleeps for 20 hours whereas the giraffe sleeps only 3 hours a day.
- The most distinctive thing about sleep is that it is accompanied by a characteristic pattern of electrical activity in the brain (as described on page 12). However, REM activity is absent in some animals, such as reptiles.

What does this tell us? There are no certain features of sleep, but all animals sleep and they all do it differently. This suggests two things: (1) sleep is necessary for survival (otherwise why would all animals do it?), and (2) the actual patterns of sleep are adaptive to each particular species (otherwise why are the patterns so different?). On the next two spreads we will look at explanations of the function of sleep, but here we start with a look at human sleep patterns over the human lifespan.

IDA THE DEVELOPMENTAL APPROACH

The lifespan approach is important because it recognises that sleep patterns are not consistent but change as we age. For a long time psychologists ignored such age-related changes and assumed that there was one sleep pattern that applied to all ages. This association between age and sleep has led to new understanding of, for example, some of the effects of ageing (as described on this spread).

The specification says 'The nature of sleep, including stages of sleep and lifespan changes in sleep'. This means that exam questions can be set on:

1. *The nature of sleep – an appropriate answer can include anything on this spread, sleep stages, explanations of sleep (pages 20–23) and/or disorders of sleep (see pages 24–27).*
2. *Stages of sleep – sleep stages are described on page 12 and evaluated on page 13. For further evaluation you could make comparisons with other biological rhythms.*
3. *Lifespan changes in sleep – described and evaluated on this spread.*

LIFESPAN CHANGES IN SLEEP

As humans grow from infancy to old age there are major changes in the amount and kind of sleep experienced.

Infancy

Babies sleep a lot more than children and adults, and also have different sleep patterns and different stages of sleep. They tend to sleep about 16 hours a day, but their sleep is not continuous. They usually wake up every hour or so because their sleep cycles are shorter than the adult 90-minute cycle. Infants have sleep stages which are similar to adult stages, called quiet sleep and active sleep; these are immature versions of **SWS** and **REM** sleep respectively. At birth there is more active sleep than adult REM sleep; about half of infant sleep is spent in active sleep. Another difference relates to going to sleep; adults can usually go fairly directly into the state of deep sleep (quiet sleep), whereas infants in the early months enter sleep through an initial period of light sleep. After twenty minutes or more they gradually enter deep sleep.

By the age of six months a circadian rhythm has become established (one main sleep-wake cycle) and by the age of one year infants are usually sleeping mainly at night, with one or two naps during the day. The periods of deep sleep lengthen and there is a reduction in the amounts of active/REM sleep. It is not known whether REM activity is accompanied by dreaming, as babies and young children cannot provide reliable subjective reports.

Childhood

By the age of five, children have EEG patterns that look like those of an adult but they are still sleeping more (about 12 hours per day) and having more REM activity (about 30% of total sleep time). Boys sleep slightly more than girls. During childhood it is not uncommon for children to experience a variety of **parasomnias** – sleep disorders, such as sleep walking or **night terrors**. These are described on pages 24–27.

Adolescence

During childhood the need for sleep decreases, but in adolescence it increases slightly, to about nine or ten hours a night. **Circadian rhythms** also change so that teenagers feel naturally more awake later at night and have more difficulty getting up early (a phase delay). One distinguishing feature of adolescent REM sleep is that in males it is sometimes accompanied by orgasm and ejaculation, which is significantly less likely at other ages.

Adulthood and old age

'Normal' adult sleep is typically for about eight hours per night, with 25% in REM sleep. Childhood **parasomnias** such as **sleep walking** are more rare in adulthood but there is an increasing frequency of other sleep disorders, such as **insomnia** and **apnoea** (see page 24).

With increasing age, total sleep time remains about the same, although older people have more difficulty going to sleep and wake up more frequently (up to six times a night). This means they may have a nap during the day to satisfy their sleep needs. Even more significant is the fact that the pattern of sleep changes; REM sleep decreases to about 20% of total sleep time and the amount of slow wave sleep is also considerably reduced to as little as 5% or even none (other kinds of NREM sleep increase). Older people also experience a phase advance of circadian rhythms – feeling sleepier early in the evening and waking up earlier.

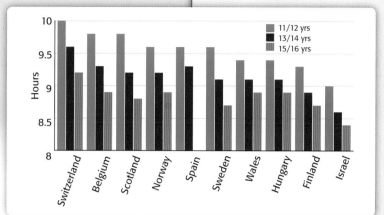

▼ Graph showing mean sleep duration for most of the countries in the study by Tynjälä et al. (1993).

CULTURAL BIAS

Psychologists make assumptions about sleep behaviour based on research that has been largely conducted with American and British samples. Such research assumes that there are no cultural influences on sleep behaviour but this may not be true.

Tynjälä et al. (1993) looked at sleep patterns in adolescents living in different cultures. Altogether over 400,000 11–16 year olds from 11 European countries were questioned. The results (see graph on left) showed significant differences. An important contributory factor was the number of evenings spent outside the home, which meant the young people went to bed late and had too little sleep because they had to get up early.

Outside of Europe other studies show differences in sleep duration. In Korea, mean sleep time was recorded as about 6.5 hours for adolescents (Shin et al., 2003) and a recent study in Iran found a mean time of 7.7 hours (Ghanizadeh et al., 2008).

Such research shows that sleep duration is influenced by cultural practices and reminds us that our view of behaviour often ignores such influences (i.e. is biased).

EVALUATION

One general comment to be made is that there are significant individual differences at any age, as well as cultural differences (see above).

Newborn babies

An evolutionary approach – Why are babies' sleep patterns so different from those of adults? One suggestion is that babies' sleep is an adaptive mechanism to make their parents' life easier – daytime sleeping means that parents can get on with their chores, enhancing survival. Nightwaking has adaptive benefits too. Babies have small stomachs and need to be fed regularly. A baby who sleeps soundly through the night might not be woken by feeling cold or hungry.

Explaining why infants are different – Infants' greater amount of active/REM sleep may be explained in terms of the relative immaturity of the infant brain, and is related to the considerable amount of learning that is taking place. REM sleep has been linked to the production of neurotransmitters and to consolidation of memories. This explains why babies have a significantly greater amount of active/REM sleep. It is further supported by the fact that premature babies (whose brains are even less mature) spend 90% of their time in active sleep.

Adolescence

Adolescent sleep can be explained by hormone changes – In adolescence hormone production changes. Hormones are primarily released at night and therefore sleep patterns are disturbed leading to sleep deprivation. Interestingly, many of the correlates of sleep deprivation are similar to those thought to be 'typical' of puberty: irritability, moodiness, changes in school performance and changes in motivation.

Hormonal changes can also explain the upset to the circadian clock, which has been described as a **delayed sleep phase syndrome** (Crowley et al., 2007). In fact some researchers have recommended that schools should begin their day later to accommodate the poor attention spans of adolescents in the early morning (e.g. Wolfson and Carskadon, 2005).

Adulthood

Too much sleep may not be a good thing – The common perception is that a good night's sleep is related to good health, but several studies have found that there is an increased mortality risk associated with *too much* sleep. For example, Kripke et al. (2002) surveyed over one million adult men and women and found that people sleeping for only six or seven hours had a reduced mortality risk, whereas those sleeping for an average of eight hours had a 15% increase in risk of death, and the risk was over 30% for people sleeping 10 hours.

It is important to recognise that this is correlational data and there may be other intervening variables that cause the link between sleep duration and mortality. For example, underlying illness may lead to increased sleep needs and to increased mortality.

Old age

Reduced sleep may not be a consequence of physiological changes – It may also be explained in terms of actual problems staying asleep, such as sleep **apnoea** or medical illnesses. Problems staying asleep are also explained by the fact that deep sleep (**SWS**) is reduced in old age, so the older sleeper is more easily woken.

Poor sleep might explain old age – The reduction in SWS leads to reduced production of **growth hormone** (because this is mainly produced in SWS), which may explain some of the symptoms associated with old age – such as lack of energy and lower bone density (van Cauter et al., 2000).

CAN YOU...?   No.**1.5**

...1 Outline, in about 200 words, the lifespan changes in sleep.

...2 Outline **one** study of lifespan changes in sleep and present **one** detailed criticism of the research methods used in this study.

...3 Identify **eight** criticisms related to the nature of sleep and lifespan changes, including **at least one** IDA topic. Each criticism should be about 50 words.

...4 Use this material to write a 600-word answer to the question: *Describe and evaluate lifespan changes in sleep.* (8 marks + 16 marks)

REAL-WORLD APPLICATION

There are useful applications of the research discussed on this spread. For example, the suggestion by Wilson and Carskadon (see above) that teenagers should start school later to accommodate delayed sleep phase syndrome. Researchers have also suggested that the effects of ageing could be reduced by improving sleep 'hygiene', i.e. improving the healthiness of sleep. For example, the habit of napping may reduce the amount of deep sleep during the night. Therefore, sleep hygiene may be improved by resisting having naps during the day.

Sleep must have some benefit, otherwise why would humans and other animals spend so much time sleeping? Animals cannot eat or mate while asleep, and are vulnerable to predation, so sleep must have some adaptive advantage or it would not be present in any animals whereas, in fact, it is found in virtually all animals. A likely explanation is that, during sleep, important biological functions take place, restoring the biological system to better working order; this is the basis of restoration theory which we will explore on this spread. This approach makes intuitive sense because most people feel refreshed after a good night's sleep.

The alternative view is that sleep actually has no specific benefit except to conserve energy or keep an animal safe from predators; this is regarded as the evolutionary approach which is considered on the next spread.

RESTORATION EXPLANATIONS

Sleep is divided into several different stages, as we have seen earlier in this chapter. Two of the stages – **slow-wave sleep (SWS)** and **REM sleep** – are associated with particular benefits. Oswald (1980) proposed that these each had different functions – SWS enables body repair and REM enables brain recovery.

Slow wave sleep (SWS)

Growth hormone is secreted during SWS. Growth hormone (GH) stimulates growth and is therefore particularly important during childhood. It is also important in adulthood because it enables protein synthesis and cell growth to take place. This is vital in the restoration of body tissue because proteins are fragile and must be constantly renewed. This constant restoration of vital proteins is part of the body's natural recovery process.

GH is secreted in pulses through the day but a significant amount is released at night and mainly during SWS. Sassin *et al.* (1969) found that, when sleep-waking cycles are reversed by 12 hours (i.e. a person goes to sleep in the morning and gets up at night), the release of GH with sleep is also reversed. This shows that GH release is controlled by neural mechanisms related to SWS. Further evidence comes from research which found that the amount of GH released correlates with the amount of SWS (van Cauter and Plat, 1996) and the decline of GH in older age has also been associated with reduced SWS (van Cauter *et al.*, 2000).

The immune system – Lack of SWS has also been associated with reduced functioning of the immune system – the body's system of defence against viruses and bacteria (Krueger *et al.*, 1985). The immune system consists of various protein molecules – antibodies – which are regenerated during cell growth and protein synthesis in SWS.

REM sleep

Brain growth – As we saw on the previous spread, the percentage of active/REM sleep is far higher in babies than adults, and even higher in premature babies. This has been explained in terms of their rapid brain growth. It has been suggested that the amount of REM sleep in any species is proportional to the immaturity of the offspring at birth; for example the platypus is immature at birth and has about eight hours of REM sleep per day, whereas the dolphin, which can swim from birth, has almost no REM sleep (Siegel, 2003). This suggests a relationship between neural development and REM sleep.

Neurotransmitter activity may be affected by REM sleep. Siegel and Rogawski (1988) suggest that REM sleep allows for a break in neurotransmitter release which in turn permits neurons to regain their sensitivity and allow the body to function properly. Support for this comes from the action of antidepressant drugs, such as **MAOIs**. These drugs aim to increase the levels of neurotransmitters of the monoamine group (such as **dopamine** and **serotonin**). A side effect is that MAOIs abolish REM activity completely. One suggestion is that these two effects are linked – the increase in monoamines means that monoamine receptors don't have to be revitalised and therefore there is no need for REM sleep.

REM sleep and memory – For a long time psychologists have proposed a link between memory and REM sleep. For example, Crick and Mitchison (1983) proposed that during REM sleep, unwanted memories are discarded, thus making more important memories accessible. A recent explosion of research on sleep and memory has found a more complex relationship between memory and sleep (Stickgold, 2005). The evidence currently suggests that REM may be important in the consolidation of procedural memory (related to skills, such as riding a bicycle), whereas SWS sleep is important for the consolidation of semantic memory (related to knowledge and the meaning of things) and episodic memory (memory for events).

'Have you seen that weedy little rat we're using to test our new growth hormone?'

Did you know that alcohol suppresses REM sleep? This might explain why people often feel very tired after a night out drinking, despite having apparently had plenty of sleep – the lack of sufficient REM sleep leads to REM deficit and tiredness.

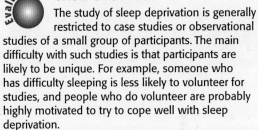

STUDIES OF TOTAL SLEEP DEPRIVATION

In order to raise money for charity, American DJ, Peter Tripp, stayed awake for a total of 201 hours, even managing to perform live during his 'wakeathon'. Three days into the experiment Tripp became unpleasant and abusive, and after five days he began to hallucinate (seeing spiders in his shoes) and to become paranoid (believing people were drugging his food). Throughout the experiment Tripp showed a continuous decline in body temperature, and by the end his waking brain-wave patterns were virtually indistinguishable from those of a sleeping person.

After 24 hours of sleep, Tripp awoke and reported himself feeling perfectly normal.

In 1965, Tripp's record was shattered by a 17-year-old American student, Randy Gardner, who managed to stay awake for an astonishing 260 hours (11 days). Unlike Tripp, he displayed no significant psychotic symptoms during his epic period of wakefulness and, like Tripp, he appeared perfectly normal after a lengthy sleep.

There are reports of individuals who have gone without sleep for years. For example, a Vietnamese man, Hai Ngoc, is reported to have stopped sleeping altogether in 1973 with no apparent ill effects.

EVALUATION

The effects of sleep deprivation

If sleep has an important restorative effect, then sleep deprivation should have clear consequences. The findings provide mixed support for this, suggesting that some kinds of sleep (REM sleep and SWS) are critical but that this is not true of all sleep

The effects of total sleep deprivation – The data has tended to be fairly anecdotal and based on individual case studies, such as those described above. The studies suggest that lack of sleep doesn't always result in long-term damage and that there is no need to recover anything like the amount of sleep that was lost. However, when participants have been deprived of sleep for more than 72 hours while being closely monitored, they invariably had short periods of **microsleep** while apparently awake. EEG recordings show that microsleep is the same as sleep (Williams *et al.*, 1959). It could be that apparent 'non-sleepers' are in fact getting the benefits of sleep while appearing to be awake.

Non-human animal studies – Various studies of non-human animals suggest that sleep deprivation may have fatal consequences. For example, Rechtschaffen *et al.* (1983) forced rats to remain physically active by rotating a disc that they were standing on every time the rat started to go to sleep. After 33 days all sleep-deprived rats died. However, it is possible that stress rather than lack of sleep was the direct cause of death. Rattenborg *et al.* (2005) conducted a similar experiment with pigeons and the pigeons suffered no ill effects.

The effects of partial sleep deprivation may lead to what is called 'REM rebound' – the need for more REM sleep after a night deprived of REM sleep. When a person is simply deprived of sleep there is not the same kind of rebound effect; it appears to be solely related to REM and SWS. To achieve REM sleep deprivation, researchers wake sleeping volunteers as soon as their eyes start to dart about. The result is that people show an increased tendency to go into REM sleep when they go back to sleep and, on recovery nights, the proportion of time spent in REM sleep increases, with this REM rebound being as much as 50% higher than normal (Empson, 2002).

SWS rebound effects have been demonstrated using acoustic stimulation which suppresses all SWS sleep by arousing a participant whenever their EEG appears to be going into deep sleep/SWS (Ferrara *et al.*, 1999).

Exercise and the need for sleep

A second consequence of 'sleep as restoration' is that increased physical exercise should lead to increased sleep in order to restore the proteins and biochemicals used, which appears to be the case in some studies. Shapiro *et al.* (1981) found that runners in a marathon race slept for about an hour more on the two nights following the race. SWS increased in particular, which fits the view that NREM sleep appears to be more associated with physical recovery.

However, in general, research has found that intense exercise does little more than make you fall asleep faster. For example, Horne and Minard (1985) gave participants numerous exhausting tasks to see if this increased their sleep duration, but it didn't. The participants went to sleep faster than usual but not for longer.

CASE STUDIES

The study of sleep deprivation is generally restricted to case studies or observational studies of a small group of participants. The main difficulty with such studies is that participants are likely to be unique. For example, someone who has difficulty sleeping is less likely to volunteer for studies, and people who do volunteer are probably highly motivated to try to cope well with sleep deprivation.

IDA — THE EVOLUTIONARY APPROACH

The main alternative to restoration theory is the evolutionary approach (discussed on the next spread). One of the strengths of the evolutionary approach is that it can account for facts that can't be explained by the restoration approach. For example, EEG studies of dolphins have found no evidence of REM sleep; if REM sleep is vital to restoration then why don't dolphins need it as well? Like dolphins, fur seals sleep one hemisphere at a time when at sea and have no REM. When back on land they switch to sleep patterns similar to those of other small mammals (i.e. their whole brain goes to sleep and they have REM sleep). Such sleep patterns may be related to the process of evolution – environmental pressures lead to differences in sleep patterns in different species.

Young (2008) suggests that the more we know about the sleep patterns of other species the more it becomes apparent that environmental pressures rather than restoration provide the key to understanding sleep.

CAN YOU...? — No.1.6

...1 Outline, in about 200 words, why restoration is the function of sleep.

...2 Identify **eight** criticisms related to restoration theory, including **at least one** IDA topic. Each criticism should be about 50 words.

...3 Use this material to write a 600-word answer to the question: *Outline and evaluate restoration explanations of the function of sleep.* (8 marks + 16 marks)

We know that sleep must be adaptive in some way, otherwise why do all animals do it despite substantial costs? Either it provides some vital biological function, as explored on the previous spread, or it provides some other benefit. Evolutionary explanations aim to suggest what other benefits might be associated with sleep. The evolutionary approach has also been called the **ecological approach**. It is called 'ecological' because it is based on observations of animals in their natural environment; 'ecology' is the study of animals in relation to their environment.

The evolutionary approach to explaining behaviour is outlined in the introduction.

EVOLUTIONARY EXPLANATIONS

Energy conservation

Warm-blooded animals (mammals), such as ourselves, need to expend a lot of energy to maintain a constant body temperature. This is particularly problematic for small animals with high metabolic rates, such as mice (metabolism refers to the chemical processes taking place in the body). All activities use energy, and animals with high metabolic rates use even more energy. Sleep, however, serves the purpose of providing a period of enforced *inactivity* (therefore using less energy) much as hibernation is a means of conserving energy. Webb (1982) described this as the **hibernation theory** of sleep.

Foraging requirements

If sleep is a necessity, the time spent sleeping may be constrained by food requirements. An animal has to gather food. Herbivores, such as cows and horses, spend their time eating plants (such as grass) that is relatively poor in nutrients. As a result, they must spend a great deal of time eating, and consequently cannot 'afford' to spend time sleeping. Carnivores, such as cats and dogs, eat food that is high in nutrients, and so do not need to eat continuously. Therefore, they can 'afford' to rest much of the time, and by resting they can conserve energy.

Predator avoidance

A further likelihood is that sleep is constrained by predation risk. If an animal is a predator, then it can sleep for longer, whereas for prey species, their sleep time is reduced as they must remain vigilant to avoid predators. Logically, to be safe they shouldn't sleep at all but if sleep is a vital function then they are best to sleep when least vulnerable.

Waste of time

Meddis (1975) was the first to propose the 'waste of time' hypothesis. He suggested that sleep helps animals to stay out of the way of predators during the parts of the day when they are most vulnerable. For most animals, this means sleeping during the hours of darkness. It also means sleeping in places where they will be hidden. According to Meddis, sleep may simply ensure that animals stay still when they have nothing better to do with their time.

Siegel (in Young, 2008) concurs with this view and points out that in fact, being awake is riskier than sleeping because an animal is more likely to be injured. Siegel's view, based on what we currently know about sleep patterns (see 'Cutting Edge'), is that the only possible explanation for sleep is that it enables both energy conservation and keeping an individual out of danger: 'in the wild, the best strategy for passing on your genes is to be asleep for as long as you can get away with … and that is exactly what you see' (Young, 2008). For example, the little brown bat is awake for a few hours each day, just when the insects that it lives on are awake. It might be expected that the bat would sleep little because it is a small mammal – but it doesn't. It is awake when it needs to be.

Evaluation PRODUCING A BETTER DATABASE

We are finding out about animal sleep habits all the time. Young (2008) reports that out of 5000 mammal species we have information about the sleep patterns of less than 150. Even this knowledge is incomplete. For example, we do not have reliable evidence of the different amounts of REM and SWS sleep, and of sleep patterns at different ages.

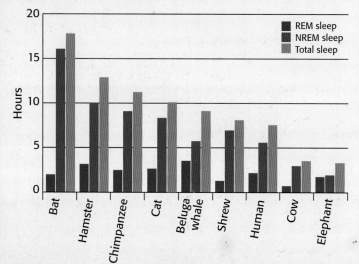

The Phylogeny of Sleep project (see www.bu.edu/phylogeny/) aims to collect data from different sources to help future understanding of sleep. The database is available for anyone to search, and highlights some of the problems with the data, e.g. it is not always reliable. In some cases there is data for one species from a number of different studies and the records are conflicting – for example the various studies of giraffes rate NREM sleep somewhere between 1.5 and 3.6 hours and REM sleep somewhere between 0.4 and 1.0 hour. The problem is that often the data is based on studies of fewer than five animals and their sleep has been studied under lab conditions where they may not be displaying natural behaviour. The animals may also have only been observed for 12 hours. The database includes information about whether data was collected in the wild or in a lab, and also rates the quality of the lab research. Until we have a fuller and more accurate record of animal sleep patterns it won't be possible to fully understand the evolution of sleep.

◀ Graph showing sleep patterns in different animals from the Phylogeny of Sleep project database.

UNILATERAL SLEEP

It isn't just sleep that is adaptive but also the pattern of sleeping. Sleep patterns differ from one species to another (although they are similar in genetically-related species). Such differences tell us something about the different **selective pressures** facing a particular species, with different sleep patterns being the adaptive response.

One example of an adaptive response is **unilateral sleep** – one hemisphere of the brain being asleep while the other is awake. This form of sleep has evolved in some marine mammals and also in migrating birds to cope with particular selective pressures. Dolphins must swim to the surface every time they need to take a breath. A dolphin that fell into a deep sleep (**SWS**) while underwater, would drown. The two hemispheres of the brain swap over about every two to three hours (Mukhametov, 1987). Migrating birds must remain awake for long periods of time when they are migrating and therefore unilateral sleep is important.

The fact that unilateral sleep has separately evolved in both of these groups of animals shows that it is a means of solving the evolutionary pressures facing these animal groups.

▲ Mallard ducks sleep with one eye open. Recordings of brain activity show that the brain hemisphere corresponding to the open eye is awake, while the hemisphere for the closed eye is in a deep sleep.

EVALUATION

Energy, foraging or predation?

Support for energy conservation
– One way to investigate the comparative costs and benefits of sleep is to compare sleep habits across different species. Zepelin and Rechtschaffen (1974) found that smaller animals, with higher metabolic rates, sleep more than larger animals. This supports the view that energy conservation might be the main reason for sleep. However, there are many exceptions, such as sloths, which are very large yet sleep for 20 hours a day.

Support for predator avoidance
– Allison and Cicchetti (1976) found that species who had a higher risk of predation did sleep less, although again there were exceptions, such as rabbits who had a very high danger rating yet slept as much as moles who had a low danger rating.

Support for foraging and predator avoidance – However, recent research by Capellini et al. (see below) suggests that the energy conservation hypothesis may be wrong, whereas the foraging and predator avoidance explanations are right.

REM and NREM sleep

When considering energy conservation there may be an important distinction between **NREM** and **REM** sleep. Interestingly the energy consumption of the brain drops only in NREM sleep; during REM sleep the brain is still relatively active. This leads to the view that it is only NREM sleep that has evolved for energy conservation, which was supported by Allison and Cicchetti (1976) who found that larger animals had less NREM sleep but not less REM sleep. This shows that it is NREM sleep that is important to energy conservation. However, the data from Capellini et al. found no correlation between body size and NREM sleep.

There is a further argument for the REM/NREM distinction. Animals that are more 'primitive', such as most reptiles, only have NREM sleep. REM sleep appears to have evolved about 50 million years ago in birds and mammals. It might be that NREM sleep evolved first for energy conservation, whereas REM sleep may have evolved later to maintain brain activity. This is supported by the greater need for REM sleep in infants whose brains are developing.

The phylogenetic signal

Perhaps the key piece of evidence for the evolutionary approach is the existence of a strong **phylogenetic signal** for sleep among mammals. 'Phylogenetic signal' means the behavioural similarities between species that are close on the phylogenetic scale (i.e. are genetically closely related). Research has found that mammalian species that are genetically close have more similar sleep patterns than would be expected by chance (Capellini et al., 2008).

IDA THE EVOLUTIONARY APPROACH

The evolutionary approach fails to address some of the key aspects of sleep, such as why we have such a strong drive for sleep when sleep deprived. Perhaps the resolution lies in a combined approach. For example, Horne (1988) proposed a theory that combines elements from both restorative and evolutionary explanations. He suggested a distinction between **core** and **optional sleep**. Core sleep is mainly SWS sleep and is the vital portion of sleep that an organism requires for essential body and brain processes. Optional sleep is mainly REM sleep and is dispensable. Horne believes that optional sleep has the function of occupying unproductive hours and, in the case of small mammals, of conserving energy.

CAN YOU...? No.1.7

...1 Provide an outline, in about 200 words, of how evolutionary explanations might account for the function of sleep.

...2 Identify **eight** criticisms related to evolutionary explanations, including **at least one** IDA topic. Each criticism should be about 50 words.

...3 Use this material to write a 600-word answer to the question: *Discuss evolutionary explanations of the function of sleep.* (8 marks + 16 marks)

Evaluation MAMMALIAN SLEEP

Capellini and her research team (2008) argued that previous research was flawed because the methods used to collect data on sleep in different animals were not standardised and therefore comparisons between species were meaningless. They carefully selected data from studies using only standardised procedures (e.g. animals habituated to lab conditions). The study focused on only land mammals because unilateral sleep in aquatic mammals involves different sleep patterns.

- They found a negative correlation between metabolic rate and sleep (smaller animals have higher metabolic rates and sleep less) which doesn't support the energy conservation hypothesis.
- However, this data supports the view that there is a trade-off between sleep and foraging – greater foraging requirements (e.g. due to higher metabolic rate or diet low in energy) creates a restraint on time available for sleeping.
- The relationship between predation risk and sleep is a complex one. Animals that sleep in exposed positions sleep less, but time spent sleeping is also reduced in species that sleep socially – yet they ought to be able to sleep longer because there is safety in numbers.

A sleep disorder is any condition that involves difficulty experienced when sleeping. One of the most common disorders is insomnia. It is not defined in terms of number of hours of sleep a person has because there are large individual differences in the amount of sleep that is 'normal' for each person. Some people who have very little sleep suffer no ill consequences whereas others who have many hours of sleep a night may feel unrefreshed and complain of insomnia.

Both length and efficiency of sleep are important. Insomnia can be transient (short term), intermittent or long term. It may involve trouble falling asleep (initial insomnia), trouble remaining asleep (middle insomnia) or waking up too early (terminal insomnia).

Insomnia affects at least 10% of the adult population, making it one of the most common psychological health complaints. Sleep deficits associated with insomnia create serious health risks, such as falling asleep while driving and accidents in the workplace.

EXPLANATIONS FOR INSOMNIA

Short-term insomnia
Some people suffer difficulties in sleeping for a short period of time – days or a few weeks. Such short-term insomnia tends to be caused by immediate worries, such as an exam or a death in the family, noises at night, jet lag or a temporary medical condition, such as a cold.

Long-term (chronic) insomnia
Chronic insomnia describes sleep difficulties lasting more than four weeks (this is the DSM definition). A distinction is then made between secondary and primary insomnia. Secondary insomnia is much more common.

Primary insomnia occurs when a person is having sleep problems that are not directly associated with any other health condition or physical cause (such as drug abuse or medications). A person may be feeling stressed or depressed but such psychological states are not the cause of the insomnia. It may be that the individual has developed bad sleep habits (e.g. staying up late) and this causes insomnia, but insomnia is the only problem. Sometimes insomnia may have had an identifiable cause but this has disappeared, yet the insomnia persists because of an expectation of sleep difficulty – in other words, the individual has come to expect that they will have sleep difficulties and these expectations lead to anxiety which then continue to cause insomnia.

Secondary insomnia is when a person is having sleep problems because of something else. There is a single, underlying medical, psychiatric or environmental cause. In such cases insomnia is a symptom of the main disorder, i.e. it is comes second, after the main disorder.

For example, insomnia is a characteristic symptom of illnesses, such as depression or heart disease. In such cases there is a medical condition first and this is the underlying cause of the insomnia experienced.

Insomnia is also typical of people who do shift work or who have **circadian rhythm** disorders, such as phase delay syndrome, where abnormal biological rhythms cause sleepiness at inappropriate times.

Older people tend to be more likely to experience insomnia because of discomfort when sleeping due to, for example, rheumatism. They also have more difficulty sleeping because of reduced deep sleep (**SWS**) and therefore are more easily awoken.

Insomnia may also be the result of environmental factors, such as too much caffeine (in coffee, tea or even chocolate) or alcohol.

Finally, other sleep disorders (parasomnias), such as sleep apnoea, can cause insomnia. Apnoea is a disorder where a person stops breathing while asleep. The pauses can last from a few seconds to minutes and might occur 5–30 times an hour, thus having a major disruptive effect on sleep. Other parasomnias include sleep walking and teeth grinding (bruxism). All such parasomnias increase the likelihood that a person will experience some loss of sleep and therefore insomnia.

TEENAGE INSOMNIA
Rachel is at high school. She feels exhausted all day and goes to bed at 10.00 pm to try to get some much-needed sleep. She reads, she writes, she gets up again. Finally at around 1.00 am she goes to sleep. Rachel is a typical example of a teenage insomniac (Kalb, 2008). Her sleep patterns suggest that her insomnia may be due to the shift in circadian rhythms which is typical of the teenage years – circadian phase disorder.

A recent study by Roberts *et al.* (2008) found that teenage insomnia is a major problem, as common as either substance abuse or depression, but given less publicity. They analysed data from over 4,000 adolescents, aged between 11 and 17, from Houston, Texas, and found that 25% of the young people had symptoms of insomnia and 5% reported that their lack of sleep interfered with their ability to function during the day. In a follow-up study of those teenagers with symptoms of insomnia, 41% were found to still have symptoms one year later. It is possible that some teenagers turn to drugs as a means of dealing with their sleep problems.

EVALUATION

Primary versus secondary insomnia

It is important to distinguish between primary and secondary insomnia because of the implications for treatment. If insomnia is a symptom of another disorder then it is important to treat the disorder rather than the insomnia. So, for example, if insomnia is the result of chronic depression it would be unhelpful to simply treat the symptom.

However, it may not be that simple to work out the cause of a person's insomnia – does depression cause insomnia or does insomnia cause depression? A study of almost 15,000 Europeans found that insomnia more often preceded rather than followed cases of mood disorders, such as depression (Ohayon and Roth, 2003). This means that, in some cases, it might be helpful to treat insomnia regardless of whether it is a primary or secondary effect.

Consequences of insomnia

The importance of understanding and being able to find ways to deal with insomnia is shown in the potentially serious, and even fatal, consequences of the disorder.

Cognitive impairment may also be a consequence, for example memory loss and poor concentration during the day. Zammit *et al.* (1999) found that patients with insomnia scored lower on the Medical Outcomes Study Cognitive Scale than control participants, demonstrating problems with concentration, memory, reasoning and problem solving.

Accidents – Sleepiness and cognitive difficulties obviously create a risk for safe driving. One study compared the performance of adults who had been deprived of one night's sleep with adults given alcohol. They found that even keeping people awake for three more hours than usual led to impairments equivalent to modest levels of alcohol (Arendt *et al.*, 2001). The National Traffic Safety Administration estimates that 1500 deaths annually are related to sleepiness/fatigue (Zammit *et al.*, 1999).

The effects of tiredness have also been linked to industrial accidents as a result of shift work (see page 17).

Psychological disturbance – As discussed above it is possible that insomnia is actually a cause of psychological problems, such as depression and anxiety disorders, rather than an effect. Breslau *et al.* (1996) found that insomnia was also associated with increased risks for drug and alcohol abuse.

Immune system underfunctioning – A Canadian study (Savard *et al.*, 2003) found fewer immune cells in the bodies of people with chronic insomnia compared with good sleepers. This would make insomniacs more vulnerable to physical illness. However, here again there is a problem with cause and effect because it could be that stress was the initial cause of insomnia and, as you know from your AS studies, stress has a negative effect on the immune system (e.g. Kiecolt-Glaser *et al.*, 1984).

A model to explain insomnia

Spielman and Glovinsky (1991) propose a useful distinction between predisposing, precipitating and perpetuating components in their 3P model of insomnia.

Predisposing factors include a genetic vulnerability for insomnia. Evidence for a genetic link comes from twin studies. For example, in one such study Watson *et al.* (2006) found that 50% of the variance in the risk for insomnia could be attributed to genetic factors. Research also suggests that physiological factors may predispose a person to develop insomnia. For example, it has been found that insomniacs are more likely to experience hyperarousal (high physiological arousal) both when awake and asleep (e.g. Bonnet and Arand, 1995). Hyperarousal would make it more difficult to get to sleep. Such factors explain why only some people develop insomnia, for example in response to stress or jet lag.

Precipitating factors are the events that trigger the disorder in a vulnerable individual. Two individuals may experience the same stressors but only one develops insomnia as a consequence because of predisposing factors. Environmental triggers for insomnia include stress at work, exams and shift work.

Perpetuating factors are also important, i.e. factors that maintain insomnia when the original causes (such as stress) have disappeared or been treated. Perpetuating factors include being tense when going to bed because of previous sleep problems. Espie (2002) suggests that such perpetuating factors are the key to chronic insomnia.

RESEARCH COMPLICATIONS

Chronic insomnia is highly complex and unlikely to be explained by one single factor. The large number of factors that may contribute to a person's insomnia makes it very difficult to conduct meaningful research because research tends to find only small effects. This means that research is unlikely to uncover clear solutions to the problem, although one possibility is described below.

IDA | **REAL-WORLD APPLICATION – THE COGNITIVE APPROACH**

One of the causes of primary insomnia is a person's belief that they are going to have difficulty sleeping. Such an expectation becomes self-fulfilling because the person is tense when trying to sleep. One clever way to treat this is a method based on attribution theory. The insomniac has learned to attribute their sleep difficulties to 'insomnia'. If they can be convinced that the source of their difficulty lies elsewhere this will end their dysfunctional attribution.

In one study, insomniacs were given a pill and told either that the pill would stimulate them or act as a sedative. Those who expected arousal actually went to sleep faster because they attributed their arousal to the pill and therefore actually relaxed (Storms and Nisbett, 1970)!

CAN YOU...? No.1.8

...1 Provide an outline of explanations for insomnia in about 200 words.

...2 Identify **eight** criticisms related to evaluation, including **at least one** IDA topic. Each criticism should be about 50 words.

...3 Use this material to write a 600-word answer to the question: *Describe and evaluate explanations of insomnia.* (8 marks + 16 marks)

On the previous spread we looked at insomnia. On this spread we examine two other sleep disorders. **Narcolepsy** is a disorder where individuals experience sudden and uncontrollable attacks of sleep at irregular and unexpected times, which may last seconds or minutes. An episode is often triggered by stressful situations. **Sleep walking** (somnambulism) is a term that covers a range of activities that take place while sleeping but are normally associated with wakefulness (such as eating, getting dressed or walking about); the person has no conscious knowledge of what they are doing.

REAL-WORLD APPLICATION

IDA

One of the things about research is that you never know when it may prove to have a real-world application. In the case of sleep walking there have been murder cases where the disorder has been claimed as a defence. The issue is whether or not the accused was actually sleep walking. In order to decide, experts on sleep walking offer their views to the court.

One such case occurred in October 2003 when a Manchester man, Jules Lowe aged 32, attacked and killed his 82-year-old father. He claimed that he had no recollection of the attack because he was sleep walking at the time.

Dr Irshaad Ebrahim, director of the London Sleep Centre, was called in to establish whether what Mr Lowe claimed was true, based on what research has told us about sleep walking.

Tests were conducted by observing Lowe while he slept. Lowe had a history of sleep walking but he had never been violent like this previously. The tests showed that he was indeed prone to sleep walking and therefore the defence case was proved.

However, there is a slight twist to the case because the judge ruled that the sleep walking (automatism) was caused by 'insanity' and therefore Lowe was sent to a psychiatric hospital for an indefinite period of time.

Adapted from http://news.bbc.co.uk/1/hi/england/manchester/4337309.stm

EXPLANATIONS OF NARCOLEPSY

Psychological explanations

A very early approach to explaining narcolepsy focused on psychological issues. For example, Lehrman and Weiss (1943) suggested that sudden attacks of sleepiness disguise sexual fantasies.

REM

One of the classic symptoms of narcolepsy is loss of muscle tone (called 'cataplexy'). This is similar to what happens during **REM sleep**. In addition, during the daytime, narcoleptics often experience intrusions of REM-type sleep (hallucinations). At night narcoleptics have abnormal REM sleep. Therefore, in the 1960s an explanation offered for narcolepsy was that it was caused by a malfunction in the system that regulates REM sleep.

HLA

In the 1980s research pointed in a new direction, suggesting that narcolepsy was linked to a mutation of the immune system. Honda *et al*. (1983) found increased frequency of one type of HLA (human leukocyte antigen) in narcoleptic patients. HLA molecules are found on the surface of white blood cells and coordinate the immune response. Recent research has found that more than 90% of people suffering from narcolepsy with cataplexy have been found to have the HLA variant HLA-DQB1*0602 (Stanford Medical Center, 2012). It is not clear how HLA would lead to narcolepsy, although one possibility is discussed on the facing page.

Hypocretin

Most recently, research has uncovered another link, this time between a neurotransmitter and narcolepsy. The neurotransmitter is **hypocretin** (also called orexin). Hypocretins regulate sleep and wakefulness through interactions with systems that regulate emotion and homeostasis in the hypothalamus (Sakurai, 2007). Normally there are about 10,000–20,000 hypocretin-producing cells in the hypothalamus but in many narcleptics a large number of these cells are missing, resulting in low levels of hypocretin.

EXPLANATIONS OF SLEEP WALKING

Incomplete arousal

Sleep walking is a disorder of arousal – a person who is sleep walking is partly awake in the sense that they are engaged in activities normally associated with the waking state, but they are also asleep. Most importantly, the kind of sleep they are in is deep sleep (called slow wave sleep, **SWS**), which means that it is very difficult to rouse the sleep walker.

Recordings of brain activity made during sleep walking show a mixture of the delta waves which are typical of SWS, plus the higher frequency beta waves which are characteristic of the awake state. So it looks as if sleep walking occurs when a person in deep sleep is awakened but the arousal of the brain is incomplete.

Risk factors

Certain factors appear to increase the likelihood of sleep walking – such as sleep deprivation, alcohol, having a fever, stress or psychiatric conditions (Plazzi *et al*., 2005). Hormonal changes during puberty and menstruation may also be triggers for sleep walking. The fact that risk factors trigger sleep walking in only some people (for example not everyone sleep walks when they have a fever) suggests that some individuals may have an inherited vulnerability for sleep walking.

Why children?

Many explanations have to been offered to explain why sleep walking is more common in childhood. One possibility is that it happens because children have more SWS than adults. A recent suggestion by Oliviero (2008) is that the system that normally inhibits motor activity in SWS is not sufficiently developed in some children, and it also may be underdeveloped in some adults. This was demonstrated in a study reported by Oliviero that examined the motor excitability of adult sleepwalkers during wakefulness. Compared to normal controls, the sleepwalkers had signs of immaturity in the relevant neural circuits.

EVALUATION

[handwritten: based on genetic biological environmental factors ignored]

REM

The REM explanation was supported by Vogel (1960) who observed REM sleep at the onset of sleep in a narcoleptic patient, whereas it more commonly occurs later in the first cycle of sleep stages. This was further supported by recordings of neuron activity in the brainstem of narcoleptic dogs. This showed that cataplexy (lack of muscle tone) co-occurred with brain cell activity that usually only occurs in REM sleep (Siegel, 1999). However, in general research support has not been convincing.

HLA

The specific HLA variant (HLA-DQB1*0602) found most commonly in narcoleptics is not found in all narcoleptics. The same HLA variant is also reasonably common in the general population (Mignot *et al.*, 1997). Both of these facts mean that the HLA variant cannot be the only cause.

Hypocretin

Evidence of lower levels – The first evidence for hypocretins came from narcoleptic dogs who were found to have a mutation in a gene on chromosome 12. This mutation had the effect of disrupting the processing of hypocretin (Lin *et al.*, 1999). The findings from narcoleptic dogs have been confirmed in human studies, for example it was found that human narcoleptics had lower levels of hypocretin than normal in their cerebrospinal fluid (Nishino *et al.*, 2000). This supports the view that lower levels of hypocretin play a role in narcolepsy.

What causes low levels of hypocretin? Despite the evidence from dogs, it appears that hypocretin loss in humans is only rarely due to a gene. Generally narcolepsy doesn't appear to be inherited. This is indicated by the fact that human narcolepsy doesn't run in families and, in cases where one twin has the disorder, it has not been found in the other twin (Mignot, 1998).

It is more likely that lower levels of hypocretin are due to brain injury, infection, diet, stress or possibly the result of an autoimmune attack (where the body's immune system turns on itself rather than fighting external infection). *[handwritten: antibodies itself]*

Linking hypocretin to HLA – The autoimmune explanation could explain the involvement of HLA in narcolepsy. Mutations of HLA affect the immune response, making autoimmune conditions more likely. This may result in reduced numbers of hypocretin cells (Mignot, 2001).

[handwritten: Nature vs Nurture]

[handwritten: hormone + immune system; only mentions bio not other factors; reductionist]

EVALUATION

Genetic basis

There is evidence that the tendency to sleep walk may be inherited. For example, Broughton (1968) found that the prevalence of sleep walking in first-degree relatives (i.e. parents, siblings and children) of an affected subject is at least 10 times greater than that in the general population. Twin studies have also been used; Lecendreux *et al.* (2003) report about 50% **concordance** in identical (MZ) twins compared to 10–15% in DZ twins, and also have identified a gene that may be critical in sleep walking (the DQB1*05 gene).

Diathesis-stress model

The diathesis-stress model proposes that genes merely provide a vulnerability (diathesis) for a disorder but the disorder will only occur in situations of environmental 'stress'. In the case of sleep walking this seems likely. For example, Zadra *et al.* (2008) studied 40 patients who were referred to a sleep lab for suspected sleep walking. In the sleep lab the participants were prevented from falling asleep. On the first night 50% of the sleepwalkers had showed signs of sleep walking, which rose to 90% on the second night. Sleep deprivation does not lead to sleep walking in normal individuals. Therefore, the sleep deprivation was acting as a 'stressor' in individuals who had a vulnerability for sleep walking.

[handwritten: more vulnerable]

The diathesis-stress model can also be used to explain the higher frequency of sleep walking in children. The higher levels of SWS in childhood acts as a diathesis, so that children are more likely than adults to have episodes of sleep walking. *[handwritten: things that make us more vulnerable]*

Psychological cause unlikely

One belief about sleep walking is that, in some way, it results when a person acts out dreams representing repressed traumas and anxieties. However, the fact that sleep walking occurs during deep (**SWS**) sleep means it is unlikely to be associated with dreaming.

REAL-WORLD APPLICATION

The fact that low hypocretin levels are implicated as a cause of narcolepsy suggests that a cure is obvious – give sufferers a dose of hypocretins. Unfortunately it is not that easy because the hypocretin molecule is relatively unstable. If given by mouth or injection it is broken down before it reaches the brain. Therefore, researchers are currently trying to create an artificial drug to replace the missing hypocretin in the brains of narcoleptics.

However, even this won't result in a cure because the condition is merely controlled by continuously taking the drug; the condition has not ended. It is possible, in the future, that transplanting hypocretin-producing cells may result in a cure (Center for Narcolepsy, 2011).

▲ The classic image of a sleepwalker is eyes closed, arms outstretched and walking – in fact a sleepwalkers' eyes are invariably open and sleep walking is a term that covers any activity characteristics of the awake state, such as sitting up in bed, getting dressed, looking out of a window and so on. In other words, it doesn't just involve walking.

CAN YOU...? No.1.9

...1 Outline explanations of narcolepsy in about 200 words.

...2 Outline explanations of sleepwalking in about 200 words.

...3 Identify **four** criticisms related to explanations of narcolepsy, including **at least one** IDA topic. Each criticism should be about 50 words.

...4 Do the same as in question 3 for the explanations of sleep walking.

...5 Use this material to write a 600-word answer to the following questions:

Discuss explanations of narcolepsy. (8 marks + 16 marks)

Discuss explanations of sleep walking. (8 marks + 16 marks)

CHAPTER SUMMARY

BIOLOGICAL RHYTHMS

CIRCADIAN RHYTHMS

SLEEP-WAKE CYCLE
- Circadian = 24 hours.
- Cycle persists despite isolation from light.

EVALUATION
- Participants not isolated from artificial light in early research.
- Demonstrated by Siffre and Aschoff and Weaver.
- External cues important too (Folkard et al.)
- Cycle length varies in individuals.

CORE BODY TEMPERATURE
- Lowest at 04:30; highest at 18:00.
- Post-lunch dip, even without food.

EVALUATION
- Linked to cognitive abilities (Folkard et al., 1977).
- Evidence that change is caused by temperature (Giesbrecht et al., 1993).
- Other research suggests link is spurious.

HORMONES
- Cortisol – lowest at midnight.
- Melatonin and growth hormone highest at midnight.

IDA
- Biological and determinist.
- Real-world application – chronotherapeutics.

INFRADIAN AND ULTRADIAN RHYTHMS

ULTRADIAN RHYTHMS
- Less than one day.
- Sleep stages: first four stages = NREM.
- Fifth stage = REM.
- BRAC = 90 minutes within 24-hour rhythm.

EVALUATION
- REM does not equal dreaming.
- BRAC important because it ensures biological processes work in unison.

INFRADIAN RHYTHMS
- Female menstrual cycle regulates ovulation.
- Males have 20-day cycle of body temperature and alertness.
- SAD – caused by melatonin during winter months.

EVALUATION
- Menstrual cycle also subject to exogenous cues.
- Some women suffer from PMS.
- SAD could also be consequence of disrupted circadian rhythms.

IDA
- Determinist (e.g. PM) but can change through willpower (Born et al.).
- Real-world application – phototherapy.

ENDOGENOUS PACEMAKERS AND EXOGENOUS ZEITGEBERS

ENDOGENOUS PACEMAKERS
- SCN – main endogenous pacemaker.
- SCN contains protein mechanism.
- Pineal gland controls melatonin secretion.

EVALUATION
- SCN evidence – 'mutant' hamsters (Morgan, 1995).
- Desynchronisation leads to symptoms similar to jet lag.

EXOGENOUS ZEITGEBERS
- Light is dominant zeitgeber.
- Social cues also important.
- Biological rhythms can be entrained by temperature.

EVALUATION
- Artificial lighting may also reset biological clock.
- Failure of biological clock leads to sleep-phase disorders.
- Biological clock is really a blend of endogenous and exogenous factors.

IDA
- Evolutionary approach – SCN lesions in chipmunks (deCoursey et al.).
- Non-human animal studies evaluated in terms of ethics and relevance.

SLEEP

LIFESPAN CHANGES

CHILDREN
- Babies sleep 16 hours a day, but not continuously.
- Babies have shorter sleep cycles than adults.
- Circadian rhythm established at six months.
- Age 5, sleep patterns like those of adults, but sleep longer.
- May experience parasomnias.

EVALUATION
- Sleep differences in babies – adaptive (for parents), and due to immature brain.

ADOLESCENCE
- Need for sleep increases (9–10 hours a night).
- Circadian rhythms change – slight phase delay.

EVALUATION
- Changes may be linked to hormone production.
- Implications for school day.

ADULTHOOD AND OLD AGE
- Increase in sleep disorders (e.g. insomnia).
- Pattern of sleep changes in old age (reduction of REM and SWS).
- Older people experience phase advance effect.

EVALUATION
- Increased mortality rate with too much sleep (Kripke et al., 2002).
- Sleep deficit in old age may explain impaired functioning in other areas.

IDA
- Developmental approach, emphasising changes in sleep patterns.
- Cultural bias – cultual differences overlooked.
- Real-world application.

RESTORATION EXPLANATIONS

SWS
- SWS = Stages 3 and 4.
- Growth hormone (GH) secreted during SWS.
- Decline of GH in older age because reduced SWS.
- Lack of SWS = poor immune functioning.

REM
- Important for brain growth.
- Important for restoring neurotransmitter sensitivity.
- Link between REM and procedural memory.

IDA
- Evolutionary approach – Young (2008) suggests that environmental pressures rather than restoration is a better explanation of why we need to sleep.

DISORDERS OF SLEEP

EXPLANATIONS FOR INSOMNIA   OTHER SLEEP DISORDERS

DISRUPTION OF BIOLOGICAL RHYTHMS

SHIFT WORK AND SHIFT LAG
- Nightworkers experience 'trough' of decreased alertness.
- Sleep deprivation due to sleeping problems during day.
- Relationship between shift work and organ disease.

EVALUATION
- Shift work effects not solely due to disruption of biological rhythms.
- More problems with rotating shifts, but forward rotating less harmful.
- Artificial lighting can reset rhythm (Boivin et al., 1996) but not dim lighting (Gronfier et al., 2007).

JET TRAVEL AND JET LAG
- Jet lag caused by disruption of circadian rhythms.
- Phase delay less disruptive than phase advance.
- Demonstrated in performance decrement studies (e.g. Recht et al., 1995).

EVALUATION
- Jet-lag symptoms may be caused by other factors associated with air travel.
- Melatonin may reduce symptoms.
- Social customs (e.g. eating at right time) also help.
- Individual differences exist in coping with disruption.

IDA
- Real-world application, e.g. artificial lighting.

SHORT-TERM INSOMNIA
- Caused by e.g. worry, noises at night, jet lag, temporary medical conditions.

LONG-TERM INSOMNIA
- Primary insomnia – not associated with any medical condition, e.g. due to bad sleep habits.
- Secondary insomnia is a symptom of a medical disorder, such as depression or heart disease, or some other issue, such as shift work, too much caffeine or other sleep disorders.

EVALUATION
- Diagnosis has implications for treatment, although may be a cause rather than effect (Ohayon and Roth, 2003).
- Consequences include cognitive impairment (Zammit et al., 1999), accidents (as potentially detrimental as alcohol, Arendt et al., 2001), psychological disturbance (may cause depression, anxiety disorders, Breslau et al., 1996) and immune system underfunctioning (Kiecolt-Glaser et al., 1984).
- Spielman and Glovinsky (1991) proposed predisposing factors (e.g. genetics), precipitating factors (e.g. environmental stressors) and perpetuating factors (e.g. expectations).

IDA
- Real-world application – the cognitive approach and attribution retraining.

EXPLANATIONS OF NARCOLEPSY
- Psychological, e.g. disguising sexual fantasies.
- Early explanations – failure of REM regulation.
- HLA mutation causes reduced immune system function.
- Low levels of neurotransmitter hypocretin in hypothalamus, affects wakefulness.

EVALUATION
- REM hypothesis – some evidence (e.g. Siegel, 1999) but not convincing.
- HLA variant cannot be sole explanation because common in general population.
- Hypocretin support from studies of dogs (Lin et al., 1999) and humans (Nishino et al., 2000).
- Low levels of hypocretin rarely inherited, most likely due to e.g. brain injury or autommune attack.
- Link to HLA.

IDA
- Real-world application – treatment with manufactured hypocretin.

EXPLANATIONS OF SLEEP WALKING
- Person wakes during SWS but brain arousal incomplete.
- Other factors – sleep deprivation, alcohol, hormone changes.
- May affect children more because underdeveloped SWS inhibition.

EVALUATION
- Evidence for genetic basis, e.g. DQB1*05 gene (Lecendreux et al., 2003).
- Diathesis-stress model, e.g. Zadra et al. (2008) found sleep deprivation triggers sleep walking in vulnerable individuals.
- Psychological cause unlikely because not in REM sleep.

IDA
- Real-world application – accepted as defence in some crimes.

EVOLUTIONARY EXPLANATIONS

EVALUATION
- Total sleep deprivation studies suggest no long-term damage, although case studies anecdotal (e.g. Peter Tripp).
- Non-human animal studies, e.g. Rechtschaffen et al. (1983).
- Partial sleep deprivation leads to rebound.
- Exercise leads to increased sleep (Shapiro et al., 1981) or just faster (Horne and Minard, 1985).

- Results from animals may not generalise to humans.

ENERGY CONSERVATION
- Sleep provides a period of inactivity to conserve energy, essential for animals with high metabolic rates.

FORAGING
- Herbivores spend less time sleeping; carnivores more, because food rich in nutrients.

PREDATOR AVOIDANCE
- Sleep constrained by predation risk. Predators sleep more, prey less.

WASTE OF TIME
- Sleep may simply be a way of staying still at times when an animal cannot forage and would be subject to predation.

EVALUATION
- 'Evidence about animal sleep patterns incomplete (Phylogeny of Sleep project).
- Evidence suggests that species with a higher metabolic rate sleep more (Zepelin and Rechtschaffen, 1974).
- Evidence suggests that species with higher predation risk sleep less (Alison and Cicchetti, 1976).
- Evidence from Capellini et al. (2008) supports foraging and predator avoidance.
- NREM evolved first for energy conservation, then REM to maintain brain activity.
- Phylogenetic signal supports evolution of sleep patterns.

IDA
- Evolutionary approach can be combined with restoration using core and optional sleep (Horne, 1988).

EXAM QUESTION WITH STUDENT ANSWER

QUESTION Discuss research relating to the disruption of biological rhythms. *(8 marks + 16 marks)*

STUDENT ANSWER

There are three kinds of biological rhythm: circadian rhythms that occur around a day, such as the sleep-wake cycle; ultradian rhythms that occur more than once a day, such as the stages of sleep and infradian rhythms that occur with less frequency, such as the menstrual cycle. All these rhythms are governed by a combination of internal mechanisms and external cues.

Many aspects of modern-day life disrupt these rhythms and cause considerable problems. It is reckoned that most major industrial accidents are caused at night which is due to the fact that people are not fully awake because they are doing shift work. For example, the Bhopal accident occurred at night and so did the Exxon Valdez disaster. It is also true that many car accidents occur at night.

When people work shifts they usually do a shift for a few days at a time. One effect of this is that shift workers become sleep deprived because they have to sleep during the day when it is light outside and more noisy. Another effect of shift working is that people become ill, for example they develop heart disease. In one study they found that individuals who worked shifts for more than 15 years were three times more likely to develop heart disease.

However, the effects of shift work may be due to factors aside from the disruption of biological rhythms. For example, shift work disrupts the pattern of family life. People who work shifts are sleeping when everyone else is awake and this may cause stress in the family. Some of the effects of shift work may be reduced if rotating shifts are used, which is an example of phase delay. A further way to improve the effects of shift work is to use pulses of bright light, as shown in a study by Gronfier et al. (2007) to entrain circadian rhythms and therefore avoid longer periods of desynchronisation.

Jet travel, like shift work, is likely to disrupt biological rhythms and lead to desynchronisation which is experienced as jet lag. The symptoms of jet lag include feeling disoriented, nauseous, tired or depressed. In fact these same symptoms are felt whenever the body's clocks are desynchronised. Jet lag is caused when a large change of time zones means that some of the body's clocks change with the exogenous cues, such as daylight, whereas other body clocks are slower to change (although they could be changed by strong light).

Evidence to demonstrate the effects of these changes comes from travelling baseball teams in America. Some of them travel from the east coast to the west coast, or vice versa, to play games. According to the belief that phase delay should be easier we would expect the teams that have a delay to do better – the teams that go from east to west. This is what the study found. This is a natural experiment, which means that we cannot draw causal conclusions from it. However, it is supported by other research.

Suggested treatments to alleviate the consequences of jet lag include the use of bright lights and also melatonin to induce sleepiness, although it is important that melatonin is taken just before bedtime or otherwise it may have a detrimental effect.

The importance of this research lies in finding ways to reduce the effects of shift work and jet lag because of the potential dangers to individuals and society at large. Our society needs shift work and jet travel so the problems are not going to go away. One thing to bear in mind, however, is that there are important individual differences. Some people are less badly affected than others by desynchronisation. One explanation is that the people who cope better are those whose rhythms are slower to adjust so they experience less desynchronisation.

[631 words]

EXAMINER COMMENTS

This introductory paragraph is a form of scene-setting but not actually relevant to the question here. It is best to avoid wasting precious examination time.

The second paragraph describes evidence relating to the disruption of biological rhythms. Research isn't specifically cited but underlies the points made, so **limited**.

This paragraph contains further description which is **detailed and accurate**. Notice, at the end of the paragraph, how a research study has been used as part of the description. No names have been given for this study; such information increases the **'detail'** of the answer (an important AO1 criterion) but there is no penalty for omitting names.

Evaluation is provided by considering other explanations for the effects, and also considering methods of reducing some of the negative effects. The evaluation provided is **sound** and the material is **coherently elaborated (AO2 criteria)**. The **line of argument** could be made clearer if specific links were made, for example pointing out how stress in the family might lead to heart disease.

Jet travel and jet lag offer a chance to further describe the effects of disruption and desynchronisation, demonstrating a good **understanding** of a **range of relevant material**.

In this paragraph research has been used as evaluation on the effects, providing **AO2** material. It is important to focus on what this research shows rather than getting too bogged down in the details of the actual study. More **AO2** opportunities can be taken by considering the methodology of the studies which is also important evidence of **IDA**.

The final paragraphs provide further evaluation (**AO2**), including a consideration of the real-world application and the effect of individual differences (an 'issue'), providing additional **IDA**.

The answer is **well-structured** and **ideas are expressed clearly**. The **line of argument** is weak at the outset but improves throughout the essay.

AO1 – Sound, **accurate** and **well-detailed**.
AO2/AO3 – Reasonable analysis and line of argument but lacks elaboration in places and therefore **not effective**. **Evidence of IDA** but IDA is rather **basic**.

Chapter 2
Perception

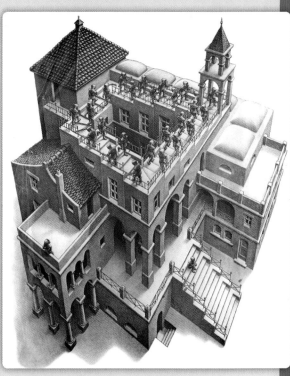

▲ An impossible drawing by M.C. Escher –
see www.mcescher.com for more of the same.

SPECIFICATION

Perception	
Theories of perceptual organisation	• Gregory's top-down/indirect theory of perception. • Gibson's bottom-up/direct theory of perception.
Development of perception	• The development of perceptual abilities, including depth/distance, visual constancies. • Perceptual development, including infant and cross-cultural research.
Face recognition and visual agnosias	• Bruce and Young's theory of face recognition, including case studies and explanations of prosopagnosia.

▲ **The hollow face illusion** – this rotating mask of Charlie Chaplin turns from being convex on the left (with features pointing towards you), to concave on the right (features pointing inwards). When we look at a hollow, concave mask it is almost impossible not to see it as convex. The reason for this is that we have such a strong tendency to 'see' faces, that our perceptual system overrides the depth information presented to us. This also explains why people often see things like a man's face on the surface of the moon.

You can see an excellent demonstration of the effects at Michael Bach's illusion site www.michaelbach.de/ot/ – look at the rotating face mask.

31

What can you see in the picture on the left? Most people can pick out the outline of a Dalmatian dog – which is strange because there is no outline. (If you can't see it, don't worry, because some people can't.)

Our visual system has a tendency to organise information so that we see patterns. The question is whether this is a **bottom-up process**, meaning that perceptions are based solely on the data received at our eyes. An alternative view is that perception is a **top-down process** – our mind generates expectations about what we are looking at and these expectations help us make sense of the mass of information that reaches our eyes.

On this spread we will start by looking at one example of a top-down theory of perception – Richard Gregory's indirect theory.

GREGORY'S INDIRECT THEORY (1974)

Gregory (1974) believed that perception is a process of construction. We construct our perceptions by combining the physical information received by the eye (direct data) with stored knowledge in the brain. Therefore, perception is indirect because it relies on the addition of this stored knowledge.

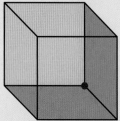

▲ **The Necker cube.** Is the red dot near you or further away?

The Necker cube illusion is an example of 'hypothesis testing'. The image suggests two possible hypotheses – the yellow face with red dot is either in front, or the dot is behind. There are no other clues to help resolve this so the yellow face moves in and out.

The hollow mask
When you see the inside of a mask, it still looks as if the features are sticking out (see page 31).

Perception as hypothesis formation

According to Gregory, perception is based on three things (1) sensory data, (2) knowledge stored in the brain and (3) an inference or hypothesis about what is out there. Your brain develops hypotheses in order to make sense of incoming sensory data. The picture on the right illustrates this process. What we 'see' is not a direct consequence of the stimulus input (three cars identical in size), but the end product of an interaction between the original stimulus, internal expectation (the same object seen at a greater distance should have a smaller **retinal image**) and inferences/hypotheses. This process is necessary, according to Gregory, because the brain must make inferences about the external environment based on frequently inadequate information supplied by the senses.

▼ The cars appear as if they are different in size but if you measure them with a ruler, you will see that they are exactly the same. They appear different because depth cues (such as overlap) create expectations of distance. We expect the same object to appear smaller when it is more distant, and adjust for this in working out the visual scene. Even when you know it is not there, it is impossible not to perceive a size difference.

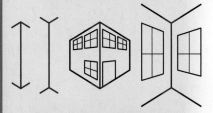

▲ **The Müller-Lyer illusion**
The two lines on the left are equal in length, but the first one appears shorter. Gregory (1990) suggested that this illusion occurs because of our experience with depth cues. The first line on the left is like the edge of a building and the second line is like the corner of a room. Our experience of the world tells us that the edge of the building is closer to us than the rest of the building and experience also tells us that the corner of the room is further away. If we view an object in the distance it produces a smaller **retinal image** than if we view the same object nearby. Therefore, the distant image represents something which is actually larger/longer. When we view the Müller-Lyer illusion our brain automatically adjusts the apparent size of the more distant object so that the second line looks longer.

The role of previous knowledge and expectation

The key element in this process of indirect perception is the knowledge stored from past experience, which produces expectations and hypotheses, and which in turn affect perception. One classic example of this was in a study by Bruner *et al.* (1951). Researchers showed false playing cards to participants (e.g. red clubs or black hearts). The participants expected black clubs or red hearts, so their perceptual systems coped by 'seeing' cards that were purple or brown, showing that expectations distorted their perceptions.

For the most part expectations produce accurate perceptions. For example, when you view a table, the image received by the eye is rarely rectangular but, because of your expectations, you 'see' a rectangular table.

Visual illusions

According to Gregory's theory, the formation of incorrect hypotheses or expectations leads to errors of perception, such as visual illusions. Visual illusions are not magic, they are quite lawful and can be explained in terms of indirect perception. The illustrations on the left show some common illusions and possible explanations for them. Gregory suggests that many visual illusions are the result of 'misapplied hypotheses', hypotheses that normally work in the 'real' world but have been misapplied. For example, converging lines are usually correct in informing us about which objects are closer or further away. These cues are used by artists when producing two-dimensional drawings of the three-dimensional world.

AUDITORY EXPECTATIONS

If you happened to listen to Led Zeppelin's song, *Stairway to Heaven*, backwards you would probably hear just a jumble of sounds (listen at jeffmilner.com/backmasking.htm). However, if you are told that there is a message saying 'Oh here's to my sweet Satan. The one whose little path would make me sad, whose power is Satan', that is probably what you would hear. Listen again and you will hear the message!

Of course there is no message, but once you expect to hear it, you will find it impossible to undo the effect of your expectations. Visit Jeff Milner's Backmasking website the hear other examples of apparent hidden messages in songs.

Evaluation **THE ROLE OF EXPECTATION**

Support for the role of expectations in perception comes from a study by Palmer (1975). Participants were shown contextual scenes (such as a kitchen) and then shown either an appropriate object (a loaf), a similar object (a mailbox – which looks like a loaf) or a different object (a drum – which does not look like a loaf). When shown a mailbox, participants frequently reported they saw a loaf. Their stored knowledge about what they would expect to find in a kitchen led them to form (in this case) an erroneous hypothesis about the object they were viewing. This effect was not evident when the object *conflicted* with the expectation, for example when shown a drum. This shows that expectations have a strong influence over what we see, supporting Gregory's theory.

EVALUATION

Research evidence

Hypothesis testing – Once a hypothesis has been formed it may be tested against reality; in fact that is how infants develop their perceptual abilities. Khorasani *et al.* (2007) found that the Müller-Lyer illusion had less effect once participants knew about the illusion. However, Shopland and Gregory (1964) found that visual reversals of the Necker cube were not prevented when participants handled a three-dimensional self-luminous model in a dark room. This suggests that hypothesis-testing may sometimes, but not always, contribute to the end perception.

The role of previous knowledge and expectation has been demonstrated in many experiments, such as Palmer's demonstration of the role of context (see above). This has been described as perceptual set because expectations prepare us to have a 'set' or fixed view of what we will see. For example, Bruner and Minturn (1955) showed that the digits 1 and 3 will be perceived as the letter B if displayed within a set of letters, but as the number 13 if seen as part of a set of numbers.

Visual illusions offer the main support for Gregory's theory. They show that tricks of perception can be explained in terms of misapplied hypotheses based on usual relationships between objects. Gregory's explanation of the Müller-Lyer illusion has received support from cross-cultural research. For example, Segall *et al.* (1963) found that people who do not live in 'carpentered' environments (e.g. they live in round huts) are less likely to perceive differences in the length of the two lines of the illusion. They would not be used to seeing the edges of buildings or the corners of rooms.

Strengths and limitations

Strengths – The indirect approach can explain the way our perceptual system deals with ambiguous situations, or situations where the retinal image is poor. Prior experience provides possible solutions (hypotheses). This approach to perception can help in the design of computer systems that can 'see' the world, because such systems have to cope with situations where the sensory input is ambiguous and/or incomplete, and therefore must be programmed to draw on 'experience'.

Limitations – Indirect theory is criticised because it is based largely on the study of perception in artificial settings and therefore fails to explain much of our real-world perception.

Another criticism is that the theory fails to explain why we continue to see visual illusions even when we know our brain is misleading us. New hypotheses should be formed which override our erroneous perceptions.

Finally there is a lack of precision regarding the key concepts. The notion of perceptual hypotheses may appear to make sense, but there are a number of unanswered questions. For example, Marr (1982) asked what determines which information is selected from the retinal image?

IDA **REAL-WORLD APPLICATION**

Our understanding of the effect of expectations is important in questioning what we think we are seeing. Here's an example from real life – in 1988 the US naval ship USS Vincennes launched a guided missile which shot down an Iranian plane killing 260 people. A military investigation blamed the radar operators aboard the Vincennes who had mistakenly convinced themselves that the plane they saw in their radar was an enemy plane. Once they had formed that perception, they interpreted the plane's flight as a direct threat to the Vincennes and were convinced that it intended to attack it (*New York Times*, 1988).

EXAM TIP: *You can use the theory of direct perception (described on the next page) as a means to evaluate Gregory's theory – but proceed with caution. If you say 'by contrast with this theory we can consider an alternative theory', and then continue to describe the second theory, this will not attract much credit as evaluation. You must use the alternative theory to highlight the strengths and/or limitations of your original theory.*

CAN YOU...? No.2.1

...1 Identify **four** key points related to Gregory's top-down/indirect theory (including examples).

...2 Use these points to write a 200-word description of the theory.

...3 Identify **eight** criticisms related to Gregory's theory, including **at least one** IDA topic. Each criticism should be about 50 words.

...4 Use this material to write a 600-word answer to the question: *Discuss Gregory's top-down (indirect) theory of perception.* (8 marks + 16 marks)

GIBSON'S BOTTOM-UP/DIRECT THEORY OF PERCEPTION

The bottom-up or direct approach suggests that the information received by the senses is sufficient for us to perceive the world around us, whereas the top-down or indirect approach suggests that this information is insufficient on its own. According to the direct approach, expectations may have a role in perception but they are not necessary. James Gibson's view was that perception, quite simply, is the detection of information. His theory of direct perception originated from the work he carried out training pilots during World War II. He found that all the information a pilot required to land an aircraft was in the total pattern of light that reached the eye: there was sufficient information from the horizon line, the runway outline, ground texture, apparent movement and so on to be able to land a plane (Gibson *et al.*, 1955).

EXAM TIP: *The specification describes Gibson and Gregory's theories as 'theories of perceptual organisation'. So, if a question says 'Discuss **one** theory of perceptual organisation' it means write about **one** of these two theories.*

▲ This picture demonstrates texture gradient, suggesting distance – objects that are more distant are less detailed and smaller.

▲ The **horizon-ratio relation**. In the picture above man number 1 appears to be the same actual size as man number 2. According to the direct theory of perception this is because their horizon-ratio is the same. Man number 3 is the same actual size as man number 1 but appears to be tiny because the horizon-ratio is different from that of the two other men.

GIBSON'S DIRECT THEORY (1979)

The optic array

Gibson (1979) suggested that the changing pattern of light that surrounds the active perceiver (the **optic array**) provides us with sufficient information for perception. The optic array is the bundle of light rays that moves towards the observer from each point in an illuminated world.

Optic flow – As we move towards a point in our visual environment, objects that are directly in front of us appear stationary (i.e. they represent a fixed point), but objects to the side appear to move towards us (the **optic flow**). The further away something is from that fixed point, the more rapid the apparent movement towards us.

The importance of movement – In order to collect this perceptual information, the perceiver has to move around the environment.

Ecological aspects of perception – Gibson believed that we cannot fully understand how our visual perception works unless we study how it operates in the real environment. For example, most objects in our visual world have texture, and the grain of this texture appears to get finer as you get further away from these objects. This produces a **texture gradient**, with closer objects having a coarser gradient and objects further away having a finer texture. As we move towards an object, its texture density changes, becoming coarser, and we are able to pick up this information from the optic array and use it to judge our distance from the object.

The role of invariants in perception – Gibson believed that whereas some aspects of the environment change as the observer moves around, other aspects do not change. These unchanging 'invariants' supply us with information that is crucial for accurate perception. The fact that changes in texture are associated with changes in distance is an invariant feature of visual perception. Another invariant feature is the **horizon-ratio** relation. In the illustration on the left you can see that man number 1 and man number 2 both show the same proportion of their bodies above and below the red horizon line. The ratio above and below the horizon line is a constant for objects of the same size standing on the same ground.

◄ The optic flow.

Making sense of the optic array

The optic array provides information, but how do we make sense of that information?

Resonance – Perceptual information is 'broadcast' in the environment in the same way that radio waves are broadcast. An animal 'tunes in' to particular aspects of the environment, just like a radio is tuned into radio waves. Both the animal and the radio *resonate* to the source i.e. pick up the signal. Perception, according to Gibson, is simply picking up information from the environment around us. **Resonance** is how we make sense of the broadcast information.

Affordance – Gibson argued that the meaning of an object can be directly perceived and this meaning communicates action potential i.e. it tells you what you can do with the object. For instance, some objects are shaped in a way that makes them look like 'seats', as in the case of a flat stone of a particular height. As a result we are more likely to sit on a flat stone than do anything else with it. Similarly a handle on a door is there for grasping. In Gibson's language the flat stone '*affords* sitting' and the handle '*affords* grasping'. The term **affordance** is the *potential* for action offered by objects; they *afford* opportunities for particular action. The concept of affordance further links perception and movement (action).

The usefulness of perception – Gibson believed that the purpose of perception is not simply the detection of information; it is the detection of *useful* information. This is why the concept of affordance is so important – the fact that objects have affordances enables an animal to respond in an appropriate or **adaptive** way to its environment.

Neisser's cyclic model – Neisser (1976) proposed a model that would involve bottom-up and top-down processes. Perception starts with the **retinal image** (data-driven) which generates a set of expectations about what things are likely in this environment. This generates a 'perceptual model' and the environment can then be searched for confirming evidence. However, in reality such a perceptual cycle would be slow and thus unlikely.

Different kinds of perception – A second way to reconcile top-down and bottom-up processes is to recognise that each are appropriate in different circumstances. Top-down processes are particularly important in ambiguous conditions, such as those created by dim lighting. Bottom-up processes operate when the optic array is rich, as in broad daylight.

What and where systems – Data is processed in the visual cortex in two separate routes or 'streams'. The so-called *ventral stream* runs from the visual cortex (area of the brain that receives sensory data) along the base of the brain. It deals with object recognition, while the *dorsal stream* (a route running along the top of the brain) deals with spatial perception and movement of objects. Norman (2002) suggests that there are strong parallels – object recognition (ventral) involves memory processes i.e. is top-down, whereas spatial perception (dorsal) is more immediate, direct and bottom-up.

WWW

A great example of biological motion can be found at www.youtube.com/watch?v=Ob BRkifC2sM

EVALUATION

Research evidence

Biological motion is the visual system's innate ability to detect movement information from sparse input and an example of how perception occurs from **ecological** data only. Johansson (1973) provided good evidence to demonstrate this. He strategically placed small lights on different parts of a person's body and filmed the lights as the person moved. Participants were able to perceive motion simply from a changing array of dots. Even young babies and non-human mammals responded appropriately when shown the sequences, suggesting this is an innate ability (Fox and McDaniel, 1982; Blake, 1993).

Time-to-contact is another aspect of perceptual performance that provides support for the idea of direct perception. 'Time-to-contact' is the ability to judge what responses need to be made when approaching an object so that, for example, you avoid colliding with someone. Such judgements can be made using visual (direct) information only. Lee *et al.* (1982) demonstrated this by videotaping long jumpers. As they approached take-off, their stride length varied, so that their final take-off footfall position was correct. Gannets (seabirds) can also account for speed in their dives into water from varying heights; they close their wings at a constant time before contacting water (Lee, 1980). These studies show that direct visual information can provide important perceptual data.

Innate perceptual abilities – On the next spread in this chapter you will find out about infants' perceptual abilities. For example, Gibson and Walk (1960) found that infants and animals perceive depth innately, thus supporting the direct explanation of perception.

Explaining visual illusions – A strength of Gregory's indirect approach is that it can explain visual illusions, but Gibson's direct theory can also explain them. For example, the Ames room illusion (see right) has been explained in terms of top-down processing (expectations about rectangular rooms) but could also be explained in terms of horizon-ratio relation because the illusion persists even without walls and floor.

Visual illusions can also be explained in terms of direct perception. For example, Wraga *et al.* (2000) found that there was no Müller-Lyer effect when participants walked around a three-dimensional display. This shows that movement is important in perception because a static display leads to the illusion. See also the Ames Room explanation on the right.

Strengths and limitations

Direct perception correctly highlights the richness of information in the optic array, and undoubtedly explains some aspects of perception. However, the theory can't explain the influence of situation and culture (as shown by studies of expectation).

The theory may explain perception from the point of view of a species' history (how perceptual abilities evolved) but not from an individual's perspective – how would an individual from the African bush know that a red pillar box affords posting a letter? Affordances inevitably involve some **top-down processes**.

▲ The Ames Room illusion makes one person look small because the room is cleverly distorted. Although the floor appears level, it is actually at an incline (the far left corner is much lower than the near right corner). So we misperceive the depth cues in this picture because our brain interprets the room as normal. However, when the walls, floor and ceiling are omitted (on right) the illusion persists. Seckel and Klarke (1997) suggest this is because of the *horizon-ratio relation*. In the absence of any horizon information we assume the horizon runs across the picture (as it also does in the Ames Room). This means that the ratio of both figures above and below the horizon is different, and therefore they do not appear to be the same size.

NATURE AND NURTURE
The question about whether perceptual abilities are largely due to nature or nurture underlies Gregory and Gibson's theories. Gregory's theory suggests that perception can be explained in terms of experience (nurture) whereas Gibson's theory is related to innate mechanisms (nature). Research on pages 36–41 can be used to support these two positions.

REAL-WORLD APPLICATION
The concept of affordance has been successfully applied to the development of autonomous robots, which are able to learn about the meaning of objects in their environment and use them appropriately (Şahin *et al.*, 2007).

CAN YOU...? No.2.2

...1 Identify **four** key points related to Gibson's bottom-up/direct theory (including examples).

...2 Use these points to write a 200-word description of the theory.

...3 Identify **eight** criticisms related to Gibson's theory, including **at least one** IDA topic. Each criticism should be about 50 words.

...4 Use this material to write a 600-word answer to the question: *Discuss Gibson's bottom-up/direct theory of perception.* (8 marks + 16 marks)

PERCEPTUAL DEVELOPMENT: INFANT STUDIES

To what extent are our perceptual abilities **innate**? Are we born with perceptual abilities, such as depth perception and the perception of constancies, or do they develop through experience? **Nature** or **nurture**? One of the ways to resolve this question is to look at infants' perceptual abilities, to see what they can and can't do from birth.

EXAM TIP: The specification requires you to study perceptual development and four subtopics are identified – the development of depth perception and visual constancies based on both infant and cross-cultural studies. This means you need to be prepared for a variety of different exam questions. You might, for example, be asked about infant studies of perceptual development or about research related to the development of depth perception.

INFANT STUDIES

Depth perception

Monocular cues – Responsiveness to dynamic cues appears earlier than to static cues. Dynamic cues are cues such as **motion parallax** (objects that are closer move more quickly across our field of vision) which rely on movement, whereas static cues, such as **occlusion** (when one object blocks another it appears closer), are depth cues viewed from a stationary position. In the classic study by Gibson and Walk (1960) (see far right) the most probable cue used by the infants was motion parallax. Hofsten *et al.* (1992) demonstrated the use of motion parallax in three-month-old infants, using the **habituation method** – this means showing an infant a display until the infant gets used to it (habituates). If the same display is shown again, the infant should show less interest than when looking at a novel display. In this study the infants habituated to a display of three rods while being moved about in a chair. The three rods were at the same distance but the middle one was moved in synchrony with the infant so it created a motion parallax effect. The infant was then shown two further displays – one of three rods at the same distance from the infant and the other with the middle rod further away (matching the effect of the motion parallax). The infants showed more interest in the three equidistant rods (a new display as far as the infant was concerned), demonstrating that they had the ability to use motion parallax. Responsiveness to static cues appears later, for example Granrud and Yonas (1984) found that the response to the depth cue of occlusion developed around the age of six months.

Binocular cues – The use of **retinal disparity** (the closer an object is to the viewer, the more separate the image is viewed from our two eyes) was tested in infants by presenting different information to each eye, so an image appeared three-dimensional (Bower *et al.*, 1970). Infants as young as one week old responded by trying to grasp the object, thus demonstrating fairly precise depth perception based on retinal disparity.

Age-related changes were demonstrated in a study by Yonas *et al.* (2001) testing whether human infants use shadows as a cue to depth. Infants were shown two toys, both equidistant from them but one appeared to be closer because of added shadows. The infants also had one eye covered to remove binocular information for depth. Older infants (average age 30 weeks) were more likely to reach towards the apparently closer toy than younger infants (average age 21 weeks), suggesting that the ability to use shadows as a cue to depth develops with age.

▶ An illustration of visual constancy. A door looks like a door from any angle.

Visual constancy

Shape constancy – Bower (1966) used an **operant conditioning** technique where infants received a reward when they viewed one object; therefore they should prefer that object in future (preference was indicated if the infant turned its head, measured by pressure sensors on the infant's headrest). Infants aged about two months were conditioned to prefer a rectangle that was slanted at a 45-degree angle: the retinal image this creates looks like a trapezoid. The infants were then shown a variety of other objects, either a rectangle (same objective shape but different retinal image) or a trapezoid (new objective shape but same retinal shape). The infants preferred the rectangle, demonstrating shape constancy.

Size constancy was studied by Slater *et al.* (1990) using the habituation method. Each newborn infant was shown a series of different-sized cubes to habituate them to the cubes. Infants were then shown two cubes side-by-side, the larger one more distant so that both cubes had the same retinal size. All infants looked longer at the cube they were *not* familiarised with, indicating they recognised this as novel. These findings showed that the infants differentiated between the cubes despite the fact that they looked the same size, therefore displaying size constancy.

Pattern perception

A fascinating area of research concerns face recognition in infants. Newborn infants have been found to show a preference for a face-like pattern rather than a non-face pattern (see page 40). They also generally show a greater interest in images that are more complex. For example, Brennan *et al.* (1966) showed infants checkerboard patterns of increasing complexity (2 × 2, 8 × 8 or 24 × 24 squares). One-month-old infants preferred the simple stimulus, whereas three-month-olds preferred the most complex one. The youngest infants do not have sufficient **visual acuity** to see the smaller squares in a 24 × 24 display, but the preference of the older infants indicates a preference for more complex visual stimuli.

THE VISUAL CLIFF

Eleanor Gibson (wife of James) and her colleague Richard Walk (1960) devised the **'visual cliff'** technique and demonstrated that 6-month-old infants would refuse to crawl to their mothers if they had to cross an apparent cliff edge. Gibson and Walk also found that day-old chicks and goats avoided the deep side. The researchers concluded that this showed that depth perception was innate.

However, the infants tested had plenty of sensorimotor experience and so may have learned to use depth cues. Support for Gibson and Walk comes from Campos *et al.* (1978) who placed 2-month-old infants on the deep side of the visual cliff and found that their heart rate was slower than when on the shallow side, indicating interest and thus awareness of the change in depth.

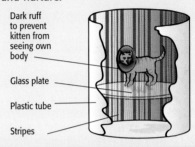
EVALUATION

The research described on this spread certainly seems to suggest that many key perceptual abilities are present at birth or, if they are not present, they appear through maturation in the months after birth. This supports the view that perception is innate and largely a **bottom-up process**.

However, there are some perceptual abilities which appear later and do not appear to be due to maturation, as we will now consider.

Perceptual completion is one of these perceptual abilities. Often we have to bridge gaps in our retinal image, and this enables us to 'see' objects which are not actually there, as illustrated below. Newborn infants cannot do this. One example is the Kanizsa square.

Ghim (1990) found that infants could not detect the Kanizsa square at the age of two months. Newborn infants can detect angular relationships but they appear unable to integrate the separate angular features into the shape of a square until three months.

▶ **Perceptual completion**.
A Kanizsa's square (it appears as if a white square were in front of four black circles).
B The yellow lines are 'seen' as continuing behind the black line.
C The occlusion of one playing card by another – we still 'see' two separate cards.

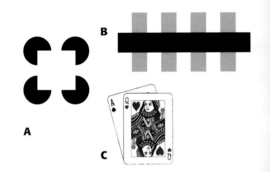

Occlusion (a monocular depth cue) is also an example of perceptual completion. When infants are shown two objects, such as two playing cards, where one is in front of the other, they act as if it is just one object. Only by around two months do they appear to perceive that the objects are separate (Slater *et al.*, 2002).

The importance of research on perceptual completion is that it supports the **top-down** theory of perception – perceptual completion requires knowledge of object properties to see a whole item, even when part is hidden. However, bottom-up theorists would argue that the ability to 'see' hidden parts is not a perceptual process, instead it is part of cognitive development (the development of thinking). This means that the distinction between top-down and bottom-up approaches may lie in deciding what counts as perceptual development and what counts as cognitive development.

CAN YOU...?   No.2.3

...1 Describe, in about 200 words, **two** infant studies related to depth perception and **two** infant studies related to visual constancy.

...2 Identify **eight** criticisms related to infant studies, including **at least one** IDA topic. Each critiscm should be about 50 words.

...3 Use this material to write a 600-word answer to the question: *Outline and evaluate infant studies of the development of perceptual abilities.* (8 marks + 16 marks)

Dark ruff to prevent kitten from seeing own body

Glass plate

Plastic tube

Stripes

STUDYING INFANTS

The assessment of infant abilities is hampered because they lack the ability to point at things or the ability to report what they are seeing. This means that researchers have to devise some ingenious methods to be able to detect what an infant is perceiving, such as the habituation method described on the left, or the visual cliff above. We cannot be certain that the results gathered by using such techniques are reliable. For example, using the habituation technique, we assume that increased interest is due to novelty, but increased interest might be due to subtle cues communicated by the experimenter. Infants may be especially susceptible to **experimenter bias**. Another problem is that lack of reaction may be due to the infant getting sleepy rather than being habituated.

Infants also have very poor visual acuity (the ability to focus) – newborns can only clearly see the top line of an eye test chart (tested using the visual preference technique). This makes one wonder what they are actually seeing when tested with relatively detailed pictures. This might of course mean that they are more capable than they appear to be.

Infant studies are one way to conduct research into the question of whether our perceptual abilities are explained mainly by **nurture** or by mainly by **nature**. A second way to investigate this question is to look at the perceptual abilities of people who live in different environments to see how their environmental experiences (a naturally varying **independent variable**) might alter the development of their perceptual abilities. If perceptual abilities are largely **innate**, then we should expect people living in different environments to develop in the same way. In fact, since the eye and brain are at the root of visual perception, we would expect people the world over to be the same in terms of their perceptual abilities.

▼ A strange illusion is created by rotating an object that looks like a window but which is a trapezium rather than a rectangle. The window appears to swing back and forth instead of going around. This illusory effect occurs because past experience leads the visual system to assume that the window is rectangular, and shape constancy leads us to expect the shortest edge to always be the one furthest away. Since it is in fact a trapezium, sometimes the shortest edge is actually closer but appears further away, which makes it appear to swing.

WWW You can view this illusion at www.exploratorium.edu/exhibits/trapezoidal_window/trap_window.html

CROSS-CULTURAL STUDIES

Depth perception

Forest dwellers – The anthropologist Colin Turnbull published the following description of what happened when a BaMbuti pygmy from the Congo, used to living in the dense Ituri forest, went with him to the plains: 'And then he saw the buffalo, still grazing lazily several miles away, far down below. He turned to me and said, "What insects are those?" At first I hardly understood, then I realised that in the forest, vision is so limited that there is no great need to make an automatic allowance for distance when judging size…. When I told Kenge that the insects were buffalo, he roared with laughter and told me not to tell such stupid lies.' (Turnbull, 1963). This suggests that Kenge's lack of experience with perspective led to his inability to use cues for distance perception to interpret size.

Testing the use of pictorial cues – Hudson (1960) studied the influence of culture on depth perception using Bantu, European and Indian children in South Africa. The children were shown a set of drawings, each with an antelope, an elephant, and a man with a spear (as in the illustrations on the right). In each of these drawings the spear is pointing at both the antelope and the elephant, but depth cues (such as **occlusion**, **linear perspective** and object size) suggest where it is *actually* pointing. The results showed that at the beginning of primary school all children had difficulty using these depth cues. By the end of primary school, nearly all of the European children were able to correctly interpret the depth cues in the drawings. However, some Bantu children still tended to see the pictures as two-dimensional, being unable to interpret the depth cues.

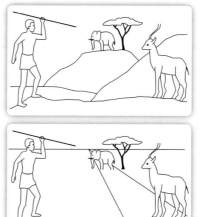

Visual constancies

Shape constancy – Allport and Pettigrew (1957) tested Zulu people in South Africa with the trapezoid window illusion (above). The Zulus living in rural areas did not have rectangular windows, and so it was expected that they would be less likely to experience the illusion, indicating that shape constancy had not been learned. This was exactly what the study found. In contrast, Zulus living in urban areas (who had experience of rectangular windows) responded in a similar way to Europeans.

Size constancy – Gregory claimed (see page 32) that the Müller-Lyer illusion can be explained in terms of misapplied hypotheses. Segall *et al.* (1963) provided support for this in a study again involving Zulu participants. These people, at the time, lived in mostly circular huts and therefore would not have learned the depth cues proposed to explain the Müller-Lyer illusion. Theirs was a round rather than a 'carpentered' world. As expected, Segall *et al.* found that the Zulus were less affected by the illusion than were Europeans and Americans.

PICTORIAL DEPTH PERCEPTION

Jahoda and McGurk (1974) devised a task to test depth perception. The participants were shown pictures of two silhouettes (one woman and one child where one was in the foreground and the other was in the background – see illustrations on right). Depth was indicated by the use of linear perspective and/or **texture gradient**. Sometimes the figures were the same actual **retinal size** and sometimes they were different in size. In the middle distance of the picture there was always a small bird.

Next, the participants were given a square board with a small bird in the middle. For each picture they were asked to place appropriately sized wooden models in their correct position. They might, for example, place a woman in the foreground and a girl in the background if that was the way they interpreted the picture.

The study tested children from Ghana and Scotland and found: (1) the more depth cues available, the better the children did in interpreting the pictures; (2) older children from both countries did better than younger children; (3) overall the Scottish children were more accurate than the Ghanaian children, but Jahoda and McGurk concluded that results did not support the view that Ghanian children are deficient in perceiving pictorial depth.

▶ Pictures used by Jahoda and McGurk, with texture gradient only (right, above) or texture gradient plus linear perspective (right, below).

METHODOLOGICAL PROBLEMS IN CROSS-CULTURAL RESEARCH

There are a number of problems inherent in cross-cultural research. For example, researchers may use tests or procedures that have been developed in one country/culture and are not valid in the other culture. This may make the individuals in the other culture appear 'abnormal' or inferior. The term that is used to describe this is an **imposed etic** – when a technique or psychological test is used (i.e. imposed) in one culture even though it was designed for use in another culture. In the case of research on perceptual abilities, an example of an imposed etic is the use of the trapezoid illusion to test people unaccustomed to three-dimensional pictures. Their lack of ability to 'see' the illusion could be explained by the fact that the means of testing shape constancy made no sense to them, rather than because they had not learned shape constancy.

A second limitation is that the group of participants may not be representative of that culture, and yet generalisations may be being made about the whole culture – or even the whole country.

A further difficulty concerns communication. We cannot be sure that participants and investigators, who rely on translators, have fully understood each other. It is possible, for example, that Turnbull misinterpreted what Kenge said to him.

Finally, much of cross-cultural research is rather anecdotal in nature, and poorly controlled. Such studies are also **natural experiments** where it is not reasonable to conclude that the independent variable (environment) has *caused* the difference in perceptual abilities but can only conclude that there is an association between experience and ability.

However, this does not mean that all cross-cultural research is useless. It provides us with many interesting insights. What we must remember is to treat the evidence with a degree of scepticism.

EVALUATION

The 'classic' cross-cultural studies described on the left suggest that experience does affect perceptual abilities – an environmental explanation, supporting the nurture position. However, subsequent research in the 1970s and 1980s found fewer cross-cultural differences, as in the study by Jahoda and McGurk (at the bottom of this spread). It is possible that the early work was mistaken.

Research methods

Language – Page (1970) changed the question used by Hudson from 'Which is nearer to the man, the antelope or the elephant?' to 'Which is nearer to *you*, the antelope or the elephant?'. The result was that Zulu participants demonstrated better abilities to perceive depth in the pictures.

Pictorial interpretation – The reason some participants may have performed poorly on the tests of depth perception is not because they didn't understand the depth cues, but because they found it difficult to understand a two-dimensional picture. Deregowski (1989) proposed that there is an important distinction between *epitomic* and **eidolic** images. Epitomic illustrations (such as silhouettes) provide no information about depth, whereas **eidolic** illustrations look three-dimensional even when they are impossible figures (such as the two-pronged trident on the right). Deregowski suggested that Hudson's pictures are more epitomic, whereas the task used by Jahoda and McGurk is more eidolic, and this explains why there were more three-dimensional responders on Jahoda and McGurk's task. For example, the task used texture gradients to communicate depth which is a 'stronger', more easily interpreted depth cue.

Effects of experience

In fact the study by Jahoda and McGurk is not in total opposition to the classic studies on the left, because correct interpretation of depth cues was found to increase with age, which suggests that experience matters but to less of an extent than originally believed. One reason is that *some* depth cues are innate (and therefore don't require experience) whereas others are actually cultural forms of expression, i.e. they are conventions developed by one culture. One example of this is the use of linear perspective, where parallel lines are depicted as meeting in the distance. This is a technique that artists started to use in fifteenth-century Europe to show depth in pictures. It is true that parallel lines converge, but only at infinity, and the horizon of our visual field is rarely at infinity (Berry *et al.*, 2002). The fact that some cultural groups find it difficult to interpret certain depth cues may well be related to experience, but it is not experience of depth cues in the real world but experience of using culturally relative depth cues in pictures.

▼ Two-pronged trident – an impossible figure.

A BIOLOGICAL APPROACH

Since perception is a physical process it might be assumed to be the same across cultures. However, the pigmentation of the retina has been found to vary with skin colour and is linked to difficulties in perceiving edges of objects. High pigmentation, found in African people, could explain why they are less likely to 'see' certain visual illusions. Some evidence has supported this retinal pigmentation hypothesis (e.g. Berry, 1971) but overall, environmental explanations have been preferred.

NON-HUMAN ANIMAL RESEARCH

Our understanding of perceptual development has also involved research using non-human animals (for example the study by Blackmore and Cooper on the previous spread). The findings from such research support human infant and cross-cultural studies. However, there are two main issues connected with the use of non-human animals. First of all there are ethical issues – animals in perceptual deprivation experiments may not suffer pain but they are left permanently impaired. The second issue relates to generalisability – non-human animal perceptual may not function the same as human perceptual systems because human behaviour generally is more influenced by cognition.

CAN YOU...? (No.2.4)

...**1** Describe **two** cross-cultural studies related to depth perception and **two** cross-cultural studies related to visual constancy in about 50 words for each study.

...**2** Identify **eight** criticisms related to cross-cultural studies, including **at least one** IDA topic. Each criticism should be about 50 words.

...**3** Use this material to write a 600-word answer to the question: *Outline and evaluate cross-cultural studies of the development of perceptual abilities.* (8 marks + 16 marks)

Y ou may be one of those people who is poor at recognising faces that you have seen before – but it probably never occurred to you that this may be due to a brain disorder! Well, probably not a disorder but a mild disability. Some people do have a disorder (called **prosopagnosia**) that results in a total inability to recognise faces. The fact that people appear to have a separate ability with respect to face recognition – they can recognise complex patterns but not faces – suggests that there is a separate part of the brain that exclusively deals with face perception. However, not all psychologists share this view, as we will see on this spread.

Groucho Marx: 'I never forget a face but I'll make an exception in your case.' (Quoted in the Guardian, 18 June 1965)

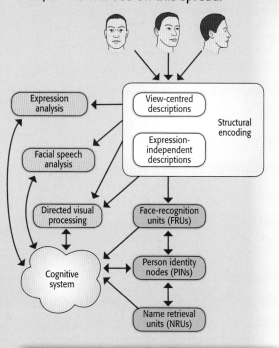

BRUCE AND YOUNG'S THEORY (1986)

Vicki Bruce and Andrew Young developed one of the most widely accepted models of face recognition. The model (see diagram on the left) essentially presents face recognition as a series of stages which are accessed one after the other (serially). At any time only some of the units (or 'nodes') are activated. There are also two paths through the model – one for familiar faces (blue boxes) and one for recognising facial expressions (yellow boxes). The model applies only to face recognition rather than general object recognition or word recognition.

Structural encoding

The process starts with structural encoding. The details of a person's face are encoded or translated into specific information about the features and about the expressions on the person's face. This information is then sent to a range of different units (coloured blue and yellow in the diagram).

Recognising familiar faces

One route through the model is concerned with the recognition of familiar faces. Face recognition units (FRUs) contain information about the faces you know. If the encoded information has a reasonable match with this information then the FRU is activated and triggers the next node, the person identity node (PIN). PINs contain information about a person's identity, such as their occupation, their interests and so on. Once a person's identity is established, then a person's name can be retrieved (name recognition unit, NRU).

Because this is a serial access model, names can only be accessed once the person has been identified; there is no direct link from face to name. This is consistent with the fact that people rarely remember a name without knowing any personal identity information, whereas the opposite is common (knowing something about a person but finding it hard to remember their name). Activation of any of these three nodes may draw on the cognitive system to decide whether the match is close enough to constitute recognition or merely a 'resemblance'.

Other aspects of face processing

The second (yellow) route of the model is concerned with the other kinds of information provided by faces, such as information about emotional state or information related to what a person is saying. Data from structural encoding is used to work out the meaning of facial expressions (expression analysis node), to use lip movements to help understand what someone is saying (facial speech analysis) and process other facial information (directed visual processing).

This route is used when dealing with unfamiliar faces, which accounts for the finding that some people with brain damage can match familiar faces but not unfamiliar faces (Malone *et al.*, 1982).

The cognitive system

All of the units/nodes (coloured in blue and yellow in the diagram above) are linked to the cognitive system (green) which provides information as required, for example information about stereotypes (e.g. actresses tend to be attractive) or information about the people we know (e.g. who you are likely to see at your local shopping centre).

This 'facial preference' finding has been replicated in a number of studies, such as Goren *et al.* (1975) (although the preference may be due to a liking for things that are symmetrical). If face preference is innate it makes sense because such a preference would have adaptive significance – a newborn who can recognise and respond to its own species will better elicit attachment and caring.

THE INVERSION EFFECT

Evaluation People find it more difficult to recognise a person's face when it is upside down (inverted), despite the same features being present. This is not true of object recognition, and suggests a unique face processor. An amusing example of this is the **Thatcher effect** (Thompson, 1980). The picture of the former Prime Minister Margaret Thatcher (below) looks fine, until you view it the right way up. The explanation is that when a face is upside down, **configural processing** cannot take place (processing where features viewed are related to each other rather than feature-by-feature detection). This means that minor feature differences are more difficult to detect and supports the notion of a unique face processor.

However, Diamond and Carey (1986) proposed an alternative hypothesis. It could be that people have become specially tuned in to seeing faces in an upright orientation, and our face expertise disappears when a face is inverted. This was supported by a study where people who were dog experts (e.g. dog-show judges) and non-dog experts, judged photos of dogs. The dog experts recognised upright photos of dogs better, showing that the inversion effect is probably the result of expertise rather than a special face processor.

EVALUATION

Research evidence

Bruce and Young's model was based on research. For example, Young *et al.* (1985) conducted a diary study where they asked 22 participants to keep a record of the mistakes they made when recognising people over an eight-week period. They found that many errors involved recalling information about a person but not recalling their name, but never recalling a name without some relevant personal identity information. The pattern of these errors is explained by the serial nature of the model (PIN comes before NRU).

Other research has also supported the model, for example Young *et al.* (1986) found that, as predicted, participants were faster at identifying whether a particular face was that of a politician than they were at identifying the politician's name.

However, not all subsequent research has confirmed the model's predictions. For example, Stanhope and Cohen (1993) found that participants could retrieve the names for faces despite having no information about personal identity (PIN).

Strengths and limitations

The main strength of the model is that it generates precise predictions that can be tested, and that can further our knowledge of face recognition. The model also spells out the differences in the way familiar and unfamiliar faces are processed. However, the details of unfamiliar face processing are vague, and other components of the model, such as the cognitive system, are also not clearly specified.

An updated model

Burton and Bruce (1993) extended the original model, developing the *IAC model* (interactive activation and competition network). This is a **connectionist** model proposing that face recognition involves a large number of nodes (FRUs, PINs, etc). These nodes have complex connections between them rather than being a set of serially-linked units. One strength of this model is that it matches the way the nervous system acts – with lots of interconnected neurons that fire when activated by sufficient incoming links.

Are faces 'special'?

The big question concerns whether face recognition is actually a separate skill or just an example of object recognition in general. The Bruce and Young model is irrelevant if face recognition is not special.

***Face recognition* is special** – One line of support comes from infant preferences for faces (see far left). Another line of support comes from studies of people with prosopagnosia, described on the next spread. A further line of support is that it makes sense to have a dedicated face processor because face recognition has such important social functions, for example recognising an enemy or recognising one's child. Decoding facial expressions is also important in adaptive terms to understand emotion.

The final source of support comes from recent neurophysiological studies which have used scanning techniques and found that the *fusiform face area (FFA)* is active when processing faces, but not as active when identifying other objects, especially in the right hemisphere (e.g. Sergent *et al.*, 1992, Kanwisher and Yovel, 2006).

***Face recognition* isn't special** – Findings related to the FFA have not all supported unique face processing. For example, Gauthier *et al.* (2000) found that the FFA was also active when experts were asked to distinguish between different types of bird or different types of car, and also if they were trained to be experts in distinguishing between computer-generated nonsense figures called *Greebles*.

It may be that expertise is what activates the FFA – a similar conclusion to that reached by Diamond and Carey (above); face processing may simply be a form of expert object recognition. Pike and Brace (2005) concluded that the processes involved in face recognition are not unique – but this may not be the end of the story … which continues over the page.

▲ Margaret Thatcher may look the same in both pictures, but try viewing the page upside down. What does this tell you about face perception?

CAN YOU...? **No.2.5**

...1 Identify **five** key topics related to Bruce and Young's theory and write about 40 words for each.

...2 Identify **eight** criticisms related to Bruce and Young's theory, including **at least one** IDA topic. Each criticism should be about 50 words.

...3 Use this material to write a 600-word answer to the question: *Describe and evaluate Bruce and Young's theory of face recognition.* (8 marks + 16 marks)

AN EXAMPLE OF VISUAL AGNOSIA: PROSOPAGNOSIA

Prosopagnosia is a form of **visual agnosia** where an individual typically can describe a person's face and its expression but cannot recognise whose face it is unless they use other non-facial information, such as hair, gait, clothing or voice. A common complaint of prosopagnosics is that they have trouble following the plot of movies, because they cannot keep track of the actors' identity. Despite their difficulty with face recognition, prosopagnosics can usually recognise objects.

The study of prosopagnosia is valuable for two reasons. It can help our understanding of the normal process of face recognition and can also help identify the regions of the brain involved in face recognition.

▶ People with prosopagnosia cannot recognise familiar faces – the features are identifiable but the whole configuration makes no sense. In extreme cases patients have even failed to recognise themselves.

Visual agnosia

Visual agnosia refers to being able to see things but not recognise them; the visual cortex functions normally but the person cannot extract meaning from what they see. Sigmund Freud (1891) was the first person to recognise that such disabilities were not due to faulty vision but rather to some malfunctioning of the brain.

Traditionally visual agnosias have been divided into apperceptive and associative agnosia. Apperceptive agnosia is related to an inability to perceive the form of the object. Patients are typically unable to draw the object, match objects or describe component parts. Associative agnosia is a failure that occurs at a later stage in the object recognition process. In contrast with apperceptive agnosia, patients with associative agnosia can draw objects, match similar objects and describe the component parts. However, they cannot associate these details with stored knowledge about the objects in order to recognise them.

There are other kinds of agnosia related to other senses, such as tactile agnosia (inability to recognise objects by touch) and auditory agnosia (inability to recognise sounds).

CASE STUDIES OF PROSOPAGNOSIA

Inability to recognise faces – Cases of prosopagnosia that solely involve a lack of face recognition (object recognition is intact) are rare. However, Busigny *et al.* (2010) studied one such case, a 52-year-old woman (PS) injured in a bus accident. An MRI scan showed damage to the lateral part of the occipital and temporal lobes in both hemispheres. She was unable to recognise familiar faces, even her own face in photographs – but sometimes she managed to appear as if she could by using peripheral cues, such as haircut or glasses, as well as a person's posture and voice. She had no difficulty recognising objects, scoring in the normal range on tests of object recognition.

Inability to recognise both faces and objects – Much more common are cases of prosopagnosia where, in addition to problems with face recognition, a patient also has varying levels of difficulty with object recognition. For example, Delvenne *et al.* (2004) studied NS, aged 40, whose brain was damaged in a cycling accident. An MRI scan showed damage to both sides of his brain in the occipito-temporal junction area. After his accident NS was unable to recognise either faces or objects. His colour perception and acuity remained perfect and he could perform some object and face recognition tasks normally, such as identifying an unfamiliar target face from a selection of faces. He also did not experience the inversion effect (**Thatcher effect**).

Partial face recognition ability – There are a number of cases where prosopagnosic individuals have some ability to recognise faces. Bruyer *et al.* (1983) reported the case of Mr. W., a farmer who could recognise his individual cows and dogs but could not recognise people. Mr. W. could answer questions about individual facial features and could match unfamiliar faces (shown an unfamiliar face and asked to select a matching face from a selection). He couldn't, however, match photos of familiar faces and couldn't recognise himself in a video recording.

EXPLANATIONS OF PROSOPAGNOSIA

Acquired versus developmental – Most case studies relate to individuals with brain damage (acquired prosopagnosia). However, in some individuals prosopagnosia is present from birth and may even be inherited (i.e. has a genetic explanation). Duchaine *et al.* (2007) studied 10 family members who showed deficits on tasks requiring face memory and judgements of facial similarity, although they performed normally on facial emotion recognition tasks. The family members also had some difficulties with object recognition. Prosopagnosia was once thought to be a rare disorder, but Duchaine and Nakayama (2006) report that about 2% of the population is affected by developmental prosopagnosia.

Damage to a face processing unit – Case studies of acquired prosopagnosia have been able to identify the region of the brain that is damaged by using brain scanning techniques. The patient PS (see above) was worthy of particular study because she experienced difficulties solely with face recognition. fMRI scans of her brain indicated that damage to the FFA and OFA (*fusiform face area* and *occipital face area* located in the temporal and occipital lobes) in the right hemisphere underlies prosopagnosia (Rossion *et al.*, 2003). This suggests that face and object recognition have different causes.

Holistic processing failure – Farah (1991) suggested that object recognition, alexia (inability to recognise text) and prosopagnosia are not three independent conditions. She proposed instead that they all lie on a continuum. At one end of the continuum is the ability to decode structure (feature analysis, a kind of **configural process**). At the other end is the ability to compute relationships among the parts (a **holistic process**). Prosopagnosia results from problems with the latter, alexia is an example of problems with the former, difficulties with object recognition lie across both. This suggests that inability to decode faces is simply a characteristic of one end of the object recognition continuum and not an independent disorder.

EVALUATION

Case studies

Methodological issues – Evidence from case studies such as those on the facing page is very important for our understanding of prosopagnosia. However, there are many criticisms of such research, some of which are explained on the right.

Contradictory evidence – It is difficult to reach firm conclusions from case studies because there are contradictions. For example, it appears that, unlike Mr. W., some prosopagnosic farmers cannot recognise their individual cows (Assal *et al.*, 1984) or individual sheep (McNeil and Warrington, 1993).

Explanations

Support for a unique face processor – Some case studies of acquired prosopagnosia suggest that there is a unique face processor. This has been supported by research with developmental prosopagnosia. Garrido *et al.* (2009) used brain scanning techniques to compare the responses of 17 people with developmental prosopagnosia with responses from control subjects. Analysis showed a weaker response in prosopagnosics' FFA when shown faces.

Evidence challenging unique face processor view – Most prosopagnosic patients have difficulty with both face and object recognition. This has led researchers to propose that prosopagnosia is merely an extreme case of failure to recognise objects. Humphreys and Riddoch (1987) argue that faces are complex objects and therefore require more skills for recognition. This means that we would expect to find patients with severe face recognition problems but minimal object recognition difficulties, but not vice versa. This is generally what has been found.

Greebles – On the previous spread we looked at the argument that face recognition was just an example of expert object identification, which was tested using Greebles. Duchaine *et al.* (2006) tested a developmental prosopganosic, Edward. He was found to perform normally on a Greeble training task. Therefore, Duchaine *et al.* concluded that there is a brain region specific to face recognition.

Holistic processing failure – This is supported, for example, by the absence of susceptibility to the inversion effect in many prospagnosics (Busigny and Rossion, 2010). However, there is some evidence that holistic processing failure is not universal in prosopagnosics. For example, HJA showed some evidence of holistic abilities (Groome, 2006) yet face inversion did not affect his performance (Boutsen and Humphreys, 2002).

Furthermore, Busigny and Rossion (2011) tested the patient PS on a task to assess global versus local processing (called the Navon task where you are shown a large letter such as 'A' composed of lots of small Bs, and asked to identify the large letter (a global task) or the smaller letters (a local task)). They found that global functioning was intact. This suggests that lack of face recognition is not related to a failure at the level of holistic processing in general.

Supports Bruce and Young's model – There are interesting links between different cases of prosopagnosia and the Bruce and Young model. For example, Edward (see above) could describe a face but could not remember information about a face, therefore his problem was with face recognition units (FRUs). By contrast, Van der Linden *et al.* (1995) studied a patient (CB) who could say whether a person was familiar but could not provide any information about them or name them, suggesting damage to a later stage (PIN and NRU).

CASE STUDIES OF ABNORMAL INDIVIDUALS

Evaluation

There are many problems associated with the use of case studies of brain-damaged individuals as a source of empirical evidence.

First of all, when studying prosopagnosics, each case study involves an individual with unique patterns of brain damage. This makes it difficult to make generalisations about what behavioural deficits might generally be linked to which areas of the brain.

Second, just because an area of the brain (such as the FFA) is associated with an inability to recognise faces it doesn't mean that part of the brain is responsible. It may be that the FFA acts as a relay station and thus damage to the FFA has an effect. So we cannot demonstrate with certainty that one area of the brain is the causal component.

Third, it is very difficult to fully and reliably test any individual to be certain what they can and cannot do. This is due to many things, such as different methods used by different researchers lacking comparability. Brain-damaged patients may be generally slower and thus appear to have face/object recognition problems when, in fact, this is due to general cognitive impairment. Also some patients may have developed strategies to cope with their difficulties – which means that their performance may mask their true lack of ability (for example learning to identify faces using peripheral clues).

However, case studies remain a rich source of information about prosopagnosia although increasingly researchers are turning to study cases of developmental prosopagnosia and even face recognition difficulties in 'normal' people.

WWW Test your own face perception skills at www.faceblind.org/facetests/index.php

---

ETHICAL ISSUES

IDA

Case studies raise a number of ethical issues, such as privacy and harm to participants. In order to protect privacy, patients are referred to by initials although it is relatively easy to discover a person's true identity. The bigger issue is psychological and perhaps even physical harm. Individuals such as PS have been subjected to intensive testing, sitting in a laboratory for hours on end. Increasing interest in agnosia has meant that some patients are often 'over-tested' to fully establish what they can or can't do. Furthermore, these tests are likely to span a number of years – for example one patient, HJA, was first tested after his stroke in 1981 when he was 61 and, as far as we know, he is still being tested. The issue is that some brain-damaged patients might enjoy the attention but some may feel a bit like a goldfish in a bowl.

REAL-WORLD APPLICATION

IDA

One of the spin-offs of this research is offering some kind of help to people with agnosias. However, the reality is there is little that can be done, but we can offer reassurance. One woman reported that she never realised she had an identifiable problem until she read an article about prosopagnosia: 'Knowing about it comes as quite a relief' (*New Scientist*, 2008).

CAN YOU...?

No.2.6

...1 Write a description of **three** case studies of prosopagnosia, in about 200 words, and **three** explanations of prosopagnosia, in 200 words.

...2 Identify **eight** criticisms related to prosopagnosia, including **at least one** IDA topic. Each criticism should be about 50 words.

...3 Use this material to write 600-word answers to the question: *Discuss case studies of prosopagnosia.* (8 marks + 16 marks)

CHAPTER SUMMARY

THEORIES OF PERCEPTUAL ORGANISATION

GREGORY'S INDIRECT (TOP-DOWN) THEORY

PERCEPTION AS HYPOTHESIS FORMATION
- Perception based on sensory data, stored knowledge and inference.
- Inferences frequently made on basis of inadequate sensory data.

PREVIOUS KNOWLEDGE AND EXPECTATION
- Importance of stored knowledge demonstrated in Bruner (1951) study.
- Expectations usually lead to accurate perceptions.

VISUAL ILLUSIONS
- Inferences lead to incorrect perceptions, such as illusions.
- Illusions are 'misapplied hypotheses'.

EVALUATION
- Hypothesis testing – research (Shopland and Gregory, 1964) suggests hypothesis testing does not always contribute to end perception.
- Previous knowledge and expectation – demonstrated in Palmer's (1975) study of the role of context.
- Visual illusions – explanation of Müller-Lyer illusion supported by cross-cultural research.
- Strengths – can explain how perceptual system deals with ambiguous stimuli; can help in design of computer systems that can 'see'.
- Limitations – based largely on study of perception in artificial settings; lack of precision in key concepts.

IDA
- Real-world application – USS Vincennes incident.

GIBSON'S DIRECT (BOTTOM-UP) THEORY

THE OPTIC ARRAY
- Changing pattern of light that surrounds the active perceiver.
- Optic flow – objects to the side of a fixed point appear to move more rapidly.
- Ecological aspects of perception, e.g. texture gradient – closer things have coarser gradient.
- Role of invariants – unchanging aspects of environment e.g. horizon-ratio.

MAKING SENSE OF OPTIC ARRAY
- Resonance is how we make sense of 'broadcast information'.
- Affordance – the potential for action offered by objects.
- Perception is the detection of *useful* information.

EVALUATION
- Research evidence for notion of biological motion suggests innate ability.
- Time-to-contact demonstrated in long-jumpers and in gannets.
- Innate perceptual abilities demonstrated in Gibson and Walk (1960) study.
- Visual illusions can be explained in terms of direct perception (e.g. horizon-ratio in Ames room).
- Limitation – affordance must involve some top-down processes.
- Reconcile top-down and bottom-up approaches using (1) Neisser's cyclic model, (2) each suited to different circumstances, (3) what and where systems.

IDA
- Nature and nurture – Gibson's theory represents nature and Gregory's theory is nurture.
- Real-world application – affordance successfully applied in design of autonomous robots.

DEVELOPMENT OF PERCEPTION

INFANT STUDIES

DEPTH PERCEPTION
- Monocular cues e.g. motion parallax (dynamic rather than static cues).
- Demonstrated by Gibson and Walk (1960) using the visual cliff, and by Hofsten *et al.* (1992) using habituation.
- Binocular cues – retinal disparity demonstrated by Bower *et al.* (1970).
- Age-related changes – research by Yonas *et al.* (2001) showed ability to use shadow as depth cue develops with age.

VISUAL CONSTANCY
- Tendency to see properties of objects as invariant despite changes in retinal image.
- Shape constancy in infants – demonstrated in Bower (1966) study.
- Size constancy – Slater *et al.* (1990) showed newborn infants able to differentiate between different size cubes.

PATTERN PERCEPTION
- Newborn infants show preference for face-like patterns and for more complex stimuli.

EVALUATION
- Some perceptual abilities not present at birth, nor product of maturation.
- Perceptual completion – infants unable to detect Kanisza square.
- Occlusion – example of perceptual completion task that confuses infants.
- Perceptual completion research important – supports top-down theory.
- Gibson and Walk (1960) study criticised because infants may have learned to use depth cues therefore conclusions inappropriate.
- Studying infants is difficult – techniques used may not be reliable.

IDA
- Studying nature and nurture – difficult to disentangle nature and nurture e.g. abilities may be due to experience (nurture) or maturing visual system (nature).
- Nature–nurture debate – Blakemore and Cooper (1970) visual deprivation in kittens shows it is nature shaped by experience.
- Real-world application – treating children with squints (Banks *et al.*, 1975).

FACE PERCEPTION

FACE RECOGNITION

BRUCE AND YOUNG (1986)
- Face recognition consists of a series of stages that are distinct from general object recognition.
- Structural encoding – details of face encoded into information about features and expression.
- Face Recognition Units – information about familiar faces ‹ Person Identity Node ‹ Name Recognition Unit.
- Second route – data from structural encoding used to work out expression; used with unfamiliar faces.
- The cognitive system – may add information based on stereotypes.

EVALUATION
- Supported by research evidence, e.g. Young et al. (1985 and 1986), although other research (Stanhope and Cohen, 1993) challenges main assumptions.
- Strength – generates precise predictions that can be tested.
- Limitation – some aspects of model vague and not clearly specified.
- Updated model – Burton and Bruce (1993) developed IAC model with network of links between units, not just serial connections.
- Is face recognition special? Support from Fantz's study, studies of prosopagnosia, scanning studies (demonstrating importance of FFA), inversion effect (Thatcher illusion).
- Face recognition isn't special. FFA active in other types of perception. Face processing may simply be a form of expert object recognition.

IDA
- Real-world application – e.g. in development of face recognition systems (facial cognitive biometric systems).

CROSS-CULTURAL STUDIES

DEPTH PERCEPTION
- Anthropological studies suggest some cultures unable to use distance cues to interpret size.
- Testing use of pictorial cues – Hudson (1960) found that Europeans better able to use pictorial cues to interpret depth.

VISUAL CONSTANCIES
- Shape constancy – Allport and Pettigrew (1957) found Zulus in rural areas less likely to be influenced by trapezoidal window illusion than Zulus living in urban environments.
- Size constancy – Segall et al. (1963) found rural Zulus also less affected by Müller-Lyer illusion than people living in 'carpentered' world.

EVALUATION
- Later research has found fewer cultural differences (e.g. Jahoda and McGurk, 1974).
- Language – changing the nature of question in Hudson study led to more Zulus displaying depth perception.
- Pictorial interpretation – Deregowski suggests important distinction between epitomic and eidolic images which explains different results.
- Experience of depth cues appears to matter, but less than originally believed.
- Cross-cultural research – problems include tests and procedures developed in one country that may not be valid in another (imposed etic).
- Other problems include lack of representativeness of participants, communication problems, anecdotal nature of some research.

IDA
- Biological approach – retinal pigmentation hypothesis has some support but environmental explanations preferred.
- Non-human animal research: issues about ethics of permanent damage and generalisability of findings.

AN EXAMPLE OF VISUAL AGNOSIA: PROSOPAGNOSIA

CASE STUDIES
- Inability to recognise faces – rare condition, e.g. PS (Busigny et al., 2010).
- Inability to recognise both faces and objects – more common, e.g. NS (Delvenne et al., 2004), also no inversion effect.
- Partial face recognition, e.g. Mr. W. (Bruyer et al., 1983) could recognise his individual cows but not faces.

EXPLANATIONS
- Acquired versus developmental – Duchaine et al. (2007) 10 family members with inherited/developmental prosopagnosia, possibly affects 2% of the population.
- Damage to a face processing unit – fMRI scans of PS, damage to right FFA and OFA.
- Prosopagnosia is a holistic processing failure (Farah, 1991) whereas alexia is a configural failure and lack of object recognition is a mixture of both.

EVALUATION
- Case studies – low generalisability (unique patterns of brain damage), no certainty about causal connections, problems with reliable testing of brain-damaged individuals.
- Contradictory evidence, e.g. some patients can't recognise their cows (Assal et al., 1984).
- Evidence from developmental prosopagnosiacs also indicated activity in the FFA unique to faces (Garrido et al., 2009).
- May just be an extreme case of failure to recognise objects, faces are very complex objects (Humphreys and Riddoch, 1987).
- Greeble testing showed that this was unaffected, supporting unique face processor (Duchaine et al., 2006).
- Holistic processing not supported by all evidence, e.g. PS coped on Navon task (Busigny and Rossion, 2011).
- Supports Bruce and Young – patients with damage to FRUs (Duchaine et al., 2006) or PINs and NRUs (Van der Linden et al., 1995).

IDA
- Ethical issues – privacy and potential harm through extensive testing.
- Real-world application – implications for treatment, although currently little help available.

EXAM QUESTION WITH STUDENT ANSWER

QUESTION Discuss research relating to the development of depth/distance perception. *(8 marks + 16 marks)*

STUDENT ANSWER

[607 words]

The study by Gibson and Walk (1960) investigated the development of distance and depth perception. In this study they used a visual cliff apparatus where one side appeared to be deeper than the other. (There was a checkerboard pattern to show this.) The infants were encouraged to crawl over to the deep side because their mothers were standing at the end (in fact there was glass covering the apparent deep side so they were in no danger). Gibson and Walk found that most infants aged six months refused thus showing innate depth perception.

One problem with this conclusion is that the infants were six months old and therefore had plenty of visual experience already. Therefore, their depth perception may not have been innate. However, the original finding has been supported by other studies that found a way to test depth perception in younger infants.

There is also further support from Gibson and Walk who used their apparatus to test young animals and found that goats and chicks only a day old avoided the deep side, suggesting that depth perception was innate.

Another study of depth/distance perception again with infants was conducted by Bower et al. (1970). They showed infants as young as one week old a three-dimensional shape by presenting different information to each eye. If the infants weren't using binocular depth cues they wouldn't have perceived depth but they reached out for the objects. This shows innate depth perception because of the age of the infants.

Depth/distance perception has also been investigated using cross-cultural studies. A classic study by Turnbull in the 1960s described the experience of an African pygmy who had lived in a forest all his life and never had to use depth perception. When he saw buffalo grazing on the plains he thought they were insects because they were so small. This study suggests that depth perception is not innate but is learned.

It is supported by another study again conducted in the 1960s in Africa. Hudson showed pictures to African and European children and asked them questions about what was happening. The pictures of course were two dimensional but showed depth/distance using pictorial clues, such as overlap and size. Hudson found that when the children were quite young they all had difficulty interpreting the pictorial clues but as they got older the European children could do it although the African children didn't do it very well.

This study again suggests that experience contributes to the development of depth/distance vision. However, there are a number of problems with cross-cultural studies. One of them is that the people in another culture don't properly understand the task or the instructions. This is an example of an imposed etic, a kind of cultural bias where we assume that things mean the same the world over.

So it is possible that the children in Hudson's study were underperforming. This is supported by a later study by Page where they slightly changed the questions used and the result was that the African children did better. This does suggest that the findings might have been an experimental artefact.

This research is relevant to the nature–nurture debate because it considers the question of whether depth/distance perception is innate (nature) or learned (nurture). The evidence presented above doesn't have a clear answer. One solution has been suggested in research on the visual system by Blakemore and Cooper that showed that the innate visual system is altered through experience because visual cells disappeared if not used.

This has important real-world applications for children born with squints. If the squint is not treated early in life this may affect the innate visual system.

EXAMINER COMMENTS

In this first paragraph there is perhaps **too much detail** on Gibson and Walk's study (nearly 100 words). It is difficult to reduce details of some studies but is something you should practise. Too much detail here means less breadth overall in the essay.

Reasonable elaboration of **AO2** point although it would be better to name the study and perhaps provide a few details.

Gibson and Walk's findings used as additional evaluation (**AO2**) shows how you can use the same material as description or evaluation, it just depends on the way it is introduced.

Brief but **detailed** description of an appropriate study with a conclusion drawn at the end ('This shows ...', **AO2**).

Cross-cultural research is also appropriate in this essay. Description is again **detailed** and followed by a **rudimentary AO2** comment ('This study suggests ...').

The paragraph starts off as evaluation ('This is supported ...') but the paragraph is actually descriptive. It is well-detailed, in fact it is again too **well-detailed** because the essay balance is wrong. This student knows a lot about the studies but is in danger of leaving insufficient time for evaluation.

A welcome evaluation paragraph, with **some evidence** of **elaboration**. The use of the term 'imposed etic' is good for gaining credit with **quality of written communication** (use of psychological terminology is one of the criteria).

Further interpretation (**AO2**) and use of other research evidence to give a contrasting view.

The final two paragraphs focus on **IDA topics**, both of which are **reasonably effective** in terms of contextualisation. The real-world application point **lacks elaboration**.

AO1 – **accurate** and **well-detailed**. An appropriate **range** of material covered and is **substantial**. The essay is **coherent**.

AO2/AO3 – Very little until last four paragraphs. So, even though the evaluation is **elaborated**, **effective** and **focused**, overall it is described as **basic** rather than reasonable.

Chapter 3
Relationships

SPECIFICATION

Relationships	
The formation, maintenance and breakdown of romantic relationships	• Theories of the formation, maintenance and breakdown of romantic relationships: for example reward/need satisfaction, social exchange theory.
Evolutionary explanations of human reproductive behaviour	• The relationship between sexual selection and human reproductive behaviour. • Sex differences in parental investment.
Effects of early experience and culture on adult relationships	• The influence of childhood on adult relationships. • The influence of culture on romantic relationships.

We may prefer to think of the development of romantic relationships as being based on deep feelings and shared emotions, rather than simple reinforcement or similarity. Social psychologists, however, are not usually known for such romantic views of relationships. The scientific study of how relationships form has shown that, in the initial stages at least, this process may have little to do with shared emotions, and more to do with self-interest.

▲▼ Some relationships develop because they are associated with happy times, but the most successful long-term relationships seem to be those where couples have similar attitudes and personalities.

REWARD/NEED SATISFACTION THEORY
(Byrne and Clore, 1970)

If we ask someone why they are attracted to their partner, they might respond that their partner is attentive, supportive, loving or just good fun. This suggests that we are attracted to people who we find satisfying or gratifying to be with. Most stimuli in our lives can be viewed as being rewarding or punishing in some way, and we are motivated to seek rewarding stimuli and avoid punishing stimuli. The sort of things we find rewarding tend to reflect our unmet needs (e.g. the need for company, financial security, an attractive partner and so on). Mutual attraction occurs when each partner meets the other person's needs. One person might have the need for financial security, while the other craves love.

Rewards and punishments

Rewarding stimuli produce positive feelings in us (e.g. they make us happy), and punishing stimuli produce negative feelings (e.g. they make us unhappy). Given that some of these stimuli are other people, it follows that some people make us happy, and some do not. According to the principles of **operant conditioning**, we are likely to repeat any behaviour that leads to a desirable outcome and avoid behaviours that lead to an undesirable outcome. Byrne and Clore's

theory suggests, therefore, that we enter into relationships because the presence of some individuals is directly associated with reinforcement (i.e. the person creates positive feelings in us), which makes them more attractive to us.

Attraction through association

As well as liking people with whom we share a pleasant experience, we also like people who are *associated* with pleasant events. If we meet someone when we are feeling happy (positive mood), we are much more inclined to like them than if we meet them when we are feeling unhappy (negative mood). In this way, a previously neutral stimulus (e.g. someone we had not previously met and therefore have no real feelings about) can become positively valued because of their **association** with a pleasant event (i.e. we learn to like people through the process of **classical conditioning**). Byrne and Clore believed that the balance of positive and negative feelings was crucial in relationship formation. Relationships where the positive feelings outweigh the negative feelings were more likely to develop and succeed, whereas relationships where the negative feelings outweighed the positive were likely to fail.

SIMILARITY (Byrne, Clore and Smeaton, 1986)

The essence of this view is that similarity promotes liking. According to this model, there are two distinct stages in the formation of relationships. People first sort potential partners for *dissimilarity*, avoiding those whose personality or attitudes appear too different from their own. Then, from those remaining, they are most likely to choose somebody who is similar to themselves. Byrne *et al.*'s model emphasises similarity of *personality* and of *attitudes*.

Personality

Research has consistently demonstrated that people are more likely to be attracted to others who have similar personality traits than they are to those who have dissimilar or complementary traits (Berscheid and Reis, 1998). For example, two people who are serious and hardworking are more likely to be attracted to each other than a serious, hardworking person and someone whose main interests are having fun and avoiding responsibility.

Of course this is not always the case. We all know couples who are complete opposites of each other, but research suggests that similarity is more often the rule, particularly in long-term relationships. For example, Caspi and Herbener (1990) found that married couples with similar personalities tend to be happier than couples with less similar personalities.

Attitudes

What if people find they disagree on something important? For example, dating partners may discover that they differ in their attitudes to holidays. One partner might like activity holidays while the other likes relaxing beach holidays. Research suggests that a process of 'attitude alignment' often occurs, with partners modifying their attitudes so they become more similar. In order for the relationship to develop, one or both partners may modify their attitudes, otherwise they may end up taking holidays on their own for many years to come!

DO SIMILARITY AND RECIPROCAL LIKING REALLY MATTER?

In a laboratory experiment, Lehr and Geher (2006) studied 24 male and 32 female students to test the importance of attitude similarity and reciprocal attraction in liking. Knowing that someone likes you is particularly rewarding, and so is more likely to result in mutual liking for the other person. Participants were given a description of a stranger, with varying degrees of similarity of the stranger's attitudes to the participant's. Inserted in each description was a statement that the stranger either liked or did not like the participant. The **dependent variables** included measures of liking for the bogus stranger (e.g. degree of liking and likelihood of dating). Researchers found significant effects for attitude similarity (similar people were liked more) and liking (which was more likely to be reciprocated).

Having a partner with similar attitudes to our own is in itself reinforcing, so similarity can be seen as an extension of the reward/need satisfaction theory.

EVALUATION

Research support

Evidence for the importance of reward – The theory proposes that we like some individuals because they provide direct reinforcement. Support for this claim comes from Griffitt and Guay (1969). Participants were evaluated on a creative task by an experimenter and then asked to rate how much they liked the experimenter. This rating was highest when the experimenter had positively evaluated (i.e. rewarded) the participant's performance on the task.

Evidence for need satisfaction through Facebook use – Sheldon et al. (2011) discovered that greater Facebook use was positively correlated with both positive (feelings of 'connectedness') and negative indicators of relationship satisfaction (feelings of 'disconnectedness'). Relationally 'connected' people tend to be those whose sociability motivates their Facebook use and satisfies their relational needs to reach out to others. 'Disconnected' people may lack need satisfaction through face-to-face relationships, so are likely to use Facebook more as a coping strategy.

Physiological support – Research by Aron et al. (2005) found that participants who measured very high on a self-report questionnaire of romantic love also showed strong activity in particular areas of the brain, including the ventral tegmental area. Early-stage, intense romantic love was associated with elevated levels of activity in subcortical reward regions of the brain, rich in the neurotransmitter dopamine.

How important *are* rewards?

Cate et al. (1982) asked 337 individuals to assess their current relationships in terms of reward level and satisfaction. Results showed that reward level was superior to all other factors in determining relationship satisfaction. However, a basic problem with the reward/need satisfaction theory is that it only explores the *receiving* of rewards, whereas Hays (1985) found that we gain satisfaction from giving as well as receiving.

CULTURAL BIAS

The reward/need satisfaction theory does not account for cultural and gender differences in the formation of relationships. For example, Lott (1994) suggests that in many cultures women are more focused on the needs of others rather than receiving reinforcement. This suggests that this theory is not a universal explanation of relationship formation and therefore culturally biased.

AN EVOLUTIONARY EXPLANATION

Aron et al. (2005) suggest that the brain reward system associated with romantic love most probably evolved to drive our ancestors to focus their courtship energy on specific individuals. Love at first sight is a basic mammalian response that our ancestors inherited to speed up the mating process.

MUNDANE REALISM

Most of the studies carried out in this area are laboratory studies, and therefore do not necessarily show that the principles of need satisfaction and similarity apply to real life (i.e. such studies lack **mundane realism**). However, some studies (for example Caspi and Herbener (1990)) have been conducted on real-life couples, and have tended to support these claims.

EVALUATION

Similarity or dissimilarity?

Rosenbaum (1986) suggested that dissimilarity rather than similarity was the more important factor in determining whether a relationship will develop. This *dissimilarity-repulsion hypothesis* has been tested in a number of different cultures e.g. Singh and Tan (1992) in Singapore, and Drigotas (1993) in the USA. These studies established that participants were first attracted to each other because of similarity of attitudes, and that, as they got to know each other better, those who discovered more *dissimilarities* than similarities became less attracted to each other.

Limitations

Research on similarity has only dealt with attitude and personality similarities. Yoshida (1972) pointed out that this represents only a very narrow view of factors important in relationship formation, with factors such as similarity of self-concept, economic level and physical condition being equally important. For example, research by Speakman et al. (2007) found that people often choose partners with similar levels of body fat.

Why is similarity so important?

Similarity is important in the formation of relationships for two main reasons. First, we assume that people similar to us will be more likely to like us. By ruling out dissimilar people, we lessen the chance of being rejected as a partner (Condon and Crano, 1988). Second, when other people share our attitudes and beliefs, it tends to validate them, which in turn is rewarding (see reward/need satisfaction theory above).

CAN YOU...? No.3.1

...1 Describe, in about 200 words, each of the **two** theories described opposite, and also outline each in about 100 words.

...2 Identify **four** criticisms for each theory, including **at least one** IDA topic. Each criticism should be about 50 words. Remember that criticisms can be positive as well as negative.

...3 Use this material to write a 600-word answer to the question: *Describe and evaluate **two** theories of the formation of relationships.* (8 marks + 16 marks).

Psychologists are not only interested in why relationships form, but also what keeps them going. Some relationships never seem to flourish, while others are extremely successful and long-lasting. Maintaining a relationship is not a one-way process, but involves an interaction between the two partners, each with their own needs and expectations. In a sense, the two theories on this spread represent a kind of marketplace, where each member of a romantic partnership must serve their own needs, but also satisfy the needs of their partner.

▲ Investing in each other? Equity theory suggests that the most successful relationships are those where levels of giving and receiving are balanced.

SOCIAL EXCHANGE THEORY (Thibaut and Kelley, 1959)

Profit and loss

At the centre of this theory is the assumption that all social behaviour is a series of exchanges; individuals attempt to maximise their rewards and minimise their costs. In our society, people exchange resources with the expectation (or at least the hope) that they will earn a 'profit', i.e. that rewards will exceed the costs incurred. Rewards that we may receive from a relationship include being cared for, companionship and sex. Costs may include effort, financial investment and time wasted (i.e. missed opportunities with others because of being in that particular relationship). Rewards minus costs equal the outcome (a profit or a loss). Social exchange, in line with other 'economic' theories of human behaviour, stresses that commitment to a relationship is dependent on the profitability of this outcome.

Comparison level

In order to judge whether one person offers something better or worse than we might expect from another, Thibaut and Kelley proposed that we develop a **comparison level** – a standard against which all our relationships are judged. Our comparison level (CL) is a product of our experiences in other relationships together with our general views of what we might expect from this particular exchange. If we judge that the potential profit in a new relationship exceeds our CL, the relationship will be judged as worthwhile, and the other person will be seen as attractive as a partner. If the final result is negative (profit is less than our CL), we will be dissatisfied with the relationship and the other person is thus less attractive. A related concept is the **comparison level for alternatives**, where the person weighs up a potential increase in rewards from a different partner, minus any costs associated with ending the current relationship. A new relationship can take the place of the current one if its profit level is significantly higher.

EQUITY THEORY (Walster et al., 1978)

Inequity and distress

In social exchange theory, we learned that all social behaviour is a series of exchanges, with individuals attempting to maximise their rewards and minimise their costs. Equity theory is an extension of that underlying belief, with its central assumption that people strive to achieve fairness in their relationships and feel distressed if they perceive unfairness (Messick and Cook, 1983). According to equity theory, any kind of inequity has the potential to create distress. People who give a great deal in a relationship and get little in return would perceive inequity, and therefore would be dissatisfied in the relationship. However, the same is true of those who receive a great deal and give little in return. This is also an inequitable relationship, with the same consequence for both partners – dissatisfaction. As you might imagine, the greater the perceived inequity, the greater the dissatisfaction, and the greater the dissatisfaction, the greater the distress.

Ratio of inputs and outputs

An important point to bear in mind when considering this theory is that equity does not necessarily mean equality. It is possible for each partner to contribute (and receive) very different amounts and for the relationship still to be equitable. What is considered 'fair' in a relationship, in terms of input and output, is largely a subjective opinion for each partner. Thus, although one partner perceives themselves as putting in less than the other, the relationship will still be judged fair if they get less out of the relationship (relative to the other person). This is explained in terms of a person's perceived ratio of inputs and outputs, a subjective assessment of the relative inputs of each partner relative to the outcomes for that partner. Deciding whether a relationship is equitable therefore involves some fairly complicated mathematics. An equitable relationship should, according to the theory, be one where one partner's benefits minus their costs equals their partner's benefits less their costs. If we perceive inequality in our relationship, then we are motivated to restore it. This can be achieved in several different ways. For example, we may change the amount we put into a relationship, the amount we demand from the relationship, or our perceptions of relative inputs and outputs, in order to restore the appearance of equity. We may also compare our relationship to our comparison level for other relationships to see if it is worth continuing our investment in the current relationship or whether we should end it and begin a new one.

EQUITY AND SATISFACTION

Stafford and Canary (2006) asked over 200 married couples to complete measures of equity and relationship satisfaction. Findings revealed that satisfaction was highest for spouses who perceived their relationships to be equitable, followed by over-benefited partners and lowest for under-benefited partners. These findings are consistent with predictions from equity theory. Couples also completed measures of five maintenance strategies – positivity, openness, assurances, social networks and sharing tasks. Under-benefited husbands reported significantly lower levels of three of these compared to equitable or over-benefited husbands.

EVALUATION

Profit and loss

The notion of exchange has been used to explain why some women stay in abusive relationships. Rusbult and Martz (1995) argue that when investments are high (e.g. children, financial security) and alternatives are low (e.g. nowhere else to live, no money) this could still be considered a profit situation and a woman might choose to remain in such a relationship.

Comparison level

Support can be found by looking at how people in a relationship deal with potential alternatives; one way of dealing with such potential threats is to reduce them as a means of protecting the relationship. Simpson et al. (1990) asked participants to rate members of the opposite sex in terms of attractiveness; those participants who were already involved in a relationship gave lower ratings. However, social exchange theory does not explain why some people leave relationships despite having no alternative, nor does it suggest how great the disparity in CL has to be to become unsatisfactory.

Limitations

Social exchange theory has been criticised for focusing too much on the individual's perspective and ignoring the social aspects of a relationship, such as how partners communicate and interpret shared events (Duck and Sants, 1983). The main criticism, however, focuses on the selfish nature of the theory. Are people only motivated to maintain relationships out of hedonistic (selfish) concerns? It is possible that such principles only apply in **individualist** cultures, if at all (see 'Cultural bias in equity and exchange' above).

IDA **CULTURAL BIAS IN EQUITY AND EXCHANGE**

Moghaddam (1998) suggests that such 'economic' theories only apply to Western relationships and even then only to certain short-term relationships among individuals with high mobility. One group of people who fit this description are students in Western societies. They are typically very mobile and experience many short-term romantic relationships. When there is little time to develop long-term commitment, it makes sense to be concerned with give-and-take. However, long-term relationships within other less mobile population groups, particularly in non-traditional societies, are more likely to value security than personal profit.

IDA **REAL WORLD APPLICATION – RELATIONSHIP THERAPY**

Individuals in unsuccessful marriages frequently report a lack of positive behaviour exchanges with their partner and an excess of negative exchanges. Gottman and Levenson (1992) found that in successful marriages the ratio of positive to negative exchanges was around 5:1, but in unsuccessful marriages this ratio was much lower at around 1:1 or less. A primary goal of relationship therapy, therefore, might be to increase the proportion of positive exchanges within a relationship and decrease the proportion of negative exchanges. Integrated Behavioural Couples Therapy (IBCT) (Jacobson et al., 2000) helps partners to break the negative patterns of behaviour that cause problems thus making each other happier. Christensen et al. (2004) treated over 60 distressed couples using IBCT, and found that about two-thirds reported significant improvements in the quality of their relationships as a result.

EVALUATION

Exchange and communal relationships

Clark and Mills (1979) disagreed with the claim that all relationships are based on economics. They distinguished between exchange relationships (e.g. between colleagues or business associates) and communal relationships (e.g. between friends or lovers). Although exchange relationships may involve keeping track of rewards and costs, communal relationships are governed more by a desire to respond to the needs of the partner. There is still some concern with equity, but partners tend to believe things will balance out in the long run.

The role of relationship inequity in marital disruption

If equity is so important in relationships, what happens in the case of inequitable relationships? DeMaris (2007) investigated whether marital inequity is associated with later marital disruption. Using 1500 couples as part of the *US National Survey of Families and Households*, he found that the only subjective index of inequity associated with disruption is women's sense of being under-benefited, with greater under-benefit raising the risk of divorce.

Equity: an insufficient theory

Ragsdale and Brandau-Brown (2007) reject the claim that equity is a key determinant of relationship satisfaction. They argue that this represents '…an incomplete rendering of the way in which married people behave with respect to each other', and that equity theory is, therefore, an insufficient theory to explain marital maintenance.

Evaluation **GENDER DIFFERENCES**

Research suggests that men and women might judge the equity of a relationship differently. For example, Steil and Weltman (1991) found that, among married working couples, husbands who earned more than their wives rated their own careers as more important than their wives' careers. In such couples the women generally also rated their husbands' careers as more important than their own. However, in couples where the woman's income exceeded the man's, neither partner rated their career as more important. Researchers concluded that 'wives' tendency to seek less for themselves than comparable men making comparable contributions… impeded the achievement of equality at home'.

CAN YOU...? No.3.2

…1 Describe exchange and equity theories in 200 words each and outline each in about 100 words.

…2 Identify **four** criticisms for each theory, including **at least one** IDA topic. Each criticism should be about 50 words. Remember that criticisms can be positive as well as negative.

…3 Use this material to write a 600-word answer to the following questions:

*Outline and evaluate **two** theories of the maintenance of relationships.* (8 marks + 16 marks)

*Describe and evaluate **one** theory of the maintenance of relationships.* (8 marks + 16 marks)

THE BREAKDOWN OF RELATIONSHIPS

Some relationships flourish, some survive in name alone and some fail completely. In our culture, relationships are considered 'successful' if partners stay together, and those relationships that end 'prematurely' are considered failures. This is despite the fact that many so-called successful relationships continue even though neither partner is really committed to the relationship. Likewise, ending an unhappy relationship may help each partner to find a new and happy life elsewhere with a new partner. As Steve Duck (2007) suggests, relationships are a little like cars, in that they can have 'accidents' for many reasons. Sometimes it is the 'driver's' fault, sometimes it is a mechanical failure that causes the accident and sometimes it is the actions of other road users. Like a car, a poorly maintained relationship is more at risk of breakdown.

REASONS FOR RELATIONSHIP BREAKDOWN (Duck, 1999)

Lack of skills

For some people, relationships are difficult because they lack the interpersonal skills to make them mutually satisfying. Individuals lacking social skills may be poor conversationalists, poor at indicating their interest in other people, and are likely to be generally unrewarding in their interactions with other people (Duck, 1991). The lack of social skills, therefore, means that others perceive them as not being interested in relating, so a relationship tends to break down before it really gets going.

Lack of stimulation

According to social exchange theory (see page 50), people look for rewards in their relationships, one of which is 'stimulation'. We would expect, therefore, that lack of stimulation would be a reason why relationships break down. There is evidence (e.g. Baxter, 1994) that lack of stimulation (i.e. boredom or a belief that the relationship wasn't going anywhere) is often quoted when breaking off a relationship. People expect relationships to change and develop, and when they do not this is seen as sufficient justification to end the relationship or begin a new one (i.e. have an affair).

Maintenance difficulties

There are clearly some circumstances where relationships become strained simply because partners cannot see each other enough. Going away to university, for example, places a great strain on existing relationships, and is often responsible for their breakdown (Shaver et al., 1985). While enduring romantic relationships *can* be strong enough to survive the pressures of decreased daily contact, it is evident that for many this isn't the case. In these cases, the maintenance difficulties become overwhelming, and the relationships break down.

A MODEL OF BREAKDOWN (Rollie and Duck, 2006)

Keeping it personal

The first phase of Rollie and Duck's model begins when one of the partners becomes distressed with the way the relationship is conducted. As we saw on the previous spread, inequitable relationships are more likely to create dissatisfaction than equitable relationships, so this realisation may be the first step in the eventual *breakdown* of the relationship.

This leads to an *intrapsychic* process characterised by a brooding focus on the relationship. During this process, nothing is said to the partner, although the dissatisfied partner may express their dissatisfaction in other ways, e.g. in a personal diary entry.

Some people will end relationships without ever discussing their dissatisfaction with their partner. The promises of 'I'll call you' or 'Let's stay friends' often disguise a deeper dissatisfaction with the other person as a romantic partner. In the *dyadic* process, people confront their partners and begin to discuss their feelings and the future. At this stage the relationship might be saved or partners begin to involve others in their dissatisfaction with the relationship.

BREAKDOWN
Dissatisfaction with relationship
Threshold: I can't stand this anymore

INTRAPSYCHIC PROCESSES
Social withdrawal; 'rumination' resentment
Brooding on partner's 'faults' and relational 'costs'
Re-evaluation of alternatives to relationship
Threshold: I'd be justified in withdrawing

DYADIC PROCESSES
Uncertainty, anxiety, hostility, complaints
Discussion of discontents
Talk about 'our relationship'; equity, roles
Reassessment of goals, possibilities, commitments
Threshold: I mean it

SOCIAL PROCESSES
Going public; support seeking from third parties
Denigration of partner, alliance building
Social commitment, outside forces create cohesion
Threshold: It's now inevitable

GRAVE-DRESSING PROCESSES
Tidying up memories; making relational histories
Stories prepared for different audiences
Saving face
Threshold: Time to get a new life

RESURRECTION PROCESSES
Recreating sense of own social value
Defining what to get out of future relationships
Preparation for a different sort of relational future
Reframing of past relational life:
What I learned and how things will be different

▲ A summary of Rollie and Duck's model of relationship breakdown.

Going public

Up to this point, partners might have kept their dissatisfaction fairly private, but it now spills over to a network of friends and family as it reaches the *social* process. Others may take sides, offer advice and support, or may help in mending any disputes between the two sides. The involvement of others may even speed the partners towards dissolution through revelations about one or other of the partners.

Having left a relationship, partners attempt to justify their actions. This process is important, as each partner must present themselves to others as being trustworthy and loyal, key attributes for future relationships. Partners strive to construct a representation of the failed relationship that does not paint their contribution to it in unfavourable terms. In this *grave-dressing* process, people may strategically reinterpret their view of the partner. For example, they may have been attracted to their 'rebellious' nature, but now label that characteristic irresponsible. In the final *resurrection* process each partner prepares themselves for new relationships by redefining themselves and building on past mistakes and experiences.

The importance of social skills deficits in relationship breakdown has led to the development of training programmes that attempt to *enhance* relationship skills in distressed couples. The Couples Coping Enhancement Training (CCET) programme aims to sensitise couples to issues of equity and respect within their relationship and to improve communication and problem-solving skills. Cina *et al.* (2003) compared 50 couples (average length of relationship 12 years) who received CCET training with a control group who did not. Results showed that the CCET group reported much higher marital quality after training compared to the control group.

Women are more likely to stress unhappiness and incompatibility as reasons for dissolution, whereas men are particularly upset by 'sexual withholding' (Brehm and Kassin, 1996). Women have more desire to stay friends after a relationship has broken up, whereas men want to 'cut their losses' and move on (Akert, 1998).

EVALUATION

Extramarital affairs

A major reason why relationships break down is that one or both partners have an extramarital affair. Boekhout *et al.* (1999) showed how such affairs might be a direct reaction to the perceived lack of skills and/or stimulation in the current relationship. They asked undergraduates to rate various sexual and emotional reasons for men and women to be unfaithful in a committed relationship. Participants judged that sexual reasons for infidelity (e.g. sexual excitement, boredom, variety) would be more likely to be used by men, whereas emotional reasons for infidelity (e.g. lack of attention, lack of commitment, emotional satisfaction) would be more likely to be used by women.

Maintenance difficulties

Long-distance romantic relationships (LDRR) and long-distance friendships (LDF) are perhaps more common than we think. One study found that 70% of students sampled had experienced at least one LDRR and that 90% said had experienced one LDF (Rohlfing, 1995). The fact that in our mobile society people do have to move, and do become separated from family, friends and/or partners, means that it is useful to understand the management strategies that people use. For example, Holt and Stone (1988) found that there was little decrease in relationship satisfaction as long as lovers are able to reunite regularly.

▲ 'I hate him!' Bridget Jones reflects on her frustration with Mark Darcy in the film *Bridget Jones's Diary*. In the initial stages of breakdown, relationship dissatisfaction may be restricted to personal brooding and resentment.

EVALUATION

Research support

Rollie and Duck's model is supported by observations of real-life break-ups. Tashiro and Frazier (2003) surveyed undergraduates who had recently broken up with a romantic partner. They typically reported that they had not only experienced emotional distress, but also personal growth. These students reported that breaking up with their partner had given them new insights into themselves and a clearer idea about future partners. Through grave-dressing and resurrection processes they were able to put the original relationship to rest and get on with their lives.

Implications for intervention

Rollie and Duck's model stresses the importance of *communication* in relationship breakdown. Paying attention to the things that people say, the topics that they discuss and the ways in which they talk about their relationship offers both an insight into their stage and also suggests interventions appropriate to that stage.

If the relationship was in the intrapsychic stage for example, repair might involve re-establishing liking for the partner, perhaps by re-evaluating their behaviour in a more positive light. In the later stages, different strategies of repair are appropriate. For example, people outside the relationship may help the partners patch up their differences.

Carrying out research in this sensitive area raises particular issues of vulnerability (participants may experience distress when revisiting the issues that led to breakdown), privacy (many such issues are of an intensely personal nature) and confidentiality. For example, a woman in an abusive relationship may fear recrimination from her abuser should he discover her participation in the research. Ultimately the researcher faces a choice of pursuing valuable information or terminating their involvement with a participant to prevent any further harm befalling them.

CAN YOU...? No.3.3

...1 Outline each of the **two** 'theories' of relationship breakdown in approximately 100 words each, and **one** theory in 200 words.

...2 Identify **four** criticisms for each theory, including **at least one** IDA topic. Each criticism should be about 50 words.

...3 Use this material to write a 600-word answer to the question: *Discuss **two** theories of the breakdown of relationships.* (8 marks + 16 marks)

Sensitive research limits info collected *validity*

social desirability

Reductionism *determinism* *theory based on research with problems*

53

SEXUAL SELECTION

Reproductive success is at the very heart of the evolutionary process. Among early humans, those who failed to mate also failed to become ancestors. For our ancestors, successful mating was a complex business, involving selecting the right mate, out-competing rivals and then engaging in all the right behaviours for successful conception and child-rearing. It follows then, that modern-day humans have a similarly complex array of psychological adaptations specifically dedicated to the task of mating.

'Sexual selection depends not on a struggle for existence in relation to other organic beings or to external conditions, but on a struggle between the individuals of one sex, generally the males, for possession of the other sex.' (Darwin, 1871)

THE NATURE OF SEXUAL SELECTION

Inter- and intra-sexual selection

An important feature of most sexually reproducing species is that males are more brightly coloured than their female counterparts; the classic example of this is the peacock's tail. One would expect such disadvantageous traits not to be naturally selected – unless they enhanced reproductive success in some way. To explain this, Darwin (1874) came up with his theory of **sexual selection**, describing two processes through which it took place. The two processes are:

Intrasexual selection (mate competition) – Members of one sex (usually males) compete with each other for access to members of the other sex. The victors are able to mate and so pass on their genes, whereas the losers do not. Whatever traits lead to success in these same-sex contests will be passed on to the next generation.

Intersexual selection (mate choice) – This form of selection involves the preferences of one sex for members of the opposite sex who possess certain qualities. For example, if females prefer tall males, over time there would be an increase in the number of tall males in the population. The preferences of one sex, therefore, determine the areas in which the other sex must compete. This may be in terms of plumage (as in the case of the peacock), or economic resources (in the case of humans). These indicators reveal traits that could be passed on to offspring (i.e. selection for 'good genes'), as well as information about the chances of the mate being able to give protection and support to offspring (i.e. selection for 'good parents'). Human beings are perceptually 'pre-programmed' to attend to displays of these important indicators, which in turn increases their willingness to mate with the individual who possesses them.

▲ Males of all species strive to attract females by advertising their quality as a potential mate.

SEX DIFFERENCES IN HUMAN MATE PREFERENCES

Supporting evidence for universal sex differences in long-term mate preferences comes from Buss (1989). Buss explored what males and females looked for in a marriage partner. The study involved over 10,000 people from 37 different cultures.

Among the main results were the following:

- Women more than men desired mates who were 'good financial prospects'. This translated into a desire for men with resources, or qualities that were linked to resource acquisition, such as ambition.
- Men placed more importance on physical attractiveness. Research has consistently shown that physical appearance provides a wealth of cues to a woman's health and hence her fertility and reproductive value.
- Men universally wanted mates who were younger than them – an indication that men valued increased fertility in potential mates.
- Both sexes wanted mates who were intelligent (linked to skill at parenting), kind (linked to an interest in long-term relationships) and dependable (linked to willingness to help a mate in times of trouble).

Short-term mating preferences

Human beings possess a menu of different mating strategies, some of which evolved specifically for short-term mating success. According to **parental investment theory** (see next spread), men evolved a greater desire for casual sex, and would ideally seek sex earlier in a relationship. Female behaviour would not be subjected to the same evolutionary pressures. Over the period of one year, for example, a male who managed to impregnate a large number of females would have passed on more copies of his genes than a less successful male. On the other hand, a female who had sex with the same number of men in the same time period would only produce a single child. The less time a man permits to elapse before he has sexual intercourse with a woman, the larger the number of women he can impregnate in a given time (Buss, 2007). In contrast to women, men appear to lower their standards in the context of short-term mating opportunities (Buss and Schmitt, 1993) and then show a marked *decrease* in attraction following sex – an evolved adaptation to bring about a hasty departure which prevents them spending too long with one woman.

Long-term mate preferences

In long-term mating, both sexes typically invest heavily in any offspring. As a consequence of this, sexual selection should favour high levels of choosiness in *both* sexes. Poor long-term mate choice could be disastrous for both sexes because they would have wasted valuable resources. As women have an obligatory biological investment in their children, they are predicted to be very particular about their choice of mate. This means being attracted to males who (i) are able to invest resources in her and her children, (ii) are able to physically protect her and her children, (iii) show promise as a good parent and (iv) are sufficiently compatible to ensure minimal costs to her and her children (Buss, 2003). However, people do not give away their resources indiscriminately, therefore males would be most attracted to females who display signals of fertility, an indication of their reproductive value. Buss's research (see left) explored sex differences in long-term mate choice and found universal trends in male and female preferences.

EVALUATION

The logic of sexual selection

Why do mechanisms for mate choice evolve? Being choosy requires time and energy, and the costs of mate choice can even impair survival in some cases. The rationale behind sexual selection is that random mating is essentially stupid mating. It pays to be choosy, as the genetic quality of a mate will determine half the genetic quality of any offspring. Low-quality mates (e.g. those who are unattractive and unhealthy) will be more likely to produce unattractive, unhealthy offspring. By joining forces with an attractive, high-quality mate, offspring are higher quality and an individual's genes are much more likely to be passed on.

Mate choice and the menstrual cycle

Research by Penton-Voak et al. (1999) suggests that far from being constant, female mate choice varies across the menstrual cycle. They found that women chose a slightly feminised version of a male face as 'most attractive' for a long-term relationship. However, for a short-term sexual relationship, during the high conception risk phase of the menstrual cycle, the preferred face shape was more masculinised. Sexual selection may well have favoured females who pursue a mixed mating strategy under certain conditions. A female might choose a main partner whose feminised appearance suggests kindness and cooperation in parental care, but might also copulate with a male with a more masculine appearance when conception is most likely. Such males are likely to have higher levels of the sex hormone testosterone, which suppresses the immune system. A male who is healthy despite this must, therefore, have a highly efficient immune system – a very valuable characteristic to pass on to offspring.

Male preferences for younger women

One of the most striking conclusions from Buss's study of 37 cultures (see left) was that men have a distinct preference for younger women, a finding consistent with the theory of sexual selection because the younger the woman, the greater the fertility. However, some critics have tried to explain this preference in terms of social power – younger women are easier to control, and therefore are preferred as mates. Kenrick et al. (1996) effectively rejected this hypothesis. They found that teenage males are most attracted to women who are five years older than them, despite the fact such women usually show no interest in them, and are certainly not more easily controlled by adolescent males!

CAN YOU...? No.3.4

...1 Outline, in about 50 words, what is meant by sexual selection in the context of human behaviour.

...2 Describe the relationship between sexual selection and human reproductive behaviour in about 200 words.

...3 Identify **eight** criticisms related to this relationship, including **at least one** IDA topic. Each criticism should be about 50 words.

...4 Use this material to write a 600-word answer to the question: *Discuss the relationship between sexual selection and human reproductive behaviour.* (8 marks + 16 marks)

PARENTAL INVESTMENT

Parental investment (PI) is defined as 'any investment by a parent in an offspring that increases the chance that the offspring will survive at the expense of that parent's ability to invest in any other offspring (alive or yet to be born)' (Trivers, 1972).

At the heart of Trivers' theory is the fact that in most species males and females do not invest equally. Females' initial investment is far greater because female gametes (eggs) are less numerous and more costly to produce than male gametes (sperm). A female can have only a limited number of offspring, whereas a male can (potentially) have a virtually unlimited number.

As a result of this biological inequity, females must be much choosier concerning potential mates. Males mainly compete for *quantity* of females, whereas females select for *quality* of males and their resources.

Investment by grandparents

Consistent with predictions based on paternity uncertainty, differences in investment between maternal and paternal grandparents have been found in historical and modern societies (Michalski and Shackelford, 2005). Typically, maternal grandmothers invest most (e.g. in terms of attentive care and protectiveness) in their grandchildren, followed by maternal grandfathers, and paternal grandmothers, with paternal grandfathers investing least. Similar differences have also been found for uncles and aunts (Pashos, 2007), therefore, in general, individuals appear to invest more in the maternal line than in the paternal line.

SEX DIFFERENCES IN PARENTAL INVESTMENT

The most obvious sex difference in human parental investment is that human males can opt out of parental investment in a way that females cannot. By expending a relatively large part of their reproductive effort on courtship and mating, males of most species can afford to devote rather little, in comparison to females, to parental care (Daly and Wilson, 1978). Parental investment theory states that the sex that makes the larger investment will, therefore, be the more sexually discriminating, whereas the sex that makes the smaller obligatory parental investment will compete for access to the higher-investing sex. In humans, because females invest more in their offspring, this means that they will be more discriminating in their choice of partner, and males will compete with other males for access to the higher-investing females.

Maternal investment

The investment made by human females is considerably greater than that made by males. For example, the female produces far fewer gametes (eggs) over the course of her lifetime than the male produces (sperm). The greater investment made by females may also be explained in terms of parental certainty. Because a characteristic of human reproduction is internal fertilisation, this means that unlike males, who cannot be certain that they are the father, females can be certain that they are the true parent of their child.

Why do human females invest more? As brain size increased in response to adaptive pressures among our distant ancestors, this resulted in a more difficult childbirth because of the enlargement of the skull. To compensate for this, childbirth in humans occurs earlier in development, meaning that human infants are born relatively immature compared to other animals. In common with other mammals, human females breastfeed their young, and so are more burdened by the extended period of childcare that results from this prolonged immaturity. Human mothers therefore not only make the greater prenatal contribution of resources (through pregnancy), but also make the larger postnatal contribution as well.

The costs of maternal investment – In human females, the costs of childcare are especially high. For our distant female ancestors, the minimum parental investment would have been a nine-month pregnancy followed by years of feeding and carrying. The minimum paternal investment on the other hand would have been a few moments of copulation and a teaspoonful of semen (Symons, 1979). The result is an enormous difference in the potential maximum reproductive success of the sexes, so making random mating all the more costly for human females.

Paternal investment

The minimum obligatory investment made by human males is considerably less than that of females. There are several reasons for this, including the fact that a woman can produce only a limited number of offspring, whereas a man can potentially father an unlimited number. Similarly, whereas the female must carry the developing embryo inside her for nine months and then wean the child for years afterwards, the human male can simply walk away having achieved the task of fertilisation. Therefore, indiscriminate mating could cost a woman a great deal in terms of time and resources, whereas indiscriminate mating tends to be much less costly for a man (Goetz and Shackelford, 2009).

Paternal investment and cuckoldry – When males do invest parentally (e.g. through their resources), they are under pressure to protect themselves from the possibility of cuckoldry (i.e. investing in offspring that are not their own). Because human males make a considerable investment in their children, they have a greater concern than females about the fidelity of their mates (Miller, 1998). As a result, they try to ensure that their care is not misdirected towards non-relatives, e.g. through adultery laws that define the offence in terms of the woman's marital status rather than the man's.

Sexual and emotional jealousy – The possibility of sexual infidelity posed different adaptive problems for males and females. A man whose mate was unfaithful risked investing in offspring that were not his own, whereas a woman whose mate was unfaithful risked the diversion of resources away from her and the family. Sexual jealousy, therefore, may have evolved as a solution to these problems (Buss, 1995). Men are more jealous of the sexual act (to avoid cuckoldry) while women are more jealous of the shift in emotional focus (and consequent loss of resources).

RESEARCH EVIDENCE: ARE MALES LESS 'PREPARED' THAN FEMALES TO INVEST?

In 2008, Conservative MP Michael Gove claimed that 'lads' mags' such as *Zoo* and *Nuts* reinforce a 'shallow approach' to women, and linked them to a rise in feckless fatherhood and family breakdown. Could this be the case, or are male attitudes to parenting more shaped by biological forces (as predicted by parental investment theory)? Geher *et al.* (2007) studied 91 non-parent undergraduates. Each completed a parental investment perception scale, which included statements, such as: 'I believe that I am very prepared to raise a child at this time in my life'. They were additionally exposed to various parenting related scenarios, such as: 'You are the parent of a three-year-old girl who has an ear infection. Your plans for the day have completely changed, as you now have to look after her'. Although there were no sex differences in self-report responses to parenting on the parental investment perception scale, there were clear differences in **ANS** arousal to the different parenting scenarios. Males showed significantly increased heart rate when presented with scenarios that emphasised the costs of parenting (e.g. that they would be unable to work). Researchers concluded that, consistent with predictions from parental investment theory, males are biologically less prepared than females to confront issues associated with parenting.

EVALUATION

The consequences of greater investment by females

Extra-marital affairs – The expense of childrearing means that females want to ensure good quality offspring so they don't waste their efforts. One way to achieve this is to marry a man who has good resources and is caring, but shop around for good genes through extramarital affairs with 'studs' – attractive men advertising good genes but no resources. Although accurate data for mistaken paternity are notoriously elusive, there is some evidence of this from a magazine survey of over 2700 UK women. From the results of this survey, Baker and Bellis (1990) estimated that as many as 14% of the population were products of extramarital matings.

The benefits and risks of cuckoldry – Some women may attempt to offset their greater parental investment by cuckolding their partners. The benefits women could obtain by this type of behaviour include receiving additional social support from another male and perhaps higher-quality genes for her children. However, for the woman, cuckolding her partner is not without risks. These include the possibility of abandonment and the use of mate-retention strategies (e.g. threats or actual violence against the female or the other male) by the current partner (Daly and Wilson, 1988).

Commentary on paternal investment

Males *do* invest – Joint parental care is desirable because of the obvious benefits of successful reproduction. In any situation where males can increase the success of childrearing, it will pay them to do so (Dunbar, 1995). In humans, males may restrict their reproductive opportunities and invest more in each individual offspring. Research (e.g. Reid, 1997) supports the claim that human males do contribute to parenting by providing resources (e.g. a stable food supply), and this investment allows the family to live in healthier environments, resulting in a decrease in infant and child mortality.

Parental certainty is not always an issue for human males – Parental investment theory would predict that investment by fathers would always be greater if they know the child is biologically theirs. They would not want to spend time and resources bringing up another man's child. However, some studies have contradicted this assumption. Anderson (1999) measured the resources invested by fathers and stepfathers (i.e. time spent with the child and financial support given). Men appeared not to discriminate between children born to their current partner from a previous relationship (i.e. stepchildren) and their own children from a previous relationship (i.e. their biological offspring).

Evidence for sex differences in jealousy – In line with PI theory predictions about sex differences in type of jealousy, Buss *et al.* (1992) found that male US students indicated more concern about sexual infidelity, whereas female students expressed more concern about emotional infidelity. This was supported by physiological responses when respondents were asked to imagine scenes of sexual or emotional infidelity – the men showed much more distress for sexual than emotional infidelity. However, Harris (2003) found that men tended to respond with greater arousal to any sexual imagery, which challenges the view that sex differences in jealousy are an adaptive response in males and females.

IDA PATERNAL INVESTMENT: INSIGHTS FROM NON-HUMAN SPECIES

We can better understand the origins of patterns of human parental behaviour by making a comparative analysis of parental investment in closely related species. The two most closely related (in evolutionary terms) species are chimpanzees and bonobos (pygmy chimpanzees). In both of these species, males show little or no parental investment. This suggests that the emergence of male parenting in humans represents either a dramatic evolutionary change over our primate ancestors or the contribution of cultural learning.

CAN YOU...? No.3.5

...1 Outline sex differences in parental investment (i.e. male and female investment) in about 200 words.

...2 Identify **eight** criticisms relating to sex differences in parental investment, including **at least one** IDA topic. Each critical point should be about 50 words.

...3 Choose **at least one** IDA topic relevant to this area and elaborate on these in 50 words each.

...4 Use this material to write a 600-word answer to the question: *Discuss sex differences in parental investment.* (24 marks)

IDA EVOLUTIONARY EXPLANATIONS ARE REDUCTIONIST

Rowe (2002) suggests that an explanation of paternal investment based on evolutionary factors alone is severely limited. Men's parental behaviour depends on various personal and social conditions, including the quality of the relationship with the mother, the characteristics of the child and the personality characteristics of the father. Belsky (1991) also claims that childhood experiences such as parental divorce tend to correlate with the degree to which men invest in the upbringing and care of their own children.

THE INFLUENCE OF CHILDHOOD ON ADULT RELATIONSHIPS

Childhood provides us with many different experiences, each of which shapes how we interact with the world when we are older. During childhood we learn to understand other people and ourselves. It is this last point that we are interested in here. Although everybody's childhood is unique, psychologists have identified persistent themes in childhood experiences that predispose us towards particular types of relationship as adults.

ATTACHMENT DISORDERS

Some children find the closeness of relationships with others very difficult indeed. These children resist or reject the mutual intimacy of loving family relationships and may be suffering from an attachment disorder. The specific causes of attachment disorder are unknown, but a common thread appears to be abuse or neglect during infancy. As a consequence, at times of stress, they lack someone with whom they have developed a close relationship and who can comfort and reassure them. The child's resulting behaviour and emotions create a disturbed way of relating to others, which may involve a lack of responsiveness or excessive over-familiarity. The pervasive nature of attachment disorder means that it can interfere with subsequent interpersonal relationships, such as the development of normal peer relations and ultimately romantic relationships in adulthood.

PARENT–CHILD RELATIONSHIPS

Attachment, caregiving and sexuality

Shaver et al. (1988) claimed that what we experience as romantic love in adulthood is an integration of three behavioural systems acquired in infancy – attachment, caregiving and sexuality systems. The first system, attachment, is related to the concept of the **internal working model** which you may remember from your AS studies of John Bowlby's theory of attachment. According to Bowlby (1969), later relationships are likely to be a continuation of early attachment styles (secure or insecure) because the behaviour of the infants' primary attachment figure promotes an internal working model of relationships which leads the infant to expect the same in later relationships. In some extreme cases a child's internal working model leads them to develop an **attachment disorder** (see box below left).

The caregiving system is knowledge about how one cares for others, learned by modelling the behaviour of the primary attachment figure. The sexuality system is also learned in relation to early attachment; for example individuals who suffered from an **avoidant attachment** are more likely to hold the view that sex without love is pleasurable.

Effects of childhood abuse on later relationships

Physical abuse in childhood has a number of negative effects on adult psychological functioning. For example, individuals who have experienced physical abuse in childhood are subsequently more likely to report increased rates of depression, anger and anxiety than non-abused individuals (Springer et al., 2007). Childhood sexual abuse has also been associated with psychological impairment in adult life. Research suggests that many victims of sexual abuse experience difficulties forming healthy relationships in adulthood.

Individuals who have experienced both forms of abuse in childhood develop a damaged ability to trust people and a sense of isolation from others (Alpert et al., 1998). Distancing and self-isolation can inhibit the development of romantic attachments in adulthood. van der Kolk and Fisler (1994) found that individuals who suffered childhood abuse also had difficulty forming healthy attachments and formed disorganised attachments instead. These disorganised patterns of attachment lead to a difficulty in regulating emotions, a key aspect in forming and maintaining healthy relationships.

INTERACTION WITH PEERS

Childhood friendships

Qualter and Munn (2005) have shown that children also learn from their experiences with other children. The way that a child thinks about himself and others is determined at least in part by specific experiences, which then become internalised. As a result, children may develop a sense of their own value as a result of interactions with others, which in turn determines how they approach adult relationships. Nangle et al. (2003) claim that children's friendships are training grounds for important adult relationships. Close friendships are characterised by affection, a sense of alliance and intimacy, and the sharing of secrets and personal information. The experience of having a friend to confide in promotes feelings of trust, acceptance and a sense of being understood – characteristics that are also important in later romantic relationships.

Adolescent relationships

In the later stages of childhood, attachment usually shifts from parents to peers. Romantic relationships in adolescence serve a number of purposes. First, they help to achieve the goal of separation from parents. Having shifted their attachment focus from parents to peers, adolescents can redirect intense interpersonal energy towards their romantic partner. Second, romantic relationships allow the adolescent to gain a type of emotional and physical intimacy that is quite different from that experienced with parents. Madsen (2001) tested the effects of dating behaviour in adolescence (ages 15–17½) on the quality of young adult romantic relationships (ages 20–21). She found that moderate or low dating frequency predicted higher-quality young adult relationships, whereas heavy dating predicted poorer quality young adult relationships. This suggests that some dating in adolescence is advantageous for adult relationship quality, but too much can be maladaptive.

EVALUATION

Parental relationships – research support

The relationship between attachment style and later adult relationships has been demonstrated in a number of studies. For example, Fraley (1998) conducted a **meta-analysis** of studies, finding correlations from .10 to .50 between early attachment type and later relationships. Fraley suggested that one reason for low correlations may be because insecure-anxious attachment is more unstable.

However, one key question concerns the stability of attachment types. It could be that an individual's attachment type is determined by the current relationship, which is why happily married individuals are secure. Attachment theory does suggest that significant relationship experiences may alter attachment organisation, for example Kirkpatrick and Hazan (1994) found that relationship break-ups were associated with a shift from secure to insecure attachment.

Research support for the influence of childhood abuse

Research by Berenson and Andersen (2006) provides support for the claim that abused children have a difficult time developing adult relationships. They found that adult women who had been abused in childhood later displayed negative reactions toward another person (such as the expectation of rejection and emotional distancing) but only with people who reminded them of their abusive parent. No such pattern of behaviour occurred with people who bore no resemblance to the abusive parent. Berenson and Andersen concluded that this process of transference could lead individuals abused in childhood to use inappropriate behavioural patterns learned from their relationship with an abusive parent in their subsequent interpersonal relationships.

EVALUATION

Gender differences

Gender differences in childhood relationships have been found in a number of studies. For example, Richard and Schneider (2005) found that girls have more intimate friendships than boys, and are more likely to report care and security in their relationships with other girls. Other research (e.g. Erwin, 1993) has found that boys' relationships tend to be more competitive, a fact attributed to the greater emphasis on competitive play activities. In contrast, girls are more likely to engage in cooperative and sharing activities. However, Erwin claims that sex differences in the experience of childhood relationships have been over-emphasised, and that the many similarities tend to be overlooked.

Negative effects

Although research suggests that romantic relationships in adolescence can be healthy for later adult relationships, it has also shown the potential for some negative effects. Haynie (2003) found that romantic involvement increased some forms of deviance in adolescents by as much as 35%, and Neemann et al. (1995) found that romantic involvement in early to middle adolescence was associated with decreases in academic achievement and increases in conduct problems. In late adolescence, romantic involvement was no longer related to these negative outcomes, suggesting that it is the *timing* of romantic relationships in adolescence that determines what influence, if any, they will have.

Madsen's finding that heavy dating patterns during adolescence are associated with poorer quality adult relationships is challenged by the research of Roisman et al. (2004). They found no effect of romantic experiences at age 20 on romantic relationships at age 30, suggesting that there is no consistent evidence that adolescent romantic relationships are the 'building blocks' of adult relationships.

CAN YOU…? No.3.6

…1 Outline (in 100 words each) the influence of parent–child experiences on adult relationships and interactions with peers on adult relationships.

…2 Identify **eight** criticisms related to the influence of childhood on adult relationships, including **at least one** IDA topic. Each criticism should be about 50 words.

…3 Use this material to write a 600-word answer to the question: *Discuss the influence of childhood on adult relationships.* (8 marks + 16 marks)

THE INFLUENCE OF CULTURE ON ROMANTIC RELATIONSHIPS

In our experiences of romantic relationships, we tend to view the whole process from the perspective of our own culture. In particular, our exposure to cultural stories of love structure what we might expect and how we should act in our relationships with others. However, all cultures are not the same, therefore we might expect many differences in how relationships are viewed and how they are acted out. Psychologists have discovered important differences between Western cultures, such as the US and UK, and non-Western cultures, such as India and China.

CULTURE AND ROMANCE

Love and romance are viewed as being the stuff that long-term relationships are made of. Indeed, 'falling in love' is viewed as an important part of the process of growing up. Erikson (1968) believed that the establishment of an intimate relationship is an essential task of young adulthood which, if unsuccessful, will lead to social isolation.

Marrying for love is seen as a vital component of long-term relationships in the West, but for Chinese couples, romance and love are less important and are only considered in the light of responsibility towards parents and the family. Spontaneous expression of love, especially in terms of sex outside marriage, is not considered appropriate in Chinese society (Ho, 1986).

Moore and Leung (2001) tested this predicted cultural difference in an Australian study. They compared 212 Anglo-Australian students (born in Australia, New Zealand or the UK) and 106 Chinese-Australian students (born in Hong Kong or China) to see if the 'romantic conservatism' of Chinese students would manifest itself in different attitudes toward romance and different romantic styles.

- Of the two groups, 61% of the Anglo-Australian students were in a romantic relationship, compared to just 38% of Chinese students.
- Anglo-Australian males were less romantic (and more casual about relationships) than were females. In contrast, Chinese males were as romantic as Chinese females.
- Contrary to the stereotypical view that romance is a characteristic only of Western cultures, positive attitudes to romantic love were endorsed by both groups.

WESTERN AND NON-WESTERN RELATIONSHIPS

Voluntary or non-voluntary relationships

A distinguishing feature of many Western cultures is that we live in predominantly urban settings, with relatively easy geographical and social mobility. This ensures that, on a daily basis, we voluntarily interact with a large number of people, many of whom are first acquaintances. Western cultures, therefore, appear to be characterised by a high degree of choice in romantic relationships and a greater 'pool' of potential relationships. Non-Western cultures, on the other hand, have fewer large urban centres, and less geographical and social mobility, and people therefore have less choice about whom they interact with on a daily basis. Interactions with strangers are rare, and relationships are frequently tied to other factors, such as family or economic resources.

Individual or group-based relationships

Western cultures place great importance on the rights and freedom of the individual, with individual happiness and pleasure seen as fundamentally important. Such cultures are described as **individualist** because of their focus on the individual rather than the group. In non-Western cultures, the group tends to be the primary unit of concern. Members of such **collectivist** cultures are encouraged to be interdependent rather than independent. The cultural attitudes of individualist cultures, where individual interests are more highly regarded than group goals and interests, are consistent with the formation of romantic relationships that are based on freedom of choice, whereas collectivism leads to relationships that may have more to do with the concerns of family or group (Moghaddam *et al.*, 1993).

The importance of love in romantic relationships

Because relationships in Western cultures are typically based on freedom of choice, we might expect to find differences between Western and non-Western cultures regarding the importance of love in romantic relationships. Levine *et al.* (1995) investigated love as a basis for marriage in 11 countries. Respondents were asked whether they would be willing to marry someone who had all the qualities they desired in a marriage partner but whom they did not love. The US respondents expressed a reluctance to marry in the absence of love (only 14% said they might marry someone they did not love). However, the figures from collectivist cultures such as India (24%) and Thailand (34%) were higher, suggesting a higher proportion of people in these cultures were prepared to marry in the absence of love. This suggests that in such cultures the extended family is of greater importance and romantic love is considered a comparative luxury. The different attitude toward love across cultures is explored further in the box on the left.

Cultural differences in loneliness

Cultures that promote a strong desire for romantic relationships can greatly influence feelings of romantic loneliness in young people not involved in a romantic relationship. Seepersad *et al.* (2008) suggested that young adults in Western cultures such as the UK and US would experience a greater degree of loneliness because of a high desire for romantic relationships, compared to young adults from non-Western cultures, such as China and Korea. Seepersad *et al.*'s study revealed that in a sample of 227 US and Korean students, US students reported significantly higher levels of romantic loneliness than did Koreans when they were not in a romantic relationship. Their results suggest that a strong emphasis on the importance of romantic relationships in Western cultures may unduly amplify individuals' feelings of loneliness. Seepersad *et al.*'s study also showed that Korean students relied more heavily on their families to fulfill their social network needs, while American students relied more on friends and significant others.

◄ What's love got to do with it? Left: In Eritrea, a Rashaidan wedding guest arrives on camelback accompanied by his three wives. In Rashaidan culture, young men and woman have few chances to meet of their own accord, so marriages are usually arranged by families. Brides as young as sixteen may be married to men of fifty or more, who can afford the large dowry of jewelry, camels or cash. Right: a Surma bride from Ethiopia wears a clay lip plate inserted six months before marriage. Successive stretching is achieved by placing increasingly larger plates into the lip. The final size of the plate is an indication of the number of cattle required by the girl's family for her hand in marriage. This plate is worth seventy-five head of cattle.

EVALUATION

Voluntary or non-voluntary relationships

Voluntary relationships aren't necessarily better – In some societies, 'non-voluntary' or arranged marriages make good sense and seem to work well. Divorce rates are low, and, even more surprising, in perhaps about half of them the spouses report that they have fallen in love with each other (Epstein, 2002). Myers *et al.* (2005) studied individuals in India living in arranged marriages. No differences in marital satisfaction were found when compared to individuals in non-arranged marriages in the US.

Love and marital satisfaction – However, in some rapidly developing cultures, such as China, there has been a noticeable increase in 'love matches', i.e. a move away from traditional 'arranged' marriages. In China, instances in which parents dominate the process of partner choice have declined from 70% prior to 1949, to less than 10% in the 1990s. What effect has this had on marital satisfaction? A study of women in Chengdu, China, found that women who had married for love felt better about their marriages (regardless of duration) than women who experienced arranged marriages (Xiaohe and Whyte, 1990).

Individual or group-based relationships

Although we might expect relationships based on love to produce more compatible partners, this may not necessarily be the case. Parents may be in a better position to judge compatibility in the long-term, whereas young people may be 'blinded by love' and overlook areas of personal incompatibility that will become apparent later. However, contrary to this traditional view, in Xiaohe and Whyte's study freedom of mate choice appeared to promote marital *stability* rather than instability.

The consequences of increasing urbanisation

Research suggests that attitudes toward love and romantic relationships generally may be better explained by the greater urbanisation and mobility found in Western cultures rather than by Western/non-Western cultural differences. For example, there has been a sharp increase in divorce rates in India in recent years despite India being generally regarded as a traditional, collectivist culture. As most of those being divorced are members of India's thriving urban middle class, this suggests that their aspirations and attitudes to relationships are radically different to those of their parents and grandparents.

Cultural bias in relationship research

Methodological problems – Research into cultural differences in relationships may be limited by the research method adopted. If any aspect of the methodology is interpreted differently in one culture than in another, then this creates a cultural bias that can invalidate any conclusions from a cross-cultural study. For example, measures of 'love' or 'satisfaction' that have been developed in Western cultures might not be valid in other cultures.

Indigenous psychologies – This has led some psychologists (e.g. Kim and Berry, 1993) to suggest that we should aim to develop more *indigenous* psychologies (i.e. explanations and research methods that are not transported from other cultures, and that are designed for one specific culture). This means that we could then study aspects of relationships that are seen as important and meaningful within a particular culture rather than imposing aspects from our own culture.

IDA CULTURAL BIAS IN REPRESENTATIONS OF ROMANTIC RELATIONSHIPS

Psychologists believe that the influence of US romantic comedies creates a warped sense of the 'perfect' relationship and presents a culturally-biased view of romance to young people in the UK. Children and adolescents who are repeatedly exposed to these highly idealised views of relationship come to perceive them as normal. This could then have an adverse effect on their satisfaction with their own future relationships. Johnson and Holmes (2009) spent a year analysing 40 top box office films released between 1995 and 2005. They then asked hundreds of people to fill out a questionnaire to describe their beliefs and expectations concerning romantic relationships. The researchers found that fans of films such as 'My Best Friend's Wedding' and 'How to Lose a Guy in 10 Days' were more likely to have views of relationships that reflected the themes portrayed in the films. For example, the films suggested that love and commitment exist from the moment people meet, whereas in real life these are qualities that normally take years to develop.

Evaluation IS LOVE A UNIVERSAL EVOLUTIONARY ADAPTATION?

Pinker (2008) views romantic love as a 'human universal' that has evolved to promote survival and reproduction among human beings. Being in a long-term committed relationship offers lower mortality rates, increased happiness, and decreased stress. As a result, there is a clear adaptive value to being in a long-term relationship, but how necessary is love? For romantic love to be an evolved adaptation, it should be experienced everywhere among human groups. Research has shown that romantic love is not exclusive to Western cultures, but is also found in many non-Western cultures. For example, Jankowiak and Fischer (1992) searched for evidence of romantic love in a sample of non-Western tribal societies. They found clear evidence of romantic love in 90% of the 166 cultures studied. Evidence for the universality of romantic love also comes from Bartels and Zeki (2000), who claim to have discovered a 'functionally specialised system', that lights up during fMRI scans of the brains of people who claim to be in love.

CAN YOU...? No.3.7

...1 Describe (in about 200 words) the nature of relationships in non-Western cultures.

...2 Identify **eight** criticisms related to the influence of culture on romantic relationships, including **at least one** IDA topic. Each criticism should be about 50 words.

...3 Use this material to write a 600-word answer to the question: *Discuss the influence of culture on romantic relationships*. (8 marks + 16 marks)

CHAPTER SUMMARY

ROMANTIC RELATIONSHIPS

FORMATION

REWARD/NEED SATISFACTION
- We are attracted to people who provide us with direct reinforcement.
- We are attracted to people associated with pleasant events.

EVALUATION
Research support from:
- Griffitt and Guay (1969), Cate et al. (1982), Lehr and Geher (2006).
- Physiological support – Aron et al. (2005).
- Need satisfaction through Facebook use (Sheddon et al. 2011).

SIMILARITY
- We sort people first for dissimilarity and then similarity.
- We are attracted to people with similar personalities and attitudes.

EVALUATION
- Rosenbaum (1986) – dissimilarity more important than similarity.
- Yoshida (1972) – represents a narrow view of important factors.
- Important because lessens chances of rejection and validates our beliefs.
- Studies may lack mundane realism, but some support from study of real-life couples.

IDA
- Cultural bias – reward/need satisfaction not relevant in some cultures.
- Evolutionary explanation – love is an adaptation to focus courtship energy on specific individuals.

MAINTENANCE

SOCIAL EXCHANGE THEORY
- Commitment to a relationship dependent on profitability.
- To judge if relationship worthwhile, we use CL and CL for alternatives.

EVALUATION
- Profit and loss – explains women in abusive relationships.
- Research support from Simpson et al. (1990).
- Focuses only on selfish concerns.

EQUITY THEORY
- Dissatisfaction = inequitable relationship, Satisfaction = equitable relationship.
- Equity judged by perceived ratio of inputs and outputs.

EVALUATION
- Equity less important in long-term relationships.
- DeMaris – women's sense of being under-benefited most important
- Equity insufficient as theory of real-life married relationships.

IDA
- Cultural bias – 'economic' theories only apply to relationships in Western cultures.
- Gender bias – Steil and Weltman (1991) – married men and women judge equity differently.
- Real-world application – relationship therapy.

BREAKDOWN

REASONS FOR BREAKDOWN
Duck (1999) suggests:
- lack of skills,
- lack of stimulation,
- maintenance difficulties.

EVALUATION
- Some affairs may be a reaction to perceived lack or skills/stimulation.
- Success of skills training shows importance of relationship skills.
- Many LDRs prosper despite maintenance difficulties.

MODEL OF BREAKDOWN
Rollie and Duck (2006) – Five 'processes' of breakdown: Intrapsychic → Dyadic → Social → Grave dressing → Resurrection.

EVALUATION
- Support from real-life relationships (Tashiro and Frazier, 2003).
- Model stresses importance of communication and possibility of effective intervention.
- Gender difference – men and women stress different reasons for breakdown (Brehm and Kassin, 1996).

IDA
- Ethical issues – 'breakdown' research a sensitive area with very vulnerable participants.
- Real-world application – CCET.

EFFECTS OF EARLY EXPERIENCE AND CULTURE

CHILDHOOD

PARENT–CHILD RELATIONSHIPS
- Adult romantic love a product of attachment, caregiving and sexuality systems from infancy.
- Abuse and/or neglect in infancy can lead to development of attachment disorder.
- Physical and sexual abuse in childhood make adult relationships more difficult.

EVALUATION
- Research support – meta-analysis (Fraley, 1998) showed link between attachment type and later relationships.
- Simpson et al. (2007) – emotional styles in adulthood can be traced back to infancy.
- Berenson and Andersen (2006) – support that abused children have a difficult time developing adult relationships.

INTERACTION WITH PEERS
- Childhood friendships – children learn about relationships and develop sense of their own value from interacting with close friends.
- Adolescent relationships allow separation from parents and development of sexual and emotional intimacy through dating.

EVALUATION
- Research suggests gender differences in childhood relationships – girls are more intimate and caring, boys more competitive.
- Negative effects – early dating linked to deviance and lack of achievement, although findings inconsistent on this association.

IDA
- Support from studies of non-human animals show importance of interactions with peers for later development (Suomi and Harlow, 1978).
- Determinism – Simpson et al. claim that despite their findings, this does not indicate that an individual's past unalterably determines the future course of their relationships.

HUMAN REPRODUCTIVE BEHAVIOUR

SEXUAL SELECTION

NATURE OF SEXUAL SELECTION
- Intrasexual = mate competition.
- Intersexual = mate choice.
- Sex differences in short-term mating strategies (e.g. males show preference for casual sex).
- Long-term mate preferences – females attracted to males who have resources, good parenting skills and are protective. Males attracted to females who display signals of fertility.

EVALUATION
- Logic of sexual selection – random mating costly.
- Mate choice and menstrual cycle – women choose different types of male at different stages of cycle.
- Male preferences for younger women – challenged by 'social power' explanation but this challenge is not supported (Kenrick et al., 1996).
- Validity problems – Buss's study measured preferences rather than actual choices, but results also supported in real marriages (Buss, 1989).

RESEARCH SUPPORT
- Buss (1989) – universal differences in long-term mate preferences.
- Sex differences in short-term mating strategies supported by Clarke and Hatfield's (1989) campus study.
- Importance of fertility in mate choice supported by lap dancer study (Miller et al., 2007).

IDA
- Gender bias – short-term mating (e.g. casual sex) may also benefit females, e.g. mate switching.

SEX DIFFERENCES IN PARENTAL INVESTMENT

MATERNAL INVESTMENT
- Female investment greater than male investment – internal fertilisation.
- Human females invest more because infants born relatively helpless.
- Costs of maternal investment makes random mating costly for females.

EVALUATION
- Greater investment may lead to search for 'good genes' through extramarital affairs.
- Cuckolding male partner carries risks – e.g. abandonment or violence against the female.

PATERNAL INVESTMENT
- Males invest less as costs of indiscriminate mating less for males.
- Males must protect themselves from risk of cuckoldry therefore concerned about sexual infidelity in female partner.
- Sexual jealousy evolved as solution to problem of possible cuckoldry.

EVALUATION
- Human males do invest – leads to decrease in infant mortality.
- In terms of investment, parental certainty may not be an issue for human males.
- Buss et al. (1992) – evidence for sex differences in jealousy.
- Physiological measures support limited male investment (Geher et al., 2007).

IDA
- Support from studies of comparative species show little paternal investment in chimpanzees and bonobos.
- Evolutionary explanations are reductionist as ignore personal and social conditions that determine paternal investment.

CULTURE

WESTERN AND NON-WESTERN RELATIONSHIPS
- Western relationships more voluntary, non-Western less so.
- Western cultures emphasise individual rights and freedom, non-Western cultures emphasise importance of family or group in decisions about romantic relationships.
- Importance of love – members of Western cultures less likely to marry in absence of love compared to members of non-Western cultures.
- Loneliness – members of Western cultures more likely to experience loneliness in absence of romantic relationships (Seepersad et al., 2008).
- Research (Moore and Leung, 2001) – found sex differences in attitudes to romantic love between Australian and Chinese students.

EVALUATION
- Non-voluntary relationships also characterised by love (Myers et al., 2005) although move away from arranged marriages in China associated with higher levels of marital satisfaction (Xiaohe and Whyte, 1990).
- Non-voluntary relationships may produce more compatible partners in long term.
- Change from permanent to temporary relationships associated with increasing urbanisation rather than cultural differences.
- Love is an evolutionary adaptation, supported by the finding that most cultures have some evidence of romantic love (Jankowiak and Fischer, 1992).

IDA
- US romantic comedies represent culturally-biased view of romantic relationships (Johnson and Holmes, 2009).
- Cultural bias in relationship research – need for indigenous psychology to overcome different meanings of measures used.

EXAM QUESTION WITH STUDENT ANSWER

QUESTION (a) Outline and evaluate **one** theory of the formation of romantic relationships. *(4 marks + 8 marks)*
(b) Outline and evaluate **one** theory of the breakdown of romantic relationships. *(4 marks + 8 marks)*

STUDENT ANSWER

(a) *One theory of the formation of romantic relationships is the reward-satisfaction theory by Byrne and Clore (1970). This theory suggests that we learn to have an affection for someone as a consequence of either operant or classical conditioning. With operant conditioning the person experiences rewards from another person, either directly or indirectly, and this increases their liking for that person.*

This has research support, for example a study by Griffitt and Guay showed that people did express more liking for an experimenter who rewarded them.

With classical conditioning, we develop a liking for someone because we associate them with pleasant experiences. This also has research support from Griffitt and Guay because they found that someone who was an onlooker in the experiment was also liked more if they were present when the experimenter was rewarding the participant.

However, one criticism of this theory is that it is very determinist because it suggests that we like people because of external factors such as rewards, whereas there is also evidence that people have more complex reasons for forming relationships than just liking people. Hays says that we gain satisfaction from giving as well as receiving rewards.

(b) *One theory of the breakdown of relationships is the model proposed by Rollie and Duck (2006). This model has six stages which are:*

1. Breakdown – at first a person is dissatisfied with their relationship.
2. Intrapsychic processes – when a person thinks about what has gone wrong, and considers the costs and possible alternatives.
3. Dyadic processes – now they start to talk about the difficulties.
4. Social processes – seeking support from other people.
5. Grave-dressing processes – preparing stories about what went wrong in order, for example, to save face.
6. Resurrection processes – preparing for future relationships.

All these processes have thresholds where the person tips over into the next stage. For example, Stage 2 ends when the person feels they are justified in ending the relationship, so then they start to talk about it more publicly.

There is research support for this theory. For example, in one study, undergraduates who had recently experienced a break-up were asked about their experiences, and they said that breaking up had given them new insights, which supports the resurrection phase. However, this study, like a lot of studies on relationships, is limited because it dealt with students who had not had very long-term relationships so we cannot really generalise such findings to adults who have been married for a long time and with children. Also, a lot of the research was done in America and does not tell us about people from other cultures.

One strength of this model is that it can be used to help with marriage guidance to work out the stage a couple is at in order to address the specific problems that might be occurring.

A criticism of Rollie and Duck's model is that it is largely descriptive – it just describes the stages a person goes through rather than explaining why the breakdown might have happened. Duck provided a different kind of approach in his reasons for relationship breakdown (Duck, 1999). For example, he suggested that often a relationship will break down because of lack of stimulation – one partner gets bored. Or it may be lack of social skills where one partner is not very good at getting on with the other partner because he/she is just not very good with people. However, some of these explanations again are more appropriate for short-term relationships in individualist cultures.

[590 words]

EXAMINER COMMENTS

In an exam it is fine to plunge straight into your answer without any elegant introduction. Marks are awarded for **knowledge**, **understanding**, **analysis**, **evaluation** – and an **elaboration** of all the points you make, as illustrated in this answer where each point is identified and then explained.

Reward-satisfaction theory is given a brief explanation – but the question only requires an outline. Perhaps the commentary is overbrief, although it does include mention of a **'debate'** (determinism).

AO1 – sound, **accurate** and **well-detailed**.
AO2/AO3 – somewhat limited analysis and evaluation, **basic** reference to **IDA**.

The description of the theory is well-balanced, although brief. Each of the stages has been identified but is given a rather superficial description. However, as there are only six marks available for description in this essay, the basic outline constitutes a **thorough** description.

This additional descriptive paragraph clinches the full marks for **AO1** because it shows that little bit extra **detail** to distinguish this answer from a simple outline.

More attention has been paid to the **evaluation** than the description, which is reasonable given the fact that there are more marks available for **AO2/AO3** material. Research evidence is used effectively – the study is not named but it has been well elaborated. Comments are included about the research methodology.

IDA is demonstrated by making reference to practical applications of the theory.

The final paragraph includes a criticism of the 'model' approach, contrasting it with Duck's other approach to understanding relationship breakdown – the reasons for breakdown. Some of this material borders on being too descriptive, which needs to be avoided when writing evaluation.

AO1 – accurate and **detailed**.
AO2/AO3 – substantial and **thorough, reasonably effective**, including some **IDA**.

Chapter 4
Aggression

SPECIFICATION

Aggression		
Social psychological approaches to explaining aggression	• Social psychological theories of aggression, for example social learning theory, deindividuation. • Institutional aggression.	
Biological explanations of aggression	• Neural and hormonal mechanisms in aggression. • Genetic factors in aggressive behaviour.	
Evolution and human aggression	• Evolutionary explanations of human aggression, including infidelity and jealousy. • Evolutionary explanations of group display in humans, for example sport and warfare.	

SOCIAL LEARNING THEORY

Aggressive behaviour is viewed as one of the most disturbing forms of human social behaviour. Some psychologists believe that aggression is a legacy of our evolutionary ancestry, while others believe it is best explained in physiological terms, e.g. an imbalance in hormones or neurotransmitters in the brain. Social psychological theories, however, see the cause of our aggressive behaviour arising out of our interactions with others in our social world.

SOCIAL LEARNING THEORY

Bandura and Walters (1963) believed that aggression could not be explained using traditional learning theory where only *direct* experience was seen as responsible for the acquisition of new behaviours. **Social learning theory (SLT)** suggests that we also learn by observing others. We learn the specifics of aggressive behaviour (e.g. the forms it takes, how often it is enacted, the situations that produce it and the targets towards which it is directed). This is not to suggest that the role of biological factors is ignored in this theory, but rather that a person's biological make-up creates a potential for aggression and it is the actual *expression* of aggression that is learned. Bandura *et al.*'s classic study (see left) illustrates many of the important principles of this theory.

Observation

Children primarily learn their aggressive responses through *observation* – watching the behaviour of role models and then *imitating* that behaviour. Whereas Skinner's **operant conditioning** theory claimed that learning takes place through direct reinforcement, Bandura suggested that children learn just by observing role models with whom they identify.

Children also observe and learn about the consequences of aggressive behaviour by watching others being reinforced or punished. This is called indirect or **vicarious reinforcement**. Children witness many examples of aggressive behaviour at home and at school, as well as on television and in films. By observing the *consequences* of aggressive behaviour for those who use it, a child gradually learns something about what is considered appropriate (and effective) conduct in the world around them. Thus they learn the behaviours (through observation) and they also learn whether and when such behaviours are worth repeating (through vicarious reinforcement).

Mental representation

Bandura (1986) claimed that in order for social learning to take place, the child must form mental representations of events in their social environment. The child must also represent possible rewards and punishments for their aggressive behaviour in terms of *expectancies* of future outcomes. When appropriate opportunities arise in the future, the child will display the learned behaviour *as long as* the expectation of reward is greater than the expectation of punishment.

Production of behaviour

Maintenance through direct experience – If a child is rewarded (i.e. gets what he wants or is praised by others) for a behaviour, he or she is likely to repeat the same action in similar situations in the future. A child who has a history of successfully bullying other children will therefore come to attach considerable value to aggression.

Self-efficacy expectancies – In addition to forming expectancies of the likely outcomes of their aggression, children also develop confidence in their ability to carry out the necessary aggressive actions. Children for whom this form of behaviour has been particularly disastrous in the past (e.g. they weren't very good at it) have less confidence (lower sense of **self-efficacy**) in their ability to use aggression successfully to resolve conflicts, and therefore may turn to other means.

EXAM TIP: *Beware of exam questions that ask for **theories** of aggression. Bandura et al.'s Bobo doll study can be used as research support for the prediction of the **theory**, but it is the material elsewhere on this spread that explains the theory of social learning.*

EVALUATION

Research support

The role of punishment – In the Bandura and Walters study on the left, did the children in Group 2 show low levels of aggression because the punishment prevented *learning* or did the punishment prevent *performance* of the behaviour? To test this, Bandura (1965) repeated the study but now, after exposure to the model, offered rewards to all the children for performing the model's aggressive behaviours. In this case all three groups performed a similar number of imitative acts. This shows that learning does take place regardless of reinforcements but that *production* of behaviours is related to selective reinforcements.

Applicability to adults – The studies on this spread have involved children, but does SLT explain adult behaviour as well? Phillips (1986) found that daily homicide rates in the US almost always increased in the week following a major boxing match, suggesting that viewers were imitating behaviour they watched and that social learning is evident in adults as well as children.

Strengths

The role of vicarious learning – A major strength of SLT is that, unlike operant conditioning theory, it can explain aggressive behaviour in the *absence* of direct reinforcement. Although Bandura *et al.*'s (1963) participants behaved more aggressively after observing an aggressive model, at no point were the children directly rewarded for any action, either aggressive or non-aggressive. Consequently, the concept of vicarious learning is necessary to explain these findings.

Individual differences in aggressive behaviour – A second strength of this theory is that it can explain differences in aggressive and non-aggressive behaviour both *between* and *within* individuals. The 'culture of violence' theory (Wolfgang and Ferracuti, 1967), for example, proposes that, in large societies, some subcultures develop norms that sanction violence to a greater degree than the dominant culture. Some cultures may emphasise and model *non*-aggressive behaviour, producing individuals that show low levels of aggression (see 'cultural differences' box). Differences *within* individuals can be related to selective reinforcement and **context-dependent learning**. People respond differently in different situations because they have observed that aggression is rewarded in some situations and not others, i.e. they learn behaviours that are appropriate to particular contexts.

Evaluation CULTURAL DIFFERENCES

Social learning theory can be used to explain cultural differences in aggression. Among the !Kung San of the Kalahari Desert, aggression is comparatively rare, so why is this the case?

The answer lies in the child-rearing practices of the !Kung San. First, when two children argue or fight, parents neither reward nor punish them, but physically separate them and try to distract their attention onto other things. Second, parents do not use physical punishment, and aggressive postures are avoided by adults and devalued by the society as a whole. The absence of direct reinforcement of aggressive behaviour as well as the absence of aggressive models means there is little opportunity or motivation for !Kung San children to acquire aggressive behaviours.

Evaluation VALIDITY

It is possible that the children in Bandura's studies were aware of what was expected of them (**demand characteristics**). In fact Noble (1975) reports that one child arriving at the laboratory for the experiment said: 'Look Mummy, there's the doll we have to hit.' These studies also focus on aggression towards a doll rather than a real person (who tends to hit back). However, responding to this criticism, Bandura produced a film of a young woman beating up a live clown. When the children went into the other room, there was the live clown! They proceeded to punch him, kick him, hit him with hammers, and so on.

CAN YOU...? No.4.1

...1 Describe the social learning theory of aggression in approximately 200 words, and then produce a summary in about 100 words.

...2 Identify **eight** criticisms related to the social learning theory of aggression, including **at least one** IDA topic. Each criticism should be about 50 words.

...3 Use this material to write a 600-word answer to the question: *Discuss **one** social psychological theory of aggression.* (8 marks + 16 marks)

DEINDIVIDUATION

Not all aggressive behaviour is between individuals. Psychologists have explored the idea that membership of large, anonymous groups leads individuals to behave in a more antisocial manner than they would on their own. To explain this, Zimbardo (1969) introduced the theory of **deindividuation**, whereby people, when part of a relatively anonymous group, lose their personal identity and hence their inhibitions about violence. Deindividuation theory has been used as an explanation of the collective behaviour of violent crowds, mindless hooligans and social atrocities, such as genocide. In some countries, deindividuation has even been accepted as grounds for extenuating circumstances in murder trials (Colman, 1991).

'Sure this robe of mine doth change my disposition.'

William Shakespeare – The Winter's Tale

DEINDIVIDUATION THEORY

Deindividuation theory is based, to a large extent, on the classic crowd theory of Gustave Le Bon (1895). Le Bon described how an individual was transformed when part of a crowd. He claimed that, in a crowd, the combination of anonymity, suggestibility and contagion mean that a 'collective mind' takes possession of the individual. As a consequence, the individual loses self-control and becomes capable of acting in a way that goes against personal or social norms.

The nature of deindividuation

Deindividuation is a psychological state characterised by lowered self-evaluation and decreased concerns about evaluation by others. This leads to an increase in behaviour that would normally be inhibited by personal or social norms. The psychological state of deindividuation is aroused when individuals join crowds or large groups. Factors that contribute to deindividuation include anonymity (e.g. wearing a uniform) and altered consciousness due to drugs or alcohol (Zimbardo, 1969). Although Zimbardo has stressed that these same conditions may also lead to an increase in *prosocial* behaviours (for example crowds at music festivals and large religious gatherings), the focus of deindividuation theory has been almost exclusively on **antisocial** behaviour.

The process of deindividuation

People normally refrain from acting in an aggressive manner partly because there are social norms inhibiting such 'uncivilised' behaviour and partly because they are easily identifiable. Being anonymous (and therefore effectively unaccountable) in a crowd has the psychological consequence of reducing inner restraints and increasing behaviours that are usually inhibited.

According to Zimbardo, being part of a crowd can diminish awareness of our own individuality. In a large crowd, each person is faceless and anonymous – the larger the group, the greater the anonymity. There is diminished fear of negative evaluation of actions and a reduced sense of guilt. Conditions that increase anonymity also minimise concerns about evaluation by others, and so weaken the normal barriers to antisocial behaviour that are based on guilt or shame.

Research on deindividuation

Anonymity – Zimbardo (1969) carried out a series of experiments that were instrumental in the development of deindividuation theory. One of these studies is described in the box below. This study led to the suggestion that anonymity, a key component of the deindividuation process, increased aggressiveness. Rehm *et al.* (1987) investigated whether wearing a uniform when part of a sports team also increased aggressive behaviour. They randomly assigned German schoolchildren to handball teams of five people, half the teams wearing the same orange shirts, and the other half their normal street clothes. The children wearing orange (who were harder to tell apart) played the game consistently more aggressively than the children in their everyday clothes.

The faceless crowd – Mullen (1986) analysed newspaper cuttings of sixty lynchings in the United States between 1899 and 1946. He found that the more people there were in the mob, the greater the savagery with which they killed their victims. Another example of the deindividuated crowd can be seen in Mann's 'baiting crowd' research (see far right).

Reduced private self-awareness

Prentice-Dunn *et al.* (1982) offer an alternative perspective to Zimbardo's conclusion that anonymity is an important determinant of deindividuation. They claim that it is reduced self-awareness, rather than simply anonymity, that leads to deindividuation. If an individual is self-focused, they tend to focus on, and act according to, their internalised attitudes and moral standards, thus reducing the likelihood of antisocial behaviour. If the individual submerges themselves within a group, they may lose this focus, becoming less privately self-aware, and therefore less able to regulate their own behaviour.

GENDER BIAS

Cannavale *et al.* (1970) found that male and female groups responded differently under deindividuation conditions reflecting a gender bias in the theory. An increase in aggression was obtained only in the all-male groups. This was also the finding of Diener *et al.* (1973), who found greater **disinhibition** of aggression (i.e. removal of the normal inhibitions concerning aggression) in males. Thus, evidence indicates that males may be more prone to disinhibition of aggressive behaviour when deindividuated, than females.

EVALUATION

The importance of local group norms

Johnson and Downing (1979) explored the idea that rather than deindividuation automatically increasing the incidence of aggression, any behaviour produced could be a product of local group norms. They used the same experimental conditions as Zimbardo (see below), but this time participants were made anonymous by means of a mask and overalls (reminiscent of the Ku Klux Klan), or by means of nurses' uniforms. Participants shocked more than a control condition when dressed in the Ku Klux Klan uniforms, but actually shocked less than the controls when dressed as nurses. This finding illustrates that, as was the case in Zimbardo *et al.*'s Stanford Prison Experiment (1972), people respond to normative cues associated with the social context in which they find themselves. In this study, participants dressed as Ku Klux Klansmen clearly felt that aggressive behaviour was more appropriate than did the participants dressed as nurses.

Lack of support for deindividuation

Evidence for deindividuation theory is mixed. A **meta-analysis** of 60 studies of deindividuation (Postmes and Spears 1998) concludes that there is insufficient support for the major claims of deindividuation theory. For example, Postmes and Spears found that **disinhibition** and antisocial behaviour are not more common in large groups and anonymous settings. Nor was there much evidence that deindividuation is associated with reduced self-awareness, or that reduced self-awareness increases aggressive behaviour.

Prosocial consequences of deindividuation

Deindividuation can increase prosocial behaviour – Although most of the research on this spread has attempted to find a relationship between deindividuation and antisocial behaviour, some studies have shown that deindividuation may also increase the incidence of *pro*social behaviour. Spivey and Prentice-Dunn (1990) found that deindividuation could lead to either prosocial or antisocial behaviour depending on situational factors. When prosocial environmental cues were present (such as a prosocial model), deindividuated participants performed significantly more altruistic acts (giving money) and significantly fewer antisocial acts (giving electric shocks) compared to a control group.

Online deindividuation – The desirable effects of deindividuation can also be found in cyberspace. Adolescents reported feeling significantly more comfortable seeking help with mental health problems under the deindividuated circumstances of Internet chatrooms compared to the individuated circumstances of a personal appointment with a health professional (Francis *et al.*, 2006).

REAL-WORLD APPLICATION – THE BAITING CROWD AND SUICIDE JUMPERS

'When darkness fell,
Excitement kissed the crowd
And made them wild,
In an atmosphere of freaky holiday
When the spotlight hit the boy,
The crowd began to cheer
He flew away'. (Simon and Garfunkel – 'Save the life of my child')

Mann (1981) used the concept of deindividuation to explain a bizarre aspect of collective behaviour – the 'baiting crowd'. The baiting crowd lends support to the notion of the crowd as a deindividuated 'mob'. Mann analysed 21 suicide leaps reported in US newspapers in the 1960s and 1970s. He found that in 10 of the 21 cases where a crowd had gathered to watch, baiting had occurred (i.e. the crowd had urged the potential suicide to jump). These incidents tended to occur at night, when the crowd was large and some distance from the person being taunted (particularly when the 'jumper' was high above them). All these features were likely to produce a state of deindividuation in the members of the crowd.

CULTURAL DIFFERENCES

Dramatic support for the deadly influence of deindividuation comes from a study by anthropologist Robert Watson (1973). He collected data on the extent to which warriors in 23 societies changed their appearance prior to going to war and the extent to which they killed, tortured or mutilated their victims. As can be seen from the figures below, those societies where warriors changed their appearance (e.g. through war paint, tribal costumes, etc.) were more destructive toward their victims compared to those who did not change their appearance. As Zimbardo (2007) comments, when we want '...usually peaceful young men to harm and kill other young men...it is easier to do so if they first change their appearance to alter their usual external façade'.

▲ Comparative levels of killing, torture and mutilation in warriors who significantly change their appearance when going to war and those who don't.

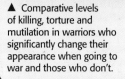

	No change	Changed
Low	7	3
High	1	12

Source: Watson, 1973.

CAN YOU...? No.4.2

...1 Describe the deindividuation theory of aggression in approximately 200 words, and then produce a summary in about 100 words.

...2 Identify **eight** criticisms related to deindividuation theory and aggression, including **at least one** IDA topic. Each criticisms should be about 50 words.

...3 Use this material and the material on the previous spread to write a 600-word answer to the question: *Outline and evaluate **two** social psychological theories of aggression*. (8 marks + 16 marks).

EXAM TIP: *Exam questions will never ask for 'deindividuation' as this is only an example in the specification. You may be asked to discuss one theory – and you can use deindividuation as the one theory. Alternatively, you may be asked to discuss two theories – in which case you must only write 4 marks + 8 marks worth for each theory. If deindividuation is your 'second' theory then you only need a 4 + 8 mark version.*

INSTITUTIONAL AGGRESSION

Human aggression occurs at both interpersonal and institutional levels. Interpersonal aggression involves direct actions against a specific individual and is restricted to a specific place and time. On the previous two spreads we have looked at explanations of interpersonal aggression, but we now turn our attention to aggression at an institutional or group level.

Institutional aggression may occur *within* groups or institutions, such as the armed forces, prisons or mental institutions, or *between* different groups. Thus it involves more complex processes and conditions than interpersonal aggression, and can, on occasion, lead to the most terrible consequences for its victims.

STAGES IN THE PROCESS OF GENOCIDE

1 Difficult social conditions, leading to…
2 Scapegoating of a less powerful group, leading to…
3 Negative evaluation and dehumanisation of the target group, leading to…
4 Moral values and rules becoming inapplicable, and the killing begins.
5 The passivity of bystanders (e.g. the UN) enhances the process.

Staub (1999)

► A Tutsi survivor of the Rwandan genocide clearly shows the machete scars inflicted on him by Hutu extremists.

INSTITUTIONAL AGGRESSION WITHIN GROUPS: PRISONS

Prisons are dangerous places. Statistics released by the Howard League for Penal Reform in 2010 showed that recorded assault incidents rose by 61% between 2000 and 2009. In the US, a 2007 report by the Bureau of Justice Statistics estimated that as many as 70,000 inmates are victims of sexual violence while behind bars (Beck and Harrison, 2007).

The importation model

Interpersonal factors – Irwin and Cressey (1962) claim that prisoners bring their own social histories and traits with them into prison, and this influences their adaptation to the prison environment. Irwin and Cressey argue that prisoners are not 'blank slates' when they enter prison, and that many of the normative systems developed on the outside would be 'imported' into the prison.

Gang membership – Within prison environments, gang membership is consistently related to violence and other forms of antisocial behaviour. Several studies (e.g. Allender and Marcell, 2003) have found that gang members disproportionately engage in acts of prison violence. Pre-prison gang membership appears to be an important determinant of prison misconduct. Members of street gangs offend at higher levels than their non-gang counterparts and account for a disproportionate amount of serious and violent crime. For example, Huff (1998) found that gang members in the US were ten times more likely to commit a murder and three times more likely to assault someone in public than were non-gang members of a similar age and background.

Situational factors – the 'deprivation model' – This model argues that prisoner or patient aggression is the product of the stressful and oppressive conditions of the institution itself (Paterline and Peterson, 1999). These include crowding, assumed to increase fear and frustration levels, and staff experience. For example, Hodgkinson et al. (1985) found that trainee nurses are more likely to suffer violent assault than experienced nurses, and in the prison setting, length of service was also a significant factor, with more experienced officers being less likely to suffer an assault (Davies and Burgess, 1988).

The 'pains of imprisonment' – Sykes (1958) described the specific deprivations that inmates experience within prison and which might be linked to an increase in violence. These included the loss of liberty, the loss of autonomy and the loss of security. For example, Sykes found that the potential threat to personal security increased anxiety levels in inmates, even if the majority of prisoners posed no significant threat to them. Inmates may cope with the pains of imprisonment in several ways. Some choose to withdraw through seclusion in their cell or living space, whereas others choose to rebel in the form of violence against other prisoners or against staff.

INSTITUTIONAL AGGRESSION BETWEEN GROUPS: GENOCIDE

In some cases, the 'institution' may refer to a whole section of society, defined by ethnicity, religion or some other significant feature. Violence may occur when one institution's relationship with another is characterised by hatred and hostility. The murder of six million Jews by Nazis during World War II, and more recently the murder of 800,000 Tutsi and moderate Hutu by Hutu extremists in Rwanda in 1994, are examples of this special form of institutional aggression. Staub (1999) outlined five stages in the process of genocide (see above) that explain how difficult social conditions such as those found in pre-war Germany can rapidly escalate into victimisation of a target group.

Dehumanisation – Although human beings usually have moral inhibitions about killing fellow humans, this changes if the target group is dehumanised so that its members are seen as worthless animals and therefore not worthy of moral consideration. In the Rwandan genocide, the influential Hutu-controlled 'hate' radio station RTLM encouraged Hutu listeners to murder their Tutsi neighbours by referring to the minority Tutsi as 'cockroaches'.

Obedience to authority

'The Nazi extermination of European Jews is the most extreme instance of abhorrent immoral acts carried out by thousands of people in the name of obedience'. (Milgram, 1974)

Milgram believed that the Holocaust was primarily the result of situational pressures that forced Nazi soldiers to obey their leaders regardless of any personal moral repugnance. If, he argued, so many participants in his study could administer painful electric shocks to a victim simply because they were told to do so by someone in authority, the mighty Nazi regime would have no trouble making soldiers kill innocent, unarmed people.

EVALUATION

Institutional aggression within groups: Prisons

The importation model – This model has received some research support, particularly in terms of individual factors, such as age, education level and race. For example, Harer and Steffensmeier (2006) collected data from 58 US prisons and found that black inmates had significantly higher rates of violent behaviour but lower rates of alcohol-related and drug-related misconduct than white inmates. These patterns parallel racial differences in these behaviours in US society and so support the importation model.

Gang membership – Evidence from DeLisi *et al.* (2004) challenges the claim that pre-prison gang membership predicts violence whilst in prison. They found that inmates with prior street gang involvement were no more likely than other inmates to engage in prison violence. This lack of a correlation between the two might, however, be explained by the fact that violent gang members tend to be isolated from the general inmate population, therefore greatly restricting their opportunities for violence. For example, Fischer (2001) found that isolating known gang members in a special management unit reduced the rates of serious assault by 50%.

The deprivation model – There is substantial research evidence to support the claim that peer violence is used to relieve the deprivation imposed by institutional cultures, such as prisons. McCorkle *et al.* (1995) found that overcrowding, lack of privacy and the lack of meaningful activity all significantly influence peer violence. However, research in this area is not consistent in its findings. Research in psychiatric institutions, for example Nijman *et al.* (1999), found that increased personal space failed to decrease the level of violent incidents among patients.

Combining deprivation and importation models – Jiang and Fisher-Giorlando (2002) found support for both the deprivation and importation models as explanations of prison violence. They found that the deprivation model was better able to explain violence against prison staff, whereas the importation model was better able to explain violence against other inmates. The deprivation model is also challenged by research by Poole and Regoli (1983). They found that the best indicator of violence among juvenile offenders was pre-institutional violence regardless of any situational factors in the institution.

Institutional aggression between groups: genocide

The importance of bystanders
– Staub's model emphasises the importance of bystander intervention in preventing genocide. Doing nothing, it appears, merely allows the killing to continue unabated, and may even escalate it by signalling apathy or consent. However, bystander intervention does not necessarily end institutional aggression, as there is an important difference between the effect of intervention on duration and on *severity* of violence. In international or civil conflict, although intervention by outside agencies such as the UN can shorten a conflict, it might also hasten perpetrators to step up their genocidal policy within that period of time. In the Rwandan genocide, for example, 800,000 people died in just 100 days, a staggering rate of 8,000 deaths per day.

Dehumanisation – Evidence for the destructive consequences of dehumanisation can be seen in many conflicts (Jews in the Holocaust, Bosnians in the Balkan wars and Tutsis in Rwanda). However, dehumanisation may also explain violence against immigrants, seen by some as 'polluting threats to the social order' (O'Brien, 2003). This claim is examined in more detail in the 'Real-world application' above.

Obedience to authority – Mandel (1998) rejects Milgram's claims that obedience to authority was sufficient to explain the behaviour of Holocaust perpetrators. He argues that Milgram's account is *monocausal* (i.e. ignores other possible causes) and simply does not match the historical record. For example, Goldhagen (1996) suggests that the main causal factor in the atrocities was a form of anti-Semitism so deeply entrenched in the German people at that time that they implicitly condoned the elimination of millions of innocent Jews.

▲ A stereotypical view of asylum seekers. Young Iraqi Kurds wait in Calais before trying to smuggle themselves into the UK.

CAN YOU...? No.4.3

...1 Describe **two** types of institutional aggression, giving **two** explanations for each. Altogether you should write about 200 words.

...2 Identify **eight** criticisms related to institutional aggression, including **at least one** IDA topic. Each criticism should be about 50 words.

...3 Use this material to write a 600-word answer to the question: *Discuss psychological explanations of **two or more** forms of institutional aggression.* (8 marks + 16 marks)

NEURAL AND HORMONAL MECHANISMS IN AGGRESSION

Biological explanations of aggression offer a completely different perspective to the social psychological explanations we have looked at so far. Biological models assume that aggression is located within the biological make-up of the individual rather than in the environment around them. Many research studies in the last 30 years have shown that violent criminals were high in the hormone testosterone, encouraging some people to conclude that castration of highly aggressive males would stop them from killing or injuring innocent people. However, the relationship between biological mechanisms and aggressive behaviour is not that simple.

NEUROTRANSMITTERS

Neurotransmitters are chemicals that enable impulses within the brain to be transmitted from one area of the brain to another. There is some evidence that at least two of these neurotransmitters, serotonin and dopamine, are linked to aggressive behaviour. **Serotonin** and **dopamine** are of particular interest because low levels of serotonin and high levels of dopamine have been associated with aggression in animals and humans.

Serotonin

Serotonin is thought to reduce aggression by inhibiting responses to emotional stimuli that might otherwise lead to an aggressive response. Low levels of serotonin in the brain have been associated with an increased susceptibility to impulsive behaviour, aggression, and even violent suicide. Some drugs are thought to alter serotonin levels and thus increase aggressive behaviour. Mann *et al.* (1990) gave 35 healthy subjects *dexfenfluramine*, which is known to deplete serotonin. Using a questionnaire to assess hostility and aggression levels, they found that *dexfenfluramine* treatment in males (but not females) was associated with an increase in hostility and aggression scores.

Dopamine

Although the link between high levels of dopamine and aggressive behaviour is not as well established as with serotonin, there is some evidence to suggest that such a link exists. For example, increases in dopamine activity via the use of amphetamines have also been associated with increases in aggressive behaviour (Lavine, 1997). Antipsychotics, which reduce dopamine activity in the brain, have been shown to reduce aggressive behaviour in violent delinquents (Buitelaar, 2003).

RESEARCH SUPPORT

A **meta-analysis** of 29 studies published before 1992 (Scerbo and Raine, 1993), examined **neurotransmitter** levels in antisocial children and adults. These studies consistently found lower levels of serotonin in individuals described as being aggressive, but found no significant rise or fall in dopamine levels. Indications of reduced levels of serotonin were found in all antisocial groups, but were particularly marked in those individuals who had attempted suicide. This suggests that serotonin depletion leads to impulsive behaviour, which in turn may lead to aggressive behaviour in various forms.

RESEARCH SUPPORT

Two meta-analyses have established a weak but positive relationship between testosterone and aggression.

- Archer (1991) analysed the results of 230 males over five studies and found a low positive correlation between testosterone and aggression. However, the type of participant, and the form and measurement of aggression, differed substantially between studies.

- A larger meta-analysis of 45 studies (Book *et al.*, 2001) established a mean correlation of 0.14 between testosterone and aggression, although Archer *et al.* (2005) claims that methodological problems with this study meant that a correlation of 0.08 was more appropriate.

HORMONAL MECHANISMS

Testosterone

The male sex hormone **testosterone** is thought to influence aggression from young adulthood onwards due to its action on brain areas involved in controlling aggression. Evidence for this association comes from a number of sources.

Research studies – Dabbs *et al.* (1987) measured salivary testosterone in violent and non-violent criminals. Those with the highest testosterone levels had a history of primarily violent crimes, whereas those with the lowest levels had committed only non-violent crimes. Studies of non-prison populations have found similar trends. Lindman *et al.* (1987) found that young males who behaved aggressively when drunk had higher testosterone levels than those who did not act aggressively.

The challenge hypothesis (Wingfield *et al.*, 1990) proposes that, in **monogamous** species, testosterone levels should only rise above the baseline breeding level in response to social challenges, such as male–male aggression or threats to status. As the human species is considered to be monogamous, this would predict that male testosterone levels would rise sharply in response to such challenges. In such situations, a testosterone surge is to be expected, with a consequent increase in aggression, provided the threat is deemed relevant to reproductive competition, e.g. a dispute over a female.

Cortisol

Cortisol appears to have a mediating effect on other aggression-related hormones such as testosterone, possibly because it increases anxiety and the likelihood of social withdrawal (Dabbs *et al.*, 1991). High levels of cortisol inhibit testosterone levels and so inhibit aggression. Studies have reported low levels of cortisol in habitual violent offenders (Virkkunen, 1985) and in violent schoolchildren (Tennes and Kreye, 1985). This suggests that although relatively high testosterone is the primary biochemical influence on aggression, low cortisol also plays an important role by increasing the *likelihood* of aggressive behaviour.

EVALUATION

↑ tryptophan ↓ aggr
↓ tryptophan ↑ aggress

Serotonin

3 Evidence from non-human studies – Raleigh *et al.* (1991) have added support for the importance of serotonin in aggressive behaviour in a study of vervet monkeys. They found that individuals fed on experimental diets high in tryptophan (which increases serotonin levels in the brain) exhibited decreased levels of aggression. Individuals fed on diets that were low in tryptophan exhibited increased aggressive behaviour, suggesting that the difference in aggression could be attributed to their serotonin levels. Other evidence for the importance of serotonin in aggression has shown that in animals that are selectively bred for domestication and for increasingly docile temperaments, there is a corresponding increase, over generations, in brain concentrations of serotonin (Popova *et al.*, 1991).

4 Evidence from antidepressants – If low levels of serotonin are associated with low impulse control and aggressive behaviour, drugs that clinically raise serotonin levels should produce a concurrent lowering in aggression. Bond (2005) has established that this is exactly what happens in clinical studies of antidepressant drugs that elevate serotonin levels. She established that such drugs do tend to reduce irritability and impulsive aggression.

Dopamine

Although research is fairly inconclusive about the *causal* role of dopamine in aggression, recent research suggests that its influence might be as a *consequence* instead. Couppis and Kennedy (2008) found that in mice, a reward pathway in the brain becomes engaged in response to an aggressive event and that dopamine is involved as a positive reinforcer in this pathway. This suggests that individuals will intentionally seek out an aggressive encounter solely because they experience a rewarding sensation from it.

EVALUATION

Testosterone

6 Inconsistent evidence – Albert *et al.* (1993) claim that despite many studies showing a positive correlation between testosterone and aggression, other studies find no such relationship, particularly those that have compared testosterone levels of aggressive and less aggressive individuals. In addition, most studies showing a positive correlation have involved small samples of men within prisons, using either self-report measures of aggression or judgements based solely on the severity of the crime committed.

Aggression or dominance? – Mazur (1985) suggests we should distinguish aggression from *dominance*. Individuals act aggressively when their intent is to inflict injury, whereas they act dominantly if their wish is to achieve or maintain status over another. Mazur claims that aggression is just one form of dominance behaviour. In non-human animals the influence of testosterone on dominance behaviour might be shown in aggressive behaviour. In humans, however, the influence of testosterone on dominance is likely to be expressed in more varied and subtle ways (e.g. through status-striving behaviour).

Cortisol

The moderating effect of cortisol on aggressive behaviour is supported in a four-year study of boys with behavioural problems (McBurnett *et al.*, 2000). Those boys with consistently low cortisol levels began antisocial acts at a younger age and exhibited three times the number of aggressive symptoms compared to boys with higher or fluctuating cortisol levels. Researchers concluded that cortisol levels were 'strongly and inversely related to aggressive conduct disorder'.

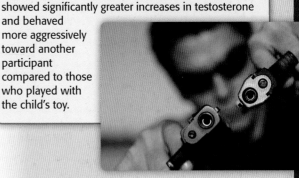

CAN YOU...? No.4.4

...1 Outline (in about 100 words each) the neural and hormonal mechanisms in aggression.

...2 Identify **eight** criticisms related to neural and hormonal mechanisms in aggression, including **at least one** IDA topic. Each criticism should be about 50 words.

...3 Use this material to write a 600-word answer to the question: *Discuss neural and hormonal mechanisms in human aggression.* (8 marks + 16 marks)

The biological approach to aggression includes the belief that the propensity for aggressive behaviour lies in an individual's genetic make-up. Researchers must try to establish whether genetically related individuals are more similar in their aggressive tendencies than non-related individuals. This also has important implications for understanding the origins of violent crime. Although the question of genetic influences for aggression and violent crime has perhaps not interested researchers quite as much as the general public, research suggests that aggressive tendencies may, at least in part, be inherited.

Why are meta-analyses so important? They provide a way of summarising the results of many different studies, and so give us a more accurate overall view of genetic influences.

IS AGGRESSION INHERITED?

Trying to determine the role of genetic factors in aggression is essentially a question of **nature** and **nurture**. To disentangle the relative contributions of nature (genetic inheritance) and nurture (environmental influences), researchers have employed a variety of methodological techniques, including twin and adoption studies, studies of individual genes and studies of violent populations.

Twin studies

Monozygotic (identical) twins share all of their genes, while **dizygotic** (non-identical) twins share only 50%. In twin studies, researchers compare the degree of similarity for a particular trait (such as aggression) between sets of monozygotic (MZ) twins to the similarity between sets of dizygotic (DZ) twins. If the MZ twins are more alike in terms of their aggressive behaviour, then this should be due to genes rather than environment (both types of twin share the same environment as each other but monozygotic twins are more genetically alike). Most twin studies have focused on criminal behaviour generally, but one of the few studies to specifically study aggressive behaviour using adult twin pairs found that nearly 50% of the variance in direct aggressive behaviour (i.e. aggression toward others) could be attributed to genetic factors (Coccaro *et al.*, 1997).

Adoption studies

Adoption studies can help to untangle the relative contributions of environment and heredity in aggression. If a positive correlation is found between aggressive behaviour in adopted children and aggressive behaviour in their biological parents, a genetic effect is implied. If a positive correlation is found between the adoptee's aggressive behaviour and the rearing family, then an environmental effect is implied. A study of over 14,000 adoptions in Denmark found that a significant number of adopted boys with criminal convictions had biological parents (particularly fathers) with criminal convictions (Hutchings and Mednick, 1975), providing evidence for a genetic effect.

A gene for aggression?

The role of MAOA – Although no individual gene for aggression has been identified in humans, a gene responsible for producing a protein called monoamine oxidase A (MAOA) has been associated with aggressive behaviour. MAOA regulates the metabolism of **serotonin** in the brain, and low levels of serotonin are associated with impulsive and aggressive behaviour (page 72). In the 1980s, a study of a Dutch family found that many of its male members behaved in a particularly violent and aggressive manner, and a large proportion had been involved in serious crimes of violence, including rape and arson. These men were found to have abnormally low levels of MAOA in their bodies, and a defect in this gene was later identified (Brunner *et al.*, 1993).

Gene-environment interaction – A second study (Caspi *et al.*, 2002), linking MAOA to aggressive behaviour, involved 500 male children. Researchers discovered a variant of the gene associated with high levels of MAOA and a variant associated with low levels. Those with low levels of MAOA were significantly more likely to grow up to exhibit antisocial behaviour but *only* if they had been maltreated as children. Children with high levels of MAOA who were maltreated, and those with low levels who were not maltreated, did not display antisocial behaviour. This shows that it is the *interaction* between genes and environment that determines behaviours, such as aggression.

Genetics and violent crime

Researchers do not suggest that there is a gene for violent crime per se. Rather it is claimed that inherited temperamental or personality characteristics place some individuals more at risk of committing violent crime. Adoption studies have shown that the highest rates of criminal violence in adopted children occur when both biological *and* adoptive parents have a history of violent crime – clear evidence of a gene-environment interaction. However, a series of adoption studies in which the criminal history of an adopted male was compared with the criminal history of both his biological and his adoptive fathers, found that genetic influences were significant in cases of property crime but *not* in cases of violent crime (Brennan and Mednick, 1993).

PROBLEMS OF SAMPLING

Many of the studies in this area have focused on individuals convicted of violent crime. Two particular difficulties arise when trying to draw meaningful conclusions from these studies. The first problem lies with the participants themselves. Convictions for violent crime are relatively few compared to the vast number of violent attacks by individuals that never result in a conviction. They therefore represent just a small minority of those regularly involved in aggressive behaviour. Second, contrary to popular belief, offenders designated as 'violent' on the basis of a court conviction are not necessarily the most serious, persistent offenders. For example, a convicted murderer would be designated as violent for one offence despite, perhaps, having otherwise had a lifetime free from crime. This might explain why so many studies have found little or no evidence of heritability for violence.

EVALUATION

Difficulties of determining the role of genetic factors

We have discussed the role of genetic factors in aggression, but what does this really mean? The connection between genetic factors and aggression is far from straightforward because of problems determining what is, and what is not, a product of genetic inheritance. It is difficult to establish genetic contributions to aggressive behaviour for the following reasons:

- More than one gene usually contributes to a given behaviour.
- As well as genetic factors there are many non-genetic (i.e. environmental) influences on the manifestation of aggressive behaviour.
- These influences may interact with each other. Genetic factors may affect which environmental factors have an influence, and *vice versa* (gene-environment interaction).

This last point is clearly demonstrated in the study by Caspi *et al.* (2002) described on the facing page.

Problems of assessing aggression

Many of the reported studies of aggression have relied on either parental or self-reports of aggressive behaviour, whereas other studies have made use of observational techniques. In the Miles and Carey meta-analysis reported on the left, mode of assessment was found to be a significant moderator of aggressive behaviour in the 24 studies that made up their analysis. They found that genetic factors explained a large proportion of the variance in aggressive behaviour in studies that had used parental or self-reports. However, those that had made use of observational ratings showed significantly *less* genetic contribution and a greater influence of environmental factors. For example, in a replication of Bandura *et al.*'s Bobo doll study (see page 66), twin pairs were encouraged to act aggressively towards the doll by being exposed to an adult model who also acted aggressively towards it. Researchers found no difference in correlations between monozygotic and dizygotic twin pairs, suggesting that individual differences in aggression were more a product of environmental influences (e.g. family upbringing) than genetic influences (Plomin *et al.*, 1981).

The inheritance of criminal violence

Methodological limitatios – Studies that have investigated the role of genetic factors often fail to distinguish between violent and non-violent crime, making it more difficult to untangle the role of genetic factors in specifically *aggressive* violence. These studies also often fail to distinguish between criminals who are *habitually* violent and those for whom their violent crime is a one-off (see research methods box above).

Inconclusive evidence – The evidence for violent crime being inherited is also far from conclusive. A meta-analysis of studies in this area (Walters, 1992) found only a low to moderate correlation between heredity and crime, with better designed and more recently published studies providing less support for the gene-crime hypothesis than more poorly designed and earlier published studies. A more recent review of published studies of youth crime (Surgeon General's report on youth violence, 2001) concluded: 'The data do not suggest a strong role for heredity in violence'.

REAL-WORLD APPLICATION

IDA Although studies of the biological basis of aggression interest nearly everyone, research findings are far too uncertain to be valuable in understanding the causal factors affecting those who engage in violent activities. Nevertheless, there have been suggestions that public policy should be informed by the results of this research. If people *are* predisposed towards aggressive behaviour or violent crime, then questions about the *treatment* of such behaviours inevitably arise. Some commentators advocate **genetic engineering** but others go much further. As long as violence remains at the forefront of public concern, ways of dealing with it that address the problem more directly (e.g. through 'chemical castration') remain an attractive option to many. Given the extremely tentative nature of conclusions that can be reached from this research and the far-reaching ethical consequences of labelling an individual as a threat to society on the basis of their genetic inheritance, an awareness of the limitations of these studies is extremely important.

THE VALUE OF ANIMAL RESEARCH

IDA Studies of aggressive behaviour in non-human animals have an important role in helping us understand aggressive behaviour in humans. For example, rodents offer the advantage of experimental manipulation to test the effects of specific genes on aggressive behaviour. Manipulations may involve **selective breeding programmes** and 'knockout' techniques (where a single gene is eliminated from a group of experimental animals in order to study its effect). An example of such a study that has potential for an understanding of human aggression was by Young *et al.* (2002). These researchers claim to have identified a genetic mutation that causes violent behaviour in mice. This mutation, nicknamed 'fierce', has a range of effects on mice, including extremely violent behaviour towards other mice. A counterpart of this gene does exist in humans, although its precise function is not known.

CAN YOU...? No.4.5

...1 Outline (in about 200 words) genetic factors in aggressive behaviour.

...2 Identify **eight** criticisms related to factors in agressive behaviour, including **at least one** IDA topic. Each criticism should be about 50 words.

...3 Use this material to write a 600-word answer to the question: *Discuss genetic factors in aggressive behaviour.* (8 marks + 16 marks)

EVOLUTIONARY EXPLANATIONS OF HUMAN AGGRESSION

Evolutionary psychologists argue that the different reproductive challenges faced by our ancestors led to a number of evolved sex differences, including sex differences in jealousy. Male sexual jealousy as a result of real or suspected infidelity is a frequently cited cause of violence in interpersonal relationships. In many cultures, the murder of an adulterous wife or her lover is not only condoned but encouraged. Among the Nuer people of East Africa, for example, a man caught in adultery runs the risk of death at the hands of the woman's husband. As recently as 1974, in the US state of Texas, a man who killed his wife's lover 'while in the act', would remain unpunished. On this spread we examine evolutionary explanations for this phenomenon.

▲ Could violence towards women have adaptive value for some males?

JEALOUSY

Daly and Wilson (1988) claim that men have evolved several different strategies to deter their female partners from committing adultery (i.e. having sex with an extra-marital partner). These range from vigilance to violence, but all are fueled by male sexual jealousy, an adaptation that evolved specifically to deal with the threat of paternal uncertainty.

Cuckoldry and sexual jealousy

Unlike women, men can never be entirely certain that they are the fathers of their children, as fertilisation is hidden from them, inside the woman. As a result, men are always at risk of **cuckoldry**, the reproductive cost that might be inflicted on a man as a result of his partner's infidelity. The consequence of cuckoldry is that the man might unwittingly invest his resources in offspring that are not his own. The adaptive functions of sexual jealousy, therefore, would have been to deter a mate from sexual infidelity, thereby minimising the risk of cuckoldry.

Mate retention and violence

Buss (1988) suggests that males have a number of strategies that have evolved specifically for the purpose of keeping a mate. These include restricting their partners' autonomy ('direct guarding') and 'negative inducements' in the form of violence or threats of violence to prevent her from straying. Because sexual jealousy is a primary cause of violence against women, those who are perceived by their partner to be threatening infidelity (e.g. by looking at another man), are more at risk of violence than those who are not. Studies of battered women, for example, have shown that in the majority of cases, women cite extreme jealousy on the part of their husbands or boyfriends as the key cause of the violence directed toward them (Dobash and Dobash, 1984).

Sexual jealousy and extreme violence

Male sexual jealousy is claimed to be the single most common motivation for killings in domestic disputes in the US (Daly *et al.*, 1982) and Dell (1984) concluded that sexual jealousy accounted for 17% of all cases of murder in the UK. Men are predominantly the perpetrators and the victims. A summary of eight studies of same-sex killings involving 'love-triangles' found that 92% were male–male murders and only 8% were female–female murders.

▶ In July 2002, a Thai court freed a man who admitted battering his wife to death in a jealous rage after discovering she had visited a former sweetheart.

Pipat Lueprasitkul, a former university lecturer, was given a two-year suspended prison sentence after the court took into account his background and the young age of his children. The court also considered that Pipat attacked his wife Wannee in a fit of jealousy, an explanation that outraged women's groups.

According to a World Health Organisation study, nearly half of all women in Thailand are subjected to physical or sexual violence at some point in their lives.

INFIDELITY

Another problem linked to mate violence is sexual infidelity – i.e. voluntary sexual relations between an individual who is married and someone who is not the individual's spouse. Research suggests that the detection or suspicion of infidelity is a key predictor of partner violence (Daly *et al.*, 1982). Although a 2006 BBC online survey (*The Love Map*, BBC, 2006) found that men are more likely to engage in extra-marital affairs than women, it also discovered that one in ten women admitted to be being unfaithful to their husbands.

Sexual coercion

A consequence of men's perceptions or suspicions of their wives' sexual infidelity is sexual coercion or partner rape (Goetz *et al.*, 2008). Camilleri (2004) found that sexual assault of a female by her male partner was directly linked with the perceived risk of her infidelity. Shields and Hanneke (1983) also found that female victims of partner rape were more likely to have reported engaging in extra-marital sex than women who had not been raped by their male partner.

Violence toward pregnant partners

Sexual infidelity by a woman may sometimes lead to pregnancy. From the perspective of her long-term mate, if the child is born, he risks investing in the offspring of another male and consequently lowering his own reproductive success. When a woman becomes pregnant with another man's child, therefore, the function of violence directed towards her may be to terminate the pregnancy, thus eliminating the potential offspring of a rival and leaving her free to bear offspring for him.

Uxorocide (wife-killing)

Men can guard against their partner's infidelity either by conferring benefits or by inflicting costs, including violence. As not all men possess resources that might be used to provide benefits, some men are especially prone to using violence, or the threat of violence (Shackelford *et al.*, 2000). According to Daly and Wilson (1988), death of the partner from physical violence may be an unintended outcome of an evolutionary adaptation that was designed for control rather than death (see the story of Pipat Lueprasitkul, on the left).

MATE RETENTION AND VIOLENCE AGAINST WOMEN

Shackelford *et al.* (2005) used a survey method to test evolutionary psychology predictions concerning mate retention strategies. They used 461 men and 560 women in the US. All participants were in committed, heterosexual relationships. Male participants answered questions about their use of mate retention techniques, and were assessed on how often they performed each of 26 different types of violent act against their partners. Female participants answered questions concerning their partners' use of male retention techniques and the degree to which their partners used violence against them.

Men's use of two broad types of retention technique (intersexual negative inducements and direct guarding) was positively correlated with their violence scores. In addition, use of emotional manipulation (e.g. saying they would kill themselves if their partner left) as a specific tactic appeared to consistently predict men's violence against women. Results from female participants confirmed this trend, with reports of direct guarding and intersexual negative inducements being positively correlated with their experience of female-directed violence. In addition, women reported that those partners who frequently used specific mate retention tactics of vigilance and emotional manipulation were most likely to use violence against them. As with males, age relationship duration made no difference to the reported trends.

PROBLEMS WITH SURVEYS

In the Shackelford *et al.* study on the left, data was collected using a survey technique. **Surveys** are a form of self-report technique that have particular problems, especially when used in sensitive areas, such as violence against a spouse. Answers may not be truthful because of the **social desirability** bias – a tendency to respond in a way that will be viewed favourably by others. This takes the form of over-reporting desirable behaviour and under-reporting undesirable behaviour.

EVALUATION

Jealousy

Research support – The predictions concerning mate retention techniques and female-directed violence have been tested in the Shackelford *et al.* study above. This study shows a clear relationship between sexual jealousy, mate-retention strategies by males, and violence towards women. Other research also supports this connection. Buss and Shackelford (1997) found that men who suspected that their wives might be unfaithful over the next year exacted greater punishment for a known or suspected infidelity than men who did not anticipate future infidelities. This finding is consistent with the claim in evolutionary psychology that mate retention strategies are evoked only when a particular adaptive problem is faced, in this case the belief that the wife's infidelity is likely.

Practical applications – An important implication of research such as Shackelford *et al.*'s is that particular tactics of mate retention used by males can be an early indicator of violence against the female partner. The findings from these studies can potentially be used to alert friends and family members to the danger signs, the specific acts that can lead to future violence in relationships. At this point, help can be sought or offered before the violence ever happens.

A physiological basis for jealousy based aggression – The claim that male sexual jealousy is linked to aggression is supported in a study by Takahashi *et al.* (2006). They showed that the neural response to imagined scenes depicting sexual infidelity (e.g. their partner having sex) and emotional jealousy (e.g. their partner falling in love) was different for men and women. Using brain imaging techniques, they discovered that men showed much greater activation in the amygdala and hypothalamus (brain areas associated with aggression), when presented with scenes depicting sexual infidelity in their mate.

Research doesn't tell the whole story – Edlund and Sagarin (2009) claim that our understanding of the relationship between sexual jealousy and aggression is limited. For example, research doesn't tell us whether the perceived locus of responsibility (e.g. whether the perceived infidelity is initiated by the female partner or the male rival) moderates the jealous response. Nor does research tell us whether the degree of perceived infidelity is important (e.g. whether sexual intercourse provokes a greater degree of jealousy than some other action).

Infidelity

Research support – The link between infidelity and partner violence is supported by the finding that the risk of a partner's infidelity predicts sexual coercion among males, but not among females (Camilleri, 2004). This is significant because males, but not females, are at risk of cuckoldry, i.e. unwittingly investing resources in genetically unrelated offspring. In another study supporting this link, Camilleri and Quinsey (2009) found that men convicted of raping their partners were more likely to have experienced cuckoldry risks prior to their offence compared to men convicted of non-sexual partner abuse.

Violence toward pregnant partners – There is some supporting evidence for the hypothesis that a man who suspects that his partner is pregnant with another man's child is likely to inflict violence upon her. Burch and Gallup (2004) found that the frequency of violent acts toward pregnant mates was roughly double that directed toward partners who were not pregnant, with sexual jealousy characterising those men who committed violence against their pregnant partners. Likewise, Taillieu and Brownridge (2010) found that women abused while pregnant were more likely to be carrying the child of a man other than her current mate. A Nicaraguan study found that half of a sample of pregnant women physically abused by their partners had suffered from blows directed at their abdomen, specifically designed to increase the probability of aborting the foetus (Valladares *et al.*, 2005).

Limitations of evolutionary explanations of partner violence – An evolutionary perspective on violence cannot explain why people react in different ways when faced with the same adaptive problem. Buss and Shackelford (1997) suggest that it cannot account for why different males, when faced with their partner's infidelity, respond in different ways. Some men may resort to aggressive mate-retention strategies, others to murder whilst others will get drunk.

GENDER BIAS

IDA

Most studies of infidelity have focused solely on men's mate retention strategies and men's violence against women. However, women also engage in mate retention tactics and sometimes behave violently towards their partners. Research suggests that women initiate and carry out physical assaults on their partners as often as men do. For example, Felson (1997) examined 2,060 murders in the US and found that women were twice as likely to murder out of jealousy as were men.

CAN YOU...? (No.4.6)

...1 Outline (in 200 words) evolutionary explanations of **two** forms of human aggressive behaviour (including jealousy/infidelity).

...2 Identify **eight** criticisms related to evolutionary explanations of human aggression, including **at least one** IDA topic. Each criticism should be about 50 words.

...3 Use this material to write a 600-word answer to the question: *Discuss evolutionary explanations of human aggression based on infidelity and jealousy.* (8 marks + 16 marks)

GROUP DISPLAY AS AN ADAPTIVE RESPONSE

Social psychological theories such as **deindividuation** do not tell the whole story about the origins of aggression in groups. Aggressive group displays are a product of some external stimulus that triggers the behaviour in question (known as the proximate cause). However, this may conceal the **adaptive** or 'real' reason *why* the behaviour evolved in the first place, known as its ultimate cause. Aggressive group displays emerged among our distant ancestors due to the fact that they increased their fitness in some way. Nowadays, similar situations trigger the same response, even though the original function of the behaviour may no longer be relevant.

The term 'group display' does not have any specific meaning within evolutionary theory when applied to humans, but loosely refers to the collective behaviours of groups. In an exam question your task would be to explain such behaviours in the context of aggression using the principles of evolutionary theory.

SPORTS

Xenophobia

Wilson (1975) claims that xenophobia (a fear and hatred of strangers or foreigners) has been documented in 'virtually every group of animals displaying higher forms of social organisation'. **Natural selection**, it appears, has favoured those genes that caused human beings to be altruistic toward members of their own group but intolerant towards outsiders. Shaw and Wong (1989) argue that the mechanisms that prompt suspicion towards strangers would have been favoured by natural selection. This would have enabled our ancestors to avoid attack, and so leave behind more offspring. MacDonald (1992) suggests that from an evolutionary perspective, it is adaptive to exaggerate negative stereotypes about outsiders, as the overperception of threat is less costly than its underperception.

Xenophobic displays on the terraces – Podaliri and Balestri (1998) have found evidence of xenophobic tendencies in their analysis of the group displays of Italian football crowds. In the 1980s, xenophobic political organisations such as the Northern League led to the growth of extreme right-wing movements characterised by racist chants and openly anti-Semitic banners. In April 2005, during a Serie A match between Lazio and Livorno, Paolo Di Canio (then a Lazio player) performed the 'Roman salute' in the direction of Lazio's extremist fans, the *Irriducibili*. This gesture, originally associated with the fascist dictator Benito Mussolini, was intended as an expression of solidarity with the far-right attitudes of the Lazio fans, and as a provocative gesture toward the Livorno fans, known for their extreme left-wing political attitudes.

Territoriality

Threat displays – Another explanation for the evolution of group displays in sport is based on territoriality, the protective response to an invasion of one's territory. Territorial behaviour is common in many animal species, which typically show threat displays toward outsiders and attack with greater vigour when defending a home territory (Huntingford and Turner, 1987). This form of territorial display has its human equivalent in the aggressive displays of sports teams prior to a match. For example, Samoa adopted the *manu siva tau* war chant before the 1991 Rugby World Cup. These displays intimidate opponents and make the home team more aggressive towards them. Aggressive displays would have been adaptive for our distant ancestors because they allowed groups to defend valuable resources associated with their territory.

Testosterone and territorial behaviour – As we saw on page 72, animals (including humans) display more aggression when they have higher testosterone levels. Might sports teams also display more collective aggression when defending home 'territory', and do they have higher testosterone levels when doing so? Neave and Wolfson (2003) found that football teams playing at home were far more likely to win than the visiting team partly because players have the benefit of a huge surge in testosterone before a match. They believed this could be due to an evolved drive to defend home territory, which led to more aggressive displays when playing at home. This increase in testosterone levels before home games (compared with levels before training) did not occur before away games. Team members who subjectively felt that the burden of 'defending the territory' lay with them (e.g. goalkeepers) had higher levels of testosterone compared to other players.

WARFARE

War is undoubtedly dangerous and costly, therefore it is difficult to see why any organism, selected to survive, should engage in behaviours associated with such extremes of personal cost and danger. An evolutionary explanation, therefore, would lead us to expect that any behaviour associated with warfare would have evolved because of the adaptive benefits for the individual and their offspring.

Benefits of aggressive displays

Sexual selection – In societies that experience frequent warfare, males are far more likely to escape infanticide than females because of their potential usefulness in battle. As a result, since there are relatively few women compared to men in these societies, men must compete with each other for mates, with those who do well in battle being 'rewarded' by access to female mates (Divale and Harris, 1976). Displays of aggressiveness and bravery are attractive to females, and their absence reduces the attractiveness of individual males. For example, male warriors in traditional societies tend to have more sexual partners and more children suggesting a direct reproductive benefit (Chagnon, 1988).

Acquisition of status within the group – Displays of ferocity and aggressiveness by individual warriors would also lead peers to respect them more and so strengthen the bond between them and other males in the group. Because cooperation between males is so important to an individual's status in the group, fleeing from battle would make an individual appear a 'coward', thus losing the respect of their peers. According to this perspective, therefore, displays of aggressiveness and bravery in battle means that individuals are more likely to share the benefits associated with status, which in turn would increase their reproductive fitness.

Costly displays signal commitment

Signals of commitment – Anthropologists suggest that one of the primary functions of ritual displays is the promotion of group solidarity, particularly in times of collective action. Irons (2004) claims that the costliness of permanent displays such as scars and mutilation means that they serve as honest signals of commitment to the group. By engaging in such displays, individuals demonstrate their commitment and loyalty to the group and so can benefit from the profits of warfare against another group.

Minimising the likelihood of defection – During battle, each individual has an incentive to keep himself out of harm's way which, as a result, exposes others to a greater risk of injury or death. Therefore, in groups where war against other groups is relatively frequent, displays, such as permanent scars or piercings, would be important for the survival of the group. This is because such permanent displays minimise the ability of males to abscond to another group and increase their commitment to the group of which they are a member (Thorpe, 2003).

▲ Fascist sections among the supporters of AS Roma display their xenophobic tendencies

EVALUATION

Sports

Research support for xenophobic displays – Foldesi (1996) provides evidence to support the link between xenophobia and violent displays among Hungarian football crowds. He found that the racist conduct of a core of extremist supporters led to an increase of spectators' violence in general, and xenophobic outbursts in particular. Violent incidents based on racist or xenophobic attitudes were observed at all stadia, with gypsies, Jews and Russians the usual targets.

Territoriality – Lewis *et al.* (2005) found that, among football fans, crowd support was rated as the most significant factor contributing to a home advantage. Through their displays of support, fans felt responsible for inspiring their team to victory and took credit for distracting opponents. However, the precise way in which displays of support have an effect has been difficult to pinpoint. For example, the relationship with crowd size is unclear as the advantage has been shown to operate even with very small crowds (Pollard and Pollard, 2005). Likewise, it is not known whether the primary effect of crowd displays is to 'psych up' the home team or distract the away team, all of which suggests that the original adaptive function of such displays may no longer be relevant.

Does a home advantage really exist? – A study by Moore and Brylinsky (1993) challenges the claim that home crowd displays provide a territorial advantage. A measles epidemic resulted in a quarantine that caused 11 American basketball games for two teams to be played in the absence of spectators. For one team, the Siena Saints from New York, nine away games were analysed. Five were played with spectators present and four with no spectators. For the other team, the Hartford Hawks from Connecticut, 11 home games were used, four with no spectators and seven with spectators. Siena scored an average of 76.25 points when playing in front of spectators and 86.20 in the absence of spectators. Likewise, Hartford scored an average of 64.29 in front of spectators yet 71.25 without spectators, suggesting that the displays of support from home crowds did not increase the performance of the teams.

Warfare

Sexual selection – Research has provided support for the importance of aggressive displays in determining the sexual attractiveness of male warriors. Palmer and Tilley (1995) found that male youth street gang members have more sexual partners than ordinary young males. Leunissen and Van Vugt (2010) also found that military men have greater sex appeal but only if they have been observed showing bravery in combat.

War is not 'in the genes' – War emerged when humans shifted from a nomadic existence to a settled one and were tied to agriculture or fishing sites. Because of this, people could no longer walk away from trouble and had far more to lose, and to fight over, than their hunter–gatherer forebears. So rather than being an evolved adaptation, it looks as if warfare emerged as a rational response to a changing lifestyle. This suggests that warfare, and the aggressive displays associated with warfare, are not biological compulsions but are a consequence of environmental changes, such as rising populations and dwindling food supplies (LeBlanc and Register, 2004).

Limitations of an evolutionary explanation of warfare – Explanations of displays of aggression that are based on mating success, status or commitment fail to explain the astonishing levels of cruelty that are often found in human wars yet not among non-human species. For example, why do humans torture or mutilate their opponents when they have already been defeated and no longer pose a threat? Anthropological evidence (e.g. Watson, 1973, see page 69) suggests this may be more a consequence of **deindividuation** effects than of evolutionary adaptations.

IDA **GENDER BIAS IN EXPLANATIONS OF WARFARE**

Evolutionary explanations for warfare may demonstrate a gender bias as they do not adequately reflect the behaviour of women in this process. Adams (1983) claimed that the idea of the woman warrior is almost unheard of within most societies. Even within those societies that allow women to participate in war, they are always the rare exception. Women would have considerably less to gain from fighting in near certain-death situations and considerably more to lose (in terms of loss of their reproductive capacity). This is fundamental to women's exclusion from warfare, as women simply do not increase their fitness nearly as much as men do. Our understanding of the displays typically found in warfare, therefore, is limited to the behaviour of males rather than females.

CAN YOU...? No.4.7

...**1** Outline, in about 200 words, evolutionary explanations of group displays in humans.

...**2** Identify **eight** criticisms related to evolutionary explanations of group displays in humans, including **at least one** IDA topic. Each criticism should be about 50 words.

...**3** Use this material to write a 600-word answer to the question: *Discuss evolutionary explanations of group display in humans.* (8 marks + 16 marks)

CHAPTER SUMMARY

SOCIAL PSYCHOLOGICAL EXPLANATIONS OF AGGRESSION

SOCIAL LEARNING THEORY

OBSERVATION
- Learning takes place through the observation of models.
- Seeing others reinforced or punished acts as vicarious reinforcement.

MENTAL REPRESENTATION
- Individual forms mental representations of events.
- Also forms expectations of possible rewards or punishments.

PRODUCTION OF BEHAVIOUR
- Aggression maintained through direct reinforcement.
- Likelihood of aggression increased if high self-efficacy for production.

EVALUATION
- SLT demonstrated in young children observing aggressive adult model (Badura et al., 1961).
- Imitated model, but only if model was rewarded for their behaviour, Bandura and Walters (1963).
- Learning takes place regardless of outcome, but production linked only to reinforcement.
- SLT also applies to aggression in adults e.g. Phillips (1986) – homicide rates and boxing matches.
- Strength – can explain aggression in absence of direct reinforcement.
- Can also explain individual differences and context-dependent learning.
- Problem of demand characteristics in Bobo doll study.
- Cultural differences – absence of aggressive models among !Kung San.

IDA
- Ethical issues make SLT explanation difficult to test scientifically.

DEINDIVIDUATION

NATURE OF DEINDIVIDUATION
- Reduced self-evaluation; decreased concern about evaluation by others.
- Leads to an increase in antisocial behaviour.
- More likely when anonymous, in a large crowd or drunk.

PROCESS OF DEINDIVIDUATION
- Social norms usually inhibit antisocial behaviour.
- Inhibitions removed when deindividuated.
- Conditions that increase anonymity weaken barriers to antisocial behaviour.

RESEARCH ON DEINDIVIDUATION
- Faceless crowd – lynchings more savage when large crowds (Mullen, 1986); baiting crowd (Mann, 1981).

REDUCED PRIVATE SELF-AWARENESS.
- Reduced self-awareness more important than anonymity.
- In large crowds, less able to self-regulate behaviour.

EVALUATION
- Anonymity – Zimbardo (1969) found longer shocks when anonymous.
- Local group norms – people respond to normative cues within the social context.
- Meta-analysis (Postmes and Spears, 1998) – insufficient support for claims of theory.
- Evidence of online aggression when deindividuated (Francis et al., 2006)
- Deindividuation may increase prosocial behaviour in some situations.
- Cultural difference – cultures that change appearance more brutal in war (Watson, 1973).

IDA
- Gender bias – males more likely to become aggressive when deindividuated (Cannavale et al., 1970).
- Real-world application – the baiting crowd.

INSTITUTIONAL AGGRESSION

PRISON VIOLENCE
- Importation model – prisoners 'import' their violent behaviours into prison.
- Gang membership – pre-prison gang membership an important determinant of prison misconduct.
- Deprivation model – a reaction to stressful conditions of prison.
- Sykes (1958) – specific deprivations within prison linked to increase in violence.

EVALUATION
- Importation model – support from studies of US prisons (Harer and Steffensmeier, 2006).
- DeLisi et al. (2004) challenges the claim that pre-prison gang membership predicts violence.
- Deprivation model – support from prison studies but not psychiatric institutions.
- Deprivation model explains violence against staff – importation model explains violence against other inmates (Jiang and Fisher-Giorlando, 2002)

GENOCIDE
- Staub (1999) – five stages of genocide.
- Dehumanisation – removal of moral restraints against killing other humans (e.g. Tutsi 'cockroaches').
- Milgram believed situational pressures could coerce people into destructive obedience.

EVALUATION
- Bystanders – non-intervention allows killing to continue.
- Dehumanisation – may explain violence against immigrants.
- Obedience – ignores other factors (e.g. anti-Semitism).

IDA
- Real-world application – reversing conditions of deprivation led to reduction of violence at HMP Woodhill (Wilson, 2010).
- Real-world application – dehumanisation can explain violence towards refugees through social dominance orientation (SDO).

EVOLUTION AND HUMAN AGGRESSION

EVOLUTIONARY EXPLANATIONS

JEALOUSY
- Men experience sexual jealousy due to threat of paternal uncertainty.
- Sexual jealousy deters mate from infidelity and avoid cuckoldry.
- Mate retention strategies (e.g. direct guarding and negative inducements).
- Dobash and Dobash (1984) – study of battered wives discovered sexual jealousy main cause of assault.
- Dell (1984) – jealousy accounted for 17% of murders in the UK.

EVALUATION
- Mate retention strategies and violence supported by Shackelford et al. (2005).
- Surveys – problem of social desirability bias.
- Application – use of mate retention strategies is early indication of the need for intervention.
- Takahashi et al. (2006) – jealousy activates amygdala and hypothalamus in males.
- Edlund and Sagarin (2009) – research ignores moderators in jealousy aggression relationship.
- Problems with surveys – social desirability bias may make responses less truthful.

IDA
- Gender bias – most studies of jealousy and infidelity have focused on men's retention strategies and men's violence against women. However, women twice as likely to murder out of jealousy than men (Felson, 1997).

INFIDELITY
- Infidelity key predictor of partner violence (Daly et al., 1982).
- Infidelity may lead to sexual coercion or partner rape.
- Violence toward pregnant partners – may be to terminate the pregnancy.
- Uxoricide – unintended outcome of an adaptation designed for control.

EVALUATION
- Risk of partner's infidelity predicts sexual coercion in males (cuckoldry risk) but not females (Camilleri, 2004).
- Men convicted of raping partners had cuckoldry risks (Camilleri and Quinsey, 2007).
- Violent acts toward pregnant mates due to sexual jealousy (Burch and Gallup, 2004).
- Women abused in pregnancy carrying the child of other man (Taillieu and Brownridge, 2010).
- Evolutionary perspective unable to account for differences in partner response to infidelity.

BIOLOGICAL EXPLANATIONS OF AGGRESSION

NEURAL AND HORMONAL EXPLANATIONS

NEUROTRANSMITTERS

- Low levels of serotonin and high levels of dopamine associated with aggressive behaviour.
- Serotonin normally inhibits responses to emotional stimuli that might lead to aggressive response.
- Mann (1990) - dexfenfluramine depletes serotonin in brain, and led to increased aggression in males but not in females.
- Amphetamines increase dopamine activity – also increase aggressive behaviour (Lavine, 1997).
- Antipsychotics reduce dopamine activity – also reduce aggressive behaviour (Buitelaar, 2003).

EVALUATION

- Meta-analysis (Scerbo and Raine, 1993) found evidence for serotonin-aggression link, but not dopamine-aggression link.
- Animal studies suggest lower levels of serotonin associated with aggression and dominance.
- Research support from antidepressants that raise serotonin levels.
- Dopamine may be a consequence rather than a cause of aggression.

HORMONAL MECHANISMS

- Testosterone influences aggression through action on brain areas associated with aggressive behaviour.
- Dabbs *et al.* (1987) – testosterone levels high among violent criminals.
- Challenge hypothesis – testosterone levels rise in response to social challenges.
- Cortisol – high levels inhibit testosterone and so inhibit aggression.

EVALUATION

- Meta-analyses established weak, positive correlation between testosterone and aggression (Archer, 1991; Book *et al.*, 2001).
- Inconsistent evidence for testosterone-aggression link.
- Influence of testosterone linked to dominance rather than aggression (Mazur, 1985).
- Cortisol – link supported in boys with behaviour problems (McBurnett *et al.*, 2000).

IDA

- Reductionism – human social behaviour more complex, therefore biological factors represent an incomplete picture.
- Gender bias – research tends to focus on males, but studies of females also show important role for testosterone.
- Real-world application – link between presence of guns and increased testosterone levels.

GENETIC FACTORS

TWIN STUDIES

- MZ twins genetically identical, more similar levels of aggressive behaviour than DZ twins indicates genetic influence.
- Coccaro *et al.* (1997) – genetic factors account for 50% of variance in aggressive behaviour.

ADOPTION STUDIES

- Possible to disentangle genetic and environmental factors by comparing adopted children and biological parents.
- Hutchings and Mednick (1975) – children with criminal convictions had fathers with criminal convictions.

GENE FOR AGGRESSION

- Gene for MAOA associated with aggressive behaviour.
- MAOA regulates serotonin in brain, low levels of serotonin associated with aggression.
- Brunner *et al.* (1993) – violent men had low levels of MAOA.
- Caspi *et al.* (2002) – MAOA linked to aggression in children.

GENETICS AND VIOLENT CRIME

- Inherited temperament or personality characteristics place some individuals at risk of committing violent crime.
- Brennan and Madnick(1993) – genetic influences significant in property crime but not violent crime.

EVALUATION

- Miles and Carey (1997) – meta-analysis suggests 50% variance in aggression due to genetic factors.
- Difficult to determine what is a product of genetic inheritance.
- More than one gene contributes, as do environmental factors, and there is an interaction between the two.
- Problems of measuring aggression (self-reports vs observation).
- Individual differences in aggression due to environmental rather than genetic influences.
- Studies of youth violence do not suggest a strong role for heredity.
- Research support from meta analyses, although these do not discount role of other factors.
- Problems of sampling – violent criminals represent tiny minority of people involved in aggression.
- Some violent criminals are not generally 'aggressive'.

IDA

- Animal studies – allow experimental manipulation and selective breeding, e.g. 'fierce' mutation.
- Possibility of genetic engineering creates ethical issues.

EXPLANATIONS OF GROUP DISPLAY

SPORTS

- Distinction between ultimate and proximate levels of explanation.
- Xenophobia – suspicion of strangers favoured by natural selection.
- Podaliri and Balestri (1998) – xenophobic displays in behaviour of Italian football crowds.
- Territorial displays – e.g. Samoan *manu siva tau*.
- Neave and Wolfson (2003) – home support shows raised testosterone levels.

EVALUATION

- Foldesi (1996) – evidence to support the link between xenophobia and violent displays among Hungarian football crowds.
- Wolfson *et al.* (2005) – crowd support rated as most significant factor contributing to home advantage.
- Moore and Brylinsky (1993) challenge claim that home crowd displays of support provide a territorial advantage.

WARFARE

- Males who display aggressiveness are more attractive to females (Divale and Harris, 1976) and have more sexual partners (Chagnon, 1988).
- Displays of aggressiveness result in increased status and acceptance by other males.
- Signals of commitment – Irons (2004), costliness of rituals signal commitment to group.
- Permanent displays minimise likelihood of defection.

EVALUATION

- Palmer and Tilley (1995) – male youth street gang members have more sexual partners. Leunissen and Van Vugt (2010) – military men have greater sex appeal but only if they have been observed showing bravery in combat.
- Warfare emerged in response to a changing lifestyle.
- Anthropological evidence (e.g. Watson, 1973) suggests cruelty in war more a consequence of deindividuation effects.

IDA

- Real-world application – the power of xenophobia to invoke violence has motivated football clubs to take steps to minimise its influence e.g. 'Show Racism the Red Card'.
- Gender bias – women warriors almost unheard of within most societies (Adams, 1983).

EXAM QUESTION WITH STUDENT ANSWER

> **QUESTION** Outline and evaluate **two social psychological theories of aggression.** *(8 marks + 16 marks)*

STUDENT ANSWER

In this essay I will describe and evaluate the social learning explanation and deindividuation theory which both explain aggressiveness from a social psychological point of view. The opposite point of view is that people (and other animals) are aggressive because it is in their genes. This is the biological approach – together these two approaches are an example of the nature–nurture debate because according to the social psychological position aggression is learned (nurture) and the biological view suggests aggression is innate (nature). This debate is no longer a debate as such because it is recognised that nature and nurture interact rather than it being one or the other.

In a sense this can be seen in social learning theory. Bandura proposed that aggression is learned through direct and indirect reinforcement but he did acknowledge the role of biology which supplies the urge to aggress. What is learned is when and how to express this aggression. Bandura suggested that people learn about aggression by observing other people behaving aggressively. If such behaviour is rewarded (vicarious reinforcement) this increases the likelihood that such behaviour will be imitated. However, if such imitation is not further reinforced then the behaviour is less likely to be repeated in the future. What is learned is an expectancy of future outcomes which is learned both indirectly and directly.

The second theory is deindividuation which refers to loss of individuality. In a crowd a person loses their sense of personal responsibility and therefore is more likely to behave in an antisocial or aggressive manner. Zimbardo suggests that deindividuation results from anonymity which can happen in a crowd or when a person is wearing a uniform.

Both theories have been supported by research studies. Bandura conducted a study with a Bobo doll and showed that children who observed a model behaving aggressively towards the life-sized doll were later more aggressive and imitated specific acts when they were allowed to play with toys, including a Bobo doll. Furthermore, in a later study, Bandura and others showed that this only happened if the model was positively reinforced for their actions. If they were punished then the children did not imitate the behaviour. This shows that people may learn a behaviour but will only imitate it if they experience vicarious reinforcement. There have, however, been quite a few criticisms of this study. For one thing it is about children and may not explain adult behaviour because children are more impressionable. Another criticism has been that the children's behaviour towards the Bobo doll was the result of demand characteristics – the doll invited aggressive behaviour and one child even commented spontaneously that they should hit the doll.

Zimbardo (1969) demonstrated the effects of deindividuation in a study similar to Milgram's experiment and found that participants delivered more electric shocks if they were anonymous (no name tags, wearing a hood). However, in another study by Johnson and Downing (1979) there were two sets of deindividuated participants – wearing gowns like the Ku Klux Klan or wearing nurses' uniforms. The participants wearing nurses uniforms actually gave fewer shocks than control participants which shows that deindividuation can lead to prosocial as well as antisocial effects. In fact it seems that deindividuation orients people towards group norms rather than simply increasing aggression.

In fact Prentice-Dunn et al. (1982) have suggested that deindividuation is caused by reduced self-awareness, rather than by anonymity. When a person is aware of themselves they act according to personal moral standards. In a group situation people lose their self-awareness and respond to group norms, which may lead to antisocial behaviour.

[594 words]

EXAMINER COMMENTS

The first sentence offers a general introduction to the essay, which is not strictly necessary. Such introductions rarely attract any marks as they do not demonstrate knowledge and understanding. The rest of the paragraph offers a useful evaluation on the contrast with biological explanations and on the nature–nurture debate, evidence of **IDA**.

The second paragraph begins with some extra evaluation on the nature/nurture elements of social learning theory, attracting further **AO2** credit.

  This paragraph contains a competent outline of social learning theory, making use of **psychological terminology** and also providing evidence of **organisation** and **structure**, which are both important criteria for **AO1** marks.

The second social psychological theory is outlined here. Note that words have not been wasted on introducing this second theory, for example saying: 'The second theory I will look at is deindividuation'. This outline is somewhat **basic**, although sufficient in this situation where an outline only is required.

The next two paragraphs present research support plus various other critical points, demonstrating the **effective evaluation**. In total, three studies have been selected and for each there is minimal description of the actual study. Some description is necessary but if there is too much then the material ceases to be evaluation.

  Most importantly the student has made it clear what the study demonstrated and thus has shown **sound analysis**.

  Further **AO2** credit is given to the criticisms of Bandura's study. Both critical points have been reasonably **elaborated** so the student's understanding is obvious.

The study by Johnson and Downing is used to provide **evaluation** of the basic theory of deindividuation and this criticism is further developed in the final paragraph which contains a mixture of **AO1** (further description of the theory of deindividuation) and **AO2** (contrast with earlier explanation related to anonymity).

> **AO1** – **sound**, **accurate** and sufficiently **detailed** for an outline.
>
> **AO2/AO3** – **sound** analysis and line of argument, however **evidence of IDA** is **not substantial** and used only **'reasonably effectively'**.

Chapter 5
Eating behaviour

SPECIFICATION

Note that in this chapter you have a choice about which eating disorders to study – we have covered both anorexia nervosa and bulimia nervosa but not obesity. You need to study only one of these three disorders.

Eating behaviour	
Eating behaviour	• Factors influencing attitudes to food and eating behaviour, for example cultural influences, mood, health concerns. • Explanations for the success and failure of dieting.
Biological explanations of eating behaviour	• Neural mechanisms involved in controlling eating behaviour. • Evolutionary explanations of food preference.
Eating disorders	• Psychological explanations in relation to either anorexia nervosa or bulimia nervosa or obesity. • Biological explanations, including neural and evolutionary explanations.

ATTITUDES TO FOOD AND EATING BEHAVIOUR

M ost of us take food for granted, even taking into account the odd food fad or healthy eating regime. However, for a substantial number of people, their attitudes to food and the consequent eating behaviours might be described as 'disordered'. What distinguishes 'disordered' eaters from 'faddy' eaters is the purpose and consistency of the behaviour and whether or not the person maintains some degree of control over their eating behaviour. When we begin to use food to resolve an underlying emotional issue, for example, there is a problem. Where these distinctive attitudes to food and eating come from is open to question, and so on this spread we examine some possible explanations.

► Unhealthy eating? Chef Jamie Oliver tries shock tactics to persuade us to abandon convenience foods in favour of a new healthy eating regime.

EXPLANATIONS OF ATTITUDES TO FOOD AND EATING BEHAVIOUR

Social learning

Social learning, theory (see page 66) emphasises the impact that observing other people (i.e. models) has on our own attitudes and behaviour.

Parental modelling – One way in which children acquire their eating behaviour and attitudes to food is by observing the behaviour of their parents. Parental attitudes to food inevitably affect children because parents control the foods bought and served in the home. However, research also suggests an association between parents' and children's attitudes to food generally. For example, Brown and Ogden (2004) reported consistent correlations between parents and their children in terms of snack food intake, eating motivations and body dissatisfaction.

Media effects – The role of social learning is evident in the impact of television and other media (such as magazines) on attitudes to eating. MacIntyre *et al.* (1998) found that the media have a major impact both on *what* people eat, and also their attitudes to certain foods. However, the researchers also state that many eating behaviours are limited by personal circumstances, such as age, income and family circumstances. Thus, people appear to learn from the media about healthy eating, but must place this information within the broader context of their lives. It was precisely this problem that led chef Jamie Oliver to set up his BBC 'Ministry of Food' experiment in 2008 (see above).

Cultural influences

Much of the research into attitudes to food and eating behaviour has focused on body dissatisfaction, i.e. negative feelings and cognitions about the body that influence people's attitudes toward their eating behaviour. The causes of body dissatisfaction and the consequent influence on eating behaviour include the following:

- ***Ethnicity*** – Research suggests that body dissatisfaction and related eating concerns and disorders (e.g. bulimia nervosa) are more characteristic of white women than black or Asian women (Powell and Khan, 1995). Ball and Kenardy (2002) studied over fourteen thousand women between the ages of 18 and 23 in Australia. Results showed that for all ethnic groups, the longer the time spent in Australia, the more the women reported attitudes and eating behaviours similar to women born in Australia (known as the 'acculturation effect').

- ***Social class*** – A number of studies have found that body dissatisfaction, dieting behaviour and eating disorders are more common in higher-class individuals. For example, Dornbusch *et al.* (1984) surveyed 7000 American adolescents, and concluded that higher-class females had a greater desire to be thin, and were more likely to diet to achieve this, than their lower-class counterparts were. A recent study (Goode *et al.*, 2008) used data from the 2003 Scottish Health Survey and established that, in general, income was positively associated with healthy eating.

Mood and eating behaviour

Some explanations of eating behaviour, particularly of **binge-eating**, see it as a temporary escape from negative mood (such as sadness or anxiety).

Binge-eating – Research has shown that individuals with **bulimia nervosa** complain of anxiety prior to a binge. Self-monitoring studies (e.g. Davis *et al.*, 1988) have shown that one hour before a binge, bulimic individuals had more negative mood states than one hour before a normal snack or meal. The same relationship between low mood and binge-eating appears to hold for **sub-clinical** (below the threshold for clinical diagnosis) populations. Wegner *et al.* (2002) had students record their eating patterns and mood states over a two-week period. Binge days were characterised by generally low mood compared to non-binge days, but there was no difference in mood before and after a binge. This suggests that although low mood may make binge-eating more likely, it does not alleviate the low mood state.

Comfort-eating – For many of us, the experience of eating junk food when feeling a little low strikes a familiar chord. The Garg *et al.* study on the left offers an explanation for this particular relationship between mood and eating behaviour.

LOW MOOD AND COMFORT-EATING

Garg *et al.* (2007) observed the food choices of 38 participants as they watched either an upbeat, funny movie (*Sweet Home Alabama*) or a sad, depressing one (*Love Story*). Participants were offered buttered popcorn and seedless grapes throughout the films.

Those watching the sad film consumed 36% more popcorn than those watching the upbeat film, but the upbeat film group ate far more grapes than the other group.

Garg *et al.* claim that people who feel sad or depressed want to 'jolt themselves out of the dumps', therefore they are more likely to go for a snack that tastes good to give them a sudden rush of euphoria. Happy people want to extend their upbeat mood and so choose healthy foods.

However, when participants were presented with nutritional information about the foods (among other information) prior to viewing, consumption of the relatively unhealthy foods dropped dramatically. Perhaps, suggest the researchers, when we eat to comfort ourselves, we would do well to check the nutritional information on the foods we indulge in!

CULTURAL DIFFERENCES

Rozin *et al.* (1999) claim that food functions differently in the minds and lives of people from different cultures. Adults and college students from Belgium, France, U.S.A. and Japan completed a survey dealing with food-related issues, including beliefs about the diet–health link, consumption of 'healthy' foods (e.g. reduced in salt or fat) and satisfaction with the healthiness of their own diets. In all areas except beliefs about the importance of diet for health, they found substantial cultural (and usually gender) differences. In all four countries, females, more than males, showed a pattern of attitudes that was more like the American and less like the French (i.e. food associated with health rather than with pleasure). The researchers concluded that these differences may influence health and may partially account for national differences in rates of cardiovascular disease.

▼ The Disney-Pixar film *Ratatouille,* the story of a rat skilled in fine cuisine, reflects the French obsession with the pleasures of food.

EVALUATION

Social learning

Research support – The importance of social learning in attitudes to food was demonstrated in a study by Meyer and Gast (2008). They surveyed 10–12-year-old girls and boys and found a significant positive correlation between peer influence and disordered eating. The 'likeability' of peers was considered the most important factor in this relationship. The role of social learning is also supported in a study of mothers and daughters by Birch and Fisher (2000). They found that the best predictors of the daughters' eating behaviour were the mothers' dietary restraint and their perception of the risks of the daughters becoming overweight.

Much more than learning – A social learning explanation of eating behaviour focuses explicitly on the role of fashion models in influencing the food attitudes of young people. However, attitudes to food are clearly a product of much more than social learning alone. Evolutionary explanations of food preferences for example (see page 97), suggest that our preference for fatty and sweet foods is a direct result of an evolved adaptation among our distant ancestors over two million years ago.

Cultural influences

Ethnicity – Although some research has found that a preoccupation with dieting and disordered eating are more common among white females than black or Asian women, other studies have found the complete opposite. For example, Mumford *et al.* (1991) found that the incidence of bulimia was greater among Asian schoolgirls than among their white counterparts. Similarly, Striegel-Moore *et al.* (1995) found more evidence of a 'drive for thinness' among black girls than among white girls.

Social class – Research suggests that the relationship between social class and eating behaviour is not that straightforward. In direct contrast to Dornbusch *et al.*'s (1984) study described on the left, Story *et al.* (1995) found that in a sample of American students, higher social class was related to greater *satisfaction* with weight and *lower* rates of weight control behaviours, such as vomiting. Other studies have found no relationship between social class and weight dissatisfaction, the desire for thinness and eating disorders.

Mood and eating behaviour

Binge-eating and reinforcement – A number of studies have supported the claim that a period of lowered mood or anxiety precedes an episode of binge-eating. However, although a binge-eating episode might offer immediate gratification for the individual, any reinforcement is fleeting at best, and many studies report a *drop* in mood immediately after the binge.

It is unclear, however, *why* a binge-eating episode might be reinforcing for the individual, particularly as any benefit appears to be fleeting at best, and many studies report a mood *decrement* immediately after the binge.

Chocolate – the ultimate comfort food? Chocolate has long been seen as the ultimate comfort food. Our attitudes towards chocolate appear to be influenced by its ability to popular claims that it can lift our mood. However, a recent study by Parker *et al.* (2006) found that, although chocolate has a slight antidepressant effect for some people, when consumed as an emotional eating strategy (e.g. when feeling down), it is more likely to *prolong* rather than alleviate the negative mood, particularly if used repeatedly.

IDA — GENDER BIAS

Most studies have concentrated only on women's attitudes to eating behaviour, particularly in terms of body dissatisfaction and disordered eating. However, studies have shown that in men, homosexuality is a risk factor in the development of disordered eating attitudes and behaviour, including body dissatisfaction and higher levels of dieting (Siever, 1994). These findings have been attributed to the male gay subculture, which places great emphasis on the lean, muscular body ideal. This suggests that studies that concentrate only on women offer a limited view of attitudes to food and eating behaviour.

Evaluation — PROBLEMS OF GENERALISABILITY

The studies on this spread come from a variety of groups, some clinical (i.e. diagnosed with an eating disorder, such as bulimia nervosa), some with sub-clinical conditions, and others who represent a **non-clinical population** who experience a temporarily depressed mood (e.g. comfort-eaters). This puts limitations on the degree to which we can generalise from one group to another, and therefore the degree to which these studies offer a *universal* understanding of causal factors in eating behaviour.

CAN YOU...? — No.5.1

...1 Describe **two** explanations of the origins of attitudes to food and eating behaviour. Write about 100 words for each.

...2 Identify **eight** criticisms related to explanations of the origins of attitudes to food and eating behaviour, including **at least one** IDA topic. Each criticism should be about 50 words.

...3 Use this material to write a 600-word answer to the question: *Discuss attitudes to food and/or eating behaviour.* (8 marks + 16 marks)

EXPLANATIONS FOR THE SUCCESS AND FAILURE OF DIETING

A consequence of body dissatisfaction is the need to diet as an attempt to modify body size and shape to fit in with perceived cultural ideals. Three basic forms of dieting have been identified: (1) restricting the total amount of food eaten (2) refraining from eating certain *types* of food and (3) avoiding eating for long periods of time. The potential to influence weight change then becomes the primary (in many cases the *exclusive*) criterion for food selection. Dieting may also be associated with a particular mentality or mindset, characterised by a pervasive concern with body size, shape and weight (Higgins and Gray, 1999). On this spread we examine the psychological reasons why dieting sometimes succeeds but often fails.

▶ Research, such as the Kern *et al.* study on the right, suggests that for some people, dieting will always be difficult because of a genetic predisposition to obesity.

EXPLANATIONS OF THE IMPACT OF DIETING

Restraint theory

Restrained eating has become synonymous with dieting. Research suggests that as many as 89% of the female population in the UK consciously restrain their food intake at some point in their lives (Klesges *et al.*, 1987). Restraint theory (Herman and Mack, 1975) was developed as an attempt to explain both the causes and consequences associated with the cognitive restriction of food intake. Herman and Mack suggest that attempting not to eat actually *increases* the probability of overeating. Wardle and Beales (1988) carried out an experiment to test this prediction (see bottom left). Their study showed that the overeating shown by many dieters is actually caused by their attempts to diet.

The boundary model – In an attempt to explain why dieting might lead to overeating, Herman and Polivy (1984) developed the boundary model. According to this model, hunger keeps intake of food above a certain minimum, and satiety (satisfaction of hunger) works to keep intake below some maximum level. Between these two levels, psychological factors have the greatest impact on consumption. Dieters tend to have a larger range between hunger and satiety levels as it takes them longer to feel hungry and more food to satisfy them (see right). In addition, restrained eaters have a self-imposed *desired* intake. Once they have gone over this boundary they continue to eat until they reach satiety, i.e. beyond the maximum level imposed as part of their diet.

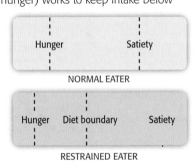

NORMAL EATER: Hunger — Satiety

RESTRAINED EATER: Hunger — Diet boundary — Satiety

▲ Comparison of boundaries for normal and restrained eaters (from Ogden, 2007).

RESTRAINT AND OVEREATING

Support for the claim that dietary restraint can lead to overeating comes from Wardle and Beales (1988). They randomly assigned 27 obese women to either a diet group (focusing on restrained eating patterns), an exercise group, or a non-treatment group for seven weeks. At weeks four and six, all participants were assessed under laboratory conditions.

At week four, food intake and appetite were assessed before and after a 'preload' (i.e. a small snack, such as a milkshake or chocolate bar). At week six, food intake was assessed under stressful conditions.

Results showed that at both assessment sessions, women in the diet condition ate more than women in the exercise and non-treatment groups.

The role of denial

Research in cognitive psychology has shown that attempting to suppress or deny a thought frequently has the opposite effect, making it even more prominent. For example, Wegner *et al.* (1987) asked some participants *not* to think about a white bear, but to ring a bell if they did, and others to think about the bear. Results showed that those told *not* to think about the bear rang their bells far more often than participants instructed to think about the bear. Wegner (1994) refers to this phenomenon as the 'theory of ironic processes of mental control' because it represents a paradoxical effect of thought control, i.e. denial often backfires.

The theory of ironic processes of mental control – Central to any dieting strategy is the decision not to eat certain foods, or to eat less of them. This results in a similar state of denial to the example above, as dieters try to suppress thoughts about foods deemed to be 'forbidden' as part of their diet. According to this theory, therefore, attempts to suppress thoughts of foods such as pizza and chocolate only serve to increase the dieters' preoccupation with the very foods they are trying to deny themselves. As soon as a food is denied, therefore, it simultaneously becomes more attractive.

Detail – the key to a successful diet

So far on this spread we have concentrated on the reasons why diets fail, but recent research by Redden (2008) suggests that the secret of *successful* dieting lies in the attention we pay to what is being eaten. He claims that people usually like experiences less as they repeat them. When it comes to dieting, this makes it harder to stick to a particular regime. To overcome this, suggests Redden, instead of thinking 'not another salad', we should focus on the details of the meal (e.g. rocket, tomato, apple, etc.). By focusing on the specific details of each meal, people get bored less easily and so are better able to maintain their diet.

The jelly beans experiment – To test this theory, Redden gave 135 people 22 jelly beans each, one at a time. As each bean was dispensed, information about it was flashed onto a computer screen. One group saw general information (e.g. 'bean number 7') whereas the other group saw specific flavour details (e.g. 'cherry flavour number 7'). Participants got bored with eating beans faster if they saw the general information, and enjoyed the task more if they saw the specific flavour details.

EVALUATION

Restraint theory

Implications for obesity treatment – Restraint theory suggests that restraint leads to excess, yet the treatment of obesity commonly recommends restraint as a solution to excessive weight gain. However, failed attempts to diet can leave obese individuals depressed, feeling a failure and unable to control their weight. Although obesity may not necessarily be caused by overeating, overeating may be a *consequence* of obesity if restraint is recommended as a treatment (Ogden, 1994).

Limited relevance – Restraint theory proposes an association between food restriction and overeating. However, Ogden (2007) points out that although dieters, bulimics and some anorexics report episodes of overeating, the behaviour of restricting anorexics (see page 92) cannot be explained using this theory. If trying not to eat results in overeating, says Ogden, then how do anorexics manage to starve themselves?

The theory of ironic processes of mental control

Research support – Soetens *et al.* (2006) provided experimental support for this theory. Participants were divided into restrained and unrestrained eaters, and the restrained group was then subdivided into those who were either high or low on disinhibition. The disinhibited restrained group (i.e. those who tried to eat less but who would often overeat) used more thought suppression than the other groups, and also showed a rebound effect (i.e. thought more about food) afterwards. This study shows that restrained eaters who tend to overeat try to suppress thoughts about food more often, but when they do, think more about food afterwards.

Limited experimental effects – Wegner (1994) admits that the 'ironic effects' observed in research are not particularly huge. As experimental effects go, they are detectable but far from overwhelming. However, as such effects may underlie more serious pathological forms of eating behaviour, their influence could be considered overwhelming in terms of everyday human cost.

Anti-dieting programmes

Concerns about the ineffectiveness and potentially damaging effects of many diet programmes has led to the development of programmes aimed at replacing dieting with conventional healthy eating. These programmes emphasise regulation by body hunger and satiety signals and the prevention of inappropriate attitudes to food (e.g. comfort-eating or food avoidance). A **meta-analysis** of the effectiveness of anti-dieting programmes (Higgins and Gray, 1999) found that participation in these programmes was associated with improvements in both eating behaviour and psychological wellbeing and with weight *stability* rather than weight *change*.

CAN YOU...? No.5.2

...**1** Describe **two** explanations for why diets succeed and fail. Each explanation should be about 100 words.

...**2** Identify **eight** criticisms related to why dieting might succeed and fail, including **at least one** IDA topic. Each criticism should be about 50 words.

...**3** Use this material to write a 600-word answer to the question: *Discuss **two or more** explanations for the success and failure of dieting*. (8 marks + 16 marks)

NEURAL MECHANISMS IN EATING BEHAVIOUR

We are so dependent on food that hunger is one of the most compelling of human motives. The need to eat shapes our daily lives and many of our activities. Our television screens and newspapers are crammed with food-related products, and a walk down any high street will leave you in no doubt about the importance of food in our everyday experience. It comes as no surprise then to discover that human beings have developed a sophisticated physiology for dealing with the related states of hunger (signalling a need for nutrients and the energy they provide) and satiation (signalling the satisfaction of these needs).

THE ROLE OF NEURAL MECHANISMS

Homeostasis

Homeostasis involves mechanisms which both *detect* the state of the internal environment (e.g. whether the body has enough nutrients) and also *correct* the situation to restore that environment to its optimal state. There is, however, a significant time lag between mechanisms operating to restore equilibrium, and the body registering their effect. By the time an individual has eaten enough to restore energy levels, only a small amount of food has been digested, therefore the receptors responsible for detecting nutrient levels have insufficient 'data' to turn off eating.

The body has evolved two separate systems, one for turning eating 'on' and one for turning it 'off'. Among humans, glucose levels probably play the most important role in producing feelings of hunger. Hunger increases as glucose levels decrease. A decline in glucose levels in the blood activates a part of the brain called the **lateral hypothalamus**, resulting in feelings of hunger. This causes the individual to search for and consume food, which causes glucose levels to rise again. This rise in glucose levels activates the **ventromedial hypothalamus**, which leads to feelings of satiation, which in turn inhibits further feeding. In some animals however, this does not happen, as can be seen from studies of the protein leptin (see below).

The lateral hypothalamus

Investigation into the role of the hypothalamus in eating behaviour began in the 1950s, when researchers discovered that damage to the lateral hypothalamus (LH) in rats caused a condition called **aphagia** (from the Greek meaning 'absence of eating'). Researchers also found that stimulation of the LH elicits feeding behaviour. These opposing effects of injury and stimulation led researchers to conclude that they had discovered the 'on' switch for eating behaviour. A **neurotransmitter** found in the hypothalamus, called **neuropeptide Y (NPY)**, is particularly important in turning on eating. When injected into the hypothalamus of rats, NPY causes them to immediately begin feeding, even when satiated (Wickens, 2000). Repeated injections of NPY into the hypothalamus of rats produces obesity in just a few days (Stanley et al., 1986).

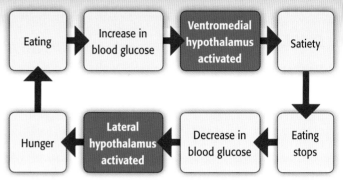

The ventromedial hypothalamus

In contrast to the effect of damage to the lateral hypothalamus, researchers also discovered that damage to the ventromedial hypothalamus (VMH) caused rats to overeat, leading to a condition called **hyperphagia**. Similarly, stimulation of this area inhibited feeding. This led researchers to conclude that the VMH signals 'stop eating' as a result of the many glucose receptors in this area. However, damage to the nerve fibres passing through the VMH tends to also damage another area of the hypothalamus, the **paraventricular nucleus** (PVN), and it is now believed that damage to the PVN alone causes hyperphagia (Gold, 1973). The PVN also detects the specific foods our body needs, and consequently seems to be responsible for many of our 'cravings'.

Neural control of cognitive factors

We have probably all experienced situations where simply thinking about a food makes us feel hungry. This cognitive aspect of food includes not only the images of food we have in our memory, but also food-related sights and smells (e.g. when we walk past an Indian restaurant). The neural control of these cognitive factors in hunger probably originates in two main brain areas, the **amygdala** and the **inferior prefrontal cortex**.

The amygdala – The role of the **amygdala** is thought to be primarily in the selection of foods on the basis of previous experience. For example, Rolls and Rolls (1973) found that surgically removing the amygdala in rats would cause the animals to consume both familiar and novel (i.e. unfamiliar) foods indiscriminately, whereas amygdala-intact rats would initially avoid novel foods and consume only the more palatable familiar foods instead.

The inferior frontal cortex receives messages from the olfactory bulb (part of the brain responsible for smell). Because odours influence the taste of foods, damage to the inferior prefrontal cortex is thought to decrease eating because of diminished sensory responses to food odour, and also probably to taste (Kolb and Whishaw, 2006).

LEPTIN AND OBESITY

Research with mice has shown that some mice receive two copies of the gene for obesity (abbreviated *ob*). These *ob/ob* mice have a tendency to overeat, especially foods high in fat or sugar. Zhang et al. (1994) discovered that *ob/ob* mice have defective genes for the protein **leptin**. Leptin is normally produced by fat tissue and secreted into the bloodstream where it travels to the brain and other tissues, causing fat loss and decreased appetite. In *ob/ob* mice, this process does not happen. Injecting *ob/ob* mice with leptin causes them to lose weight dramatically. Leptin treatment for obese human patients is still in its infancy, but research in genetics has made it possible to identify a predisposition to obesity, and treat this accordingly.

▶ Both these mice have the *ob/ob* gene pairing that predisposes them to obesity, but the mouse on the right has been treated with leptin injections which have restored normal weight levels.

EVALUATION

Limitations of a homeostatic explanation

For a hunger mechanism to be **adaptive** it must both anticipate and *prevent* energy deficits, not just react to them. As a result, the theory that hunger and eating are triggered only when the energy resources fall below their desired level, is incompatible with the harsh reality in which such systems would have evolved. For such a mechanism to be truly adaptive, it must promote levels of consumption that maintain bodily resources well above the optimal level to act as a buffer against future lack of food availability.

The role of the lateral hypothalamus

The view that the LH served as an 'on switch' for eating turned out to have a few problems. For example, damage to the LH caused deficits in other aspects of behaviour (e.g. thirst and sex) rather than just hunger. Also, more recent research has shown that eating behaviour is controlled by neural circuits that run throughout the brain, and not just by the hypothalamus. Although the LH undoubtedly plays an important role in controlling eating behaviour, it is not, as previously thought, the brain's 'eating centre' (Sakurai *et al.*, 1998).

Neuropeptide Y – Recent research on NPY has cast doubt on whether its normal function is to influence feeding behaviour. Marie *et al.* (2005) genetically manipulated mice so that they did not make NPY. They found no subsequent decrease in their feeding behaviour. The researchers suggest that the hunger stimulated by injections of NPY may actually be an experimental artefact, in that the flood of NPY during experimental manipulations could cause behaviour not like that caused by normal amounts of the neurotransmitter. The role of NPY in human obesity is discussed in the 'Real-world application' box above.

The role of the ventromedial hypothalamus

Early researchers found that lesions or damage to the VMH resulted in hyperphagia and obesity in a number of different species, including humans. This led them to designate the VMH as the 'satiety centre' in eating behaviour. However, Gold (1973) found that lesions restricted to the VMH alone did *not* result in hyperphagia and only produced overeating when they included other areas, such as the paraventricular nucleus (PVN). However, subsequent research has failed to replicate Gold's findings, with most studies showing that, compared to lesions in other brain areas such as the PVN, animals with VMH lesions ate substantially more and gained substantially more weight.

Neural control of cognitive factors

Klüver-Bucy syndrome – Damage to the amygdala and inferior prefrontal cortex could explain the feeding abnormalities observed in **Klüver–Bucy syndrome**. Patients with this syndrome typically show increased appetite, indiscriminate eating, and even attempts to eat non-food items. Research on the effects of damage to these brain areas suggests that food cues no longer accurately represent their real reward value to the individual.

Research support – Zald and Pardo (1997) have provided physiological evidence to support the claim that the amygdala participates in the emotional processing of olfactory stimuli. They exposed healthy adult participants to aversive olfactory (smell) stimuli while measuring blood flow to the **amygdala** by means of a **PET scan**. Exposure to unpleasant odours produced significant blood flow increases to the amygdala whereas non-aversive odours did not cause increased blood flow. Increased blood flow to the amygdala was also associated with subjective ratings of the perceived unpleasantness of the stimuli.

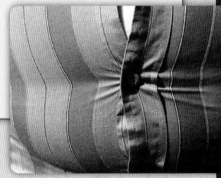

CAN YOU...? No.5.3

...**1** Describe **at least two** ways in which eating behaviour is controlled by neural mechanisms. Your response should be about 200 words.

...**2** Identify **eight** criticisms related to neural mechanisms in eating behaviour, including **at least one** IDA topic. Each criticism should be about 50 words.

...**3** Use this material to write a 600-word answer to the question: *Discuss **two or more** ways in which eating behaviour is controlled by neural mechanisms.* (8 marks + 16 marks)

EVOLUTIONARY EXPLANATIONS OF FOOD PREFERENCE

The goal of any evolutionary explanation is to discover the adaptive function of a particular behaviour. Since the mechanisms that make up human nature were designed by natural selection millions of years ago, we need to consider the problems faced by our distant ancestors to discover why behaviours such as food preferences evolved in the first place. We only have to look at the sugar, fat and salt served up in fast-food restaurants to get an idea what these adaptive problems might have been.

THE EVOLUTION OF FOOD PREFERENCES

▼ Hunter–gatherers such as these in Botswana still rely on catching animals to provide an energy-rich meat diet.

The environment of evolutionary adaptation (EEA)

To understand the adaptive problems faced by our distant ancestors, we must understand the environment in which they lived. The **environment of evolutionary adaptation (EEA)** refers to the environment in which a species first evolved.

Human beings first emerged as a separate species some two million years ago on the African savannah, and natural selection favoured adaptations geared toward survival in that particular environment. For most of our evolutionary history we have probably lived in hunter–gatherer societies, and it therefore makes sense to begin our quest there.

▼ Our modern preferences for calorie-rich foods can be traced back to the adaptive problems faced by our ancestors.

Early diets

Early humans were hunter–gatherers whose diet included the animals and plants that were part of their natural environment. Preferences for fatty food would have been adaptive for early humans, because conditions in the EEA meant that energy resources were vital in order to stay alive and also to find the next meal. Although modern human beings are more concerned with the nutritious value of food (i.e. containing vitamins, minerals and other substances necessary for a healthy diet), instead what we eat is often rich in calories but not particularly nutritious. In the EEA, calories were not as plentiful as they are today, so it makes sense that humans and other animals have evolved a distinct preference for foods that are particularly rich in calories.

Preference for meat

Human ancestors began to include meat in their diets to compensate for a decline in the quality of plant foods caused by receding forests two million years ago. Fossil evidence from groups of hunter–gatherers suggests that their daily diet was derived primarily from animal-based foods, in particular animal organs, such as liver, kidneys, and brains that are extremely rich sources of energy. A meat diet, full of densely packed nutrients, provided the catalyst for the growth of the brain. Without animals, claims Milton (2008), it is unlikely that early humans could have secured enough nutrition from a vegetarian diet to evolve into the active and intelligent creatures they became. Meat supplied early humans with all the essential amino acids, minerals and nutrients they required, allowing them to supplement their diet with marginal, low-quality, plant-based foods that have few nutrients but lots of calories (e.g. rice and wheat).

Taste aversion

Bait shyness (Taste aversion) was first discovered by farmers trying to rid themselves of rats. They found that it was difficult to kill the rats by using poisoned bait because rats would only take a small amount of any new food, and if they became ill, would rapidly learn to avoid it. For this reason, taste aversion was originally known as 'bait shyness'. Garcia et al. (1955) were the first to study taste aversion in the laboratory. Rats who had been made ill through radiation shortly after eating saccharin, developed an aversion to it and very quickly associated their illness with the saccharin.

The adaptive advantages of taste aversion – Despite the name 'taste' aversion, subsequent research has found that not only taste but also the *odour* of food can be linked to illness and consequently to the development of a food aversion. The development of taste aversions would have helped our ancestors to survive because, if they were lucky enough to survive eating poisoned food, they would not make the same mistake again. Taste aversion learning has other properties that would also have enhanced survival in the EEA. A taste aversion can still be acquired up to 24 hours after the consumption of food, as the reaction to poisoned food in the natural environment is often delayed. Once learned, such aversions are very hard to shift – an adaptive quality designed to keep our ancestors alive.

The 'medicine effect' – There is also evidence that animals can learn a preference that makes them healthier, with any food eaten just before recovery from illness being preferred in the future. This is known as the 'medicine effect'. For example, Garcia et al. (1955) found that when a distinctive flavour is presented to a thiamine-deficient rat and then followed by an injection of thiamine, the animal will acquire a preference for that flavour.

> ### REAL-WORLD APPLICATION
> Research on the adaptive origins of taste aversion has been helpful in understanding the food avoidance that can sometimes occur during the treatment of cancer. Some cancer treatments, such as radiation and chemotherapy, can cause gastrointestinal illness. When this illness is paired with food consumption, taste aversions can result. For example, Bernstein and Webster (1980) gave patients a novel-tasting ice cream prior to their chemotherapy and the patients acquired an aversion to that ice cream. These findings have resulted in the development of the 'scapegoat technique', which involves giving cancer patients a novel food along with some familiar food just prior to their chemotherapy. The patient forms an aversion to the novel food and not to the familiar, usual food. This is consistent with an adaptive avoidance of novel (i.e. unfamiliar) foods known as **neophobia**.

TESTING EVOLUTIONARY HYPOTHESES

Evaluation

A common way of testing evolutionary hypotheses is through comparison with a different species. We might, for example, question whether the same eating preferences are found in other species. Although we cannot travel back to the EEA to see what adaptive problems were faced by our ancestors, we *can* study a related species (e.g. chimpanzees) who face similar adaptive problems today. Alternatively we may look for modern-day human products that reflect our evolved food preferences. For example, hamburgers, pizza and sugary foods sell well because they correspond to and exploit evolved desires for fat, sugar, etc. However, a search for 'ultimate' causes in food preferences may mask more 'proximate' causes, such as advertising, availability, laziness and so on.

▼ A group of chimpanzees sharing a red colobus monkey after they have hunted and killed it.

EVALUATION

The importance of calories in early diets

Gibson and Wardle (2001) provided evidence to support the importance of calories in an ancestral diet. They showed that the best way to predict which fruit and vegetables would be preferred by four-to-five-year-old children was not in terms of how sweet they were, nor how much protein they contained, nor even how familiar they were, but in how dense they were in calories. Bananas and potatoes are particularly calorie-rich, and were more likely to be chosen by the children, demonstrating an evolved preference for calorie-rich foods.

Could early humans have been vegetarian?

Cordain *et al.* (2006) argued that early humans consumed most of their calories from sources other than saturated animal fats. This has led to the intriguing suggestion that our distant ancestors were healthy eaters and may even have been vegetarian. The evidence, however, does not support this hypothesis. Anthropological evidence (e.g. Abrams, 1987) shows that all societies display a preference for animal foods and fats. Nor would it have been possible for early humans to be completely vegetarian because they would not have been able to get sufficient calories from the plants and grains available.

Are all food preferences a product of evolution?

Many food preferences can be traced back to the adaptive pressures of the EEA, but this is not always the case. A trait that is beneficial today (e.g. consumption of low cholesterol foods) would not have evolved because of its beneficial effects for our ancestors. Many things that were important to our ancestors (such as saturated animal fats) are harmful in modern environments, so we are more likely to *avoid* them in order to survive and lead a healthy life.

Taste aversion

Explaining taste aversion in humans – Seligman (1970) claimed that different species evolved different learning abilities, something he called **biological preparedness**. This natural selection of differential learning has occurred so that each species has the ability to learn certain associations more easily than others, particularly those associations that help individuals survive.

Detecting toxins – Scientists have long assumed that bitter taste evolved as a defence mechanism to detect potentially harmful toxins in plants. An American study provides the first direct evidence in support of this hypothesis. Sandell and Breslin (2006) screened 35 adults for the *hTAS2R38 bitter taste receptor gene*. Participants rated the bitterness of various vegetables, some of which contained *glucosinolates* and others that did not. Glucosinolates are well known for their toxic effects at high doses. Those with the sensitive form of the gene rated the glucosinolate-containing vegetables as 60% more bitter than those with the insensitive form of the gene. The ability to detect and avoid naturally-occurring glucosinolates would confer a selective advantage on our ancestors, which would explain why such genes are widespread today.

EVIDENCE FROM OTHER PRIMATES

Evaluation

For our ancestors in the EEA, meat was an important source of saturated fat. Fat was vital for survival, yet was not readily available in early human environments. Anthropologist Craig Stanford's observations of chimpanzees in Tanzania's Gombe National park showed that these animals face the same problems today as our ancestors did millions of years ago. After coming close to starvation for much of the year, when they do manage a kill (usually a colobus monkey), they go straight for the fattiest parts (e.g. the brain and bone marrow) rather than the tender, more nutritious flesh (Stanford, 1999).

CULTURAL DIFFERENCES IN FOOD PREFERENCES

Evaluation

Despite evidence of evolved food preferences, the vast majority of specific food likes and dislikes appear not to be predetermined. This doesn't mean that evolved preferences are unimportant – the strong affinity that children show for very sweet foods, and the persistence of liking for the taste of fatty and salty foods throughout life, appear to be universal. However, innate responses do not account for the broad range of food likes and dislikes that develop beyond infancy. The pungency of spicy foods, for example, is initially rejected, yet across the world chilli is second only to salt in its popularity as a food spice. Although evolved factors are clearly important in food selection, these are modified by our experience with different foods, with culture partly determining the extent of such experiences. However, if our ancestors had eaten inappropriately and so failed to get the nutrition they required for survival, they would have died off, and any built-in preference for inappropriate foodstuffs would have gone with them. Therefore, cultural differences in food preferences may exist, but these are usually a fine-tuning of the evolved preferences discussed on this spread.

CAN YOU...? No.5.4

...1 Describe **at least two** evolutionary explanations of food preferences. Each explanation should be about 100 words.

...2 Identify **eight** criticisms related to evolutionary explantions of food preference, including **at least one** IDA topic. Each criticism should be about 50 words.

...3 Use this material to write a 600-word answer to the question: *Discuss **two or more** evolutionary explanations of food preferences.* (8 marks + 16 marks)

PSYCHOLOGICAL EXPLANATIONS FOR ANOREXIA NERVOSA

Many Western cultures appear preoccupied with food, so it is hardly surprising to find that many people are overweight, even obese. As a consequence, we have developed an obsession with losing weight. This obsession with food, coupled with an obsession for losing weight has led to the emergence of disorders associated with food and eating. In 1694, Richard Morton published the first medical case history of **anorexia nervosa (AN)** and in 1870, Sir William Gull gave it its name, which means 'nervous loss of appetite'.

You are required to study either anorexia nervosa or bulimia nervosa for the examination. There is a third choice (obesity), but we have decided not to cover that here.

CLINICAL CHARACTERISTICS OF ANOREXIA NERVOSA

DSM-IV-TR lists four criteria for anorexia.

1 Anxiety
A key characteristic of anorexia is the anxiety associated with the disorder, and excessive fear of being fat. People with anorexia are not simply obsessed with weight but fearful of weight gain.

2 Weight
Weight loss is considered abnormal when it drops below 85% of the individual's normal weight, based on age and height. People with anorexia develop unusual eating habits, such as avoiding food and meals or carefully weighing and portioning food. Individuals may repeatedly check their body weight, and many engage in techniques to control their weight, such as compulsive exercise.

3 Body-image distortion
People with anorexia do not see their own thinness and deny the seriousness of their low body weight. They often continue to see themselves as fat despite their bones being clearly visible. Thinness is vital to their self-esteem.

4 Amenorrhoea
'Amenorrhoea' means cessation of menstrual periods. The absence of periods for more than three months is a clinical characteristic of anorexia in girls who have begun menstruation. The lack of a menstrual cycle is caused in these cases by inadequate nutrition.

PSYCHOLOGICAL EXPLANATIONS

Cultural ideals and the media

Cultural ideals – It is a widely held belief that Western standards of attractiveness are an important contributory factor to the development of AN. Numerous studies have reported that many teenagers, especially girls, are dissatisfied with their weight and have a distorted view of their body image. *The National Diet and Nutrition Survey of Young People* (Gregory et al., 2000) found that 16% of 15–18 year old girls in the UK were 'currently on a diet'.

Media influences – The media are a major source of influence for the body image attitudes maintained by Western adolescents. For example, the portrayal of thin models on television and in magazines is a significant contributory factor in body image concerns and the drive for thinness among Western adolescent girls. The media does not influence everyone in the same way, for example individuals with low self-esteem are more likely to compare themselves to idealised images portrayed in the media (Jones and Buckingham, 2005).

Ethnicity and peer influences

Ethnicity – Other cultural groups do not place the same value on thinness as an ideal for women. The incidence of AN in non-Western cultures and in black populations in Western cultures is much lower than within a white Western population. In a meta-analysis of 98 studies, Grabe and Hyde (2006) found a difference between African-American and Caucasian and Hispanic females. African-Americans reported significantly less body dissatisfaction than the other two groups. In many non-Western cultures (e.g. Fiji and the Caribbean), there are more positive attitudes toward large body sizes, which are associated with attractiveness, fertility and nurturance (Pollack, 1995).

Peer influences – Peer acceptance is particularly important during adolescence, so adolescents may be particularly susceptible to peer influence on patterns of disordered eating. A US study found that dieting among friends was significantly related to unhealthy weight control behaviours, such as the use of diet pills or purging (Eisenberg et al., 2005). A specific mechanism of peer influence is teasing. Jones and Crawford (2006) found that overweight girls and underweight boys were most likely to be teased by their peers, suggesting that through teasing, peers serve to enforce gender-based ideals.

Hilde Bruch (1973) claimed that the origins of AN are in early childhood. She distinguished between *effective* parents who respond appropriately to their child's needs (e.g. feeding them when hungry) and *ineffective* parents who fail to respond to their child's internal needs. If a child cries because they are anxious, an ineffective parent may feed them, or conversely, may comfort them when actually they are hungry. Children of ineffective parents may grow up confused about their internal needs, becoming overly reliant on their parents. Adolescence increases a desire to establish autonomy, but adolescents are often unable to do so, feeling that they do not own their own bodies. To overcome their sense of helplessness they can take excessive control over their body shape and size by developing abnormal eating habits.

Personality

Personality traits, the enduring characteristics that define who we are, are thought to play an important causal role in the development and maintenance of AN.

Perfectionism (e.g. concern for mistakes) is often found in individuals with AN and other eating disorders. Strober et al. (2006) retrospectively evaluated personality traits in teenage boys and girls receiving treatment for AN. They found high levels of perfectionism in 73% of the girls and 50% of the boys.

Impulsiveness – Although most studies have linked impulsiveness with bulimia nervosa, recent research has shown that individuals with AN act more impulsively than they self-report. Butler and Montgomery (2005) found that, compared to a normal control group, patients with AN responded rapidly (but inaccurately) to a performance task, indicating behavioural impulsiveness, despite their low self-reported impulsiveness.

EVALUATION

Cultural ideals and media influences

Cultural ideals – Hoek et al. (1998) set out to test the view that anorexia is rare in non-Western cultures. The researchers examined the records of 44,192 people admitted to hospital between 1987 and 1989 in Curacao, a non-Westernised Caribbean island where it is acceptable to be overweight. They found six cases, a rate that they claim is within the range of rates of AN reported in Western countries.

Media influences – Evidence for the role of the media in shaping perceptions of body image comes from studies of societies where television has been introduced. Eating attitudes and behaviours were studied among adolescent Fijian girls following the introduction of television in 1995 (Becker et al., 2002). The girls stated a desire to lose weight to become more like Western television characters. However, other research has shown that instructional intervention prior to media exposure to idealised female images *prevents* the adverse effects of exposure (Yamamiya et al., 2005).

Ethnicity and peer influences

Ethnicity – Not all studies have found differences in the incidence of AN between black and white groups. For example, Cachelin and Regan (2006) found no significant differences in prevalence of disordered eating between African-American and white Caucasian participants. The stereotypical view that white populations have a higher incidence of AN than black populations appears to be true only in older adolescents (Roberts et al., 2006).

Peer influences – Research does not always show a significant relationship between peer influence and development of AN. Shroff and Thompson (2006) found no correlation among friends on measures of disordered eating in an adolescent sample. Although Jones and Crawford (see left) found that overweight girls and underweight boys were more likely to be teased, these gender differences do not emerge until adolescence. A study of 10-year-olds found a positive correlation between body mass index (BMI) and teasing for both boys *and* girls (Lunde et al., 2006).

Bruch's psychodynamic explanation

Bruch's theory is supported by observations that parents of adolescents with AN have a tendency to define their children's physical needs rather than allowing their children to define their own (Steiner et al., 1991). Bruch found that many of these parents claimed to 'anticipate' their children's needs rather then ever letting them 'feel' hungry (Bruch, 1973). Research also supports Bruch's claim that people with AN rely excessively on the opinions of others, worry about how others view them and feel a lack of control over their lives (Button and Warren, 2001).

Personality

Perfectionism – The study by Halmi et al. (see right) highlights the importance of perfectionism as a risk factor for AN. A recent longitudinal study (Nilsson et al., 1999) also shows the importance of perfectionism in the *duration* of AN. Individuals who had short illness duration had lower levels of perfectionism, and those with high levels were more at risk of long illness duration.

Methodological problems – The study of personality in AN is fraught with methodological problems. These include separating out lasting personality traits from short-lived states that may be caused by starvation. In addition there is a frequent reliance on clinically diagnosed samples, which represents a biased view of the relationship between personality and disordered eating.

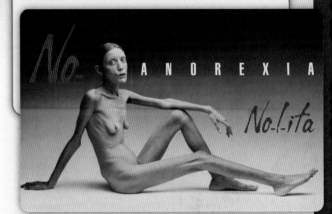

▲ Model Isabelle Caro featured in an anti-anorexia campaign in 2007. She died in 2010, aged just 28.

Evaluation **PERFECTIONISM AND ANOREXIA NERVOSA**
The link between perfectionism and AN is supported by research (Halmi et al., 2000) investigated the relationship between perfectionism and anorexia nervosa in 322 women with a history of AN across Europe and the United States. Prior to this study, much of the available data on the relationship between perfectionism and AN had been anecdotal.

The results of this study showed that those individuals who had a history of AN scored significantly higher on the *Multidimensional Perfectionism Scale* when compared to a comparison group of healthy women. In addition, the extent of perfectionism was directly related to the severity of AN experienced by the women.

As part of the study, researchers included patients with relatives who also suffered from AN, and enlisted them for the study. The results of this study showed that perfectionism as a personality trait appears to run in families and therefore represents a genetic vulnerability (i.e. a diathesis) for the development of AN.

CAN YOU...? No.5.5

...1 Describe **two** psychological explanations of anorexia nervosa. Each should be about 100 words.

...2 Identify **eight** criticisms related to psychological explanations of anoresxia nervosa, including **at least one** IDA topic. Each criticism should be about 50 words.

...3 Use this material to write a 600-word answer to the question: *Discuss **two or more** psychological explanations of anorexia nervosa.* (8 marks + 16 marks)

BIOLOGICAL EXPLANATIONS FOR ANOREXIA NERVOSA

Many of the early explanations of **anorexia nervosa (AN)** concentrated on the influence of psychological factors, but more recent work has highlighted the importance of biological factors in this disorder. These include 'neural' explanations (i.e. relating to changes in the nervous system) and 'evolutionary' explanations (i.e. relating to the adaptive function of AN). The prominence of recent biological explanations of AN is a direct result of more sophisticated methodologies that were not available to researchers twenty years ago. Most of the studies on this page reflect this new-found sophistication.

NEURAL EXPLANATIONS

Neurotransmitters

Serotonin – Disturbances in levels of the neurotransmitter serotonin appear to be a characteristic of individuals with eating disorders. Bailer *et al.* (2007) compared serotonin activity in women recovering from *restricting-type anorexia* (restricted food intake) and *binge-eating/purging type* (periods of restrictive eating and binge-eating/purging) with healthy controls. They found significantly higher serotonin activity in the women recovering from the binge-eating/purging type. In addition they found the highest levels of serotonin activity in women who showed the most anxiety, suggesting that persistent disruption of serotonin levels may lead to increased anxiety, which may trigger AN.

Dopamine – Recent studies suggest a role for dopamine in AN. Kaye *et al.* (2005) used a **PET scan** to compare dopamine activity in the brains of 10 women recovering from AN, and 12 healthy women. In the AN women, they found overactivity in dopamine receptors in a part of the brain known as the **basal ganglia**, where dopamine plays a part in the interpretation of harm and pleasure. Increased dopamine activity in this area appears to alter the way people interpret rewards. Individuals with AN find it difficult to associate good feelings with the things that most people find pleasurable (such as food).

Neurodevelopment

Pregnancy and birth complications – Lindberg and Hjern (2003) found a significant association between premature birth and development of AN. Birth complications may lead to brain damage caused by hypoxia (lack of oxygen), impairing the neurodevelopment of the child. Nutritional factors may be implicated if mothers have an eating disorder. Bulik *et al.* (2005) suggest that mothers with AN expose their offspring to a 'double disadvantage' – transmission of a genetic vulnerability to AN, *and* inadequate nutrition during pregnancy.

Season of birth – Research also suggests that individuals with AN are more likely to have been born during the spring months (Eagles *et al.*, 2001). Explanations for this intriguing association include intrauterine infections during pregnancy and temperature at time of conception. For example, a study by Willoughby *et al.* (2005) found that among patients with AN in equatorial regions of the world (where it is constantly hot), there was no seasonality effect in the development of AN.

EVOLUTIONARY EXPLANATIONS

The reproductive suppression hypothesis

Surbey (1987) suggests that adolescent girls' desire to control their weight represents an evolutionary adaptation in which ancestral girls delayed the onset of sexual maturation in response to cues about the probability of poor reproductive success. The ability to delay reproduction is **adaptive** because it enables a female to avoid giving birth at a time when conditions are not conducive to her offspring's survival. This model is based on the observation that in a number of species puberty is delayed or reproduction suppressed in females when they are subjected to stress or are in poor physical condition. Surbey argues that AN is a 'disordered variant' of the adaptive ability of females to alter the timing of reproduction at a time when they feel unable to cope with the biological, emotional and social responsibilities of womanhood.

The 'adapted to flee' hypothesis (AFFH)

An adaptive response to famine conditions – The AFHH (Guisinger, 2003) proposes that the typical AN symptoms of food restriction, hyperactivity and denial of starvation, reflect the operation of adaptive mechanisms that once caused migration in response to local famine conditions. Normally, when a person begins to lose weight, physiological mechanisms conserve energy and increase desire for food. These adaptations facilitate survival in hard times. However, among ancestral nomadic foragers, when extreme weight loss was due to a severe depletion of local food resources, this adaptation must be turned off so that individuals can increase their chances of survival by migrating to a more favourable environment. Food restriction is a common feature of many species when feeding competes with other activities, such as migration or breeding.

Migratory restlessness – The hyperactivity typically found in anorexics may be a form of 'migratory restlessness' as many species increase activity in times of food shortage and prior to migration. In the **EEA** those starving foragers who deceived themselves about their physical condition would have been more confident about moving on to a more favourable (in terms of food availability) environment, and so would have been more likely to survive. Therefore, for modern-day individuals, among those who are genetically vulnerable to AN, losing too much weight may trigger these ancestral mechanisms.

▲ **Holy anorexia – St. Catherine of Siena.** An assumption of the reproduction suppression hypothesis is that anorexic symptoms should be evident throughout human history. During the Middle Ages, many pious women fasted excessively, leading to what has now become known as 'holy anorexia' (Bell, 1985). In fact, the Roman Catholic church canonised over 85 very thin saints who were recognised, in part, for their seemingly miraculous ability to live with very little food.

Catherine Benincasa (St. Catherine of Siena) lived in the fourteenth century. As a youth she fasted rigorously but at the time of her conversion to radical holiness she restricted her diet to bread, uncooked vegetables and water. In her later years she ate even less, leading some to believe that she must be possessed by the devil. Her abstemiousness went far beyond the austere fasting of even the holiest men and women, and was in direct violation of the directions and advice of those around her. She was eventually canonised in 1461.

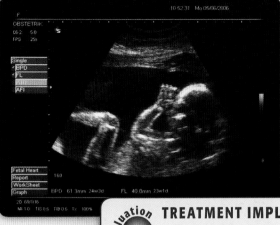

REAL-WORLD APPLICATION
An unlikely application of research in this area has been its implication for insurance payouts for psychiatric conditions. In the US, for example, treatment for AN is restricted under many insurance plans because it is not considered to be 'biologically based'. However, research such as that considered on ths spread creates a case for insurance companies to consider AN in the same way as other psychiatric conditions (such as schizophrenia) that *are* considered to be biologically based.

◀ A safe environment? Research suggests that exposure to infections while in the womb may be a risk factor for the later development of eating disorders, such as AN.

EVALUATION

Neurotransmitters

Serotonin – A problem for this explanation is that **SSRIs**, which alter levels of available brain serotonin, are ineffective when used with AN patients. Kaye *et al.* (2001), however, found that when used with recovering AN patients, these drugs *were* effective in preventing relapse. Malnutrition-related changes in serotonin function may negate the action of SSRIs, which only become effective when weight returns to a more normal level.

Dopamine – Castro-Fornieles *et al.* (2006) found that adolescent girls with AN had higher levels of homovanillic acid (a waste product of dopamine) than a control group. Improvement in weight levels was associated with normalisation of homovanillic levels. Research has also shown *lower* than normal levels of dopamine receptors in the brains of obese individuals (Wang *et al.,* 2001). Levels of dopamine appear to be inversely related to body weight, although whether this is a cause or a consequence is not yet clear.

Neurodevelopment

Obstetric complications – A recent prospective birth study (following a group of children from birth to adulthood) provides support for the contribution of obstetric complications. Favaro *et al.* (2006) found that perinatal (i.e. immediately before or after birth) complications significantly associated with risk of developing AN were placental infarction (obstructed blood supply in the placenta), early eating difficulties and a low birth weight.

Season of birth – This explanation is supported by a study of family composition (Eagles *et al.*, 2005). They found that anorexic individuals tend to be later in birth order compared with healthy individuals. The more elder siblings a child has while he/she is still in the womb, the more likely it is that the mother will be exposed to common infections, and the more likely these will be passed to the unborn child. The critical period for brain development is the second trimester of pregnancy, so for a spring birth the second trimester would occur at the time of year when infections are more likely.

Evolutionary explanations

The reproduction suppression hypothesis – This hypothesis is supported by the observation that menarche (the onset of puberty) is delayed in prepubertal girls with AN. Additionally, since amenorrhoea is a typical characteristic of AN, this means that reproduction is effectively suspended in anorexic females.

Treatment implications of the AFHH – Guisinger claims that the AFHH 'relieves therapists of the need to search for familial reasons for AN'. A struggle for control between those with AN and those who want them to get better, is an often reported characteristic of AN. This struggle is explained in terms of the 'worried and uncomprehending family' on the one hand, and the anorexic's powerful biological urge to avoid food and to exercise. Awareness of this causal influence can help treatment, and encourage parents to be more compassionate toward an anorexic child.

Problems associated with evolutionary explanations – We might question how the symptoms of AN might be passed on by natural selection, particularly as they decrease fertility and could even kill the individual with this condition. AN would have functioned more effectively in ancestral conditions, yet outside the ecological setting in which it evolved disorders such as AN can be deadly.

TREATMENT IMPLICATIONS
Biological explanations of AN offer the promise of a range of treatment possibilities, including drug therapies to normalise neurotransmitter levels and even gene-replacement therapy. Bulik *et al.* (2006) suggests that if we could use an individual's genetic profile to indicate level of risk, it would be possible to develop specially tailored prevention programmes for those most susceptible to developing AN. An additional advantage of treatments linked to biological explanations is that people then realise they are dealing with a dysfunctional *biology* (which is treatable) rather than a dysfunctional *family* (which often is not). Perhaps the most important implication of this is that it reduces the guilt generated by the view that it is *parents* who cause the development of eating disorders in their children.

GENDER BIAS
Most studies of eating disorders have concentrated on the study of women but, according to recent statistics, 25% of adults with eating disorders are men. Whether that figure indicates that more men nowadays suffer from disordered eating compared to ten years ago, or whether previously boys and men escaped attention, is not yet clear. However, what this does show is that eating disorders such as AN are not exclusively a female problem.

CAN YOU...? No.5.6

...1 Describe **one** neural and **one** evolutionary explanation of anorexia nervosa. Each should be about 100 words.

...2 Identify **eight** criticisms related to biological explanations for anorexia nervosa, including **at least one** IDA topic. Each criticism should be about 50 words.

...3 Use this material to write a 600-word answer to the question: *Discuss **two or more** biological explanations of anorexia nervosa.* (8 marks + 16 marks)

PSYCHOLOGICAL EXPLANATIONS FOR BULIMIA NERVOSA

Bulimia nervosa (BN) is an eating disorder characterised by recurrent binge-eating followed by self-induced vomiting or another compensatory behaviour (purging). BN is relatively common among young women, and is three times as common as AN (Cooper *et al.*, 2004). Bulimia is similar to anorexia in many ways – individuals are fearful of being obese and are driven to be thin. Bulimia is more common than anorexia, and usually starts when people are a little older.

▲ Princess Diana publicly admitted suffering from bulimia nervosa in a TV interview with Martin Bashir in 1995. It was, she claimed, a consequence of her unhappy relationship with Prince Charles.

CLINICAL CHARACTERISTICS OF BULIMIA NERVOSA

DSM-IV-TR lists five criteria for bulimia.

1. Binge – People with bulimia engage in recurrent episodes of secret binge-eating. Bingeing involves eating an excessive amount of food within a short period of time and feeling a lack of control over eating during the episode.

2. Purge – After bingeing the individual with bulimia is likely to purge her/himself to compensate for the overindulgence and in order to prevent weight gain. This is achieved by self-induced vomiting or by misuse of laxatives or other medications. Alternatively the individual with bulimia may stop eating for a long period as a means of purging.

3. Frequency – In order to be diagnosed as suffering from bulimia, an individual should have been displaying binge-eating and inappropriate compensatory behaviours, on average, at least twice a week for three months.

4. Body image – Like people with anorexia, the bulimic's self-image and self-esteem are unduly influenced by body shape and weight. Someone suffering from bulimia has an inappropriate perception of his/her own body.

5. Different from anorexia – As purging or other compensatory behaviour follows the binge-eating episodes, people with bulimia are usually within the normal weight range for their age and height. However, like individuals with anorexia, they fear becoming obese, have a strong desire to lose weight, and feel intensely dissatisfied with their bodies. People with bulimia often perform the behaviours in secret, feeling disgusted and ashamed when they binge, yet relieved once they purge.

COGNITIVE EXPLANATIONS

Cooper *et al.*'s cognitive model

Developmental factors – Most people who suffer from BN have experienced early trauma or life events that may not be obvious to other people. As a result, these individuals conclude that they are unacceptable to those around them, thinking of themselves as unlovable or worthless (Cooper *et al.*, 2004). As these individuals grow older they become exposed to dieting and to criticisms about their weight and shape. These criticisms may be direct, in the form of comments from friends or family, or implied in the form of exposure to media representations of thin, 'beautiful' people. Cooper believes that the bulimic learns from these experiences that fat = bad and thin = good, and so they inevitably start to diet. Unlike normal dieters, the BN individual diets because they believe that by losing weight they will overcome their bad thoughts about themselves. They typically have thoughts, such as: 'If I lose weight, everybody will like me'.

Maintaining factors – Cooper *et al.*'s model explains the maintenance of BN as a 'vicious circle' of thoughts, e.g. an individual with BN may believe that binge-eating will make them feel better, or that they are unable to control their eating. These kinds of thoughts trigger a binge, which might continue until thoughts such as 'I will get fat' take over. This then triggers the purge phase of BN, and the individual may then begin vomiting to reduce the harm done by binge-eating. This then leads to feelings of worthlessness, which may be (temporarily) reduced by eating, then purging, and so the whole process repeats itself.

The functional model

Polivy *et al.* (1994) suggested that individuals engage in the binge-eating associated with BN as a way of coping with identity problems, particularly those associated with self-image. By overeating, the person can attribute any resulting distress to the overeating rather than to the more serious underlying issues associated with threats to their emotional well-being. This led to the view that bulimic binge behaviour was purposeful or 'functional' for individuals dealing with life stressors.

Bulimia and identity – Polivy *et al.*'s model assumes that individuals with BN engage in binge-eating as a way of avoiding identity issues. Wheeler *et al.* (2001) proposed that negative self-image and a desire to escape from difficult life issues predicted the onset of bulimic behaviour, the consequence of which was a '*diffuse-avoidant identity style*'. Individuals in this state feel externally controlled, use emotion-focused rather than problem-focused coping strategies, and avoid the exploration of identity issues. Consequently they maintain a negative self-image and feel socially isolated.

RELATIONSHIP PROCESSES

Anxious attachment in intimate relationships

Boskind-Lodahl (1976) drew an analogy between women with BN and the story of Cinderella's stepsisters to illustrate the link between attempts to change one's body and a desire to please a partner. Women attempt to change themselves in order to meet some perceived ideal held by men about what is considered 'attractive'. Anxious attachment in adult intimate relationships is characterised by a strong desire for closeness and a fear of abandonment (Hazan and Shaver, 1987), and people with an anxious attachment style blame themselves for rejection, whether it be perceived or real. Research has shown a relationship between anxious attachment style and BN as women (and some men) try to lose weight to avoid rejection (Evans and Wertheim, 2005).

Bodily self-consciousness

Cash (2002) suggested that women who are dissatisfied with their physical appearance are likely to become self-conscious about their bodies and worry about being accepted by their partners. Although self-consciousness during sexual activity has not been studied as a cause of BN, Ackard *et al.* found that women who experienced body dissatisfaction (a major component of BN) were more likely to express less confidence in their ability as a sexual partner. Similarly, Allerdissen *et al.* (1981) found that women with BN reported more fear about meeting their partner's sexual expectations than did a sample of healthy participants.

EVALUATION

Cooper et al.'s cognitive model

Supporting evidence – Cooper et al.'s cognitive model of BN is consistent with evidence from published studies of the disorder. For example, Leung et al. (2000) found that a lack of parental bonding was linked to the development of dysfunctional core beliefs (e.g. the belief that one is unacceptable to others) among bulimics. These dysfunctional beliefs have also been linked to bingeing and vomiting symptoms in a number of studies (e.g. Waller et al., 2000). Again, consistent with the claims of this theory, there is ample evidence that binge-eating in BN is preceded by considerable distress. Feelings of loneliness, for example, have been found to precede or trigger bingeing (Abraham and Beumont, 1982).

Implications for treatment – A major implication of any cognitive model of abnormal behaviour is that because the disorder is cognitively based, it should be possible to treat it successfully by using a cognitively based therapy. While the use of **cognitive behavioural therapy** (CBT) has been reasonably successful in the treatment of BN, it is evident that not everyone with BN gets better at the end of cognitive treatment, with many patients still having episodes of binge-eating and self induced vomiting (Cooper et al., 2004). A follow-up study of patients who had received CBT for their BN found that at the end of treatment, only 50% were symptom free, and 37% still met the diagnostic criteria for an eating disorder (Fairburn et al., 1995).

The functional model

Supporting evidence – Polivy et al. (1994) provided evidence for the claim that BN is a functional response in an experimental study of the effects of stress on dieters. Compared to ordinary dieters, stress-induced dieters consumed larger quantities of food *regardless* of its palatability. This lends support to the claim that the primary purpose of binge-eating is to alleviate identity-related stress, rather than the attractiveness or palatability of any foods consumed during a bingeing episode.

Implications for treatment – According to this model, a consequence of BN is the development of a diffuse-avoidant identity style. This has been shown to make such individuals susceptible to a variety of health and social problems, including self-harm (Adams et al., 2001). Targeting the initial symptoms that lead to BN (such as self-consciousness and depression), can both avoid BN *and* prevent the development of the potentially harmful diffuse-avoidant style.

Relationship processes

Bulimia or depression? – It is possible that these adverse relationship processes are not specifically associated with the characteristic bulimic symptoms that distinguish bulimia from other disorders (i.e. binge-eating and purging). Rather they could be part of a more general psychopathology that accompanies bulimic symptoms (e.g. depression or low self-esteem) such that the characteristic anxious attachment and self-consciousness are more a product of this *general* psychopathology than BN specifically.

Limitations of the Schembri and Evans study – The landmark study in this area is described on the right. The researchers conclude that, like Cinderella's stepsisters, women with bulimia are making an attempt to change themselves to fit in with their perception of the ideal held by men, in order to be accepted and loved by their male partner. However, being a correlational design, no causal conclusions can be drawn from this study.

Evaluation BULIMIA AND INTIMATE RELATIONSHIPS

Recent research by Schembri and Evans (2008) tested the link between relationship processes and bulimic symptoms. Two hundred and twenty five women aged 18–63 in intimate relationships completed questionnaires on eating behaviours, opinions of self and their current relationships. Approximately 8% of the women were receiving professional help for eating disorders.

Results showed that self-consciousness during sexual activity was the strongest predictor of bulimic symptoms, followed by anxious attachment.

These findings support the claim that adverse relationship processes, reflecting a definition of self in terms of others' expectations, are a significant risk factor for the development of bulimia nervosa.

▶ Recent research suggests that for some women, bulimia is a consequence of them trying to fit what they believe their intimate partner sees as attractive in a mate.

CAN YOU...? No.5.7

...1 Describe **two** psychological explanations of bulimia nervosa in about 100 words each.

...2 Identify **eight** criticisms related to psychological explanations for bulimia nervosa, including **at least one** IDA topic. Each criticism should be about 50 words.

...3 Use this material to write a 600-word answer to the question: *Discuss **two or more** psychological explanations of bulimia nervosa.* (8 marks + 16 marks)

BIOLOGICAL EXPLANATIONS FOR BULIMIA NERVOSA

As with **anorexia**, biological explanations of **bulimia nervosa (BN)** emphasise the influence of neural (i.e. the nervous system and its chemical messengers) influences on this behaviour. While most people accept that bulimia arises from pressures to be thin, coupled with a dysfunctional nervous system, few people have asked why such pressures exist in the first place. Evolutionary theories provide an *ultimate* explanation for bulimia, (i.e. what was its adaptive advantage to our ancestors?), whereas biological mechanisms represent a more *proximate* explanation, based on the individual's life history.

REPRESENTATIONS OF 'NUBILITY' IN THE MEDIA

The sexual competition hypothesis (see right) argues that the most 'nubile' females are those who conform to a standard waist to hips ratio, and that women can advertise their reproductive potential by conforming to this 'ideal' form. In Western cultures, there is the additional problem of the 'pseudo-nubile' older woman, so there is increased pressure on young women to lose even more weight to convince potential mates of their superior reproductive potential.

This trend is promoted by, and reflected in, representations of 'attractive' women. Sypeck *et al.* (2006) examined the covers of four popular fashion magazines from 1959 to 1999 and found that there was a significant decrease in the body size of models during the 1980s and 1990s, together with an increasing focus on the body rather than the face.

NEURAL EXPLANATIONS

Serotonin

The fact that depression and BN occur together suggests that they have a common cause. Both have been linked to imbalances in the **neurotransmitter serotonin**. Serotonin plays an important role in controlling anxiety levels as well as perceptions of hunger and appetite. A study by Kaye *et al.* (2001) compared levels of the neurotransmitters serotonin, dopamine and noradrenaline in recovered bulimics and a control group of people who had never experienced bulimia. Levels of **dopamine** and **noradrenaline** were the same in both groups, but levels of serotonin were abnormal in the recovered bulimics.

How are they linked? – Low levels of serotonin result in depression, while high levels can result in anxiety. Binge-eating may increase serotonin levels, which relieves feelings of depression and restores well-being. However, binge-eating may raise serotonin levels too high, leading to intense feelings of anxiety. The bulimic tends to associate these anxious feelings with eating and weight gain. To counter these feelings and to prevent weight gain, they purge. Purging reduces anxiety levels, but may lower serotonin levels too much, causing depression, and starting the cycle all over again.

Nitric oxide

Nitric oxide (NO) is a **neurotransmitter** involved in the regulation of food intake. Neurotransmitters transmit information to other neurons, thus altering their activities. NO is 'delivered' to recipient neurons by plasma nitrite where it causes the production of cGMP (*cyclic guanosine monophosphate*). Most of the actions of NO are due to the production of cGMP, and together they regulate much of our eating behaviour. NO mediates the action of several hormones involved in weight control, for example **leptin** and **ghrelin** (see pages 88–9).

Research on NO and bulimia – Vannacci *et al.* (2006) assessed the effect of NO in bulimia. They studied 62 female patients referred to an outpatients department for treatment for an eating disorder. Of these, 50% were diagnosed as suffering from BN. The researchers measured plasma nitrite and cGMP levels among the patients and a corresponding group of healthy women. Both plasma nitrite and cGMP levels were significantly higher in the BN patients than they were in the healthy women. Among the BN patients, nitrite levels correlated positively with the frequency of binge-eating episodes. For this group, nitrite and cGMP levels were also positively correlated with the *degree* of pathological impairment.

EVOLUTIONARY EXPLANATIONS

The sexual competition hypothesis

Abed (1998) suggests that BN is a direct consequence of the evolved need to compete with other females in order to attract a mate. An obsession with weight loss, he argues, is an evolved adaptation to preserve a shape that is attractive to potential mates.

Evolution of nubility – Males and females have distinctive body shapes. Research has shown that in women, waist to hips ratio (WHR) determines judgements of attractiveness for both males and females. The most attractive WHR appears to be between 0.7 and 0.8 (Singh, 1994). Ridley (1993) claims that among our distant ancestors, to avoid rearing another man's child (**cuckoldry**), males must have developed an aversion to even the slightest thickening of the waist (an indication of pregnancy). Abed proposes, therefore, that the traditional 'hour glass' female figure was designed by **sexual selection**, through the differential reproductive success of those who possessed this trait compared to those who did not.

Sexual competition – The function of this adaptation within the ancestral environment was twofold. It ensured that such 'nubile' (i.e. sexually mature and attractive) females differentiated themselves from older (lower reproductive potential) females. It also helped females compete with other nubile females in the vicinity for the best long-term mates. The adaptation is designed to work through scanning other females in the environment and setting the desired shape at a level which is thinner than the older, less nubile females and broadly the same as other nubile females in the vicinity. Abed suggests that at a critical time during development (probably in early puberty), females must set this desired shape into a mental template based on their visual evidence of the body shapes of surrounding females. Because in the West there are large numbers of 'pseudo-nubile' females (i.e. older women who have maintained or recreated their nubile shape), younger females must 'go one better', in order to mark themselves out as having higher reproductive potential. Consequently they must set the desired shape much lower than it would have been in the ancestral environment, which leads to a drive for thinness and thus the development of eating disorders, such as BN.

IDA

AGEISM IN RESEARCH – NEVER TOO OLD FOR BULIMIA?

Research on the causes and development of BN have focused almost exclusively on youth: adolescent girls and young women (although increasingly males have also been the focus of research interest). However, recent research suggests that body dissatisfaction continues into old age. Mangweth-Matzek et al. (2006) analysed the responses from a sample of 475 60–70-year-old women. Eighteen of these (3.8% of the sample) met the diagnostic criteria for eating disorders. This research concludes that although eating disorders and body dissatisfaction are typical for young women, they also occur in the female elderly and should be considered when such women show excessive weight loss and vomiting.

EVALUATION

Neural explanations

Serotonin and SSRIs – If BN is a product of abnormal serotonin levels, then it should be able to treat the disorder using drugs that specifically target serotonin levels. **SSRIs** such as *fluoxetine* raise levels of serotonin in the brain, and so should inhibit the incidence of binge-eating episodes. A study by Walsh et al. (2000) provided support for this association. They treated 22 patients with BN who had not responded to a course of **cognitive behavioural therapy**. Each patient was given a course of fluoxetine or a **placebo** (a drug with no pharmacological action). Significant improvements were found in the fluoxetine group, particularly in terms of decreased incidence of binge-eating and purging.

Tryptophan – A study by Smith et al. (1999) provides an explanation for the specific relationship between binge-eating and the raising of serotonin levels. Women who had suffered from BN and recovered were compared to a control group of normal women. Both groups were given identical-looking snacks and fruit drinks, some with **tryptophan**, an amino acid that occurs naturally in many foods and is used by the body to make serotonin, and some without. After being deprived of tryptophan for 17 hours, the recovered bulimics showed greater dips in mood, were more concerned about their body image and feared losing control over their eating. This study shows that lowered brain serotonin can trigger some of the characteristic features of BN even among recovered bulimics, who remain vulnerable to the disorder.

The sexual competition hypothesis

Fits the statistics – This explanation is able to account for the fact that BN affects mostly young females (although see 'ageism' feature above), and particularly the fact that adolescent girls and young women (i.e. highest reproductive potential) are most at risk. BN is an eating disorder where there is a particularly uneven sex ratio between males and females. In a ten-year study in Minnesota, USA, researchers found an annual incidence of BN in females that was 33 times greater than in males (Soundy et al., 1995).

Bulimia and gay men – This explanation would predict that homosexual males have a higher incidence of eating disorders because they are subject to similar mate selection strategies to heterosexual females (Symons, 1979). This would not mean a 'search for nubility', but it *would* lead males to rely on visual evidence for mate attraction in a similar way to heterosexual females. This is consistent with statistics in some studies, that among males with eating disorders, approximately 25% are homosexual, compared to an incidence of homosexuality in the general population of less than 10% (Woodside and Kennedy, 1995).

Is BN universal? – Cross-cultural statistics suggest that BN is more a characteristic of Western cultures (American Psychiatric Association, 2000), and in non-Western cultures the characteristic preoccupation with thinness is absent. However, some studies suggest that the BN 'syndrome' is similar in Western *and* non-Western cultures. This is important for this explanation as it proposes that BN arises because of a universal female trait of 'concern for physical attractiveness'. If this was absent in some cultures it would pose a serious challenge to the sexual competition hypothesis.

Evaluation

EFECTIVE DRUG TREATMENTS

Additional support for the biological origins of bulimia has been obtained from the application of drug therapies in its treatment. Treatments using a variety of antidepressant drugs (which alter the levels of neurotransmitter activity in the brain) have shown significant decreases in the episodes of binge-eating associated with bulimia. Some studies (e.g. Walsh et al., 1997) have compared the effectiveness of psychotherapy (a *psychological* treatment) and drug therapy (a *biological* treatment) for the management of bulimia. Although these studies typically show little short-term improvement from psychotherapy *plus* medication compared to medication alone, long-term follow-up studies have found that combined treatment is more effective than psychotherapy alone. The success of drug therapies for bulimia, compared to the limited success of similar drug treatments for anorexia, has made the case for a *biological* basis for bulimia that bit more convincing.

IDA

THE MYTH OF GENETIC DETERMINISM

Evolutionary explanations are frequently criticised for appearing to suggest that particular behaviours (such as BN) are genetically *determined* (i.e. fixed by genes and therefore unchangeable). Most evolutionary explanations, including the sexual competition hypothesis discussed on this spread, acknowledge the equally important influences of genes *and* environment in the development of BN. Evolutionary explanations do not *compete* with psychological explanations of BN, but supplement them by providing an understanding of the adaptive function of this behaviour.

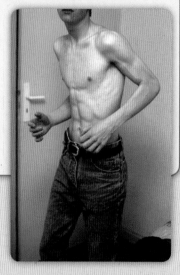

▶ Bulimia does not only affect women. A recent study (Hudson et al., 2007) found that 25% of those with AN or BN were men.

CAN YOU...?   No.5.8

...1 Describe **one** neural and **one** evolutionary explanation of bulimia nervosa. Each should be about 100 words.

...2 Identify **eight** criticisms related to biological explanations of bulimia nervosa, including **at least one** IDA topic. Each criticism should be about 50 words.

...3 Use this material to write a 600-word answer to the question: *Discuss biological explanations of bulimia nervosa.* (8 marks + 16 marks)

CHAPTER SUMMARY

EATING BEHAVIOUR

ATTITUDES TO FOOD

SOCIAL LEARNING
- Children acquire attitudes to food by observing behaviour in parents.
- The media influences what people eat and attitudes to food.

EVALUATION
- Meyer and Gast (2008) – positive correlation between peer influence and eating behaviours.
- Evolutionary explanations – food preferences more than just social learning.
- Problems of generalisability as some studies use clinical groups, others focus on sub-clinical groups.

CULTURAL INFLUENCES
- Eating concerns more likely in white rather than Asian or black women.
- Acculturation effect influences attitudes and behaviour.
- Body dissatisfaction and eating disorders more common in higher-class individuals.

EVALUATION
- Some studies contradict claim that disordered eating mainly found in white women.
- Others suggest higher social class = *greater* body satisfaction.
- Cultural differences – may influence attitude to food.

MOOD AND EATING BEHAVIOUR
- Binge-eating – anxiety tends to precede binge episodes.
- Garg *et al.* (2007) – people snack when sad or depressed to experience feelings of euphoria.

EVALUATION
- Not clear why binge-eating is reinforcing.
- Chocolate may prolong rather than alleviate negative mood.

IDA
- Gender bias – tendency to focus erroneously on women alone.

SUCCESS AND FAILURE OF DIETING

RESTRAINT THEORY
- Attempting not to eat increases probability of overeating.
- Boundary model – dieters have larger range between hunger and satiety levels.

EVALUATION
- Implication for treatment – overeating may occur if restraint recommended.
- Behaviour of restricting anorexics not explained using this theory.
- Anecdotal evidence – less trustworthy compared to scientific studies.
- Green (1999) – dieting may lead to slower information processing.
- Wardle and Beales (1988) – women in diet condition ate more than those in non-diet.

ROLE OF DENIAL
- Theory of ironic processes – denial of food thoughts may backfire.
- Attempts to suppress thoughts of food makes them more prominent.

EVALUATION
- Soetens *et al.* (2006) – group that tried to suppress thoughts of food thought about it more.
- Effects small but significant in pathological forms of eating behaviour.

DETAIL
- Successful dieting by focusing on specific details of each meal.
- Jelly beans experiment – focused on flavours rather than just numbers.

EVALUATION
- Concern about dieting ineffectiveness led to healthy-eating programmes.
- Meta-analysis showed significant improvement in well-being and weight stability.

IDA
- Free will or determinism – high levels of LPL = greater weight gain.
- Cultural bias – Asian adults more prone to obesity than Europeans.

EATING DISORDERS – ANOREXIA NERVOSA

PSYCHOLOGICAL EXPLANATIONS

PSYCHOLOGICAL EXPLANATIONS
- Cultural ideals – Western standards of attractiveness contribute to AN.
- Portrayal of thin models on TV contributes to drive for thinness.
- Comparisons with media images more likely if self-esteem is low.
- Ethnicity – incidence of AN in non-Western cultures much lower.
- Meta-analysis – less body dissatisfaction among African-Americans.
- Peer influences – adolescents susceptible to disordered eating.
- Teasing is key mechanism of peer influence.
- Bruch (1973) – children of ineffective parents become overly reliant on them.
- Adolescents take excessive control over body shape to gain autonomy.
- Perfectionism often found in individuals with AN.
- Impulsiveness linked with BN *and* AN.

EVALUATION
- Hoek *et al.* (1998) – similar rates of AN in some non-Western cultures.
- Media influences – Becker *et al.* (2002): eating disorders in Fiji increased after introduction of TV.
- Ethnicity – not all studies find cultural or subcultural differences.
- Some studies – no influence of peer influence on development of AN.
- Bruch – supported by clinical observations of parental behaviour.
- Support for claim that people with AN rely on opinions of others.
- Perfectionism link supported by Halmi *et al.* (2000).
- Study of personality in AN has methodological problems (e.g. personality trait or state caused by starvation).

IDA
- Ethical issues in study of AN on Internet (e.g. privacy, confidentiality).
- Real-world application – French fashion industry charter to promote healthy body image in young women.

BIOLOGICAL EXPLANATIONS

NEURAL EXPLANATIONS
- More serotonin activity in binge-eating/purging type AN.
- Disruption of serotonin → increased anxiety → triggers AN (Bailer *et al.*, 2007).
- AN linked to overactivity of dopamine receptors in basal ganglia (Kaye *et al.*, 2005).
- Increased dopamine activity alters interpretation of rewards.
- Possible neurodevelopmental factors include premature birth and hypoxia.
- Season of birth – spring months more associated with AN (Eagles *et al.*, 2001).

EVALUATION
- Serotonin – SSRIs that alter serotonin levels are *ineffective* with AN.
- Dopamine – supported by finding that homovanillic acid levels higher in AN group.
- Obstetric complications – supported by research (Favaro *et al.*, 2006).
- Season of birth supported – AN children more exposed to common infections while in womb.

EVOLUTIONARY EXPLANATIONS
- Reproductive suppression hypothesis (Surbey, 1987) – ancestral girls had reduced onset of maturation during conditions of lowered reproductive success.
- 'Adapted to flee' hypothesis (Guisinger, 2003) – AN part of an ancestral adaptation of self-deception about physical condition prior to migration.

EVALUATION
- Reproduction suppression supported by observation that onset of menarche delayed in girls with AN.
- Treatment implications – awareness of evolved causes encourages compassion towards person with AN.
- AN functional in ancestral conditions, but deadly outside these conditions.

IDA
- Real-world application – research may influence insurance companies to regard AN as 'biologically based'.
- Gender bias – recent statistics suggest 25% of those with AN are male.

BIOLOGICAL EXPLANATIONS

ROLE OF NEURAL MECHANISMS

HOMEOSTASIS
- Body's tendency to maintain constant internal state.
- Decline in glucose levels in blood activates LH.
- Rise in glucose levels in blood activates VMH.

EVALUATION
- For hunger to be adaptive, must anticipate and prevent energy deficits, not just react to them.

LATERAL (LH) AND VENTROMEDIAL HYPOTHALAMUS (VMH)
- Damage to LH leads to aphagia, stimulation to feeding behaviour.
- NPY 'turns on eating' if injected into LH.
- Damage to VMH causes animals to overeat (hyperphagia).
- Stimulation of VMH inhibits feeding.
- Research suggests that damage to PVN alone causes hyperphagia.

EVALUATION
- Damage to LH does not only affect feeding.
- Eating behaviour controlled by neural circuits throughout the brain.
- Influence of NPY may be overstated (Marie *et al.*, 2005).
- Body produces ghrelin in response to stress; also boosts appetite.

NEURAL CONTROL OF COGNITIVE FACTORS
- Amygdala – selection of foods on basis of previous experience.
- Inferior frontal cortex – damage decreases eating because of decreased sensory responses.

EVALUATION
- Klüver-Bucy syndrome – damage to brain areas leads to increased appetite and indiscriminate eating.
- Zald and Pardo (1997) – physiological evidence to support role in emotional processing of olfactory stimuli.

IDA
- Evolutionary approach - primary stimulus for hunger and eating is food's positive-incentive value.
- Real-world application – NPY also produced by abdominal fat, which leads to more eating and more fat.

EVOLUTIONARY EXPLANATIONS OF FOOD PREFERENCE

THE EEA
- Environment in which human beings first emerged as separate species.
- Natural selection favoured adaptations that promoted survival in EEA.

EARLY DIETS
- Fatty foods adaptive for energy resources.
- Evolved preference for foods rich in calories.

PREFERENCES FOR MEAT
- Fossil evidence suggests early diet mainly animal-based foods.
- Unlikely early humans would have had enough energy from meat-free diet.

TASTE AVERSION
- Animals who became ill after eating developed aversion to that food.
- Development of taste aversions helped ancestors to survive.
- Taste aversions difficult to shift once learned.
- Medicine effect – animals learn preference for foods that make them healthier.

EVALUATION
- Importance of calorie-rich foods demonstrated in studies of young children.
- Anthropological evidence dismisses suggestion that ancestors were vegetarian.
- Some food preferences have not been a product of evolution.
- Taste aversion explained by concept of biological preparedness.
- Preference for fatty foods reflected in success of fast-food restaurants.
- Comparative evidence – chimps in Gombe National Park.
- Evolved preferences are modified by cultural factors.
- Sandell and Breslin (2006) – evidence for adoptive value of bitter taste.

IDA
- Real-world application – understanding of taste aversions acquired during chemotherapy.

EATING DISORDERS – BULIMIA NERVOSA

PSYCHOLOGICAL EXPLANATIONS

COGNITIVE EXPLANATIONS
- Cooper et al. (2004) – most BN sufferers experienced early trauma.
- Develop belief that fat=bad and that thin=good.
- Maintenance of BN as 'vicious circle' of binge to feel better → purge to relieve guilt → feelings of worthlessness → binge.
- Functional model – individual can attribute distress to overeating rather than underlying problems.
- Diffuse-avoidant identity style common in BN.

EVALUATION
- Cooper's model – lack of parental bonding associated with dysfunctional beliefs in BN sufferers.
- Evidence - binge-eating in BN preceded by distress.
- Implications for treatment – only about 50% get better after CBT.
- Functional model supported by fact that stress-induced dieters eat regardless of palatability.
- Targeting initial symptoms of BN can prevent BN and potentially harmful identity style.

RELATIONSHIP PROCESSES
- Relationship between anxious attachment style and BN in attempt to avoid rejection.
- BN may result from bodily self-consciousness during sexual activity.

EVALUATION
- Adverse relationship processes part of general psychopathology rather than BN specifically.
- Schembri and Evans (2008) - self-consciousness during sexual activity strongest predictor of BN, but correlational data only.

IDA
- Cultural bias – BN 'culture-bound syndrome'.
- Heterosexual bias – Feldman and Meyer (2007) estimate 15% of gay or bisexual men suffer from eating disorder compared to 8% of heterosexual women.

BIOLOGICAL EXPLANATIONS

NEURAL EXPLANATIONS
- Low levels of serotonin result in depression, high levels in anxiety.
- Binge-eating increases serotonin levels – relieves depressive symptoms.
- If levels too high, increases anxiety – person then purges.
- Nitric oxide regulates eating behaviour through production of cGMP.
- Vannacci et al. (2006) – cGMP levels higher in BN patients.

EVALUATION
- Walsh *et al.* (2000) – course of SSRIs improved BN symptoms.
- Characteristic symptoms of BN provoked by tryptophan depletion, supporting importance of serotonin.
- Combined psychological/ biological treatment more effective.

EVOLUTIONARY EXPLANATIONS
- Sexual competition hypothesis – BN consequence of evolved need to compete with other females to attract a mate.
- Presence of 'pseudo-nubile' females means shape set lower than in ancestral environment.

EVALUATION
- Fits the data – US study, female BN 33 times higher than male BN.
- Gay men subject to similar mate selection strategies as heterosexual females.
- BN 'syndrome' similar in all cultures, so possibly universal.

IDA
- Ageism in research, BN can also affect much older women.
- Myth of genetic determinism – evolutionary explanations supplement rather than compete with psychological explanations.

EXAM QUESTION WITH STUDENT ANSWER

> **QUESTION** **(a)** Outline and evaluate **one** explanation for the success and failure of dieting.
> *(3 marks + 6 marks)*
> **(b)** Discuss **one** evolutionary explanation for food preference. *(5 marks + 10 marks)*

STUDENT ANSWER

(a) *One reason that people fail when dieting is because it involves restricting the amount they eat. This is called restraint theory. The evidence shows that when people restrain what they are eating this may have the opposite effect to weight loss. For example, Wardle and Beales (1988) studied overweight women and found that those who were put on a diet actually ended up eating more than those who were in an exercise group or had no treatment.*

It is important to understand why diets fail because people who fail to lose weight when they are trying their hardest may then become depressed and this leads to them eating even more. If we understand how dieting fails then we can help people so they avoid a self-perpetuating cycle.

*However, there are criticisms of the 'failure of restraint' view because it doesn't explain the behaviour of anorexics who also restrain their eating but in their case it **does** result in weight loss. This suggests that failure to lose weight when restraining intake is more complex. One possibility is that it is related to genes. For example, Kern et al. (1990) studied the effect of the gene that codes for LPL. Levels of LPL are higher in obese people and this may affect their ability to lose weight later.*

(b) *One evolutionary explanation for food preferences is that people have evolved a preference for those foods that are beneficial to them, such as foods that are high in calories. This would happen because starvation would be a major problem faced by our ancestors in the EEA when they were hunter–gatherers and dependent on what food they could find. When they did find food it would be important to eat food that had the highest calorific value to sustain them as long as possible. Thus food preference for calories was adaptive and may explain why people today have a preference for fat-rich foods, such as pizzas.*

Calories would not be the only factor that was important. It would be important to eat foods high in nutritional value such as meat because it is an important source of energy for the brain. Milton (2008) argues that without a meat diet humans would not have had enough energy to use their brains effectively and evolve into what they are. In contrast to meat, plants are often high in calories but low in nutrients, therefore it was important to have a meat diet.

There is evidence to support the importance of calories. One source of evidence comes from studying animals. Researchers have observed how chimpanzees in the Gombe National Park will first eat the brain and bone marrow of an animal they have killed. These parts have the highest calories whereas the flesh is more nutritious but lower in calories.

Other evidence comes from studies with humans. For example, Gibson and Wardle (2001) looked at the vegetable preferences of children aged 4–5 years. The most significant factor was calories rather than sweetness or familiarity. As the participants were children this study particularly supports calories as innate food preferences.

The importance of meat is questioned by vegetarians, some of whom believe that humans were originally not meat-eaters. This is unlikely, because before humans had fires they couldn't cook vegetables, and vegetables are often poisonous in their uncooked form.

However, evolutionary explanations can't account for all our food preferences because there are marked cultural differences and also, as people grow up their preferences change which suggests that experience plays a role. For example, spicy food is very popular but universally disliked by children.

[604 words]

EXAMINER COMMENTS

In part (a) of this essay the student is required to **outline** and **evaluate** one explanation. The answer begins with a brief description of one explanation for diet failure. In fact restraint theory is an explanation of how people diet, but the explanation has been appropriately turned into an explanation for failure.

In the second paragraph there is a brief comment on the importance of this kind of research, i.e. a look at an **application** of research – part of the **AO2** component of this answer.

The final paragraph offers an evaluation of this explanation as well as additional evidence that should be considered. Looking at a genetic explanation offers a different **approach** to understanding failure to diet, and thus is evidence of further **IDA**.

> **AO1** – **accurate** and **reasonably detailed**.
> **AO2/AO3** – **thorough**, **effective** and **some** evidence of IDA.

The essays starts with one explanation, outlining the evolutionary argument of adaptiveness in the EEA. This description is **accurate** and **reasonably detailed**, providing evidence of **depth**.

The explanation continues with reference to another aspect of adaptive behaviour – the preference for food high in nutritional value. This further paragraph increases the **breadth** of the descriptive element of the essay.

The remainder of the essay offers **evaluation** on the explanations, beginning with evidence from observational studies. This evidence is used **effectively** and has been well **elaborated** by going on to explain why the chimpanzees don't eat flesh.

The evaluation in this paragraph is improved by the final sentence which offers some additional, thoughtful evaluation on the study – providing more **elaboration**.

The final paragraph offers some useful **IDA** comments.

> **AO1** – **accurate** and **detailed**.
> **AO2/AO3** – **clear** line of argument, **coherent** elaboration and **some** evidence of **IDA**.

Chapter 6
Gender

◀ What are little girls made of? Sugar and spice and all things nice.

▼ What are little boys made of? Slugs and snails and puppy dogs' tails.

SPECIFICATION

Gender	
Psychological explanations of gender development	• Cognitive developmental theory, including Kohlberg. • Gender schema theory.
Biological influences on gender	• The role of hormones and genes in gender development. • Evolutionary explanations of gender roles. • The biosocial approach to gender development, including gender dysphoria.
Social contexts of gender role	• Social influences on gender role, for example the influence of parents, peers, schools and media. • Cultural influences on gender role.

THE ROLE OF GENES AND HORMONES

I f I ask 'who are you?', one of your first answers might be to say 'a boy' or 'a girl'; gender is a key aspect of your sense of who you are. In fact psychologists distinguish between 'sex' and 'gender'. **Sex** is a biological fact – whether a person is a genetic male or female. **Gender** refers to a person's sense of who they are – their sense of maleness or femaleness. In this chapter we are concerned with the development of gender, which is due in part to biology (nature) and in part to life experiences (nurture). We begin by looking at some biological explanations for gender development on this spread and the next spread.

► Genetic males have a pair of chromosomes described as XY, which are shown here. The picture has been taken using an electron microscope.

THE ROLE OF GENES IN GENDER DEVELOPMENT

Each person has 23 pairs of chromosomes (in each cell of the body). Each of these chromosomes carries hundreds of **genes** containing instructions about physical and behavioural characteristics, such as eye colour and predisposition to certain mental illnesses.

One pair of chromosomes are called the sex chromosomes because they determine an individual's sex. In the case of a female this pair is called XX because both chromosomes are shaped like Xs. The male chromosome pair is described as XY. The Y chromosome carries very little genetic material although it does determine the sex of a child.

There is usually a direct link between an individual's chromosomal sex (XX and XY) and their external genitalia (vagina or penis) and internal genitalia (ovaries or testes).

During prenatal development all individuals start out the same – a few weeks after conception both male and female embryos have external genitalia that look essentially feminine. When the foetus is about three months old, if it is to develop as a male, the testes normally produce the male hormone **testosterone** which causes external male genitalia to develop.

Genetic transmission explains how individuals acquire their sex. It may also explain some aspects of gender (a person's sense of whether they are male or female) because of the link between genes and genitalia and hormones.

AIS – ANDROGEN INSENSITIVITY SYNDROME

Androgens, such as testosterone, are male hormones. Some XY individuals have an insensitivity to such hormones, i.e. their bodies' tissues do not respond to the effects of the hormone. In extreme cases the consequence is that no external male genitalia develop. Such individuals are usually identified as females at birth and raised as girls, although some are identified and raised as boys.

One classic case of androgen insensitivity was reported in one family from the Dominican Republic (Imperato-McGinley *et al.*, 1979). Four children in the Batista family were born with external female genitalia and raised as girls. The large amounts of testosterone produced during puberty caused their male genitalia to appear. These children were genetically XY but had not developed male genitalia because of an inherited gene that caused androgen insensitivity.

It is interesting to note that the girls seemed to accept their change of sex without difficulty. One explanation offered is that they had never really taken on the feminine role because a number of their relatives had had similar experiences, and therefore they expected to eventually become boys.

WWW You can take the sex ID test to find out the sex of your brain, see: www.bbc.co.uk/science/humanbody/sex/add_user.shtml

THE ROLE OF HORMONES IN GENDER DEVELOPMENT

Chromosomes initially determine a person's sex but most gender development is actually governed by **hormones**. These are produced both prenatally (e.g. testosterone as described on the left) and in adolescence (a surge of hormones during puberty leads to secondary sexual characteristics, such as pubic hair). Hormones influence the development of genitalia and/or affect the development of the brain, both of which influence gender behaviour.

Development of genitalia

The role of hormones in gender development can be seen by studying individuals who have been exposed prenatally to abnormal hormone levels (**intersex** individuals). Normally external genitalia are in accord with genetic sex (e.g. a genetic male develops a penis). However, in some cases a genetic male embryo is exposed to too little male hormone and the result is that the newborn appears externally to be female (read about **androgen insensitivity syndrome** (AIS) and the Batista family on the left).

Conversely, genetic females may be exposed prenatally to relatively large doses of male hormones (for example when pregnant mothers have been given drugs containing male hormones). The result is ambiguous genitalia (swollen labia resembling a penis). Such individuals are usually identified as girls at birth and are usually content with this gender assignation, although research (e.g. Berenbaum and Bailey, 2003) has indicated that they are often interested in male-type activities and are tomboyish, presumably because of the influence of the male hormones.

Brain development

Sex differences explained – Male brains are different from female brains in many ways. For example, girls generally appear to be better at social skills (such as **empathising**) than boys, and are more talkative, less good at spatial navigation and so on (Hoag, 2008). Geschwind and Galaburda (1987) were the first to suggest that such sex differences may be caused by the effects of testosterone levels on the developing brain. Male brains are exposed prenatally to more testosterone than female brains and this leads to the development of a masculinised brain. If the brain of a genetic female is exposed to testosterone prenatally the effect may be to masculinise the brain. This may explain, for example, why David Reimer (see facing page) 'felt' he was a boy even though he was raised as a girl and also can explain why girls exposed prenatally to male hormones grow up to be tomboyish.

Animal studies – The effects of testosterone on brain development have been confirmed in non-human animals. For example, Quadagno *et al.* (1977) found that female monkeys who were deliberately exposed to testosterone during prenatal development later engaged in more rough-and-tumble play than other females and were more aggressive.

IDA **NATURE AND NURTURE**
The theme throughout this chapter is **nature** and **nurture**, which means that evidence on later spreads will form useful IDA evaluation for the explanations on this spread – providing alternative approaches (such as social explanations) which counterbalance the more biological view.

▼ David Reimer (also called 'Bruce'), born a boy, raised as a girl because of a botched circumcision.

EVALUATION

The importance of genetic factors

John Money (Money and Ehrhardt, 1972) claimed that biological sex was not the main factor in gender development. He argued that sex of rearing was much more important and recommended that **intersex** individuals, such as David Reimer (right) could be successfully raised as either a boy or a girl. However, his famous case study of David Reimer did not support this. This outcome has been further supported by subsequent research, for example that of Reiner and Gearhart (2004) who studied 16 genetic males born with almost no penis. Two were raised as males and remained as males. The remaining 14 were raised as females, and of these, eight re-assigned themselves as males by the age of 16. Such research suggests that biological factors have a key role in gender development.

Biological determinism

However, genes and hormones are not the whole story either. Genetic sex does not match external genitalia in cases of abnormal hormone exposure, as we have seen, and even hormones do not produce a simple formula for establishing gender. The eventual outcome for each individual is what appears to be a complex and unpredictable combination of genes, hormones, sex of rearing and socialisation. The outcome is described as 'unpredictable' because there do not appear to be any simple rules. For example, **congenital adrenal hyperplasia (CAH)** occurs when XX females have prenatally high levels of male hormones resulting in varying degrees of external male genitalia. Research appears to indicate that whatever gender is assigned at birth seems to be accepted by some individuals but not others (see studies on page 111). Thus gender development is in part biologically determined (nature) but experience, personal qualities and socialisation (nurture) also have a key role.

IDA **REAL-WORLD APPLICATION**
An interesting slant on the issue of biological determinism is shown in a dilemma faced by the International Olympics Committee. Since 1968 it has tested the genetic sex of all athletes and excluded all but XX females and XY males, which meant that AIS individuals couldn't compete. In 1991 there was a ruling that genetic sex would no longer determine entry to the games; individuals are now excluded from women's events only if they are obviously physically male (Bown, 1992). In other words genetic sex no longer determines gender.

RESEARCH METHODS
You will see on this spread that much evidence comes from case studies or small samples of abnormal individuals. Such research is fraught with problems that you will be familiar with from your AS studies. The main problem is lack of generalisability from abnormal individuals to the wider 'normal' population.

A further criticism of the research is that intersexes may be more vulnerable to social influences than 'normal' individuals because their biological ambiguities mean they have to search harder for clues to their identity, and this is another reason why this research may lack generalisability.

Evaluation **AS NATURE MADE HIM**
Dr John Money argued against the biological approach to gender development. He proposed that gender is learned – as long as a child is young enough they can be socialised to be a boy or girl, biological sex didn't matter. He used the case study of David Reimer as evidence to support this theory. David started life as Bruce Reimer and had an identical twin, Brian. When the twins were 6 months old they were circumcised to cure a urination problem. Tragically the operation on Bruce was botched and Bruce's penis was all but burned off. Bruce's parents sought advice from Dr Money, who said that Bruce should have his penis and testes removed so he looked like a girl and he should be raised as Brenda.

Over the next 10 years the twins, now Brian and Brenda, visited Money regularly because he took a great interest in the case which would allow him to test his theory – this was a unique natural experiment, a normal XY male raised as a female with a identical twin brother as a control. Money regularly reported on the twins he called John and Joan, claiming that the gender assignment had been a success and advising that this was the way forward for many intersex cases.

However, in 2000 John Colapinto wrote a book called *As Nature Made Him*, which told the world the true story. In adolescence Brenda received female hormone treatments so she would develop breasts, continuing her outward female development. However, inwardly she/he was in turmoil. Throughout childhood Brenda had been an outcast at school and became increasingly depressed. Her parents decided to tell her the true story of her life and Brenda's response was 'I was relieved. Suddenly it all made sense why I felt the way I did. I wasn't some sort of weirdo.' Her difficulties in being a girl were because she wasn't a girl. Brenda immediately reverted to her/his true sex and called himself David. He had an operation to remove his breasts and further operations to construct a penis. He married and raised three stepchildren. Therefore, David's case seems to suggest that, at least in some cases, biological sex is the primary factor in one's sense of gender.

Unfortunately the story ends sadly. In 2002 David's wife left him and in 2004 David killed himself.

CAN YOU...? No.6.1

...1 Write a description (in about 100 words) of the role of genes in gender development.

...2 Write a description (in about 100 words) of the role of hormones in gender development.

...3 Identify **eight** criticisms related to the role of genes and/or hormones in gender development, including **at least one** IDA topic. Each criticism should be about 50 words.

...4 Use this material to write a 600-word answer to the question: *Discuss the role of genes **and** hormones in gender development.* (8 marks + 16 marks)

On the first spread of this chapter you read that biology is an important factor in an individual's sense of their own gender. We are now moving from gender to **gender roles** – the different attitudes, interests and behaviours that members of each sex adopt. For example, women usually look after babies while men are the providers. Evolutionary psychologists argue that this gender role division appeared as an adaptation to the challenges faced by ancestral humans in the **EEA**. Therefore, the role differences we observe are more a product of our biological inheritance than acquired through socialisation. On this spread we will consider to what extent these traditional roles can be explained from an evolutionary perspective.

The EEA *or environment of evolutionary adaptation refers to the environment to which a species is adapted and the set of selection pressures that operated at this time. This is generally regarded as the time when our ancestors were hunter–gatherers on the African savannah over 10,000 years ago.*

▲ Neanderthals – no division of gender roles here. Is that the reason they disappeared?

▲ Disney's Cinderella shows the ideal characteristics of physical attractiveness – plentiful hair, red lips and a thin waist advertise that she is young and healthy – and therefore likely to be fertile. You can read more about mate choice on pages 54–5.

THE EVOLUTIONARY PERSPECTIVE

Division of labour

The traditional picture is of man the hunter and woman the gatherer-cum-domestic goddess. The role division may have evolved because women would have spent most of their adult life either pregnant or producing milk or both; if a woman spent time hunting, this would reduce the group's reproductive success. However, women could contribute to the important business of providing food by growing vegetables, milling grain, making clothing and shelter, and so on. Not only does this complementary division of labour enhance reproductive success but it is also important in avoiding starvation – a further **adaptive** advantage.

Kuhn and Stiner (2006) suggest that this gender division of labour might actually explain why humans (*homo sapiens*) survived, whereas the Neanderthals (*homo neanderthalensis*) did not. The Neanderthal diet was mainly animals, and men and women both hunted – there is evidence for this from the fact that male and female skeletons showed injuries which occurred while hunting, and also there is no evidence that Neanderthals were farmers. Neanderthals were large and needed high calorie foods; when hunting was unsuccessful the groups starved. A more adaptive division of labour evolved in humans but didn't in Neanderthals.

Mate choice

The key to adaptive behaviour is reproductive success, therefore it is not surprising to find that many gender role behaviours are related to reproductive strategies. In terms of mate choice, men look for partners who are physically attractive whereas women are additionally interested in the resources a partner might be able to provide (Buss, 1989, see page 54 for details of this study). The evolutionary explanation for this is again related to the way males and females maximise their reproductive success. Males do well to mate as frequently as they can and select women who are more fertile (young) and healthy – smooth skin, glossy hair, red lips and thin waist are all indicators of youthfulness and healthiness, and add up to what we see as 'physical attractiveness'. Females also seek signs of fertility and healthiness in their partner, but are more concerned to find a partner who can provide resources. Therefore, in terms of gender role differences, we expect that men will seek physical attractiveness and women will seek to enhance their physical attractiveness; women seek a partner who is wealthy and powerful, and men advertise their status, for example by owning powerful cars or a large herd of cattle.

Cognitive style

E-S theory – Research has shown that women are better at **empathising** (understanding what other people think and feel) whereas men are better at **systematising** (understanding and building systems, i.e. complex sets of relating things). Baron-Cohen (2002) calls this E-S theory (empathising-systematising) and has proposed that this gender difference may be the result of a selection pressure for males, who develop better hunting strategies, and females, who are focused on rearing children. He suggests that males who were able to systematise with greater precision would have gained an evolutionary advantage.

Tend and befriend – Women may not just be better at empathising but may also be more focused on interpersonal concerns, i.e. the relationships between people. Taylor *et al.* (2000) have proposed that this may stem from the different challenges faced by men and women when dealing with stress in the EEA. Ancestral males would deal with threats (from, for example, an attacking animal) by getting ready to fight or flee. In contrast, the adaptive response for females as the primary caregivers would be to protect themselves and their young in their role as primary caregivers to children. It would also be adaptive to group together with family units. This leads to a female tendency to 'tend and befriend' at times of stress, whereas men are more likely to become defensive.

EVALUATION

Speculative theories

There are a number of common criticisms made of evolutionary explanations, such as accusations that they ignore social explanations and are determinist (see above and right). Another key criticism is that evolutionary explanations are speculative, i.e. they do not have a firm factual basis. For example, the appearance of gender-related division of labour may be a plausible explanation for the disappearance of Neanderthals, but we have no direct evidence. Other theories for their disappearance are equally plausible, for example climate change in Europe around 30,000 BC (Tzedakis *et al.*, 2007).

Research support

Many evolutionary explanations are speculative, but this is by no means true of all such explanations; in some cases there is research support.

Mate choice – The predicted difference in how males and females advertise themselves to the opposite sex was confirmed in a study by Waynforth and Dunbar (1995). The researchers used personal ads to assess what men and women were seeking and also what they were advertising, claiming that such ads are particularly interesting because they represent the writer's ideal bid in the lengthy process of mate selection. The results were as predicted – 44% of males sought a physically attractive partner compared with 22% of women; 50% of women offered attractiveness whereas only 34% of males did.

Tend and befriend – Ennis *et al.* (2001) conducted a natural experiment to test male–female differences in stress responses. They sampled levels of **cortisol** (the stress hormone) a week before students took examinations (low stress) and immediately before the examination (high stress). In the male participants there was a significant increase in cortisol levels, whereas in females there was a significant decrease, supporting the view that women respond to the stress of others in a different way to men. Other research by Taylor *et al.* (2000) showed that, in women, levels of **oxytocin** – a hormone that reduces anxiety and makes people more sociable (tend and befriend) – increased with stress.

Implications

One means of evaluating explanations is to consider implications.

The meat-sharing hypothesis – When humans turned from a vegetarian diet to one that included meat, men became the hunters because of selective pressures. An outcome of this may be that men used meat as a means of attracting female interest (Stanford, 1999). Studies of modern hunter–gatherer societies have found that men use meat as a means of gaining access to women (Hill and Kaplan, 1988).

Autism – Baron-Cohen (2004) has proposed that autism may be an example of the extreme male brain which excels at systematising and lacks the ability to empathise. Autism is characterised by difficulties with social relationships and social communication, and appears to be particularly strongly linked to an inability to understand what other people are thinking/feeling (called a **Theory of Mind**). Baron-Cohen (2004) has found that autistics score high at systematising and low on empathising, i.e. they have an extreme male brain.

RESEARCH METHODS

Evaluation

Support for evolutionary explanations comes from a number of sources, such as the use of historical records, experiments, observations, questionnaires, comparative studies (comparing the behaviour of humans with non-humans) and cross-cultural studies.

Cross-cultural studies are used to test whether behaviours are universal (and therefore presumed to be innate) or influenced by cultural practices (and therefore related to nurture). One of the main difficulties with such research is the degree to which data collected actually represents the behaviour of people from different cultures. For example, one difficulty is that people do not always represent themselves honestly in questionnaires and, in the case of research conducted in other cultures, some of the questions may not make sense.

COGNITIVE STYLE

Evaluation

Baron-Cohen (2004) has conducted research to demonstrate that men and women do think in different ways which align with predicted differences in cognitive style. He developed a *Systematising Quotient Questionnaire* with questions, such as: 'When I read a newspaper, I am drawn to tables of information, such as football scores or stock-market indices' or 'When I watch a film I prefer to be with a group of friends, rather than alone.' (You can see the questionnaire at www.glenrowe.net.BaronCohen/SystemizingQuotient/SystemizingQuotient.aspx.) Participants were asked to indicate how strongly they agreed or disagreed with the statements. Baron-Cohen found that males tended to be systematisers and females tended to be empathisers – only about 17% of men had a female empathising brain and the same percentage of women had a male systematising brain.

CAN YOU...?   No.6.2

...**1** Write a description (in about 200 words) of evolutionary explanations of gender roles.

...**2** Identify **eight** criticisms related to evolutionary explanations of gender roles, including **at least one** IDA topic. Each criticism should be about 50 words.

...**3** Use this material to write a 600-word answer to the question: *Describe and evaluate evolutionary explanations of gender roles.* (8 marks + 16 marks)

THE BIOSOCIAL APPROACH TO GENDER DEVELOPMENT

The biosocial approach is exactly what it says – an approach encompassing both biological and social influences. Gangestad *et al.* (2006) note that there are two facts to consider in relation to gender (1) there are significant universals in gender behaviour, and (2) there are significant cultural variations in gender differences. A comprehensive theory must account for both cultural similarities (universals) and cultural differences.

The genetic approach and the evolutionary approach (on the previous two spreads) are largely focused on biological (universal) influences, however they do not *exclude* social factors. The biosocial approach includes biological factors but places more emphasis on social factors. Is the biosocial approach more successful than the evolutionary one?

'One is not born a woman but rather becomes one. No biological, psychological, or economic fate determines the figure that the human female presents in society: it is civilization as a whole that produces this creature, intermediate between male and eunuch, which is described as feminine.'
Simone de Beauvoir in *The Second Sex* (1952).

BIOSOCIAL THEORIES

Biosocial theory (Money and Ehrhardt, 1972)

John Money, in collaboration with Anke Ehrhardt, produced a classic book in 1972 called *Man and woman, boy and girl*. In this book they set out their theory that once a biological male or female is born, social labelling and differential treatment of boys and girls interact with biological factors (such as prenatal exposure to **testosterone**) to steer development. This theory was an attempt to integrate the influences of nature and nurture. Essentially they argued that it is sex of rearing that is the pivotal point in gender development. Biology is likely to determine sex of rearing as a baby is sexed at birth and everything else follows from that. However, as we have seen, some individuals are **intersexes** and may be mistyped at birth. Money and Ehrhardt predicted that, if a genetic male is mislabelled as a girl and treated as a girl before the age of three, he would acquire the gender identity of a girl. Thus the key to gender development, according to Money and Ehrhardt, is the label that a person is given.

▶ Who said women don't hunt? In Roman mythology Diana was the Goddess of the Hunt. Both evolutionary theory and social role theory explain that men rather than women are likely to become the hunters in any society because women are better designed to look after children, and hunting is incompatible with looking after children. However, in some cultures today women *are* the hunters, for example the Agta in the Philippines and the Aka Pygmy in Central Africa. In both these societies animals are available close to home and therefore women can hunt accompanied by their children.

The phrase 'sex differences' rather than 'gender differences' is now preferred by researchers. 'Gender differences' was a phrase first introduced by Money et al. (1955) to distinguish between biological and social factors but current research has led to the understanding that biological and social contributions to development should be the end point rather than the starting point. Therefore, 'sex differences' is a more appropriate term (Wood, 2008).

Social role theory (Eagly and Wood, 1999)

Alice Eagly and Wendy Wood's approach has also been described as a biosocial one. It is not linked to the earlier biosocial theory from Money and Ehrhardt but it does have similarities. Eagly and Wood argue that the evolutionary explanation of gender development is not fully correct. Evolutionary theory proposes that selective pressures caused both physical and psychological sex differences. By contrast, Eagly and Wood's social role theory suggests that selective pressures do not cause both physical and psychological differences; they only cause physical differences, and these lead to sex role allocations which in turn create psychological sex differences. This means that psychological sex differences are seen as the consequence of the different roles to which men and women are assigned rather than *vice versa* – the evolutionary view suggests that social roles grow out of biologically determined psychological differences.

Consider the following example. According to evolutionary theory, selective pressures meant that men took on the role of hunter, while women took on the role of homemaker. These are psychological differences. According to social role theory, evolved physical differences between men and women (men are stronger, women bear children) mean that men are assigned the social role of hunter, and women are assigned the social role of homemaker. Psychological differences then emerge from these social role assignments, such as greater aggressiveness or the tendency to be empathic.

Division of labour – Social role theory argues that the biologically-based physical differences between men and women allow them to perform certain tasks more efficiently. For example, childbearing and nursing of infants mean that women are well placed to care for young children but are less able to take on roles which require extended absence from home, such as hunting. Men's greater speed and upper-body strength facilitate their efficient performance of tasks that require intensive bursts of energy and strength.

In addition, according to social role theory, in societies where strength is not required for occupational roles outside the home and/or societies where there is alternative care for children, social roles will be more similar between men and women, and psychological differences reduced.

Mate choice – Social role theory proposes that what men and women seek in a partner can be related to their social roles rather than to the reproductive value of certain traits (the evolutionary view). The physical differences between men and women create social roles – men are the providers and women take on a domestic role. Women maximise their outcomes by selecting a man who is a good wage earner, and men maximise their outcomes by seeking a mate who is successful in the domestic role. Therefore, different social roles can explain sex differences in mate choice.

Hormonal differences – Eagly and Wood (2002) have further suggested that hormonal differences between men and women may be the outcome of social roles and psychological sex differences rather than the cause. For example, they propose that the male hormone testosterone is not the cause of greater male versus female aggressiveness, but instead it is the effect of the fact that men (because of their strength) engage in more athletic and competitive events and this creates higher levels of testosterone than in women.

The final two spreads of this chapter look at research studies related to social influence – how parents, peers, the media and culture generally set the social context for gender development. Such research can be used to discuss the social part of the biosocial approach.

▼ The differences between traditional evolutionary theory and Eagly and Wood's social role theory are illustrated below.

Evolutionary theory Selective pressure led to:	Social role theory Selective pressure led to:
Physical differences • Men have greater upper body strength, faster • Women designed to look after children	**Physical differences** • Men have greater upper body strength, faster • Women designed to look after children
Psychological differences • Men are more aggressive • Women are more nurturing	**Social roles** • Man the hunter/provided • Woman the domestic goddess
Social roles • Man the hunter/provided • Woman the domestic goddess	**Psychological differences** • Men are more aggressive • Women are more nurturing

IDA A SOCIAL CONSTRUCTIONIST APPROACH

The approach taken by Eagly and Wood is a **social constructionist** one, an approach which suggests that much of human behaviour is an invention or outcome of a particular society or culture. There is no objective reality, such as a real difference between men and women – or if there is one, it is not really relevant. According to this approach, behaviours are best understood in terms of the social context in which they occur.

EVALUATION

Biosocial theory

Lack of evidence – As we have seen earlier in this chapter, Money and Ehrhardt's theory took a considerable blow from the outcome of the John/Joan study (see page 105) which they had hoped would be definitive evidence in favour of the importance of sex typing.

Sample bias – Money and Ehrhardt had collected other evidence to support their theory yet it was still all derived from the study of abnormal individuals, such as the study of genetic females exposed to male hormones prenatally because of drugs taken by their mothers. Such evidence may not be relevant to understanding normal gender development.

Social role theory

Eagly and Wood's theory was put forward as an alternative to the evolutionary approach. There is no doubt that social factors are important in gender development, and that, increasingly, such influences have reduced the division between male and female gender roles. However, Luxen (2007) argues that evolutionary theory can explain this and provides a simpler theory which is preferable for a number of reasons, such as:

- *Selective pressure* – Luxen argues that behaviour is at least as important as physical characteristicsm and therefore selective pressure would act directly on behaviour to create psychological as well as physical sex differences.
- *Sex differences without socialisation* – Luxen also points to research that has shown that very young children and even animals display sex differences in their toy preferences. This suggests that such preferences would be biological rather than psychological because sex role socialisation is unlikely to have occurred in very young children and animals.

IDA REAL-WORLD APPLICATION

In the last 100 years the feminist movement has succeeded in bringing about great changes in opportunities for women in the UK – from gaining the vote for women to ensuring equal pay and maternity cover. The evolutionary approach has been seen as a force against gender equality since it might be seen to imply that sex differences are innate and cannot be changed by altering social context. The value of the social role approach is that it supports the feminist view that changes in social roles will lead to changes in psychological differences between men and women. In addition it has high ethical appeal because sex roles are perceived as social and therefore more flexible (Luxen, 2007).

Evaluation BUSS'S STUDY OF 37 CULTURES RE-EXAMINED

Eagly and Wood (1999) re-examined the data from Buss's study of 37 cultures (see page 54) and suggested that the pattern of sex differences can be just as well explained by social roles. Buss's evidence showed that in all cultures women seek men with resources, while men prefer younger, physically attractive women. Given that women generally have had less earning capacity it is no wonder that, universally, women seek men with resources. Along with resources, men have power and dominance. Men want younger women not because of their fertility but because they will be more obedient.

Eagly and Wood supported this identification of power as the root of mate choice by re-analysing Buss's data using the *Gender Empowerment Measure* to identify which cultures had greater or less gender equality. They found that when women had a higher status, and male–female division of labour was less pronounced, sex differences in mating preferences become less pronounced. This further suggests that social roles are the driving force in psychological sex differences.

However, this conclusion was challenged by Gangestad *et al.* (2006) who conducted a further analysis of the same data, adding some additional controls, such as affluence and social structure. The finding was that gender equality was not related to sex differences, and thus they concluded that evolutionary theory can provide a better explanation for the joint effects of biology and culture.

CAN YOU...? No.6.3

...**1** Write a description (in about 200 words) of **one or more** theories that illustrate the biosocial approach to gender development.

...**2** Identify **eight** criticisms related to gender development, including **at least one** IDA topic. Each criticism should be about 50 words.

...**3** Contrast **one** biosocial theory with any other account of gender development (for example consider **one** similarity and **one** difference).

...**4** Use this material to write a 600-word answer to the question: *Describe and evaluate the biosocial approach to gender development.* (8 marks + 16 marks)

GENDER DYSPHORIA

The term gender dysphoria describes an individual's experience of feeling uncomfortable with the gender assigned to them at birth, which may lead to a sex change operation or gender reassignment. Other terms are used to refer to the same condition, such as transgender or transsexual or gender identity disorder (see right).

Gender dysphoria was traditionally thought to be a purely psychological condition, however more recent research has found evidence of biological causes, especially those related to the development of gender identity before birth. For example, during prenatal development a genetic male is usually exposed to male hormones (e.g. testosterone). However, for various reasons, this isn't always the case and a possible consequence of the lack of exposure to testosterone is a genetic male without a male gender identity.

Gender dysphoria affects both males and females – males to females (MtF) outnumber females to males (FtM) by about 5 to 1 (NHS, 2012).

*The term **gender identity disorder (GID)** is a psychiatric classification for people experiencing gender dysphoria. This condition is only diagnosed in cases where a person does not have any physical intersex condition, such as **AIS** or **CAH**. Such **intersex** conditions are recognised as a separate psychiatric category. None of these classifications are related to homosexuality where both men and women are content with their sex assignments.*

A PHANTOM LIMB PHENOMENON

One intriguing explanation for gender dysphoria is related to the phenomenon of a phantom limb. People who have a limb amputated often report they feel as if the limb was still there, for example they feel itches in the limb or even try to pick things up. Ramachandran et al. (1995) demonstrated that this occurs because the brain is 'crosswired'. The part of the brain that received input from the amputated limb gets taken over by a different part of the body, such as the cheek. Stroking the person's cheek then feels as if the limb is being stroked.

Ramachandran (2008) suggested that gender dysphoria is an innate form of phantom limb syndrome. This is based on evidence that two-thirds of FtM transsexuals report the sensation of a phantom penis from childhood onwards, including phantom erections. This suggests they have been born with some cross-wiring that makes them feel they ought to have a penis.

This is further supported by the findings that nearly two-thirds of non-transsexual males who have a penis surgically removed experience the sensation of a phantom penis, whereas only one-third of MtF transsexuals do after sex reassignment surgery, i.e. there was something wrong with their original 'wiring'.

EXPLANATIONS OF GENDER DYSPHORIA

Psychosocial explanations

Mental illness – A number of psychologists have proposed that gender dysphoria is related to mental illness, which in turn is linked to some childhood trauma or maladaptive upbringing. For example, Coates et al. (1991) produced a case history of a boy who developed GID, proposing that this was a defensive reaction to the boy's mother's depression following an abortion. The trauma occurred when the boy was three, a time in development when a child is particularly sensitive to gender issues. Coates et al. suggest that the trauma may have led to a cross-gender fantasy as a means of resolving the ensuing anxiety.

Mother–son relationships – Stoller (1975) proposed that GID results from distorted parental attitudes. In clinical interviews with individuals diagnosed with GID Stoller observed that they displayed overly close mother–son relationships. This would be likely to lead to greater female identification and confused gender identity.

Biological explanations

Mismatch between hormones and genetic sex – Prenatal hormone levels may be affected by genetic conditions and this may lead to a mismatch between hormones and genetic sex, as we saw at the beginning of this chapter. AIS (**androgen insensitivity syndrome**) and CAH (**congenital adrenal hyperplasia**) may result in an **intersex** condition when external genitalia do not match genetic sex, and an individual may be assigned to the wrong sex at birth.

Transsexual gene – A recent study (Hare et al., 2009) looked at the DNA of 112 MtF transsexuals and found they were more likely to have a longer version of the *androgen receptor gene* than in a 'normal' sample. The effect of this abnormality is reduced action of the male sex hormone **testosterone** and this may have an effect on gender development in the womb (e.g. under-masculinising the brain).

The brain-sex theory of transsexualism is based on the fact that male and female brains are different and perhaps transsexuals' brains do not match their genetic sex. One region of the brain that has been studied is the BSTc (*bed nucleus of the stria terminalis*), which is located in the thalamus. On average, the BSTc is twice as large in heterosexual men as in heterosexual women and contains twice the number of neurons. The explanation may be that the size of the BSTc correlates with preferred sex rather than biological sex. Two Dutch studies (Zhou et al., 1995 and Kruijver et al., 2000) found that the number of neurons in the BSTc of MtF transsexuals was similar to that of the females. By contrast, the number of neurons in a FtM transsexual was found to be in the male range.

▶ The BSTc is located in the thalamus and may be associated with sex differences.

Environmental effects – Not all biological causes are internal. One external possibility is that environmental pollution may be causing problems. For example, the insecticide DDT contains **oestrogens** which may mean that males are prenatally exposed to unduly high levels of these female hormones causing a mismatch between genetic sex and hormone influences.

◀ Gender dysphoria is probably much more common than most people realise. *The Gender Identity Research and Education Society* (GIRES) estimates that about 1 in 4,000 of the British population is receiving medical help for gender dysphoria – to get a sense of the meaningfulness of this, compare to rates of about 1 in 1,000 for autism.

 REAL-WORLD APPLICATION

Colapinto (2000) reports that 1 in 2,000 people are born with anomalous genitals (external genitals that do not match genetic sex) and may be given an erroneous gender assignation. Research on gender dysphoria is very important in providing information about the effects of such erroneous assignations and determining the best solutions.

Organisations such as oii (*Organisation Intersex International*) campaign for the rights of intersex individuals. Their view is that all infants born as intersexes (i.e. no clear sex) should have the right to determine their own sexual identity once they are old enough. In order to do this our society needs to place less emphasis on sex, recognising that many gender characteristics are socially constructed. Again, psychological research is important in supplying research evidence to support such arguments.

EVALUATION

Increasingly, biological factors are implicated in gender identity, however, no clear explanations have emerged despite intensive research. One issue is that gender dysphoria may not be one single condition (see box on right below).

Psychosocial explanations

Mental illness – Cole *et al.* (1997) studied 435 individuals experiencing gender dysphoria and reported that the range of psychiatric conditions displayed was no greater than found in a 'normal' population, which suggests that gender dysphoria is generally unrelated to trauma or pathological families.

Mother–son relationships – Zucker *et al.* (1996) studied 115 boys with concerns about their gender identity and their mothers. Of the boys who were eventually diagnosed with GID, 64% were also diagnosed with separation anxiety disorder, compared to only 38% of the boys whose symptoms were subclinical. This points to some kind of disordered attachment to a mother as a factor in GID, but it does only explain MtF transsexuals.

General psychological influences – In some cases it has been suggested that persistently dressing a young boy in girl's clothing (or vice versa) may cause transsexualism. Diamond (1996) claims that there is no evidence to support this.

Biological explanations

Prenatal hormonal abnormalities – Dessens *et al.* (2005) studied 250 genetic females with CAH who were raised as females. Despite prenatal exposure to male hormones 95% were content with their female gender role. The remaining 5% did experience gender dysphoria but generally prenatal exposure to male hormones did not show a clear relationship with dysphoria.

Criticisms of brain-sex theory – The theory was seriously challenged by Chung *et al.* (2002) who noted that the differences in BSTc volume between men and women does not develop until adulthood, whereas most transsexuals report that their feelings of gender dysphoria began in early childhood (e.g. Lawrence, 2003). This suggests that the difference found in the BSTc could not be the cause of transsexualism but might perhaps be an effect.

In addition, Hulshoff Pol *et al.* (2006) found that transgender hormone therapy does influence the size of the BSTc and the individuals in the Dutch studies (see facing page) had been receiving hormone therapy. Therefore, it may be the hormones that caused the difference in transsexuals such that their brain sex was more similar to their gender identity rather than their biological sex.

Support for brain-sex theory – There is other evidence that does continue to support transsexualism as a sexual differentiation disorder. For example, Rametti *et al.* (2011) studied the brains of FtM transsexuals before they started transgender hormone therapy. In terms of amounts of white matter in their brains, the FtM individuals had a more similar pattern to individuals who share their gender identity (males) than those who share their biological sex (females).

Environmental effects – A number of studies have produced supporting evidence for environmental effects. For example, a group of Dutch researchers (Vreugdenhil *et al.*, 2002) reported that boys born to mothers who were exposed to dioxins (which can promote oestrogen) displayed feminised play.

ETHICS: SOCIALLY SENSITIVE RESEARCH

Research on gender dysphoria has potential social consequences for individuals represented by the research. The question is whether they are better off with or without the research. If a biological cause is identified this may help other people to be more accepting about the needs of transsexuals (it is not their 'fault', it is simply in their biology).

On the other hand if a biological cause is identified this might harm individuals born with the abnormality because it might be assumed (wrongly) that transsexualism is inevitable. The evidence, for example from CAH cases, is that a simple cause and effect (determinist) relationship is unlikely. Either way the outcome of research has social consequences for individuals represented by this research.

DIFFERENT KINDS OF GENDER DYSPHORIA AND SEXUAL ORIENTATION

People often confuse sexual orientation and gender identity believing, for example, that FtM transsexuals are simply lesbians. With regards to MtF transsexuals, Blanchard (1985) has proposed two distinct groups: 'homosexual transsexuals', who wish to change sex because they are attracted to men, and 'non-homosexual transsexuals', who wish to change sex because they are *autogynephilic* (sexually aroused by the thought or image of themselves as a woman).

These groups are so different that it is almost impossible to imagine that they could have the same etiology. Therefore, it is quite likely that there are a number of different explanations for gender dysphoria.

CAN YOU...? No.6.4

...1 Outline **two or more** explanations of gender dysphoria in about 200 words.

...2 Identify **eight** criticisms related to explanations of gender dysphoria, including **at least one** IDA topic. Each criticism should be about 50 words.

...3 Use this material to write a 600-word answer to the question: *Discuss explanations of gender dysphoria*. (8 marks + 16 marks)

There are three main approaches to explaining gender development: biological, psychological and social. On this spread and the next we will examine two psychological explanations. Kohlberg's theory is an example of the cognitive developmental approach which emphasises the role of thinking (cognition) in the process of development. The cognitive developmental approach is not just used as an explanation of gender development – Kohlberg used the same approach to explain moral development (see page 152) and the most famous example is Piaget's theory of how each of us develops from a child, with little understanding of the way the world works, to an adult, who is full of knowledge and capable of logical thinking.

GENDER CONSTANCY THEORY (KOHLBERG, 1966)

Background

Piaget's influence – Lawrence Kohlberg's theory draws on the Piagetian idea that the way we think changes as we get older because of physical changes in the brain (Piaget's theory is described on page 146). The brain becomes capable of increasingly complicated and abstract thinking. This means that changes in gender thinking are solely the outcome of age-related changes in a child's cognitive capabilities.

The consequence of this is that development occurs in stages (it is called a 'stage theory'). Children naturally progress from one stage to the next as their way of thinking matures, i.e. when they are 'ready'. It is useful to recognise that this progression through stages is a gradual process rather than one of sudden transitions.

Stages

Stage 1: gender labelling – The first stage occurs between the ages of two and three. Children of this age label themselves and others as a boy or a girl, a man or woman. This label is based on outward appearance only, such as hairstyle or what a person is wearing. Children will change the gender labels as appearances change ('He has long hair now so must be a girl'). Towards the end of this stage children not only can label others but will also label themselves as a girl or boy.

A child's way of thinking at this stage has been described by Piaget as **pre-operational**, i.e. it lacks internal logic (see page 146). It has a kind of superficial logic but is not internally consistent.

Stage 2: gender stability – At the age of around four, children recognise that gender is something that is consistent over time, boys grow into men and girls grow into women. Thus their gender concept is one of stability but it does not yet recognise consistency. They do not understand that gender is also consistent across situations, believing instead that males might change into females if they engage in female activities.

Children under the age of seven are still swayed by outward appearances – an example of Piaget's concept of **conservation** (see right). In terms of gender, children of this age believe that a person must be a girl if they are wearing a dress, i.e. if they appear to be a girl then they must be a girl. They lack the ability to conserve. For example, McConaghy (1979) found that when young children were shown a line drawing of a doll where the male genitals were visible through the doll's dress children under the age of five judged the doll to be female because of its external appearance despite the contrary evidence that it was a boy.

Stage 3: gender consistency – In the final stage of gender development, around the age of six, children come to realise that gender is consistent across situations. Thus they have now developed full gender constancy (constant across time and situations). The key feature of this stage is that it is only at this point, when a child has acquired gender constancy, that they start to learn about gender-appropriate behaviour. Up until the stage of constancy such information is not really relevant because the child believes that his/her gender may change.

Conservation refers to the ability to understand that, despite superficial changes in appearance, basic properties of an object remain unchanged. This ability appears around the age of six or seven. For example, that if you roll out a lump of clay so it looks longer, the quantity remains unchanged (i.e. is conserved).

The inability to conserve happens because young children cannot distinguish between appearance and reality – they believe that what you see represents what is true. For example, if a young child watches someone put a dog's mask on a cat the young child will believe it is now a dog (DeVries, 1969).

Evaluation

GENITAL KNOWLEDGE

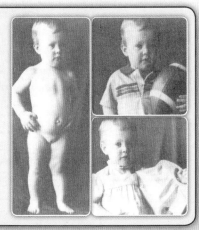

Sandra Bem (1989) argues that it is genital knowledge rather than gender constancy that lies at the root of gender development. To demonstrate this she showed children a picture of a toddler in the nude (see right) and then asked each child to identify the toddler's sex when dressed gender inappropriately (bottom) and appropriately (top).

She found that 40% of 3–5 year olds were capable of conserving gender. She then tested those children who didn't conserve gender and found that most of these (77%) also failed a genital knowledge test! They simply didn't know what opposite sex genitalia looked like. They couldn't conserve anything because they didn't know it had changed!

In any case, Bem argued that the basic task is nonsense – when children are asked to resolve a contradiction between genitals and clothing, the child goes for the cue which is most relevant in our society – we demarcate gender through hairstyle and clothing. Children who resolve this contradiction by identifying gender on the basis of clothing are simply showing that they have learned about our world.

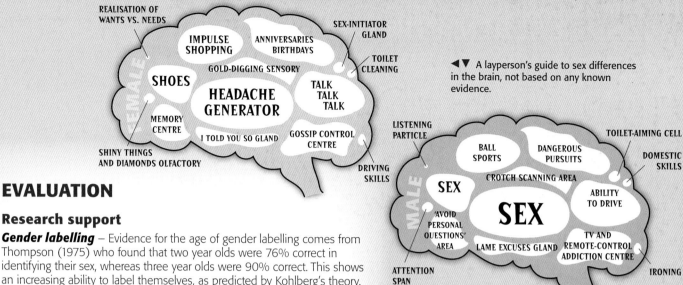

Labels on the female brain:
REALISATION OF WANTS VS. NEEDS
IMPULSE SHOPPING
ANNIVERSARIES BIRTHDAYS
SEX-INITIATOR GLAND
TOILET CLEANING
GOLD-DIGGING SENSORY
SHOES
HEADACHE GENERATOR
TALK TALK TALK
MEMORY CENTRE
I TOLD YOU SO GLAND
GOSSIP CONTROL CENTRE
SHINY THINGS AND DIAMONDS OLFACTORY
DRIVING SKILLS

▲▼ A layperson's guide to sex differences in the brain, not based on any known evidence.

Labels on the male brain:
LISTENING PARTICLE
BALL SPORTS
DANGEROUS PURSUITS
TOILET-AIMING CELL
DOMESTIC SKILLS
SEX
CROTCH SCANNING AREA
ABILITY TO DRIVE
SEX
'AVOID PERSONAL QUESTIONS' AREA
LAME EXCUSES GLAND
TV AND REMOTE-CONTROL ADDICTION CENTRE
ATTENTION SPAN
IRONING

EVALUATION

Research support

Gender labelling – Evidence for the age of gender labelling comes from Thompson (1975) who found that two year olds were 76% correct in identifying their sex, whereas three year olds were 90% correct. This shows an increasing ability to label themselves, as predicted by Kohlberg's theory.

Gender stability was investigated by Slaby and Frey (1975). They asked young children questions, such as: 'Were you a little girl or a little boy when you were a baby?' and 'When you grow up will you be a mummy or daddy?' The answers given by children showed that they did not recognise that these traits were stable over time until they were three or four years old, as Kohlberg predicted.

Gender consistency was also supported by Slaby and Frey. This time they asked a different set of questions, such as: 'If you played football would you be a boy or a girl' and 'Could you be a boy/girl if you wanted to be'. They found that children who scored high on both stability and consistency (i.e. they had achieved gender constancy) showed greatest interest in same-sex models. This suggests, as Kohlberg predicted, that an increasing sense of constancy leads children to pay more attention to gender-appropriate models, furthering gender development.

Criticisms of Kohlberg's theory

Age underestimated – Slaby and Frey (1975) did find that gender consistency appeared at a younger age than Kohlberg had suggested, as young as five. This is not a direct challenge to the theory but suggests that adjustments are necessary to the ages.

Gender difference – Slaby and Frey also found that boys tended to exhibit gender consistency before girls and Huston (1985) points out that it is relatively easy to get girls to take on masculine-type activities but the same cannot be said of boys who generally resist, for example, dressing up as a girl.

This difference can be explained in terms of **social learning theory**. The role models that boys identify with tend to be more powerful (males in our society have greater power). Power is one factor that determines how likely a person is to identify with a role model. Therefore, girls are less likely to identify with their role models because, even though the role models are gender appropriate they are less powerful.

A second reason may be that boys are more likely to be punished for gender inappropriate behaviour than girls and therefore learn appropriate gender behaviour more rapidly (Langlois and Downs, 1980). This means that Kohlberg's theory is incomplete because social learning theory principles are also involved.

Methodology – Bem (see facing page) has criticised the way children's gender constancy is measured. She claims that all that is being assessed is a child's understanding of our social cues for indicating gender, i.e. what you are wearing.

Slaby and Frey's methods have also been criticised. Martin and Halverson (1983) analysed children's responses to the questions used by Slaby and Frey and judged that children were adopting a 'pretend' mode and answering the questions based on this rather than what they really thought.

Gender schema theory (GST) is discussed on the next spread. In contrast to Kohlberg's theory, GST suggests that children can acquire information about gender-appropriate behaviours before gender constancy is achieved. Martin and Little (1990) presented evidence to support this (see next spread).

IDA OTHER APPROACHES

Cognitive developmental theory is only one approach to explaining gender development. As we have seen, the biological approach proposes that the key factor in gender role is your genes and hormones.

The cognitive developmental approach makes no mention of the influence of hormones and genes. It suggests that changing the way people think can alter gender behaviours (e.g. changing their stereotypes) but the evidence suggests that while thinking may change, behaviour doesn't. For example, many couples theoretically agree to sharing domestic duties but in practice this doesn't happen (Durkin, 1995). Perhaps this is because the division of gender roles has a biological rather than psychological basis.

Alternatively such gender roles may be learned through reinforcement, which is the social approach (examined later in this chapter). The cognitive developmental approach emphasises the active role of children in acquiring their gender concepts. In contrast, the social approach views gender development as a more passive process, the outcome of direct and indirect reinforcement from parents, peers and the media.

CAN YOU...? No.6.5

...1 Write a description of Kohlberg's theory in about 200 words.

...2 Identify **eight** criticisms related to Kohlberg's cognitive developmental theory, including **at least one** IDA topic. Each criticism should be about 50 words.

...3 Contrast the psychological approach with another approach to explaining gender development (for example consider **one** similarity and **one** difference).

...4 Use this material to write a 600-word answer to the question: *Describe and evaluate Kohlberg's cognitive developmental theory of gender development.* (8 marks + 16 marks)

113

GENDER SCHEMA THEORY

◀ Is this gender-inappropriate play?

This spread concerns a second psychological approach to explaining gender development. Both gender schema theory and Kohlberg's gender constancy theory take a cognitive approach, emphasising the role of a child's *thinking* in their gender development.

   Carol Martin and Charles Halverson, like Kohlberg, believed that the key to gender development is seeking to acquire information about one's own gender, as distinct from learning about gender behaviour through reinforcement and punishment – which is the social cognitive perspective (to be studied next).

WHAT IS A SCHEMA?

Think of a bank robbery and write down all the words that come into your mind associated with it.

   These words represent your schema of a bank robbery.

   A schema is a mental representation of an aspect of the world. It's a cluster of related items that together represent a concept. The term 'stereotype' is often used instead of schema. However, a schema involves more than a stereotype, being more complex and generating inferences and expectations.

WHEN DO GENDER PREFERENCES APPEAR?

Evaluation

   Martin and Halverson suggest that gender-typed preferences appear once a child is aware of which gender category they belong to (i.e. being able to label themselves as a boy or a girl). There has been some debate on this issue.

   According to Kohlberg this would be around the age of two or three years. This was confirmed in a study by Bauer (1993) who found that children as young as 25 months copied gender appropriate behaviours but not inappropriate behaviours.

   However, there is more recent evidence that children show gender typed preferences even earlier than this (i.e. before gender identity) which was seen as a challenge to gender schema theory (Bandura and Bussey, 2004). In defence of gender schema theory Zosuls *et al.* (2009) provided evidence that children can label their gender group earlier than indicated in previous studies. They recorded samples of children's language and observed them at play in order to identify when they first started labelling themselves as a boy or girl. They concluded that children were using gender labels by the age of 19 months.

GENDER SCHEMA THEORY (MARTIN AND HALVERSON, 1981)

Martin and Halverson propose two key factors that differentiate their theory from Kohlberg's. First, they argue that the process of acquiring gender-relevant information happens *before* gender consistency/constancy is achieved. They claim that basic gender identity (gender labelling) is sufficient for a child to identify him/herself as boy/girl and take an interest in what behaviours are appropriate. Kolberg claimed this did not happen until after gender constancy was achieved.

   Second, Martin and Halverson go further than Kohlberg in suggesting how the acquisition of stereotypes/schema affects later behaviour, especially in terms of memory and attention.

Schemas – The main concept in Gender Schema Theory (GST) is the concept of a **schema** (see left). Children learn schemas related to gender from their interactions with other children and adults, as well as from television programmes or videos.

   Such schema or stereotypes have the function of organising and structuring other information that is presented to children. They learn about what toys are appropriate for each gender, what clothes to wear and so on. In a sense, these gender schemas are like 'naïve' (i.e. personal rather than scientific) theories about appropriate behaviour for men and women.

Ingroup and outgroup schema – The term **ingroup** refers to the groups with which a person identifies. Being a girl means that you identify yourself with that group. You are also in many other groups (such as the town you come from, the football team you support, the boy bands you like and so on). Once a child has identified with a group this leads them to positively evaluate their own group and negatively evaluate the **outgroup**.

   In turn, this evaluation motivates a child to be like their own group and avoid behaviours of the other group. It also leads them to actively seek information about what their ingroup does, i.e. to acquire ingroup schemas. According to GST, from an early age, before gender constancy, children focus on ingroup schemas and avoid behaviours that belong to outgroup schemas.

Resilience of gender beliefs – An important aspect of GST is that it can explain the power of gender beliefs. Gender beliefs lead children to hold very fixed gender attitudes because they ignore any information they encounter that is not consistent with ingroup information. For example, if a boy sees a film with a male nurse, this information is ignored because the man is not behaving consistently with the boys' ingroup schema. Therefore, the boy does not alter his existing schema. In this way gender schema have a profound effect on what is remembered.

IDA   REAL-WORLD APPLICATION

The fact that gender schemas lead to misremembering or even distorting information (see facing page) has important implications for efforts to reduce gender stereotypes. It means that even when children are exposed to counter-stereotypes they don't remember them accurately. This suggests that the use of counter-stereotypes may not be the best way to reduce children's gender schema.

Sigmund Freud's theory of personality development includes an explanation of gender development. Freud proposed that around the age of three, a boy becomes sexually aware and attracted to his mother. This makes him wish his father dead so he can have his mother to himself. Such wishes make the boy feel guilty but ultimately are resolved through gender identification with his father. If the conflict is not resolved the boy may have gender identity problems. A similar process happens in girls.

It is interesting to note that there are some similarities between this and GST. Freud's critical age is closer to GST than Kohlberg's gender constancy and Freud suggested that identification with the ingroup (same-sex parent) was important in taking on gender attitudes.

EVALUATION

Research support

Gender stereotypes without constancy – Martin and Little (1990) found that children under the age of four showed no signs of gender stability let alone signs of constancy, but did display strong gender stereotypes about what boys and girls were permitted to do. This shows that they have acquired information about gender roles *before* Kohlberg suggested, in line with gender schema theory.

Effect on memory – If gender schemas are important in acquiring information about ingroup gender then we would expect children to pay greater attention to information consistent with gender schemas and to remember this information better. Indeed, Martin and Halverson (1983) found that when children were asked to recall pictures of people, children under six recalled more of the gender-consistent ones (such as a male firefighter or female teacher) than gender-inconsistent ones (such as a male nurse or female chemist).

Furthermore, children appear to pay greatest attention to ingroup rather than outgroup schema. Bradbard *et al.* (1986) told four to nine year olds that certain gender neutral items (e.g. burglar alarms, pizza cutter) were either boy or girl items. Participants took a greater interest in toys labelled as ingroup (i.e. a boy was more interested in a toy labelled as a boy's toy). Also, one week later, they were able to remember more details about ingroup objects. This shows how gender schema are related in particular to memory (organisation of information).

Gender schemas may distort information – Aside from just not remembering inconsistent information, gender schema may also lead children to actually distort this kind of information. This was shown in Martin and Halverson's study. When children were shown consistent or inconsistent (counter-stereotypical) pictures they distorted the information, e.g. shown a boy holding a gun (consistent) or a boy holding a doll (inconsistent). When children were asked to describe the picture they insisted, for example, that the doll was held by a girl.

Resilience of children's stereotypes explains why children are frequently highly sexist despite the best efforts of parents (insisting on Barbie dolls and toy guns) – because they actively seek to acquire gender-appropriate schema. However, Hoffman (1998) reports that children whose mothers work have less stereotyped views of what men do, suggesting that children are not entirely fixed in their views but are receptive to some gender inconsistent ideas.

▶ Research suggests that if children see a gender inconsistent picture they just remember it incorrectly – they are more likely to recall this as a man. This memory bias makes it difficult to change gender stereotypes using counter-stereotypes (see Real-world application on facing page).

GENDER CONSTANCY VERSUS SCHEMATA

The critical difference between the two theories presented on this spread lies in terms of when they predict that children will begin to absorb gender-relevant knowledge. Kohlberg claims this can't happen until gender constancy is achieved, whereas Martin and Halverson say it starts as soon as a child has some awareness of which group they belong to (boy or girl). Ruble *et al.* (2007) suggest that constancy is 'one of the most compelling yet controversial ideas in gender research', however a number of studies do not support Kohlberg's idea. For example, Bussey and Bandura (1992) found that boys and girls age four said they felt good about playing with gender-appropriate toys and awful about playing with gender-inappropriate ones. Kohlberg would predict this couldn't happen until later.

A compromise – Stangor and Ruble (1989) have proposed a means of unifying the two approaches. They argue that gender schema and gender constancy may represent different processes. Gender schema are concerned with organisation of information and therefore should affect cognitive variables such as memory, whereas gender constancy is more concerned with motivation (once you realise you are always going to be a girl you are especially motivated to find out about this role) and should thus be associated with things like activity choice. Stangor and Ruble tested children aged four to ten years and found that (a) memory (organisation) for gender-consistent pictures increased with age (supporting gender schema theory), and (b) that preference (motivation) for same-sex toys increased with increased gender constancy (supporting gender constancy theory).

CAN YOU...? No.6.6

...1 Write a description of gender schema theory in about 200 words.

...2 Identify **eight** criticisms related to gender schema theory, including **at least one** IDA topic. Each criticism should be about 50 words.

...3 Contrast gender schema theory with another approach to explaining gender development (for example consider **one** similarity and **one** difference).

...4 Use this material to write a 600-word answer to the question: *Describe and evaluate gender schema theory.* (8 marks + 16 marks)

SOCIAL INFLUENCES ON GENDER ROLE

In this chapter so far we have examined biological and psychological influences on gender development. Now we turn to social influences on gender role. Social cognitive theory explains how social factors lead children to learn about gender-appropriate and gender-inappropriate behaviours. These in turn dictate gender role behaviour – behaving in a feminine or masculine way. The source of social influence includes parents, peers and the media.

SOCIAL COGNITIVE THEORY

Albert Bandura renamed **social learning theory** as 'social cognitive theory' to emphasise the role of cognitive factors in learning. In this theory the source of information is social (parents, peers and so on) and what is learned is a cognition, something stored in the mind. Bandura (1991) proposed that gender role development is the result of learning from social agents who model and reinforce gender role behaviours.

Indirect reinforcement – Children observe the behaviour of others and learn the consequences of the behaviour (**vicarious reinforcement**). This information is stored as an expectancy of future outcome. Learning such behaviours results in imitation or **modelling**.

Direct reinforcement – Although boys and girls may learn the characteristic behaviours of both sexes, they do not perform everything they learn. For example, boys may learn a great deal about the homemaking role through repeated observation of their mothers but rarely adopt such activities in their everyday life (Bussey and Bandura, 1999).

Direct tuition – Children learn through **vicarious reinforcement** (indirect) but also through explicit (direct) instructions about appropriate gender behaviour. Direct tuition begins as children acquire linguistic skills and serves as a convenient way of informing children about appropriate or inappropriate styles of conduct.

SOURCES OF SOCIAL INFLUENCE

The influence of parents

There is considerable evidence for differential reinforcement from parents, i.e. that they reinforce gender-appropriate behaviour but not gender-inappropriate behaviour. For example, Smith and Lloyd (1978) observed mothers playing with an infant who was either presented as a boy (in terms of name and clothing), or as a girl. The mothers selected gender-appropriate toys (e.g. a doll for girls or squeaky hammer for boys) and also responded more actively when a 'boy' showed increased motor activity.

Furthermore, such differential reinforcement does affect behaviour. For example, Fagot et al. (1992) found that parents who show the clearest patterns of differential reinforcement have children who are quickest to develop strong gender preferences.

The influence of peers

As a child's social world expands outside the home, peer groups become another source of gender development. Peers are important because they offer a model of gender-appropriate behaviours. This was demonstrated in a study by Perry and Bussey (1979) who showed film clips to children aged eight and nine. In the film boys and girls were seen selecting an apple or pear, both gender-neutral items. Later the children were given a choice of fruit. Boys selected the fruit they had seen another boy selecting, and the same for girls.

Peers also provide feedback when a friend steps outside of what is accepted as 'appropriate' behaviour for that gender, reinforcing each other for gender-appropriate activities as well as punishing gender conduct that is considered inappropriate for their gender (Lamb et al., 1980). This may involve 'direct tuition', for example saying 'Don't be a cissy'.

The influence of the media

The media (books, films, TV, commercials, toys and so on) generally portrays males as independent, directive, and pursuing engaging occupations and recreational activities. By contrast, women are usually shown as acting in dependent, unambitious and emotional ways (Bussey and Bandura, 1999). Men are also more likely to be shown exercising control over events, whereas women are frequently shown to be more at the mercy of others (Hodges et al., 1981). Not surprisingly, those who have a higher exposure to these differential gender representations tend to display more stereotypic gender role conceptions than do light viewers (McGhee and Frueh, 1980).

The media does more than simply model gender typical behaviours, as it also gives information about the likely outcomes of those behaviours for males and females. Seeing people similar to oneself succeed raises a person's beliefs in their own capabilities (**self-efficacy**), whereas the failure of similar others produces self-doubt about one's own ability to master similar activities.

Evaluation

NOTEL, UNITEL AND MULTITEL

In the 1970s, a valley of Canada surrounded by high mountains had never been able to receive a television signal. This community, code named *Notel*, offered Tannis Williams (1985) an opportunity to study the effects of exposure to TV. In addition to *Notel* there were two further towns that were studied – *Unitel* was a town with only one Canadian TV channel (CBC), whereas *Multitel* had access to a number of American channels.

The behaviour and attitudes of children in these towns were assessed in various ways, including questionnaires about their gender stereotypes (e.g. asking them what characteristics were more typical of boys or girls).

Williams found that children in *Notel* and *Unitel* had weaker sex-typed views than the children in *Multitel*. This was especially true for the girls. The children were re-assessed two years after the introduction of TV in *Notel*, and it was found that their views had become significantly more sex-typed.

EVALUATION

Social cognitive theory

Evidence to support modelling – Bandura's initial source of evidence for both learning and modelling was the Bobo doll studies, which demonstrated the effects of an adult model on children's aggressive behaviour (see page 66). These effects have also been demonstrated for gender. For example, the study by Perry and Bussey (see facing page) demonstrated the effect of modelling on gender development. However, the children only modelled same-sex behaviour as long as the behaviour was not counter to gender stereotypes (e.g. a man wearing a dress). So it seems that the effects of modelling are limited by existing stereotypes.

Direct tuition may be more effective than modelling – Research has shown that children do not always model their behaviour on a same-sex model and that direct tuition may be more important. For example, Martin *et al.* (1995) found that preschool boys played with toys labelled 'boy's toys' (a kind of 'direct tuition' because they were told the toy is for boys). They did this even if they saw girls playing with them. However, they didn't play with toys labelled girls' toys even when they saw boys playing with them (i.e. they didn't model same-sex behaviour when 'told' that it was a girl's toy). This suggests that direct instruction is more important than modelling, at least in preschool children.

However, 'instructors' (such as parents and teachers) do not always practise what they preach, and the impact of this tuition is weakened when what is being taught is contradicted by what is modelled (Hildebrandt *et al.*, 1973).

Sources of social influence

Gender differences – Mothers and fathers appear to behave differently with regard to reinforcement. Langlois and Downs (1980) found that fathers were more openly disapproving of their sons' inappropriate gender behaviour (e.g. playing with dolls), whereas mothers simply reinforced gender-appropriate play and did not punish gender-inappropriate play in sons or daughters.

Langlois and Downs also found a similar pattern of behaviour in peer reinforcement – the boys reacted negatively to gender-inappropriate behaviour in peers whereas girls were more tolerant.

Such behaviour may be due to the fact that female behaviour has a lower value and therefore gender-inappropriate behaviour in females may be desirable (acting like a boy), whereas a boy acting like a girl is undesirable.

Peer influences – Some psychologists (e.g. Maccoby, 1998) take the view that peers are the prime socialising agency of gender development. However, peers are unlikely to be important in early childhood when important aspects of gender development are taking place.

Later on in childhood it is likely that peer behaviour does not create gender role stereotypes but simply reinforces existing ones. For example, Lamb and Roopnarine (1979) observed preschool children at play and found that when male-type behaviour was reinforced in girls the behaviour continued for a shorter time than when male-type behaviour was reinforced in boys. This suggests that peer reinforcement mainly acts as a reminder.

Demonstrating media influence – It is difficult to demonstrate the effects of media stereotypes because almost all children watch some television and therefore there are no control groups for comparison – except for the rare cases of communities that have no television, as in the study by Williams described on the facing page. This study shows that exposure to the media can have significant effects on gender attitudes.

Media effects may be insignificant – Another study that looked at the effects of TV on a community previously without it (Charlton *et al.*, 2000) found no changes in aggressive behaviour and concluded that this was because of pre-existing community values that reduced the effect of exposure to the media.

This latter study did concern aggression and not gender but does suggest that simply exposing children to stereotypes is not sufficient to change attitudes. In general, it seems that the media's effect is simply to reinforce the status quo. For example, Signorelli and Bacue (1999) examined over 30 years of TV programming and found very little change in gender stereotypes.

▶ **Liberate me!**
In 1993 the Barbie Liberation Organisation (BLO) was horrified to find that Barbie had been programmed to say 'Math is hard!' and 'I love shopping!' Such comments reinforce gender stereotypes, so the BLO operated on some 300 'GI Joes' and Barbies so that the Barbies now said 'Eat lead, Cobra' and 'Dead men tell no lies'. The GI Joes were full of their love of shopping.

IDA | **THE BIOLOGICAL APPROACH**
Bandura did not deny the role of biological factors in social learning. In terms of gender he recognised that the starting point for social learning is knowing which sex you are – as we have seen in this chapter, this is largely based on biology (gender identification at birth).

IDA | **REAL-WORLD APPLICATION**
Research has shown that exposure to non-stereotypical information in the media can change expectations. For example, Pingree (1978) found that stereotyping was reduced when children were shown commercials with women in non-traditional roles. This has led to pressure on programme makers to try to use this knowledge to alter such attitudes.

However, not all research has supported the effectiveness of this approach. Pingree also found that pre-adolescent boys displayed *stronger* stereotypes after exposure to the non-traditional models. This 'backlash' may occur because boys of this age want to take a view that is counter to the view held by the adults.

There is also the issue, raised by Martin and Halverson (see previous spread), that gender-inconsistent messages are mis-remembered and therefore have no effect.

CAN YOU...? No.6.7

...1 Write an outline, in about 200 words, of social influences on gender role.

...2 Identify **eight** criticisms related to social influences on gender role, including to **at least one** IDA topic. Each criticism should be about 50 words.

...3 Contrast this approach to understanding gender role development with one other approach presented in this chapter (for example consider **one** similarity and **one** difference).

...4 Use this material to write a 600-word answer to the question: *Describe and evaluate social influences on gender role.* (8 marks + 16 marks)

CULTURAL INFLUENCES ON GENDER ROLE

The study of cultural influences on gender role helps us increase our understanding of the relative contributions of biology and socialisation. If biology is the main factor in determining gender role then we would expect to find cultural similarities in the division of labour. If socialisation is the main factor then we should observe variation between cultures in the different roles taken on by men and women.

In fact we already know that there are many cultural similarities in the division of labour as well as significant cultural variations in the differences between genders (see, for example, page 108). On this spread we will look at further research and consider the implications.

What is culture? *It is the rules, customs, morals, childrearing practices and so on, that bind a group of people together. There is a distinction made between* **individualist** *cultures, where members are more focused on their own interests and on independence, and* **collectivist** *cultures, where group interests come first.*

CULTURAL SIMILARITIES AND VARIATIONS

Cultural similarities: Division of labour

Cross-cultural studies of gender show that every society has some division of labour and behaviour by gender (Munroe and Munroe, 1975). For example, food preparation and childcare is predominantly carried out by females in all societies. It is sometimes shared, but in no society is it the major responsibility of males. Girls are socialised more towards compliance (nurturance, responsibility and obedience) and boys are raised more for assertiveness (independence, self-reliance and achievement).

There are three studies in particular that stand out: Mead's classic study of gender roles in three primitive societies (left), Williams and Best's study conducted in 27 countries (below), and Buss's (1989) analysis of 37 cultural groups (discussed on pages 54 and 109). The message from all these studies is that there are considerable cultural similarities in the direction of division of labour across genders.

Cultural variations: Magnitude of sex differences

Despite such similarities, there are also some significant variations, which Mead described as cultural relativism. For example, Berry *et al.* (2002) looked at male superiority on spatial perceptual tasks in 17 societies. They found that this superiority is only found in relatively tightly knit, sedentary societies, but absent or even reversed in 'looser' nomadic societies. This shows that sex differences on spatial perceptual tasks interact with ecological and cultural factors.

The same pattern emerges with conformity. Across cultures there is a general consensus that women are more conformist than men. However, this difference varies considerably, again, with culture. Berry *et al.* report that conformity is highest in tight, sedentary societies, with a correlation between this sex difference and an **ecocultural index** of +.78.

We can also include historical changes when considering the magnitude of sex differences. In the UK, women continue to perform more domestic duties than men and to occupy less powerful positions. However, this gender gap has been decreasing, which supports the role of changing social influences (www.statistics.gov.uk/focuson/gender/archive 2004/).

Evaluation — SEX AND TEMPERAMENT IN THREE PRIMITIVE SOCIETIES

Margaret Mead (1935) conducted a classic study of social groups in Papua New Guinea, providing evidence of cultural role differences. She found the *Arapesh* men and women to be gentle, responsive and cooperative. The *Mundugumor* men and women were violent and aggressive, seeking power and position. By contrast the *Tchambuli* exhibited gender role differences: the woman were dominant, impersonal and managerial whereas the men were more emotionally dependent.

Her research has not been without criticism, in particular from Freeman (1984) who himself worked with native Samoans and was told that they had provided Mead with the information she wanted to hear. However, Freeman's version has also been criticised for being inaccurate (e.g. Appell, 1984).

▲ Margaret Mead with native Samoans.

Evaluation — MEASURING SEX STEREOTYPES

John Williams and Deborah Best (1990a) produced evidence of cultural similarities in gender stereotypes. They tested 2,800 students in 30 different countries using a 300-item adjective checklist. Participants were asked to decide for each adjective whether it was more frequently associated with men or women. There was a broad consensus across countries. Men were seen as more dominant, aggressive and autonomous, whereas women were more nurturant, deferent and interested in affiliation. This suggests there are universal gender stereotypes about male–female characteristics.

However, several things should be noted. First the task was a forced choice one – participants had to select male or female; there was no 'equal' category, although participants were allowed to respond 'cannot say'. This means that the division between male and female stereotypes may be exaggerated.

Second, the task was related to stereotypes and not to actual behaviours. It can be argued that such stereotypes have a significant effect on socialisation within the culture and thus are related to behaviour, but the data from this study does not demonstrate this.

Third, the participants were university students who share common attributes – they are well educated and may be exposed to similar global influences, such as books, films, etc. This might explain the high level of consensus.

▶ Europeans and Americans classify individuals as male or female, a dichotomy that causes problems for **intersex** individuals. By contrast, other cultures recognise a third sex. For example, it is estimated that there are over 5 million *hijras* in India, individuals who are neither male nor female. In 2005 the Indian passport system changed to allow people to class themselves as M, F or E (for Eunuch).

Native Americans use the term 'two spirit' to refer to people who have both a male and a female spirit. Gender (male, female or two spirit) is decided by each child at puberty and at that time they chose what clothing to wear to physically display their gender choice (Lang, 1998).

EVALUATION

Cultural similarities

The fact that labour divisions are the same in most cultures suggests that biology rather than culture explains the development of gender roles. However, what we don't know is whether this division is the direct outcome of biological differences (as proposed by the evolutionary approach), or whether it is a more indirect outcome of biological differences (as proposed by Eagly and Wood (see page 108) who argued that all cultures shape their socialisation processes along the lines of inborn biological tendencies).

In fact, the picture is more complicated. Labour divisions are the same in *most* but not all cultures. For example, Sugihara and Katsurada (2002) found that Japanese men do not seek to be 'macho' like Americans, but instead value being well-rounded in the arts, a trait normally regarded as feminine.

Cultural differences

Spatial perception – The evidence suggests that the magnitude of sex differences is linked to culture and ecology; for example the magnitude of male superiority on spatial tasks was highest in tight sedentary societies. In such societies the division of labour is greatest because women stay at home while men hunt, whereas in nomadic societies both men and women travel and hunt and there is less division of labour (Van Leeuwen, 1978). Where there is a strong division of labour, men will be given practice from early childhood in skills related to hunting and this would enhance their spatial-perceptual skills, thus offering an explanation for the magnitude of differences across different cultures.

This interpretation indicates that it is social factors that underlie cross-cultural differences in divisions of labour. However, Kimura (1999) offers an alternative biological interpretation, suggesting that in hunting societies those with poor spatial perception are likely to die, thus eliminating such genes from the gene pool. This would explain why, in societies where both men and women hunt (nomadic societies) there would be less gender difference in spatial abilities.

Conformity – In societies where women contribute a lot to food accumulation (such as the nomadic societies), women are highly valued, allowed more freedom and generally regarded less as objects for male sexual and reproductive needs (Schlegel and Barry, 1986). This means that women occupy a higher position within the social group and therefore have more power and less need to conform to the demands of the powerful members of society.

Historical changes – More generally, wealth is associated with greater role equality; the greater the socioeconomic development of a society, the less difference there is between male and female roles (Williams and Best, 1990b). This relationship was also reported in Eagly and Wood's analysis of cross-cultural data (page 108) – they reported that, in societies where women had a higher status (which occurs with increased socioeconomic development), male–female division of labour was less pronounced.

Culture or biology?

The fact that there are universals points to biology, but the fact that there are differences within these universals points to the role of social factors as being equally important as biological factors. The final conclusion is that there is a complex interaction between both factors.

DETERMINISM AND RELATIVISM

Mead concluded that the data on the facing page demonstrated **cultural determinism**, the position that male and female differences are determined by social factors rather than biological ones.

However, Mead (1949) later changed her view to one of **cultural relativism**. In re-analysing her original data she realised that although both sexes of the Arapesh were non-aggressive, and both sexes of Mundugumor were aggressive, in all three societies the men were more aggressive than the women. This suggests that some behaviours are innate and universal but the degree to which these behaviours are expressed is *relative* to the particular culture.

CULTURAL BIAS

The evidence examined on this spread has largely been collected by Western researchers working in a mixture of Western and non-Western cultures, leaving scope for cultural bias. Researchers (indigenous or not) use tests and other measures developed by Western psychology (such as the adjective checklist used by Williams and Best, see facing page). Such measures are described as **imposed etics**. The results of such imposed etics are likely to be meaningless unless conducted with the cultural group for which they are designed. The outcome is that conclusions are produced that are culturally biased in favour of the culture who designed the test.

Berry *et al.* (2002) believe that most cross-cultural studies are driven by the interests of Western psychologists, using concepts rooted in Western thinking about human behaviour. They recommend the use of more genuine indigenous research to avoid such biases. Just using indigenous researchers doesn't solve the problem because they may still be using Western tests.

CAN YOU...?   No.6.7

...1 Write a description of cultural influences on gender role in about 200 words.

...2 Identify **eight** criticisms related to the social learning approach to gender, including **at least one** IDA topic. Each criticism should be about 50 words.

...3 Use this material to write a 600-word answer to the question: *Describe and evaluate cultural influences on gender role.* (8 marks + 16 marks)

CHAPTER SUMMARY

BIOLOGICAL INFLUENCES

GENES AND HORMONES	EVOLUTIONARY EXPLANATIONS	BIOSOCIAL APPROACH	GENDER DYSPHORIA

THE ROLE OF GENES
- Female XX, male XY chromosomes determine biological sex of person.
- Direct link between chromosomal sex and external/internal genitalia.
- In males, testes produce testosterone.

THE ROLE OF HORMONES
- Gender development governed by prenatal hormones.
- Intersex individuals exposed prenatally to abnormal hormone levels.
- Androgen insensitivity syndrome (AIS) – some individuals do not respond to XY hormones so no external genitalia develop.
- Genetic females exposed prenatally to large doses of male hormones then develop ambiguous genitalia.
- Sex differences in male and female brains (e.g. males – spatial navigation; females – language and social skills).
- Some evidence that sex differences are caused by testosterone exposure in developing brain.
- Animal studies (e.g. Quadagno et al., 1977) confirm this relationship.

EVALUATION
- Importance of biological factors – demonstrated in case of David Reimer and by subsequent research (Reiner and Gearhart, 2004).
- Biological determinism – outcome for each individual is a combination of genes, hormones, sex or rearing and socialisation.
- Illustrated by congenital adrenal hyperplasia (CAH), when XX females exposed prenatally to high levels of male hormones.
- Research methods – research may lack generalisability (e.g. reliance on case studies of abnormal development).

IDA
- Nature and nurture – genes and hormones represent *nature*.
- Real-world application – International Olympic Committee ruling that genetic sex no longer determines eligibility.

DIVISION OF LABOUR
- Complimentary division of labour enhances reproductive success and important in avoiding starvation.
- May explain why humans survived and Neanderthals did not.

MATE CHOICE
- Many gender role behaviours linked to reproductive strategies.
- Males seek physical attractiveness, females seek males with resources.
- Gender role behaviours linked to enhancement of these characteristics.

COGNITIVE STYLE
- Empathising (females)/ systematising (males) linked to different selection pressures.
- Tend and befriend (female trait) – Taylor et al. propose this is due to different challenges from those faced by males in the EEA.

EVALUATION
- Evolutionary explanations not supported by *direct* evidence.
- Research support – mate choice claims supported by study of personal ads (Waynforth and Dunbar, 1995).
- Tend and befriend – supported by research on responses to stress, males show increase in cortisol, females show increases in oxytocin.
- Implications – meat sharing hypothesis (Stanford, 1999) and autism (Baron-Cohen, 2004).
- Baron-Cohen (2004) – men and women think in different ways according to evolved cognitive style.
- Research methods – cross-cultural methods create specific problems making direct comparisons difficult.

IDA
- Approaches – evolutionary approach is an example of nature approach.
- Determinism – genes do not *determine*, but rather *predispose* us to behave in certain ways.

BIOSOCIAL THEORY
- Social labelling and differential treatment of boys and girls, with biological factors, steer development.
- Individuals mislabelled as male or female would acquire the gender identity of the opposite sex.

SOCIAL ROLE THEORY
- Selective pressures cause only physical differences.
- These lead to sex role allocations which create psychological sex differences.
- Thus psychological sex differences are the *consequence* of assigned roles.
- Division of labour – a product of biologically based physical differences.
- Mate choice preferences determined by social roles performed by males and females.
- Eagly and Wood (2002) suggest hormonal differences may be the outcome of social roles and psychological differences between sexes.

EVALUATION
- Biosocial theory challenged by David Reimer study.
- Study of abnormal individuals may not reflect normal gender development.
- Luxen (2007) argues that evolutionary theory is a simpler explanation of gender role differences.
- Selective pressure would act on behaviour as well as physical factors.
- Research suggests gender role differences arise without socialisation.

IDA
- Social constructionism – differences in gender role not inevitable.
- Real-world application – value of social role approach is that it leads to changes in social roles and so to changes in psychological differences.

PSYCHOSOCIAL EXPLANATIONS
- Caused by childhood trauma leading to e.g. cross-gender fantasy (Coates et al., 1991).
- Overly close mother–son relationship (Stoller, 1975).

EVALUATION
- Psychiatric conditions in those with gender dysphoria no greater than norm (Cole et al., 1997).
- MtF transsexuals do tend to have disordered attachment (Zucker et al., 1996).

BIOLOGICAL EXPLANATIONS
- Mismatch between hormones and genetic sex, e.g. AIS and CAH.
- Transsexual gene (androgen receptor) more common in MtF transsexuals (Hare et al., 2009).
- Brain sex theory – BSTc smaller in normal females and transsexuals.
- Environmental cause – DDT contains oestrogen.
- Innate form of phantom limb syndrome (Ramachandran, 2008).

EVALUATION
- CAH – 95% content with female gender assignment (Dessens et al., 2005).
- BSTc size difference appears in adulthood so cannot be the cause of dysphoria (Chung et al., 2002), however Rametti et al. (2011) found support.
- Feminised play in boys exposed to dioxins (Vreugdenhil et al., 2002).
- Different kinds of gender dysphoria require different explanations.

IDA
- Real-world application – provide advice on relatively common problem of intersex (1 in 2000).
- Ethics (socially sensitive) – identifying a biological cause may harm or help.

PSYCHOLOGICAL EXPLANATIONS

KOHLBERG'S COGNITIVE DEVELOPMENTAL THEORY

BACKGROUND
- Kohlberg (1966) suggested that changes in gender thinking are a product of changes in cognitive capabilities as child ages.
- Related to Piaget's ideas about maturation of the mind and conservation (appearance-reality).

STAGES
- Gender labelling – gender identification based on outward appearance only.
- Gender stability – gender is consistent over time but not across situations, so gender might change if a person engages in different gender behaviour.
- Gender constancy – gender is consistent across time and situations, leads to interest in gender-appropriate information.

EVALUATION
- Gender labeling – children aged 3 more accurate at identifying own sex than those age 2 (Thompson, 1975).
- Gender stability – Slaby and Frey (1975) found that children recognised stability of gender over time.
- Gender consistency – children high in gender constancy showed more interest in same sex models (Slaby and Frey).
- Age underestimated – Slaby and Frey consistency appeared earlier.
- Gender difference – boys show gender consistency earlier, because men have more power and this encourages identification.
- Methodology criticised, e.g. actually testing genital knowledge rather than gender constancy (Bem, 1989) and questions answered in pretend mode (Martin and Halverson, 1983).
- Contrast with gender schema theory.

IDA
- Other approaches – biological factors may explain why people resist changing gender behaviours.

GENDER SCHEMA THEORY

- Martin and Halverson (1981) basic gender identity sufficient for child to absorb gender schema.
- Schema affect cognitive processes, such as memory and attention.
- Children learn gender schemas from interactions with others.
- More interested in ingroup (same sex) than outgroup (other sex) schemas.
- Gender beliefs are resilient to change.

EVALUATION
- Do gender preferences appear before gender identity? Gender identity appears by 19 months (Zosuls et al., 2009).
- Martin and Little (1990) – children under 4 had strong gender stereotypes even though no gender stability.
- Memory – children recall more gender-consistent information (Martin and Halverson, 1983) and pay more attention to ingroup schema (Bradbard et al., 1986).
- Gender schema may lead to distortion of inconsistent information (Martin and Halverson, 1983).
- Children may be receptive to some gender stereotype changes (Gibbons et al., 1996).
- Reconcile the two cognitive theories – gender schema = organisation, gender constancy = motivation.

IDA
- Real-world application – counter-stereotypes don't work because information distorted.
- Freudian approach – ingroup identification leads to gender development.

SOCIAL CONTEXTS OF GENDER ROLE

SOCIAL INFLUENCES ON GENDER ROLE

SOCIAL COGNITIVE THEORY
- Indirect reinforcement – children learn gender role behaviour through vicarious reinforcement.
- Cognitive – experiences stored as expectancies of future outcomes.
- Direct reinforcement – children don't perform everything they learn.
- Direct tuition – begins when children acquire linguistic skills.

EVALUATION
- Perry and Bussey (1979) – effects of modelling limited by existing gender stereotypes.
- Martin et al. (1995) – preschool children were more influenced by direct tuition than modelling.
- Direct tuition may be contradicted by parental modeling (Hildebrandt et al., 1973).

SOURCES OF INFLUENCE
- Parents provide differential reinforcement (Smith and Lloyd, 1978) which affects behaviour (Fagot et al., 1992).
- Peers model gender-appropriate behaviours (Perry and Bussey, 1978) and give feedback when gender-inappropriate behaviour shown (Lamb et al., 1980).
- Media – stronger gender role conceptions in more frequent viewers (McGhee and Frueh, 1980). May also increase feelings of self-efficacy.

EVALUATION
- Gender differences, e.g. fathers and male peers more disapproving (Langlois and Downs, 1980).
- Peers reinforce existing stereotypes (Lamb and Roopnarine, 1979).
- The coming of TV to 'Notel' led to more sex-typed behaviour (Williams, 1985).
- TV doesn't always have this effect (Charlton et al., 2000), may simply reinforce the status quo (Signorelli and Bacue, 1999).

IDA
- Biological approach not ignored.
- Real-world application for TV programme makers to reduce stereotyping.

CULTURAL INFLUENCES ON GENDER ROLE

CULTURAL SIMILARITIES
- All societies have some gender division of labour and behaviour.
- Demonstrated in studies by Mead (1935) in Papua New Guinea, Williams and Best (1990) and Buss (1989).

EVALUATION
- Uncertain whether division of gender roles is direct outcome of biological differences or shaped by socialisation.
- But...labour divisions are the same in most but not all cultures.

CULTURAL VARIATIONS
- Male/female superiority on certain tasks relative to the type of culture.
- Historical changes important in magnitude of sex differences, e.g. decreasing gender gap supports changing social influences.

EVALUATION
- Alternative biological explanation for spatial perception – in hunting societies males and females with poor spatial perception would die out.
- In some societies, where women are more highly valued, they have more social power and less need to conform.
- Research suggests the greater the socioeconomic development of a culture, the less difference between male and female gender role.
- Williams and Best (1990) – evidence of universal gender stereotypes about male–female characteristics.
- Rigid demarcation between sexes not evident in all cultures. In some cultures a 'third' sex is recognised (e.g. *hijras* in India).
- Complex interaction between biology and culture.

IDA
- Cultural bias created by using concepts rooted in Western thinking (imposed etic).
- Mead moved from position of cultural determinism (male-female differences due to social factors) to one of cultural relativism.

EXAM QUESTION WITH STUDENT ANSWER

> **QUESTION** Outline and evaluate **two** psychological explanations of gender development.
> *(8 marks + 16 marks)*

STUDENT ANSWER

Gender is the sociocultural equivalent of being male or female. Gender identity is knowing 'I am a boy' or 'I am a girl'. Gender constancy is one theory used to explain how gender identity develops. Gender constancy is knowing that this is permanent despite superficial changes. Kohlberg suggested that children identify gender constancy when they are able to 'conserve'. Children are found to begin conserving at the age of about 6 years. Kohlberg identified three stages of gender development. The first is basic gender labelling which is when a child knows that they are a boy or a girl. The second stage is gender stability which is knowing males remain males and females remain females over time. The final stage, which occurs after the age of 6, is gender consistency when a child realises that gender is constant i.e. it is permanent regardless of gender inappropriate hair or clothing. After these stages, the child is ready to learn about the gender 'stereotypes' of society (e.g. males being domineering, competitive and women being sensitive and caring). Until a child has achieved gender constancy there is no point learning about these things because the child's gender is not certain.

This explanation suggests that cognitive development works alongside gender development and most research agrees. There are studies which show the changes that Kohlberg predicted at the ages he predicted.

Another explanation is gender schema theory by Martin and Halverson (1981). This theory proposes that children start to acquire gender-appropriate concepts at a much earlier age than Kohlberg had suggested. Martin and Halverson said a child does not need to have achieved gender constancy in order to attend to gender-related schemas. They suggest that as soon as a child takes on a basic gender identity (around the age of 3 or 4), the child will attend especially to ingroup schemas and these lead them to acquire gender concepts.

One of the strengths of this theory is that it can explain why children have rather fixed gender stereotypes – it is because they attend just to ingroup schemas which means they are only affected by these.

Both theories are supported by research evidence but one study is especially interesting because it shows that both views may be correct. Stangor and Ruble (1989) gave children a variety of tasks. They found that children's memory for gender-appropriate items increased with age which supports gender schema theory. However, they also found that children's preference for gender-appropriate items increased with age which supports gender constancy theory. This suggests that memory and preferences are two separate things explained by two separate processes – schema and constancy.

Cognitive developmental theory differs from various other accounts of gender development. For example, the biological approach explains that gender identity is mainly influenced by genes and hormones. Hormones may influence brain development so a person's brain is masculinised or feminised and this could lead to gender role behaviours rather than these being acquired by learning about gender schemas. The evolutionary view, which is also biological, suggests that gender role behaviours are adaptive. In contrast the cognitive developmental view is that gender-appropriate behaviours are learned by seeing what other people of the same gender are doing.

Another approach to gender development is the social learning approach. Cognitive developmental theory is better because it can explain why children don't learn opposite-sex behaviours even if they are reinforced. For example, a boy might be praised for playing with dolls but is unlikely to take on this behaviour because it is gender-inappropriate. According to social learning theory any behaviour that is reinforced should be learned but according to cognitive developmental theory this only works when it is gender-appropriate.

[608 words]

EXAMINER COMMENTS

The first paragraph of this essay contains a fairly **well-detailed** description of Kohlberg's theory, demonstrating **sound** knowledge and understanding. The student has added some good elaboration. However, considering the fact that more marks are available for **AO2**, perhaps less time should have been spent outlining the theory and more on evaluating it. The student may well have prepared a description of Kohlberg's theory appropriate for a question that asked for just one cognitive developmental theory. However, when a question asks for two theories it is important to present an outline rather than the full description to leave yourself enough time for the other requirements of the question.

This evaluation of this theory is **rudimentary**. The material is relevant but **incomplete**.

A briefer explanation of the second theory is presented, again demonstrating a good level of **knowledge and understanding**. It is not uncommon for students to focus too much on **AO2** and fail to pick up the easier **AO1 marks**, but this student knows the theories well and has demonstrated this.

A brief comment on a strength of the theory attracts some further **AO2** credit.

Evidence is presented that is relevant to both theories and counts as both description and evaluation. In this case the study has been used in a **reasonably effective manner** and demonstrates **reasonable analysis**.

The final two paragraphs make an important contribution to this essay. First, they provide evidence of **IDA** as well as evidence of using other **approaches effectively**. Notice that the student has avoided spending time on *description* of the approaches (which would not be relevant in this essay) and focused on using other approaches as contrasts to the cognitive developmental approach.

Second, these paragraphs increase the **AO2/AO3** content of the essay which otherwise would otherwise be described as **basic**.

AO1 – sound, **accurate** and sufficiently **detailed** for an outline.

AO2/AO3 – sound analysis and **line of argument**, evidence of **IDA** is bordering on being **effective** and **substantial**.

Chapter 7
Intelligence and learning

SPECIFICATION

Intelligence and learning	
Theories of intelligence	• Psychometric theories, for example Spearman, Cattell, Thurstone. • Information processing theories, for example Sternberg, Gardner.
Animal learning and intelligence	• Simple learning (classical and operant conditioning) and its role in the behaviour of non-human animals. • Intelligence in non-human animals, for example self-recognition, social learning, Machiavellian intelligence.
Human intelligence	• Evolutionary factors in the development of human intelligence, for example ecological demands, social complexity, brain size. • Genetic and environmental factors associated with intelligence test performance, including the influence of culture.

PSYCHOMETRIC THEORIES

The **psychometric** approach refers to the practice of measuring psychological characteristics in a person. It could apply to almost anything, but the most common examples are personality and intelligence. The history of this approach stretches back over 100 years, although the use of intelligence tests came under intense attack in the 1960s and such tests became less popular, when it was claimed that test results were being used to discriminate against job applicants and students applying to institutions. Psychometric theories of intelligence have as their central assumption the belief that intelligence is a stable characteristic that can be measured accurately by intelligence tests.

PSYCHOMETRIC THEORIES OF INTELLIGENCE

General intelligence

In the early days of intelligence testing, **intelligence** was something measured by testing for particular purposes, such as educational applications or the recruitment of military personnel. This changed when psychologists such as Charles Spearman were able to analyse correlations between different test results using a statistical technique called **factor analysis**. He came up with the idea of a general factor underlying intelligence that determined how people fared in such tests. Spearman called this the *general factor*, or simply *g*, and by his own research was able to provide compelling evidence that all intelligent behaviour was derived from one 'pool' of mental energy.

Spearman's two-factor theory – Using factor analysis, Spearman (1927) discovered that individuals who do well on one test of intelligence (**IQ test**) tended to also do well on others. Similarly, people who did poorly on one test also did poorly on others. This led Spearman to propose two factors that together could explain why this was the case:

- **Specific abilities (s)** – Individuals performed consistently well (or badly) on specific aspects of intelligence, such as vocabulary and mathematical intelligence, but not on other aspects.
- **General intelligence (g)** – Spearman believed that what explained the positive correlation between different test performances and the specific abilities that make up these tests, was a general intelligence (or *g*), which determined performance on all types of intelligence test.

HIGH *G* AND LOW *G* TASKS

The task shown in **A** below is highly correlated with general intelligence (*g*), as it requires conscious effort to work out that the third pair, unlike the other pairs, is asymmetrical, with the darker part of the shape being on the same side of each figure rather than on opposite sides like the other pairs. The task in **B** is, by way of contrast, a much simpler one, with the solution appearing to 'leap out' without much conscious effort on the part of the reader. Tasks requiring focused problem-solving tend to correlate strongly with *g*, whereas simpler tasks such as **B** below, do not.

▶ Which figure does not belong with the others?

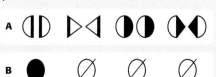

Multifactor theorists

Later theorists also used factor analysis to separate out different aspects of intelligence. Because of their focus on multiple factors in intelligence rather than just one underlying 'general' intelligence, they are known as **multifactor** theorists.

Cattell's Gf–Gc theory – Although Cattell (1943) acknowledged Spearman's work on *g*, he suggested that it actually comprises two distinct components, **crystallised intelligence** and **fluid intelligence**, which represented different aspects of underlying intelligence or *g*.

- **Crystallised intelligence (Gc)** refers to acquired knowledge and skills, such as the factual knowledge that we pick up as a result of our cultural and educational experiences, and which is stored in memory. Our vocabulary, language comprehension and general knowledge would all be aspects of *Gc*.
- **Fluid intelligence (Gf)** refers to reasoning and problem-solving ability. It is our 'on the spot' reasoning ability, a skill not basically dependent on our experience (Belsky, 1990). *Gf* is seen as providing the 'raw material' for the development of *Gc*.
- **The relationship between Gc and Gf** – People with a high capacity for *Gf* tend to acquire *Gc* knowledge at faster rates – a phenomenon referred to as '*investment*'. Cattell's *investment theory* (Cattell, 1987) describes *Gf* as the inborn capacity that, when invested in through education, experience and effort, leads to a greater level of *Gc*.

Thurstone's Primary Mental Abilities (PMA) – Thurstone (1938) disagreed with Spearman, arguing that a single IQ score based on one major underlying factor did not have much value in the assessment of intelligence. He believed that intelligence was made up from a primary group of mental abilities. Each person had their own pattern of strengths and weaknesses, and these could be measured. On the basis of a battery of 57 tests administered to 240 students at the University of Chicago, he was able to identify seven intelligence factors. He referred to these as 'primary abilities', and together they made up each individual's 'intelligence'.

- **Verbal comprehension** – The ability to understand and define words, e.g. when reading a book.
- **Verbal fluency** – The ability to produce words appropriate to a particular context, e.g. when writing an essay.
- **Number** – The ability to solve arithmetic problems, e.g. working out the correct amount of change from a transaction.
- **Spatial ability** – The ability to visualise relationships between objects, e.g. when packing suitcases into a car boot.
- **Memory** – The ability to memorise and recall information, e.g. remembering people's faces and names.
- **Perceptual speed** – The ability to judge similarities and differences between objects, e.g. when proofreading a document looking for errors.
- **Inductive reasoning** – The ability to draws inferences from observations in order to make rules, e.g. being able to complete a number series.

EVALUATION

▶ Ruben Bolling's cartoon nicely demonstrates the logical flaw in research that has found evidence of race differences in IQ scores.

General intelligence

Neurophysiological evidence – Support for the idea of an underlying general intelligence (*g*) comes from Duncan *et al.* (2000) using **PET scans**. Researchers presented participants with tasks that either correlated highly with tests of *g* or did not. They then watched to see which areas of the brain 'lit up'. Regardless of whether the tasks were visual or verbal, tasks associated with general intelligence consistently led to activation of the same areas of the **frontal lobes**, whereas 'non-*g*' tasks did not.

The 'reification' of intelligence – Gould (1981) claims that Spearman committed the logical error of *reification* (i.e. an abstract concept is treated as a concrete 'thing'). Spearman took an abstract correlation and reified it as a 'thing' with a location in the brain. It is then easy to make another logical error, circular reasoning, where the only evidence for an explanation of some phenomenon is the phenomenon itself. In Spearman's case, the only evidence for *g* was the positive correlation between test performances on different tests, even though it was those correlations he was trying to explain in the first place.

Multifactor theorists

Cattell's Gf-Gc theory – Cattell's theory has a number of advantages over theories that advocate one underlying general intelligence – (*g*). Whereas *g* holds constant over many years, crystallised intelligence (*Gc*) tends to rise over the lifespan, and fluid intelligence usually falls (McArdle *et al.*, 2000). Some researchers (e.g. Stankov, 1988) suggest that changes in attentional processes with age (e.g. concentration) play an important part in the age-related changes associated with fluid intelligence. To rely totally on one unchanging general intelligence therefore underestimates the complexity of cognitive changes throughout the lifespan.

The Flynn effect – Flynn (1987) provides evidence that IQ scores have been increasing over the past 50 years. He discovered this effect by analysing changes in test scores over the years. The so-called **Flynn effect** was illustrated for scores on measures of fluid intelligence, but measures of *crystallised intelligence* have been largely ignored. Raven (2000), in addition to documenting the effects observed by Flynn, found much smaller increases in adult vocabulary scores (a measure of crystallised intelligence) from the 1940s to the 1990s, even finding a *decline* in the vocabulary scores of young adults.

Thurstone's theory of intelligence was well supported when tests were given to university undergraduates (who did not differ significantly in terms of their general intelligence). However, when Thurstone administered his tests to an intellectually diverse group of schoolchildren, he failed to find evidence that the seven primary abilities were entirely separate. Instead he found more evidence of *g*, with the children differing not so much in terms of their primary mental abilities, but in terms of their general underlying intelligence. Thurstone managed to resolve these apparently contradictory results with a compromise to his original theory that accounted for the presence of both the seven primary abilities and a general factor.

Application of Thurstone's theory – Thurstone's tests have largely dropped out of use because the initial hope that they would be able to predict academic and occupational performance better than tests of general intelligence was never fulfilled. However, his view of intelligence as a series of differing abilities was shown to have some importance in the selection and classification of pilots, navigators and other aircrew during World War II (Flanagan, 1948).

CULTURAL BIAS IN IQ TESTING

IDA
IQ tests based on the psychometric approach tend to be culturally biased. Robert Yerkes (1921) persuaded the US army to test the intelligence of 1.75 million men using psychometric tests. Literate recruits were given the *Army Alpha Test* (a written examination), whereas illiterates were given the *Army Beta Test*, which was based on pictures. The tests showed that European immigrants fell slightly below white Americans in terms of IQ, and African Americans were at the bottom of the scale with the lowest mental age. However, the European immigrants could not answer some questions on the examination because they were about American food, sports, etc., and the African Americans could not answer the questions because the objects in the test represented a white middle-class American culture. Despite this, Yerkes never came to the conclusion that the poor scores on his tests were a result of the cultural bias of the tests used. Test results such as these have lent scientific credibility to the prevailing prejudice and thereby led to popular stereotypes concerning race and IQ.

CAN YOU...?   No.7.1

...1 Describe **three** psychometric approaches to intelligence in about 100 words each.

...2 Identify **eight** criticisms related to psychometric theories of intelligence, including **at least one** IDA topic. Each criticism should be about 50 words.

...3 Use this material to write a 600-word answer to the question: *Discuss* **two or more** *psychometric theories of intelligence.* (8 marks + 16 marks)

Psychometric theories of intelligence describe how people differ in terms of intelligence, but tell us little about why people vary in terms of their mental abilities. Psychometric theories are more concerned with quantifying these abilities whereas, by contrast, information-processing theories, such as Sternberg's triarchic theory, explore the cognitive processes that underlie intelligent behaviour.

The theory of multiple intelligence was proposed by Howard Gardner in 1983. Gardner claimed that the traditional view of intelligence ignored other 'less traditional' forms of intelligence, such as interpersonal intelligence.

WWW Learn more about MI and assess your own intelligence profile at: http://surfaquarium.com/MI/

THE TRIARCHIC THEORY OF INTELLIGENCE

Sternberg's triarchic theory of intelligence addresses the underlying processes of intelligence *and* the many different forms that intelligence can take (Sternberg, 1988). Sternberg first identified only componential (or analytical) intelligence, but later expanded his theory to include three distinct aspects (or *subtheories*) of intelligence as follows:

Analytical (componential) intelligence is the ability to combine the most appropriate mental mechanisms, or 'components' when applying intelligence to a problem. *Metacomponents* act as the overall executor of intelligent behaviour, in that they recognise and determine the exact nature of a problem, develop strategies to solve it, allocate appropriate resources, and then monitor the success of that strategy. *Performance components* are the cognitive processes that are actually involved in solving a problem, and *knowledge-acquisition components* are used to acquire and learn new material by sifting out relevant from irrelevant information.

Practical (contextual) intelligence is the ability to make a 'considered' response to a problem dependent on the context in which the problem occurs, judging which response is likely to be the most appropriate in that situation. Sternberg believes that intelligent behaviour 'in context' requires three important dimensions – adaptation, shaping and selection. For example, you will have adapted to the demands of A-level psychology by learning what constitutes intelligent behaviour in this context (e.g. writing essays, passing exams, etc.). If you are no good at exams, an intelligent response would be to shape your behaviour in such a way that you improve your exam skills (e.g. by seeking help). Selection involves making the response that is most likely to bring success, for example choosing an exam question you are more likely to be able to answer well.

Creative (experiential) intelligence helps an individual identify when a problem is a new one, requiring intelligent behaviour to solve it. It also helps to identify when they have so much experience of a particular problem that an automatic response is more appropriate.

For example, in an exam you may find a question type that is completely new, but through your previous experience, you are able to construct an intelligent response. This is the *novelty* aspect of experiential intelligence. *Automisation*, on the other hand, refers to the performance of an action that has been carried out many times and can now be achieved with little or no thought.

MULTIPLE INTELLIGENCES (MI)

Gardner believed that many different abilities could count as 'intelligence' if they resolved genuine problems within a particular cultural setting. He believed that each of these intelligences are independent of each other and reside in separate parts of the brain. However, they can and do interact with each other when needed. For example, being able to sing and dance at the same time requires a certain level of both musical and bodily-kinaesthetic intelligence.

Criteria for inclusion as an 'intelligence'

Gardner proposed a number of criteria that he uses to identify whether a specific ability is sufficiently distinct to be regarded as an 'intelligence'. These include the following:

Neuropsychological evidence – Gardner argues that people have multiple intelligences because they have distinct neural modules. Damage to one area of the brain may impair one intellectual skill, while others remain at least partially intact. For example, a brain-damaged musician may have impaired speech, yet retain the ability to play music.

Existence of individuals with exceptional talent in one area (e.g. child prodigies or autistic savants – see left) suggests a distinct form of intelligence. For example, Mozart could write music before he could read, suggesting that the neural systems involved in musical intelligence must be separate from those involved in language processing.

A distinct developmental history – For some skills there is a characteristic developmental history. For example, spoken language develops quickly and to reasonably high levels of competence in most people. By contrast, although most normal individuals can count, few attain an understanding of higher mathematics even after formal schooling.

Research evidence – Research suggests that a person engaged in a crossword puzzle is less able to carry on a conversation effectively, because both tasks demand the attention of linguistic intelligence, which creates interference. Dancing and talking creates less interference, suggesting they rely on different types of underlying intelligence.

GARDNER'S EIGHT INTELLIGENCES

Using these criteria, Gardner (1983) initially identified seven types of intelligence and, in 1999, added an eighth – *natural* intelligence.

1 **Linguistic intelligence** (language skills, such as the ability to learn languages and express oneself).

2 **Logical-mathematical intelligence** (numerical skills, such as the ability to carry out mathematical operations and investigate issues scientifically).

3 **Spatial intelligence** (understanding relationships in space, for example being able to read a map).

4 **Bodily-kinaesthetic intelligence** (using the body, for example using mental abilities to coordinate bodily movements).

5 **Musical intelligence** (skills, such as playing an instrument or composing music). As a young man, Gardner himself was a serious pianist.

6 **Interpersonal intelligence** (understanding and relating to others, for example understanding the intentions and motivations of other people).

7 **Intrapersonal intelligence** (understanding oneself, including an appreciation of feelings, fears and motivations).

8 **Natural intelligence** (showing an expertise in the recognition and classification of the different species of flora and fauna that form the natural environment).

CULTURAL BIAS IN MI

Although Gardner never actually claimed that each of the eight intelligences would be valued equally in different cultures, it is clear from research that some intelligences are valued more highly than others by members of different cultures, resulting in a cultural bias to the theory. Chan (2004) found that mathematical intelligence was most valued among parents and children in Hong Kong, while bodily-kinaesthetic and naturalist intelligences were rated the lowest. The Hong Kong school system, like most Asian school systems, values logic and rote learning to the exclusion of other forms of intelligence. A study by Furnham *et al.* (2005) among Polish adults found that ratings of intrapersonal intelligence predicted ratings of overall intelligence. The conclusion we can draw from this is that, in some cultures, such as Poland, when someone can speak freely and openly about their own feelings, they are considered to be intelligent.

EVALUATION

The triarchic theory

Evidence for Sternberg's triarchic theory – Berg and Sternberg (1985) provided evidence consistent with both the predictions of the triarchic theory *and* the generally acknowledged decline in cognitive abilities associated with ageing. They found that younger adults were superior in most of the metacomponents and performance components associated with intelligence. Older adults had more difficulty defining the problems to be solved, managing their attention to solve those problems and monitoring the effectiveness of any solutions. However, Cunningham and Tomer (1990) suggest that knowledge-acquisition components that are based on experience do not necessarily decline with age, especially if exercised by an older person trying to cope with new situations.

Applications of triarchic theory – Sternberg's theory has been successfully applied to education at both school and university level. For example, Sternberg *et al.* (1999) have shown that teaching 'triarchically' tends to result in significant improvements in academic achievement. Williams *et al.* (2002) assessed the impact of the *Practical Intelligence for School* (PIFS) intervention, in which all three types of intelligence are emphasised. Where PIFS was used as a major part of the curriculum, significant improvements in practical intelligence were obtained.

Criticisms of triarchic theory – Critics of Sternberg's theory, such as Gottfredson (2003), claim that Sternberg has failed to provide sufficient evidence to support his assertion that practical intelligence is distinct from general intelligence (*g*), and his assertion that it equals or exceeds *g* in its ability to predict academic achievement and everyday success. In response to these criticisms Sternberg acknowledges that, as yet, there is no published test of triarchic abilities, and that this is an ongoing theory rather than a completed piece of work (Sternberg, 2004).

Multiple intelligences

Empirical support – To date, there have been very few published studies that offer evidence of the **validity** of multiple intelligences theory. Gardner himself admitted that MI theory has few enthusiasts among those of a traditional psychological background because they require 'psychometric or experimental evidence that allows one to prove the existence of the several intelligences' (Gardner, 2004). Research support is, however, beginning to filter through. For example, Douglas *et al.* (2008) found that, compared to direct instruction, teaching methods that focused on the development of *multiple* intelligences produced significant increases in several areas of importance to a student's academic, social, and emotional wellbeing.

Implications for assessment – Gardner (1993) claimed that the assessment of intelligence should involve the use of multiple measures. Relying on a single **IQ** score from a psychometric test does the individual a disservice and produces insufficient information for those who provide educational interventions. This does not mean that Gardner is against the use of assessment in education, rather that he feels its primary purpose should be to *help* students rather than to classify or rank them. Gardner also believed that assessment should focus on specific types of intelligence: for example, spatial intelligence could be assessed by having an individual navigate themselves through unfamiliar territory.

Positive implications of MI theory – A major strength of this approach to intelligence is that it gives hope to individuals. MI theory outlines a whole set of ways in which any individual might succeed both educationally and in life generally. It does not adhere to narrow traditional views of intelligence but rather assumes that there are many different ways to approach a problem using a variety of intelligences. As a result, if educators accept the possibilities offered by multiple intelligences, children are likely to improve their skills and feel better about themselves in the process.

CULTURAL BIAS IN THE TRIARCHIC THEORY

Researchers must be careful how they define and measure 'intelligence' in different cultures as this may lead to a culturally biased view of intelligence. Sternberg and Grigorenko (2002) tested intelligence in Kenyan children using a test based on the triarchic model of intelligence. Kenyan culture prioritises children's learning, but those children who know a great deal about their indigenous culture (e.g. have a high practical knowledge of medicinal herbs) don't appear to learn well in school and *vice versa*. Therefore, standard tests of intelligence may not accurately assess a Kenyan child's true cognitive abilities. Sternberg claims that we cannot assume that the cognitive skills we value or label as intelligence are those valued or labelled in another culture.

CAN YOU...? (No.7.2)

...1 Describe **two** information-processing theories of intelligence in about 100 words each.

...2 Identify **eight** criticisms related to information processing theories of intelligence, including **at least one** IDA topic. Each criticism should be about 50 words.

...3 Use this material to write a 600-word answer to the question: *Discuss **two or more** information-processing theories of intelligence.* (8 marks + 16 marks)

CLASSICAL CONDITIONING

Classical conditioning was discovered by Russian physiologist Ivan Pavlov in 1927. Pavlov was investigating the salivary reflex in dogs when he noticed that the animals not only salivated when food was placed in their mouths, but also reacted to stimuli that coincided with the presentation of the food, such as the presence of a food bowl or the person who fed them. This chance observation led him to develop the theory of **classical conditioning** (sometimes referred to as Pavlovian conditioning in Pavlov's honour).

CLASSICAL CONDITIONING

BEFORE CONDITIONING

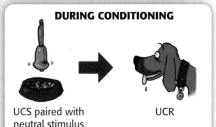

UCS → UCR

Neutral stimulus → No salivation

UCS automatically produces UCR. Neutral stimulus does not produce salivation

DURING CONDITIONING

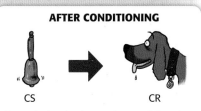

UCS paired with neutral stimulus → UCR

UCS is paired with neutral stimulus. UCS produces UCR.

AFTER CONDITIONING

CS → CR

Neutral stimulus is now the conditioned stimulus. It produces CR, salivation, which is similar to the UCR produced by the food.

CHARACTERISTICS OF CLASSICAL CONDITIONING

The essence of this theory is that all animals are born with a number of natural reflexes (such as salivation when food is placed in the mouth). Reflexes are made up of a stimulus (in our example this would be the food) and its naturally associated response (salivation). By regularly pairing another 'neutral' stimulus (such as a buzzer) with the food, Pavlov discovered that this new stimulus eventually triggered the same response (salivation) even when presented *without* the original stimulus.

Acquisition

In classical conditioning, the researcher selects a naturally occurring reflex and then consistently presents an artificial stimulus (i.e. one that normally does not trigger the reflex) either at the same time as the natural stimulus, or shortly before it. Pavlov used specific terms to describe the different components of this process. The natural stimulus in any reflex is referred to as the *unconditioned stimulus* or UCS (where 'unconditioned' can be considered equivalent to 'unlearned'). The natural response to this stimulus is correspondingly referred to as the *unconditioned response* or UCR. During the acquisition phase of conditioning, the artificial stimulus is referred to as a *neutral stimulus* or NS. Prior to conditioning, the NS does not bring about a reflex response by itself, but after many pairings of the NS and UCS, the situation changes. When the NS is able to produce the same response in the absence of the UCS, it is referred to as a *conditioned stimulus* or CS. At this point, the animal's response when presented with the CS alone is referred to as the *conditioned response* or CR.

Timing

The precise timing of the NS-UCS pairing is important in determining whether the NS will become a reliable CS, leading in turn to a CR. If the NS precedes the UCS, but overlaps with it, then conditioning tends to be strong, as the response elicited by the UCS extends backwards because it becomes associated with the NS. However, the longer the delay between the onset of the NS and the onset of the UCS, the weaker the strength of any conditioning that might develop. If the NS and UCS occur at the same time, conditioning also tends to be weaker, as the NS cannot be used to *predict* the onset of the UCS. If the NS occurs *after* the UCS, conditioning tends to be ineffective, as the UCS has already produced a response which is not dependent on any relationship between NS and UCS.

Extinction and spontaneous recovery

Natural reflexes such as the food-salivation reflex are almost permanent features of the animal's behavioural repertoire, and therefore show little change over the animal's lifetime. However, Pavlov discovered some important differences between the UCR and the CR. Unlike the UCR, he found that the CR does not become permanently established as a response – in fact it does not last very long after the removal of the UCS. In Pavlov's experiment, the dog could be conditioned so that it eventually salivated to the sound of a bell, but this conditioned salivary response rapidly diminished in the absence of the food. This is because the bell no longer *predicts* the coming of food, therefore the association between the two stimuli is no longer a useful one.

Pavlov called this process *extinction*, which is not the same as forgetting. The CR is always liable to reappear if the CS and UCS are paired together once more. This time the link between them is made much more quickly, suggesting that the association is not lost, but merely inhibited. The sudden reappearance of the CR in response to the CS is called *spontaneous recovery*.

Stimulus generalisation and discrimination

Pavlov introduced the term *stimulus generalisation* to describe what happens when a stimulus is presented that is similar to the CS, but not identical to it. For example, if a dog was conditioned to salivate to the sound of a specific bell, it would also salivate to the sound of other bells. The more similar the sound of the new bell to the original bell, the more similar are the responses to this bell and the original bell. Likewise, the more different the new stimulus to the original CS, the weaker the response it produces. In contrast to this, if during the conditioning procedure other similar stimuli are presented *without* being followed by the UCS, then eventually the animal will respond only to the CS, and *not* to other similar stimuli. The animal has learned to discriminate between the CS and similar stimuli – some predict the onset of a UCS, while others do not. Pavlov called this process *stimulus discrimination*.

Would classical conditioning work on cats? Try putting 'Eddie Izzard – Pavlov's cat' in Youtube and find out!

REAL-WORLD APPLICATION: ADVERTISING

Just as Pavlov's dogs learned to associate the sound of a bell with food, humans can be conditioned to associate stimuli, such as advertising messages of quality, fun or 'sexiness', with different products and brands. As in Pavlov's experiments, these stimuli must be paired with the product several times in order to be effective (hence the frequent exposure to particular adverts). So, at the time of writing, we are exposed *ad nauseam* to adverts associating George Clooney with coffee or Keira Knightley with perfume. Advertisers also have to deal with the problem of stimulus generalisation. A particular stimulus may end up driving a consumer to buy a similar product, because the association has generalised to other 'similar' stimuli (e.g. other types of coffee). To deal with this, advertisers may then use stimulus discrimination techniques where they urge consumers not to buy 'cheap imitations' because the results will not be what they expect.

So here's a task for you, the next time you watch the adverts, don't let them wash over you, but try to appreciate the classical conditioning techniques that may be in operation.

EVALUATION

How neutral is the 'neutral stimulus'?

For classical conditioning to occur in the natural environment of an animal rather than in the artificial setting of a laboratory, CS-UCS pairings must be a feature of that environment. For that to be the case, suggests Domjan (2005), the CS *cannot* be unrelated to the UCS. In the natural environment, an arbitrary stimulus such as a bell or buzzer is unlikely to occur prior to a UCS. If it does, it is likely to be coincidental, and there will be many occasions when such a stimulus appears *without* being followed by the UCS. It is unlikely, therefore, that conditioning would occur simply because some totally random stimulus happens to appear prior to a natural reflex. As a result, although CS-UCS associations undoubtedly *do* develop during conditioning, they are likely to reflect physical relationships between the CS and UCS that exist in the natural environment of the animal rather than being a random association between a truly 'neutral' stimulus and a UCS.

Taste aversion learning

The problem of taste aversion – Taste aversion, a type of classical conditioning, challenges the assumptions of this theory because it does not require that the CS and UCS occur closely together in time, nor does it require many repetitions of the NS-UCS association for conditioning to take place. For example, an animal may eat poisoned food and later become ill. After just one experience, and despite a long interval (hours rather than seconds) between the NS (the taste of the food) and the UCS (becoming ill), the animal learns to avoid all foods with that particular taste. This learned association is remarkably resistant to extinction, and persists for a considerable time despite the absence of the UCS.

Why does this challenge Pavlov's theory? – This type of learning challenges Pavlov's theory in three ways. First, the number of times the NS and UCS must appear together. In classical conditioning there must be many associations for conditioning to take place, while in food aversion conditioning, just one association is necessary. Second, the delay between the NS and UCS is critical in classical conditioning. For conditioning to be effective, they should overlap. However, in taste aversion conditioning, timing is less important, and conditioning can still be extremely strong despite several hours between NS and UCS. Third, in classical conditioning, the withdrawal of the UCS means that extinction sets in rapidly, yet in taste-aversion, the time period before extinction sets in is far beyond what we would normally expect. It is possible to explain these discrepancies if we view classical conditioning from an evolutionary perspective (see right).

Is classical conditioning universal?

Different species differ in terms of their motives, their cognitive capacities and, of course, the degree to which their life depends on learning. As a result, we must be cautious about making generalisations from one species to another. The evolutionary perspective (see right) suggests that each species' genetic make-up would place limitations on its learning abilities. This would mean that the principles of classical conditioning cannot be applied in the same way across all species or even all situations. What an animal can learn, therefore, appears to be as much a product of its evolutionary history as its learning opportunities. However, given that the environment is constantly changing, those species that have the capacity to modify their genetically predetermined reflexes have a better chance of survival and reproduction. As a result, we might expect learning through classical conditioning to become widespread across different species, if not universal across all species.

AN EVOLUTIONARY PERSPECTIVE – BIOLOGICAL 'PREPAREDNESS'

Different species face different challenges to survive, so have different capabilities to learn in any given situation. Relationships between the CS and UCS tend to be more difficult to establish for some species than for others. To accommodate this, Seligman (1970) proposed the concept of 'preparedness'.

- Animals are *prepared* to learn associations that are significant in terms of their survival needs, e.g. a dog will readily learn to associate the smell of meat with the presence of food.

- Animals are *unprepared* to learn associations that are not significant in this respect, e.g. a dog will find it harder to associate the sound of a bell with food.

- If learning never occurs, despite many associations between NS and UCS, the animal is said to be *contraprepared* to learn, e.g. no matter how many times you leave a note for the dog saying 'your food is in the fridge,' it is unlikely to respond!

CAN YOU...? No.7.3

...1 Outline, in about 200 words, the main features of classical conditioning.

...2 Identify **eight** criticisms related to classical conditioning, including **at least one** IDA topic. Each criticism should be about 50 words.

...3 Use this material to write a 600-word answer to the question: *Describe and evaluate classical conditioning as an explanation of learning.* (8 marks + 16 marks)

OPERANT CONDITIONING

This approach to learning can be traced back to the work of Edward Thorndike (1911), whose *law of effect* stated that any behaviour that leads to a positive outcome, such as the solution of a problem or a feeling of satisfaction, will tend to be repeated more often in the future. Each time this behaviour is produced in the future (provided it has the same positive effect) the behaviour is reinforced, and then becomes part of the animal's behavioural repertoire. It is this concept of 'reinforcement' that lies at the core of B.F. Skinner's later reworking of Thorndike's law of effect in a theory now known as **operant conditioning**. This describes how an animal *operates* on its environment, and the results of these operations determine the likelihood of a behaviour recurring in the future.

CHARACTERISTICS OF OPERANT CONDITIONING

The basic idea behind Skinner's theory of operant conditioning is that behaviour is spontaneously produced by the organism rather than being elicited by the environment. These spontaneous behaviours (or *operants*), produce reactions in other organisms or in the environment, i.e. they have *consequences*. Whether or not a particular behaviour will appear again is largely due to the nature of these consequences. Some behaviours may become more frequent because they produce desirable consequences, some less frequent because they lead to undesirable consequences.

WILL PRESS LEVER FOR FOOD

Don't be distracted by the words 'positive' and 'negative' in this context. 'Positive' simply means adding something and 'negative' means taking something away. Both positive and negative reinforcement increase the frequency of a behaviour, while both positive and negative punishment decrease it.

Reinforcement

Reinforcement means just what the word implies, i.e. something in the environment (including other organisms) that strengthens or 'reinforces' a behaviour. A reinforcer, therefore, is an environmental consequence that appears as a result of the behaviour and makes it more likely to recur.

Positive reinforcement occurs when behaviour produces a consequence that is satisfying or pleasant for the organism. For example, **primary reinforcers** such as food to a hungry animal or water to a thirsty animal, are so important that any behaviour that leads to their presentation will be reinforced. Other **secondary reinforcers**, such as praise to a child or money to an A-level student acquire their reinforcing qualities because of their association (through **classical conditioning**) with unlearned needs, such as the need for security, the need for status and so on.

Negative reinforcement – Behaviour terminates an aversive (i.e. unpleasant) stimulus. For example, nothing is more annoying first thing in the morning than the invasive ring of an alarm clock, yet hitting the off button restores peace and calm. The act of hitting the off button is thus reinforced and so is more likely to recur whenever we hear the alarm. Negative reinforcers, therefore, strengthen a particular behaviour because they remove an aversive stimulus. The alarm example is an instance of *escape learning*, where an animal acts to escape from the aversive stimulus. However, through the process of classical conditioning, animals may learn to respond to any stimulus that precedes (and therefore predicts) the aversive situation, and thus can avoid it (avoidance conditioning).

Schedules of reinforcement

It would be difficult to praise children every time they were well-behaved. Instead they may be reinforced on a *partial* reinforcement schedule. Intuitively we might expect continuous reinforcement to be more effective. Although this tends to be true during the acquisition phase of a response (presumably because this makes the connection between a behaviour and its consequence clear and predictable), partial reinforcement is usually more effective at maintaining that behaviour. Partial reinforcement schedules include:

- *Fixed-ratio schedules* – An organism receives reinforcement for a fixed proportion of the responses it produces, for example, every third or fifth response.
- *Variable-ratio schedules* – An organism receives reinforcement for a fixed percentage of responses (e.g. 60%), but the number of responses required before each reinforcement is unpredictable. This is the principle of the 'one-arm bandit' machine where the reward percentage might be fixed at a certain level, but the machine may pay out two or more times on the trot, with a long gap before the next payout.
- *Fixed-interval schedules* – An organism is reinforced after a fixed period of time (e.g. every 10 minutes), provided it performs the behaviour at some point during that interval.
- *Variable-interval schedules* – reinforcement is delivered on average at certain time intervals (e.g. four per hour, but not necessarily at 15-minute intervals), and as with variable ratio schedules, the organism cannot predict when that might be.

Punishment

Reinforcement *increases* the likelihood of a behaviour recurring, whereas punishment *decreases* it. As with reinforcement, punishment can be either positive or negative. In this context, positive means adding something, and negative means taking away. Thus a *positive* punishment may involve spanking a naughty child or locking up a criminal, whereas *negative* punishment involves taking away something the individual finds pleasant, such as confiscating a child's mobile phone for using it in class, or 'grounding' a teenager because of a poor report from school. A longitudinal study of Australian children found that outgoing children were more likely to develop behavioural problems if their parents used high levels of punishment, and were more likely to be well-adjusted if parents used positive reinforcement to channel their exuberance (Hemphill and Sanson, 2001).

provided, of course, he remains hungry, otherwise food would no longer be a reinforcer. If the food pellets stop, the rat presses the lever a few more times, and then abandons it (*extinction*). Skinner also found that by sending a small electric shock through the floor of the cage, he could terminate the bar-pressing behaviour by *punishment* (see right).

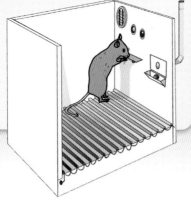

EVALUATION

Instinctive drift

The effectiveness of operant conditioning is limited by the characteristics of the species being conditioned. Some behaviours are more easily learned by some species than by others. Breland and Breland (1951) used operant conditioning techniques to train many different types of animals to perform 'tricks' for reward. However, despite initial success, in some species the conditioned behaviour could not be maintained. In one case, they trained pigs to pick up large wooden coins in their mouth and deposit them in a 'piggy bank'. For doing this the pigs received a reward of food. However, after a few months of performing this trick for food, the pigs appeared to lose interest, preferring instead to push the coin along with their snout, throw it up in the air, then push it along the ground again. The Brelands believed that even after conditioning, behaviours drift back towards instinct after a time. Pigs usually engage in 'rooting' behaviour where they unearth their food from the ground by pushing it with their snouts, and this was the behaviour they were now associating with food.

Problems with punishment

Because reinforcement cannot, by itself, eliminate undesirable behaviours, punishment has become commonplace in our society. However, it is frequently used in ways that render it ineffective.

The person not the action – The individual may come to fear the person doing the punishing rather than the action that led to the punishment. For example, a person punished for 'mucking about' during lessons may avoid that teacher in future rather than changing their ways.

Physical punishment leads to physical aggression – If children are punished physically, they may learn that problems can be solved with violence, which legitimises it, and makes *them* more likely to use violence in their own lives. Research by Dodge *et al.* (1997) supports this claim. They found that the more physical punishment parents use, the more aggressively their children behave at home and at school.

Angry punishment – People tend to use punishment more when they are angry. Therefore, if punishment depends more on mood than the type of behaviour parents want to discourage, children may find it difficult to learn what behaviour is being punished, and under what circumstances it is being punished.

Behaviour modification

The power of operant conditioning has been demonstrated in **behaviour modification** (replacing undesirable with desirable behaviours) techniques. For example, operant conditioning techniques have been used to help people avoid obesity, give up smoking and engage in healthier lifestyles. The 'toilet training in a day' method pioneered by Azrin and Foxx (1974) makes use of operant conditioning techniques to achieve toilet training in difficult-to-train children – positive reinforcement is provided at every instance of correct toileting skills. A **meta-analysis** of 34 studies comparing the Azrin and Foxx method with conventional methods of toilet training found the use of operant conditioning techniques particularly effective for children with learning difficulties (Kiddoo, 2006).

Evaluation
CROSS-CULTURAL DIFFERENCES
Research suggests that cultures vary considerably in their reliance on the use of operant conditioning strategies. Westen *et al.* (2006) suggest that this, in part, reflects the dangers that confront a particular society. For example, the Gusii of Kenya have a history of tribal warfare, and additionally face constant threats from wild animals. Gusii parents rely more on punishment and fear than rewards to shape the behaviour of their children. Caning (positive punishment) and withdrawing food and shelter (negative punishment) are common ways of bringing about compliance in such a dangerous environment.

IDA
THE ILLUSION OF FREE WILL
Being able to decide between different courses of action may suggest to individuals that they have free will. However, Skinner believed that all behaviour was the result of either positive or negative reinforcement, and therefore the existence of free will was merely an illusion. What we may think of as behaviours chosen by free will, suggests Skinner, are really behaviours chosen by external influences within our culture. He argued that we are all controlled by the world in which we live, and so free will is not as important as our ability to withstand the control that we are under.

Evaluation
SKINNER AND THE EXPERIMENTAL METHOD
The experimental psychologist carries out tests under controlled conditions in an attempt to discover a causal relationship between two or more variables. Skinner's reliance on the experimental method, exemplified by the Skinner box, was a good example of the experimental method in practice. By manipulating the consequences of behaviour (the **independent variable**), he was able to accurately measure the effects on the rat's (or pigeon's) behaviour, thus allowing him to establish a cause and effect relationship between the consequences of a behaviour and its future frequency of occurrence.

IDA
THE USE OF NON-HUMAN ANIMALS
Animal research has been the major contributor to our knowledge of basic learning processes. However, Skinner's reliance on rats and pigeons for his experiments has led some critics to suggest that such studies can neither confirm nor refute hypotheses about *human* behaviour. They can, at best, only suggest new hypotheses that might be relevant to humans.

CAN YOU...? No.7.4

...**1** Outline, in 200 words, the main features of operant conditioning.

...**2** Identify **eight** criticisms related to operant conditioning, including **at least one** IDA topic. Each criticism should be about 50 words.

...**3** Use this material to write a 600-word answer to the question: *Describe and evaluate operant conditioning as an explanation of learning.* (8 marks + 16 marks)

CONDITIONING AND THE BEHAVIOUR OF ANIMALS

The ability to modify behaviour in the light of environmental changes is clearly a sign of intelligence, and gives animals a selective advantage over those with more fixed repertoires. Although much of the research on **classical conditioning** and **operant conditioning** has been carried out in laboratories, its principles also apply to the behaviour of animals in the natural environment.

CLASSICAL CONDITIONING

Training animals for release

Several situations necessitate training wild animals held in captivity prior to release. These include the study of animals for research (e.g. dolphins) as well as the hand-rearing of orphaned animals (e.g. otters). In each of these cases, there is the problem that the animals become dependent on humans, e.g. learning that feeding is associated with human presence.

Simple conditioning – Among captive dolphins, feeding patterns mean that food and eating almost always occur when in the presence of humans, and rarely in their absence. In simple classical conditioning terms, food can be considered a **UCS (unconditioned stimulus)**, and because human presence predicts the coming of food, this becomes a **CS (conditioned stimulus)**. This suggests that dolphins would consequently learn a strong association between humans and food reward, something that may well put them in danger when back in the wild.

Compound conditioning – The problem of inappropriate conditioning in wild animals can be overcome by using a simple classical conditioning model combined with a compound CS. If human presence is combined with a more appropriate stimulus (such as an auditory signal), then together they form a compound stimulus, where one part of the stimulus (in this case the auditory signal) overshadows the other (human presence – see top right). Overshadowing occurs when one stimulus interferes with a potential learned association with another stimulus. For captive dolphins, humans are a less reliable predictor of food (e.g. they frequently appear *without* food) but auditory signals *always* predict the coming of food, thus are more likely to become a learned CS. Kleiman (1989) described how field assistants carried backpacks containing food, which they distributed in the habitat of golden lion tamarins. The tamarins eventually learned to associate the sound of the backpack zippers with food, but not with the humans themselves. The sound of an opening backpack zipper was a more reliable predictor of the coming of food, and therefore overshadowed the association of food with human presence.

Reproductive success

Researchers have long explored *how* the conditioned response has developed, but not really *why* it develops. From an evolutionary perspective, the primary task of any organism is to pass on its genes to subsequent generations. If classical conditioning evolved because it increases **reproductive fitness**, we should find that males exposed to a conditioned stimulus (CS) prior to mating, sire more offspring than males not exposed to a CS. The Matthews *et al.* study (left) explores this possibility. If males receiving a CS prior to mating *are* more successful (in terms of number of offspring they leave behind), then this suggests that an advantage of the CS is that it functions to predict potential mating opportunities, and therefore increases an animal's reproductive success.

MATING SUCCESS

Matthews *et al.* (2007) provided support for the importance of classical conditioning in mating. They placed male quail in one of two distinctive chambers. One chamber signalled access to a receptive female (i.e. it acted as a CS), whereas the other did not (i.e. it remained as a neutral stimulus). In the test trials, each female mated with two males in succession, but for only one of each pair had the pre-mating chamber (CS) been previously associated with the UCS (mating). They found that 72% of the eggs laid by the females had been fertilised by the males who had received the CS signal prior to mating.

▶ Male (left) and female (right) quail

PRT TECHNIQUES

Desensitisation By pairing positive rewards with any object or event that causes fear, the fearful entity gradually becomes less frightening and less stressful.

Cooperative feeding PRT can reduce aggression and increase affiliative behaviours among socially housed animals by reinforcing dominant animals (for allowing subordinates to feed or receive attention) and subordinates for being 'brave' enough to accept food and attention in the presence of dominant animals.

OPERANT CONDITIONING

Positive reinforcement training (PRT)

The Animal Welfare Act of 2006 dictates that all the welfare needs of animals used in research must be met. These include the need to protect against pain and suffering and to allow animals the opportunity to exhibit normal behaviour patterns. Following the success of *positive reinforcement training (PRT)* to teach dolphins and other marine mammals to perform numerous 'tricks' at parks such as Sea World in Florida, there has been increased interest in the use of PRT to enhance the care and wellbeing of animals used in research. Training laboratory animals to cooperate voluntarily in veterinary and research procedures makes these events less stressful and less frightening for the animals, and training can enhance animal welfare by providing animals with the opportunity to work for food and even achieve greater control over daily events in their environment. All of these events have been associated with enhanced psychological wellbeing (Laule *et al.*, 2003). Some PRT techniques are detailed in the box on the left.

Foraging

Animals are subject to the principles of operant conditioning as they forage in their environment. For example, woodpeckers must find insects to eat. They find these by pecking holes in trees with their beaks. If a woodpecker finds a tree that offers an abundant supply of insects, then its behaviour (i.e. pecking at that particular tree) is *reinforced* and so the woodpecker is likely to return to that tree time and time again. When the supply of insects from that tree is exhausted, the pecking response is gradually extinguished and the woodpecker looks elsewhere. Food patches in an animal's habitat vary in quality, therefore when the quality drops below a certain marginal level (in terms of its reinforcement value), the animal gives up on that patch and searches for a better one.

► **Compound conditioning** – Training methods for minimising associations between humans and food present humans as part of a compound stimulus with other stimuli and so reduce the association between humans and food. The association is further minimised if humans are also present when no food is given.

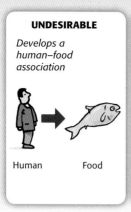 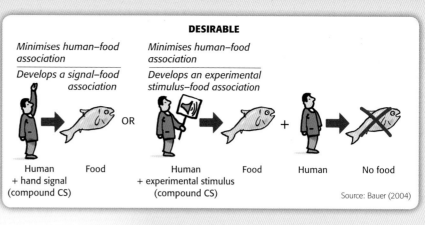

Source: Bauer (2004)

EVALUATION

Training animals for release

Contact with humans – Although training using compound stimuli (as demonstrated above) may be desirable in animals that will eventually be released back into the natural environment, it would be difficult, and even undesirable, to totally isolate many species from humans. Goldblatt (1993), in a review of research literature on captive animal stress, concluded that understimulating environments were more likely to be associated with stress responses in a wide range of animals, including marine mammals.

The necessity of training – Bauer (2004) suggests that as long as animals are going to be in captivity (for whatever reason), interacting with humans, it is beneficial to find out as much as we can about them, in an attempt to protect both them and their environment. To accomplish this requires behavioural training. However, a critical objective in caring for animals in captivity is to ensure that they do not learn responses that they will transfer to the wild and that will endanger them.

Reproductive success

For classical conditioning to be an **adaptive** trait, it must occur under natural circumstances, in other words the CS-UCS pairings that are necessary for classical conditioning occur together regularly in the natural environment. However, an arbitrary CS (such as that used in the Matthews *et al.* study opposite) may coincide with a UCS under natural circumstances only occasionally if at all. Such accidental pairings are bound to be rare (Domjan, 2005). In addition, an accidental pairing is likely to be preceded or followed by many occasions where that CS is *not* accompanied by the UCS in question, which would undermine any learned association.

EVALUATION

Positive reinforcement training

In groups of captive chimpanzees, some dominant animals routinely chase more subordinate animals and steal their food. This creates many problems, including dominant animals that become overweight, and subordinate animals who may not receive proper nutrition. Bloomsmith *et al.* (1994) used PRT to train dominant chimpanzees not to chase and steal subordinates' food by reinforcing them for sitting in one spot during feeding, a behaviour incompatible with chasing and stealing. This had the desired effect of decreasing aggression from dominants and submission from subordinates to levels equivalent to non-feeding periods. The Clay *et al.* study (see right) demonstrates how desensitisation can reduce fear responses to human handlers.

Foraging

Research supports the importance of operant conditioning in foraging strategies among non-human animals. Agetsuma (1999) manipulated the quality of food patches in the environment of Japanese monkeys by making the probability of reinforcement higher in one condition (representing a high-quality food patch) than the other (representing a lower quality patch). Consistent with prediction, subsequent responses were much higher in the high-quality patch.

IDA **ETHICAL ISSUES IN ANIMAL RESEARCH**

The use of conditioning techniques in the training of non-human animals may both create and alleviate problems faced by the animals who participate in scientific research. For animals that are eventually released into the wild, reliance on human beings for food may create learned patterns of behaviour that prevent their subsequent post-release adjustment. The use of compound conditioning procedures may go some way to preventing this.

The use of PRT techniques has alleviated many of the stressors associated with research participation, and has both satisfied the requirements of the Animal Welfare Act *and* acknowledged the often unique needs of different species used in research.

DESENSITISATION AS PRT

Clay *et al.* (2009) provided support for the effectiveness of desensitisation as a PRT. They randomly allocated male rhesus macaques to either a desensitisation training group or a control group. Over six weeks of training, macaques in the desensitisation group received a total of 125 minutes of positive reinforcement whenever they were in the laboratory environment. The macaques in the control group were simply exposed to the same environment without accompanying reinforcement. Macaques in the desensitisation group showed a significant reduction in both the rate and duration of fearful cringing behaviour shown toward humans compared to the control group, following training. Results of this study support the claim that PRT training can enhance the welfare of captive animals.

CAN YOU...? **No.7.5**

...1 Describe **two** ways in which classical conditioning and **two** ways in which operant conditioning are involved in the behaviour of animals. Each 'way' should be about 50 words.

...2 Identify **eight** criticisms related to the role of classical conditioning, including **at least one** IDA topic. Each criticism should be about 50 words.

...3 Use this material to write a 600-word answer to the question: *Discuss the role of classical and/or operant conditioning in the behaviour of non-human animals.* (8 marks + 16 marks)

INTELLIGENCE IN NON-HUMAN ANIMALS

The **intelligence** of animals is a difficult concept to quantify. We all have anecdotal stories of smart pets and the amazing skills of wild animals, but does this constitute *intelligence*? Most species are able to learn by simple conditioning, and are therefore able to adapt their behaviour as a result of experience. This constitutes a basic form of intelligence. Alternatively we can think of intelligence as the ability to think flexibly to solve problems. An example of this approach is the idea of 'social' intelligence, which is an adaptation to the complexities of *social* life rather than practical problems, such as finding food. On this spread we examine an example of this, the 'Machiavellian intelligence' hypothesis, and another ability requiring advanced cognitive abilities, notably self-recognition.

WHO'S A PRETTY ELEPHANT THEN?

Recent research by Plotnik *et al.* (2006) suggests that elephants are also able to recognise themselves in a mirror, and even use their reflections to explore hidden parts of themselves. The test required the construction of a large mirror at the Bronx Zoo in New York. Although the provision of mirrors for zoo animals is not new, most animals act as though the reflection they see is another animal. They seem incapable of learning that *their* behaviour is the source of what they see in the mirror.

In the experiments with the three Bronx Zoo Asian elephants, the animals first explored the mirror, reaching behind it and even trying to get into it, gathering clues that what they were seeing was an image, not another elephant. This realisation was followed by the animal making slow rhythmic movements which they watched being mimicked in the mirror. All three elephants used the mirror to look inside their mouths, and one female, Maxine, even used her trunk to pull her ear closer to the mirror so she could get a good look at it. Another female, Happy, passed the most difficult test of self-recognition, the **mark test** (developmental psychologists call this the rouge test – see page 154). The researchers painted a large white cross on the side of her head, visible only in the mirror. She stood in front of the mirror and repeatedly touched the mark, not the mirror, a clear indication that she realised that the image she saw in the mirror was indeed her own.

ANIMAL INTELLIGENCE

Machiavellian intelligence

Intelligence may be an adaptation to social problem-solving in large groups. Individual animals able to manipulate others in their social group without causing aggression would be at an advantage, and this ability could be passed on to their offspring, thus becoming widespread. Whiten and Byrne (1988) refer to this as **Machiavellian intelligence** (after a novel called *The Prince* by Niccolò Machiavelli, which tells the story of an Italian courtesan who schemed his way to power).

Manipulation and deception – Among social-living animals, individuals can use behavioural tactics to manipulate those who are not allies into unwitting help. The ability to understand and plan deception appears to be restricted to the great apes, although other primates seem to be able to learn such tactics by watching. Manipulative tricks include the management of attention, in which the target's attention is diverted towards or away from something to profit the agent of deception (the animal doing the deceiving), and 'creating an image', in which deception serves to change how other animals view that individual (see facing page).

Forming alliances – Power in complex social groups is often determined more by having the right allies than by physical strength. Harcourt (1992) suggests that although other animals form alliances, only the catarrhine primates (such as baboons, apes and humans) cultivate alliances based on an individual's ability to provide useful help in the future. Among rhesus macaques, males form alliances with more powerful individuals, and females act in Machiavellian ways when it comes to reproduction: by having sex with the dominant alpha male, they increase the chance that he will later protect the newborn infants.

Self-recognition

The ability for animals to recognise themselves in a mirror is usually accepted as indicating a form of intelligence. Human babies are able to do this by the time they are two years old (see page 152), as are adult chimpanzees, bonobos and orangutans. **Monkeys**, on the other hand, a more distant relative of human beings, never appear to catch on. The only other non-ape species to possess this skill are bottle-nosed dolphins, killer whales and possibly elephants (see left).

Research into self-recognition

- **Chimpanzees** – Gallup (1970) discovered that chimpanzees may also be able to recognise themselves in a mirror. After becoming accustomed to the mirrors, the chimpanzees were anaesthetised, and a red mark placed on their foreheads and ears. After recovering from the anaesthetic, none of the animals showed any interest in the marks until seeing their reflections in the mirror. This caused them to touch the marks on their faces, using the mirror to direct their responses.
- **Dolphins** – To test for dolphin self-recognition, Reiss and Marino (2001) exposed two bottlenose dolphins to reflective surfaces after marking them with black ink, a water-filled marker (sham-marking) or not marking them at all. The dolphins appeared to recognise their reflections, and spent more time in front of the mirror when marked, even selecting the best reflective surface in which to view their markings.
- **Killer whales** – A similar study with killer whales, using a mirror and the mark test, has also suggested that killer whales and false killer whales, like dolphins, appear to possess the cognitive abilities necessary for self-recognition (Delfour and Marten, 2001).

Why do some species have self-recognition? – It is possible that self-recognition may result from large brains and advanced cognitive ability, rather than being a by-product of primate-specific factors. Dolphins and primates differ a great deal in their brain organisation and evolutionary histories, but both exhibit this unusual ability, suggesting a form of cognitive convergence between the two species that can be attributed to the development of large, highly developed brains (Reiss and Marino, 2001).

Machievellian intelligence in action. The agent of the deception (A) grooms the dominant animal (T) in order to snatch a prized food resource.

EVALUATION

Machiavellian intelligence

Agonistic buffering – Support for the existence of Machiavellian intelligence among primates comes from studies of agonistic buffering. This was first described by Deag and Crook (1971) in their study of Barbary macaques. They found that an infant monkey was frequently 'used' by males in social interactions with other individuals, usually males. Their interpretation of this phenomenon was that subordinate males carry an infant when approaching a higher-ranking male to reduce the likelihood of being attacked. More recently, Casanova *et al.* (2008) have found evidence of agonistic buffering in a colony of captive chimpanzees. They found that the whole colony supported an individual with an infant who had previously been the subject of aggression from the dominant alpha male.

Not restricted to primates – The idea that intelligence and social complexity are linked dates back to Charles Darwin (1871). Since then, research has suggested a central role for the cerebral cortex, particularly the neocortex (see right) in the rise of social or 'Machiavellian' intelligence in primates. However, Burish *et al.* (2004) have also provided evidence that this relationship is not restricted to primates, but may also be found in birds, where the degree of social complexity correlates strongly with the relative size of a specific area of the brain, the telencephalon, which in birds is equivalent to the cortex in primates.

Implications of 'social' intelligence – An important consequence of social intelligence (such as Machiavellian intelligence) is that a more highly developed social intellect in some individuals will exert selection pressures on others, so that over evolutionary time, there will be an 'arms race' of social intelligence within a particular species.

Self-recognition

Self-recognition in elephants – It is possible that during Reiss *et al.*'s study of the mark test in elephants (see far left), subjects might have touched the cross merely because they could feel the mark on their skin, rather than see it in the mirror. To control for this possibility, researchers also placed a transparent mark on the elephant's cheek, which could not be seen in the mirror. Although Happy touched the white mark during the mirror test, during the 'sham mark' control, she did not touch the mark despite the fact it would have felt the same on her skin.

Lack of research support – The view that animals other than humans might possess powers of self-recognition is not shared by all researchers. Heyes (1998) argues that there is little reliable evidence that this ability is present in all primate species. In particular, evidence that primates such as chimpanzees are able to use a mirror to explore their own bodies is unconvincing, and does not, according to Heyes, indicate the possession of a self-concept or any other aspect of self-recognition that might be equivalent to the cognitive abilities of human beings.

Implications of self-recognition research – The rarity of self-recognition among non-human species, coupled with the fact that it is more common among animals reported as helping other animals in need (e.g. elephants and dolphins) suggests that self-recognition is an indication of a certain level of consciousness in these species. This in turn emphasises the need to protect species such as the Asian elephant, which is currently endangered due to hunting and habitat destruction.

CAN YOU...? No.7.6

...1 Describe findings from research studies about **two** types of animal intelligence, in abou 100 words each.

...2 Identify **eight** criticisms related to intelligence in non-human animals, including **at least one** IDA topic. Each criticism should be about 50 words.

...3 Use this material to write a 600-word answer to the question: *Discuss evidence for intelligence in non-human animals.* (8 marks + 16 marks)

Why did humans need to become so intelligent – what were the evolutionary pressures that prompted the evolution of intelligence in humans and the other great apes? Humans, like other primates, have faced the demands of living in complex social groups, but most explanations have focused on the demands of dealing with the *physical* environment, such as those related to finding sufficient food. Dealing with environmental and social complexity also requires an efficient memory system, which requires a large brain, so we might also expect that large brain size is linked to a more highly developed intelligence.

THE WASON PROBLEM

'If a card has a vowel on one side, then it has an even number on the other'.

Which of the cards above must you turn over to test this statement?

This apparently simple task usually produces the wrong solution, as only the E and the 7 need be turned over to disconfirm the relationship. However, if these are replaced by cards with Beer, Coke, 19 and 16, and the question is…

'If a person is drinking alcohol, then they must be over 18 years of age',

…then most people get it right. Cosmides (1989) offers an explanation: In social groups, our ancestors must have evolved a 'cheat detection' mechanism which enabled them (and us) to recognise those who take the benefits of social membership, yet defect on its rules.

EVOLUTIONARY FACTORS IN INTELLIGENCE

The central idea of an evolutionary explanation is that heritable characteristics (such as intelligence) are changeable rather than fixed, and that change is likely to be caused either by **natural selection** (i.e. individuals adapt to the changing demands of their environment – those that are best adapted survive and reproduce) or **sexual selection** (individuals compete for access to mates – those that are successful leave behind more offspring). The measure of evolutionary success is **reproductive fitness** – i.e. an individual's reproductive outcomes (usually number of offspring) relative to other individuals in the group.

Ecological demands

Finding food – Dunbar (1992) suggests that intelligence evolved because of an increased cognitive demand on *frugivores* (fruit eaters) to monitor a food supply that was available only at certain times and in certain places. Frugivores must remember the location of their food supply, evaluate ripeness, develop a harvesting plan and decide how they will survive in the interim. *Foliovores* (leaf-eaters) on the other hand, have much smaller home ranges and can therefore monitor food availability more easily. As a result, there is less pressure for the development of complex cognitive abilities among this group. Early **hominids** fit into the frugivore category, as do modern chimpanzees.

Extracting food: tool use – Mercader *et al.* (2002) studied chimpanzees in a remote West African rainforest, where they used stones and branches as hammers to crack open nuts when foraging. Mercader *et al.* claimed that many of the stone by-products of chimpanzee nut cracking are similar to those found in early human archaeological sites in East Africa. Some of the most successful human hunter–gatherers, such as the !Kung San, use highly elaborate tools, whereas less successful groups, such as the Tasmanian Aborigines, used only very simple tools. Tool use is thus an indication of intelligence in both human and non-human species, as, by using tools, individuals can solve many of the problems they face when trying to extract food.

Social complexity

Humphrey (1976) argues that social objects (members of the same species) offer a different form of complexity from the physical environment. Individuals who best deal with these demands would be more successful at increasing their reproductive fitness.

Machiavellian intelligence – The concept of **Machiavellian Intelligence** (Whiten and Byrne, 1988) suggests that the evolution of human intellect was primarily driven by selection for social expertise within groups where the most challenging problem faced by early humans was dealing with their companions. An example of such an adaptation can be seen in the 'search for cheats' explanation of the Wason problem (see left).

The meat-sharing hypothesis – For our ancestors in the **EEA**, meat was an important source of saturated fat, which was vital for survival. Stanford (1999) believes that strategic sharing of meat paved the way for human intelligence. Meat could be used to forge alliances and persuade females to mate, particularly as males did most of the hunting. Stanford believes that strategic meat-sharing required considerable cognitive abilities, as males had to recognise individuals and keep a 'running score' of debts and credits.

Brain size and intelligence

MRI measures of brain size – Broman *et al.* (1987) showed that head perimeter at birth and at age seven significantly predicted later IQ. The development of sophisticated brain scanning techniques such as **MRI** has allowed researchers to estimate brain size more directly. A number of studies (e.g. Andreasen *et al.*, 1993) have found significant correlations of around 0.40 between brain size and IQ using this method.

Evolutionary factors in the development of large brains – Some of the pressure to develop large brains would have arisen from the primate life style that required early humans to forage and hunt animals, but there are other explanations.

- Innovation, social learning and tool use – Reader and Laland (2002) searched the major primate journals for evidence of innovation (displaying novel solutions to environmental or social problems), social learning (acquisition of information from others) and tool use. This provided a measure of the behavioural flexibility of a species and therefore an ecologically valid measure of intelligence. They found that the frequency of all three was significantly correlated with brain size in 116 primate species.

- Sexual selection – Miller (1998) suggests that large brains evolved in humans because they enhanced reproductive success. Intelligence, therefore, is attractive to members of the opposite sex. This explains why people so often place intelligence high on the list of characteristics they seek in a partner, why men have larger brains (men compete to be selected) and why the human brain has trebled in size in a relatively short period of time (because it directly affects reproductive success).

EVALUATION

Ecological demands

Foraging versus social theories of intelligence – Dunbar (1992) compared environmental *and* social complexity with **neocortex** volume. Although he found a significant positive relationship between social complexity and neocortex volume, the same was not true for environmental complexity (e.g. area of home range and reliance on fruit and grains) and neocortex volume. This seems to uphold a social rather than ecological origin of primate intelligence. Group size alone, however, cannot explain why apes are more intelligent than monkeys (Byrne, 1995), as both live in groups of similar size and complexity. Byrne suggests that environmental challenges may be more significant to apes than they are to monkeys, leading to higher intelligence.

Intelligence comes at a cost – As early humans moved from plant-eating to fruit- and meat-eating, this led to significant improvements in brain size and function. However, this came at a cost, with a significant increase in the incidence of what we would now call **schizophrenic** behaviours. Horrobin (1998) suggests that these dietary changes led to biochemical differences which improved neural connectivity and thereby led to creative intelligence, but also produced a number of disordered behaviour patterns, such as paranoia (a symptom of some types of schizophrenia). These were kept in check by a diet rich in essential fatty acids but, Horrobin claims, because they are largely absent in the modern diet, the incidence of disorders like schizophrenia has become more common.

Social complexity

Meat sharing – Studies of human societies confirm the 'meat for sex' hypothesis. Hill and Kaplan (1988) found that among the men of the Ache people of Paraguay, plant food and insect grubs are not shared outside the immediate family, although meat is. Skilled hunters are often rewarded not only with the majority of the hunting spoils, but also with disproportionate sexual favours from women, who frequently directly exchange sex for meat. However, Wrangham (1975) suggests that a simpler explanation might suffice. Males must expend considerable energy defending a kill from others or chasing scavengers. By sharing with others, they can eat without interruption.

Machiavellian intelligence – Mitani and Watts (2001) provide support for the importance of alliances (a key aspect of Machiavellian intelligence) *and* the role of meat sharing among primates. They found that male chimpanzees in Uganda shared meat with each other more than with any females. This was important in forging alliances because hunting was more successful when done in groups. So, it may be 'meat for alliance' rather than 'meat for sex' that explains the significance of meat sharing.

Brain size and intelligence

Problems associated with large brain size – If large brains gave early humans a significant advantage when it came to finding food and dealing with the complexity of social living, then we might ask why all species don't have large brains. However, animals with such large brains (relative to body size) are comparatively rare, probably because of the costs associated with large increases in brain size. A large brain is extremely demanding in terms of energy, and must compete with other body organs for resources. A large brain takes a long time to mature, which means that infants are heavily dependent on their parents for much longer, which in turn limits the rate at which they can reproduce. We might therefore expect that there would have been selective pressure *against* the development of large brains.

We are not alone – Despite the costs associated with large brains, progressively larger brains have evolved in all primates, not just in humans. Reader and Laland's research challenges the belief that large brains arose in human beings because of the unique problems faced during human evolution. They argue that specific human accomplishments, such as the development of language, may have played a smaller role in the evolution of our large human brains than was previously thought, as other primates have brains of a similar relative size, yet lack this uniquely human characteristic.

IDA CULTURAL BIAS

Explanations that focus on the relationship between brain size and intelligence without taking account of cultural factors may be culturally biased. Beals *et al.* (1984) analysed over 20,000 skulls from around the world, and concluded that there are significant differences in cranial volume between East Asians (1,415 cm³), Europeans (1,362 cm³) and Africans (1,268 cm³). Rushton (1995) has suggested an evolutionary explanation for these differences – the **'out-of-Africa' hypothesis**. He argued that as early humans left the EEA, they encountered more cognitively demanding problems, such as finding food and surviving the harsh winters. In addition, among East Asians, for example, intelligence is culturally valued, a fact that by itself could explain why East Asians tend to score higher in IQ tests than other cultural groups.

IDA GENDER BIAS

The assumption that large brains = higher intelligence may reflect a gender bias in our understanding of this relationship. Ankney (1992) examined autopsy data on 1261 American men and women, discovering that the brains of men were heavier than those of women, regardless of ethnic or cultural origin. However, such findings cannot account for the fact that women have the same IQ scores as men (Peters, 1993). Although male brains are larger, female brains may be better organised. Johnson *et al.* (1996) report that females have a larger *corpus callosum* (the bundle of nerve fibres that connect the two brain hemispheres), which would lead to improved communication between the hemispheres.

▶ Research suggests that brain organisation may be more important than brain size. Research that focuses solely on the latter may, therefore, be gender biased.

CAN YOU...? No.7.7

...1 Describe **two** factors that are important in the evolution of human intelligence in about 100 words each.

...2 Identify **eight** criticisms related to evolutioinary factors in human intelligence, including **at least one** IDA topic. Each criticism should be about 50 words.

...3 Use this material to write a 600-word answer to the question: *Discuss the role of evolutionary factors in human intelligence.* (8 marks + 16 marks)

GENETIC FACTORS IN INTELLIGENCE-TEST PERFORMANCE

Nowhere has the **nature** versus **nurture** argument been more keenly fought than in the study of **intelligence**. The notion that intelligence could be genetically influenced to any great extent goes against the fundamental belief that we are all born equal. However, as we have already seen, human intelligence has been inexorably shaped by both natural and sexual selection, so it makes sense that we should find a major role for genetics in the development of this trait. Although there are cultural differences in what might be described as 'intelligent behaviour', in the West, intelligence is commonly equated to performance on intelligence tests, which gives an individual an intelligence quotient (or **IQ**) score. In this section, intelligence and IQ are therefore used interchangeably.

THE HERITABILITY OF INTELLIGENCE

In explaining the origins of intelligence, there are only two dimensions that determine intelligence-test performance. The first is genetics (i.e. characteristics inherited from parents) and the second is environment (e.g. family background, educational experiences, etc.). These two components will always add up to 100% of the variation in intelligence scores between two people. Hence if researchers calculate that the genetic part is 40%, then that would mean 60% could be attributed to the environment. The extent to which a particular characteristic (such as eye colour, temperament or intelligence) is passed from parents to children purely by means of their genes is known as **genetic heritability**. Traditionally, psychologists have used studies of twins and adoption studies to assess the relative contributions of genetics and environment in intelligence-test performance, i.e. to a person's IQ.

Twin and adoption studies

Twin studies – There are two types of twin. Non-identical **dizygotic (DZ)** twins share 50% of their genes, and are therefore genetically related by 0.5. **Monozygotic (MZ)** twins are genetically identical, and therefore have a degree of genetic relatedness of 1.0. It follows, therefore, that if genetic factors are important in intelligence, MZ twins should be more alike than DZ twins. It is difficult to disentangle the relative influences of genes and environment when twins are reared together. However, the real indication of the importance of genetic factors in intelligence comes from studies that have assessed the degree of similarity in twins reared *apart*, i.e. in situations where for one reason or another, twins have been separated at birth and brought up in entirely different environments. Research (e.g. Bouchard and McGue, 1981) has shown that the closer similarity of the MZ twins in terms of IQ scores is still evident even when they are reared apart. Bouchard and McGue estimated an average concordance rate of IQ (i.e. the degree to which intelligence level was the same for two individuals) for DZ twins reared *together* of 60% (or .60), yet for MZ twins reared *apart*, the concordance rate was much higher, at 72% (or .72).

Adoption studies – Finding large numbers of MZ twins who have been reared apart is (thankfully) relatively rare, but there is another important source of data for the assessment of the role of genetic factors. Adoption studies compare the IQ of adopted children with other members of their adoptive families *and* members of their biological families. If genetic factors influence intelligence, research should find a similarity between the IQ levels of adopted children and their biological families. The Texas Adoption Project (Horn *et al.*, 1979) tested members of 300 Texan families who had adopted children shortly after their birth from a home for unwed mothers. When the children were first assessed, there were higher correlations between the children's IQs and those of their adoptive mothers than with their biological mothers. However, when the researchers tracked down many of the participants 10 years later, the only correlations that remained above .20 were between the children and their biological relatives (Loehlin *et al.*, 1989). This finding has been evident in many other studies – the impact of family influences tends to *decrease* with age, while genetic influences tend to *increase*.

Is there a gene for intelligence?

IGF2R – Hill *et al.* (1999) tested children between the ages of 6 and 15 and living in the UK. They then divided the children into two groups. In one group (the 'super-bright' group), the average IQ was 136, and in the other (the average IQ group) it was 103. The researchers examined each child's chromosome 6, and discovered that a specific form of the gene IGF2R (insulin-like growth factor 2 receptor) occurred in twice as many children in the high-IQ group as in the average group – 32% versus 16%. They concluded that it is this form of the IGF2R gene (called allele 5), that contributes to intelligence.

Genetic markers for intelligence – In a more recent study, Curtis *et al.* (2008) took cheek swabs and from these scanned the genes of more than 7,000 children with a device called a *microarray* – a small chip that can recognise half a million distinctive snippets of DNA. This device enabled the researchers to detect genes that had only a tiny effect on the variation in IQ scores. They found only six genetic markers (i.e. genes or fragments of DNA associated with particular traits) that showed any sign of having an influence on IQ test scores. However, when they ran stringent statistical tests, only one gene passed, accounting for just 0.4% of the variation in IQ scores.

▶ A mother and children living in poor conditions in Tower Hamlets, London.

EVALUATION

Are twins a representative group?

A criticism of twin studies is that twins, particularly those drawn from Western cultures, may not constitute a representative group, and so may lead to an over- or under-estimation of the heritability of intelligence particularly with reference to a non-twin population. Voracek and Haubner (2008) addressed this issue through a meta-analysis of published studies comparing twins and singletons (non-twins). This analysis compared more than 30,000 twins with nearly 1.6 million singletons across six different countries and a variety of intelligence tests. They found that on average, twins score 4.2 IQ points less than singletons, although it is not clear whether this effect persists over the lifespan. Likely causes of the effect appear to be prenatal and perinatal factors (e.g. reduced foetal growth and shorter gestation for twins) although the researchers acknowledge that this difference is likely to disappear in more recent studies in modern industrialised societies.

A gene for intelligence

IGF2R – Although the IGF2R gene appears to be associated with high IQ, it is not sufficient on its own to cause high IQ. Of Plomin's high IQ group, a larger proportion of the high IQ children did *not* have the IGF2R gene than did have the gene. Similarly, some of the average IQ group *did* have the gene, but still had only average IQ. Presumably this is because intelligence, if it *is* influenced by genetic factors, requires a combination of many different genes, each of which is responsible for only a small variation in overall intelligence. A further problem is that others have failed to replicate Plomin *et al.*'s study, effectively rendering the results scientifically meaningless.

Genetic markers – Not everybody is enthusiastic about the search for genetic markers of intelligence. Members of the 'Campaign for Real Intelligence' argue that IQ is only one element of mental ability, and should not be taken as the sole measure of a person's intelligence. They warn that the discovery of any genes connected with IQ could divide society by marginalising people who lack these 'IQ genes'.

Gene-environment interactions

Breastfeeding and IQ – Caspi *et al.* (2007) found that children with one version of the FADS2 gene scored seven points higher in IQ tests if they were breastfed, whereas children with another variant of this gene showed no such benefits associated with breastfeeding. This study is significant because it appears to show how genes can alter the effect that a particular environmental influence (in this case breastfeeding) has on intelligence.

Genes can mould the environment – Genes may also influence behaviour in terms of how intelligence develops, by moulding the intellectual environment in particular ways. For example, genes may cause us to seek out some experiences rather than others, which in turn affects our intelligence for better or worse. This might explain why the influence of genes on IQ performance becomes more pronounced as people get older. As people grow up and take control of their own lives, they are free to act in a way that is consistent with their psychological make-up. Thus, the influence of their genes becomes stronger, and the influence of family background becomes weaker.

ENVIRONMENTAL FACTORS IN INTELLIGENCE-TEST PERFORMANCE

The list of potential environmental factors that might influence **intelligence** is endless. It includes family factors, such as parental occupation and birth order, and cultural influences, such as peer groups, ethnicity and educational opportunities. We can also throw into the pot such immeasurables as environmental luck, e.g. who you sit next to at school, or even a chance comment from a teacher.

▶ Research suggests that environmental factors such as socioeconomic class and family size can have a significant influence on measured intelligence.

THE HIGH SCOPE/PERRY PRESCHOOL PROJECT

The High Scope/Perry Preschool Project provided evidence for the effectiveness of compensatory education and therefore the importance of environmental influences in intelligence. This study carried out from 1962 to 1967, provided high-quality preschool education to three- and four-year-old African-American children living in poverty and at high risk of school failure. The study randomly allocated 128 children either to a programme group (who received high-quality preschool education each weekday morning) or a control group that did not receive the programme. For the programme group, teachers also provided a weekly home visit to each mother and child, designed to involve the mother in the educational process. Initial improvements were encouraging, with 67% of the programme group having IQ levels in excess of 90 when they began school (100 is 'average'), compared to just 28% of the non-programme group.

The children were followed up at age 27 (Schweinhart *et al.*, 1993), at which point the programme group was compared to the control group. The programme group:

- had completed an average of almost one year more of schooling (11.9 years versus 11 years)
- spent an average of 1.3 fewer years in special education for mental or learning impairment (3.9 years versus 5.2 years)
- had a higher rate of high school graduation (65% versus 45%).

ENVIRONMENTAL FACTORS IN INTELLIGENCE

Family environment

Socioeconomic status (SES) – A family's SES is based on many things, including parental occupations and income, status, educational level of the parents and so on. In the UK, **socioeconomic status (SES)** is determined by parental occupation, and is graded from Class I (professional occupations) to Class V (unskilled occupations). Mackintosh (1998) used evidence from the *British National Child Development Study* (NCDS), showing that even when factors such as financial hardship and area of residence are taken into account, children with fathers in Class I occupations scored 10 points higher than children of Class V fathers.

Birth-order and family size – Belmont and Marolla (1973) looked at the relationship between family size, birth order and **IQ** in a sample of 386 nineteen-year-old Dutch men. They found that, even when SES was controlled for, children from larger families had lower IQ than children from smaller families, and first-born children typically had higher IQ levels than later-born children. A recent Norwegian study (Bjerkedal *et al.*, 2007) also found that first-born children had higher IQs than later-born children, and also that if the first-born child had died, the second child 'moved up a place' scoring closer to an IQ level of the average first-born child.

The influence of culture

Group socialisation theory – Harris (1995) claims that experiences outside the home may be more important in developing people's intelligence than experiences within it. As children get older, they become less influenced by their family life, and more influenced by life outside the home. Children identify with a number of different groups, and the shared norms within these groups dictate much of their subsequent development (e.g. the degree to which they engage in 'intellectual' pastimes, such as reading books or going on to university).

Ethnicity and IQ – Herrnstein and Murray (1994) compared IQ test scores for different groups in the US. Among their findings was that immigrants coming into the US had IQ levels that were significantly lower than resident Americans. Controversially, they argued that as more and more immigrants came into the country, this caused a downward pressure on intelligence levels and an increase in the social problems associated with people with low IQ.

School effects – The relationship between formal education and intelligence test scores is often taken for granted, but is there evidence that school *boosts* intelligence? There have been many studies testing this claim, and Ceci's **meta-analysis** of such studies (Ceci, 1991) concluded that children who attend school regularly score higher than those who attend less regularly: that IQ scores decrease over the long summer holidays, and that there is a rise of 2.7 IQ points for each year of formal schooling.

Compensatory education – Early attempts to boost the IQs of disadvantaged children by a period of preschool education were somewhat disappointing. The most famous of these, *Head Start*, which began in the 1960s was an attempt to break the cycle of poverty for disadvantaged children in the US. Although there were some initial gains in IQs, in the longer term, its effectiveness has been questioned, with some studies showing positive gains from participation but others reporting no significant gains. However, the findings from another major US study (see left) have been far more encouraging.

STATISTICAL FALLACIES

Maltby *et al.* (2007) argue that much research in this area is misleading because the statistics themselves are misleading. Research that studies, for example, the relationship between birth order and IQ must also take into account family size, education, region of the country and so on. It would be inappropriate to draw conclusions concerning birth order and IQ by comparing a first-born child raised in a small, professional family in an affluent area of Surrey and a second-born from the large family of an unskilled migrant worker in South Wales. It would be impossible to determine which, if any, of these environmental factors was responsible for any differences in IQ. Such erroneous conclusions based on simple comparisons are known as '*statistical fallacies*'.

REAL-WORLD APPLICATION – IMPROVING INTELLIGENCE

Research suggests that socioeconomic status can affect IQ, so would improvements in SES produce a corresponding improvement in IQ? Wahlsten (1997) cites adoption studies in France, where an infant has been moved from a low SES family to one where the parents have higher socioeconomic status. On average, the child's score improves between 12–16 points. Similar gains have been noted in studies in the US, where significant improvements in terms of financial resources and additional day-care provision for disadvantaged children has produced the same magnitude of gain.

EVALUATION

Family environment

Socioeconomic status – SES undoubtedly affects measured intelligence, but why? One reason is that families with high SES are better able to prepare their children for school because they have better access to resources and information that enhance children's cognitive and intellectual development. For example, the *National Statistics Omnibus Survey* found that in 2000, 71% of Class I households in the UK had Internet access compared to just 26% of Class V households.

Birth-order and family size – In the Bjerkedal *et al.* study described on the facing page, one finding was that first-born children typically have IQ scores three points higher than second-born children. In societies where such a discrepancy could make a huge difference to a child's life (e.g. the difference between an elite university and a less elite institution) such a finding is bound to provoke anxiety. But is there any evidence that such differences *persist*? A 1989 study (Blake, 1989) of more than 100,000 people, which found that in small and medium-sized families, birth order had no effect on how far children progressed in education.

The influence of culture

Conflicting conclusions – Herrnstein and Murray (1994) and Ceci (1991) reach sharply contrasting conclusions about the potential for education to increase the intelligence of individuals. Herrnstein and Murray's conclusion is that 'the story of attempts to raise intelligence is one of high hopes, flamboyant claims and disappointing results'. In contrast, Ceci concludes that 'schooling exerts a substantial influence on IQ formation and maintenance'. How do we explain such different conclusions from the same research studies? Perhaps the answer lies in a failure to define what constitutes an *improvement*. Both Herrnstein and Murray *and* Ceci would presumably agree that education has *some* effect, but the issue appears to be more to do with the *size* of the effect and the circumstances in which it manifests itself.

Problems in assessing effectiveness – A second problem concerns the generally accepted belief that *g* (see page 124) is both a meaningful concept and can be accurately measured by traditional IQ tests. This position has been challenged by theorists such as Robert Sternberg and Howard Gardner (see page 126), who both argue that intelligence is multidimensional, and that any attempts to measure it using a simple psychometric test, or to assess the success of an educational programme in the same way is a meaningless exercise.

Group socialisation theory – Harris's claim that intelligence, like many other characteristics, is more a product of peer group than family influences is rejected by Pinker (2002). He sees the interaction between genes and peers as a possible explanation for some behaviours, such as smoking, but not for intelligence.

Cultural bias in IQ tests – Greenfield (1997) argues that assessing the IQ of people from cultures other than the one in which the test was developed represents a cultural bias that will inevitably influence any results. In societies where formal schooling is common, for example, students gain an early familiarity with organising items into rows and columns, which gives them an advantage over test-takers in cultures where formal schooling is rare. Likewise, media technologies such as television and video games give test-takers from cultures where such media are commonplace an advantage on visual IQ tests.

A PHYSIOLOGICAL EXPLANATION FOR POVERTY AND INTELLIGENCE

Recent research by Kishiyama *et al.* (2008) found that children with different levels of socioeconomic status also had detectable differences in the efficiency of their **prefrontal cortex**, a part of the brain that is important in problem-solving and creativity. They tested 26 normal children aged 9 and 10, half from families with low incomes, and half from families with high incomes. For each child, the researchers measured brain activity using an **EEG** while the child was engaged in a simple task – watching a sequence of triangles projected on a screen. The children were instructed to click a button when a slightly skewed triangle flashed up. The researchers discovered that children from low socioeconomic backgrounds showed a lower prefrontal cortex response to the unexpected novel stimuli. Kishiyama *et al.* suggest that children from poor backgrounds might not be getting full brain development because of the stressful and relatively impoverished environment associated with low socioeconomic status. They believe that this brain difference, while not inevitable among children from poor backgrounds, can be eliminated by appropriate intervention, and are currently collaborating with neuroscientists, who are developing games to improve prefrontal cortex function, and thus the reasoning ability, of school-age children.

CAN YOU...? No.7.9

...**1** Describe, in about 200 words, research into the role of environmental and cultural factors in intelligence-test performance.

...**2** Identify **eight** criticisms related to the role of environmental and cultural factors, including **at least one** IDA topic. Each criticism should be about 50 words.

...**3** Use this material to write a 600-word answer to the question: *Discuss the role of environmental factors (cultural factors) in intelligence-test performance.* (8 marks + 16 marks)

CHAPTER SUMMARY

THEORIES OF INTELLIGENCE

PSYCHOMETRIC THEORIES

GENERAL INTELLIGENCE
- Spearman believed that all intelligent behaviour derived from one 'pool' of mental energy.
- Two-factor theory – proposed two factors to explain intelligence.
- Specific abilities (s) – explain consistent performance on specific tests.
- General intelligence (g) – explains positive correlation in performance across all tests.

EVALUATION
- Duncan et al. (2000) – PET scans for g and non-g tasks reveal different patterns of activation.
- Reification of intelligence – abstract notion made into a concrete 'thing'.

MULTIFACTOR THEORISTS – CATTELL (1942)
- Crystallised intelligence (Gc) – acquired knowledge and skills result from experience.
- Fluid intelligence (Gf) – reasoning and problem-solving ability, not dependent on experience.
- People with high capacity for Gf acquire Gc knowledge at faster rates.

MULTIFACTOR THEORISTS - THURSTONE
- Identified seven primary mental abilities (PMA) that made up a person's intelligence.
- Includes verbal fluency, spatial ability and perceptual speed.

EVALUATION
- McArdle et al. (2000) – evidence that Gc rises over lifespan, Gf falls.
- Flynn effect – IQ scores rising over last 50 years but Gf only, not Gc.
- Failed to find evidence for separate PMA when tested on schoolchildren.
- Has been useful in selection of aircrew.
- IQ tests may not be 'fair' because of issue of coaching.

IDA
- Cultural/racial biases in testing, which discriminates against some groups.

INFORMATION-PROCESSING THEORIES

TRIARCHIC THEORY
- Analytical intelligence involves combination of three components – metacomponents, performance and knowledge acquisition.
- Practical intelligence – making a response dependent on context – involves adaptation, shaping and selection.
- Creative intelligence – identification of whether task requires intelligence behaviour or automatic response.

EVALUATION
- Berg and Sternberg (1985) – evidence for theory and for decline in cognitive abilities with age.
- Applications of triarchic theory, including PIFS intervention.
- Criticisms include relative lack of evidence to support assertions.

MULTIPLE INTELLIGENCES (MI)
- Gardner identified seven types of intelligence and later added an eighth. Included linguistic, logical mathematical, spatial, interpersonal and natural intelligence.
- Criteria for inclusion – neuropsychological evidence, existence of individuals with exceptional talent, distinct developmental history and experimental evidence.

EVALUATION
- Very little empirical support for theory.
- Implications for assessment – should involve multiple measures specific to each type of intelligence.
- Positive implications of MI – offers hope for individuals who do not do well on one type of intelligence may be able to do well on another.
- Difficult to assess MI scientifically, which limits acceptability as 'scientific' theory of intelligence.

IDA
- Cultural bias in triarchic theory – cognitive skills labelled as intelligence in one culture may not have the same value in other cultures.
- Cultural bias in MI – some forms of intelligence more highly valued in different cultures.

ANIMAL LEARNING AND INTELLIGENCE

CLASSICAL CONDITIONING

ACQUISITION
- Exploits naturally occurring association between UCS and UCR.
- Combination of NS and UCS eventually leads to CS-CR association.

TIMING
- Conditioning stronger if NS precedes UCS but overlaps with it.
- The longer the delay between NS and UCS, the weaker the conditioning.
- If NS occurs after UCS, conditioning is ineffective.

EXTINCTION AND SPONTANEOUS RECOVERY
- CR extinguished if UCS removed, as no CR no longer predicts UCS.
- If CS-UCS link re-established, CR reappears very quickly.

STIMULUS GENERALISATION AND DISCRIMINATION
- Organism also responds to stimuli that are similar to CS.
- The more similar, the stronger the response.
- Generalisation can be overcome with stimulus discrimination training.

EVALUATION
- NS learning may only reflect NS-CS relationships that exist in nature.
- Taste aversion challenges classical conditioning because (1) one pairing enough, (2) timing less important, (3) resistant to extinction.
- Species that can modify reflexes more likely to survive, therefore classical conditioning likely to be universal.

IDA
- Real-world application – advertisements associate products with attractive celebrities, but suffer problem of stimulus generalisation.
- Evolutionary perspective – CS-UCS pairings more difficult to establish in some species, and reflect degrees of biological preparedness.

OPERANT CONDITIONING

REINFORCEMENT
- Reinforcement strengthens behaviour, making it more likely to recur.
- Positive reinforcement – adding satisfying or pleasant consequence following a behaviour.
- Negative reinforcement – terminating something unpleasant as a consequence of behaviour.

SCHEDULES OF REINFORCEMENT
- Continuous reinforcement most effective during acquisition.
- Partial reinforcement effective in maintaining conditioned behaviour.
- Fixed- and variable-ratio; fixed- and variable-interval.

PUNISHMENT
- Punishment decreases likelihood of a behaviour recurring.
- Can be positive (add unpleasant consequence) or negative (remove positive stimulus).

EVALUATION
- Conditioned behaviours may drift back towards instinct after time.
- Problems with punishment – may fear punisher rather than action.
- Physical punishment may increase likelihood of physical aggression.
- Angry punishment – punishment more likely to be used when angry.
- Power of operant conditioning demonstrated in behaviour modification.
- Advantage of experiments include cause and effect.
- Cultures vary in their reliance on operant conditioning strategies.

IDA
- Illusion of free will – all behaviours are a result of reinforcement.
- Use of non-human animals – reliance on animal studies can neither confirm not refute hypotheses about human behaviour.

HUMAN INTELLIGENCE

EVOLUTIONARY FACTORS IN HUAMN INTELLIGENCE

ECOLOGICAL DEMANDS
- Dunbar (1992) suggests intelligence evolved because of demands of finding food.
- Tool use is an indication of intelligence – linked to success of hunter–gatherer cultures.

EVALUATION
- Dunbar (1992) found no significant positive correlation with environmental complexity.
- Intelligence related to increased incidence of schizophrenic behaviours.

SOCIAL COMPLEXITY
- Machiavellian intelligence – main selective pressure is dealing with companions.
- Strategic sharing of meat, to forge alliances and persuade females to mate, paved way for human intelligence.

EVALUATION
- Studies confirm 'meat for sex' hypothesis, but alternative explanation is that sharing allows hunter to eat without interruption.
- Evidence in chimps that meat sharing more important in forging alliances than for sex.

BRAIN SIZE AND INTELLIGENCE
- Reader and Laland (2002) – brain size correlated with innovation, social learning and tool use.
- Large brains and intelligence evolved because they enhanced reproductive success.

EVALUATION
- Problems associated with large brain size so some selective pressure *against* development of large brains.
- Large brains evolved in all primates, therefore not linked to unique problems faced by humans.

IDA
- Cultural bias – Rushton (1995) – 'out-of-Africa' explanation for brain size differences between different racial groups.
- Gender bias – male brains larger, but female brains better organised.

GENETIC FACTORS IN IQ TEST PERFORMANCE

TWIN AND ADOPTION STUDIES
- MZ twins genetically identical, DZ twins share 50% of genes.
- MZ twins more similar in terms of IQ, even when reared apart.
- Texas Adoption Project – initially higher correlations between adopted children and their adoptive parents, 10 years later higher correlation with *biological* parents.

EVALUATION
- Twins not representative group, may lead to over- or under-estimation of heritability of intelligence.
- Twins different to singletons e.g. score 4.2 IQ points less.
- Meta-analysis of studies suggested 48% of variance in IQ attributed to genes.
- Problems with interpretation of twin studies – e.g. greater shared environment than singletons may influence similarity of IQ.

A GENE FOR INTELLIGENCE
- Hill *et al.* (1999) – specific version of IGF2R more likely to occur in highly intelligent children.
- Curtis *et al.* (2008) scanned genes of 7,000 children. Only one gene influenced IQ, but just accounted for 0.4% of variation in scores.

EVALUATION
- Limitations of IGF2R study – higher proportion of highly intelligent children did *not* have the gene than had it.
- Discovery of genes for IQ may marginalise those who don't have these genes.
- Genes interact with environment – e.g. children with one version of FADS2 gene scored higher in IQ tests if breast-fed, but those with another version did not.
- Genes can mould environment – we seek some experiences rather than others.

IDA
- Real-world application – genetic engineering, may be possible to boost human intelligence by modifying DNA of human embryo.
- Sub-cultural bias – Turkheimer *et al.* (2003) – influence of genetic factors masked by environmental deprivation in some social groups.

ENVIRONMENTAL FACTORS

FAMILY ENVIRONMENT
- Socioeconomic status (SES) is a key determinant of intelligence.
- Children from larger families have lower IQ than children from small families; first-born higher IQ than later-born.

EVALUATION
- SES linked to higher IQ because high SES parents better access to resources.
- Birth-order effect not evident in study of 100,000 people (Blake, 1989).

CULTURE
- Harris (1995) – experiences outside home more important in shaping intelligence than experiences within it.
- Herrnstein and Murray (1994) – immigrants coming into US had lower IQs than resident Americans, lowered national IQ.
- Ceci (1991) meta-analysis – children who attend school regularly score higher on IQ.
- Compensation education programme (e.g. Headstart) attempt to boost IQs of disadvantaged children.

EVALUATION
- Theorists disagree over potential for education to boost IQ, but disagreement appears to be over what constitutes *improvement*.
- Problems include ability to test IQ using traditional tests to assess success.
- Some notable successes at boosting IQ (e.g. High Scope/Perry Preschool Project).
- Harris's view rejected by Pinker (2002) – peer influence not important in shaping intelligence.
- Cultural bias of test influences results. Some cultures benefit more from certain kinds of test.

IDA
- Real-world application – improvements in SES have led to positive changes in IQ in France and the US.
- Physiological approach – children with lower SES – lower prefrontal cortex response to unexpected novel stimuli (Kishiyama *et al.*, 2008).

CONDITIONING AND ANIMAL BEHAVIOUR

CLASSICAL CONDITIONING
- Training animals for release, e.g. in research or when hand-reared.
- Simple conditioning – dolphins learn association between humans and food.
- Compound conditioning – human presence combined with more appropriate stimulus, leads to overshadowing.

EVALUATION
- Compound conditioning desirable in animals for release but stimulating environment better with captive animals.
- Trade-off between learning from animals and not endangering them.
- Reproductive success: CS-UCS pairings must occur under natural circumstances to be adaptive.
- Males exposed to CS prior to mating sire more offspring (Matthews *et al.*, 2007).

OPERANT CONDITIONING
- PRT – makes procedures less stressful and frightening.
- Link between reinforcement value of a food patch and frequency of foraging.

EVALUATION
- PRT – effective in reducing aggression during feeding in captive animals (Bloomsmith *et al.*, 1994).
- Agetsuma (1999) manipulated quality of food patches – subsequent responses higher in high-quality patch.
- Desensitisation as PRT can improve welfare of animals (Clay *et al.*, 2009).

IDA
- Ethical issues – use of PRT satisfies requirements of Animal Welfare Act.

INTELLIGENCE IN NON-HUMAN ANIMALS

MACHIAVELLIAN INTELLIGENCE
- Ability to manipulate group members without causing aggression.
- Adaptation to social problem-solving in large groups.
- Manipulation and deception – tricks include management of attention.
- Power in complex social groups determined by making alliances rather than by physical strength.

EVALUATION
- Support for Machiavellian intelligence comes from studies of agonistic buffering in Barbary macaques and chimpanzees.
- Not restricted to primates – also evident in birds (Burish *et al.*, 2004).
- Implications of social intelligence – development of 'arms race'.

SELF-RECOGNITION
- Ability to recognise oneself in a mirror indicates self-awareness.
- Chimpanzees, bonobos and orang-utans have this ability.
- Dolphins and killer whales also appear to show self-recognition.
- Plotnik *et al.* (2006) – Asian elephants may also be able to pass the 'mark test'.
- Self-recognition a result of large brains and advanced cognitive ability.

EVALUATION
- Elephants – possibility of 'feeling' the mark, but dismissed by use of transparent mark.
- Heyes (1998) – little reliable evidence for self-recognition in primates.
- Self-recognition – indication of level of self-consciousness in species.
- Maestripieri (2007) – rhesus macaques show Machiavellian intelligence but no self-recognition.

IDA
- Biological perspective – Machiavellian intelligence linked to developments in neocortex. Neocortical enlargement correlates with typical group size in primates.

EXAM QUESTION WITH STUDENT ANSWER

QUESTION (a) Briefly outline **one psychometric theory of intelligence.** *(3 marks)*
(b) **Evaluate the psychometric theory outlined in part (a).** *(10 marks)*
(c) **Discuss the role of genetic factors associated with intelligence-test performance.**
(5 marks + 6 marks)

STUDENT ANSWER

(a) *Spearman's two-factor theory claimed that people have two types of intelligence. The first of these is called g and refers to general underlying intelligence. This explains why people who do well on one test of intelligence also do well on other tests of intelligence. Spearman also claimed that people have specific abilities(s) that explain why individuals perform consistently well on specific aspects of intelligence (e.g. vocabulary) but not on others.*

(b) *There have been many criticisms of Spearman's theory. Some of them are positive while others are negative. I will present a few of each of them here.*

On the positive side there is evidence from brain scans to support the existence of the g factor. When people are given a variety of different tasks to perform, those that have been classified as g factor tasks led to activation of certain areas of the brain regardless of the specific abilities involved.

Also on the positive side this approach has helped the development of IQ tests, which are extremely widely used in education, job assessment and so on.

On the negative side, these tests are not thought to be a fair assessment because some children are coached, which can raise their intelligence test performance artificially. They may then struggle to keep up with the demands of a grammar school education.

Another criticism is that the g factor suggests that there is a real thing called g whereas it is really only an abstract concept. This is known as reification, making something abstract real.

(c) *Research suggests that intelligence is related to genetic factors. For example, twin studies have shown that MZ twins (genetically identical) have more similar IQs than DZ (non-identical) twins even when they have been reared apart (Bouchard and McGue, 1981). It is important to study twins reared apart because this excludes the influence of a shared environment which is likely to be a greater influence in the case of MZ twins than DZ twins because MZs are treated more similarly.*

Other evidence of the role of genetic factors comes from adoption studies. For example, the Texas Adoption study followed a group of 300 children who were adopted at birth. Initially the children showed closer IQ correlations with their adopted mothers, but as they got older these correlations were reduced and the closest correlations were with their biological relatives. It seems that environmental influences decrease with age whereas genetic influences increase.

Such genetic evidence has led researchers to look for the actual genes that may be involved. Plomin identified a version of one gene, IGF2R, which was more common in highly intelligent children than those with an average IQ. However, the figures were rather small – only 32% of the superbright children had this version (allele) of the gene and in fact the allele was present in some of the average children. Furthermore the findings have not been replicated in other studies.

Plomin has done further research looking for genetic IQ markers but the results were rather unpromising.

There is some worry about the implications of research into such genetic factors. In America researchers have already experimented with genetically modifying mice by inserting genes into a developing animal to improve learning abilities. In future scientists might try to do this with humans which leads us to question the ethics of such research.

[549 words]

EXAMINER COMMENTS

Some examination questions may span several topic areas rather than focusing on just one. In such cases it is important that you produce the right amount of material for the marks available rather than, for example, writing your full 24-mark essay on the psychometric approach.

The answer to this part of the question is just about right for the mark allocation – you should write about 25 words per mark available. The outline of Spearman's theory is **accurate** and **detailed**.

This section of the answer is quite weak although well organised. It starts with a wasted paragraph which will attract no credit, as it simply outlines the content. It is better to simply get on and present the content.

The evaluation based on brain scan research is **reasonable**, but key information has been omitted such as the area of the brain associated with *g* (the frontal lobes) and the source of the research (e.g. Duncan *et al.*, 2000).

The next three paragraphs raise relevant critical points but none of them have been well **elaborated** in order to demonstrate that the student really understands the points being made.

Finally, there is no attempt to refer to methodology, issues, debates, etc. (**IDA points**), which are an important part of **AO2**.

The injunction 'discuss' means a combination of **AO1** and **AO2** and in this case it is in equal measures because part (a) was all **AO1** and part (b) all **AO2**.

Overall there is a good balance between description (**AO1**) and evaluation (**AO2**) in this answer. In the first two paragraphs there is clear description of appropriate evidence, and both paragraphs end with evaluation (**AO2**). In the first paragraph this includes a discussion of the methodology with **reasonable elaboration**.

In the third paragraph the same pattern has been followed – description followed by evaluation. The description of the research by Plomin is **accurate** and **detailed**, and the evaluation has been **well elaborated** and **used effectively**. However, the brief report of Plomin's subsequent research in the fourth paragraph **lacks detail** and would attract little credit.

In the final paragraph an important ethical issue has been raised, forming part of an **effective** and **IDA** evaluation.

AO1 – In parts (a) and (c) of this essay the content demonstrates **substantial** knowledge and understanding.

AO2/AO3 – In part (b) the evaluation is **basic**, whereas in part (c) it is **thorough**, showing a **clear line** of argument and **effective** IDA.

Chapter 8
Cognition and development

SPECIFICATION

Cognition and development	
Development of thinking	• Theories of cognitive development, including Piaget and Vygotsky. • Applications of cognitive development theories to education.
Development of moral understanding	• Kohlberg's theory of moral understanding.
Development of social cognition	• Development of the child's sense of self, including Theory of Mind. • Development of children's understanding of others, including perspective-taking, for example Selman. • Biological explanations of social cognition, including the role of the mirror neuron system.

PIAGET'S THEORY OF COGNITIVE DEVELOPMENT

Jean Piaget (1926, 1954) proposed that **cognitive development** was equivalent to the development of *logical* thinking, and that this developed over four major stages, stretching from birth to early adolescence. Before Piaget developed his theory, psychologists regarded cognitive development as the acquisition of knowledge – children were simply adults who knew less. Piaget's two main contributions to understanding cognitive development were, first, to suggest that the *way* children think changes qualitatively as they get older (rather than that they just gain more knowledge) and second, that these changes are mainly driven by biological development.

▲ Jean Piaget (1896–1980)

PIAGET'S THEORY

The mechanisms of cognitive development

Piaget believed that cognitive development was a result of two influences: **maturation** and the environment. Maturation refers to the effects of ageing. As children get older, certain mental operations become possible and at the same time, through interactions with the environment, their understanding of the world becomes more complex.

Schema are self-constructed mental structures that can be *behavioural* (such as grasping an object) or *cognitive* (such as classifying objects). Rather like individual computer programmes, **schema** are 'programmes' that people construct for dealing with the world. When a child is born it has few schema, but these are developed over time as a consequence of the child's interaction with its environment.

Assimilation – A child initially tries to understand any new information in terms of their existing knowledge about the world. For example, a baby who is given a new toy car to play with may grasp or suck that toy in the same way that they grasped or sucked a rattle. **Assimilation** occurs when an existing schema (such as sucking) is used on a new object (such as a toy car). Assimilation, therefore, involves the incorporation of new information into an existing schema.

Accommodation occurs when a child adapts existing schema in order to understand new information that doesn't appear to fit. Learning to drive a manual car involves developing a convenient schema for working the three pedals. What would happen if you drove an automatic car (no clutch pedal)? Assimilation into your existing schema would not work, so **accommodation** must (quickly!) occur.

Equilibration – According to Piaget, cognitive development is driven by the need for equilibrium in cognitive structures. When a child is aware of shortcomings in existing thinking, they experience an imbalance between what is understood and what is encountered. They try to reduce these imbalances by developing new schema or adapting old ones until equilibrium is restored, a process Piaget called **equilibration**.

Operations – You will notice in the stages below that the term 'operations' is frequently used. Piaget used this term to describe logical mental rules, such as the rules of arithmetic. Schemas and operation are 'variant' processes i.e. they change as a child matures, whereas assimilation and accommodation are invariant processes because they remain the same throughout a person's lifetime.

Stages in cognitive development

Stage 1: sensorimotor stage – Children learn to co-ordinate sensory input (e.g. what they see) with motor actions (i.e. with their hand movements) through **circular reactions** where they repeat the same action over and over to test sensorimotor relationships. The key development of this stage is **object permanence** – very young infants lose interest in an object when it is hidden behind a pillow because they assume it has ceased to exist. Around eight months they realise that objects that are out of sight still exist.

Stage 2: pre-operational stage – Children's thought becomes increasingly symbolic as they begin to represent their world with words, images, and drawings. They are, however, not capable of *reversibility of thought*. For example, they fail to understand that the physical properties of an object (e.g. its mass, volume, area and weight) remain the same despite changes in its appearance. This, Piaget thought, was due to the child's reliance on perceptual rather than logic-based reasoning i.e. based on the appearance of a situation rather than reality (the **appearance-reality distinction**). The child has a logical system based on what they see rather than any internally consistent rules. Children at this stage are also **egocentric** in their thinking. They only see the world from their position and are not aware of other perspectives.

Stage 3: concrete operational stage – Children acquire the rudiments of logical reasoning, and display skills of reversibility and **decentration** (no longer focusing on just one aspect of a task). This means that they are now able to conserve quantities (see facing page). Conservation involves recognising that quantities don't change even if they look different. Piaget believed that **conservation** was the single most important achievement of the concrete operational stage because it provides evidence of the child's command of logical operations.

Stage 4: formal operational stage – Children can now solve abstract problems. They can solve problems using **hypothetico-deductive reasoning**, thinking like a scientist – for example developing hypotheses and testing them to determine causal relationships. Children also display **idealistic thinking** – they are no longer tied to how things are but are able to imagine how things might be if certain changes are made (e.g. thinking about an ideal world).

AGES AND STAGES

Many students focus on the 'ages and stages' of Piaget's theory, shown in this table, but do remember that there is a lot more to his theory than this.

Stage and approximate age	Typical ways of thinking and achievements
Sensorimotor (0–2 years)	Circular reactions Object permanence
Pre-operational (2–7 years)	Lacking internally consistent logic and lacking reversibility of thought Egocentric (three mountains experiment)
Concrete operations (7–11 years)	Use of logical mental rules but only in concrete context Conservation, decentration
Formal operations (11+ years)	Abstract, adult thinking Hypothetico-deductive reasoning and idealistic thought

EVALUATION

The mechanisms of development

There is actually little research to support Piaget's ideas about the effects of disequilibrium. Inhelder *et al.* (1974) did show that children's learning was helped when there was a mild conflict between what they expected to happen and what did happen, but this wasn't really the sort of conflict that Piaget was talking about (Bryant, 1995).

Stages in development

Sensorimotor stage – Nativists claim that infants have more knowledge about the world than Piaget suggested. For example, Baillargeon and DeVos (1991) showed that infants as young as three to four months *did* display object permanence. They used tasks such as the *rolling car task*, where a large carrot or a small carrot is placed on a toy train set and rolled along a track. At one point the train and carrot go behind a screen with a large window. The large carrot should be visible as it passes behind the window, whereas the small carrot (not as broad) should remain hidden. The infants looked longer at the large carrot when it didn't appear, presumably expecting the top half to be visible, i.e. they had object permanence.

Pre-operational stage – Piaget illustrated pre-operational thinking using the *three mountains task* (see illustration on right). Children were shown a set of pictures and asked to choose the one which showed the dolls' perspective. Four-year-old children tended to choose their own perspective, rather than the perspective of the doll. However, Hughes (1975) showed that young children could cope with the task if it was more realistic, for example using a naughty boy doll who was hiding from a toy policeman.

▲ The three mountains task.

Concrete operational stage – Piaget demonstrated conservation by showing children various displays of quantity, such as rows of counters, cylinders of plasticine or beakers of water (as on the right). If the display was transformed so that the quantity *appeared* to have increased (e.g. the counters were spread out or the cylinder was squashed flat or water poured in a taller beaker) younger children could not conserve the quantity i.e. they did not think it had remained the same, if it looked bigger it *was* bigger. Only around the age of seven were children able to recognise that the quantities stayed the same even after their appearance had changed.

A   B

Formal operational stage – Piaget and Inhelder (1956) used the *beaker problem* to demonstrate how children apply logical thinking to problem-solving. Children were shown five liquid-filled beakers and asked to work out how to turn the liquid yellow by combining various liquids. Young children tried random combinations whereas children at the stage of formal operations developed a logical strategy. However, Dasen (1994) claims that only a third of adults ever reach this stage and even then not during adolescence.

Strengths and limitations

Limitations – The studies we have reviewed on this spread suggest that Piaget underestimated children's abilities at younger ages, and may have overestimated the ability to use abstract logic in the formal operational stage. In general his theory focuses too much on logic and generally ignores social factors, such as the benefit of cooperative group work. A further criticism is that the methods he used to research children's behaviour were flawed (see research methods above right). However, the evidence still supports the view that there are qualitative changes in cognitive development as a child matures.

Strengths – Despite the wealth of criticisms, Piaget remains one of the most influential psychologists of the twentieth century. His theory has had an enormous influence on education (discussed on page 150) and on psychological research. Bryant (1995) reminds us that Piaget's key contribution was to highlight the radical differences in the way young children and adults think.

Evaluation

PIAGET'S RESEARCH METHODS

Piaget's research methods are both admired and criticised. Bryant (1995) describes them as simple yet ingenious investigations of quite complex topics. On the negative side, one issue is that his studies involved children from European academic families who valued certain aspects of cognitive development, such as logical thinking; in other cultures and social classes greater value may be placed on, for example, a more basic level of concrete operations (i.e. making things rather than thinking about abstract ideas).

The second major criticism is that the design of many of the experiments may have confused younger children in particular, which may explain why they appeared to be less capable. For example, in the conservation experiments it was the way the questions were asked which made the task difficult for children. Samuel and Bryant (1984) showed that younger children did better when they were only asked once (after the transformation) if the two displays were the same, instead of Piaget's standard two questions (before and after).

McGarrigle and Donaldson (1974) argued that the deliberate transformation in the conservation experiment acted as a **demand characteristic**, demanding an alternative response. When a 'naughty teddy' toy accidentally messed up the counters making one row longer, younger children coped better because the change was 'explained' by naughty teddy's behaviour, eliminating demand characteristics (i.e. that the apparent change needed an explanation).

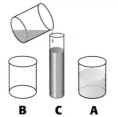

◀ **Conservation of volume.** Children are shown the two glasses, A and B, and asked whether they contain the same amount of water. The researcher then pours the contents of B into C and again asks whether the quantity is the same. Pre-operational children are dominated by what they see and therefore say 'No'.

B   C   A

IDA

NATURE AND NURTURE

Piaget's theory combines **nature** (biological maturation) with **nurture** (experience) to explain cognitive development. Piaget's conception of 'nurture' is more focused on the *physical* environment whereas Vygotsky emphasised the *social* environment (see box on page 149 comparing Piaget and Vygotsky.

CAN YOU...?   No.8.1

...**1** Write a description, in about 200 words, of Piaget's theory of cognitive development.

...**2** Produce a shortened version of the theory in about 100 words.

...**3** Identify **eight** criticisms related to Piaget's theory, including **at least one** IDA topic. Each criticism should be about 50 words.

...**4** Use this material to write a 600-word answer to the question: *Discuss Piaget's theory of cognitive development.* (8 marks + 16 marks)

Russian psychologist Lev Vygotsky agreed with Piaget that a child's thinking is qualitatively different from an adult's. However, he placed much greater emphasis on the importance of the social context of children's learning. Vygotsky (1934) believed that *culture* is the prime determinant of individual development. **Cognitive development** is driven by a child's biological maturation, but is also a product of their interactions with others. Cognitive development occurs when children internalise the tools of thinking through social interactions with those who currently know more than they do.

'Culture' *is defined as the things that bind a group of people together – the rules, customs, morals, and childrearing practices – and this includes language.*

Vygotsky uses the term 'culture' to refer to shared meanings and the social context in which each of us grows up.

◄ Lev Vygotsky (1896-1934). Piaget and Vygotsky were born in the same year but worlds apart – Vygotsky was Russian, whereas Piaget was Swiss. They never met, although Vygotsky read about Piaget's theory. Piaget was only able to read Vygotsky's works in 1958 when they were first translated into English.

ZONE OF PROXIMAL DEVELOPMENT (ZPD)

The **ZPD** is a key concept in Vygotsky's theory. He defined it as 'the distance between the actual development level as determined by independent problem-solving and the level of potential development as determined through problem-solving under adult guidance or in collaboration with more capable peers.... What the child can do in cooperation today, he can do alone tomorrow'. (Vygotsky, 1934).

Unlike Piaget, Vygotsky believed that learning *precedes* development. According to Vygotsky, learning or cognitive *development* does not take place in the area of current *development* (i.e. where the child already is), nor does it take place too far ahead of what the child can already do independently. In the former instance, nothing new would be learned, and in the latter, the new challenges would be too far from the child's current knowledge to be useful.

VYGOTSKY'S THEORY

The major theme of Vygotsky's theory is that social interaction plays a fundamental role in cognitive development. Vygotsky believed that every aspect of a child's cognitive development appears first at a *social* level (i.e. between the child and others), and later, at an *individual* level (i.e. inside the child).

Mental processes

Elementary and higher mental functions – Vygotsky proposed that children are born with *elementary* mental functions, such as perception and memory. These are transformed into *higher* mental functions (such as use of mathematical systems) by the influence of culture. Lower mental functions are biological and a form of natural development. Higher mental functions are exclusively human. The role of culture is to transform elementary mental functions into higher mental functions.

What to think and how to think – Culture, in the form of exposure to others, makes two types of contributions to a child's cognitive development. Through culture, children acquire much of the *content* of their thinking, i.e. their *knowledge*. The surrounding culture also provides a child with the *processes* of their thinking, i.e. the tools of intellectual adaptation. In short, culture teaches children both *what* to think and also *how* to think.

The process of cultural influence

Cultural influences affect cognitive development in several ways, for example:

The role of others: experts – A child learns through problem-solving experiences shared with someone else, usually a parent or teacher but also more competent peers. All people with greater knowledge are called '*experts*'. Initially, the person interacting with the child assumes most of the responsibility for guiding the problem-solving activity, but gradually this responsibility transfers to the child.

Semiotics and the role of language – Vygotsky believed that culture is transmitted by experts using semiotics i.e. the signs and symbols developed within a particular culture. Language is the semiotic system of foremost importance, but mathematical symbols are valuable too. Conversations between expert and learner enable adults to transmit the rich body of knowledge that exists in the culture. To begin with, language takes the form of shared dialogues between the adult and child (*pre-intellectual speech*), but as they develop the skill of mental representation, children begin to communicate with themselves in the same way that they would communicate with others. Children also begin using language to solve problems around the age of two, and frequently talk out loud when trying to solve problems, a type of speech known as *egocentric* speech. At around age seven this gives way to silent or *inner* speech, but these inner dialogues continue to be used as a way of reflecting upon and solving problems.

The social and individual level – According to Vygotsky, every function in the child's cognitive development appears twice: first, on the *social* level (between people), and later on the *individual* level (inside the child). The child converts these social relations into higher mental functions through mediation. Language is the most important kind of mediation (called **semiotic mediation**) for the acquisition of higher mental processes, because it frees children from the constraints of their immediate environment.

The zone of proximal development (ZPD) – A child's ZPD is the region where cognitive development takes place (see left). The learner is aided by cultural influences (e.g. experts and language). At first, learning is between people (social) and later it becomes internalised (individual) – a process called 'internalisation'; this mirrors the distinction between the social and individual level described above.

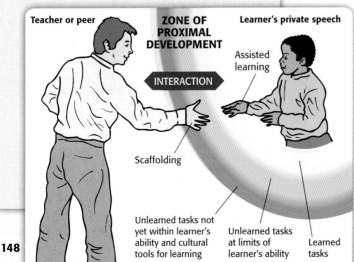

| Teacher or peer | ZONE OF PROXIMAL DEVELOPMENT | Learner's private speech |

INTERACTION

Assisted learning

Scaffolding

Unlearned tasks not yet within learner's ability and cultural tools for learning

Unlearned tasks at limits of learner's ability

Learned tasks

APE TALK

Vygotsky proposed that higher mental functions were uniquely human. However, research over the past 20 years suggests that he was wrong. For example, Savage-Rumbaugh *et al.* (1998) taught several pygmy chimpanzees (notably Kanzi) to use human language (using a symbol system called *lexigrams*). The process of teaching them has been called 'enculturation' i.e. the chimpanzees are exposed to the human culture around them and moved through their ZPD.

EVALUATION

Research evidence

The role of culture – Vygotsky's claims about the effects of culture have been supported in cross-cultural research. For example, Gredler (1992) pointed to the primitive counting system used in Papua New Guinea as an example of how culture can limit cognitive development. Counting is done by starting on the thumb of one hand and going up the arm and down to the other fingers, ending at 29. This system makes it very difficult to add and subtract large numbers, a limiting factor for development in this culture.

The role of language – A cornerstone of Vygotsky's theory is the role of language in cognitive development. Vygotsky believed that language and thought are at first independent, but become interdependent. He suggested that the acquisition of a new word was the *beginning* of the development of a concept. This is supported in a classic study by Carmichael *et al.* (1932) who gave participants one of two labels for certain drawings. For example, they were shown a kidney shape and told either that their drawing was a kidney bean or that it was a canoe. When participants were subsequently asked to draw the shape, it differed according to which label they had been given. This shows that words can affect the way we remember things.

On the other hand, Sinclair-de-Zwart (1969) tried to teach children who could not conserve to use comparative terms, such as bigger and shorter – terms they didn't have in their vocabulary. She found very little improvement in their ability to conserve, a finding that does not support Vygotsky because his theory suggests that cultural tools (such as language) should lead to cognitive development.

The role of the ZPD – Evidence for the ZPD was produced in a study by McNaughton and Leyland (1990). They observed young children working with their mothers on jigsaw puzzles of increasing difficulty, and then a week later observed the children working on their own. The children reached a higher of level of difficulty with their mothers (their potential ability) than when working on their own (their current ability) so defining their ZPD. The ZPD was related to the method of instruction used by the mothers. When the children were doing puzzles that were too easy for them (below the child's ZPD) the mothers were mainly concerned with keeping the child on task. At the second level (within the child's ZPD), the mothers focused on helping the children solve the puzzle for themselves. At the third level (beyond the child's ZPD), the emphasis was on completing the puzzle by whatever means. Vygotsky predicted that the greatest teaching input will occur at the edge of the ZPD, the point lying between the second and third level, at which the child can still cope, which is the same as the findings of McNaughton and Leyland.

Strengths and limitations

Limitations – Despite the number of studies discussed here, there has been relatively little research related to Vygotsky's theory compared with the abundance of research on Piaget's theory. This is partly because Vygotsky's theory doesn't lend itself as readily to experimentation, as the concepts are more difficult to **operationalise**.

A further limitation relates to the social emphasis in Vygotsky's theory. Whereas Piaget underplayed social influences, Vygotsky may have overplayed the importance of the social environment – if social influence was all that was needed to advance cognitive development then learning would be a lot faster than it is. Vygotsky's emphasis on social factors also led him to largely ignore biological factors. Finally, his theory has been criticised for lacking detail although this is in part due to the fact that he died at such a young age and did not have time to fully develop his theory (Lindblom and Ziemke, 2003).

Strengths – The Vygotskian approach provides a bridge between social and cognitive domains. It is a more positive approach than Piaget's because it offers ways that others can be actively involved in assisting a learner. In this way Vygotsky's theory may potentially have *more* educational applications than Piaget's theory.

CAN YOU...?   No.8.2

...1 Write a description, in about 200 words, of Vygotsky's theory of cognitive development.

...2 Produce a shortened version of the theory in about 100 words.

...3 Identify **eight** criticisms related to Vygotsky's theory, including **at least one** IDA topic. Each criticism should be about 50 words.

...4 Use this material to write a 600-word answer to the question: *Discuss Vygotsky's theory of cognitive development.* (8 marks + 16 marks)

COMPARING APPROACHES

The differences between Piaget's and Vygotsky's approaches reflect differences between the two men. Vygotsky was a Communist believing in the power of community, and thus valued the role of society in the development of the individual; Piaget was a product of **individualist** European society. Apart from their different cultural backgrounds, the two men may also represent rather different kinds of learner: Piaget's child is an introvert whereas Vygotsky's child is an extrovert, and this may be a reflection of the men themselves (Miller, 1994). Thus the two views can be reconciled because they are talking about different styles of learning and different kinds of learner. It is also possible to reconcile the theories by taking the view that they are not that different at their central core (Glassman, 1999). If one contrasts these theories with others in psychology, such as those by Freud, Pavlov or Skinner, we can see that there are similarities. They both place cognition at the centre of the theory; both emphasise the complex interactionist nature of development; both see abstract, scientific thought as the final stage of development; and both see the learner as active rather than passive.

Similarities & differences	Piaget	Vygotsky
Learning is	Solitary	Social
What drives development?	Maturation, conflict	Learning is enjoyable and this motivates more learning
Role of language	Thought drives language	Language drives thought
Role of biology	Maturation dictates pace of cognitive development	Elementary mental functions are innate
Child is active	Child actively organises cognitive schemes to maintain equilibration	Child is active in providing feedback to the parent/instructor

149

APPLICATIONS OF COGNITIVE DEVELOPMENT THEORIES TO EDUCATION

Although Piaget's theory is not a theory of education as such, its relevance to learning and education is obvious. The Piagetian classroom might be thought of as a construction zone where children are actively involved in the formation of knowledge. Vygotsky's perspective on learning requires teacher and learners to collaborate with each other to create meaning in ways that children are then able to make their own. The Vygotskian classroom would be structured to promote collaboration, effectively becoming a community of learning. Both applications have one thing in common – they advocate an *active* approach to education, emphasising the necessity for the learner to be a true participant in the learning process, in contrast with traditional teaching methods where the learner is passive (just sits back and takes information in).

Vygotsky suggested that collaborative learning and working with more knowledgeable others (MKOs) enables students to move through their ZPD whereas, in Piaget's view, learning should be a more independent process and personal discovery is vital for complete understanding.

'Each time one prematurely teaches a child something he could have discovered for himself, that child is kept from inventing it and consequently from understanding it completely'. (Piaget, 1970)

'What the child is able to do in collaboration today he will be able to do independently tomorrow.' (Vygotsky, 1987).

▼ Processes involved in scaffolding (Wood *et al.*, 1976)

Recruitment	*Engage interest and encourage* Gaining the learner's interest in the task and ensuring they stick to the specific requirements of the task.
Reduction in degrees of freedom	*Simplify* Simplifying the task by reducing the number of acts required to reach a solution, reducing alternative choices.
Direction maintenance	*Keep up motivation* Ensuring learning stays on task, in line with the original objectives, despite distractions, such as new problems emerging.
Marking critical features	*Highlight relevant features of task* The tutor makes sure that the relevant features of the task are kept in the foreground, providing information about what has been achieved.
Frustration control	*Reducing frustration* Making sure the learner doesn't experience frustration and also doesn't develop too much dependency on the tutor.
Demonstration	*Modelling solutions to tasks* The tutor provides a model of idealised task performance.

APPLYING PIAGET'S THEORY TO EDUCATION

Readiness – According to Piaget, each stage of cognitive development appears through the natural process of ageing. Therefore, his view is that you cannot teach a child to perform certain activities before they are biologically 'ready'. For example, it would be difficult to teach a pre-operational child to perform abstract mathematical calculations. For *real* learning to take place (as opposed to rote learning with little understanding), Piaget proposed that activities should be at the appropriate level for a child's age. If a child is not mature enough, they may acquire skills superficially but in order to truly understand and become competent it is important to wait until they are ready.

Stages of development – The concept of readiness means that educational programmes should be designed along the lines of Piaget's stages of development. For example, children in the concrete operational stage should be given concrete materials to manipulate (e.g. an abacus to development numerical skills).

Motivation to learn – Piaget suggested that cognitive growth comes from the desire to resolve the disequilibrium caused by cognitive conflict. A teacher's task is to create an environment where the learner is challenged to accommodate current schemas to cope with new information. The teacher's role is not to impart knowledge but to ask questions and in this way a child's knowledge develops through discovery learning.

Logical thinking – Piaget argued that logical thinking is the spur to cognitive development and needs to be taught. He believed that logical thinking was not 'innate'. Therefore, it is important to have logic, maths and science subjects on the curriculum to facilitate cognitive development.

APPLYING VYGOTSKY'S THEORY TO EDUCATION

Vygotsky maintained that learners construct knowledge through interaction with their social environment. He agreed with Piaget that children must construct understanding and knowledge in their own minds, but Vygotsky placed greater emphasis on how this process is facilitated by collaboration with others.

Collaborative learning refers to a method of learning in which students at various performance levels work together in small groups toward a common goal. Group members are responsible for one another's learning as well as their own, so the success of one student helps other students to be successful. When people work collaboratively, they bring their own perspectives to the activity, and so are better able to generate a solution through shared understanding.

Peer tutoring and the **more knowledgeable other** (MKO) refers to someone who has a better understanding, with respect to a particular task or concept, than the learner. Although the MKO is often a teacher or older adult, this is not necessarily the case. A child's peers may be the individuals with more knowledge or experience, and therefore may act as the MKO. This is called **peer tutoring**.

Scaffolding – Jerome Bruner and his colleagues (Wood *et al.*, 1976) were the first to introduce the term **scaffolding** to describe the Vygotskian process of assisting a learner through the **ZPD** (explained on page 148). Scaffolding is a 'process that enables a … novice to solve a problem, carry out a task, or achieve a goal which would be beyond his unassisted efforts' (Wood *et al.*, 1976). The expert or tutor creates a 'scaffold' (i.e. temporary support), which is gradually withdrawn as the child is more able to work independently.

The motivation to learn – Scaffolding provides the motivation to learn. A learner is motivated to move through their zone of proximal development (ZPD) by MKOs who encourage a learner to tackle increasingly difficult tasks, taking control when necessary and handing over responsibility to the learner whenever they are ready.

EVALUATION

Readiness – The notion of readiness implies that practice on a task should *not* lead to improved performance until a child is sufficiently mature. There is evidence for and against this. Bryant and Trabasso (1971) showed that pre-operational children could be trained to solve certain logical tasks. They argued that children's failure was due to memory restrictions rather than a lack of operational (logical) thinking. When pre-operational children practiced solving simple problems and gradually built up to more complex tasks, they could cope, showing that practice rather than readiness mattered.

In contrast, Danner and Day (1977) found that practice made no difference. Students aged 10 and 13 were tutored on three formal operational tasks and showed no improvement, whereas 17-year-olds' performance was improved as we would expect because they should be sufficiently mature. However, even when practice does improve performance, this doesn't mean the child has *understood* the principles of the operation – they may be just repeating certain actions and will not be able to transfer this knowledge to a novel situation.

Limitations – Sylva (1987) suggests that the criticisms of Piaget's theory undermine its educational application. Other critics feel that Piagetian discovery activities are often at the expense of content knowledge and may lead to backwardness in reading and writing because they spent too little time practising these skills (Modgil *et al.*, 1983). Furthermore the Piagetian view may be culture-biased. It suggests that the child is the sole agent of his learning which is an **individualist** approach.

EVALUATION

Collaborative learning – Research has found support for the value of collaborative learning. For example, Gokhale (1995) found that students who participated in collaborative learning subsequently performed better on an individual critical-thinking test than students who studied individually.

Many studies have shown that peer tutoring leads to improvements in both tutees' and tutors' academic and social development (e.g. Cohen *et al.*, 1982). However, a consistent finding is that it is most effective for peer tutors (Cloward, 1967). This makes sense because the best way to understand something better is to teach it. One note of caution with these studies is that experimental groups often receive peer tutoring in *addition* to normal lessons, and having extra lessons may be the reason for greater success (Slavin, 1991).

Maximising the value of scaffolding – Wood and Middleton (1975) found that successful scaffolding depends on something they called 'contingent regulations'. They watched mothers and their three-to-four-year-old children assembling a three-dimensional pyramid puzzle, a task that was beyond the children's current abilities. They found that task mastery was related to contingent regulations – when a mother responded to her child's failure by providing more explicit instructions (e.g. identifying what particular piece needs to be moved) and responded to success by providing less explicit instructions (e.g. just praising the strategy that has just been used). This shows that the teaching (from MKO) needs to respond differentially to a learner's responses to enhance learning success.

IDA — CULTURAL BIAS

On page 149 we discussed the cultural differences between Piaget and Vygotsky's approach. Such differences may lead to a cultural bias because we assume that they apply to all cultures but this may not be the case. Vygotsky's approach may be more appropriate in collectivist settings because true sharing is the basis of such cultures. This is not to say that group work is not possible in individualist societies but in settings where children are encouraged to be more competitive and self-reliant, group work may be less effective. For example, Stigler and Perry (1990) compared American and Asian schools and found in the latter that maths was more effectively taught by group work than in individualist American schools.

Evaluation — ASSESSING TEACHING METHODS

It is difficult to assess real learning because learning is so complex. There are problems with selecting suitable outcome measures (i.e. ways of measuring whether learning has taken place). In addition, the goals of one method are different from the goals of another, and therefore each would select different outcome measures. Also, two teachers may ostensibly be using the same method, but there may be significant differences in what they do in practice.

Evaluation — GENERAL EVALUATION

Discovery learning – Both theories place importance on the active role of the learner and have had a major influence on education. For example, the British *Plowden Report* (1967) drew extensively on Piaget's theory and led to major changes in primary school education in the UK. However, this active approach is by no means new. The psychologist John Dewey advocated child-centred education in the 1920s, as did the Greek philosopher Plato in the 4th century BC. Walkerdine (1984) suggests that theories of cognitive development are simply used to provide 'after the fact' justifications for a new educational idea, rather than being the original driving force.

Comparison with 'traditional' methods – A classic study compared the more formal, teacher-oriented approach with active learning methods derived from Piaget and Vygotsky (Bennett, 1976) and found that, in general, children taught via formal methods did better on reading, maths and English. However, the best results of all were produced by some teachers using more informal, child-centred methods. The general lack of success for active learning may be due to the fact that teachers in formal classrooms spend more time on the core topics, and that is why children do better when assessed in this way. A further reason may be that active learning requires much more sensitivity and experience from teachers in knowing how and when to guide pupils. Therefore, it is not the method, but the application of it that is the problem.

Emotion – Both theories are mainly concerned with the development of problem-solving abilities and ignore the importance of emotional intelligence. Projects such as SEAL (social and emotional aspects of learning) have been developed in English schools to redress the balance.

CAN YOU...? (No.8.3)

...1 Write an outline (in about 200 words) of the application of both Piaget and Vygotsky's theories to education.

...2 Identify **eight** criticisms related to applications of cognitive development theories to education, including **at least one** IDA topic. Each criticism should be about 50 words.

...3 Use this material to write a 600-word answer to the following two questions:

(a) Outline **one** theory of cognitive development. (4 marks)
(b) Discuss the application of this theory to education. (4 marks + 16 marks)

Discuss the application of **one or more** theories of cognitive development to education. (8 marks + 16 marks)

KOHLBERG'S THEORY OF MORAL UNDERSTANDING

Respect and concern for others has long been an essential requirement for civilised groups. Moral understanding has both an *emotional* component (in that we might empathise with the suffering of another person or feel guilty for causing it) and a *cognitive* component (cognitive maturity allows us to make more sophisticated judgements about right and wrong). The theory covered on this spread emphasises the cognitive component.

KOHLBERG'S THEORY

Lawrence Kohlberg began studying moral development in the 1950s. At that time there were two dominant approaches in psychology. The first was the **behaviourist** approach, explaining moral development in terms of rewards and punishments – children learn to behave in ways regarded as morally 'good' because they receive rewards, and avoid behaviour regarded as morally 'bad' as a consequence of being punished. The second dominant approach was Piaget's theory of moral development. Piaget (1932) proposed that children's moral thinking changes as a consequence of maturity – a similar idea to his theory of cognitive development.

Kohlberg's approach was inspired by Piaget's theory although Kohlberg focused particularly on the way children *think* about moral decisions, rather than on their moral *behaviour*. Kohlberg (1966) constructed a stage theory based on extensive interviews that he conducted with boys aged 10–16 (see above). The key features of the theory are:

- The stages are *invariant* and *universal* – people everywhere go through the same stages in the same order.
- Each new stage represents a more *equilibriated* form of moral understanding, resulting in a more logically consistent and morally mature form of understanding.
- Each stage forms an *organised whole* – a qualitatively different pattern of moral understanding that is applied across all situations.
- Moral maturity is achieved through (1) biological *maturation*, (2) *disequilibrium* (noticing weaknesses in the existing style of thinking) and (3) gains in *perspective-taking* (understanding another's point of view).

REAL-WORLD APPLICATION

IDA

Kohlberg observed that children raised on Israeli kibbutzim were morally more advanced than those not raised on kibbutzim, which led him to suggest that belonging to a democratic group and being involved in making moral judgements facilitated moral development. With Carol Gilligan, he set up a number of *Cluster Schools* (also called 'just' communities) in a number of schools, and even one in a prison. Members had the power to define and resolve disputes within the group, encouraging moral development.

KOHLBERG'S MORAL DILEMMAS

Kohlberg (1958) collected data on the thinking behind moral decisions by using a moral judgement interview. He created nine hypothetical moral dilemmas (such as the one below) which presented a conflict between two moral issues. A total of 84 boys aged 10, 13 or 16 were interviewed. Each boy was asked to discuss three of these dilemmas, prompted by a set of ten or more open-ended questions, such as: 'Why do you think that would be right or wrong?', or ,'What does the word morality mean to you?'. The focus was not on the boys' actual moral decision but the thinking behind the decision. The boys' answers were analysed and common themes were identified so that the stage theory could be constructed.

▲ Lawrence Kohlberg (1927–1987)

AN EXAMPLE OF KOHLBERG'S MORAL DILEMMA

The Heinz moral dilemma – *In Europe, a woman was near death from cancer. There was one drug the doctors thought might save her. A druggist in the same town had discovered it, but he was charging ten times what the drug cost him to make. The sick woman's husband, Heinz, went to everyone he knew to borrow money, but he could only get together half of what it cost. The druggist refused to sell it cheaper or let Heinz pay later. So Heinz got desperate and broke into the man's store to steal the drug for his wife.*

KOHLBERG'S STAGES OF MORAL DEVELOPMENT

THE PRE-CONVENTIONAL LEVEL Children accept the rules of authority figures and judge actions by their consequences. Actions that result in punishments are bad, those that bring rewards are good.	**Stage 1** The punishment and obedience orientation	This style of morality ignores the intentions behind a behaviour and focuses on obeying rules that are enforced by punishment (e.g. 'Heinz shouldn't steal the drug because he might get caught and sent to prison').
	Stage 2 The instrumental purpose orientation	Children view actions as 'right' if they satisfy their own needs (e.g. 'Stealing is OK because Heinz had to do it to save his wife').
THE CONVENTIONAL LEVEL Individuals continue to believe that conformity to social rules is desirable, but this is not out of self-interest. Maintaining the current social system ensures positive human relationships and social order.	**Stage 3** Interpersonal cooperation	This is a 'good boy – good girl' orientation. What is right is defined by what is expected by others (e.g. 'People would think Heinz inhuman if he didn't save his wife').
	Stage 4 The social-order-maintaining orientation	This marks the shift from defining what is right in terms of role expectations to defining right in terms of norms established by the larger social system (e.g. 'Even if his wife is dying, it's still his duty as a citizen to obey the law').
THE POST-CONVENTIONAL (PRINCIPLED) LEVEL The post-conventional individual moves beyond unquestioning compliance with the norms of their own social system. They now define morality in terms of abstract moral principles that apply to all societies and situations.	**Stage 5** The social-contract orientation	Laws are seen as relative and flexible. Where they are consistent with individual rights and the interests of the majority, they are upheld (to preserve social order), otherwise they can be changed (e.g. 'Although there is a law against stealing, the law wasn't meant to violate a person's right to life').
	Stage 6 The universal ethical principles orientation	Morality is defined in terms of self-chosen abstract moral principles. Laws usually conform to these principles, but where this is not the case, the individual acts in accordance with their moral principles (e.g. 'It doesn't make sense to put respect for property above respect for life itself').

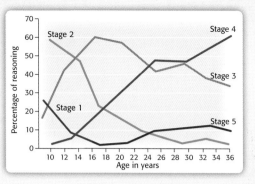
EVALUATION

Moral behaviour

One problem with Kohlberg's theory is that it concerns moral thinking rather than behaviour (and it is behaviour that people are ultimately interested in, e.g. why do some people commit crimes while others don't). Kohlberg did predict that those who reason in a more mature fashion should be inclined to more morally mature behaviour and he found some support for this (Kohlberg, 1975). When students were given the opportunity to cheat on a test, he found that only 15% of college students at the post-conventional stage cheated, whereas 70% of those at the pre-conventional stage did. However, Burton (1976) found that people only behave consistently with their moral principles on some *kinds* of moral behaviour, such as cheating or sharing toys, and concluded that generally it is likely that factors other than moral principles affect moral behaviour, such as the likelihood of punishment or the nature of the situation.

Moral consistency

A further issue is that participants do not make consistent judgements when given moral dilemmas i.e. they might judge one dilemma using Stage 1 arguments and another using Stage 3 arguments. Krebs and Denton (2005) suggest that the reason for this is that moral principles are only one factor in moral behaviour and may be overridden by more practical factors, such as making personal financial gains. In fact Krebs and Denton found, when analysing real-life moral decisions, that moral principles were used to justify behaviour *after* it had been performed.

Different moral perspectives

A further criticism of Kohlberg's theory is that he had a restricted view of morality. Gilligan argued (see 'gender bias' above right) that Kohlberg favoured a morality of justice rather than of care. Eisenberg (1982) also claimed that Kohlberg's view of morality was restricted by ignoring the effect of emotional factors. Eisenberg suggested that moral decision making matures as children develop the ability to empathise with others.

Strengths

Kohlberg's theory has remained an important influence on our understanding of moral development, especially in terms of its emphasis on the universal nature of at least some kinds of moral reasoning and the the way that moral reasoning progresses with age.

GENDER BIAS

Kohlberg's dilemmas deal with wrongdoing. The result is that his classification system is based on a morality of *justice*. There are other criteria on which moral decisions are based, such as being more concerned with relationships. Carol Gilligan (1982) found that women tend to be more focused on relationships ('caring'), than justice when making moral decisions. This suggests that Kohlberg's theory was gender-biased and restricted to only one type of morality. However, many psychologists have come to recognise that Gilligan's critique was more of an expansion of Kohlberg's theory than an alternative to it (Jorgensen, 2006). The core concepts put forward by Kohlberg remain unchallenged, such as the invariant sequence of development and the importance of social interactions.

CULTURAL BIAS

Kohlberg claimed that his stages were universal, and cited evidence from Mexico, Turkey, India and Kenya that supported his findings (Colby and Kohlberg, 1987). Snarey (1985) also reviewed studies using Kohlberg's dilemmas conducted in 27 different countries, all reporting the same sequence of development. However, other research has found that post-conventional understanding occurs mainly in more developed, industrialised societies and is much less usual in rural communities (Snarey and Keljo, 1991). This may be related to Kohlberg's concept that moral maturity is achieved through *disequilibrium*. More diverse communities pose more conflicts, and this may promote moral development because individuals have to question moral standards.

REALISM

Gilligan (1982) also criticised Kohlberg's research because the evidence was not based on real-life decisions. The moral dilemmas were hypothetical scenarios which may have made little sense, especially to young children. Gilligan's own research involved interviewing people about their own moral decisions, such as the decision about whether to have an abortion.

CAN YOU...?   No.8.4

...1 Write a description, in about 200 words, of Kohlberg's theory of moral understanding.

...2 Produce a shortened version of the theory in 100 words.

...3 Identify **eight** criticisms related to Kohlberg's theory, including **at least one** IDA topic. Each criticism should be about 50 words.

...4 Use this material to write a 600-word answer to the question: *Discuss Kohlberg's theory of moral understanding.* (8 marks + 16 marks)

The final three spreads of this chapter are concerned with the development of **social cognition** – our ability to predict, monitor and interpret the behaviours and mental states of other people. This is something that adults do effortlessly, using, for example, the tone of someone's voice or minimal changes in a person's facial expression. Learning to understand these signals begins with the child's development of self, enabling them to distinguish self from other. This distinction leads on to a **Theory of Mind** – the comprehension that someone else's thoughts are separate from your own.

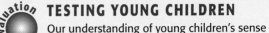

Evaluation | **TESTING YOUNG CHILDREN**

Our understanding of young children's sense of self involves inferring what is going on in their minds on the basis of outward behaviours. Psychologists have devised some ingenious ways of doing this, such as the **mirror test** and the **false-belief task**, but such measures are not perfect and may possibly underestimate what children can actually do.

▲ Around the age of 18 months an infant first recognises that its reflection in the mirror is actually of itself. This is demonstrated using the mirror test.

THE MIRROR TEST

Gallup (1970) and Amsterdam (1972) independently developed a test of self-awareness using monkeys and human babies respectively. The test involves placing a smudge of rouge or red colouring on the individual's nose and then seeing what they do when shown their reflection in a mirror. If they possess self-awareness they will touch their own nose, otherwise they will touch the mirror. To this day the **'mirror test'** (or 'rouge test') is regarded as the best way to assess self-awareness (Bard *et al.*, 2006).

Amsterdam (1972) tested 88 babies, obtaining reliable data from 16 of them (many didn't want to play). She found that babies between 6 and 12 months behaved as if the baby in the mirror is someone else. Between 13 and 24 months, babies looked warily at the image in the mirror, possibly displaying some self-awareness. By 24 months, babies clearly recognised themselves.

A CHILD'S SENSE OF SELF

Subjective self-awareness

Some aspects of self-awareness are present from birth, such as sensations of warmth and fullness. By two months, infants have a sense of 'personal agency', in that they recognise that they are responsible for the movement of their limbs. For example, Bahrick and Watson (1985) demonstrated that five-month-olds had an awareness of what their legs were doing. The infants responded differently to a video taken in real time of their leg movements (so video and current movements were synchronised) and a video of their leg movements taken at an earlier time.

Around the same time infants can also recognise their own faces, for example Legerstee *et al.* (1998) found that five- to eight-month-old infants looked longer at pictures of other children than at pictures of themselves.

Lewis (1991) argues that this is a subjective rather than objective sense of self. *Subjective* self-awareness refers to the ability to *perceive* oneself as distinct from others, which is different from the ability to reflect upon oneself – an *objective* sense of self.

Objective self-awareness and self-recognition

The ability to reflect upon oneself (objective self-awareness) is regarded as a milestone in development and a key feature of human behaviour (see discussion on far right). When an infant responds to a rouge mark on its nose by touching its nose rather than the mirror image, this suggests an understanding that the mirror image is of itself, demonstrating objective self-awareness. Amsterdam's findings (see research study on left) have been confirmed in a number of other studies. For example, the classic study by Lewis and Brooks-Gunn (1979) found that 19% of babies touched their nose by the age of 15 months and 66% did it by 24 months. Around the same age, babies are beginning to use personal pronouns, such as 'me' and 'mine' (Slater and Lewis, 2002).

Psychological self

Visual or physical self-recognition is only the beginning of a child's self-concept: young children still lack a psychological concept of who they are. When asked to describe themselves, children aged four years are likely to mention physical features, such as: 'I've got black hair' or 'I can ride my bike' (Damon and Hart, 1988). However, they are beginning to develop a psychological self. Eder (1990) used questions to elicit insight into the child's psychological self (e.g. asking children to choose between 'I like to play by myself' and 'I like to play with my friends'). The choices young children made were stable over time, showing that they have some rudimentary psychological insights.

A further development is **self-esteem**, the value that a person attaches to their self-concept. Signs of this also begin to appear around the age of four.

Distinguishing between self and others – Theory of Mind

Theory of Mind (ToM) is not an actual theory like Piaget's theory of cognitive development. It is an intuitive set of beliefs (or 'theory') developed by each individual – the understanding that someone else has a separate mind to your own and therefore does not see or experience the world as you do.

Newborns can distinguish between humans and other objects, therefore displaying a knowledge of others (Legerstee, 1992). By the age of two, children display some understanding of the mental state of others, for example they comfort others and begin to use deceit which requires an understanding of what someone else believes to be true (Dunn, 1991). However, a distinction is made between knowing about someone else's internal state and knowing about how they experience the world. The latter is a true Theory of Mind (Wellman and Woolley, 1990). Infants are capable of social interaction but social *relationships* require ToM.

ToM first appears around the age of three or four years. At this time children also start using terms like 'think' and 'know' when referring to others. The typical task used to demonstrate ToM is the **false-belief task** (see above).

FALSE-BELIEF TASK

The classic **false-belief** task is called the **Sally Anne Test**, a story about two dolls (see right). A child with ToM can answer the final question correctly – and would respond that Sally would look in the basket despite the fact that the child knows the ball is in the box. A child without ToM cannot separate their own knowledge from Sally's, and would therefore say that Sally will look in the box because that is where the child would look. ToM enables us to recognise that others can have beliefs about the world that are wrong (i.e. false beliefs).

The test was first used by Wimmer and Perner (1983) who found that nearly all three-year-olds say the ball is in the box, whereas from four years on children give the correct answer (a false belief).

Other tasks have been devised to test false beliefs, such as the appearance-reality task. For example, in the *Smartie tube test* a child is shown a tube of Smarties and asked what is inside. The child is then shown that in fact a pencil is inside. Finally they are asked what another child will say when shown the tube. A child without ToM says 'a pencil'. This makes an interesting link to Piaget's appearance-reality distinction because both concern a child's ability to distinguish between superficial appearance and reality, based on logical reasoning (see page 146).

Sally puts her ball in her basket and leaves the room.

Anne moves the ball to her box.

Sally returns. Where will she look for the ball?

EVALUATION

Subjective self-awareness

The view that infants are born with a rudimentary sense of self, or a least an ability to distinguish themselves from others, is not shared by all psychologists. Freudians such as Mahler *et al.* (1973) present a contrasting view. They argue that, at birth, an infant has no sense of separateness from his/her mother. Individuation (the infant's recognition of self as distinct from others) is something that develops over the first few months of life.

Objective self-awareness

Emotional development – One of the *consequences* of the development of objective self-awareness is the ability to display emotions. Very young children display the basic emotions of pleasure, sadness, fear, and surprise, but the development of the conscious awareness of self is an important step in emotional development and leads to self-conscious emotions, such as empathy, jealousy and embarrassment.

Individual differences – Research has found that the development of self-recognition is faster in **securely attached** infants (Pipp *et al.*, 1992) and also in babies who have been encouraged to be independent (Borke *et al.*, 2007). This makes an interesting link to cultural differences (see right) because in Western cultures attachment is about *independence*; infants are given more object stimulation and less body contact. By contrast, the norm in non-Western cultures is *interdependence* (Borke *et al.*, 2007).

Psychological self

The development of self-esteem, a key aspect of the psychological self, is also related to attachment, and this creates individual differences. For example, Verschueren and Marcoen (1999) found that securely attached children rated themselves more favourably and that this was stable over time (Verschueren *et al.*, 2001).

Theory of mind

Autism – Simon Baron-Cohen has taken a particular interest in the concept of ToM as an explanation for the childhood disorder of **autism**. One of the typical characteristics of individuals with autism is that they find social interaction difficult. Baron-Cohen *et al.* (1985) used the **Sally Anne Test** (see above) to demonstrate that autistic children lacked a ToM whereas children with Down's syndrome coped normally, showing that social abnormalities typical of autism are not linked to low IQ but to a specific ToM deficit.

ToMM – Baron-Cohen (1995) has proposed a ToM module (ToMM) which is a specific mechanism that matures in the brain around the age of four and explains an individual's ability to understand the mental states of other people. Alternatively, it is possible that **mirror neurons** underlie ToM (see page 158).

Individual differences – ToM Is not solely determined by biology. Research shows that it appears earlier in children from large families (Perner *et al.*, 1994). Having a large family and especially older siblings means that a child is challenged to think about the intentions of others when resolving conflicts. Research has also shown that discussion about motives and other mental states promotes the development of ToM (Sabbagh and Callanan, 1998).

IDA **USE OF NON-HUMAN ANIMALS**
When considering the use of non-human animals in psychological research, one argument concerns the extent to which animals *experience* pain. The argument is that there is an important difference between being in an emotional state and experiencing an emotion. The difference lies in consciousness, a self-reflexive ability often regarded as uniquely human. Psychologists have sought to establish consciousness in other animals by using the **mirror test**. This is discussed on page 134.

IDA **CULTURAL BIAS**
Descriptions of the development of a child's sense of self assume that children all over the world follow a similar sequence, whereas research shows that this is a culturally biased perspective. For example, Van den Heuvel *et al.* (1992) compared Dutch, Turkish and Moroccan children aged 10–11 years. As predicted, Western (**individualist**) children used many more psychological statements than the non-Western (**collectivist**) children, whereas the non-Western children used more references to the social aspects of self.

Liu *et al.* (2004) compared over 300 Chinese and North American children in terms of ToM. They found a similar sequence of development in both groups, but the timing differed by as much as two years in different communities supporting the role of biological and experiential factors.

CAN YOU...? No.8.5

...1 Write a description, in about 200 words, of the development of the child's sense of self.

...2 Outline, in about 100 words, Theory of Mind with reference to its role in the development of a child's sense of self.

...3 Identify **eight** criticisms related to the development of the child's sense of self, including **at least one** IDA topic. Each criticism should be about 50 words.

...4 Use this material to write a 600-word answer to the question: *Discuss the development of the child's sense of self, including Theory of Mind.* (8 marks + 16 marks)

DEVELOPMENT OF A CHILD'S UNDERSTANDING OF OTHERS

The development of a child's sense of self is the beginning of the development of their understanding of others. The concept of self is a fundamental aspect of social development because such knowledge is necessary in order to identify oneself as human and interact meaningfully with other humans (Lewis, 1990).

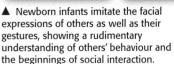

▲ Newborn infants imitate the facial expressions of others as well as their gestures, showing a rudimentary understanding of others' behaviour and the beginnings of social interaction.

A CHILD'S UNDERSTANDING OF OTHERS

Wellman and Woolley (1990) distinguished between knowing about someone else's internal state and knowing about their representations of the world, i.e. a true **Theory of Mind (ToM)**. Psychologists have charted the stages in the child's ultimate development of this true ToM, and these stages are described below.

Early development

Imitation – The first evidence of children's understanding of others is shown in their ability to imitate other people's expressions. Meltzoff and Moore (1977, 1989) found that even newborns who are less than 72 hours old are able to imitate an experimenter's facial gestures of mouth opening, lip protrusion and tongue protrusion, as well as manual gestures, such as the opening of the hand (see illustrations above).

Intentions – In order to interact with others it is necessary to understand their intentions, although this is still a simpler mental ability than understanding the *thoughts* of others. Infants as young as three months will follow a person's gaze to nearby objects, which indicates an understanding of communicative intent (D'Entrement *et al.* 1997). Around the age of one, infants reliably follow gaze and pointing gestures to more distant objects (Carpenter *et al.*, 1998). Carpenter *et al.* (2001) used the same test with autistic children aged two-and-a-half to five years and found little difference with normal children, which suggests that understanding intentions is a separate ability to ToM.

Perspective-taking

Egocentricity – Piaget described the **pre-operational** child as 'egocentric' i.e. unable to take another's perspective, and demonstrated this using the three mountains experiment (see page 147). He suggested that this was typical of children under the age of four, although other researchers found that younger children could cope if the task was set in a social context (e.g. involving a naughty boy hiding from a policeman).

It is important to distinguish this *perceptual* perspective-taking ability from the *conceptual* perspective-taking ability required by the **Sally Anne test** which is used to assess ToM (see previous spread). The three mountains task relies solely on visuo-spatial skills and doesn't involve understanding the beliefs of others.

Role-taking – Role-taking (conceptual perspective-taking) is a cognitive skill involving a child's comprehension about other people's internal experiences. It is strongly related to ToM. Robert Selman, a psychoanalyst by training, used dilemmas similar to Kohlberg (see page 152). Selman's dilemmas explore children's reasoning when faced with conflicting feelings. He used children's answers to construct a stage model of the development of perspective-taking (see below). As children grow older they develop the ability to analyse the perspectives of several people and can even imagine how different cultural values would influence objective perception.

Role-taking and social development – Selman (1980) argued that role-taking was the central dynamic of social development. This enables a child to understand the perspective and feelings of another person. Ultimately this leads to **prosocial behaviour**.

Deception – An interesting outcome of role-taking is the ability to deceive. Children are first able to plant a **false belief** in someone else's mind around the age of three. For example, Cole (1986) found that children of this age were able to hide their disappointment when they received the worst present (rather than the best one) if they were being watched by others, but they did show disappointment when filmed secretly on their own.

SELMAN'S ROLE-TAKING DILEMMAS

Selman (1976) used dilemmas, such as the one below, to assess the ability of children to take the perspective of others.

AN EXAMPLE OF SELMAN'S PERSPECTIVE-TAKING DILEMMA

Holly is an eight-year-old girl who likes to climb trees. She is the best tree climber in the neighbourhood. One day while climbing a tree she falls off the bottom branch but does not hurt herself. Her father sees her fall, and is upset. He asks her to promise not to climb trees any more, and Holly promises.

Later that day, Holly and her friends meet Sean. Sean's kitten is caught up a tree and cannot get down. Something has to be done right away or the kitten may fall. Holly is the only one who climbs trees well enough to reach the kitten and get it down, but she remembers her promise to her father.

Selman then asked children a series of role-taking questions: If Holly climbs the tree, should she be punished? Will her father understand if she climbs the tree? Will Sean understand if Holly refuses?

SELMAN'S STAGE THEORY OF PERSPECTIVE OR ROLE-TAKING

Stage 0: Undifferentiated Approx 3–6 years	Children can distinguish between self and others but are largely governed by their own perspective (e.g. whatever is right for Holly is the same as what will be right for others).
Stage 1: Social-informational 6–8 years	Children are aware of perspectives that are different from their own, but assume that is because others have different information (e.g. Holly's father would not be angry if he realised why she did it).
Stage 2: Self-reflective 8–10 years	Children can now understand that two people with the same information may form different views. Aware of other's perspective and also aware that other people can understand their perspective – but can't consider two perspectives at the same time.
Stage 3: Mutual 10–12 years	Can step outside a two-person situation and imagine how the self and other are viewed from the point of view of a third, impartial party (e.g. can view both Holly and her father's perspectives as well as Holly's view of her father's feelings and vice versa).
Stage 4: Societal 12–15+ years	Personal decisions are now made with reference to social conventions (e.g. Holly shouldn't be punished because the humane treatment of animals is important).

► Children often display coyness – deliberately looking cute. This is another behaviour that requires some understanding of another person's point of view, because the child is presuming that his behaviour has a particular effect on the observer.

EVALUATION

The evidence suggests that there is a clear progression in the development of children's abilities to understand others, starting with imitation and understanding intention, and ending with true ToM (understanding the thoughts and feelings of others i.e. a **mentalistic** state). The question is to what extent these abilities are separate or are interdependent i.e. is the shift to a 'higher' ability dependent on previous stages, or are they functionally separate?

Separate modules

One view is that there are separate biological modules for different abilites, which mature at different rates. On the next spread we will look at neurophysiological evidence for a unique, innate ToM module which is activated around three years of age. Behavioural support for a separate ToM module comes from the fact that autistic children can understand the intentions of others but do not develop ToM (see far left). This is further supported by Hobson (1984) who found that autistic children performed at the same level as children of the same mental age on the three mountains task – so they could cope with *perceptual* perspective-taking but ultimately do not develop *conceptual* perspective-taking.

Interdependence

On the other hand, there is evidence that points more to a continuum, starting with imitation and moving through perceptual perspective-taking to ToM (conceptual perspective-taking). Perceptual perspective-taking is a necessary (but not sufficient) condition of ToM. Research has shown that children with sensory impairments (such as hearing or visual difficulties) usually experience delays in the development of ToM (Eide and Eide, 2006). For example, some hearing-impaired children do not develop ToM until adolescence. It is possible that their restricted sensory experiences slow down the development of perceptual perspective-taking and this, in turn, slows down the normal development of ToM.

The importance of role-taking skills

Role-taking skills are a critical component of moral understanding. In fact they are fundamentally important in all social behaviour, for example popular children have better role-taking skills (Schaffer, 2002) which suggests that social success is related to understanding the mental states of others.

Another social behaviour, deception, may not appear to be an important outcome of role-taking skills but in terms of evolution it is. In general, ToM is an ability that has evolved because it is part of group living and social interaction – in order for any animal to interact with other members of its species, each individual needs to have an ability to understand the mental states of others. However, hand in hand with this is the evolution of the ability to deceive or manipulate others (sometimes called **Machiavellian intelligence**). Anyone capable of deceiving their conspecifics (members of the same species) has an evolutionary advantage (see page 134).

IDA NATURE AND NURTURE

Throughout this chapter we have looked at a number of stage theories. The key feature of stage theories is that they describe an invariant developmental sequence i.e. all children are expected to go through the stages in the same order. Each stage is an outcome of the previous stage such that the behaviours associated with later stages build on behaviours developed in earlier stages. The invariant nature of the stages implies some biological mechanism. Biological maturation sets the bottom limits so that children below a certain age, for example, cannot develop ToM or abstract logical thinking. However, **nurture** as well as **nature** is important. The speed of development is related to experience (nurture), for example deaf children are slower to develop ToM.

IDA REAL-WORLD APPLICATION

The evidence we have examined shows that perspective or role-taking skills can be fostered by experience, and this has a number of important implications for schools, therapy and the treatment of criminals. Selman (2003) argues that facilitation of role-taking is one of the fundamental missions of primary schools today, and that it should be woven into many of the daily activities. One way to do this with younger children is through play, as this is the natural way in which role-taking skills are learned (Smith and Pellegrini, 2008). *Social skills training* (SST) programmes are used with older children. SST is also used in therapeutic settings with people with mental disorders or emotional problems.

One explanation offered for antisocial, criminal behaviour is that some criminals lack empathy and role-taking skills, and this may explain their 'willingness' to harm others directly or indirectly (Hoge *et al.*, 2008). Therefore, SST programmes have been developed where prisoners are taught role-taking skills to increase their empathic concern for others and their prosocial behaviour on release from prison.

There is a final interesting application of perspective-taking research. In one study, researchers (Sommerville *et al.*, 2005) used 'sticky mittens' to enable very young infants to manipulate objects (the mittens had Velcro on them so that infants were able to pick objects up). The interesting thing was that these infants then showed earlier-than-usual abilities to understand the intentions of others, suggesting that if you give infants earlier-than-normal experiences this may speed up the development of understanding intentions and ultimately of perspective-taking. The researchers said that there was no current plan to market their sticky mittens for keen parents who wish to encourage social and cognitive development.

CAN YOU...?   No.8.6

...1 Write a description, in about 200 words, of the development of a child's understanding of others.

...2 Identify **eight** criticisms related to the development of the child's sense of self, including **at least one** IDA topic. Each criticism should be about 50 words.

...3 Use this material to write a 600-word answer to the question: *Discuss the development of the child's understanding of others.* (8 marks + 16 marks)

157

As we have seen, more than 20 years ago Simon Baron-Cohen proposed that a biological mechanism might underlie the ability to develop a **Theory of Mind (ToM)**. Since that time psychologists have searched for neurophysiological evidence for this ToM module (ToMM) and produced an extensive list of possible locations, including the superior temporal areas, the **amygdala** and the **orbitofrontal cortex** (OFC) (Stone, 2007). This long list suggests that ToM is served by a number of components, some of which are domain-general (i.e. relate to a number of abilities including ToM but not exclusive to it) and some which are domain-specific (i.e. specific to ToM).

However, in the 1990s the discovery of **mirror neurons (MNs)** overshadowed the search for a ToMM (see page 154) and offered a new kind of explanation for ToM. Mirror neurons are nerve cells that react when a person performs an action and also when another individual performs the same action. This means that an observer experiences the actions of another as if it were his own. The neurologist V.S. Ramachandran (2000) predicted that 'mirror neurons will do for psychology what DNA did for biology: they will provide a unifying framework and help explain a host of mental abilities that have hitherto remained mysterious and inaccessible to experiments'.

A TEA PARTY

Evaluation

Iacoboni *et al.* (2005) conducted a study to demonstrate that MNs might encode more than the *what* of an action but also the *why* i.e. the understanding of a person's intentions. In this study, 23 participants were shown three different types of a movie clip related to a 'tea party' and fMRI was used to record neuron activity.

- **Context clip** – scene one was before tea (tea cup full, table clean), scene two after (crumbs on table).
- **Action clip** – scene one showed a hand grasping the cup as if to drink from it, scene two showed the hand grasping the cup as if to clear it away. There was no context in this clip, just a hand.
- **Intention clip** – combined context and action.

Iacoboni *et al.* found the highest level of MN activity in the inferior **frontal cortex** from the intention clip. This shows that this area of the brain is concerned with understanding *why* a person was behaving in a certain way, because otherwise there would have been a similar level of activity from the other clips.

THE ROLE OF THE MIRROR NEURON SYSTEM

Mirror neurons (MNs) were discovered accidentally by Rizzolatti *et al.* (1996). The researchers were recording neural activity in the **motor cortex** of macaque monkeys when they found that certain neurons in the F5 area of the **premotor cortex** became active when the monkey wasn't doing anything but was watching another monkey or an experimenter perform an action (such as tearing up paper). The same neurons then became active if the monkey repeated the action itself.

Imitation

What had been discovered was a system that could explain, at the most basic level, how one individual imitates another. A mirror neuron encodes the activity of another as if the observer were acting out the same activity.

Such imitation is important in the acquisition of skilled behaviours, where an observer watches how someone else performs an action and then models that behaviour. Imitation, as we have seen on the previous spread, is also the beginning of the development of social cognition.

Another aspect of imitation is behavioural regulation. MN response is generally 'off-line', i.e. watching someone else's performance doesn't immediately result in imitation, although sometimes we find it difficult to resist, for example yawning when someone else does. Research has found that individuals who have damage to their frontal cortex (the part of the brain involved in inhibitory control) display compulsive imitation (Lhermitte *et al.*, 1986).

Understanding intention

Research subsequently found that MNs recorded more than the mere imitation of motor activity. It appears that MNs also represent intentions, i.e. not just what a person is doing but what they intend to do. Iacoboni *et al.* (see left) demonstrated this in humans.

The progression from imitation to intention is similar to the development of social cognition in children (see previous spread). The next step is the ability to take the perspective of others.

Perspective taking and ToM

Gallese and Goldman (1998) claimed that MNs may be seen as 'a part of, or a precursor to, a more general mind-reading ability' because they enable us to experience someone else's actions as if they are our own. This means that MNs are the mechanism by which we understand another person's perspective, i.e. when we develop a **Theory of Mind** (ToM, see page 154).

This may also lead to empathy – the ability to do more than just understand what someone else is thinking but to also understand how they are feeling. Eisenberg (2000) suggested that empathy is likely to be the basis for **prosocial behaviour**.

Language acquisition

Language is an important part of social behaviour and MNs may play a role in its development. For example, the beginning of learning to use language involves the imitation of speech sounds. This is likely to involve MNs (Rizzolatti and Arbib, 1998).

Further indication of a link between language and MNs comes from Binkofski *et al.* (2000). Using brain imaging techniques, they found evidence of MNs in Broca's area. This area of the brain is involved in speech production. It is also the human equivalent of the F5 area where MNs were found in macaque monkeys.

NATURE OR NURTURE

IDA

Gopnik (2007) suggests that MNs could offer a different kind of explanation. She proposes that MNs might arise as a result of experience (**nature**) rather than being innate (**nature**). Neurons learn by association – when two events are associated the neurons for each event form a connection ('cells that fire together wire together'). An infant's first experience is to see a hand moving (its own) and at the same time experience that hand moving. This would create a mirror connection.

NEUROIMAGING

None of the research on human MNs would be possible without modern neuroimaging techniques, such as functional magnetic resonance imaging (**fMRI**). This works by highlighting the areas of the brain that are rich in oxygenated blood. Such areas represent the more active areas of the brain.

EVALUATION

Simulation theory

The discovery of MNs has been seen as support for **simulation theory** (ST). According to this theory we read other people's minds by experiencing what they are experiencing and use this to predict the other's actions and feelings.

The alternative view is **'theory' theory** (TT), which suggests that we infer mental states from observations, and construct a 'theory' about what the other person is thinking on the basis of all available information. We infer states on the basis of reasoning. ToM is essentially a 'theory' theory.

The discovery of MNs offered a neurological basis for ST because MNs suggest that the way we experience others is by having an internal, off-line representation. However, not everyone agrees with this. For example, Borg (2007) argues that there remains a difference between experiencing the actions of another person and reading their mind. Borg likens the MN approach to **behaviourism** where it is assumed that, for example, crying (a behaviour) is all there is to being sad (a mental state).

Lack of supporting evidence

There is some supporting evidence (see box on right) but generally the confirmation has been weak for the more major claims of MNs. For example, the brain regions that are active when people experience emotions or active when watching someone else experiencing emotions are not the ones identified for mirror neurons (Lamm *et al.*, 2007).

On the other hand Gazzola *et al.* (2006) have produced evidence that people high in empathy (as measured by self-report) show greater activity in the MN brain regions.

Is it all a myth?

Alison Gopnik (2007) suggests that mirror neurons have taken on the status of a scientific myth. She argues that the major claims made for the role of mirror neurons have little foundation in reality. First of all much of the evidence is derived from non-human animal studies and this evidence may not generalise to humans since most non-human animals do not have ToM (see page 157 for evidence). Second, Gopnik argues that it is inconceivable that systems as complex as moral behaviour could be explained simply by mirror neurons. They may form the basis of ToM but a lot more would have to be involved.

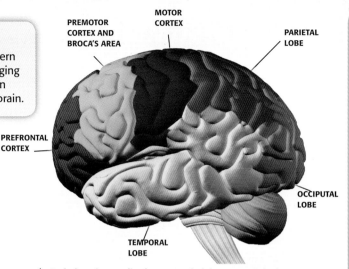

▲ Brain imaging studies have revealed the areas of the human brain rich in MNs. The inferior frontal lobe is the lower part of the blue area which has been linked to emotional MNs (Wicker *et al.*, 2003) and Broca's area (language production). Areas in the temporal lobe may be related to auditory MNs (Gazzola *et al.*, 2006) and in the occipital, parietal and temporal lobe to visual input. Decety (2007) has identified the frontopolar cortex (in the frontal lobe) and the right inferior parietal lobule as key areas.

Evaluation EVIDENCE FROM NEURONS

Our understanding of mirror neurons and the role they may play in human behaviour is an area of research in its infancy. The early excitement of researchers remains to be matched by hard evidence. It is not easy to gain direct evidence of human neural activity as such research requires placing electrodes inside the brain.

Much of the evidence so far has been based on non-human animal studies where it is possible to use electrodes in individual neurons. Where there has been research on humans, this has involved imaging studies. Such studies can only tell us about the activity of thousands of neurons, not individual cells. This makes it difficult to draw meaningful conclusions.

However, recently, Iacoboni (Slack, 2007) was able to observe the activity of individual neurons in epileptic patients wired up to locate the starting point of their seizures. The research team recorded the actions of 286 individual neurons in the frontal lobes of the subjects' brains and then asked them to perform simple actions and to observe short films of others executing the same actions. The study identified 34 mirror neurons, which were activated by both performance and observation. They also identified different kinds of MN – one kind actually becomes suppressed when watching a film, which might explain why we don't imitate everything we see and how we can distinguish between our own and someone else's behaviour.

IDA REAL-WORLD APPLICATION

Various studies have produced evidence that autistic individuals may have some sort of MN malfunction. For example, Williams *et al.* (2001) suggest that MN abnormalities may well underlie the fact that people with autism often have difficulty copying actions. Dapretto *et al.* (2006) used brain-scanning techniques to observe what parts of the brain were used by autistic and non-autistic children as they watched faces showing anger, fear, happiness, sadness or no emotion. The only difference was that the autistics showed reduced activity in a part of the inferior frontal gyrus, a section of the brain that has been identified as part of the mirror neuron system. Slack (2007) suggests that it might be possible to help autistic individuals by strengthening their MNs through activities that require the imitation of others.

CAN YOU...?   No.8.7

...1 Write a description, in about 200 words, of biological explanations of social cognition, including the role of mirror neurons.

...2 Identify **eight** criticisms related to the biological explanations of social cognition, including **at least one** IDA topic. Each criticism should be about 50 words.

...3 Use this material to write a 600-word answer to the question: *Discuss biological explanations of social cognition.* (8 marks + 16 marks)

CHAPTER SUMMARY

DEVELOPMENT OF THINKING

PIAGET'S THEORY

MECHANISMS
- Cognitive development is the result of maturation and experience.
- Children develop schema (behavioural or cognitive) for dealing with the world.
- Assimilation – existing schema used on new information.
- Accommodation – existing schema adapted to fit new information.
- Equilibration – child develops new schema or adapts existing ones to restore equilibrium.
- Operations – logical mental rules.

STAGES
- Sensorimotor – sensory input co-ordinated with motor actions. Key development is object permanence.
- Pre-operational – thinking becomes increasingly symbolic. Characterised by egocentricity and lack of reversibility.
- Concrete operational – logical operations, such as reversibility, decentration and conservation.
- Formal operational – can solve abstract problems using hypothetico-deductive reasoning.

EVALUATION
- Little support for Piaget's disequilibrium claim.
- Sensorimotor stage – evidence that children at three months display object permanence.
- Pre-operational stage – children able to display decentration if task more realistic.
- Concrete operational stage – Piaget's claims about number conservation challenged in 'naughty teddy' study.
- Formal operational stage – only one third of adults reach this stage.
- Limitations – Piaget underestimated children's abilities at younger ages and used flawed methods.
- Strengths – influence on education; highlighted qualitative differences between child and adult thinking.

IDA
- Piaget's theory represents combination of nature (maturation) and nurture (experience).

VYGOTSKY'S THEORY

MENTAL PROCESSES
- Social interaction plays fundamental role in cognitive development.
- Elementary mental functions transformed into higher mental functions through culture.
- Culture contributes content (knowledge) and *processes* of thinking.

PROCESS OF CULTURAL INFLUENCE
- Child initially learns through shared problem-solving with 'experts'.
- Culture transmitted through language, from pre-intellectual to egocentric to inner speech.
- Social relations converted into higher mental processes through semiotic mediation.
- ZPD – what child can do in cooperation today, can do alone tomorrow.

EVALUATION
- Claims for importance of culture supported in cross-cultural research (e.g. Gredler, 1992).
- Importance of language in instruction demonstrated in Carmichael *et al.* study (1932).
- Evidence for ZPD in jigsaw completion study.
- Limitations include relatively little supporting research; role of biological factors underestimated.
- Non-human animal research suggests higher mental functions *not* uniquely human.
- Strengths – more positive approach than Piaget's in terms of experience, therefore more educational implications.

IDA
- Differences between Piaget and Vygotsky's theories reflect background – Piaget individualist Swiss, Vygotsky Communist Russian.

DEVELOPMENT OF SOCIAL COGNITION

DEVELOPMENT OF SENSE OF SELF

SUBJECTIVE SELF-AWARENESS
- Two months – children have sense of 'personal agency'.
- Five months – infants recognise their own faces.
- Ability to perceive oneself as distinct rather than ability to reflect upon oneself (objective self-awareness).

EVALUATION
- Alternative view – Mahler *et al.* (1973) suggest infants have no sense of separateness from mother.
- Difficult to infer mental states of young children from behaviour.

OBJECTIVE SELF-AWARENESS
- In 'mirror test', children 6–12 months act as if reflection is someone else; by 24 months children recognise that reflection was their own (Gallup, 1970; Amsterdam, 1972).
- At same age, children begin to use personal pronouns (me, mine).

EVALUATION
- Objective self-awareness leads to ability to display emotions.
- Development of self-recognition faster in securely attached infants.

PSYCHOLOGICAL SELF
- Age 4, children develop a psychological self, with psychological insights about themselves.
- Develop self-esteem, which is the value a person attaches to their self-concept.

EVALUATION
- Positive self-esteem related to secure attachment (Verschueren and Marcoen, 1999).

THEORY OF MIND (ToM)
- The understanding that other people have separate mental states and see the world differently.
- Social relationships require ToM, which starts to appear at age 3-4 years.

EVALUATION
- Autistic individuals find social interaction difficult because of ToM deficit.
- Baren-Cohen (1995) – development of ToM module (ToMM) explains individual's ability to understand mental states of others.
- Individual differences – ToM appears earlier in children from large families (Perner *et al.*, 1994).

IDA
- Non-human animals – experience of emotions requires consciousness. Consciousness found in other species with mirror test.
- Cultural bias, e.g. individualist cultures – more psychological statements of self; collectivist cultures – more social statements.

KOHLBERG'S THEORY OF MORAL UNDERSTANDING

APPLICATIONS TO EDUCATION

PIAGET'S THEORY
- Readiness – activities must match children's maturational age.
- Educational programmes should match child's stage of development.
- Motivation to learn through disequilibrium and discovery learning.
- Logical thinking – needs to be taught through maths and science.

EVALUATION
- Concept of readiness – evidence for (Danner and Day, 1977) and against (Bryant and Trabasso, 1971).
- Sylva (1987) claims criticisms of Piaget's theory undermine its educational application.

VYGOTSKY'S THEORY
- Collaborative learning – students at different levels work in small group toward common goal.
- Importance of 'more knowledgeable other' (MKO) and peer tutoring.
- Scaffolding – offering assistance to learner when necessary.
- Learner motivated to move through their ZPD by MKO.

EVALUATION
- Research support for collaborative learning (Gokhale, 1995) and peer tutoring (Cohen et al., 1982).
- Success of scaffolding depends on contingent relations (Wood and Middleton, 1975).

GENERAL EVALUATION
- Difficulties of assessing learning include selection of suitable outcome measures; individual differences among teachers.
- The active approach existed without the theoretical underpinning.
- More formal methods of instruction – teachers spend more time on core topics, so children do better when assessed this way.
- No mention of emotional factors.

IDA
- Cultural bias – Vygotsky's approach more appropriate to collectivist cultures.

NATURE OF THE THEORY
- Focus on the way children *think* about moral decisions rather than moral *behaviour*.
- Used moral dilemmas to discover thinking behind answers.

STAGES OF MORAL DEVELOPMENT
- Three levels, each divided into two stages:
  I *Preconventional* – accept rules of authority figures, actions judged by their consequences (stage 1: punishment and obedience, stage 2: instrumental purpose).
  II *Conventional*. Interest in maintaining positive relationships and social order (stage 3 interpersonal cooperation, stage 4: social order maintaining).
  III *Postconventional* – Morality now defined in terms of abstract moral principles that apply across all situations (stage 5: social-contract, stage 6: universal ethical principles).
- Stages invariant and universal.
- New stage is more logical and mature understanding.
- Each stage is qualitatively different from the preceding one.
- Moral maturity achieved through: biological maturation; disequilibrium and gains in perspective-taking.

EVALUATION
- Colby et al. (1983) – longitudinal study showed Stage 1 and 2 reasoning decrease with age, 4 and 5 increase.
- Theory concerns moral thinking rather than moral behaviour; thinking consistent with behaviour only in some situations.
- Lack of consistency across different dilemmas, moral decisions may be overridden by practical factors.
- Restricted perspective – morality of justice rather than care and lacks reference to emotional factors.
- Moral stories lack realism, unlike Gilligan's research.
- Remains a key theory.

IDA
- Real-world application – cluster schools enabled moral thinking.
- Gender bias – theory restricted to a justice (male)-based morality. Gilligan (1982) – different 'moral voice' of women.
- Evidence for universality of moral reasoning (Colby and Kohlberg, 1987), but postconventional reasoning rare in rural communities.

CHILD'S UNDERSTANDING OF OTHERS

EARLY DEVELOPMENT
- Children's understanding of others first evident in imitation – demonstrated at 72 hours.
- Following gaze of others indicative of understanding of communicative intent – evident at 3 months.
- Research with autistic children suggests understanding intent separate from ToM.

PERSPECTIVE-TAKING
- Pre-operational children lack ability to take another's perspective.
- Role-taking – cognitive skill involving child's comprehension about other's internal experiences.
- Selman – role-taking important in social development.
- Selman's stage theory of role taking – undifferentiated → social-informational → self-reflective → mutual → societal.
- Deception – ability to plant false belief in another's mind, appears around age 3.

EVALUATION
- Clear progression in development of social abilities – imitation → understanding intention → ToM.
- May be separate biological modules for different abilities, which mature at different rates.
- Other evidence suggests continuum – e.g. children with sensory impairments usually experience delays in development of ToM.
- Importance of role-taking skills – popular children have better role-taking skills.
- Ability to deceive others – adaptive value (Machiavellian intelligence).

IDA
- Real-world application: role-taking skills in SST training programmes in schools and prisons.
- Invariant sequence of stages (nature) and experience (nurture).

BIOLOGICAL EXPLANATIONS OF SOCIAL COGNITION

ROLE OF MIRROR NEURONS
- Accidental discovery in macaque monkeys (Rizzolatti et al., 1996) – neurons in cortex fired when monkeys performed action or observed another monkey perform same action.
- Imitation based on MN activity – important in acquisition of skilled behaviours and in behavioural regulation.
- Understanding intention – Iacoboni et al. (2005) demonstrated in humans.
- Leads to general mind-reading ability (perspective-taking and Theory of Mind) and to empathy (important for prosocial behaviour).
- Language acquisition – Binkoski et al. (2000) MNs in Broca's area.

EVALUATION
- Simulation theory – 'read' others' minds by experiencing what they are experiencing. 'Theory' theory – infer mental states from observations of actions.
- Lack of support, e.g. Lamm et al. (2007) found mismatch between MNs for emotion and brain areas active during emotional processing, but Gazzola et al. (2006) found opposite.
- Gopnik (2007) – MNS a scientific myth. Most evidence derived from animal studies, complex behaviours unlikely to be explained by MNs.
- Support for MNs – 34 MNs identified when recording electrical activity in epileptics' brains; also different kinds, e.g. one suppressed while watching a film (Slack, 2007).

IDA
- Real-world application – Williams et al. (2001) autistic individuals may have some sort of MN malfunction.
- MNs may be innate (nature) or created through association (nurture).

QUESTION **(a) Describe and evaluate Piaget's theory of cognitive development.** *(4 marks + 8 marks)*

(b) Discuss biological explanations of social cognition. *(4 marks + 8 marks)*

STUDENT ANSWER

(a) *Piaget's theory consists of four stages of development: sensorimotor stage, pre-operational stage, concrete operations and formal operations. A child moves through these stages in a fixed order and at predictable ages.*

In the first stage the child learns to co-ordinate sensory input with their own movements. A typical development during this stage is object permanence, where an infant comes to realise that objects that can't be seen still exist.

The second stage of cognitive development is the pre-operational stage, which happens between the ages of 2 and 7. 'Pre-operational' refers to the fact that children of this age are not capable of using systematic mental rules and their thinking lacks internally-consistent logic. During this period children's thought becomes increasingly symbolic but it lacks reversibility of thought, for example in Piaget's conservation tasks children of this age think that if you change the physical properties of an object (such as rolling out a ball of clay), the quantity has actually changed. Children of this age are also described as egocentric and can only see the world from their position and are not aware of other perspectives.

Piaget used the three mountains experiment to demonstrate egocentric thinking. Children in the pre-operational stage choose their own perspective when asked what view a doll would be seeing that was placed at various positions around the model of mountains. However, this method has been criticised because it was quite unrealistic. Another psychologist (Hughes, 1975) showed that young children can understand another person's perspective if tested with something more realistic – like a naughty boy doll hiding from a toy policeman. This doesn't actually mean that Piaget was wrong; he just underestimated what children of a certain age can do.

The same point can be shown in his conservation experiments. When other psychologists repeated this but used one question instead of two they found that younger children could conserve (Samuel and Bryant, 1984). They still found age-related differences – the very youngest children couldn't conserve, but children younger than 7 were able to conserve.

A key criticism of Piaget's approach has been that he overemphasised biological processes (nature) and didn't place enough emphasis on experiential factors. He did acknowledge that experience plays a key role in creating new mental structures (the process of assimilation and accommodation) but he didn't mention the ways that culture may have influenced this process but Vygotsky did.

Piaget's theory has had important real-world application to education, influencing the way children are taught especially in primary school. The emphasis is on concrete operations because that is what Piaget found out about the way that children of this age think.

(b) *One biological explanation of social cognition is the mirror neuron system. This was discovered in research with monkeys where they found that certain cells in the pre-motor cortex became active even when the monkey either performed an action or observed another monkey or an experimenter performing the same task. This led neuropsychologists to find similar mirror neurons (MNs) in humans using brain scanning techniques.*

Another biological explanation is the ToM module (ToMM). Baron-Cohen (1995) proposed that there is specific mechanism that matures in the brain around the age of four and explains an individual's ability to understand the mental states of other people. It could be that MNs are involved in the ToMM.

Evidence for mirror neurons was initially from animal studies and then from brain scanning in humans. Both techniques do not give us precise information about how mirror neurons might actually function in humans. But recently there has been an attempt to directly measure activity in individual neurons and this appears to support the MN system.

[603 words]

EXAMINER COMMENTS

It is important to divide your time, when answering a question like this, according to the marks available. A glance at the answer on the left shows that the student has not done this – spending considerably more time on part (a) than part (b), even though part (b) is worth the same marks. Furthermore, in both parts the student has presented too much description. In order to maximise essay marks it is crucial to strictly organise your answer according to the AO1/AO2 split.

(a) The first three paragraphs offer a **well-detailed** description of Piaget's stages (considering that only 4-marks worth are required). Two stages are presented in outline but two are more detailed than necessary for a brief outline. Other aspects of the theory have not been included. Students generally have a lot to write about Piaget's theory which causes problems in a essay where only 4 marks are available for description. It makes sense to practise writing 4- and 8-mark descriptions (about 100 and 200 words respectively) in order to be prepared.

The fourth paragraph provides evaluation. It begins with a brief **description** of research which is then evaluated. This evaluation is **coherently elaborated** and the **line of argument** is clear. Notice how the methodological criticism has been linked back to Piaget's theory. Many students fail to do this and therefore don't receive **AO2** credit.

The evaluation is continued in the next paragraph. The final two paragraphs of part (a) cover **IDA** topics. Both of them have been well contextualised, i.e. they are **effective**.

AO1– Accurate, well-detailed and **coherent**. There is more than 200 words of description.

AO2 – There is a similar amount of evaluation (about 200 words), which is appropriate for the 8 marks available. **It is well-focused** and there is **effective** use of issues, debates and approaches (**IDA**).

(b) This part of the question requires more than one explanation and two have been provided here. The same could have been achieved by looking at different aspects of social cognition (e.g. intention, language acquisition). Both descriptions are **reasonable** but not enough for 4 marks.

Sadly, this student has left little time for any **evaluation**. What has been given is rather superficial, and would be improved by the addition of some more precise details and/or references.

AO1 – Overall the knowledge and understanding covered is **basic** and there is insufficient **breadth** and **depth**.

AO2 – Rudimentary, material not used **effectively**, some evidence of **elaboration**. No **IDA**.

Chapter 9
Psychopathology: Schizophrenia

SPECIFICATION

Psychopathology

Candidates will be expected to study one of the following disorders:
- *schizophrenia*
- *depression*
- *phobic disorders*
- *obsessive compulsive disorder*

Schizophrenia	
Overview	• Clinical characteristics of schizophrenia. • Issues surrounding the classification and diagnosis of schizophrenia, including reliability and validity.
Explanations	• Biological explanations of schizophrenia, for example genetics, biochemistry. • Psychological explanations of schizophrenia, for example behavioural, cognitive, psychodynamic and socio-cultural.
Therapy	• Biological therapies for schizophrenia, including their evaluation in terms of appropriateness and effectiveness. • Psychological therapies for schizophrenia, for example behavioural, psychodynamic and cognitive-behavioural, including their evaluation in terms of appropriateness and effectiveness.

The opening voice-over of the 1976 horror film *Schizo* (right) demonstrates two of the most common misconceptions that many people have about **schizophrenia**. Schizophrenia is neither 'split personality' nor 'multiple personality'. People with schizophrenia are not perpetually incoherent nor do they constantly display **psychotic** (loss of contact with reality) behaviour. Schizophrenia is, however, a severe mental disorder characterised by a profound disruption of cognition and emotion. This affects a person's language, thought, perception, affect and even their sense of self. The schizophrenic believes things that cannot be true (delusions) or hears voices or sees visions where there are no sensory stimuli to create them (hallucinations). Schizophrenia ranks among the top 10 causes of disability worldwide and affects about one in 100 people at some point in their lives (Mathers *et al.*, 1996).

▶ **Misleading media**
Schizophrenia is often misrepresented in the medi[a]
The voice-over in the '70s fi[lm]
'Schizo' erroneously refers to
'...a mental disorder, somet[imes]
known as multiple or split
personality, characterised by [loss]
of touch with the environm[ent]
and alternation
between
violent and
contrasting
behaviour
patterns'.

CLINICAL CHARACTERISTICS OF SCHIZOPHRENIA

Positive and negative symptoms – the symptoms of schizophrenia are typically divided into positive and negative symptoms. Positive symptoms are those that appear to reflect an excess or distortion of normal functions. Negative symptoms are those that appear to reflect a diminution or loss of normal functions, which often persist during periods of low (or absent) positive symptoms. Under DSM-IVR, the diagnosis of schizophrenia requires at least a one-month duration of two or more positive symptoms.

A: Positive symptoms

- **Delusions** – bizarre beliefs that seem real to the person with schizophrenia, but they are not real. Sometimes these delusions can be paranoid (i.e. persecutory) in nature. Delusions may also involve inflated beliefs about the person's power and importance.
- **Experiences of control** – the person may believe they are under the control of an alien force that has invaded their mind and/or body.
- **Hallucinations** are bizarre, unreal perceptions of the environment that are usually auditory (hearing voices) but may also be visual (seeing lights, objects or faces), olfactory (smelling things) or tactile (e.g. feeling that bugs are crawling on or under the skin).
- **Disordered thinking** – the feeling that thoughts have been inserted or withdrawn from the mind. In some cases the person may believe their thoughts are being broadcast so that others can hear them. Tangential, incoherent or loosely associated speech is used as an indicator of thought disorder.

B: Negative symptoms

- **Affective flattening** – a reduction in the range and intensity of emotional expression, including facial expression, voice tone, eye contact and body language.
- **Alogia** – poverty of speech, characterised by the lessening of speech fluency and productivity. This is thought to reflect slowing or blocked thoughts.
- **Avolition** – the reduction of, or inability to initiate and persist in, goal-directed behaviour (for example sitting in the house for hours every day, doing nothing); it is often mistaken for apparent disinterest.

Adapted from the American Psychiatric Association (2000) DSM-IVR criteria for the diagnosis of schizophrenia.

ISSUES OF RELIABILITY AND VALIDITY

Reliability

Reliability refers to the consistency of a measuring instrument, such as a questionnaire or scale, to assess, for example, the severity of their schizophrenic symptoms. Reliability of such questionnaires or scales can be measured in terms of whether two independent assessors give similar diagnoses (**inter-rater reliability**) or whether tests used to deliver these diagnoses are consistent over time (**test–retest reliability**).

Inter-rater reliability – The publication of DSM-III in 1980 was specifically designed to provide a much more reliable system for classifying psychiatric disorders. In a review of the success of DSM-III, Carson (1991) claimed that DSM-III had fixed the problem of inter-rater reliability once and for all. Psychiatrists now had a reliable classification system, so this should have led to much greater agreement over who did, or did not, have schizophrenia.

Test–retest reliability – Cognitive screening tests such as RBANS (Repeatable Battery for the Assessment of Neuropsychological Status) are important in the diagnosis of schizophrenia as they measure the degree of neuropsychological impairment. Wilks *et al.* (2003) administered two alternate forms of the test to schizophrenic patients over intervals varying from 1–134 days. The test–retest reliability (correlation of scores across the two test periods) was high at .84.

Validity

Validity refers to the extent that a diagnosis represents something that is real and distinct from other disorders and the extent that a classification system such as **ICD** or DSM measures what it claims to measure. Reliability and validity are inextricably linked because a diagnosis cannot be valid if it is not reliable.

Comorbidity – **Comorbidity** is an important issue for the validity of diagnosis of mental illness. It refers to the extent that two (or more) conditions co-occur. Psychiatric comorbidities are common among patients with schizophrenia. These include substance abuse, anxiety and symptoms of depression. Buckley *et al.* (2009) estimate that comorbid depression occurs in 50% of patients, and 47% of patients also have a lifetime diagnosis of comorbid substance abuse. Such comorbidity creates difficulties in the diagnosis of a disorder and also in deciding what treatment to advise.

Positive or negative symptoms? – Klosterkötter *et al.* (1994) assessed 489 admissions to a psychiatric unit in Germany to determine whether positive or negative symptoms were more valid for a diagnosis of schizophrenia. They found that positive symptoms were more useful for diagnosis than were negative symptoms.

Prognosis – People diagnosed as schizophrenic rarely share the same symptoms, nor is there evidence that they share the same outcomes. The prognosis for patients varies with about 20% recovering their previous level of functioning, 10% achieving significant and lasting improvement, and about 30% showing some improvement with intermittent relapses (Bentall *et al.*, 1988). A diagnosis of schizophrenia, therefore, has little **predictive validity** – some people never appear to recover from the disorder, but many do.

EVALUATION

Reliability

Inter-rater reliability – Despite the claims for increased reliability in DSM-III (and later revisions), over 30 years later there is still little evidence that DSM is routinely used with high reliability by mental health clinicians. Recent studies (e.g. Whaley, 2001) have found inter-rater reliability correlations in the diagnosis of schizophrenia as low as +.11. Further problems with the inter-rater reliability of diagnosis of schizophrenia are illustrated in the Rosenhan study on the right.

Unreliable symptoms – For a diagnosis of 'schizophrenia', only one of the characteristic symptoms is required 'if delusions are bizarre'. However, this creates problems for diagnosis. When 50 senior psychiatrists in the US were asked to differentiate between 'bizarre' and 'non-bizarre' delusions, they produced inter-reliability correlations of only around +.40, forcing the researchers to conclude that even this central diagnostic requirement lacks sufficient reliability for it to be a reliable method of distinguishing between schizophrenic and non-schizophrenic patients (Mojtabi and Nicholson, 1995).

Test–retest reliability – Measures of cognitive functioning are vital in the diagnosis of schizophrenia, therefore must have test–retest reliability to be useful in this role. Prescott et al. (1986) analysed the test–retest reliability of several measures of attention and information processing in 14 chronic schizophrenics. Performance on these measures was stable over a 6-month period.

Comparing DSM and ICD – Cheniaux et al. (2009) investigated the inter-rater reliability of the diagnosis of schizophrenia according to both DSM-IV and ICD-10. Although the inter-rater reliability was above +.50 for both classificatory systems, schizophrenia was more frequently diagnosed according to ICD-10 than DSM-IV criteria.

Validity

Comorbidity and medical complications – The poor levels of functioning found in many schizophrenics may be less the result of their psychiatric disorder and more to do with their untreated comorbid physical disorders. A US study (Weber et al., 2009) examined nearly 6 million hospital discharge records to calculate comorbidity rates. Psychiatric and behaviour related diagnoses accounted for 45% of comorbidity. However, the study also found evidence of many comorbid non-psychiatric diagnoses. Many patients with a primary diagnosis of schizophrenia were also diagnosed with medical problems, including hypothyroidism, asthma, hypertension and type 2 diabetes. The authors concluded that a consequence of being diagnosed with a psychiatric disorder such as schizophrenia is that patients tend to receive a lower standard of medical care, which in turn adversely affects their prognosis.

Comorbidity and suicide risk – Persons with schizophrenia pose a relatively high risk for suicide, with comorbid depression being the major cause for suicidal behaviour. For example, among patients in the National Comorbidity Survey (NCS) (Kessler et al., 1994) the rate for attempted suicide rose from 1% for those with schizophrenia alone to 40% for those with at least one lifetime comorbid mood disorder.

Ethnicity may lead to misdiagnosis – Research suggests that within the UK and elsewhere, rates of schizophrenia among African–Caribbeans are much higher when compared with white populations. For example, Harrison et al. (1997) reported that the incidence rate for schizophrenia was eight times higher for African–Caribbean groups (46.7 per 100,000) than for white groups (5.7 per 100,000). Some of this increase can be explained as a result of poor housing, higher rates of unemployment and social isolation. However, there also remains the possibility that misdiagnosis may, in part, result from factors, such as cultural differences in language and mannerisms and difficulties in relating between black patients and white clinicians.

Symptoms – Despite the belief that identification of the symptoms of schizophrenia would make for more valid diagnoses of the disorder, many of these symptoms are also found in many other disorders, such as depression and bipolar disorder. Ellason and Ross (1995) point out that people with **dissociative identity disorder** (**DID**) actually have more schizophrenic symptoms than people diagnosed as being schizophrenic!

▶ The absurdity of psychiatric diagnosis is dramatically captured in the 1975 film 'One Flew Over the Cuckoo's Nest', starring Jack Nicholson.

CAN YOU...? No.9.1

...**1** Outline clinical characteristics of schizophrenia in about 200 words.

...**2** Outline issues relating to reliability and validity in the diagnosis of schizophrenia in about 200 words.

...**3** Choose **eight** critical points relevant to issues of reliability and validity in the diagnosis and/or classification of schizophrenia. Elaborate each point in about 50 words.

...**4** Use this material to write answers to the following questions:

Outline clinical characteristics of schizophrenia. (8 marks) [200-word answer]

Discuss issues of reliability and validity associated with the classification and diagnosis of schizophrenia. (8 marks + 16 marks) [600-word answer]

There are many different explanations for the disorder that we call **schizophrenia**, but it is the biological explanations that have received the most research support to date (Comer, 2003). The importance of biological explanations of schizophrenia does not, however, deny the important role that psychological factors play in the onset of this disorder. Current thinking is that a '**diathesis-stress**' relationship may be at work, with a biological predisposition (the diathesis) for schizophrenia only developing into the disorder if other significant psychological stressors are present in the person's life (Gottesman and Reilly, 2003).

*What is a **concordance rate**? In a sample of, for example, 100 twin pairs, one twin of each pair has schizophrenia. The number of times their other twin also shows the illness determines the concordance rate, so if 40 have schizophrenia, then the concordance rate is 40%.*

▲ Studies of identical twins have provided valuable insights into the genetic origins of schizophrenia

EVIDENCE FROM TREATMENT

Evaluation

Much of the evidence supporting the dopamine hypothesis comes from the success of drug treatments that attempt to change levels of dopamine activity in the brain. The basic mechanism of antipsychotic drugs is to reduce the effects of dopamine and so reduce the symptoms of schizophrenia. For example, Davis *et al.* (1980) carried out a meta-analysis of 29 studies that analysed the effectiveness of antipsychotic treatment compared with a **placebo**. They found that at the end of the clinical trial, relapse occurred in 55% of the patients whose drugs were replaced by a placebo, but only 19% of those who remained on the drug.

BIOLOGICAL EXPLANATIONS

Genetic factors

Family studies – Family studies (e.g. Gottesman, 1991) find individuals who have schizophrenia and determine whether their biological relatives are similarly affected more often than non-biological relatives. Family studies have established that schizophrenia is more common among biological relatives of a person with schizophrenia, and that the closer the degree of genetic relatedness, the greater the risk. For example, children with two schizophrenic parents have a concordance rate of 46%, children of one schizophrenic parent 13% and siblings 9%.

Twin studies – Twin studies offer a unique opportunity for researchers to investigate the relative contributions of **genetic** and environmental influences. If **monozygotic** (identical) twins, who share 100% of their genes, are more concordant (similar) in terms of a trait like schizophrenia than **dizygotic** (fraternal) twins who share only 50% of their genes, then this suggests that the greater similarity is due to genetic factors. Joseph (2004) calculated that the pooled data for all schizophrenia twin studies carried out prior to 2001 shows a concordance rate for monozygotic twins of 40.4% and for dizygotic twins of 7.4%. More recent, methodologically sound studies (e.g. those using 'blind' diagnoses where researchers do not know whether the twin they are assessing is MZ or DZ) have tended to report a lower concordance rate for monozygotic twins. However, despite this, twin researchers still argue that even these findings support the genetic position, because they provide a monozygotic concordance rate that is many times higher than the dizygotic concordance rate.

Adoption studies – Because of the difficulties of disentangling genetic and environmental influences for individuals who share genes *and* environment, studies of genetically related individuals who have been reared *apart* are used. Probably the most methodologically sound study of this type was carried out by Tienari *et al.* (2000) in Finland. Of the 164 adoptees whose biological mothers had been diagnosed with schizophrenia, 11 (6.7%) also received a diagnosis of schizophrenia, compared to just four (2%) of the 197 control adoptees (born to non-schizophrenic mothers). The investigators concluded that these findings showed that the genetic liability to schizophrenia had been 'decisively confirmed'.

The dopamine hypothesis

Dopamine is one of the many different **neurotransmitters** that operate in the brain. The **dopamine hypothesis** states that messages from neurons that transmit dopamine fire too easily or too often, leading to the characteristic symptoms of schizophrenia. Schizophrenics are thought to have abnormally high numbers of D_2 **receptors** on receiving neurons, resulting in more dopamine binding and therefore more neurons firing. Dopamine neurons play a key role in guiding attention, so disturbances in this process may well lead to the problems relating to attention, perception and thought found in people with schizophrenia (Comer, 2003). The key role played by dopamine in schizophrenia was highlighted in three sources of evidence:

- ***Amphetamines*** – Amphetamine is a drug with special relevance for our understanding of schizophrenia. It is a dopamine **agonist**, stimulating nerve cells containing dopamine causing the **synapse** to be flooded with this neurotransmitter. Large doses of the drug can cause the characteristic hallucinations and delusions of a schizophrenic episode.
- ***Antipsychotic drugs*** – Although there are many different types of antipsychotic drug, they all have one thing in common – they block the activity of dopamine in the brain. By reducing stimulation of the dopamine system, these drugs eliminate symptoms, such as hallucinations and delusions. The fact that these drugs (known as dopamine **antagonists** because they block its action) alleviated many of the symptoms of schizophrenia, strengthened the case for being a significant contributory factor in this disorder.
- ***Parkinson's disease*** – Low levels of dopamine activity are found in people who suffer from Parkinson's disease, a degenerative neurological disorder. It was found that some people who were taking the drug *L-dopa* to raise their levels of dopamine were developing schizophrenic-type symptoms (Grilly, 2002).

► Founding member of the band Pink Floyd, Syd Barrett, developed schizophrenia in his early twenties. It has been speculated that his symptoms were made worse by drug abuses. He died of pancreatic cancer in 2006.

EVALUATION

Genetic factors

Family studies – Research has shown that schizophrenia appears to run in families, supporting the argument for a genetic basis for the disorder. However, many researchers now accept that the fact that schizophrenia appears to run in families may be more to do with common rearing patterns or other factors that have nothing to do with heredity. For example, research on **expressed emotion** (see page 168) has shown that the negative emotional climate in some families may lead to stress beyond an individual's coping mechanisms, thus triggering a schizophrenic episode.

Twin studies – A crucial assumption underlying all twin studies is that the environments of monozygotic (MZ) twins and dizygotic (DZ) twins are equivalent. It is assumed, therefore, that the greater concordance for schizophrenia between MZ twins is a product of greater *genetic* similarity rather than greater environmental similarity. However, as Joseph (2004) points out, it is widely accepted that MZ twins are treated more similarly, encounter more similar environments (i.e. are more likely to do things together) and experience more 'identity confusion' (i.e. frequently being treated as 'the twins' rather than as two distinct individuals) than DZ twins. As a result, argues Joseph, there is reason to believe that the differences in concordance rates between MZ and DZ twins reflect nothing more than the environmental differences that distinguish the two types of twin.

Adoption studies – A central assumption of adoption studies is that adoptees are not 'selectively placed', i.e. adoptive parents who adopt children with a schizophrenic biological parent are no different from adoptive parents who adopt children whose background is normal. Joseph (2004) claims that this is unlikely to have been the case, particularly in the early studies. In countries like Denmark and the US, potential adoptive parents would have been informed of the genetic background of children prior to selection for adoption. As Kringlen (1987, cited in Joseph, 2004) points out – 'Because the adoptive parents evidently received information about the child's biological parents, one might wonder who would adopt such a child'.

The dopamine hypothesis

Post-mortem studies – A major problem for the dopamine hypothesis is the fact that drugs used to treat schizophrenia by blocking dopamine activity can actually increase it as neurons struggle to compensate for the sudden deficiency. Haracz (1982), in a review of post-mortem studies of schizophrenics, found that most of those studied who showed elevated dopamine levels had received antipsychotic drugs shortly before death. Post-mortems of schizophrenics who had not received medication, on the other hand, showed that these individuals had normal levels of dopamine.

Evidence from neuroimaging research – The development of sophisticated neuroimaging techniques such as **PET scans** has allowed researchers to investigate dopamine activity more precisely than in previous studies that had relied on measures of the metabolites (waste products) associated with dopamine activity. However, neuroimaging studies have, as yet, failed to provide convincing evidence of altered dopamine activity in the brains of individuals with schizophrenia (Copolov and Crook, 2000).

CAN YOU...?   No.9.2

...1 Describe **two** biological explanations of schizophrenia in 100 words each.

...2 Outline **four** critical points for each explanation, including **(a)** the critical point being made, **(b)** your evidence for this criticism, and **(c)** how this criticism affects that explanation.

...3 Use this material to write a 600-word answer to the question: *Discuss **two or more** biological explanations of schizophrenia.* (8 marks + 16 marks)

PSYCHOLOGICAL EXPLANATIONS OF SCHIZOPHRENIA

Although biological explanations of **schizophrenia** have attracted the most research support in recent years, psychological explanations of this disorder abound. Some of these explanations are considered *psychological* in that they arise from the major psychological perspectives, while others are considered *socio-cultural*, in that they stress the role of social and family relationships in the development of schizophrenia. Both are 'psychological' in the broader sense of the word, and so are relevant to 'psychological' explanations of schizophrenia.

YOU'VE REACHED THE SCHIZOPHRENIA SOCIETY. NO NEED TO LEAVE US A MESSAGE. WE HEAR YOUR VOICE.

www.reneelevy.com

PSYCHOLOGICAL THEORIES

Psychodynamic

Freud (1924) believed that schizophrenia was the result of two related processes, regression to a pre-ego stage and attempts to re-establish ego control. If the world of the schizophrenic has been particularly harsh, for example if his or her parents were cold and uncaring, an individual may regress to this early stage in their development before the ego was properly formed and before he or she had developed a realistic awareness of the external world. Schizophrenia was thus seen by Freud as an infantile state, with some symptoms (e.g. delusions of grandeur) reflecting this primitive condition, and other symptoms (e.g. auditory hallucinations) reflecting the person's attempts to re-establish ego control.

Cognitive — Mention more

This explanation of schizophrenia acknowledges the role of biological factors in causing the initial sensory experiences of schizophrenia, but claims that further features of the disorder appear as individuals attempt to understand those experiences. When schizophrenics first experience voices and other worrying sensory experiences, they turn to others to confirm the validity of what they are experiencing. Other people fail to confirm the reality of these experiences, so the schizophrenic comes to believe that others must be hiding the truth. They begin to reject feedback from those around them and develop delusional beliefs that they are being manipulated and persecuted by others.

SOCIO-CULTURAL FACTORS *Mention more*

Life events and schizophrenia

A major stress factor that has been associated with a higher risk of schizophrenic episodes is the occurrence of stressful life events. These are discrete stresses, such as the death of a close relative or the break-up of a relationship. For example, a study by Brown and Birley (1968) found that, prior to a schizophrenic episode, patients who had previously experienced schizophrenia reported twice as many stressful life events compared to a healthy control group (see below left). The mechanisms through which stress factors trigger schizophrenia are not known, although high levels of physiological arousal associated with neurotransmitter changes are thought to be involved (Falloon *et al.*, 1996).

Family relationships

Double-bind theory – Bateson *et al.* (1956) suggest that children who frequently receive contradictory messages from their parents are more likely to develop schizophrenia. For example, if a mother tells her son that she loves him, yet at the same time turns her head away in disgust, the child receives two conflicting messages about their relationship on different communicative levels, one of affection on the verbal level, and one of animosity on the non-verbal level. The child's ability to respond to the mother is incapacitated by such contradictions because one message invalidates the other. These interactions prevent the development of an internally coherent construction of reality, and in the long run, this manifests itself as schizophrenic symptoms (e.g. flattened affect and withdrawal). These ideas were echoed in the work of psychiatrist R.D. Laing, who argued that what we call schizophrenia is actually a reasonable response to an insane world.

Expressed emotion – Another family variable associated with schizophrenia is a negative emotional climate, or more specifically, a high degree of expressed emotions. **Expressed emotion (EE)** is a family communication style that involves criticism, hostility, and emotional over-involvement. High levels of EE are most likely to influence relapse rates. A patient returning to a family with high EE is about four times more likely to relapse than a patient returning to a family with low EE (Linszen *et al.*, 1997). In a study of the relapse rates among schizophrenics in Iran, Kalafi and Torabi (1996) found that the high prevalence of EE in Iranian culture (overprotective mothers and rejective fathers) was one of the main causes of schizophrenic relapses. It appears that the negative emotional climate in these families arouses the patient and leads to stress beyond his or her already impaired coping mechanisms, thus triggering a schizophrenic episode.

Labelling theory

The *labelling theory* of schizophrenia, popularised by Scheff (1999), states that social groups construct rules for members of their group to follow. The symptoms of schizophrenia (e.g. hallucinations and delusions, and bizarre behaviour) are seen as deviant from the rules we ascribe to 'normal' experience. If a person displays these unusual forms of behaviour, they are considered deviant, and the label of 'schizophrenic' may be applied. Once this diagnostic label is applied it becomes a self-fulfilling prophecy that promotes the development of other symptoms of schizophrenia (Comer, 2003).

*In all these psychological explanations, it is likely that only vulnerable individuals (i.e. those who are in some way biologically predisposed to develop schizophrenia) are sufficiently affected by the psychological or sociocultural factors to develop schizophrenia. This is the **diathesis-stress model**.*

EXPRESSED EMOTION AND CULTURE

Although findings on expressed emotion have been replicated cross-culturally, expressed emotion is much less common in families of people with schizophrenia outside the West (Jenkins and Karno, 1992). One possible explanation for this is that non-Western cultures are less **individualist** and less committed to concepts of personal responsibility than Western societies, such as the US and UK. Thus, they are less likely to blame someone with schizophrenia for their actions.

▶ Psychiatrist R.D. Laing believed schizophrenia was a response to intolerable stresses in the family and in society.

EVALUATION OF PSYCHOLOGICAL THEORIES

Psychodynamic explanations – There is no research evidence to support Freud's specific ideas concerning schizophrenia, except that subsequent psychoanalysts have claimed, like him, that disordered family patterns are the cause of this disorder. For example, Fromm-Reichmann (1948) described '*schizophrenogenic mothers*' or families who are rejecting, overprotective, dominant and moralistic, as important contributory influences in the development of schizophrenia. Studies have shown that parents of schizophrenic patients do behave differently from parents of other kinds of patient, particularly in the presence of their disturbed offspring (Oltmanns *et al.*, 1999) but this is as likely to be a consequence of their children's problems as a cause.

Cognitive explanations – There is much evidence of a physical basis for the cognitive deficits associated with schizophrenia, for example research by Meyer-Lindenberg *et al.* (2002), which found a link between excess **dopamine** in the **prefrontal cortex**, and **working memory**. The suggestion that 'madness' is a consequence of disbelieving others, receives curious support from a recent suggestion for treatment. Yellowlees *et al.* (2002) have developed a machine that produces virtual hallucinations, such as hearing the TV tell you to kill yourself, or one person's face morphing into another. The intention is to show schizophrenics that their hallucinations are not real. As yet there is no evidence that this will provide a successful treatment.

CAN YOU...? No.9.3

...**1** Describe **four** psychological explanations of schizophrenia in about 50 words each.

...**2** Outline **eight** critical points for psychological explanations of schizophrenia, including **(a)** the critical point being made, **(b)** your evidence for this criticism, and **(c)** how this criticism affects that explanation.

...**3** Use this material to write a 600-word answer to the question: *Discuss **two or more** psychological explanations of schizophrenia.* (8 marks + 16 marks)

EVALUATION OF SOCIO-CULTURAL FACTORS

Life events and schizophrenia – Not all evidence supports the role of life events. For example, van Os *et al.* (1994) reported no link between life events and the onset of schizophrenia. Patients were not more likely to have had a major stressful life event in the three months preceding the onset of their illness. In a prospective part of the study, those patients who had experienced a major life event went on to have a *lower* likelihood of relapse.

Evidence that does suggest a link between life events and the onset of schizophrenia is only correlational. It could be that the beginnings of the disorder (e.g. erratic behaviour) were the cause of the major life events. Furthermore, life events after the onset of the disorder (e.g. losing one's job, divorce) may be a consequence rather than a cause of mental illness.

Family relationships – The importance of family relationships in the development of schizophrenia is supported by an adoption study by Tienari *et al.* (1994). In this study those adopted children who had schizophrenic biological parents were more likely to become ill themselves than those children with non-schizophrenic biological parents. However, this difference only emerged in situations where the adopted family was rated as disturbed. In other words the illness only manifested itself under appropriate environmental conditions. Genetic vulnerability alone was not sufficient.

Double-bind theory – There is some evidence to support this particular account of how family relationships may lead to schizophrenia. Berger (1965) found that schizophrenics reported a higher recall of double-bind statements by their mothers than non-schizophrenics. However, this evidence may not be reliable, as patients' recall may be affected by their schizophrenia. Other studies are less supportive. Liem (1974) measured patterns of parental communication in families with a schizophrenic child and found no difference when compared to normal families. Hall and Levin (1980) analysed data from various previous studies and found no difference between families with and without a schizophrenic member in the degree to which verbal and non-verbal communication were in agreement.

Expressed emotion – The effects of expressed emotion have received much more universal empirical support than the double-bind theory. However, there is the issue of whether EE is a cause or an effect of schizophrenia. Either way it has led to an effective form of therapy where high-EE relatives are shown how to reduce levels of expressed emotion. Hogarty *et al.* (1991) found that such therapy can significantly reduce relapse rates. However, as with all therapies, it is not clear whether the EE intervention was the key element of the therapy or whether other aspects of family intervention may have helped.

Labelling theory – In a review of the evidence, Scheff (1974) evaluated 18 studies explicitly related to labelling theory. He judged 13 to be consistent with the theory and 5 to be inconsistent, thus concluding that the theory was supported by the evidence. A study which he assessed as supporting labelling theory was the Rosenhan study, described on page 165 (Rosenhan, 1973). Rosenhan found that once the 'label' of schizophrenia had been applied, the 'diagnosis' continued to influence the behaviour of staff toward the patient, even when this was no longer warranted.

Prior to the introduction of antipsychotic drugs in the 1950s, there was no effective treatment for **schizophrenia**. Following the discovery of **dopamine** in 1952, drugs were developed that had a direct effect on the action of this **neurotransmitter**. Some drugs, such as the amphetamines, were found to create the symptoms of schizophrenia in healthy people, while others markedly reduced these symptoms in people who were severely ill. Drugs that had the latter effect consequently became known as antipsychotics.

BIOLOGICAL THERAPIES

Antipsychotic medication

Drugs that are effective in treating the most disturbing forms of **psychotic** illness, such as schizophrenia and **bipolar disorder**, are called *antipsychotics*. Antipsychotic medication helps the person with the disorder function as well as possible in their life, as well as increasing their feelings of subjective wellbeing. *Conventional* antipsychotics (such as *chlorpromazine*) are used primarily to combat the positive symptoms of schizophrenia – such as hallucinations and thought disturbances – products of an overactive dopamine system. The *atypical* antipsychotic drugs (such as *clozapine*) also combat these positive symptoms of schizophrenia (see page 164), but there are claims that they have some beneficial effects on negative symptoms as well.

Conventional antipsychotic drugs –

The basic mechanism of conventional antipsychotic drugs is to reduce the effects of dopamine and so reduce the symptoms of schizophrenia. Conventional antipsychotics are dopamine **antagonists** in that they bind to dopamine receptors (particularly the D_2 receptors) but do not stimulate them, thus blocking their action

Biological therapies are any form of treatment focused on producing physical changes in the brain, and so decreasing the symptoms of schizophrenia. Drugs are most commonly used nowadays, with ECT less likely to be the first choice of treatment. You should make this point when constructing an essay in this area.

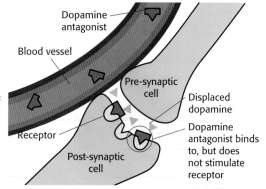

Dopamine antagonist

Blood vessel

Pre-synaptic cell

Displaced dopamine

Receptor

Dopamine antagonist binds to, but does not stimulate receptor

Post-synaptic cell

(see diagram on right). By reducing stimulation of the dopamine system in the brain, antipsychotic drugs such as *chlorpromazine* can eliminate the hallucinations and delusions experienced by people with schizophrenia. The effectiveness of the dopamine antagonists in reducing these symptoms led to the development of the **dopamine hypothesis** (see page 166) of schizophrenia.

Atypical antipsychotic drugs – Atypical antipsychotic drugs also act on the dopamine system, but are thought to block **serotonin** receptors in the brain too. Kapur and Remington (2001), however, suggest that these drugs do not involve serotonin or other neurotransmitters, but only the dopamine system, and the D_2 receptors in particular. They help by only temporarily occupying the D_2 receptors and then rapidly dissociating to allow normal dopamine transmission. It is this characteristic of atypical antipsychotics that is thought to be responsible for the lower levels of side effects (such as *tardive dyskinesia* – involuntary movements of the mouth and tongue) found with these drugs compared to conventional antipsychotics.

Electroconvulsive therapy (ECT)

Historical origins – The idea that schizophrenia could somehow be cured by inducing seizures followed reports that *dementia praecox* (an early name for what we now know as schizophrenia) was rare in patients with severe epilepsy, and that seizures in patients with dementia praecox somehow reduced the symptoms of the disorder. The first studies of the clinical use of this technique specifically for the treatment of schizophrenia were disappointing, with lower rates of recovery for ECT patients compared to those who did not receive ECT (Karagulla, 1950).

What happens in ECT? – An electric current is passed between two scalp electrodes to create a seizure. An electrode is placed above the temple of the non-dominant side of the brain, and a second in the middle of the forehead (unilateral ECT). The patient is first injected with a short-acting barbiturate, so they are unconscious before the electric shock is administered. They are then given a nerve-blocking agent, paralysing the muscles of the body to prevent them contracting during the treatment and causing fractures. A small amount of electric current (approximately 0.6 amps), lasting about half a second, is passed through the brain. This produces a seizure lasting up to one minute, which affects the entire brain. A patient usually requires between 3 and 15 treatments. The use of ECT as a treatment for schizophrenia is described in the box on the left.

ECT AND SCHIZOPHRENIA

Evaluation

Tharyan and Adams (2005) carried out a review of 26 studies which included 798 participants in total, in order to assess whether ECT resulted in any meaningful benefit for schizophrenic patients (e.g. in terms of hospitalisation, change in mental state and behaviour).

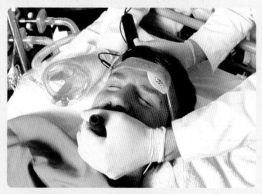

They included a range of studies that compared ECT with a **placebo** condition, with 'simulated', or 'sham' ECT and with antipsychotic medication.

They found that when ECT was compared with placebo or simulated ECT, more people improved in the real ECT condition. However, there was no indication that this advantage was maintained over the medium- or long-term. When ECT was compared with antipsychotic medication treatment, results favoured the medication groups. There was some limited evidence to suggest that when ECT was *combined* with antipsychotic medication, this resulted in a greater improvement in mental state. The authors conclude that a combination of ECT and medication may be appropriate when rapid reduction of symptoms is required, or when patients show limited response to medication alone.

EVALUATION

Effectiveness of conventional antipsychotics

Relapse rates – Many studies that have evaluated the effectiveness of antipsychotic medication have done so by comparing the relapse rates of those on medication with those on a **placebo**. For example, a review by Davis *et al.* (1980) found a significant difference in terms of relapse rates between treatment and placebo groups in every study reviewed, thus demonstrating the therapeutic effectiveness of these drugs (see above right).

Other factors are important – One of the studies in the Davis *et al.* review (Vaughn and Leff, 1976) found that antipsychotic medication *did* make a significant difference, but only for those living with hostility and criticism in their home environment. In such conditions, the relapse rate for those on medication was 53%, but for those in the placebo condition the relapse rate was 92%. For individuals living in more supportive home environments, however, there was no significant difference between those on medication (12% relapse rate) and those in a placebo condition (15% relapse rate).

Appropriateness of conventional antipsychotics

Tardive dyskinesia – Conventional antipsychotics have many worrying side effects, including *tardive dyskinesia* (uncontrollable movements of the lips, tongue, face, hands and feet). About 30% of people taking antipsychotic medication develop tardive dyskinesia, and it is irreversible in 75% of cases (Hill, 1986).

Motivational deficits – Ross and Read (2004) argue that being prescribed medication reinforces the view that there is 'something wrong with *you*'. This prevents the individual from thinking about possible stressors (such as life history or current circumstances) that might be a trigger for their condition. In turn this reduces their motivation to look for possible solutions that might alleviate these stressors and reduce their suffering.

Effectiveness of atypical antipsychotics

Atypical versus conventional antipsychotics – Although the introduction of the new 'atypical' antipsychotics raised expectations for the outcomes possible with medication, a **meta-analysis** of studies published in 1999 revealed that the superiority of these drugs compared to conventional antipsychotics was only moderate (Leucht *et al.*, 1999). This analysis found that two of the new drugs tested were only 'slightly' more effective than conventional antipsychotics, while the other two were no more effective.

Effectiveness with negative symptoms – The claim that atypical antipsychotics are particularly effective with the negative symptoms of schizophrenia also has very marginal support. In the Leucht *et al.* study, two of the atypical drugs were 'slightly' more effective than conventional antipsychotics, one was 'as effective' and one 'slightly worse'.

Appropriateness of atypical antipsychotics

Lower likelihood of tardive dyskinesia – One of the main claims of the atypical antipsychotics is the lower likelihood of tardive dyskinesia. This claim was supported in a study by Jeste *et al.* (1999), which found *tardive dyskinesia* rates in 30% of people after nine months of treatment with conventional antipsychotics, but just 5% for those treated with atypical antipsychotics.

Fewer side effects – Atypical antipsychotics may ultimately be more appropriate in the treatment of schizophrenia because there are fewer side effects, which in turn means that patients are more likely to continue their medications and therefore see more benefits.

Effectiveness of ECT

An *American Psychiatric Association* review in 2001 listed 19 studies that had compared ECT with 'simulated ECT' (patients are given general anaesthesia but no ECT). It concluded that ECT produced results that were no different from or worse than antipsychotic medication. However, an Indian study (Sarita *et al.*, 1998) found no difference in symptom reduction between 36 schizophrenia patients given either ECT or simulated ECT.

Appropriateness of ECT

Because there are significant risks associated with ECT, including memory dysfunction, brain damage and even death, the use of this technique as a treatment for schizophrenia has declined. In the UK, the decline between 1979 and 1999 was 59% (Read, 2004).

PSYCHOLOGICAL THERAPIES FOR SCHIZOPHRENIA

Although the use of **antipsychotic** drugs is crucial in the treatment of **schizophrenia**, many people do not experience the benefits they offer because they fail to take the medications prescribed (often because of the side-effects of these drugs). Even if they are compliant with their medication, a significant proportion of patients still suffer from distressing symptoms. As a result, some believe that additional psychological treatments (psychotherapy) are needed if improvement is to be sustained. There are many forms of psychotherapy, two of the most commonly used being **family intervention** (reducing stress within the family environment), and **CBT**, a currently very popular therapy with a specific, shorter-term, problem-solving approach, sometimes used in treating schizophrenia.

Cognitive therapy: Example of a delusional belief

- **Event:** See a man outside house.
- **Interpretation:** He's following me.
- **Feeling:** Scared, paranoid.
- **Behaviour:** Take evasive action, avoid going out.

▲ Clear thinking is good for you. The schizophrenic's inability to think clearly about their problems tends to make their symptoms worse. In cognitive therapy, disordered and delusional thinking can be replaced with thought processes that are more constructive and more in line with reality.

PSYCHOLOGICAL THERAPIES

Cognitive-behavioural therapy (CBT)

The basic assumption of CBT is that people often have distorted beliefs which influence their behaviour in maladaptive ways. For example, someone with schizophrenia may believe that their behaviour is being controlled by someone or something else. Delusions are thought to result from faulty interpretations of events, and cognitive therapy is used to help the patient to identify and correct these.

CBT techniques – In CBT, patients are encouraged to trace back the origins of their symptoms in order to get a better idea of how the symptoms might have developed. They are also encouraged to evaluate the content of their delusions or of any internal voices they hear, and to consider ways in which they might test the **validity** of their faulty beliefs. Patients might also be set behavioural assignments with the aim of improving their general level of functioning. The learning of maladaptive responses to life's problems is often the result of distorted thinking by the schizophrenic, or mistakes in assessing cause and effect (for example assuming that something terrible has happened because they wished it). During CBT, the therapist lets the patient develop their own alternatives to these previous maladaptive beliefs, ideally by looking for alternative explanations and coping strategies that are already present in the patient's mind.

Outcome studies – Outcome studies measure how well a patient does after a particular treatment, compared with the accepted form of treatment for that condition. Outcome studies of CBT suggest that patients who receive cognitive therapy experience fewer hallucinations and delusions and recover their functioning to a greater extent than those who receive antipsychotic medication alone. Drury et al. (1996) found benefits in terms of a reduction of positive symptoms and a 25-50% reduction in recovery time for patients given a combination of antipsychotic medication and CBT. A subsequent study by Kuipers et al. (1997) confirmed these advantages, but also noted that there were lower patient drop-out rates and greater patient satisfaction when CBT was used in addition to antipsychotic medication.

Family Intervention

In the 1970s, research discovered that the family environment had a potential role in influencing the course of schizophrenia. Schizophrenics in families that expressed high levels of criticism, hostility or over involvement had more frequent relapses than people with the same problems who lived in families that were less expressive in their emotions (Brown et al.,1972). The main aim of family intervention, therefore, is to attempt to make family life less stressful and so reduce re-hospitalisation.

Family intervention strategies – By reducing levels of expressed emotion and stress, and by increasing the capacity of relatives to solve related problems, family intervention attempts to reduce the incidence of relapse for the person with schizophrenia.

Family intervention makes use of a number of strategies including:

- Forming an alliance with relatives who care for the person with schizophrenia.
- Reducing the emotional climate within the family and the burden of care for family members.
- Enhancing relatives' ability to anticipate and solve problems.
- Reducing expressions of anger and guilt by family members.
- Maintaining reasonable expectations among family members for patient behaviour.
- Encouraging relatives to set appropriate limits whilst maintaining some degree of separation when needed.

Family interventions form part of an overall treatment package and are commonly used in conjunction with routine drug treatment and outpatient clinical care.

A META-ANALYSIS OF FAMILY INTERVENTION STUDIES

Pharoah et al. (2012) reviewed 53 studies published between 2002 and 2010 to investigate the effectiveness of family intervention. Studies were conducted in Europe, Asia and North America. The studies compared outcomes from family intervention to 'standard' care alone. The main results were:

- **Mental state** – the overall impression was mixed. Some studies reported an improvement in the overall mental state of patients compared to those receiving standard care, whereas others did not.
- **Compliance with medication** – compared to those who received standard care, the use of family intervention increased patients' compliance with medication.
- **Social functioning** – although appearing to show some improvement on general functioning, family intervention did not appear to have much of an effect on more concrete outcomes such as living independently or employment.

EVALUATION

Effectiveness of CBT

Supporting research – Research has tended to show that CBT has a significant effect on improving the symptoms of patients with schizophrenia. For example, Gould *et al.* (2001) found that all seven studies in their **meta-analysis** reported a statistically significant decrease in the positive symptoms of schizophrenia after treatment.

How much is due to the effects of CBT alone? Most studies of the effectiveness of CBT have been conducted with patients treated at the same time with antipsychotic medication. It has been difficult, therefore to assess the effectiveness of CBT independent of antipsychotic medication.

Appropriateness of CBT

Negative symptoms – CBT for schizophrenia works by trying to generate less distressing explanations for psychotic experiences, rather than trying to eliminate them completely. Negative symptoms may well serve a useful function for the person and so can be understood as 'safety behaviours'. For example, within a psychiatric setting, the strong expression of emotions might lead to increases in medication or hospital admission. Similarly, inactivity and withdrawal might be seen as a way of avoiding making positive symptoms worse. CBT, therefore, offers some hope of alleviating these maladaptive thought processes.

Who benefits? The use of CBT in conjunction with medications seems to have benefits, but it is commonly believed within psychiatry that not everyone with schizophrenia may benefit from CBT. For example, in a study of 142 schizophrenic patients in Hampshire, Kingdon and Kirschen (2006) found that many patients were not deemed suitable for CBT because psychiatrists believed they would not fully engage with the therapy. In particular they found that older patients were deemed less suitable than younger patients.

Effectiveness of family intervention

Supporting research – A meta-analysis involving 32 studies and nearly 2500 participants found significant evidence for the effectiveness of family intervention in the treatment of schizophrenia (NICE, 2009). When compared with patients receiving standard care alone, there was a reduction in hospital admissions during treatment and in the severity of symptoms both during and up to 24 months following the intervention. The relapse rate in the family intervention condition was 26% and in the control (standard care) condition it was 50%.

Why is it effective? – The Pharoah et al. (2012) meta-analysis (see previous page) established that family intervention may be effective in improving clinical outcomes such as mental state and social functioning. However, the authors suggest that the main reason for its effectiveness may have less to do with any improvements in these clinical markers and more to do with the fact that it increases medication compliance. Patients are more likely to reap the benefits of medication because they are more likely to comply with their medication regime.

Appropriateness of family intervention

Economic benefits – The NICE review of family intervention studies (NICE, 2009) demonstrated that family intervention is associated with significant cost savings when offered to people with schizophrenia in addition to standard care. The extra cost of family intervention is offset by a reduction in costs of hospitalisation because of the lower relapse rates associated with family intervention. There is also evidence that family intervention reduces relapse rates for a significant period after completion of the intervention. This means that the cost savings associated with family intervention would be even higher.

Cultural limitations – Research evidence has begun to show the effectiveness of family interventions as an addition to antipsychotic medication. However, most of this evidence comes from studies conducted outside the UK, principally from China. The NICE study (NICE, 2009) expressed the view that hospitalisation levels may differ significantly across countries, depending on clinical practice within those countries. Therefore data on hospitalisation rates from non-UK countries might not be applicable to the UK setting

CAN YOU...? No.9.5

...1 Describe **two** psychological therapies for schizophrenia in 100 words each.

...2 Outline **four** critical points for each therapy, including **(a)** its effectiveness **(b)** its appropriateness.

...3 Use this material to write a 600-word answer to the question: *Discuss **two or more** psychological therapies for schizophrenia.* (8 marks + 16 marks)

CHAPTER SUMMARY

OVERVIEW OF SCHIZOPHRENIA

CLASSIFICATION AND DIAGNOSIS

BIOLOGICAL THERAPIES

CLINICAL CHARACTERISTICS
- Profound disruption of cognition and emotion – affects language, perception, affect and sense of self.
- Diagnosis of schizophrenia – under DSM-IVR, diagnosis of schizophrenia requires at least a one-month duration of two or more positive symptoms.
- Positive symptoms – excess or distortion of normal symptoms e.g. delusions (bizarre beliefs), experiences of control (e.g. by alien force), hallucinations (unreal perceptions), disordered thinking (e.g. thought insertion).
- Negative symptoms – diminution or loss of normal functions, e.g. affective flattening (reduction in emotional expression), alogia (poverty of speech), avolition (lack of goal-directed behaviour).

ECT
- First studies of ECT as treatment for schizophrenia were disappointing (Karagulla, 1950), with recovery lower than control group.
- Combination of medication and ECT effective for rapid reduction of symptoms.

EVALUATION
- Effectiveness of ECT is inconsistent. APA study found no difference between effects of ECT and antipsychotic medication.
- Sarita et al. (1998) – no difference in symptom reduction between ECT and simulated ECT.
- Because of risks of ECT (e.g. memory dysfunction, brain damage) use has declined.
- Tharyan and Adams (2005) – review of 26 studies found 'real' ECT more effective than 'sham' ECT.

RELIABILITY
- Inter-rater reliability – DSM-III and later versions claim increased reliability of diagnosis.
- Test–retest reliability – screening tests such as RBANS show high test–retest reliability (Wilks et al., 2003).

EVALUATION
- Inter-rater reliability – despite claims for increased reliability, there is still little evidence that DSM is routinely used with high reliability by mental health clinicians.
- 'On being sane in unsane places' – demonstrated unreliability of diagnosis (Rosenhan, 1973).
- Unreliable symptoms – diagnosis based on 'bizarre' delusions not a reliable method of distinguishing between schizophrenic and non-schizophrenic patients (Mojtabi and Nicholson, 1995).
- Test–retest reliability (Prescott et al., 1986) performance on measures of cognitive deficits associated with schizophrenia stable over a 6-month period.
- Comparing DSM and ICD – schizophrenia was more frequently diagnosed according to ICD-10 than DSM-IV criteria (Cheniaux et al., 2009).
- Reliability of diagnosis challenged by difference between US and UK diagnoses (Copeland, 1971).

VALIDITY
- Psychiatric comorbidities are common among patients with schizophrenia and create difficulties in diagnosis of schizophrenia.
- Klosterkötter et al. (1994) – positive symptoms more useful for diagnosis than negative symptoms.
- Prognosis – people diagnosed as schizophrenic rarely share the same symptoms, nor the same outcomes.

EVALUATION
- Comorbidity and medical complications – Weber et al. (2009) found evidence of many comorbid non-psychiatric diagnoses among patients with schizophrenia, which affects prognosis.
- Comorbidity and suicide risk – persons with schizophrenia at risk for suicide, with comorbid depression the major cause for suicidal behaviour (Kessler et al., 1994).
- Ethnicity and misdiagnosis – rates of schizophrenia among African–Caribbeans much higher than white populations (Harrison et al., 1997), which in part may be a product of misdiagnosis.
- Symptoms – schizophrenic symptoms also found in many other disorders, including depression and DID (Ellason and Ross, 1995).

EXPLANATIONS OF SCHIZOPHRENIA

BIOLOGICAL EXPLANATIONS

GENETIC FACTORS
- Schizophrenia more common among biological relatives of person with schizophrenia (Gottesman, 1991).
- Twin studies – Joseph (2000) pooled data shows concordance rate for MZ twins of 40% and DZ twins 7%.
- Use of 'blind' diagnoses produces lower concordance rate for MZ twins, but still much higher than DZ.
- Adoption study by Tienari et al. (2000) – if biological mother schizophrenic, 6.7% of adoptees also schizophrenic (2% of controls).

EVALUATION
- Environments of MZ twins may be more similar than for DZ twins.
- Differences in concordance rates may reflect environmental similarity rather than role of genetic factors.
- The fact that schizophrenia runs in families may be due to factors that have nothing to do with heritability (e.g. 'expressed emotion').
- Adopted children from schizophrenic backgrounds may be adopted by particular type of adoptive parent, making conclusions difficult to draw.
- Many studies have to include 'schizophrenia spectrum disorders' to show genetic influences.
- Evolutionary perspective – schizophrenia may have adaptive advantage (e.g. group splitting hypothesis).

DOPAMINE HYPOTHESIS
- Neurons that transmit dopamine fire too easily or too often, leading to symptoms of schizophrenia.
- Schizophrenics – abnormally high levels of D_2 receptors.
- Evidence from large doses of amphetamines (dopamine agonist) causes hallucinations and delusions.
- Antipsychotic drugs – block dopamine and eliminate symptoms.
- Parkinson's disease – treatment with L-dopa raises dopamine levels and can therefore also trigger schizophrenic symptoms.

EVALUATION
- Drugs can increase schizophrenia symptoms as neurons try to compensate. Haracz (1982) found elevated dopamine levels in post-mortems of schizophrenics who had taken medication.
- Neuroimaging studies failed to provide convincing evidence for altered dopamine activity in schizophrenics.

BIOLOGICAL THERAPIES cont'd

PSYCHOLOGICAL THERAPIES

ANTIPSYCHOTIC MEDICATION

- Conventional antipsychotics reduce effects of dopamine and so reduce symptoms of schizophrenia.
- Bind to D_2 dopamine receptors but do not stimulate them.
- Atypical antipsychotics only temporarily occupy D_2 receptors then dissociate to allow normal dopamine transmission.
- Leads to lower levels of side effects, such as tardive dyskinesia.

EVALUATION

- Davis et al. (1980) – higher relapse rate in patients whose drug replaced with placebo than those who remained on drug.
- Antipsychotic medication more effective for those living with hostility and criticism.
- Conventional antipsychotics – 30% develop tardive dyskinesia.
- Being prescribed medication creates motivational deficits which prevents positive action against illness.
- Meta-analysis (Leucht et al., 1999) – superiority of atypical over conventional antipsychotics only moderate.
- Atypical antipsychotics – only marginal support for effectiveness with negative symptoms.
- Lower rates of tardive dyskinesia with atypical antipsychotics supported by Jeste et al. (1999).
- Patients more likely to continue with medication if fewer side effects.
- Ross and Read (2004) – placebo studies not a fair test because proportion of relapses explained by withdrawal effects.
- Ethical issues – human rights issues associated with use of antipsychotic medication (e.g. tardive dyskinesia).

CBT

- Patients: 1) trace origins of symptoms to understand how they might have developed and 2) evaluate content of delusions/hallucinations.
- Patients allowed to develop own alternatives to maladaptive beliefs.
- Outcome studies show that patients receiving CBT experience fewer hallucinations and delusions than those receiving antipsychotic medication alone.
- Lower patient drop-out rates and greater patient satisfaction with CBT than antipsychotic medication.

EVALUATION

- Effectiveness – meta-analysis found significant decreases in positive symptoms after CBT treatment.
- Most CBT studies also involve antipsychotic medication, therefore difficult to assess effects of CBT alone.
- CBT works by generating less distressing explanations for psychotic experiences rather than trying to eliminate them.
- Psychiatrists believe that older patients are less likely to benefit from CBT.
- Ethical issues arise in placebo condition where patients are denied effective treatment.

FAMILY INTERVENTION

- Based on the assumption that a stressful family environment can increase risk of relapse.
- Main aim is to make family life less stressful and reduce incidence of relapse.
- Strategies include forming an alliance with the relatives who provide care, reducing emotional climate in family and increasing capacity of relatives to solve problems.
- Commonly used in conjunction with drug treatment and clinical care.

EVALUATION

- Meta-analysis (Pharoah et al., 2012) – some improvements in mental state, compliance with medication and social functioning.
- Methodological limitations of Pharoah et al. study include problem of randomization and lack of blinding.
- NICE study (2009) found reduction in hospital admissions and severity of symptoms.
- Main influence may be that family intervention increases medication compliance.
- NICE study demonstrated significant economic benefits due to reduction in costs of hospitalization.
- Evidence may not be applicable to UK as most is from countries where levels of hospitalisation differ from UK.

PSYCHOLOGICAL EXPLANATIONS

PSYCHOLOGICAL THEORIES

- Psychodynamic view of schizophrenia – result of regression to pre-ego stage and attempts to re-establish ego control.
- Some schizophrenic symptoms reflect infantile state, other symptoms are an attempt to re-establish control.
- Further features of disorder appear as individuals attempt to understand their experiences.
- They may reject feedback from others and develop delusional beliefs.

EVALUATION

- Very little evidence to support psychodynamic view of schizophrenia.
- Behaviour of parents assumed to be key influence in development of schizophrenia but may be consequence rather than cause.
- Cognitive explanation supported by neurophysiological evidence (Meyer-Lindenberg et al., 2002).

SOCIO-CULTURAL FACTORS

- Prior to schizophrenic episode, patients report twice as many stressful life events.
- Double-bind theory – contradictory messages from parents prevent coherent construction of reality, leads to schizophrenic symptoms.
- Expressed emotion – family communication style involving criticism, hostility and emotional over-involvement.
- Leads to stress beyond impaired coping mechanisms and so schizophrenia.
- Labelling theory – symptoms of schizophrenia seen as deviant from rules ascribed to normal experience. Diagnostic label leads to self-fulfilling prophecy.

EVALUATION

- Some evidence challenges link between life events and schizophrenia. Evidence for link is only correlational, not causal.
- Importance of family relationships in development of schizophrenia shown in adoption study by Tienari et al. (1994).
- Double-bind theory supported by Berger (1965) – schizophrenics recalled more double-bind statements from mothers.
- Expressed emotion – has led to effective therapy for relatives.
- Scheff (1974) – 13 of 18 studies consistent with predictions of labelling theory.
- Link supported in both retrospective (Brown and Birley, 1968) and prospective (Hirsch et al., 1996) studies.
- Expressed emotion effects much less common in non-individualist cultures.

EXAM QUESTION WITH STUDENT ANSWER

Question (a) Outline and evaluate **one or more** biological explanations of schizophrenia. *(4 marks + 10 marks)*
(b) Outline and evaluate **one** psychological therapy used as a treatment for schizophrenia. *(4 marks + 6 marks)*

STUDENT ANSWER

(a) *Schizophrenia is a severe disorder that is characterised by disturbances in thoughts, emotions and behaviour. One of the problems in the classification of schizophrenia is that the range of symptoms is so wide that sometimes, different patients have no symptoms in common at all. A classic study carried out by Rosenhan (on being sane in insane places) also showed that psychiatrists were all too willing to diagnose the disorder despite very limited information about a patient's symptoms.*

One explanation of schizophrenia is that it is caused by excessive activity of the neurotransmitter dopamine. In schizophrenics, neurons that use dopamine fire too often and transmit too many messages. As a result of this, the symptoms associated with schizophrenia appear.

Evidence for the 'dopamine hypothesis' comes from the use of antipsychotic drugs (the dopamine antagonists) that block receptor sites for dopamine and so reduce its activity. This reduces the symptoms of schizophrenia. Other drugs, such as amphetamines increase dopamine activity and may lead to schizophrenic-like symptoms. Low dopamine activity is found in people who suffer from Parkinson's disease but some patients who take drugs to increase their dopamine levels experience schizophrenia-like symptoms.

There are problems with the dopamine hypothesis. Only about half of all patients respond to the dopamine antagonists, and usually the beneficial effects take a week to kick in. This suggests that the key factor in improvement is not the immediate blocking of the dopamine receptors brought about by the drug.

A second explanation is a genetic one, i.e. that people inherit the disorder. Twin studies have shown that genetics is likely to a n important factor. For example, when researchers compare concordance rates between identical and non-identical twins they find much higher concordance in identical twins. However, the rates are certainly never 100% and more often around 50%, which suggests a significant contribution of other factors.

One of the problems with twin studies is that we don't know whether similarities of identical twins may be because identical twins are treated more alike. Twin studies don't separate environment and genetics very well. A different way to study genetic effects is to use adoption studies. One of the best was conducted by Tienari et al. in Finland. Those adoptees whose mothers developed schizophrenia were more likely to develop it themselves (about 7%) compared to adoptees whose mothers were non-schizophrenic (about 2%).

(b) *One of the common therapies that is used for schizophrenia, from a psychological approach, is CBT (cognitive-behavioural therapy). This kind of therapy is a mixture of cognitive and behavioural techniques. A patient's thoughts or beliefs (cognitive) are challenged and then the therapist tries to change the behaviours. With schizophrenic patients they are encouraged to think back to their childhood and the origin of their symptoms. In particular they are challenged to consider the content of their delusions that may have developed at that time. They are also encouraged to consider their maladaptive behaviours and unlearn these, replacing them with more adaptive behaviours.*

Research has shown that CBT has a positive effect. For example, studies that look at the outcome of CBT have found reduced hallucinations and delusions in schizophrenic patients, i.e. their maladaptive behaviours have been reduced. Research also shows that this outcome is better than when drugs (antipsychotics) are used, although patients who use antipsychotics and CBT do best of all (Drury et al.).

[557 words]

EXAMINER COMMENTS

A glance at this answer tells us one thing straight away – there is a lot less written for part (b). Part (a) is about the right length whereas part (b) is really too brief for ten marks.

The first paragraph is completely **uncreditworthy**. Students frequently begin essays on explanations with an introduction about schizophrenia in general which is not relevant to the actual question.

The essay really begins in the second paragraph with an accurate, but rather brief explanation of the dopamine hypothesis – the student could have added some more about D_2 receptors and the general effects of dopamine.

This paragraph provides evidence to support the dopamine hypothesis. Such evidence can be credited as description or as evaluation depending on the manner in which it is presented. In this case it is a mainly descriptive paragraph and therefore will count towards the **AO1** mark.

Clearly this paragraph concerns **evaluation**. Essentially only one point is made, but it shows coherent **elaboration**.

In the final two paragraphs of part (a) the student has described and evaluated a second explanation. The descriptive element is provided by describing twin and adoption studies; the latter are **more detailed** than the former which is a rather general (although informed) overview of the topic.

Unfortunately the quality of the description has rather taken over and there is little room for important evaluation marks. The evaluation is **rudimentary**.

AO1 – Knowledge and understanding of two explanations is **accurate** and **well-detailed**. A **good range** of relevant material has been included.
AO2/AO3 – There is a mixture of **effective** and **rudimentary** evaluation, making the answer basic overall.

In part (b) the student has done well to focus on CBT in relation to schizophrenia instead of simply presenting a description of CBT.

The second paragraph contains some **clear** and **effective** evaluation. However, there simply isn't enough of it for the 6 marks available.

AO1 – **Well-detailed**.
AO2/AO3 – Not enough material to take this above a **basic** response.

Chapter 10

Psychopathology: Depression

SPECIFICATION

Psychopathology

Candidates will be expected to study one of the following disorders:
- *schizophrenia*
- *depression*
- *phobic disorders*
- *obsessive compulsive disorder*

Depression	
Overview	• Clinical characteristics of depression. • Issues surrounding the classification and diagnosis of depression, including reliability and validity.
Explanations	• Biological explanations of depression, for example genetics, biochemistry. • Psychological explanations of depression, for example behavioural, cognitive, psychodynamic and socio-cultural.
Therapy	• Biological therapies for depression, including their evaluation in terms of appropriateness and effectiveness. • Psychological therapies for depression, for example behavioural, psychodynamic and cognitive-behavioural, including their evaluation in terms of appropriateness and effectiveness.

Depression is classified under DSM-IV-TR as a mood disorder. Mood disorders affect a person's emotional state and include **major depressive disorder** (depression) and **bipolar disorder**. Most people with a mood disorder suffer only from depression whereas others experience states of mania that alternate with their depression (hence bipolar disorder). There are many symptoms of depression, including low mood, feelings of hopelessness, lack of energy and low self-esteem. The more symptoms a person has, the more likely they are to suffer from depression. In its mildest form, depression can just involve being in low spirits but at its most severe, major depression can be life-threatening, because it can make people simply give up the will to live. The Global Burden of Disease Project (Lopez *et al.*, 2006) established that depression ranks first among the top 10 causes of worldwide disability.

▶ **A case study of drepression**

Since I left school a few months ago I seem to feel lonely all the time and sometimes I find myself sobbing for no reason at all. My parents are going through a divorce and life at home is just awful. I can't get enthusiastic about anything and even going shopping feels overwhelming. The routine that I used to know in my life has gone and now I feel completely lost. I've always been described as 'outgoing' and 'bubbly', but not any more. Nowadays I feel I have no energy and no interest in anything. I just want my life to return to normal.

CLINICAL CHARACTERISTICS OF MAJOR DEPRESSIVE DISORDER

Diagnosis – the formal diagnosis of 'major depressive disorder' requires the presence of five of the following symptoms (including either depressed mood or loss of interest and pleasure). The symptoms must also cause clinically significant distress or impairment in general functioning and not be better accounted for by bereavement. For a diagnosis of depression, these symptoms should be present all or most of the time, and should persist for longer than 2 weeks.

- **Sad, depressed mood** – as indicated by either subjective report (feeling sad or empty) or observation made by others (e.g. appears tearful).
- **Loss of interest and pleasure in usual activities** – as indicated by either subjective account or observation made by others.
- **Difficulties in sleeping (insomnia)** – some patients have a desire to sleep all the time (hypersomnia).
- **Shift in activity level, becoming either lethargic or agitated** – observable by others, not merely subjective feelings or restlessness or being slowed down.
- **Poor appetite and weight loss, or increased appetite and weight gain** – significant weight loss when not dieting or a significant decrease (or increase) in appetite.
- **Loss of energy and great fatigue**.
- **Negative self-concept, feelings of worthlessness and guilt** – feelings of worthlessness or excessive or inappropriate guilt (which may be delusional).
- **Difficulty in concentrating**, such as slowed thinking and indecisiveness.
- **Recurrent thoughts of death or suicide** – major depressive disorders account for about 20–35% of all deaths by suicide (Angst *et al.*, 1995).

Adapted from the American Psychiatric Association (2000) DSM-IVR criteria for the diagnosis of major depressive disorder.

ISSUES OF RELIABILITY AND VALIDITY

Reliability

Reliability refers to the consistency of a measuring instrument such as a questionnaire or scale to assess, for example, the severity of depressive symptoms. Reliability of questionnaires or scales can be measured in terms of whether two independent assessors give similar diagnoses (**inter-rater reliability**) or whether tests used to deliver these diagnoses are consistent over time (**test–retest reliability**). Kraemer *et al.* (2012) note that much research has been carried out on the evaluation of medical treatments, but little attention has been paid to an evaluation of the quality of the diagnoses themselves.

Inter-rater reliability – Low levels of inter-rater reliability related to any classification procedure suggest that it might lead to faulty diagnosis and inappropriate treatment. Lobbestael *et al.* (2011) assessed the inter-rater reliability of the *Structured Clinical Interview* for the assessment of major depressive disorder in a mixed sample of patients and non-patient controls. Results revealed moderate agreement with an inter-rater reliability coefficient of .66.

Test–retest reliability – Field trials of the latest version of **DSM** (DSM-V, due for release in 2013), have emphasised the importance of test–retest reliability and have this as a major goal of the new system. Current measurement scales such as the *Beck Depression Inventory* (BDI) have been assessed for their test–retest reliability. The BDI is a 21-item self-report questionnaire designed to measure the severity of symptoms in individuals diagnosed with depression. It is thus able to distinguish between different types of depression, such as major depressive disorder and **dysthymia**. Beck *et al.* (1996) studied the responses of 26 outpatients tested at two therapy sessions one week apart using the BDI. There was a correlation of .93 indicating a significant level of test–retest reliability.

Validity

Validity refers to the extent that a diagnosis represents something that is real and distinct from other disorders and the extent that a classification system such as ICD or DSM measures what it claims to measure. Reliability and validity are inextricably linked because a diagnosis cannot be valid if it is not reliable.

Comorbidity is an important issue for the validity of diagnosis of mental illness. It refers to the extent that two (or more) conditions co-occur. For example, research has shown that the presence of an anxiety disorder is the single biggest clinical risk for the development of depression. The experience of anxiety serves as a compounding stressor that leads (especially in patients with a genetic vulnerability) to major depression.

Content validity refers to whether the items in a test are representative of that which is being measured. The BDI is considered to be high in **content validity** because it was constructed as a result of a consensus among mental health clinicians concerning symptoms found among psychiatric patients.

Concurrent validity is a measure of the extent to which a test concurs with already existing standard ways of assessing the characteristic in question. Research (e.g. Beck *et al.*, 1988) has consistently demonstrated **concurrent validity** between the BDI and other measures of depression, such as the Hamilton Depression Scale.

EVALUATION

Reliability

Research evidence for the DSM diagnosis of depression – Research (e.g. Keller *et al.*, 1995, see right) on the reliability of diagnoses using the DSM classification system suggests that inter-rater reliability is 'fair to good' and test–retest reliability is 'fair' at best. This was also the conclusion reached by Zanarini *et al.* (2000), who, although finding an inter-rater reliability correlation of .80 for major depressive disorder, found a test–retest correlation of just .61 with one week between diagnosis sessions.

Reasons for low reliability – Keller *et al.* suggest a number of possible reasons why DSM diagnoses of depression might lack reliability. These include the fact that for major depression to be diagnosed, a minimum of five out of nine symptoms must be present. When the severity of the disorder is such that it is just at the diagnostic threshold, a one item disagreement (e.g. considering that an individual is sufficiently lethargic that it satisfies the symptom of shift in activity levels) makes the difference between a diagnosis of major depressive disorder or a less serious illness.

Simplifying diagnosis – Zimmerman *et al.* (2010) claim that the DSM-IV criteria for major depressive disorder are unnecessarily lengthy, and that treatment doctors frequently have difficulty recalling all nine symptoms, which could lead to unreliable diagnoses. In a study of 2,500 GPs in Australia and New Zealand, Krupinski and Tiller (2001) found that only one-quarter could list even five of the nine symptoms listed in DSM-IV. Zimmerman *et al.* developed a briefer definition of major depressive disorder composed only of the mood and cognitive symptoms of the DSM-IV criteria. They found in excess of 95% agreement of diagnoses using the simplified and full DSM-IV definitions. They suggest that, compared to DSM diagnosis, the new simpler definition is easier to apply with medically ill patients because it is free of somatic symptoms that are difficult to apply in patients who also have medical illnesses.

Validity

Are there distinct types of depression? – The diagnosis of depression requires clinicians to differentiate among several distinct subtypes of this disorder. However, when McCullough *et al.* (2003) compared 681 outpatients with various types of depression (including major depressive disorder and dysthymia), they found few differences on a range of clinical, psychosocial and treatment response variables. This suggests that distinctions between the different subtypes of depression may not be valid.

Are GP diagnoses valid? For most people a diagnosis of depression is given by their local GP. However, van Weel-Baumgarten *et al.* (2006) suggests that diagnoses made by GPs (rather than secondary care 'specialists') are made against a background of previous patient knowledge and so could be biased as a result.

The consequences of comorbidity – The presence of comorbidity has been repeatedly shown to have a negative impact on social and occupational functioning and a poorer response to treatment for patients with depression. For example, Goodwin *et al.* (2001) found that the odds of having suicidal thoughts was five times higher in patients with major depression alone, compared to patients with no psychiatric disorder. However, patients with major depression comorbid with panic disorder had triple that ratio.

DSM versus ICD – Does it make a difference to the accuracy of diagnosis according to the classification system used? In depression, the classifications are very similar and research has shown that the concordance between the two is above 75%. The major difference is that ICD-10 but not DSM-IV requires, in the diagnosis of depression, that there must be two of the three key symptoms of depression (sad depressed mood, loss of interest or lack of energy). However, Andrews *et al.* (1999) demonstrated that this difference in the classification systems does not produce a high number of discrepant diagnoses and that therefore one system relative to the other cannot be regarded as more 'valid' in the diagnosis of depression.

CAN YOU...?   No.10.1

...**1** Outline clinical characteristics of depression in about 200 words.

...**2** Outline issues relating to reliability and validity in the diagnosis and/or classification of depression in about 200 words.

...**3** Choose **eight** critical points relevant to issues of reliability and validity in the diagnosis and/or classification of depression. Elaborate each point in about 50 words.

...**4** Use this material to write answers to the following questions:

Outline clinical characteristics of depression. (8 marks) [200-word answer]

Discuss issues of reliability and validity associated with the classification and diagnosis of depression. (8 marks + 16 marks) [600-word answer]

BIOLOGICAL EXPLANATIONS OF DEPRESSION

Depressive disorders are the most common of the mental disorders, with about 1 person in 10 in the UK having a diagnosable depressive condition at some time in their lives. It makes sense that such a widespread disorder should have some biological basis. Hammen (1997) suggests four different aspects of depression that support that belief:

- The symptoms of depression include *physical* changes (e.g. sleep disturbances, fatigue).
- Depression appears to run in families.
- The success of antidepressant medication is consistent with a biological process in depression.
- Particular kinds of illness, injury or even medication may give rise to depression.

BIOLOGICAL EXPLANATIONS

Genetic factors

Family studies – Having a **first-degree relative** (parent or sibling) with depression appears to be a risk factor for depression. Family studies select people who already have depression (the **probands**), and examine whether other members of their family have been, or might be, diagnosed with depression. If there is a genetic link for this disorder, the probands' relatives should show higher rates of depression than the rest of the population. Research has found that around 20% of such relatives have depression compared to a figure of around 10% for the population at large (Harrington *et al.*, 1993).

Twin studies – The basis of twin studies is that identical (or **monozygotic**) twins are naturally occurring clones of each other, having all their genes in common. On the other hand, fraternal (or **dizygotic**) twins share just half of their genes. If we assume that the environment shared by twins is roughly the same for both types of twin, then any greater similarities in identical pairs, compared to fraternal pairs, shows the action of genes. McGuffin *et al.* (1996) studied 177 probands with depression and their same-sex co-twins. The **concordance rate** was 46% for identical twins and 20% for fraternal twins, suggesting that depression has a substantial heritable component.

Adoption studies – Wender *et al.* (1986) studied the biological relatives of adopted individuals who had been hospitalised for severe depression. They found a much higher incidence of severe depression in the biological relatives of the depressed group than in the biological relatives of a non-depressed control group.

Genes as diatheses – Genetic factors are thought to act as *diatheses* in a **diathesis-stress** relationship. Such a view would see a genetic predisposition for depression interacting with environmental stressors to produce a depressive reaction. We might expect, therefore, such environmental stressors to affect those *with* the genetic predisposition differently to those *without* it. Kendler *et al.* (1995) found that women who were the co-twin of a depressed sibling were more likely to have become depressed than those without this presumed genetic vulnerability. Most significantly, the highest levels of depression were found in the group who were exposed to significant negative **life events** *and* were most genetically at risk for depression.

Neurotransmitter dysfunction

Noradrenaline – In the 1960s, it was proposed that depression stems from a deficiency of the **neurotransmitter noradrenaline** in certain brain circuits. Among the findings linking low levels of noradrenaline to depression was the discovery that indirect markers of noradrenaline levels in the brain (e.g. by-products found in urine) were often low in depressed individuals (Bunney *et al.*, 1965). In addition, post-mortem studies revealed increased densities of certain noradrenaline receptors in the brains of depressed suicide victims. When transmitter molecules become unusually scarce in synapses, postsynaptic cells often expand receptor numbers in a compensatory attempt to pick up whatever signals are available (a process known as '*up-regulation*').

Serotonin – Among the findings supporting a link between low synaptic **serotonin** levels and depression is that cerebrospinal fluid in depressed, and especially suicidal, patients contains reduced amounts of a major serotonin by-product, signifying reduced levels of serotonin in the brain itself (McNeal and Cimbolic, 1986). The introduction of *Prozac* and other antidepressant drugs that selectively block serotonin re-uptake confirmed the association between low serotonin and depression. Furthermore, Delgado *et al.* (1990) gave depressed patients who were receiving antidepressant medication a special diet that lowered their levels of one of the precursors of serotonin – tryptophan. The majority of patients experienced a return of their depressive symptoms, which disappeared again when their diet was returned to normal.

Cortisol hypersecretion

A number of studies have found evidence of elevated levels of the stress hormone **cortisol** among depressed individuals. These high levels of cortisol usually reduce to a normal level once the depression disappears. Cortisol is one of the hormones released by the adrenal glands during times of stress, and stressful events have been shown to trigger depression. The mechanism appears to be that elevated cortisol levels, caused by stressful life events, reduce brain serotonin levels which in turn leads to the development of a depressive state.

Dexamethasone suppression test – Evidence for the role of cortisol in depression comes from the administration of *dexamethasone*, a drug that temporarily suppresses cortisol secretion in normal people. For depressed people, however, dexamethasone does not appear to maintain cortisol suppression for as long as it does in non-depressed people. This suggests that over-activity in the **hypothalamic-pituitary-adrenal axis** is a characteristic of the depressed state, particularly as, when the depressive state ends, dexamethasone is again able to suppress cortisol activity.

EVALUATION

Genetic factors

Research support – A mutant gene that starves the brain of serotonin has been found to be 10 times more prevalent in depressed patients than in control individuals (Zhang *et al.*, 2005). The mutant gene codes for the brain enzyme, *tryptophan hydroxylase-2*, which makes serotonin, and can result in an 80% reduction of normal serotonin levels in the brain. Caron *et al.* found that this version of the gene was carried by 9 out of 87 depressed patients, but only 3 of 219 healthy controls. Patients with the mutation failed to respond well to SSRI medications, which work via serotonin, suggesting that the mutation may underlie a treatment-resistant subtype of depression.

Comorbidity – The relatively low genetic concordance rates for depression may be explained in terms of **comorbidity**, when two or more mental illnesses occur together and perhaps have some common cause. It is possible that people inherit a vulnerability for a wider range of disorders than depression alone. If this were the case we would expect to see higher concordance when looking at a range of disorders in related individuals. There is some research support for this. For example, Kendler *et al.* (1992) found a higher incidence of mental disorders in twins when looking at depression *and* generalised anxiety disorder than when looking at depression alone. This suggests that some disorders, such as depression, are a product of genes that underlie a number of different disorders. The actual symptoms (and disorder) that develop could be related to environmental triggers (the diathesis-stress model).

Neurotransmitter dysfunction

Noradrenaline and depression – This link was supported by the fact that drugs that lower noradrenaline levels bring about depressive states, while those that increase noradrenaline levels show antidepressant effects (Leonard, 2000). Kraft *et al.* (2005) studied 96 patients with major depression who were treated for six weeks with a dual *serotonin-noradrenaline re-uptake inhibitor* (SNRI). The patients showed a significantly more positive response than those treated with a **placebo**, thus strengthening the link between the depletion of these neurotransmitters and the development of depressive symptoms.

Serotonin and depression – The link between the two is not that straightforward. Some studies have used patients whose depression is currently in remission. The patients are given a tryptophan-deficient amino acid mixture that temporarily decreases serotonin levels in the brain. They experience a brief relapse of symptoms during tryptophan depletion, suggesting that a lowering of serotonin levels results in depression (Ruhe *et al.*, 2007). However, individuals who had never been depressed nor had a family history of depression tended not to show any mood changes following tryptophan depletion, despite the fact that tryptophan depletion alters the activity of the same mood-regulating regions of the brain, such as the **amygdala**, in these individuals as it does in patients with depression. Thus, lowering serotonin levels does not induce depression in all people. Aan het Rot *et al.* (2009) suggest that it is possible that a depressive episode alters the serotonin system in such a way that a person becomes more vulnerable to the effects of *future* changes in serotonin levels.

Cortisol hypersecretion

Conflicting research evidence – Strickland *et al.* (2002) found no evidence of increased cortisol levels in a large group of women with depression or in the majority of those who were vulnerable to depression through adverse social or personal circumstances. This finding poses serious problems for an explanation linking elevated cortisol levels to lowered brain serotonin function and to depression. They did find, however, elevated cortisol levels in some participants who had experienced recent severe life events, yet were not depressed. It appears that stressful life events can result in elevated cortisol levels but this does not necessarily lead to the development of depression.

Cortisol, depression and pregnancy – O'Keane and Marsh (2007) claim that during pregnancy, higher levels of cortisol are necessary for the normal development of the baby. However, if the cortisol levels are too high – for example if a woman is depressed during pregnancy – this can lead to premature birth, which is the leading cause of infant death and postnatal illness.

Evaluation · DEPRESSION AND ADOLESCENTS

Our understanding of the genetics of depression among adolescents is limited. In adults, about 40% of the risk for *Major Depressive Disorder* (MDD) is attributable to genetic factors, but little data exist on the heritability of adolescent MDD. Glowinski *et al.* (2003) sampled 3416 female adolescent twins (mean age 15.5 years) for MDD using a structured telephone interview that included a DSM-IV based section for the assessment of MDD.

Results showed that the lifetime occurrence of self-reported MDD ranged from 1% for girls under the age of 12, to over 17% at age 19 and older. The proportion of risk for MDD due to genetic factors was approximately 40%, with the remaining risk attributable to environmental factors. The genetic and environmental contributions to risk of MDD in female adolescent twins are very close to findings from adult samples. The authors acknowledge, however, that any conclusions about the heritability of MDD among adolescents can only be tentative because male twins were not included in the sample.

► Kelly Holmes has claimed that the depression she suffered in 2003 made her a stronger person. A year after her depression she achieved double-gold performance at the 2004 Olympics.

Evaluation · AN EVOLUTIONARY PERSPECTIVE

Support for the view that depression has a genetic basis comes from evolutionary theory. The fact that depression is so widespread among humans suggests that it may have some evolutionary significance, i.e. it may be **adaptive**. For example, Buist-Bouwman *et al.*, (2004) found that individuals reported higher levels of psychological functioning *after* their depression than beforehand. Evolutionary explanations of depression suggest that as it is costly (both to the individual *and* their close social partners), it serves as an 'honest' signal of need, with the result that others in the social network are more likely to provide much-needed help and support which strengthens the individual.

CAN YOU...? No.10.2

...1 Describe **two** biological explanations of depression in 100 words each.

...2 Outline **eight** critical points for biological explanations of depression, including **(a)** the critical point being made, **(b)** your evidence for this criticism, and **(c)** how this criticism affects that explanation.

...3 Use this material to write a 600-word answer to the question: *Discuss **two or more** biological explanations of depression.* (8 marks + 16 marks)

PSYCHOLOGICAL EXPLANATIONS OF DEPRESSION

Although biological explanations of depression have attracted the most research support in recent years, *psychological* explanations have also been influential. The most common psychological explanations have been grouped into three models: psychodynamic, cognitive and socio-cultural. How all these different explanations fit together is not clear – it is possible, for example, that some factors *cause* the development of depression in the first place, whereas others maintain it. It is also possible that two or more factors are needed for the development of depression. For example, it is possible that people only become depressed if they have low levels of serotonin (a biological explanation), feel helpless *and* blame themselves for the negative events that happen to them (a psychological explanation) (Comer, 2003).

PSYCHOLOGICAL EXPLANATIONS

Psychodynamic

Mourning and melancholia – In his essay '*On Mourning and Melancholia*', Freud (1917) explained how, when a loved one is lost (through bereavement or, for children, separation or withdrawal of affection) there is first a mourning period and then, after a while, life returns to normal. For some people, however, the mourning period never seems to come to an end. They continue to exist in a state of permanent melancholia (Freud's term for what we now call depression). Freud stated that mourning and melancholia are very much the same – they can both be reactions to the loss of a loved person – but whereas mourning was a natural process, melancholia was a pathological illness.

The pathology of depression – Freud believed that we unconsciously harbour some negative feelings towards those we love. When we lose a loved one these feelings are turned upon ourselves, and in addition we may resent being deserted by them. This period is followed by a period of mourning where we recall memories of the person lost, and gradually separate ourselves from them. In some cases this process may go astray, and we continue a pattern of self-abuse and self-blame because anger against the lost person is directed inwards. Depression, according to this view, is 'anger turned against oneself'.

Evaluation

VULNERABILITY FACTORS IN DEPRESSION

Brown and Harris (1978) provided evidence for the claim that that episodes of depression were almost always preceded by a major **life event**. After studying depressed women in Camberwell, London, they concluded that two circumstances appeared to increase a person's vulnerability to severe life events. The first of these was the presence of long-term difficulties, such as being in a long-standing difficult relationship. The second was the existence of vulnerability factors, such as having three or more children under the age of 14 years, not working outside the home, or the lack of a close confiding relationship.

Cognitive

Beck's theory of depression – Aaron Beck (1967) believed that depressed individuals feel as they do because their thinking is biased towards negative interpretations of the world. Depressed people have acquired a negative **schema** – a tendency to adopt a negative view of the world – during childhood. This may be caused by a variety of factors, including parental and/or peer rejection and criticisms by teachers. These negative schema (e.g. expecting to fail) are activated whenever they encounter a new situation (e.g. an examination) that resembles the original conditions in which these schema were learned. Negative schema are subject to *cognitive biases* in thinking (e.g. over-generalisation – drawing a sweeping conclusion regarding self-worth on the basis of one small piece of negative feedback). Negative schema and cognitive biases maintain what Beck calls the *negative triad*, a pessimistic view of the self, the world and the future.

Learned helplessness (Seligman, 1975) – Depression may be learned when a person tries but fails to control unpleasant experiences. As a result they acquire a sense of being unable to exercise control over their life, and so become depressed. This **learned helplessness** then impairs their performance in situations that *can* be controlled – a characteristic of many depressives who fail to initiate coping strategies in the face of stress. Seligman also discovered that depressed people thought about unpleasant events in more pessimistic ways than non-depressed people, tending to hold themselves responsible. The '*reformulated helplessness theory*' (Abramson *et al.*, 1978) suggests that the depressed person thinks the cause of such events is *internal* ('it's my fault, I'm stupid'), *stable* ('People will never want to be my friend'), and *global* ('Everything I do goes wrong'). A person prone to depression is thus thought to show a depressive **attributional style**, where they attribute bad outcomes to personal, stable and global character faults.

Hopelessness – Abramson *et al.* (1989) modified the helplessness theory into a still broader *hopelessness* theory. This explains depression on the basis of pessimistic *expectations of the future*. Some people with a negative attributional style don't become depressed (by avoiding traumatic experiences) and some go through these experiences without becoming depressed (by avoiding negative thinking). The hopeless person, however, *expects* bad rather than good things to happen in important areas of his/her life (pessimism) and doesn't believe they have the resources to change that situation.

Sociocultural factors

Life events and depression – Life events may act as a trigger in individuals who have a genetic vulnerability for depression. As we saw on the previous spread (Kendler *et al.*, 1995), the highest levels of depression were found in women who had been exposed to recent negative life events and who were most genetically at risk for depression. Cognitive models believe that the presence of a depressive attributional style acts as a 'diathesis' that predisposes the person to interpret the event and its consequences in ways that facilitate depression. In this way, even relatively minor events may trigger depressive episodes if they are subjected to the biased interpretation that arises from this cognitive vulnerability (Hammen, 1997).

Social networks and social skills – Depressed individuals tend to report having sparse social networks providing little social support. This in turn makes them less able to handle negative life events and so more vulnerable to continuing depression (Billings *et al.*, 1983). Research has also shown that the behaviour of depressed people reflects a deficit in social skills (e.g. poor interpersonal problem solving, lack of eye contact) and frequently elicits rejection from others (Joiner *et al.*, 1992).

GENDER DIFFERENCES AND DEPRESSION

Evaluation

Women have a lifetime likelihood of depression of 20% compared to 10% in men, and depression in women occurs at younger ages, lasts longer, and is more frequently associated with stressful life events than depression in men (Aneshensel, 1985). One possible explanation for this statistic is that gender differences in social roles and in life experiences (e.g. pregnancy and childrearing) contribute to women's greater risk for depression. Another possibility is that gender differences in depression rates may be the result of men developing different disorders in response to stress, such as antisocial behaviour and alcohol abuse. Nolen-Hoeksema (1987) suggests that men and women even respond differently to depression; women focus on the negative emotions associated with depression, and are more likely to seek professional help, while men use distractions (e.g. alcohol) to cope with their mood state.

EVALUATION

Psychodynamic

Research support – There is some research support for the role of early loss in later depression. For example, studies have found that many people who have suffered depression describe their parents as 'affectionless' (Shah and Waller, 2000) supporting Freud's concept of 'loss' through withdrawal of affection. Barnes and Prosen (1985) found that men who had lost their fathers through death during childhood scored higher on a depression scale than those whose fathers had not died. Bifulco *et al.* (1992) found evidence that children whose mothers died in childhood were more likely than other children to experience depression later in life. However, they found that the association could be explained by the lack of care from parents and parent substitutes following the loss, rather than the loss itself.

Limitations – Loss probably only explains a relatively small percentage of cases of depression. It is estimated that only 10% of those who experience early loss later become depressed (Paykel and Cooper, 1992). Another weakness of the Freudian psychoanalytic approach is that the associated therapy (**psychoanalysis**) has not proved very effective with cases of depression (Comer, 2002). However, this may be, in part, because people who are depressed find it difficult to communicate in the way required by psychoanalysis.

Sociocultural factors

Life events and depression – The link between early bereavement and later depression can be used to support the life events approach, as bereavement is a major life event. One criticism of the research by Brown and Harris is that the sample was only women (and British). The life events that affected these women may apply only to this group of people. There is evidence, for example, that women rely more on social support (Frydenberg and Lewis, 1993), and are therefore more likely to be adversely affected by its absence. Stress may cause depression, but depression also causes stress, thus leading to a spiralling depression. For example, a partner who is depressed may cause greater problems in a marriage, and this then produces greater stress for the depressed individual (Hammen, 1997).

Social networks and social skills – Are social skills deficits a *cause* or a *consequence* of depression? It is easy to see how they may be a consequence of depression (e.g. low mood makes it more difficult to interact with others) but there is evidence that they do play a causal role in the onset of depression. For example, low social competence has been found to predict the onset of depression in primary age children (Cole, 1990), and poor interpersonal problem-solving skills has been found to predict increases in depression among adolescents (Davila *et al.*, 1995).

Cognitive

By contrast, cognitive explanations are associated with successful therapies for depression. Butler and Beck (2000) reviewed 14 **meta-analyses** that have investigated the effectiveness of Beck's cognitive therapy and concluded that about 80% of adults benefited from the therapy compared to controls who had no treatment. The therapy was more successful than drug therapies and had a lower relapse rate, thus lending support to the proposition that depression has a cognitive basis.

Beck's theory of depression is further supported by research that bears out many of Beck's predictions. For example, Hammen and Krantz (1976) found that depressed women made more errors in logic when asked to interpret written material than non-depressed participants. Bates *et al.* (1999) found that depressed participants who were given negative automatic-thought statements became more and more depressed. However, as with so many explanations, the fact that there is a link between negative thoughts and depression does not mean that the former *caused* the latter.

Learned helplessness – Although Seligman's initial research was based on the study of animals, learned helplessness has subsequently been supported by many human studies. For example, Hiroto and Seligman (1975) showed that college students who were exposed to uncontrollable aversive events were more likely to fail on cognitive tasks. Another study by Miller and Seligman (1974) found that depressed students performed worst of all on a similar task. These findings show that having some degree of control and not feeling completely helpless greatly improves performance, especially for those who are depressed. These findings also support the learned helplessness-depression model.

Hopelessness – Kwon and Laurenceau (2002) provided evidence to support the hopelessness model. Participants were assessed on a weekly basis and they found that those with a higher negative attributional style also showed more of the symptoms associated with depression when stressed. It is possible that a negative attributional style is more common in women than men. This is because, throughout their social development, women are often taught to think in a negative way about themselves (Notman and Nadelson, 1995). This might explain why many more women suffer from depression than men.

CAN YOU...? (No.10.3)

...1 Outline **two or more** psychological explanations of depression in about 100 words each.

...2 Outline **eight** critical points relating to psychological explanations of depression, including **(a)** the critical point being made, **(b)** your evidence for this criticism, and **(c)** how this criticism affects that explanation.

...3 Use this material to write a 600-word answer to the question: *Discuss **two or more** psychological explanations of depression.* (8 marks + 16 marks)

The frequency with which depression occurs, and the suffering it can cause, together with the increasing evidence for the biological *causes* of this disorder, has led to pressure to develop effective forms of treatment that are likewise biological in nature. The most well-established forms of treatment and the most widely used are antidepressant drugs, such as *Prozac* (fluoxetine) and, for the most severe cases of depression, **electro-convulsive therapy** or ECT.

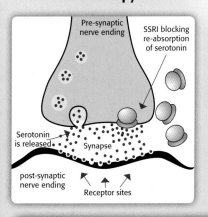

◀ SSRIs block the re-uptake of serotonin at the presynaptic membrane, increasing serotonin concentration at receptor sites on the postsynaptic membrane.

A CASE STUDY OF ECT FOR DEPRESSION (RAPOPORT *et al.*, 1998)

A 37-year-old woman was treated for a severe major depressive episode. Her depressive symptoms had first appeared following her separation from her husband, and had persisted for one year. During that time, she had attempted suicide four times, including deliberately crashing her car in an attempt to kill herself.

Psychotherapy and antidepressants had little effect on her symptoms. Her mental status examination revealed a woman who was 'tearful with soft speech, depressed mood, a restricted range of affect, depressive cognitions and suicidal thoughts'. Her BDI score was 30 (see page 178). An overdose of *clomipramine* (a tricyclic antidepressant) and *lorazepam* (an anti-anxiety drug) several weeks after admission led to eight sessions of right unilateral ECT, over 3 weeks.

Although after three sessions of ECT there was little change, by the final session of ECT she showed a significant improvement in her depressive symptoms with a Beck score of 7, and no additional suicidal thoughts. After further treatment with antidepressants she was discharged, and at a four-month follow-up, she showed normal social and occupational functioning.

BIOLOGICAL THERAPIES

Antidepressants

Antidepressants are drugs that relieve the symptoms of depression. There are several different types, although we will only focus on the older 'tricyclic' antidepressants and the newer 'SSRIs' (*Selective Serotonin Re-uptake Inhibitors*) here. These drugs are used to treat moderate to severe depressive illnesses. Antidepressants are typically taken for at least four to six months, although in some cases, they are needed for a longer time.

How do they work? Depression is thought to be due to insufficient amounts of **neurotransmitters** such as **serotonin** and **noradrenaline** being produced in the nerve endings to activate their neighbouring cells. In normal brains, neurotransmitters are constantly being released from the nerve endings, stimulating the neighbouring cells. To terminate their action, neurotransmitters are re-absorbed into the nerve endings or are broken down by an enzyme. Antidepressants work either by reducing the rate of re-absorption or by blocking the enzyme which breaks down the neurotransmitters. Both of these mechanisms increase the amount of neurotransmitter available to excite neighbouring cells.

Tricyclics block the transporter mechanism that re-absorbs both serotonin and noradrenaline into the pre-synaptic cell after it has fired. As a result, more of these neurotransmitters are left in the **synapse**, prolonging their activity, and making transmission of the next impulse easier.

Selective serotonin re-uptake inhibitors (SSRIs) work in much the same way as the tricyclics but, instead of blocking the re-uptake of different neurotransmitters, they block mainly serotonin and so increase the quantity available to excite neighbouring brain cells, thus reducing the symptoms of depression. The best known of these drugs is *Prozac* (fluoxetine).

Phases of treatment – The treatment of depression has three distinct phases. The treatment of current symptoms takes place during the *acute* phase of treatment. Once symptoms have diminished, treatment enters the *continuation* phase for approximately four to six months, after which medication is gradually withdrawn in order to prevent relapse. A third phase, the *maintenance* phase is recommended for individuals who have a history of recurrent depressive episodes.

Electroconvulsive therapy (ECT)

ECT is generally used in severely depressed patients for whom psychotherapy and medication have proved ineffective. ECT can also be used for patients with schizophrenia or those experiencing severe manic episodes. It is used when there is a risk of suicide, because ECT often has much quicker results than antidepressant drugs. The *National Institute for Clinical Excellence* (2003) suggests that ECT should only be used in cases where all other treatments have failed or when the condition is considered to be potentially life-threatening.

The use of ECT – An electrode is placed above the temple of the non-dominant side of the brain, and a second in the middle of the forehead (*unilateral* ECT). Alternatively, one electrode is placed above each temple (*bilateral* ECT). The patient is first injected with a short-acting general anaesthetic, so that they are unconscious before the electric shock is administered, and given a nerve-blocking agent, paralysing the muscles of the body to prevent them contracting during the treatment and causing fractures. Oxygen is given to the patient, to compensate for their inability to breathe. A small amount of electric current (approximately 0.6 amps), lasting about half a second, is passed through the brain. This current produces a seizure lasting up to one minute, which affects the entire brain. ECT is usually given three times a week, with the patient requiring between 3 and 15 treatments.

The mechanism of ECT – Exactly how or why ECT works is not completely understood, but what is clear is that it is the *seizure* rather than the electrical stimulus that generates improvement in depressive symptoms. The seizure appears to restore the brain's ability to regulate mood. It may do this by enhancing the transmission of neurochemicals, or by improving blood flow in the brain.

EVALUATION

Effectiveness of antidepressants

Severity of depression– Kirsch *et al.* (2008) reviewed clinical trials of SSRI antidepressants and concluded that only in cases of the most severe depression was there any significant advantage to using SSRIs. However, this is not the whole story, as what they found was that only for the most severely depressed group was there a difference between drug treatment and the **placebo**. In other words, even the placebo appeared to benefit *moderately* depressed individuals presumably because it 'offered them hope', which contributed to a lessening of their symptoms. For the most severely depressed group, presumably the expectation of anything working was lessened, thus diminishing any 'placebo effect' and increasing the apparent difference between treatment and control conditions.

SSRIs versus non-SSRIs – For some patients who fail to respond to treatment with an SSRI antidepressant, there may be some advantage in switching to an alternative non-SSRI antidepressant. However, in a **meta-analysis** of studies which compared the effectiveness of SSRI versus non-SSRI treatment, there was no significant difference in outcomes for the two treatment groups (Papakostas *et al.*, 2008).

Appropriateness of antidepressants

Children and adolescents – Despite their role in the treatment of adults, antidepressants appear less useful when given to children and adolescents (Hammen, 1997). **Double-blind** studies (e.g. Geller *et al.*, 1992) have consistently failed to demonstrate the superiority of antidepressant medications over placebo conditions. Ryan (1992) suggests that this may well have something to do with developmental differences in brain neurochemistry.

Risk of suicide – There has been concern about the safety of SSRIs, particularly the possibility that their use may increase suicidal thoughts in vulnerable people. A review of studies comparing SSRIs with other treatments or with a placebo condition, (Ferguson *et al.*, 2005) found that those treated with SSRIs were twice as likely to attempt suicide. A later review of studies (Barbui *et al.*, 2008) found that although the use of SSRIs increased the risk of suicide among adolescents, this risk was *decreased* among adults. Among adults aged 65 or older, exposure to SSRIs appeared to have a protective effect against suicide attempts.

The effectiveness of ECT

ECT versus 'sham' ECT – There is a substantial body of evidence to support the effectiveness of ECT. Studies (e.g. Gregory *et al.*, 1985) that have compared ECT with 'sham' ECT (i.e. where the patient is anaesthetised but does not receive ECT) have found a significant difference in outcome in favour of real ECT. ECT has also been found to be effective in cases of treatment-resistant depression (Folkerts *et al.*, 1997) although there are also studies that have shown no difference in response to ECT in treatment-resistant depression (Hussain, 2002).

ECT versus antidepressants – A review of 18 studies with 1144 patients comparing ECT with drug therapy showed that ECT is more effective than drug therapy in the short-term treatment of depression (Scott, 2004). However, none of these trials compared ECT with newer antidepressant medications, such as the SSRIs.

The appropriateness of ECT

Side effects – Possible physical side effects include impaired memory, cardiovascular changes and headaches (Datto, 2000). In a review of research, Rose *et al.* (2003) concluded that at least one-third of patients complained of persistent memory loss after ECT. Weiner (1980) found a general slowing of cognition following ECT that takes weeks to disappear. The *Department of Health report* (2007) found that among those receiving ECT within the last two years, 30% reported that it had resulted in permanent fear and anxiety.

Unilateral versus bilateral ECT – One way of minimising the cognitive problems associated with ECT is to use unilateral ECT (where electrodes are placed on one side of the skull) rather than bilateral ECT (where electrodes are placed on each side). Studies (e.g. Sackeim *et al.*, 2000) have found that unilateral ECT is less likely to cause cognitive problems than bilateral ECT, yet may be just as effective.

AGE BIAS AND TREATMENT

Benek-Higgins *et al.* (2008) claim that depression in elderly people is often misdiagnosed because its symptoms are masked by natural changes in these individuals and their lifestyles. As a result, antidepressant medication is less likely to be prescribed even when needed. There is the additional problem that elderly people are less likely to seek help for depressive symptoms because they fear the stigma attached to mental illness or that they will lose their independence. ECT is also effective and well tolerated in the elderly. A meta-analysis found a significant improvement in 83% of cases where ECT was used with elderly patients (Mulsant *et al.*, 1991).

PUBLICATION BIAS

Turner *et al.* (2008) claim that there is evidence of a **publication bias** towards studies which show a positive outcome of antidepressant treatment, thus exaggerating the benefits of antidepressant drugs. The authors found that, not only were positive results more likely to be published, but studies that were not positive were often published in a way that conveyed a positive outcome. The authors consider that such selective publication can lead doctors to make inappropriate treatment decisions that may not be in the best interest of their patients.

ETHICAL ISSUES IN BIOLOGICAL THERAPIES

- **Antidepressants and the use of placebos** – A fundamental requirement of research ethics is that if effective treatments exist, they should be used as control conditions when new treatments are tested. Substituting a placebo for an effective treatment does not satisfy this duty as it exposes individuals to a treatment known to be inferior.
- **ECT and informed consent** – The DOH report (1999) found that of 700 patients who received ECT when sectioned under the Mental Health Act, 59% had not consented to treatment. Where patients receive treatment voluntarily there remains the issue of being fully *informed* about possible side effects (see left).

CAN YOU...? (No.10.4)

...1 Describe **two** biological therapies for depression in 100 words each.

...2 Outline **four** critical points for each therapy, including **(a)** its effectiveness, and **(b)** its appropriateness.

...3 Use this material to write a 600-word answer to the question: *Discuss **two or more** biological therapies for depression.* (8 marks + 16 marks)

Psychotherapy is the treatment of mental disorders through the use of psychological rather than physical means. It is sometimes referred to as a 'talking cure' because it involves talking to a therapist. **Cognitive behavioural therapies (CBTs)** are based on the fact that the way we feel is partly dependent on the way we *think* about events (i.e. cognition). Treatment involves identifying maladaptive thinking and then developing coping strategies (i.e. *behavioural* change). Although the weight of published evidence for CBT suggests that this is the main alternative to the use of antidepressants, research also shows that psychodynamic therapy can be effective in the treatment of depression.

PSYCHOLOGICAL THERAPIES

Cognitive-behavioural therapy (CBT)

Originally developed by psychiatrist Aaron Beck (Beck, 1967), CBT emphasises the role of maladaptive thoughts and beliefs in the origins and maintenance of depression. When people think negatively about themselves and their lives, they become depressed (see page 182). The aim of CBT is to identify and alter these maladaptive cognitions (the cognitive part of therapy) as well as any dysfunctional behaviours that might be contributing to depression (the behavioural part). CBT is intended to be relatively brief (usually between 16 and 20 sessions) and is focused on current problems and current dysfunctional thinking. Although there are many ingredients involved in CBT (including 'homework'), two of the main ones are 'thought catching' and 'behavioural activation', as described below (Hammen, 1997).

Thought catching – Individuals are taught how to see the link between their thoughts and the way they feel. They might, as part of their 'homework' be asked to record any emotion-arousing events, the automatic 'negative' thoughts associated with these events, and then their 'realistic' thoughts that might challenge these negative thoughts. For example, they may feel distressed about something they overhear, automatically assuming that the person was talking about them. During CBT they are taught to challenge this association by asking themselves questions, such as: 'Where's the evidence that they *were* talking about me? Might they have been talking about someone else? What is the worst that can happen if they were?'. By challenging these dysfunctional thoughts, and replacing them with more constructive ones, clients are trying out new ways of behaving.

Behavioural activation – This is based on the commonsense idea that being active leads to rewards that act as an antidote to depression. A characteristic of many depressed people is that they no longer participate in activities that they previously enjoyed (see below). In CBT, therapist and client identify potentially pleasurable activities and anticipate and deal with any cognitive obstacles (e.g. 'I won't be able to achieve that').

The belief that changing behaviour can go some way to alleviating depression is supported by a study on the beneficial effects of exercise.

Babyak *et al.* (2000) studied 156 adult volunteers diagnosed with major depressive disorder. They were randomly assigned to a four-month course of aerobic exercise, drug treatment (an SSRI) or a combination of the two. Patients in all three groups exhibited significant improvement at the end of the four months. Six months after the end of the study, those in the exercise group had significantly lower relapse rates than those in the medication group, particularly among those who had continued with an exercise regime on their own.

PIT IN PRACTICE
Evaluation

Paley *et al.* (2008) investigated the effectiveness of PIT in a routine clinical practice setting. Sixty-two patients received a course of PIT over a 52-month period. Outcomes were assessed using a variety of measures, including the Beck Depression Inventory (BDI) described on page 178.

There were significant differences in scores on the BDI in the pre- and post-treatment phases. Clinically significant change was achieved by 34% of clients as measured by scores on the BDI.

Although these results were less favourable than those obtained during clinical trials, they are roughly equivalent to changes in depressive symptoms reported with other therapies, such as CBT. This shows that PIT can be an effective treatment for depression in routine clinical settings, such as hospitals or surgeries.

Psychodynamic interpersonal therapy (PIT)

PIT was first developed by Robert Hobson (1985) as an attempt to move away from the traditional psychoanalytic approach of a one-sided relationship between therapist and client. It was originally called the 'conversational model' to emphasise the fact that the mutual task of therapist and client was to engage in a therapeutic 'conversation'. In this 'conversation' problems are not only talked about as past events, but are also actively relived in the present and resolved within the therapeutic relationship. Hobson believed that the symptoms of depression arise from disturbances in interpersonal relationships. These disturbances can only be explored and modified effectively from within another relationship – the therapeutic one. The *quality* of the relationship is therefore crucial.

Components of PIT – The model has seven interlinking components, some of which are generic to all psychotherapy.

- **Exploratory rationale** – Interpersonal difficulties in the individual's life are identified, and the therapist tries to find a rationale for the individual that links their current symptoms with these difficulties.
- **Shared understanding** – The therapist tries to understand what the individual is really experiencing or feeling, by saying, for example: 'This is what I am hearing you say. Have I got it right?'.
- **Staying with feelings** – Rather than talking about feelings in an abstract way, an attempt is made to recreate them in the therapeutic environment.
- **Focus on difficult feelings** – The individual may express an emotion (such as anger) of which they are unaware, or may not display an appropriate emotion, e.g. they appear calm or disinterested when discussing something of great emotional significance.
- **Gaining insight** – The therapist points out patterns in different types of relationship (e.g. between child and adult relationships or relationships with other adults).
- **Sequencing of interventions** – Different aspects of the model must be used in a coherent manner (e.g. establishing the context of feelings before sharing insights).
- **Change** – The therapist acknowledges and encourages changes made during therapy.

THE PROBLEM OF ATTRITION
Evaluation
Participant attrition refers to the tendency of people undergoing psychotherapy to drop out of the study during treatment. Hunt and Andrews (2007) examined five **meta-analyses** and found the median drop-out rate was 8%. If participants drop out because they feel therapy isn't helping, then the outcomes for the remaining participants will appear artificially positive. The remaining participants are more likely to be highly motivated and to show greater improvement. Dropping out of therapy *after* improvement also biases results, as those remaining are probably doing less well.

PHONE PSYCHOTHERAPY
Evaluation

It is generally the rule that in psychotherapy, therapist and patient meet face to face, but research suggests that this does not necessarily have to be the case. Mohr *et al.* (2005) carried out a meta-analysis of 12 studies and found that psychotherapy carried out over the phone significantly reduced the symptoms of depression when compared to control conditions (no therapy), although it was only about half as effective as face-to-face psychotherapy. Therapy is effective only when patients continue long enough to receive the benefit. This is the major advantage of phone psychotherapy. Mohr found that only 8% of patients dropped out of phone psychotherapy whereas 47% dropped out of face-to-face psychotherapy. As a result, the greater likelihood of patients *completing* phone-based psychotherapy may make it as effective as face-to-face therapy.

EVALUATION

Effectiveness of CBT

Research support – A meta-analysis by Robinson *et al.* (1990) found that CBT was superior to no-treatment control groups. However, when these control groups were subdivided into waiting list (i.e. no treatment at all) and **placebo** groups, CBT was not significantly more effective than the placebo condition at reducing depressive symptoms.

Therapist competence – Therapist competence appears to explain a significant amount of the variation in CBT outcomes. Kuyken and Tsivrikos (2009) lend support to this claim, concluding that as much as 15% of the variance in outcome may be attributable to therapist competence.

The importance of homework – Research suggests that clients' engagement with 'homework' predicts their outcomes and that therapists who are able to improve clients' engagement with homework have associated benefits in terms of outcomes (Bryant *et al.*, 1999).

Appropriateness of CBT

Who is it suitable for? CBT has been successfully applied to many different client groups, including elderly populations, juveniles and depressed adolescents (see below). The cognitive aspect of CBT has also been administered by computer and shown to be as effective as other forms of psychotherapy treatment (Selmi *et al.*, 1990). A particular advantage of computer-based and phone-based psychotherapy (see above), is the relatively low level of drop-out compared to face-to-face CBT.

Who isn't it suitable for? CBT appears to be less suitable for people who have high levels of dysfunctional beliefs that are both rigid and resistant to change (Elkin *et al.*, 1985). CBT also appears to be less suitable in situations where high levels of stress in the individual reflect realistic stressors in the person's life that therapy cannot resolve (Simons *et al.*, 1995).

Effectiveness of PIT

Research support – Paley *et al.* (2008) have shown that as a treatment for depression, outcomes for PIT are at least equivalent to those achieved with CBT (see box on facing page). However, they acknowledge that changes in significant **life-events** were not monitored during the study, therefore any observed clinical gains (or lack of them) could not be attributed solely to the therapeutic intervention.

The Collaborative Psychotherapy Project (CPP) (Barkham *et al.*, 1996) found that PIT and CBT were equally effective in reducing the severity of depression (as measured on the BDI, see page 178). However, after 12 months, those treated with PIT *or* CBT showed a tendency for symptoms to recur, thus limiting its long-term effectiveness.

Appropriateness of PIT

The importance of relational processes – Guthrie (1999) argues that explanations (and their related therapies) that concentrate solely on cognitive processes in the development of depression, neglect the important role of interpersonal relationships. This makes PIT particularly important in the treatment of cases of depression that result from dysfunctional relationships (e.g. between parent and child). As a result, research has consistently shown that the quality of the relationship between *therapist* and client is a central determinant of the outcomes of therapy (e.g. Horvath and Bedi, 2002).

Brief intervention – NHS psychotherapy patients were randomly allocated to receive 12 weeks' PIT (by psychiatry trainees) or to remain as waiting-list controls for that period. Fifty-four patients entered the study, of whom 33 completed. Significant improvement was observed in patients who completed therapy, suggesting that even brief treatment by inexperienced therapists can be effective in alleviating the symptoms of depression. However, high **attrition** rates were found between waiting list and completion of therapy (see box above).

CBT IN DEPRESSED ADOLESCENTS
Evaluation

The fear that some antidepressant drugs might increase the risk of suicide, has led researchers to explore the possibility that combining antidepressants with CBT might reduce this risk.

The Treatments for Adolescents with Depression Study (March *et al.*, 2007) enrolled 327 adolescents aged between 12 and 17 who were diagnosed with major depression. They were randomly assigned to either fluoxetine (a SSRI antidepressant) alone, CBT alone, or fluoxetine combined with CBT.

After 12 weeks, 62% had responded positively to the drug treatment alone, 48% to CBT alone and 73% to a combination of the two. After 36 weeks, 81% were responding positively to either the drug treatment or the CBT alone, and 86% to the combination treatment.

However, on further analysis, March *et al.* found that CBT had significantly reduced suicidal thoughts and behaviour. When patients began the study, 30% expressed thoughts about suicide. At the end of the study, this figure had dropped to under 15% for those on the drug treatment, compared to 6% for those who had received CBT.

CAN YOU...? No.10.5

...1 Describe **two** psychological therapies for depression in 100 words each.

...2 Outline **four** critical points for each therapy, including **(a)** its effectiveness, and **(b)** its appropriateness.

...3 Use this material to write a 600-word answer to the question: *Discuss **two** psychological therapies for depression.* (8 marks + 16 marks)

CHAPTER SUMMARY

OVERVIEW OF DEPRESSION

CLASSIFICATION AND DIAGNOSIS

CLINICAL CHARACTERISTICS
Under DSM-IVR, diagnosis of 'major depressive disorder' requires the presence of five out of nine symptoms, including either depressed mood or loss of interest and pleasure.

RELIABILITY
- Inter-rater reliability – Lobbestael et al. (2011) reported moderate inter-rater reliability using Structured Clinical Interview.
- Test–retest reliability – high levels of test–retest reliability using Beck Depression Inventory (Beck et al., 1996).

EVALUATION
- Evidence for reliability – Keller et al. (1995) and Zanarini et al. (2000) found generally 'good' inter-rater reliability for diagnoses using DSM but 'fair' at best for test–retest reliability.
- Reasons for lack of reliability – include subjectivity of interpretation of symptoms.
- Simpler diagnoses – Zimmerman et al. (2010) argue that using only mood and cognitive symptoms produced more reliable diagnosis.

VALIDITY
- Comorbidity – presence of an anxiety disorder is the single biggest clinical risk for the development of depression.
- Content validity – BDI considered high in content validity because a result of a consensus among mental health clinicians concerning symptoms.
- Concurrent validity – high between BDI and measures, such as Hamilton Depression Scale (Beck, 1998).

EVALUATION
- McCullough et al. (2003) found considerable overlap in symptoms, making it difficult to justify different forms of depressive illness.
- Diagnoses made by GPs less objective than those made by 'specialists'.
- Consequences of comorbidity include increased risk of suicide when combined with panic disorder (Goodwin et al., 2001).
- DSM vs ICD – Andrews et al. (1999) compared the two systems and concluded no differences in validity in diagnosis of depression.
- Depression less likely to be accepted as an 'illness' among Asians compared to Europeans because of stigma attached to illness (Karasz, 2005).

BIOLOGICAL THERAPIES

ANTIDEPRESSANTS
- Tricyclics block mechanism that reabsorbs serotonin and noradrenaline into presynaptic cell. Results in more being available in the synapse.
- SSRIs selectively block the reabsorption of serotonin and so increase amount available to excite neighbouring brain cells.
- Treatment phases – acute, continuation and maintenance.

EVALUATION
- Kirsch et al. (2008) – SSRIs only effective in the most severe cases of depression. Placebos had some effect on moderately depressed group because it 'offered them help'.
- SSRI versus non-SSRI treatment, no significant difference in outcomes.
- Antidepressants less appropriate for children and adolescents which may reflect differences in brain neurochemistry.
- Risk of suicide when taking SSRIs may be greater for adolescents but reduced for adults.
- Age bias – depression in old people may be ignored because symptoms put down to natural changes in old age.
- Publication bias – tendency to publish studies with positive outcomes, thus exaggerating benefits of antidepressant drugs.

EXPLANATIONS OF DEPRESSION

BIOLOGICAL EXPLANATIONS

GENETIC FACTORS
- Relatives of probands with depression have 20% risk of disorder (10% in general population).
- Concordance rate for MZ twins 46%, for DZ twins 20%.
- Adoption studies – higher incidence of depression in biological relatives of depressed group than relatives of non-depressed group.

EVALUATION
- Zhang et al. (2005) – gene that starves brain of serotonin 10 times more likely in depressed patients.
- Relatively low concordance rates for depression may be explained by idea of comorbidity i.e. inherit vulnerability to number of disorders.
- Genetic and environmental contributions to depression similar for adolescents and adults (Glowinski et al., 2003).
- Evolutionary approach – adaptive value of depression may be as an honest signal of need, which increases social support from others.

NEUROTRANSMITTER DYSFUNCTION
- Deficiency in noradrenaline – support from reduced levels of byproducts in urine and increased density of receptors (up-regulation).
- Low levels of serotonin – support from reduced level of byproducts in cerebrospinal fluid in suicide victims and improvements from SSRIs.

EVALUATION
- Support – drugs which lower noradrenaline levels bring on depressive states, those which raise noradrenaline then show antidepressant effects.
- Tryptophan depletion produces relapse of symptoms when recovering from depression, but not in those with no history of depression.
- Serotonin disturbances also associated with exposure to insecticides.

CORTISOL HYPERSECRETION
- Depression associated with elevated levels of stress hormone cortisol which lower serotonin levels in the brain.
- Supported by dexamethasone test, suggesting over-activity in HPA axis characteristic of depressed state.

EVALUATION
- Strickland et al. (2002) – no evidence of increased cortisol levels in a group of depressed women.
- Depression during pregnancy → high cortisol levels → increased risk of premature birth.

THERAPIES FOR DEPRESSION

BIOLOGICAL THERAPIES cont'd

ECT

- Small amount of electric current passed through the brain, resulting in a seizure, which appears to restore brain's ability to regulate mood.
- Used for severely depressed patients for whom psychotherapy and medication are ineffective.
- Can be effective where suicide is a possibility because quicker acting than antidepressants.

EVALUATION

- Significant difference between ECT and 'sham' ECT. ECT proven effective in treatment-resistant depression.
- Comparison with antidepressant treatments found ECT more effective in short-term treatment, but comparison did not include SSRIs.
- Side effects of ECT include impaired memory and cardiovascular changes. Many report permanent fear and anxiety.
- Cognitive problems may be minimised with unilateral rather than bilateral ECT.
- Ethical issues – problem of using placebo treatment which does not satisfy duty of care. Many people receiving ECT do not consent to treatment.

PSYCHOLOGICAL THERAPIES

CBT

- Aim of CBT is to identify and alter maladaptive cognitions and any dysfunctional behaviour that contributes to depression.
- Thought catching – patients taught to identify and challenge dysfunctional thoughts, and replace them with more constructive ones.
- Behavioural activation – identify potentially pleasurable activities that would lead to rewards that act as an antidote to depression.
- Illustrated in study of adults on regime of aerobic exercise (Babyak *et al.*, 2000) – lower relapse rates than those on medication.

EVALUATION

- Meta-analysis (Robinson *et al.*, 1990) – CBT superior to non-treatment control groups, but not superior to placebo groups.
- Therapist competence plays significant role in effectiveness of CBT.
- Improving client's engagement with 'homework' improves outcomes.
- CBT effective for many different client groups and also works when administered by computer or over phone.
- Less suitable for people with high levels of dysfunctional beliefs or severe life stressors.
- March *et al.* (2007) – CBT effective at reducing thoughts of suicide.
- Phone psychotherapy also effective (Mohr *et al.*, 2005).
- Problem of attrition – if patients drop out because therapy not working, may give a false result based on those remaining.

PSYCHODYNAMIC INTERPERSONAL THERAPY (PIT)

- Symptoms of depression thought to arise from disturbances in interpersonal relationships.
- Therapist and client thus develop a 'therapeutic relationship' to relive and resolve these disturbances.
- Quality of therapeutic relationship is crucial.
- Components of PIT are – exploratory rationale, shared understanding, staying with feelings, focus on difficult feelings, gaining insight, sequencing of interventions and change.

EVALUATION

- In Paley *et al.* study, changes in life events not monitored during study, could contribute to outcomes.
- CPP study – PIT and CBT equally effective in reducing severity of depression.
- Because PIT emphasises therapeutic relationship, particularly effective when depression results from dysfunctional relationships.
- Even brief PIT intervention from psychiatry trainees effective when compared to waiting list group.
- Paley *et al.* (2008) – significant changes in BDI for people receiving PIT.

PSYCHOLOGICAL EXPLANATIONS

PSYCHOANALYTIC EXPLANATION

- Freud (1917) believed that depression (melancholia) was a reaction to the loss of a loved one.
- We unconsciously harbour negative feelings to loved ones. When they are lost, negative feelings are turned inwards.
- Depression is anger turned against oneself.

EVALUATION

- Some support for link between loss and depression, but only about 10% of those who suffer early loss become depressed.
- Weakness is that psychoanalysis therapy is not effective in treatment of depression.

COGNITIVE EXPLANATIONS

- Beck (1967) – negative interpretations of the world, caused by parental rejection, criticisms by teachers, etc., which lead to development of negative schema.
- Learned helplessness – when individuals feel unable to take control of their lives and develop depression; person shows a depressive attributional style.
- Hopelessness theory – person has pessimistic expectations of the future and doesn't believe they have resources to change situation.

EVALUATION

- Cognitive therapies *are* effective in treatment of depression e.g. meta-analysis by Butler and Beck (2000).
- Some evidence to show link between logical errors and depression, but does not demonstrate *causal* link.
- Learned helplessness initially demonstrated in animals, but also evident in humans (e.g. Hiroto and Seligman, 1975).
- Hopelessness theory may explain gender incidence of depression in women because of socialisation differences.

SOCIO-CULTURAL FACTORS

- Life events act as trigger for depression.

EVALUATION

- Research support (e.g. Brown and Harris, 1978 found episodes of depression preceded by major life event).
- Depressed individuals report having sparse social networks, which makes them more vulnerable to life events.
- Brown and Harris studied only women who suffer more from lack of social support, therefore more vulnerable to depression.
- Stress → depression → stress, therefore spiralling depression.
- Social skills deficits may be a consequence or a cause of depression.
- Gender differences in depression may be result of men and women developing different disorders in response to stress (Nolen-Hoeksema, 1987).
- Women twice as likely to develop depression than men. Men may develop different disorders in response to stress (e.g. antisocial behaviour or alcohol abuse).

EXAM QUESTION WITH STUDENT ANSWER

> **QUESTIONS** (a) Outline the clinical characteristics of depression. *(4 marks)*
> (b) Outline and evaluate **one or more** psychological explanations of depression. *(4 marks + 16 marks)*

STUDENT ANSWER

(a) Depression is a mood disorder. It comes in several forms – you can just have depression (unipolar disorder) or a combination of depression and mania (bipolar disorder). In unipolar disorder or major depressive disorder (MDD) the main clinical characteristics are:

- *Feeling sad or depressed.*
- *Loss of interest and pleasure in usual activities.*
- *Difficulties in sleeping, either too much or too little sleep.*
- *Change in activity level, becoming either lethargic or agitated.*
- *Change in appetite (increased or decreased).*
- *Loss of energy and tiredness.*
- *Feelings of worthlessness and guilt that may be inappropriate.*
- *Difficulty in concentrating.*
- *Recurrent thoughts of death or suicide.*

For a diagnosis of MDD to be made five of the symptoms above should be present and have persisted for at least 2 weeks. Some of the symptoms rely on self-report (such as feeling sad) whereas other symptoms may be observed by others (e.g. change in activity level).

(b) The two psychological explanations that I will present are the psychodynamic explanation and the cognitive explanation.

Freud proposed that depression arises because a person has experienced loss early in life (which might be withdrawal of affection or death of a parent). This creates negative feelings towards the loved one that later becomes turned towards oneself.

Some studies have indeed found an association between early experience of loss and later depression. For example, Shah and Waller (2000) found that people who experienced affectionless parents later became depressed and Bifulco et al. (1992) found that children whose mothers died in childhood were more likely to become depressed. However, Bifulco also found that the women had experienced a lack of care during childhood, presumably because of having no mother or a difficult relationship with a stepmother, and this might explain later depression rather than the loss of their mother/affection.

A problem with the 'loss' explanation is that it doesn't apply to everyone who becomes depressed. Some people who become depressed have no experiences of loss during childhood. Therefore, at best, it is a partial explanation. A further weakness with the psychodynamic approach is that, if it was correct, we would expect psychoanalysis to help reduce depression in patients with the disorder but it has not been very effective. However, the lack of success may be due to other reasons, such as the fact that depressed individuals may find communication with a psychotherapist quite difficult.

The second psychological explanation is the cognitive one. There are actually several different cognitive ones, such as Beck's concept of the negative triad. He suggested that depressed people view the world, themselves and the future in a negative way and this creates depression and prevents recovery.

Beck's ideas have been supported in research. For example, Hammen and Krantz (1976) found that women who were depressed were more likely to make errors on logical reasoning tasks than non-depressed women. This supports the view that they were prone to using faulty logic.

Beck himself found that when he gave depressed patients negative-thoughts they became more depressed, suggested that such thoughts are the cause of the depression. However, we cannot be certain that negative thoughts are the initial cause of depression. They could also be an effect of being depressed.

[536 words]

EXAMINER COMMENTS

The student answer for part (a) begins with background information that can be described as 'scene-setting'. Such information is unlikely to attract many (if any) marks so it is best left out and time spent instead on directly answering the question.

The student has provided a bulleted list of the symptoms used in a diagnosis of depression. It is perfectly acceptable to use bulleted lists as long as each point contains sufficient information to convey **knowledge and understanding**. There is no need to include all these symptoms. Less breadth and more depth would have been more appropriate.

The answer ends with some important information about how this list of symptoms is used to provide a diagnosis, although no comment is made about the necessity of the first two bullet points when making a diagnosis.

> **AO1** – Knowledge and understanding is **accurate** although **lacks detail (depth)**. A **good range of material** has been selected but far too much for the 4 marks available for (a).

In this exam question, part (b) is predominantly **AO2/AO3** (evaluation). Students often find this difficult to comply with because it seems unnatural to provide minimal description and yet so much evaluation. The student has managed to get the balance between **AO1** and **AO2** more or less right here and has restricted their description of the two explanations to a very brief outline (perhaps a little too brief). Aiming for 50 words per explanation would have been better.

Paragraph 3 provides some excellent and informed evaluation on the psychodynamic explanation of depression – demonstrating **sound analysis** and **coherent elaboration**. Elaboration is demonstrated through the explanation of each point made, as well as the presentation of an alternative explanation for the findings.

Further evaluation is provided in the following paragraph, including some **evaluative** material in the reference to individual differences (not everyone becomes depressed because of loss) and also in considering the treatment of depression.

The next paragraph is a brief outline of the second explanation, which again could be a little less concise.

The final two paragraphs contain further **effective AO2** material as well as some **rudimentary** critical consideration of research issues – the question of whether the research does demonstrate a cause.

> **AO1** – The temptation to provide too much descriptive detail has been avoided. Whilst the content is **accurate**, it lacks sufficient **detail** for the full 4 marks available.
>
> **AO2/AO3** – The ideas in this answer are **well-structured** and **expressed clearly**. Overall, the answer demonstrates **reasonable analysis** although these ideas could have been elaborated more for higher marks.

Chapter 11
Psychopathology: Phobic disorders

SPECIFICATION

Psychopathology

Candidates will be expected to study one of the following disorders:
* *schizophrenia*
* *depression*
* *phobic disorders*
* *obsessive compulsive disorder*

Phobic disorders	
Overview	• Clinical characteristics of phobic disorders. • Issues surrounding the classification and diagnosis of phobic disorders, including reliability and validity.
Explanations	• Biological explanations of phobic disorders, for example genetics, biochemistry. • Psychological explanations of phobic disorders, for example behavioural, cognitive, psychodynamic and socio-cultural.
Therapy	• Biological therapies for phobic disorders, including their evaluation in terms of appropriateness and effectiveness. • Psychological therapies for phobic disorders, for example behavioural, psychodynamic and cognitive-behavioural, including their evaluation in terms of appropriateness and effectiveness.

CLASSIFICATION AND DIAGNOSIS OF PHOBIC DISORDERS

Phobic disorders are included in diagnostic manuals (e.g. **DSM** and **ICD**) within the category of 'anxiety disorders', a group of mental disorders that share the primary symptom of extreme anxiety. Phobic disorders, or '**phobias**', are instances of irrational fears that produce a conscious avoidance of the feared object or situation. This includes agoraphobia (fear of being trapped in a public place where escape is difficult), social phobia (anxiety related to social situations) and specific phobias (fears about specific objects, such as spiders or snakes, or specific situations, such as heights or the dark).

▶ Most people associate 'phobias' with fear of spiders or snakes, but take a look at phobialist.com which lists every imaginable phobia from ablutophobia (fear of washing) to zemmiphobia (fear of the great mole rat – pictured on the right).

CLINICAL CHARACTERISTICS OF SPECIFIC PHOBIC DISORDERS

An individual shows a marked and persistent fear that is excessive or unreasonable. The fear is cued by the presence or anticipation of a specific object or situation (e.g. flying, heights, seeing blood).

Exposure to the phobic stimulus almost invariably provokes an immediate anxiety response, such as a panic attack. In children the anxiety may be expressed as crying, tantrums, freezing or clinging.

A key characteristic is that the person recognises that their fear is excessive or unreasonable, although this feature may be absent in children. This characteristic distinguishes between a phobia and a delusional mental illness (such as schizophrenia) where the individual is not aware of the unreasonableness of their behaviour.

The avoidance or distress in the feared situation interferes significantly with the person's normal routine, occupation, social activities or relationships, and there is marked distress about having the phobia. This distinguishes phobias from more everyday fears that do not interfere with normal day-to-day living.

Panic attacks are a common symptom associated with phobias, especially agoraphobia. A panic attack (or panic disorder) involves physical symptoms, such as a pounding heart, difficulty breathing, dizziness and stomach upset.

In individuals under age 18 years the duration is at least 6 months.

The anxiety, panic attacks or phobic avoidance should not be better accounted for by another mental disorder, such as obsessive compulsive disorder or post-traumatic stress disorder.

Adapted from the American Psychiatric Association (2000) DSM-IVR criteria for the diagnosis of specific phobia.

Rosenhan (1973) conducted a classic study on the unreliability of psychiatric diagnoses. This study is described on page 165. You can refer to this as long as a link is clearly made to phobic disorders.

ISSUES OF RELIABILITY AND VALIDITY

Reliability

Reliability refers to the *consistency* of a measuring instrument, such as a questionnaire or scale to assess how fearful a person is about certain objects/experiences. Reliability of such questionnaires or scales can be measured in terms of whether two independent assessors give similar scores (**inter-rater reliability**) or whether the test items are consistent (**test–retest reliability**).

Inter-rater reliability – Skyre *et al.* (1991) assessed inter-rater reliability for diagnosing social phobia by asking three **clinicians** to assess 54 patient interviews obtained using the *Structured Clinical Interview* (SCID-I). There was high inter-rater agreement (+.72) showing that the diagnosis of phobia is reliable.

Test–retest reliability – Scales such as SCID take 1–2 hours to complete. The alternative is to use shorter, structured, self-administered scales. These are popular for specific phobias, for example the *Munich Diagnostic Checklist* (MDC). Hiller *et al.* (1990) reported satisfactory to excellent diagnostic agreement in a test–retest study using the MDC.

Validity

Validity refers to the extent that a diagnosis represents something that is real and distinct from other disorders and the extent that a classification system such as ICD measures what it claims to measure. Reliability and validity are inextricably linked because a diagnosis that is not reliable is meaningless (i.e. not valid).

Comorbidity is an important issue for the validity of diagnosis. It refers to the extent that two (or more) conditions co-occur. Research has found high levels of **comorbidity** between social phobias, animal phobias, generalised anxiety disorder and depression (e.g. Kendler *et al.*, 1993). Such comorbidity suggests that these conditions are not separate entities and therefore the diagnostic category is not very useful, e.g. when deciding what treatment to advise.

Concurrent validity – Questionnaires and interviews are used in the diagnosis of phobic disorders. One way to demonstrate that they are measuring what they intended to measure is to use **concurrent validity**. Concurrent validity establishes the value of a new measure of phobic symptoms by correlating it with an existing one. For example, Herbert *et al.* (1991) established the concurrent validity of the *Social Phobia Anxiety Inventory* (SPAI) by giving the test and various other standard measures to 23 social phobics. The SPAI correlated well with the other measures.

Construct validity is also used to assess diagnostic questionnaires and interviews. This measures the extent that a test for phobic disorders really does measure a target construct (symptom) of phobias. To do this clinicians identify possible target behaviours that we would expect in someone with a phobic disorder and see if people who score high on the test for phobic disorders also exhibit the target behaviour.

For example, patients with social phobia might tend to underestimate their ability to cope in social situations (which would lead to higher levels of anxiety in such situations). **Construct validity** would then be demonstrated by showing that people who score high on the test of phobic disorders also underestimate their ability to cope in social situations.

EVALUATION

Reliability

Research evidence – SCID is a semi-structured interview requiring extensive training to administer, which may explain the high reliability. However, reliability has not always been found to be high. Kendler *et al.* (1999) used face-to-face and telephone interviews to assess individuals with phobias. Over a one-month interval (test–retest) they found a mean agreement of +.46. Reliability over the long term (8 years) was even lower at +.30.

On the other hand, Picon *et al.* (2005) found good test–retest reliability (better than +.80) with a Portuguese version of the Social Phobia and Anxiety Inventory (SPAI) over a 14-day interval. This indicates that reliability can be good at least in the short-term.

Reasons for low reliability – Kendler *et al.* (1999) suggest that the low reliability found in their study might be due to several factors. First, test–retest reliability might be due to the poor recall by participants of their fears, for example people tend to over-exaggerate fears when recalling previous distress.

Second, low inter-rater reliability might be due to the different decisions made by interviewers when deciding if the severity of a symptom does or does not exceed the clinical threshold for a symptom. For example, one clinician might conclude that a symptom is clinically significant whereas another could conclude that the severity does not exceed the clinical threshold and therefore a diagnosis is not made.

Validity

Comorbidity – The findings on comorbidity have been supported in many other studies. For example, Eysenck (1997) reported that up to 66% of patients with one anxiety disorder are also diagnosed with another anxiety disorder. The implication is that a diagnosis should simply be 'anxiety disorder' rather than phobia or obsessive compulsive disorder (OCD).

Further support comes from Vasey and Dadds (2001) who reported that treatment success of anxiety disorders was unrelated to the original diagnosis of a specific phobia. The same treatments worked equally well which means there is no benefit in making a specific diagnosis of one kind of anxiety disorder.

Support for concurrent validity – Mattick and Clarke (1998) showed that their *Social Phobia Scale* (SPS) correlated well with other standard measures (varying between +.54 and +.69). This indicates that there are methods of diagnosis that agree and therefore appear to be measuring something real.

Support for construct validity – The *Social Phobia and Anxiety Inventory* (SPAI) correlates well with behavioural measures of social phobia (e.g. discomfort with public speaking). It also doesn't correlate with behaviours related to other anxiety disorders (Beidel *et al.*, 1989).

However, perhaps this is not surprising because the inventory includes questions about cognitions and behaviours across a range of fear-producing situations. This means it is likely to correlate with behaviours associated with social phobias.

The implications of low reliability and/or validity – In order to conduct research on the effectiveness of treatments for phobic disorders researchers require a reliable and valid means of assessing the disorders in the first place. Therefore, diagnosis and classification is critical in what we will consider on the following spreads.

▲ The Japanese recognise a unique social phobia – *taijin-kyofusho* – which is the fear of embarrassing others in a social situation.

CAN YOU…? No.11.1

…**1** Outline clinical characteristics of phobic disorders in about 200 words.

…**2** Outline issues relating to reliability and validity in the diagnosis and/or classification of phobic disorders in about 200 words.

…**3** Choose **eight** critical points relevant to issues of reliability and validity in the diagnosis and/or classification of phobic disorders. Elaborate each point in about 50 words.

…**4** Use this material to answer the following questions:
Outline clinical characteristics of phobic disorders. (8 marks) [200-word answer]

Discuss issues of reliability and validity associated with the classification and diagnosis of phobic disorders. (8 marks + 16 marks) [600-word answer]

Phobias are among the most common mental disorders. Statistics suggest that about 4% of the adult population suffer from phobias, although this rate varies from 2% (ONS, 2000) to 13% in one US survey (Stern, 1995).

Anxiety and fear are natural and adaptive responses, and therefore have a biological basis (part of the study of stress AS level). This might lead us to expect that abnormal fears and anxieties are also biologically based. This spread looks at the evidence for inheriting phobic disorders and the evolutionary explanation for such disorders.

*What is a **concordance rate**? In a sample of, for example, 100 twin pairs, one twin of each pair has a phobic disorder. The number of times the other twin also shows the illness determines the concordance rate, so if 40 have phobic disorders, then the concordance rate is 40%.*

BIOLOGICAL EXPLANATIONS

Genetic factors

Family studies – Research shows that having a family member with a phobic disorder increases the risk that an individual develops a similar disorder. (The family member who already has the disorder is called the **proband**). For example, Fyer *et al.* (1995) found that probands had three times as many relatives who also experienced phobias as normal controls. Solyom *et al.* (1974) found that 45% of phobic patients had at least one relative with the disorder, compared to a rate of 17% of non-phobic controls. Relatives usually have the same disorder as the proband, for example Ost (1989) found that 64% of blood phobics had at least one relative with the same disorder.

Twin studies – Comparisons can be made between identical (or **monozygotic**, **MZ**) twins and non-identical (or **dizygotic**, **DZ**) twins. As MZ twins are genetically identical, a closer **concordance rate** between MZ twins and DZ twins is evidence for a genetic basis for phobic disorders. Torgersen (1983) compared MZ and same-sex DZ twin pairs (total number of twins was 85) where one twin (the proband) had an anxiety disorder with panic attacks. Such disorders were five times more frequent in MZ twin pairs.

What is inherited? It may be that people inherit an oversensitive fear response. People with phobias often respond to normal situations with abnormal levels of anxiety, for example having panic attacks. Once an individual has experienced a panic attack in a particular situation this creates further anxiety that the same will happen in the future.

The oversensitive fear response can be explained in terms of the functioning of the **autonomic nervous system** (ANS). In some individuals there may be abnormally high levels of arousal in the ANS which leads to increased amounts of **adrenaline**. This is called the *adrenergic theory*. Additional theories concern **dopamine** pathways in the brain that predispose some people to be more readily conditioned to acquire phobias easily (see the behavioural explanation of phobias on the next spread). Finally, abnormally high **serotonin** activity has been suggested as a cause of oversensitive fear response because it affects those areas of the brain involved in the fear response, such as the amygdala.

An evolutionary approach

There are three explanations that each offer a way to explain the uneven distribution of phobias, i.e. that some fears are more common than others.

Ancient fears and modern minds – Some stimuli are more likely to be feared than others, such as snakes, heights, storms, darkness, strangers, separation and leaving the home range. These might be referred to as *ancient fears*, in that these stimuli reflected very real danger to our ancestors. Most modern-day phobias are exaggerations of these ancient fears (Marks and Nesse, 1994). Many other stimuli, such as leaves, stones and shallow water, were also part of our ancestral environment, yet because they posed no significant danger, are rarely feared. By the same token, things that are dangers today, such as motor cars, electricity or guns, rarely develop into phobias because they have not been around enough to have influenced our adaptive selection.

Prepotency – Experiencing anxiety *after* an event has happened would not be an **adaptive** response, therefore animals have evolved to respond to *potential* threats. Those ancestors who were able to respond appropriately to 'ancient' threats were more likely to survive and pass on their genes to subsequent generations. **Natural selection**, therefore, has shaped our nervous system so that we attend more to certain cues than others. For example, we may respond more anxiously to sudden noises or to visual stimuli that are more snake-like, a phenomenon known as **prepotency** (something that has power prior to direct experience). Prepotent fears are more likely to develop into phobias.

Preparedness – In addition to the idea of prepotency, it is a more flexible arrangement to have an innate readiness to *learn* about dangerous situations rather than inheriting rigid behavioural responses to specific situations. The concept of **biological preparedness** (Seligman, 1970) accounts for this. Seligman argued that animals, including humans, are biologically prepared to rapidly learn an association between particular (i.e. potentially life-threatening) stimuli and fear. Once learned, this association is difficult to extinguish. What is inherited is therefore the predisposition to form certain associations rather than others, instead of inheriting a fixed fear of certain things. For example, when an infant sees a stranger, they first look at their mother to gauge her response. Fear in the mother is likely to produce a fearful reaction from the infant (Marks, 1987). The infant has inherited a predisposition to learn this fear through observation rather than having an innate fear of strangers. However, such learning does not take place in response to all stimuli. Rhesus monkeys rapidly develop a fear of snakes if they see another rhesus monkey showing fear towards a snake, however the same rapid association is not made if another rhesus monkey shows fear towards a flower (Mineka *et al.*, 1984).

◄ The caterpillar of the convolvulus hawk moth has snake-head markings on its back end, an example of a prepotent signal which deters predators.

Bennett-Levy and Marteau (1984) have suggested that prepotent signalling in humans is achieved by an innate readiness to fear animals whose form is most different from that of humans, in terms of texture of skin and number of limbs. However, they found, when asking participants to rate a list of animals for fearfulness, ugliness and strangeness, that some animals (such as a slug) should have been highly feared, but weren't.

BEHAVIOURAL INHIBITION

Kagan (1994) identified an infant temperamental type that he described as *'behavioural inhibition'* – infants who tend to withdraw from unfamiliar people, objects and situations. He suggested that this behaviour had a genetic basis.

Longitudinal studies have followed children who showed signs of behavioural instability at birth. At primary school age such children were found to have higher ANS activity and also the largest number of specific fears. Similar results were found when looking at children whose parents suffered from panic disorder. Further follow-up studies found that both these groups of children developed significantly more anxiety disorders, supporting the hypothesis that behavioural inhibition to unfamiliar things or situations is genetically based and a risk factor for anxiety disorders (Biederman *et al.*, 1993).

CULTURAL DIFFERENCES

There are significant differences in the *kind* of phobias reported by different cultural groups. For example, Brown *et al.* (1990) found that phobic disorders were more common among African American than white American participants even when socioeconomic factors were controlled. This shows that environmental/social factors are important in determining aspects of phobias.

EVALUATION

Genetic factors

Family and twin studies provide modest support for the genetic basis of phobic disorders. However, there is considerable variability between disorders – Kendler *et al.* (1992) estimated a 67% **heritability** rate for agoraphobia, 59% for blood/injury, 51% for social phobias and 47% for animal phobias. However, other studies find even less support for genetic explanations. Torgerson (see facing page), for example, actually only found 31% concordance for MZ twins in terms of anxiety disorders, and almost no concordance for DZ twins.

One of the problems with family and twin studies is that they fail to control for shared environmental experiences. For example, MZ twins are likely to share more similar experiences (environments) than DZ twins because, for example, they are likely to have more similar interests. One way to control for shared environment is to use studies of twins reared apart, but such studies have not been conducted with phobic disorders.

The diathesis-stress model – Even at the highest rates it is clear that phobic disorders are not solely genetic and have some considerable experiential component. This combination can be explained by the **diathesis-stress model** – genetic factors predispose an individual to develop phobias but life experiences play an important role in triggering such responses. It is important to remember the comorbidity between phobias and depression (discussed on the previous spread), which means that genetic factors may actually predispose individuals to a range of different mental disorders.

What is inherited? Evidence has been accumulated to support the possible physiological differences between phobic and normal individuals. For example, brain-scanning techniques have been used to measure the density of dopamine re-uptake sites (i.e. areas in the brain where dopamine levels are controlled). Tiihonen *et al.* (1997) found a significantly lower number of such sites in patients with social phobia than in normal controls. This low number of sites would be likely to lead to abnormally low levels of dopamine.

Additional support comes from studies of behavioural inhibition (see box above) and the fact that successful drug therapies for phobics include drugs that block activity of the adrenergic system (**beta-blockers**) and thus reduce the symptoms of anxiety. However, none of this is evidence that such differences actually *cause* the disorder in the first place. Drugs may, for example, be treating symptoms that have arisen as an effect rather than the cause of phobias.

An evolutionary approach

Prepotency – Öhman and Soares (1994) provided supporting evidence for prepotency effects. 'Masked' pictures were constructed of feared objects (snakes or spiders) in such a way that the animals in the pictures were not immediately recognisable. Participants who were fearful of snakes or spiders showed greater **GSR** (indicates arousal of the **autonomic nervous system**) when briefly shown 'masked' pictures compared to viewing neutral pictures or when compared to non-phobic participants. This shows that important components of phobic responses are set in motion before the phobic stimulus is represented in awareness, and these could be prepotent signals.

Preparedness – The two important predictions arising from the concept of preparedness are (a) that we learn certain fears more readily, and (b) that such fears are harder to unlearn. Laboratory studies typically condition fear responses by pairing an *unconditioned stimulus* (e.g. electric shock) with a *conditioned stimulus*. The conditioned stimulus is either a photograph of a 'prepared' stimulus (e.g. snake) or an 'unprepared' stimulus (e.g. flowers). McNally (1987) concluded that although there was firm evidence for enhanced resistance to extinction of fear responses conditioned by 'prepared' stimuli, evidence for rapid acquisition was, at best, equivocal.

This led Davey (1995) to propose a simpler explanation – *expectancy biases*. An expectancy bias is an expectation that fear-relevant stimuli (such as dangerous situations or past experience of unpleasantness) will produce negative consequences in the future. There is therefore no need to invoke past evolutionary history. This explains certain anomalous data, such as the lack of rapid acquisition of phobias and the acquisition of 'modern' phobias (e.g. phobia of hypodermic needles).

Clinical phobias – Do the concepts of prepotency and preparedness explain anxiety disorders? Much of the research we have looked at is concerned with avoidance responses rather than clinical disorders (i.e. phobias that fulfil the clinical characteristics for phobic disorders). Studies of patients suffering from disabling disorders do not support the preparedness explanation. For example, Merckelbach *et al.* (1988) found that most of the clinical phobias in their sample were rated as non-prepared rather than prepared. In addition, research has found that clinical phobias do not display the suddenness of onset and resistance to treatment predicted by preparedness (de Silva *et al.*, 1977).

CAN YOU...? No.11.2

...**1** Describe **two** biological explanations of phobic disorders in 100 words each.

...**2** Outline **eight** critical points for biological explanations of phobic disorders, including **(a)** the critical point being made, **(b)** your evidence for this critical point, and **(c)** how this criticism affects the explanation. Each criticism should be about 50 words.

...**3** Use this material to write a 600-word answer to the question: *Discuss **two or more** biological explanations of phobic disorders.* (8 marks + 16 marks)

PSYCHOLOGICAL EXPLANATIONS OF PHOBIC DISORDERS

We have seen that biological explanations for **phobias** have reasonable support, however, as you will see, there is a considerable psychological component in the development of phobic disorders. The **diathesis-stress** model proposes that some individuals have a genetic vulnerability to acquire phobic disorders, but such disorders only develop when the vulnerable individuals are exposed to psychological triggers.

Evaluation · LITTLE HANS

The case study of a five-year-old boy, 'Little Hans', was used by Freud as support for his psychodynamic explanation of the development of phobias. Hans had become terrified of horses pulling a laden cart. Freud (1909) suggested that Hans' phobia developed for several reasons. First of all Hans once heard a man saying to a child: 'Don't put your finger to the white horse or it'll bite you'. Hans also once asked his mother if she would like to put her finger on his penis. His mother told him this would not be proper, leading Hans to worry that his mother might leave him. Hans projected one source of anxiety onto another – he became afraid of being bitten by a white horse, whereas he was really scared that his mother would leave him (the two events were linked by touching something with your finger).

Second, Hans saw a horse with a laden cart fall down and thought it was dead. The horse symbolised his wish that his father (big whiskers and glasses similar to horses' blinkers) would die and the laden cart symbolised his mother pregnant with his sister, and when it fell over this was like giving birth. Therefore, the laden cart symbolised his father dying and his mother giving birth – both events that filled him with anxiety.

Evaluation · LITTLE ALBERT

It is possible that Hans' phobia may have been the result of **classical conditioning** – the accident with the horse made him experience fear which then became associated with horses.

Watson and Rayner (1920) sought to provide experimental evidence that fear could be learned in this way. They worked with an 11-month-old boy called 'Little Albert'. They first tested his responses to white fluffy objects: a white rat, a rabbit, and white cotton wool. He showed no fear response.

Next they set about creating a conditioned response to these previously neutral objects. To do this they used a steel bar that was four feet long. When he reached out for the rat they struck the bar with a hammer behind Albert's head to startle him. They repeated this three times, and did the same a week later. After this, when they showed the fluffy rat to Albert, he began to cry. They had conditioned a fear response to fluffy white objects in Little Albert.

▶ Rosalie Rayner and John B. Watson conditioning fear in Little Albert.

PSYCHOLOGICAL EXPLANATIONS

Psychodynamic

Sigmund Freud was the first to offer a psychological explanation for the origins of phobias. He proposed that a phobia was the conscious expression of **repressed** conflicts. The **ego** deals with conflict by protecting itself and repressing the emotions into the unconscious mind. Freud believed that such repressed conflicts continued to create anxiety which the mind deals with in various ways. These include expressing repressed thoughts in dreams, or displacing the repressed anxieties onto a neutral object or situation, such as a dog or social situations. Therefore, the individual displays a fear of dogs or social situations rather than expressing their real fear.

He illustrated this explanation with the case study of Little Hans described on the left. Hans recovered from his phobia once he was able to understand and accept his real anxieties about his father, mother and sister. According to Freud this demonstrated that the source of the phobia was the repressed anxiety.

Behavioural

The behavioural approach proposes that phobias are acquired through conditioning, i.e. learning.

Classical conditioning – Fears are acquired when an individual associates a neutral stimulus, such as a fluffy bunny, with a fear response, as demonstrated by Little Albert (see left). In this case the original *unconditioned stimulus* (UCS) is a loud noise, and the *unconditioned response* (UCR) is fear. By pairing the loud noise with the fluffy object, the fluffy object (now a *conditioned stimulus*, CS) acquired the same properties, so that when Albert saw a white fluffy object he cried, presumably because he was scared. The same process can explain, for example, why someone develops a fear of dogs after being bitten (bite creates fear, dog associated with bite and therefore dog produces fear response) or develops a fear of social situations after having a panic attack in such a situation.

Operant conditioning – Mowrer (1947) proposed that learning phobias involves more than **classical conditioning**. He described the acquisition of phobias in his *two-process theory*. The first stage is classical conditioning and then, in a second stage, **operant conditioning** occurs. The avoidance of the phobic stimulus reduces fear and is thus reinforcing (an example of **negative reinforcement**). The person avoids the anxiety created by, for example, the dog or social situation by avoiding them entirely. The fact that no anxiety is experienced from this avoidance behaviour is positively reinforcing.

Social learning – Extreme fears (phobias) may also be acquired through **modelling** the behaviour of others. For example, seeing a parent responding to a spider with extreme fear may lead a child to acquire a similar behaviour because the behaviour appears rewarding i.e. the fearful person gets attention.

Cognitive

Phobias may develop as the consequence of irrational thinking. For example, a person in a lift may think: 'I could become trapped in here and suffocate' (an irrational thought). Such thoughts create extreme anxiety and may trigger a phobia. Aaron Beck (Beck *et al.*, 1985) proposed that phobias arise because people become afraid of situations where fears may occur. He suggested, for example, that a social phobia may develop because 'a person develops the dysfunctional belief that no one likes them'. This belief develops into a fear of social rejection and the individual avoids situations which are likely to produce fear. Beck also argued that phobics tend to overestimate their fears, increasing the likelihood of phobias.

EVALUATION

Psychodynamic

Little Hans – Freud only provided one piece of evidence to support his explanation for phobias, the case study of Little Hans. There are two main problems with this – first Hans' phobia could just as easily be explained in terms of classical conditioning and second, a case study concerns one unique individual and therefore can't be generalised to the wider population. The Hans study has been further criticised because of lack of objectivity – both Hans' father and Freud interpreted the evidence according to their expectations about the origins of phobias.

Research support – The psychodynamic explanation, however, has received some further research support. For example, Bowlby (1973) found that agoraphobics often had early experiences of family conflict. He suggested that such conflict leads a young child to feel very anxious when separated from their parents (**separation anxiety**). Such fears are suppressed but later emerge as agoraphobia.

Whiting *et al.* (1966) studied the occurrence of phobias in other cultures and concluded that they were more common in societies that had a structured form of child-rearing. The reason may be because stricter, structured parenting might lead to children having to repress desires, thus supporting the psychodynamic explanation.

Further support comes from the fact that therapies that simply target the symptoms of phobia (such as **systematic desensitisation**, discussed on page 200) are not 100% successful, maybe because they fail to deal with the underlying causes of the phobias.

Behavioural

Conditioning – People with phobias often do recall a specific incident when their phobia appeared, for example being bitten by a dog or experiencing a panic attack in a social situation (Sue *et al.*, 1994). This supports the behavioural explanation of phobias – except that not everyone who has a phobia can recall such an incident. It is possible that such traumatic incidents did happen, but have since been forgotten (Öst, 1987).

In addition, not everyone who is bitten by a dog develops a phobia of dogs (Di Nardo *et al.*, 1988). This could be explained by the diathesis-stress model – only those with a genetic vulnerability for developing anxiety disorders would become phobic after such an event.

Biological preparedness – The fact that phobias do not always develop after a traumatic incident may be explained in terms of **biological preparedness** (discussed on the previous spread). For example, Bregman (1934) failed to condition a fear response in infants aged 8 to 16 months by pairing a loud bell with wooden blocks. It may be that fear responses are only learned with living animals, a link with ancient fears (see page 194).

Social learning – An experiment by Bandura and Rosenthal (1966) supported the social learning explanation. In the experiment, a model apparently experienced pain every time a buzzer sounded. Later on, participants who observed this showed an emotional reaction to the buzzer, demonstrating an acquired 'fear' response.

Conclusion – Sue *et al.* (1994) suggest that different phobias may be the result of different processes. For example, **agoraphobics** were most likely to explain their disorder in terms of a specific incident, whereas arachnophobics (people who are scared of spiders) were most likely to cite modelling as the cause. In addition it is clear that behavioural explanations alone cannot explain phobias – they work in combination with biological, psychodynamic and cognitive explanations.

Cognitive

Dysfunctional assumptions – There is support for the view that phobics have dysfunctional assumptions. For example, Gournay (1989) found that phobics were more likely than normal people to overestimate risks, which might mean that they are generally more fearful and this results in them being more predisposed to develop phobias.

The success of cognitive behavioural therapy as a treatment for phobia (see page 200) can be seen as support for the explanation – it can be argued that, if a therapy changes the dysfunctional assumptions a person has and this leads to a reduction in their phobia, then the dysfunctional assumptions may originally have caused the disorder.

▶ Now-retired Arsenal footballer Dennis Bergkamp developed a fear of flying after a false bomb scare on a plane during the 1994 World Cup. He had an agreement with the club that he would never be required to fly as part of his job, even if it meant missing out on away matches.

SOCIO-CULTURAL EXPLANATIONS

According to this view, the occurrence of phobias can be explained in terms of specific social and cultural attitudes that differ from one social group to another. There is certainly evidence of such differences – see Whiting's study (left) and also evidence described on the previous spread. The behaviourist approach can account for cultural differences because, for example, each society offers its own culture-specific role models which influence which phobias might be acquired.

REDUCTIONIST AND DETERMINIST

There is a tendency in all these psychological (and biological) explanations to suggest that phobias can be reduced to a simple set of principles (i.e. **reductionist**), such as repressed anxieties or classical conditioning. It is important to recognise that the 'real' explanations are likely to be a combination of a number of different explanations.

A further issue lies with the extent to which these explanations are **determinist**. For example, the behavioural view suggests that traumatic experiences lead to phobias. The evidence suggests, however, that phobias are not inevitable (i.e. not a determinist relationship).

CAN YOU...? No.11.3

...1 Describe **two or more** psychological explanations of phobic disorders. Each explanation should be about 100 words.

...2 Outline **eight** critical points for psychological explanations of phobic disorders, including **(a)** the critical point being made, **(b)** your evidence for this critical point, and **(c)** how this criticism affects the explanation. Each criticism should be about 50 words.

...3 Use this material to write a 600-word answer to the question: *Discuss **two or more** psychological explanations of phobic disorders.* (8 marks + 16 marks)

Phobias are mainly treated using psychological rather than biological methods. However, biological therapies have their place – they can help reduce the high level of anxiety experienced by phobics, allowing a patient to return to a more normal life (such as being able to go outdoors again). Alternatively, biological therapies may be useful in conjunction with psychological therapies in reducing anxiety levels in order for a patient to tackle the more psychological causes of their disorder.

BIOLOGICAL THERAPIES

Chemotherapy

Two types of drugs are used in the treatment of phobic disorders – anti-anxiety drugs and antidepressants, both of which aim to lower the anxiety levels associated with phobias and to enable a patient to lead a near-normal life.

Anti-anxiety drugs – Benzodiazepines (BZs) are commonly used to reduce anxiety (as covered in the AS-level stress topic). They are sold under various trade names, such as *Librium*, *Xanax*, *Valium*, and *Diazepam*. BZs slow down the activity of the central nervous system by enhancing the activity of **GABA** (gamma-amino-butyric-acid), a **neurotransmitter** that, when released, has a general quietening effect on many of the neurons in the brain. It does this by reacting with special sites (called GABA receptors) on the outside of receiving neurons. When GABA locks into these receptors it opens a channel which increases the flow of *chloride ions* into the neuron. Chloride ions make it harder for the neuron to be stimulated by other neurotransmitters, thus slowing down its activity and making the person feel more relaxed.

Beta-blockers are also used to reduce anxiety. They work by reducing the activity of **adrenaline** and **noradrenaline** which are part of the **sympathomedullary response** to stress. **Beta-blockers** bind to receptors on the cells of the heart and other parts of the body that are usually stimulated during arousal. By blocking these receptors, it is harder to stimulate cells in these parts of the body, so the heart beats slower and with less force, and blood vessels do not contract so easily. This results in a fall in blood pressure, and so less stress on the heart. The person taking the medication will feel calmer and less anxious.

Antidepressants are also used to reduce anxiety. **SSRIs** (see page 184) are currently the preferred drug for treating anxiety disorders (Choy and Schneier, 2008). SSRIs, such as *Zoloft*, *Paxil* and *Prozac*, increase levels of the neurotransmitter **serotonin** which regulates mood and anxiety.

Another antidepressant, **MAOI** (*monamine oxidase inhibitor*), has been used for anxiety disorders. They are an older class of antidepressants and rarely used now, but there are some patients who respond better to them than they do to the newer ones (Lader and Petursson 1983). *Monoamine oxidase* is the enzyme responsible for breaking down monoamine neurotransmitters (such as serotonin, noradrenaline and **dopamine**) so an inhibitor prevents this happening, leading to higher levels of monoamines.

◀ American singer, actress and director Barbra Streisand developed a social phobia while giving a concert during which she forgot the words to several songs. For 27 years she avoided any public engagements. During an interview in 2006 with Oprah Winfrey, Barbra revealed that she overcame her social phobia through the use of anti-anxiety drugs and gradually exposing herself to more public performances, starting with a small warm-up show, then a national tour and finally performing in front of a large television audience.

Psychosurgery

Psychosurgery is a surgical intervention that aims to treat a behaviour for which no pathological cause can be established (surgery to remove a brain tumour, for example, is not an example of psychosurgery because there is a pathological cause). In the case of psychosurgery it is believed that an area of the brain is malfunctioning, and if the connection to this part of the brain is severed, then psychological symptoms may be relieved.

Capsulotomy and cingulotomy are the two operations performed to treat anxiety disorders. They functionally remove the *capsule* and the *cingulum* – 'functional' removal means that no organ is removed but the connections with the organ are severed so the effect is the same as if the organ had been removed. The capsule and the cingulum are both parts of the **limbic system**, the region of the brain associated with emotion. Such operations are irreversible and only performed as a last resort.

Deep brain stimulation (DBS) involves placing wires in target areas of the brain (see description on left). When the current is on, this interrupts target ciruits in the brain resulting in a reduction of symtoms.

Transcranial magnetic stimulation is another reversible, non-invasive method (see page 212).

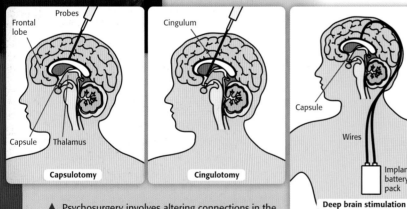

▲ Psychosurgery involves altering connections in the brain. In a **capsulotomy** the surgeon inserts a probe through the top of the skull and pushes it to the capsule, which is located deep in the brain. The leading tip of the probe burns away small portions of tissue. The same procedure is followed for a **cingulotomy**, this time targeting a nearby area, the cingulum. **Deep brain stimulation** involves no destruction of tissue although the wires are permanent. The wires are attached to a battery and when this is switched on it interferes with the brain circuits in the region of the capsule and cingulum, having a similar effect to the surgical operations.

EVALUATION

Effectiveness of chemotherapy

Anti-anxiety drugs – Kahn *et al.* (1986) found that BZs were more effective than a **placebo** treatment in reducing anxiety, and Hildalgo *et al.* (2001) found that BZs were more effective than antidepressants (in contrast to the view expressed by Choy and Schneider on the facing page). Research studies have shown that beta-blockers can also provide an effective means of anxiety control (e.g. Liebowitz *et al.*, 1985). However, some studies have shown that the benefits may be largely explained in terms of **placebo** effects. For example, Turner *et al.* (1994) found no difference between a beta-blocker and placebo group in terms of reduced heart rate, feelings of nervousness and so on.

Antidepressants – By contrast, MAOIs have been found to be more effective than placebos and more effective in the reduction of anxiety than beta-blockers (Liebowitz *et al.*, 1992). A further study compared the use of SSRIs and placebo treatment. The study found improved levels of self-rated anxiety (Katzelnick *et al.*, 1995). A survey of research by Aouizerate *et al.* (2004) concluded that SSRIs provide relief for social phobics in 50-80% of cases, a level fairly similar to BZs. However, SSRIs are often considered preferable because there are fewer side effects.

Appropriateness of chemotherapy

Not a cure – Generally drugs have not been considered to be the primary treatment for specific phobias, probably because such phobias tend to interfere less with day-to-day life than, for example, social phobias. Chemotherapy, however, is appropriate when panic attacks accompany specific phobias and also for social phobia, although drugs cannot provide a complete treatment as they simply focus on symptoms.

Side effects – The possible side effects of BZs include increased aggressiveness and long-term impairment of memory – although recent research has suggested that such negative effects might be turned to positive use (see 'Fearful memories', above right). Beta-blockers have few, if any, side effects whereas there are many problems associated with the use of antidepressants. SSRIs have been linked to increased suicides (see page 185) and MAOIs have a list of related issues, such as dizziness insomnia, drowsiness and blurred vision.

Addiction can be a problem with BZs, even when only low doses are given. For this reason the recommendation is that they should be used for a maximum of four weeks (Ashton, 1997).

Effectiveness of psychosurgery

The study by Ruck *et al.* (below) gives some indication of the success of psychosurgery for treating a range of anxiety disorders, including social phobias. However, any benefits clearly have to be weighed against the potential for negative effects.

Appropriateness of psychosurgery

Psychosurgery is rarely suitable for phobias and then only for extreme cases that have proved otherwise untreatable, and that interfere with normal day-to-day functioning. Szasz (1978) criticised psychosurgery generally because a person's psychological self is not something physical and therefore it is illogical to suggest that it can be operated on.

A STUDY OF CAPSULOTOMY

Research support comes from a study by Ruck *et al.* (2003) involving 26 patients with non-obsessive anxiety disorders (13 with generalised anxiety disorder, eight with panic disorder and five with social phobia). All patients had been suffering for more than five years, had experienced considerable reduction of their psychosocial functioning and had tried numerous other treatment options. After a capsulotomy was performed, assessments were conducted by independent personnel. The mean pre-operative anxiety score (using the *Brief Scale for Anxiety*) was 22.0. When 25 of the patients were followed up a year later the score had dropped to 4.6, indicating a successful outcome.

However, the negative symptoms were greater than expected. For example, seven patients attempted to commit suicide after surgery and there were two recorded cases of epileptic seizures. The researchers concluded that while capsulotomy may be effective, it is expensive and has the potential for extremely adverse effects.

REAL-WORLD APPLICATION

Research has found that it may be possible to erase fearful memories, which could be a useful method of treating phobias. Stehberg *et al.* (2009) have blocked memory consolidation in rats using a form of deep brain stimulation, and suggest this could lead to a novel treatment for the traumatic memories that underlie anxiety disorders.

A different study (Kindt *et al.*, 2009) looked at the effects of beta-blockers on memory. In this study fearful memories of spiders were created in participants by pairing pictures of a spider with an electric shock. In the following part of the experiment some participants were given a beta-blocker while others received a placebo; those who had the beta-blocker showed a reduced fear response after 24 hours. Those given the placebos did not. The researchers suggest that memories are always being reconsolidated, and the beta-blockers interfere in particular with the emotional content of the memories. This interference might eradicate anxiety-causing memories.

ETHICS

Biological treatments raise important ethical issues. First, there is an issue related to studying the effectiveness of drugs. A fundamental requirement of research ethics is that, if effective, treatments exist, then they should be used as controls when new treatments are tested. Substituting a placebo for an effective treatment does not satisfy this duty as it exposes individuals to a treatment known to be inferior.

Second, there is the issue of informed consent, or lack of it. Most patients are not informed about the comparative success of drugs versus placebos. They expose themselves to unpleasant side effects even though the pharmacological effects of the drugs may be slim.

Finally, we might consider the ethics of irreversible forms of psychosurgery. The case of Mary Lou Zimmerman, described on page 213, highlights again the dangers of such operations and the issue of obtaining truly informed consent.

CAN YOU...? No.11.4

...1 Describe **two** biological therapies for phobic disorders in 100 words each.

...2 Outline **eight** critical points for biological therapies for phobic disorders, including **(a)** the critical point being made, **(b)** your evidence for this critical point, and **(c)** how this criticism affects the explanation. Each criticism should be about 50 words.

...3 Use this material to write a 600-word answer to the question: *Discuss **two or more** biological therapies for phobic disorders.* (8 marks + 16 marks)

PSYCHOLOGICAL THERAPIES FOR PHOBIC DISORDERS

Psychological therapies aim to treat mental disorders through psychological rather than physical (biological) techniques, although in practice there is not always a clear distinction. For example, systematic desensitisation (below) involves the use of relaxation (a biological method) and, in some cases, patients use anti-anxiety drugs (another biological method) to reduce levels of distress when learning to deal with their phobias with psychological methods.

▶ Franklin Roosevelt, the 32nd President of the United States, famously said in his inauguration speech of 1933: 'The only thing we have to fear is fear itself' (referring to the troubles of the Great Depression). Little did he know it, but he was taking a cognitive approach to fear.

PSYCHOLOGICAL THERAPIES

Behavioural therapy: Systematic desensitisation (SD)

An individual might learn that their feared stimulus is not so fearful after all – if only they could re-experience the feared stimulus, But this doesn't happen because the anxiety it creates blocks any attempt to re-experience the stimulus. Joseph Wolpe developed a technique in the 1950s where phobics were introduced to the feared stimulus *gradually*.

Counterconditioning – The diagram below shows the steps of systematic desensitisation (SD). The process begins with learning relaxation techniques. The eventual aim is to acquire a new stimulus-response link, moving from responding to a stimulus with fear to responding to the feared stimulus with relaxation. This is called **counterconditioning** because the patient is taught a new association that runs counter to the original association. Wolpe also called this '*reciprocal inhibition*' because the relaxation inhibits the anxiety.

Desensitisation hierarchy – The diagram below shows how the therapy proceeds through gradual steps that are determined at the beginning of therapy when the patient and therapist work out a hierarchy of feared stimuli.

Different forms of SD – In the early days of SD, patients would learn to confront their feared situations directly (*in vivo* desensitisation), by learning to relax in the presence of objects or images that would normally arouse anxiety. In more recent years, however, rather than actually presenting the feared stimulus, the therapist asks the subject to *imagine* the presence of it (**covert desensitisation**).

HOW DOES IT WORK?

▲ **Problem** – Patient is terrified whenever she sees a spider.

▼ **Result** – After SD, patient has overcome her fear of spiders and feels relaxed in their presence.

Step 1: Patient is taught how to relax their muscles completely. (A relaxed state is incompatible with anxiety.)

Step 2: Therapist and patient together construct a desensitisation hierarchy – a series of imagined scenes, each one causing a little more anxiety than the previous one.

Step 3: Patient gradually works his/her way through desensitisation hierarchy, visualising each anxiety-evoking event while engaging in the competing relaxation response.

Step 4: Once the patient has mastered one step in the hierarchy (i.e. they can remain relaxed while imagining it), they are ready to move onto the next.

Step 5: Patient eventually masters the feared situation that caused them to seek help in the first place.

Cognitive therapy: REBT

Rational-Emotive Behaviour Therapy (*REBT*) was developed by Albert Ellis in the 1950s. It is a cognitive approach because psychological problems are seen as the result of irrational thinking. In the case of phobias it is not the stimulus object itself that is the problem but the irrational beliefs related to it. Therefore, the phobia aims to tackle the irrational thoughts and turn them into 'rational' ones (therefore *rational* EBT). The words 'emotive' and 'behaviour' are used because the therapy focuses on resolving emotional and behavioural problems.

ABC model – Ellis (1957) proposed that the way to deal with irrational thoughts was to identify them using the ABC model. 'A' stands for the activating event – a situation that results in feelings of frustration and anxiety. Such events lead to irrational beliefs (B) and the beliefs lead to self-defeating consequences (C). For example:

A → A friend ignores you in the street.
B → He must have decided he doesn't like you; no one likes you and you are worthless.
C → Avoid social situations in the future.

Disputing – It is not the activating events that cause unproductive consequences, it is the beliefs that lead to the self-defeating consequences. Therefore, REBT focuses on challenging or disputing the beliefs and replacing them with effective, rational beliefs. For example:

- **Logical disputing** – Self-defeating beliefs do not follow logically from the information available (e.g. 'Does thinking in this way make sense?').
- **Empirical disputing** – Self-defeating beliefs may not be consistent with reality (e.g. 'Where is the proof that this belief is accurate?').
- **Pragmatic disputing** – Emphasises the lack of usefulness of self-defeating beliefs (e.g. 'How is this belief likely to help me?').

Effective disputing changes self-defeating beliefs into more rational beliefs. The individual can move from *catastrophising* ('No one will ever like me') to more rational interpretations of events ('My friend was probably thinking about something else and didn't even see me'). This in turn helps them to feel better, and eventually become more self-accepting.

EVALUATION

Effectiveness of SD

Research has found that SD is successful for a range of phobic disorders. For example, McGrath *et al.* (1990) reported that about 75% of patients with phobias respond to SD. The key to success appears to lie with actual contact with the feared stimulus, so *in vivo* techniques are more successful than covert ones (Menzies and Clarke, 1993). Often a number of different exposure techniques are involved – *in vivo*, covert and also modelling, where the patient watches someone else who is coping well with the feared stimulus (Comer, 2002).

However, Öhman *et al.* (1975) suggest that SD may not be as effective in treating phobias that have an underlying evolutionary survival component (e.g. fear of the dark, fear of heights or fear of dangerous animals), than in treating phobias that have been acquired as a result of personal experience.

Appropriateness of SD

Strengths – Behavioural therapies for dealing with phobias are generally relatively fast and require less effort on the patient's part than other psychotherapies (such as REBT), where patients must play a more active part in their treatment. A further strength of SD is that it can be self-administered, a method that has proved successful with, for example, social phobia (Humphrey, 1973).

Symptom substitution – SD may *appear* to resolve a problem but simply eliminating or suppressing symptoms can result in other symptoms appearing (called *symptom substitution*). Langevin (1983), however, claims that there is no evidence to support this objection.

Is relaxation necessary? It may be that the success of SD is more to do with exposure than relaxation. It might be that the expectation of being able to cope with the feared stimulus is most important. For example, Klein *et al.* (1983) compared SD with supportive psychotherapy for patients with either social or specific phobias. They found no difference in effectiveness (those receiving supportive psychotherapy had also done well), suggesting that the 'active ingredient' in SD or CBT may simply be the generation of hopeful expectancies that the phobia can be overcome.

Effectiveness of REBT

REBT has generally been shown to be effective in outcome studies (i.e. studies designed to measure responses to treatment). For example, in a **meta-analysis** Engels *et al.* (1993) concluded that REBT is an effective treatment for a number of different types of disorder, including social phobia. Ellis (1957) claimed a 90% success rate, taking an average of 27 sessions. In the UK, *The National Institute for Clinical Excellence* (2004) identified cognitive behaviour therapy (CBT), of which REBT is an example, as the first-line approach in treating anxiety disorders. However, Emmelkamp *et al.* (1988) concluded that REBT was less effective than *in vivo* exposure treatments at least in the treatment of **agoraphobia**.

Appropriateness of REBT

Not suitable for all – Like all psychotherapies, REBT does not always work. Ellis (2001) believed that sometimes people who *claimed* to be following REBT principles were not putting their revised beliefs into action and therefore the therapy was not effective. Ellis also explained lack of success in terms of suitability – some people simply do not want the direct sort of advice that REBT practitioners tend to dispense. They prefer to share their worries with a therapist, without getting involved with the cognitive effort that is associated with recovery (Ellis, 2001).

The theoretical basis for the therapy has received research attention showing, for example, that people who hold irrational beliefs form inferences that are significantly less functional than those formed by people who hold rational beliefs (Bond and Dryden, 2002). On the other hand it may be that irrational beliefs are counterproductive but realistic. Alloy and Abrahmson (1979) found that depressed people gave more accurate estimates of the likelihood of a disaster than 'normal' controls (calling it the *'sadder but wiser'* effect).

Does all this sound familiar? Both SD and CBT were part of the stress module of your AS studies, so you have studied them before.

ANIMAL RESEARCH

Wolpe's inspiration for SD came from experiments with cats. The issue is, to what extent can we generalise from animal behaviour to humans?

The original research by Masserman (1943) showed how phobias developed. Cats were given an electric shock when they were put in a box and thereafter displayed extreme anxiety when placed in the box. This disappeared if they were fed in the box. Therefore, fear in cats could be reduced through forming new associations (conditioning).

However, subsequent research does suggest that in humans, fear is not so simply reduced to conditioned associations because expectations contribute less to the stress response in cats. Forming new associations is not always sufficient to overcome a learned fear association.

FEAR OF FLYING

Capafóns *et al.* (1998) assessed the effectiveness of SD with a group of 41 aerophobics recruited through a media campaign in Spain offering free treatment. Twenty-one participants were assigned to a waiting-control group while the others received SD immediately. Treatment consisted of two one-hour sessions per week over a 12–15 week period. Both imagination and *in vivo* techniques were used. Various measures were used to assess recovery, such as self-report scales and physiological measures of anxiety. Aerophobics who received treatment reported lower levels of fear (compared to the control group) *and* lower physiological signs of fear during a flight simulation. However, one person in the control group showed similar levels of improvement (evidence of spontaneous recovery) and two patients in the treatment group showed no recovery, demonstrating that SD is not 100% effective.

CAN YOU...? (No.11.5)

...**1** Describe **two** psychological therapies for phobic disorders in 100 words each.

...**2** Outline **eight** critical points for psychological therapies for phobic disorders, including **(a)** the critical point being made, **(b)** your evidence for this critical point, and **(c)** how this criticism affects the explanation. Each criticism should be about 50 words.

...**3** Use this material to write a 600-word answer to the question: *Discuss **two or more** psychological therapies for phobic disorders.* (8 marks + 16 marks)

CHAPTER SUMMARY

OVERVIEW OF PHOBIC DISORDERS

CLASSIFICATION AND DIAGNOSIS

BIOLOGICAL THERAPIES

CLINICAL CHARACTERISTICS
- An anxiety disorder, including agoraphobia, social phobias and specific phobias.
- Marked and persistent fear that is excessive, cued by presence or anticipation of specific object or situation.
- Person is aware that fear is excessive.
- The distress and avoidance of feared situation interferes significantly with the person's day-to-day living.
- The phobic situation is avoided or endured with intense anxiety or distress.
- Panic attacks are associated with phobias.
- Duration of 6 months or more.
- Diagnosis of phobic disorder only made if no possible physiological cause or better accounted for by another disorder.

RELIABILITY
- Refers to consistency of measuring instrument or scale to assess fear ratings.
- Measured by degree of agreement over symptoms (inter-rater reliability) and consistency of scores on different occasions (test–retest reliability).
- Skyre et al. (1991) – high inter-rater reliability for diagnosis of phobias using SCID-1.
- Hiller et al. (1990) – high test–retest reliability for diagnosis of specific phobias using MDC.

EVALUATION
- SCID requires extensive training and this enhances reliability.
- Some studies have found lower levels of test–retest reliability, particularly over longer-term intervals (Kendler et al., 1999).
- Picon et al. (2005) found high test–retest reliability (more than +.80).
- Low reliability may be due to poor recall of fears or different criteria used by interviewers.
- Reliability improved using computerised scales because less opportunity for interviewer effects (Kobak et al., 1992).

VALIDITY
- Extent to which diagnosis represents something real and distinct from other disorders, and measures what it claims to measure.
- Comorbidity with other disorders is high, suggesting that diagnostic category is not useful when deciding on treatments.
- Concurrent validity – compares one method of diagnosis with another.
- Construct validity – extent to which test measures target construct, e.g. phobics might underestimate coping in social situations.

EVALUATION
- Comorbidity supported, e.g. Eysenck (1997) found 66% comorbid and Vasey and Dadds (2001) reported little relationship between diagnosis and treatment success.
- Concurrent validity demonstrated, e.g. Mattick and Clarke (1998) – SPS correlated well with other measures.
- Construct validity demonstrated, e.g. SPAI correlates well with behavioural measures of social phobia (Beidel et al., 1989), although may not be surprising since behaviours mentioned in the scale.
- Validity may be compromised when using computer-based diagnosis, because it lacks ability to facilitate disclosure of troubling information (Heimberg et al., 1999).
- Cultural differences in diagnosis means cultural norms determine what is 'normal' functioning and what is 'abnormal' – e.g. taiijin-kyofusho found only in Japan.

CHEMOTHERAPY
- Anti-anxiety drugs – BZs reduce anxiety by enhancing activity of GABA, thus making a person feel more relaxed in phobic situation.
- Beta-blockers reduce anxiety by reducing activity of adrenaline and noradrenaline – resulting in fall in blood pressure and feelings of calm.
- Antidepressants – SSRIs currently the preferred method of treating anxiety disorders by regulating mood and anxiety.

EVALUATION
- Kahn et al. (1986) – BZs more effective than placebo in reducing anxiety.
- Beta-blockers also effective means of anxiety control (Liebowitz et al., 1985) although some benefits explained in terms of placebo effects.
- Kindt et al. (2009) – beta-blockers able to block fearful memories.
- Survey of research (Aouizerate et al., 1995) – SSRIs provide relief for social phobics in 50-80% of cases.
- However, drugs do not provide a complete cure as they focus only on symptoms not underlying problem.
- BZs have side effects (e.g. memory loss) and possibility of addiction, while SSRIs have been linked to increased risk of suicide among adolescents.

EXPLANATIONS OF PHOBIC DISORDERS

BIOLOGICAL EXPLANATIONS

GENETIC FACTORS
- Having family member with phobic disorder increases risk that an individual develops similar disorder.
- Fyer et al. (1995) – probands had three times as many relatives who experienced phobias than normal controls.
- Twin studies – Torgersen (1983) found that, where one twin had phobic disorder, MZ twin five times more (than DZ) likely to develop phobia.
- People may inherit oversensitive fear response, e.g. abnormally high levels of arousal in ANS, leading to increased levels of adrenaline.
- Alternatively, abnormal levels of dopamine and serotonin implicated in fear response.

EVALUATION
- Variability between disorders for role of genetic factors, e.g. 67% for agoraphobia and 47% for animal phobias (Kendler et al., 1992).
- Problem for family and twin studies – they fail to control for shared environmental experiences.
- Diathesis-stress model – genetic factors predispose individual to develop phobias but life experiences trigger them.
- Brain-scanning techniques suggest abnormally low levels of dopamine in socially phobic individuals.
- Kagan (1994) – genetically-based infant temperamental type predisposes infants to withdraw from unfamiliar people, and later to develop anxiety disorders.

AN EVOLUTIONARY APPROACH
- Ancient fears and modern minds – modern phobias are exaggerations of responses to stimuli that reflected very real fears to our ancestors.
- Prepotency – animals evolved to respond to potential threats rather than after event has happened.
- Preparedness – humans are biologically prepared to learn association between, and fear for, some types of stimuli more readily than others.

EVALUATION
- Öhman and Soares (1994) provided evidence for prepotency effects – greater GSR response to 'masked' pictures of feared animals.
- Preparedness – McNally (1987) found evidence for enhanced resistance of extinction of fear responses to prepared stimuli but not for rapid acquisition.
- Clinical phobias – Merckelbach et al. (1988) found that most clinical phobias in their sample rated as 'non' prepared rather than prepared.
- Cultural differences in types of phobias reported by different cultural groups.

BIOLOGICAL THERAPIES cont'd

PSYCHOLOGICAL THERAPIES

PSYCHOSURGERY

- Based on belief that an area of the brain is malfunctioning – if connection to this area is severed, symptoms may be relieved.
- Capsulotomy – removes *capsule*, part of the limbic system associated with emotion.
- Cingulotomy – removes *cingulum*, also part of the limbic system.
- Deep brain stimulation – current interrupts target circuits in the brain.

EVALUATION

- Ruck *et al.* (2003) studied 26 capsulotomy patients operated on for various anxiety disorders – positive outcomes, but serious side effects, including attempted suicide.
- Rarely suitable for phobias, and only then for extreme cases that have proved otherwise untreatable.
- Ethical issues of withholding treatment in placebo conditions, as well as exposure to unpleasant side effects due to treatment.

BEHAVIOURAL THERAPY: SD

- Systematic desensitisation – phobics are introduced to the feared stimulus gradually while also relaxing.
- Counterconditioning – responding to a stimulus with fear, changes to responding with relaxation. Patient taught new association that runs counter to original association.
- Desensitisation hierarchy – learning proceeds through gradual steps that reflect hierarchy of feared stimuli.
- May confront fears directly (in vivo desensitisation) or imagine feared stimulus (covert desensitisation).

EVALUATION

- McGrath *et al.* (1990) – 75% of patients with phobias respond to SD.
- Key to success appears to be contact with feared stimulus, so in vivo more successful than covert.
- Öhman *et al.* (1975) – SD not as effective with phobias that have underlying survival component.
- SD generally faster and requires less patient effort than cognitive therapies and may be self-administered.
- SD may *appear* to solve a problem, but only addresses symptoms rather than underlying problem.
- Relaxation may not be important, research suggests that exposure alone is as effective (Klein *et al.*, 1983).
- Early research by Wolpe (1958) used animals which raises issues of whether this research can be generalised to humans.
- Real-world application – Capafóns *et al.* (1998) used SD effectively in treatment of fear of flying.

COGNITIVE THERAPY: REBT

- REBT – based on idea that it is the irrational beliefs associated with an object that presents the problem, not the object itself.
- REBT aims to tackle irrational beliefs and turn them into rational ones.
- ABC model – activating event ‹ beliefs ‹ self-defeating consequences.
- Disputing – REBT challenges irrational beliefs e.g. by logical disputing (does this make sense?) or empirical disputing (where is the evidence?).

EVALUATION

- Meta-analysis of studies of REBT (Engels *et al.*, 1993) concluded that REBT is effective for social phobia.
- NICE (2004) identified CBT as first-line treatment for anxiety disorders, although Emmelkamp *et al.* (1988) found REBT less effective for agoraphobia than in vivo treatments.
- REBT does not work for all, e.g. those who are uncomfortable with the direct approach of cognitive therapists.
- Irrational beliefs may be irrational but realistic ('sadder but wiser' effect).

PSYCHOLOGICAL EXPLANATIONS

PSYCHODYNAMIC

- Freud believed phobias to be the conscious expression of repressed conflicts.
- Repressed anxieties may be displaced onto neutral objects or situations.

EVALUATION

- Supported by case study of Little Hans – recovered from phobia of horses once he understood his real anxieties about father, mother and sister.
- Only one piece of evidence for this view – Little Hans case study, which can be explained through simple classical conditioning.
- Case studies about one individual – problem of generalising onto a wider population.
- Bowlby (1973) – agoraphobics had early experiences of family conflict, which led to separation anxiety (suppressed but then later emerged as agoraphobia).
- Occurrence of phobias can be explained in terms of specific social and cultural attitudes that differ from one group to another.

BEHAVIOURAL

- Operant conditioning – Mowrer (1947) proposed two-stage theory, avoidance of feared object reduces fear and is thus negatively reinforcing.
- Social learning – phobias acquired through modelling behaviour of others.

EVALUATION

- Classical conditioning – fears acquired when individual associates a neutral stimulus with a fear response (e.g. Little Albert).
- Conditioning – people with phobias often do recall a specific incident when their phobia appeared (Sue *et al.*, 1994), although not always but may have been forgotten (Öst, 1987).
- Phobias do not always appear after traumatic incident – explained by biological preparedness.
- Sue *et al.* (1994) – different phobias, different processes, e.g. agoraphobia explained by specific incident whereas, arachnophobia due to modelling.
- Psychological explanations of phobias may be reductionist (e.g. explanations based on conditioning) and determinist (e.g. traumatic experiences lead to phobias).

COGNITIVE

- Phobias may develop as result of irrational thinking.
- Beck *et al.* (1985) – phobias arise because people become afraid of situations where fears *may* occur.
- Phobics tend to overestimate their fears, increasing the likelihood of a phobia.

EVALUATION

- Gournay (1989) – support for claim that phobics have dysfunctional assumptions.
- CBT successful as treatment for phobia, supporting claim that dysfunctional thinking involved.

EXAM QUESTION WITH STUDENT ANSWER

QUESTIONS **(a) Outline and evaluate two psychological explanations for phobic disorders.** *(4 marks + 8 marks)*

(b) Outline and evaluate one biological therapy used in the treatment of phobic disorders. *(4 marks + 8 marks)*

STUDENT ANSWER

(a) *The first psychological explanation is the psychodynamic one. Freud suggested that phobias develop because people repress their fears and anxieties into the unconscious and then project these fears onto something neutral but linked, which then becomes a phobia. Freud used the case study of Little Hans to explain this. Hans developed a fear of white horses but really he was afraid that his mother would leave him. The link occurred because he heard someone say you shouldn't touch horses because they bite and, because he desired his mother, he asked her to touch his penis but she said you shouldn't.*

Freud's explanations sound fairly incredible but there is support for them aside from his own case study of Little Hans. For example, Bowlby found that agoraphobics had actually experienced more early conflict than normal – such conflict would make a child feel more anxious when separated from parents (and home), which would be repressed and might be expressed later as agoraphobia (a fear of being away from the safety of home).

A different psychological explanation comes from the behavioural approach that explains phobias in terms of conditioning. Mowrer proposed a two stage process. In the first stage an individual acquires a phobia because of a fearful experience with an otherwise neutral object. For example, Little Albert (Watson and Raynor) became afraid of fluffy white objects because he learned to associate them with a loud noise which created fear. In the second stage operant conditioning occurs where a person avoids the feared object, which has a positive outcome thus reinforcing (negative reinforcement) the phobic behaviour.

The study with Little Albert supports the classical conditioning of phobias, however research has found that people with phobias can't always recall a particular incident that led to their phobia. And also some people who do have a traumatic experience (such as being bitten by a dog) don't develop a phobia. This supports the diathesis-stress model which proposes that it is only people who have a genetic vulnerability to develop certain mental disorders that would develop a phobia.

One criticism that is made about all of these explanations is that they are reductionist in that they reduce human behaviour to a simple set of principles, such as repressed desires or conditioning. At least the diathesis-stress model suggests a more complex set of principles as the cause for mental disorder.

(b) *One example of a biological therapy is the use of drugs to reduce the anxiety associated with phobia. Two kinds of drugs are used – anti-anxiety drugs and antidepressants. Benzodiazepine (BZ) is an anti-anxiety drug that quietens the nervous system by enhancing the production of GABA, the body's natural form of anxiety relief.*

Beta-blockers are also used to reduce anxiety, often by athletes or public speakers or musicians to calm their nerves before performing. They reduce arousal in the sympathetic nervous system by blocking activity at the heart and other parts of the body that usually respond to adrenaline.

SSRIs are a common form of antidepressant. These increase levels of the neurotransmitter serotonin which regulates mood and anxiety. Another kind of antidepressant, MAIO, increases the levels of monamines, such as serotonin and adrenaline).

The advantage of drugs is that they are easy to use, not requiring any effort from the patient. However, all drugs have side effects and may also lead to addiction (especially BZs) so they are really only useful for short periods and don't offer a permanent cure.

[572 words]

EXAMINER COMMENTS

The mark split for this question indicates that equal amounts should be written for both parts of this question. It is tempting to write more for part (a) since two explanations are required, but that would probably result in reduced marks overall.

In the first paragraph the student wisely moves straight into the question instead of wasting time describing the characteristics of phobic disorders – a common mistake (see answer on page 176).

The description is **reasonable** but would have benefited from the use of more precise concepts, such as reference to the role of the ego.

The second paragraph provides some **evaluation** of the psychodynamic explanation – **limited in breadth** but **well elaborated**.

In the next paragraph we move on to the second psychological explanation, containing another reasonable description. The student has provided names of researchers but not dates, which may detract from the overall **detail** of the answer.

The description of the two-process theory is **coherent,** although brief. In an exam there isn't time for a full explanation but perhaps this is just a little too brief.

A good range of critical points are raised and each elaborated sufficiently for the points to be **reasonably effective.**

In the final paragraph a further criticism is made in terms of reductionism. However, this criticism lacks contextualisation.

> **AO1** – The descriptive content is **reasonably detailed**, certainly better than basic. There is evidence of both **breadth and depth**. The structure of the answer is **coherent**.
> **AO2/AO3** – The evaluation shows **reasonable elaboration**.

In part (b) chemotherapy has been selected as the form of biological therapy and four different kinds of drug are outlined. A considerable amount of **detail** has been provided in relatively limited space, demonstrating **sound** knowledge and understanding.

The information about antidepressants is a little less **detailed**.

In the final paragraph a succession of quick evaluative points are made which would require greater **elaboration** to attract high marks.

> **AO1** – **Good range** of relevant material and mostly **well-detailed**.
> **AO2/AO3** – Evaluation is **rudimentary** although it is **relevant** and **focused**.

Chapter 12
Psychopathology: Obsessive compulsive disorder

▲ David Beckham is one of 2% of the population who has OCD. He explained: 'I have to have everything in a straight line or everything has to be in pairs… I'll go into a hotel room – before I can relax I have to move all the leaflets and all the books and put them in a drawer. Everything has to be perfect.' (*Daily Mail*, 2006)

SPECIFICATION

Psychopathology

Candidates will be expected to study one of the following disorders:
* *schizophrenia*
* *depression*
* *phobic disorders*
* *obsessive compulsive disorder*

Obsessive compulsive disorder (OCD)	
Overview	• Clinical characteristics of OCD. • Issues surrounding the classification and diagnosis of OCD, including reliability and validity.
Explanations	• Biological explanations of OCD, for example genetics, biochemistry. • Psychological explanations of OCD, for example behavioural, cognitive, psychodynamic and socio-cultural.
Therapy	• Biological therapies for OCD, including their evaluation in terms of appropriateness and effectiveness. • Psychological therapies for OCD, for example behavioural, psychodynamic and cognitive-behavioural, including their evaluation in terms of appropriateness and effectiveness.

CLASSIFICATION AND DIAGNOSIS OF OCD

One of the broad categories of mental disorder is anxiety disorders, which includes **obsessive compulsive disorder** (OCD) as well as phobic disorders (discussed in chapter 11). Anxiety disorders are a group of conditions that share extreme or pathological anxiety as the principal disturbance of mood. For people with OCD, the obsessions and repetitive execution of what are essentially irrational actions (such as constant hand washing) are both a source of considerable anxiety, hence OCD is regarded as an anxiety disorder.

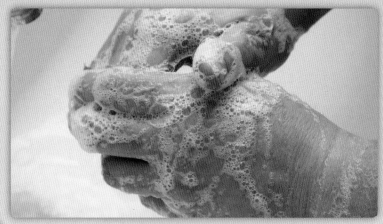

▲ One of the most common obsessions relates to fear of contamination. For example, the Y-BOCS (see facing page) lists 'concerns or disgust with bodily waste or secretions', 'concerns with dirt or germs' and 'excessive concerns with animals'.

It follows that compulsions are frequently related to cleaning and washing. For example, one item on the Padua Inventory (PI) is: ' I wash my hands more often and longer than necessary (0 not at all, 4 = very much).

CLINICAL CHARACTERISTICS OF OCD

The main characteristic of OCD is anxiety, which can arise from both obsessions and compulsions. The disorder typically begins in young adult life and is equally common among men and women.

Obsessions – create anxiety.

- They are recurrent, intrusive thoughts or impulses that are perceived as inappropriate or forbidden. Common obsessional themes include *ideas* (e.g. that germs are everywhere), *doubts* (e.g. the worry that something important has been overlooked), *impulses* (e.g. to shout out obscenities) or *images* (e.g. fleeting sexual images).
- The thoughts, impulses or images are not simply excessive worries about everyday problems.
- They are seen as uncontrollable, which creates anxiety.
- The person recognises that the obsessional thoughts or impulses are a product of his or her own mind (rather than 'thought insertion' as is typical of **schizophrenia**).
- The person attempts to ignore or suppress such thoughts, impulses or images, or to neutralise them with some other thought or action.

Compulsions – aim to reduce the anxiety created by obsessions.

- They are repetitive behaviours, including both overt behaviours, such as hand washing or checking, and mental acts, including counting or praying.
- The compulsive behaviours or mental acts either are not connected in a realistic way with what they are designed to neutralise or prevent or are clearly excessive.

Further criteria – At some point during the course of the disorder, the person does recognise that the obsessions or compulsions are excessive or unreasonable. This does not apply to children.

The obsessions and/or compulsions cause marked distress, are time consuming (take more than one hour a day) and/or significantly interfere with the person's normal routine, occupational (or academic) functioning, or usual social activities or relationships.

No other mental disorder is present and the disturbance is not due to the direct physiological effects of a substance (e.g. a drug of abuse, a medication) or a general medical condition.

Adapted from the American Psychiatric Association (2000) DSM-IVR criteria for the diagnosis of specific phobia.

ISSUES OF RELIABILITY AND VALIDITY

Reliability

Reliability refers to the *consistency* of a measuring instrument, such as a questionnaire or scale to assess how fearful a person is about certain objects/experiences. Reliability of such questionnaires or scales can be measured in terms of whether two independent assessors give similar scores (**inter-rater reliability**) or whether the test items are consistent (**test–retest reliability**).

Inter-rater reliability – There is a range of different scales and inventories used to assess the severity and frequency of OCD symptoms. The Y-BOCS (see top of facing page) is one of the most popular, returning reasonable scores for reliability. For example, Woody *et al.* (1995) assessed 54 patients with OCD using Y-BOCS and found good internal consistency, although this was improved if items related to resistance were removed.

The children's version (CY-BOCS) has also been shown to have good inter-rater reliability (Scahill *et al.*, 1997).

Test–retest reliability for Y-BOCS was also reported by Woody *et al.* Over a relatively long period (average between test and retest was 48.5 days) the reliability was .64 for the obsessions subscale and .56 for the compulsions subscale. They describe this as 'lower than desirable' for diagnosing patients as opposed to when using the scale for research purposes.

Validity

Validity refers to the extent that a diagnosis represents something that is real and distinct from other disorders and the extent that a classification system such as **ICD** measures what it claims to measure. Reliability and validity are inextricably linked because a diagnosis cannot be valid if it is not reliable.

Comorbidity is an important issue for the validity of diagnosis. It refers to the extent that two (or more) conditions co-occur. Rosenfeld *et al.* (1992) found that patients diagnosed with OCD had higher Y-BOCS scores than patients with other anxiety disorders and normal controls, i.e. it does distinguish OCD patients from others.

Internal validity of questionnaires – A key issue that reduces the validity of diagnosis is the extent to which people produce honest answers to questionnaires about their obsessive/compulsive symptoms. This means the questionnaire is not measuring what it intends to measure. For example, patients may be embarrassed or feel afraid that an interviewer will take symptoms as a sign of deeper psychosis. Therefore, they underplay their symptoms.

MEASURING OBSESSIONS AND COMPULSIONS

Scales such as ADIS-IV and SCID (see page 192) are used to assess general anxiety levels whereas there are specific scales for the assessment of obsessions and compulsions. According to Rush *et al.* (2007) the best available measure is the *Yale-Brown Obsessive Compulsive Scale* (Y-BOCS) devised by Goodman *et al.* (1989). This is a **semi-structured interview** that can be used to assess symptom severity and also monitor response to treatment. There are three sections; the first two sections ask patients to identify which obsessions and compulsions have been experienced now or in the past. The final section consists of 10 short questions (referred to as Y-BOCS-10), for example concerning the extent that obsessions/compulsions interfere with everyday life, and the extent that patients are able to resist obsessions/compulsions and patients' perceived control over their symptoms. There is a children's version of this scale and online versions (see, for example, www.brainphysics.com/ybocs.php). More recently, Goodman has developed a new scale, the *Florida Obsessive Compulsive Inventory* (Storch *et al.*, 2007).

EVALUATION

Reliability

Research evidence – In contrast with the findings about long-term test–retest reliability, other studies have reported good test–retest reliability for Y-BOCS over the shorter term (2 weeks) (e.g. Kim *et al.*, 1990). Short-term assessments may be more appropriate when considering reliability because we might expect patients' symptoms to change over longer periods of time.

Computerised versions of Y-BOCS have been developed that appear to yield reliability scores similar to interviewer-administered versions (Baer *et al.*, 1993). It is useful to know this because such scales have benefits (e.g. ease of use), although face-to-face interviews have other strengths (see below).

Validity

Comorbidity – Not all research studies have found that OCD is a condition distinct from other disorders. For example, Woody *et al.* (1995) found poor discrimination with depression, i.e. patients diagnosed with OCD were also often diagnosed with depression. This suggests that the diagnostic category is not very useful, e.g. when deciding what treatment to advise.

Using interviews to improve internal validity – OCD patients may be fearful of handling questionnaires because they worry that the paper is contaminated (Anthony and Barlow, 2004). This means they might resist answering the questionnaire. It might generally be preferable to interview patients in order to get fuller responses.

A further benefit of interviews is that an experienced **clinician** can distinguish between obsessions and 'simple' worries that are not pathological (i.e. they are not related to a mental disorder) (Brown *et al.*, 1993). Patients, on the other hand, might not distinguish between these and end up overplaying their obsessions and compulsions.

Problems with self-report – Some patients may lack awareness of the severity and frequency of their symptoms. This means that the validity of any diagnosis is likely to be improved by interviewing close friends/partners as well as the patient themselves.

On the other hand, in contrast with other mental disorders, the symptoms of OCD are observable and concrete, and therefore are easier to identify even by a patient. In addition OCD patients have self-awareness whereas, for example, schizophrenics do not.

Using computer diagnosis to improve internal validity – Computerised scales for assessing OCD may be preferable to interviews because the presence of another person creates fears of negative evaluation (the patient underplays their symptoms to 'look' better, an example of social desirability bias).

Computerised scales also mean there is less influence of interviewer expectations on the patient's answers. An interviewer might, for example, steer a patient into overplaying their symptoms in order for the interviewer to be able to make a diagnosis (Kobak *et al.*, 1993).

ICD versus DSM – Steinberger and Schuch (2002) considered the diagnosis rates using these two classification systems. Using DSM 95% of their sample of children and adults with OCD symptoms were diagnosed with OCD whereas only 46% were using ICD. They suggest this is because the criteria used for ICD are less detailed, which challenges the validity of this measure.

CULTURAL BIAS IN DIAGNOSING OCD

Evaluation

The incidence of OCD tends to be about the same in most countries/cultures (about 2–3% lifetime prevalence – OCD Centre, 2002). However, the symptoms are often shaped by the patient's culture of origin. For example, a patient from a Western country may have a contamination obsession that is focused on germs, whereas a patient from India may fear contamination by touching a person from a lower social caste.

The problem of cultural differences may lead to difficulties when using diagnostic scales because the symptom checklist is culturally-based. For example, Williams *et al.* (2005) demonstrated that there were significant differences between normal populations of black and white Americans in the scores for contamination obsessions. The researchers suggest that black Americans produce higher scores because of, for example, the fact that they interact less with animals and therefore have a greater concern about contamination from animals. This would then increase the likelihood of an OCD diagnosis.

By contrast, Matsunaga *et al.* (2008) studied Japanese OCD patients and found symptoms remarkably similar to those in the West, concluding that this disorder transcends culture.

CAN YOU...? No.12.1

...1 Outline clinical characteristics of OCD in about 200 words.

...2 Outline issues relating to reliability and validity in the diagnosis and/or classification of OCD in about 200 words.

...3 Choose **eight** critical points relevant to issues of reliability and validity in the diagnosis and/or classification of OCD. Elaborate each point in about 50 words.

...4 Use this material to answer the following questions:

Outline clinical characteristics of obsessive compulsive disorder. (8 marks) [200-word answer]

Discuss issues of reliability and validity associated with the classification and diagnosis of obsessive compulsive disorder. (8 marks + 16 marks) [600-word answer]

Researchers studying **obsessive compulsive disorder (OCD)** are split over its exact cause. On one side are those who believe that it is a psychological disorder, while on the other are those who believe that OCD is caused by abnormalities in the brain. Anxiety and fear are natural and adaptive responses, and therefore have a biological basis, which you learned about when studying stress at AS level. This might lead us to expect that *abnormal* fears and anxieties are also biologically based. This spread looks at the biological explanations for OCD, including evolutionary explanations.

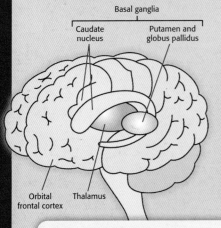

Basal ganglia

Caudate nucleus

Putamen and globus pallidus

Orbital frontal cortex

Thalamus

◀ A three-dimensional view of the brain showing the regions that have been linked to OCD. These areas may be overactive in people with the disorder, and form a 'worry circuit'.

NEUROANATOMICAL ABNORMALITIES

Several areas in the frontal lobes of the brain are thought to be abnormal in people with OCD. The **caudate nucleus** (located in the **basal ganglia**) normally suppresses signals from the **orbitofrontal cortex (OFC)**. In turn, the OFC sends signals to the **thalamus** about things that are worrying, such as a potential germ hazard. When the caudate nucleus is damaged, it fails to suppress minor 'worry' signals and the thalamus is alerted, which in turn sends signals back to the OFC, acting as a worry circuit.

This is supported by **PET** scans of patients with OCD, taken while their symptoms are active (e.g. when a person with a germ obsession holds a dirty cloth). Such scans show heightened activity in the OFC.

Serotonin and dopamine are linked to these regions of the frontal lobes. Comer (1998) reports that serotonin plays a key role in the operation of the OFC and the caudate nuclei, and therefore it would appear that low serotonin would cause these areas to function poorly.

Dopamine is also linked to this system, as it is the main neurotransmitter of the basal ganglia. High levels of dopamine lead to overactivity of this region (Sukel, 2007).

BIOLOGICAL EXPLANATIONS

Genetic factors

Family and twin studies – Evidence for the genetic basis of OCD comes from evaluations of first-degree relatives and twin studies. Nestadt *et al.* (2000) identified 80 patients with OCD and 343 of their **first-degree relatives** and compared them with 73 control patients without mental illness and 300 of their relatives. The results showed a strong familial link for the most common form of this disorder. They found that people with a first-degree relative with OCD (parents or siblings) had a five times greater risk of having the illness themselves at some time in their lives, compared to the general population.

A **meta-analysis** of 14 twin studies of OCD found that, on average, identical (**monozygotic, MZ**) twins were more than twice as likely to develop OCD if their co-twin had the disorder than was the case for non-identical (**dizygotic, DZ**) twins (Billett *et al.*, 1998).

The COMT gene – Karayiorgou *et al.* (1997) discovered that variation in the expression of a specific gene may contribute to OCD. This genetic alteration reduces the production of the enzyme *catechol-O-methyltransferase* (COMT), which helps terminate the action of the neurotransmitter **dopamine** (linked to OCD, see left). The researchers collected DNA samples from 73 people diagnosed with OCD and 148 who had not experienced any mental disorder. The variation in the COMT gene's usual sequence, inherited from both parents, occurred in nearly half of the men suffering from OCD, whereas only 10% of women with OCD displayed the same genetic trait, as did about 17% of the men and women who displayed good mental health.

What is inherited? Genetic factors may lead to abnormal functioning of areas of the brain (e.g. the caudate nucleus, see left). They may also lead to abnormal levels of certain **neurotransmitters** (e.g. **serotonin** and **dopamine**). Low levels of serotonin are implicated because **antidepressant** drugs that increase serotonin have been shown to reduce OCD symptoms (Pigott *et al.*, 1990), whereas antidepressants that have less effect on serotonin do not reduce OCD symptoms (Jenicke, 1992). In contrast with serotonin, dopamine levels are thought to be abnormally high in people with OCD. This is based on animal studies – high doses of drugs that enhance levels of dopamine, induce stereotyped movements resembling the compulsive behaviours found in OCD patients (Szechtman *et al.*, 1998).

An evolutionary approach

The adaptive nature of obsessions and compulsions – The ritual behaviours associated with this type of anxiety disorder can be considered an exaggeration of the behaviours that more usually serve an **adaptive** function. Marks and Nesse (1994) suggest the following examples of adaptive behaviours that may lead to obsessive compulsive behaviours:

- **Grooming behaviour** – In mammals, parasitism is reduced by grooming, and in some primate species, grooming smoothes social interaction. Many obsessive compulsives wash and groom endlessly.
- **Concern for others** – Ignoring the needs of other members of the group increases the likelihood of ostracism from the group. Many obsessive compulsives are overly concerned with fear of harming or embarrassing others.
- Hoarding – This guards against future shortages and protects the individual from periods when that resource might be scarce. Hoarding (e.g. collecting food or other items) may become grossly exaggerated in some obsessive compulsives.

Harm-avoidance strategies – Abed and de Pauw (1998) have suggested a particular adaptive function underlying OCD. They suggest that a particular **mental module** evolved – the *Involuntary Risk Scenario Generating System* (IRSGS) – which allows individuals to imagine certain potential risks before they happen and thus be able to deal more effectively with them when they do happen. An extremely sensitive IRSGS would lead to OCD.

TOURETTE'S SYNDROME

Tourette's syndrome is a neurological disorder characterised by tics – sudden involuntary movements or vocalisations (such as swear words) that are repeated excessively. These tics occur in spasms and may appear many times a day or only occasionally throughout a year. There may be long spells without any tics. Individuals have some control over the tics but usually feel a compulsion to produce them. If the person tries to hold back the tics, this leads eventually to a strong outburst. Between 45 and 90% of Tourette's patients also have obsessions and compulsions.

*What is a **concordance rate**? In a sample of, for example, 100 twin pairs, one twin of each pair has a phobic disorder. The number of times their other twin also shows the illness determines the concordance rate, so if 40 have phobic disorder, then the concordance rate is 40%.*

EVALUATION

Genetic factors

Research evidence suggests quite a high inheritance factor for OCD, certainly when compared with other disorders. For example, Carey and Gottesmann (1981) found an 87% **concordance rate** in **MZ twins** for OCD, whereas McGuffin *et al.* (1996) found a concordance rate for schizophrenia in MZ twins of 46%.

However, these concordance rates are not 100%, which means that environmental factors must play a role too. Indeed it is the occurrence of OCD that seems to run in families rather than the specific symptoms (such as obsession with dirt), which also indicates an environmental contribution.

Tourette's syndrome and other disorders – Pauls and Leckman (1986) studied patients with Tourette's syndrome, and their families, and concluded that OCD is one form of expression of the same gene that determines Tourette's. The obsessional behaviour of OCD and Tourette's patients is also found in **autistic** children, who display stereotyped behaviours and rituals as well as compulsions. In addition, obsessive behaviour is typical of **anorexia**, and is one of the characteristics distinguishing individuals with anorexia from individuals with bulimia. Furthermore, it is reported that two out of every three patients with OCD also experience at least one episode of depression (Rasmussen and Eisen, 1992).

The COMT gene – A study by Schindler *et al.* (2002) confirmed the association between OCD and the COMT gene but didn't support the gender differences found by Karayiorgou *et al.* (see facing page). Other candidate genes are being discovered all the time. For example, Wendland *et al.* (2008) identified a variation in a gene involved in serotonin production (SLC6A4) in OCD patients. Welch *et al.* (2007) found that mice lacking the SAPAP3 gene (a gene also present in humans) compulsively groomed themselves to the point of self-injury and showed greater anxiety than normal mice.

Biochemical explanations are supported by research studies of the effects of drugs. For example, Kim *et al.* (2007) found that drugs that raised levels of serotonin (e.g. SSRIs) also reduced dopamine levels in the right basal ganglia. Reduction in dopamine levels was positively correlated with a reduction of obsessive compulsive symptoms assessed using Y-BOCS (see page 206).

Neuroanatomical explanations are also supported by research evidence. For example, **PET scans** indicate that OCD patients exhibit increased glucose metabolism in the OFC-caudate nuclei loop. When compared with control subjects, people with OCD burn energy more rapidly in this network. This increased metabolism is also correlated with the severity of OCD. Further support comes from studies of SSRIs, such as *Prozac*, that reduce OCD symptoms, and also reduce this abnormally high metabolism (Schwartz *et al.*, 1996).

However, a recent study (Moritz *et al.*, 2009) has questioned the role of the OFC, because OCD patients did not perform abnormally on cognitive tasks related to the OFC. The researchers conclude that OFC dysfunction may be more subtle than previously claimed.

Evolutionary explanations

Less prone to risk-taking – Abed and de Pauw suggest that the strength of their theory is that it generates a number of testable hypotheses. For example, they suggest that obsessional patients should be less prone to risk-taking because overactivity of IRSGS would alert an individual to the dangers associated with risky activities and thus lead to risk avoidance. Evidence from Osborn (1998) suggests that this is the case.

Increased risk at critical life stages – Another prediction is that there should be an increased risk of OCD at biologically critical life stages (e.g. having just had a baby) because that would be the time when the IRSGS would be generating lots of new risks. Again there is evidence to support this, such as increased risk for OCD during pregnancy (Buttolph *et al.*, 1998).

GENES AND NEUROANATOMY

Support for both genetic and neuroanatomical explanations comes from a study by Menzies *et al.* (2007). They used **MRI** to produce images of brain activity in OCD patients and their immediate family members without OCD (a sibling, parent or child) and also a group of unrelated healthy people. OCD patients and their close relatives had reduced grey matter in key regions of the brain, including the OFC. This supports the view that anatomical differences are inherited and these may lead to OCD in certain individuals. Menzies *et al.* concluded that, in the future, brain scans may be used to detect OCD risk.

All participants were also given a computer test where they had to rapidly press an arrow each time it appeared but had to stop when a beeping noise was heard. This assessed their ability to stop repetitive behaviours. The OCD patients and their relatives scored lower on the test, finding it more difficult to control repetitive responses and further supporting the view that the tendency to develop OCD is genetic.

REAL-WORLD APPLICATION

The mapping of the human genome has led to the hope that specific genes could be linked to particular mental and physical disorders. For example, it might be that people who possess the COMT gene could have their fertilised eggs screened, thus giving them the choice of whether to abort those with the gene. Alternatively gene therapy may produce a means of turning certain genes 'off' so that a disorder is not expressed. Both raise important ethical issues.

This presumes, of course, that there is a relatively simple relationship between a disorder, such as OCD and genes. There may well be more than one gene involved, which will make it difficult to identify someone who is a candidate for OCD.

CAN YOU...? (No.12.2)

...**1** Describe **two** biological explanations of OCD in 100 words each.

...**2** Outline **eight** critical points for biological explanations therapies for OCD, including **(a)** the critical point being made, **(b)** your evidence for this critical point, and **(c)** how this criticism affects the explanation. Each criticism should be about 50 words.

...**3** Use this material to write a 600-word answer to the question: *Discuss **two or more** biological explanations of OCD.* (8 marks + 16 marks)

PSYCHOLOGICAL EXPLANATIONS OF OCD

We are all taught to be careful and clean, and many of us have repetitive worries or fixed routines that we recognise to be not entirely rational. In people suffering from **obsessive compulsive disorder (OCD)** however, such concerns are all-consuming and self-destructive. As we have seen on the previous spread, biological explanations of OCD are well-established, and the therapeutic success of **serotonin** treatments have further reinforced the underlying biological basis of this disorder. Psychological explanations, on the other hand, typically emphasise the way a sufferer has learned to avoid certain situations and learned to carry out compulsions that perpetuate the condition.

PSYCHOLOGICAL EXPLANATIONS

Psychodynamic

Freud (1917) suggested that OCD arises when unacceptable wishes and impulses coming from the **id** are only partially **repressed** (driven out of consciousness) and so provoke anxiety. People with OCD use **ego-defence** mechanisms to reduce the anxiety associated with these wishes and impulses. The main defence mechanisms common to OCD are:

- **Isolation** – People attempt to isolate themselves from, or disown, these undesirable wishes and impulses. Sometimes the defence mechanism predominates, at other times it is the id that predominates. When the forces of the id are dominant, the impulses intrude as obsessional thoughts.
- **Undoing** – When isolation is about to fail, the secondary defence of undoing produces compulsive acts. Someone who compulsively washes their hands may be symbolically undoing their unacceptable id impulses (Comer, 2003).
- **Reaction formation** – This involves adopting behaviours and character traits that are exactly the opposite of the unacceptable impulses. Compulsive kindness towards others may be a way of countering unacceptable aggressive impulses. Often these patterns appear to an observer to be highly exaggerated and even inappropriate.

Evaluation: THE EFFECT OF INTRUSIVE THOUGHTS

The effect of intrusive thinking on the development of OCD was demonstrated by Pleva and Wade (2006), in particular how the *misinterpretation of intrusive thoughts* (MIT) leads to self-blame.

In the study, 300 students were divided into an obsessive compulsive group (OC) and a control group, on the basis of their scores on a scale measuring OC symptoms. The students were also rated on two other scales. One scale (*Responsibility Interpretations Questionnaire*, RIQ) measured interpretation of intrusive thoughts by providing a list of common intrusive thoughts (e.g. images of attacking someone or suddenly thinking your hands are dirty), and asking participants to identify and rate those they had experienced in the previous two weeks.

The other scale (*Responsibility Attitude Scale*, RAS) assessed attitudes towards responsibility (self-blame). For example, there were statements to comment on, such as: 'I often feel responsible when things go wrong'.

A close positive correlation was found between the RIQ and RAS in students classified as having OC symptoms, but not in the other students. This supports the cognitive explanation that self-blame (responsibility) underlies the obsessions of OCD.

Behavioural

Obsessions – Mowrer (1960) suggested that the acquisition of fears is a two-step process. First, a particular neutral stimulus becomes associated with anxiety through **classical conditioning**. For example, a child is told that eating food that has been dropped on the floor is disgusting and this creates anxiety for the child. Thereafter, when the child thinks of any dirty object, feelings of anxiety are created.

The second part of the process is that the anxiety then associated with these stimuli is maintained over time by avoidance – avoiding a feared stimulus leads to positive outcomes and is thus reinforced. Any action that enables the individual to avoid a negative event is said to be **negatively reinforcing** – one of the principles of **operant conditioning**.

Compulsive behaviour – Compulsive rituals are learned because of an association between the anxiety-associated obsessions and the reduction of that anxiety. As a result, ritualistic behaviour is reinforced, and the person may link whatever act they have performed with changing the fearful situation. In this way accidental associations are formed and may become compulsive whenever the individual faces thoughts or situations that provoke anxiety.

Cognitive

Intrusive thoughts – Cognitive explanations of OCD stress that everybody has unwanted or intrusive thoughts from time to time (e.g. harming others or being contaminated by germs), but these thoughts can be ignored or dismissed fairly easily. For some people, however, these thoughts are misinterpreted and lead to self-blame and the expectation that terrible things will happen (Salkovskis, 1998). These thoughts continue because the person cannot stop or ignore them easily. This is often because they also have depression, which weakens their ability to distract themselves from the intrusive thoughts (Frost and Steketee, 2002).

Neutralising anxiety through compulsive acts – In order to avoid the anticipated consequences of these thoughts, the individual must 'neutralise' them, for example washing their hands after feeling contaminated by dirty objects. However, such behaviours provide only temporary relief and then anxiety builds up again. Every time a neutralising thought or action is repeated it becomes harder to resist because of the temporary relief it provides, and eventually it becomes, by definition, a compulsion (Comer, 2003). Over time, people become more convinced that these intrusive thoughts are dangerous, and therefore their fear of them increases. In this way, the thoughts turn into obsessions, and the need to reduce the anxiety associated with them becomes even more acute. The pattern of behaviour characteristic of OCD is, therefore, rather like an addiction – the more you do it, the more you have to do it again.

◄ Leonardo di Caprio played one of the richest men in the world, Howard Hughes, in the film *The Aviator*. This is ironic, as both men have suffered from OCD. Howard Hughes developed various obsessions, including a fear of germs, which meant that he used tissues to pick things up or open doors. He also became obsessed with the film *Ice Station Zebra* and is said to have watched it over 150 times. In addition to OCD he suffered from social phobia and towards the end of his life disappeared from public view.

Di Caprio says he has to force himself not to step on every piece of squashed chewing gum when walking down a pavement, and fights urges to walk through a doorway several times, because he doesn't want his condition taking over his life.

USING A NON-CLINICAL POPULATION

Evaluation

One problem with research into OCD is that it tends to use people who are just 'OCD-like', i.e. they have more obsessions/compulsions than 'normal' people. This is described as a *non-clinical* group. 'Normal' participants are given a questionnaire, such as Y-BOCS (see page 206), and separated into an OC group (those who score high in terms of obsessive compulsive symptoms) and a control group. The study by Pleva and Wade (facing page) and the study by Tracy *et al.* (below) used non-clinical, OCD-like participants. It may not be appropriate to generalise the data from such studies to understanding *clinical* cases of OCD.

EVALUATION

Psychodynamic

Evidence – Freud produced supporting evidence to support his explanation. In one of his classic case studies he analysed the 'Rat Man' who had obsessive fears about harm coming to his fiancée and her father, for example that pots of rats were going to be fastened to their buttocks and then gnaw into their anuses (Freud, 1909). The Rat Man tried to fend off his obsessional fantasies with compulsive acts. For example, he jumped into the path of a carriage to remove a rock that he thought was in its way. Freud suggested two reasons for his patient's obsessions: that they were the result of conflicting thoughts about his fiancée and her father (for example loving the father but also wishing him dead so he could inherit his money) and that they stemmed from childhood conflicts.

Negative effects – Salzman (1980) suggests that the therapy derived from Freud, **psychoanalysis**, may actually have a *negative* effect on OCD recovery, which challenges the Freudian explanation. An alternative is to use a short-term psychodynamic therapy. These tend to be more direct and action-oriented and therefore reduce the OCD patients' tendency to 'think too much'.

Behavioural

Conditioning – Tracy *et al.* (1999) suggest that Mowrer's theory would predict that OCD patients are predisposed to rapid conditioning, a prediction supported by a study they conducted using students. The student participants were divided into an 'OCD-like' group and a control group, on the basis of responses to an obsessive compulsive symptom checklist. They did find that in some conditions the OCD-like students were conditioned more rapidly (they used an eye blink task – when a puff of air is blown in the eye, the unconditioned response is to blink; if a bell is rung along with the puff, a person acquires a conditioned response of blinking to the sound of the bell).

Compulsive behaviour – If the performance of compulsive acts relieves the anxiety associated with obsessional thoughts, then blocking these acts should cause a rise in anxiety. Rachman and Hodgson (1980) carried out a series of experiments that demonstrated the anxiety-reducing properties of compulsive acts in OCD. In these studies, OCD patients were asked to carry out some 'prohibited' activity (such as touching something dirty) that would cause a rise in anxiety and an accompanying urge to perform whatever compulsive action was relevant for this feared situation. Patients were then allowed to carry out their compulsive act, and a consequent reduction in anxiety was noted. If, however, patients were asked to *delay* carrying out the compulsive activity, their anxiety levels were found to persist for a while then gradually decline. Rachman (1998) suggests that compulsive behaviours serve an important function, because they provide *quicker* relief from anxiety than would be the case with spontaneous decay alone.

Link with biological explanations – Behavioural explanations for compulsive behaviours can be used in conjunction with biological explanations. If genetic factors cause obsessive behaviour then the anxiety associated with such obsessions may be reduced by, for example, performing various rituals (i.e. compulsive acts). Such rituals are thus rewarding and will be repeated.

Cognitive

Intrusive thoughts – People with OCD appear to have different patterns of thinking, such as believing that they can and should have total control over their world (Bouchard *et al.*, 1999). This can explain why an individual who is vulnerable to developing an anxiety or mood disorder might end up with OCD. It is because they react to their obsessions and anxieties with maladaptive thought patterns. Indeed, it appears that people with OCD do have more intrusive thoughts than 'normal' people (Clark, 1992) and that people with OCD report trying to do things that will neutralise unwanted thoughts (Freeston *et al.*, 1992). Such findings support the cognitive view.

Neutralising anxiety – The evidence from Rachman and Hodgson (described left) demonstrated that compulsive acts can reduce or neutralise anxiety, which supports cognitive explanations because it suggests that compulsive acts may well develop as a means of neutralising anxiety.

CAN YOU...? No.12.3

...**1** Describe **three** psychological explanations of OCD in about 70 words each.

...**2** Outline **eight** critical points for psychological explanations for OCD, including **(a)** the critical point being made, **(b)** your evidence for this critical point, and **(c)** how this criticism affects the explanation. Each criticism should be about 50 words.

...**3** Use this material to write a 600-word answer to the question: *Discuss **two or more** psychological explanations of OCD.* (8 marks + 16 marks)

GENDER BIAS

Evaluation

The descriptions of OCD assume that the disorder has the same origins in men and women. However, Lochner and Stein (2001) suggest that there are some interesting gender issues raised by the differential rates of OCD and associated mental disorders. In males it appears that early brain injury may be associated with OCD and **Tourette's**, whereas in females, OCD and *trichotillomania* (pulling hair out) often appear after childbirth and pregnancy. This suggests that *obsessive compulsive spectrum disorders* may have different triggers in men and women.

BIOLOGICAL THERAPIES FOR OCD

Biological therapies are not new to you – you studied, for example, the use of drugs (**chemotherapy**) during your AS course. Biological therapies are often used in conjunction with psychological therapies because they reduce the anxiety levels associated with OCD, allowing a patient to engage in psychotherapy. The *American Psychiatric Association* (2007) has recently recommended that drugs should only be used in severe cases or in conjunction with psychotherapy; psychotherapy should be the treatment of preference.

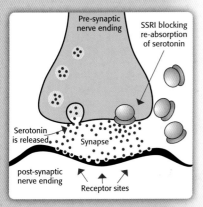

▲ SSRIs block the re-uptake of serotonin at the presynaptic membrane, increasing serotonin concentration at receptor sites on the postsynaptic membrane.

▲ Transcranial magnetic stimulation (TMS) uses an electromagnetic coil to pass a painless electric current through the scalp to stimulate areas of the brain associated with OCD and mood regulation.

BIOLOGICAL THERAPIES

Chemotherapy

Drug therapy is currently the most commonly used treatment for OCD (Gava *et al.*, 2007). The most commonly used drugs are **antidepressants**, although **anti-anxiety** drugs may be used.

Antidepressants are used to reduce the anxiety associated with OCD. **SSRIs** (see page 184) are currently the preferred drug for treating anxiety disorders (Choy and Schneier, 2008). SSRIs, such as *Zoloft*, *Paxil* and *Prozac*, increase levels of the **neurotransmitter serotonin** which regulates mood and anxiety. Low levels of serotonin are implicated in the 'worry circuit' described on page 208. Increasing levels of serotonin may therefore normalise this circuit.

Another antidepressant, the **tricyclic** *clomipramine* (brand name *Anafranil*) was the first antidepressant used for OCD and today is primarily used in the treatment of OCD rather than depression. Tricyclics block the transporter mechanism that re-absorbs both serotonin and **noradrenaline** into the pre-synaptic cell after it has fired. As a result, more of these neurotransmitters are left in the **synapse**, prolonging their activity, and easing transmission of the next impulse.

SSRIs work in much the same way as the tricyclics but, instead of blocking the re-uptake of different neurotransmitters, they block the re-uptake of serotonin and so increase the quantity available to excite neighbouring brain cells, thus reducing the symptoms of depression and anxiety (see diagram on left).

Anti-anxiety drugs – Benzodiazepines (BZs) are commonly used to reduce anxiety, as you learned in your AS level course. They are manufactured under various trade names, such as *Librium*, *Xanax*, *Valium*, and *Diazepam*. BZs slow down the activity of the central nervous system by enhancing the activity of **GABA** (gamma-amino-butyric-acid), a neurotransmitter that, when released, has a general quietening effect on many of the neurons in the brain. It does this by reacting with special sites (called GABA receptors) on the outside of receiving neurons. When GABA locks into these receptors it opens a channel which increases the flow of *chloride ions* into the neuron. *Chloride ions* make it harder for the neuron to be stimulated by other neurotransmitters, thus slowing down its activity and making the person feel more relaxed.

Other drugs – Recent research has found that D-Cycloserine has an effect on reducing anxiety and thus may be an effective treatment for OCD, particularly when used in conjunction with psychotherapy (see page 215). D-Cycloserine is an antibiotic used in the treatment of tuberculosis. It also appears to enhance the transmission of GABA and thus reduce anxiety (Kushner *et al.*, 2007).

Psychosurgery

If damage to areas of the brain is a cause of at least some of the symptoms of OCD, this means that removal or deconnection of these areas may be a way to reduce undesirable symptoms. **Psychosurgery** is a surgical intervention that aims to treat a behaviour for which no pathological cause can be established (surgery to remove, for example, a brain tumour is not an example of psychosurgery because there is a pathological cause).

Capsulotomy and cingulotomy are the two operations that are performed for anxiety disorders (see diagram on page 198). Such operations remove the *capsule* and the *cingulum* respectively. The cingulum links the orbitofrontal cortex to the caudate nucleus. The capsule is part of the **limbic system** involved with emotion and anxiety.

Deep brain stimulation (DBS) involves placing wires in target areas of the brain. The wires are connected to a battery in the patient's chest. When the current is on, this interrupts the target circuits in the brain, such as the 'worry' circuit (see page 208).

Transcranial magnetic stimulation (TMS) is another technique which, like DBS, avoids destruction of brain tissue and has recently been used with OCD patients. There are various similar techniques but, in general, a large electromagnetic coil is placed above the scalp near the forehead. This creates painless electric currents that stimulate the **frontal cortex**, a region of the brain associated with OCD and mood regulation.

EVALUATION

Effectiveness of chemotherapy

SRRIs – There is considerable evidence for the effectiveness of SSRIs for the treatment of OCD. For example, Soomro et al. (2008) reviewed 17 studies of the use of SSRIs with OCD and found them to be more effective than **placebos** in reducing the symptoms of OCD as measured with Y-BOCS up to three months after treatment i.e. in the short-term. One of the issues regarding the evaluation of treatment is that most treatment studies are only of three to four months' duration, and therefore little long-term data exists (Koran et al., 2007).

Tricyclics – *Clomipramine*, a tricyclic antidepressant, is often regarded as more effective than SSRIs (Koran et al., 2007). However, tricyclic antidepressants tend to have more side effects (such as hallucinations and irregular heartbeat) than SSRIs so they are more likely to be used as a second-line treatment i.e. in cases where SSRIs were not effective. However, some studies have found SSRIs to be comparable in effectiveness to clomipramine (and to placebos) (Zohar and Judge, 1996).

Appropriateness of chemotherapy

Lacks lasting effects – Koran et al. (2007), in a comprehensive review of treatments for OCD sponsored by the *American Psychiatric Association* (APA), suggested that although drug therapy may be more commonly used, psychotherapies such as **CBT** should be tried first. Drug therapy may require little effort and also may be relatively effective in the short term but it does not provide a lasting cure, as indicated by the fact that patients relapse within a few weeks if medication is stopped (Maina et al., 2001). In addition there are considerable side effects. For example, nausea, headache and insomnia are common side effects of SSRIs (Soomro et al., 2008).

Behavioural therapy plus chemotherapy – Even when chemotherapy is the preferred option it may be best to also engage in some kind of psychotherapy to help reduce compulsions. In fact, it has been found that behavioural therapy can have the same effect on the brain as drugs. Schwartz et al. (1996) found that patients who were given *response prevention therapy* (where compulsive responses are prevented) all showed reduced activity in the **caudate nucleus**, as did those given antidepressants.

Effectiveness of psychosurgery

Cingulotomy – Dougherty et al. (2002) found that up to 45% of the patients studied (total 44) who were previously unresponsive to medication and behavioural treatments for OCD, were at least partly improved after cingulotomy. Jung et al. (2006) found similar recovery rates in a sample of 17 patients and reported no adverse long-term effects on follow-up.

However, Koran et al. (2007) suggest that such studies may be biased because they are 'unblinded' i.e. the researchers know the treatment received by patients, and their expectations may influence their judgement. A further criticism is that psychosurgery may affect behaviour more globally, for example reducing motivation and energy levels (Sachdev and Hay, 1995). This, rather than the surgery, may explain reduced OCD symptoms.

TMS – Greenberg et al. (1997) used TMS to treat 12 OCD patients. Two frontal sites were stimulated for 20 minutes resulting in a significant reduction in compulsive urges lasting at least eight hours. However, another study found less impressive effects for TMS. When OCD patients were given either TMS or **sham TMS** there was no measurable difference afterwards as assessed using Y-BOCS (Rodriguez-Martin et al., 2003). This suggests that the earlier success might be due to a placebo effect.

Appropriateness of psychosurgery

Ablative psychosurgery (where permanent changes are made to the brain by either severing connections or removing the whole region) is associated with severe side effects ranging from personality changes and seizures to transient mania. However, there is some evidence that such side-effects are not long-lasting. Nyman et al. (2001) conducted a follow-up study of all OCD patients treated with a capsulotomy at the Karolinska Hospital in Sweden between 1978 and 1990. Their IQ test performance, in general, remained intact. Some functioning had been adversely affected at the time of the operation, but recovery took place over time.

Evaluation ETHICS

Biological treatments for OCD raise important ethical issues. First, there is an issue related to studying the effectiveness of drugs. A fundamental requirement of research ethics is that if effective treatments exist, they should be used as controls when new treatments are tested. Substituting a placebo for an effective treatment does not satisfy this duty as it exposes individuals to a treatment known to be inferior.

Second, there is the issue of informed consent, or lack of it. Most patients are not informed about the comparative success of drugs versus placebos. They expose themselves to unpleasant side-effects even though the pharmacological effects of drugs may be slim.

Finally, we might consider the ethics of irreversible forms of psychosurgery. The case of Mary Lou Zimmerman (below) highlights the potential dangers of such operations and again the issue of obtaining truly informed consent.

Evaluation CAN PSYCHOSURGERY BE JUSTIFIED?

Some people believe that the use of psychosurgery is justified in extreme cases, where mental disorder appears untreatable by other means. However, this was not the view of the jury in the case brought by the family of Mary Lou Zimmerman. Mrs Zimmerman had suffered for many years from OCD (compulsive handwashing) and depression, which was not relieved by drugs or other therapies. As a last resort she was referred to the Cleveland Clinic in Ohio, US, which claimed a 70% success rate, with the remaining 30% of patients unchanged but unharmed. The doctors decided to perform both a capsulotomy and cingulotomy on Mrs Zimmerman. The result of the operation, in her case, was that afterwards she was unable to walk, stand, eat or use the toilet by herself. In June 2002, a jury in Ohio awarded Zimmerman and her husband, Sherman, $7.5 million in damages because it was claimed that they had not been sufficiently informed of the dangerous and experimental nature of the surgery (Carey, 2003).

The point of describing this case history is to provide an illustration of the problems of informed consent and the all-too-real dangers of psychosurgery.

CAN YOU...? No.12.4

...**1** Describe **two** biological therapies for OCD in 100 words each.

...**2** Outline **eight** critical points for biological therapies for OCD, including **(a)** the critical point being made, **(b)** your evidence for this critical point, and **(c)** how this criticism affects the explanation. Each criticism should be about 50 words.

...**3** Use this material to write a 600-word answer to the question: *Discuss **two or more** biological therapies for OCD.* (8 marks + 16 marks)

PSYCHOLOGICAL THERAPIES FOR OCD

Although the use of drugs is popular in the treatment of OCD, research has shown that the most effective treatments use a combination of medication and psychotherapy. This is partly because drugs only offer temporary relief whereas psychotherapeutic treatments may provide a longer-term solution. On this spread we will focus on the two most common forms of psychotherapy used in the treatment of OCD – behavioural therapy and cognitive therapy – but will also briefly consider psychoanalysis.

PSYCHOLOGICAL THERAPIES

Behavioural therapy – Exposure and Response Prevention (ERP) therapy

According to the behavioural explanation for OCD (see page 210) both obsessions and compulsions have been acquired through conditioning and therefore, in order to recover, patients must unlearn these behaviours. However, obsessions are maintained over time by avoidance (**negative reinforcement**) and this prevents relearning taking place. Equally, compulsive rituals have become associated with anxiety reduction and prevent relearning. Thus ERP therapy aims to provide opportunities for re-conditioning. ERP consists of two components:

1 **Exposure** – In the exposure element the patient is repeatedly presented with the feared stimulus until anxiety subsides (called 'habituation'). Exposures may be at first imagined and later experienced *in vivo* (e.g. actually touching dirty objects). Exposures may move gradually from least to most threatening in a manner similar to **systematic desensitisation** (see page 200). If the pace is too slow, patients may lose motivation. The underlying principle is that anxieties persist because of negative reinforcement – avoidance of an anxiety-producing stimulus is reinforcing. This cycle can be broken by forcing the patient to experience the stimulus and learn, through association with relaxation, that it no longer produces anxiety.

2 **Response prevention** – At the same time, the patient is also prohibited from engaging in the usual compulsive response. This is important in order for the patient to recognise that anxiety can be reduced without the compulsive ritual. For example, a woman obsessed about cleanliness might be given a list of therapeutic rules she must accept, such as not cleaning her house for a week and then only spending half an hour vacuuming it. Or, in an institutional setting, hospital staff may work out a strict routine to restrict patients' compulsive behaviours, such as only allowing them to flush the toilet twice. If a patient can control their behaviour, then they learn that those obsessions that previously created anxiety no longer produce this response.

Mode of action – At the beginning of therapy the psychiatrist can identify a list of target symptoms, including obsessions and compulsions, using Y-BOCS (see page 206). A list of items can then be ranked by the patient from least to most anxiety-provoking. Typically, ERP consists of 13–20 weekly sessions although severely ill patients may require longer treatment and/or more frequent sessions (March *et al.*, 1997). Once patients have made progress in treatment, they are encouraged to continue using the ERP techniques they have learned, and to apply them to new situations as they arise. Sometimes monthly booster sessions are added for up to six months to prevent relapse.

Cognitive therapy (CT)

Cognitive therapies focus on changing *thoughts* in contrast to behavioural therapies which focus on changing *behaviour*. CT aims to identify, challenge and modify dysfunctional beliefs.

Obsessions – The therapist questions how patients interpret their beliefs, including why they think they are true and why they think the obsessions developed. For example, the person who fears shaking hands may believe the action will pass on germs that may cause them to become ill. Such beliefs can then be challenged and re-interpreted so that shaking hands is no longer experienced as an anxiety-producing activity.

Compulsions – A CT therapist also questions patients about the value of their compulsive behaviour(s). For example, a person who compulsively washes his or her hands for 30 minutes at a time may believe that he or she is doing so to guard against infection. When this belief is challenged and confronted as false, it can help control the behaviour.

Thought records are used to help patients consider their dysfunctional beliefs about obsessions and compulsions. Patients are required to keep a daily record of their intrusive (unwelcome) thoughts. This might include details of where they were when they had the thought, details of what the thought meant to them, what they felt, and what they did in response to the intrusive thought. A thought record might also include information about what they did to challenge the intrusive thoughts and compulsive responses.

The therapist can then discuss the thought record with the patient and challenge unrealistic beliefs so that the patient will come to recognise the irrational nature of their beliefs and responses.

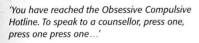

'You have reached the Obsessive Compulsive Hotline. To speak to a counsellor, press one, press one press one…'

Some psychologists classify ERP as a form of cognitive-behavioural therapy (CBT) because the 'exposure' element may include challenging irrational thoughts. CBT differs from cognitive therapy (CT) because there is usually greater emphasis on the final behavioural outcome.

◄ Katz (2008) suggests that many people think OCD is like the more everyday obsessions and compulsions people talk about, or the 'minstrel-show version' of the disorder as portrayed by Jack Nicholson in *As Good as it Gets*. One patient interviewed by Katz described his experience of OCD as being like living in an Escher print – you just go round and round. 'You've just parked the car. You hop out, grab your bag, and head towards the gym. But wait. Did you lock the car? You head back to make sure you did. Yup, it's locked, problem solved.' But a person with OCD doesn't stop there. 'I went and checked the car, but did I really check it? I'm looking at my hand turning the key in the lock, but is that perception really clear enough? Did I hear the click, or do I just remember hearing the click, or did I hear the click last time I checked this?'

EVALUATION

Effectiveness of ERP

Success rates – Albucher *et al.* (1998) report that between 60 and 90% of adults with OCD have improved considerably using ERP. Research has found that the effectiveness of ERP was improved when integrated with discussions of feared consequences and dysfunctional beliefs i.e. cognitive therapy (Huppert and Franklin, 2005). In particular this may help prevent relapse.

Combined with drug treatments – ERP is also often combined with drug treatments although this may or may not improve effectiveness. In one review of research (Foa and Kozak, 1996) ERP alone was found to be as effective as ERP with medication. In both conditions (without or with drugs) patients were doing equally well at a two-year follow-up. However, some more recent studies have found evidence for the effectiveness of ERP combined with drug therapy. For example, Foa *et al.* (2005) found that a combination of *clomipramine* (an **antidepressant**) and ERP was more effective than either alone. Wilhem *et al.* (2008) also found that simultaneous administration of *d-cycloserine* (an antibiotic that enhances the transmission of **GABA**) substantially improves effectiveness of ERP.

Self-directed ERP – For people with mild OCD, self-directed ERP may be a reasonably effective alternative to therapist-led ERP. One computer-based program, BT STEPs, was found to be more effective than relaxation training alone, but less effective than therapist-guided ERP (Greist *et al.*, 2002).

Appropriateness of ERP

Not all patients are helped by this therapy. ERP alone is not successful with patients who are severely depressed (Gershuny *et al.*, 2002) nor with patients who have certain types of OCD, such as severe hoarding behaviour (Steketee and Frost, 2003).

The success of ERP depends on the effort made by the patient, e.g. their willingness to do their 'homework' – not all patients are willing to commit to this kind of effort. This leads to a substantial refusal rate that may artificially elevate the apparent success of therapy because only those patients who are willing to 'be helped' may agree to participate.

Effectiveness of CT

CT is rarely used on its own, although a few studies have looked at the effectiveness of CT alone. For example, Wilhelm *et al.* (2005) found a significant improvement in 15 patients who used CT alone over 14 weeks, as measured on Y-BOCS. Jones and Menzies (1998) found a 20% improvement in symptoms from group CT over eight sessions.

Appropriateness of CT

Not suitable for all – Cognitive therapy, like ERP, also involves considerable patient effort and is therefore not suitable for all patients. Ellis (2001) believed that sometimes people who *claimed* to be following the principles of CT were not putting their revised beliefs into action, and therefore the therapy was not effective. Ellis also explained lack of success in terms of suitability – some people simply do not want the direct sort of advice that CT practitioners tend to dispense. They prefer to share their worries with a therapist without getting involved with the cognitive effort that is associated with recovery (Ellis, 2001).

The theoretical basis for the therapy has received research attention showing, for example, that people who hold irrational beliefs tend to produce thoughts that are more dysfunctional than those formed by people who hold rational beliefs (Bond and Dryden, 2002). On the other hand it may be that irrational beliefs are counterproductive but realistic. Alloy and Abrahmson (1979) found that depressed people gave more accurate estimates of the likelihood of a disaster than 'normal' controls (calling it the '*sadder but wiser*' effect).

ⓔ ETHICAL ISSUES IN RESEARCH

In some studies the effectiveness of ERP is determined by comparing symptom reduction in patients given therapy with that in patients on a waiting list who have not yet received therapy. For example, O'Kearney *et al.* (2006) examined four studies where **cognitive behavioural therapy** (ERP combined with CT) was compared to either a **placebo** therapy or no treatment (waiting list) – two of the studies found no lessening in symptoms as a result of the therapy. A fundamental requirement of research ethics is that if effective treatments exist, they should be used as control conditions when new treatments are tested. Substituting a placebo for an effective treatment, or leaving patients on a waiting list, does not satisfy this duty as it exposes individuals to a treatment known to be inferior.

ⓔ ERP VERSUS CT

Koran *et al.* (2007) point out that in many instances ERP inevitably involves some informal cognitive techniques (i.e. not directed by a cognitive psychotherapist). In fact in most therapeutic studies it is not possible to be sure of the extent to which a therapist has adhered to treatment protocols. This means that it is difficult to state whether any one particular therapeutic approach is more effective. However, Koran *et al.* concluded that ERP combined with CT probably produces the best results of all.

CAN YOU...? No.12.5

...**1** Describe **two** psychological therapies for OCD in 100 words each.

...**2** Outline **eight** critical points for pychological therapies for OCD, including **(a)** the critical point being made, **(b)** your evidence for this critical point, and **(c)** how this criticism affects the explanation. Each criticism should be about 50 words.

...**3** Use this material to write a 600-word answer to the question: *Discuss **two or more** psychological therapies for OCD*. (8 marks + 16 marks)

CHAPTER SUMMARY

OVERVIEW OF OCD

CLASSIFICATION AND DIAGNOSIS

BIOLOGICAL THERAPIES

CLINICAL CHARACTERISTICS
- Obsessions create anxiety.
- They are recurrent, intrusive thoughts or impulses perceived as inappropriate or forbidden. Perceived as uncontrollable which creates anxiety, recognised as the product of patient's own mind.
- Compulsions aim to reduce anxiety.
- Repetitive behaviours or mental acts that are recognised as unreasonable by sufferer but they believe terrible consequences if behaviours not performed.
- Obsessions/compulsions recognised as unreasonable and cause marked distress.
- No known physiological cause or symptoms better explained by another disorder.

VALIDITY
- Extent to which diagnosis represents something real and distinct from other disorders, and measures what it claims to measure.
- Y-BOCS does distinguish OCD from other anxiety disorders (Rosenfeld et al., 1992).
- Responses to questionnaires might not be honest, e.g. patient embarrassed.

EVALUATION
- Co-morbdity – inconsistent results, some studies show OCD not distinct from other disorders, e.g. similar pattern of symptoms to depression (Woody et al., 1995).
- Fear of handling questionnaires, interviews may be better (Anthony and Barlow, 2004).
- Experienced clinician interviewers can distinguish between obsessions and simple worries (Brown et al., 1993).
- Self-report improved by interviewing relatives because patients may lack awareness of severity of symptoms.
- However, OCD patients do have insight and symptoms are 'concrete'.
- Use of computer scales reduces fears of negative evaluation and effects of interviewer's expectations, enhancing validity.
- Different diagnosis rates with ICD and DSM (Steinberger and Schuch, 2002), 46% versus 95%, challenges validity of ICD.
- Symptoms of OCD may be shaped by culture of origin, e.g. Williams et al. (2005) – differences between black and white Americans in scores for contamination obsessions.

RELIABILITY
- Refers to consistency of measuring instrument or scale to assess fear ratings.
- Measured by degree of agreement over symptoms (inter-rater reliability) and consistency of scores on different occasions (test–retest reliability).
- Y-BOCS and CY-BOCS show good inter-rater reliability (Woody et al., 1995; Scahill et al., 1997), but better when items on resistance were removed.
- Long-term test–retest (average 48.5 days) lower than desirable (Woody et al., 1995).

EVALUATION
- Good short-term reliability (2 weeks) (Kim et al., 1990).
- Computerised versions of Y-BOCS reliable (Baer et al., 1993) but lack some of advantages of interviews.

CHEMOTHERAPY
- Antidepressants used to reduce anxiety associated with OCD.
- SSRIs increase levels of serotonin – increasing serotonin thought to normalise 'worry circuit' in brain.
- Tricyclics block re-uptake of serotonin and noradrenaline into pre-synaptic cell, leaving more available in the synapse.
- Anti-anxiety drugs such as BZs also used to reduce anxiety by enhancing activity of GABA. D-Cycloserine also enhances GABA activity.

EVALUATION
- Soomro et al. (2008) – supporting evidence for effectiveness of SSRIs in treatment of OCD, although little long-term data exists.
- Tricyclics often regarded as more effective in treatment of OCD, but have more side effects than SSRIs.
- Drug therapies do not provide lasting cure for OCD and may have side effects compared to psychotherapies.
- Behavioural therapy may also have physiological effects, e.g. response prevention therapy reduces activity in caudate nucleus.

EXPLANATIONS OF OCD

BIOLOGICAL EXPLANATIONS

GENETIC FACTORS
- Nestadt et al. (2000) – people with first degree relatives with OCD show five times greater risk of developing disorder than general population.
- Meta-analysis of twin studies – MZ twins twice as likely (compared to DZ twins) to develop OCD if other twin had OCD.
- Variation in COMT gene in 50% of men with OCD, and in 10% of women.
- What is inherited? Low levels of serotonin implicated because SSRI antidepressants reduce OCD symptoms whereas non SSRIs do not. High levels of dopamine also implicated.
- Neuroanatomical abnormalities – OFC-caudate nucleus link important in suppressing 'worry signals', which take over when circuit is damaged.

EVALUATION
- Research supports high inheritance factor for OCD, but concordance rates not 100% therefore environmental factors also important.
- OCD may be one form of expression of the gene that causes Tourette's, and OCD symptoms are part of other disorders.
- Schindler et al. (2002) supported link between COMT and OCD, but not gender differences found previously.
- Support for biochemical explanations – Kim et al. (2007) found that drugs that raise serotonin levels also reduced dopamine levels in basal ganglia leading to reduction in OCD symptoms.
- OCD-caudate nucleus link supported by PET scans showing increased activity in this area for OCD sufferers.
- Real-world application – mapping of human genome presents possibility of gene therapy for disorders, such as OCD (e.g. if OCD version of COMT gene present).
- Brain scans show reduced grey matter in OFC of OCD patients and family (Menzies et al., 2007).

AN EVOLUTIONARY APPROACH
- Marks and Nesse (1994) – adaptive behaviours that may lead to obsessive compulsive behaviours include grooming behaviour, concern for others, and hoarding.
- Harm-avoidance strategies (Abed and de Pauw, 1998) – the IRSGS is a mental module that allows individuals to imagine risks before they happen and so deal with them more effectively.

EVALUATION
- IRSGS would predict that OCD patients less likely to take risks than non-OCD individuals – supported by Osborn (1998).
- Increased risk at critical life stages – supported by Buttolph et al. (1998).

THERAPIES FOR OCD

BIOLOGICAL THERAPIES cont'd

PSYCHOSURGERY
- Capsulotomy removes *capsule* – part of limbic system involved with emotion and anxiety.
- Cingulotomy removes *cingulum* – links orbitofrontal cortex to caudate nucleus.
- Deep brain stimulation interrupts 'worry circuit' in the brain.
- TMS – painless electric currents stimulate frontal cortex, which is associated with OCD and mood regulation.

EVALUATION
- Dougherty *et al.* (2002) – 45% of OCD sufferers who were unresponsive to medication improved after cingulotomy.
- However, studies such as this are not 'blind' in terms of treatment type – therefore expectation of researchers may influence their judgement.
- TMS – inconsistent results in research studies. Early success may have been due to placebo effect.
- Some studies find severe side effects with psychosurgery whereas others find such effects are not long-lasting.
- Ethical issues include need to provide effective treatment rather than placebo, and issue of informed consent (e.g. Mary Lou Zimmerman).

PSYCHOLOGICAL THERAPIES

BEHAVIOURAL THERAPY: ERP
- ERP therapy provides opportunities for re-conditioning:
- Exposure – patient presented with feared stimulus, perhaps through systematic desensitisation.
- Response prevention – patient prohibited from engaging in usual compulsive response, which shows anxiety can be reduced without ritual.
- Mode of action – 13-20 weekly sessions, then encouraged to use ERP techniques in new situations.

EVALUATION
- Albucher *et al.* (1998) – between 60 and 90% of adults with OCD improve considerably using ERP.
- ERP often combined with drug treatments although doesn't always improve effectiveness.
- ERP not successful with patients who are also severely depressed nor those with hoarding behaviour.
- Ethical issues involved in denying treatment to OCD sufferers by using a placebo instead of effective treatment.

COGNITIVE THERAPY: CT
- Focus on changing thoughts by identifying, challenging and modifying dysfunctional beliefs.
- Obsessions – therapist questions patient's interpretation.
- Compulsions – therapist questions value of compulsive behaviours.
- Thought records – patient keeps daily record of intrusive thoughts for discussion with therapist.

EVALUATION
- CT rarely used on its own, although Wilhelm *et al.* (2005) found significant improvement in patients who used CT alone.
- Not all patients put in the effort required for success, and some people do not want the direct approach of a CT therapist.
- Irrational beliefs may be counterproductive but may also be realistic ('sadder but wiser effect').
- ERP versus CT – difficult to assess extent to which therapist has adhered to treatment protocols. Combination of both approaches produces the best results.

PSYCHOLOGICAL EXPLANATIONS

PSYCHODYNAMIC
- OCD arises when unacceptable impulses coming from the id are only partially repressed and so provoke anxiety.
- Defence mechanisms used against these impulses include isolaton, undoing and reaction formation.

EVALUATION
- Freud (1909) supported claims with case study of the 'Rat man' who tried to fend off obsessional thoughts with compulsive acts.
- Salzman (1980) – psychoanalytic therapy can make OCD worse, which challenges psychoanalytic explanation.

BEHAVIOURAL
- Mowrer (1960) – acquisition of obsessional fears is a two-stage process.
- Neutral stimulus associated with fear through classical conditioning.
- Anxiety associated with stimuli maintained by avoidance – leads to positive outcomes and so is reinforced (operant conditioning).
- Ritualistic behaviour is reinforced because it reduces anxiety. Accidental associations are formed which then become compulsive.

EVALUATION
- Tracy *et al.* (1999) – supported claim that OCD patients are predisposed to rapid conditioning.
- Methodological problems associated with use of non-clinical participants (have OCD-like symptoms) – may not be generalisable to OCD populations.
- Performance of compulsive acts relieves anxiety, so blocking them should raise anxiety levels – supported by Rachman and Hodgson (1980) study.

COGNITIVE
- Intrusive thoughts cannot be dismissed in some people, particularly if they suffer from depression – weakens ability to distract from these thoughts.
- To avoid anticipated consequences of intrusive thoughts, person must neutralise them through compulsive behaviours – gradually become harder to resist, as fear of 'dangerous' thoughts increases.
- Pleva and Wade (2006) – misinterpretation of intrusive thoughts leads to self-blame which underlies the obsessions of OCD.

EVALUATION
- Bouchard *et al.* (1999) – supporting evidence that people with OCD react to obsessions and anxieties with maladaptive thought patterns.
- Rachman and Hodgson (1980) – compulsive acts reduce anxiety, supporting cognitive view that obsessional thoughts misinterpreted.
- Gender bias – obsessive compulsive spectrum disorders may have different triggers in men and women.

EXAM QUESTION WITH STUDENT ANSWER

Question **(a) Explain issues associated with the classification and diagnosis of obsessive compulsive disorder.** *(8 marks)*

(b) Discuss one biological and one psychological explanation of obsessive compulsive disorder. *(8 marks + 8 marks)*

STUDENT ANSWER

(a) *The two main issues related to classification and diagnosis are reliability and validity. Obsessions and compulsions may be assessed using a variety of different scales but the 'gold standard' is Y-BOCs (the Yale-Brown Obsessive Compulsive Scale devised by Goodman et al. (1989). One of the sections of this scale (Y-BOCS-10) is often used on its own and contains 10 short questions concerning, for example, the extent to which obsessions/ compulsions interfere with everyday life and patients' perceived control over their symptoms. There is a children's version of this scale and online versions as well.*

The reliability of Y-BOCS has been reported as excellent in terms of inter-rater reliability and also test–retest over a two-week period. Over longer periods the test–retest scores were lower than desirable although it is possible that this is because of spontaneous changes in obsessions and compulsions.

The use of rating scales has some problems in relation to validity. Some people may not give honest answers to questionnaires about their obsessive/compulsive symptoms because they may be embarrassed or feel afraid that an interviewer will take symptoms as a sign of deeper psychosis.

There are also cultural issues in dealing with rating scales because certain obsessions are more normal in some cultures than others, such as black people in America being more concerned about animal contamination (Williams et al., 2005). This means that such people may appear to have OCD when they are just expressing normal concerns.

(b) *The biological explanation of OCD focuses on the role of genetics. It has been suggested that you are 10 times more likely to develop OCD if a family member has the disorder. This is supported by family and twin studies. In family studies, the presence of OCD in close genetic relatives supports the fact that it might be inherited. In twin studies, an identical twin is more likely to have OCD if their co-twin has it, than is the case with a non-identical twin. However, this fails to recognise the importance of learning in the development of compulsive behaviours.*

The biological explanation of OCD suggests that it is more to do with an 'abnormal' brain structure in OCD sufferers. It suggests that the caudate nuclei and orbitofrontal cortex in OCD sufferers is different from that on non-OCD sufferers. This might be to do with a difficult birth experience involving oxygen starvation. Therefore, the biological explanation suggests that it is the brain structure 'abnormality' in OCD sufferers that contributes to the faulty thinking as described in cognitive explanations. Biological explanations are also supported by research findings that show that low levels of serotonin cause these areas of the brain to malfunction.

The behavioural explanation focuses on OCD being learned and reinforced and does not look at the past as the psychodynamic explanation does. The behavioural explanation suggests that repetitive and compulsive behaviours are reinforced each time an OCD sufferer performs a 'ritual' such as a checking behaviour. This then suggests that a behaviour could be reinforced which lessens anxiety (an acceptable behaviour), whereas the psychodynamic explanation would suggest looking at the past in order to establish a cause and therefore find an effective treatment. Behavioural treatments include ERP therapy, where people are exposed to situations that trigger their obsessions, but are prevented from performing their compulsive acts. The fact that this type of treatment helps so many people supports the idea that OCD is learned.

[561 words]

EXAMINER COMMENTS

(a) This answer begins with a lengthy paragraph describing Y-BOCs, which is not relevant to the focus of the question and therefore is only **marginally creditworthy** as 'scene-setting'.

The remaining three paragraphs deal with a variety of issues related to diagnosis and classification. The question requires an 'explanation' of the issues which is regarded as all **AO2**. This has been done **reasonably** well in the paragraph on reliability, although this would have been improved with reference to actual studies and perhaps a discussion of why reliability is important.

The second paragraph is rather **superficial**, while the final paragraph is **more effective**, although again there is a **lack** of explanation/elaboration.

AO2/AO3 – In terms of the **breadth** of issues covered, this answer is **reasonable**, which balances the lack of elaboration in places.

In part (b), both description (**AO1**) and evaluation (**AO2**) are required, although there is a greater emphasis on AO2.

In the first paragraph there is a mixture of **AO1** and **AO2**. The AO1 material is accurate and **reasonably detailed** whereas the AO2 is **basic**.

In the second paragraph, a second biological explanation is presented – explaining OCD in terms of abnormal neuroanatomy. This could have been linked to the genetic explanation (e.g. OCD sufferers may inherit abnormal neuroanatomy) but this student has not made the link, so credit can only be given to one of the biological explanations (the question only asks for one).

The second paragraph contains **less detail** than the first paragraph – there is little information about the relationship between the orbitofrontal cortex and the caudate nuclei, and the same is true of the role of serotonin in OCD. Furthermore there is almost **no evaluation** in this paragraph.

This paragraph presents a fairly **basic** description of the behavioural explanation. This could be improved by providing a more explicit account of how obsessions and compulsions are learned and reinforced. **Evaluation** is achieved through making comparison with the psychodynamic approach and also using the success of the therapy derived from the explanation.

AO1 – The two creditworthy paragraphs jointly provide a **reasonable** description, although only just 'reasonable'.

AO2/AO3 – The analysis and evaluation is **superficial** even though there is some evidence of **elaboration**.

Chapter 13
Media psychology

SPECIFICATION

Media psychology	
Media influences on social behaviour	• Explanations of media influences on prosocial and antisocial behaviour. • The positive and negative effects of computers and video games on behaviour.
Media and persuasion	• The application of Hovland-Yale and Elaboration Likelihood models in explaining the persuasive effects of media. • Explanations for the persuasiveness of television advertising.
The psychology of celebrity	• The attraction of 'celebrity', including social-psychological and evolutionary explanations. • Research into intense fandom, including celebrity worship and celebrity stalking.

MEDIA INFLUENCES ON PROSOCIAL BEHAVIOUR

Studies of media effects primarily focus on the relationship between media violence and aggression. The possible **prosocial** influences of the media, therefore, are often overlooked. Most research in this area has studied media influences on altruism (helping someone else at some cost to the helper), as well as the development of empathy and the reversal of gender and cultural stereotyping. The effect of prosocial media is not as widely studied as **antisocial** media, largely because it does not engender moral panics as violent media do. This does not detract, however, from its potential educational and social implications.

▶ Remember any of these? Early children's programmes were designed to be watched with the parent as co-viewer.

EXPLANATIONS FOR MEDIA INFLUENCES ON PROSOCIAL BEHAVIOUR

Exposure to prosocial behaviour

A commonly reported statistic is the high prevalence of violent acts shown on television. In one **content analysis** two-thirds of the children's programmes sampled contained at least one act of violence (Kunkel *et al.*, 1996). But what about the prosocial content of such programmes? Despite the moral panic over the antisocial content of popular television programmes, there is clear evidence of a comparable level of prosocial content as well. Greenberg (1980) analysed popular children's programmes in the US and found an equivalent number of prosocial and antisocial acts in any hour.

Acquisition of prosocial behaviours and norms

The major claim of **social learning theory** (Bandura, 1962) is that we learn by observation how to do things and when it is acceptable to do them. We may then imitate those behaviours, and the consequence of our behaviour will determine the likelihood of us repeating the behaviours. Unlike the depiction of *antisocial* acts on television (e.g. murder and fighting), prosocial acts are more likely to represent established social norms (e.g. helping others). Such prosocial acts are likely to *reinforce* our social norms rather than contrast with them. This also means that we are more likely to be rewarded for imitating prosocial acts than for antisocial acts.

Developmental factors

Research suggests that many of the skills that are synonymous with prosocial behaviour (e.g. perspective-taking, empathy, moral reasoning) develop throughout childhood and into adolescence (Eisenberg, 1990). Consequently, we might expect strong developmental differences in the degree to which children of different ages are influenced by the prosocial content they view on television (or in other media). This means that younger children may be less affected by prosocial portrayals in the media than older children.

Parental mediation

Although an increasing number of children watch television on their own, for many the effect of television viewing is *mediated* by the presence of a parent (as co-viewer). The significance of parental mediation was recognised by the BBC with early children's programmes, such as '*Watch with Mother*'. Austin (1993) argued that effective mediation involves the parent discussing the programme with the child, explaining any ambiguous or disturbing material and following up the concepts presented in the programme. Parental mediation has been shown to enhance the learning effect of *Sesame Street* (Rice *et al.*, 1990). Rosenkoetter (1999) suggested that with parental mediation, children as young as seven were able to understand even complex moral messages contained in adult sitcoms.

RESEARCH STUDIES OF PROSOCIAL MEDIA

Mares (1996) examined research published between 1966 and 1995 considering four main behavioural effects of prosocial television. These are described below:

Altruism (e.g. sharing, offering help) – Studies of the effects of television on altruistic behaviour typically involve explicit modelling of very specific behaviours. Sprafkin *et al.* (1975) showed that young children who watched an episode of *Lassie* where a child rescued a dog were more likely to help puppies in distress than children who watched a neutral TV programme. Mares concluded that children who saw prosocial content behaved more altruistically than those who viewed neutral or antisocial content.

Self-control (e.g. resistance to temptation, task persistence) – Mares found that when exposed to a TV model demonstrating self-control, children subsequently showed higher levels of self-control in their own behaviour. Friedrich and Stein (1973) found that four-year-old children who watched *Mister Rogers' Neighbourhood* over four weeks subsequently showed more task persistence and obedience to rules than those who watched aggressive cartoons (such as *Batman*) or neutral programmes over the same period.

Positive interaction (e.g. friendly interactions, peaceable conflict resolution) – In the study by Freidrich and Stein, observers watched the children at play, counting the number of aggressive acts, friendly behaviours, expressions of affection, etc. Those who had watched the prosocial programme behaved more positively towards each other than those who had seen the neutral programme.

Anti-stereotyping (e.g. counter-stereotypes of gender) – A typical study was Johnston and Ettema (1982), who conducted a large-scale study involving several thousand 9–12-year-old children. The children watched the television series, *Freestyle* (a programme designed to reduce sex-role stereotypes), once a week for 13 weeks. Overall, there were moderate positive effects in studies such as this, which featured counter-stereotypical themes, with children becoming less stereotyped or prejudiced in their attitudes or beliefs.

PROSOCIAL EFFECTS OF OTHER MEDIA

Research focuses almost exclusively on the effects of TV; however, Mares and Woodard (2001) considered how other media could have important prosocial effects. Children's stories have traditionally carried prosocial messages (such as Snow White, who looked after the dwarves and triumphed over the bad stepmother).

Young children are especially fond of reading such stories over and over again which reinforces the message (Mares, 1996). For an increasing number of children, computer software and the Internet are an important form of entertainment, but not yet focused on prosocial content.

EVALUATION

Exposure to prosocial behaviour

Are children exposed to prosocial programming? Woodard (1999) found that US programmes for preschool children did have high levels of prosocial content; 77% of programmes surveyed contained at least one prosocial lesson. However, the survey also found that only four of the top 20 most watched TV programmes for under 17s contained any prosocial lessons.

Acquisition of prosocial behaviours and norms

Some studies of prosocial effects (such as the study by Sprafkin *et al.* on the facing page) looked at one-shot exposures to a prosocial model. In general, the findings are that children are most affected when they are shown the exact steps for positive behaviour, such as being shown someone donating tokens (Mares and Woodard, 2001). This may be because they can remember concrete acts better than abstract ones.

Learning prosocial *norms* (rather than specific behaviours) from the media may be less common, except possibly when viewing is accompanied by follow-up discussion. For example, in the study by Johnston and Ettema (on left) the largest effects were found when the programme was viewed in the classroom and accompanied by teacher-led discussions. However, there are cases where this doesn't work. Rubenstein and Sprafkin (1982), in a study of adolescents hospitalised for psychiatric problems, found that post-viewing discussion led to *decreased* altruism. This possibly happened because adolescents have a tendency to take up a view counter to that held by adults.

Developmental factors

Despite the expectation that younger children would be least affected by prosocial programming, the **meta-analysis** by Mares (1996) found that the weakest effect was for adolescents and the strongest effect for primary-school children. Effects for preschool children were intermediate. The expectation that media may have an effect at all on the development of prosocial reasoning may be unrealistic, not just because children might not be ready to absorb such information, but because they are likely to be more strongly affected by home experiences than by media exposure.

SESAME STREET

First broadcast in 1969, *Sesame Street* was designed with deliberately prosocial aims in mind (e.g. increasing interracial harmony) and was particularly aimed at inner-city children. However, research suggests that, counter to the programme's objectives, it was children from *higher* socioeconomic backgrounds who benefited the most, presumably because of the parental mediation effects described on the facing page.

Parental mediation

Valkenburg *et al.* (1999) suggest that only some forms of parental mediation would be effective in enhancing the prosocial messages in television programmes. They found that in 'social co-viewing', parents and children might watch together but do not discuss the content. This type of mediation, they argue, is largely ineffective as a means of modifying children's interpretation of television. Only in conditions of 'instructive mediation', which involves discussion and explanation, can the parent be described as an effective mediator between TV and the child.

Prosocial versus antisocial effects

Lack of generalisation – The Mares study described opposite found that children are more likely to generalise after watching aggressive acts than after watching prosocial acts on television. In other words, they may watch a specific violent act on television and then express their own aggressive behaviour in a totally different way. Prosocial acts, on the other hand, tend to be imitated directly, with little evidence of generalisation to other forms of prosocial behaviour. This lack of generalisation therefore limits the overall effectiveness of prosocial messages in the media.

The problem of mixed messages – Lovelace and Huston (1983) suggested that prosocial effects can be achieved by setting prosocial goals against antisocial ones in the same programme. However, it seems that mixing prosocial and antisocial messages somehow reduces the effectiveness of the prosocial message. Mares and Woodards' meta-analysis (2001), for example, found that children who watched mixed messages behaved more aggressively than children who watched aggression only!

CAN YOU...?   No.13.1

...1 Outline **four** explanations of the prosocial effects of the media in about 50 words each.

...2 Outline, in 100 words, the main conclusions of research into the prosocial effects of the media.

...3 Outline **eight** critical points relating to explanations/research into the prosocial effects of the media. Each criticism should be about 50 words.

...4 Use this material to answer the following question: *Outline and evaluate media influences on prosocial behaviour.* (4 marks + 8 marks) [300-word answer]

...5 Answer the following 'apply your knowledge' question:

Consider advice that may be given to a TV production company looking to increase prosocial behaviour in viewers. (6 marks) [150-word answer]

MEDIA INFLUENCES ON ANTISOCIAL BEHAVIOUR

The question of how media violence might influence viewer aggression has been the subject of intense research for at least the last 50 years. Many studies have demonstrated an association between television viewing and subsequent aggression, yet no clear-cut answers have yet emerged about *how* television has such an influence. Edgar (1988) notes that in every country where television exists, it has generated social concern, and that public opinion, in spite of the uncertain nature of any research findings, tends to unequivocally blame the media for any rise in levels of aggressive behaviour in young people.

PSYCHOLOGICAL EXPLANATIONS FOR MEDIA INFLUENCES ON ANTISOCIAL BEHAVIOUR

Huesmann and Moise (1996) suggest five ways that exposure to media violence might lead to aggression in children.

Observational learning and imitation

Children observe the actions of media models and may later imitate these behaviours, especially when the child admires and identifies with the model. Television may also inform viewers of the positive and negative consequences of violent behaviour. Children can be expected to imitate violent behaviour that is successful in gaining the model's objectives. The more *real* children perceive violent televised scenes to be, and the more they believe the characters are like them (identification), the more likely they will be to try out the behaviour they have learned. Proponents of this explanation often point to the evidence from 'natural experiments' as testimony to the link. For example, Philips (1983) examined crime statistics for the 10-day period following televised heavyweight boxing contests, and found a significant rise in the number of murders during that period. There was no such rise after televised SuperBowl contests (American football).

Cognitive priming

This refers to the activation of existing aggressive thoughts and feelings, and explains why children observe one kind of aggression on television and commit another kind of aggressive act afterwards. Immediately after a violent programme, the viewer is primed to respond aggressively because a network of memories involving aggression is retrieved. Frequent exposure to scenes of violence may lead children to store scripts for aggressive behaviour in their memories, and these may be recalled in a later situation if any aspect of the original situation (even a superficial one) is present.

Desensitisation

This argument assumes that under normal conditions, anxiety about violence inhibits its use. Media violence, however, may stimulate aggressive behaviour by *desensitising* children to the effects of violence. The more televised violence a child watches, the more acceptable aggressive behaviour becomes for that child. Frequent viewing of television violence may cause children to be less anxious about violence. Someone who becomes desensitised to violence may therefore perceive it as more 'normal', and be more likely to engage in violence themselves.

Lowered physiological arousal

Large-scale studies of this explanation have consistently found that there are stronger desensitisation effects for males than there are for females (Giles, 2003). Huesmann and Moise report that boys who are heavy television watchers show lower-than-average physiological arousal in response to new scenes of violence. The arousal stimulated by viewing violence is unpleasant at first, but children who constantly watch violent television become used to it, and their emotional and physiological responses decline. As a result, they do not react in the same way to violent behaviour, and so are less inhibited in using it.

Justification

Violent behaviours on television may provide a justification for a child's own violent behaviour, or they may provide moral guidelines concerning what is acceptable and what is unacceptable. The ability to judge issues involving harm to others is primarily acquired through social transmission, including exposure to moral messages on television and in other media. The justification of violence in the media is, therefore, one of the ways in which children can infer standards of acceptable behaviour. Children who behave aggressively may also watch violent television programmes to relieve their guilt and justify their own aggression. When violence is justified or left unpunished on television, the viewer's guilt or concern about consequences is also reduced. The child then feels less inhibited about aggressing again. Viewing television violence may also produce attitude change and suggest that problems can be solved through aggressive behaviour.

⭐ Evaluation META-ANALYSIS (PAIK AND COMSTOCK, 1994)

A substantial number of laboratory and field experiments over the past half-century have examined whether children exposed to violent behaviour on film or television behave more aggressively afterwards. A **meta-analysis** of media violence research (Paik and Comstock, 1994) suggests that they do. They examined 217 studies of the relationship between media violence and aggressive behaviour. The studies were carried out between 1957 and 1990, with an age range from 3 to 70 years of age. They found a highly significant relationship between television violence and aggressive behaviour. The greatest effect was evident in preschool children, and the effect for males was slightly higher than it was for females.

► The 1971 film *Clockwork Orange* typified the moral panics associated with violent media. Its director, Stanley Kubrick, fed up with constantly denying the link between film violence and criminal behaviour, eventually withdrew the film from general release. It was re-released in 2000, after Kubrick's death.

Being the adventures of a young man whose principal interests are rape, ultra-violence and Beethoven.

STANLEY KUBRICK'S

CLOCKWORK ORANGE

EVALUATION

METHODOLOGICAL PROBLEMS WITH RESEARCH

Among the methodological problems with experimental studies such as Bandura's is the likelihood of **demand characteristics**. For example, Noble quotes one four-year-old who, on her first visit to the laboratory was heard to whisper to her mother: 'Look, mummy! There's the doll we have to hit!' (Noble, 1975). Laboratory experiments such as Bandura's began to die out in the 1980s, largely because of ethical concerns about subjecting children to violent media content which might then encourage increased aggressive behaviour in the child.

EVALUATION

Observational learning – Bandura's research (see pages 66–7) supports the view that children learn specific acts of aggression and also learn increased aggressiveness through imitating models, even when such models are not real – Bandura also found moderate levels of aggression when the model was a cartoon character. However, such imitation is actually quite rare outside of Bandura-style studies using specially prepared videos. There have been anecdotal claims of copycat acts of violence but no real evidence for this. For example, the two boys who murdered James Bulger (1993) were said to be inspired by the video *Child's Play*, but Cumberbatch (2001) reports that no known link was ever found.

Cognitive priming – The importance of cognitive priming was demonstrated in a study by Josephson (1987) where hockey players were deliberately frustrated and then shown a violent or non-violent film where an actor held a walkie-talkie. In a subsequent hockey game the boys behaved most aggressively if they had seen the violent film and the referee in their game was holding a walkie-talkie. Presumably the walkie-talkie acted as a cue for aggression.

Desensitisation – Cumberbatch (2001) argues that people might get 'used' to screen violence but that this does not mean a person will also get used to violence in the real world. He claims that screen violence is more likely to make children 'frightened' than 'frightening'.

Lowered physiological arousal – It has also been claimed that watching violence leads to increased arousal and thus more aggression. The *excitation-transfer model* suggests that arousal creates a readiness to aggress if there are appropriate circumstances (Zillmann, 1988). Furthermore some theorists (e.g. Feshbach and Singer, 1971) believe that watching violence has beneficial, cathartic effects – arousal allows one to release pent-up aggressive energies.

Justification – Many TV programmes have mixed **prosocial** and **antisocial** messages, for example the 1980s television series *The A Team* portrayed good guys behaving violently. Liss and Reinhardt (1979) suggest that the negative effects of such programmes support the concept of justification. The use of aggression by prosocial characters lends an aura of moral justification to their violence, with which children readily identify.

The anti-effects lobby

There is growing concern that the media are unreasonably the focus of blame for violent behaviour. The evidence, however, does not universally support the hypothesis that media violence leads to violent behaviour. Belson (1978), for example, interviewed over 1500 adolescent boys, and found that those who watched least television when they were younger were least aggressive in adolescence. However, boys who watched most television were *less* aggressive (by about 50%) than boys who watched moderate amounts. This suggests that the link between watching television and aggression is unpredictable.

A NATURAL EXPERIMENT – THE ST. HELENA STUDY

A study in St. Helena, a British Colony in the South Atlantic Ocean, which received television for the first time in 1995, contradicts many of our expectations about its harmful effects (Charlton *et al.*, 2000). Despite expectations that the introduction of television would produce an increase in antisocial behaviour, the researchers concluded that very little changed following television's arrival. The vast majority of the measures used to assess prosocial and antisocial behaviour showed no differences in either behavioural type after the introduction of television. Those measures that did show a difference were fairly equally split between positive and negative changes. Five of these showed decreases in prosocial behaviour in boys and girls, but two showed increases (boys only). There were only two significant changes in antisocial behaviour scores – both of which were *lower* after the introduction of television.

GENDER BIAS IN MEDIA EFFECTS RESEARCH

Research into media effects may demonstrate a pronounced gender bias in several ways (Boyle, 1999), including the following:

- Effects research has primarily focused on acts of male-on-male physical violence, frequently viewed within the artificial setting of the psychology laboratory. There is also no conception of how this focus on on-screen violence may affect male and female viewers' responses to the characters and situations depicted.
- Effects research has frequently used unrepresentative samples (e.g. male students) and then made generalisations about all viewers. The inherent gender bias in these studies is often hidden behind gender-neutral terms such as 'college students' or 'viewers' when describing the population from which the sample is drawn.

CAN YOU...? No.13.2

...1 Outline **four** explanations of the antisocial effects of the media in about 50 words each.

...2 Outline, in 100 words, the main conclusions of research into the antisocial effects of the media.

...3 Outline **six** critical points relating to explanations/research into the antisocial effects of the media. Each criticism should be about 50 words.

...4 Use some of this material to write 300-word answers to the following questions:

Outline and evaluate media influences on antisocial behaviour. (4 marks + 8 marks)

*Outline and evaluate **two** arguments that could be used to support the view that violent media do not lead to antisocial behaviour. Use your knowledge of psychological research in this area to justify these arguments.* (4 marks + 8 marks)

THE EFFECTS OF COMPUTERS AND VIDEO GAMES

Video games are increasingly becoming a part of the lives of children, adolescents and young adults. Violent games have raised concerns in the media and among regulatory bodies about the possible link between excessive game play and violent or antisocial behaviour in real life. This concern is based on a few studies that suggest that playing violent video games can lead to increases in violent behaviour. As is the case with other forms of media, computers have the potential for positive as well as negative outcomes. Research suggests that playing certain video games may have a range of positive effects, including increasing prosociality and civic responsibility. Our increasing reliance on computers to conduct relationships has also led to an explosion of interest in social networking sites, such as Facebook.

FACEBOOK USE AND COLLEGE GRADES

In a study at Ohio State University, Karpinski (2009) found that the majority of students who use Facebook every day underachieved by as much as an entire grade compared with those who do not use the site. The report also found that Facebook users spent between one and five hours a week studying, while non-users of the site studied between 11 and 15 hours a week. The link between lower grades and Facebook use was found even in graduate students.

THE NEGATIVE EFFECTS

Video games and aggression

Experimental studies – Lab experiments have found short-term increases in levels of physiological arousal, hostile feelings and aggressive behaviour following violent game play compared to non-violent game play (Gentile and Stone, 2005). Aggressive behaviour cannot be studied directly, as this is not permitted on ethical grounds, therefore other forms of behaviour must be used instead. For example, participants blasted their opponents with white noise (a random, multi-frequency sound) for longer and rated themselves higher on the *State Hostility Scale* after playing *Wolfenstein 3D* (a violent 'first person shooter' game) compared to those who played *Myst* (a slow-paced puzzle game) (Anderson and Dill, 2000).

Longitudinal studies – Anderson *et al.* (2007) surveyed 430 children aged between seven and nine at two points during the school year. Children who had high exposure to violent video games became more verbally and physically aggressive and less prosocial (as rated by themselves, their peers and their teachers).

Meta-analyses on the video games and aggression link – Several meta-analyses have found a consistent link between violent game play and aggressive behaviour. This association appears to hold for children and adults (Gentile and Anderson, 2003). It might be expected that there would be larger effects with newer studies as violent video games have become more violent over time. In the Gentile and Anderson study, this was the pattern found, with earlier studies showing smaller effect sizes than more recent studies.

Computers: Facebook use

Facebook friends and stress – Charles (2011) used focus group and interview techniques to investigate the Facebook habits of 200 undergraduate students in Scotland. A significant number (12%) experienced anxiety linked to their use of the social networking site. The majority who reported anxiety had significantly more friends than other Facebook users. They reported stress from deleting unwanted contacts, the constant pressure to be humorous and entertaining and worrying about the proper type of etiquette toward different friends. Of the students surveyed, 32% stated that rejecting friend requests made them feel guilty and uncomfortable and 10% reported that they disliked receiving friend requests.

THE POSITIVE EFFECTS

Video games and prosocial behaviour

Helping behaviour – Research has also shown that playing a prosocial (relative to a violent or neutral) game can increase helping behaviour. Greitemeyer and Osswald (2010) demonstrated that participants who played the prosocial video game *Lemmings*, (where they had to ensure the safety of the lemmings) subsequently displayed significantly more prosocial behaviour than those who played an aggressive game (*Lamers*), or a neutral game (*Tetris*). After playing the respective video games for eight minutes, participants saw the researcher accidentally knock a cup of pencils off a table and onto the floor. Of those who played the prosocial game, 67% helped pick up the pencils, whereas only 33% of those who had played the neutral game and 28% of those who played the aggressive game helped.

Multiplayer games and social commitment – Games that involve other players offer the possibility of social outcomes, including learning about a problem in society, or exploring a social issue. Kahne *et al.* (2008) found that the majority of those who listed *The Sims* (a life simulation game) as a favourite game said they learned about problems in society and explored social issues while playing computer games. Lenhart *et al.* (2008) carried out a large-scale US survey to investigate the influence of multiplayer game play on social commitment. They found that 64% of those who played multiplayer games such as *Halo* (where players must battle to save humankind) or *The Sims* were committed to civic participation (compared to 59% of 'solo' players), and 26% had tried to persuade others how to vote in an election (compared to 19% of solo players). They also found that those who regularly took part in social interaction related to the game (e.g. on websites or discussion boards) were more committed civically and politically.

Computers: Facebook use

Facebook and self-esteem – Gonzales and Hancock (2011) argue that Facebook walls can have a positive influence on our self-esteem, because feedback posted on them by others tends to be overwhelmingly positive. In a study at Cornell University in the US, students were given three minutes to (1) use their Facebook page, (2) look at themselves in the mirror, or (3) do nothing. Those who had interacted with their Facebook page subsequently gave much more positive feedback about themselves than the other two groups.

EVALUATION

The negative effects of video games

Problems with research evidence – A major weakness of lab experiments in this area is that researchers cannot measure 'real-life' aggression. They therefore must use measures of aggressive behaviour that have no relationship to real-life aggression, and can only measure short-term effects. Longitudinal studies are able to observe real-life patterns of behaviour and document both short-term and long-term effects. However, a problem for most longitudinal studies in this area is that participants may be exposed to other forms of media violence (e.g. on television) during the course of the study, meaning that the effect from violent video game exposure alone is uncertain.

Why might there be an effect? – Research has yet to establish a reliable causal link between violent game play and aggressive behaviour. A 'bi-directional model' (Gentile *et al.*, 2004) has been proposed whereby, although playing violent video games may cause an increase in aggressive behaviour, it is just as likely that people who already possess personality traits that orientate them towards aggressive behaviour, preferentially select violent video games for recreational purposes.

The negative effects of Facebook use

Facebook use and college grades – Karpinski acknowledges that her study does not suggest that excessive Facebook use directly *causes* lower grades, merely that there is some relationship between the two. She suggests that other personality factors are likely to be involved, and perhaps Facebook users are simply prone to distraction. However, other psychologists have gone further. Greenfield (2009), in a presentation to the House of Lords, argued that social networks such as Facebook 'infantilise' the brain by shortening the attention span and providing constant instant gratification although, as yet, she has failed to provide the evidence to support this claim.

Facebook use and stress – The stress associated with Facebook use has been supported in a case study of an 18-year-old asthmatic man whose condition was stable until he split up with his girlfriend and she erased him from her Facebook page (D'Amato *et al.*, 2010). He became depressed and changed his Facebook name in order to become 'friends' with her again, but after logging on to the site and seeing her picture, his maximum breath force was reduced, a sign of his asthma worsening. This case indicates that social networking sites such as Facebook could be a significant source of psychological stress, and a triggering factor in depressed asthmatic individuals.

EVALUATION

The positive effects of video games

Why don't prosocial video games have more of an effect? – Greitemeyer and Osswald (2010) suggest that as 85% of video games involve some kind of violence. Therefore, although the content of prosocial games can cause behavioural shifts in an altruistic direction, people who play video games are much less likely to experience this type of game, partly because they are seen as less attractive. Consequently, the video game industry is less likely to produce such games for purely commercial reasons (i.e. they are less likely to sell).

Methodological limitations – A problem for surveys in game research concerns the lack of controls for young people's prior civic commitments and prosocial activities. The lack of random exposure to civic gaming opportunities (i.e. young people choose these games rather than being randomly allocated to them) also limits our ability to make causal claims about how games or features of games influence the development of social and civic responsibilities.

Therapeutic applications of video games – Video games have been successfully used in the treatment of post-traumatic stress. For example, the *Virtual Iraq* computer 'game' is a 'fully-immersive' computer simulation, which allows soldiers suffering post-traumatic stress disorder to relive and confront psychological trauma in a low threat context. Researchers have also discovered that playing the game *Tetris* minimises the mind's tendency to flash back to memories of traumatic events (see 'Real Life Application').

The positive effects of Facebook use

How does Facebook increase self-esteem? – One explanation for the relationship between Facebook use and positive self-esteem comes from the Hyperpersonal Model (Walther, 1996). This claims that self-selection of the information we choose to represent ourselves (e.g. through photos, personal details and witty comments) can have a positive influence on self-esteem. Computer mediated communication (such as through the medium of Facebook) offers people such an opportunity for positive self-esteem as feedback left on their 'wall' is invariably positive.

REAL-WORLD APPLICATION

Research has shown that playing the computer game *Tetris* can help to reduce memory flashbacks after traumatic events. Holmes *et al.* (2010) showed volunteers traumatic images of personal injury (e.g. from traffic accidents). Thirty minutes later, some volunteers played *Tetris* for 10 minutes, some played *Pub Quiz* and some did nothing. In a second experiment, the wait between viewing the film and playing the computer games was extended to four hours. In both experiments, those who played *Tetris* had significantly fewer flashbacks from the film compared to the other groups. *Tetris* was effective as long as it was played within a four-hour 'window' after the traumatic event. This was achieved without altering the person's ability to make sense of the event. The researchers concluded that playing the game interfered with the way that traumatic memories are formed in the mind. It is thought that games like *Tetris* reduce flashbacks because they compete with the same sensory channels that are needed to form the memory.

CAN YOU...? No.13.3

...**1** Outline **two** positive and **two** negative effects of computers and/or video games in 100 words each.

...**2** Outline **two** critical points concerning positive effects and **two** for negative effects. For each, include (a) the critical point being made, (b) your evidence for this criticism, and (c) how this criticism affects that explanation.

...**3** Use some of this material to write a 250-word answer to the question: *Discuss **two or more** positive effects of computers and/or video games*. (5 marks + 5 marks)

...**4** Answer the following 'apply your knowledge' question:

A school wants to produce a leaflet about the possible effects of video games and computers on young people. Suggest what information should be included in the leaflet. Use your knowledge of psychological research in this area to justify your advice. (10 marks) [250-word answer]

EXPLAINING THE PERSUASIVE EFFECTS OF MEDIA

According to Schwerin and Newell (1981), behavioural change (e.g. living a healthier lifestyle or changing our buying habits) cannot occur without attitude change having first taken place. To alter consumer or public attitudes psychologists have developed the science of persuasion.

MAJOR FINDINGS FROM HOVLAND *ET AL.*

Source factors	Experts are more effective because they are more credible than non-experts.
	Popular and attractive sources are more effective than unpopular or unattractive sources.
Message factors	Messages are more effective if we think they are not intended to persuade.
	A message can be more effective if it creates a moderate level of fear.
Audience factors	Low- and high-intelligence audiences are less easily persuaded than those with moderate intelligence.
	With intelligent audiences, presenting both sides of an argument is more effective.

CENTRAL AND PERIPHERAL ROUTES TO PERSUASION

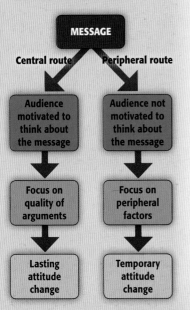

THE HOVLAND-YALE MODEL

Carl Hovland's team discovered that effective persuasion could be achieved by focusing on *who* says *what* to *whom*, i.e. the communicator (who), the persuasive message (what) and the audience (to whom). The work of this team was described in the book *Communication and Persuasion* (Hovland *et al.*, 1953). Some of the main findings of Hovland and subsequent researchers in this area are explained below and summarised on the left.

Applying the Hovland-Yale model

The source – One important source characteristic is the attractiveness of the communicator. Social psychological research has shown that attractive communicators are more persuasive than less attractive communicators (Petty and Cacioppo, 1986). For example, Bono, the lead singer of U2, has become the best known spokesperson for the plight of African nations. Celebrities such as Cheryl Cole and George Clooney appear in advertisements in order to persuade audiences to buy a particular type of make-up or drink a particular brand of coffee.

The message: do fear appeals work? Putwain and Symes (2011) investigated whether classroom fear appeals (relating to the timing of an upcoming examination) influenced examination performance among a sample of secondary school students. When fear appeals emphasised a 'mastery' approach (e.g. they included advice about how to make the most of the time before the exam), their frequency was positively related to examination performance. However, when they were perceived as *threatening* (i.e. creating greater test anxiety), they were negatively related to examination performance.

The audience – Younger people are more susceptible to persuasive messages than adults or the elderly. This has implications for the use of children as witnesses, for example in child abuse cases, when their attitudes can readily be altered by misleading information (Loftus, 2003). Children also appear to be more susceptible to the persuasive power of advertising. Martin (1997) found that whereas older children had a good understanding of the persuasive intent of advertisements (i.e. to sell products), younger children did not.

THE ELABORATION-LIKELIHOOD MODEL (ELM)

Petty and Cacioppo (1981) suggested two different routes to persuasion, depending on whether the audience is likely to focus on the message itself or on other factors, such as how attractive or credible the source appears to be. If an audience is likely to focus on the arguments (e.g. if they are of personal interest to them), then a central route to persuasion is more appropriate. If they focus more on the context of the message than the message itself, then a peripheral route is more likely to be effective. When processing by this route, individuals are influenced more by contextual cues (such as celebrity endorsement of a product or the mood created). Cacioppo and Petty (1982) suggest that some people enjoy analysing arguments (high need for cognition) and are more likely to focus on the quality of the arguments than their context.

Applying the ELM

Online shopping – Lin *et al.* (2011) asked 263 Taiwanese students to take part in an online shopping study in a virtual shopping mall. Each student had to select (for purchase) a mobile phone based on consumer reviews that had previously been selected from the Amazon.com website. The reviews for each phone differed in terms of *quality* (for example high-quality reviews were objective and supported with relevant facts, low-quality reviews were subjective and based more on emotional reaction) and the *quantity* of reviews. Students also completed a 'need for cognition' measure. Both quality and quantity of reviews positively influenced purchasing intention – students were more likely to buy a phone that had a large number of high-quality reviews. However, consistent with the predictions of the ELM, high need for cognition students placed a greater importance on review *quality* rather than quantity of reviews when making their decision to purchase.

Health campaigns – Vidrine *et al.* (2007) showed that need for cognition (NC) is also a relevant factor in real-life health campaigns. Students were exposed either to a fact-based (central route) or emotion-based (peripheral route) smoking risk campaign. Those with higher NC were more influenced by the fact-based message (i.e. the central route), whereas participants with low NC were more influenced by the emotion-based message (the peripheral route). What is also clear from research on the ELM is that when people lack expertise about an issue (e.g. HIV risks or healthy eating), they are more likely to employ the peripheral route as they consider a health message. This helps to explain why health claims unsupported by research findings (e.g. that organic food is healthier than non-organic food) are often appealing to many people.

EVALUATION

Attractive sources are not necessarily the most influential – Research on product endorsement (see pages 228–9) suggests that celebrities are not as effective as we might imagine, given the predictions of the Hovland-Yale model. O'Mahony and Meenaghan (1997) found that celebrity endorsements were not regarded as particularly convincing or believable, and Hume (1992) concluded that celebrity endorsement of a product does not significantly increase the persuasive communication of the advert. Sometimes the celebrity can overshadow the product so that people remember the celebrity but persuasion fails because they can't remember the product! This happened with the ill-fated ITV Digital TV adverts, where Johnny Vegas and Monkey became instant celebrities, but their popularity failed to rub off on the service they were promoting. ITV Digital folded in 2002 (unlike Vegas and Monkey who are still going strong!).

Fear appeals do work – Research has shown that fear appeals can be persuasive if they do not petrify the audience with fear and if the audience is informed how to avoid the danger. This was supported in a real-life anti-drug campaign. In 2008, the Australian government launched phase 4 of a campaign to warn young people about the dangers of crystal methamphetamine or 'ice' – *'Don't let ice destroy you'*. The ICE campaign used moderate fear: through explicit images, scenes and consequences (e.g. family abuse, skin abnormalities and criminal behaviour). However, it also emphasised choice, as well as opportunities for positive attitude formation and change. Although this phase is ongoing, an earlier phase (covering marijuana, ecstasy and amphetamines) found that 78% of 13–24 year olds felt that the campaign had changed how they felt about drugs.

Gender bias in persuasion research – Research suggests that women are more susceptible to persuasive communications than men. Eagly and Carli (1981) explained this in terms of socialisation differences – women are socialised to conform and therefore are more open to social influence. Sistrunk and McDavid (1971) claimed that studies find women more easily persuaded because in most cases the topic used was one with which men were more familiar. Women, they argued, would not be so susceptible to persuasive communications if the topic was one with which they were familiar (and men were not). Karabenick (1983) provided evidence to support this claim, finding that influence varied with item content: males were influenced more with feminine content, females more with masculine content.

METHODOLOGICAL PROBLEMS WITH THE HOVLAND-YALE APPROACH

Much of the early research carried out by Hovland *et al.* to develop this model used students and army personnel. As Hovland himself pointed out, it is perhaps inappropriate to generalise from these samples to the general population. These groups had an age, wealth and education profile which was untypical of the general public. The experimenters were also in a position to cut off other stimuli and demand the complete attention of study participants, something that real-life sources rarely have.

EVALUATION

Online shopping: lessons learned – Lin *et al.*'s research finding contributes to a better understanding of the effect of online reviews. For marketing executives, the peripheral route perspective demonstrates the importance of generating as many reviews as possible for a low need for cognition audience. Knowledge of the demographic profile of a target audience, e.g. their level of need for cognition can also guide Internet marketers to design appropriate promotional materials and review formats in order to influence online shoppers effectively.

Peripheral route influence may only be temporary – On 7 November 1991, the prominent US basketball player, Earvin 'Magic' Johnson Jr, announced that he was HIV positive. At the time of this announcement, psychologists Louis Penner and Barbara Fritzsche had just finished collecting data on participants' willingness to help a person with the AIDS virus. They found that that no university students volunteered when asked to help an AIDS victim carry out a school project. However, one week after Magic Johnson announced that he was a victim, the helping rate soared to 83%. Four and a half months after the announcement, helping was back to preannouncement levels, indicating that although the peripheral route influence (in this case a celebrity role model) can be considerable, there is a strong likelihood that any change produced by this route is likely to be temporary (Penner and Fritzsche, 1993).

Why do people sometimes take the peripheral route? – Fiske and Taylor (1984) claim that most human beings are essentially cognitive misers in that they frequently rely on simple and time-efficient strategies when evaluating information and making decisions. If the content of a message is not personally important, then individuals are more likely to be influenced by contextual cues (such as celebrity endorsement of a product or the mood created). However, when the content is more important, they are better motivated to process the message more carefully (i.e. take a central route). Thus, we may be influenced by Gary Lineker endorsing crisps, but not if he was endorsing mortgages or bank loans.

► Earvin 'Magic' Johnson Jr announced that he was HIV positive in 1991, resulting in a surge in positive attitudes towards people infected with HIV.

CAN YOU...? No.13.4

...1 Outline **two** applications each of the Hovland-Yale and Elaboration-Likelihood models in 75 words each.

...2 Outline **two** critical points for each of these two models in about 50 words each. For each, include (a) the critical point being made, (b) your evidence for this criticism, and (c) how this criticism affects that explanation.

...3 Use some of this material to write a 250-word answer to the question: *Discuss **two** applications of the Hovland-Yale model of persuasion.* (5 marks + 5 marks).

...4 Use your knowledge of psychology to answer the following questions:

*Discuss **two or more** applications of the Elaboration-Likelihood model of persuasion.* (5 marks + 5 marks) [250-word answer]

An online charity wants people to donate regularly to their cause. With reference to psychological research, explain two insights from the Hovland-Yale model that might help them to achieve this aim. (6 marks) [150-word answer]

EXPLANATIONS FOR THE PERSUASIVENESS OF TELEVISION ADVERTISING

Television is an important part of our daily lives. The average daily TV viewing figures over the last quarter of 2008 were at their highest level since 2004, standing at 3.9 hours per individual (IPA, 2009). If the role of television is more than just to entertain, we might also expect it to play an important role in shaping our attitudes, beliefs and ultimately our behaviours. On this spread we look at some of the different explanations for the persuasiveness (or not) of television advertising.

WWW

Are you a high or low self-monitor? Take a test at: www.outofservice.com/self-monitor-censor-test/

THE PERSUASIVENESS OF TELEVISION ADVERTISING

Television advertising has long been used as a means of persuading viewers to buy a particular product or service. Research has focused on the persuasiveness of advertising by looking at how it has shaped consumer behaviour, although this is usually measured in terms of how much consumers *like* the product after advertising rather than whether they have actually bought it.

Hard-sell and soft-sell advertising – On page 226, we covered the idea of central route and peripheral route persuasion. Advertisers sometimes refer to this distinction as 'hard sell' (presenting factual information about a product) and 'soft sell' (using more subtle and creative persuasive techniques). Snyder and DeBono (1985) found that hard-sell and soft-sell approaches had different effects on different types of people. People who scored highly on a test of 'self-monitoring' (i.e. regulating their behaviour so that they would be perceived by others in a favourable manner) had more favourable attitudes to soft-sell advertisements. People low in self-monitoring (i.e. less image conscious) preferred more factual, hard-sell approaches.

Product endorsement – Fowles (1996) estimated that in 1990, 20% of TV commercials used celebrity product endorsements. Giles (2003) suggests that celebrities provide a familiar face – a reliable source of information that we feel we can trust because of the **parasocial relationship** (see the following pages) that we have built up with that celebrity. Celebrities are also seen as a neutral source of information and so perform the function of 'rubber stamping' the advertiser's claims. O'Mahony and Meenaghan (1997) found that in general, celebrity endorsements were not regarded as overly convincing or believable, with perceived credibility and expertise of the endorser being the two 'source' characteristics with the greatest influence on any consumer purchase intentions.

Children and advertising – Do children understand that the purpose of advertisements is to persuade us to buy? Martin (1997), in a **meta-analysis** of studies, found a strong **positive correlation** between age and understanding of persuasive intent. Older children could discriminate better between commercials and regular programming, and better understood the persuasive intent of the commercials and trusted them less.

'Pester power' – It is a commonly accepted belief that advertising to young children increases the degree to which they 'pester' their parents (and others) for the products they have seen on TV. In an ingenious test of this belief, Pine and Nash (2001) studied the relationship between the amount of commercial TV watched and the number of advertised items on children's letters to Santa (see facing page). There was, needless to say, a strong positive correlation.

The importance of congruence – Bushman (2007) suggests that TV advertisements may be better remembered if there is a congruence between the programme content and the content of the ad. For example, people may be more likely to remember advertisements if they are embedded within programmes with the same type of content. This relationship can be explained in terms of the viewer's motives for watching a particular TV programme. For example, an individual may watch a programme with cognitively involving content (such as a documentary or the news) in order to gain knowledge. This motive persists throughout the whole programme so that commercials that are consistent with this motive (i.e. are also cognitively involving) would be easier to recall, and therefore their message would be more persuasive. Commercials that are inconsistent with this motive would, as a consequence, be less persuasive.

Sex, violence and persuasive advertisements – Advertisers are especially interested in making their commercials persuasive for viewers in the 18–34 years age bracket. These viewers are believed to be more susceptible to commercial influence because they have less well established purchasing habits and more disposable income that do older viewers (Hamilton, 1998). Because younger viewers also watch less television than older viewers, advertisers tend to embed their commercial messages in programmes that younger viewers like to watch, such as those that contain violence or sex. However, research suggests that advertising during this type of programme may backfire for advertisers. The content of these programmes appears to impair memory for advertising shown during the commercial breaks (Bushman, 2005), thus reducing their abilty to persuade their audience to buy.

Most research has focused on neutral adverts embedded in this type of programme, but it is possible that people would pay more attention to adverts that also have a violent or sexual theme. Research on violence in advertising is rare, but sexual appeals are a common theme in TV advertising (Bushman, 2007). There appears to be an assumption among advertisers that sex attracts attention, which increases sales. However, although sexual adverts do appeal to younger audiences, brand recall is poorer for sexual adverts than it is for neutral ones (Alden and Crowley, 1995).

Evaluation — ARE SEX AND VIOLENCE PERSUASIVE IN ADVERTISING?

Bushman (2007) tested whether sex and violence increased or decreased persuasiveness of television advertisements. Student participants were assigned randomly to watch either a violent, sexually explicit or neutral television programme. Each 40–45 minute programme was accompanied by three commercial breaks containing a total of nine advertisements, three with a violent theme, three with a sexual theme and three neutral ones. Participants were then asked to recall the adverts when the programme was over. They were less likely to remember the advertised brands when their adverts were embedded in a violent or sexual programme than when they were embedded in a neutral programme. Within these programmes, violent adverts were the least memorable and therefore the least persuasive. This study suggests that if advertisers want to increase the persuasiveness of their messages, they should avoid embedding them in programmes containing violence or sex.

To determine how 'persuasive' a television advertisement has been, researchers typically measure how much viewers *like* a product after viewing, or measure their *intention* to buy. However, for an advertisement to have been persuasive, it should lead to an *actual* purchase of the product being advertised. This, according to Giles (2003), is the major problem of this type of research. What is being measured is not the actual *behaviour* (i.e. product purchase) but a related *attitude* (liking, intention, etc.) that may, or may not, lead to a purchase.

► A Gillette advert featuring Roger Federer, Thierry Henry and Tiger Woods, was named the worst TV advert of 2008 by advertising industry magazine, *Campaign*. Research suggests that adverts such as this, which would have cost millions of pounds to make, may not be that effective in actually persuading consumers to buy.

EVALUATION

Hard- versus soft-sell advertising – Okazaki *et al.* (2010) carried out a meta-analysis of over 75 investigations to test whether 'hard-sell' or 'soft-sell' advertisements were more persuasive in terms of attitude toward a product. They found that as hard-sell techniques focus on specific, factual information (whereas soft-sell techniques are more diffuse and general), viewers generally find them more believable. However, as soft-sell techniques are focused more on generating positive emotions, they are associated with more positive attitudes toward the product than hard-sell techniques. Okazaki *et al.* also established that hard-sell techniques have a greater capacity to irritate viewers by being more direct, provocative or confrontational, thus decreasing their ability to persuade.

Does product endorsement work? – Research on celebrity endorsement suggests that it is not as persuasive as we may think. A study by Martin *et al.* (2008) found that their student participants were more convinced by a television endorsement from a fictional fellow student when buying a digital camera than by one from a celebrity. The researchers claimed that young people like to make sure their product is fashionable among people who resemble them, rather than approved by celebrities. In a study of the 'persuasiveness' of over 5,000 TV commercials, Hume (1992) concluded that celebrity endorsement did not significantly increase the persuasive communication of the advert.

Limitations of celebrity endorsement research – Erfgen (2011) claims that research on the persuasiveness of celebrity endorsement has tended to focus more on the characteristics of the celebrity and less on the characteristics of the message communicated by the advertisement. Erfgen argues that a celebrity might be portrayed as endorsing a product in a number of different ways. For example, they may endorse it in an explicit mode ('I endorse this product'), an implicit mode ('I use this product') or in a co-present mode (i.e. celebrity and product are depicted simultaneously without further explanation). Research has not considered these different endorsement modes in order to determine whether one type is more persuasive that the others.

Disentangling media and other effects – Pine and Nash's study (described on the right) found a positive correlation between exposure to commercial television and Christmas gift requests. However, this correlation was stronger for children who watched television on their own than for those who watched with their parents, suggesting that parents somehow mediate in the relationship between advertisement and subsequent behaviour. The influence of peers is also an important factor, as conversations with friends about the things they have seen in television adverts inevitably shape subsequent behaviour. Consequently, it becomes difficult, if not impossible, to confidently predict a direct causal relationship between exposure to advertisements and subsequent consumer behaviour among children.

The impact of advertising – Giles (2003) points out that the reason television and cinema advertising have been so successful is due to the fact that their adverts generally have a captive audience. However, unlike cinema audiences, television audiences have more options open to them when it comes to the viewing of adverts. For example, Comstock and Scharrer (1999) found that 80% of viewers were likely to leave the room when the adverts came on, and that when programmes were recorded, viewers tended to fast-forward through the adverts, thereby minimising their impact.

 CULTURAL DIFFERENCES

Pine and Nash (2001) studied children's Christmas gift requests (the number of items on their letter to Santa) in the US and in Sweden. In Sweden, television advertising aimed at under-twelves is banned by law. They found significantly fewer gift requests among Swedish children than among children from the US. Although there are a number of possible explanations for this cultural difference, the researchers suggest that the lack of direct advertising to Swedish children is a strong candidate.

 GENDER BIAS IN ADVERTISING AND ITS CONSEQUENCES

In television advertising, men are typically shown in stereotypical roles of authority and dominance (e.g. an 'expert' rather than a 'user') and, when shown attempting non-traditional gender roles such as cleaning or cooking, men are often represented as incompetent. Such gender stereotypes reinforce the traditional role of women as caretakers, wives or subordinates (Scharrer *et al.*, 2006). As a result, gender-stereotyped television advertisements promote acceptance of current social arrangements no matter how biased or inappropriate these representations are (Coltrane and Messineo, 2000).

CAN YOU...? No.13.5

...1 Outline, in 100 words each, research relating to **two** areas where psychologists have explored the persuasiveness of television advertising.

...2 Identify **eight** critical points and expand each to 50 words.

...3 Use some of this material to write a 300-word answer to the question: *Outline and evaluate the persuasiveness of television advertising.* (4 marks + 8 marks)

...4 Answer the following 'apply your knowledge' question:

*A health food company is about to make its first TV advertisement. Using your knowledge of psychology, suggest **two** things they should consider in order to make their advertisements persuasive.* (6 marks) [150-word answer]

THE ATTRACTION OF CELEBRITY

Jade Goody first entered the public consciousness in 2002 and rapidly became a household name before her death from cervical cancer seven years later. Jade's status as a celebrity was founded on little more than an appearance in the Big Brother house, and more than anyone she exemplifies our fascination with 'celebrity', a concept that has only recently become a topic of interest for media psychologists.

► Reality TV star Jade Goody, who died in 2009 at the age of 27, epitomised the new breed of 'celebrity' by being 'the girl next door'.

SOCIAL-PSYCHOLOGICAL EXPLANATIONS

Parasocial relationships

A **parasocial relationship** is one in which an individual is attracted to another individual (usually a celebrity), but the target individual is usually unaware of the existence of the person who has created the relationship (Horton and Wohl, 1956). Such relationships, common among celebrities and their fans, might be particularly appealing to some individuals because the relationships make few demands. Because a fan does not usually have a 'real' relationship with a celebrity, they do not run the risk of criticism or rejection, as might be the case in a real relationship (Ashe and McCutcheon, 2001).

What determines the likelihood of a parasocial relationship? – Schiappa *et al.* (2007) carried out a **meta-analysis** of studies of parasocial relationships. From this they concluded that parasocial relationships were most likely to form with television celebrities who were seen as *attractive* and *similar* in some way to the viewer. An important additional factor appeared to be that they were perceived as *real* or that they acted in a believable way. Schiappa *et al.* believed that if the celebrity acted in a believable way, viewers were able to compare how they would behave in similar situations. Although some researchers have claimed that such parasocial relationships are mainly an adolescent phenomenon, Schiappa *et al.* found no evidence of age being a predictor of their development.

The 'Absorption-Addiction model'

According to this model, (McCutcheon *et al.*, 2002) most people never go beyond admiring celebrities because of the celebrities' *entertainment* or *social* value. However, the motivational forces driving this absorption may eventually become addictive, leading the person to more extreme (and even delusional) behaviours in order to sustain satisfaction with the parasocial relationship they have developed with the celebrity. Giles and Maltby (2006) identify three levels in this process:

• **Entertainment-social** – Fans are attracted to a favourite celebrity because of their perceived ability to entertain and to become a source of social interaction and gossip, for example: 'Learning the life story of my favourite celebrity is a lot of fun'.

• **Intense-personal** – This aspect of celebrity worship reflects intensive and compulsive feelings about the celebrity, akin to the obsession tendencies of fans often referred to in the literature, for example: 'I consider my favourite celebrity to be my soul-mate'.

• **Borderline-pathological** – This dimension is typified by uncontrollable behaviours and fantasies about their celebrities, for example: 'If I walked through the door of my favourite celebrity's house she or he would be happy to see me'.

Giles and Maltby suggest that the *intense-personal* dimension of celebrity attraction can lead to the development of a passive parasocial relationship (e.g. 'If something bad happens to my favourite celebrity, I feel as if it happened to me'). With the *borderline-pathological* dimension, however, the relationship may go way beyond the parasocial, with the person believing there is a real relationship between themselves and the celebrity.

PARASOCIAL RELATIONSHIPS AND SELF-ESTEEM

Research by Derrick *et al.* (2008), with US undergraduates, examined the relationship between self-esteem, identification with a parasocial relationship and the perceived discrepancies between the ideal and actual self.

Those with low **self-esteem** saw their favourite celebrity as very similar to their *ideal* selves, but those with high self-esteem saw their favourite celebrity as similar to their *actual* selves. After writing an essay about their favourite celebrity those with low self-esteem reported feeling closer to their ideal selves and experienced a boost in self-esteem. For people with low self-esteem these benefits were unique to parasocial relationships and were not experienced in their real-life relationships.

EVOLUTIONARY EXPLANATIONS

Attraction to creative individuals

Human beings possess a love of novelty (known as **neophilia**). For females choosing a mate, therefore, this would have led to a demand for ever-more creative displays from potential partners. Mate choice in the **EEA** (environment of evolutionary adaptation) could well have favoured creative courtship displays, which would explain many of the characteristics that are universally and uniquely developed in humans, such as music, art and humour (Miller, 1998). Because musicians, artists and actors display these talents in abundance, we are inevitably drawn to them. Miller (2000) argued that although **natural selection** favours the development of skills that enhance survival, **sexual selection** might favour minds prone to creativity and fantasy. Celebrities represent this world of fantasy so we are attracted to them because of their association with it.

Celebrity gossip

The exchange of social information about other group members might have been **adaptive** for our ancestors when they started living in larger social groups. This exchange of information is what we now refer to as 'gossip'. De Backer (2005) suggests that gossip creates bonds within social groups and serves a similar adaptive function to social grooming by initiating and maintaining alliances. Gossip also functions to construct and manipulate reputations, particularly those of rivals, and to exchange relevant information about potential mates. However, we not only talk about people we encounter in real-life, but also gossip about individuals we encounter through the media. Barkow (1992) suggests that our minds are fooled into regarding media characters as being members of our social network, thus celebrities trigger the same gossip mechanisms that have evolved to keep up with the affairs of ingroup members.

EXPERIMENTS VERSUS SELF-REPORTS

Most of the research on parasocial relationships has simply involved asking people about their attitudes to celebrities. However, Tsao (1996) argues that experimental manipulations may be more effective in determining the causes of identification with a celebrity. For example, Noble (1975) created two viewing conditions – a cinema environment and television. He found that identification with media characters arose more readily in a darkened cinema environment where viewers were isolated from everyday reality. Television viewing did not invite identification as readily because the 'lights-on' environment made viewers more aware of their own identities, thus preventing them from 'merging' with the character(s) seen on screen.

EVALUATION

Parasocial relationships – Although it is commonly believed that parasocial relationships with celebrities are dysfunctional (formed on the basis of loneliness), research does not support that assertion. Schiappa *et al.*'s (2007) meta-analysis found that loneliness was not a predictor of the formation of parasocial relationships. In fact, some research suggests that people who are more socially active and socially motivated are more likely to engage in parasocial relationships than those who are not (Sood and Rogers, 2000).

Benefits of parasocial relationships – Parasocial interactions with celebrities offer many social benefits. They provide models of social behaviour (such as intimacy and generosity) and an opportunity to learn cultural values (such as the importance of marriage). Perse and Rubin's study of parasocial relationships with soap-opera characters (Perse and Rubin, 1989) found that, due to the fact that people are exposed to the same characters over and over again, one benefit of parasocial interaction is a perceived reduction in uncertainty about social relationships.

The absorption-addiction model: links to mental health – Maltby *et al.* (2003) used the *Eysenck Personality Questionnaire* (EPQ) to assess the relationship between level of celebrity worship and personality. They found that whereas the *entertainment-social* level was associated with extraversion, the *intense-personal* level was associated with **neuroticism**. As neuroticism is related to anxiety and depression, this provides a clear explanation of why higher levels of celebrity worship are related to poorer mental health. Maltby *et al.* suggest that future research might explore the implications of a reported connection between the *borderline-pathological* level of celebrity worship and **psychoticism**, as measured on the EPQ.

EVALUATION

Evidence for an evolved love of creativity – Shiraishi *et al.* (2006) discovered an enzyme correlated with novelty-seeking tendencies. Genetic differences mean that people produce different variations of an enzyme called **MAOA** (monoamine oxidase A). The researchers found that one form of this enzyme was significantly associated with higher scores of novelty-seeking, suggesting that there may be a genetic origin for neophilia and our attraction to creative people.

The arbitrary nature of sexual selection explanations – Suggesting that a love of novelty, and therefore an attraction to creative people, arose because early females preferred creative behaviour in potential mates tells us nothing about *why* they would prefer it. Sexual selection explanations are arbitrary because they argue that traits are preferred simply because they would have been 'attractive'. Such explanations do not provide an adequate adaptive reason to explain why traits such as creativity in music, art and humour would have been attractive to ancestral members of the opposite sex.

Research support for the adaptive role of celebrity gossip – De Backer (2007) surveyed over 800 participants to test evolutionary explanations for celebrity gossip. Participants reported that gossip was seen as a useful way of acquiring information about social group members. Media exposure was also found to be a strong predictor of interest in celebrities. De Backer concluded that media exposure would lead to the misperception that celebrities were actually a part of the social network, thus explaining the interest in celebrity gossip.

ATTACHMENT STYLE AND PARASOCIAL RELATIONSHIPS

Researchers have explained why some people are more vulnerable to the formation of parasocial relationships through the concept of attachment style. Cole and Leets (1999) reported that individuals with **anxious-ambivalent** attachment were most likely, and **avoidant** individuals least likely to enter into parasocial relationships. Anxious-ambivalent attachment is characterised by a concern that others will not reciprocate one's desire for intimacy. Coles and Leets argued that individuals with an anxious-ambivalent attachment style turn to TV characters as a means of satisfying their 'unrealistic and often unmet relational needs'. People with an avoidant attachment style, on the other hand, find it difficult to develop intimate relationships and therefore are less likely to seek real-life *or* parasocial relationships.

PARASOCIAL RELATIONSHIPS AND EATING DISORDERS

Research by Maltby *et al.* (2005) found evidence of a relationship between attitudes to celebrities and body image among female adolescents. This was strongest in girls between the ages of 14 and 16, and suggests that parasocial relationships with celebrities who are perceived as being slim and with a good body shape may lead to a poor body image in female adolescents, and consequently may predispose them to eating disorders, such as **anorexia nervosa** or **bulimia nervosa**. No relationship was found in male adolescents, and research suggests that for females, the relationship disappears in early adulthood.

► Bolivian natives gather to chew coca leaves. Gatherings such as this have for thousands of years provided an opportunity to swap gossip and gather information about other group members.

CAN YOU...? No.13.6

...1 Outline, in 100 words each, social-psychological and evolutionary explanations of the attraction of celebrity.

...2 Outline **three** critical points for each explanation and expand each to 50 words.

...3 Use some of this material to write a 300-word answer to the question: *Outline and evaluate **two** explanations of the attraction of celebrity.* (4 marks + 8 marks) [300-word answer]

The existence of celebrities has led to a related phenomenon, the behaviour of fans. Although celebrity worship can exist at fairly innocent levels, once a fan goes beyond the 'passive' interactions associated with **parasocial relationships** and begins to 'stalk' a celebrity, the relationship enters a whole new dimension, much to the distress of the victim.

CELEBRITY WORSHIP

Measuring celebrity worship

Most research on celebrity worship has used the *Celebrity Attitude Scale* (CAS), a 17-item scale with the lower scores indicating more individualistic behaviour (e.g. watching or reading about celebrities) and higher scores indicating over-identification and obsession with celebrities. Maltby *et al.* (2006) used this scale to produce the three levels of parasocial relationships described on page 230: *entertainment-social*, *intense-personal* and *borderline-pathological*.

How common is celebrity worship?

Although it is commonly assumed that celebrity worship is an uncommon phenomenon, a study by Maltby *et al.* (2003) found that over one-third of a combined sample of students and workers scored above the midpoints of the three subscales of the CAS. A later study (Maltby *et al.*, 2004) found that in a sample of 372 people aged 18–47, 15% were at the *entertainment-social* level of celebrity worship, 5% at the *intense-personal* level, and less than 2% would be considered *borderline pathological*.

Celebrity worship and developmental problems

Celebrity worship has been associated with less desirable developmental outcomes. In a telephone survey of 833 Chinese teenagers, Cheung and Yue (2003) found that 'idol worship' was associated with lower levels of work or study and lower **self-esteem** and less successful identity achievement. Those teenagers who worshipped idols from television demonstrated the lowest levels of identity achievement.

Maltby *et al.* (2001) concluded that celebrity worshippers have lower levels of psychological wellbeing than non-worshippers. Data from 307 UK adults identified that whereas scores on the *entertainment-social* subscale of the CAS predicted patterns of social dysfunction, scores on the *intense-personal* subscale predicted both depression and anxiety scores. The authors conclude that celebrity worship is a behavioural representation of poor psychological well-being, which results from failed attempts to escape from or simply cope with the pressures of everyday life (Maltby *et al.*, 2001).

PARASOCIAL BEREAVEMENT

Parasocial bereavement was described by Giles (2003) as the grief felt at the death of a celebrity. Giles and Naylor (2000) analysed tributes left on the BBC website following the death of Diana, Princess of Wales and BBC presenter Jill Dando, both of whom died in tragic circumstances. These tributes revealed the nature of the parasocial relationships (see page 230) formed with these two 'celebrities'. Many of those who posted messages wrote about how they had come to 'know' Diana and Jill, even though they had never met, and many revealed how they were 'taken aback' by the strength of their feelings following their deaths.

CELEBRITY STALKING

Although opinions vary, most people think that stalking places the person being stalked in fear for their safety. Stalking involves repeated and persistent attempts to impose unwanted communication and/or contact on another person, e.g. through telephone calls, e-mail, and by approaching and following the target person. If a fan's attempts to contact or approach a celebrity are unwanted, repetitive and provoke fear in the celebrity, then their behaviour might be labelled as criminal harassment or stalking (Meloy, 1998).

Types of celebrity stalker

Two types of stalker have been identified. About one in five stalkers develop a *love obsession* or fixation with another person (such as a celebrity) with whom they have no personal relationship. Stalkers of this type suffer from *delusional thought patterns* and many suffer from a mental disorder, such as **schizophrenia** (Meloy, 2001). Since most are unable to develop normal personal relationships through more conventional means, they retreat into a life of fantasy relationships with individuals they hardly know, if at all. They may invent fictional stories, casting celebrities in the lead role as their love interest. They then attempt to act out these fictional scripts in real life. The second, more common *simple* obsessional stalking-type is distinguished by some previous personal relationship having existed between stalker and victim before the stalking behaviour began.

Attachment style – Bartholomew and Horowitz (1991) proposed a model of adult attachment styles based on individual working models of self and others. One of these, the 'pre-occupied' attachment style, has been linked to the phenomenon of celebrity stalking. Individuals with this type of attachment style have a negative self-model and a positive other-model. They have a poor self-image and a positive image of others. Because of this, such individuals actively seek approval and personal validation from others. Meloy (1996) claims that celebrity stalking could be considered to be indicative of an abnormal attachment similar to the pre-occupied attachment style. Individuals with this type of attachment style may engage in celebrity stalking because they overvalue others and perceive that contact with celebrities will indicate that they are acceptable and valued, thus challenging their negative views of self.

▲ Robert Hoskins (above, left) was sentenced to 10 years in prison for stalking and terrorising the singer Madonna. He had even threatened to slash her throat if she did not agree to marry him.

▶ Actress Uma Thurman (right), star of the *Kill Bill* films, was stalked by an obsessed fan for two years. Jack Jordan, a 35 year-old former psychiatric patient, was arrested in 2007 after camping outside her house, trespassing on a movie set and even drawing a bizarre cartoon of Thurman digging a grave for him. Jordan sent the star a letter in which he threatened to kill himself if he ever saw her out with another man again.

EVALUATION OF CELEBRITY WORSHIP

The limited benefits of 'celebrity' worship – The Cheung and Yue study described on the facing page, found that teenagers who 'worshipped' key family members, teachers or other individuals with whom they came into regular contact tended to demonstrate higher levels of self-esteem and educational achievement than teenagers who worshipped television stars. This is understandable given that the admiration of those who are able to provide tangible benefits and inputs to the adolescents' lives would be more likely to provide a greater positive impact than those celebrities with whom they enjoy only a parasocial relationship.

Negative consequences of celebrity worship – Research (e.g. Phillips, 1974) has shown that high-profile celebrity suicides are often followed by increased numbers of suicides among the general population. Sheridan *et al.* (2007) make the point that pathological worshippers are often drawn to more entertaining, even antisocial celebrities, so we might, therefore, expect fans of more rebellious celebrities such as the late Amy Winehouse or Pete Doherty to seek to emulate them, with negative consequences for the worshipper. As celebrity deaths are more likely than non-celebrity deaths, Wasserman (1984) warns that when reporting celebrity suicides, the media should not let the glamour associated with that individual obscure any mental health or drugs problems from which they may have been suffering.

An evolutionary explanation for celebrity worship – Evolutionary psychologists suggest that it is natural for humans to look up to those individuals who receive attention because they have succeeded in our society. For our ancestors, this would have meant respecting good hunters and elders. Because hunting is no longer an essential skill, we may look to celebrities, whose fame and fortune we would like to emulate. It makes a good deal of evolutionary sense to value individuals according to how successful they are, because whoever is getting more of what everybody wants is probably using above-average methods to get them, therefore would serve as a valuable role model.

EVALUATION OF CELEBRITY STALKING

Anti-stalking legislation – Although laws that address stalking have emerged, a continuing problem is that many of the strategies employed by celebrity stalkers, such as being in the same place as the victim, are basic rights and freedoms that are guaranteed by law. Similarly, as fans are encouraged to be adoring it becomes difficult to assess when fan behaviour actually becomes stalking. The impact of stalking behaviour on its victims has led to the development of anti-stalking laws in the UK and US. Perhaps not surprisingly, given the number of celebrities who live there, California has the broadest set of anti-stalking laws. For example, in 1996 Robert Hoskins was given a ten-year prison sentence after he was convicted of stalking Madonna in her Hollywood home.

Stalking as an indication of attachment difficulties – Tonin (2004) provided evidence to support the proposition that celebrity stalking might be explained in terms of abnormal attachment. She measured stalkers' retrospective childhood attachment styles and their current adult attachment using two self-report measures. In order to see if stalkers detained under the Mental Health Act were less securely attached than non-stalkers, she compared them to two other groups: 24 people detained in the same way but with no history of stalking, and a non-clinical community sample of 33. It was found that the stalkers had significantly more evidence of insecure adult attachment styles than the control group.

Real-world application: psychological profiles and clinical interventions – Roberts (2007) found that individuals with low self-esteem who were motivated to approach others for self-validation, were also more prone to celebrity stalking. This pattern of attachment is typical of the preoccupied attachment style identified by Bartholomew and Horowitz (1991), and supports an association between preoccupied attachment and the likelihood of approach behaviour towards celebrities. Roberts suggests that this finding has a number of important implications, including the police being able to draw a psychological profile of an unknown offender after persistent and unwanted attempts to contact a particular celebrity. Similarly, for persistent stalking offenders, clinical interventions may then be designed to help them overcome their attachment difficulties.

▶ People who are drawn to 'notorious' celebrities such as Pete Doherty (right) may seek to emulate their bad behaviour.

Evaluation — CELEBRITY WORSHIP AND RELIGIOSITY

'You shall not make for yourself an idol'

Within the Christian religion, the Ten Commandments forbid the worship of anyone other than God. We might expect, therefore, that there would be a negative relationship between celebrity worship and **religiosity** (i.e. strength of religious adherence). To test this hypothesis, Maltby *et al.* (2002) compared participants' scores on different religiosity measures against scores on the *Celebrity Attitude Scale* (CAS). They did indeed find that as religiosity *increased* (for both men and women), the tendency to worship celebrities *decreased*.

Evaluation — THE PSYCHOPATHOLOGY OF STALKERS

Maltby *et al.* (2006) claim that the tendency to engage in stalking behaviour may actually be indicative of an underlying psychopathology. They found that scores on a measure of obsessive compulsive disorder (OCD) correlated significantly with revised measures of the CAS-intense-personal and CAS-borderline-pathological (but not the entertainment-social subscale). Stalkers sometimes behave irrationally towards their victims, in ways that clearly reflect an underlying psychopathology (Cupach and Spitzberg, 1998). For example, those who score high on the borderline-pathological subscale of the CAS endorse irrational items such as: 'If I were lucky enough to meet my favorite celebrity, and he/she asked me to do something illegal as a favour, I would probably do it.'

CAN YOU...? No.13.7

...1 Outline, in 100 words each, research into celebrity worship and celebrity stalking.

...2 Outline **four** critical points for each of these two examples of intense fandom and expand each to 50 words.

...3 Use some of this material to answer the following questions:

*Outline and evaluate research into **two** areas of intense fandom.* (4 marks + 8 marks) [300-word answer]

*Outline **one** methodological and **one** ethical issue you might face in using a questionnaire to measure celebrity worship among the students in your class, and explain how you would overcome these issues.* (6 marks) [150-word answer]

CHAPTER SUMMARY

MEDIA INFLUENCES ON SOCIAL BEHAVIOUR

MEDIA INFLUENCES ON PROSOCIAL BEHAVIOUR

EXPLANATIONS FOR MEDIA INFLUENCES
- Equivalent number of prosocial and antisocial acts on children's TV.
- Prosocial TV reflects prosocial norms – prosocial behaviours more likely to be reinforced.
- Younger children less able to understand prosocial messages on TV.
- Effective parental mediation – discussing programmes with child.

RESEARCH STUDIES
- Mares (1996) meta-analysis – children exposed to prosocial content:
  - Behaved more altruistically.
  - Showed higher levels of social control in own behaviour.
  - Prosocial effects from other forms of media e.g. children's stories (Mares and Woodard, 2001).
  - Acted more positively towards each other.
  - Became less stereotyped in attitudes and beliefs.

EVALUATION
- TV for preschool children contained few prosocial lessons.
- Prosocial depictions more effective when concrete than abstract.
- Post-viewing discussion may enhance prosocial norms, but does not always work.
- Strongest effects for pre-school children, weakest for adolescents.
- 'Instructive mediation' effective, 'social co-viewing' ineffective.
- Mixing prosocial and antisocial messages reduces the effectiveness of prosocial message.
- Zimmerman *et al.* (2007) - Baby Einstein (italics) DVDs may lead to poorer outcomes.
- Real-world application – *Sesame Street* is more effective for children of higher socioeconomic class, possibly due to parental mediation effects.

MEDIA INFLUENCES ON ANTISOCIAL BEHAVIOUR

OBSERVATIONAL LEARNING	EVALUATION
• Children observe actions of models and may later imitate them. • More likely to be imitated if perceived as real.	• Bandura (1963) – artificial situation, little evidence of real-world 'copycat' violence. • St Helena – no increases in aggression after introduction of TV.

COGNITIVE PRIMING	EVALUATION
• Activation of existing aggressive thoughts and feelings. • Frequent exposure leads to stored scripts for violent behaviour.	• Josephson (1987) – walkie-talkie acted as cue for aggression.

DESENSITISATION	EVALUATION
• Media violence desensitises children to its effects. • Media violence represents violent behaviour as 'normal'.	• Cumberbatch (2001) – fact that children get used to screen violence does not mean they get used to real-life violence.

LOWERED PHYSIOLOGICAL AROUSAL	EVALUATION
• Heavy TV violence viewers – lower arousal levels to scenes of violence. • Don't react in normal way to violence and less inhibited about using it.	• Excitation-transfer – violence creates readiness to aggress. • Catharsis – watching violence causes release of emotions.

JUSTIFICATION	EVALUATION
• Violent TV may justify what is acceptable behaviour. • Unpunished TV violence decreases concerns about own behaviour.	• Negative effects of exposure to violent characters on TV supports justification model. • Belson (1978) – unpredictable link between violent TV and aggression.

EVALUATION
- Problem of demand characteristics, and ethical issues of making aggression more likely.
- Gender bias – most research has concentrated on males and says little about effect on females.

THE PSYCHOLOGY OF 'CELEBRITY'

ATTRACTION OF CELEBRITY

SOCIAL-PSYCHOLOGICAL EXPLANATIONS
- Parasocial relationships (PR) – individual attracted to celebrity even though celebrity is unaware.
- Because of this, no risk of criticisms or rejection.
- Formed with those seen as attractive and similar – raises self-esteem.
- Allows person to imagine how they would act in similar situations.
- Absorption-addiction model – three levels of attraction: entertainment-social, intense-personal, borderline-pathological.

EVALUATION
- Research does not support idea that PR are dysfunctional (Schiappa *et al.*, 2007).
- PR offer benefits of models of behaviour and reduction in uncertainty over social relationships.
- Intense-personal level associated with neuroticism, borderline-pathological associated with psychoticism.
- Experimental manipulation to demonstrate importance of 'lights-off' situation in development of PR.
- Link with attachment theory – anxious attachment style and PR.
- PR with celebrities perceived as slim may lead to poor body image.

EVOLUTIONARY EXPLANATIONS
- Human beings possess love of novelty (neophilia).
- Would have led to neophilia as criterion for female choice and so evolution of these characteristics in males (sexual selection).
- Celebrities represent the creative world, so we are attracted to them.
- Exchange of social information useful for ancestors.
- No distinction between social network and familiar media, hence celebrity gossip.

EVALUATION
- Shiraishi *et al.* (2006) – genetic variations of MAOA enzyme associated with preferences for neophilia.
- Sexual selection explanations arbitrary – do not explain *why* these traits were attractive to ancestors.
- De Backer (2007) – survey provides support that celebrities misperceived as part of social network, explaining interest in gossip.

COMPUTERS AND VIDEO GAMES

NEGATIVE EFFECTS OF GAME PLAY
- Increases in aggression (Gentile and Stone, 2005) and white noise blast (Anderson and Dill, 2000).
- Longitudinal studies (Anderson et al., 2007) – high exposure to violent video games, more aggression.
- Consistent link between violent game play and aggressive behaviour (Gentile and Anderson, 2003).

EVALUATION
- Researchers cannot measure 'real-life' aggression.
- Longitudinal studies – participants exposed to other forms of media violence.
- 'Bi-directional model' (Gentile et al., 2004) explains link between game play and aggression.

NEGATIVE EFFECTS OF COMPUTERS
- Charles (2011) – anxiety linked to their use of social networking site Facebook.
- Karpinski (2009) – link between lower grades among students and Facebook use.

EVALUATION
- Karpinski study doesn't indicate causal relationship.
- Greenfield (2009) – Facebook 'infantilises' the brain.
- Link between Facebook use and stress supported in real life study (D'Amato et al., 2010).

POSITIVE EFFECTS OF COMPUTERS
- Gonzales and Hancock (2011) – Facebook walls can have a positive influence on self-esteem.

EVALUATION
- Hyperpersonal Model (Walther, 1996) explains relationship between Facebook use and positive self-esteem.

POSITVE EFFECTS OF GAME PLAY
- Playing prosocial game can increase helping behaviour (Greitemeyer and Osswald, 2010).
- Multiplayer games and social issues (Kahne et al., 2008) and social commitment (Lenhart et al., 2008).

EVALUATION
- Greitemeyer and Osswald (2010) – video game industry less likely to produce altruistic games as less likely to sell.
- Methodological limitations of surveys.
- Therapeutic applications of video games, e.g. *Virtual Iraq* and *Tetris* (Holmes et al., 2010)

EXPLAINING THE PERSUASIVE EFFECTS OF MEDIA

HOVLAND-YALE MODEL
Source factors
- Experts more effective because more credible.
- Popular and attractive sources more persuasive (e.g. Bono, Cheryl Cole).

Message factors
- Messages more effective if we think they are not intended to persuade.
- Message can be more effective if it creates moderate level of fear and linked to mastery approach (Putwain and Symes, 2011).

Audience factors
- Low-intelligence audiences less likely to process content of message so less easily influenced.
- Both sides of an argument more effective with intelligent audiences.
- Younger people susceptible to persuasive power of advertising (Martin, 1997).

EVALUATION
- O'Mahony and Meenaghan (1997) – celebrity endorsements not convincing or believable. Hume (1992) – celebrity endorsement not persuasive.
- Fear appeals persuasive if audience informed how to avoid danger (ICE campaign).
- Women more susceptible to persuasive communications (Eagly and Carli, 1981) but due to topic used in research (Karabenick, 1983).
- Methodological problems with the Hovland-Yale approach – limited research sample and artificial conditions.

ELABORATION-LIKELIHOOD MODEL (ELM)
- Central route – audience motivated to focus on message, produces lasting attitude change.
- Some people high in 'need for cognition' (NC) therefore more likely to choose this route, e.g. high NC students placed greater importance on review quality rather than quantity in online shopping.
- Vidrine et al. (2007) – NC relevant factor in real-life health campaigns, e.g. smoking risk.
- Peripheral route – audience not motivated to think about message, produces temporary attitude change.

EVALUATION
- Lin et al.'s study contributes to a better understanding of the effect of online reviews for different audiences.
- Peripheral route influence may only be temporary – 'Magic' Johnson and attitude to AIDS victims (Penner and Fritzsche, 1993).
- Fiske and Taylor (1984) – human beings are cognitive misers so may be motivated to take peripheral route with adverts.

PERSUASIVENESS OF TELEVISION ADVERTISING

ADVERTISING
- Hard sell (factual) and soft sell (subtle) techniques.
- High self-monitors prefer soft sell, low self-monitors hard sell.
- Celebrity endorsement provides someone who can be trusted but not as credible as 'experts'.
- Martin (1997) – meta-analysis found strong positive correlation between age and understanding of persuasive intent.
- Pester power of children – demonstrated in Pine and Nash (2001) study.

EVALUATION
- Hume (1992) concluded that celebrity endorsement did not significantly increase persuasive communication of adverts.
- Difficult to determine impact of exposure to commercial TV because of parental mediation and peer influence.
- Cinema advertising may be more effective than TV advertising because audience can leave room in latter.

HEALTH-RELATED BEHAVIOUR CHANGE
- Erfgen (2011) – research on celebrity endorsement ignores different modes of endorsement.
- Bushman (2007) – TV ads more persuasive if congruence between the programme content and the content of the ad.
- Brand recall poorer for sexual ads than for neutral ads (Alden and Crowley, 1995).

EVALUATION
- Sex and violence impairs persuasiveness of ads (Bushman, 2005).
- Hard-sell ads more believable but less likely to create positive attitdes and more irritating (Okazaki et al., 2010)
- Problems of measurement – in advertising research, what is measured is *attitude* rather than purchasing *behaviour*.
- Cultural differences in pester power – lower in Sweden (where direct advertising to children under 12 is banned).
- Gender-stereotyped adverts promote acceptance of current social arrangements no matter how inappropriate.
- Bushman (2007) – less likely to remember and be persuaded by ads embedded in violent or sexual programmes.

INTENSE FANDOM

CELEBRITY WORSHIP
- Measured using 'Celebrity Attitude Scale' (CAS) – produced three levels of PR.
- Maltby et al. (2003) – one-third of sample scored above midpoint of CAS, although most at entertainment-social level.
- Celebrity worship associated with lower levels of academic work and lower levels of psychological well-being.
- Parasocial bereavement experienced after death of celebrity.

EVALUATION
- Higher self-esteem experienced if 'worship' towards those who provide positive impact on person's life.
- Negative consequences of celebrity worship – copying bad or suicidal behaviour of celebrities.
- Adaptive for individuals to look up to those who receive attention for being successful.
- Celebrity stalking may be indicative of underlying psychopathology (Maltby et al., 2006).

CELEBRITY STALKING
- Love-obsessional stalkers – many suffer from delusional thought patterns, retreating to fantasy world.
- Simple-obsessional stalkers – distinguished by previous relationship with target.
- Bartholomew and Horowitz (1991) – pre-occupied attachment style linked to celebrity stalking.
- Meloy (1996) – This type of attachment style = low self-esteem and overvaluation of others.

EVALUATION
- Impact of stalking includes development of anti-stalking legislation.
- Tonin (2004) – stalkers show more evidence of insecure attachment styles.
- Roberts (2007) – individuals with low self-esteem and motivated to approach others more prone to stalking.
- Implications for police profiling and clinical intervention.
- Mullen et al. – identified five types of stalker, each linked to a different form of psychopathology.

QUESTION
(a) Describe and evaluate explanations of media influences on prosocial behaviour. *(4 marks + 10 marks)*
(b) Outline the Elaboration-likelihood model (ELM). Explain how a car manufacturer might use knowledge of the ELM in a campaign to market a new model. *(4 marks + 6 marks)*

STUDENT ANSWER

(a) *Media influences on prosocial behaviour can be explained in terms of norm acquisition. In other words, watching someone else behaving prosocially sets an expectation of what counts as 'normal' behaviour and this then affects the viewer's behaviour. However, the acquisition of new norms is a slow process and likely to be counteracted by the norms that exist within the child's own life.*

A different explanation might be in terms of social learning theory and modelling. This is supported by a study by Sprafkin et al. (1975) who showed a video of children being helpful. Children who saw the video later modelled the same behaviour (helping puppies).

Age is another explanation for media influences. Media influences vary depending on age. Younger children should be less likely to be affected by what they experience on television and in the media generally because they are still developing their own views and are therefore not ready to acquire information about, for example, perspective-taking. However, Mares (1996) found that in fact adolescents were least affected and younger children were most affected.

Another explanation for media influences is that parents tend to mediate what children watch and can emphasise prosocial information. Watching prosocial videos is likely to be most effective when it is accompanied by discussions about the actors' behaviour. For example, parental involvement has been shown to increase the prosocial message of a programme like Sesame Street (Rice et al., 1990). Rubenstein and Sprafkin (1982) found that this doesn't always work with adolescents. They found that some adolescents actually became less prosocial after such discussions, although this may be because they wished to take up a contrary position.

There are fewer explanations of the prosocial effects of the media than antisocial effects. This may be because prosocial effects tend to be more abstract, whereas aggressive acts are more concrete and easier to explain. It also seems that children do not generalise prosocial acts as much as antisocial acts – they imitate specific things they have seen but don't apply them to other situations. In the case of antisocial behaviour, for example, one of the effects is general desensitisation to aggressive behaviour whereas this doesn't seem to happen with prosocial effects.

(b) *The elaboration-likelihood model claims there are two routes to persuasion. The first of these is the central route. This focuses more on presenting information and arguments and is more effective at persuading an audience if they are motivated to think about the presented information. The second route is the peripheral route, which focuses more on the context of a message, for example by having a celebrity endorse a particular product. This works when an audience is more likely to be swayed by the context of a message than the message itself.*

A car manufacturer may also have different audiences, for example companies buying fleet cars as well as private owners. For the trade customers, messages would be more persuasive if they took the central route emphasising things like fuel economy and cost of servicing. Fleet buyers would be more likely to consider this information to be vital when making a buying decision, so a central route would be more effective.

A private owner often buys a car for very different reasons. They may be more interested in image, how other people will view them if they drive a particular car, and whether driving a particular car would be viewed as a measure of personal success. As a result, things like celebrity endorsement would be important when making a decision, so a peripheral route would be more effective.

[591 words]

EXAMINER COMMENTS

Both parts of this question require **AO1** and **AO2** content.

The first explanation is described in **reasonable detail**. The **evaluation** is **basic**, although **reasonably effective**. It could be improved by explaining the concept of 'norms that exist in the child's own life'.

The second explanation is very brief but supported by clearer **evaluation** (in the form of research evidence).

In the third paragraph a further explanation is offered, thus increasing the **breadth** of this essay and beginning to counterbalance the **lack of depth**. The trade-off between depth and breadth is important in gaining top marks – there needs to be evidence of both. The explanation is **reasonably detailed** and the **evaluation** again makes use of research evidence, but shows little **evidence** of **elaboration**.

The fourth explanation is supplemented by the example from *Sesame Street*, making the description **reasonable**, although it needs research evidence to extend the explanation.

The final paragraph offers some further **evaluation**.

This student has presented antisocial explanations as a contrast to prosocial explanations, thus maintaining their **AO2** nature.

AO1 – The rather **basic** descriptions are offset by a **good range** of explanations, making the description **reasonable**.

AO2/AO3 – The **evaluation** has been elaborated in places, but often not, which averages out as a **reasonable** answer but tending towards **basic**, as the fact there are far more marks available for AO2 appears to have been ignored.

The first paragraph deals effectively and efficiently with the **AO1** requirement of the question. There is an appropriate amount of detail and there is due regard to the number of marks available for this component of the question.

The ELM is explicitly used to explain when and why the two different routes might be taken within this particular context and why they would be effective with the two different audiences.

For the **AO1** component, the answer is **coherent**, with knowledge and understanding **accurate and well-detailed**.

AO2/AO3 – **Well-focused** and **effective** application of knowledge (**AO2**), demonstrating **sound analysis** and **understanding**.

Chapter 14
The psychology of addictive behaviour

SPECIFICATION

The psychology of addictive behaviour	
Models of addictive behaviour	• Biological, cognitive and learning approaches to explaining initiation, maintenance and relapse, and their applications to smoking and gambling.
Vulnerability to addiction	• Risk factors in the development of addiction, including stress, peers, age and personality. • Media influences on addictive behaviour.
Reducing addictive behaviour	• The theory of planned behaviour as a model for addiction prevention. • Types of intervention and their effectiveness, including biological, psychological and public health interventions.

THE BIOLOGICAL APPROACH

Biological models of addiction emphasise the influence of **genetic** and **neurochemical** factors in the onset, maintenance and relapse of addictive behaviours. Addiction to smoking occurs when an individual has developed an uncontrollable dependence on cigarettes such that they find it almost impossible to stop smoking. Researchers tend to use the term 'pathological gambling' to indicate a progressive addiction characterised by increasing preoccupation with gambling, a need to bet more money more frequently, 'chasing' losses, and loss of control over gambling behaviour.

BIOLOGICAL EXPLANATIONS OF GAMBLING

Pathological gambling is a major psychiatric disorder. DSM-IV-TR diagnostic criteria focus on three areas: (1) the individual demonstrates a loss of control of gambling behaviour; (2) they exhibit a progressive increase in gambling frequency, time spent thinking about gambling, etc.; (3) they also continue to gamble despite negative repercussions on their life.

Initiation

The role of genetics – Studies have shown that pathological gambling runs in families. Although many attribute this to social-modelling influences, it is also possible that it could be due to genetic as well as environmental factors. A twin study by Shah et al. (2005) found evidence of genetic transmission of gambling in men. Black et al. (2006) found that the **first-degree relatives** of pathological gamblers were more likely to suffer from pathological gambling than were more distant relatives, thus demonstrating a strong genetic link.

Maintenance

The pituitary-adrenal response – Recent research suggests that pathological gambling is associated with an underactive pituitary-adrenal response to gambling stimuli. Paris et al. (2010) measured gamblers' **cortisol** (the stress hormone associated with the pituitary-adrenal response) levels before and after watching a video of their preferred mode of gambling (e.g. slot machines, lottery tickets), and a video of neutral stimuli (a rollercoaster ride). Recreational gamblers had significantly increased salivary cortisol levels after both videos, whereas pathological gamblers demonstrated no salivary cortisol increase in response to either video.

Sensation-seeking – Zuckerman (1979) claimed that there are individual differences in the need for optimal amounts of stimulation. Sensation seekers look for varied or novel experiences. High sensation-seekers have a lower appreciation of risk and anticipate arousal as more positive than do low sensation-seekers, and therefore are more likely to gamble.

Relapse

Boredom avoidance – The pathological gambler is seen as a person who needs this intense stimulation and excitement. Blaszczynski et al. (1990) found that poor tolerance for boredom may contribute to repetitive gambling behaviour. Pathological gamblers had significantly higher boredom proneness scores than a control group of non-gamblers. There were no significant differences between the different types of gambling (e.g. betting on horses, slot machines, etc.).

BIOLOGICAL EXPLANATIONS OF SMOKING

Initiation

The role of genetics – Family and twin studies estimate the **heritability** of tobacco smoking to be between 39% and 80%. Vink et al. (2005) studied 1,572 Dutch twin pairs. They found that for both males and females individual differences in smoking initiation were explained by genetic (44%) and environmental (56%) influences. Likewise, a US study of 348 identical twin pairs and 321 same-sex fraternal twin pairs estimate the heritability for regular smoking to be 42% (Boardman et al. 2008).

Maintenance

The effects of nicotine – Vink et al. also reported that nicotine dependence was influenced primarily by genetic (75%) factors. This suggests that although the initiation of smoking might be influenced more by environmental factors, regular tobacco use is linked more strongly to individual differences in nicotine metabolism. Nicotine affects brain chemistry by activating *nicotinic acetylcholine* receptors (nAchRs) in the brain, which leads to the release of **dopamine**. These chemical reactions create short-lived feelings of pleasure for the smoker, who then experiences impairment of mood and concentration within hours of their last cigarette as nicotine level drops in the blood. These effects can be alleviated by smoking another cigarette. Smokers repeat this cycle many thousands of times in order to avoid withdrawal symptoms when not smoking.

Pre-natal exposure to nicotine – Research suggests that mothers who smoked heavily while pregnant were more likely to have children who, should they start smoking, were more likely to become addicted (see box below).

Relapse

Twin studies suggest that the ability to quit smoking is also subject to genetic influences. For example, Xian et al. (2003) carried out a twin study to test whether genetic risk factors contributed to failed attempts to quit smoking. They found that 54% of the risk for quit failure could be attributed to heritability. Research (e.g. Uhl et al. 2008) has also attempted to identify the specific gene clusters associated with quit success and with nicotine dependence, with the aim of matching specific antismoking treatments with the smokers most likely to benefit from them.

SMOKING IN PREGNANCY AND LATER ADDICTION

Buka et al. (2003) found that although an expectant mother's smoking during pregnancy did not increase the likelihood that her child will later try smoking or become a regular smoker, women who smoked heavily during pregnancy doubled the risk of their child becoming addicted to tobacco if they did begin smoking. They collected data from 1,248 women aged 17 to 39, between 1959 and 1966.

Children of women who smoked at least 20 cigarettes a day during pregnancy were more likely to become addicted to nicotine or progress from regular smoking to addiction as adults, compared with children of women who smoked fewer than 20 cigarettes a day. Associations between maternal smoking during pregnancy and offspring's future smoking were independent of **socioeconomic** status, maternal age at pregnancy and sex of offspring.

EVALUATION

Gambling

Explaining individual differences – Genetic explanations can explain why some people develop pathological gambling yet others who have the same environmental experiences and life pressures do not. Some people are more vulnerable to develop an addiction because of their genetic predisposition (i.e. the diathesis-stress model). This idea of genetic vulnerability may also explain why some people are more resistant to treatment for their addictive behaviours, and more likely to relapse.

Ignores environmental and situational factors – Explaining pathological gambling in terms of biological factors alone ignores the importance of external factors in the development of gambling behaviour. These include factors such as accessibility to gambling opportunities, incentives to gambling (such as free bets and peer pressure) and the provision of alcoholic drinks while gambling. Therefore, it is more likely that addictive gambling is a product of biological factors, which may predispose them to excessive gambling, plus external factors, together with the interaction between them.

Explanatory limitations of the biological approach – Explanations based on genetics or sensation-seeking cannot explain why some types of gambling (e.g. online and video gambling) are more addictive than others. For example, Breen and Zimmerman (2001) found that men and women who got hooked on video gambling became compulsive gamblers in about one year. In other forms of gambling, such as betting on horses or sports, it tended to take over 3½ years before gamblers were at risk of developing compulsive gambling addiction.

Smoking

Supporting research evidence – Supporting evidence for genetic influence on smoking behaviour comes from an Icelandic study (Thorgeirsson et al., 2008). They identified a specific gene variant on chromosome 15 that influenced the number of cigarettes smoked per day, nicotine dependence and the risk of developing smoking-related diseases. Smokers who smoked less that ten cigarettes a day were less likely to have this variant of the gene than those who smoked more than ten a day. This suggests that genetic factors may not determine smoking initiation, but make it more likely that some smokers will become dependent on nicotine once they do start smoking.

Limitations of biological explanations – A problem for biological explanations of addiction is that they neglect other possible determining factors, including the social context of smoking behaviour (see 'reductionism' feature above). However, by regarding smoking addiction as a biological problem, this creates the possibility that it may be treated by various pharmacological methods.

Implications for treatment – Genomic medicine involves screening people to identify those who carry genes that increase their susceptibility to specific diseases or addictions. Individuals who are found to have a higher genetic risk of smoking addiction could then be advised to change their behaviour (e.g. stop smoking) or seek medical treatment to reduce their chances of developing smoking related diseases. Smoking does appear to be a good candidate for this approach, given the large public health burden caused by smoking, as well as the increasing evidence of a genetic contribution. However, Gartner et al. (2009) suggest that, at present, screening for genetic susceptibility to smoking is unlikely to be successful, given the relatively small associations between specific genes and smoking addiction that have been reported to date.

CAN YOU...? No.14.1

...**1** Outline the biological approach to smoking addiction and the biological approach to gambling addiction in 200 words each.

...**2** Outline **four** critical points for each of these explanations. Each criticism should be about 50 words.

...**3** Outline, in about 75 words each, biological explanations for the initiation, maintenance and relapse of smoking and gambling addiction.

...**4** Answer the following 'apply your knowledge' questions:

Gareth started playing poker with his friends just for fun, now he finds himself increasingly drawn into a world of online betting and casino gambling that is getting out of control.

(a) *Using your knowledge of psychology, explain some of the likely reasons why Gareth finds it difficult to give up his gambling.* (6 marks) [150-word answer]

(b) *Using your knowledge of psychology, suggest what advice might be given to smokers on how they might prevent relapse.* (6 marks) [150-word answer]

THE COGNITIVE APPROACH

So far we have viewed addiction purely in terms of the biological mechanisms involved. A cognitive view of addiction, by contrast, emphasises habitual ways of thinking and of interpreting events that might lead to the development of addictive behaviour. From this perspective, the development of an addiction does not depend on the properties of the drug or activity alone, but also on the reasons for taking it or engaging in the activity. A person may come to rely on smoking or gambling as a way of coping with life's problems. When these coping mechanisms are used excessively, they may create more problems than they solve.

COGNITIVE BIAS IN FRUIT MACHINE GAMBLING

Griffiths (1994) set out to discover whether regular gamblers thought and behaved differently to non-regular gamblers. He compared 30 regular and 30 non-regular gamblers in terms of their verbalisations as they played a fruit machine ('*Fruitskill*').

Regular gamblers believed they were more skilful than they actually were, and were more likely to make irrational verbalisations during play (e.g. 'Putting only a quid in bluffs the machine'). They tended to treat the machine as if it were a person (e.g. 'This 'fruity' isn't in a good mood'). Regular gamblers also explained away their losses by seeing 'near misses' as 'near wins', i.e. they weren't constantly losing, but constantly 'nearly winning', something that justified their continuation.

COGNITIVE EXPLANATIONS OF GAMBLING

Initiation: self-medication

This model (Gelkopf *et al.*, 2002) proposes that individuals *intentionally* use different forms of pathological behaviour (e.g. alcohol, drugs, binge eating and pathological gambling) to treat the psychological symptoms from which they suffer. The particular activity an addict chooses is not selected at random, but tends to be one that is perceived as helping with a particular problem. For example, some activities may be chosen because they help the individual overcome anxiety, whereas others, such as gambling, appear to help with the depression associated with poverty and so on. Gambling might not actually make things better, but needs only to be judged as doing so by the individual to become an addiction.

Maintenance: the role of irrational beliefs

Cognitive distortions or irrational beliefs play a role in the maintenance of pathological gambling specifically (Oei and Gordon, 2008). Despite the objective probability of failure related to any games based on chance, problem gamblers frequently have irrational perceptions about their ability to influence the outcomes of their gambling. Cognitive distortions associated with gambling include the 'gambler's fallacy', i.e. the belief that completely random events such as a coin toss are somehow influenced by recent events. For example, runs of a particular outcome (two or three heads in a row) will be balanced out by the opposite outcome (the same number of tails). Illusions of control are demonstrated through the performance of superstitious behaviours, which the gambler believes helps them to manipulate the event outcome in their favour. Pathological gamblers may also show an exaggerated self-confidence in their ability to 'beat the system' and influence chance (see box on left). This is in part due to the different attributions that many gamblers make about their gambling, with success being attributed to their personal ability or skill, and failure attributed to chance factors, such as bad luck.

Relapse: recall bias and the 'just world' hypothesis

Pathological gamblers often suffer from a 'recall bias', i.e. the tendency to remember and overestimate wins while forgetting about, underestimating or rationalising losses (Blanco *et al.*, 2000). Consequently, a string of losses does not always act as a disincentive for future gambling. Such individuals believe they will eventually be rewarded for their efforts and could be motivated to return on subsequent occasions because of a belief that they 'deserve' to win, having lost so often on previous occasions (the 'just world' hypothesis).

COGNITIVE EXPLANATIONS OF SMOKING

Initiation: expectancy theory

Addicts differ from non-addicts in terms of their expectancies about the positive versus negative effects of a behaviour. Expectancy theories (e.g. Brandon *et al.*, 1999) propose that a behaviour escalates into addiction because of the expectations that an individual has about the costs and benefits of that activity. Adolescent smokers commonly report smoking when they are experiencing negative moods (Kassel *et al.*, 2007) and expect that smoking will decrease the intensity of their negative mood (Brandon and Baker, 1991). The expectancy of positive mood states (such as relaxation and increased self-confidence) has also been shown to be reasons for adolescents beginning to smoke (Mermelstein *et al.*, 2009).

Maintenance: automatic processing

Brandon *et al.* (1999) suggests that as an addiction develops, the activity is influenced less by conscious expectancies and more by unconscious expectancies involving automatic processing. This would explain the loss of control that many addicts experience in their addictive behaviour and the difficulties they experience in abstaining. Expectancies can also be manipulated to prevent relapse. Tate *et al.* (1994) told smokers that they should expect no negative experiences during a period of abstinence. This led to fewer reported somatic effects (e.g. the 'shakes') and psychological effects (e.g. mood disturbance) than a control group who were not so primed. Those told to expect somatic but not psychological problems later experienced more numerous and more severe somatic complaints than a control group who had not been told to expect this.

Relapse: assessing costs and benefits

Expectations of the costs and benefits of smoking affect an individual's readiness to quit and also the likelihood of them relapsing after they have quit. Several studies have demonstrated that smokers' perceptions of the pros and cons of smoking and of quitting affect their quitting behaviour (DeVries and Backbier, 1994). According to this perspective, those individuals who perceive smoking to have many benefits and quitting to have relatively few are the ones most likely to relapse and revert to smoking after embarking on a quit attempt.

EVALUATION

Gambling

Research support – Li *et al.* (2008) provided research support for the self-medication model. They found that, compared to pathological gamblers who gambled for pure pleasure, pathological gamblers who gambled to escape the painful reality of life were significantly more likely to have other substance dependencies. They also found that these 'self-medicating' gamblers were less likely to commit crimes to finance their gambling behaviours compared with other types of pathological gamblers. Pathological gamblers motivated by self-medication usually have substitute means to satisfy their goal, whereas those who gamble for pure pleasure do not.

Non-supporting research – Despite the logic underlying cognitive explanations of pathological gambling, research suggests that possessing relevant knowledge does not make people less susceptible to cognitive distortions. For example, Benhsain and Ladouceur (2004) administered a gambling-related cognition scale to two groups of university students, one group trained in statistics and the other in a non-statistical field. They found no difference between the two groups in their susceptibility to irrational gambling-related cognitions. Likewise, Delfabbro *et al.* (2006) found that pathological gamblers were more irrational in some forms of gambling-related cognition, but were just as accurate as non-gamblers in estimating the odds of winning.

Problems of cause and effect – The self-medication model argues that some form of psychological distress must precede drug use, as the one necessitates the use of the other. There is some evidence to support this, for example research has shown that a major depressive disorder is evident in the majority of pathological gamblers (Becona *et al.*, 1996). However, this correlation between depression and gambling does not necessarily mean that depression is the *cause* of gambling. Indeed, it is equally possible that depression is a consequence of the personal and financial costs of pathological gambling.

Smoking

Addiction or excess? – Much of the research relating to expectancy theory is concerned more with *excesses* of a particular behaviour rather than addiction to it. Research might focus on 'problematic behaviour', such as heavy smoking or excessive gambling, but rarely does it consider 'loss of control'. Addiction normally involves the individual being unable to control their behaviour, in which case it is not clear what role expectancies might play in the development of this loss of control.

Research support for the relationship between expectancies and relapse – Studies on the effectiveness of nicotine patch treatment on smoking cessation and relapse have revealed inconsistent findings, with some studies (e.g. Hurt *et al.*, 2000) finding that use of nicotine patches did not improve cessation rates among adolescents. Moolchan *et al.* (2005) showed that use of nicotine patches could increase cessation rates and reduce relapse rates, but only when accompanied by **cognitive behavioural therapy** to change the positive expectancies of smoking behaviour.

The importance of expectancies – Juliano and Brandon (2004) found that smokers reported greater expectancies that cigarettes alleviate negative mood states and craving, and had a positive effect on weight control compared with the different forms of nicotine replacement therapy (NRT) available. Therefore, smokers' positive expectancies for the effects of smoking do not appear to generalise to NRT, which might explain its relatively modest success rate for smoking cessation.

CAN YOU...? No.14.2

...1 Outline the cognitive approach to smoking addiction and the cognitive approach to gambling addiction in 200 words each.

...2 Outline **four** critical points for each of these explanations. Each criticism should be about 50 words.

...3 Outline, in about 75 words each, cognitive explanations for the initiation, maintenance and relapse of smoking and gambling addiction.

...4 Answer the following 'apply your knowledge' question:

Laura has smoked since age 14. She claims that she feels a lot calmer after a cigarette and believes that smoking keeps her slim.

Using your knowledge of psychology, explain some of the likely reasons why Laura might find it difficult to give up smoking. (6 marks) [150-word answer]

THE LEARNING APPROACH

Learning theories explain addictive behaviour without involving any conscious evaluation of the costs or benefits of a particular activity. Individuals will typically learn to perform behaviours because they are associated with the onset of something pleasant (e.g. feelings of euphoria) or the termination of something unpleasant (e.g. feelings of tension or depression). As a result, impulses to engage in behaviours such as gambling or smoking may become so powerful that they can overwhelm conscious desires to restrain these activities.

GENDER BIAS IN SMOKING ADDICTION RESEARCH

Nerín de la Puerta and Jané (2007) argue that there is an inherent gender bias in much of the research relating to smoking addiction. The onset of smoking and development of smoking addiction follows a different pattern in men and women according to López et al. (1994). They found that women start smoking later than men, and that there are gender-related differences in relation to both the stages and context of smoking. Explanations of smoking addiction generally fail to address these gender differences.

LEARNING EXPLANATIONS OF GAMBLING

Initiation

Operant conditioning proposes that any behaviour that produces a consequence that the individual finds rewarding, then becomes more frequent. Griffiths (2009) argues that gamblers playing slot machines may become addicted because of the *physiological* rewards (e.g. getting a buzz from winning), *psychological* rewards (e.g. the near miss), *social* rewards (e.g. peer praise) as well as *financial* rewards if they win. This may seem strange given that the gambler generally loses but, as Delfabbro and Winefield (1999) point out, gamblers are not always rational in their thinking, and greater weight may be given to the experience of winning.

Maintenance

Intermittent reinforcement – The operant conditioning model proposes that people continue to gamble because of the intermittent (i.e. occasional) reinforcement that is characteristic of most types of gambling. As a result, they become used to long periods without reward and their gambling behaviour is reinforced by the occasional payout.

Social approval – This type of behaviour may also be maintained because reinforcement is provided in the form of social approval from others. Lambos et al. (2007) found that peers and family members of problem gamblers were more likely to approve of gambling. Respondents who received this form of reinforcement for their gambling not only gambled more than other respondents, but also intended to continue doing so in the future.

Relapse

Conditioned cues – Addicts learn (through classical conditioning) to associate other stimuli with their gambling behaviour (e.g. the sights and sounds of a casino or the presence of other gamblers). These stimuli act as triggers for gambling because they have the ability to increase arousal. If, after a period of abstinence, an individual comes into contact with one of these conditioned cues, they are at a higher risk of relapse.

Approach-avoidance conflict – Because gambling has both positive and negative consequences for the individual, they are motivated to *approach* and to *avoid* situations where gambling is involved. This creates an approach-avoidance conflict, where motivation fluctuates between wanting to gamble and wanting to stop. Whether or not the gambler will gamble when faced with an urge to do so is related to their ability to control the increased arousal and delay their need for reinforcement.

LEARNING EXPLANATIONS OF SMOKING

Initiation

Availability of role models – Social learning theory explanations of experimental smoking propose that young people begin smoking as a consequence of the social models they have around them who smoke (Kandel and Wu, 1995). From this perspective, experimental smoking is primarily a function of parental and peer role modeling and the vicarious reinforcement that leads young people to expect positive physical and social consequences from smoking.

Popularity as a positive reinforcer – Popularity among peers may also serve as a positive reinforcer in the initiation of smoking. Mayeux et al. (2008) found a positive relationship between smoking at age 16 and boys' popularity two years later.

Maintenance

The repetition of the act of smoking thousands of times a year eventually leads to a strong conditioned association between the sensory aspects of smoking (the sight of cigarettes, smell of the smoke, etc.) and the reinforcing effects of nicotine. Although the effects of nicotine in the brain are important when first starting smoking, smoking-related sensory cues rapidly become conditioned stimuli and so activate the same brain areas, making cessation more difficult (Franklin et al., 2007).

Relapse

Conditioned cues – Cues associated previously with receiving nicotine, such as the availability of cigarettes or the smell of cigarette smoke, increase the likelihood that the smoker will respond by smoking. Hogarth et al. (2010) found that the amount of craving increased significantly when a conditioned stimulus related to smoking was presented to a smoker.

Refusal self-efficacy – A concept related to the social learning explanation of smoking is self-efficacy, a person's belief in his or her ability to succeed in a particular situation. Among adults, those who smoke more frequently have less confidence in their ability to abstain (Lawrance and Rubinson, 1989) and so are more likely to relapse.

EVALUATION

Gambling

Can't explain all forms of gambling – A problem for explanations of gambling based on operant conditioning is that it is difficult to apply the same principles to all different forms of gambling. For example, some forms of gambling have a short time-period between the behaviour and the consequence (e.g. scratch cards) whereas others (such as sports betting) have a much longer period between bet and outcome, which is also less to do with chance and more to do with the skill of the individual.

Different pathways – Blaszczynski and Nower (2002) claim different pathways for gambling that predict the likelihood of treatment being successful. Gamblers in the 'behaviourally conditioned' pathway may have begun gambling because of exposure to gambling through role models or peer groups. They tend to show the least severe gambling and gambling-associated difficulties of any pathological gamblers, are motivated to enter treatment and are more likely to be successful in curbing their gambling as a result. However, a second subgroup tends to have accompanying anxiety and/or depression, a history of poor coping skills, as well as negative background experiences and life events. These factors produce an 'emotionally vulnerable gambler', who uses gambling primarily to relieve their aversive emotional states. Unlike the behaviourally conditioned group, the accompanying psychological dysfunction in the emotionally vulnerable group makes them more resistant to change and necessitates treatment that addresses the underlying vulnerabilities as well as the gambling behaviour.

Fails to explain why only some people become addicted – This explanation of pathological gambling explains addiction in terms of the consequences of the gambling behaviour. Although this may explain why some people initially take potentially addictive drugs or engage in potentially addictive behaviour, there are aspects of addiction that are not dealt with by this explanation. Although many people gamble at some time during their lives and experience the reinforcements associated with this behaviour, relatively few become addicts. This suggests, therefore, that there are other psychological factors involved in the transition from gambling *behaviour* to gambling *addiction*.

Smoking

Role models – Many of the claims of social learning influences on the development of addictive behaviours have been supported by research evidence. For example, peer group influences have been found to be the primary influence for adolescents who smoke or use drugs (DiBlasio and Benda, 1993). Those adolescents who smoked were more likely to 'hang out' with other adolescents who also smoked. Karcher and Finn (2005) found that youth whose parents smoked were 1.88 times more likely to take up smoking. If their siblings smoked, they were 2.64 times more likely to smoke, and if close friends smoked they were up to 8 times more likely to smoke than if their parents, siblings and friends did not smoke.

Conditioned cues – Thewissen *et al.* (2008) tested the importance of environmental contexts in the urge to smoke. In one room, they repeatedly presented 33 smokers with a cue predicting smoking, whilst in a second room they presented a cue predicting smoking unavailability. Consistent with expectations, results supported the view that a cue predicting smoking later led to a greater urge to smoke than did a cue associated with smoking unavailability.

Implications for treatment – Drummond *et al.* (1990) propose a treatment approach based on the idea that the cues associated with smoking or other forms of drug taking are an important factor in the maintenance of that habit. The proposed treatment, *cue exposure*, involves presenting the cues *without* the opportunity to engage in the smoking behaviour. This leads to a phenomenon known as stimulus discrimination, as without the reinforcement provided by the actual nicotine, the association between the cue and smoking is extinguished, thereby reducing the craving for cigarettes that arises when exposed to that particular cue.

⟳ᵘᵃᵗⁱᵒⁿ THE SIGNIFICANCE OF OCCASIONAL REINFORCEMENT

Learning explanations propose that people become 'hooked' on specific activities (such as smoking or gambling) because when they engage in them it leads to some desired consequence (e.g. feeling less depressed). In real life this positive consequence is likely to be occasional rather than consistent (see page 130), as smoking a cigarette (or engaging in gambling behaviour) will not always produce a desired positive mood state or relieve a negative one.

As the world is an unpredictable place, organisms tend to learn adaptive behaviours that work to their advantage on average. Provided engaging in a particular behaviour produces the desired consequences now and then (e.g. making the person feel better), then a pattern of addictive behaviour will become established and maintained.

▲ Associations with other drug-users have been shown to explain a variety of drug habits including smoking, with imitation the major reason why young adolescents use cigarettes or other drugs.

⟳ᵘᵃᵗⁱᵒⁿ REAL-WORLD APPLICATION

Botvin (2000) suggests that effective forms of drug prevention programme should target beginner adolescents. It is at this crucial developmental period that adolescents are most vulnerable to the influences of peers in particular, and therefore most in need of drug resistance skills and social skill development. Resistance training not only teaches adolescents how to refuse drugs such as cigarettes, but also informs them of the influences of peers and adults on drug use. Botvin argues that it is imperative to equip adolescents with the anti-smoking and anti-drug messages and arguments needed to counter the pro-smoking and pro-drug messages received from their environments.

CAN YOU...? No.14.3

...1 Outline the learning approach to smoking addiction and the learning approach to gambling addiction in 200 words each.

...2 Outline **four** critical points for each of these explanations. Each criticism should be about 50 words.

...3 Outline, in about 75 words each, learning explanations for the initiation, maintenance and relapse of smoking and gambling addiction.

...4 Use some of this material to answer the following question in about 250 words:

'Over two-thirds of smokers relapse in the first three months after trying to give up.'

Discuss reasons why so many smokers relapse after trying to give up. (5 marks + 5 marks)

In the first part of this chapter we considered explanations for how addictive behaviour is initiated and maintained, and why relapse can occur. Alongside these explanations is the question of why some people are more vulnerable to addiction – for example, many people drink alcohol but only some people become addicted. One reason might be because only those individuals who are very stressed become addicted. Or perhaps it can be explained in terms of peer pressure, age or personality. On this spread we examine these four possible risk factors.

PERSONALITY AND MOBILE PHONE ADDICTION

'They were brought in after spending an average of six hours a day on their phones, talking, texting or playing games. Their parents became concerned that the children, aged 12 and 13, were unable to carry out normal activities without their handsets. They were failing at school and deceiving relatives in an attempt to obtain more money for phone cards'. (*The Daily Telegraph*, 2008)

When we think of addiction we usually think of smoking, alcohol and substance abuse but addiction applies to a wide range of substances and activities, one of which is mobile phone use. Takao *et al.* (2009) looked at the relationship between personality and *problem mobile phone use* (where people do not refrain from using their mobile phones despite the fact that its use is banned). This kind of mobile phone use can be considered to be an addiction-like behaviour.

Takao *et al.* issued questionnaires to over 400 college students and found that the problematic mobile phone user tended to be low in self-esteem and high in self-monitoring (the tendency to monitor and regulate how other people see you – your public self). This supports the view that people who become addicted share certain personality characteristics.

RISK FACTORS

Stress

Everyday stress – People report that they drink, smoke, use drugs, gamble, etc. as a means of coping with daily hassles, such as relationship problems, money worries and workplace stress. Such stressors may contribute to initiation and continuation of addictions, as well as to relapse even after long periods of abstinence (NIDA, 1999).

Traumatic stress – People exposed to severe stress are more vulnerable to addictions, especially children who have experienced, for example, parental loss or child abuse. PTSD (**post-traumatic stress disorder**) is also linked to addiction. For example, Driessen *et al.* (2008) found that 30% of drug addicts and 15% of alcoholics also suffered from PTSD.

Peers

Peer pressure is cited as a reason for why adolescents start taking drugs or smoking. Among adolescents, smokers tend to befriend smokers, and non-smokers befriend other non-smokers (Eiser *et al.*, 1991). Transitions to increased levels of smoking are linked to peers' encouragement and approval, together with the message that smoking is an activity that promotes popularity (McAlister *et al.*, 1984). Two theories are particularly relevant to the development of smoking.

Social learning theory (Bandura, 1977) – Behaviours are learned through the observation of others and subsequent modelling of this behaviour. Young people are most likely to imitate the behaviour of those with whom they have the most social contact. Once they have started smoking, experiences with the new behaviour determine whether it persists.

Social identity theory (Abrams and Hogg, 1990) – This assumes that group members adopt those norms and behaviours that are central to the social identity of the group to which they belong. In peer groups where status as 'smoker' or 'non-smoker' is central to the social identity of the group, individuals are likely to be similar to one another in their smoking habits.

Age

The influence of peers on smoking and drug use appears to wane in later adolescence and the role of close friends, and particularly romantic partners, becomes increasingly important as an influence on attitudes and behaviours, especially those that are health-related (Brown *et al.*, 1997). The social crowd (e.g. peers) might have a greater impact on smoking and drug use for young adolescents, while the best friend and/or romantic partner plays a greater role later on.

Personality

The concept of an 'addictive personality' is appealing because (like all risk factors) it can explain why some people become addicted when others don't, despite the fact that both try the same experience (such as smoking). It can also explain why some people become addicted to a range of things, such as gambling, food, exercise, work and even relationships.

Neuroticism and psychoticism – Eysenck (1967) proposed a biologically based theory of personality based on three dimensions:

- *Extraversion-introversion* – extraverts are chronically under-aroused and bored, and seek external stimulation to increase their cortical (brain) arousal.
- *Neuroticism* – people high in neuroticism experience negative affect (depression, anxiety).
- *Psychoticism* – related to hostility and impulsivity (reacting with little forethought).

Francis (1996) has found a link between addiction and high scores on both neuroticism and psychoticism.

Tri-dimensional theory of addictive behaviour – Cloniger (1987) proposed three personality traits that predispose individuals towards substance dependence:

- *Novelty seeking* – trying to engage in new experiences.
- *Harm avoidance* – which includes worrying and being pessimistic.
- *Reward dependence* – the extent to which an individual learns quickly from rewarding experiences and repeats behaviours that have been rewarded.

Gambling, especially online, is big business. So it is not surprising that a number of websites concerned with selling gambling services have latched on to a 'Canadian study' that apparently demonstrates that gambling can have beneficial effects. The websites claim this study shows that cortisol levels drop by as much as 17% when players are enjoying online poker because gamblers become so wrapped up in the thrill of their poker game that they forget about external stresses and direct their mind toward other thought processes.

The issue is – what is this study? No precise reference is given and we have been unable to locate it. Without access to the actual research we cannot ascertain the validity of the methods. This is an example of 'bad science' because 'research' is used to seduce people into regarding this evidence as fact.

EVALUATION

Stress

Do addictions decrease stress? On page 240 we noted that, despite the fact that many smokers say they smoke to reduce stress, smoking actually *increases* stress levels. So stress may be a risk factor for smoking addiction but the addiction doesn't have the desired effect. Although, paradoxically, once a smoker has taken up smoking it may *become* stress reducing because the desire to have another cigarette is stressful and therefore when the smoker has one, stress is reduced (Hajek *et al.*, 2010).

Individual differences – Stress may create vulnerability in some but not all people. Cloniger (1987) suggested that there are two different kinds of alcoholics: type 1 individuals primarily drink to reduce tension (and are more likely to be female and prone to anxiety/depression), type 2 alcoholics drink primarily to relieve boredom (and have a tendency towards risk taking). Therefore, stress may explain vulnerability for some (the type 1s) but not all people.

Peers

Social learning theory – Many of the hypotheses consistent with the importance of social context in smoking have been supported by research. For example, research supports the claim that exposure to peer models increases the likelihood that teenagers will begin smoking (Duncan *et al.*, 1995). Likewise there is plentiful support for the claim that perceived rewards such as social status and popularity are instrumental in why adolescents begin smoking and remain important while they continue to smoke (Eiser *et al.*, 1989).

Social identity theory – Although there is evidence to support the claim that adolescents are motivated to begin smoking because of the stereotypes they hold of specific social crowds (Michell, 1997), little is known about the extent to which these groups influence their members to smoke. Nor do we know whether adolescents are impervious to the demands of their social group when these evidently conflict with their own concerns to maintain a healthy lifestyle.

Personality

Causality – One issue with the concept of an addictive personality relates to the fact that research is correlational only. Certain personality traits may be common amongst addicts, however this does not mean they predict addictive behaviour, i.e. the two are simply correlated.

Even if there is a causal relationship, the question is whether the personality trait or the addiction comes first. Teeson *et al.* (2002) suggest it is difficult to disentangle the effects of personality on addiction from the effects of addiction on personality.

Evidence for personality as a cause – Research has found evidence, at least in rats, that personality comes first. Belin *et al.* (2008) placed rats in a device where they could self-administer doses of cocaine. One group of rats were sensation-seekers and they immediately started taking large doses. A second group were high in impulsiveness; they started with lower doses but they, rather than the sensation-seekers, were the ones to become addicted.

Impulsivity rather than sensation-seeking – Another study, this time with humans, supports the role of impulsivity in addiction. Weintraub *et al.* (2010) assessed individuals suffering from Parkinson's disease. Such individuals are treated with drugs that increase **dopamine** levels to combat their symptoms. A side effect appears to be a 3.5 fold increase in impulse-control disorders, including gambling and sex addiction. We saw earlier in this chapter that addiction is linked to dopamine (see biological and learning models of addiction) and this study suggests that high levels of dopamine lead to impulsivity and also may cause addiction.

Role of the dopamine system – A recent study (Buckholtz *et al.*, 2010) also indicated that addictions may simply be more rewarding for people with certain personality types because those people (e.g. people high in impulsivity and sensation-seeking) have a more hypersensitive dopamine response system. Buckholtz *et al.* speculate that that a heightened response to an anticipated reward could make such individuals less fearful about the consequences of their behaviour.

▲ **Relationship addiction**
In 2007, media regulator Ofcom revealed that, for the first time, females between 25 and 49 years of age were spending more time on the Internet than men. David Smallwood, an addictions expert with the Priory Clinic in London, believes that social networking sites are to blame for the new phenomenon of 'friendship addiction'. Smallwood suggests that women are particularly vulnerable because their self-esteem stems from relationships with others, and Facebook compels them to 'acquire' hundreds of friends.

Lee (1993) suggests that research in sensitive areas creates ethical issues for the researcher. One of these is the 'threat of sanction', which involves the possibility that research may reveal information that is incriminating in some way. An example might be interviewing people with a drug addiction who may reveal illegal behaviours as part of the interview. Researchers must weigh up the potential benefits (e.g. possibilities for intervention) against the potential risks (e.g. further discrimination).

CAN YOU...? No.14.4

...1 Outline **four** risk factors for addiction in about 50 words each.

...2 Outline **two** critical points concerning each of these risk factors. Each of these points should be about 50 words.

...3 Use some of this material to write a 250-word answer to the question: *Discuss **two or more** risk factors for addiction*. (5 marks + 5 marks)

...4 Answer the following 'apply your knowledge' question:

'Jack's parents are going through a divorce. He shuts himself in his room for hours at a time playing online computer games with his friends and shunning social contact. His mother is worried because she experienced the same pattern of behaviour with her husband's online gambling some years earlier'.

Use your knowledge of risk factors in the development of addiction to explain Jack's addiction to online gaming. (6 marks) [150-word answer]

MEDIA INFLUENCES ON ADDICTIVE BEHAVIOUR

In April 2009, a new test-tube shaped drink, Rampant TT, was removed from supermarket shelves after the industry watchdog claimed that publicity for the vodka-based drink on the company's website promoted 'down-in-one' drinking and showed a 'profound disregard' for responsible drinking. Our reliance on popular media such as the Internet, television and magazines for information and lifestyle choices, has promoted widespread concern about promoting potentially addictive behaviours, such as alcohol and drug abuse. The media may also portray addictions in a glamorised way, hiding the true costs of the addictions being represented.

MEDIA AND ADDICTIVE BEHAVIOUR

Sulkunen (2007) argues that although the notion of 'addiction' is increasingly used in everyday language, there is no universally accepted understanding of what it means. He believes that the media are a rich source of lay beliefs about substance use and misuse. In the 1990s, for example, use of recreational drugs inspired a number of drug-related films, including the film *Trainspotting*. The success of films such as *Trainspotting* revealed that the world of the heroin addict, although dark and disturbing as depicted here, was nonetheless fascinating for a mainstream audience.

Research into film representations of addiction

Sulkunen (2007) collected 140 scenes from 47 films. These scenes represented various addictions, including alcohol, drugs, tobacco, gambling and sex. Because of the difficulties of spotting addiction in films that were not specifically about addiction, this left 61 scenes to be analysed. Films about drug-users, such as *Trainspotting* (1996), *American Beauty* (1999) and *Human Traffic* (1999), presented scenes of drug competence and enjoyment of the effects. This enjoyment was frequently contrasted with the dullness of ordinary life. The competent use of drugs was also represented as a way of alleviating a particular problem. In the film *Human Traffic*, for example, the use of ecstasy is portrayed as a way of resolving relationship problems for two of the main characters. In other films, such as *Traffic* (2000), drugs are represented as a legitimate way of protesting against parental hypocrisy.

Representation of smoking in film

– New research suggests that media representation of smoking does influence teenagers to take up the habit. Waylen et al. (2011) examined 360 of the top US box office films released between 2001 and 2005, including those that depicted smoking (for example *Bridget Jones' Diary*). They found that teenagers who watched films showing actors smoking were more likely to start smoking themselves. Even after controlling for social factors such as whether their parents or peers smoked, the researchers found a significant relationship between adolescent smoking and the number of films they had seen depicting smoking.

The role of the media in changing addictive behaviour

The treatment of drug and alcohol addiction is often hampered by factors, such as the limited number of professionals able to administer treatment, the motivation of addicts to attend treatment sessions and so on. This has prompted a search for other ways of providing support and education for these individuals. Television and the Internet have been identified as media that could potentially be used to provide this form of intervention. Television is increasingly being used to promote healthy lifestyles and behaviour change, such as smoking cessation and physical exercise.

Television support for problem drinking – The television series entitled *Psst....the Really Useful Guide to Alcohol*, (six 30-minute instalments broadcast by the BBC in 1989) was evaluated by Bennett et al. (1991). Viewers of the series were compared with matched controls who did not watch the series. Although the results showed an improvement in alcohol-related knowledge, they did not show any change in attitude or in actual alcohol consumption. In a more recent study carried out in the Netherlands, Kramer et al. (2009) assessed the effectiveness of *Drinking Less? Do it Yourself!*, a five-week television self-help intervention designed to reduce problem drinking. They found that the intervention group was more successful than a control group in achieving low-risk (rather than high-risk) problem drinking, a difference that was maintained at a three-month follow up.

Anti-drug campaigns – In 2008, a television and Internet advertising campaign was launched in the UK to warn teenagers of the dangers of cocaine use. The adverts feature a fictional dog called Pablo, who is used by drug dealers to carry cocaine. The dog seeks out cocaine users to find out what happens to them after taking the drug. In one advert, he watches a young woman have a heart attack after taking cocaine. Although we might expect such dramatic representations to work, evidence about the effectiveness of such campaigns is far from conclusive (see right).

▲ The 1996 film, *Trainspotting*, directed by Danny Boyle and starring Ewan McGregor, follows a group of heroin addicts in a deprived area of Edinburgh. This was one of many films released around that time which, some claim, glamorised heroin addiction for mainstream audiences.

> **Evaluation**
>
> ## DO ANTI-DRUG CAMPAIGNS WORK?
>
> Between 1998 and 2004, The US Congress invested nearly $1 billion in the US National Youth Anti-Drug Media Campaign. This had three goals:
>
> - To educate and enable US youth to reject illegal drugs.
> - To prevent youths from initiating use of drugs.
> - To convince occasional users to stop.
>
> The messages included resistance skills and raising **self-efficacy** as well as the negative consequences of drug use. These were transmitted through a variety of media channels, including television, radio, magazines, movie theatres and the Internet. Hornik et al. (2008) examined the effects of this campaign, claiming that not only did the campaign fail to accomplish its goals but may also have led to delayed unfavourable effects, particularly in terms of increased marijuana use.

ETHICAL GUIDELINES FOR THE MEDIA REPRESENTATION OF DRUGS IN FILM AND ON TELEVISION

In the US, the *Office for Substance Abuse Protection* (OSAP) has developed guideline materials about drugs for film and television writers. These recommend that writers should communicate that all illegal drug use is 'unhealthy and harmful for all persons', that addiction should be presented as a disease, and that abstinence is the 'viable choice for everyone'. These guidelines also note that there should be no references to 'recreational use of drugs', since no drug use is 'recreational'.

EVALUATION

Film representations of addiction

Research support – Although a number of studies have documented the way addictions are represented in film media, very few have assessed whether such representations actually have an effect on viewers. Sargent and Hanewinkel (2009) tested whether adolescents' exposure to smoking in the movies influenced their initiation into smoking. They surveyed a total of 4384 adolescents aged 11–15 who were re-surveyed a year later. They found that in those individuals who had not smoked when first surveyed, exposure to movie smoking over the intervening year was a significant and strong predictor of whether they had begun to smoke when re-surveyed one year later.

An alternative perspective – Contrary to the claim that films portray addiction in a positive, and at times glamorous way, Boyd (2008) argues that films frequently *do* represent the negative consequences of alcohol and drug dependence. For example, illegal drug use and addiction, claims Boyd, are depicted by physical deterioration (e.g. unkempt bodies and hair), sexual degradation (e.g. prostitution and rape), violence and crime (e.g. theft and murder) and moral decline (e.g. stealing from loved ones). In the US, filmmakers are provided with script-to-screen advice about how to represent drug use and addiction in films and offered financial incentives if they do so in a negative way.

The importance of film representations of addiction – Byrne (1997) argues that films such as *Trainspotting* are particularly important, partly because of their widespread appeal, but also because such films provide enduring stereotypes of drug addicts, both for the addicts themselves and also for the general public. He draws a parallel with the fact that the dominant image of **electroconvulsive therapy (ECT)** comes not from the public information literature of the Royal College of Psychiatrists, but from the 1975 film *One Flew Over the Cuckoo's Nest*.

The role of the media in changing addictive behaviour

Methodological problems with the Kramer et al. study – This study (see left) involved an intervention group that watched the *Drinking Less* series, and a control group that remained on the waiting list for the same treatment. There are two main problems with this approach. First, the intervention group received weekly visits from the researchers so that the extra attention may well have worked in favour of a positive outcome for this group. Second, the waiting-list group was aware that it would receive treatment soon, so may well have postponed its behavioural change, thereby artificially inflating the magnitude of the difference between the two groups.

Why didn't the US anti-drug campaign work? – Hornik *et al.* (2008) suggest two main reasons why this very expensive media campaign failed to produce significant reductions in drug use. First, given all the anti-drug messages to which youths in the US are exposed, and the fact that the messages in the campaign were not particularly novel, it is unsurprising that effects were minimal. Second, anti-drug advertising contains an implicit message that drug use is commonplace. Johnston *et al.* (2002) found that youths who saw the campaign ads took from them the message that their peers were using marijuana, and were then more likely to imitate marijuana use themselves.

CREATIVITY AND ADDICTION

An analysis by Belli (2009) offers support for the claim that addiction and the media are linked although in a rather different way. Brian Wilson was the creative genius behind the iconic 1960s US group, The Beach Boys. Wilson employed novel approaches in composition and musical techniques that were both unconventional and bizarre, and he was consistently named as one of the most creative and influential figures in the medium of popular music.

Wilson's addiction to drugs throughout the 1960s and 1970s is widely documented. He enjoyed the perceptual experiences offered by cannabis, and cites its creative influence in his decision to use bigger, denser sounds in music production. The other drug Wilson used with creative intent was LSD, citing it as being greatly influential on The Beach Boys' most famous album, *Pet Sounds*. His use of cocaine, to which he quickly became addicted, no longer contributed to the creative process, but was used as a form of self-medication as he struggled with the pressures of writing and touring. Brian Wilson's addiction to drugs offers an insight into how being part of a competitive media drives some people to experiment with drugs as a creative influence, but then become victims of the drugs' addictive power.

▶ The Beach Boys with Brian Wilson (in the centre of the picture). Recent research suggests that Wilson's addiction may have been driven in part by the pressures of being at the forefront of a creative media (i.e. the music industry).

CORRELATION ISN'T THE SAME AS CAUSALITY

Most of the evidence about media effects on addictive behaviour is correlational, i.e. exposure to depictions of drug and alcohol use in films and on television is related to addictive behaviour. However, this does not indicate a *causal* relationship between exposure and addiction.

CAN YOU...? (No.14.5)

...1 Describe, in 100–150 words each, **two** ways in which the media has a role in addictive behaviour.

...2 Outline **four** critical points related to media influences on addictive behaviour. Each criticism should be about 50 words.

...3 Use some of this material to write a 300-word answer to the question: *Discuss the role of the media in explaining addictive behaviour.* (4 marks + 8 marks)

...4 Answer the following 'apply your knowledge' question: 'The more that young people see smoking on television and in the cinema, the more likely they are to begin smoking themselves.'

Using your knowledge of psychology, explain why exposure to smoking in the media might encourage young people to start smoking. (4 marks) [100-word answer]

THEORY OF PLANNED BEHAVIOUR

Changing or preventing risky or unhealthy behaviour, such as addiction, has become a major concern of health professionals and governments alike. One way to approach change or prevention is to consider the factors that contribute to a person's intention to change an unhealthy behaviour. In addition, any model must consider how that intention might be transformed into an actual behaviour.

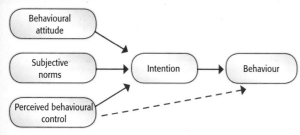

▲ The Theory of Planned Behaviour (Ajzen, 1989)

TPB as a model for addiction prevention

The TPB can be used as an explanatory framework for understanding the processes that lead to addiction but also as a means to understand prevention and treatment. Thus it can be used to help develop appropriate programmes to bring about long-lasting changes in addiction behaviour.

Changing behavioural attitude – The US *Office of National Drug Control Policy* (ONDCP) launched a campaign in 2005 to lower teenage marijuana use. A review of the effectiveness of this campaign attributes its success to its influence on attitudes. Previously campaigns had focused on the risk of abuse but many teenagers are not risk avoidant. The campaign ONDCP launched 'Above the influence' (and several other similar ONDCP campaigns) has tried to create a different attitude toward the effect of marijuana use, namely that it is inconsistent with being autonomous and achieving aspirations. This target on attitudes may be key to the success of the current campaign (Slater *et al.*, 2011).

Changing subjective norms – Anti-drug campaigns often seek to give adolescents actual data about the percentage of people engaging in risky behaviour. This is done in order to change subjective norms. For example, adolescents who smoke are usually part of a peer group who smoke and therefore might believe that smoking is the norm for teenagers. However, generally most adolescents do not smoke, therefore exposure to accurate statistical information should correct subjective norms and should form part of any effective campaign (Wilson and Kolander, 2003).

Perceived behavioural control – Godin *et al.* (2002) examined the extent to which the TPB could explain smoking intentions and behaviours in adults intending to give up smoking. Data was collected using questionnaires and also at home using trained interviewers. Participants were surveyed at the start of the study and again six months later.

THE THEORY OF PLANNED BEHAVIOUR (TPB)

Main assumptions

The Theory of Planned Behaviour (Ajzen, 1989) is one of several cognitive theories about the factors that lead to a person's decision to engage in a particular behaviour. According to this theory, an individual's decision to engage in a *particular* behaviour (e.g. to take drugs, or to give up alcohol) can be directly predicted by their intention to engage in that behaviour. Intention is a function of three factors:

1 *Behavioural attitude* – A product of personal views; the individual's *attitude* toward the behaviour (i.e. how desirable it seems to be). This attitude is formed on the basis of beliefs about the consequences of performing the behaviour (e.g. I will feel good; I will get my life back together), and an appraisal of the value of these consequences (i.e. whether they will be good or bad).

2 *Subjective norms* – A product of social influence; the individual's subjective awareness of *social norms* relating to that particular behaviour, i.e. not simply social norms but the individual's own beliefs about what we think significant others feel is the right thing to do (the 'injunctive norm') as well as perceptions of what other people are actually doing (the 'descriptive norm').

3 *Perceived behavioural control* is assumed to act either on the intention to behave in a particular way, or directly on the behaviour itself. This is because:

a The more control people believe themselves to have over the behaviour in question, the stronger their intention to actually perform that behaviour will be.

b An individual with higher perceived behavioural control is likely to try harder and to persevere for longer than someone with low perceived behavioural control.

The researchers found that the three elements of the TPB (attitudes, subjective norms and perceived behavioural control) helped to explain *intentions*, whereas perceived behavioural control was the most important predictor of ultimate *behaviour*.

The researchers concluded that prevention programmes should help smokers to focus on the willpower required to give up smoking and also alert smokers to the effort that is required to modify smoking behaviour.

Self-efficacy – The TPB proposes, as part of perceived behavioural control, that intentions to change behaviour will be stronger in people who have an increased sense of control. Such self-efficacy has been shown to be important in many aspects of addiction prevention, such as relapse prevention programmes. For example, Majer *et al.* (2004) investigated the role of cognitive factors, including self-efficacy, on abstinence. They found that encouraging an addict's belief in their ability to abstain was related to optimism and ultimately a positive outcome. Therefore, they concluded that enhancing self-efficacy should form a primary goal of treatment plans.

Using the Internet to promote health behaviour change – The Internet is being increasingly used to promote health behaviour change, such as giving up smoking or quitting gambling. Webb *et al.* (2010) analysed 85 studies of such interventions and concluded that those based on a theoretical model, especially the TPB, tended to have greater success. This suggests that the TPB can have an important role in the development of Internet prevention programmes.

Addiction to sun – White *et al.* (2008) examined the sun protection intentions and behaviours of young people in Queensland, Australia. Over 1,000 participants, aged 12–20, completed a questionnaire assessing the TPB predictors. Participants reported their sun protection behaviour for the previous fortnight. Results showed that the TPB components were significant predictors of intentions to engage in sun protection, and these intentions were significant predictors of actual sun protection behaviour.

EVALUATION

Too rational – The TPB has been criticised as being too rational, failing to take into account emotions, compulsions or other irrational determinants of human behaviour (Armitage *et al.*, 1999). When completing a questionnaire about attitudes and intention, people might find it impossible to anticipate the strong desires and emotions that compel their behaviour in real life. The presence of strong emotions may help to explain why people sometimes act irrationally by failing to carry out an intended behaviour (e.g. stop drinking) even when it is in their best interest to do so (Albarracín *et al.*, 2005).

Ignores other factors – Asides from emotion, there are many other influential factors that are ignored by the TPB. For example, Topa and Moriano (2010) suggest that group variables, such as identification with peers, could play a mediating role in the relation with tobacco addiction or indeed any addictive behaviour.

Another element that is missing from the TPB is motivation. Klag (2006) studied 350 substance abusers in Australia and found that recovery was consistently more successful in individuals who had decided themselves to give up rather than people who were coerced (e.g. because of a court sentence). *Self-determination theory*, according to Klag, is preferable to the TPB because it emphasises the importance of self-motivation (i.e. intrinsic motivation).

Intention and expectation – It has been argued that a distinction should be made between behavioural *intention* which refers to a person's plans about their future behaviour, and behavioural *expectation*, which refers to the perceived likelihood of performing a particular behaviour (Warshaw and Davis, 1985). For example, a smoker may think it likely that they will have given up smoking in five years' time (expectation) without having a definite plan to give up (intention). Although intention may have a causal effect on behaviour, a behavioural expectation is less likely to do so (Armitage and Conner, 2001).

Predicts intention rather than behaviour change – Armitage and Conner's **meta-analysis** of studies using the TPB found that this model was successful in predicting *intention* to change rather than actual behavioural change. This pattern of results is typically found in the prediction of health behaviours that involve the adoption of difficult behavioural change, such as stopping using drugs of abuse, eating a healthy diet and so on. This suggests that the TPB is primarily an account of intention formation rather than specifying the processes involved in translating the intention into action (Ajzen and Fishbein, 2005). In the context of changing risky behaviours such as drug taking or gambling, therefore, we can make a distinction between a motivational phase that results in the formation of a behavioural intention, and a post-decisional phase which involves behavioural initiation and maintenance (Abraham *et al.*, 1998).

The influence of alcohol and drugs – The influence of alcohol or drugs can produce a discrepancy between measured intention and actual behaviour. Attitudes and intentions tend to be measured when sober, whereas risky behaviours such as gambling or unprotected sex may be performed when under the influence of alcohol or drugs. This is consistent with the idea of **alcohol myopia** (Steele and Josephs, 1990), the tendency for alcohol to decrease cognitive capacity so that only the most obvious characteristics of a situation are attended to. Indeed, MacDonald *et al.* (1996) found that alcohol intoxication actually *increased* measured intention to engage in unprotected sex and other risky behaviours.

When is perceived control important? Perceived behavioural control takes on a more important role when issues of control are associated with the performance of a task. Thus, control has been found to contribute very little to the prediction of intentions to consume convenience food, but is an important predictor of the intention to lose weight (Netemeyer *et al.*, 1991).

▲ Why don't smokers change their behaviour?

METHODOLOGICAL ISSUES

Self-report techniques
A major issue is that research tends to rely on self-report despite evidence to suggest the vulnerability of such data to self-presentational biases (e.g. Paulhus, 2002).

In studies of the TPB, attitudes and intentions that are assessed by questionnaires may, according to Albarracín *et al.* (2005), turn out to be poor representations of the attitudes and intentions that eventually exist in the behavioural situation, and thus poor predictors of actual behaviour. For example, a smoker may develop a negative attitude toward cigarettes based on their threat to his or her health, and intend to give them up. However, their actual intention and behaviour may differ greatly when they find themselves in a group of heavy smokers with all the associated sights and smells of smoking.

Studies using correlational analysis
A second major issue is that the research on the TPB is almost entirely correlational, linking positive (or negative) outcomes to certain behaviours. This means it is not clear that, for example, behavioural attitudes have *caused* any change.

CAN YOU...? No.14.6

...1 Outline, in about 100 words, the Theory of Planned Behaviour.

...2 Outline **at least three** examples of how the TPB has been used as a model for addiction prevention.

...3 Identify **four** critical points relating to how the TPB has been used as a model for addiction prevention. Each criticism should be about 50 words.

...4 Use some of this material to write a 375-word answer to the question: *Discuss the theory of planned behaviour as a model for addiction prevention.* (5 marks + 10 marks)

...5 Answer the following 'apply your knowledge' question:

Using your knowledge of psychology, explain how the theory of planned behaviour might be used to prevent either smoking addiction or gambling addiction. (6 marks) [150-word answer]

TYPES OF INTERVENTION

Because addiction causes so much personal distress and can create social problems such as crime and poverty, psychologists have tried to find effective ways to intervene in the cycle of addictive behaviour. Some of these are biological (e.g. drug treatments) and others involve psychological interventions, such as counselling or cognitive therapy. On this final spread we examine the effectiveness of such interventions in changing addictive behaviour.

TYPES OF INTERVENTION IN ADDICTIVE BEHAVIOUR

Biological interventions

Heroin addiction and methadone – *Methadone* is a synthetic drug widely used in the treatment of heroin addiction. *Methadone* mimics the effects of heroin but is less addictive. Like heroin, it produces feelings of euphoria, but to a lesser degree. Initially, a drug abuser is prescribed slowly increasing amounts of methadone to increase **tolerance** to the drug. The dose is then slowly decreased until the addict no longer needs either methadone or heroin.

Drug treatments for gambling addiction – No drug has yet been approved for use in the UK to treat pathological gambling, but research suggests that drug treatments can have beneficial effects. There is, for example, evidence to support **serotonin** dysfunction in pathological gambling (George and Murali, 2005), and in a study by Hollander *et al.* (2000), gamblers treated with **SSRIs** to increase serotonin levels showed significant improvements compared to a control group. Administration of *naltrexone*, which is a **dopamine** receptor **antagonist**, works by reducing the rewarding and reinforcing properties of gambling behaviour, thus reducing the urge to gamble.

Psychological interventions

Reinforcement – One way to reduce addictive behaviour is to give people rewards for not engaging in the behaviour in question. Sindelar *et al.* (2007) investigated whether the provision of monetary rewards would produce better patient outcomes for people on *methadone* treatment programmes. Participants were randomly allocated to either a reward or no-reward condition in addition to both groups receiving their usual care (i.e. a methadone dose daily and individual and group counselling). Participants in the rewards condition drew for prizes of various monetary value each time they tested negative for drugs. Drug use dropped significantly for participants in the rewards condition, with the number of negative urine samples being 60% higher compared to the control condition.

Cognitive-behavioural therapies – Cognitive behavioural therapy (CBT) is based on the idea that addictive behaviours are maintained by the person's thoughts about these behaviours. The main goal of CBT is to help people change the way they think about their addiction, and to learn new ways of coping more effectively with the circumstances that led to these behaviours in the past (e.g. coping with difficult situations or when exposed to peer pressure). In gambling addiction, for example, cognitive errors such as the belief that the individual can control and predict outcomes plays a key part in the maintenance of gambling. CBT attempts to correct these errors in thinking, thus reducing the urge to gamble.

Public health interventions

The NIDA study – Government-sponsored intervention studies such as the US *National Institute on Drug Abuse (NIDA) Collaborative Cocaine Treatment Study* (see below) are designed to intervene in the cycle of personal and social problems associated with drug abuse. In this study, the provision of a combination of group and individual drug counselling significantly reduced cocaine use, with an associated reduction in other behaviours (e.g. the incidence of unprotected sex among addicts).

Telephone smoking Quitline services – A meta-analysis by Stead *et al.* (2006), including over 18,000 participants, found that people who received repeated telephone calls from a counsellor increased their odds of stopping smoking by 50% compared to smokers who only received self-help materials and/or brief counselling. They concluded that multiple call-back counselling improves the long-term probability of cessation for smokers who contact *Quitline* services.

Prevention of youth gambling – There is growing concern that adolescents and young adults represent the highest risk group for gambling problems. Messerlian *et al.* (2005) proposed a prevention model based on research into pathological gambling in this age group. This framework applies denormalisation, protection, prevention, and harm-reduction principles. For example, programmes based on prevention attempt to avert at-risk youth from escalating towards pathological gambling and includes early identification strategies. Programmes founded on a harm-reduction approach inform youth of the risks and dangers associated with gambling and help them develop the necessary skills to remain in control.

> **Evaluation**
>
> ### THE NIDA STUDY
>
> The US *National Institute on Drug Abuse (NIDA) Collaborative Cocaine Treatment Study* (Crits-Christoph *et al.* 2003) enrolled 487 patients who were randomly assigned to one of four interventions:
>
> - **Group drug counselling (GDC) alone** – Learn about stages of recovery; engage in group problem-solving.
> - **Cognitive behavioural therapy/GDC** – Recognise and change distorted thinking about drug use, (plus GDC).
> - **Supportive-expressive psychotherapy/GDC** – Learn how addiction affects relationships and how to improve interpersonal relations, (plus GDC).
> - **Individual drug counselling/GDC** – Learn how to avoid drug triggers and adopt more positive behaviours, (plus GDC).
>
> All treatments decreased days of drug use in the previous month, from a mean of 10 days at the start of the study to three days a year later.
>
> The intervention combining individual drug counselling (IDC) and group drug counselling (GDC) worked best. At the six-month mark, for example, 39% of people in the IDC-GDC intervention reported using cocaine in the previous month, compared with 57% of people who underwent cognitive behavioural therapy and GDC, 49% of those who received supportive-expressive psychotherapy and GDC, and 52% of those receiving GDC alone.

◀ British troops on patrol in Iraq. Studies suggest that the stress of deployment increases smokers' dependence on cigarettes.

34
34
32 4
2 4
2 6
68
82

18
5
54

REAL-WORLD APPLICATION

Evaluation

Dealing with increased nicotine dependence in returning troops has become an important health issue. In a study of British military personnel deployed in Iraq (Boos and Croft, 2004), 29% of pre-existing regular smokers significantly increased their cigarette consumption while deployed. Furthermore, 7% of respondents reported starting to smoke for the first time as a result of deployment. The use of telephone counselling for dependent smokers (*Quitline* services) has been reported to be effective in reducing smoking dependence in military veterans.

Beckham *et al.* (2008) took a sample of 24 US military veterans who had returned from deployment in either Iraq or Afghanistan, and gave them a combination of *Quitline* counselling services and nicotine replacement therapy. Research has shown that tobacco users are more likely to quit with therapy that includes a combination of counselling and medication. Of these 24, eleven (46%) had stopped smoking by their agreed 'quit date', with nine still abstaining two months later.

EVALUATION

Biological interventions

Problems with methadone treatment – Some drug addicts can become as reliant on methadone as they were on heroin, thereby substituting one addiction for another. The use of methadone remains controversial, with *UK Statistics Authority* figures showing that methadone was responsible for the deaths of over 300 people in the UK in 2007. Because for the majority of addicts, methadone consumption is unsupervised, it has created a black market in methadone, with addicts sometimes selling their doses for only £2.

Drug treatments for gambling addiction – In the Hollander study described on the facing page, the sample size was very small (N=10), and of relatively short duration (16 weeks). A larger and longer study (Blanco *et al.*, 2002), involving 32 gamblers over six months, failed to demonstrate any superiority for SSRI treatment over a placebo. Support for the effectiveness of *naltrexone* comes from a study that found significant decreases in gambling thoughts and behaviours after six weeks of treatment (Kim and Grant, 2001).

Psychological interventions

Reinforcement interventions do not address the underlying problem – Although research such as the Sindelar *et al.* study have shown the effectiveness of reinforcement therapies for reducing addictive behaviour, such interventions do nothing to address the problem that led to the addiction in the first place. This means that although a specific addictive behaviour might have been reduced, there is the possibility that the person may simply engage in a different addictive behaviour instead. A drug addict may, for example, turn to alcohol, but in most cases new addictions tend to be subtle, including compulsive spending or even developing dependent relationships.

Research support for CBT – Ladouceur *et al.* (2001) randomly allocated 66 pathological gamblers either to a **cognitive therapy** group or to a waiting list control group. Of those who completed treatment, 86% no longer fulfilled the **DSM** criteria for pathological gambling. They also found that after treatment, gamblers had a better perception of control over their gambling problem and increased **self-efficacy**, improvements that were maintained at a one-year follow-up. Other treatments have combined cognitive and behavioural aspects of gambling, and attempted to alter gamblers' cognitions and behaviours. Sylvain *et al.* (1997) evaluated the effectiveness of cognitive behavioural treatments in a sample of male pathological gamblers. Treatment included cognitive therapy, social skills training and relapse prevention. They found significant improvements after treatment, with these gains maintained at a one-year follow-up.

Public health interventions

Public health interventions – An additional and very important finding from the NIDA study described opposite (Crits-Christoph *et al.*, 2003) was that there was a marked reduction in HIV risk associated with reduction in cocaine use. This appeared to be primarily due to a reduction in the frequency of unprotected sex that was otherwise associated with high levels of cocaine use. The use of telephone *Quitline* services for smokers has also been shown to be effective in reducing nicotine dependence (see 'real-world application' above).

The importance of public health interventions into youth gambling – A public health approach to youth gambling is important because it is a proactive approach to addressing a potentially devastating social issue. Research has demonstrated that problem gambling during adolescence can lead to adverse outcomes, such as strained relationships, delinquency and criminal behaviour, depression and even suicide (Derevensky and Gupta, 2004).

Conclusions

Research has not tended to show that any one type of psychological treatment is superior to any other. This implies that relationship factors (i.e. the relationship between therapist and client) are more important than the specific characteristics of the individual therapy. In addition, psychological therapies appear more effective when combined with a pharmacological treatment (see 'real-world application' above) and, according to Woody and Crits-Christoph (2007), this approach may well improve treatment outcomes as more effective medications become available to treat cocaine and alcohol dependence.

INTERVENTION BIAS

Evaluation

Cohen and Cohen (1984) describe a phenomenon called 'the clinician's illusion'. They argue that many clinicians believe that alcoholism and drug addiction are extremely difficult to treat – more difficult than research suggests. The lack of routine screening for alcohol or drug problems means that many clinicians only come across addicts when their condition is well advanced, and in many cases too severe to effectively respond to treatment. The view of addiction as 'incurable' among the general public is further strengthened by biased media reports which rarely comment on celebrities who *used* to have an addiction problem, but who are now doing well.

CAN YOU...?   No.14.7

...1 Outline, in 100 words each, **three** types of intervention for addictive behaviour.

...2 Identify **three** critical points relating to each type of intervention. Each criticism should be about 50 words.

...3 Use some of this material to produce a 300-word answer to the following question: *Outline and evaluate two or more types of intervention for addictive behaviour.* (4 marks + 8 marks)

...4 Using your knowledge of psychology, answer the following 'apply your knowledge' question.

'Gambling has increased to its highest levels since the 1990s, as has the proportion of 'problem gamblers'.

With reference to psychological and public-health interventions, consider how the issue of 'problem gambling' might be addressed. (8 marks) [200-word answer]

CHAPTER SUMMARY

MODELS OF ADDICTIVE BEHAVIOUR

THE BIOLOGICAL APPROACH

GAMBLING
- Initiation – evidence of genetic transmission of gambling in men (Shah et al., 2005); first degree relatives of gamblers more likely to gamble than distant relatives (Black et al., 2006).
- Maintenance – pathological gambling associated with underactive pituitary-adrenal system (Paris et al., 2010). Individual differences in optimal amounts of stimulation (Zuckerman, 1979).
- Blaszczynski et al. (1990) – poor boredom tolerance may contribute to repetitive gambling.

EVALUATION
- Can explain individual differences in gambling addiction through diathesis-stress model.
- Biological approach ignores importance of external factors in development of gambling addiction.
- Cannot explain why some types of gambling (e.g. online and video gambling) are more addictive than others (Breen and Zimmerman, 2001).
- Sensation seeking explains racetrack gambling but not café gambling (Bonnaire et al., 2006).
- Biological explanations are reductionist.

SMOKING
- Initiation – individual differences in smoking initiation 42–44% genetic (Boardman et al., 2008; Vink et al., 2005)
- Maintenance – Vink et al. estimate nicotine dependence 75% genetic and linked to individual differences in nicotine metabolism. Pre-natal exposure to nicotine important in determining later addiction (Buka et al., 2003).
- Relapse – Xian et al. (2003) found ability to quit smoking is also substantially heritable. Uhl et al. (2008) attempted to identify gene clusters associated with quit success and nicotine dependence.

EVALUATION
- Supporting evidence for genetic influence on smoking – Thorgeirsson et al. (2008) identified gene variant on chromosome 15.
- Biological explanations neglect other possible determining factors, including social context of smoking.
- Genomic medicine – screening to identify those with genes that increase susceptibility to smoking addiction. Gartner et al. (2009) – screening for susceptibility unlikely to be practical.
- Asp40 variant less likely to quit with low dose NRT – genetic testing might allow therapists to match cessation therapy with genotype (Lerman et al., 2004).

THE COGNITIVE APPROACH

GAMBLING
- Initiation – self-medication model (Gelkopf et al., 2002) – individuals intentionally use different forms of pathological behaviour to treat their psychological symptoms.
- Maintenance – cognitive distortions (e.g. gamblers' fallacy) play a role in the maintenance of pathological gambling (Oei and Gordon, 2008). Griffiths (1994) – regular gamblers believed they were more skilful than they were, and more likely to make irrational verbalisations.
- Relapse – pathological gamblers suffer from a 'recall bias' (Blanco et al., 2000) and belief in 'just world' hypothesis.

EVALUATION
- Li et al. (2008) – self-medicating pathological gamblers more likely to have other substance dependencies than pleasure-seeking gamblers.
- Relevant knowledge does not make people less susceptible to cognitive distortions (Benhsain and Ladouceur, 2004). Delfabbro et al. (2006) – pathological gamblers more irrational in some forms of gambling-related cognition but not others.
- Evidence to support self-medication model (Becona et al., 1996), but correlational only.
- Differing approaches to helping in treatment for pathological gambling, depending on motivations.

SMOKING
- Initiation – Brandon et al., (1999), behaviour escalates into addiction because of expectations of costs and benefits. Negative moods alleviated by smoking (Kassel et al., 2007, Brandon and Baker, 1991) plus expectation of positive mood states (Mermelstein et al., 2009).
- Maintenance – as addiction develops, activity influenced more by unconscious expectancies involving automatic processing (Brandon et al., 1999). Tate et al. (1994) manipulated expectations during abstinence.
- Expectations of costs and benefits of smoking affect individual's readiness to quit and likelihood of them relapsing after they have quit (De Vries and Backbier, 1994).

EVALUATION
- Addiction or excess? – research relating to expectancy theory concerned more with excesses than with addiction.
- Research support for influence of expectancies on relapse – Hurt et al. (2000), use of nicotine patches alone did not improve cessation rates. Moolchan et al. (2005) nicotine patches worked only when accompanied by CBT.
- Juliano and Brandon (2004) – smokers' positive expectancies for effects of smoking do not generalise to NRT.
- Research in this area may suffer from publication bias and also problems collecting objective data (addicts reports vary depending who they are talking to).

THE LEARNING APPROACH

GAMBLING
- Initiation – gamblers playing slot machines may become addicted because of rewards associated with playing (Griffiths, 2009). Delfabbro and Winefield (1999) – greater weight given to winning than losing.
- Maintenance – gambling continues because of intermittent reinforcement and approval of others (Lambos et al., 2007).
- Occasional reinforcement – organisms tend to learn adaptive behaviours that work to their advantage on average.
- Relapse – gamblers experience approach-avoidance conflict and relapse likely because of exposure to cues associated with gambling.

EVALUATION
- Difficult to apply the same learning principles to all different forms of gambling, because of time period and skill differences.
- Blaszczynski and Nower (2002) distinguish between behaviourally conditioned and emotionally vulnerable gamblers.
- Fails to explain why only some people become addicted despite similar level of exposure.
- The significance of occasional reinforcement – tendency to learn adaptive behaviours that work to our advantage on average.
- Real-world application – Botvin (2000) suggests effective forms of smoking prevention programme should target beginner adolescents.

SMOKING
- Initiation – availability of role models in home and peer group (Kandel and Wu, 1995) determines who will smoke. Popularity among peers may serve as positive reinforcer in initiation of smoking (Mayeux et al., 2008).
- Maintenance – smoking-related sensory cues become conditioned stimuli and activate the same brain areas (Franklin et al., 2007).
- Relapse – made difficult because of presence of conditioned cues (Hogarth et al., 2010) and low refusal self-efficacy (Lawrance and Rubinson, 1989).

EVALUATION
- Social learning influences supported by research evidence – peer group influences (DiBlasio and Benda, 1993) and family influences (Karcher and Finn, 2005).
- Role of conditioned cues supported by Thewissen et al. (2008) study.
- Implications for treatment – cue exposure therapy (Drummond et al., 1990).
- Botvin (2000) – effective forms of smoking prevention programme should target beginner adolescents because of need to resist peer pressure.
- Gender differences/bias?

THE THEORY
- Behaviour directly predicted by intention to engage.
- Behavioural attitude – formed on basis of beliefs about consequences of performing behaviour.
- Subjective norms = injunctive norm + descriptive norm.
- Perceived behavioural control acts either on intention to behave, or directly on behaviour.

AS A MODEL FOR BEHAVIOUR CHANGE
- ONDCP – effectiveness of campaign attributed to its influence on attitudes (Slater et al., 2011).
- Exposure to accurate statistical information corrects subjective norms (Wilson and Kolander, 2003).
- Perceived behavioural control most important predictor for giving up smoking (Godin et al., 2002).
- Self-efficacy – important in relapse prevention programmes (Majer et al., 2004).
- Webb et al. (2010) – Internet interventions based on TPB had greater success.
- White et al. (2008) – TPB predictors significant in sun protection intentions and behaviour.

FACTORS AFFECTING ADDICTIVE BEHAVIOUR

RISK FACTORS FOR ADDICTION

STRESS
- Everyday stress – addiction associated with relieving anxiety. Stressors contribute to initiation and continuation of addictions, and to relapse (NIDA, 1999).
- Traumatic stress – people exposed to severe stress more vulnerable to addictions. PTSD also linked to addiction (e.g. Driessen et al., 2008 – 30% drug addicts and 15% alcoholics also had PTSD).

EVALUATION
- Addictions may sometimes reduce stress, e.g. by smoking (Hajek et al., 2010) but this tends to be temporary.
- Stress may create vulnerability in some but not all people, e.g. Cloniger (1987) suggested stress explains vulnerability in type 1 but not type 2 alcoholics.

PEERS
- Peer pressure – reason why adolescents start taking drugs or smoking (Eiser et al., 1991) and associated with increased levels of smoking (McAlister et al, 1984).
- Social learning theory (Bandura, 1977) – behaviours are learned through the observation of others and subsequent modelling of this behaviour.
- Social identity theory (Abrams and Hogg, 1990) – individuals adopt norms and behaviours that are central to the social identity of the group to which they belong.

EVALUATION
- SLT – research support, e.g. exposure to peer models increases likelihood that teenagers begin smoking (Duncan et al., 1995); social status and popularity instrumental in adolescents' smoking behaviour (Eiser et al., 1989).
- SIT – evidence supports claim that adolescents motivated to begin smoking because of the peer stereotypes they hold (Michell, 1997) but little known about extent to which these groups influence members to smoke.

AGE
- Peer group has greater impact on smoking and drug use for young adolescents, but this wanes in later adolescence.
- Romantic partners become increasingly important as an influence on health-related attitudes and behaviours (Brown et al., 1997).

EVALUATION
- Sensitive research – Lee (1993) suggests research in sensitive or illegal areas (such as drug taking) creates ethical particular issues, e.g. 'threat of sanction'.
- Bad science – poor 'research' used to seduce people into regarding all 'evidence' as fact.

PERSONALITY
- Francis (1996) found link between addiction and high scores on neuroticism and psychoticism.
- Cloniger (1987) – personality traits that predispose people to addiction: novelty seeking, harm avoidance, reward dependence.
- Takao et al. (2009) – mobile phone addiction associated with low self-esteem and high self-monitoring.

EVALUATION
- Lack of causality – research on relationship between personality and addiction is correlational only.
- Difficult to disentangle effects of personality on addiction from the effects of addiction on personality.
- Belin et al. (2008), rats high in impulsiveness rather than sensation-seekers more likely to become addicted.
- Weintraub et al. (2010) supports the role of impulsivity in addiction in humans rather than sensation-seeking.
- Buckholtz et al. (2010) claim addictions more rewarding for people with certain personality types because of hypersensitive dopamine response system.

MEDIA INFLUENCES ON ADDICTIVE BEHAVIOUR

FILM REPRESENTATIONS OF ADDICTION
- Sulkunen (2007) – films with scenes of drug enjoyment, contrasted with dullness of ordinary life.
- Waylen et al. (2011) found that teenagers who watched films showing actors smoking were more likely to start smoking themselves.

EVALUATION
- Sargent and Hanewinkel (2009) – exposure to movie smoking was significant influence on adolescents taking up smoking.
- Boyd (2008) – movies frequently do portray negative consequences of drug and alcohol dependence.
- Films play important role in generating stereotypes of drug takers.
- Ethical guidelines for representation of drugs in film developed in US.
- Creative media led Brian Wilson to use drugs to increase creative output.
- Most evidence about media effects on addictive behaviour is correlational, not causal.

CHANGING ADDICTIVE BEHAVIOUR
- Television support for problem drinking – Bennett et al. (1991) found change in alcohol-related knowledge but not in attitudes or behaviour.
- TV self-help series (Kramer et al., 2009) – more in intervention group achieved low-risk drinking than in control group.
- Anti-drug campaigns – US study included resistance skills and raising self-efficacy.

EVALUATION
- Kramer et al. study – intervention group also received regular visits from researchers (extraneous variable was extra attention).
- US study didn't work because messages not novel, and may contain message that drug taking is commonplace, encouraging marijuana use.

REDUCING ADDICTIVE BEHAVIOUR

THEORY OF PLANNED BEHAVIOUR

EVALUATION
- Fails to take into account irrational determinants of behaviour.
- Ignores other factors, e.g. identification with peers (Topa and Moriano, 2010). Klag (2006) suggests self-determination theory preferable.
- Distinction between behavioural intention and behavioural expectation (Warshaw and Davis, 1985).
- TPB explains intention formation rather than processes involved in translating intention into action.
- Distinction made between motivational phase and post-decisional phase.
- Alcohol or drugs can produce discrepancy between intention and actual behaviour.
- Perceived behavioural control more important when associated with performance of a task.
- Self-report techniques subject to self-presentational biases. Questionnaires are poor representations of attitudes and intentions.
- TPB research mostly correlational – not clear that behavioural attitudes have caused change.

TYPES OF INTERVENTION

BIOLOGICAL
- Methadone mimics effects of heroin but is less addictive.
- Drug treatments for gambling include SSRIs to increase serotonin levels and naltrexone to reduce reinforcing properties of gambling.

EVALUATION
- Some addicts also become reliant on methadone.
- Methadone use has resulted in black market for drug.
- Support for use of SSRIs for gambling inconclusive, but effectiveness supported by Kim and Grant (2001).
- Clinician's illusion – addiction perceived as difficult to treat because only advanced cases seen.

PSYCHOLOGICAL
- Addictive behaviour reduced by reinforcement (Sindelar et al., 2007).
- CBT changes way people think about their addiction.

EVALUATION
- Reinforcement interventions do not address the problem that led to addiction.
- CBT supported in studies of pathological gamblers (Sylvain et al., 1997).
- Telephone 'Quitlines' successful in returning military personnel (Beckham et al., 2008).

PUBLIC HEALTH
- NIDA study – combination of individual and group drug counselling worked best.
- 'Quitlines' increased odds of stopping smoking by 50%.
- Legislation in 2007 led to creation of more supportive environment for stopping smoking.

EVALUATION
- NIDA study – reduction in cocaine use accompanied by reduction in HIV risk (less unprotected sex).
- Messerlian et al. (2005) – youth gambling prevention treatments (e.g. harm reduction approach).

EXAM QUESTION WITH STUDENT ANSWER

QUESTION | **(a)** Outline and evaluate **one** approach to the initiation and maintenance of smoking and/or gambling addiction. *(4 marks + 8 marks)* | **(b)** Discuss **two or more** risk factors in vulnerability to addiction. *(4 marks + 8 marks)*

STUDENT ANSWER

(a) *One explanation of the initiation of addiction is the biological model. This claims that people become addicted because of their genetics. A study by Vink et al. (2005) found that initiation of smoking was about 40% inherited and 60% environmental. Research has also shown that gambling addiction might be inherited. For example, Black et al. (2006) found that close relatives of gamblers were more likely to gamble themselves and distant relatives were not. Another study by Shah et al. (2005) also found that there was strong genetic influence in male gamblers. The maintenance of smoking is because the nicotine in cigarettes leads to the release of dopamine in the brain. Dopamine causes feelings of pleasure for the smoker, but these effects are only temporary for the smoker and so they must repeat the action to have the same effect. Gambling might be maintained because some people are high in sensation-seeking so gambling is a way of experiencing arousal through risk taking.*

One criticism that is made of biological explanations of addiction are that they are reductionist as they reduce a complex phenomenon such as addiction down to a relatively simple level of explanation, i.e. an imbalance of brain chemicals or the influence of specific genes. This criticism is both positive and negative – it is positive because it leads to a useful way to research addiction and treat it with biological methods. However, there is a danger of ignoring other possible influences, which are also important, as shown by the fact that heritability rates are not anything like 100%. A problem with the biological explanation of addiction is that it ignores environmental factors in addictive behaviour. For example, people may be more likely to gamble because of seeing their family gamble or because of peer pressure. Also people might smoke because of peer pressure or the desire to look tough. This means that although biological factors may be important in determining who has the potential for addiction, environmental factors might be the reason that people actually take up smoking or gambling.

(b) *Vulnerability to addiction can be explained in terms of stress factors. Smoking and gambling might be used as a way of coping with stressors, such as relationship problems or work stress. People who experience extreme stress, for example soldiers serving in Iraq or Afghanistan, are also more vulnerable to developing addictive behaviours, such as smoking or drug taking. This claim is supported in a study by Driessen et al. (2008), who found that 30% of drug addicts also suffered from PTSD, suggesting that their PTSD had made them vulnerable to drug addiction.*

Another vulnerability factor is the influence of peers – the friends you spend your time with increase the likelihood that you experiment with drugs or begin gambling. This can be explained in terms of social learning theory – we observe other people enjoying themselves and model our own behaviour on this. It can also be explained in terms of social identity theory (SIT). We create our social identity through group membership and in order to do this we adopt the norms and behaviours of the group. For example, if we are in a group of friends who take drugs regularly we are more likely to adopt the same behaviour because we identify with them. A problem for the importance of peers as a vulnerability factor is that there are methodological problems with collecting data to support the importance of peers. These methodological problems include the social desirability bias (in the case of smoking or gambling) and the ethical issues associated with asking questions about illegal behaviour (in the case of drug taking).

[605 words]

EXAMINER COMMENTS

Part (a) of this question does not specify which approach, so that is your choice. This student has chosen the biological model and, although not required, they have included both smoking *and* gambling. This is commendable, although a consequence of this approach is that there is far too much AO1 content for the 4 marks available.

The first paragraph is entirely **AO1**, which is a neat solution to dividing up the different requirements of the question. The research studies included here have been used only as description but, as there is far too much of this, at least one of these studies could have been diverted into the more important (in terms of marks available) **AO2**. The trick is to precede the content with a suitable **AO2** phrase, for example 'The claim that gambling is a product of genetic influences is supported in a study by Shah *et al.* (2005), who found that …'

In the second part of this paragraph the student introduces important information about maintenance since the question requires that both initiation and maintenance should be addressed. Without this, the answer would be **basic**.

The second paragraph is entirely **AO2**, which is a good way separating the two component parts efficiently. There are two main critical points made here. The first concerns reductionism, which is linked effectively to the biological model of addiction. The second is the contrasting role of environmental factors. There is always a danger that an alternative perspective is simply described without being embedded within a critical commentary. This has been avoided by the final sentence in this paragraph.

AO1 – A **good range** of material has been selected, and it is **reasonably detailed**.

AO2/AO3 – The evaluation is **reasonable** with a **reasonable** level of elaboration.

It looks as if this candidate has spent too long on part (a), leaving insufficient time for part (b) – poor time management. It is difficult, in exam conditions, to select material appropriately – but it is crucial in order to maximise your marks.

In the first paragraph, stress is proposed as a vulnerability factor. The **AO1** descriptive content is nicely developed, but the more important **AO2** material is brief and underdeveloped.

This pattern is reproduced in the second paragraph, with detailed **AO1** content but less detailed **AO2** content. An additional problem for the **AO2** comments made here is that they haven't been made explicitly relevant to this particular vulnerability factor. For example, social desirability bias is mentioned but not in terms of peer group influences.

AO1 – Certainly enough relevant material for the full 4 marks.

AO2/AO3 – Fairly **basic** with some **elaboration** although not as **effective** as it might have been.

Chapter 15

Anomalistic psychology

▲ The Roper Poll (Hopkins *et al.*, 1992) found that about 1 in 50 Americans claimed to have had an experience of alien abduction (that's nearly four million of them). A *CNN/Time* poll (1997) found that 64% of Americans believed that aliens had made contact with humans.

SPECIFICATION

Anomalistic psychology	
The study of anomalous experience	• Pseudoscience and the scientific status of parapsychology. • Methodological issues related to the study of paranormal cognition (ESP, including Ganzfeld) and paranormal action (psychokinesis).
Explanations for anomalous experience	• The role of coincidence and probability judgements in anomalous experience. • Explanations for superstitious behaviour and magical thinking. • Personality factors underlying anomalous experience.
Research into exceptional experience	• Psychological research into and explanations for psychic healing, near-death and out-of-body experiences, and psychic mediumship.

This chapter is concerned with **anomalous experience**. The term 'anomalous' literally means something that is irregular and doesn't fit into existing explanations. The term has been used since the 1970s as a way to refer to **paranormal** or **psi phenomenon**.

There are two kinds of evidence for anomalous experiences – personal evidence and scientific evidence. Personal evidence consists of reports by individuals of their own experiences or experiences they have witnessed. Such reports have a powerful influence and, for some people, count as sufficient evidence. However, for over a century paranormal psychologists have sought to provide objective scientific evidence for anomalous experiences. We start by considering the issue of whether paranormal psychology is, in reality, a science or a pseudoscience.

The key elements of science are discussed on page 274 (in Chapter 16 'Psychological research and scientific method').

The term 'psi' is a letter from the Greek alphabet and is related to the Greek word 'psyche' meaning 'mind' or 'soul'.

▲ **Evidence seen with you own eyes**
'Pareidolia' is the term used to describe the human tendency to see recognisable patterns and images where there are none. Some might believe that a wisp of smoke looks like a ghost, or a pattern on a piece of toast resembles the Virgin Mary (as did Diana Duyser, above). Some people take this as evidence of the supernatural. Others explain this in terms of the human perceptual system.

JEALOUS PHENOMENA AND OCCAM'S RAZOR

Paranormal psychologists have suggested that the lack of positive results in studies of psi phenomena such as ESP occurs because the presence of sceptics causes the phenomena to go away – they say that the phenomena are 'jealous'. They further claim that an experimenter who insists on highly controlled research is demonstrating his lack of belief in the phenomena by requiring rigorous control and this lack of belief means that nothing will be found.

There is of course a simpler explanation, i.e. that the phenomena don't exist. **Occam's razor** is the principle of simplicity (attributed to the medieval philosopher William of Occam) – if there are two competing explanations, and all other things are equal, then the simpler one is to be preferred. Many paranormal explanations are extremely convoluted in which case, according to Occam's razor, a simpler, probably non-paranormal, explanation should be preferred.

PSEUDOSCIENCE IN PARAPSYCHOLOGY

Pseudoscience is the term used to described a 'false' science. It is a field of study where researchers claim to be scientific in their research and adopt some of the procedures of science but fail to fulfil the criteria effectively. There are features of parapsychology that suggest it is a pseudoscience (Hines, 2003):

Lacks falsifiability – The aim of the **scientific method** is to test **hypotheses**. It is not possible to prove a hypothesis correct but you can prove it is wrong (i.e. **falsify** it – see page 275 for a further explanation). In some cases, however, this is not possible. For example, a study may find no evidence of ESP (i.e. reading someone else's mind). This would appear to prove the hypothesis that ESP exists is wrong. However, some paranormal psychologists then claim the lack of supporting evidence occurs because sceptics are present and the phenomena disappear under such conditions (see 'Jealous phenomena and Occam's razor' below left). The end result is a non-falsifiable hypothesis. Many of the hypotheses related to anomalous experience are of this nature. This makes them pseudoscientific.

Lacks carefully controlled, replicable research – There are many studies of paranormal phenomenon that claim to be highly controlled but aren't. The Ganzfeld studies (discussed on the next spread) are an example of this, where experimenters may encourage particular answers.

There are also many examples of failure to replicate studies in parapsychology, especially by non-believers. Recently, Bem (2011) produced evidence that people can sense future events before they happen. His research involved testing participants' recall of words. Normally a person would be able to remember words that were previously rehearsed better than those not rehearsed. In this experiment Bem demonstrated that people remember words better if they rehearsed them afterwards, so a future event was affecting the present.

However, a team of three UK sceptical researchers separately failed to replicate this result despite using the exact same procedure (Ritchie et al., 2012). The fact that sceptics invariably fail to get the same results as believers challenges the objective nature of the research.

Lacks theory to explain the effects – The aim of scientific research is to construct theories. Most paranormal phenomena have not, as yet, been given theoretical explanations. For example, exactly how does **ESP** happen or what is it that some people have got that makes them able to move objects without touching them. The *Society for Psychical Research* (SPR) acknowledges this, saying 'Psychical research will not attain scientific respectability until it has some agreed theoretical basis' (SPR, 2012).

Burden of proof misplaced – Supporters of psi phenomena argue that the burden of proof is not theirs and say it is up to sceptics to disprove the reality of psi phenomena (see 'The Cottingley fairies' on facing page). Such disproof is difficult because, for example, it is not always easy to prove that a photo is fake. In science, as opposed to paranormal investigations, the burden of proof usually lies with the believer not the sceptic.

Lack ability to change – A key characteristic of science is that explanations are adapted as a result of hypothesis testing. If a scientist fails to find support for a hypothesis, the response is to develop a new explanation/hypothesis. This is not the case with psi phenomena which have continued to be explained in the same way for centuries despite a lack of evidence.

THE COTTINGLEY FAIRIES

The photograph on the right was regarded as definite proof of the existence of fairies. One of its notable believers was Sir Arthur Conan Doyle, who wrote the Sherlock Holmes stories. There were five photographs taken between 1916 and 1920 by cousins Elsie Wright and Frances Griffiths who lived in Cottingley near Bradford, England. The girls claimed to play with fairies but no one believed them so they produced photographic evidence. Various attempts to prove that the photos were fake failed and it was not until 1983 that the women admitted the hoax (www.cottingleyconnect.org.uk).

People continue to accept photographic evidence as proof for anomalous phenomena (such as photos of unidentified flying objects and photos of ghosts) despite the fact that photographs are easily faked. The burden of proof is placed on the sceptic who is asked by a believer: 'Well you explain this photograph then.' In scientific research the burden of proof is on the believer to provide supporting evidence or an explanation.

EVALUATION

Paranormal research is not the only pseudoscience – It is not fair to suggest that paranormal research is alone in masquerading as a science. The same accusations have been made, for example, about Freud's theory. Some of his hypotheses are unfalsifiable, as is the case for his view that all men have repressed homosexual tendencies. This cannot be disproved – if you do find men who appear to have no homosexual tendencies then it could be argued that they have them, it's just they are so repressed they are not apparent.

It could also be argued that psychology itself is not scientific. In 1992 Koch reviewed the state of psychological research and concluded that such research has resulted in verifiable *descriptions* of behaviour but the explanations derived from such research are more opinion than fact.

It is appears to be that paranormal research should not be singled out as pseudoscience as it is no better (or worse) than many other areas of psychological enquiry that are commonly accepted as being scientific.

Respectable research – Mousseau (2003) considered the question of whether parapsychology is a science or a pseudoscience by comparing articles in peer-reviewed parapsychology journals with journal articles covering respectable mainstream science. She concluded that parapsychology journals came out better because, for example, they did report negative findings (a necessary part of the scientific process). She found no mainstream articles that reported negative findings, a distinct case of selective reporting.

She also found that 43% of parapsychology journal articles produced empirical data, a reasonable figure (mainstream rates were higher at 64%). And she found that 24% of the parapsychology articles used the experimental method (compared to 57% in mainstream journals). This suggests that mainstream research is 'more scientific', but nevertheless a significant proportion of parapsychological research is embracing the goals of science.

Parapsychology as a science – The *American Association for the Advancement of Science* (AAAS), the largest general scientific society in the world, allowed the *Parapsychological Association* (PA) to become an affiliated member in 1969. This appears to confirm the scientific status of parapsychology. The PA is an international organisation with about 300 members, a relatively small professional organisation.

Where's the harm? There are three reasons to be concerned about paranormal research. First, some people make a lot of money out of unfounded claims, such as psychics who tour the country claiming to make contact with dead relatives.

Second, as a society we should be encouraged to ask for evidence rather than respond to trends and superstitions which, in the past, have resulted in the persecution of witches or the punishment of mental patients.

Third, on the positive side, thorough creditable research may lead to valuable discoveries. For example, acupuncture is now accepted as a valuable therapy due to research that has demonstrated replicable results.

WWW The web is full of relevant material. For example, look at the website of the Parapsychological Association (www.parapsych.org/index.html) that contains information, research and various online psi tests and questionnaires. There is also the James Randi Educational Foundation (JREF) (www.randi.org) that aims to promote critical thinking by providing reliable information about paranormal and supernatural ideas. The JREF sponsors the million dollar challenge, offering a prize of one million dollars to anyone who can demonstrate evidence of any paranormal, supernatural or occult power or event, under test conditions agreed to by both parties. As of this time, no one has claimed the prize.

Jonathan Miller (1983), a physician, actor and director, suggests that psychologists have deluded themselves about being scientists. Just because they use the appropriate terms and methods is no more than 'dressing up'. The same criticisms could be made of parapsychology.

CAN YOU...? No.15.1

...1 Explain, in about 100 words, what is meant by pseudoscience.

...2 Explain how the study of anomalous experience might be regarded as a pseudoscience. You should write about 100 words.

...3 Evaluate your explanation(s) in question 2. Each criticism should be elaborated to about 50 words.

...4 Answer the following 'apply your knowledge' question:

Sara is annoyed that her friend Sophie believes in ghosts and other paranormal phemonena. Sara is a true sceptic and wants to see good scientific evidence. She tells her friend that parapsychology is a pseudoscience.

(a) *Use your psychological knowledge to suggest what evidence Sara might give to convince Sophie that it is pseudoscientific?* (6 marks) [150-word answer]

(b) *Suggest a response that Sophie might make to justify her views.* (6 marks) [150-word answer]

METHODOLOGICAL ISSUES

When considering the scientific status of paranormal research, a key issue is the validity of the methods used in its investigation. On this spread we will consider some of the methodological issues in two key areas of paranormal research: **extrasensory perception** (ESP), an example of paranormal cognition, and **psychokinesis** (PK), an example of paranormal action.

ESP refers to the perception of objects or events without any of the known physical senses being involved, thus 'extra sensory' ('outside of the known senses'). It includes telepathy (ESP between two minds), clairvoyance (ESP at a distance with no other mind involved) and precognition (knowing about events in the future).

Psychokinesis (PK) is the movement or manipulation of objects or events without any physical contact. It literally means movement with the mind. The phenomenon can include distorting an object, such as spoon bending (called macro-PK) or influencing the output of probabilistic systems, such as dice throwing or random number generators (micro-PK).

GANZFELD STUDIES

Honorton (1974) developed the Ganzfeld technique because he (and other researchers) believed that the previous lack of success in ESP research occurred because psi is such a weak force as it is normally drowned out by our other senses. Ganzfeld (German for 'whole field') aims to create a situation of sensory deprivation to suppress sensory input, so a subject is better able to use their ESP and receive telepathic messages.

The subject (receiver) is typically isolated in a red-lit room with halved table-tennis balls taped over their eyes and earphones playing white noise.

The sender is in another room and chooses one of (usually) four images to send telepathically. The choice of image to send should be random.

Afterwards the receiver is shown a set of images and asked to select the target image from several. Alternatively, the receiver describes the image and an independent judge matches the description to one of the images.

INVESTIGATING MICRO PK

A random event generator (REG) is often used to investigate micro-PK. A REG is, essentially, a kind of electronic coin flipper that produces an equal number of heads and tails over a number of coin 'flips'. Micro-PK is demonstrated by asking volunteers to influence REG by coming up with more heads than tails, or vice versa.

Researchers have also looked at other random events. For example, Stevens (1998) conducted an experiment using the web where remote participants were invited to try to influence the activity of a split-beam laser. A comparison was made between participants in the experimental condition who did try to change the beam and those in a control condition who did nothing. Laser output was more active in the experimental condition.

Ganzfeld studies of ESP

Researcher bias – Wooffitt (2007) analysed Ganzfeld interviews and found evidence of researcher bias. He observed that sceptical researchers were much less encouraging when asking 'receivers' to elaborate their images whereas interviewers who believed in psi elicited lengthier responses that led to more positive results. Thus research expectations appear to have biased the results. The differential effect of beliefs on outcomes is called the *sheep–goat effect*.

Biased analysis – Expectations may affect other aspects of the research process. One of the key researchers on ESP, Charles Honorton (1985), published an analysis of 28 Ganzfeld studies, concluding that performance was significantly above chance. However, non-believers appear to find the opposite. For example, Ray Hyman (1985) re-analysed Honorton's data using a different method and found that results were not significant. In this case the researcher's beliefs influenced the method of analysis chosen, resulting in results that supported the researcher's beliefs.

The file–drawer effect – Many reports are reviews (**meta-analyses**). The outcomes of such reviews change if some studies are removed – this is a publication bias called the *file–drawer effect*, referring to researchers filing away (i.e. not publishing) studies with negative outcomes. The researcher's beliefs are again relevant because they influence which studies are left in or out.

Lack of control – Criticisms have been made about poor controls, for example poor soundproofing of the receiver's room would mean that, when videos are used as the stimuli to be sent, these could be heard by the receiver. A second criticism has been made about order of presentation of the target selections. There is generally a bias towards selecting the first one displayed. Therefore, presentation should be randomised to average out this bias.

Psychokinesis (PK)

The effect of expectations has been found in PK studies as well. For example, Wiseman and Greening (2005) demonstrated this in a study where participants were shown a video where a fake psychic placed a bent key on a table. In one condition (the 'expectation' condition) the participants heard him say that the key was continuing to bend – these participants later were more likely to report further bending than participants in a no-expectation condition. This shows that expectations make it more likely that a person reports a paranormal effect.

Lack of control – Hansel (1989) reported that well-controlled studies tended to produce no support for PK 30. Ideal controls for a conclusive PK test are having two researchers, true randomisation of targets and using independent recording of targets (a standard laid down by the earliest researcher, J.B. Rhine, in the 1950s). Hansel found that, out of the 30 PK studies he examined, only 13 produced positive results, none of which were adequately controlled. On the other hand, many of the studies returning negative results did apply controls. Therefore, the reason for positive findings would appear to be flawed methodology.

Ecological validity – The use of random number generators, such as REG, has led some paranormal researchers to suggest that this is an inappropriate way to investigate psychokinesis – inappropriate because the original claims for psychokinesis were about observable physical changes and REG concerns unobservable changes. It may be that PK doesn't function at the unobserved level.

► A horse with exceptional powers – it was claimed that Lady Wonder (above) could read people's minds and was studied by the ESP researcher J.B. Rhine (1929). Probably a case of researcher bias – the owner communicated expectations.

EVALUATION

Ganzfeld studies of ESP

Researcher bias – It could be argued that positive results from non-sceptical researchers are due to the fact that jealous phenomena (phenomena that disappear when observed by non-believers) only appear when in the presence of a non-sceptic. However, Hyman (1985) argued that, even if significant effects are found, these are meaningless unless some explanation can be offered about how this happens.

Improving control – The autoganzfeld technique was developed to deal with the early methodological criticisms about poor control. This procedure uses an automated computer system to select and display the targets. This means that the experimenter is blind as to which target has been selected and therefore cannot unconsciously influence the target selected by a judge as a match. The receiver is also placed in a soundproof steel-walled and electromagnetically shielded room. These changes dealt with the major objections.

Conflicting findings continue – Despite the use of more controlled techniques, the conflicting findings have continued. Honorton *et al.* (1990) reported the results of 11 autoganzfeld studies involving eight different researchers. The studies produced a hit rate of 34% (a statistically significant effect). However, sceptics Milton and Wiseman (1999) reviewed 30 further, well-controlled Ganzfeld studies and concluded that these studies showed no significant effects. In turn, this review was subsequently criticised because it included studies that had not followed the Ganzfeld protocol. When these inconsistent studies were removed, and some more recent studies added, a significant result was again obtained (Bem *et al.*, 2001).

Psychokinesis

Lack of control – Radin and Nelson (2003) conducted a meta-analysis of over 500 studies of micro-PK conducted between 1959 and 2000. They assessed the methodological quality (e.g. size of sample) of each study and correlated this with the outcomes, finding no significant relationship. This is further supported by a neutral research team (Bosch *et al.*, 2006) who looked at the highest quality studies and still found no significant effects. This suggests that quality is not a factor in obtaining significant effects.

Number of investigators – The positive findings of micro-PK studies may be due to the involvement of only a small number of investigators. However, the review by Radin and Nelson (2003) of 500 studies suggests this is not the case. In their sample 91 investigators were involved; about half of the studies were conducted by 10 investigators. They conclude that this suggests that the overall significant effect cannot be attributed to a small group of investigators gaining significant results.

File–drawer effect – Positive PK results have been attributed to selective reporting. Radin and Nelson (2003) calculated that there would need to be 10 unpublished studies with negative effects for each of the 500 published studies in order to nullify the effect.

There have been disagreements about how this figure can be calculated (e.g. Schub, 2006) but further support comes from Radin *et al.* (2006). They conducted a survey and found that the average number of unreported studies per investigator was only about one. Therefore, the file–drawer effect is unlikely to explain the positive findings.

Effect size – Bierman (2000) analysed a large number of paranormal studies conducted since the time of J.B. Rhine, including micro-PK studies. He concluded that there has been a steady decline in the effect size. Usually, if there is a real effect, the size of an effect should become greater over time because scientists are progressively better able to identify and control extraneous variables. By contrast, increasing control has had the opposite effect in paranormal research – effect sizes have been getting smaller, which suggests that the phenomena are not real.

CAN YOU...? No.15.2

...1 Explain, in about 100 words, how psychologists investigate paranormal cognition (ESP).

...2 Explain, in about 100 words, how psychologists investigate paranormal action (psychokinesis).

...3 Describe methodological issues related to the study of paranormal cognition (Ganzfeld), in about 100 words.

...4 Describe methodological issues related to the study of paranormal action (psychokinesis), in about 100 words.

...5 Outline **three** critical points for each of the topics in questions 3 and 4. For each you should include evidence to support the point being made. Each point should be about 50 words.

...6 Answer the following 'apply your knowledge' question:

A class of psychology students plan to study ESP. Outline methodological issues that they need to be aware of and suggest how they might deal with these. (8 marks)

On the previous spread we looked at evidence for anomalous experiences. Now we are going to put aside the question of whether anomalous experiences are real or not, and consider why some people have anomalous experiences and beliefs whereas others do not. Two possible explanations are examined on this spread: the way different people deal with coincidence and their ability to make probability judgements.

Evaluation

ILLUSION OF CONNECTION: SEEING FACES THAT AREN'T THERE

There may be biological support for the tendency to make connections that aren't real. Brugger *et al.* (1990) (in Philips, 2002) found that people with high levels of **dopamine** in their brain are more likely to find significance in coincidence, and pick out meaning when there is none. This might explain what sets believers apart from non-believers. In this study believers and non-believers were briefly shown real and scrambled faces and real and made-up words on a screen. The believers were more likely to see a face or word when there wasn't one, whereas the non-believers were more likely to *miss* a real face or word.

In the next part of the study both groups of participants were given the drug *L-dopa* which increases dopamine levels in the brain. The result was that the non-believers acted more like the believers, i.e. they saw more real faces/words when there were none. The drug had no effect on the believers.

◀ One explanation for the role of coincidence is that people interpret what they see erroneously by making links that aren't there. In the photo of the moon some people claim to see a face.

Evaluation

IS THERE A DIFFERENCE BETWEEN SHEEP AND GOATS?

Evidence that probability misjudgement may not explain paranormal beliefs comes from Susan Blackmore (1997). She asked over 6,000 participants to identify which of 10 statements were true for them (e.g. 'There is someone called Jack in my family', 'I have a scar on my left knee'). Participants were also asked to imagine how many statements would be identified as true for a person selected at random in the street. Blakemore found that people identified on average 2.42 statements as true for themselves and 3.57 as true for others, i.e. they overestimated the number true for others.

Blackmore found that people who believed in ESP generally gave higher answers for themselves and for others but the difference between self and other was about the same for believers and non-believers, suggesting that probability misjudgement does not explain paranormal belief.

THE ROLE OF COINCIDENCE

Illusion of causality – A coincidence is when two events happen at about the same time (they are co-incidents). Rightly or wrongly people often assume that one causes the other. In some situations it is obvious that there isn't a causal relationship, for example you think of your friend and it starts to rain – no likely link there. In other situations you might think there is a causal link, for example you think of your friend and at that same moment she phones you. It might be that people who believe in anomalous experience are more likely to think that such co-incidents have a causal link.

Illusion of control – Explanations for coincidence mean that people feel they control things that, in fact, they have no control over. This illusion of control makes the world seem a more orderly place. Research (e.g. Ayeroff and Abelson, 1976) has found that believers are more likely to express an illusion of control when engaged on a **psi** task.

General cognitive ability or intelligence might be lower in believers and thus they are less able to accurately judge whether a paranormal event, in fact, has a normal explanation. Some research has found that believers have significantly lower levels of academic performance than sceptics (e.g. Gray, 1987). Research has also found that believers perform less well on tests of *syllogistic reasoning* (e.g. all men are mortal, Tom is a man, therefore can we conclude that Tom is mortal?).

THE ROLE OF PROBABILITY JUDGEMENTS

'Probability' refers to the likelihood of an event occurring, such as the likelihood that a horse will win a race. Believers ('sheep') may underestimate the probability that certain events may simply happen by chance. Therefore, they reject coincidence as an explanation for paranormal events and attribute causality when, in fact, the events are simply random. Blackmore and Troscianko (1985) suggested that paranormal experiences are a kind of 'cognitive illusion' resulting from a failure to accurately judge probability. To test this, researchers have used a variety of probabilistic reasoning tasks, such as:

- ***Repetition avoidance*** – Participants are asked to produce a string of random numbers and the number of repetitions is counted. In a true series of random numbers there are consecutive repetitions but people who underestimate probability are less likely to produce such repetitions. Brugger *et al.* (1990) found that 'sheep' avoid producing repetitions more than 'goats'.

- ***Questions about probability*** – Blackmore and Troscianko (1985) asked participants various questions including the birthday party paradox – how many people would you need at a party to have a 50:50 chance that two of them will have the same birthday (not counting year)? More goats than sheep got this right when asked a multiple choice question containing the right answer of 23.

- ***Conjunction fallacy*** – Rogers *et al.* (2009) tested probability judgement by giving participants 16 'conjunction vignettes' (descriptions of occasions where two events co-occur, such as getting food poisoning after eating eggs). Participants were asked to indicate the probability of such events co-occurring. Sheep made more conjunction errors than goats.

What is it that separates the sheep (believers) from the goats (non-believers)? Are they less intelligent? Are they worse at probability judgements? Do they have flawed personalities? These questions are examined on this spread and the following two spreads.

EVALUATION

The illusion of causality may have adaptive significance – Causal thinking evolved because it allows people to understand and control their environment, for example being able to predict that eating a particular mushroom results in death. This causal thinking is adaptive but may sometimes lead to **Type 1 errors**: the null hypothesis is that 'mushrooms have no effect' whereas the alternative hypothesis (a causal one) is 'mushrooms cause death'. The Type 1 error is rejecting the null hypothesis when it is true. Such Type 1 errors are tolerated in order to avoid **Type 2 errors** (eating a mushroom that is actually poisonous). Foster and Kokko (2009) argue that the adaptive advantage will persist as long as the occasionally correct response has a large adaptive benefit.

Illusion of connection – Brugger *et al.* (see facing page) point out that the tendency to see things that aren't there also has an adaptive advantage – it's always better to think you see a tiger that is hidden in the grassland than miss it. This ability may also underlie creativity. In fact researchers have found a link between creativity and paranormal beliefs. For example, Thalbourne (1998) found that believers are more creative whereas non-believers are not and may even lose out because they fail to detect meaningful connections.

Illusion of control – This was supported in a study where illusion of control was experimentally manipulated. Whitson and Galinsky (2008) found that reduced control led participants to detect patterns where there were none and form illusory correlations between unrelated events (see details of this study on the next spread).

General cognitive ability – The finding that poor cognitive ability is associated with paranormal experience/beliefs hasn't been confirmed in all studies. In fact some researchers have actually found the opposite (e.g. Jones *et al.*, 1977).

Surveys also suggest that even amongst the scientific community belief is high, for example when *New Scientist* readers (who are mainly scientists and engineers and thus presumably high in cognitive ability) were questioned 67% said they regarded ESP either as an 'established fact' or 'a likely possibility' (Evans, 1973). Wiseman and Watt (2006) concluded from a general survey of research that believers and non-believers only differ in terms of syllogistic reasoning rather than cognitive ability generally.

EVALUATION

Contrasting research evidence – Not all research has found a difference between believers and non-believers in terms of their probability judgements (e.g. Blackmore, 1997, see facing page). One reason for the different findings from various studies may lie in the way that 'belief' is determined, as discussed top right. In many studies a general scale is used whereas in Blackmore's 1997 study there was simply one question about whether the participant believed in ESP.

Correlation is not cause – The research evidence largely suggests that there is a link between probability misjudgement and paranormal beliefs, but such a link doesn't mean we are justified in concluding that difficulties in making appropriate probability judgements cause the paranormal beliefs. There may be an intervening factor, such as cognitive ability.

Cognitive ability – Cognitive ability may explain the link between probability misjudgement and paranormal beliefs. Musch and Ehrenberg (2002) controlled for differences in general cognitive ability and found this reduced the performance difference between believers and non-believers on probability judgement tasks to zero. So it may be that poor probability judgements are due to low cognitive ability rather than directly causing a tendency to believe in psi phenomena (although research discussed above challenges this).

Not misjudgement, simply a different heuristic – A different approach to probability misjudgement is offered by Kahneman and Tversky (1972). They suggest that people use various heuristics (strategies to solve problems). One of these **heuristics** is representativeness – some people understand that short runs of tossing a coin will not be *representative* of a theoretical probability of 50:50 whereas other people expect short runs to match theoretical probability. This is referred to as the **gambler's fallacy**, for example believing that if you throw a coin and get three heads in succession it is more likely that tails will come up next (it isn't – the probability remains the same).

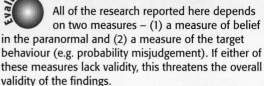

VALIDITY OF RESEARCH

All of the research reported here depends on two measures – (1) a measure of belief in the paranormal and (2) a measure of the target behaviour (e.g. probability misjudgement). If either of these measures lack validity, this threatens the overall validity of the findings.

Measuring belief in the paranormal usually involves a set of statements about psi phenomena. Some scales are restricted to 'core' phenomena, such as the *Australian Sheep–Goat Scale* – ASGS (Thalbourne and Delin, 1993), which mainly concerns ESP and PK. Other scales are broader, such as the *Paranormal Belief Scale* – PBS (Tobacyk and Milford, 1983), which covers an extensive range of paranormal phenomena, including UFOs, superstition and the Loch Ness monster. Blakemore (facing page) used a simpler measure – just asking people whether or not they believed in ESP.

The choice of measurement can have an important effect on the results because some characteristics (such as locus of control) only correlate positively if you use a narrow scale.

CAN YOU...? No.15.3

...1 Outline, in about 100 words, the role of coincidence in anomalous beliefs.

...2 Outline, in about 100 words, the role of probability judgements in anomalous beliefs.

...3 Outline **two or three** critical points for each of the topics in questions 1 and 2. For each you should include evidence to support the point being made. Each point should be about 50 words.

...4 Use some of this material to write a 200-word answer to each of the following questions:

Discuss the role of coincidence in anomalous beliefs. (4 marks + 6 marks)

Discuss the role of probability judgements in anomalous beliefs. (4 marks + 6 marks)

...5 Answer the following 'apply your knowledge' question:

Betty likes to read her horoscope. Last week it said she would have an argument with a close friend. She was astonished the following week when she did have an argument with her friend.

How could you use the concepts of coincidence and probability judgements to explain to Betty that the horoscope did not actually cause the argument? (8 marks) [200-word answer]

SUPERSTITIOUS BEHAVIOUR AND MAGICAL THINKING

Superstition and magical thinking may be the core cognitions that drive paranormal beliefs, according to Lindeman and Aarnio (2007). They are both examples of irrational thinking where a causal relationship has been assumed between events that are merely correlated, for example when a footballer believes that wearing odd socks causes good luck.

The distinction between superstitions and magical thinking is not always clear because the latter often underlies the former.

▲ A Chinese good luck pig.

EXPLANATIONS FOR SUPERSTITIOUS BEHAVIOUR

Superstitions are beliefs that are not based on reason or knowledge, such as believing that the number 7 is lucky.

Type 1 and 2 errors – Superstitions arise from making unjustified causal links. On the previous spread we explained that a preference for making a causal link between two unrelated events was adaptive. It is better to erroneously assume causality between unrelated events that co-occur (**Type 1 error**) than occasionally miss a genuine one (a **Type 2 error** believing no causal link when there is one).

Behaviourist explanation – Skinner (1947) proposed that superstitions develop through **operant conditioning** where an accidental stimulus–response link is learned (see 'Skinner's superstitious pigeons' on facing page). In fact, there are two components to this learning process. First, the superstition is acquired through operant conditioning. Second, it is maintained through **negative reinforcement** – every time you repeat the superstitious behaviour (for example don't walk under the ladder) anxiety is reduced, thus the superstitious belief is reinforced.

Illusion of control – Superstitions develop in situations where people feel a lack of control, such as sitting exams or playing in a football match. In order to gain some feeling of control, superstitious rituals are used to bring good luck. Whitson and Galinsky (2008) illustrated this with an experiment. In this study participants were first asked to recall situations in their lives – one group was asked to recall situations where they felt in control and the others were asked to recall instances where they felt a lack of control. Later, all participants were given stories involving a superstitious behaviour (e.g. stamping one's foot three times before entering a meeting) and asked to judge how much this affected the eventual outcome of the meeting. Participants who had been made to feel less in control were more likely to believe that the superstitious behaviour affected the eventual outcome.

EXPLANATIONS FOR MAGICAL THINKING

In the case of magical thinking, meaning is attached to objects or actions so that the objects/actions gain special (magical) properties. For example, some people believe that an ordinary glove gains special properties because Michael Jackson wore it.

Psychodynamic explanation – Freud (1913) identified magical thinking as a form of childlike thought where inner feelings are projected onto the outer world. For example, a person might believe that, if they think badly about a person, then that might cause the person's death. In adults, such behaviour is a **defence mechanism** where they regress as a means of coping with anxiety.

Dual processing theory – Even those who don't agree with Freud's formulation acknowledge that magical thinking is based on a child's mode of thought. Such thinking is intuitive, i.e. lacking internal logic. Adult thinking is logical (internally-consistent reasoning), however adults continue to use intuitive thinking in some situations (thus there are two processes, in other words dual processing.).

Animism – Piaget (1954) also considered the intuitive nature of young children's thought (see page 146). In the **pre-operational stage** a characteristic mode of thinking is *animism*, where children ascribe feelings to physical objects (e.g. a bed 'hurts' when you jump on it). Lindeman and Aarnio (2007) relate magical thinking to animism, for example *feng shui* assumes that positive feelings come from arrangements of furniture.

Nominal realism – A further characteristic of pre-operational thought, according to Piaget, is *nominal thinking* where children have difficulty separating the names of things from the things themselves. This carries on in adult thinking. For example, Rozin *et al.* (1986) poured sugar in two glasses labelled as 'sugar' or 'cyanide'. Participants who observed the pouring still were reluctant to drink from the glass labelled as poison.

Law of contagion states that things having been in contact continue to act on each other even after physical contact ceases. This can be extended to magical thinking, such as believing that a thing from someone special confers special powers. Nemeroff and Rozin (1994) relate this to our evolved fear of contagion. It would be adaptive to avoid touching something that had been in contact with a diseased person, leading to the belief that psychological and physical properties can pass between people via the things they touch.

EVALUATION

Behaviourist explanation – Skinner's study (see right) and explanation were challenged by Staddon and Simmelhag (1971), who repeated the study. They observed similar ritual behaviours but realised that these behaviours were unrelated to the food. A detailed record of the birds' behaviour showed that around the time of the food presentation, all the animals were behaving in the same way. The idiosyncratic rituals occurred at other times and were produced as frequently before any reinforcement had taken place. Schnur (2008) concludes that the pigeons' behaviour was not the result of accidental or 'adventitious' reinforcement.

However, a study with humans does support the role of such reinforcement. Matute (1996) exposed participants to uncontrollable noises being emitted from a computer in a library. The participants pressed various buttons to try to stop the noise – which did eventually stop but not because of the participants' activity. When the noise started again, the participants tried to press the key they had been pressing when the noise stopped the first time. They assumed cause where there was none.

Personal versus cultural superstitions – The explanations on the facing page only account for how individuals acquire *personal* superstitions. There are also culturally transmitted superstitions, for example the number 7 is lucky in the UK, whereas in Thailand it's the lucky number 9. This suggests that people sometimes adopt superstitions through indirect learning perhaps as a means of gaining a sense of control.

Illusion of control – Whitson and Galinsky (on facing page) suggest that the illusion of control brings benefits because it means we actively confront unpredictable circumstances rather than withdraw from them. The value of self-belief was demonstrated by Damisch *et al.* (2010). They found that the activation of good-luck-related superstitions led to enhanced performance on a variety of tasks (such as motor dexterity and memory) and suggest that such superstitions increase one's self-efficacy (belief in your own competence).

SKINNER'S SUPERSTITIOUS PIGEONS

Skinner's explanation for superstition is supported by an experiment with hungry pigeons in a cage (Skinner, 1947). For a few minutes each day, food pellets appeared at regular intervals. The bird's behaviour had no effect on the timing of the food. However, inevitably, certain random behaviours immediately preceded the food (and therefore *seemed* to cause the appearance of food). These behaviours then persisted as 'ritualistic behaviours'. For example, one bird repeatedly turned anti-clockwise and another developed a pendulum movement of the head.

The explanation offered by Skinner was that the random behaviours were reinforced by the arrival of food. The random behaviour did not cause the arrival of the food but appeared to cause it and therefore the food acted as a reinforcer for the behaviour.

You might think that when the birds later repeated their 'superstitious' behaviour – turning and nodding – and no food was immediately forthcoming, this would lead to 'unlearning'. It seems not, the fact that food did continue to appear occasionally would presumably maintain the 'superstition'.

WWW Test your own tendency towards magical thinking at www.goformegamall.com/forms/magic_ideation_scale.html

EVALUATION

Benefits of magical thinking – As with superstitions, magical thinking may lead people to deal more confidently with their environment because they expect good things to happen as a result of their beliefs and actions. Self-efficacy is one explanation, another is increased expectations similar to the placebo effect. Magical thinking acts like a placebo – it creates a positive expectation and this alone can account for improvements. This is called a *self-fulfilling prophecy* – things turn out as we expected just because of our expectations (Rosenthal and Jacobsen, 1968).

Costs of magical thinking – At the other extreme is the fact that magical thinking is associated with a number of mental disorders; too much is not a good thing. Magical thinking is sometimes listed as one of the characteristics for **schizophrenia** (Weinberger and Harrison, 2011), which suggests it might be an element in the separation from reality experienced by schizophrenics. Magical thinking is also a critical factor in **obsessive compulsive disorder** (OCD) (Yorulmaz *et al.*, 2011). OCD patients with a strong belief in magical thinking also reported more checking symptoms (e.g. checking all car doors are locked).

Lack of magical thinking may also have a cost. People who are depressed generally show less magical thinking, called *depression realism*. This suggests that a fully accurate assessment of one's own abilities may not be good for you (Hutson, 2008). A lack of magical thinking, as well as *anhedonia* (the inability to experience pleasure) has been linked to low levels of **dopamine**, a neurotransmitter that is high in both schizophrenics and believers in the paranormal (Mohr *et al.*, 2005).

CAN YOU...?   No.15.4

...1 Outline, in about 100 words, explanations for superstitious behaviour.

...2 Outline, in about 100 words, explanations for magical thinking.

...3 Outline **two or three** critical points for each of the topics in questions 1 and 2. For each you should include evidence to support the point being made. Each point should be about 50 words.

...4 Answer the following 'apply your knowledge' question:

Some people believe they can create good luck by wearing a 'good luck charm'.

Use your knowledge of psychology to explain why people might believe in good luck charms. (8 marks)

REAL-WORLD APPLICATION

Lives can be saved through the donation of organs for transplant after your death, however donation rates remain low. One possible explanation can be related to magical thinking. Vamos (2010) suggests that decisions may be based on the law of contagion – we link donation with the image of our dead body, therefore just thinking about the decision to carry a donor card creates negative emotions and discourages people from volunteering. Vamos suggests that donation rates might increase if more focus was made on the association between donation and giving someone else an extended life, so that the act of donation gains positive magical properties!

On the previous two spreads we have considered why some people have anomalous experiences whereas others do not – our predispositions to have paranormal beliefs are related to how we deal with coincidence and probability judgements, and our susceptibility for superstitious behaviour and magical thinking.

We now turn to a different kind of explanation, looking at the role of personality factors in anomalous experiences. 'Personality' refers to a person's consistent and relatively enduring set of behaviours, attitudes, feelings, capabilities and so on.

▶ There is a difference between anomalous experiences and anomalous belief. A lot of research is about beliefs as opposed to actual experiences but there is an assumption that the two are linked. People who have had paranormal experiences are likely to be believers and vice versa, but it is difficult to know which comes first, the experience or the belief.

▲ Unidentified flying object or observation platform?

Gow *et al.* (2004) found that people who reported the experience of seeing 'flying saucers' had higher levels of fantasy proneness and also were more likely to be believers.

THERE ARE MANY OTHER PERSONALITY FACTORS

Locus of control can also be considered as a personality characteristic. Research has shown a correlation between external locus of control and paranormal belief (e.g. Allen and Lester, 1994).

Hergovich (2003) found a positive correlation with field dependence and paranormal beliefs, which is possibly because such people rely less on detail.

Kumar *et al.* (1993) found that people with higher sensation-seeking personality scores had higher ratings for belief in the paranormal and also reported more such experiences. *Sensation seeking* is associated with high levels of extraversion.

Dissociation has also been linked to paranormal belief (Gow *et al.*, 2004). Dissociation refers to a separation of feelings, thoughts and experiences into separate streams of consciousness.

PERSONALITY FACTORS

Eysenck's personality factors

Eysenck (1967) proposed a biologically based theory of personality, based on three dimensions: neuroticism, extraversion and psychoticism. Research has linked the first two with paranormal beliefs.

Neuroticism is the tendency to experience negative emotional states (such as anger, anxiety and depression) rather than positive emotional states. Paranormal beliefs may create a distance from reality as a **defence mechanism** to reduce such negative emotional states. Various studies have found a positive relationship between neuroticism and paranormal beliefs. For example, Williams *et al.* (2007) tested nearly 300 Welsh school children and found a significant correlation (+.32) between paranormal beliefs and neuroticism. In this study no correlation was found between paranormal beliefs and either extraversion or psychoticism.

Extraversion is characterised by positive emotions and the tendency to seek extra stimulation to increase brain arousal levels. Peltzer (2002) found that extraversion was associated with paranormal beliefs but neuroticism and psychoticism were not. Honorton *et al.* (1992) conducted a **meta-analysis** of 60 published studies relating extraversion to ESP performance and found an overall positive correlation. One possible explanation for this link is that extraverts respond better to new stimuli than introverts and therefore are more open to paranormal experiences, which increases their belief.

A more imaginative personality

There are a number of personality characteristics linked to paranormal belief that can be considered under the general heading of 'imagination'.

Fantasy proneness refers to the tendency to become so deeply absorbed in a fantasy that it feels as if it is actually happening. Evidence suggests that paranormal believers are more fantasy prone. For example, research has found a link between belief in the paranormal and mental imagination (Dixon *et al.*, 1996).

A study by Wiseman *et al.* (2003) showed how becoming very involved in a task (deep absorption) may enable people to overlook the facts and believe in events they know are not true. In this study the researchers set up a 'mock' séance, in other words, everyone knew it wasn't real and that they were simply acting as if it were a real séance. During this séance one actor suggested that a table was levitating (it wasn't). After the séance more believers than non-believers reported that the table had moved. It might be that the believers were more deeply absorbed and this led them to believe despite knowing it to be fake. This might explain why, in general, believers are more easily 'fooled'.

Suggestibility is the inclination to accept the suggestions of others. People who are suggestible are more easily hypnotised. Hergovich (2003) proposed that suggestibility might also be linked to paranormal experience/belief because at least some paranormal phenomena are the result of deceptions (e.g. psychic mediums or the apparent spoon bending abilities of Uri Geller, which have been demonstrated to be fakes). Suggestible people might be more prone to accept such phenomena as real. To demonstrate this Hergovich tested participants' suggestibility by trying to hypnotise them and found a positive correlation between this and their score on a paranormal belief scale.

Creative personality – Thalbourne (1998) conducted a meta-analysis of relevant studies and found a correlation between creative personality and paranormal beliefs. People who are more creative may be more able to make links between unrelated items, a characteristic that may underlie paranormal experiences (see page 260).

EVALUATION

Different types of paranormal belief

Methods used to measure belief – A persistent issue raised by critics is that the correlations found between personality factors and paranormal belief depend on how the latter is measured. Many studies use the *Paranormal Belief Scale* (PBS) which consists of attitudes towards a range of different paranormal events, such as traditional religious belief, psi, witchcraft, superstition, spiritualism, extraordinary life forms and precognition (these are the seven sub-scales). Each of these sub-scales may produce different correlations, as we will see below.

Neuroticism – Wiseman and Watt (2004) focused on just the superstition sub-scale of the PBS (see box on right). One of their findings was that neuroticism was only related to paranormal beliefs relating to bad luck, in other words neuroticism doesn't explain all paranormal beliefs.

The mechanism underlying belief in good luck superstitions is likely to promote optimism unlike bad luck superstitions which indeed could create negative emotional states.

Psychoticism – There is evidence that this is linked to some paranormal beliefs. Francis *et al.* (2010) tested about 20,000 UK children aged 13–15 years and found that high psychoticism did correlate with unconventional paranormal beliefs, such as astrology and psychokinesis.

Locus of control – It may be that only some forms of psi (such as superstition) correlate positively with an external locus of control, whereas others (such as PK) correlate negatively (Wolfradt, 1997). This might explain why some studies (e.g. Davies and Kirkby, 1985) have found a positive correlation between an internal locus of control and paranormal belief. The unreliability of results may be, at least in part, due to the type of paranormal belief that is measured. Groth-Marnat and Pegden (1998) found that greater external locus of control was associated with spirituality and precognition, whereas internality was associated with superstition.

A more imaginative personality

Susceptibility – Clancy *et al.* (2002) found that people who claimed to have experienced an alien abduction also were found to be more susceptible to the suggestions of others, in particular more susceptible to false memories, when compared to people who hadn't had such an experience. It may be that some reports of paranormal experiences are actually false memories.

Link to false memories – Paranormal experience and belief may occur because people who have strong imaginations (e.g. those who are more creative) create a memory of events, such as sightings of UFOs, and then they believe them to be true, i.e. hold a false memory. A false memory is a memory that didn't happen but feels as if it is real.

There is evidence to support this. French and Wilson (2006) gave 100 participants a questionnaire. Four of the five items were about real events but one was fictitious (it was a CCTV footage of the first Bali bombing); 36% of the participants claimed that they did see the fictitious footage. These participants had scored higher on a test of paranormal belief and experience.

The final section of this chapter concerns research (studies and explanations) into various examples of exceptional experience – **psychic healing** and **psychic mediumship** on this spread. In considering these exceptional experiences you can also draw on other research in this chapter on the factors underlying anomalous experience as well as methodological issues involved in this kind of research.

▲ The Catholic Church concluded that psychic healing (in particular therapeutic touch) cannot be supported on the basis of an extensive review of relevant scientific research (Guinan, 2004).

PSYCHIC HEALING

Psychic healing refers to treatments used to deal with health problems by purely mental means. Such methods can be face-to-face, over the telephone or remotely. Methods include faith healing and laying on hands (therapeutic touch).

Explanations

Energy fields – Therapeutic touch (TT) is explained by supporters in terms of the ability to detect a patient's aura (energy field) without touching their body. Health is restored by re-aligning the patient's energy field. It is a popular treatment having been taught to at least 10,000 nurses in the US alone (Solfvin *et al.*, 2005).

Anxiety reduction – Psychic healing might be explained in terms of the beneficial effects of contact with a sympathetic person. Social support is known to reduce stress and anxiety, and enhance the effectiveness of the immune system (e.g. Kiecolt-Glaser *et al.*, 1984).

Placebo effect – Success might also be due to the **placebo** effect, i.e. real, measurable improvement that occurs as a result of believing that an effective treatment has been received. These beliefs may be based on the fact that some cases of psychic healing are apparently successful. Such apparent success may be due to spontaneous recovery or because recovery is only temporary and later the patient relapses, but such relapses are not reported.

Research studies

Therapeutic touch (TT) – Wirth (1990) conducted a study of patients with wounds who were either treated with TT or no treatment. The patients were not aware of the treatment they received, thus eliminating placebo effects. Wirth found that patients treated with TT healed faster.

Rosa *et al.* (1998) tested 21 TT practitioners. Each sat on one side of a screen and placed their hands through two holes in the screen. On the other side an experimenter placed one of her hands about four inches above the practitioner's right or left hand. TT practitioners should be able to detect the energy field of the hand but they were correct only 44% of the time (less than chance).

The effects of prayer – Wirth was involved in another study that looked at the effect of prayer on infertile women (Cha *et al.*, 2001). The researchers arranged for a group of Christian strangers to pray for some of the infertile women. As far as we know no one prayed for the other women. Those infertile women who were prayed for were twice as likely to become pregnant.

PSYCHIC MEDIUMSHIP

Psychic mediums claim to be able to communicate with people in the afterlife or spirit world.

Explanations

Sensitivity to cues – There are many clues that can help a talented medium produce accurate information (called **cold reading**). Even without sight of their 'sitter' they can pick up information from the sitter's tone of voice and the sitter's replies to previous statements.

The Barnum effect – A cold reader starts with some general statements that could apply, e.g. 'I see a recent loss of life' or 'I see the letter J' (Barnum statement), which elicit responses from the sitter. The responses can be used later in the conversation to convince listeners of the psychic's abilities (Wiseman and O'Keeffe, 2001). The willingness of sitters to elaborate on limited information helps the medium appear to have special powers.

Fraud – Spiritualism is big business, which means that people resort to complex and convincing strategies. For example, a medium might hire an accomplice to visit a regular sitter. During the visit, the accomplice asks to use the toilet and is able to steal a treasured possession. Later the medium asks if the person has lost something treasured and tells her where it can be found (Hines, 2003).

Research studies

TV test – Schwartz *et al.* (2001) tested five mediums, filmed by an American TV network. Two women were 'sitters' (one of them only saw two of the mediums). Both sitters were unknown to the mediums, were over 40 and had experienced a number of deaths recently. The mediums could not see the sitters and the sitters were only allowed to answer yes or no. The two women judged the accuracy of mediums' statements as 83% and 77% (respectively). When the same statements were given to a group of undergraduates, 36% were rated as accurate, suggesting that the mediums' performance was well above chance with the original sitters.

Rock and Beischel (2008) tested the belief that mediums can report specific and accurate information about deceased persons without cues. They tested this using two conditions. Six mediums spoke on the phone to a sitter (an experimenter). They were given no information about the sitter or the sitter's loved ones except names, and the only conversation consisted of the sitter asking questions about their loved one (e.g. what were their hobbies). In one condition the loved one was deceased and in the other condition the loved one was living. The medium was blind to the conditions yet significant differences in the information retrieved were found between the two conditions.

EVALUATION

Explanations

Sheep–goat effect – The study by Lyvers *et al.* (see right) suggests that belief in psychic healing may explain at least some of its success. Belief creates positive expectations, acting like a placebo.

Lack of support for the placebo effect – Benson *et al.* (2006) studied patients recovering from cardiac surgery. One group of patients acted as a control and the other two groups were told prayers were being said for them. In fact only one group was prayed for; the other group were the placebo group (they expected benefits). There was no benefit from the placebo effect. In fact the only group to suffer more complications were those who were prayed for (i.e. there was actually a negative effect).

Research studies

Therapeutic touch (TT) – TT supporters have criticised the Rosa *et al.* study because it was designed by a nine-year-old girl, although this is not necessarily a problem and the article was published in the reputable, peer-reviewed *Journal of the American Medical Association*. TT supporters have also claimed the study was invalid because the experimenter was not ill, which might affect their aura (Hines, 2003).

Replication – Long *et al.* (1999) repeated the Rosa *et al.* study using ordinary people instead of TT practitioners and found that, when the experimenter's hand was only about three inches away, the results were better than chance. Long *et al.* suggest that this was due to the ability to detect heat from the experimenter's hand. Glickman and Gracely (1998) designed a study that eliminated body heat, and the results were at the chance level, supporting the heat explanation.

Wirth's research has attracted criticism. He failed to replicate his own research on wound healing (Wirth *et al.*, 1997) and researchers who wished to discuss his research have failed to be able to contact him (Solfvin *et al.*, 2005). The study on the power of prayer has also been questioned by Flamm (2004), leading one of the authors to withdraw his name saying he had nothing to do with the study. Subsequently Wirth has been convicted of criminal fraud and given a five-year prison sentence, and the final author, Cha, has been accused of plagiarism in another journal. Nevertheless, worryingly, the study continues to be cited and taken as evidence for the power of prayer (Flamm, 2005).

▶ Derek Acorah, billed as TV's number 1 medium. Derek claims to access the spirit world through a guide called Sam whom he first met 2,000 years ago. However, many people don't believe he has special powers. Derren Brown has shown how easy it is to fake spirit readings (see YouTube for examples). Further challenges to Acorah's authenticity have been made by one of the TV shows' parapsychologists, Dr Ciaran O'Keeffe, who claimed to invent a spirit called Kreed Kafer (an anagram of Acorah faker). Acorah later became possessed by this character.

THE POWER OF BELIEF

A team of psychologists was invited by an Australian TV company to test the powers of a well-known Australian psychic. Lyvers *et al.* (2006) recruited 20 volunteers, who were all suffering from chronic back pain, through newspaper adverts and randomly assigned them to a treatment or control group (the volunteers didn't know which group they were in).

During the experiment all participants were told that the psychic was focusing on them, although in fact the psychic only focused on the treatment group. The TV broadcast showed the psychic seated in a separate room looking at a photo of each participant in turn.

The effect of the psychic healing was assessed using the *McGill Pain Questionnaire*. No overall reduction in pain was recorded in either the treatment or control groups.

However, what was interesting was that there was a correlation between belief and final pain score. All participants filled in a pre-treatment questionnaire about belief in psychic healing and this correlated positively with the extent to which pain was reduced irrespective of the group they were in. This suggests that belief plays a central role in the success of psychic healing.

EVALUATION

Explanations

Willingness to be deceived – Roe (1996) reports that many sitters are aware that mediums are just using general statements but nevertheless remain convinced. This is supported by the mock séance study (Wiseman *et al.*, 2003, see page 264). Even though participants knew the séance was fake, believers had a tendency to be taken in by events.

Research studies

Contradictory evidence – O'Keeffe and Wiseman (2005) arranged for five mediums to give readings for five sitters. Each sitter read all of the 25 readings produced and rated the personal relevance of each statement. The ratings were actually lowest for the statements written for them. This well-controlled study, conducted by sceptics, showed no evidence of mediumship.

Criticism – Schwartz *et al.* (facing page) used undergraduates to determine a baseline for the accuracy of the cold readings. Each undergraduate considered how accurately each statement reflected their own feelings. Since the statements were written to apply to older women who had experienced deaths in recent years, it is likely that the undergraduates would find the statements low in accuracy.

The sheep–goat effect – In general the quality of research conducted on mediumship is poor. Most people are content to believe in it without scientific proof so there is less motivation to conduct well-controlled research. What research is conducted tends to show the usual pattern of positive findings from believers (e.g. Rock and Beischel) and negative findings from sceptics.

CAN YOU...? (No.15.6)

...**1** Outline, in about 100 words, each of the following: studies related to psychic healing, explanations of psychic healing, studies related to psychic mediumship and explanations of psychic mediumship.

...**2** Outline **two or more** critical points for each of the above four topics. For each you should include evidence to support the point being made, writing about 50 words.

...**3** Answer the following 'apply your knowledge' question:

Many people pay to see psychic mediums perform on stage.

Use your knowledge of psychology to explain why people are prepared to spend money to do this. (8 marks)

OUT-OF-BODY AND NEAR-DEATH EXPERIENCES

Out-of-body experiences (OOBEs) and **near-death experiences** (NDEs) share certain characteristics, such as experiencing a detachment from one's physical body. However, NDEs are clearly linked to death or other stressful experiences, whereas OOBEs are associated with relaxation.

Unlike the other paranormal phenomena covered in this chapter, OOBEs and NDEs have a reasonably sound scientific pedigree. Controlled, replicated research has indicated real physiological explanations for these experiences, however a link with the paranormal remains (for example NDEs are seen by some as evidence of the existence of the soul).

You can use explanations as a way to evaluate the research studies and vice versa.

▲ In an OOBE the second body is called the 'parasomatic' body which may be experienced as an exact replica, like an identical twin, or experienced as a white weightless cloud or just a sense of pure consciousness. In rare cases (3.5%) there is a cord connecting the two bodies (Green, 1968). You could try your own qualitative analysis using first-hand accounts of OOBEs at www.oberf.org/stories_obe.htm

OUT-OF-BODY EXPERIENCE (OOBE)

Out-of-body experience refers to the sensation of being awake and seeing your own body from a location outside your physical body. About 15–20% of people claim to have experienced an OOBE (Blackmore, 1982).

Explanations

Paranormal explanations suggest that something beyond our current understanding is happening. The only possible way to explain how you can physically leave your body is by separating mind and body (see 'reductionism' below).

Biological explanations suggest that OOBEs are related to sensory disturbance. For example, Blackmore (1982) suggests that normally we view the world as if we were behind our eyes. In situations where sensory input breaks down, the brain attempts to reconstruct what we are seeing using memory and imagination. Memory images are often bird's-eye views so the constructed image usually appears to be viewing oneself from above.

Research studies

Naturally-occurring OOBEs – Green (1968) studied 400 personal accounts of OOBEs and classified them as parasomatic (about 20% of the accounts) or sometimes asomatic (no sense of another body). She also found, for example, that 25% of the cases were associated with some kind of psychological stress and 12% occurred during sleep.

Artificially induced OOBEs – Alvarado (1982) reviewed a range of lab studies where OOBEs were induced by various means (e.g. relaxation, hypnosis, audio-visual stimulation). The participants were then asked to identify target objects out of sight of their physical body. In one experiment a Miss Z was able to read out a randomly selected five-digit number placed in another room (Tart, 1968). Overall Alvarado considered that the evidence was weak although there were some striking results.

Biological studies – Blanke *et al.* (2002) induced OOBEs accidentally by electrically stimulating the *temporal-parietal junction* (TPJ) in a woman who suffered epilepsy in that region. This led them to study neurologically normal subjects as well (Blanke *et al.*, 2005). Stimulation of the TPJ using **transcranial magnetic stimulation** resulted in OOBEs whereas stimulation of other areas did not.

NEAR-DEATH EXPERIENCE

Near-death experiences (NDEs) occur when a person is close to death and also after fainting or simply in stressful or threatening situations.

Explanations

Psychological explanations – Some people hold paranormal beliefs and this leads them to interpret events in terms of paranormal explanations, for example viewing NDEs as spiritual experiences.

Biological explanations – One suggestion is that endorphins are released at times of pain or stress and these lead to feelings of euphoria and detachment (Carr, 1982).

More recent explanations suggest that NDEs are related to hypoxia (lack of oxygen) which may occur, for example during cardiac arrest or fainting. This hypoxia might cause **REM** intrusions which create a mixed sleep/awake state that could, like OOBEs, disrupt the integration of sensory information.

Alternatively hypoxia creates a flood of the neurotransmitter **glutamate** which causes neuronal death. As a defence, the brain creates a protective blockade to prevent neuronal death and this blockade is the source of an NDE.

Research studies

Naturally-occurring NDEs – Ring (1980) interviewed 100 people who had NDEs, finding that about 60% of survivors reported a sense of peace, 33% reported OOBEs, 25% said they entered a tunnel and a few had experienced a kind of 'life review'.

Nelson *et al.* (2006) studied 55 people with NDEs and 55 controls. He found that the NDE group were more likely to also experience 'REM intrusions'.

Artificially induced NDEs – Jansen (1993) has experimented with the drug **ketamine**, giving it to patients to observe the effects. He has found that it can produce the classic symptoms of NDEs. In addition, ketamine has been found to trigger the same blockade as glutamate (Jansen, 2009).

INDIVIDUAL DIFFERENCES

As with other paranormal experiences, OOBEs are reported more often by individuals who are paranormal believers (Irwin, 1985). People who have OOBEs are also more fantasy prone, score higher on hypnotisability and on dissociation (ability to separate different aspects of conscious activity) (Gow *et al.*, 2004; Irwin, 1985). Such characteristics go some way to explaining why such individuals have OOBEs. However, there is no evidence to suggest people with OOBEs are mentally ill, although the experience may make people feel they are losing their mind (Gabbard and Twemlow, 1984).

CREATING OOBES

Ehrsson (2007) provided support for the link between sensory disturbance and OOBEs. He did this by demonstrating that an OOBE can be created by scrambling a person's visual and touch sensations. This is done by placing a pair of video displays in front of a participant's eyes. The displays show a live film relayed by two video cameras that are two metres behind the participant (left camera to left eye, right camera to right eye). The participant sees their own back as if they were sitting behind themselves. The experimenter then places one rod on the participant's chest (out of the participant's view) and another rod on where the illusory body would be located just below the camera's view. Participants reported feeling that they were sitting behind their physical body and looking at it from that location.

Ehrrsson tested the reality of the illusion by threatening the illusory body. Participants displayed a physiological fear response (perspiration on their skin).

EVALUATION

Explanations

Paranormal explanations – The evidence does not support such explanations. For example, Alvarado's review did not find evidence that the parasomatic body had physically moved out of the physical body. He did acknowledge some exceptional cases but perhaps these can be explained in terms of suspect methodology, for example the participant might have had the opportunity to see the target object prior to the test.

Biological explanations suggest that OOBEs are related to sensory disturbance. There is support for this from the Blanke *et al.* study (facing page) that implicates activation of the TPJ. Other research shows that this area of the brain is implicated in the construction of the sense of body in space (Persinger, 2001).

Ehrsson's research (on the right) also showed a link between sensory disturbance and OOBEs.

Research studies

Artifical versus natural OOBEs – One of the problems with any research is that it is difficult to study natural OOBEs because they occur without predictability and, even if a researcher was present, the OOBE would cease as soon as the participant reported it. Therefore, most research is conducted on artificially-induced OOBEs in lab settings. Some researchers (e.g. Holden *et al.*, 2006) do not regard these as equivalent to naturally-occuring OOBEs.

EVALUATION

Explanations

Psychological explanation – The fact that NDEs are not experienced by all near-death patients means that there is likely to be a psychological component to the experience. For example, some people may expect to have such experiences and then, if they experience certain physiological changes, they label these as a spiritual event.

Spiritual explanation – van Lommel *et al.* (2001) followed 344 cardiac survivors over eight years and found that those who had experienced an NDE subsequently regarded it as a life-changing, spiritual experience. Those who didn't have an NDE continued to fear death. This suggests that it is a spiritual *experience* but that doesn't mean that it is caused by spiritual factors.

Cultural differences – Augustine (2008) presented a comprehensive review of NDEs in different cultures and provided examples, such as in India NDEs involve encounters with Hindu figures and in Japan there were no instances of any light appearing. There were also consistent features, such going through a tunnel, feelings of peace, OOBEs, and meeting a barrier between life and death. Such differences and similarities suggest that both psychological and physiological factors are involved.

Research studies

Early studies may have lacked appropriate controls. **Interviewer bias** may have affected the data collected as Moody (1975) reported NDEs as wonderful experiences, whereas more recent research has found that for many people they are experienced as frightening.

CAN YOU...? No.15.7

...1 Outline, in about 100 words, each of the following: studies related to out-of-body experience, explanations of out-of-body experience, studies related to near-death experience and explanations of near-death experience.

...2 Outline **two or more** critical points for each of the above four topics. For each you should include evidence to support the point being made, writing about 50 words.

...3 Answer the following 'apply your knowledge' question:

A psychology teacher has been asked to prepare a leaflet on out-of-body experiences for her local paranormal society. She wants to make it as balanced as possible, including views in favour and against the reality of such experiences.

Prepare a short leaflet that she might use, based on psychological research relating to explanations and/or studies.
(8 marks) [200-word answer]

CHAPTER SUMMARY

THE STUDY OF ANOMALOUS EXPERIENCE

PSEUDOSCIENCE AND PARAPSYCHOLOGY

- Pseudoscience – masquerading as science.
- Lacks falsifiability – hypotheses can't be disproved because they are 'jealous' phenomena.
- Lacks controlled, replicable research, e.g. Bem (2011) not replicated.
- Lacks theory to explain phenomena, e.g. ESP.
- Burden of proof misplaced on sceptic.
- Lacks ability to change explanations.
- If there are two competing explanations, simpler one is to be preferred (Occam's razor) – paranormal explanations are extremely convoluted.

EVALUATION
- Paranormal research is not the only pseudoscience – some Freudian hypotheses also unfalsifiable.
- Koch (1992) argues that psychology lacks objective theories.
- Mousseau (2003) – paranormal research often matches standards of scientific research, or even betters it (e.g. publishing negative results).
- The AAAS accepted the Parapsychological Association as a member.
- Reasons to be concerned about paranormal research include: making money out of unfounded claims, not asking for evidence.

METHODOLOGICAL ISSUES

ESP (GANZFELD)
Significant results could be due to other factors, e.g.:
- Researcher bias – sheep–goat effect in receiver's elaborations (Wooffitt, 2007).
- Expectations affect outcome of meta-analysis – Honorton (1985) vs Hyman (1985).
- File–drawer effect – results of meta-analyses change according to which studies are left out.
- Lack of control – lack of soundproofing and order of presentation.

EVALUATION
- Positive results could be due to phenomena being 'jealous'.
- Autoganzfeld improved control (e.g. random display of targets).
- This still led to positive results by Honorton et al. (1990) but not Milton and Wiseman (1999), although this was criticised by Bem et al. (2001).
- Fraudulent research by Sargent still included in data; fraud may be a particular problem in parapsychology.

PSYCHOKINESIS (PK)
- Expectations created in study by Wiseman and Greening (2005), led to macro-PK reports.
- Lack of control – well-controlled studies show no effect (Hansel, 1989).
- Ecological validity – micro-PK may not represent paranormal action.

EVALUATION
- Quality of studies not related to positive results (Radin and Nelson, 2003), same findings from non-believers (Bosch et al., 2006).
- Significant effects not due to a small group of investigators nor to file–drawer effect (Radin and Nelson, 2003).
- Bierman (2000) – steady decline in effect size over years, suggesting phenomena not real.

RESEARCH INTO EXCEPTIONAL EXPERIENCE

PSYCHIC HEALING AND MEDIUMSHIP

PSYCHIC HEALING
EXPLANATIONS
- Energy fields re-aligned by e.g. therapeutic touch.
- Reduction of anxiety through psychological support.
- Placebo effect – expectations of benefit created by success stories which could be due to spontaneous recovery.

EVALUATION
- Lyvers et al. (2006) – no evidence for psychic healing, believers improved more.
- No placebo effect for prayers for cardiac recovery (Benson et al., 2006).

RESEARCH STUDIES
- Wirth (1990) – tested patients treated with TT or no touch – former recovered faster.
- Rosa et al. (1998) – TT practitioners unable to detect 'energy field' of experimenter's hand.
- Cha et al. (2001) – effect of prayer on infertile women, twice as many became pregnant.

EVALUATION
- Rosa et al. study invalid because experimenter not ill.
- Study repeated (Long et al., 1999), results better than chance, however this may be through heat detection.
- Wirth's results haven't been replicated, and Wirth was subsequently convicted of criminal fraud.
- Power of prayer study – one researcher has withdrawn their name.

PSYCHIC MEDIUMSHIP
EXPLANATIONS
- Clues help medium produce accurate information without psychic ability (cold reading).
- Use of general statements (Barnum statements) and willingness of sitters to elaborate.
- Fraud – psychic mediumship is big business so people resort to complex and convincing strategies.

EVALUATION
- Sitters willing to be deceived.
- Supported by mock séance (Wiseman et al., 2003).

RESEARCH STUDIES
- Schwartz et al. (2001) – accuracy of medium statements about 80%.
- Rock and Beischel (2008) – mediums responding differently to dead or living loved ones.

EVALUATION
- O'Keeffe and Wiseman (2005) – five mediums gave readings to five sitters producing 25 statements which were rated by sitters as having little relevance.
- Schwartz et al. – undergraduates not suitable as control group.
- Sheep–goat effect – positive findings from believers.

OUT-OF-BODY AND NEAR-DEATH EXPERIENCES

OUT-OF-BODY EXPERIENCE (OOBE)
EXPLANATIONS
- Paranormal – mind and body separated.
- Sensory input is disturbed, reconstruction based on bird's-eye view (Blackmore, 1982).

EVALUATION
- Alvarado (1982) found no evidence of parasomatic body having physically moved.
- Link between sensory disturbance and OOBEs – Blanke et al. (2002) and Ehrsson (2007).
- Individual differences, e.g. OOBEs reported more often by believers and those prone to fantasy.

RESEARCH STUDIES
- Green (1968) – 400 personal accounts of OOBEs, 20% 'parasomatic', rest 'asomatic'.
- Use of induced OOBEs (Alvarado, 1982) – weak but occasionally startling results.
- Blanke et al. (2002) – stimulation of temporal-parie junction of the brain resulted OOBEs.

EVALUATION
- Difficult to study OOBEs scientifically because occur without predictability.
- Artificially-induced OOBEs no seen as equivalent.
- Physiological explanations are reductionist.

NEAR-DEATH EXPERIENCE (NDE)
EXPLANATIONS
- Evidence of an afterlife or 'soul' due to paranormal beliefs.
- Endorphins released at time of stress, lead to feelings of euphoria and detachment (Carr, 1982).
- REM intrusions due to hypoxia disrupt integration of sensory information.
- Hypoxia triggers a flood of glutamate which is blocked by the brain to prevent neuronal death, leading to an NDE.

EVALUATION
- Likely to be a psychological component because NDEs not experienced by all.
- Cardiac survivors regarded NDE as a spiritual experience, but this doesn't mean that spiritual factors cause NDEs.
- Cultural differences and similarities suggest that both psychological and physiological factors important.

RESEARCH STUDIES
- Ring (1980) – surviv describe NDE as peaceful and like a review.
- Nelson et al. (2006) NDE group more lik to experience REM intrusions.
- Jansen (1993) – ketamine can produ symptoms of NDEs, and ketamine has s effect as glutamate (Jansen, 2009).

EVALUATION
- Early studies poorly controlled.
- Interviewer bias ma affect data collecte

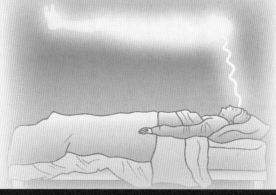

EXPLANATIONS FOR ANOMALOUS EXPERIENCE

COINCIDENCE AND PROBABILITY

SUPERSTITIOUS BEHAVIOUR AND MAGICAL THINKING

PERSONALITY FACTORS IN ANOMALOUS EXPERIENCE

THE ROLE OF COINCIDENCE
- Illusion of causality – if two things happen at same time, 'sheep' more likely to believe that one has caused the other.
- Illusion of connection – making links between unrelated items.
- Illusion of control – explanations for coincidence give sense of order in world, more likely in 'sheep' (Ayeroff and Abelson, 1976).
- General cognitive ability – lower intelligence more likely to be believers.

EVALUATION
- Adaptive significance – Type 1 errors of causal thinking tolerated in order to avoid Type 2 errors.
- Illusion of connection – may be created by higher levels of dopamine (Brugger et al., 2002).
- Making links also adaptive and may underlie creativity (Thalbourne, 1998).
- Illusion of control supported by Whitson and Galinsky (2008).
- General cognitive ability – not always confirmed in all studies, e.g. Jones et al. (1977) found complete opposite.

THE ROLE OF PROBABILITY JUDGEMENTS
- Paranormal experiences are a cognitive illusion due to attributing cause to random events (Blackmore and Troscianko, 1985).
- Tested using repetition avoidance (e.g. estimate dice throw), questions about probability (e.g. birthday party paradox), conjunction vignettes (estimate probability).

EVALUATION
- Blackmore (1997) – no difference between sheep and goats on probability task.
- Evidence shows belief is linked to probability misjudgement but not necessarily a cause.
- Probability misjudgement may be linked to low cognitive ability.
- Probability misjudgements can alternatively be explained in terms of failing to understand heuristics, such as representativeness (Kahneman and Tversky, 1972).

EXPLANATIONS FOR SUPERSTITIOUS BEHAVIOUR
- Making erroneous causal links (Type 1 error) is adaptive.
- Skinner (1947) – superstitions develop when an accidental stimulus-response link is learned, and then maintained through negative reinforcement (dual process).
- Superstitions develop to give an illusion of control (Whitson and Galinsky, 2008).

EVALUATION
- Skinner provided evidence from study of pigeons, who acquired superstitions.
- Staddon and Simmelhag (1971) repeated Skinner's experiment and found 'superstitious' behaviours unrelated to food reward.
- Matute (1996) – humans did learn to press a button despite no actual effectiveness.
- Some superstitions are learned indirectly (cultural), provide sense of control.
- Illusion of control increases self-efficacy (Damisch et al., 2010).

EXPLANATIONS FOR MAGICAL THINKING
- Freud (1915) – a form of child-like thinking, a defence mechanism in adults.
- Dual processing theory – thought is intuitive or logical.
- Animism (Piaget, 1954) – association of objects with feelings, e.g. feng shui.
- Nominal thinking – names of objects affect our feelings about them, e.g. a jar labeled cyanide (Rozin et al., 1986).
- Law of contagion – magical thinking is adaptive to avoid disease (Nemeroff and Rozin, 1994).

EVALUATION
- Experimental support with voodoo dolls – participants felt more responsible if they had bad thoughts (Pronin et al., 2006).
- May act like a placebo and provide positive expectations (e.g. Rosenthal and Jacobsen, 1968 – self-fulfilling prophecy).
- Costs – associated with mental disorder, e.g. schizophrenia and OCD.
- Benefits – avoid 'depression realism', lack of magical thinking linked to low levels of dopamine (Mohr et al., 2005).
- Real-world application – increase willingness to donate organs for transplant (Vamos, 2010).

EYSENCK'S PERSONALITY FACTORS
- Neuroticism – negative emotional states reduced by paranormal beliefs (defence mechanism).
- Extraversion – people more open to paranormal beliefs.
- Positive correlation with neuroticism (Williams et al., 2007) and with extraversion (Honorton et al., 1992).

MORE IMAGINATIVE PERSONALITY
- Fantasy proneness – becoming so deeply absorbed in fantasy to believe it real, demonstrated in fake séance (Wiseman et al., 2003).
- Suggestibility – more willing to believe fakes, link demonstrated by Hergovich (2003).
- Creative personalities make links between unrelated items (Thalbourne, 2001).

OTHER FACTORS
- Locus of control, field dependence, higher sensation seeking and dissociation.

EVALUATION
- Method used to measure paranormal beliefs affects correlations with personality factors.
- Wiseman and Watt (2004) found correlation with neuroticism only when negative beliefs of PBS measured.
- Evidence that psychoticism is linked to some paranormal beliefs (Francis et al., 2010).
- Locus of control – depends on type of paranormal belief, some correlate positively with externality, others negatively.
- Susceptibility might explain recollection of alien abductions (Clancy et al., 2002).
- Paranormal experiences may be false beliefs, more common in susceptible people, supported by French and Wilson (2006).
- Some evidence of link with mental disorder but more likely satisfies a need for some people, e.g. abuse in childhood may lead to fantasy proneness and need for a greater sense of control.

EXAM QUESTION WITH STUDENT ANSWER

QUESTION **(a) Discuss issues of pseudoscience in relation to the study of anomalous experience**
(4 marks + 6 marks)
(b) Mr Smith's wife wants to go to see a psychic healer. Mr Smith thinks such performances are just acting but Mrs Smith is a real believer. Use your knowledge of personality factors to explain why people differ in their beliefs about anomalous experience. *(4 marks)*
(c) Outline and critically evaluate research into out-of-body and/or near-death experience.
(4 marks + 6 marks)

STUDENT ANSWER

(a) *Many people have criticised studies of anomalous experience for being pseudoscientific. There are several reasons for this. One is that such studies often have hypotheses that are impossible to falsify. For example, if a hypothesis is proved to be wrong believers argue that this is actually a demonstration of 'jealous phenomena' – due to the presence of non-believers or doing research which is too highly controlled which prevents psi phenomena being displayed.*

Studies of anomalous experience also are often poorly controlled and also fail to be replicated. These are key features of scientific research. Scientists seek to demonstrate causal relationships but in order to do so they must exclude extraneous variables.

Science also aims to develop theories or explanations of the phenomena that are observed. This is a key part of the scientific process. Studies of anomalous experience have not led to convincing explanations, which is further evidence that this area of research is pseudoscientific.

A further part of the scientific process is that explanations should be adapted to explain any new evidence, whereas this is not true with paranormal research. When studies have found no support for psi phenomena changes are not made to explanations.

(b) *One suggestion is that believers are more neurotic than non-believers. It could be that people use paranormal beliefs as a way to distance themselves from reality and this reduces the negative emotional states associated with neuroticism. So Mrs Smith might be neurotic.*

Another suggestion is that believers tend to have an external locus of control. So it might be that Mr Smith has a greater sense of internal control, in other words he believes things happen because he is controlling them rather than being externally determined by a paranormal force.

(c) *Alvarado (1982) reviewed a number of studies that looked at whether people having an OOBE were actually out of their body. This was tested by seeing if they could identify objects that were out of sight of their physical body. Alvarado did find one or two cases where people were able to do this but generally there was little evidence to support the idea that a person was actually out of their body.*

One criticism of this kind of research is that, in order to study OOBEs, particularly in a controlled environment, they have to be artificially induced. This is done, for example, through relaxation or hypnosis. Some people argue that such OOBEs are not the same as naturally occurring ones (they are not as complex and may not be the same thing at all). So we can't really draw valid conclusions from these studies.

Studies of naturally occurring OOBEs generally just seek to categorise the kinds of OOBE that people have. You can't do much else really because, if a person in the middle of an OOBE starts to talk about it, the OOBE stops. So all people can do is record their OOBE experience and then people can analyse those experiences to find things that are commonplace in OOBEs. Green (1968) studied 400 personal reports and concluded that some people did not experience a second body (called asomatic cases) whereas sometimes there was another body (parasomatic) and the two bodies were sometimes linked by a cord.

Other research has focused on the physiological aspects of OOBEs. Blanke et al. (2002) found that if you stimulated a part of the brain called the TPJ people had OOBE experiences. Again we don't know whether these are actually the same as naturally occurring OOBEs but the research does support the idea that OOBEs are the result of sensory disturbance because the TPJ area of the brain is associated with experiencing the sense of our bodies in space.

[613 words]

EXAMINER COMMENTS

The answer to part (a) is well-structured and contains a number of arguments that demonstrate why studies of anomalous experience might be considered pseudoscientific. These arguments are accurate and detailed, although they would have benefitted from the use of actual examples from research into anomalous experience (as has been done in the first paragraph). This means that the descriptive element would be described as **reasonably detailed** rather than well-detailed.

The main problem is that there is no evaluation (which was required in the question). The student needed to cover fewer descriptive points and instead present some arguments against the idea that paranormal research is pseudoscientific.

AO1 – Well-structured, a **range of relevant material selected**, **accurate** and **reasonably detailed**.

AO2/AO3 – No creditworthy material.

Part (b) is an example of an 'apply your knowledge' kind of question, which is all AO2. The student has used psychological knowledge to try to explain the personality differences but there is only minimal attempt to engage with the characters in the stem of the question and no mention is made of psychic healing.

AO2 – Application is **sometimes focused**.

In part (c) the student has focused entirely on OOBEs even though NDEs are included in the question – but the question says 'and/or' and therefore full marks can be awarded if only one kind of experience is discussed.

The first two paragraphs present an **accurate** and **well-detailed** description of a study followed by **effective** criticism that demonstrates **understanding** by elaborating the critical point.

In the third paragraph there is a mixture of evaluation and then **reasonably detailed** description of research (percentages of cases could have been reported).

The final paragraph is again a mixture of description and evaluation, both are brief but **reasonably detailed** and **reasonably effective** – they are better than **basic** but only just.

AO1 – Well-structured, a **range of relevant material selected** appropriate for 4 marks.

AO2/AO3 – Ideas are **structured appropriately** and **expressed clearly**. The answer is **focused** and shows **reasonable evaluation**.

Chapter 16
Psychological research and scientific method

SPECIFICATION

This section builds on the knowledge and skills developed at AS level.

In order to gain sufficient understanding of the design and conduct of scientific research in psychology, candidates will need to practise these skills by carrying out, analysing and reporting small-scale investigations.

Psychological research and scientific method	
The application of scientific method in psychology	• The major features of science, including replicability, objectivity, theory construction, hypothesis testing, the use of empirical methods. • Validating new knowledge and the role of peer review.
Designing psychological investigations	• Selection and application of appropriate research methods. • Implications of sampling strategies, e.g. bias and generalising. • Issues of reliability, including types of reliability, assessment of reliability, improving reliability. • Assessing and improving validity (internal and external). • Ethical considerations in design and conduct of psychological research.
Data analysis and reporting on investigations	• Appropriate selection of graphical representations. • Probability and significance, including the interpretation of significance and Type 1/Type 2 errors. • Factors affecting choice of statistical test, including levels of measurement. • The use of inferential analysis, including Spearman's *Rho*, Mann-Whitney, Wilcoxon, chi-square. • Analysis and interpretation of qualitative data. • Conventions of reporting on psychological investigations.

SCIENCE

T he word science comes from the Latin word for 'knowledge'. Science is essentially a systematic approach to creating knowledge. The fact that it is systematic means we can rely on it in order to predict and control the world (e.g. build dams, create vaccines, treat schizophrenia). The method used to gain scientific knowledge is the scientific method.

There is more to scientific research than the use of experiments. This is only one of the techniques used. Scientists also use observation, questionnaires, interviews, case studies and so on.

The discussion on pseudoscience on page 256 provides some useful insight into the process of science.

EMPIRICAL METHODS

On the left is a picture of a burger from a well-known fast-food outlet. This is what you are led to expect you will get. But what about reality? You may think you know something, but unless you test this empirically you cannot know if it is true. On the right is the **empirical** evidence of what the burgers are really like. 'Empirical' refers to information gained through direct observation. Science uses empirical methods to separate unfounded beliefs from real truths.

Thanks to Professor Sergio della Sala of Edinburgh University for this tasty and memorable example of empiricism.

THE SCIENTIFIC PROCESS

Knowledge can be acquired through induction or deduction.

Induction involves reasoning from the particular to the general. For example, a scientist may observe instances of a natural phenomenon and come up with a general law or theory. Pre-twentieth-century science largely used the principles of induction, making discoveries about the world beginning with accurate observations. These were used to formulate theories based on the regularities observed. Newton's Laws are an example of this. He observed the behaviour of physical objects and produced laws that made sense of what he observed.

Deduction involves reasoning from the general to the particular, starting with a theory and looking for instances that confirm this. Darwin's theory of evolution is an example of this. He formulated a theory and set out to test its propositions by observing animals in nature. He specifically sought to collect data to prove his theory.

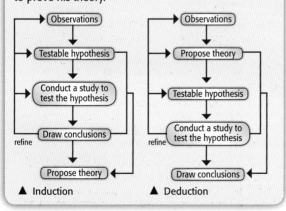

▲ Induction   ▲ Deduction

THE SCIENTIFIC METHOD

Scientific knowledge aims to be based on:

Empirical methods – Information is gained through direct observation or experiment rather than by reasoned argument or unfounded beliefs. Scientific research aims to collect facts.

This is important because people can make claims about anything (such as the truth of a theory or the benefits of a treatment or the taste of a hamburger) but the only way we know such things to be true is through direct testing, i.e. empirical evidence.

Objectivity – An important aspect of empirical data is that it should be objective, i.e. not affected by the expectations of the researcher. Systematic collection of measurable data is at the heart of the scientific method.

In order to be objective the ideal is to carefully control conditions in which research is conducted, i.e. in a laboratory. Furthermore, an experiment enables cause and effect relationships to be investigated – where we vary one factor (the **independent variable**) and observe its effect on the **dependent variable**. Therefore, the lab experiment is the best means of conducting scientific research.

Replicability – One way to demonstrate the validity of any observation or experiment is to repeat it. If the outcome is the same this affirms the truth of the original results, especially if the observations have been made by a different person. In order to achieve such replication it is important for scientists to record their procedures carefully so someone else can repeat them exactly and verify the original results.

Theory construction – Facts alone are meaningless. Explanations or theories must be constructed to make sense of the facts. A **theory** is a collection of general principles that explain observations and facts. Such theories can then help us understand and predict the natural phenomena around us.

Hypothesis testing – Theories are modified through the process of hypothesis testing. This is another essential characteristic of science where the validity of a theory is tested. A good theory must be able to generate testable expectations. These are stated in the form of a hypothesis (or hypotheses). If a scientist fails to find support for a hypothesis, then the theory requires modification, as shown in the diagrams on the left.

Hypothesis testing as we know it only developed in the twentieth century, as described in the box on **falsification** (facing page). Science as a method for discovering reliable knowledge is constantly evolving.

REDUCTIONIST AND DETERMINIST

Evaluation

The scientific approach is both **reductionist** and **determinist**. It is reductionist because complex phenomena are reduced to simple variables in order to study the causal relationships between them. It is also reductionist in the development of theories – the *canon of parsimony* or *Occam's razor* (a principle attributed to the mediaeval philosopher William of Occam) states that 'Of two competing theories or explanations, all other things being equal, the simpler one is to be preferred.'

EVALUATION

Can psychology claim to be a science?

Scientific research is desirable – In the nineteenth century, early psychologists sought to create a science of psychology because this would enable them to produce verifiable knowledge about behaviour as distinct from commonsense or 'armchair psychology'. We might claim that men are more aggressive than women or that ECT cures depression but people are not willing to accept this without proof.

Psychology uses the scientific method – Most psychologists generate models that can be falsified and conduct well-controlled experiments to test these models.

However, there is the question of whether simply using the scientific method turns psychology into a science. Miller (1983) suggests that psychologists who attempt to be scientists are doing no more than 'dressing up'. They may take on the tools of sciences such as quantified measurements and statistical analysis but that doesn't make it science. Perhaps at best it is a **pseudoscience** – but a dangerous one because psychologists can then claim their discoveries are fact.

Lack of objectivity and control – Some psychologists claim that human behaviour can be measured as objectively as the measurement of physical objects. But is this true? In psychology the object of study reacts to the researcher and this leads to problems, such as **experimenter bias** and **demand characteristics**, which compromise validity.

However, similar problems apply to the hard sciences. Heisenberg (1927) argued that it is not even possible to measure a subatomic particle without altering its 'behaviour' in doing the measurement. This *uncertainty principle* is a kind of experimenter effect: the presence of an experimenter changes the behaviour of what is being observed even in physics.

Are the goals of science appropriate for psychology?

Nomothetic versus idiographic – Some psychologists do not see the study of behaviour as a scientific pursuit. For example, the psychiatrist R.D. Laing (1960), in discussing the causes of schizophrenia, claimed it was inappropriate to view a person experiencing distress as a physical-chemical system that had gone wrong. Laing claimed that treatment could only succeed if each patient was treated as an individual case (the **idiographic** approach). Science takes the **nomothetic** approach, looking to make generalisations about people and find similarities.

Scientific methods haven't worked – Perhaps the way to decide whether science is appropriate for psychology is to look at the results of psychological research – psychological approaches to treating mental illness have had at best modest success, which suggests that the goals of science are not always appropriate.

Qualitative research – Some psychologists advocate more subjective, **qualitative** methods of conducting research (see page 296). However, **these** methods are still 'scientific' insofar as they aim to be valid. For example, data can be collected from interviews, qualitative **content analysis**, observations, etc. and then **triangulated** – the findings from these different methods are compared with each other as a means of verifying them and making them objective.

> Science is also determinist in its search for causal relationships, i.e. seeking to discover if X determines Y. If we don't take a determinist view of behaviour then this rules out scientific research as a means of understanding behaviour.
>
> Reductionism and determinism are mixed blessings. If we reduce complex behaviour to simple variables this may tell us little about 'real' behaviour, and yet without this reductionism it is difficult to pick out any patterns or reach conclusions. Determinism may also oversimplify the relationship between causes and effects but provides insights into important factors, such as the influences of nature and nurture.

▶ A good scientist is a sceptic who always asks:

- Where is the evidence?
- How good is the evidence?
- Is there other evidence?
- Does it make sense (i.e. is there an explanation for the facts?

Look at the photograph on the right. This man was apparently swallowed by a python. Do you believe this evidence? Why or why not?

FALSIFICATION

Until the 1930s scientists believed that their task was to find examples that would *confirm* their theories. Karl Popper, a philosopher of science, brought about a revolution in the way scientists thought about proof (confirming their theories). He pointed out:

> *'No matter how many instances of white swans we may have observed, this does not justify the conclusion that all swans are white'. (Popper, 1934)*

No number of sightings of white swans can prove the theory that all swans are white, whereas the sighting of just one black one will disprove it.

This proposition led to the realisation that the only way to prove a theory correct was actually to seek *disproof* (**falsification**) – i.e. look for those black swans. Therefore, we start research with what is called a **null hypothesis**: 'Not all swans in the world are white, i.e. there are black swans.'

We then go looking for swans and record many sightings but if we see no black swans this leads us to be reasonably certain (we can never be absolutely certain) that the null hypothesis is false.

We therefore can reject the null hypothesis (with reasonable certainty). If the null hypothesis isn't true this means that the alternative must be true. The alternative to the null hypothesis is 'All swans are white' – called the **alternative hypothesis**. We can accept the alternative hypothesis, with reasonable certainty!

This is, in the present state of knowledge, the best approximation to the truth.

CAN YOU...? | No.16.1

...1 Select **three** features of science and explain why each is important as a means of gaining 'true' knowledge.

...2 For each one give an example from your studies of psychology.

...3 Outline **three** criticisms of the scientific approach in psychology. Each criticism should be about 50 words.

...4 Answer the following 'apply your knowledge' question:

> *Harriet's mother is always telling her that blondes have more fun. Harriet is studying psychology and explains to her mother that something isn't true just because you believe it to be so.*
>
> *Outline how Harriet could use her knowledge of the features of science to explain what is wrong with her mother's argument. (6 marks)*

Psychology, in common with all scientific subjects, develops its knowledge base through conducting research and sharing the findings of such research with other scientists. **Peer review** is an essential part of this process whereby scientific quality is judged. It is in the interest of all scientists that their work is held up for scrutiny and any work that is flawed or downright fraudulent (as in the 'Cyril Burt Affair' below) is detected and the results of such research are ignored.

FRAUDULENT RESEARCH

The Cyril Burt affair

In the early 1950s, the eminent psychologist Sir Cyril Burt published results from studies of identical twins that was used as evidence to show that intelligence is inherited. Burt (1955) started with 21 pairs of twins raised apart, later increasing this to 42 pairs of twins. In a subsequent study Burt (1966) increased his sample to 53 pairs of identical twins raised apart, reporting an identical correlation to the earlier twin study of .771. The suspicious consistency of these correlation coefficients led Kamin (1977) to accuse Burt of inventing data. When a reporter, Oliver Gillie (1976), tried but failed to find two of Burt's research assistants this appeared to confirm the underlying fraud and Burt was publicly discredited. These accusations have been challenged (e.g. Joynson, 1989) but the most recent view is that Burt was astonishingly dishonest in his research (Mackintosh, 1995).

The Burt affair is particularly worrying because his research was used to shape social policy. Burt helped to establish the 11-Plus examination used in the UK to identify which children should go to grammar school rather than secondary moderns. He argued that since IQ was largely genetic then it was appropriate to test and segregate children into schools suitable for their abilities.

Some more recent cases of fraud

In 2010 Professor Marc Hauser of Harvard University was found responsible for scientific misconduct related to a number of published scientific papers. His main area of research concerned cotton-top tamarin monkeys and their cognitive abilities. He appears to have drawn conclusions for which he has been unable to provide evidence.

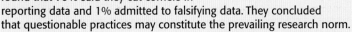

In the light of such prominent cases of professional misconduct Leslie John and colleagues (2012) surveyed over 2,000 psychologists asking them to anonymously report their involvement in questionable research practices. They found that 70% said they cut corners in reporting data and 1% admitted to falsifying data. They concluded that questionable practices may constitute the prevailing research norm.

Aftermath

Such practices raise two key issues. First, there is the issue of lack of trust. In the future people are likely to be less trusting of scientific data.

Second, is the problem that the data from such fraudulent studies remains published. Despite the fact the journals involved usually publish retractions (stating that the evidence is flawed and fraudulent), there are people who will continue to use the faulty data not knowing that it is discredited.

THE ROLE OF PEER REVIEW

Peer review (also called 'refereeing') is the assessment of scientific work by others who are experts in the same field (i.e. 'peers'). The intention of peer reviewing is to ensure that any research conducted and published is of high quality.

Peer reviewers are generally unpaid. Usually there are a number of reviewers for each application/article/ assessment. Their task is to report on the quality of the research and then their views are considered by a peer review panel.

The Parliamentary Office of Science and Technology (2002) suggests that peer review serves three main purposes:

1 **Allocation of research funding** – Research is paid for by various government and charitable bodies. The government-run Medical Research Council (MRC), for example, is one of the leading UK sources of funding for research. In 2008–9 it had £605 million to spend (Hansard, 2007) and obviously a duty to spend this responsibly. Therefore, public bodies such as the MRC require reviews to enable them to decide which research is likely to be worthwhile.

2 **Publication of research in scientific journals and books** – Scientific or scholarly journals provide scientists with the opportunity to share the results of their research. The peer review process has only been used in such journals since the middle of the twentieth century as a means of preventing incorrect or faulty data entering the public domain. Prior to peer review, research was simply published and it was assumed that the burden of proof lay with opponents of any new ideas.

3 **Assessing the research rating of university departments** – All university science departments are expected to conduct research and this is assessed in terms of quality (Research Excellence Framework, REF). Future funding for the department depends on receiving good ratings from the RAE peer review.

Peer review and the Internet

The sheer volume and pace of information available on the Internet means that new solutions are needed in order to maintain the quality of information. Scientific information is available in numerous online blogs, online journals and, of course, *Wikipedia* (an online encyclopedia). To a large extent such sources of information are policed by the 'wisdom of crowds' approach – readers decide whether it is valid or not, and post comments and/or edit entries accordingly. Several online journals (such as *ArXiv* and *Philica*) ask readers to rate articles. On Philica, papers are ranked on the basis of peer reviews. On the Internet, however, 'peer' is coming to mean 'everyone' – perhaps a more egalitarian system.

'Editors and scientists alike insist on the pivotal importance of peer review. We portray peer review to the public as a quasi-sacred process that helps to make science our most objective truth teller. But we know that the system of peer review is biased, unjust, unaccountable, incomplete, easily fixed, often insulting, usually ignorant, occasionally foolish, and frequently wrong'. (Richard Horton, 2000)

EVALUATION

It is clear why peer review is essential – without it we don't know what is mere opinion and speculation as distinct from real fact. We need to have a means of establishing the validity of scientific research.

While the benefit of peer review is beyond question, certain features of the process can be criticised. For example, Richard Smith, previous editor of the *British Medical Journal* (*BMJ*) commented: 'Peer review is slow, expensive, profligate of academic time, highly subjective, prone to bias, easily abused, poor at detecting gross defects and almost useless at detecting fraud' (Smith *et al.*, 1999). Let us pick up a few of these criticisms.

Finding an expert – It isn't always possible to find an appropriate expert to review a research proposal or report. This means that poor research may be passed because the reviewer didn't really understand it (Smith, 1999).

Anonymity – Anonymity is usually practised so that reviewers can be honest and objective. However, it may have the opposite effect if reviewers use the veil of anonymity to settle old scores or bury rival research. Research is conducted in a social world where people compete for research grants and jobs, and make friends and enemies. Social relationships inevitably affect objectivity. Some journals now favour open reviewing (where both author and reviewer know each other's identity).

Publication bias – Journals tend to prefer to publish positive results, possibly because editors want research that has important implications in order to increase the standing of their journal. This results in a bias in published research that in turn leads to a misperception of the true facts.

Furthermore, it appears that journals also avoid publishing straight replications of a study, a fundamental part of research validation. French (2011) submitted a replication of a study on paranormal phenomena (see Ritchie *et al.*, page 256) and found that it was not even considered for peer review. Ritchie *et al.* suggest that journals are as bad as newspapers for seeking eye-catching stories.

Preserving the status quo – Peer review results in a preference for research that goes with existing theory rather than dissenting or unconventional work. Richard Horton (2000), the former editor of the medical journal *The Lancet*, made the following comment: 'The mistake, of course, is to have thought that peer review was any more than a crude means of discovering the acceptability – not the validity – of a new finding.'

Science is generally resistant to large shifts in opinion. Change takes a long time and requires a 'revolution' in the way people think. Peer review may be one of the elements that slow change down.

Cannot deal with already published research – We noted on the facing page the problem that, once a research study has been published, the results remain in the public view even if they have subsequently been shown to be fraudulent or simply the result of poor research practices. For example, Brooks (2010) points to peer-reviewed research that was subsequently debunked but nevertheless continued to be used in a debate in parliament. The fact that members of parliament have such little critical understanding of the process of science emphasises the need for increased vigilance by scientists of the quality of their work.

SCHOLARLY JOURNALS

There are thousands of scholarly journals publishing over one million research papers each year. They differ from 'popular' magazines because they contain in-depth reports of research. The articles are written by academics and are peer reviewed. Several hundred such journals specifically relate to psychology, such as *The Psychologist, Archives of Sexual Behaviour, Journal of Early Adolescence* and *British Journal of Psychology*.

Academic textbooks are based on such articles – as you can see by looking in the references at the back of this book.

WIKIPEDIA

Wikipedia deals with the issue of peer review by having various levels of editor to check information posted. However, they recognise that, while it may be simple to detect incorrect information, it is more difficult to recognise 'subtle viewpoint promotion' than in a typical reference work. On the other hand, they point out that bias which would be unchallenged in a traditional reference work is more likely to be pointed out in Wikipedia. In addition, the online form of Wikipedia permits instant revision when mistakes are spotted.

CAN YOU...? No.16.2

...1 Explain what is meant by 'peer review'.

...2 Explain, in about 100 words, why peer review is essential to the process of producing valid scientific data.

...3 Outline **three** criticisms of peer review. Each criticism should be about 50 words.

...4 Answer the following 'apply your knowledge' question:

A psychologist wishes to publish his research in a mainstream psychology journal.

(a) *Explain why it is desirable for this research study to be peer reviewed before publication.* (4 marks)

(b) *The research paper is rejected for publication. Suggest **two** reasons why it may have been rejected.* (4 marks)

RESEARCH METHODS AND CONCEPTS

This chapter began with a consideration of science and the scientific process. The ideal form of scientific investigation is the laboratory experiment because it enables us to maximise **control** and identify causal relationships. However, experiments, as you know, are by no means the only form of research method used by scientists and psychologists. On this spread we will review the research methods and techniques that you studied at AS level. In addition, we will also review a number of other concepts you studied as part of the AS course. At A2 level you are expected to build on the knowledge and skills developed at AS.

EXAM TIP In the A2 Unit 4 examination there will be a set of compulsory questions on 'Psychological research and scientific method'. These questions will be worth a total of 35 marks and usually start with a brief description of a psychological study followed by a number of questions, similar to those on the facing page. There is also an example of such questions at the end of this chapter.

Experiments

All experiments involve an **IV** (**independent variable**) and **DV** (**dependent variable**). The IV is varied in order to see how this affects the DV, thus demonstrating a causal relationship. As far as possible, all other variables are controlled, so any changes in the DV are due to the IV rather than **extraneous variables**.

Laboratory experiment – An experiment conducted in a controlled environment which therefore tends to be high in terms of internal validity because many extraneous variables can be controlled. However, some (such as investigator/experimenter effects and demand characteristics) may reduce internal validity. Control also increases replicability, which is desirable, but reduces **external validity** because a highly controlled situation may be less like everyday life.

Field experiment – An experiment conducted in a more natural environment. It may be possible to control extraneous variables, although such control is more difficult than in a lab experiment. Experimenter effects are reduced because participants are usually not aware of being in a study. However, **demand characteristics** may still be problematic, for example the way an IV is operationalised may convey the experimental hypothesis to participants.

Natural experiment – An experiment which makes use of existing IVs, such as a treatment used for people with schizophrenia. Strictly speaking, an experiment involves the deliberate manipulation of an IV by the experimenter, so causal conclusions cannot be drawn from a natural experiment. In addition, participants are not randomly allocated to conditions in a natural experiment, which may reduce validity, but it is often the only way to study certain behaviours or experiences, such as the effects of privation.

Experimental design – In any experiment there are several levels of the IV. For example, in the study of eyewitness testimony by Loftus and Palmer (1974) participants were given a sentence with one of five verbs (hit, smashed, bumped, etc) so there were five levels of the IV. Experimenters have a choice – either each participant is tested on all of the IVs (**repeated measures**) or there are separate groups for each IV (**independent groups**). There is also a third possibility – the participants in each independent group can be matched with participants in the other group(s) on key variables, such as age and IQ (**matched pairs** design).

Experimental control is a balancing act

Too little control ▶ means it is difficult to draw clear conclusions because of extraneous variables – variables other than the IV which may affect the DV.

◀ Too much control means the behaviour we are studying isn't very much like everyday life (lacks mundane realism).

Self-report methods

Psychologists use **questionnaires** and **interviews** to find out what people think and feel. Interviews are essentially real-time, face-to-face (or over the phone) questionnaires, although there is the option to conduct a fairly **unstructured interview** where the questions are developed by the interviewer as a response to the answers given by the interviewee. Structured questionnaires/interviews can be more easily repeated in exactly the same way than unstructured interviews, which is an advantage.

The main problem for **self-report methods** is honesty because, for example, the social desirability bias means that respondents may provide answers to put themselves in a good light.

Questionnaires and interviews may involve **open questions** which permit a respondent to provide their own answer. Such questions can produce unexpected answers providing rich insights but they are more difficult to analyse than **closed questions**.

Observational studies

Perhaps one of the most obvious research methods is simply to watch what people do (**observational techniques**). However, it is not that simple to observe behaviour because there is so much information to collect. For this reason, psychologists use **behavioural categories** to record particular instances of behaviour, and also **sampling methods**, such as recording behaviour every 30 seconds (**time sampling**) or every time a certain behaviour occurs (**event sampling**).

Even in **naturalistic observations** (as distinct from controlled observations) structured techniques are used to study behaviour.

Observational studies provide a rich picture of what people actually do (rather than what they say they do). However, observers may be biased (**observer bias**) – their observations can be affected by their expectations.

Correlational analysis

Some studies are concerned with the relationship between two variables, such as IQ and A-level results (which we would expect to be positively correlated) or reaction time and age (which might be negatively correlated). Such studies use a **correlational analysis** which does not demonstrate a cause but is useful in identifying where relationships between co-variables exist. Such studies can be done with large data sets and can be easily replicated. However, there may be other, unknown (intervening) variables that can explain why the co-variables being studied are linked. Such studies may lack internal/external validity – for example, the method used to measure IQ may lack validity or the sample may lack generalisability.

When answering these questions you may also need to refer to your AS notes on research methods as well as the information on this spread.

...1 For each of the research methods named on this spread, identify an example from the research you are familiar with, and for each example explain **one** strength and **one** weakness of using this research method, in the context of your research example.

...2 Give an example of the following terms in the context of a named study: (a) demand characteristics, (b) pilot study, (c) social desirability bias, (d) extraneous variable, (e) longitudinal study. In each case use the study as a way to provide a clear explanation of the concept.

...3 In the box on the right, a few studies have been briefly described. Try to answer the questions below in relation to each of these studies (or use some other studies you have looked at during your Psychology course).

(a) Identify the research method(s) and/or research technique(s) used in this study and explain your choice.

(b) Write a suitable hypothesis for the study.

(c) Identify whether your hypothesis is directional or non-directional and explain why you chose this kind of hypothesis.

(d) If appropriate, identify the type of experimental design used in the study and explain why the researcher would have chosen this experimental design.

(e) Identify **one** possible extraneous variable that could be a problem in this study and explain how it could be dealt with.

...4 A psychologist intends to study the behaviour of car drivers. Suggest **three** behavioural categories that could be used when recording behaviour.

...5 The government plans a new campaign related to speeding. It decides to find out about attitudes towards speeding in order to make the campaign effective. Suggest **one** closed question and **one** open question that might help the researchers find out more about people's attitudes to speeding.

...6 Design a study to investigate the relationship between success at school and attitudes to school. You should include sufficient details to permit replication, for example a hypothesis, variables being studied, and detail of design and procedures.

RESEARCH STUDIES

Study A – Johnson and Scott (1976) conducted a study of weapon focus (eyewitness identification may be unreliable because witnesses are distracted by the weapon and take less notice of an assailant's face). In this study participants were asked to sit in a waiting room before being called for the experiment. While waiting, the participants heard a man shouting next door and then someone (a confederate) ran through the room either holding a pen and with grease on his hands, or holding a bloodied letter opener. Participants were then asked to identify the person who had run through the room. They were found to be less accurate if the confederate had been holding the knife.

Study B – Buss (1989) explored what males and females looked for in a marriage partner. The study involved over 10,000 people from 37 different cultures. Participants were asked to rate 18 characteristics (e.g. dependability, chastity, intelligence) in terms of desirability in a mate. The results from men and women were compared and they found, for example, that more women than men desired mates who were 'good financial prospects' whereas more men than women placed importance on physical attractiveness.

Study C – Rahe *et al.* (1970) investigated the relationship between stressful life events and illness by studying a large group of men in the US Navy and seeing if there was an association between the number of stressful life events they experienced over a six-month period and the number of illnesses they experienced.

Study D – Kiecolt-Glaser *et al.* (1984) also investigated stress. In this study the effects of short-term stress on the immune system were demonstrated by comparing blood samples taken from students one month prior to their exams (low stress) and during the exam period itself (high stress).

Case studies

A **case study** is a detailed study of a single individual, institution or event. It uses information from a range of sources, such as from the person concerned and also from their family and friends. Many techniques may be used, such as interviews, psychological tests, observations and experiments. Case studies are generally longitudinal: in other words they follow the individual or group over an extended period of time. The complex interaction of many factors can be studied, in contrast to experiments where many variables are held constant. However, it is difficult to generalise from individual cases as each one has unique characteristics. It is often necessary to use recollection of past events as part of the case study and such evidence may be unreliable.

Other research methods

There are numerous other methods such as content analysis, a kind of observational study; cross-cultural research, comparing the effects of different cultural practices on behaviour; and meta-analysis, which combines the results of many studies on the same topic to reach overall conclusions.

A FEW OTHER CONCEPTS

Aims and hypotheses – Researchers start by identifying what they intend to study (the **aims**) and then make a formal statement of their expectations using a **hypothesis**. A hypothesis may be **directional** or **non-directional** (i.e. the direction of a difference or relationship is or is not stated). A good hypothesis should be **operationalised** so that the variables are in a form that can be easily tested.

Investigator effects and other problems – Investigators may communicate their expectations unwittingly to participants (**investigator** or **experimenter effects**), thus leading participants to fulfil the investigator's expectations. Other problems include **demand characteristics** (features of an experiment that may cue participants to behave in predictable ways) and **social desirability bias** (participants wish to present themselves in a good light).

Pilot study – A small-scale trial run of a research study to test any aspects of the design, with a view to making improvements in the main study.

Reliability refers to how much we can depend on any particular measurement, for example the measurement of a table, the measurement of a psychological characteristic such as IQ, or the findings of a research study. In particular we want to know whether, if we repeat exactly the same measurement/test/study we can be sure that we would get the same result. If not, our measurement is unreliable.

Validity is related to reliability because, if a measurement is not reliable (consistent), then a study cannot be valid i.e. it cannot be 'true' or legitimate. For example, a researcher might measure intelligence using an intelligence test. If the same person is tested on several occasions using the same test and the results change each time then the intelligence test lacks reliability – and it also lacks validity because the scores are meaningless.

However, a measurement may be reliable but still lack validity. For example, a person may take an IQ test and then take the same test several months later. Their score may be consistent, so it is a reliable test. However, the items on the test may simply assess what a person learned at school rather than 'intelligence'. In which case the test is lacking validity (meaningfulness).

THE ISSUE OF RELIABILITY

We can consider reliability in relation to different research methods, including different *types* of reliability (internal and external), as well as looking at how reliability can be assessed and improved.

Experimental research

In the context of an experiment, reliability refers to the ability to repeat a study and obtain the same result i.e. replication. It is essential that all conditions are the same, otherwise any change in the result may be due to changed conditions.

Observational techniques

Observations should be consistent, which means that ideally two or more observers should produce the same record. The extent to which the observers agree is called inter-rater or **inter-observer reliability**, calculated by dividing total agreements by the total number of observations. A result of 0.80 or more suggests good inter-observer reliability.

The reliability of observations can be improved through training observers in the use of a coding system/behaviour checklist.

Self-report techniques

There are two different types of reliability which are particularly apparent when thinking of self-report techniques, such as questionnaires and interviews.

- Internal reliability is a measure of the extent to which something is consistent within itself. For example, all the questions on an IQ test (which is a kind of questionnaire) should be measuring the same thing.
- External reliability is a measure of consistency over several different occasions. For example, if the same interview by the same interviewer with the same interviewee was conducted one day and then again a week later, the outcome should be the same, otherwise the interview is not reliable.

Reliability also concerns whether two interviewers produce the same outcome. This is called **inter-interviewer reliability**.

There are various ways to assess reliability, such as using the **split-half method** to compare a person's performance on two halves of a questionnaire or test. If the test is assessing the same thing in all its questions then there should be a close correlation in the scores derived from both halves of the test, a measure of internal reliability. A second method of assessing reliability is the **test–retest method** where a person is given a questionnaire/interview/test on one occasion and then this is repeated again after a reasonable interval (e.g. a week or a month). If the measure is reliable the outcome should be the same every time.

THE ISSUE OF VALIDITY

All research strives to be high in validity. Any flaws must be minimised in order to draw valid conclusions from any study. There are two kinds of validity:

- **Internal validity** concerns what goes on inside a study – whether the researcher did test what he (or she) intended to test.
- **External validity** concerns things outside a study – the extent to which the results of the study can be generalised to other situations and people. The term **ecological validity** is often used as another term for external validity.

Experimental research

Internal validity is affected by extraneous variables (EVs) which may act as an alternative IV. Therefore, changes in the DV are due to EVs rather than the IV, and conclusions about the effect of the IV on the DV are erroneous.

Many people think that all **laboratory experiments** are low in external validity, and that **field experiments**, conducted in more natural surroundings, are seen as high in external validity. This is not necessarily true. In some cases the contrived, artificial nature of the laboratory setting is not particularly relevant to the behaviour being observed (such as a memory task) and therefore it can be generalised to everyday situations (external validity). Also, in some cases, field experiments can be very contrived and artificial. And, as mentioned before, more control is possible in a laboratory.

It is often more important to consider issues, such as whether the participants were aware they were being studied (which reduces the realism of their behaviour) and whether the task itself (rather than the setting) was artificial and thus low in **mundane realism**, which reduces the generalisability of the results.

Observational techniques

In terms of internal validity, observations will not be valid (nor reliable) if the coding system/behaviour checklist is flawed. For example, some observations may belong in more than one category, or some behaviours may not be codeable, which reduces the internal validity of the data collected.

The internal validity of observations is also affected by **observer bias** – what someone observes is influenced by their expectations. This reduces the objectivity of observations.

Observational studies are likely to have high ecological validity because they involve more natural behaviours – although, as we have seen, naturalistic research is not necessarily higher in ecological validity.

SAMPLING TECHNIQUES

The aim of all psychological research is to be able to make valid generalisations about behaviour. In any research project only a small number of participants are studied because larger groups involve more time and money. Psychologists use **sampling** techniques which will minimise cost while maximising generalisability.

Opportunity sample – Participants are selected by using those people who are most easily available. This is the easiest method to use but it is inevitably biased because the sample is drawn from a small part of the target population. For example, if you selected your sample from people walking around the centre of a town on a Monday morning, it would be unlikely to include professional people (because they are at work).

Volunteer sample – Participants are selected by asking for volunteers, for example placing an advertisement on a college noticeboard. This method can access a variety of participants if the advertisement is, for example, in a national newspaper, which would make the sample more representative. However, such samples are inevitably biased because participants are likely to be highly motivated and/or with extra time on their hands (= **volunteer bias**).

Random sample – Participants are selected using a random number technique. First, all members of the target population are identified (e.g. all the members of one school or all the residents of a town) and then individuals are selected either by the lottery method (numbers drawn from a 'hat') or using a random number generator.

This method is potentially unbiased because all members of the target population have an equal chance of selection, although in the end a researcher may still end up with a biased sample because some people refuse to take part.

Stratified and quota samples – Sub-groups (strata) within a population are identified (e.g. boys and girls or different age groups). Then a predetermined number of participants is taken from each sub-group in proportion to their representation in the target population, e.g. if there are twice as many boys than girls in the target population then the sample will consist of twice as many boys. In stratified sampling this is done using random techniques, in quota sampling it is done using opportunity sampling.

This method is more representative than other methods because there is proportional representation of sub-groups. However, selection within each sub-group may be biased, for example because of opportunity sampling.

Snowball sampling – In some studies it is difficult to identify suitable participants. For example, in a study of eating disorders, a useful technique is to start with one or two people with eating disorders and ask them to direct you to some other people with eating disorders and so on. This is useful when conducting research with participants who are not easy to identify, but is prone to bias because researchers may only contact people within a limited section of the population.

Self-report techniques

There are several ways to assess the internal validity of self-report techniques:

- **Face validity**: Does the test look as if it is measuring what the researcher intended to measure. For example, are the questions obviously related to the topic?
- **Concurrent validity**: This can be established by comparing performance on a new questionnaire or test with a previously established test on the same topic. If the participants' performance on both tests show a high correlation, this is evidence of high concurrent validity.

The external validity of self-report techniques is likely to be affected by the sampling strategies used, which may create a biased sample.

*Sampling techniques are also used in observational studies as we have previously discussed – **time sampling** and **event sampling** (see page 278).*

*A **systematic sample** – e.g. taking every tenth person from a register – is often mistaken for a random sample. However, it is random if the first person is selected randomly!*

CAN YOU...? No.16.4

...1 Explain what is meant by validity and reliability, internal and external validity, and internal and external reliability.

...2 In each of the following studies describe **two** features of the study that might affect the validity of the data being collected and how the validity could be improved.

(a) A psychologist conducts interviews with mothers about their attitudes towards day care.
(b) A psychologist conducts a study to see if students do more homework in the winter or spring term. To do this he asks students to keep a diary of how much time they spend on homework each week.

...3 In each of the following studies suggest how reliability could be assessed.

(a) A psychologist intends to use a repeated measures design to test participants' memories in the morning and afternoon. He uses two tests of memory.
(b) A psychologist interviews teenage girls about their dieting.

...4 Some psychology students plan to conduct an observational study on the effects of different dress styles to see if men look more at girls dressed casually or smartly.

(a) Identify **two** ways you could operationalise 'being dressed "casually"'.
(b) Identify **one** way in which you could ensure reliability among the different observers and explain how to do this.
(c) Describe what sampling technique you might use for making the observations.
(d) Explain **one** feature of the study that might affect the validity of the data being collected.

...5 On the previous spread **four** studies have been described. For each study identify an appropriate sampling technique and give **one** strength and **one** weakness of that technique in the context of the study.

...6 Why might a volunteer sample be preferable to an opportunity sample?

...7 Explain the difference between a random sample and a systematic sample.

ETHICAL CONSIDERATIONS IN PSYCHOLOGICAL RESEARCH

Any professional group, such as psychologists, doctors or solicitors, has a duty to behave in an ethical manner i.e. to behave with a proper regard for the rights and feelings of others. For psychologists this encompasses the treatment of patients, and the responsibilities of researchers towards their participants – human or non-human.

There is an important point to remember where ethical issues are concerned – there are no right or wrong answers because these are topics where there are conflicting points of view. Professional organisations such as the BPS (British Psychological Organisation) and APA (American Psychological Association) provide guidance for psychologists about how to behave. Such guidance is always being updated in order to keep up with changing viewpoints and new moral dilemmas (e.g. research on the Internet).

WWW You can read the BPS code of conduct and other statements about ethical practice at www.bps.org.uk/the-society/code-of-conduct/code-of-conduct_home.cfm

SOCIALLY SENSITIVE RESEARCH

Despite the existence of ethical guidelines, some broader ethical issues arise in 'socially sensitive' areas. Sieber and Stanley (1988) defined **socially sensitive research** as '...studies in which there are potential social consequences or implications, either directly for the participants in research or the class of individuals represented by the research' (Sieber and Stanley, 1988).

One of the most controversial avenues of research has been consideration of inter-racial differences in IQ. Some evidence suggests that, in terms of IQ, black children may be innately inferior. Even though such research may be flawed (e.g. it ignores social conditions) such 'scientific' evidence can be used to support divisive and discriminatory social policies. Other areas of social sensitivity include research on drug abuse or sexual orientation.

The ethical question concerns whether or not such research should be conducted. If research is not conducted, such groups may miss out on any potential benefits from the research (e.g. increased funding or wider public understanding). Also, ignoring these important areas of research would amount to an abdication of the 'social responsibilities' of the psychological researcher (i.e. their duty to society to study important areas of human behaviour).

An understanding of the nature of socially-sensitive research should focus psychologists more clearly on the implications of their findings and the worrying potential, as Sieber and Stanley (1988) suggest, to on occasion offer 'scientific credibility to the prevailing prejudice'.

▶ Concern for the protection of human participants in research has its roots in the Nuremberg Code (1947), a document designed to protect against the unethical Nazi practices (such as medical experiments) considered at the Nuremberg Trials following World War II. The Nuremberg Code was the first ethical code of practice. The APA produced the first code for psychologists in 1953 (a document of 170 pages).

ETHICAL ISSUES WITH HUMAN PARTICIPANTS

Ethical issues

The first main issue relates to **informed consent** and **deception**. Ideally, participants should be given the opportunity to know about all aspects of any research before agreeing to take part. This is a basic right stemming from the inhumane experiments conducted in concentration camps, such as Auschwitz-Birkenau in the Second World War. However, the issue arises because full information may compromise the integrity of a study (e.g. knowing the full aims may alter participants' behaviour, rendering the results meaningless).

The second main issue relates to **harm,** and what constitutes too much harm. For example, Ainsworth argued in her strange situation research with infants, that the distress they experienced was no greater than that experienced in everyday life (Ainsworth *et al.*, 1978).

In both cases the decision as to what is acceptable or not acceptable is open to debate.

Code of conduct

The current BPS code of ethics and conduct (BPS, 2009) identifies four ethical principles and includes advice on how these should be dealt with:

1 ***Respect*** for the dignity and worth of all persons. This includes standards of **privacy** and **confidentiality** and **informed consent**. Observations of behaviour in public without informed consent are only acceptable in situations where the people being studied would reasonably expect to be observed by strangers.

   Intentional **deception** (lack of informed consent) is only acceptable when it is necessary to protect the integrity of research and when the nature of the deception is disclosed to participants at the earliest opportunity. One way to judge deception is to consider whether participants are likely to object or show unease when debriefed (see below), in which case the deception may be judged unacceptable.

   Participants should be aware of the **right to withdraw** from the research at any time.

2 ***Competence*** – Psychologists should maintain high standards in their professional work.

3 ***Responsibility*** – Psychologists have a responsibility to their clients, to the general public and to the science of Psychology. This includes protecting participants from physical and psychological **harm** as well as **debriefing** at the conclusion of their participation to inform clients of the nature and conclusions of the research, to identify any unforeseen harm, and to arrange for assistance if needed.

4 ***Integrity*** – Psychologists should be honest and accurate. This includes reporting the findings of any research accurately and acknowledging any potential limitations. It also includes bringing instances of misconduct by other psychologists to the attention of the BPS.

Dealing with ethical issues

The code of conduct offers **ethical guidelines** for psychologists to follow. In conjunction with such guidelines psychologists deal with ethical issues by using **ethical committees** to assess research proposals, by punishing psychologists who contravene the code with disbarment from the society, and by educating students and qualified psychologists about their duties as researchers.

ETHICAL ISSUES WITH NON-HUMAN ANIMALS

Although the vast majority of investigations in psychology involve the study of *humans*, there are several reasons why psychologists may choose to carry out research using non-human animals:

- Animals may be studied simply because they are fascinating to study in their own right and such research may ultimately benefit animals.
- Animals offer the opportunity for greater control and objectivity in research procedures. Much of behaviourist theory was established using animal studies for just this reason, for example animals in the Skinner box (see page 131).
- We may use animals when we can't use humans. Animals have been exposed to various procedures and events that would simply not be possible with human beings. For example, Harlow's research (1959) with rhesus monkeys and wire 'mothers' showed that contact comfort was a more essential requirement for primates than food.
- Human beings and non-human animals have enough of their physiology and evolutionary past in common to justify conclusions drawn from experiments involving one, to the other. However, it can be argued that animals tested under stressful conditions may provide very little useful information.

Moral justification

The question still remains as to whether 'science at any cost' is justifiable.

Sentient beings – Do animals experience pain and emotions? In terms of pain there is evidence that they *respond* to pain but this may not be the same as conscious awareness. However, there is some evidence that animals other than primates have self-awareness (see page 134). In addition, some humans, such as brain-damaged individuals, lack sentience, but wouldn't be used in research without consent.

Speciesism – Peter Singer (1990) argued that discrimination on the basis of species is no different from racial or gender discrimination and thus suggests that the use of animals is an example of 'speciesism', similar to racism or sexism. However, Gray (1991) argues that we have a special duty of care to humans, then speciesism is not equivalent to, for example, racism.

Animal rights – Singer's view is a utilitarian one, i.e. whatever produces the greater good for the greater number is ethically acceptable, so if animal research can alleviate pain and suffering it is justifiable. Tom Regan (1984), on the other hand, argues that there are no circumstances under which animal research is acceptable. Regan claims that animals have a right to be treated with respect and should *never* be used in research. The issue of 'animal rights' can be challenged by examining the concept of rights – having rights is dependent on having responsibilities in society, i.e. as citizens. It can therefore be said that as animals do not have responsibilities, they have no rights.

Existing constraints

Animal research is very strictly controlled. The BPS publishes guidelines for research with animals but, more importantly, there is legislation. In the UK, the Animals (Scientific Procedures) Act (1986) requires that animal research only takes place at licensed laboratories with licensed researchers on licensed projects. Such licences are only granted if:
- Potential results are important enough to justify the use of animals.
- The research cannot be done using non-animal methods.
- The minimum number of animals will be used.
- Any discomfort or suffering is kept to a minimum by appropriate use of anaesthetics or painkillers.

The 3 Rs were proposed by Russell and Birch (1959) – reduction (use fewer animals), replacement (where possible use alternative methods, such as brain scans), and refinement (use improved techniques to reduce stress). The House of Lords (2002) endorsed the principle of the 3Rs with respect to animal research. Nevertheless, in the UK, the need for animal research continues. For example, British law requires that any new drug (such as antidepressants) must be tested on at least two different species of live mammal.

▼ When considering the use of non-human animals in psychological research, it can be helpful to put emotions to one side to consider the logic of the arguments. It is also important to remember that much *psychological* research with animals does not involve physical interventions – although psychological treatments may be equally damaging.

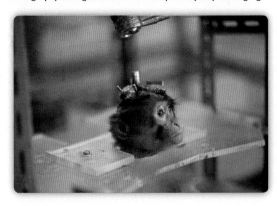

WWW If you wish to read more about animal research, the BBC website presents some excellent information – see www.bbc.co.uk/ethics/animals/

CAN YOU...? (No.16.5)

...1 For each of the following studies, identify **one** ethical issue that might arise, and suggest how the researcher might deal with it.

(a) A correlation of pupil IQ scores and GCSE results.

(b) Interviewing teenage girls about their dieting habits.

(c) An observational study of the way in which children cross the road going to and from school.

(d) A psychologist decides to conduct a field experiment to see whether people are more likely to obey someone in a uniform or dressed in a casual suit.

(e) A school decides to conduct a natural experiment to see if the students doing a new maths programme do better in their GCSE maths exam than a group of students using the traditional learning methods.

(f) An experiment to test the effect of self-esteem on performance. Participants are given a self-esteem questionnaire and then given a false score (told they either have high or low self-esteem).

(g) A teacher asks her students to take part in a research project, telling them it is about eating habits whereas it is really about eating disorders.

...2 Describe **one** example of socially sensitive research and consider the pros and cons of conducting such research.

...3 What protection exists to ensure that animals involved in psychological research are treated ethically?

...4 Identify **two** examples of psychological research that have used non-human animals and discuss the ethical issues raised by this study.

INTRODUCING INFERENTIAL TESTS

You may have heard the phrase 'statistical test' – for example, a newspaper might report that *'statistical tests show that women are better at reading maps than men'*. If we wanted to know whether women are better at reading maps than men we could not possibly test all the women and men in the world, so we just test a small group of women and a small group of men. If we find that the sample of women are indeed better with maps than the sample of men, then we *infer* that the same is true for all women and men. We can only make such inferences using statistical tests (called **inferential tests**). Such statistical tests are based on probabilities.

*In the AS Psychology course you looked at **descriptive statistics**, such as graphs and measures of central tendancy and dispersion. We can draw conclusions from descriptive statistics, such as using a graph to see that one group of participants did better than another group. But we don't know whether this difference is **significant**. Inferential statistics allows us to determine whether a difference is significant.*

UNDERSTANDING SIGNIFICANCE

Consider the following example from the psychologist and statistician Hugh Coolican (2004):

At my local chippy I am convinced that they save money by giving some people rather thin chips (because they then can get more chips from each potato). There are two chip bins under the counter – the owner of the chippy claims the two bins contain the same kind of chips but I suspect they are different. So I (sadly) tried an experiment. I asked for one bag of chips from each of the chip bins, and I measured the width of the chips in each bag.

- *Belief 1 is 'The two bins contain chips of an equal average width'.*
- *Belief 2 is 'One bin has thinner chips on average than the other'.*

In fact I found a very small difference between the average width of the chips in each bag (as you can see in the bar chart).

▼ Graph showing the mean width for both bins.

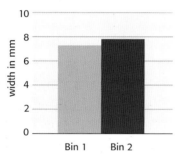

We would expect small differences between samples (bags of chips) just because things do vary a little – this is simply random variation or 'chance'. What we are looking for is a sufficiently large difference between the samples to be sure that the bins (the total population) are actually different. Otherwise we assume the bins are the same, i.e. the samples are drawn from a single population rather than from two different populations.

- The *bins* contain the populations – in the earlier example about gender differences in map reading, the population is all the map reading abilities of all the men and women in the world.
- The *bags* of chips are samples – in our other example, the 20 women and 20 men comprise our samples.
- The belief that the two bins contain chips of the same width or the belief that there is no gender difference in map reading is called the **null hypothesis (H$_0$)**. This is a statement of *no effect* – the samples are not different.
- The alternative belief is that one bin has thinner chips or that women are better than men – this is called the **alternative hypothesis (H$_1$)**. This is a statement that there is an effect – the samples are different.

Ultimately we are interested in making a statement about the population(s) from which the samples are drawn rather than just stating something about samples themselves.

PROBABILITY

In the example at the bottom of the page about boyfriends and cheating, you might have worked out the *likelihood* that the cheating was real (e.g. you might have felt 'fairly certain'). In research we need to be a bit more precise than that. In order to work out whether a difference is or is not significant we use inferential tests. Such tests permit you to work out, at a given **probability**, whether a pattern in the data from a study could have arisen by **chance** or whether the effect occurred because there is a real difference/correlation in the populations from which the samples were drawn.

But what do we mean by 'chance'? Chance refers to something with no cause. It just happens. We decide on a probability that we will 'risk'. You can't be 100% certain that an observed effect was not due to chance but you can state how certain you are. In the kissing example you might say to your friend that you are 95% sure her boyfriend is cheating. Which means you are fairly confident that you are right but nevertheless have a little bit of doubt.

In general, psychologists use a probability of 95%. This expresses the degree of uncertainty. It means that there is a 5% chance (probability) of the results occurring if the null hypothesis is true (i.e. there is nothing going on). In other words, a 5% probability that the results would occur even if there was no real difference/association between the populations from which the samples were drawn. This probability of 5% is recorded as $p = 0.05$ (where p means probability).

In some studies psychologists want to be more certain – such as when they are conducting a replication of a previous study or considering the effects of a new drug on health. Then, researchers use a more stringent probability, such as $p < 0.01$ or even $p < 0.001$. This chosen value of 'p' is called the **significance level**, which we will discuss on the next spread.

The null hypothesis
The null hypothesis is a statement of no difference or no correlation. It is a statement that 'nothing is going on'. The null hypothesis isn't as strange as it sounds. Consider this example:

It's late at night and on your way home you happen to see you best friend's boyfriend with another girl, and he's doing more than talking. You think to yourself *'How likely is it that he would be kissing her if there is nothing going on between them?'*

- Null hypothesis: 'There is nothing going on, there is no relationship between them.'
- Alternative hypothesis: 'There is something going on between them.'

It isn't very likely that he would be kissing her if there was nothing going on, therefore you reject the null hypothesis and accept the alternative hypothesis – and tell your friend that you are fairly certain that he is cheating on her.

TYPE 1 AND TYPE 2 ERRORS

In general psychologists use a 5% level of significance level. One reason for this is because it is a good compromise between Type 1 and Type 2 errors.

Type 1 and 2 errors concern whether we make a mistake about accepting/rejecting the null hypothesis. Consider the null hypothesis 'There is no difference in the map reading abilities of men and women'. We conduct a study and find a small difference between men and women. There are two correct conclusions and two possible errors (see table on right):

- In truth there is no difference between men and women but, because we use a lenient level of significance (e.g. 10%) we reject the null hypothesis. This is a **Type 1 error**. We reject a null hypothesis that is in fact true (e.g. we decide that women are better than men at reading maps whereas, in reality, this is not true).
- In truth there is a difference between men and women but, because we are using a significance level that is too stringent (e.g. 1%), we accept the null hypothesis when it is in fact

false (e.g. women are really better than men at reading maps but we mistakenly accept that there is no difference). This is a **Type 2 error**.

		Truth	
		H_1 is correct There is something going on	H_0 is correct There is nothing going on
Test result	Reject H_0	True positive	False positive (likely when p too lenient, i.e. 10%) TYPE 1 ERROR
	Accept H_0	False negative (likely when p too stringent, i.e. 1%) TYPE 2 ERROR	True negative

USING INFERENTIAL TESTS

Inferential tests help us to draw inferences about populations based on the samples tested. These tests allow us to infer that a pattern in the data is likely (or not) to be due to chance.

Observed and critical values

Each inferential test involves taking the data collected in a study and doing some calculations to produce a single number called the **test statistic**. In the case of Spearman's Rank Order Correlation Coefficient that test statistic is called *rho* whereas for the Mann-Whitney test it is *U*. The *rho* or *U* value calculated for any set of data is called the **observed value** (because it is based on the observations made). This is sometimes alternatively called the calculated value because it is the value you calculate.

To decide if the observed value is significant this figure is compared to another number (the **critical value**), found in a table of critical values. There are different tables of critical values for each different statistical test, as you will see on the following spreads. The critical value is the number that a test statistic must reach in order for the null hypothesis to be rejected.

To find the appropriate critical value in a table you need to know four pieces of information:

- **Degrees of freedom** (*df*) In most cases you get this value by looking at the number of participants in the study (*N*).
- **One-tailed or two-tailed test** – If the hypothesis was a directional hypothesis, then you use a one-tailed test, if it was non-directional you use a two-tailed test.
- **Significance level** selected, usually $p \leq 0.05$ (5% level).
- Whether the observed value needs to be greater than or less than the critical value for significance to be shown. You will find this information stated underneath each table.

Choosing which statistical test to use

Different inferential tests are used depending on (1) the research design and (2) the level of measurement. When deciding which test is appropriate in any situation you can ask yourself the questions in the diagram below:

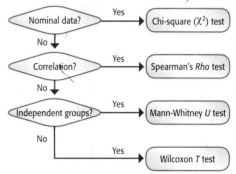

Justifying the choice of test – On each spread that follows we have provided information that will help you justify your choice of tests but *be warned that such justifications need to be adapted to suit particular circumstances*. Essentially you should:

- Identify the level of measurement with reference to the actual data.
- State whether a test of correlation or difference is required and justify this.
- If a test of difference is required, state whether it is **independent groups** or **repeated measures**, and justify this statement.

Further explanation is given on page 294.

Further explanation is given on page 294.

CAN YOU...? (No.16.6)

...**1** Explain what is meant by the phrase 'significant at $p \leq 0.05$'.

...**2** Suggest why a researcher may choose to use $p \leq 0.01$ in preference to $p \leq 0.05$. (Try to give two reasons).

...**3** What other term is used for the observed value?

...**4** Identify the **four** pieces of information used to find the critical value.

...**5** Identify the level of measurement that would be used in the examples below:

  (a) Rating how stressful certain experiences are.

  (b) Counting the days a person has had off school.

  (c) Asking people to indicate the reasons for days off school

...**6** A researcher finds that his results are significant at $p \leq 0.05$. What is the likelihood of having made a Type 1 error?

LEVELS OF MEASUREMENT

When deciding which test to use you may need to identify the level of measurement that was used. If the data are, for example, nominal, then you cannot use Spearman's test.

Nominal – The data are in separate categories, such as grouping your class into people who are tall, medium or short.

Ordinal – Data are ordered in some way, for example lining up your classmates in order of height. The 'difference' between each item is not the same.

Interval – Data are measured using units of equal intervals, such as when counting correct answers or measuring your classmates' heights.

The first inferential test we will look at is a test of correlation – Spearman's *rho*. It is used to determine whether the correlation between two co-variables is significant or not. For example, the study of stress and illness by Rahe *et al.* (1970) found a correlation of + .118 between the number of times a participant was ill and their stress score as measured by the SRRS (social readjustment rating scale). A figure of zero would be no correlation, whereas a figure of +1.0 would be a perfect positive correlation. A correlation of +.118 may sound like a rather weak correlation but in fact it is significant.

The observed value of +.118 was calculated using an inferential statistical test, such as Spearman's *rho*. This observed value is then compared to the critical value found in a table of critical values, such as the table on the far right, to see whether the observed value is significant. In this study the number of participants was over 2700 and therefore .118 was significant. (As the number of participants increases, the value needed for significance decreases.) Incidentally if the observed value had been –.118 this would still be significant – a significant *negative* correlation.

▲ **Literacy hand**
People with short ring fingers and long index fingers are better at literacy.

▲ **Numeracy hand**
People with long ring fingers and short index fingers are more likely to excel in numeracy.

FINGER LENGTH AND EXAM PERFORMANCE

A number of studies have looked at the relationship between finger length and various abilities, such as numeracy or literacy. For example, a recent study by Brosnan (2008) examined finger length in 75 British children aged between six and seven (boys and girls), and found that children with a higher digit ratio between their index and ring fingers were more likely to have a talent in maths, while those with a shorter digit ratio were more likely to have a talent in literacy.

This relationship is thought to be due to biological factors, specifically the production of **testosterone** and **oestrogen** in the brain. Male babies are exposed to more testosterone (a male hormone) during prenatal development and this affects their finger length. Testosterone also promotes the development of the areas of the brain which are often associated with spatial and mathematical skills, whereas oestrogen (a female hormone) is thought to do the same in the areas of the brain which are often associated with verbal ability.

In order to study the correlation between finger length and numeracy/literacy the researchers took photocopies of both the right and left hands of the children and measured the length of the index and ring fingers. They divided the length of the index finger by the length of the ring finger to calculate each child's 'digit ratio'.

The digit ratios were then correlated with the results from their National Standard Assessment Tests (SATs) for numeracy and literacy.

DO-IT-YOURSELF
You can repeat (replicate) this study using GCSE scores instead of SATs results, or you could use online tests of literacy and/or numeracy. In order to determine if your results are significant, follow the worked example on the facing page.

CAN YOU...? (No.16.7)

...1 Identify **two** ethical problems that might arise when conducting a study on finger length and numeracy, and state how these could be dealt with.

...2 Suggest problems that might occur when dealing with the ethical problems in the manner you suggested

...3 Identify the co-variables in the study by Brosnan (above).

...4 Identify the intervening variable in this study (the variable that links finger length to, for example, numeracy).

...5 If you were going to study the relationship between finger ratio and literacy, state a possible alternative and null hypothesis for this study.

...6 Draw a scattergram of the results on the right to check the outcome of the inferential test – does your graph show the same relationship as found by the inferential test?

...7 If you conduct a study yourself, produce a report of the study using the normal conventions (see 'Conventions for reporting psychological investigations' on page 295). Remember to use a scattergram to 'eyeball' your data as well as conducting an inferential test.

MORE DO-IT-YOURSELF IDEAS FOR STUDIES USING A CORRELATIONAL ANALYSIS

- **Stressful life events and illness**. In your AS studies you looked at the relationship between stressful life events or daily hassles and illness. You can replicate such a study and check whether your correlations were significant.
- **Reaction time and number of hours of sleep**. Does sleep deprivation have any effects? For example, it might be related to poor reaction time. You can measure reaction time using an online test.
- **Reaction time and time spent playing computer games**. Perhaps playing computer games is related to reaction time.
- **Working memory and IQ** are predicted to be positively correlated. You can find tests for both at www.bbc.co.uk.

WHEN TO USE SPEARMAN'S RANK CORRELATION (RHO) TEST

- The hypothesis states a **correlation** between two co-variables.
- The two sets of data are pairs of scores from one person or thing = i.e. they are *related*.
- The data are **ordinal** or **interval** (i.e. not nominal). See page 285 for an explanation.

You will never be required to do any calculations in an exam. The reason it is a good idea to have a go is that it gives you a better 'feel' for the test and also helps you understand how to deal with observed and critical values, and draw a conclusion. You can, however, avoid the actual calculation by using an electronic version – look online or use one in Excel (Microsoft Office).

▲ Charles Edward Spearman (1863–1945)

SPEARMAN'S RANK CORRELATION TEST – A WORKED EXAMPLE

STEP 1. State the alternative and null hypothesis

Alternative hypothesis: The digit ratio between index finger and ring finger is positively correlated to numeracy skills. (This is a directional hypothesis, therefore requiring a one-tailed test.)

Null hypothesis: There is no correlation between digit ratio and numeracy skills.

STEP 2. Record the data, rank each co-variable, and calculate the difference

- Rank A and B separately, from low to high (i.e. the lowest number receives the rank of 1).
- If there are two or more of the same number (tied ranks), calculate the rank by working out the mean of the ranks that would have been given.

Participant number	Digit ratio	Numeracy score	Rank A	Rank B	Difference between rank A and rank B (d)	d_2
1	1.026	8	10	2.5	7.5	56.25
2	1.000	16	5.5	9	−3.5	12.25
3	1.021	10	9	5	4.0	16.0
4	0.991	9	4	4	0	0
5	0.984	15	3	8	−5.0	25.0
6	0.975	14	1	7	−6.0	36.0
7	1.013	12	7	6	1	1.0
8	1.018	8	8	2.5	5.5	30.25
9	0.982	17	2	10	−8.0	64.0
10	1.000	5	5.5	1	4.5	20.25
N = 10					Σd^2 (sum of differences squared) = 261.0	

ALTERNATIVE AND NULL HYPOTHESIS

On the previous spread we introduced the **alternative** and **null hypothesis**. The term 'alternative hypothesis' (H_1) is used because it is the alternative to the null hypothesis (H_0). The null hypothesis is required because inferential tests are looking at whether our samples come from a population where there is no relationship (in which case the null hypothesis is true i.e. any relationship is due to chance) or whether our samples come from a population where there is a relationship (in which case we can reject the null hypothesis and accept the alternative).

The null hypothesis is a statement of no relationship (in a correlational analysis) or no difference. So it should always begin: 'There is no correlation between ...' or 'There is no difference between ...'.

STEP 3. Find observed value of rho (the correlation coefficient)

$$rho = 1 - \frac{6\,\Sigma d^2}{N(N^2-1)} = 1 - \frac{6 \times 261.0}{10 \times (100-1)} = 1 - \frac{1566}{990} = 1 - 1.58 = -0.58$$

STEP 4. Find the critical value of rho

N=10, the hypothesis is directional, therefore a one-tailed test is used.

Look up critical value in table of critical values (on right).

For a one-tailed test where N=10, the critical value of *rho* ($p \leq 0.05$) = 0.564

Note that the observed value is negative – when comparing this figure to the critical value, only the value, not the sign, is important. The sign does, however, tell you whether the correlation is positive or negative. If the hypothesis was one-tailed and the sign (and therefore the correlation) is not as stated, then the null hypothesis must be retained.

STEP 5. State the conclusion

As the observed value (0.58) is greater than the critical value (0.564) we could reject the null hypothesis (at $p \leq 0.05$) and therefore could conclude that digit ratio is correlated with numeracy.

Note, however, that in this case the sign is in the wrong direction – a positive correlation was stated but a negative correlation was found. This means that in fact we have to accept the null hypothesis. If we had stated a negative correlation then we could have rejected the null hypothesis – although you should also remember that there is a 5% chance that we are wrong because $p \leq 0.05$.

Level of significance for a one-tailed test	0.05	0.01
Level of significance for a two-tailed test	0.10	0.02
N = 4	1.000	
5	.900	1.000
6	.829	.886
7	.714	.786
8	.643	.738
9	.600	.700
10	.564	.648
11	.536	.618
12	.503	.587
13	.484	.560
14	.464	.538
15	.443	.521
16	.429	.503
17	.414	.485
18	.401	.472
19	.391	.460
20	.380	.447
25	.337	.398
30	.306	.362

◄ **Table of critical values of *rho***

Observed value of *rho* must be EQUAL TO or GREATER THAN the critical value in this table for significance to be shown.

Source:
J.H. Zhar (1972). Significance testing of the Spearman rank correlation coefficient. *Journal of the American Statistical Association*, 67, 578–80. (Reproduced with kind permission of the publisher.)

The second inferential test we will look at deals with **nominal data** i.e. data that is in categories. We use this test when we have counted how many occurrences there are in each category – called 'frequency data'. For example, we might be interested to find out whether men and women do actually differ in terms of their finger-length ratio. Research has found that adult women usually have ratios of one i.e. their index and ring fingers are of equal length. The average for men is lower, at 0.98, since they tend to have longer ring fingers than index fingers, suggesting greater exposure to testosterone in the womb. Of course the chi-square analysis (see below) does not *prove* this but can support this gender difference.

'Chi' is one of the letters of the Greek alphabet (pronounced as 'kie' to rhyme with 'pie'). The Greek symbol for chi is χ which is why this symbol is used for the statistic for the chi-square test.

CHI-SQUARE TEST
– A WORKED EXAMPLE FOR A 2 × 2 TABLE

STEP 1. State the alternative and null hypothesis

Alternative hypothesis: There is difference between men and women in terms of digit ratio (the ratio between the index and ring fingers). (This is a non-directional hypothesis, and therefore requires a two-tailed test.)

Null hypothesis: There is no difference between men and women in terms of digit ratio.

There are online programmes that will calculate chi-square for you, see for example http://math.hws. edu/javamath/ryan/ChiSquare. html (scroll about half way down the page). You can also use Excel.

STEP 2. Draw up a contingency table

Chi-square can be used to investigate a difference (as in the worked example on this page) or an association (as on the facing page).

	Male	Female	Totals
Digit ratio ≥1.00	5 (cell A)	12 (cell B)	17
Digit ratio <1.00	10 (cell C)	9 (cell D)	19
Totals	15	21	36

This is a 2 × 2 contingency table as there are two rows and two columns. On the facing page there is a 3 × 2 contingency table as there are three rows and two columns. The first number is always rows and the second number is columns (rows then columns, RC as in Roman Catholic).

STEP 3. Find observed value by comparing observed and expected frequencies for each cell.

The expected frequencies are calculated by working out how the data would be distributed across all cells in the table if there were no differences or pattern.

In some books Yates's correction is recommended but Coolican (1996) said that this was no longer current practice.

Many students get confused about the expected frequencies. These are not what the researcher expects – they are the frequencies that would occur if the data were distributed evenly across the table in proportion to the row and column totals.

	row × column / total = expected frequency (E)	Subtract expected value from observed value, ignoring signs (O–E)	Square previous value (O–E)^2	Divide previous value by expected value (O–E)^2/E
Cell A	17 × 15 / 36 = 7.08	5 – 7.08 = 2.08	4.3264	0.6110
Cell B	17 × 21 / 36 = 9.92	12 – 9.92 = 2.08	4.3264	0.4361
Cell C	19 × 15 / 36 = 7.92	10 – 7.92 = 2.08	4.3264	0.5463
Cell D	19 × 21 / 36 = 11.08	9 – 11.08 = 2.08	4.3264	0.3905

STEP 4. Add all the values in the final column

This gives you the observed value of chi-square as 1.984

STEP 5. Find the critical value of chi-square

Calculate degrees of freedom (df) by multiplying (rows – 1) × (columns – 1) = 1
Look up value in table of critical values (on the right). For a two-tailed test, df = 1, the critical value of χ^2 ($p \leq 0.05$) = 3.84

STEP 6. State the conclusion

As the observed value (1.984) is less than the critical value (3.84) we must accept the null hypothesis (at $p \leq 0.05$) and therefore we conclude that there is no difference between men and women in terms of digit ratio.

▼ **Table of critical values of chi-square (χ^2)**

Level of significance for a one-tailed test	0.10	0.05	0.025	0.01
Level of significance for a two-tailed test	0.20	0.10	0.05	0.02
df				
1	1.64	2.71	3.84	5.41
2	3.22	4.60	5.99	7.82
3	4.64	6.25	7.82	9.84
4	5.99	7.78	9.49	11.67

Observed value of χ^2 must be EQUAL TO or GREATER THAN the critical value in this table for significance to be shown.

Source: abridged from R.A. Fisher and F. Yates (1974). *Statistical tables for biological, agricultural and medical research* (sixth edition). Longman.

WHEN TO USE THE CHI-SQUARE (χ^2) TEST

- The hypothesis states a *difference* between two conditions or an *association* between co-variables.
- The sets of data must be *independent* (no individual should have a score in more than one 'cell').
- The data are in *frequencies* (i.e. **nominal**). Frequencies must not be percentages.

Note – This test is unreliable when the *expected* frequencies (i.e. the ones you calculate) fall below 5 in any cell i.e. you need at least 20 participants for a 2×2 contingency table.

CHI-SQUARE TEST
– A WORKED EXAMPLE FOR A 3 × 2 TABLE

STEP 1. State the alternative and null hypothesis

Alternative hypothesis: Certain parental styles are associated with higher self-esteem in adolescence. (This is a non-directional hypothesis and therefore requires a two-tailed test.)

Null hypothesis: There is no association between parental style and self-esteem in adolescence.

STEP 2. Draw up a contingency table

In this case it will be 3 by 2 (rows first then columns)

Parental style	Self-esteem		Totals
	High	Low	
Authoritarian	10 (cell A)	4 (cell B)	14
Democratic	5 (cell C)	7 (cell D)	12
Laissez-faire	8 (cell E)	2 (cell F)	10
Totals	23	13	36

STEP 3. Find observed value by comparing observed and expected frequencies

	row × column / total = expected frequency	Subtract expected value from observed value, ignoring signs |(O–E)|	Square the previous value $(O-E)^2$	Divide previous value by the expected value $(O-E)^2/E$
Cell A	14 × 23 / 36 = 8.94	10 – 8.94 = 1.06	1.1236	0.1257
Cell B	14 × 13 / 36 = 5.06	4 – 5.06 = 1.06	1.1236	0.2221
Cell C	12 × 23 / 36 = 7.67	5 – 7.67 = 2.67	7.1289	0.9294
Cell D	12 × 13 / 36 = 4.33	7 – 4.33 = 2.67	7.1289	1.6464
Cell E	10 × 23 / 36 = 6.39	8 – 6.39 = 1.61	2.5921	0.4056
Cell F	10 × 13 / 36 = 3.61	2 – 3.61 = 1.61	2.5921	0.7180

STEP 4. Add all the values in the final column
This gives you the observed value of chi-square (χ^2) = 4.0472

STEP 5. Find the critical value of chi-square (χ^2)
Calculate degrees of freedom (*df*) calculate (rows − 1) × (columns − 1) = 2
Look up critical value in table of critical values (on facing page).
For a two-tailed test, *df* = 2, the critical value of χ^2 ($p \leq 0.05$) = 5.99

STEP 6. State the conclusion
As the observed value (4.0472) is less than the critical value (5.99) we must accept the null hypothesis (at $p \leq 0.05$) and therefore conclude that there is no association between parental style and self-esteem in adolescence.

PARENTAL STYLE AND SELF-ESTEEM

Psychological research has identified three different parenting styles: authoritarian (parents dictate how children should behave), democratic (parents discuss standards with their children) and laissez-faire (parents encourage children to set their own rules). Buri (1991) found that children who experienced authoritarian parenting were more likely to develop high self-esteem.

DO-IT-YOURSELF
You can access the Parental Authority Questionnaire (PAQ) at http://faculty.sjcny.edu/~treboux/documents/parental%20authority%20questionnaire.pdf

There are various self-esteem questionnaires on the Internet.

MORE DO-IT-YOURSELF IDEAS FOR STUDIES USING A CHI-SQUARE TEST

- **Gender and conformity**. Are women more conformist than men? Some studies have found this to be true although Eagly and Carli (1981) suggest that this is only the case for male-oriented tasks. Try different types of conformity tasks and see whether they have higher or lower levels of female conformity, for example ask questions on a general knowledge test which are related to male or female interests. The answers from previous 'participants' should be shown so you can see if your real participant conforms to the majority answer.
- **Sleep and age**. Research suggests that people sleep less as they get older (see page 18). Compare older and younger participants in terms of average numbers of hours of sleep.

CAN YOU...? (No.16.8)

...**1** Draw a contingency table to show the following data – old and young participants are asked whether they sleep more or less than eight hours per night on average. Of the older people, 11 said they sleep more and 25 said they sleep less. Of the younger participants, 31 said they sleep more than eight hours and 33 said they sleep less.

...**2** State a non-directional alternative hypothesis and null hypothesis for this investigation.

...**3** The observed value of chi-square for the data from question 1 is 3.02 (two-tailed test). Is this value significant? Explain your decision and state whether this means you can reject the null hypothesis.

The final two inferential tests required in the specification are called 'tests of difference'. They enable us to consider whether two samples of data are different or not different from each other i.e. that they are drawn from the same population (the null hypothesis) or from two different populations. Tests of difference are generally used for experiments. For example, we might conduct an experiment to see if noisy conditions reduce the effectiveness of revision.

Case A – we could have two groups of participants:
- Group 1: participants revise in a silent room and are tested.
- Group 2: participants revise in a noisy room and are tested.

Case B – we might have two conditions:
- Condition 1: participants revise in a silent room and are tested.
- Condition 2: the same participants revise in a noisy room and are tested.

Case A is an **independent groups design** (we have two separate groups of participants). Case B (two conditions) is a **repeated measures design** as the same participants are tested twice.

The Mann-Whitney test is used for independent groups designs and the Wilcoxon test (on the next spread) is used for repeated measures designs.

In some experiments there are more than two conditions or groups – for example the study by Loftus and Palmer on leading questions had five different groups according to which verb was in the sentence (smashed, hit, etc.). There are other inferential tests that are used for designs with more than two conditions/groups.

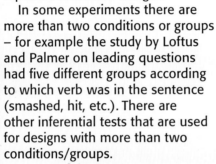

◀ The Capilano Suspension Bridge was used in the study by Dutton and Aron (see right). The bridge is narrow and long and has many arousal-inducing features: a tendency to tilt, sway, and wobble, creating the impression that one is about to fall over the side; very low handrails of wire cable contribute to this impression as well as a 230-foot drop to rocks and shallow rapids below.

CAN YOU...? — No.16.9

...1 Use descriptive statistics to summarise the results given in the worked example on the facing page, e.g. calculate measures of central tendency and dispersion, and also sketch an appropriate graph.

...2 A psychology class decides to replicate the study by White *et al.* on the right. Write an appropriate alternative and null hypothesis for this study.

...3 Is your alternative hypothesis directional or non-directional?

...4 The students check the significance of their results using the Mann-Whitney test and find that $U = 40$ (there were 9 participants in one group and 13 in a second group). State what conclusion they could draw from their results.

...5 If you were going to write a report of this study, outline what would be included in each section of it (see 'Conventions for reporting psychological investigations' on page 295).

FALLING IN LOVE

Psychologists have sought to explain the process of falling in love. One suggestion is that love is basically physiological arousal – arousal of your **sympathetic nervous system** which occurs when you are feeling scared or stressed or find someone physically attractive. Hatfield and Walster (1981) suggested that love is simply a label that we place on physiological arousal when it occurs in the presence of an appropriate object. A man or woman who meets a potential partner after an exciting football game is more likely to fall in love than he or she would be on a routine day. Likewise, a man or woman is more likely to fall in love when having experienced some bitter disappointment. The reason, in both cases, is to do with the two components of love: arousal and label.

This has been supported by various experiments, such as a memorable study by Dutton and Aron (1974). A female research assistant (unaware of the study's aims) interviewed males, explaining that she was doing a project for her psychology class on the effects of attractive scenery on creative expression. The interviews took place on a high suspension bridge (high arousal group, see left) or a narrow bridge over a small stream (low arousal). When the interview was over, the confederate gave the men her phone number and asked them to call her if they had any questions about the survey. Over 60% of the men in the high arousal condition did phone her, compared with 30% from the low arousal group, suggesting that the men had mislabelled their fear-related arousal as sexual arousal.

DO-IT-YOURSELF
Another study which investigated the two-factor theory of love (which might be easier to replicate) was conducted by White *et al.* (1981). In this experiment, high and low arousal were created by asking men to run on the spot for 2 minutes or 15 seconds respectively, and then showing a short video of a young woman. The more highly aroused men rated the woman as more attractive.

MORE DO-IT-YOURSELF IDEAS FOR STUDIES USING AN INDEPENDENT GROUPS TEST

- **Digit ratio and gender**. You can collect data on the digit ratios of men and women and analyse it using the Mann-Whitney test by comparing the scores for men and women.
- **The power of touch**. A number of studies have shown that people are more willing to comply with a request if you touch them lightly on their arm. For example, Brockner *et al.* (1982) arranged for a confederate to approach participants as they left a phone box and ask for some money which had been left behind in the phone box. If the participant was touched lightly on the arm, 98% gave the money back, compared to 63% in the no-touch group.

There are **three** kinds of experimental design – repeated measures, independent groups and finally, **matched pairs**. In a matched pairs study there are two groups of participants (as in independent groups design), however the groups are not independent, they are matched (e.g. on characteristics, such as IQ, age, etc.). Therefore, matched pairs experiments use repeated measures tests.

THE MANN-WHITNEY *U* TEST – A WORKED EXAMPLE

STEP 1. State the alternative and null hypothesis

Alternative hypothesis: Male participants interviewed on a high bridge give higher ratings of the attractiveness of a female interviewer than those interviewed on a low bridge. (This is a directional hypothesis and therefore requires a one-tailed test).

Null hypothesis: There is no difference in the ratings of attractiveness given by those interviewed on a high or low bridge.

STEP 2. Record the data in a table and allocate points

- To allocate points, consider each score one at a time.
- Compare this score (the target) with all the scores in the other group.
- Give 1 point for every score that is higher than the target score.
- Give ½ point for every equal score.

STEP 3. Find observed value of U

U is the lower total number of points. In this case it is 16.5

STEP 4. Find the critical value of U

N_1 = number of participants in group 1
N_2 = number of participants in group 2
Look up the critical value in a table of critical values (below).
For a one-tailed test, N_1= 10 and N_2=14, the critical value of U ($p \leq 0.05$) = 41

Note – when you have a one-tailed hypothesis, remember to check whether the difference is in the direction that you stated. If it is not, you cannot reject the null hypothesis.

STEP 5. State the conclusion

As the observed value (16.5) is less than the critical value (41), we can reject the null hypothesis (at $p \leq 0.05$) and therefore conclude that participants interviewed on a high bridge give higher ratings of attractiveness to a female interviewer than those interviewed on a low bridge.

The Mann-Whitney test is named after the Austrian-born US mathematician Henry Berthold Mann and the US statistician Donald Ransom Whitney who published the test in 1947. They adapted a test designed by Wilcoxon which was for equal sample sizes.

Attractiveness ratings given by high bridge group	Points	Attractiveness ratings given by low bridge group	Points
7	1.5	4	10.0
10	0	6	8.5
8	1.0	2	10.0
6	3.5	5	9.5
5	7.0	3	10.0
8	1.0	5	9.5
9	0.5	6	8.5
7	1.5	4	10.0
10	0	5	9.5
9	0.5	7	7.0
		9	3.0
		3	10.0
		5	9.5
		6	8.5
$N_1 = 10$	16.5	$N_2 = 14$	123.5

The two samples in the table above are unequal, which may happen when using an independent groups design.

▼ **Tables of critical values of *U***

CRITICAL VALUES FOR A ONE-TAILED TEST ($p \leq 0.05$)

N_2 \ N_1	2	3	4	5	6	7	8	9	10	11	12	13	14	15
2				0	0	0	1	1	1	1	2	2	2	3
3		0	0	1	2	2	3	3	4	5	5	6	7	7
4		0	1	2	3	4	5	6	7	8	9	10	11	12
5	0	1	2	4	5	6	8	9	11	12	13	15	16	18
6	0	2	3	5	7	8	10	12	14	16	17	19	21	23
7	0	2	4	6	8	11	13	15	17	19	21	24	26	28
8	1	3	5	8	10	13	15	18	20	23	26	28	31	33
9	1	3	6	9	12	15	18	21	24	27	30	33	36	39
10	1	4	7	11	14	17	20	24	27	31	34	37	41	44
11	1	5	8	12	16	19	23	27	31	34	38	42	46	50
12	2	5	9	13	17	21	26	30	34	38	42	47	51	55
13	2	6	10	15	19	24	28	33	37	42	47	51	56	61
14	2	7	11	16	21	26	31	36	41	46	51	56	61	66
15	3	7	12	18	23	28	33	39	44	50	55	61	66	72

For any N_1 and N_2 observed value of U must be EQUAL TO or LESS THAN the critical value in this table for significance to be shown.

CRITICAL VALUES FOR A TWO-TAILED TEST ($p \leq 0.05$)

N_2 \ N_1	2	3	4	5	6	7	8	9	10	11	12	13	14	15
2							0	0	0	0	1	1	1	1
3				0	1	1	2	2	3	3	4	4	5	5
4			0	1	2	3	4	4	5	6	7	8	9	10
5		0	1	2	3	5	6	7	8	9	11	12	13	14
6		1	2	3	5	6	8	10	11	13	14	16	17	19
7		1	3	5	6	8	10	12	14	16	18	20	22	24
8	0	2	4	6	8	10	13	15	17	19	22	24	26	29
9	0	2	4	7	10	12	15	17	20	23	26	28	31	34
10	0	3	5	8	11	14	17	20	23	26	29	33	36	39
11	0	3	6	9	13	16	19	23	26	30	33	37	40	44
12	1	4	7	11	14	18	22	26	29	33	37	41	45	49
13	1	4	8	12	16	20	24	28	33	37	41	45	50	54
14	1	5	9	13	17	22	26	31	36	40	45	50	55	59
15	1	5	10	14	19	24	29	34	39	44	49	54	59	64

Source: R. Runyon and A. Haber (1976). *Fundamentals of behavioural statistics* (third edition). Reading, Mass: McGraw-Hill.

INFERENTIAL TESTS: WILCOXON *T* TEST

The final inferential test you need to study is one that is appropriate for tests of difference where pairs of data are related, such as when a **repeated measures design** has been used. Each participant is tested twice and their scores are compared to see if there is any difference. **Matched pairs** is also a related design – where there are two groups of participants, but each participant in one group is matched with a participant in the other group on key variables, so in a sense it is like testing the same person twice.

▲ Frank Wilcoxon (1892–1965)

◄ Which person is more likeable? Zajonc (1968) showed that our liking for faces and objects was a function of how often we saw the face/object. Of course it might be that one of the faces is actually more likeable – you can control this extraneous variable by varying which photo you use as the 'most frequent' condition with different participants.

THE MERE EXPOSURE EFFECT

There is a saying that 'familiarity breeds contempt', but psychological research has found that the opposite is generally true – we come to like things because of their familiarity. For example. people generally like a song more after they have heard it a few times, and advertisements often aim to increase our liking for a product through repeated exposure. Things that are familiar are less strange and threatening and thus more likeable.

Zajonc (pronounced 'zie-unts') conducted various experiments to demonstrate the *mere exposure effect*. For example, in one study Zajonc (1968) told participants that he was conducting a study on visual memory and showed them a set of photographs of 12 different men (face only). Each photograph was shown for two seconds only. At the end, participants were asked to rate how much they liked the 12 different men on a scale from 0 to 6. The key element of the study is that some photos were shown more often than others, for example one photo appeared 25 times, whereas another appeared only once.

Overall, the frequencies were 0, 1, 2, 5, 10 and 25. The same experiment was repeated with invented Chinese symbols and also with Turkish words. The results are shown in the graph on the left.

DO-IT-YOURSELF
You can replicate this study but don't need to have all six conditions. The final analysis can involve just comparing two of the stimuli – one frequent and one infrequent – as shown in the worked example on the facing page.

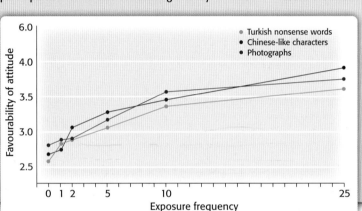

MORE DO-IT-YOURSELF IDEAS FOR STUDIES USING A REPEATED MEASURES TEST

- **Mere exposure again**. The mere exposure effect can also be used to explain the fact that people prefer pictures of themselves that are reversed as in a mirror – because that is the way you usually see yourself, and so it is more familiar (Mita *et al.*, 1977). You could take a few pictures of each participant with a digital camera and create a mirror image of each. Show them the photographs and record the ratings (on a scale of 1 to 5) for each photograph.

- **Right brain/left brain**. If you perform two tasks that involve the same brain hemisphere you should be slower on both tasks than if performing two tasks that involve the right and left hemispheres separately. For example, tap your right finger while reading a page from a book (both involve the left hemisphere). Then repeat the finger-tapping without any reading. On each occasion count how many finger taps you manage in 30 seconds and compare these scores.

- **Smiling makes you happy**. You might think that you smile because you are feeling happy, but psychological research shows it works the other way round too, i.e. you become happy because you are smiling. Laird (1974) told participants to contract certain facial muscles so he could measure facial muscular activity using electrodes. Participants who were made to smile rated cartoons as funnier than those who were made to produce a frown. You could replicate this by, for example, asking people to rate ten cartoons for humour. Ask them to smile for the first five, and frown for the next five.

WHEN TO USE THE WILCOXON *T* TEST

- The hypothesis states a *difference* between two sets of data.
- The two sets of data are pairs of scores from one person (or a matched pair) = *related*.
- The data are **ordinal** or **interval** (i.e. not nominal). See page 285 for an explanation.

THE WILCOXON *T* TEST – A WORKED EXAMPLE

STEP 1. State the alternative and null hypothesis

Alternative hypothesis: Participants rate the more frequently seen face as more likeable than the less frequently seen face. (This is a directional hypothesis and therefore requires a one-tailed test.)

Null hypothesis: There is no difference in the likeability score for faces seen more or less often.

STEP 2. Record the data, calculate the difference between scores and rank

- Once you have worked out the difference, rank from low to high, ignoring the signs (i.e. the lowest number receives the rank of 1).
- If there are two or more of the same number (tied ranks), calculate the rank by working out the mean of the ranks that would have been given.
- If the difference is zero, omit this from the ranking and reduce *N* accordingly.

Participant	Likeability for *more* frequently seen face	Likeability for *less* frequently seen face	difference	rank
1	5	2	3	9.5
2	4	3	1	3
3	3	3	omit	
4	6	4	2	6.5
5	2	3	−1	3
6	4	5	−1	3
7	5	2	3	9.5
8	3	4	−1	3
8	6	3	3	9.5
10	4	6	−2	6.5
11	5	2	3	9.5
12	3	4	−1	3

STEP 3. Find observed value of T

T = the sum of the ranks of the less frequent sign.

In this case the less frequent sign is minus, so $T = 3 + 3 + 3 + 6.5 + 3 = 18.5$

STEP 4. Find critical value of T

$N = 11$ (one score omitted). The hypothesis is directional, therefore a one-tailed test is used.

Look up critical value in table of critical values (see above right).

For a one-tailed test, $N = 11$, the critical value of T ($p \leq 0.05$) = 13

STEP 5. State the conclusion

As the observed value (18.5) is greater than the critical value (13), we must accept the null hypothesis (at $p \leq 0.05$) and conclude that there is no difference in the likeability score for faces seen more or less often.

▼ **Table of critical values of *T***

	0.05	0.01
Level of significance for a one-tailed test	0.05	0.01
Level of significance for a two-tailed test	0.10	0.02
$N = 5$	0	
6	2	0
7	3	2
8	5	3
9	8	5
10	11	8
11	13	10
12	17	13
13	21	17
14	25	21
15	30	25
16	35	29
17	41	34
18	47	40
19	53	46
20	60	52
25	100	89
30	151	137

Observed value of *T* must be EQUAL TO or LESS THAN the critical value in this table for significance to be shown.

Source: R. Meddis (1975). *Statistical handbook for non-statisticians*. London: McGraw Hill.

CAN YOU...? (No.16.10)

...1 Identify the maximum observed value of *T* that would be required for significance with a two-tailed test with 25 participants.

...2 In a psychology experiment, 15 students were given a test in the morning and a similar test in the afternoon to see at what time of day they performed better. The research expected them to do better in the morning. Write an appropriate alternative and null hypothesis for this study.

...3 Invent data for this study – you need 15 pairs of scores.

...4 Explain why the Wilcoxon test would be the appropriate test to use with this data.

...5 Follow the steps outlined above to calculate *T* and then state the conclusion you would draw about the significance of the results.

...6 One problem with this study is that the students might do better in the afternoon because they had done a similar test in the morning. Therefore, the study was conducted again using a matched pairs design. Explain how this might be done (including relevant variables that you would use for matching and explain why they are relevant).

...7 Explain how counterbalancing could be used to deal with the order effects in this study.

A good way to assess your understanding of research methods is to ask you to design a research study. Such 'design a study' questions tend to be quite challenging for students – probably because students lack the experience to think on their feet, especially under the stress of exam conditions.

Earlier in this chapter we looked at elements of research design (pages 276–80). On this spread we focus on the design decisions to be made and how you could put these into practice. This includes writing a report following the conventions used in psychological investigations.

In order to understand the research process, as well as the conventions for reporting research, have a look on the Internet at published research.

To do this, select the title of a particular research article (you can find these in the reference section of this book). Put the title into your online search engine and see if any pdf documents come up. You might have to try a few.

DESIGNING YOUR OWN STUDY

Introduction

Consider past research (theories and/or studies). The findings from such studies lead to research aims/hypotheses.

Decide on the research aims and/or hypothesis (hypotheses). This may well be provided in an exam question. Decide on whether to use a directional or non-directional hypothesis. This is related to what past research has found (for example if past research is equivocal a non-directional hypothesis might be justified).

Method

Decide on the target population and the overarching research method (e.g. experiment, questionnaire, case study, content analysis, etc.). Your choice of method should be related to the research aims and the relative advantages and disadvantages of each method. (The required method is liked to be stated in an exam question.)

In the case of an experiment or study using correlational analysis, you need to identify independent and dependent variables (IV and DV) or co-variables. Decide how these will be operationalised. You may use observational techniques or a questionnaire/interview to measure variables – so further design decisions may be involved.

Design and materials – Consider what materials you will be using, and describe these.

Consider issues related to validity and reliability and how these will be dealt with. Reliability generally concerns questionnaires, interviews and observational techniques.

For experiments – Lab, field or natural experiment? Repeated measures, independent groups or matched pairs?

For questionnaires/interviews – Structured or semi-structured or unstructured? Open and/or closed questions. Produce a sample of some of your questions.

For observations – Naturalistic or controlled? Direct or indirect (content analysis)? Structured or unstructured techniques? Overt or covert observation? Participant or non-participant observation?

Participants – Identify a suitable sampling technique and explain how it would be used. Consider size and composition of the sample. If using independent groups, explain how to assign participants to groups.

In an observational study, sampling applies to the selection of participants and also applies to how often observations are recorded (time or event sampling).

Ethics – Identify any ethical issues that might arise in the study and consider how they might be dealt with.

Procedures: what will actually be done? – The main criterion for assessment in an exam question is **replicability** – to what extent could someone else follow your instructions and repeat exactly what you did?

Outline standardised instructions given to each participant. This includes informed consent. Explain when and what materials will be given, where the participants are tested, how long they will have, etc.

Conduct a pilot study – Before conducting the full scale study, a pilot study might be conducted with a few people similar to the target population, testing the materials to be used and the standardised instructions.

Results

Consider what statistics to use. This includes descriptive and inferential statistics (including the level of significance to be used).

For a questionnaire/interview – Analysis is likely to focus on individual questions. Qualitative methods may be used with open questions.

▲ Conduct your own research into how pain thresholds can be reduced.

COURSEWORK

In the old days Psychology A Level involved producing a file of coursework which was marked and counted towards your final grade. Students had to design, conduct and report their own studies. The reporting part required using the conventions described on the facing page.

You can use some of the suggested studies in this chapter or a few more are given below.

- Names are more difficult to remember than remembering what people do (James, 2004). People remember if you are a farmer better than if someone's name is Farmer.
- Laughter increases the pain threshold (Dunbar *et al.*, 2011). Pain can be created by putting your hand in a bucket of ice cold water. People also feel less pain when they swear rather than when they say a neutral word (Stephens *et al.*, 2009).

CONVENTIONS FOR REPORTING PSYCHOLOGICAL INVESTIGATIONS

Scientific journals contain research reports that are usually organised into the following sections:

Abstract – A summary of the study covering the aims, hypothesis, the method (procedures), results and conclusions (including implications of the current study).

Introduction (including aim and hypothesis/es) begins with a review of previous research (theories and studies). The focus of this research review should lead logically to the study to be conducted so the reader is convinced of the reasons for this particular research. The introduction should be like a funnel – starting broadly and narrowing down to the particular research hypothesis. The researcher(s) states their aims, research prediction and/or hypothesis.

Method – A detailed description of what the researcher(s) did, providing enough information for replication of the study.

- *Design*, e.g. 'repeated measures' or 'covert observation'. Design decisions might be justified.
- *Participants* – Information about sampling methods and how many participants took part and their details (e.g. age, job, etc.).
- *Apparatus/materials* – Descriptions of any materials used.
- *Procedures*, including standardised instructions, the testing environment, the order of events and so on.
- *Ethics* – Significant ethical issues may be mentioned, as well as how they were dealt with.

Results – What the researcher(s) found, including:

- *Descriptive statistics* – tables and graphs showing frequencies and measures of central tendency and dispersion.
- *Inferential statistics* justified, observed value and significance level reported. Statement of whether null hypothesis accepted or rejected.

In the case of qualitative research, categories and themes are described along with examples within these categories.

Discussion – The researcher aims to interpret the results and consider their implications for future research as well as suggesting real-world applications.

- *Summary of the results* – The results are reported in brief and some explanation given about what these results show.
- *Relationship to previous research* – The results of the study are discussed in relation to the research reported in the introduction and possibly other research not previously mentioned.
- *Consideration of methodology* – Criticisms may be made of the methods used in the study, and improvements suggested.
- *Implications* for psychological theory and possible real-world applications.
- *Suggestions* for future research.

References – The full details of any journal articles or books that are mentioned.

CAN YOU...? (No.16.11)

...1 A research study discovers a positive correlation between exercise and happiness. The research team decide to conduct a further study to see if exercise actually *causes* happiness.

(a) Design a suitable consent form for this study.

(b) Describe how the research team might design an experiment to investigate this causal relationship. Include in your answer sufficient detail to enable someone to carry out this study in the future.

It is useful to refer to the following:

- Fully operationalised independent and dependent variables.
- Details of how you would control extraneous variables.
- The procedure that you would use. You should provide sufficient detail for the study to be carried out.

...2 A psychologist was researching how children's attitudes towards their family changes as they move from early adolescence (aged 12) to late adolescence (aged 18). Describe how you would collect data for this study using a questionnaire.

In your description it will be useful to refer to the following:

- The kind of questions you would use.
- The sample to be used.
- A description of the procedure that you would use. You should provide sufficient detail for the study to be carried out.

...3 People believe that football fans are very aggressive. Design an observational study to investigate the aggressiveness of spectators at a football match.

In your answer, refer to: an appropriate method of investigation and materials/apparatus and procedure. Justify your design decisions and provide sufficient detail to allow for reasonable replication of the study.

...4 TV programmes before 9pm are supposed to contain less sex and violence. Design a study that could test this by comparing programmes shown on TV from 8–9pm and 9–10pm. Your design brief should include:

- A suitable hypothesis.
- Categories that might be used in this content analysis.
- A sampling method.
- A description of the procedure that you would use. You should provide sufficient detail for the study to be carried out.

...5 Research on the effects of brain damage often involves the use of case studies. Imagine you have been asked to conduct a case study involving a patient recently involved in a car accident which resulted in him not being able to remember any new information.

Describe how you might conduct this study, including details concerning ethics and validity.

DESCRIPTIVE AND INFERENTIAL STATISTICS

O n this page we present a reminder of all the different kinds of statistical methods you should be familiar with and how you can decide which statistic(s) would be appropriate in any situation. Such decisions are not always black and white, which means that you need to take relative strengths and limitations into account.

DECIDING WHICH STATISTICS TO USE

Descriptive statistics

This is a summary of the descriptive statistics covered at AS, and their strengths and limitations.

Measures of central tendency inform us about central (or middle) values for a set of data. They are 'averages' – ways of calculating a typical value for a set of data. An average can be calculated in different ways:

- The **mean** is calculated by adding up all the scores and dividing by the number of scores. It makes use of the values of all the data in the final calculation but can be unrepresentative of the data as a whole if there are extreme values. It is *not* appropriate for nominal data.
- The **median** is the middle *value* in an *ordered* list. It is not affected by extreme scores but is not as 'sensitive' as the mean because not all values are reflected in the median. It is *not* appropriate for nominal data.
- The **mode** is the value that is *most* common in a data set. It is the only method appropriate when the data are in categories (such as number of people who like pink) i.e. nominal data, but can be used for all kinds of data. It is not a useful way of describing data when there are several modes.

Measures of dispersion inform us about the spread of data.

- **Range** – Calculated by finding the difference between the highest and lowest score in a data set. This is easy to calculate but may be affected by extreme values.
- **Standard deviation** expresses the spread of the data around the mean. This is a more precise measure because all the values of the data are taken into account. However, some characteristics of the data are not expressed, such as the influence of extreme values.

Graphs – A picture is worth a thousand words! Graphs provide a means of 'eyeballing' your data and seeing the results at a glance.

- **Bar chart** – The height of the bar represents frequency. Suitable for words and numbers i.e. all levels of measurement.
- **Scattergram** – Suitable for correlational data, a dot or cross is shown for each pair of values. If the dots form a pattern going from bottom left to top right, this indicates a **positive correlation**, whereas top left to bottom right suggests a **negative correlation**. If there is no detectable pattern there is a **zero correlation**.

Inferential statistics

Exam questions are likely to focus on three things:

1. Selecting the right test – In the exam you may be asked to select an appropriate test for a specified set of data. When deciding which test is appropriate in any situation you can use the decision tree on page 285.

The three questions to focus on are:

- Are the data nominal? (Or are they ordinal/interval?)
- Is a correlation involved? (Or is it a test of the difference between two sets of data?)
- Is the design repeated measures? (Or is it independent groups?)

The diagram on page 285 supplies the answers.

2. Justifying your choice – You may be asked to justify (i.e. say why it is the right test to use) the inferential test selected. The justifications for each test are provided on the appropriate spreads in this chapter. When answering an exam question you should try to make specific reference to the data in any particular study. Below are some examples of possible justifications that could be used. In each case, full reference to the data has been made.

Spearman – A test of correlation is needed as the hypothesis stated a correlation. The data involved ratings made by participants that are ordinal data. This means the appropriate test to use is Spearman's rho (test of correlation, ordinal data).

Chi-square – As the data have been put into categories, they are classified as nominal data. The results are independent in each cell, and the expected frequencies in each cell are greater than 4. The appropriate inferential test to use is therefore a chi-square test (test of association, independent groups, nominal data).

Mann-Whitney – A test of difference is required because the hypothesis states that there is a difference between the two groups. The design is independent groups as participants were allocated to one of two treatment groups, and the data were scores on a test (ordinal data). Therefore, the Mann-Whitney test is suitable (test of difference, independent groups, ordinal data).

Wilcoxon – A test of difference is required because the hypothesis states that there is a difference between the two conditions. The design is repeated measures as all the participants were tested twice. The data were scores on a memory test, which are interval data. Therefore, a Wilcoxon test was chosen (test of difference, related groups, interval data).

3. Stating conclusions – You may also be asked to state the conclusions that can be drawn after using an inferential test. You can see how this is done in the worked examples provided for each inferential test. See, for instance, the worked example on page 287 – the final step is a conclusion.

The key features of this conclusion are:

- State the observed value.
- Say whether this is greater than or less than the critical value.
- State whether the null hypothesis can be rejected or must be accepted. This depends on each test – for Spearman and Chi-square the value of the observed value must be greater than the critical value in order to reject the null hypothesis. For the other two tests, it is less than the critical value.
- Restate the hypothesis you are accepting.

...1 For each of the following data sets identify an appropriate measure of central tendency and dispersion and justify your choice.

(a) 8, 11, 12, 12, 14, 15, 16, 16, 17, 19, 22, 27
(b) 15, 17, 21, 25, 28, 29, 32, 34, 25, 35, 38, 41, 45
(c) yes, yes, no, no, no, yes, no, no

...2 In the following research studies, suggest a suitable alternative hypothesis for the study; briefly explain how you might conduct the study; invent a hypothetical set of data that might be produced and finally select an appropriate inferential test, justifying the reason for your choice.

(a) An experiment where reaction times are compared for each participant before and after drinking coffee.
(b) A study looking at whether old or young people watch more violence on TV.
(c) An investigation to see if reaction time is related to age.
(d) An experiment to compare stress levels in doctors and nurses.
(e) A study where two groups of participants were matched on memory ability. Each group used a different revision technique to learn a topic and then their performances were compared.
(f) A study to see whether people who have a pet are happier than those who don't.

...3 A student designed an experiment that used a repeated measures design to investigate obedience to male and female teachers. The student decided to do this by observing how pupils behaved with different teachers. She asked various friends to record student behaviours in their classrooms.

(a) State a possible directional hypothesis for this study.
(b) Suggest **two** possible extraneous variables that might be a problem for this study and describe the possible effects they could have.
(c) Suggest **three** behavioural categories that might be used to record the students' behaviours.
(d) Identify the sampling method that is likely to have been used in this study and explain why it would be chosen.
(e) Suggest some appropriate statistical measures that could be used when analysing the data (descriptive and inferential). Justify your choice.
(f) Assume that the student obtained a significant result. State the conclusion that could be drawn.
(g) The student was asked to write a report about her study. Outline the sections that it is conventional to have in a psychological report, and give a brief description of what should be included in each section (see page 295).

...4 A psychologist designs a set of questions to collect data about smokers' and non-smokers' attitudes to smoking.

(a) Write **one** open and **one** closed question he might use. [2]
(b) For each question the psychologist would like to summarise the answers that are given. Suggest **two** ways that data could be summarised from the questions you have written.
(c) Suggest **one** advantage and **one** disadvantage of presenting the questions in writing rather than conducting face-to-face interviews.
(d) Why would standardised instructions be necessary?
(e) What inferential test might be used in this study? Justify your choice.
(f) How might demand characteristics be a problem in this study?

...5 A local hospital decides to have mixed wards rather than separate wards for men and women. Before introducing this new scheme to all wards, the hospital management decides to compare the effects of mixed versus separate wards on patient wellbeing. The hospital employs a psychologist to conduct a study on patients in mixed versus single-sex wards in terms of happiness and health. Health outcomes could be determined by looking at whether patients recover more quickly in one type of ward than another, and also at whether they have better signs of health (e.g. lower blood pressure).

(a) Identify the independent variable in this study.
(b) Identify **two** possible dependent variables and suggest how you could operationalise them.
(c) Write an appropriate non-directional alternative hypothesis for this study.
(d) (i) Identify the experimental design used in this study.
(ii) Describe **one** disadvantage of this design in the context of this study.
(iii) Explain **one** way of dealing with this disadvantage.
(e) The psychologist uses a Mann-Whitney U test to check whether there is a significant difference between the recovery rates of 12 patients on mixed and 12 patients on single-sex wards.
(i) Explain why this test was chosen.
(ii) The test produced an observed (calculated) value of $U=29$. Using the table below, explain whether the results support the non-directional hypothesis that you proposed in part (c), i.e. state the conclusion.

▼ Critical values of U at 5% level ($p \leq 0.05$) for a two-tailed test

		N_1					
		10	11	12	13	14	15
N_2	10	23	26	29	33	36	39
	11	26	30	33	37	40	44
	12	29	33	37	41	45	49
	13	33	37	41	45	50	54
	14	36	40	45	50	55	59
	15	39	44	49	54	59	64

For any N_1 and N_2, the observed value of U must be EQUAL TO or LESS THAN the critical value in this table for significance to be shown.

(f) Blood pressure readings are recorded for patients on mixed and single-sex wards. Suggest **three** appropriate descriptive statistics that could be used to represent the data. Justify your choice.
(g) An alternative way to find out about people's preferences for hospital accommodation would be to conduct a survey. Write a plan for conducting this study. You should include sufficient details to permit replication, for example details of design and procedure, sampling and ethical issues.

Statistical joke: 'I read that there is about one chance in one million that someone will board an airplane carrying a bomb, so I started carrying a bomb with me on every flight I take. The way I figure it, the odds against two people having a bomb on the same plane are one in a trillion.'

ANALYSIS AND INTERPRETATION OF QUALITATIVE DATA

Descriptive and inferential statistics are methods of **quantitative data** analysis, i.e. methods of analysing numerical data. You are also familiar with **qualitative data** from your AS studies. Both quantitative and qualitative data may concern thoughts and feelings or any aspect of behaviour, the difference lies in the form the data takes. Qualitative data is data in a non-numerical form.

Quantitative and qualitative data may be produced in interviews, observational studies and case studies. Quantitative analysis involves counting responses or occurrences whereas qualitative analysis is concerned with interpreting the meaning of data, i.e. quality rather than quantity.

> **Quantitative data** is data that represents how much or how long, or how many, etc. there are of something, i.e. behaviour that is measured in numbers or quantities.
>
> **Qualitative data** is essentially anything that is not in numerical form, for example what people say or write. Qualitative data can't be counted but it can be summarised.

KEY POINTS

- Qualitative researchers believe that traditional quantitative methods do not produce results that are applicable to everyday life.

- Qualitative methods emphasise subjectiveness because they aim to represent the world as seen by the individual.

- In order to produce subjective information the qualitative researcher asks broad questions which allow a respondent to answer in their own words, or observes everyday behaviour directly or indirectly (e.g. through things that people have written or drawn).

- The data sets produced in qualitative research tend to be very large, although the samples might be quite small compared with those used in quantitative approaches.

- If a researcher is trying to produce numbers then he or she is probably not engaged in qualitative data analysis.

VALIDITY AND REFLEXIVITY

Scientific research aims to be objective. However, qualitative research, by its very nature, is subjective – it aims to view the phenomena from the perspective of those who experience it and also the process of analysis depends on the researcher's perceptions. The term **reflexivity** is used to describe the extent to which the process of research reflects a researcher's values and thoughts.

In order to enhance the scientific nature of qualitative research this inevitable subjective bias must be recognised. Instead of trying to minimise or remove subjectivity, this is dealt with by acknowledging that the subjective nature is part of the research itself.

The **validity** of qualitative research findings may be demonstrated using **triangulation**, comparing the results from a variety of different studies of the same thing or person. The studies are likely to have used different methodologies. If the results agree this supports their validity. If the results differ then this can lead to further research to enhance our understanding.

QUALITATIVE ANALYSIS

Summarising qualitative data – One problem with qualitative data is that it is difficult to summarise. *Quantitative* data can be readily summarised with measures of central tendency and measures of dispersion, and also with the use of graphs. None of these options are possible with purely descriptive findings. Instead, qualitative data is summarised by identifying repeated themes.

Inductive – Most qualitative analysis aims to be inductive or 'bottom-up' – the categories ('themes') that emerge are based in the data. The categories/themes may lead to new theories (called 'emergent theory').

A less common approach to the analysis of qualitative data is a deductive or 'top down' one, where the researcher starts with preset categories/themes. Such categories are likely to be generated by previous theories/research studies. The researcher would aim to see if the data are consistent with the previous theoretical viewpoint.

An iterative process – Qualitative analysis is a very lengthy process because it is painstaking and iterative – the data are gone through repeatedly. The main intention is to impose some kind of order on the data and ensure that the 'order' represents the participants' perspective.

Using a bottom-up approach ensures that this 'order' emerges from the data themselves rather than from any preconceptions.

There is no one method to use but the following table gives a general picture of what is done.

	General principles	**Applied to the analysis of videotaped play sessions with children**
1	Read and reread (or look at) the data transcript dispassionately, trying to understand the meaning communicated and the perspective of the participants. No notes should be made.	The play session can be transcribed, including details of what was said, describing facial expressions, etc.
2	Break the data into meaningful units – small bits of text that are independently able to convey meaning. This might be equivalent to sentences or phrases.	Each verbal and non-verbal movement would constitute a unit.
3	Assign a label or code to each unit. Such labels/codes are the initial categories that you are using. You will have developed some ideas when initially reading through the data in step 1. When a top-down approach is used the categories will be provided by existing theories. Each unit may be given more than one code/label.	Each unit is coded, for example 'playing with toy', 'sadness expressed', 'request made'.
4	Combine simple codes into larger categories/themes.	Larger categories developed, such as 'negative emotion'.
5	A check can be made on the emergent categories by collecting a new set of data and applying the categories. They should fit the new data well if they represent the topic area investigated.	
6	The final report should discuss and use quotes or other material to illustrate the emergent themes.	
7	Conclusions can be drawn, which may include new theories.	

EXAMPLES OF QUALITATIVE ANALYSIS AND INTERPRETATION

A qualitative analysis

A Finnish study considered the role of the family in adolescents' experiences with friends. Joronen and Åstedt-Kurki (2005) conducted semi-structured interviews with 19 adolescents aged 12–16, using questions, such as: 'What does your family know about your peers?' and 'How is your family involved in your school activities?' These interviews produced 234 pages of notes which were analysed using a qualitative content analysis.

1 All answers to the same questions were placed together.

2 Each statement was compressed into a briefer statement and given an identifier code.

3 These statements were compared with each other and categorised so that statements with similar content were placed together and a category identified (a thematic analysis).

4 The categories were grouped into larger units producing eight main categories, for example
   • *Enablement* e.g. 'Yeah, ever since my childhood we've always had lots of kids over visiting.' (Girl, 15 years)
   • *Support* e.g. 'They [family members] help if I have a test by asking questions.' (Boy, 13 years)
   • *Negligence* e.g. 'My sister is not at all interested in my friends.' (Girl, 16 years)

One of the conclusions drawn from this study is that schools should pay more attention to the multiple relationships that determine an adolescent's behaviour.

Collaborative research

Collier *et al.* (2005) conducted a study of how people form relationships by arranging for 10 female undergraduates, previously unacquainted, to be randomly assigned to partners and record their thoughts and feelings when forming a relationship. An essential element of this study was that the participants collaborated fully in the research; their ability to understand and reflect on their own experience means that they were the 'experts' with the researcher acting more as a 'facilitator'. Such **collaborative research** is typical of the aims of qualitative approaches.

The meetings between partners were recorded on audiotape. Each woman was interviewed over the course of the study about her thoughts, and each woman kept a weekly diary. Three of the relationships were selected for analysis because they represented rather different experiences of intimacy. The analysis looked at various aspects of relationships, for example:

• *Similarities and differences* i.e. the extent to which partners were similar to or different from each other and how these perceptions changed over time and affected relationship formation.

• *Self-disclosure* (telling someone personal information). Past research suggests that disclosure from one partner should lead to disclosure from another, but this study found that this only occurred if the disclosure communicated trust.

COMPARING QUANTITATIVE AND QUALITATIVE DATA

	Advantages	Weaknesses
Quantitative data	• Easier to analyse because data in numbers. • Produces neat conclusions.	• Oversimplifies reality and human experience (statistically significant but humanly insignificant).
Qualitative data	• Represents the true complexities of human behaviour. • Gains access to thoughts and feelings which may not be assessed using quantitative methods with closed questions. • Provides rich detail.	• More difficult to detect patterns and draw conclusions. • Subjective analysis can be affected by personal expectations and beliefs (although quantitative methods may only appear to be objective but are equally affected by bias).

DO-IT-YOURSELF IDEAS FOR STUDIES USING QUALITATIVE DATA ANALYSIS

• **Analysis of a questionnaire**. Design a questionnaire on any topic of your own choosing with a number of open-ended questions. Analyse the questions using a top-down or bottom-up approach. Summarise the findings using quotes from respondents and present some conclusions.

• **Advertisements** on TV or in magazines/newspapers. You might consider how men and women are represented in advertisements. Manstead and McCulloch (1981) looked at ads on British TV (170 ads over a one-week period, ignoring those that contained only children and animals). In each ad they looked at what the central adult figure was doing, and recorded frequencies in categories, such as whether men or women were cast in a dependent role, presented the central argument, were shown at home or at work, etc. You could produce your own categories, based on observations, and present a qualitative analysis of the ads you look at (as opposed to a frequency analysis that would be quantitative).

• **Mental disorders** – There are various websites that publish self-descriptions of people with mental disorders, such as eating disorders or depression. You could investigate by either taking a thematic approach (look for symptoms that are typical of the disorder) or a grounded theory approach (develop your own clinical characteristics by reading individual reports).

CAN YOU...? (No.16.13)

...1 Describe **one** advantage and one disadvantage of qualitative analysis over quantitative analysis.

...2 Select **one or more** studies you are familiar with and give examples of both quantitative and qualitative data collected in this study.

...3 Explain how the opinions of the participants might be represented in a qualitative analysis.

...4 Explain the concept of triangulation and how it is useful.

...5 Explain why qualitative researchers are less concerned about conducting 'valid' research.

...6 On the left is a qualitative content analysis. In what way is it a content analysis? In what way is it qualitative?

...7 The second study (by Collier *et al.*) is an example of collaborative research. Outline **one** conclusion that could be drawn from this research.

...8 A researcher conducts a case study of a child who has spent several long periods of time in hospital for a bone disorder. Suggest how this study might be conducted including some themes which might be examined and how the data might be summarised at the end of the study.

CHAPTER SUMMARY

This section builds on the knowledge and skills developed at AS level. There are a number of concepts that were included in the AS research methods chapter, that are not covered in this chapter. The concepts are listed below and you can find their definitions in the glossary/index at the back of this book:

- attrition
- cohort effects
- confederate
- control condition/group
- covert observations
- cross-sectional study
- difference studies
- double blind
- effect size
- experimental condition/group
- experimental design
- experimental realism
- Hawthorne effect
- imposed etic
- intervening variable
- interviewer bias
- participant effects
- participant variables
- presumptive consent
- protection from harm
- quasi-experiments
- random allocation
- role play
- single blind
- situational variables
- structured (systematic) observations
- unstructured interview
- unstructured observations

SCIENTIFIC METHOD

SCIENCE

THE SCIENTIFIC METHOD
- Empirical methods rather than unsupported claims.
- Objectivity and control to ensure data reliable.
- Replicability, verifies results.
- Theory construction, to predict events in the world.
- Hypothesis testing to modify theories, cannot be proved but can be falsified.
- Inductive (reasoning from particular to general) or deductive (reasoning from general to particular).

EVALUATION
- Scientific research is desirable.
- Psychology shares the goals of science, but may be just 'dressing up'.
- Lack of objectivity and control, e.g. experimenter bias and demand characteristics.
- Are goals of science appropriate? Nomothetic versus idiographic.
- Scientific methods haven't worked, e.g. treatments for mental illness.
- Qualitative approach more subjective but aims to be scientific.
- Scientific approach is reductionist – reduces complex phenomena to simple ones.
- And determinist – searches for causal relationships.

VALIDATING NEW KNOWLEDGE

PEER REVIEW
- Used in: research funding, scientific journals and university departments.
- Research published on the Internet requires new solutions.
- Protects against fraud (e.g. Burt, Hauser).

EVALUATION
- There isn't always an expert available.
- Anonymity allows honesty and objectivity or may permit dishonesty.
- Publication bias favours positive results.
- May lead to preservation of status quo.
- Can't remove flawed research from public record.

DATA ANALYSIS

INTRODUCING INFERENTIAL TESTS

SIGNIFICANCE AND PROBABILITY
- Inferential tests provide a means of assessing whether any pattern in data collected is meaningful or significant.
- They enable us to make inferences from the research sample to the population.
- Probability = likelihood that a pattern of results could arise by chance.
- Probability levels represent acceptable level of risk (e.g. $p \leq 0.05$) of making a Type 1 error.
- More important research requires more stringent significance levels.
- Type 1 error = null hypothesis rejected when true.
- Type 2 error = null hypothesis accepted when false.

INFERENTIAL TESTS
- Significance of observed value determined in table of critical values.
- Look up using (1) df, (2) one- or two-tailed test, (3) significance level, (4) greater or less than critical value.
- Directional hypothesis = one-tailed test.
- Non-directional hypothesis = two-tailed test.
- Different research designs and levels of measurement (nominal, ordinal, interval) require different tests.

INFERENTIAL TESTS

SPEARMAN'S *RHO*
Used when:
- Hypothesis states correlation between two variables.
- Each person is measured on both variables.
- Data is at least ordinal (i.e. not nominal).

CHI-SQUARE
Used when:
- Hypothesis states differences between two conditions or association between two variables.
- Data is independent.
- Data in frequencies (nominal).
- Expected frequencies in each cell must not fall below 5.

MANN-WHITNEY *U*
Used when:
- Hypothesis states difference between two sets of data.
- Independent groups design.
- Data at least ordinal (i.e. not nominal).

WILCOXON *T*
Used when:
- Hypothesis states difference between two sets of data.
- Related design (repeated measures or matched pairs).
- Data at least ordinal (i.e. not nominal).

DESCRIPTIVE STATISTICS

CENTRAL TENDENCY
- Indicates typical or 'average' score.
- Mean = sum of all scores divided by number of scores. Unrepresentative if extreme scores.
- Median = middle value in ordered list of scores. Not affected by extreme scores but not as sensitive as mean.
- Mode = most common value. Not useful if there are many modes in a set of scores.

MEASURES OF DISPERSION
- Indicate spread of scores.
- Range = difference between highest and lowest score. Not representative if extreme scores.
- Standard deviation = spread of data around mean. Precise measure but influence of extreme scores not taken into account.

GRAPHS
- Bar chart = illustration of frequency, height of bar represents frequency.
- Scattergram = illustration of correlation, suitable for correlational data. Indicates strength of correlation and direction (positive or negative).

DESIGNING PSYCHOLOGICAL INVESTIGATIONS

RESEARCH METHODS

EXPERIMENTS
- IV varied to see effect on DV.
- Laboratory experiment – high on internal validity, low on external validity.
- Field experiment – more natural environment but more issues of control than laboratory experiment.
- Natural experiment – uses naturally occurring IVs but cannot conclude causality.
- Experimental designs – repeated measures, independent groups, matched pairs.

SELF-REPORT METHODS
- Questionnaires and interviews.
- Structured interviews – more easily repeated.
- Unstructured interviews – questions that evolve are dependent on answers given.
- May involve open (respondent provides own answer) or closed (respondent chooses specific answer) questions.
- Main problem: social desirability bias.

OBSERVATIONAL STUDIES
- Observing behaviour through behavioural categories.
- Sampling methods – time and event sampling.
- Open to subjective bias – observations affected by expectations.

CORRELATIONAL ANALYSIS
- Concerned with relationship between two variables.
- Does not demonstrate causality.
- Other variables may influence any measured relationship.

CASE STUDIES
- Detailed study of individual, institution or event.
- Generally longitudinal, following individual or group over time.
- Allows study of complex interaction of many variables.
- Difficult to generalise from specific cases.

DESIGN ISSUES

RELIABILITY
- Experimental research – allows for replication of study.
- Observations – inter-observer reliability can be improved through training.
- Self-report – internal reliability (split-half) and external reliability (test–retest).

VALIDITY
- Internal validity – does study test what it was intended to test?
- External validity – can results be generalised to other situations and people?
- Laboratory experiments not necessarily low in external validity.
- If low in mundane realism, reduces generalisability of findings.
- In observations, internal validity affected by observer bias.
- Self-report techniques, issues of face and concurrent validity.

SAMPLING TECHNIQUES
- Opportunity – most easily available participants.
- Volunteer – e.g. through advert, but subject to bias.
- Random – all members of target population must have equal chance of selection.
- Stratified and quota – different subgroups within sample, leads to more representative sample.
- Snowball – researcher directed to other similar potential participants.

ETHICS

ETHICAL ISSUES WITH HUMANS
- Informed consent and deception.
- Harm – what constitutes too much?

CODE OF CONDUCT
- Respect for worth and dignity of participants.
- Right to privacy, confidentiality, informed consent and right to withdraw.
- Intentional deception only acceptable in some circumstances.
- Competence – retaining high standards.
- Protection from harm and debriefing.
- Integrity – being honest and accurate in reporting.
- Use of ethical guidelines in conjunction with ethical committees.
- Socially sensitive research – potential social consequences for participants.

ETHICAL ISSUES WITH NON-HUMANS
- Reasons for animals use – offers opportunity for greater control and objectivity; can't use humans; physiological similarities.
- Moral issues – sentience (experience pain and emotions).
- Specieism – form of discrimination against non-human species.
- Animal rights – Regan (1984), no animal research is acceptable.
- Do animals have rights if they have no responsibilities?
- Animal research subject to strict legislation (Animals Act; BPS guidelines).
- The 3Rs – Reduction, Replacement, Refinement.

QUALITATIVE DATA

KEY POINTS
- Quantitative methods not relevant to 'real life'.
- Qualitative methods represent world as seen by individual (subjective).
- Data sets tend to be large but few participants.
- Qualitative data cannot be reduced to numbers.
- Reflexivity indicates attitudes and biases of researcher.
- Validity demonstrated by triangulation.

QUALITATIVE ANALYSIS
- Summarised by identifying themes in data.
- Inductive (bottom-up) approach so themes emerge, although sometimes deductive (top-down).
- Iterative process – imposing order on the data, reflecting participants' perspective.
- (1) consider data, (2) break into meaningful units, (3) code each unit, (4) create categories/themes, (5) check themes using a new data set.

QUANTITATIVE VERSUS QUALITATIVE
- Quantitative easy to analyse and produces neat conclusions.
- But ... oversimplifies reality and human experience.
- Qualitative represents true complexities of behaviour through rich detail of thoughts, feelings, etc.
- But ... more difficult to detect patterns and subject to bias of subjectivity.

DESIGN AND REPORT YOUR OWN STUDY

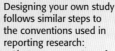

Designing your own study follows similar steps to the conventions used in reporting research:
- Abstract – summary of study.
- Introduction/aim – literature review, research aims/hypothesis(es).
- Method – includes decisions about research method, materials, design, validity, reliability, sampling methods and sample, ethics and procedures.
- Results – descriptive and inferential statistics.
- Discussion – outcomes in relation to other research, criticisms and implications of study.
- References.

QUESTIONS

There is a saying that 'hunger is the best cook'. A psychologist decided to test the relationship between hunger and the tastiness of food. He prepared a dish of scrambled eggs and toast for each participant. Before they started to eat he asked them how long it was since they had last eaten. After they had eaten the meal he asked them to rate the tastiness of the meal on a scale of 1 to 10 where 10 is very tasty.

He plotted his findings as shown in the graph on the right. The correlation coefficient is 0.15.

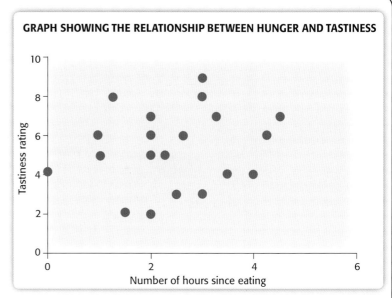

GRAPH SHOWING THE RELATIONSHIP BETWEEN HUNGER AND TASTINESS

(a) **How were hunger and tastiness operationalised?** *(2 marks)*

(b) **This study uses a correlational analysis. Describe one weakness of using this method of analysis in this study.** *(2 marks)*

(c) **(i) Describe one possible threat to the validity of this study.** *(2 marks)*

(ii) Explain how the psychologist could deal with this problem. *(2 marks)*

(d) **Tastiness is measured using a rating scale. How could you check the reliability of this scale?** *(2 marks)*

(e) **(i) The scores for hunger were 2, 2, 3, 3, 4, 4, 4, 5, 5, 5, 6, 6, 6, 6, 7, 7, 7, 8, 8, 9 (units of time without food). Suggest one suitable method of central tendency to use with this data.** *(1 mark)*

(ii) Explain how you would calculate this measure of central tendency. *(2 marks)*

(iii) Describe one advantage of this method of central tendency. *(2 marks)*

(f) **Name an appropriate statistical test for analysing this data.** *(1 mark)*

(g) **With reference to the graph above, describe the relationship between tastiness and hunger.** *(2 marks)*

(h) **(i) Write a suitable null hypothesis for this study.** *(2 marks)*

(ii) The psychologist tested a non-directional hypothesis and there were 18 participants. Identify the observed value in this study. Using the data in Table 1 below, also identify the critical value for this study, using a 5% level of significance. *(2 marks)*

▼ Table of critical values of *rho* at 5% level (*p*≤0.05)

Level of significance for a one-tailed test	0.05	0.01
Level of significance for a two-tailed test	0.10	0.02
N =		
13	.484	.560
14	.464	.538
15	.443	.521
16	.429	.503
17	.414	.485
18	.401	.472
19	.391	.460

Observed value of *rho* must be EQUAL TO or GREATER THAN the critical value in this table for significance to be shown.

(iii) State whether the null hypothesis should be rejected or accepted. *(1 mark)*

(i) **The psychologist wished to have his work published in an academic journal. Outline the sections that would be likely to be present in the report that he writes for the journal.** *(2 marks)*

(j) **The journal is peer-reviewed. Discuss the process of peer review.** *(6 marks)*

(k) **Subsequently, the psychologist decided to collect some qualitative data about the effects of hunger. Briefly outline how he might do this and how he might analyse the data he collects.** *(4 marks)*

STUDENT ANSWER	EXAMINER COMMENTS
	The answers provided on the left are all worth full marks. A few notes are provided below on the answers.
(a) *Hunger was measured in terms of time since participants last ate a meal and tastiness was measured using a rating scale.*	**(a)** Operationalisation essentially means 'how it can be measured'.
(b) *One weakness of using a correlational analysis in this study was that you can't demonstrate that it is the hunger that actually causes the changed perception of the pictures.*	**(b)** The answer has correctly been related to this particular study rather than being a general answer about studies using correlational analysis. This is always a problem for students, who will lose marks for answers that are not contextualised.
(c) (i) *One threat to validity is that some of the participants might not think scrambled eggs were very tasty no matter how hungry they were.* **(ii)** *You could deal with this by showing people about 10 pictures of different meals so there would be some they liked. This would give a better measurement of perception of food.*	**(c)** There is no single right answer to a question like this – whatever answer is chosen, it is important to give a clear explanation to the examiner so that the answer makes sense.
(d) *You could assess reliability using the test–retest method where people are asked to rate the tastiness of food and then this is repeated again about a week later with the same people who are as hungry as they were the first time. Their ratings should be the same if the measure is reliable.*	**(d)** While it is clearly necessary to say more than 'test–retest' to gain 2 marks, it is not necessary to provide as much detail as given here (although it can be useful in research methods questions to err on the side of giving too long an answer).
(e) (i) *A suitable method would be the mean.* **(ii)** *You would add all the numbers up and divide by the number of scores i.e. divide in this case by 20.* **(iii)** *The advantage of this method is that it takes all the values of the numbers into account.*	**(e)** Students will not have to perform actual calculations in an exam, nor will they be asked how to calculate an inferential statistic, but could be asked to describe how to do very easy calculations. **(iii)** Note that the key word is 'values'. All measures of central tendency use all the numbers, but only the mean uses all the values of all the numbers.
(f) *Spearman's rho.*	**(f)** No further detail is required when asked to name a suitable test.
(g) *There is possibly a small positive correlation but it doesn't look significant.*	**(g)** As this question is worth 2 marks it is necessary to say more than just 'positive correlation' or 'zero correlation' (the correlation coefficient shows it is a slight positive correlation).
(h) (i) *There is no relationship between hunger (time since eating) and tastiness (rating of the scrambled eggs).* **(ii)** *The observed value is .15 and the critical value is .401.* **(iii)** *The null hypothesis should be accepted.*	**(h)** In the case of Spearman's *rho* the null hypothesis is rejected only if the observed value is greater than the critical value (this information is given under the table of critical values).
(i) *The sections would be: abstract, introduction, method (procedures), results and a discussion. There would also be references.*	**(i)** No need for more detail.
(j) *A peer review is when an expert in the field being written about reviews the article to judge its quality. This is usually unpaid and often done anonymously to encourage objectivity and honesty although, at the same time, this may have the opposite effect – some reviewers might use it as an opportunity to prevent competing researchers from publishing work. Peer reviews may be an ideal, whereas in practice there are lots of problems, for example it slows publication down and may prevent unusual, new work being published. Some people doubt whether peer review can really prevent the publication of fraudulent research. The advent of the Internet means that a lot of research and academic comment is being published without official peer reviews than before, although systems are evolving on the Internet where everyone really has a chance to offer their opinions and police the quality of research.*	**(j)** The number of marks available for this question (6 marks) reveal that it requires a reasonably lengthy answer (1 mark is about 25 words). Throughout the research methods questions, it is important to match the length of an answer to the marks that are available. There is no point writing a lengthy answer if a question is worth just 2 marks, but, equally, it is *not* advisable to write a short paragraph when there are 6 marks available. In this question it is also important to notice the injunction 'discuss', which means describe and evaluate.
(k) *In order to collect more qualitative data the psychologist would ask people questions about what kind of things made them hungry, for example is it the way food looks or is it the smell. He would use their answers to ask further questions. He would tape-record these interviews so he could make transcripts of what people said and then he could go through these transcripts to identify key themes. It might help (improve reliability and validity) to get someone else to also analyse the data so they could compare their analyses.*	**(k)** The exam is likely to include a rather longer question about designing a study. The key is to present to the examiner as much detail as possible in the answer. There can be some benefit in scraping the barrel and including what may seem like trivial details in order to access the full marks available.

[505 words]

REFERENCES

aan het Rot, M., Mathew, S.J. and Charney, D.S. (2009). Neurobiological mechanisms in major depressive disorder. *Canadian Medical Association Journal, 180*, 305–13. ▶ page 181

Abed, R.T. (1998). The sexual competition hypothesis for eating disorders. *British Journal of Medical Psychology, 71*, 525–47. ▶ page 98

Abed, R.T. and de Pauw, K.W. (1998). An evolutionary hypothesis for obsessive compulsive disorder: a psychological immune system? *Cogprints. See* http://cognprints.org/1147/0/ocd-final.htm (accessed March 2009). ▶ page 208

Abraham, C., Sheeran, P. and Johnston, M. (1998). From health beliefs to self-regulation: theoretical advances in the psychology of action control. *Psychology and Health, 13*, 569–91. ▶ page 249

Abraham, S. and Beumont, P. (1982). How patients describe bulimia or binge eating. *Psychological Medicine, 12*, 625–35. ▶ page 97

Abrams, H.L. (1987). The preference for animal protein and fat: A cross-cultural survey. In M. Harris and E.B. Ross (eds) *Food and Evolution: Toward a Theory of Human Food Habits.* Philadelphia, PA: Temple University Press, 207–23. ▶ page 91

Abrams, D. and Hogg, M.A. (1990). An introduction to the social identity approach. In D. Abrams and M.A. Hogg (eds) *Social Identity Theory: Constructive and Critical Advances.* New York: Harvester Wheatsheaf, 1–9. ▶ page 244

Abramson, L.Y., Metalsky, F.I. and Alloy, L.B. (1989). Hopelessness depression: a theory-based subtype of depression. *Psychological Review, 96(2)*, 358–72. ▶ page 182

Abramson, L.Y., Seligman, M.E.P. and Teasdale, J. (1978). Learned helplessness in humans: critique and reformulation. *Journal of Abnormal Psychology, 87*, 49–74. ▶ page 182

Adams, D.B. (1983). Why there are so few women warriors. *Behavioral Science Research, 18*, 196–212. ▶ page 79

Adams, G.R., Munro, B., Doherty-Poirer, M., Munro, G., Petersen, A.M. and Edwards, J. (2001). Diffuse-avoidant, normative and informational identity styles: using identity theory to predict maladjustment. *Identity: An International Journal of Theory and Research, 1(4)*, 307–20. ▶ page 97

Agetsuma, N. (1999). Simulation of patch use by monkeys using operant conditioning. *Journal of Ethology, 16*, 49–55. ▶ page 133

Ainsworth, M.D.S., Blehar, M.C., Waters, E. and Wall, S. (1978). *Patterns of attachment: a psychological study of the strange situation.* Hillsdale, NJ: Lawrence Erlbaum. ▶ page 282

Ajzen, I. (1989). *Attitudes, Personality and Behaviour.* Milton Keynes, England: Open University Press. ▶ page 248

Ajzen, I. and Fishbein, M. (2005). The influence of attitudes on behavior. In D. Albarracín, B.T. Johnson and M.P. Zanna (eds) *The Handbook of Attitudes.* Hillsdale, NJ: Lawrence Erlbaum, 173–221. ▶ page 248

Akert, R. (1998). *Terminating romantic relationships: the role of personal responsibility and gender.* Unpublished manuscript, Wellesley College, MA. ▶ page 53

Albarracín, D., Johnson, B.T. and Zanna, M.P. (eds) (2005). *The Handbook of Attitudes.* Hillsdale, NJ: Lawrence Erlbaum. ▶ page 249

Albert, D.J., Walsh, M.L. and Jonik, R.H. (1993). Aggression in humans: what is its biological foundation? *Neuroscience and Biobehavioral Reviews, 17*, 405–25. ▶ page 73

Albucher, R.C., Abelson, J.L. and Nesse, R.M. (1998). Defense mechanism changes in successfully treated patients with obsessive compulsive disorder. *American Journal of Psychiatry, 155*, 558–9. ▶ page 215

Albus, H., Vansteensel, M.J., Michel, S., Block, G.D. and Meijer, J.H. (2005). A GABAergic mechanism is necessary for coupling dissociable ventral and dorsal regional oscillators within the circadian clock. *Current Biology, 15*, 886–93. ▶ page 14

Alden, D.L. and Crowley, A.E. (1995). Sex guilt and receptivity to condom advertising. *Journal of Applied Social Psychology, 25*, 1446–63. ▶ page 228

Allen, J. and Lester, D. (1994). Belief in paranormal phenomena and external locus of control. *Perceptual and Motor Skills, 79*, 226. ▶ page 264

Allender, D.M. and Marcell, F. (2003). Career criminals, security threat groups, and prison gangs: an interrelated threat. *FBI Law Enforcement Bulletin, 72*, 8–12. ▶ page 70

Allerdissen, R., Florin, I. and Rost, W. (1981). Psychological characteristics of women with bulimia nervosa (bulimerexia). *Behavior Analysis and Modification, 4*, 314–7. ▶ page 96

Allison, T. and Cicchetti, D. (1976). Sleep in mammals: ecological and constitutional correlates. *Science, 194*, 732–4. ▶ page 23

Alloy, L.B. and Abrahmson, L.Y. (1979). Judgement of contingency in depressed and non-depressed students: sadder but wiser? *Journal of Experimental Psychology, 108*, 441–85. ▶ pages 201, 215

Allport, G.W. and Pettigrew, T.F. (1957). Cultural influence on the perception of movement: the trapezoidal illusion among Zulus. *The Journal of Abnormal and Social Psychology, 55(1)*, 104–13. ▶ page 38

Alpert, E.J., Tonkin, A.E., Seeherman, A.M. and Holtz, H.A. (1998). Family violence curricula in U.S. medical schools. *American Journal of Preventative Medicine, 14*, 273. ▶ page 58

Alvarado, C.S. (1982). ESP during out-of-body experiences: a review of experimental studies. *Journal of Parapsychology, 46*, 209–30. ▶ page 268

American Psychiatric Association (2000). *Diagnostic and Statistical Manual of Mental Disorders* (4th edn, text revision) (DSM-IV-TR). Washington, DC: American Psychiatric Association. ▶ pages 164, 178, 192, 206

American Psychiatric Association (2000). *Practice Guideline for the Treatment of Patients with Eating Disorders* (2nd edn). Washington, DC: American Psychiatric Association. ▶ page 99

American Psychiatric Association (2001). *The Practice of Electroconvulsive Therapy: Recommendations for Treatment, Training and Privileging* (2nd edn), Washington, DC: American Psychiatric Association. ▶ page 171

Amr, M.M., Halim, Z.S. and Moussa, S.S. (1997). Psychiatric disorders among Egyptian pesticide applicators and formulators. *Environmental Research, 73*, 193–9. ▶ page 180

Amsterdam, B. (1972). Mirror image reactions before age two. *Developmental Psychobiology, 5*, 297–305. ▶ page 154

Anderson, C.A. and Dill, K. (2000). Video games and aggressive thoughts, feelings, and behavior in the laboratory and in life. *Journal of Personality and Social Psychology, 8(4)*, 772–90. ▶ page 224

Anderson, C.A., Gentile, D.A. and Buckley, K.E. (2007). *Violent Video Game Effects on Children and Adolescents: Theory, Research, and Public Policy.* New York: Oxford University Press. ▶ page 224

Andreasen, N.C., Flaum, M., Swayze, V., O'Leary, D.S., Alliger, R., Cohen, G., Ehrhardt, J. and Yuh, W.T. (1993). Intelligence and brain structure in normal individuals. *American Journal of Psychiatry, 150*, 130–4. ▶ page 136

Andrews, G., Slade, T. and Peters, L. (1999). Classification in psychiatry: ICD-10

versus DSM-IV. *The British Journal of Psychiatry, 174*, 3–5. ▶ page 179

Aneshensel, C.S. (1985). The natural history of depressive symptoms. *Research in Community and Mental Health, 5*, 45–74. ▶ page 183

Angst, J., Angst, F. and Stassen, H.H. (1999). Suicide risk in patients with major depressive disorder. *Journal of Clinical Psychiatry, 60(suppl. 2)*, 57–62. ▶ page 178

Ankney, C.D. (1992). Sex differences in relative brain size: the mismeasure of woman, too? *Intelligence, 16*, 329–36. ▶ page 137

Anthony, M.M. and Barlow, D.H. (eds) (2004). *Handbook of Assessment and Treatment Planning for Psychological Disorders.* London: Guildford Press. ▶ page 207

Anton, S.J., Colwell, C.S., Harmar, A.J., Waschek, J.A. and Herzog, E. (2005). Vasoactive intestinal polypeptide mediates circadian rhythmicity and synchrony in distinct subsets of mammalian clock neurons. *Nature Neuroscience, 8*, 476–83. ▶ page 15

Aouizerate, B., Martin-Guehl, C. and Tignol, J. (2004). Neurobiology and pharmacotherapy of social phobia. *Encephale, 30(4)*, 301–13. ▶ page 199

Appell, G.N. (1984). Freeman's refutation of Mead's coming of age in Samoa: the implications for anthropological inquiry. *The Eastern Anthropologist, 37*, 183–214. ▶ page 118

Archer, J. (1991). The influence of testosterone on human aggression. *British Journal of Psychology, 82*, 1–28. ▶ page 72

Archer, J., Graham-Kevan, N. and Davies, M. (2005). Testosterone and aggression: a re-analysis of Book, Starzyk and Quinsey's (2001) study. *Aggression and Violent Behaviour, 10*, 241–61. ▶ pages 72, 73

Armitage, C.J. and Conner, M. (2001). Efficacy of the theory of planned behaviour: a meta-analytic review. *British Journal of Social Psychology, 40(4)*, 471–99. ▶ page 249

Armitage, C.J., Conner, M. and Mark, N.P. (1999). Differential effects of mood on information processing: Evidence from the theories of reasoned action and planned behaviour. *European Journal of Social Psychology, 29(4)*, 419–33. ▶ page 249

Aron, A., Fisher, H., Mashe, D.J., Strong, G., Li, H. and Brown, L.L. (2005). Reward, motivation, and emotion systems associated with early-stage intense romantic love. *Journal of Neurophysiology, 94*, 327–37. ▶ page 49

Aschoff, J. and Wever, R. (1976). Human circadian rhythms: a multioscillatory system. *Federation Proceedings, 35*, 2326–32. ▶ page 10

Ashe, D.D. and McCutcheon, L.E. (2001). Shyness, loneliness, and attitude toward celebrities. *Current Research in Social Psychology, 6(9)*, 124–33. ▶ page 230

Ashton, H. (1997). Benzodiazepine dependency. In A. Baum, S. Newman, J. Weinman, R. West and C. McManus (eds) *Cambridge Handbook of Psychology, Health and Medicine.* Cambridge: Cambridge University Press. ▶ page 199

Assal, G., Favre, C. and Anderes, J.P. (1984). Non-recognition of familiar animals by a farmer – zooagnosia or prosopagnosia for animals. *Revue Neurologique, 140*, 580–4. ▶ page 43

Augustine, K. (2008). Hallucinatory near-death experiences. *See* http://www.infidels.org/library/modern/keith_augustine/HNDEs.html (accessed January 2009). ▶ page 269

Austin, E.W. (1993). Exploring the effects of active parental mediation of television content. *Journal of Broadcasting and Electronic Media, 37*, 147–58. ▶ page 220

Auton, H., Pope, J. and Seeger, G. (2003). It isn't that strange: paranormal belief and personality traits. *Social Behavior and Personality, 31*, 711–20. ▶ page 265

Ayeroff, F. and Abelson, R.P. (1976). ESP and ESB: belief in personal success at mental telepathy. *Journal of Personality and Social Psychology, 34*, 240–7. ▶ page 260

Azrin, N.H. and Foxx, R.M. (1974). *Toilet Training in Less Than a Day*. New York: Simon and Schuster. ▶ page 131

Babyak, M.A., Blumenthal, J.A., Herman, S., Khatri, P., Doraiswamy, P.M., Moore, K.A., Craighead, W.E., Baldewicz, T.T. and Krishnan, K.R. (2000). Exercise treatment for major depression: maintenance of therapeutic benefit at 10 months. *Psychosomatic Medicine, 62*, 633–8. ▶ page 186

Baer, L., Brown-Beasley, M.W. and Some, J. (1993). Computer-assisted telephone administration of a structured interview for obsessive compulsive disorder. *American Journal of Psychiatry, 150*, 1737–8. ▶ page 207

Bahrick, L.E. and Watson, J.S. (1985). Detection of intermodal proprioceptive-visual contingency as a potential basis of self-perception in infancy. *Developmental Psychology, 21*, 963–73. ▶ page 154

Bailer, U.F., Frank, G., Henry, S., Price, J., Meltzer, C., Mathis, C., Wagner, A., Thornton, L., Hoge, J., Ziolko, S.K., Becker, C., McConaha, C. and Kaye, W.H. (2007). Exaggerated 5-HT1A but normal 5-HT2A receptor. Psychopharmacology activity in individuals ill with anorexia nervosa. *Biological Psychiatry, 61*, 1090–9. ▶ page 94

Baillargeon, R. and DeVos, J. (1991). Object permanence in infants: further evidence. *Child Development, 62*, 1227–46. ▶ page 147

Baker, R.R. and Bellis, M.A. (1990). Do females promote sperm competition? Data for humans. *Animal Behavior, 40*, 997–9. ▶ page 57

Ball, K. and Kenardy, J. (2002). Body weight, body image and eating behaviors: relationship with ethnicity and acculturation in a community sample of young Australian women. *Eating Behaviors, 3*, 205–16. ▶ page 84

Bambra, C., Petticrew, M., Whitehead, M., Akers, J. and Sowden, A. (2008). Shifting schedules: the health effects of reorganising shift work. *The American Journal of Preventive Medicine, 34(5)*, 427–34. ▶ page 17

Bandura, A. (1962). Social learning through imitation. In M.R. Jones (ed.) *Nebraska Symposium on Motivation*. Lincoln, NE: University of Nebraska Press. ▶ page 220

Bandura, A. (1965). Behavioral modification through modeling practices. In L. Krasner and I. Ullman (eds) *Research in Behavior Modification*. New York: Holt, Rinehart and Winston, 310–40. ▶ page 67

Bandura, A. (1977). *Social Learning Theory*. New York: General Learning Press. ▶ page 244

Bandura, A. (1986). The social learning perspective: mechanisms of aggression. In H. Toch (ed.) *Psychology of Crime and Criminal Justice*. Prospect Heights, IL: Waveland Press. ▶ page 66

Bandura, A. (1991). Social cognitive theory of self-regulation. *Organizational Behavior and Human Decision Processes, 50*, 248–87. ▶ pages 66, 116

Bandura, A. and Bussey, K. (2004). On broadening the cognitive, motivational, and sociostructural scope of theorizing about gender development and functioning: Comment on Martin, Ruble, and Szkrybalo (2002). *Psychological Bulletin, 130*, 690–701. ▶ page 114

Bandura, A. and Rosenthal, T.L. (1966). Vicarious classical conditioning as a functioning of arousal level. *Journal of Personality and Social Psychology, 3*, 54–62. ▶ page 197

Bandura, A. and Walters, R.H. (1963). *Social Learning and Personality Development*. New York: Holt, Rinehart and Winston. ▶ page 66

Bandura, A., Ross, D. and Ross, S.A. (1961). Transmission of aggression through imitation of aggressive models. *Journal of Abnormal Social Psychology, 63*, 575–82. ▶ page 66

Bandura, A., Ross, D. and Ross, S.A. (1963). Imitation of film-mediated aggressive models. *Journal of Abnormal and Social Psychology, 66*, 3–11. ▶ page 67

Barbui, C., Furukawa, T.A. and Cipriani, A. (2008). Effectiveness of paroxetine in the treatment of acute major depression in adults: a systematic re-examination of published and unpublished data from randomized trials. *Canadian Medical Association Journal, 178*, 296–305. ▶ page 185

Barkham, M., Rees, A., Stiles, W.B., Shapiro, M.A., Hardy, G.E. and Reynolds, S. (1996). Dose effect relations in time-limited psychotherapy for depression. *Journal of Consulting and Clinical Psychology, 64*, 927–35. ▶ page 187

Barkow, J.H. (1992). Beneath new culture is old psychology: gossip and social stratification. In J.H. Barkow, L. Cosmides and J. Tooby (1992). *The Adapted Mind: Evolutionary Psychology and the Generation of Culture*. New York: Oxford University Press, 627–37. ▶ page 230

Barnes, G. and Prosen, H. (1985). Parent death and depression. *Journal of Abnormal Psychology, 94*, 64–9. ▶ page 183

Baron-Cohen, S., (1995). *Mindblindness: An Essay on Autism and Theory of Mind*. Cambridge, MA: MIT Press. ▶ page 155

Baron-Cohen, S. (2002). The extreme male brain theory of autism. *Trends in Cognitive Sciences, 6(6)*, 248–54. ▶ page 106

Baron-Cohen, S. (2004). *The Essential Difference*. London: Penguin. ▶ page 107

Baron-Cohen, S., Leslie, A.M. and Frith, U. (1985). Does the autistic child have a 'theory of mind'? *Cognition, 21*, 37–46. ▶ page 155

Bartels, A. and Zeki, S. (2000). The neural basis of romantic love. *NeuroReport, 11*, 3829–34. ▶ page 61

Bartholomew, K. and Horowitz, L.M. (1991). Attachment styles among young adults: a test of a four-category model. *Journal of Personality and Social Psychology, 61*, 226–44. ▶ pages 232, 233

Bates, G.W., Thompson, J.C. and Flanagan, C. (1999). The effectiveness of individual versus group induction of depressed mood. *Journal of Psychology, 133(3)*, 245–52. ▶ page 183

Bateson, G., Jackson, D.D., Haley, J. and Weakland, J.H. (1956). Towards a theory of schizophrenia. *Behavioural Science, 1(4)*, 251–64. ▶ page 168

Baucom, D.H., Besch, P.K. and Callahan, S. (1985). Relation between testosterone concentration, sex role identity and personality among females. *Journal of Personality and Social Psychology, 48*, 1218–26. ▶ page 73

Bauer, G.B. (2004). Research training for releasable animals. *Conservation Biology, 19(6)*, 1779–89. ▶ page 133

Bauer, P.J. (1993). Memory for gender-consistent and gender-inconsistent event sequences by 25 month old children. *Child Development, 64(1)*, 285–97. ▶ page 114

Baxter, L.A. (1994). A dialogic approach to relationship maintenance. In D.J. Canary and L. Stafford (eds) *Communication and Relational Maintenance*. New York: Academic Press. ▶ page 52

Beals, K.L., Smith, C.L. and Dodd, S.M. (1984). Brain size, cranial morphology, climate, and time machines. *Current Anthropology, 25*, 301–30. ▶ page 137

Beck, A.J. and Harrison, P.M. (2007). *Sexual Victimization in State and Federal Prisons Reported by Inmates, 2007*. Washington, DC: Bureau of Justice Statistics. ▶ page 70

Beck, A.T. (1967). *Depression: Causes and Treatment*. Philadelphia: University of Pennsylvania Press. ▶ pages 182, 186

Beck, A.T., Emery, G. and Greenberg, R.L. (1985). *Anxiety Disorders and Phobias: A Cognitive Perspective*. New York: Basic Books. ▶ page 196

Beck, A.T., Steer, R.A. and Brown, G.K. (1996). *Manual for the Beck Depression Inventory* (2nd edn). San Antonio, TX: The Psychological Corporation. ▶ page 178

Becker, A.E., Burwell, R.A., Gilman, S.E., Herzog, D.B. and Hamburg, P. (2002). Eating behaviours and attitudes following prolonged exposure to television among ethnic Fijian adolescent girls. *British Journal of Psychiatry, 180*, 509–14. ▶ page 93

Beckham, J.C., Becker, M.E., Hamlett-Berry, K.W., Drury, P.D., Kang, H.K., Wiley, M.T., Calhoun, P.S., Moore, S.D., Bright, M.A. and McFall, M.E. (2008). Preliminary findings from a clinical demonstration project for veterans returning from Iraq or Afghanistan. *Military Medicine, 173(5)*, 448–51. ▶ page 251

Becona, E., Del Carmen, L.M. and Fuentes, M.J. (1996). Pathological gambling and depression. *Psychological Reports, 78*, 635–40. ▶ page 241

Beidel, D.C., Turner, S.M., Jacob, R.G. and Cooley, M.R. (1989). Assessment of social phobia: reliability of an impromptu speech task. *Journal of Anxiety Disorders, 3*, 149–58. ▶ page 193

Belin, D., Mar, A.C., Dalley, J.W., Robbins, T.W. and Everitt, B.J. (2008). High impulsivity predicts the switch to compulsive cocaine-taking. *Science, 320(5881)*, 1352–5. ▶ page 245

Bell, R. (1985). *Holy Anorexia*. Chicago: University of Chicago Press. ▶ page 94

Belli, S. (2009). A psychobiographical analysis of Brian Douglas Wilson: creativity, drugs, and models of schizophrenic and affective disorders. *Personality and Individual Differences, 46*, 809–19. ▶ page 247

Belmont, L. and Marolla, F.A. (1973). Birth order, family size and intelligence. *Science, 182*, 1096–101. ▶ page 140

Belsky, J., Steinberg, L. and Draper, P. (1991). Childhood experience, interpersonal development, and reproductive strategy: an evolutionary theory of socialization. *Child Development, 62*, 647–70. ▶ page 57

Belsky, J.K. (1990). *The Psychology of Aging Theory, Research, and Interventions*. Pacific Grove, CA: Cole Publishing Company. ▶ page 124

Belson, W.A. (1978). *TV Violence and the Adolescent Boy*. Westmead: Saxon House. ▶ page 223

Bem, D.J. (2011). Feeling the future: experimental evidence for anomalous retroactive influences on cognition and affect. *Journal of Personality and Social Psychology, 100*, 407–25. ▶ page 256

Bem, D.J., Palmer, J. and Broughton, R.S. (2001). Updating the Ganzfeld database: a victim of its own success? *Journal of Parapsychology, 65*, 207–18. ▶ page 259

Bem, S.L. (1989). Genital knowledge and gender constancy in preschool children. *Child Development, 60*, 649–662. ▶ page 112

Bem, D.J. and Honorton, C. (1994). Does psi exist? Replicable evidence for an anomalous process of information transfer. *Psychological Bulletin, 115*, 4–18. ▶ page 259

Benek-Higgins, M.B., McReynolds, C.J., Hogan, E. and Savickas, S. (2008). Depression and the elder person: the enigma of misconceptions, stigma and treatment. *Journal of Mental Health Counseling, 30(4)*, 283–96. ▶ page 185

Benhsain, K. and Ladouceur, R. (2004). Knowledge in statistics and erroneous perceptions in gambling. *Gambling Research, 16*, 25–31. ▶ page 241

Bennett, N. (1976). *Teacher Styles and Pupil Progress*. London: Open Books. ▶ page151

Bennett, P., Smith, C., Nugent, Z. and Panter, C. (1991). Pssst… the really useful guide to alcohol: evaluation of an alcohol education television series. *Health Education Research, 6(1)*, 57–64. ▶ page 246

Bennett-Levy, J. and Marteau, T. (1984). Fear of animals: what is prepared? *British Journal of Psychology, 75*, 37–42. ▶ page 194

Benson, H., Dusek, J.A., Sherwood, J.B., Lam, P., Bethea, C.F., Carpenter, W., Levitsky, S., Hill, P.C., Clem, D.W. Jr., Jain, M.K., Drumel, D., Kopecky, S.L., Mueller, P.S., Marek, D., Rollins, S. and Hibberd, P.L. (2006). Study of the therapeutic effects of intercessory prayer (STEP) in cardiac bypass patients: a multicenter randomised trial of uncertainty and certainty of receiving intercessory prayer. *American Heart Journal, 151(4)*, 934–42. ▶ page 267

Bentall, R.P., Claridge, G. and Slade, P.D. (1989). The multi-dimensional nature of schizotypal traits: a factor-analytic study with normal subjects. *British Journal of Clinical Psychology, 28*, 363–75. ▶ page 265

Bentall, R.P., Jackson, H.F. and Pilgrim, D. (1988). Abandoning the concept of 'schizophrenia': some implications of validity arguments for psychological research into psychotic phenomena. *British Journal of Clinical Psychology, 27*, 303–24. ▶ page 164

Berenbaum, S.A. and Bailey, J.M. (2003). Effects on gender identity of prenatal androgens and genital appearance: evidence from girls with congenital adrenal hyperplasia. *The Journal of Clinical Endocrinology and Metabolism, 88(3)* (copyright © 2003 The Endocrine Society), 1102–6. ▶ page 104

Berenson, K.R. and Andersen, S.M. (2006). Childhood physical and emotional abuse by a parent: transference effects in adult interpersonal relationships. *Personality and Social Psychology Bulletin, 33*, 1509–22. ▶ page 59

Berg, C.A. and Sternberg, R.J. (1985). A triarchic theory of intellectual development during adulthood. *Developmental Review, 5*, 334–70. ▶ page 127

Berger, A. (1965). A test of the double-bind hypothesis of schizophrenia. *Family Process, 4*, 198–205. ▶ page 169

Bernstein, I.L. and Webster, M.M. (1980). Learned taste aversions in humans. *Physiology and Behavior, 25*, 363–6. ▶ page 90

Berry, J.W. (1971). Müller-Lyer susceptibility: culture, ecology or race? *International Journal of Psychology, 6*, 193–7. ▶ page 39

Berry, J.W., Poortinga, Y.H., Segall, M.H. and Dasen, P.R. (2002). *Cross-cultural Psychology* (2nd edn). Cambridge: Cambridge University Press. ▶ pages 39, 118, 119

Berscheid, E. and Reis, H.T. (1998). Attraction and close relationships. In D.T. Gilbert, S.T. Fiske and G. Lindzey (eds) *The Handbook of Social Psychology* (4th edn, vol. 2). New York: McGraw-Hill, 193–281. ▶ page 48

Beseler, C. and Stallones, L. (2008). A cohort study of pesticide poisoning and depression in Colorado farm residents. *Annals of Epidemiology, 8(10)*, 768–74. ▶ page 180

Biederman, J., Rosenbaum, J.F., Bolduc-Murphy, E.A., Faraone, S.V., Chaloff, J., Hirshfeld, D.R. and Kagan, J. (1993). A 3-year follow-up of children with and without behavioral inhibition. *Journal of the American Academy of Child and Adolescent Psychiatry, 32(4)*, 814–21. ▶ page 195

Bierman, D.J. (2000). On the nature of anomalous phenomena: another reality between the world of subjective consciousness and the objective world of physics? In P. Van Loocke (ed.) *The Physical Nature of Consciousness*. New York: Benjamins Publishing. ▶ page 259

Bifulco, A., Harris, T. and Brown, G.W. (1992). Mourning or early inadequate care? Re-examining the relationship of maternal loss in childhood with adult depression and anxiety. *Development and Psychopathology, 4*, 433–49. ▶ page 183

Billett, E.A., Richter, M.A. and Kennedy, J.L. (1998). Genetics of obsessive compulsive disorder. In R.P. Swinson, M.M. Antony, S. Rachman and M.A. Richter (eds) *Obsessive Compulsive Disorder: Theory, Research and Treatment*. New York: Guilford. ▶ page 208

Binkofski, F., Amunts, K., Stephan, K.M., Posse, S., Schormann, T., Freund, H.-J., Zilles, K. and Seitz, R.J. (2000). Broca's region subserves imagery of motion: a combined cytoarchitectonic and fMRI study. *Human Brain Mapping, 11*, 273–85. ▶ page 158

Birch, L.L. and Fisher, J.O. (2000). Mothers' child-feeding practices influence daughters' eating and weight. *American Journal of Clinical Nutrition, 71*, 1054–61. ▶ page 85

Bjerkedal, T., Kristensen, P., Skjeret, G. and Brevik, J. (2007). Birth order and intelligence. *Intelligence, 35(5)*, 503–14. ▶ page 140

Black, D.W., Monahan, P.O. and Temkit, M. (2006). A family study of pathological gambling. *Psychiatry Research, 141*, 295–303. ▶ page 238

Blackmore, S.J. (1982). *Beyond the Body: An Investigation into Out-of-Body Experiences*. London: Heinemann. ▶ page 259

Blackmore, S.J. (1987). Out-of-the-body experience. In R.L. Gregory (ed.) *The Oxford Companion to the Mind*. Oxford: Oxford University Press. ▶ page 259

Blackmore, S.J. (1997). Probability misjudgment and belief in the paranormal: a newspaper survey. *British Journal of Psychology, 88*, 683–9. ▶ page 261

Blackmore, S. and Troscianko, T. (1985). Belief in the paranormal: probability judgments, illusory control, and the 'chance baseline shift'. *British Journal of Psychology, 81*, 455–68. ▶ page 260

Blake, J. (1989). *Family Size and Achievement*. Berkeley, CA: University of California Press. ▶ page 141

Blake, R. (1993). Cats perceive biological motion. *Psychological Science, 4*, 54–7. ▶ page 35

Blakemore, C. and Cooper, G.F. (1970). Development of the brain depends on the visual environment. *Nature, 228*, 477–8. ▶ page 37

Blanchard, R. (1985). Typology of male-to-female transsexualism. *Archives of Sexual Behavior, 14*, 247–61. ▶ page 111

Blanco, C., Ibanez, A., Saiz-Ruiz, J., Blanco-Jerez, C. and Nunes, E.V. (2000). Epidemiology, pathophysiology and treatment of pathological gambling. *CNS Drugs, 13(6)*, 397–407. ▶ page 240

Blanco, C., Petkova, E., Ibanez, A. and Saiz-Ruiz, J. (2002). A pilot placebo-controlled study of fluvoxamine for pathological gambling. *Annals of Clinical Psychiatry, 14*, 9–15. ▶ page 251

Blanke, O., Mohr, C., Michel, C.M., Pascual-Leone, A., Brugger, P., Seeck, M., Landis, T. and Thut, G. (2005). Linking out-of-body experience and self processing to mental own-body imagery at the temporoparietal junction. *Journal of Neuroscience, 25(3)*, 550–7. ▶ page 268

Blanke, O., Ortigue, S., Landis, T. and Seeck, M. (2002). Stimulating illusory own-body perceptions: the part of the brain that can induce out-of-body experiences has been located. *Nature, 419(6904)*, 269–70. ▶ page 268

Blaszczynski, A. and Nower, L. (2002). A pathways model of problem and pathological gambling. *Addiction, 97*, 487–99. ▶ page 243

Blaszczynski, A., McConaghy, N. and Frankova, A. (1990). Boredom proneness in pathological gambling. *Psychological Reports, 67(1)*, 35–42. ▶ page 238

Bloomsmith, M.A., Laule, G.E., Alford, P.L. and Thurston, R.H. (1994). Using training to moderate chimpanzee aggression during feeding. *Zoo Biology, 13*, 557–66. ▶ page 133

Boardman, J.D., Blalock, C.L. and Button, T.M.M. (2008). Sex differences in the heritability of resilience. *Twin Research and Human Genetics, 11(1)*, 12–27. ▶ page 238

Boekhout, B., Hendrick, S. and Hendrick, C. (1999). Relationship infidelity: a loss perspective. *Journal of Personal and Interpersonal Loss, 4*, 97–123. ▶ page 53

Boivin, D.B. and James, F.O. (2002). Phase-dependent effect of room light exposure in a 5-hour advance of the sleep-wake cycle: implications for jet lag. *Journal of Biological Rhythms, 17*, 266–76. ▶ page 17

Boivin, D.B., Duffy, J.F., Kronauer, R.E. and Czeisler, C.A. (1996). Dose-response relationships for resetting of human circadian clock by light. *Nature, 379(6565)*, 540–2. ▶ pages 15, 16, 17

Bond, A.J. (2005). Antidepressants and human aggression. *European Journal of Pharmacology, 526*, 218–25. ▶ page 73

Bond, F.W. and Dryden, W. (2000). How rational beliefs and irrational beliefs affect people's inferences: an experimental investigation. *Behavioural and Cognitive Psychotherapy, 28*, 33–43. ▶ pages 201, 215

Bonnaire, C., Bungener, C. and Varescon, I. (2006). Pathological gambling and sensation seeking. How do gamblers playing games of chance in cafés differ from those who bet on horses at the racetrack? *Addiction Research and Theory, 14*, 619–29. ▶ page 239

Bonnet, M.H. and Arand, D.L. (1995). Twenty-four-hour metabolic rate in insomniacs and matched normal sleepers. *Sleep, 18*, 581–8. ▶ page 25

Book, A.S., Starzyk, K.B. and Quinsey, V.L. (2001). The relationship between testosterone and aggression: a meta-analysis. *Aggression and Violent Behaviour, 6*, 579–99. ▶ page 72

Boos, C.J. and Croft, A.M. (2004). Smoking rates in the staff of a military field hospital before and after wartime deployment. *Journal of the Royal Society of Medicine, 97*, 20–2. ▶ page 251

Borg, E. (2007). If mirror neurons are the answer, what was the question? *Journal of Consciousness Studies, 14*, 5–19. ▶ page 159

Borke, J., Eickhorst, A. and Keller, H. (2007). Father-infant interaction, paternal ideas about early childcare, and the consequences for the development of children's self-recognition. *The Journal of Genetic Psychology, 168(4)*, 365–79. ▶ page 155

Born, J., Hansen, K., Marshall, L., Mölle, M. and Fehm, H.L. (1999). Timing the end of nocturnal sleep. *Nature, 397*, 29–30. ▶ page 13

Bosch, H., Steinkamp, F. and Boller, E. (2006). Examining psychokinesis: the interaction of human intention with random number generators. A meta-analysis. *Psychological Bulletin, 132*, 497–523. ▶ page 259

Boskind-Lodahl, M. (1976). Cinderella's step-sisters: a feminist perspective on anorexia nervosa and bulimia. *Signs: Journal of Women in Culture and Society, 2*, 342–56. ▶ page 96

Botvin, G.J. (2000). *Preventing Drug Abuse and Violence Through Life Skills Training: Lessons Learn from a Large-scale Dissemination Initiative*. Invited paper presented at the Annual Meeting of the Society for Prevention Research, Montreal. ▶ page 243

Bouchard, T.J. Jr. and McGue, M. (1981). Familial studies of intelligence: a review. *Science, 212*, 1055–9. ▶ page 138

Bouchard, T.J. Jr., McGue, M., Lykken, D. and Tellegen, A. (1999). Intrinsic and extrinsic religiousness: genetic and environmental influences and personality correlates. *Twin Research, 2(2)*, 88–98. ▶ page 211

Boutsen, L. and Humphreys, G.W. (2002). Face context interferes with local part processing in a prosopagnosic patient. *Neuropsychologia, 40*, 2305–513. ▶ page 43

Bower, T.G.R. (1966). The visual world of infants. *Scientific American, 215*, 80–92. ▶ page 36

Bower, T.G.R., Broughton, J.M. and Moore, M.K. (1970). The co-ordination of visual and tactual input in infants. *Perception and Psychophysics, 8*, 51–3. ▶ page 36

Bowlby, J. (1969). *Attachment and love. Vol. 1: Attachment*. London: Hogarth. ▶ page 58

Bowlby, J. (1973). *Attachment and loss. Vol. 2: Separation, Anxiety and Anger*. London: Hogarth Press. ▶ page 197

Bown, W. (1992). Sex-test confusion could create havoc at Olympics. *New Scientist, 133(1804)*, 14, 14 January. ▶ page 105

Boyd, S.C. (2008). *Hooked: Drug War Films in Britain, Canada, and the U.S.* New York: Routledge. ▶ page 247

Boyle, K. (1999). *Screening Violence: A Feminist Critique of the Screen Violence Debate.* Paper presented at Women's Worlds 99, International Interdisciplinary Congress on Women, Tromsø. ▶ page 223

Bradbard, M.R., Martin, C.L., Endsley, R.C. and Halvesron, C.F. (1986). Influence of sex stereotypes on children's exploration and memory: a competence versus performance distinction. *Developmental Psychology, 22*, 481–6. ▶ page 115

Brandon, T.H. and Baker, T.B. (1991). The smoking consequences questionnaire: the subjective expected utility of smoking in college students. *Psychological Assessment: A Journal of Consulting and Clinical Psychology, 3*, 484–91. ▶ page 240

Brandon, T.H., Juliano, L.M. and Copeland, A.C. (1999). Expectancies for tobacco smoking. In I. Kirsch (ed.) *How Expectancies Shape Experience.* Washington, DC: American Psychological Association, 263–99. ▶ page 240

Brandon, T.H., Herzog, T.A., Irvin, J.E. and Gwaltney, C.J. (2004). Cognitive and social learning models of drug dependence: implications for the assessment of tobacco dependence in adolescents. *Addiction, 99*, 51–77. ▶ page 240

Breen, R.B. and Zimmerman, M. (2001). Rapid onset of pathological gambling in machine gamblers. *Journal of Gambling Studies, 18(1)*, 31–43. ▶ page 239

Bregman, E.O. (1934). An attempt to modify the emotional attitudes of infants by the conditioned response technique. *Journal of Genetic Psychology, 45*, 169–98. ▶ page 197

Brehm, S.S. and Kassin, S.M. (1996). *Social Psychology* (3rd edn). Boston: Houghton Mifflin. ▶ page 53

Breland, K. and Breland, M. (1951). A field of applied animal psychology. *American Psychologist, 6*, 202–4. ▶ page 131

Brennan, P.A. and Mednick, S.A. (1993). Genetic perspectives on crime. *Acta Psychiatrica Scandinavica, 370(suppl.)*, 19–26. ▶ page 74

Brennan, W.M., Ames, E.W. and Moore, R.W. (1966). Age differences in infants' attention to patterns of different complexity. *Science, 151*, 354–6. ▶ page 36

Breslau, N., Roth, T., Rosenthal, L. and Andreski, P. (1996). Sleep disturbance and psychiatric disorders: a longitudinal epidemiological study of young adults. *Biological Psychiatry, 39*, 411–18. ▶ page 25

Brockner, J., Pressman, B., Cabitt, J. and Moran, P. (1982). Nonverbal intimacy, sex, and compliance: a field study. *Journal of Nonverbal Behavior, 6*, 253–8. ▶ page 290

Broman, S.H., Nichols, P.L., Shaughnessy, P. and Kennedy, W. (1987). *Retardation in Young Children.* Hillsdale, NJ: Lawrence Erlbaum. ▶ page 136

Brooks, M. (2010). We need to fix peer review now. New Scientist blog. *See* http://www.newscientist.com/blogs/thesword/2010/06/we-need-to-fix-peer-review-now.html (accessed February 2012). ▶ page 277

Brosnan, M. (2008). Digit ratio as an indicator of numeracy relative to literacy in 7-year-old British school children. *British Journal of Psychology, 99*, 75–85. ▶ page 286

Broughton, R.J. (1968). Sleep disorders: disorders of arousal? Enuresis, somnambulism, and nightmares occur in confusional states of arousal, not in 'dreaming sleep'. *Science, 159*, 1070–8. ▶ page 27

Brown, B.B., Dolcini, M.M. and Leventhal, A. (1997). Transformations in peer relationships at adolescence: implications for health-related behavior. In J. Schulenberg, J.L. Maggs and K. Hurrelmann (eds) *Health Risks and Developmental Transitions During Adolescence.* New York: Cambridge University Press, 161–89. ▶ page 244

Brown, G.W and Birley, J.L.T. (1968). Crises and life: changes and the onset of schizophrenia. *Journal of Health and Social Behaviour, 9*, 203–14. ▶ page 168

Brown, G. W., Birley, J. L. and Wing, J. K. (1972). Influence of family life on the course of schizophrenic disorders: a replication. *British Journal of Psychiatry, 121 (562)*, ▶ page 241–258

Brown, G.W. and Harris, T.O. (1978). *Social Origins of Depression.* London: Tavistock. ▶ page 182

Brown, J. and Ogden, J. (2004). Children's eating attitudes and behaviour: a study of the modelling and control theories of parental influence. *Health Education Research: Theory and Practice, 19*, 261–71. ▶ page 84

Brown, T., Moras, K., Zinbarg, R. and Barlow, D.H. (1993). Differentiating generalized anxiety disorder and obsessive compulsive behavior. *Behavior Therapy, 24*, 227–40. ▶ page 207

Bruce, V. and Young, A.W. (1986). Understanding face recognition. *British Journal of Psychology, 77*, 305–27. ▶ page 40

Bruch, H. (1973). *Eating disorders: Obesity, Anorexia Nervosa and the Person Within.* New York: Basic Books. ▶ pages 92, 93

Brunner, H., Nelen, M., Breakefield, X., Ropers, H. and van Oost, B. (1993). Abnormal behavior associated with a point mutation in the structural gene for monoamine oxidase A. *Science, 262*, 578–80. ▶ page 74

Bruner, J.S. and Minturn, A.L. (1955). Perceptual identification and perceptual organisation. *Journal of General Psychology, 53*, 21–8. ▶ page 33

Bruner, J.S., Postman, L. and Rodrigues, J. (1951). Expectations and the perception of colour. *American Journal of Psychology, 64*, 216–27. ▶ page 32

Bruyer, R., Laterre, C., Seron, X., Feyereisen, P., Strypstein, E., Pierrard, E. and Rectem, D. (1983). A case of prosopagnosia with some preserved covert remembrance of familiar faces. *Brain and Cognition, 2*, 257–84. ▶ page 42

Bryant, M.J., Simons, A.D. and Thase, M.E. (1999). Therapist skill and patient variables in homework compliance: controlling an uncontrolled variable in cognitive therapy outcome research. *Cognitive Therapy and Reearch, 23(4)*, 381–99. ▶ page 187

Bryant, P. (1995). Jean Piaget. In R. Fuller (ed.) *Seven Pioneers of Psychology.* London: Routledge. ▶ page 147

Bryant, P.E. and Trabasso, T. (1971). Transitive inferences and memory in young children. *Nature, 232*, 456–8. ▶ page 151

Buckholtz, J., Treadway, M., Cowan, R., Woodward, N., Benning, S., Li, R., Ansari, M., Baldwin, R., Schwartzman, A., Shelby, E., Smith, C., Cole, D., Kessler, R. and Zald, D. (2010). Mesolimbic dopamine reward system hypersensitivity in individuals with psychopathic traits. *Nature Neuroscience, 13(4)*, 419–21. ▶ page 245

Buckley, P.F., Miller, B.J., Lehrer, D.S. and Castle, D.J. (2009). Psychiatric comorbidities and schizophrenia. *Schizophrenia Bulletin, 35(2)*, 383–402. ▶ page 164

Buist-Bouwman, M.A., Ormel, J., De Graaf, R. and Vollebergh, W.A.M. (2004). Functioning after a major depressive episode: complete or incomplete recovery? *Journal of Affective Disorders, 82*, 363–71. ▶ page 181

Buitelaar, J.K. (2003). Review: atypical antipsychotics and psychosocial interventions, alone or in combination, may reduce youth aggression. *Evidence-based Mental Health. 26(3)*, 79. ▶ page 72

Buka, S.L., Shenassa, E.D. and Niaura, R. (2003). Elevated risk of tobacco dependence among offspring of mothers who smoked during pregnancy: a 30-year prospective study. *American Journal of Psychiatry, 160*, 1978–84. ▶ page 238

Bulik, C.M., Reba, L., Siega-Riz, A.M. and Reichborn-Kjennerud, T. (2005). Anorexia nervosa: definition, epidemiology and cycle of risk. *International Journal of Eating Disorders, 37*, S2–S9. ▶ page 94

Bulik, C.M., Sullivan, P.F., Tozzi, F., Furberg, H., Lichtenstein, P. and Pedersen, N.L. (2006). Prevalence, heritability and prospective risk factors for Anorexia nervosa. *Archives of General Psychiatry, 63*, 305–12. ▶ page 95

Bunney, W.E. and Davis, J.M. (1965). Norepinephrine in depressive reactions. A review. *Archives of General Psychiatry, 13*, 483–94. ▶ page 180

Bunting, B.P. and Mooney, E. (2001). The effects of practice and coaching on test results for educational selection at eleven years of age. *Educational Psychology, 21(3)*, 243–53. ▶ page 125

Burch, R.L. and Gallup, G.G. Jr. (2004). Is pregnancy a stimulus for domestic violence? *Journal of Family Violence, 19(4)*, 243–7. ▶ page 77

Buri, J.R. (1991). Parental authority questionnaire. *Journal of Personality Assessment, 57(1)*, 110–19. ▶ page 289

Burish, M.J., Kueh, H.Y. and Wang, S.-H. (2004). Brain architecture and social complexity in birds and dinosaurs. *Brain, Behavior and Evolution, 63(2)*, 107–24. ▶ page 135

Burt, C.L. (1955). The evidence for the concept of intelligence. *British Journal of Psychology, 25*, 158–77. ▶ page 276

Burt, C.L. (1966). The genetic determination of differences in intelligence: a study of monozygotic twins reared together or apart. *British Journal of Psychology, 57*, 137–53. ▶ page 276

Burton, A.M. and Bruce, V. (1993). Naming faces and naming names: exploring an interactive activation model of person recognition. *Memory, 1*, 457–80. ▶ page 41

Burton, R.V. (1976). Honesty and dishonesty. In T. Lickona (ed.) *Moral Development and Behaviour.* New York: Holt, Rinehart and Winston. ▶ page 153

Bushman, B.J. (2005). Violence and sex in television programs do not sell products in advertisements. *Psychological Science, 16*, 702–8. ▶ page 228

Bushman, B.J. (2007). That was a great commercial, but what were they selling? Effects of violence and sex on memory for products in television commercials. *Journal of Applied Social Psychology, 37(8)*, 1784–96. ▶ page 228

Busigny, T. and Rossion, B. (2010). Acquired prosopagnosia abolishes the face inversion effect. *Cortex, 46*, 965–81. ▶ page 43

Busigny, T. and Rossion, B. (2011). Holistic processing impairment can be restricted to faces in acquired prosopagnosia: evidence from the global/local Navon effect. *Journal of Neuropsychology, 5*, 11–14. ▶ page 43

Busigny, T., Graf, M., Mayer, E. and Rossion, B. (2010). Acquired prosopagnosia as a face-specific disorder: ruling out the general visual similarity account. *Neuropsychologia, 48*, 2051–67. ▶ page 42

Buss, D.M. (1988). From vigilance to violence: tactics of mate retention in American undergraduates. *Ethology and Sociobiology, 9*, 291–317. ▶ page 76

Buss, D.M. (1989). Sex differences in human mate preferences: evolutionary hypotheses tested in 37 cultures. *Behavioral and Brain Sciences, 12*, 1–49. ▶ pages 54, 55, 106

Buss, D.M. (1995). Psychological sex differences: origins through sexual selection. *American Psychologist, 50*, 164–8. ▶ page 56

Buss, D.M. (2003). *The Evolution of Desire: Strategies of Human Mating.* New York: Basic Books. ▶ page 54

Buss, D.M. (2007). The evolution of human mating. *Acta Psychologica Sinica, 39(3)*, 502–12. ▶ page 54

Buss, D.M. and Schmitt, D.P. (1993). Sexual strategies theory: an evolutionary perspective on human mating. *Psychological Review, 100*, 204–32. ▶ page 54

Buss, D.M. and Shackleford, T.K. (1997). From vigilance to violence: mate retention tactics in married couples. *Journal of Personality and Social Psychology, 72*, 346–61. ▶ page 77

Buss, D.M., Larsen, R., Western, D. and Semmelroth, J. (1992). Sex differences in jealousy: evolution, physiology, and psychology. *Psychological Science, 3*, 251–5. ▶ page 57

Bussey, K. and Bandura, A. (1992). Self-regulatory mechanisms governing gender development. *Child Development, 63*, 1236–50. ▶ pages 115, 116

Bussey, K. and Bandura, A. (1999). Social cognitive theory of gender development and differentiation. *Psychological Review, 106*, 676–713. ▶ page 116

Butler, A.C. and Beck, J.S. (2000). Cognitive therapy outcomes: a review of meta-analyses. *Journal of the Norwegian Psychological Association, 37*, 1–9. ▶ page 183

Butler, G.K. and Montgomery, A.M. (2005). Subjective self-control and behavioural impulsivity coexist in anorexia nervosa. *Eating Behaviors 2005, 6*, 221–7. ▶ page 92

Buttolph, M.L., Peets, K.E. and Holland, A.M. (1998). Obsessive compulsive disorder symptoms and medication treatment in pregnancy. In M.A. Jenike, L. Baer and W.E. Minichiello (eds) *Obsessive Compulsive Disorders: Practical Management*. St. Louis, MO: Mosby. ▶ page 209

Button, E.J. and Warren, R.L. (2001). Living with anorexia nervosa: the experience of a cohort of sufferers from anorexia nervosa 7.5 years after initial presentation to a specialized eating disorders service. *European Eating Disorders Review, 9*, 74–96. ▶ page 93

Byrne, D. and Clore, G.L. (1970). A reinforcement model of evaluative responses. *Personality: An International Journal, 1*, 103–28. ▶ page 48

Byrne, D., Clore, G.L. and Smeaton, G. (1986). The attraction hypothesis: do similar attitudes affect anything. *Journal of Personality and Social Psychology, 51*, 1167–70. ▶ page 48

Byrne, P. (1997). Trainspotting and the depiction of addiction. *Psychiatric Bulletin, 21*, 173–5. ▶ page 247

Byrne, R.W. (1995). *The Thinking Ape: Evolutionary Origins of Intelligence*. Oxford: Oxford University Press. ▶ page 137

Byrne, R.W. and Corp, N. (2004). Neocortex size predicts deception in primates. *Proceedings of the Royal Society B, 271*, 1693–9. ▶ page 135

Cachelin, F.M. and Regan, P.C. (2006). Prevalence and correlates of chronic dieting in a multi-ethnic US community sample. *Eating and Weight Disorders, 11(2)*, 91–9. ▶ page 93

Cacioppo, J.T. and Petty, R.E. (1982). The need for cognition. *Journal of Personality and Social Psychology, 42*, 116–31. ▶ page 226

Camilleri, J.A. (2004). *Investigating Sexual Coercion in Romantic Relationships: A Test of the Cuckoldry Risk Hypothesis*. Unpublished master's thesis, University of Saskatchewan, Saskatoon, Saskatchewan, Canada. ▶ pages 76, 77

Camilleri, J.A. and Quinsey, V.L. (2009). Individual differences in the propensity for partner sexual aggression. *Sexual Abuse, 21*, 111–129. ▶ page 77

Campbell, S.S. and Murphy, P.J. (1998). Extraocular circadian phototransduction in humans. *Science, 279*, 396–9. ▶ page 14

Campos, J., Hiatt, S., Ramsay, D., Henderson, C. and Svejda, M. (1978). The emergence of fear on the visual cliff. In M. Lewis and L. Rosenblum (eds) *The Development of Affect*. New York: Plenum, 149–82. ▶ page 36

Cannavale, F.J., Scarr, H.A. and Pepitone, A. (1970). Deindividuation in the small group: further evidence. *Journal of Personality and Social Psychology, 16*, 141–7. ▶ page 69

Capafóns, J.I., Sosa, C.D. and Avero, P. (1998). Systematic desensitisation in the treatment of fear of flying. *Psychology in Spain, 2(1)*, 11–16. ▶ page 201

Capellini, I., Barton, R.A., McNamara, P. and Preston, B.T. (2008). Phylogenetic analysis of the ecology and evolution of mammalian sleep. *Evolution, 62–7*, 1764–76. ▶ page 123

Carey, B. (2003). New surgery to control behaviour. *Los Angeles Times*, 4 August. *See* http://articles.latimes.com/2003/aug/04/health/he-psychsurgery4 (accessed March 2009). ▶ page 213

Carey, G. and Gottesmann, I.I. (1981). Twin and family studies of anxiety, phobic, and obsessive disorders. In D.F. Klein and J.G. Rabkin (eds) *Anxiety: New Research and Changing Concepts*. New York: Raven. ▶ page 209

Carpenter, M., Nagell, K. and Tomasello, M. (1998). Social cognition, joint attention, and communicative competence from 9 to 15 months of age. *Monographs of the Society for Research in Child Development, 63(4)*, Serial No. 255. ▶ page 156

Carpenter, M., Pennington, B.F. and Rogers, S.J. (2001). Understanding of others' intentions in children with autism and children with developmental delays. *Journal of Autism and Developmental Disorders, 31*, 589–99. ▶ page 156

Carr, D. (1982). Pathophysiology of stress-induced limbic lobe dysfunction: a hypothesis relevant to near-death experiences. *Anabiosis: The Journal of Near-death Studies, 2*, 75–89. ▶ page 268

Carson, R.C. (1991). Dilemmas in the pathway of the DSM-IV. *Journal of Abnormal Psychology, 100*, 302–7. ▶ page 164

Casanova, C., Mondragon-Ceballos, R. and Lee, P. (2008). Innovative social behavior in chimpanzees (Pan troglodytes). *American Journal of Primatology, 70(1)*, 54–62. ▶ page 135

Cash, T.F. (2002). The management of body image problems. In C. Fairburn and K. Brownell (eds) *Eating Disorders and Obesity: A Comprehensive Handbook* (2nd edn). New York: Guilford Press, 599–603. ▶ page 96

Caspi, A. and Herbener, E.S. (1990). Continuity and change: assortative marriage and the consistency of personality in adulthood. *Journal of Personality and Social Psychology, 58(2)*, 250–8. ▶ page 48

Caspi, A., McClay, J., Moffitt, T.E., Mill, J., Martin, J. and Craig I.W. (2002). Role of genotype in the cycle of violence in maltreated children. *Science, 297*, 851–4. ▶ page 74

Caspi, A., Williams, B., Kim-Cohen, J., Craig, I.W., Milne, B.J., Poulton, R., Schalkwyk, L.C., Taylor, A., Werts, H. and Moffitt, T.E. (2007). Moderation of breastfeeding effects on the IQ by genetic variation in fatty acid metabolism. *Proceedings of the National Academy of Sciences of the United States of America, 104*, 18860–5. ▶ page 139

Castro-Fornieles, J., Bargallo, N., Lazaro, L., Andres, S., Falcon, C., Plana, M.T. and Junque, C. (2006). Adolescent anorexia nervosa: cross-sectional and follow-up frontal gray matter disturbances detected with proton magnetic resonance spectroscopy. *Journal of Psychiatric Research, 41*, 952–8. ▶ page 95

Cate, R.M., Lloyd, S.A., Henton, J. and Larson J. (1982). Fairness and rewards as predictors of relationship satisfaction. *Social Psychology Quarterly, 45*, 177–81. ▶ page 49

Cattell, R.B. (1943). The measurement of adult intelligence. *Psychological Bulletin, 40*, 153–93. ▶ page 124

Cattell, R.B. (1987). *Intelligence: Its Structure, Growth and Action*. Amsterdam: North-Holland Press. ▶ page 124

Ceci, S. (1991). How much does schooling influence general intelligence and its cognitive components? A reassessment of the evidence. *Developmental Psychology, 27*, 703–22. ▶ page 140

Center for Narcolepsy, Tanford School of Medicine (2011). *See* http://med.stanford.edu/school/Psychiatry/narcolepsy/faq1.html#13 (accessed February 2011).

Cha, K.Y., Wirth, D.P. and Lobo, R.A. (2001). Does prayer influence the success of in vitro fertilization-embryo transfer? *Journal of Reproductive Medicine, 46*, 781–7. ▶ page 266

Chagnon, N.A. (1988). Life histories, blood revenge, and warfare in a tribal population. *Science, 239*, 985–92. ▶ page 78

Chan, D.W. (2004). Multiple intelligences of Chinese gifted students in Hong Kong: perspectives from students, parents, teachers, and peers. *Roeper Review, 27(1)*, 18–25. ▶ page 127

Charles, K. (2011). Facebook stress linked to number of 'friends'. *See* http://staff.napier.ac.uk/News/pages/Newsdetails.aspx?NewsID=460 (accessed April 2011). ▶ pages 224

Charlton, T., Gunter, B. and Hannan, A. (eds) (2000). *Broadcast Television Effects in a Remote Community*. Hillsdale, NJ: Lawrence Erlbaum. ▶ pages 117, 223

Cheniaux, E., Landeira-Fernandez, J. and Versiani, M. (2009). The diagnoses of schizophrenia, schizoaffective disorder, bipolar disorder and unipolar depression: interrater reliability and congruence between DSM-IV and ICD-10. *Psychopathology, 42(5)*, 293–8. ▶ page 165

Cheung, C.K. and Yue, X.D. (2003). Identity achievement and idol worship among teenagers in Hong Kong. *International Journal of Adolescence and Youth, 11(1)*, 1–26. ▶ page 232

Chicurel, M. (2001). Mutant gene speeds up the human clock. *Science, 291(5502)*, 226–7. ▶ page 15

Choy, Y. and Schneier, F.R. (2008). New and recent drugs for anxiety disorders. *Primary Psychiatry, 15(12)*, 50–6. ▶ pages 198, 212

Christensen, A., Atkins, D.C., Berns, S., Wheeler, J., Baucom, D.H. and Simpson, L.E. (2004). Traditional versus integrative behavioral couple therapy for significantly and chronically distressed married couples. *Journal of Consulting and Clinical Psychology, 72*, 176–91. ▶ page 51

Chung, W.C., De Vries, G.J. and Swaab, D.F. (2002). Sexual differentiation of the bed nucleus of the stria terminalis in humans may extend into adulthood. *The Journal of Neuroscience, 22(3)*, 1027–33. ▶ page 111

Cina, A., Bodenmann, G. and Blattner, D. (2003). *The Effects of the CCET in Enhancing Parenting Skills*. Paper presented at the 2nd Family Congress, Munich, Germany. ▶ page 53

Clancy, S.A., McNally, R.J., Schachter, D.L., Lenzenweger, M. and Pitman, R.K. (2002). Memory distortion in people reporting abduction by aliens. *Journal of Abnormal Psychology, 111*, 455–461. ▶ page 265

Clark, D.A. (1992). Depressive, anxious and instrusive thoughts in psychiatric inpatients and outpatients. *Behaviour, Research and Therapy, 30*, 93–102. ▶ page 211

Clark, M.S. and Mills, J. (1979). Interpersonal attraction in exchange and communal relationships. *Journal of Personality and Social Psychology, 37*, 12–24. ▶ page 51

Clarke, D. (1993). Self-actualisation and paranormal beliefs: an empirical study. *Journal of the Society for Psychical Research, 59*, 81–8. ▶ page 265

Clarke, R.D. and Hatfield, E. (1989). Gender differences in receptivity to sexual offers. *Journal of Psychology and Human Sexuality, 2*, 39–55. ▶ page 55

Clay, A.W., Bloomsmith, M.A., Marr, M.J. and Maple, T.L. (2009). Habituation and desensitization as methods for reducing fearful behavior in singly housed rhesus macaques. *American Journal of Primatology, 71(1)*, 30–9. ▶ page 133

Cloniger, C.R. (1987). Neurogenetic adaptive mechanisms in alcoholism. *Science, 236(4800)*, 410–16. ▶ pages 244, 245

Cloward, R.D. (1967). Studies in tutoring. *Journal of Experimental Education, 36(1)*, 14–25. ▶ page 151

CNN/Time poll (1997). *Poll: US Hiding Knowledge of Aliens*. *See* http://www.cnn.com/US/9706/15/ufo.poll (accessed January 2009). ▶ page 255

Coates, S., Friedman, R.C. and Wolfe, S. (1991). The etiology of boyhood Gender Identity Disorder: a model for integrating temperament, development, and psychodynamic. *Psychological Dialogues, 1*, 481–523. ▶ page 110

Coccaro, E.F., Bergman, C.S., Kavoussi, R.J. and Seroczynski, A.D. (1997). Heritability of aggression and irritability: a twin study of the Buss-Durkee Aggression Scales in adult male subjects. *Biological Psychiatry*, 41, 273–84. ▶ page 74

Cohen, P. and Cohen, J. (1984). The clinician's illusion. *Archives of General Psychiatry*, 41, 1178–82. ▶ page 251

Cohen, P.A., Kulik, J.A. and Kulik, C.L.C. (1982). Educational outcomes of tutoring: a meta-analysis of findings. *American Educational Research Journal*, 19, 237–48. ▶ page 151

Colapinto, J. (2000). *As Nature Made Him: The Boy Who was Raised as a Girl*. New York: Quartet Books. ▶ pages 105, 111

Colby, A. and Kohlberg, L. (1987). *The Measurement of Moral Judgement. Vol. I: Theoretical Formulations and Research Validation. Volume II: Standard Issue Scoring Manual*. Cambridge: Cambridge University Press. ▶ page 153

Colby, A., Kohlberg, L., Gibbs, J. and Lieberman, M. (1983). A longitudinal study of moral judgement. *Monographs of the Society for Research in Child Development*, 48(1–2), Serial No. 200. ▶ page 153

Cole, C.M., O'Boyle, M., Emory, L.E. and Meyer III, W.J. (1997). Co-morbidity of gender dysphoria and other major psychiatric diagnoses. *Archives of Sexual Behaviour*, 26, 13–26. ▶ page 111

Cole, D.A. (1990). Relation of social and academic competence to depressive symptoms in childhood. *Journal of Abnormal Psychology*, 99, 422–9. ▶ page 183

Cole, P. (1986). Children's spontaneous expressive control of facial expression. *Child Development*, 57, 1309–21. ▶ page 156

Cole, T. and Leets, L. (1999). Attachment styles and intimate television viewing: insecurely forming relationships in a parasocial way. *Journal of Social and Personal Relationships*, 16(4), 495–511. ▶ page 231

Collier, K.M., Faidley, A. and Schilling, K.M. (2005). No longer 'absent when the picture was taken': putting relationships into relational research. *Humanistic Psychologist*, 33(3), 213–46. ▶ page 299

Colman, A.M. (1991). Crowd psychology in South African murder trials. *American Pfsychologist*, 46, 1071–9. ▶ page 68

Coltrane, S. and Messineo, M. (2000). The perpetuation of subtle prejudice: race and gender imagery in 1990s' television advertising. *Sex Roles*, 42(5–6), 363–89. ▶ page 229

Comer, R.J. (1998). *Abnormal Psychology* (2nd edn). New York: WH Freeman. ▶ page 208

Comer, R.J. (2002). *Fundamentals of Abnormal Psychology* (3rd edn). New York: Worth. ▶ pages 183, 201

Comer, R.J. (2003). *Abnormal Psychology* (5th edn). New York: Worth. ▶ pages 166, 168, 182, 210

Comstock, G. and Scharrer, E. (1999). *Television: What's On, Who's Watching, and What it Means*. San Diego, CA: Academic Press. ▶ page 229

Condon, J.W. and Crano, W.D. (1988). Inferred evaluation and the relation between attitude similarity and interpersonal attraction. *Journal of Personality and Social Psychology*, 54, 777–89. ▶ page 49

Coolican, H. (1996). *Introduction to Research Methods and Statistics in Psychology*. London: Hodder and Stoughton. ▶ page 284

Coolican, H. (2004). Personal communication. ▶ page 284

Cooper, P.J., Whelan, E., Woolgar, M., Morrell, J. and Murray, L. (2004). Association between childhood feeding problems and maternal eating disorder: role of the family environment. *The British Journal of Psychiatry*, 184(3), 210–5. ▶ pages 96, 97

Copolov, D. and Crook, J. (2000). Biological markers and schizophrenia. *Australian and New Zealand Journal of Psychiatry*, 34, S108–S112. ▶ page 167

Cordain, L. (2006). Saturated fat consumption in ancestral human diets: implications for contemporary intakes. In M.S. Meskin, W.R. Bidlack and R.K. Randolph (eds) *Phytochemicals, Nutrient-gene interactions*. Boca Raton, FL: CRC Press, 115–26. ▶ page 91

Cosmides, L. (1989). The logic of social exchange: has natural selection shaped how humans reason? Studies with the Wason selection task. *Cognition*, 31, 187–276. ▶ page 136

Couppis, M.H. and Kennedy, C.H. (2008). The rewarding effect of aggression is reduced by nucleus accumbens dopamine receptor antagonism in mice. *Psychopharmocology*, 197(3), 449–56. ▶ page 73

Crick, F. and Mitchison, G. (1983). The function of dream sleep. *Nature*, 304, 111–14. ▶ page 20

Crits-Christoph, P., Gibbons, M.B., Barber, J.P., Gallop, R., Beck, A.T. and Mercer, D. (2003). Mediators of outcome of psychosocial treatments for cocaine dependence. *Journal of Consulting and Clinical Psychology*, 71, 918–25. ▶ pages 250, 251

Crowley, S.J., Acebo, C. and Carskadon, M.A. (2007). Sleep, circadian rhythms and delayed phase in adolescents. *Sleep Medicine*, 8(6), 602–12. ▶ page 19

Cumberbatch, G. (2001). *Video Violence, Villain or Victim*. Borehamwood: Video Standards Council. ▶ page 223

Cunningham, W. and Tomer, A. (1990). Intellectual abilities and age: concepts, theories and analyses. In E.A. Lovelace (ed.) *Aging and Cognition: Mental Processes, Self-awareness and Interventions*. New York: Elsevier, 379–406. ▶ page 127

Cupach, W.R. and Spitzberg, B.H. (1998). Obsessive relational intrusion and stalking. In B.H. Spitzberg and W.R. Cupach (eds) *The Dark Side of Close Relationships*. Hillsdale, NJ: Lawrence Erlbaum, 233–63. ▶ page 233

Curtis, C.J.C., Meaburn, E.L., Craig, I.W. and Plomin, R. (2008). Comparison of whole-genome amplification methods using a 10K microarray platform. *American Society of Human Genetics*. ▶ page 138

Czeisler, C.A., Duffy, J.F., Shanahan, T.L., Brown, E.N., Mitchell, J.F., Rimmer, D.W., Ronda, J.M., Silva, E.J., Allan, J.S., Emens, J.S., Dijk, D.J. and Kronauer, R.E. (1999). Stability, precision, and near 24-hour period of the human circadian pacemaker. *Science*, 284, 2177–81. ▶ page 11

Dabbs, J. Jr., Frady, R., Carr, T. and N. Besch. (1987). Saliva testoterone and criminal violence in young adult prison inmates. *Psychosomatic Medicine*, 49, 174–82. ▶ page 72

Dabbs, J., Jurkovic, G. and Frady, R. (1991). Salivary testosterone and cortisol among late adolescent male offenders. *Journal of Abnormal Child Psychology*, 19, 469–78. ▶ page 72

Dalton, K. (1964). *The Premenstrual Syndrome*. Springfield, IL: Charles C. Thomas. ▶ page 13

Daly, M. and Wilson, M. (1978). *Sex, Evolution and Behavior*. Boston: Willard Grant Press. ▶ pages 56, 57

Daly, M. and Wilson, M. (1988). *Homicide*. New York: Aldine de Gruyter. ▶ page 76

Daly, M., Wilson, M. and Weghorst, S. (1982). Male Sexual Jealousy. *Ethology and Sociobiology*, (3), 11–27. ▶ page 76

D'Amato, G., Liccardi, G., Cecchi, L. Pellegrino, F. and D'Amato, M. (2010). Facebook: a new trigger for asthma? *The Lancet*, 376(9754), 1740. ▶ page 225

Damisch, L., Stoberock, B. and Mussweiler, T. (2010). Keep your fingers crossed! How superstition improves performance. *Psychological Science*, 21(7), 1014–20. ▶ page 263

Damon, W. and Hart, D. (1988). *Self-understanding in Childhood and Adolescence*. New York: Cambridge University Press. ▶ page 154

Danner, F.W. and Day, M.C. (1977). Eliciting formal operations. *Child Development*, 48, 1600–06. ▶ page 157

Dapretto, M., Davies, M.S., Pfeifer, J.H., Scott, A.A., Sigman, M., Bookheimer, S.Y. and Iacoboni, M. (2006). Understanding emotions in others: mirror neuron dysfunction in children with autism spectrum disorders. *Nature Neuroscience*, 9, 28–30. ▶ page 159

Darlington, T.K., Wager-Smith, K., Ceriani, M.F., Staknis, D., Gekakis, N., Steeves, T.D.L., Weitz, C.J., Takahashi, J.S. and Kay S.A. (1998). Closing the circadian loop: CLOCK-induced transcription of its own inhibitors per and tim. *Science*, 280(5369), 1599–603. ▶ page 14

Darwin, C. (1871). *The Descent of Man and Selection in Relation to Sex*. London: Murray. ▶ pages 54, 135

Darwin, C. (1874). *The Descent of Man and Selection in Relation to Sex* (2nd edn). Chicago: Rand McNally. ▶ page 54

Dasen, B. (1994). Culture and cognitive development from a Piagetian perspective. In W.J. Lonner and R. Malpass (eds) *Psychology and Culture*. Boston: Allyn & Bacon. ▶ page 147

Davey, G. (1995). Preparedness and phobias: specific evolved associations or a generalised expectancy bias? *Brain and Behavioural Sciences*, 18(2), 289–325. ▶ page 195

Davidson A.J. (2006). Search for the feeding-entrainable circadian oscillator: a complex proposition. *American Journal of Physiology. Regulatory, Integrative and Comparative Physiology*, 290(6), 1524–6. ▶ page 14

Davies, J.B. (1992). *The Myth of Addiction: An Application of the Psycholoical Theory of Attribution to Illicit Drug Use*. Philadelphia: Harwood Academic Publishers. ▶ page 241

Davies, M.F. and Kirkby, H.E. (1985). Multidimensionality of the relationship between perceived control and belief in the paranormal: spheres of control and types of paranormal phenomena. *Personality and Individual Differences*, 6, 661–3. ▶ page 265

Davies, W. and Burgess, P.W. (1988). The effects of management regime on disruptive behaviour: an analysis within the British orison system. *Medicine, Science and the Law*, 28, 243–7. ▶ page 70

Davila, J., Hammen, C., Burge, D., Paley, B. and Daley, S.E. (1995). Poor interpersonal problem-solving as a mechanism of stress generation in depression among adolescent women. *Journal of Abnormal Psychology*, 104, 592–600. ▶ page 183

Davis, J.M., Schaffer, C.B., Killian, G.A., Kinnard, C. and Chan, C. (1980). Important issues in the drug treatment of schizophrenia. *Schizophrenia Bulletin*, 6, 70–87. ▶ pages 166, 171

Davis, R., Freeman, R.J. and Garner, D.M. (1988). A naturalistic investigation of eating behavior in bulimia nervosa. *Journal of Consulting and Clinical Psychology*, 56, 273–9. ▶ page 84

De Backer, C. (2005). *Media Gossip in Evolutionary Perspective*. Human Nature and Society Conference, University of California, Los Angeles, CA. ▶ page 230

De Backer, C. (2007). *Like Belgian Chocolate for the Universal Mind: Interpersonal and Media Gossip from an Evolutionary Perspective*. News release, University of Leicester. ▶ page 231

de Beauvoir, S. (1952). *The Second Sex*. New York: Bantham. ▶ page 108

Deag, J.M. and Crook, J.H. (1971). Social behaviour and 'agonistic buffering' in the wild Barbary macaque (Macaca sylvana L.). *Folia Primatologica*, 15, 183–200. ▶ page 135

Decety, J. (2007). A social cognitive neuroscience model of human empathy. In E. Harmon-Jones and P. Winkielman (eds) *Social Neuroscience: Integrating Biological and Psychological Explanations of Social Behavior*. New York: Guilford Publications, 246–70. ▶ page 159

DeCoursey, P.J., Walker, J.K. and Smith, S.A. (2000). A circadian pacemaker in free-living chipmunks: essential for survival? *Journal of Comparative Physiology*, 186, 169–80. ▶ page 15

Delfabbro, P.H. and Winefield, A.H. (1999). Poker machine gambling: an analysis of within session characteristics. *British Journal of Psychology, 90*, 425–39. ▶ page 242

Delfabbro, P., Lahn, J. and Grabosky, P. (2006). It's not what you know, but how you use it: statistical knowledge and adolescent problem gambling. *Journal of Gambling Studies, 22*, 179–93. ▶ page 241

Delfour, F. and Marten, K. (2001). Mirror image processing in three marine mammal species: killer whales (*Orcinus orca*), false killer whales (*Pseudorca crassidens*) and California sea lions (*Zalophus californianus*). *Behavioural Processes, 53(3)*, 181–90. ▶ page 134

Delgado, P.L., Charney, D.S., Price, L.H., Aghajanian, G.K., Landis, H. and Heninger, G.R. (1990). Serotonin function and the mechanism of antidepressant action: reversal of antidepressant-induced remission by rapid depletion of plasma tryptophan. *Archives of General Psychiatry, 47*, 411–18. ▶ page 180

Dell, S. (1984). *Murder into Manslaughter*. Oxford: Oxford University Press. ▶ page 76

DeLisi, M., Berg, M.T. and Hochstetler, A. (2004). Gang members, career criminals and prison violence: further specification of the importation model of inmate behavior. *Criminal Justice Studies, 17(4)*, 369–83. ▶ page 71

Delvenne, J.-F., Seron, X., Coyette, F. and Rossion, B. (2004). Evidence for perceptual deficits in associative visual (prosop)agnosia: a single-case study. *Neuropsychologia, 42*, 597–612. ▶ page 42

DeMaris, A. (2007). The role of relationship inequity in marital disruption. *Journal of Social and Personal Relationships, 24*, 177–95. ▶ page 51

Dement, W.C. and Kleitman, N. (1957). The relation of eye movements during sleep to dream activity: an objective method for the study of dreaming. *Journal of Experimental Psychology, 53*, 339–46. ▶ page 13

Department of Health (2007). *Electroconvulsive Therapy*. Survey covering the period from January 2002 to March 2002. London: Department of Health. ▶ page 185

Deregowski, J.B. (1989). Real space and represented space: cross-cultural perspectives. *Behavioural and Brain Sciences, 12*, 51–119. ▶ page 39

Derevensky, J. and Gupta, R. (eds) (2004). *Gambling Problems in Youth: The Theoretical and Applied Perspectives*. New York: Kluwer Academic Publishers. ▶ page 251

Dessens, A.B., Slijper, F.M.E. and Drop, S.L.S. (2005). Gender dysphoria and gender change in chromosomal females with congenital adrenal hyperplasia. *Archives of Sexual Behaviour, 34*, 389–97. ▶ page 111

DeVries, R. (1969). Constancy of generic identity in the years three to six. *Monographs of the Society for Child Development, 34* (Serial No. 127). ▶ page 112

DeVries, H. and Backbier, E. (1994). Self-efficacy as an important determinant of quitting among pregnant women who smoke – the phi pattern. *Preventive Medicine, 23*, 167–74. ▶ page 240

Di Nardo, P.A., Guzy, L.T. and Bak, R.M. (1988). Anxiety response patterns and etiological factors in dog-fearful and non-fearful subjects. *Behaviour Research and Therapy, 26(3)*, 245–51. ▶ page 197

Diamond, M. (1996). Self-testing among transsexuals: a check on sexual identity. *Journal of Psychology & Human Sexuality, 8(3)*, 61–82. ▶ page 111

Diamond, R. and Carey, S. (1986). Why faces are and are not special: an effect of expertise. *Journal of Experimental Psychology: General, 115(3)*, 107–17. ▶ page 41

DiBlasio, F.A. and Benda, B.B. (1993). Adolescent sexual intercourse: family and peer influences. *School Social Work Journal, 18*, 17–31. ▶ page 243

Diener, E., Westford, K.L., Dineen, J. and Fraser, S.C. (1973). Beat the pacifist: the deindividuating effects of anonymity and group presence. *Proceedings*

of the 81st Annual Convention of the American Psychological Association, 8, 221–2. ▶ page 69

Divale, W.T., and Harris, M. (1976). Population, warfare, and the male supremacist complex. *American Anthropologist, 78*, 521–38. ▶ page 78

Dixon, M., Labelle, L. and Laurence, J.R. (1996). A multivariate approach to the prediction of hypnotic susceptibility. *International Journal of Clinical and Experimental Hypnosis, 44*, 250–64. ▶ page 264

Dobash, R.E. and Dobash, R.P. (1984). The nature and antecedents of violent events. *British Journal of Criminology, 24*, 269–88. ▶ page 76

Dodge, K.A., Pettit, G.S. and Bates, J.E. (1997). How the experience of early physical abuse leads children to become chronically aggressive. In D. Cicchetti and S. Toth (eds) *Rochester Symposium on Developmental Psychopathology. Vol. 8: The Effects of Trauma on the Developmental Process*. Rochester, NY: University of Rochester Press, 263–8. ▶ page 131

Domjan, M. (2005). Pavlovian conditioning: a functional perspective. *Annual Review of Psychology, 56*, 179–206. ▶ pages 129, 133

Dornbusch, S.M., Carlsmith, S.M., Duncan, P.D., Gross, R.T., Martin, J.A., Ritter, P.L. and Siegel-Gorelick, B. (1984). Sexual maturation, social class, and the desire to be thin among adolescent females. *Journal of Behavioural and Developmental Pediatrics, 5*, 308–14. ▶ page 84

Dougherty, D.D., Baer, L., Cosgrove, G.R., Cassem, E.H., Price, B.H., Nierenberg, A.A., Jenike, M.A. and Rauch, S.L. (2002). Prospective long-term follow-up of 44 patients who received cingulotomy for treatment-refractory obsessive compulsive disorder. *Journal of Psychiatry, 59(2)*, 269–75. ▶ page 213

Douglas, O., Burton, K.S. and Reese-Durha, N. (2008). The effects of the multiple intelligence teaching strategy on the academic achievement of eighth grade math students. *Journal of Instructional Psychology, 35(2)*, 182–7. ▶ page 127

Driessen, M., Schulte, S., Luedecke, C., Schaefer, I., Sutmann, F., Ohlmeier, M., Kemper, U., Koesters, G., Chodzinski, C., Schneider, U., Broese, T., Dette, C. and Havemann-Reinicke, U. (2008). Trauma and PTSD in patients with alcohol, drug, or dual dependence: a multi-center study. *Alcholism: Clinical and Experimental Research, 32(3)*, 481–8. ▶ page 244

Drigotas, S.M. (1993). Similarity revisited: a comparison of similarity-attraction versus dissimilarity-repulsion. *British Journal of Social Psychology, 32*, 365–77. ▶ page 49

Drummond, D.C., Cooper, T. and Glautier, S.P. (1990). Conditioned learning in alcohol dependence: implications for cue exposure treatment. *British Journal of Addiction, 85*, 725–43. ▶ page 243

Drury, V., Birchwood, M., Cochrane, R. and MacMillan, F. (1996). Cognitive therapy and recovery from acute psychosis: a controlled trial. *British Journal of Psychiatry, 169*, 593–601. ▶ page 172

Duchaine, B. and Nakayama, K. (2006). The Cambridge Face Memory Test: results for neurologically intact individuals and an investigation of its validity using inverted face stimuli and prosopagnosic subjects. *Neuropsychologia, 44(4)*, 576–85. ▶ page 42

Duchaine, B., Germine, L. and Nakayama, K. (2007). Family resemblance: ten family members with prosopagnosia and within-class object agnosia. *Cognitive Neuropsychology. 24*, 419–430. ▶ page 42

Duchaine, B., Yovel, G., Butterworth, E. and Nakayama, K. (2006). Prosopagnosia as an impairment to face-specific mechanisms: elimination of the alternative explanations in a developmental case. *Cognitive Neuropsychology, 23*, 714–47. ▶ page 43

Duck, S.W. (1991). *Friends for Life*. Hemel Hempstead: Harvester Wheatsheaf. ▶ page 52

Duck, S.W. (1999). *Relating to Others* (2nd edn). Chicago: Dorsey. ▶ page 52

Duck, S.W. (2007). *Human Relationships* (4th edn). London: Sage. ▶ page 52

Duck, S.W. and Sants, H. (1983). On the origins of the specious: are personal relationships really interpersonal states? *Journal of Social and Clinical Psychology, 1*, 27–41. ▶ page 51

Duffy, J.F., Rimmer, D.W. and Czeisler, C.A. (2000). Association of intrinsic circadian period with morningness-eveningness, usual wake time, and circadian phase. *Behavioural Neuroscience, 115(4)*, 8959. ▶ page 11

Dunbar, R. (1995). The mating system of callitrichid primates. I: conditions for the co-evolution of pair bonding and twinning, *Animal Behavior, 50*, 1057–70. ▶ page 57

Dunbar, R.I.M. (1992). Neocortex size as a constraint on group size in primates, *Journal of Human Evolution, 22*, 469–93. ▶ pages 135, 136, 137

Dunbar, R.I.M., Baron, R., Frangou, A., Pearce, E., van Leeuwen, E.J.C., Stow, J., Partridge, G., MacDonald, I., Barra, V. and van Vught, M. (2011). Social laughter is correlated with an elevated pain threshold. *Proceedings of the Royal Society, 279(1373)*, 1161–7. ▶ page 294

Duncan, J., Seitz, R.J., Kolodny, J., Bor, D., Herzog, H., Ahmed, A., Newell, F.N. and Emslie, H. (2000). A neural basis for general intelligence. *Science, 289(5478)*, 457–60. ▶ page 135

Duncan, T.E., Tildesley, E., Duncan, S.C. and Hops, H. (1995). The consistency of family and peer influences on the development of substance use in adolescence. *Addiction, 90*, 1647–60. ▶ page 245

Durkin, K. (1995). *Developmental Social Psychology: From Infancy to Old Age*. Oxford: Blackwell. ▶ page 113

Dutton, D.G. and Aron, A.P. (1974). Some evidence for heightened sexual attraction under conditions of high anxiety. *Journal of Personality and Social Psychology, 30*, 510–17. ▶ page 290

Eagles, J.M., Andrew, J.E., Johnston, M.I., Easton, E.A. and Millar, H.R. (2001). Season of birth in females with anorexia nervosa in Northeast Scotland. *International Journal of Eating Disorders, 30*, 167–75. ▶ page 94

Eagles, J.M., Johnston, M.I. and Millar, H.R. (2005). A case-control study of family composition in anorexia nervosa. *International Journal of Eating Disorders, 38(1)*, 49–54. ▶ page 95

Eagly, A.H. and Carli, L.L. (1981). Sex of researchers and sex-typed communications as determinants of sex differences in influenceability: a meta-analysis of social influence studies. *Psychological Bulletin, 90*, 1–20. ▶ page 289

Eagly, A.H. and Wood, W. (1999). The origins of sex differences in human behavior: evolved dispositions versus social roles. *American Psychologist, 54*, 408–23. ▶ page 108

Eagly, A.H. and Wood, W. (2002). Cross-cultural analysis of the behaviour of women and men: implications for the origins of sex differences. *Psychological Bulletin, 128*, 699–727. ▶ page 108

Eastman, C.I., Young, M.A., Fogg, L.F., Liu, L. and Meaden, P.M. (1998). Bright light treatment of winter depression: a placebo-controlled trial. *Archives of General Psychiatry, 55(10)*, 861–2. ▶ page 13

Eder, R.A. (1990). Uncovering young children's psychological selves: individual and developmental differences. *Child Development, 61*, 849–63. ▶ page 154

Edgar, P. (1988). The role of the mass media in community violence: what research is able to tell us. *Submission to Parliament of Victoria Social Development Committee Inquiry into strategies to deal with the issue of community violence, first report*. Melbourne, Australia. ▶ page 222

Edlund, J.E. and Sagarin, B.J. (2009). Sex differences in jealousy: misinterpretation of nonsignificant results as refuting the theory. *Personal Relationships, 16*, 67–78. ▶ page 77

Ehrsson, H.H. (2007). The experimental induction of out-of-body experiences. *Science, 317(5841)*, 1048. ▶ **page 269**

Eide, B. and Eide, F. (2006). *The Mislabeled Child: How Understanding your Child's Unique Learning Style can Open the Door to Success*. New York: Hyperion. ▶ **page 157**

Eisenberg, M.E., Neumark-Sztainer, D., Story, M. and Perry, C. (2005). The role of social norms and friends' influences on unhealthy weight-control behaviors among adolescent girls. *Social Science and Medicine, 60*, 1165–73. ▶ **page 92**

Eisenberg, N. (1990). Prosocial development in early and mid adolescence. In R. Montemayor, G.R. Adams and T.P. Gullotta (eds) *From Childhood to Adolescence: A Transitional Period?* Newbury Park, CA: Sage. ▶ **page 220**

Eisenberg, N. (2000). Emotion, regulation and moral development. *Annual Review of Psychology, 51*, 665–97. ▶ **page 158**

Eisenegger, C., Haushofer, J. and Fehr, E. (2011). The role of testosterone in social interaction. *Trends in Cognitive Sciences, 15*, 263–71. ▶ **page 73**

Eiser, J.R., Morgan, M., Gammage, P., Brooks, N. and Kirby, R. (1991). Adolescent health behaviour and similarity-attraction: friends share smoking habits (really), but much else besides. *British Journal of Social Psychology, 30*, 339–48. ▶ **page 244**

Eiser, J.R., Morgan, M., Gammage, P. and Gray, E. (1989). Adolescent smoking: attitudes, norms and parental influence. *British Journal of Social Psychology, 28*, 193–202. ▶ **page 245**

Elkin, I., Parloff, M.B., Hadley, S.W. (1985). NIMH treatment of depression collaborative research program: background and research plan. *Archives of General Psychiatry, 42*, 305–16. ▶ **page 187**

Ellason, J.W. and Ross, C.A. (1995). Positive and negative symptoms in dissociative identity disorder and schizophrenia: a comparative analysis. *Journal of Nervous and Mental Disease, 183(4)*, 236–41. ▶ **page 165**

Ellis, A. (1957). *How to Live with a 'Neurotic'*. Hollywood, CA: Wilshire Books. ▶ **pages 200, 201**

Ellis, A. (2001). *Overcoming Destructive Beliefs, Feelings, and Behaviors: New Directions for Rational Emotive Behavior Therapy*. New York: Prometheus Books. ▶ **pages 201, 215**

Emmelkamp, P.M., Visser, S. and Hoekstra, R.J. (1988). Cognitive therapy vs. exposure in vivo in the treatment of obsessive compulsives. *Cognitive Therapy and Research, 12*, 103–14. ▶ **page 201**

Empson, J. (2002). *Sleep and Dreaming* (3rd edn). London: Palgrave. ▶ **page 21**

Empson, J.A.C. (1977). Periodicity in body temperature in man. *Experientia, 33*, 342–3. ▶ **page 12**

Engels, G.I., Garnefski, N. and Diekstra, R.F.W. (1993). Efficacy of rational-emotive therapy: a quantitative analysis. *Journal of Consulting and Clinical Psychology, 61*, 1083–90. ▶ **page 201**

Ennis, M., Kelly, K.S. and Lambert, P.L. (2001). Sex differences in cortisol secretion during anticipation of a psychological stressor: possible support for the tend-and-befriend hypothesis. *Stress and Health, 17*, 253–61. ▶ **page 107**

Erfgen, C. (2011). *Impact of Celebrity Endorsement on Brand Image: A Communication Process Perspective on 30 Years of Empirical Research*. Research papers on marketing and retailing, University of Hamburg. ▶ **page 229**

Erikson, E.H. (1968). *Identity: Youth and Crisis*. New York: Norton. ▶ **page 60**

Erwin, P. (1993). *Friendship and Peer Relations in Children*. Chichester: Wiley. ▶ **page 59**

Espie, C.A. (2002). Insomnia: conceptual issues in the development, persistence and treatment of sleep disorder in adults. *Annual Review of Psychology, 53*, 215–43. ▶ **page 25**

Esses, V.M., Veenviet, S., Hodson, G. and Mihic, L. (2008). Justice, morality, and the dehumanization of refugees. *Social Justice Research, 21*, 4–25. ▶ **page 71**

Evans, C. (1973). Parapsychology – what the questionnaire revealed. *New Scientist, 25 January*, 209–10. ▶ **page 261**

Evans, L. and Wertheim, E. (2005). Attachment styles in adult intimate relationships: comparing women with bulimia nervosa symptoms, women with depression and women with no clinical symptoms. *European Eating Disorders Review, 13*, 285–93. ▶ **page 96**

Eysenck H.J. (1967). *Biological Basis of Personality*. Springfield, IL: Thomas. ▶ **pages 244, 264**

Eysenck, M.W. (1997). *Anxiety and Cognition: A Unified Theory*. Hove: Psychology Press. ▶ **page 193**

Fagot, B.I., Leinbach, M.D. and O'Boyle, C. (1992). Gender labeling, gender stereotyping and parenting behaviours. *Developmental Psychology, 28*, 225–30. ▶ **page 116**

Fairburn, C.G., Norman, P.A., Welch, S.L., O'Connor, M.E., Doll, H.A. and Peveler, R.C. (1995). A prospective study of outcome in bulimia nervosa and the long-term effects of three psychological treatments. *Archives of General Psychiatry, 52*, 304–12. ▶ **page 97**

Falloon, I.R.H., Kydd, R.R., Coverdale, J.H. and Laidlaw, T.M. (1996). Early detection and intervention for initial episodes of schizophrenia. *Schizophrenia Bulletin, 22(2)*, 271–82. ▶ **page 168**

Farah, M. (1991). Patterns of co-occurence among the associative agnosias: implications for visual object representations. *Cognitive Neuropsychology, 8*, 1–19. ▶ **page 42**

Favaro, A., Tenconi, E. and Santonastaso, P. (2006). Perinatal factors and the risk of developing anorexia nervosa and bulimia nervosa. *Archives of General Psychiatry, 63(1)*, 82–8. ▶ **page 95**

Feldman, M.B. and Meyer, I.H. (2007). Childhood abuse and eating disorders in gay and bisexual men. *International Journal of Eating Disorders, 40(5)*, 418–23. ▶ **page 97**

Felson, R.B. (1997). Anger, aggression, and violence in love triangles. *Violence and Victims 12*, 345–62. ▶ **page 77**

Ferguson, S., Cisneros, F., Gough, B., Hanig, J. and Berry, K. (2005). Chronic oral treatment with 13-cis-retinoic acid (isotretinoin) or all-trans-retinoic acid does not alter depression-like behaviors in rats. *Toxicological Sciences, 87*, 451–9. ▶ **page 185**

Ferrara, M., De Gennaro, L. and Bertini, M., (1999). Selective slow-wave sleep (SWS) deprivation and SWS rebound: do we need a fixed SWS amount per night? *Sleep Research Online, 2(1)*, 15–19. ▶ **page 21**

Feshbach, S. and Singer, R.D. (1971). *Television and aggression: an experimental field study*. San Francisco: Jossey-Bass. ▶ **page 223**

Fischer, D.R. (2001). *Arizona Department of Corrections: Security Threat Group (STG) Program Evaluation, Final Report*. Washington, DC: US Department of Justice, Office of Justice Programs, National Institute of Justice. ▶ **page 71**

Fiske, S.T. and Taylor, S.E. (1984). *Social Cognition*. Reading, MA: Addison-Wesley. ▶ **page 227**

Flamm, B.L. (2004). The bizarre Columbia University 'Miracle' study saga continues. *Skeptical Inquirer, 31(3)*, 19–20. ▶ **page 267**

Flamm, B.L. (2005). The Columbia University 'Miracle' study: flawed and fraud. *Skeptical Inquirer, 29(2)*, 52–3. ▶ **page 267**

Flanagan, J.C. (1948). (ed.) The Aviation Psychology Program in the Army Air Forces. *AAF Aviation Program Research Reports, 1*. Washington, DC: GPO. ▶ **page 124**

Flynn, J.R. (1987). Massive IQ gains in 14 nations: what IQ tests really measure. *Psychological Bulletin, 101*, 171–91. ▶ **page 125**

Foa, E.B. and Kozak, M.J. (1996). Psychological treatment for obsessive compulsive disorder. In M.R. Mavissakalian and R.F. Prien (eds) *Long-term Treatments of Anxiety Disorders*. Washington, DC: American Psychiatric Press. ▶ **page 215**

Foa, E.B., Liebowitz, M.R., Kozak, M.J., Davies, S., Campeas, R., Franklin, M.E., Huppert, J.D., Kjernisted, K., Rowan, V., Schmidt, A.B., Simpson, H.B. and Tu, X. (2005). Randomized, placebo-controlled trial of exposure and ritual prevention, clomipramine, and their combination in the treatment of obsessive compulsive disorder. *American Journal of Psychiatry, 162*, 151–61. ▶ **page 215**

Foldesi, G.S. (1996). Football, racism, and xenophobia in Hungary: racist and xenophobic behaviour of football spectators. In U. Merkel and W. Tokarski (eds) *Racism and Xenophobia in European Football*. Aachen: Meyer & Meyer Verlag. ▶ **page 79**

Folkard, S. (1996). Bags of time to play. *Daily Express*, 28 September. ▶ **page 15**

Folkard, S., Hume, K.I., Minors, D.S., Waterhouse, J.M. and Watson, F.L. (1985). Independence of the circadian rhythms in alertness from the sleep/wake cycle. *Nature, 313*, 678–9. ▶ **page 10**

Folkard, S., Monk, T.H., Bradbury, R. and Rosenthall, J. (1977). Time-of-day effects in school children's immediate and delayed recall of meaningful material. *British Journal of Psychology, 68*, 45–60. ▶ **page 11**

Folkerts, H.W., Michael, N. and Tolle, R. (1997). Electroconvulsive therapy v. paroxetine in treatment-resistant depression: a randomized study. *Acta Psychiatrica Scandinavica, 96*, 334–42. ▶ **page 185**

Foster, K.R. and Kokko, H. (2009). The evolution of superstition and superstition-like behaviour. *Proceedings of the Royal Society, 276(1654)*, 31–7. ▶ **page 261**

Fowles, J. (1996). *Advertising and Popular Culture*. Thousand Oaks, CA: Sage. ▶ **page 228**

Fox, R. and McDaniel, C. (1982). The perception of biological motion by human infants. *Science, 218*, 486–7. ▶ **page 35**

Fraley, R.C. (1998). *Attachment Continuity from Infancy to Adulthood: Meta-analysis and Dynamic Modeling of Developmental Mechanisms*. Colloquium speaker. University of California, Berkeley. ▶ **page 59**

Francis, K., Boyd, C.P., Aisbett, D.L., Newnham, K. and Newnham, K. (2006). Rural adolescents' perceptions of barriers to seeking help for mental health problems. *Youth Studies Australia, 25*, 22–49. ▶ **page 69**

Francis, L.J. (1996) The relationship between personality and attitude toward substance. *Addiction, 88*, 665–72. ▶ **page 265**

Francis, L.J., Williams, E. and Robbins, M. (2010). Personality, conventional Christian belief and unconventional paranormal belief: a study among teenagers. *British Journal of Religious Education, 32(91)*, 31–9. ▶ **page 265**

Franklin, T.R., Wang, Z., Wang, J., Sciortino, N., Harper, D., Li, Y., Ehrman, R., Kampman, K., O'Brien, C.P., Detre, J.A. and Childress, A.R. (2007). Limbic activation to cigarette smoking cues independent of nicotine withdrawal: a perfusion fMRI study. *Neuropsychopharmacology 32*, 2301–9. ▶ **page 242**

Freeman, D. (1984). *Margaret Mead and Samoa: The Making and Unmaking of an Anthropological Myth*. Cambridge, MA: Harvard University Press. ▶ **page 118**

Freeston, M.H., Ladouceur, R., Thibodeau, N. and Gagnon, F. (1992). Cognitive intrusions in a non-clinical population. II: associations with depressive, anxious, and compulsive symptoms. *Behaviour Research and Therapy, 30*, 263–71. ▶ **page 211**

French, C.C. and Wilson, K. (2006). Incredible memories: how accurate are reports of anomalous events? *European Journal of Parapsychology, 21*, 166–81. ▶ **page 265**

French, C. (2011). Failing the future? *The Skeptic, 22(4)/23(1)*, 13. ▶ **page 277**

French, C.C. and Kerman, M.K. (1996). Childhood trauma, fantasy proneness and belief in the paranormal. British Psychological Society London Conference at the Institute of Education, London, 17–18 December. Abstract published in *Proceedings of the British Psychological Society, 5(1)*, 54. ▶ page 265

Freud, S. (1891). *Zur Auffassung der aphasien.* Leipzig: Deuticke. [Available in English] *On Aphasia: A Critical Study.* Translated by E. Stengel (1953). Madison, CT: International Universities Press. ▶ page 42

Freud, S. (1909). Analysis of phobia in a five-year-old boy. In J. Strachey (ed. and trans.) (1976) *The Complete Psychological Works of Sigmund Freud: The Standard Edition, Volume 10.* New York: W.W. Norton and Co. ▶ page 194

Freud, S. (1909). Notes upon a case of obsessional neurosis. In *The Standard Edition of the Complete Works of Sigmund Freud, Volume 10.* London: Hogarth Press, 151–249. ▶ pages 196, 211

Freud, S. (1913). Totem and taboo. In J. Strachey (ed. and trans.) (1976) *The Complete Psychological Works of Sigmund Freud: The Standard Edition, Volume 13.* New York: W.W. Norton and Co. ▶ page 262

Freud, S. (1917). Introductory lectures on psychoanalysis. In J. Strachey (ed. and trans.) (1976) *The Complete Psychological Works of Sigmund Freud: The Standard Edition, Volume 16.* New York: W.W. Norton and Co. ▶ page 210

Freud, S. (1917). Mourning and melancholia. In *Collected papers* (vol. 4). London: Hogarth and the Institute of Psychoanalysis. ▶ page 182

Freud, S. (1924). Neurosis and psychosis: the essentials of psychoanalysis. In A. Freud (ed.) (trans. J. Strachey) (1991). *The Definitive Collection of Sigmund Freud's Writing.* London: Penguin, 563–7. ▶ page 168

Friedman, S. and Fisher, C. (1967). On the presence of a rhythmic, diurnal, oral instinctual drive cycle in man: a preliminary report. *Journal of the American Psychoanalytic Association, 15*, 317–43. ▶ page 12

Friedrich, L.K. and Stein, A.H. (1973). Aggressive and procosocial television programs and the natural behavior of preschool children. *Monographs of the Society for Research in Child Development, 38(4)*, serial no. 151. ▶ page 220

Fromm-Reichmann, F. (1948). Notes on the development of treatment of schizophrenics by psychoanalytical psychotherapy. *Psychiatry, 11*, 263–73. ▶ page 169

Frost, R.O. and Steketee, G. (2002). *Cognitive Approaches to Obsessions and Compulsions: Theory, Assessment, and Treatment.* Oxford: Elsevier Science. ▶ page 210

Frydenberg, E. and Lewis, R. (1993). Boys play sport and girls turn to others: age, gender and ethnicity as determinants of coping. *Journal of Adolescence, 16*, 253–66. ▶ page 163

Fuller, P.M., Lu, J. and Saper, C.B. (2008). Differential rescue of light- and food-entrainable circadian rhythms. *Science, 320(5879)*, 1074–7. ▶ page 17

Furnham, A., Wytykowska, A. and Petrides, K.V. (2005). Estimates of multiple intelligences: a study in Poland. *European Psychologist, 10*, 51–9. ▶ page 127

Fyer, A.J., Manuzza, S., Chapman, T.G., Martin, L.Y. and Klein, D.F. (1995). Specificity in familial aggregation of phobic disorder. *Archives of General Psychiatry, 52*, 564–73. ▶ page 194

Gabbard, G.O. and Twemlow, S.W. (1984). *With the Eyes of the Mind: An Empirical Analysis of Out-of-body States.* New York: Praeger Scientific. ▶ page 269

Gallese, V. and Goldman, A. (1998). Mirror neurons and the simulation theory of mind-reading. *Trends in Cognitive Sciences, 12*, 493–501. ▶ page 158

Gallup, G.G. Jr. (1970). Chimpanzees: self-recognition. *Science, 167*, 86–7. ▶ pages 134, 154

Gangestad, S.G., Haselton, M.G. and Buss, D.M. (2006). Evolutionary foundations of cultural variation: evoked culture and mate preferences. *Psychological Inquiry, 17(2)*, 75–95. ▶ pages 108, 109

Garcia, J., Kimeldorf, D.J. and Koelling, R.A. (1955). Conditioned aversion to saccharin resulting from exposure to gamma radiation. *Science, 122*, 157–8. ▶ page 90

Gardner, H. (1983). *Frames of Mind: The Theory of Multiple Intelligences.* New York: Basic Books. ▶ page 126

Gardner, H. (1993). *Multiple Intelligences: The Theory in Practice.* New York: Basic Books. ▶ page 127

Gardner, H. (2004). *Changing Minds: The Art and Science of Changing our Own and Other People's Minds.* Boston: Harvard Business School Press. ▶ page 127

Garg, N., Wansink, B. and Inman, J.J. (2007). The influence of incidental affect on consumers' food intake. *Journal of Marketing, 71(1)*, 194–206. ▶ page 84

Garrido, L., Furl, N., Draganski, B., Weiskopf, N., Stevens, J., Tan, G.C.-Y., Driver, J., Dolan, R. and Duchaine, B. (2009). VBM reveals reduced gray matter volume in the temporal cortex of developmental prosopagnosics. *Brain, 132*, 3443–55. ▶ page 43

Gartner, C.E., Barendregt, J.J. and Hall, W.D. (2009). Multiple genetic tests for susceptibility to smoking do not outperform simple family history. *Addiction, 104*, 118–26. ▶ page 239

Gauthier, I., Skudlarski, P., Gore, J.C. and Anderson, A.W. (2000). Expertise for cars and birds recruits brain areas involved in face recognition. *Nature Neuroscience, 3(2)*, 191–7. ▶ page 41

Gava, I., Barbui, C., Aguglia, E., Carino, D., Churchill, R., De Vanna, M. and McGuire, H. (2007). Psychological treatments versus treatment as usual for obsessive compulsive disorder (OCD). *Cochrane Database of Systematic Reviews, 2*, Article no. CD005333 ▶ page 212

Gazzola, V., Aziz-Zadeh, L. and Keysers, C. (2006). Empathy and the somatotopic auditory mirror system in humans. *Current Biology, 16(18)*, 1824–9. ▶ page 159

Geher, G., Fairweather, K., Mollette, N., Ugonabo, U., Murphy, J.W. and Wood, N. (2007). Sex differences in response to cues of parental investment: an evolutionary social psychological perspective. *Journal of Social, Evolutionary and Cultural Psychology, 1*, 18–34. ▶ page 57

Gelkopf, M., Levitt, S. and Bleich, A. (2002). An integration of three approaches to addiction and methadone maintenance treatment: the self-medication hypothesis, the disease model and social criticism. *Israel Journal of Psychiatry and Related Sciences, 39(2)*, 140–51. ▶ page 240

Geller, B., Cooper, T.B., Graham, D.L., Fetner, H.H., Marsteller, F.A. and Wells, J.M. (1992). Pharmacokinetically designed double-blind placebo-controlled study of nortriptyline in 6–12 year olds with major depressive disorder. *Journal of the American Academy of Child and Adolescent Psychiatry, 31*, 34–44. ▶ page 185

Gentile, D.A. and Anderson, C.A. (2003). Violent video games: the newest media violence hazard. In D.A. Gentile (ed.) *Media Violence and Children.* Westport, CT: Praeger, 131–52. ▶ page 224

Gentile, D.A. and Stone, W. (2005). Violent video game effects on children and adolescents: a review of the literature. *Minerva Pediatrica, 57*, 337–58. ▶ page 224

Gentile, D.A., Lynch, P.J., Linder, J.R. and Walsh, D.A. (2004). The effects of violent video game habits on adolescent aggressive attitudes and behaviors. *Journal of Adolescence, 27*, 5–22. ▶ page 225

George, S. and Murali, V. (2005). Pathological gambling: an overview of assessment and treatment. *Advances in Psychiatric Treatment, 11*, 450–6. ▶ page 250

Gershuny, B.S., Baer, L., Jenike, M.A., Minichiello, W.E. and Wilhelm, S. (2002). Comorbid posttraumatic stress disorder: impact on treatment outcome for obsessive compulsive disorder. *American Journal of Psychiatry, 159*, 852–4. ▶ page 215

Geschwind, N. and Galaburda, A.M. (1987). *Cerebral Lateralization: Biological Mechanisms, Associations and Pathology.* Cambridge, MA: MIT Press. ▶ page 104

Ghanizadeh, A., Kianpoor, M., Rezaei, M., Rezaei, H., Moini, R., Aghakhani, K., Ahmadi, J. and Moeini, S.R. (2008). Sleep patterns and habits in high school students in Iran. *Annals of General Psychiatry, 7(1)*, 5. ▶ page 19

Ghim, H.R. (1990). Evidence for perceptual organisation in infants: perception of subjective contours by young infants. *Infant Behaviour and Development, 13*, 221–48. ▶ page 37

Gibson, E.J. and Walk, R.D. (1960). The 'visual cliff'. *Scientific American, 202(4)*, 64–71. ▶ pages 35, 36

Gibson, E.L. and Wardle, J. (2001). Effect of contingent hunger state on development of appetite for a novel fruit snack. *Appetite, 37*, 97–101. ▶ page 91

Gibson, J.J. (1979). *The Ecological Approach to Visual Perception.* Boston: Houghton Mifflin. ▶ page 34

Gibson, J.J., Olum, P. and Rosenblatt, F. (1955). Parallax and perspective during aircraft landings. *American Journal of Psychology, 68*, 372–85. ▶ page 34

Giesbrecht, G.G., Arnet, J.L., Vela, E. and Bristow, G.K. (1993). Effect of task complexity on mental performance during immersion hypothermia. *Aviation, Space and Environmental Medicine, 64*, 206–11. ▶ page 11

Giles, D. (2003). *Media Psychology.* Hillsdale, NJ: Lawrence Erlbaum. ▶ pages 222, 228, 229, 232

Giles, D. and Maltby, J. (2006). Praying at the altar of the stars. *The Psychologist, 19*, 82–5. ▶ page 230

Giles, D.C. and Naylor, G.C.Z. (2000). *Self-construal and the Private Bedroom: The Effect of Domestic Environment on Idiocentrism-allocentrism in British Adolescents.* Poster presentation, BPS Developmental Section Annual Conference, University of Bristol. ▶ page 232

Gillie, O. (1976). Crucial data faked by eminent psychologist. *Sunday Times*, 24 October 1976: London. ▶ page 276

Gilligan, C. (1982). *In a Different Voice: Psychological Theory and Women's Development.* Cambridge, MA: Harvard University Press. ▶ page 153

Glassman, N. (1999). All things being equal: the two roads of Piaget and Vygotsky. In P. Lloyd and C. Fernyhough (eds) *Lev Vygotsky: Critical Assessments: Vygotsky's Theory* (vol. I). New York: Routledge, 282–310. ▶ page 149

Glickman, R. and Gracely, E.J. (1998). Therapeutic touch: investigation of a practitioner. *The Scientific Review of Alternative Medicine, 2(1)*, 43–7. ▶ page 267

Glowinski, A.L., Madden, P.A., Bucholz, K.K., Lynskey, M.T and Heath, A.C. (2003). Genetic epidemiology of self-reported lifetime DSM–IV major depressive disorder in a population-based twin sample of female adolescents. *Journal of Child Psychology and Psychiatry, 44*, 988–96. ▶ page 181

Godin, G., Valois, P., Lepage, L. and Desharnais, R. (1992). Predictors of smoking behaviour: an application of Ajzen's theory of planned behavior. *British Journal of Addiction, 87*, 1335–43. ▶ page 248

Goetz, A.T. and Shackelford, T.K. (2009). Sexual conflict in humans: evolutionary consequences of asymmetric parental investment and paternity uncertainty. *Animal Biology, 59*, 449–56. ▶ page 56

Goetz, A.T., Shackelford, T.K., Starratt, V.G. and McKibbin, W.F. (2008). Intimate partner violence. In J.D. Duntley and T.K. Shackelford (eds), *Evolutionary Forensic Psychiatry.* New York: Oxford University Press, 65–78. ▶ page 76

Gokhale, A.A. (1995). Collaborative learning enhances critical thinking. *Journal of Technology Education, 7(1)*, 22–30. ▶ page 151

Gold, D.R., Rogacz, S., Bock, N., Tosteson, Tor-D., Baum, T.M., Speizer, F.E. and Czeisler, C.A. (1992). Rotating shift-work, sleep and accidents related to sleepiness in hospital nurses. *American Journal of Public Health, 82*, 1011–14. ▶ page 17

Gold, R.M. (1973). Hypothalamic obesity: the myth of the ventromedial nucleus. *Science, 182*, 488–90. ▶ pages 88, 89

Goldblatt, A. (1993). Behavioural needs of captive marine mammals. *Aquatic Mammals, 5*, 15–17. ▶ page 133

Goldhagen, D. (1996). *Hitler's Willing Executioners: Ordinary Germans and the Holocaust.* New York: Vintage Books. ▶ page 71

Gonzales, A.L. and Hancock, J.T. (2011). Mirror, mirror on my Facebook Wall: effects of exposure to Facebook on self-esteem. *Cyberpsychology, Behavior, and Social Networking, 14(1–2)*, 79–83. ▶ page 224

Goode, A., Mavromaras, A. and Smith, M. (2008). *Intergenerational Transmission of Healthy Eating Behaviour and the Role of Household Income.* Bonn: Institute for the Study of Labor. ▶ page 84

Goodman, W.K., Price, L.H., Rasmussen, S.A., Mazure, C., Fleischmann, R.L., Hill, C.L., Heninger, G.R. and Charney, D.S. (1989). The Yale-Brown Obsessive Compulsive Scale. I: development, use and reliability. *Archives of General Psychiatry, 46(11)*, 1006–11. ▶ page 207

Goodwin, R., Olfson, M., Feder, A., Fuentes, M., Pilowsky, D.J. and Weissman, M.M. (2001). Panic and suicidal ideation in primary care. *Depress Anxiety, 14*, 244–6. ▶ page 179

Gopnik, A. (2007). Cells that read minds? What the myth of mirror neurons gets wrong about the human brain. *See* http://www.slate.com/id/2165123/pagenum/all (accessed November 2008). ▶ page 159

Gopnik, A. and Meltzoff, A.N. (1997). *Words, Thoughts, and Theories.* Cambridge, MA: Bradford, MIT Press. ▶ page 158

Goren, C.G., Sarty, M. and Wu, P.Y.K. (1975). Visual following and pattern discrimination of face-like stimuli by newborn infants. *Pediatrics, 56(4)*, 544–9. ▶ page 40

Gottesman, I.I. (1991). *Schizophrenia Genesis.* New York: W.H. Freeman. ▶ page 166

Gottesman, I.I. and Reilly, J.L. (2003). Strengthening the evidence for genetic factors in schizophrenia (without abetting genetic discrimination). In M.F. Lenzenweger and J.M. Hooley (eds) *Principles of Experimental Psychopathology.* Washington, DC: American Psychological Association, 31–44. ▶ page 166

Gottfredson, L. (2003). Dissecting practical intelligence theory: its claims and its evidence. *Intelligence, 31*, 343–97. ▶ page 127

Gottman, J.M. and Levenson, R.W. (1992). Marital processes predictive of later dissolution: behavior, physiology and health. *Journal of Personality and Social Psychology, 63*, 221–33. ▶ page 51

Gould, R.A., Mueser, K.T., Bolton, E., Mays, V. and Goff, D. (2001). Cognitive therapy for psychosis in schizophrenia: an effect size analysis. *Schizophrenia Research, 48*, 335–42. ▶ page 173

Gould, S.J. (1981). *The Mismeasure of Man.* New York: Norton. ▶ page 125

Gournay K.J.M. (1989). *Agoraphobia: Current Perspectives on Theory and Treatment.* London: Routledge. ▶ page 197

Gow, K., Lang, T. and Chant, D. (2004). Fantasy proneness, paranormal beliefs and personality features in out-of-body experiences. *Contemporary Hypnosis, 21(3)*, 107–25. ▶ pages 264, 269

Grabe, S. and Hyde, J.S. (2006). Ethnicity and body dissatisfaction among women in the United States: a meta-analysis. *Psychological Bulletin, 132*, 622–40. ▶ page 92

Granrud, C.E. and Yonas, A. (1984). Infants' perception of pictorially specified interposition. *Journal of Experimental Child Psychology, 37*, 500–11. ▶ page 36

Gray, G. (1991). On the morality of speciesism. *The Psychologist, May*, 196–8. ▶ page 283

Gray, T. (1987). Educational experience and belief in paranormal phenomena. In F.B. Harrold and R.A. Eve (eds) *Cult Archaeology and Creationism: Understanding Pseudoscientific Beliefs About the Past.* Iowa City, IA: University of Iowa Press. ▶ page 260

Gredler, M. (1992). *Learning and Instruction Theory into Practice.* New York: Macmillan Publishing. ▶ page 149

Green, C.E. (1968). *Out-of-the-body Experiences.* London: Hamish Hamilton. ▶ page 268

Greenberg, B.D., George, M.S., Martin, J.D., Benjamin, J., Schlaepfer, T.E., Altemus, M., Wassermann, E.M., Post, R.M. and Murphy, D.L. (1997). Effect of prefrontal repetitive transcranial magnetic stimulation in obsessive compulsive disorder: a preliminary study. *American Journal of Psychiatry, 154*, 867–9. ▶ page 213

Greenberg, B.S. (1980). *Life on Television: Content Analysis of US TV Drama.* Norwood, NJ: Ablex. ▶ page 220

Greenfield, S. (2009). Facebook and Bebo risk 'infantilising' the human mind. *See* http://www.guardian.co.uk/uk/2009/feb/24/social-networking-site-changing-childrens-brains (accessed April 2011). ▶ page 225

Gregory, J., Lowe, S., Bates, C.J., Prentice, A., Jackson, L.V., Smithers, G., Wenlock, R., Farron, M. (2000). *National Diet and Nutrition Survey: Young People Aged 4–18 Years* (vol. 1). London: The Stationery Office. ▶ page 92

Gregory, R.L. (1974). *Concepts and Mechanisms of Perception.* London: Duckworth. ▶ page 32

Gregory, R.L. (1990). *Eye and Brain.* London: Weidenfeld and Nicolson. ▶ page 32

Gregory, S., Shawcross, C.R. and Gill, D. (1985). The Nottingham ECT study: a double-blind comparison of bilateral, unilateral and simulated ECT in depressive illness. *British Journal of Psychiatry, 146*, 520–4. ▶ page 183

Greiling, H. and Buss, D.M. (2000). Women's sexual strategies: the hidden dimension of extra-pair mating. *Personality and Individual Differences, 28*, 929–63. ▶ page 55

Greist, J.H., Marks, I.M., Baer, L., Kobak, K.A., Wenzel, K.W., Hirsch, M.J., Mantle, J.M. and Clary, C.M. (2002). Behavior therapy for obsessive compulsive disorder guided by a computer or by a clinician compared with relaxation as a control. *Journal of Clinical Psychiatry, 63*, 138–45. ▶ page 215

Greitemeyer, T. and Osswald, S. (2010). Effects of prosocial video games on prosocial behavior. *Journal of Personality and Social Psychology, 98(2)*, 211–21. ▶ pages 224, 225

Griffitt, W. and Guay, P. (1969). Object evaluation and conditioned affect. *Journal of Experimental Research in Personality, 4*, 1–8. ▶ page 49

Griffiths, M. (1994). The role of cognitive bias and skill in fruit machine gambling. *British Journal of Psychology, 85*, 351–69. ▶ page 240

Griffiths, M. (2009). Studies in the psychology of gambling: a personal overview, *Psychology Review, 15(1)*. ▶ page 242

Grilly, D.M. (2002). *Drugs and Human Behavior.* Boston: Allyn & Bacon. ▶ page 166

Gronfier, C., Wright, K.P. Jr., Kronauer, R.E. and Czeisler, C.A. (2007). Entrainment of the human circadian pacemaker to longer-than-24-hour days. *Proceedings of the National Academy of Science USA, 104(21)*, 9081–6. ▶ page 17

Groome D. (2006). *An Introduction to Cognitive Psychology: Processes and Disorders* (2nd edn). Hove: Psychology Press. ▶ page 43

Groth-Marnat, G. and Pegden, J.A. (1998). Personality correlates of paranormal belief: locus of control and sensation seeking. *Social Behavior and Personality, 26*, 291–6. ▶ page 265

Guinan, P. (2004). Therapeutic touch is not a Catholic hospital pastoral practice. *Linacre Quarterly, February*, 5–14. ▶ page 266

Guisinger, S. (2003). Adapted to flee famine: adding an evolutionary perspective on anorexia nervosa. *Psychological Review, 110(4)*, 745–61. ▶ page 94

Gupta, S. (1991). Effects of time of day and personality on intelligence test scores. *Personality and Individual Differences, 12(11)*, 1227–31. ▶ page 11

Guthrie, E. (1999). Psychodynamic interpersonal therapy. *Advances in Psychiatric Treatment, 5*, 135–45. ▶ page 187

Hajek, P., Taylor, T. and McRobbie, H. (2010). The effect of stopping smoking on perceived stress levels. *Addiction, 105(8)*, 1466–71. ▶ page 245

Hall, J.A. and Levin, S. (1980). Affect and verbal-non-verbal discrepancy in schizophrenic and non-schizophrenic family communication. *British Journal of Psychiatry, 137*, 78–92. ▶ page 169

Halmi, K.A., Sunday, R.R., Strober, M., Kaplan, A., Woodside, D.B., Fichter, M., Treasure, J., Berrentini, W.H. and Kaye, W.H (2000). Perfectionism in anorexia nervosa: variation by clinical subtype, obsessionality, and pathological eating behavior. *American Journal of Psychiatry, 157*, 1799–1805. ▶ page 93

Hamilton, J.T. (1998). *Television Violence and Public Policy.* Ann Arbor, MI: University of Michigan Press. ▶ page 228

Hammen, C. (1997). *Depression.* Hove: Psychology Press. ▶ pages 180, 182, 183, 185, 186

Hammen, C.L., and Krantz, S. (1976). Effect of success and failure in depressive cognitions. *Journal of Abnormal Psychology, 85*, 577–86. ▶ page 183

Hansard (2007). *See* http://www.publications.parliament.uk/pa/cm200607/cmhansrd/cm071024/text/71024w0028.htm (accessed December 2008). ▶ page 276

Hansel, C.E.M. (1989). *The Search for Psychic Power: ESP and Parapsychology Revisited.* Amherst, NY: Prometheus Books. ▶ page 258

Haracz, J.L. (1982). The dopamine hypothesis: an overview of studies with schizophrenic patients. *Schizophrenia Bulletin, 8(3)*, 438–69. ▶ page 167

Harcourt, A.H. (1992). Coalitions and alliances: are primates more complex than non-primates? In A.H. Harcourt and F.B.M. de Waal (eds) *Coalitions and Alliances in Human and Other Animals.* Oxford: Oxford University Press. ▶ page 134

Hare, L., Bernard, P., Sanchez, F., Baird, P., Vilain, E., Kennedy, T. and Harley, V. (2009). Androgen receptor repeat length polymorphism associated with male-to-female transsexualism. *Biological Psychiatry, 65(1)*, 93–6. ▶ page 110

Harer, M.D. and Steffensmeier, D.J. (1996). Race and prison violence. *Criminology, 34*, 323–55. ▶ page 71

Harrington, R.C., Fudge, H., Rutter, M.L., Bredenkamp, D., Groothues, C. and Pridham, J. (1993). Child and adult depression: a test of continuities with data from a family study. *British Journal of Psychiatry, 162*, 627–33. ▶ page 180

Harris, C.R. (2003). A review of sex differences in sexual jealousy, including self-report data, psychophysiological responses, interpersonal violence, and morbid jealousy. *Personality and Social Psychology Review, 7*, 102–28. ▶ page 57

Harris, J.R. (1995). Where is the child's environment? A group socialization theory of development. *Psychological Review, 102*, 458–89. ▶ page 140

Harrison, G., Glazebrook, C., Brewin, J., Cantwell, R., Dalkin, T., Fox, R., Jones, P. and Medley, I. (1997). Increased incidence of psychotic disorders in migrants from the Caribbean to the United Kingdom. *Psychol Med, 27(4)*, 799–806. ▶ page 165

Hatfield, E. and Walster, G.W. (1981). *A New Look at Love.* Reading, MA: Addison-Wesley. ▶ page 290

Haynie, D. (2003). Contexts of risk? Explaining the link between girls' pubertal development and their delinquency involvement. *Social Forces, 82(1)*, 355–97. ▶ page 59

Hays, R.B. (1985). A longitudinal study of friendship development. *Journal of Personality and Social Psychology*, 48, 909–24. ▶ page 49

Hazan, C. and Shaver, P.R. (1987). Romantic love conceptualized as an attachment process. *Journal of Personality and Social Psychology*, 5, 511–524. ▶ page 96

Heimberg, R.G., Mennin, D.S. and MacAndrew, S.J. (1999). Computer-assisted rating scales for social phobia: reliability and validity may not be what they appear to be. *Depression and Anxiety*, 9, 44–5. ▶ page 193

Heisenberg, W. (1927). Über den anschlauchichen Inhalt der quantentheoretischen Kinetik und Mechanik. *Zeitschrift für Physik*, 43, 172–98. ▶ page 275

Hemphill, S. and Sanson, A. (2001). Matching parenting to child temperament. *Family Matters*, 59, 42–7. ▶ page 130

Herbert, J.D., Bellack, A.D. and Hope, D.A. (1991). Concurrent validity of the social and phobia anxiety inventory. *Journal of Psychopathology and Behavioural Assessment*, 13(4), 357–68. ▶ page 192

Hergovich, A. (2003). Field dependence, suggestibility and belief in paranormal phenomena. *Personality and Individual Differences*, 34, 195–209. ▶ page 264

Herman, C.P. and Mack, D. (1975). Restrained and unrestrained eating. *Journal of Personality*, 43, 646–60. ▶ page 86

Herman, C.P. and Polivy, J. (1984). A boundary model for the regulation of eating. In A.J. Stunkard and E. Stellar (eds) *Eating and its Disorders*. New York: Raven Press, 141–56. ▶ page 86

Herrnstein, R.J. and Murray, C. (1994). *The Bell Curve: Intelligence and Class Structure in American Life*. New York: The Free Press. ▶ page 140

Herxheimer, A. and Petrie, K.J. (2002). Melatonin for the prevention and treatment of jet lag. *The Cochrane Database of Systematic Reviews 2002*, Issue 2, Art. No. CD001520. ▶ page 17

Heyes, C.M. (1998). Theory of mind in non-human primates. *Behavioral and Brain Sciences*, 21(1), 101–34. ▶ page 135

Higgins, L. and Gray, W. (1999). What do anti-dieting programs achieve? A review of research. *Australian Journal of Nutrition and Dietetics*, 56(3), 128–36. ▶ pages 86, 87

Hildebrandt, D.E., Feldman, S.E., and Ditrichs, R.A. (1973). Rules, models, and self-reinforcement in children. *Journal of Personality and Social Psychology*, 25, 1–5. ▶ page 117

Hill, D. (1986). Tardive dyskinesia: a worldwide epidemic of irreversible brain damage. In N. Eisenberg and D. Glasgow (eds) *Current Issues in Clinical Psychology*. Aldershot: Gower. ▶ page 171

Hill, K. and Kaplan, H. (1988). Trade-offs in male and female reproductive strategies among the Ache: Part 1 – Males. In L. Betzig, P. Turke and M. Borgerhoff Mulder (eds) *Human Reproductive Behavior*. Cambridge: Cambridge University Press, 277–89. ▶ pages 107, 137

Hill, L., Craig, I.W., Chorney, M.J., Chorney, K., and Plomin, R. (1999). IGF2R and cognitive ability in children. *Molecular Psychiatry*, 4(suppl. 108). ▶ page 138

Hiller, W., von Bose, M., Dichtl, G. and Agerer, D. (1990). Reliability of checklist-guided diagnoses for DSM-III-R affective and anxiety disorders. *Journal of Affective Disorders*, 20, 235–47. ▶ page 192

Hines, T. (2003). *Pseudoscience and the paranormal* (vol. 2). New York: Prometheus Books. ▶ pages 256, 259, 266, 267

Hiroto, D.S., and Seligman, M.E.P. (1975). Generality of learned helplessness in man. *Journal of Personality and Social Psychology*, 31, 311–27. ▶ page 183

Hirsch, S., Bowen, J. and Enami, J. (1996). A one-year prospective study of the effect of life events and medication in the aetiology of schizophrenic relapse. *British Journal of Psychiatry*, 168, 49–56. ▶ page 168

Ho, D.Y.F. (1986). Chinese patterns of socialization: a critical review. In M. Bond (ed.) *The Psychology of the Chinese People*. Hong Kong: Oxford University Press, 1–37. ▶ page 60

Hoag, H. (2008). Brains apart: the real difference between the sexes. *New Scientist*, 16 July, 28–31. ▶ page 104

Hobson, J.A. and McCarley, R.W. (1977). The brain as a dream state generator: an activation-synthesis hypothesis of the dream process. *American Journal of Psychiatry*, 134, 1335–48. ▶ page 13

Hobson, P.R. (1984). Early childhood autism and the question of egocentrism. *Journal of Autism and Developmental Disorders*, 14, 85–104. ▶ page 157

Hobson, R.F. (1985). *Forms of Feeling*. London: Tavistock. ▶ page 186

Hodges, K.K., Brandt, D.A. and Kline, J. (1981). Competence, guilt and victimization: sex differences in ambition of causality in television dramas. *Sex Roles*, 7, 537–46. ▶ page 116

Hodgkinson, P.E., Mcivor, L. and Philips, M. (1985). Patients' assaults on staff in a psychiatric hospital: a two-year retrospective study. *Medicine, Science and the Law*, 25, 288–94. ▶ page 70

Hoek, H.W., van Harten, P.N. and van Hoeken, D. (1998). Lack of relation between culture and anorexia nervosa – results of an incidence study on Curacao. *New England Journal of Medicine*, 338(17), 1231–2. ▶ page 93

Hoffman, L. (1998). The effects of mother's employment on the family and the child. *See* http://parenthood.library.wisc.edu/Hoffman/Hoffman.html (accessed June 2012). ▶ page 115

Hofsten, C. von, Kellman, P. and Putaansuu, J. (1992). Young infants' sensitivity to motion parallax. *Infant Behaviour and Development*, 15, 245–64. ▶ page 36

Hogarth L., Dickinson A., Duka, T. (2010). The associative basis of cue-elicited drug taking in humans. *Psychopharmacology*, 208, 337–51. ▶ page 242

Hogarty, G.E., Anderson, C.M., Reiss, D.J., Kornblith, S.J., Greenwald, D.P., Ulrich, R.F. and Carter, M. (1991). Family psychoeducation, social skills training and maintenance chemotherapy in the aftercare treatment of schizophrenia. II: two-year effects of a controlled study on relapse and adjustment. Environmental-Personal Indicators in the Course of Schizophrenia (EPICS) research group. *Archives of General Psychiatry*, 48, 340–7. ▶ page 169

Hoge, R.D. Guerra, N. and Boxer, P. (2008). *Treating the juvenile offender*. New York: The Guilford Press. ▶ page 157

Holden, J.M., Long, J. and MacLurg, J. (2006). Out-of-body experiences: all in the brain? *Journal of Near-Death Studies*, 25(2), 99–107. ▶ page 269

Hollander, E., Buchalter, A.J. and DeCaria, C.M. (2000). Pathological gambling. *The Psychiatric Clinics of North America*, 23(3), 629–42. ▶ page 250

Holmes, E., James, E., Kilford, E., and Deeprose, C. (2010). Key steps in developing a cognitive vaccine against traumatic flashbacks: visuospatial Tetris versus verbal pub quiz. *PLoS ONE*, 5(11). ▶ page 225

Holt, P.A. and Stone, G.L. (1988). Needs, coping strategies and coping outcomes associated with long-distance relationships. *Journal of College Student Development*, 29, 136–41. ▶ page 53

Honda, Y., Asake, A., Tanaka, Y. and Juji, T. (1983). Discrimination of narcolepsy by using genetic markers and HLA. *Sleep Research*, 1(2), 254. ▶ page 26

Honorton C. (1974). Psi-conducive state of awareness. In J. White (ed.) *Psychic Exploration: A Challenge for Science*. New York: G.P. Putnam's Sons. ▶ page 258

Honorton, C. (1985). Meta-analysis of psi Ganzfeld research: a response to Hyman. *Journal of Parapsychology*, 49, 51–91. ▶ page 258

Honorton, C., Berger, R.E., Varvoglis, M.P., Quant, M., Derr, P., Schechter, E.I. and Ferrari, D.C. (1990). Psi communication in the ganzfeld: experiments with an automated testing system and a comparison with a meta-analysis of earlier studies. *Journal of Parapsychology*, 54, 99–139. ▶ page 259

Honorton, C., Ferrari, D.C. and Bem, D.J. (1992). Extraversion and ESP performance: a meta-analysis and a new confirmation. In L.A. Henkel and G.R. Schmeidler (eds) *Research in Parapsychology*. Metuchen, NJ: Scarecrow Press, 35–8. ▶ page 264

Hopkins, B., Jacobs, D.M. and Westrum, R. (1992). *Unusual Personal Experiences: An Analysis of Data from Three National Surveys Conducted by the Roper Organisation*. Nevada: Bigelow Holding Corporation. ▶ page 255

Hord, D.J. and Thompson, R. (1983). Cognitive performance change during a six-hour hike at low temperature in simulated rain, at controlled walking rates. *See* http://stinet.dtic.mil/cgi-bin/GetTRDoc?AD=ADA138358&Location=U2&doc=GetTRDoc.pdf (accessed August 2008). ▶ page 11

Horn, J.M., Loehlin, J.C. and Willerman, L. (1979). Intellectual resemblance among adoptive and biological relatives: the Texas adoption project. *Behaviour Genetics*, 9, 177–207. ▶ page 138

Horne, J. (1988). *Why we Sleep: The Functions of Sleep in Humans and Other Mammals*. Oxford: Oxford University Press. ▶ page 23

Horne, J.A., and Minard, A. (1985). Sleep and sleepiness following a behaviourally 'active' day. *Ergonomics*, 28, 567–75. ▶ page 21

Hornik, R., Jacobsohn, L., Orwin, R., Piesse, A. and Kalton, G. (2008). Effects of the National Youth Anti-Drug Media Campaign on youths. *American Journal of Public Health*, 98(12), 2229–36. ▶ pages 246, 247

Horrobin, D.F. (1998). Schizophrenia: the illness that made us human. *Medical Hypotheses*, 50, 269–88. ▶ page 137

Horton, D. and Wohl, R.R. (1956). Mass communication and para-social interaction, *Psychiatry*, 19, 215–29. ▶ page 230

Horton, R. (2000). Genetically modified food: consternation, confusion and crack up. *Medical Journal of Australia*, 172, 148–9. ▶ page 277

Horvath, A.O. and Bedi, R.P. (2002). The alliance. In J.C. Norcross (ed.) *Psychotherapy Relationships that Work: Therapist Contributions and Responsiveness to Patients*. New York: Oxford, 37–69. ▶ page 187

House of Lords (2002). Select Committee on Animals In Scientific Procedures. *See* http://www.publications.parliament.uk/pa/ld/ldanimal.htm (accessed December 2008). ▶ page 283

Hovland, C.I., Janis, I.L. and Kelley, H.H. (1953). *Communication and Persuasion: Psychological Studies of Opinion Change*. New Haven: Yale University Press. ▶ page 226

Hubel, D.H. and Wiesel, T.N. (1970). The period of susceptibility to the physiological effects of unilateral eye closure in kittens. *Journal of Physiology*, 206, 419–36. ▶ page 37

Hudson, J.I., Hiripi, E., Pope, H.G. and Kessler, R.C. (2007). The prevalence and correlates of eating disorders in the national comorbidity survey replication. *Biological Psychiatry*, 61, 348–58. ▶ page 99

Hudson, W. (1960). Pictorial depth perception in subcultural groups in Africa. *Journal of Social Psychology*, 52, 183–208. ▶ page 38

Huesmann, L.R. and Moise, J. (1996). Media violence: a demonstrated public threat to children. *Harvard Mental Health Letter*, 72(12), 5–7. ▶ page 222

Huff, C.R. (1998). *Criminal Behavior of Gang Members and At-risk Youth*. Research Preview. ▶ page 70

Hughes, M. (1975). *Egocentrism in Preschool Children*. Unpublished PhD thesis, University of Edinburgh. ▶ page 147

Hulshoff Pol, H.E., Cohen-Kettenis, P.T., Van Haren, E.N., Peper, J.S., Brans, R.G., Cahn, W., Schnack,

H.G., Gooren, L.J. and Kahn, R.S. (2006). Changing your sex changes your brain: influences of testosterone and estrogen on adult human brain structure. *European Journal of Endocrinology, 155(suppl. 1)*, S107–S114. ▶ page 111

Hume, S. (1992). Best ads don't rely on celebrities. *Advertising Age, 25 May*, 20. ▶ pages 227, 229

Humphrey, J.H. (1973). *Stress Education for College Students*. Hauppauge, NY: Nova. ▶ page 201

Humphrey, N. (1976). The social function of intellect. In R. Bryne and A. Whiten (eds) (1988) *Machiavellian Intelligence*. Oxford: Oxford University Press. ▶ page 136

Humphreys, G.W. and Riddoch, M.J. (1987). The fractionation of visual agnosia. In G.W. Humphreys and M.J. Riddoch (eds) *Visual Object Processing: A Cognitive Neuropsychololgical Approach*. Hove: Lawrence Erlbaum. ▶ page 43

Hunt, C. and Andrews, G. (2007). Drop-out rate as a performance indicator in psychotherapy. *Acta Psychiatrica Scandinavica, 85(4)*, 275–8. ▶ page 187

Huntingford, F.A. and Turner, A.K. (1987). *Animal Conflict*. London: Chapman and Hall. ▶ page 78

Huppert, J.D. and Franklin, M.E. (2005). Cognitive behavioral therapy for obsessive compulsive disorder: an update. *Current Psychiatry Reports, 7*, 268–73. ▶ page 215

Hurt, R.D., Croghan, G.A., Beede, S.D., Wolter, T.D., Croghan, I.T. and Patten, C.A. (2000). Nicotine patch therapy in 101 adolescent smokers: efficacy, withdrawal symptom relief, and carbon monoxide and plasma cotinine levels. *Archives of Pediatric Adolescent Medicine, 154*, 31–7. ▶ page 241

Hussain, S.S. (2002). *Electroconvulsive Therapy in Depressive Illness that has not Responded to Drug Treatment*. MPhil thesis, University of Edinburgh. ▶ page 185

Huston, A.C. (1985). The development of sex typing: themes from recent research. *Developmental Review, 5*, 1–17. ▶ page 113

Hutchings, B. and Mednick, S.A. (1975). Registered criminality in the adoptive and biological parents of registered male criminal adoptees. In R.R. Fieve, D. Rosenthal and H. Brill (eds) *Genetic Research in Psychiatry*. Baltimore, MD: Johns Hopkins University Press, 105–22. ▶ page 74

Hutson, M. (2008). Magical thinking. *Psychology Today, 1 March. See* www.psychologytoday.com/articles/200802/magical-thinking (accessed April 2011). ▶ page 263

Hyman, R. (1985). The ganzfeld psi experiment: a critical appraisal. *The Journal of Parapsychology, 49(1)*, 3–50. ▶ page 258

Iacoboni, M., Molnar-Szakacs, I., Gallese, V., Buccino, G., Mazziotta, J.C. and Rizzolatti, G. (2005). Grasping the intentions of others with one's own mirror neuron system. *PLoS Biology 3, e79*, 1–7. ▶ page 158

Imperato-McGinley, J., Guerro, L., Gautier, T. and Peterson, R.E. (1974). Steroid 5-reductase deficiency in man: an inherited form of male pseudohermaphroditism. *Science, 186*, 1213–16. ▶ page 104

Inhelder, B., Sinclair, H. and Bovet, M. (1974). *Learning and the Development of Cognition*. London: Routledge. ▶ page 147

Irons, W. (2004). An evolutionary critique of the created co-creator concept. *Zygon: Journal of Religion and Science, 39*, 773–90. ▶ page 78

Irwin, H.J. (1985). A study of the measurement and the correlates of paranormal belief. *Journal of the American Society for Psychical Research, 79*, 301–26. ▶ page 269

Irwin, H.J. and Green, M.J. (1999). Schizotypal processes and belief in the paranormal: a multidimensional study. *European Journal of Parapsychology, 14*, 1–15. ▶ page 265

Irwin, J. and Cressey, R. (1962). Thieves, convicts, and the inmate culture. *Social Problems, 10*, 142–55. ▶ page 70

Jacobson, N.S., Christensen, A., Prince, S.E., Cordova, J., and Eldridge, K. (2000). Integrative behavioral couple therapy: an acceptance-based, promising new treatment for couple discord, *Journal of Consulting and Clinical Psychology, 68*, 351–5. ▶ page 51

Jahoda, G. and McGurk, H. (1974). The development of pictorial depth perception: the role of figural elevation. *British Journal of Psychology, 65(3)*, 367–76. ▶ page 38

James, L.E. (2004). Meeting Mr Famer versus meeting a farmer: specific effects of ageing on learning proper names. *Psychology and Aging, 19(3)*, 515–22. ▶ page 294

Jankowiak, W. and Fischer, E. (1992). Romantic love: a cross-cultural perspective, *Ethnology, 31(2)*, 149–55. ▶ page 61

Jansen, K.L.R. (1993). Non-medical use of ketamine. *British Medical Journal, 298*, 4708–9. ▶ page 268

Jansen, K.L.R. (2009). *The Ketamine Model of the Near Death Experience: A Central Role for the NMDA Receptor. See* http://leda.lycaeum.org/Documents/The_Ketamine_Model_of_the_Near_Death_Experience.9264.shtml (accessed January 2009). ▶ page 268

Jenicke, M.A. (1992). New developments in treatment of obsessive compulsive disorder. In A. Tasman and M.B. Riba (eds) *Review of Psychiatry* (vol. 11). Washington, DC: American Psychiatric Press. ▶ page 208

Jenkins, J.H. and Karno, M. (1992). The meaning of expressed emotion: theoretical issues raised by cross-cultural research. *American Journal of Psychiatry, 149*, 9–21. ▶ page 169

Jeste, D., Lacro, J.P., Nguyen, H.A., Petersen, M.E., Rockwell, E. and Sewell, D.D. (1999). Lower incidence of tardive dyskinesia with risperidone compared with haloperidol in older patients. *Journal of the American Geriatric Society, 47*, 716–9. ▶ page 171

Jiang, S. and Fisher-Giorlando, M. (2002). Inmate misconduct: a test of the deprivation, importation and situational models. *The Prison Journal, 82*, 335–58. ▶ page 71

Johansson, G. (1973). Visual perception of biological motion and a model for its analysis. *Perception and Psychophysics, 14*, 201–11. ▶ page 35

John, L.K., Loewenstein, G. and Prelec, D. (2012). Measuring the prevalence of questionable research practices with incentives for truth-telling. *Psychological Science* (in press). ▶ page 276

Johnson, C. and Scott, B. (1976). *Eyewitness Testimony and Suspect Identification as a Function of Arousal, Sex of Witness, and Scheduling of Interrogation*. Paper presented at the annual convention of the American Psychological Association, Washington, DC, September 1976. ▶ page 279

Johnson, K.R. and Holmes, B.M. (2009). Contradictory messages: a content analysis of Hollywood-produced romantic comedy feature films. *Communication Quarterly, 57(3)*, 352–73. ▶ page 61

Johnson, R. and Downing, L. (1979). Deindividuation and valence of cues: effects on prosocial and antisocial behavior. *Journal of Personality and Social Psychology, 37*, 1532–8. ▶ page 69

Johnson, T. (1987). Premenstrual syndrome as a western culture-specific disorder. *Culture, Medicine, and Psychiatry, 11*, 337–56. ▶ page 13

Johnson, V.P., Swayze II, V.W., Sato, Y. and Andreasen, N.C. (1996). Fetal alcohol syndrome: craniofacial and central nervous system manifestations. *American Journal of Medical Genetics, 61(4)*, 329–39. ▶ page 137

Johnston, J. and Ettema, J.S. (1982). *Positive Images: Breaking Stereotypes with Children's Television*. Beverly Hills, CA: Sage. ▶ page 220

Johnston, L.D., O'Malley, P.M., Bachman, J.B., Schulenberg, J.E. and Yamaguchi, R. (2002). Youth, Education, and Society (YES!) results on school policies and programs: overview of key findings, 2001. Ann Arbor, MI: Institute for Social Research. ▶ page 247

Joiner T.E. Jr., Alfano, M.S. and Metalsky, G.I. (1992). When depression breeds contempt: reassurance-seeking, self-esteem, and rejection of depressed college students by their room-mates. *Journal of Abnormal Psychology, 101*, 165–73. ▶ page 182

Jones, A.M. and Buckingham, J.T. (2005). Self-esteem as a moderator of the effect of social comparisons on women's body image. *Journal of Social and Clinical Psychology, 24(8)*, 1164–87. ▶ page 92

Jones, D.C. and Crawford, J.K. (2006). The peer appearance culture during childhood: gender and body mass variation. *Journal of Youth and Adolescence, 35*, 257–69. ▶ page 92

Jones, M.K. and Menzies, R.G. (1998). Danger ideation reduction therapy (DIRT) for obsessive compulsive washers: a controlled trial. *Behaviour Research and Therapy, 365*, 959–70. ▶ page 215

Jones, W.H., Russell, D.W. and Nickel, T.W. (1977). Belief in the paranormal scale: an objective instrument to measure belief in magical phenomena and causes. *Catalog of Selected Documents in Psychology, 7*, 100 (MS. No. 1577). Washington, DC: American Psychological Association. ▶ page 261

Jorgensen, G. (2006). Kohlberg and Gilligan: duet or duel? *Journal of Moral Education, 35(2)*, 179–96. ▶ page 153

Joronen, K. and Åstedt-Kurki, P. (2005). Adolescents' experiences of familial involvement in their peer relations and school attendance. *Primary Health Care Research & Development, 6(3)*, 190–8. ▶ page 299

Joseph, J. (2004). Schizophrenia and heredity: why the emperor has no genes. In J. Read, L. Mosher and R. Bentall (eds) *Models of Madness: Psychological, Social and Biological Approaches to Schizophrenia*. Andover: Taylor & Francis, 67–83. ▶ pages 166, 167

Josephson, W.L. (1987). Television violence and children's aggression: testing the priming, social script and disinhibition predictions. *Journal of Personality and Social Psychology, 53*, 882–90. ▶ page 223

Joynson, R.B. (1989). *The Burt Affair*. London: Routledge. ▶ page 276

Jung, H.H., Kim, C.H., Chang, J.H., Park, Y.G., Chung, S.S. and Chang, J.W. (2006). Bilateral anterior cingulotomy for refractory obsessive compulsive disorder: long-term follow-up results. *Stereotactic and Functional Neurosurgery, 84*, 184–9. ▶ page 213

Kagan, J. (1994). *Galen's Prophecy: Temperament in Human Nature*. New York: Basic Books. ▶ page 195

Kahn, R.J., McNair, D.M., Lipman, R.S., Covi, L., Rickels, K., Downing, R., Fisher, S. and Frankenthaler, L.M. (1986). Imipramine and chlordiazepoxide in depressive and anxiety disorders. II: efficacy in anxious outpatients. *Archives of General Psychiatry, 43*, 79–85. ▶ page 199

Kahne, J., Middaugh, E. and Evans, C. (2008). The civic potential of video games: an occasional paper of the John D. and Catherine T. MacArthur Foundation Digital Media and Learning Program. *See* http://www.civicsurvey.org/White_paper_link_text.pdf (accessed April 2011). ▶ page 224

Kahneman, D. and Tversky, A. (1972). Subjective probability: a judgement of representativeness. *Psychology Review, 93*, 136–53. ▶ page 261

Kalafi, Y. and Torabi, M. (1996). The role of parental 'expressed emotion' in relapse of schizophrenia. *Iranian Journal of Medical Science, 21(1&2)*, 46. ▶ page 168

Kalb, C. (2008). Plight of the teenage insomniacs. *Newsweek, 151(14)*, 10. ▶ page 24

Kamin, L.J. (1977). *The Science and Politics of IQ*. Harmondsworth: Penguin. ▶ page 276

Kamin, L.J. and Goldberger, A.S. (2002). Twin studies in behavioral research: a skeptical view. *Theoretical Population Biology, 61*, 83–95. ▶ page 139

Kandel, D.B. and Wu, P. (1995). The contributions of mothers and fathers to the intergenerational transmission of cigarette smoking n adolescence. *Journal of Research on Adolescence, 5(2)*, 225–52. ▶ **page 242**

Kanwisher, N. and Yovel, G. (2006). The fusiform face area: a cortical region specialised for the perception of faces. *Philosophical Transactions Royal Society B, 361*, 2109–28. ▶ **page 41**

Kapur, S. and Remington, G. (2001). Dopamine D$_2$ receptors and their role in atypical antipsychotic action: still necessary and may even be sufficient. *Biological Psychiatry, 50*, 873–83. ▶ **page 170**

Karabenick , S.A. (1983). Sex-relevance of content and influenceability: Sistrunk and McDavid revisited. *Personality and Social Psychology Bulletin, 9(2)*, 243–52. ▶ **page 227**

Karagulla, S. (1950). Evaluation of electric convulsive therapy as compared with conservative methods of treatment in depressive states. *Journal of Mental Science, 96*, 1060–91. ▶ **page 170**

Karasz, A., (2005). Cultural differences in conceptual models of depression. *Social Science and Medicine, 60*, 1625–35. ▶ **page 179**

Karayiorgou, M., Altemus, M., Galke, B.L., Goldman, D., Murphy, D.L., Ott, J. and Gogos, J.L. (1997). Genotype determining low catechol-O-methyltransferase activity as a risk factor for obsessive compulsive disorder. *Proceedings of the National Academy of Science, 94*, 4572–5. ▶ **page 208**

Karcher, M.J. and Finn, L. (2005). How connectedness contributes to experimental smoking among rural youth: developmental and ecological analyses. *The Journal of Primary Prevention, 26*, 25–36. ▶ **page 243**

Karpinski, A.C. (2009). *A Description of Facebook Use and Academic Performance Among Undergraduate and Graduate Students*. Paper presented at the Annual Meeting of the American Educational Research Association, San Diego, California. ▶ **page 224**

Kassel, J.D., Greenstein, J.E., Evatt, D.P., Wardle, M.C., Yates, M.C., Veilleux, J.C. et al. (2007). Smoking topography in response to denicotinized and high-yield nicotine cigarettes in adolescent smokers. *Journal of Adolescent Health, 40*, 54–60. ▶ **page 240**

Katz, J. (2008). Are you crazy enough to succeed? Obsessive and compulsive behaviors can make you – or break you. *Men's Health. See* http://www.msnbc.msn.com/id/25415322 (accessed March 2009). ▶ **page 215**

Katzelnick, D.J., Kobak, K.A., Greist, J.H., Jefferson, J.W., Mantle, J.M., and Serlin, R.C. (1995). Sertraline for social phobia: a double-blind, placebo-controlled crossover study. *American Journal of Psychiatry, 152*, 1368–71. ▶ **page 199**

Kaye, W.H., Bailer, U.F., Frank, G.K., Wagner, A. and Hentry, S.E. (2005). Brain imaging of serotonin after recovery from anorexia and bulimia nervosa. *Physiology and Behavior, 86(1–2)*, 15–17. ▶ **page 94**

Kaye, W.H., Nagata, T., Weltzin, T.E., Hsu, L.K.G., Sokol, M.S., McConaha, C., Plotnikov, K.H., Weise, J. and Deep, D. (2001). Double-blind placebo-controlled administration of fluoxetine in restricting- and restricting-purging-type anorexia nervosa. *Biological Psychiatry, 49*, 644. ▶ **pages 95, 98**

Keel, P.K. and Klump, K.L. (2003). Are eating disorders culture-bound syndromes? Implications for conceptualizing their etiology. *Psychological Bulletin, 129(5)*, 747–69. ▶ **page 97**

Keller, M.B., Klein, D.N., Hirschfeld, R.M., Kocsis, J.H., McCullough, J.P., Miller, I., First, M.B., Holzer III, C.P., Keitner, G.I. and Marin, D.B. (1995). Results of the DSM-IV mood disorders field trial. *American Journal of Psychiatry, 152*, 843–9. ▶ **page 179**

Kendler, K.S., Karkowski, L.M. and Prescott, C.A. (1999). Fears and phobias: reliability and heritability. *Psychological Medicine, 29(3)*, 539–53. ▶ **page 193**

Kendler, K.S., Kessler, R.C. and Walters, E.E. (1995). Stressful life events, genetic liability and onset of an episode of major depression in women. *American Journal of Psychiatry, 152*, 833–42. ▶ **pages 180, 182**

Kendler, K.S., Neale, M.C. and Kessler, R.C. (1992). Major depression and generalized anxiety disorder. Same genes, (partly) different environments? *Archives of General Psychiatry, 49*, 716–22. ▶ **page 181**

Kendler, K.S., Neale, M.C., Kessler, R.C., Heath, A.C. and Eaves, L.J. (1992). The genetic epidemiology of phobias in women: the interrelationship of agoraphobia, social phobia, situational phobia, and simple phobia. *Archives of General Psychiatry, 49*, 273–81. ▶ **page 195**

Kenrick, D.T., Keefe, R.C., Gabrielidis, C. and Cornelius, J.S. (1996). Adolescents' age preferences for dating partners: support for an evolutionary model of life-history strategies. *Child Development, 67*, 1499–511. ▶ **page 55**

Kern, P.A., Ong, J.M., Saffari, B. and Carty, J. (1990). The effects of weight loss on the activity and expression of adipose-tissue lipoprotein lipase in very obese humans. *New England Journal of Medicine, 322*, 1053–9. ▶ **page 87**

Kessler, R.C., McGonagle, K.A., Zhao, S., Nelson, C.B., Hughes, M., Eshleman, S., Wittchen, H.-U. and Kendler, K.S. (1994). Lifetime and 12-month prevalence of DSM-III-R psychiatric disorders in the United States: results from the National Comorbidity Study. *Archives of General Psychiatry, 51*, 8–19. ▶ **page 165**

Kety, S.S., Rosenthal, D., Wender, P.H. and Schulsinger, F. (1968). The types and prevalence of mental illness in the biological and adoptive families of adopted people with schizophrenia. In D. Rosenthal and S.S. Kety (eds) *The Transmission of Schizophrenia*. New York: Pergamon Press. ▶ **page 167**

Khorasani, A.S., Fadardi, J.A., Cox, W.M. and Sharif, J.T. (2007). Effect of practice versus information on the visual illusion. *Neuroscience Bulletin, 23(1)*, 30–4. ▶ **page 33**

Kiddoo, D., Klassen, T.P., Lang, M.E., Friesen, C., Russell, K., Spooner, C. and Vandermeer, B. (2006). *The Effectiveness of Different Methods of Toilet Training for Bowel and Bladder Control. Evidence Report/Technology Assessment No. 147*. Rockville, MD: Agency for Healthcare Research and Quality. ▶ **page 131**

Kiecolt-Glaser, J.K., Garner, W., Speicher, C.E., Penn, G.M., Holliday, J. and Glaser, R. (1984). Psychosocial modifiers of immunocompetence in medical students. *Psychosomatic Medicine, 46*, 7–14. ▶ **pages 25, 266, 279**

Kim, C.H., Cheon, K.A., Koo, M.-S., Ryu, Y.H., Chang, J.W., and Lee, H.S. (2007). Dopamine transporter in the basal ganglia in obsessive compulsive disorder, measured with IPT SPECT before and after treatment with serotonin re-uptake inhibitors. *Neuropsychobiology, 55*, 3–4. ▶ **page 209**

Kim, S.W. and Grant, J.E. (2001). An open naltrexone treatment study in pathological gambling disorder. *International Clinical Psychopharmacology, 16(5)*, 285–9. ▶ **page 251**

Kim, S.W., Dysken, M.W. and Kuskowski, M. (1990). The Yale-Brown Obsessive Compulsive Scale: a reliability and validity study. *Psychiatry Research, 34*, 99–106. ▶ **page 207**

Kim, U. and Berry, J.W. (eds) (1993). *Indigenous Psychologies: Research and Experience in Cultural Context*. London: Sage. ▶ **page 61**

Kimura, D. (1999). *Sex and Cognition*. Cambridge, MA: MIT Press. ▶ **page 119**

Kindt , M., Soeter, M. and Vervliet, B. (2009). Beyond extinction: erasing human fear responses and preventing the return of fear. *Nature Neuroscience, 12*, 256–8. ▶ **page 199**

Kingdon, D.G. and Kirschen, H. (2006). Who does not get cognitive behavioural therapy for schizophrenia when therapy is readily available? *Psychiatric Services, 57*, 1792–4. ▶ **page 173**

Kirkpatrick, L.A. and Hazan, C. (1994). Attachment styles and close relationships: a four-year prospective study. *Personal Relationships, 1(2)*, 123–42. ▶ **page 59**

Kirsch, I., Deacon, B.J., Huedo-Medina, T.B., Scoboria, A., Moore, T.J. and Johnson, B.T. (2008). Initial severity and antidepressant benefits: a meta-analysis of data submitted to the food and drug administration, *PLoS Medicine, 5(2)*, e45 EP. ▶ **page 185**

Klag, S. (2006). Self-determination theory and the theory of planned behaviour applied to substance abuse treatment in a therapeutic community setting. *See* http://www4.gu.edu.au:8080/adt-root/public/adt-QGU20070112.144521/index.html (accessed April 2011). ▶ **page 249**

Kleiman, D.G. (1989). Reintroduction of captive mammals for conservation. *Bioscience, 39*, 152–61. ▶ **page 132**

Klein, D.F., Zitrin, C.M., Woerner, M.G. and Ross, D.C. (1983). Treatment of phobias: II. Behavior therapy and supportive psychotherapy: are there any specific ingredients? *Archives of General Psychiatry, 40*, 139–45. ▶ **page 201**

Klesges, R.C., Mizes, J.S. and Klesges, L.M. (1987). Self-help dieting strategies in college males and females. *International Journal of Eating Disorders, 6(3)*, 409–17. ▶ **page 86**

Klinesmith, J., Kasser, T. and McAndrew, F.T. (2006). Guns, testosterone, and aggression: an experimental test of a mediational hypothesis. *Psychological Science, 17*, 568–71. ▶ **page 76**

Klosterkötter, J., Albers, M., Steinmeyer, E.M., Hensen, A. and Sass, H. (1994). Positive or negative symptoms: which are more reliable in the diagnosis of schizophrenia? *Der Nervenarzt, 65(7)*, 444–53. ▶ **page 164**

Knutsson, A., Åkerstedt, T., Jonsson, B.G. and Orth-Gomér, K. (1986). Increased risk of ischaemic heart disease in shift workers. *Lancet, 2(8498)*, 89–92. ▶ **page 16**

Kobak, K.A., Reynolds, W.R. and Greist, J.H. (1993). Development and validation of a computer-administered version of the Hamilton Anxiety Scale. *Psychological Assessmenti, 5*, 487–92. ▶ **pages 193, 207**

Koch, S. (1992). The nature and limits of psychological knowledge. In S. Koch and D.E. Leary (eds) *A Century of Psychology as a Science*. Washington, DC: American Psychological Association. ▶ **page 257**

Kohlberg, L. (1958). *The Development of Modes of Moral Thinking and Choice in the Years 10–16*. Unpublished doctoral dissertation, University of Chicago. ▶ **page 152**

Kohlberg, L. (1966). A cognitive-developmental analysis of children's sex-role concepts and attitudes. In E.E. Maccoby (ed.) *The Development of Sex Differences*. Stanford, CA: Stanford University Press. ▶ **page 152**

Kohlberg, L. (1975). The cognitive developmental approach to moral education. *Phi Delta Kappan*, 670–7. ▶ **page 153**

Kolb, B. and Whishaw, I.Q. (2006). *Introduction to Brain and Behavior* (2nd edn). New York: Freeman-Worth. ▶ **page 88**

Koran, L.M., Hanna, G.L., Hollander, E., Nestadt, G. and Simpson, H.B. (2007). Practice guideline for the treatment of patients with obsessive compulsive disorder. *American Journal of Psychiatry, 164(7)*, 5–53. *See* http://www.psychiatryonline.com (accessed March 2009). ▶ **page 213**

Kraft, J., Slager, S., McGrath, P. and Hamilton, S. (2005). Sequence analysis of the serotonin transporter and associations with antidepressant response. *Biological Psychiatry, 58*, 374–81. ▶ page 181

Kramer, J., Riper, H., Lemmers, L., Conijn, B., van Straten, A. and Smit, F. (2009). Television-supported self-help for problem drinkers: a randomized pragmatic trial. *Addictive Behaviors, 34*, 451–7. ▶ page 246

Kraemer, H.C., Kupfer, D.J., Clarke, D.E., Narrow, W.E. and Regier, D.A. (2012). DSM-5: how reliable is reliable enough? *American Journal of Psychiatry, 169,* 13–15. ▶ page 178

Kripke, D.F., Garfinkel, L., Wingard, D.L., Klauber, M.R. and Marler, M.R. (2002). Mortality associated with sleep duration and insomnia. *Archives of General Psychiatry, 59(2),* 131–6. ▶ page 19

Kruijver, F.P.M., Zhou, J.N., Pool, C.W., Hofman, M.A., Gooren, L.J. and Swaab, D.F. (2000). Male-to-female transsexuals have female neuron numbers in a limbic nucleus. *Journal of Clinical Endocrinology & Metabolism, 85(5),* 2034. ▶ page 110

Krupinski, J. and Tiller, J.W.G. (2001). The identification and treatment of depression by general practitioners. *Australian and New Zealand Journal of Psychiatry, 35*, 827–32. ▶ page 179

Kuhn, S. and Stiner, M. (2006). What's a mother to do? A hypothesis about the division of labor among neandertals and modern humans in Eurasia. *Current Anthropology, 47(6)*, 953–80. ▶ page 106

Kuipers, E., Garety, P., Fowler, D., Dunn, G., Bebbington, P., Freeman, D. and Hadley, C. (1997). London-East Anglia randomised controlled trial of cognitive-behavioural therapy for psychosis. I: effects of the treatment phase. *British Journal of Psychiatry, 171*, 319–27. ▶ page 172

Kumar, V.K., Pekala, R.J. and Cummings, J. (1993). Sensation seeking, drug use and reported paranormal beliefs and experiences. *Personality and Individual Differences, 14(5),* 685–91. ▶ page 264

Kunkel, D., Wilson, B.J. and Linz, D. (1996). *National Television Violence Study.* Thousand Oaks, CA: Sage. ▶ page 220

Kushner, M.G., Kim, S.W., Donahue, C., Thuras, P., Adson, D., Kotlyar, M., McCabe, J., Peterson, J. and Foa, E.B. (2007). D-cycloserine augmented exposure therapy for obsessive compulsive disorder. *Biological Psychiatry, 62*, 835–8. ▶ page 212

Kuyken, W. and Tsivrikos, D. (2009). Therapist competence, co-morbidity and cognitive-behavioral therapy for depression. *Psychotherapy and Psychosomatics, 78*, 42–8. ▶ page 187

Kwon, P. and Laurenceau, J.-P. (2002). A longitudinal study of the hopelessness theory of depression: testing the diathesis-stress model within a differential reactivity and exposure framework. *Journal of Clinical Psychology, 58*, 1305–21. ▶ page 183

Ladouceur, R., Sylvain, C., Boutin, C., Lachance, S., Doucet, C. and Leblond, J. (2001). Cognitive treatment of pathological gambling. *Journal of Nervous and Mental Disorders, 189*, 766–73. ▶ page 251

Laing, R.D. (1960). *The Divided Self: An Existential Study in Sanity and Madness.* Harmondsworth: Penguin. ▶ page 275

Laird, J.D. (1974). Self-attribution of emotion: the effects of facial expression on the quality of emotional experience. *Journal of Personality and Social Psychology, 29*, 475–86. ▶ page 292

Lamb, M.E. and Roopnarine, J.L. (1979). Peer influences on sex-role development in preschoolers. *Child Development, 50*, 1219–22. ▶ page 117

Lamm, C., Batson, C.D. and Decety, J. (2007). The neural substrate of human empathy: effects of perspective-taking and cognitive appraisal. *Journal of Cognitive Neuroscience, 19(1),* 42–58. ▶ page 159

Lamb, M.E., Easterbrooks, M.A. and Holden, G.W. (1980). Reinforcement and punishment among preschoolers: characteristics, effects and correlates. *Child Development, 51*, 1230–6. ▶ page 116

Lambos, C., Delfabbro, P.H. and Pulgies, S. (2007). *Adolescent Gambling in South Australia.* Report prepared for the Independent Gambling Authority of South Australia, Adelaide. ▶ page 242

Lang, S. (1998). *Men as Women, Women as Men: Changing Gender in Native American Cultures.* Austin, TX: University of Texas Press. ▶ page 119

Langevin, R. (1983). *Sexual Strands: Understanding and Treating Sexual Anomalies in Men.* Hillsdale, NJ: Lawrence Erlbaum. ▶ page 201

Langlois, J.H. and Downs, A.C. (1980). Mothers, fathers, peers as socialization agents of sex-stereotyped play behaviours in young children. *Child Development, 51*, 1217–47. ▶ pages 113, 117

Laule, G.E., Bloomsmith, M.A. and Schapiro, S.J. (2003). The use of positive reinforcement training techniques to enhance the care, management, and welfare of primates in the laboratory. *Journal of Applied Animal Welfare Science, 6(3),* 163–73. ▶ page 132

Lavine, R. (1997). Psychopharmacological treatment of aggression and violence in the substance-using population. *Psychoactive Drugs, 29*, 321–9. ▶ page 72

Lawrance, L. and Rubinson, L. (1989). Self-efficacy as a predictor of smoking behavior in young adolescents. *Addictive Behaviors, 11*, 367–82. ▶ page 242

Lawrence, A.A. (2003). Factors associated with satisfaction or regret following male-to-female sex reassignment surgery. *Archives of Sexual Behavior, 32*, 299–315. ▶ page 111

Le Bon, G. (1995). *The Crowd: A Study of the Popular Mind.* London: Transaction Publishers. (Original work published in 1895.) ▶ page 68

LeBlanc, S.A. and Register, K.E. (2004). *Constant Battles: Why We Fight.* New York: St. Martin's Griffin Press. ▶ page 79

Lecendreux, M., Bassetti, C., Dauvilliers, Y., Mayer, G., Neidhart, E. and Tafti, M. (2003). HLA and genetic susceptibility to sleepwalking. *Molecular Psychiatry, 8*, 114–17. ▶ page 27

Lee, D.N. (1980). Visuo-motor coordination in space-time. In G.E. Stelmach and J. Requin (eds) *Tutorials In Motor Behaviour.* North Holland. ▶ page 35

Lee, D.N., Lishman, J.R. and Thomson, J.A. (1982). Regulation of gait in long-jumping. *Journal of Experimental Psychology: Human Perception and Performance, 8*, 448–59. ▶ page 35

Lee, R. (1993). *Doing Research on Sensitive Topics*, London: Sage. ▶ page 245

Legerstee, M. (1992). A review of the animate-inanimate distinction in infancy: implications for models of social and cognitive knowing. *Early Development and Parenting, 1*, 57–67. ▶ page 154

Legerstee, M., Anderson, D. and Schaffer, M. (1998). Five- and eight month-old infants recognize their faces and voices as familiar and social stimuli. *Child Development, 69*, 37–50. ▶ page 154

Lehr, A.T. and Geher, G. (2006). Differential effects of reciprocity and attitude similarity across long-versus short-term mating contexts. *The Journal of Social Psychology, 146*, 423–39. ▶ page 49

Lehrman, S.R. and Weiss, E.J. (1943). Schizophrenia in cryptogenic narcolepsy. *Psychiatric Quarterly, XVII*, 135–44. ▶ page 26

Lenhart, A., Kahne, J., Middaugh, E., Rankin Macgill, A., Evans, C. and Vitak, J. (2008). *Teens, Video Games, and Civics: Teens' Gaming Experiences are Diverse and Include Significant Social Interaction and Civic Engagement.* Pew Internet & American Life Project. ▶ page 224

Leonard, B.E. (2000). Evidence for a biochemical lesion in depression. *Journal of Clinical Psychiatry, 61(suppl. 6),* 12–17. ▶ page 181

Lerman C., Wileyto E.P., Patterson F., Rukstalis M., Audrain-McGovern J., Restine S. et al. (2004). The functional muopioid receptor (OPRM1) Asn40Asp variant predicts short-term response to nicotine replacement therapy in a clinical trial. *Pharmacogenomics Journal, 4*, 184–92. ▶ page 239

Leucht, S., Pitschel-Walz, G., Abraham, D. and Kissling, W. (1999). Efficacy and extrapyramidal side-effects. *Schizophrenia Research, 35(1),* 51–68. ▶ page 171

Leung, N., Thomas, G. and Waller, G. (2000). The relationship between parental bonding and core beliefs in anorexic and bulimic women. *British Journal of Psychology, 39*, 205–13. ▶ page 97

Leunissen, J. and Van Vugt, M. (2010). I love the man in the uniform: why women prefer male warriors. *Unpublished Manuscript*: University of Kent. ▶ page 79

Levine, R., Sato, S., Hashimoto, T. and Verma, J. (1995). Love and marriage in eleven cultures. *Journal of Cross-Cultural Psychology, 26*, 554–571. ▶ page 60

Lewis, M. (1990). Social knowledge and social development. *Merril-Palmer Quarterly of Behaviour and Development, 36*, 93–116. ▶ page 156

Lewis, M. (1991). Ways of knowing: objective self-awareness or consciousness. *Developmental Review, 11*, 231–43. ▶ page 154

Lewis, M. and Brooks-Gunn, J. (1979). *Social Cognition and the Acquisition of Self.* New York: Plenum Press. ▶ page 154

Lewis, M., Wolfson, S. and Wakelin, D. (2005). Football supporters' perceptions of their role in the home advantage. *Journal of Sports Sciences, 23*, 365–74. ▶ page 79

Lhermitte, F., Pillon, B. and Serdaru, M. (1986). Human autonomy and the frontal lobes. Part I: imitation and utilization behavior: a neuropsychological study of 75 patients. *Annals of Neurology, 19(4),* 326–34. ▶ page 158

Li, X., Lu, Q. and Miller, R. (2008). Self-medication versus pure pleasure seeking compulsive consumption. In A.Y. Lee and D. Soman (eds) *Advances in Consumer Research, 35*, 845–6. ▶ page 241

Liebowitz, M.R., Gorman, J.M., Fyer, A.J. and Klein, D.F. (1985). Social phobia: review of a neglected anxiety disorder. *Archives of General Psychiatry, 42(7),* 729–36. ▶ page 199

Liebowitz, M.R., Schneier, P., Campeas, R., Hollander, E., Hatterer, J., Fyer, A., Gorman, J., Papp, L., Davies, S., Gully, R. and Klein, D.F. (1992). Phenelzine vs atenolol in social phobia: a placebo-controlled trial. *Archives of General Psychiatry, 49*, 290–300. ▶ page 199

Liem, J. (1974). Effects of verbal communications of parents and children: a comparison of normal and schizophrenic families. *Journal of Consulting and Clinical Psychology, 42*, 438–50. ▶ page 169

Lin, C.-L., Lee, S.-H. and Horng, D.-J. (2011). The effects of online reviews on purchasing intention: the moderating role of need for cognition. *Social Behavior and Personality, 39(1),* 71–82. ▶ page 226

Lin, L., Faraco, J., Li, R., Kadotani, H., Rogers, W., Lin, X., Qiu, X., de Jong, P., Nishino, S. and Mignot, E. (1999). The sleep disorder canine narcolepsy is caused by a mutation in the hypocretin (orexin) receptor 2 gene. *Cell, 98(3),* 365–76. ▶ page 27

Lindberg, L. and Hjern, A. (2003). Risk factors for anorexia nervosa: a national cohort study. *International Journal of Eating Disorders, 34*, 397–408. ▶ page 94

Lindblom, J. and Ziemke, T. (2003). Social situatedness of natural and artificial intelligence: Vygotsky and beyond. *Adaptive Behaviour, 11(2),* 79–96. ▶ page 149

Lindeman, M. and Aarnio, K. (2007). The origin of superstition, magical thinking and paranormal beliefs: an integrative model. *Skeptic, 13(1),* 58–65. ▶ page 262

Lindman, R., Jarvinen, P. and Vidjeskog, J. (1987). Verbal interactions of aggressively and nonaggressively predisposed males in a drinking situation. *Aggressive Behavior, 13*, 187–96. ▶ page 72

Linszen, D.H., Dingemans, P.M.A.J., Nugter, M.A., Van der Does, A.J.W., Scholte, W.F. and Lenior, M.E. (1997). Expressed emotion and patient attributes as risk factors for psychotic relapse. *Schizophrenia Bulletin, 23*, 119–30. ▶ page 168

Liss, M.B. and Reinhardt, L.C. (1979). *Behavioral and Attitudinal Responses to Prosocial Programs.* Paper presented at the meeting of the Society for Research in Child Development, San Francisco, CA. ▶ page 223

Liu, D., Wellman, H.M., Tardif, T. and Sabbagh, M.A. (2004). *Development of Chinese and North American Children's Theory of Mind.* Paper presented at the 28th International Congress of Psychology, Beijing, China. ▶ page 154

Lobbestael, J., Leurgans, M. and Arntz, A. (2011). Inter-rater reliability of the Structured Clinical Interview for DSM-IV Axis I Disorders (SCID I) and Axis II Disorders (SCID II). *Clinical Psychology & Psychotherapy, 18(1)*, 75–9. ▶ page 178

Lochner, C. and Stein, D.J. (2001). Gender in obsessive compulsive disorder and obsessive compulsive spectrum disorders. *Archives of Women's Health, 4*, 19–26. ▶ page 211

Loehlin, J.C., Horn, J.M. and Willerman, L. (1989). Modeling IQ change: evidence from the Texas Adoption Project. *Child Development, 60*, 993–1004. ▶ page 138

Loftus, E.F. (2003). Our changeable memories: legal and practical implications. *Nature Reviews Neuroscience, 4*, 231–4. ▶ page 226

Loftus, E.F. and Palmer, J.C. (1974). Reconstruction of automobile destruction: an example of the interaction between language and memory. *Journal of Verbal Learning and Verbal Behavior, 13*, 585–9. ▶ page 278

Lopez, A.D., Collishaw, N.E. and Piha, T. (1994). A descriptive model of the cigarette epidemic in developed countries. *Tobacco Control, 3*, 242–7. ▶ page 247

Lopez, A.D., Mathers, C.D., Ezzati, M., Jamison, D.T. and Murray, C.J.L. (2006). *Global burden of disease and risk factors.* Washington (DC): World Bank. ▶ page 178

Lott, B.E. (1994). *Women's Lives: Themes and Variations in Gender Learning* (2nd edn). Pacific Grove, CA: Brooks/Cole Publishing. ▶ page 49

Lovelace, V. and Huston, H.C. (1983). Can television teach prosocial behavior? *Prevention in Human Services, 2*, 93–106. ▶ page 221

Lunde, C., Frisén, A. and Hwang, C.P. (2006). Ten-year-old girls' and boys' body composition and peer victimization experiences: prospective associations with body satisfaction. *Body Image, 4(1)*, 11–28. ▶ page 93

Lutter, M., Sakata, I., Osborne-Lawrence, S., Rovinsky, S.A., Anderson, J.G., Jung, S., Birnbaum, S., Yanagisawa, M., Elmquist, J.K., Nestler, E.J. and Zigman, J.M. (2008). The orexigenic hormone ghrelin defends against depressive symptoms of stress. *Nature Neuroscience, 11*, 752–3. ▶ page 89

Luxen, M.F. (2007). Sex differences, evolutionary psychology and biosocial theory: biosocial theory is no alternative. *Theory and Psychology, 17*, 383–94. ▶ page 109

Lyvers, M., Barling, N. and Harding-Clark, J. (2006). Effect of belief in 'psychic healing' on self-reported pain in chronic pain sufferers. *Journal of Psychosomatic Research, 60(1)*, 59–61. ▶ page 267

McAlister, A.L., Krosnick, J.A. and Milburn, M.A. (1984). Causes of adolescent cigarette smoking: tests of a structured equation model. *Social Psychology Quarterly, 47*, 24–36. ▶ page 244

McArdle, J.J., Hamagami, F., Meredith, W. and Bradway, K.P. (2000). Modeling the dynamic hypotheses of Gf-Gc theory using longitudinal life-span data. *Learning and Individual Differences, 12*, 53–79. ▶ page 125

McBurnett, K., Lahey, B.B., Rathouz, P.J. and Loeber, R. (2000). Low salivary cortisol and persistent aggression in boys referred for disruptive behavior. *Archives of General Psychiatry, 57*, 38–43. ▶ page 73

Maccoby, E.E. (1998). *The Two Sexes: Growing up Apart, Coming Together.* Cambridge, MA: Belknap Press. ▶ page 117

McConaghy, M.J. (1979). Gender permanence and the genital basis of gender: stages in the development of constancy of gender identity. *Child Development, 50*, 1223–6. ▶ page 112

McCorkle, R.C., Miethe, T.D. and Drass, K.A. (1995). The roots of prison violence: a test of the deprivation, management and 'not-so-total' institution models. *Crime and Delinquency, 41(3)*, 317–31. ▶ page 71

McCullough, J.P.J., Klein, D.N., Borian, F.E., Howland, R.H., Riso, L.P., Keller, M.B. and Banks, P.L.C. (2003). Group comparisons of DSM-IV subtypes of chronic depression: validity of the distinctions, part 2. *Journal of Abnormal Psychology, 112*, 614–22. ▶ page 179

McCutcheon, L.E., Lange, R. and Houran, J. (2002). Conceptualization and measurement of celebrity worship. *British Journal of Psychology, 93*, 67–87. ▶ page 230

MacDonald, J.F. (1992). *Blacks and White TV: African Americans in Television Since 1948.* Chicago: Nelson-Hall. ▶ page 78

MacDonald, T., Zanna, M.P. and Fong, G.T. (1996). Why common sense goes out the window: effects of alcohol on intentions to use condoms. *Personality and Social Psychology Bulletin, 22*, 763–75. ▶ page 249

McGarrigle, J. and Donaldson, M. (1974). Conservation accidents. *Cognition, 3*, 341–50. ▶ page 147

McGhee, P. and Frueh, T. (1980). Television viewing and the learning of sex-role stereotypes. *Sex Roles, 6*, 179–88. ▶ page 116

McGrath, T., Tsui, E., Humphries, S. and Yule, W. (1990). Successful treatment of a noise phobia in a nine-year-old girl with systematic desensitization in vivo. *Educational Psychology, 10*, 79–83. ▶ page 201

McGuffin, P., Katz, R., Rutherford, J. and Watkins S. (1996). The heritability of DSM-IV unipolar depression: a hospital-based twin register study. *Archives of General Psychiatry, 53*, 129–36. ▶ pages 180, 209

MacIntyre, S., Reilly, J., Miller, D. and Eldridge, J. (1998). Food choice, food scares, and health: the role of the media. In A. Murcott (ed.) *The Nation's Diet: The Social Science of Food Choice.* New York: Longman, 228–49. ▶ page 84

Mackintosh, J. (ed.) (1995). *Cyril Burt: Fraud or Framed?* Oxford: Oxford University Press. ▶ page 276

Mackintosh, N. (1998). *IQ and Human Intelligence.* Oxford: Oxford University Press. ▶ page 140

McNally, R.J. (1987). Preparedness and phobias: a review. *Psychological Bulletin, 101*, 283–303. ▶ page 195

McNaughton, S. and Leyland, J. (1990). Maternal regulation of children's problem-solving behaviour and its impact on children's performance. *Child Development, 61*, 113–26. ▶ page 149

McNeal, E.T. and Cimbolic, P. (1986). Antidepressants and biochemical theories of depression. *Psychological Bulletin, 99*, 361–74. ▶ page 180

McNeil, J.F. and Warrington, E.K. (1993). Prosopagnosia: a face-specific disorder. *Quarterly Journal of Experimental Psychology, 46(1)*, 1–10. ▶ page 43

Madsen, S.D. (2001). *The Salience of Adolescent Romantic Experiences for Romantic Relationships in Young Adulthood.* Unpublished dissertation, University of Minnesota. ▶ page 58

Maestripieri, D. (2007). Gestural communication in three species of macaques (*Macaca mulatta, M. nemestrina, M. arctoides*): use of signals in relation to dominance and social context. (51–66). In K. Liebal, C. Müller and S. Pika (eds) *Gestural communication in Nonhuman and Human Primates*, Amsterdam: John Benjamins. ▶ page 135

Mahler, M.S., Pine, F. and Bergman, A. (1973). *The Psychological Birth of the Human Infant.* New York: Basic Books. ▶ page 155

Maina, G., Albert, U. and Bogetto, F. (2001). Relapses after discontinuation of drugs associated with increased resistance to treatment in obsessive compulsive disorder. *International Clinical Pharmacology, 16(1)*, 33–8. ▶ page 213

Majer, J.M., Jason, L.A. and Olson, B.D. (2004). Optimism, abstinence self-efficacy, and self-mastery among Oxford House residents: a comparative analysis of cognitive resources. *Assessment, 11(1)*, 57–63. ▶ page 248

Malone, D.R., Morris, H.H., Kay, M.C. and Levin, H.S. (1982). Prosopagnosia: a double dissociation between the recognition of familiar and unfamiliar faces. *Journal of Neurology, Neurosurgery, and Psychiatry, 45*, 820–2. ▶ page 40

Malouff, J.M., Rooke, S.E. and Schutte, N.S. (2008). The heritability of human behavior: results of aggregating meta-analyses. *Current Psychology, 27(3)*, 153- 61. ▶ page 138

Maltby, J., Day, E. and Macaskill, A. (2007). *Personality, Individual Differences and Intelligence.* Harlow: Pearson. ▶ page 140

Maltby, J., Day, L., McCutcheon, L.E., Gillett, R., Houran, J. and Ashe, D. (2004). Celebrity worship using an adaptational-continuum model of personality and coping. *British Journal of Psychology, 95*, 411–28. ▶ page 232

Maltby, J., Day, L., McCutcheon, L.E., Houran, J. and Ashe, D. (2006). Extreme celebrity worship, fantasy proneness and dissociation: developing the measurement and understanding of celebrity worship within a clinical personality context. *Personality and Individual Differences, 40*, 273–83. ▶ pages 232, 233

Maltby, J., Giles, D.C., Barber, L. and McCutcheon, L.E. (2005). Intense personal celebrity worship and body image: evidence of a link among female adolescents. *British Journal of Health Psychology, 10*, 17–32. ▶ page 231

Maltby, J., Houran, J., Lange, R., Ashe, D. and McCutcheon, L.E. (2002). Thou shalt worship no other gods – unless they are celebrities. *Personality and Individual Differences, 32*, 1157–72. ▶ page 233

Maltby, J., Houran, M.A. and McCutcheon, L.E. (2003). A clinical interpretation of attitudes and behaviors associated with celebrity worship. *Journal of Nervous and Mental Disease, 191*, 25–9. ▶ pages 231, 232

Maltby, J., McCutcheon, L.E., Ashe, D.D. and Houran, J. (2001). The self-reported psychological well-being of celebrity worshippers. *North American Journal of Psychology, 3*, 441–52. ▶ page 232

Mandel, D.R. (1998). The obedience alibi: Milgram's account of the Holocaust reconsidered. *Analyse and Kritik, 30*, 74–94. ▶ page 71

Mangweth-Matzek, B., Rupp, C., Hausmann, A., Assmayr, K., Marlacher, E. and Kemmler, G. (2006). Never too old for eating disorders or body dissatisfaction: a community study of elderly women. *International Journal of Eating Disorders, 39(7)*, 583–6. ▶ page 99

Mann, J., Arango, V. and Underwood, M. (1990). Serotonin and suicidal behavior. *Annals of the New York Academy of Science, 600*, 476–84. ▶ page 72

Mann, L. (1981). The baiting crowd in episodes of threatened suicide. *Journal of Personality and Social Psychology, 41*, 703–9. ▶ page 69

Manstead, A.R. and McCulloch, C. (1981). Sex-role stereotyping in British television advertisements. *British Journal of Social Psychology, 20*, 171–80. ▶ page 299

March, J.S., Frances, A., Carpenter, D. and Kahn, D.A. (1997). The expert consensus guideline series: treatment of obsessive compulsive disorder. *Journal of Clinical Psychiatry, 58(suppl. 4)*, 3–72. ▶ page 214

March, J.S., Silva, S., Petrycki, S., Curry, J., Wells, K., Fairbank, J., Burns, B., Domino, M., McNulty, S., Vitiello, B. and Severe, J. (2007). The treatment for adolescents with depression study: long-term effectiveness and safety outcomes. *Archives of General Psychiatry, 64(10)*, 1132–43. ▶ page 187

Mares, M. (1996). The role of source confusions in television's cultivation of social reality judgments. *Human Communication Research, 23(2)*, 278–97. ▶ pages 220, 221

Mares, M. and Woodard, E.H. (2001). Prosocial effects on children's social interactions. In D.G. Singer and J.L. Singer (eds) *Handbook of Children and the Media*. Thousand Oaks, CA: Sage. ▶ pages 220, 221

Marie, L. Ste., Luquet, S., Cole, T.B. and Palmiter, R.D. (2005). Modulation of neuropeptide Y expression in adult mice does not affect feeding. *Proceedings of the National Academy of Science, 102*, 18632–7. ▶ page 89

Marks, I.M. (1987). *Fears, Phobias and Rituals*. New York: Oxford University Press. ▶ page 194

Marks, I.M. and Nesse, R.M. (1994). Fear and fitness: an evolutionary analysis of anxiety disorders. *Ethology and Sociobiology, 15*, 247–61. ▶ pages 194, 208

Marr, D. (1982). *Vision: A Computational Investigation into the Human Representation and Processing of Visual Information*. San Francisco, CA: W.H. Freeman. ▶ page 33

Martin, B., Wentzel, D. and Tomczak, T. (2008). Effects of susceptibility to normative influence and type of testimonial on attitudes toward print advertising. *Journal of Advertising, 37(1)*, 29–43. ▶ page 229

Martin, C.L. and Halverson, C.F. (1983). The effects of sex-typing schemas on young children's memory. *Child Development, 54*, 563–74. ▶ page 113

Martin, C.L. and Halverson, C.F. Jr. (1983). Gender constancy: a methodological and theoretical analysis. *Sex Roles, 9(7)*, 775–90. ▶ page 115

Martin, C.L. and Little, J.K. (1990). The relation of gender understanding to children's sex-typed preferences and gender stereotypes. *Child Development, 61*, 1427–39. ▶ page 115

Martin, C.L., Eisenbud, L. and Rose, H. (1995). Children's gender-based reasoning about toys. *Child Development, 66*, 1453–71. ▶ page 117

Martin, M.C. (1997). Children's understanding of the intent of advertising: a meta-analysis. *Journal of Public Policy and Marketing, 16*, 205–16. ▶ pages 226, 228

Martino, T.A., Oudit, G.Y., Herzenberg, A.M., Tata, N., Koletar, M.M., Kabir, G.M., Belsham, D.D., Backx, P.H., Ralph, M.R. and Sole, M.J. (2008). Circadian rhythm disorganization produces profound cardiovascular and renal disease in hamsters. *American Journal of Physiology – Regulatory, Integrative and Comparative Physiology, 294*, 1675–83. ▶ page 16

Masserman, J.H. (1943). *Behaviour and Neurosis*. Chicago: University of Chicago Press. ▶ page 201

Mathers, C.D., Stein, C. and Shibuya, K. (1996). *The Global Burden of Disease: A Comprehensive Assessment of Mortality and Disability from Diseases, Injuries, and Risk Factors in 1990 and Projected to 2020*. Cambridge, MA: Harvard University Press. ▶ page 164

Matsunaga, H., Maebayashi, K., Hayashida, K., Okino, K., Matsui, I., Iketani, T., Kiriike, N. and Stein, D.J. (2008). Symptom structure in Japanese patients with obsessive compulsive disorder. *American Journal of Psychiatry, 165*, 251–3. ▶ page 207

Matthews, R.N., Domjan, M., Ramsey, M. and Crews, D. (2007). Learning effects on sperm competition and reproductive fitness. *Psychological Science, 18(9)*, 758–62. ▶ page 132

Mattick, R.P and Clarke, J.C. (1998). Development and validation of measures of social phobia scrutiny fear and social interaction anxiety. *Behaviour Research and Therapy, 36(4)*, 455–70. ▶ page 193

Matute, H. (1996). Illusion of control: detecting response-outcome in analytic but not realistic conditions. *Psychological Science, 7*, 289–93. ▶ page 263

Mayeux, L., Sandstrom, M.J. and Cillessen, A.H.N. (2008). Is being popular a risky proposition? *Journal of Research on Adolescence, 18(1)*, 49–74. ▶ page 242

Mazur, A. (1985). A biosocial model of status in face-to-face primate groups. *Social Forces, 64*, 377–402. ▶ page 73

Mead, M. (1935). *Sex and Temperament in Three Primitive Societies*. New York: Morrow. ▶ page 118

Mead, M. (1949). *Male and Female*. New York: Morrow. ▶ page 119

Meddis, R. (1975). On the function of sleep. *Animal Behaviour, 23*, 676–91. ▶ page 22

Meloy, J.R. (1996). Stalking (obsessional following): a review of some preliminary studies. *Aggression and Violent Behaviour, 1*, 147–62. ▶ page 232

Meloy, J.R. (1998). *The Psychology of Stalking: Clinical and Forensic Perspectives*. San Diego, CA: Academic Press. ▶ page 232

Meloy, J.R. (2001). Threats, stalking, and criminal harassment. In G.-F. Pinard and L. Pagani (eds) *Clinical Assessment of Dangerousness: Empirical Contributions*. New York: Cambridge University Press. ▶ page 232

Meltzoff, A.N. and Moore, M.K. (1977). Imitation of facial and manual gestures by human neonates. *Science, 198*, 75–8. ▶ page 156

Meltzoff, A.N. and Moore, M.K. (1989). Imitation in newborn infants: exploring the range of gestures imitated and the underlying mechanisms. *Developmental Psychology, 25*, 954–62. ▶ page 156

Menzies, L., Achard, S., Chamberlain, S.R., Fineberg, N., Chen, C.-H., del Campo, N., Sahakian, B.J., Robbins, T.W. and Bullmore, E. (2007). Neurocognitive endophenotypes of obsessive compulsive disorder. *Brain, 130(12)*, 3223–36. ▶ page 209

Menzies, R.G. and Clarke, J.C. (1993). A comparison of in vivo and vicarious exposure in the treatment of childhood water phobia behaviour. *Behaviour Research and Therapy, 35*, 667–81. ▶ page 201

Mercader, J., Panger, M. and Boesch, C. (2002). Excavation of a chimpanzee stone tool site in the African rainforest. *Science, 296(5572)*, 1452–5. ▶ page 136

Merckelbach, H., van den Hout, M.A., Hoekstra, R. and Van Oppen, P. (1988). Many stimuli are frightening but some are more frightening than others: the contribution of preparedness, dangerousness, and unpredictability to making a stimulus fearful. *Journal of Psychopathology and Behavioural Assessment, 10*, 355–66. ▶ page 195

Mermelstein, R.J., Colvin, P.J. and Klingemann, S.D. (2009). Dating and changes in adolescent cigarette smoking: does partner smoking behavior matter? *Nicotine and Tobacco Research, 11(10)*, 1226–30. ▶ page 240

Messerlian, C., Derevensky, J. and Gupta, R. (2005). Youth gambling problems: a public health perspective. *Health Promotion International, 20(1)*, 69–79. ▶ page 250

Messick, D.M. and Cook, K.S. (1983). *Equity Theory: Psychological and Sociological Perspectives*. New York: Praeger. ▶ page 50

Meyer, T.A. and Gast, J. (2008). The effects of peer influence on disordered eating behavior. *The Journal of School Nursing, 24(1)*, 36–42. ▶ page 85

Meyer-Lindenberg, A., Miletich, R.W. and Kohn, P. (2002). Prefrontal cortex dysfunction predicts exaggerated striatal dopamine uptake in schizophrenia. *Nature Neuroscience, 5*, 1809–17. ▶ page 169

Michalski, R.L . and Shackelford, T.K. (2005). Grandparental investment as a function of relational uncertainty and emotional closeness with parents. *Human Nature, 16*, 292–304. ▶ page 56

Michell, L. (1997). Loud, sad or bad: young people's perceptions of peer groups and smoking. *Health Education Research, 12*, 1–14. ▶ page 245

Mignot, E. (1998). Genetic and familial aspects of narcolepsy. *Neurology, 50(suppl. 1)*, S16–S22. ▶ page 27

Mignot, E. (2001). A hundred years of research. *See* http://med.stanford.edu/school/Psychiatry/narcolepsy/narcolepsyhistory.html (accessed August 2008). Originally published in *Archives Italiennes de Biologie (2001), 39(3)*, 207–20. ▶ page 27

Mignot, E., Hayduk, R., Grumet, F.C., Black, J. and Guilleminault, C. (1997). HLA DQB1*0602 is associated with cataplexy in 509 narcoleptic patients. *Sleep, 20(11)*, 1012–20. ▶ page 27

Miles, D.R. and Carey, G. (1997). Genetic and environmental architecture of human aggression. *Journal of Personality and Social Psychology, 72*, 207–17. ▶ page 74

Miles, L.E.M., Raynal, D.M. and Wilson, M.A. (1977). Blind man living in normal society has circadian rhythms of 24.9 hours. *Science, 198*, 421–3. ▶ page 11

Milgram, S. (1974). *Obedience to Authority: An Experimental View*. New York: Harper and Row. ▶ page 70

Miller, G., Tybur, J.M. and Jordan, B.D. (2007). Ovulatory cycle effects on tip earnings by lap dancers: economic evidence for human estrus? *Evolution and Human Behavior, 28*, 375–81. ▶ page 55

Miller, G.F. (1998). How mate choice shaped human nature: a review of sexual selection and human evolution. In C. Crawford and D. Krebs (eds) *Handbook of Evolutionary Psychology: Ideas, Issues, and Applications*. Hillsdale, NJ: Lawrence Erlbaum, 8/–129. ▶ pages 56, 136, 149, 230

Miller, G.F. (2000). Sexual selection for indicators of intelligence. In G. Bock, J. Goode and K. Webb (eds) *The Nature of Intelligence*. Novartis Foundation Symposium, 233. New York: Wiley, 260–75. ▶ page 230

Miller, J. (1983). *States of Mind*. London: BBC. ▶ pages 257, 275

Miller, L. (1994). *See* http://www.radix.net/~reimann/enet/VC94/Msg/msg34.html (accessed March 2003). ▶ page 149

Miller, W. and Seligman, M.E.P. (1974). Depression and learned helplessness in man. *Journal of Abnormal Psychology, 84*, 228–38. ▶ page 183

Milton, J. and Wiseman, R. (1999). Does psi exist? Lack of replication of an anomalous process of information transfer. *Psychological Bulletin, 125(4)*, 387–91. ▶ page 259

Milton, K. (2008). Back to basics: why foods of wild primates have relevance for modern human health. *Nutrition, 16(7–8)*, 480–3. ▶ page 90

Mineka, S., Davidson, M., Cook, M. and Kuir, R. (1984). Observational conditioning of snake fear in rhesus monkeys. *Journal of Abnormal Psychology, 93*, 355–72. ▶ page 194

Misra, A., Khurana, L., Vikram, N.K., Goel, A. and Wasir, J.S. (2007). Metabolic syndrome in children: current issues and South Asian perspective. *Nutrition, 23*, 895–910. ▶ page 87

Mita, T.H., Dermer, M. and Knight, J. (1977). Reversed facial images and the mere-exposure hypothesis. *Journal of Personality and Social Psychology, 35*, 597–601. ▶ page 292

Mitani J. and Watts, D. (2001). Why do chimpanzees hunt and share meat? *Animal Behavior, 61*, 915–24. ▶ page 137

Modgil, S., Modgil, M. and Brown, G. (1983). *Jean Piaget: An Interdisciplinary Critique*. London: Routledge. ▶ page 151

Moghaddam, F.M. (1998). *Social Psychology: Exploring Universals Across Cultures*. New York: W.H. Freeman. ▶ page 51

Moghaddam, F.M., Tayler, D.M. and Wright, S.C. (1993). *Social Psychology in Cross-cultural Perspective*. New York: W.H. Freeman. ▶ page 60

Mohr, C., Landis, T., Bracha, H.S., Fathi, M. and Brugger, P. (2005). Levodopa reverses gait assymetries related to anhedonia and magical ideation. *European Archives of Psychiatry and Clinical Neurosciences, 255*, 33–9. ▶ **page 187**

Mohr, D.C., Hart, S.L., Julian, L., Catledge, C., Honos-Webb, L., Vella, L. and Tasch, E.T. (2005). Telephone-administered psychotherapy for depression. *Archives of General Psychiatry, 62(9)*, 1007–14. ▶ **page 263**

Mojtabi, R. and Nicholson, R. (1995). Interrater reliability of ratings of delusions and bizarre delusions. *American Journal of Psychiatry, 152*, 1804–8. ▶ **page 165**

Money, J. and Ehrhardt, A.A. (1972). *Man and Woman, Boy and Girl*. Baltimore, MD: Johns Hopkins University Press. ▶ **pages 105, 108**

Moody, R.A. (1975). *Life After Life*. Charlottesville, VA: Hampton Roads. ▶ **page 269**

Moolchan, E.T., Robinson, M.L., Ernst, M., Cadet, J.L., Pickworth, W.B., Heishman, S.J. et al. (2005). Safety and efficacy of the nicotine patch and gum for the treatment of adolescent tobacco addition. *Pediatrics, 115*, 407–14. ▶ **page 241**

Moore, J.C. and Brylinsky, J.A. (1993). Spectator effect on team performance in college basketball. *Journal of Sport Behavior, 16*, 77–83. ▶ **page 79**

Moore, S.M. and Leung, C. (2001). Romantic beliefs, styles, and relationships among young people from Chinese, Southern European, and Anglo-Australian backgrounds. *Asian Journal of Social Psychology, 4*, 53–68. ▶ **page 60**

Moore-Ede, M. (1993). *The 24-hour Society*. Reading, MA: Addison-Wesley. ▶ **page 17**

Morgan, E. (1995). Measuring time with a biological clock. *Biological Sciences Review, 7*, 2–5. ▶ **page 15**

Moritz, S., Jelinek, L., Hottenrott, B., Klinge, R. and Randjbar, S. (2009). No evidence for object alternation impairment in obsessive compulsive disorder. *Brain and Cognition, 69(1)*, 176–9. ▶ **page 209**

Mousseau, M. (2003). Parapsychology: science or pseudo-science? *Journal of Scientific Exploration, 17(2)*, 271–282. ▶ **page 257**

Mowrer, O.H. (1947). On the dual nature of learning: a re-interpretation of 'conditioning' and 'problem-solving'. *Harvard Educational Review, 17*, 102–48. ▶ **page 196**

Mowrer, O.H. (1960). *Learning Theory and Behavior*. New York: Wiley. ▶ **page 210**

Mukhametov, L.M. (1987). Unihemispheric slow-wave sleep in the Amazonian dolphin, *Inia geoffrensis*. *Neuroscience Letters, 79*, 128. ▶ **page 23**

Mullen, B. (1986). Atrocity as a function of lynch mob composition: a self-attention perspective. *Personality and Social Psychology Bulletin, 12*, 187–97. ▶ **page 68**

Mulsant, B.H., Rosen, J. and Thornton, J.E. (1991). A prospective naturalistic study of electroconvulsive therapy in late-life depression. *Journal of Geriatric Psychiatry and Neurology, 4*, 3–13. ▶ **page 185**

Mumford, D.B., Whitehouse, A.M. and Platts, M. (1991). Sociocultural correlates of eating disorders among Asian schoolgirls in Bradford. *British Journal of Psychiatry, 158*, 222–8. ▶ **page 85**

Munroe, R.L. and Munroe, R.H. (1975). *Cross-cultural Human Development*. Monterey, CA: Brooks/Cole. ▶ **page 118**

Murray, A.L. (2011). The validity of the meta-analytic method in addressing the issue of psi replicability. *Journal of Parapsychology, Fall 2011. See http://readperiodicals.com/201110/2591274471.html#b (accessed April 2011).* ▶ **page 259**

Musch, J. and Ehrenberg, K. (2002). Probability misjudgment, cognitive ability, and belief in the paranormal. *British Journal of Psychology, 93*, 169–77. ▶ **page 261**

Myers, J.E., Madathil, J. and Tingle, L.R. (2005). Marriage satisfaction and wellness in India and the United States: a preliminary comparison of arranged marriages and marriages of choice. *Journal of Counselling and Development, 83*, 183–90. ▶ **page 61**

Nangle, D.W., Erdley, C.A., Newman, J.E., Mason, C.A. and Carpenter, E.M. (2003). Popularity, friendship quantity, and friendship quality: interactive influences on children's psychological adjustment. *Journal of Clinical Child and Adolescent Psychology, 32*, 546–55. ▶ **page 58**

National Institute for Clinical Excellence (2003). *Electroconvulsive Therapy (ECT): Guidance, Technology Appraisal 59*, London: National Institute for Clinical Excellence. ▶ **page 184**

National Institute for Clinical Excellence (2004). Anxiety: management of anxiety (panic disorder, with or without agoraphobia, and generalized anxiety disorder) in adults in primary, secondary and community care. *See www.nice.org.uk/CG022quickrefguide (accessed 7 October 2007).* ▶ **page 201**

Neave, N. and Wolfson, S. (2003). Testosterone, territoriality and the 'home advantage'. *Physiology and Behavior, 78*, 269–75. ▶ **page 78**

Neemann, J., Hubbard, J. and Masten, A.S. (1995). The changing importance of romantic relationship involvement to competence from late childhood to late adolescence. *Development and Psychopathology, 7*, 727–50. ▶ **page 59**

Neisser, U. (1976). *Cognition and Reality*. San Francisco, CA: W.H. Freeman. ▶ **page 35**

Nelson, K.R., Mattingly, M., Lee, S.A. and Schmitt, F.A. (2006). Does the arousal system contribute to near death experience? *Neurology, 66*, 1003–9. ▶ **page 268**

Nemeroff, C. and Rozin, P. (1994). The contagion concept in adult thinking in the United States: transmission of germs and interpersonal influence. *Ethos, 22*, 158–86. ▶ **page 262**

Nerín de la Puerta, I. and Jané, M. (2007). *Libro Blanco Sobre Mujeres Y Tabaco. Abordaje con una Perspectiva de Genero*. Comite Nacional para la Prevencion del Tabaquismo, Ministerio de Sanidad y Consumo, Madrid. ▶ **page 242**

Nestadt, G., Samuels, J., Riddle, M., Bienvenu III, O.J., Liang, K.-Y., LaBuda, M., Walkup, J., Grados, M. and Hoehn-Saric, R. (2000). A family study of obsessive compulsive disorder. *Archives of General Psychiatry, 57*, 358–63. ▶ **page 208**

Netemeyer, R., Burton, S. and Johnston, M. (1991). A comparison of two models for the prediction of volitional and goal-directed behaviors: a confirmatory analysis approach. *Social Psychology Quarterly, 54(2)*, 87–100. ▶ **page 249**

New Scientist (2008). *See www.newscientist.com/article.ns?id=dn7174 (accessed August 2008).* ▶ **page 43**

New York Times (1988). Errors by a tense US crew led to downing of Iran jet, Navy inquiry said to find, August 3. ▶ **page 33**

NICE (2009). Schizophrenia: Core Interventions in the Treatment and Management of Schizophrenia in Adults in Primary and Secondary Care. NICE clinical guideline 82. Available at www.nice.org.uk/CG82 [NICE guideline]

NIDA (1999). Studies link stress and drug addiction. *NIDA notes, 14(1). See http://archives.drugabuse.gov/NIDA_Notes/NNVol14N1/Stress.html (accessed April 2011).* ▶ **page 244**

Nijman, H.L.I. and Rector, G. (1999). Crowding and aggression on inpatient psychiatric wards. *Psychiatric Services, 50*, 830–1. ▶ **page 71**

Nijman, H.L., á Campo, J.M., Ravelli, D.P. and Merckelbach, H.L. (1999). A tentative model of aggression on inpatient psychiatric wards. *Psychiatric Services, 50(6)*, 832–34. ▶ **page 71**

Nilsson, J.E., Paul, B.D., Lupini, L.N. and Tatem, B. (1999). Cultural differences in perfectionism: a comparison of African American and White college students. *Journal of College Student Development, 40*, 141–50. ▶ **page 93**

Nishino, S., Ripley, B., Overeem, S., Lammers, G.L. and Mignot, E. (2000). Hypocretin (orexin) transmission in human narcolepsy. *The Lancet, 355*, 39–40. ▶ **page 27**

NHS (2012). *See http://www.nhs.uk/conditions/gender-dysphoria/Pages/Introduction.aspx (accessed June 2012).* ▶ **page 110**

Noble, G. (1975). *Children in Front of the Small Screen*. London: Constable. ▶ **pages 67, 223, 231**

Nolen-Hoeksema, S. (1987). Sex differences in unipolar depression: evidence and theory. *Psychological Bulletin, 101*, 259–82. ▶ **page 183**

Norman, J. (2002). Two visual systems and two theories of perception. *Behavioral and Brain Sciences, 25(1)*, 73–144. ▶ **page 35**

Notman, M.T. and Nadelson, C.C. (1995). Gender, development and psychopathology: a revisited psychodynamic view. In M.V. Seeman (ed.) *Gender and Psychopathology*. Washington, DC: American Psychiatric Press. ▶ **page 183**

Nyman, H., Andréewitch, S., Lundbäck, E. and Mindus, P. (2001). Executive and cognitive functions in patients with extreme obsessive compulsive disorder treated with capsulotomy. *Applied Neuropsychology, 8(2)*, 91–8. ▶ **page 213**

O'Brien, G.V. (2003). Indigestible food, conquering hordes and waster materials: metaphors of immigrants and the early immigration restriction debate in the US. *Metaphor and Symbol, 18(1)*, 33–47. ▶ **page 71**

OCD Centre (2002). OCD: get informed. *See http://www.ocdcentre.com/pages/informed.htm (accessed September 2004).* ▶ **page 207**

Oei, T.P.S. and Gordon, L.M. (2008). Psychosocial factors related to gambling abstinence and relapse in members of Gamblers Anonymous. *Journal of Gambling Studies, 24(1)*, 91–105. ▶ **page 240**

Ogden, J. (1994). Restraint theory and its implications for obesity treatment. *Clinical Psychology and Psychotherapy, 1*, 191–201. ▶ **page 87**

Ogden, J. (2007). *Health Psychology: A Textbook* (4th edn). Buckingham: McGraw Hill/Open University Press. ▶ **pages 86, 87**

Ohayon M.M. and Roth, T. (2003). Place of chronic insomnia in the course of depressive and anxiety disorders. *Journal of Psychiatric Research, 37(1)*, 9–15. ▶ **page 25**

Öhman, A. and Soares, J.J.F. (1994). 'Unconscious anxiety': phobic responses to masked stimuli. *Journal of Abnormal Psychology, 103*, 231–40. ▶ **page 195**

Okazaki, S., Mueller, B. and Taylor, C.R. (2010). Measuring soft-sell versus hard-sell advertising appeals. *Journal of Advertising, 39(2)*, 5–20. ▶ **page 229**

O'Keane, V. and Marsh, M.S. (2007). Depression during pregnancy. *British Medical Journal, 334*, 1003–5. ▶ **page 181**

O'Kearney, R.T., Anstey, K.J. and von Sanden, C. (2006). Behavioural and cognitive behavioural therapy for obsessive compulsive disorder in children and adolescents. *Cochrane Database of Systematic Reviews 2006*, issue 4. ▶ **page 215**

O'Keeffe, C. and Wiseman, R. (2005). Testing alleged mediumship: methods and results. *The British Journal of Psychology, 96(2)*, 165–79. ▶ **page 267**

Oliviero, A. (2008). In 'Why do some people sleepwalk?' by the Editors, *Scientific American*, February 2008. *See http://www.scientificamerican.com/article.cfm?id=why-do-some-people-sleepwalk (accessed June 2012* ▶ **page 26**

Oltmanns, T.F., Neale, J.M. and Davison, G.C. (1999). *Case Studies in Abnormal Psychology* (5th edn). Chichester: Wiley. ▶ **page 169**

O'Mahony, S. and Meenaghan, T. (1997). Researching the impact of celebrity endorsements on consumers. *New Ways for Optimizing Integrated Communications*. The Netherlands: ESOMAR. ▶ **pages 227, 228**

ONS (Office for National Statistics) (2000). Psychiatric morbidity among adults living in private households in Great Britain. *See* http://www.statistics.gov.uk/STATBASE/Product.asp?vlnk=8258 (accessed February 2009). ▶ page 194

Osborn, I. (1998). *Tormenting Thoughts and Secret Rituals*. New York: Pantheon Books. ▶ page 209

Öst, L.G. (1987). Age of onset in different phobias. *Journal of Abnormal Psychology, 96*, 223–9. ▶ page 197

Öst, L.G. (1989). *Blood Phobia: A Specific Phobia Subtype in DSM-IV*. Paper requested by the Simple Phobia subcommittee of the DSM-IV Anxiety Disorders Work Group. ▶ page 194

Oswald, I. (1980). Sleep as a restorative process: human clues. *Progress in Brain Research, 53*, 279–88. ▶ page 20

Page, H.W. (1970). Pictorial depth perception: a note. *South African Journal of Psychology, 1*, 45–8. ▶ page 39

Paik, H. and Comstock, G. (1994). The effects of television violence on antisocial behavior: a meta-analysis. *Communication Research, 21(4)*, 516–46. ▶ page 222

Paley, G., Cahill, J., Barkham, M., Shapiro, D., Jones, J., Patrick, S. and Reid, E. (2008). The effectiveness of psychodynamic-interpersonal therapy in routine clinical practice: a benchmarking comparison. *Psychology and Psychotherapy: Theory, Research and Practice, 81(2)*, 157–75. ▶ pages 186, 187

Palmer, S.E. (1975). The effects of contextual scenes on the identification of objects. *Memory and Cognition, 3*, 519–26. ▶ page 33

Palmer, C.T. and Tilley, C.F. (1995). Sexual access to females as a motivation for joining gangs: an evolutionary approach. *Journal of Sex Research, 32*, 213–17. ▶ page 79

Papakostas, G.I., Nelson, J.C., Kasper, S. and Möller, H.J. (2008). A meta-analysis of clinical trials comparing reboxetine, a norepinephrine re-uptake inhibitor, with selective serotonin re-uptake inhibitors for the treatment of major depressive disorder. *European Neuropsychopharmocology, 18(2)*, 122–7. ▶ page 185

Paris, J.J., Franco, C., Sodano, R., Frye, C.A. and Wulfert, E. (2010). Gambling pathology is associated with dampened cortisol response among men and women. *Physiology and Behaviour, 99(2)*, 230–3. ▶ page 238

Park, Y.W., Allison, D.B., Heymsfield, S.B. and Gallagher, D. (2001). Larger amounts of visceral adipose tissue in Asian Americans. *Obesity Research, 9*, 381–7. ▶ page 87

Parker, G., Parker, I. and Brotchie, H. (2006). Mood state effects of chocolate. *Journal of Affective Disorders, 92*, 149–59. ▶ page 85

Parliamentary Office of Science and Technology (2002). Postnote: *Peer Review September 2002, 182*. *See* http://www.parliament.uk/post/pn182.pdf (accessed December 2008). ▶ page 276

Parnia, S. (2009). Near death experiences in cardiac arrest and the mystery of consciousness. *See* http://www.scimednet.org/library/articlesN75+/N76Parnia_nde.htm (accessed January 2009). ▶ page 268

Pashos, A. (2007). Asymmetric kin investment of grandparents, aunts and uncles: a two-generation-study from Pittsburgh. In È.B. Bodzsár and A. Zsákai (ed.). *New Perspectives and Problems in Anthropology*. Newcastle upon Tyne: Cambridge Scholars Publishing, 57–66. ▶ page 56

Paterline, B.A. and Petersen, D.M. (1999). Structural and social psychological determinants of prisonization. *Journal of Criminal Justice, 27(5)*, 427–41. ▶ page 70

Paulhus, D.L. (2002). Socially desirable responding: the evolution of a construct. In H. Braun, D.N. Jackson and D.E. Wiley (eds) *The Role of Constructs in Psychological and Educational Measurement*. Hillsdale, NJ: Lawrence Erlbaum, 67–88. ▶ page 248

Pauls, D.L. and Leckman, J.F. (1986). The inheritance of Gilles de la Tourette's syndrome and associated behaviours. Evidence for autosomal dominant transmission. *New England Journal of Medicine, 315(16)*, 993–7. ▶ page 209

Paykel, E.S. and Cooper, Z. (1992). Life events and social stress. In E.S. Paykel (ed.) *Handbook of Affective Disorders*. London: Guilford Press, 149–70. ▶ page 183

Peltzer, K. (2002). Paranormal beliefs and personality among black South African students. *Social Behavior and Personality, 30*, 391–398. ▶ page 264

Penner, L.A. and Fritzsche, B.A. (1993). Magic Johnson and reactions to people with AIDS: a natural experiment. *Journal of Applied Social Psychology, 23*, 1035–50. ▶ page 227

Penton-Voak, I.S., Perrett, D.I., Castles, D.L., Kobayashi, T., Burt, D.M. and Murray, L.K. (1999). Menstrual cycle alters face preference. *Nature, 399*, 741–2. ▶ page 55

Perner, J., Ruffman, T. and Leekam, S. (1994). Theory of mind is contagious: you catch it from your sibs. *Child Development, 65*, 1228–38. ▶ page 155

Perry, D.G. and Bussey, K. (1979). The social learning theory of sex differences: imitation is alive and well. *Journal of Personality and Social Psychology, 37*, 1699–712. ▶ page 116

Perse, E.M. and Rubin, R.B. (1989). Attribution in social and parasocial relationships. *Communication Research, 16*, 59–77. ▶ page 231

Persinger, M.M. (2001). The neuropsychiatry of paranormal experiences. *Neuropsychiatric Practice and Opinion, 13(4)*, 521–2. ▶ page 269

Peters, M. (1993). Still no convincing evidence of a relation between brain size and intelligence in humans. *Canadian Journal of Experimental Psychology, 47*, 751–6. ▶ page 137

Petty, R.E. and Cacioppo, J.T. (1981). *Attitudes and persuasion: classic and contemporary approaches*. Dubuque, IA: Wm. C. Brown. ▶ page 226

Pharoah, F., Mari, J.J., Rathbone, J. and Wong, W. (2012). Family intervention in schizophrenia: A review. *The Cochrane Collaboration*. John Wiley.

Philips, H. (2002). Paranormal beliefs linked to brain chemistry. *New Scientist, 24 July*, 17. ▶ page 260

Phillips, D.P. (1974). The influence of suggestion on suicide: substantive and theoretical implications of the Werther effect. *American Sociological Review, 39*, 340–54. ▶ page 233

Phillips, D.P. (1983). The impact of mass media violence on U.S. homicides. *American Sociological Review, 48*, 560–8. ▶ page 222

Phillips, D.P. (1986). The found experiment: a new technique for assessing the impact of mass media violence on real-world aggressive behavior. *Public Communication and Behavior, 1*, 260–307. ▶ page 67

Piaget, J. (1926). *The Language and Thought of the Child*. New York: Harcourt Brace Jovanovich. ▶ page 146

Piaget, J. (1932). *The Moral Judgement of the Child*. Harmondsworth: Penguin. ▶ page 152

Piaget, J. (1954). *The Construction of Reality in the Child*. New York: Basic Books. ▶ pages 146, 262

Piaget, J. and Inhelder, B. (1956). *The Child's Conception of Space*. London: Routledge and Kegan Paul. ▶ page 147

Picon, P., Gauer, G.J.C., Hirakata, V.N., Haggström, L.M., Beidel, D.C., Turner, S.M. and Manfro, G.G. (2005). Reliability of the social phobia and anxiety inventory (SPAI) Portugese version in a heterogenous sample of Brazilian university students. *Revista Brasileira de Psiquiatria, 27(2)*, 124–30. ▶ page 193

Pigott, T.A., Pato, M.T., Bernstein, S.E., Grover, G.N., Hill, J.L., Tolliver, T.J. and Murphy, D.L. (1990). Controlled comparisons of clomipramine and fluoxetine in the treatment of obsessive compulsive disorder. *Archives of General Psychiatry, 47*, 926–32. ▶ page 208

Pike, G. and Brace, N. (2005). Recognition. In N. Braisby and A. Gellatly (eds) *Cognitive Psychology*. Oxford: Oxford University Press. ▶ page 41

Pine, K. and Nash, A. (2001). *The Effects of Television Advertising on Young Children*. Paper presented at the British Psychological Society Centenary Conference, SECC, Glasgow. ▶ pages 228, 229

Pingree, S. (1978). The effects of nonsexist television commercials and perceptions of reality on children's attitudes about women. *Psychology of Women Quarterly, 2*, 262–77. ▶ page 117

Pinker, S. (2002). *The Blank State: The Modern Denial of Human Nature*. New York: Penguin. ▶ page 141

Pinker, S. (2008). Crazy love. *Time Magazine*, 28 January. ▶ page 61

Pipp., S., Easterbrooks, M.A. and Harmon, R.J. (1992). The relation between attachment and knowledge of self and mother in one- to three-year-old infants. *Child Development, 63*, 738–50. ▶ page 155

Playfair, G.L. (2009). PSI and fraud. *See* http://www.skepticalinvestigations.org/observer/psi_fraud.htm (accessed January 2009). ▶ page 259

Plazzi, G., Vetrugno, R., Provini, F. and Montagna, P. (2005). Sleepwalking and other ambulatory behaviours during sleep. *Journal of Neurological Sciences, 26*, 193–8. ▶ page 26

Pleva, J. and Wade, T.D. (2006). The mediating effects of misinterpretation of intrusive thoughts on obsessive compulsive symptoms. *Behaviour Research and Therapy, 44*, 1471–9. ▶ page 210

Plomin, R., Foch, T.T. and Rowe, D.C. (1981). Bobo clown aggression in childhood: environment, not genes. *Journal of Research in Personality, 15*, 331–42. ▶ page 75

Plotnik, J.M., de Waal, F.B.M. and Reiss, D. (2006). Self-recognition in an Asian elephant. *Proceedings of the National Academy of Sciences, USA, 103(45)*, 17053–7. ▶ page 134

Podaliri, C. and Balestri, C. (1998). The Ultràs, racism and football culture in Italy. In A. Brown (ed.) *Fanatics! Power, Identity and Fandom in Football*. London: Routledge. ▶ page 78

Polivy, J., Herman, P.C. and McFarlane, T. (1994). Effects of anxiety on eating: does palatability moderate distress-induced overeating in dieters? *Journal of Abnormal Psychology, 103*, 505–10. ▶ page 96

Pollack, N.J. (1995). Social fattening patterns in the Pacific: the positive side of obesity – a Nauru case study. In I. de Garine and N.J. Pollack (eds) *Social Aspects of Obesity*. Amsterdam: Gordon and Breach Publishers, 87–110. ▶ page 92

Pollard, R. and Pollard G. (2005). Long-term trends in home advantage in professional team sports in North America and England (1876–2003). *Journal of Sports Science, 23*, 337–50. ▶ page 79

Poole, E.D. and Regoli, R.M. (1983). Violence in juvenile institutions: a comparative study. *Criminology, 21*, 213–32. ▶ page 71

Popper, K.R. (1934). *The Logic of Scientific Discovery*. English translation, 1959, London: Hutchinson. ▶ page 275

Postmes, T. and Spears, R. (1998). Deindividuation and anti-normative behaviour: a meta-analysis. *Psychological Bulletin, 123*, 238–59. ▶ page 69

Powell, A.D. and Khan, A.S. (1995). Racial differences in women's desire to be thin. *International Journal of Eating Disorders, 17*, 191–5. ▶ page 84

Prentice-Dunn, S., Rogers, R.W., Spivey, C.B. and Traweek, S.J. (1982). *Public and Private Self-awareness and Collective Aggression: A Revision of Deindividuation*. Paper presented at the meeting of the Southeastern Psychological Association, New Orleans, LA. ▶ page 68

Prescott, C.A., Strauss, M.E. and Tune, L.E. (1986). Test–retest reliability of information-processing measures among chronic schizophrenics. *Psychiatry Research, 17(3)*, 199–202. ▶ page 165

Putwain, D. and Symes, W. (2011). Perceived fear appeals and examination performance: facilitating or debilitating outcomes? *Learning and Individual Differences, 21(2)*, 227–32. ▶ page 226

Pronin, E., Wegner, D.M., McCarthy, K. and Rodriguez, S. (2006). Everyday magical powers: the role of apparent mental causation in the overestimation of personal influence. *Journal of Personality and Social Psychology, 91(2)*, 216–31. ▶ page 262

Quadagno, D.M., Briscoe, R. and Quadagno, R.S. (1977). Effect of perinatal gonadal hormones on selected nonsexual behavior patterns: a critical assessment of the non-human and human literature. *Psychological Bulletin, 84*, 62–80. ▶ page 104

Qualter, P. and Munn, P. (2005). The friendships and play partners of lonely children. *Journal of Social and Personal Relationships, 22*, 379–97. ▶ page 58

Rachman, S. (1998). A cognitive theory of obsessions: elaborations. *Behaviour Research and Therapy, 36*, 385–401. ▶ page 211

Rachman, S.J. and Hodgson, R.J. (1980). *Obsessions and Compulsions.* Englewood Cliffs, NJ: Prentice-Hall. ▶ page 211

Radin, D.I. and Nelson, R.D. (2003). Meta-analysis of mind-matter interaction experiments: 1959–2000. In W. Jonas and C. Crawford (eds) *Healing, Intention and Energy Medicine.* London: Harcourt Health Sciences. ▶ page 259

Radin, D., Nelson, R.D., Dobyns, Y. and Houtkooper, J. (2006). Reexamining psychokinesis: commentary on the Bösch, Steinkamp and Boller meta-analysis. *Psychological Bulletin, 132*, 529–32. ▶ page 259

Ragsdale, J.D. and Brandau-Brown, F.E. (2007). Could relational maintenance in marriage really be like grocery shopping? A reply to Stafford and Canary. *Journal of Family Communication, 7(1)*, 47–60. ▶ page 51

Rahe, R.H., Mahan, J. and Arthur, R. (1970). Prediction of near-future health-change from subjects' preceding life changes. *Journal of Psychosomatic Research, 14*, 401–6. ▶ page 279

Raleigh, M.J., McGuire, M.T. and Brammer, G.L. (1991). Serotonergic mechanisms promote dominance acquisition in adult male vervet monkeys. *Brain Research, 559*, 181–90. ▶ page 73

Ramachandran, V.S. (2000). Mirror neurons and imitation learning as the driving force behind 'the great leap forward' in human evolution. See http://www.edge.org/3rd_culture/ramachandran/ramachandran_p1.html (accessed November 2008). ▶ page 158

Ramachandran, V.S. (2008). Phantom penises in transsexuals. *Journal of Consciousness Studies, 15(1)*, 5–16. ▶ page 110

Ramachandran, V.S., Rogers-Ramachandran, D.C. and Cobb, S. (1995). Touching the phantom. *Nature, 377(6549)*, 489–90. ▶ page 110

Rametti, G., Carrillo, B., Gómez-Gil, E., Junque, C., Segovia, S., Gomez, A. and Guillamon, A. (2011). White matter microstructure in female to male transsexuals before cross-sex hormonal treatment. A diffusion tensor imaging study. *Journal of Psychiatric Research, 45(2)*, 199–204. ▶ page 111

Rasmussen, S.A. and Eisen, J.L. (1992). The epidemiology and clinical features of obsessional compulsive disorder. *Psychiatric Clinics of North America, 15*, 743–58. ▶ page 209

Rattenborg, N.C., Obermeyer, W.H., Vacha, E. and Benca, R.M. (2005). Acute effects of light and darkness on sleep in the pigeon (Columba livia). *Physiology and Behavior, 84*, 635–40. ▶ page 21

Raven, J. (2000). The Raven's progressive matrices: change and stability over culture and time. *Cognitive Psychology, 41(1)*, 1–48. ▶ page 125

Read, J. (2004). Electroconvulsive therapy. In J. Read, L.R. Mosher and R.P. Bentall (eds) *Models of Madness.* London: Routledge, 86–99. ▶ page 171

Reader, S.M. and Laland, K.N. (2002). Social intelligence, innovation, and enhanced brain size in primates. *Proceedings of the National Academy of Science, USA, 99*, 4436–41. ▶ page 136

Recht, L.D., Lew, R.A. and Schwartz, W.J. (1995). Baseball teams beaten by jet lag. *Nature, 377(6550)*, 583. ▶ page 16

Rechtschaffen, A., Gilliland, M., Bergmann, B. and Winter, J. (1983). Physiological correlates of prolonged sleep deprivation in rats. *Science, 221*, 182–4. ▶ page 21

Redden, J.P. (2008). Reducing satiation: the role of categorization level. *Journal of Consumer Research, 34*, 624–34. ▶ page 86

Regan, T. (1984). *The Case for Animal Rights.* New York: Routledge. ▶ page 283

Rehm, J., Steinleitner, M. and Lilli, W. (1987). Wearing uniforms and aggression: a field experiment. *European Journal of Social Psychology, 17*, 357–60. ▶ page 68

Reinberg, A., Andlauer, P., DePrins, J., Malberg, W., Vieux, N. and Baurdeleau, P. (1984). Desynchronisation of the oral temperature circadian rhythm and intolerance to shift work. *Nature, 308(5956)*, 272–5. ▶ page 16

Reiner, W.G. and Gearhart, M.D. (2004). Discordant sexual identity in some genetic males with cloacal exstrophy assigned to female sex at birth. *New England Journal of Medicine, 350*, 333–641. ▶ page 105

Reiss, D., and Marino, L. (2001). Mirror self-recognition in the bottlenose dolphin: a case of cognitive convergence. *Proceedings of the National Academy of Science USA, 98*, 5937–42. ▶ page 134

Rhee, S.H. and Waldman, I.D. (2002). Genetic and environmental influences on antisocial behavior: a meta-analysis of twin and adoption studies. *Psychological Bulletin, 128*, 490–529. ▶ page 74

Rhine, J.B. (1929). An investigation of a 'mind-reading horse'. *Journal of Abnormal and Social Psychology, 23*, 449–66. ▶ page 259

Rhine, J.B. (1974). Comments: a new case of experimenter unreliability. *Journal of Parapsychology, 38*, 215–25. ▶ page 258

Rice, M.L., Huston, A.C., Truglio, R. and Wright, J. (1990). Words from Sesame Street: learning vocabulary while viewing. *Developmental Psychology, 26*, 421–8. ▶ page 220

Richard, J.F. and Schneider, B.H. (2005). Assessing friendship motivation during pre- and early adolescence. *Journal of Early Adolescence, 25*, 367–85. ▶ page 59

Ridley, M. (1993). *The Red Queen: Sex and the Evolution of Human Nature.* New York: Viking. ▶ page 98

Ring, K. (1980). *Life at Death: A Scientific Investigation of the Near-death Experience.* New York: Coward, McCann and Geoghegan. ▶ page 268

Ritchie, S.J., Wiseman, R. and French, C.C. (2012). Failing the future: three unsuccessful attempts to replicate Bem's 'retroactive facilitation of recall' effect. *PLoS ONE, 7(3)*, e33423. doi:10.1371/journal.pone.0033423. ▶ page 256

Rizzolatti, G. and Arbib, M.A. (1998). Language within our grasp. *Trends in Neuroscience, 21*, 188–94. ▶ page 158

Rizzolatti, G., Fadiga, L., Fogassi, L. and Gallese, V. (1996). Premotor cortex and the recognition of motor actions. *Cognitive Brain Research, 3*, 131–41. ▶ page 158

Roberts, K.A. (2007). Relationship attachment and the behaviour of fans towards celebrities. *Applied Psychology in Criminal Justice, 3(1)*, 54–74. ▶ page 233

Roberts, B.W., Walton, K.E. and Viechtbauer, W. (2006). Patterns of mean-level change in personality traits across the life course: a meta-analysis of longitudinal studies. *Psychological Bulletin, 132*, 3–27. ▶ page 93

Roberts, R.E., Roberts, C.R. and Duong, H.T. (2008). Chronic insomnia and its negative consequences for health and functioning of adolescents: a 12-month prospective study. *Journal of Adolescent Health, 42*, 294–302. ▶ page 24

Robinson, L., Berman, J. and Neimeyer, R. (1990). Psychotherapy for the treatment of depression: a comprehensive review of controlled outcome research. *Psychological Bulletin, 108*, 30–49. ▶ page 187

Rock, A.J. and Beischel, J. (2008). Quantitative analysis of mediums' conscious experiences during a discarnate reading versus a control task: a pilot study. *Australian Journal of Parapsychology, 8(2)*, 157–79. ▶ page 266

Rodriguez-Martin, J.L., Barbanoj, J.M., Pérez, V. and Sacristan, M. (2003). Transcranial magnetic stimulation for the treatment of obsessive compulsive disorder. *Cochrane Database of Systematic Reviews, 2.* See http://onlinelibrary.wiley.com/doi/10.1002/14651858.CD003387/full (accessed June 2012). ▶ page 213

Roe, C.A. (1996). Clients' influence in the selection of elements of a psychic reading. *The Journal of Parapsychology, 60*, 43–70. ▶ page 267

Rogers, P., Davis, T. and Fisk, J. (2009). Paranormal belief and susceptibility to the conjunction fallacy. *Applied Cognitive Psychology, 23*, 524–42. ▶ page 260

Rohlfing, M.E. (1995). Doesn't anybody stay in one place anymore? An exploration of the understudied phenomenon of long-distance relationships. In J.T. Wood and S.W. Duck (eds) *Understudied Relationships: Off the Beaten Track.* Thousand Oaks, CA: Sage, 173–96. ▶ page 53

Roisman, G.I., Masten, A.S., Coatsworth, D. and Tellegen, A. (2004). Salient and emerging developmental tasks in the transition to adulthood. *Child Development, 75(1)*, 123–33. ▶ page 59

Rollie, S.S. and Duck, S.W. (2006). Stage theories of marital breakdown. In J.H. Harvey and M.A. Fine (eds) *Handbook of Divorce and Dissolution of Romantic Relationships.* Hillsdale, NJ: Lawrence Erlbaum, 176–93. ▶ page 52

Rolls, E.T. and Rolls, B.J. (1973). Altered food preferences after lesions in the basolateral region of the amygdala. *Journal of Comparative Physiology and Psychology, 83*, 248–59. ▶ page 88

Rosa, L., Rosa, E., Sarner, L. and Barrett, S. (1998). A close look at therapeutic touch. *The Journal of the American medical Association, 279(13)*, 1005–10. ▶ page 266

Rose, D., Fleischmann, P., Wykes, T., Leese, M. and Bindman, J. (2003). Patients' perspectives on electroconvulsive therapy: systematic review. *British Medical Journal, 326*, 1363–5. ▶ page 185

Rosenbaum, M.E. (1986). The repulsion hypothesis: on the nondevelopment of relationships. *Journal of Personality and Social Psychology, 51*, 1156–61. ▶ page 49

Rosenfeld, R., Dar, R., Anderson, D., Kobak, K.A. and Greist, J.H. (1992). A computer-administered version of the Yale-Brown Obsessive Compulsive Scale. *Psychological Assessment, 4*, 329–32. ▶ page 206

Rosenhan, D.L. (1973). On being sane in insane places. *Science, 179*, 250–8. ▶ pages 165, 169, 192

Rosenhan, D.L. and Seligman, M.E.P. (1989). *Abnormal psychology* (2nd edn). London: Norton. ▶ page 201

Rosenkoetter, L.I. (1999). The television situation comedy and children's prosocial behavior. *Journal of Applied Social Psychology, 29*, 979–93. ▶ page 220

Rosenthal, R. and Jacobson, L. (1968). *Pygmalion in the Classroom: Teacher Expectations and Pupils' Intellectual Development.* New York: Holt, Rinehart and Winston. ▶ page 263

Ross, C.A. and Read, J. (2004). Antipsychotic medication: myths and facts. In J. Read, L.R. Mosher and R.P. Bentall (eds) *Models of Madness.* London: Routledge. ▶ page 171

Rossion, B., Caldara, R., Seghier, M., Schuller, A.-M., Lazeyras, F. and Mayer, E. (2003). A network of occipito-temporal face-sensitive areas besides the right middle fusiform gyrus is necessary for normal face processing. *Brain, 126*, 2381–95. ▶ page 42

Rowe, D.C. (2002). What twin and adoption studies reveal about parenting. In J.G. Borkowski, S.L. Ramey and M. Bristol-Power (eds) *Parenting* and the Child's World: Influences on Academic, Intellectual, and Social-emotional Development. Hillsdale, NJ: Lawrence Erlbaum, 21–34. ▶ page 57

Rozin, P., Fischler, C., Imada, S., Sarubin, A. and Wrzesniewski, A. (1999). Attitudes to food and the role of food in life in the USA, Japan, Flemish Belgium and France: possible implications for the diet-health debate. *Appetite*, 33, 163–80. ▶ page 85

Rozin, P., Millman, L. and Nemeroff, C. (1986). Operation of the laws of sympathetic magic in disgust and other domains. *Journal of Personality and Social Psychology*, 50, 703–12. ▶ page 262

Rubenstein, E.A. and Sprafkin, J.N. (1982). Television and persons in institutions. In D. Pearl, L. Bouthilet and J. Lazar (eds) *Television and Behavior: Ten Years of Scientific Progress and Implications for the Eighties*. US Department of Health and Human Services, Public Health Service, Alcohol, Drug Abuse and Mental Health Administration, Rockville, MD: National Institute of Mental Health, 322–30. ▶ page 221

Ruble, D.N., Taylor, L., Cyphers, L., Greulich, F.K., Lurye, L.E. and Shrout, P.E. (2007). The role of gender constancy in early gender development. *Child Development*, 78(4), 1121–36. ▶ page 115

Ruck, C., Andreewitch, S., Flyckt, K., Edman, G., Nyman, H., Meyerson, B.A., Lippitz, B.E., Hindmarsh, T., Svanborg, P., Mindus, P. and Asberg, M. (2003). Capsulotomy for refractory anxiety disorders: long-term follow-up of 26 patients. *American Journal of Psychiatry*, 160, 513–21. ▶ page 199

Ruhe, H.G., Mason, N.S. and Schene, A.H. (2007). Mood is indirectly related to serotonin, norepinephrine and dopamine levels in humans: a meta-analysis of monoamine depletion studies. *Molecular Psychiatry*, 12, 331–59. ▶ page 181

Rusbult, C.E. and Martz, J.M. (1995). Remaining in an abusive relationship: an investment model analysis of non-voluntary commitment. *Personality and Social Psychology Bulletin*, 21, 558–71. ▶ page 51

Rush, A., First, M.B. and Blacker, D. (2007). *Handbook of Psychiatric Measures*. Arlington, VA: American Psychiatric Publishing. ▶ page 207

Rushton, J.P. (1995). *Race, Evolution, and Behavior: A Life-history Perspective*. New Brunswick, NJ: Transaction. ▶ page 137

Russell, M.J., Switz, G.M. and Thompson, K. (1980). Olfactory influences on the human menstrual cycle. *Pharmacology, Biochemistry and Behaviour*, 13, 737–8. ▶ page 13

Russell, W.M.S. and Birch, R. (1959). *The Principles of Humane Experimental Technique*. London: Methuen. ▶ page 283

Ryan, N.D. (1992). The pharmacologic treatment of child and adolescent depression. *Psychiatric Clinics of North America*, 15, 29–40. ▶ page 185

Sabbagh, M.A. and Callanan, M.A. (1998). Metarepresentation in action: children's theories of mind developing and emerging in parent-child conversations. *Developmental Psychology*, 34, 491–502. ▶ page 155

Sachdev, P. and Hay, P. (1995). Does neurosurgery for obsessive compulsive disorder produce personality change? *Journal of Nervous and Mental Disease*, 183, 408–13. ▶ page 213

Sackeim, H.A., Prudic, J. and Devanand, D.P. (2000). A prospective, randomized, double-blind comparison of bilateral and right-unilateral electroconvulsive therapy at different stimulus intensities. *Archives of General Psychiatry*, 57(5), 425–34. ▶ page 185

Şahin, E., Çakmak, M., Doğar, M.R., Uğur, E. and Üçoluk, G. (2007). To afford or not to afford: a new formalisation of affordances towards affordance-based robot control. *Adaptive Behaviour*, 15(4), 447–72. ▶ page 35

Sakurai, T. (2007). The neural circuit of orexin (hypocretin): maintaining sleep and wakefulness. *Nature Reviews Neuroscience*, 8, 171–81. ▶ page 26

Sakurai, T., Amemiya, A., Ishii, M., Matsuzaki, I., Chemelli, R.M., Tanaka, H., Williams, S.C., Richardson, J.A., Kozlowski, G.P., Wilson, S., Arch, J.R., Buckingham, R.E., Haynes, A.C., Carr, S.A., Annan, R.S., McNulty, D.E., Liu, W.S., Terrett, J.A., Elshourbagy, N.A. and Bergsma, D.J. (1998). Orexins and orexin receptors: a family of hypothalamic neuropeptides and G protein-coupled receptors that regulate feeding behavior. *Cell*, 92, 573–85. ▶ page 89

Salkovskis, P.M. (1998). Psychological approaches to the understanding of obsessional problems. In R.P. Swinson, M.M. Anthony, S. Rachmen and M.A. Richter (eds) *Obsessive Compulsive Disorder: Theory, Research and Treatment*. New York: Guilford Press. ▶ page 210

Salzman, L. (1980). *Psychotherapy of the Obsessive Personality*. New York: Jason Aronson. ▶ page 211

Samuel, J. and Bryant, P. (1984). Asking only one question in the conservation experiment. *Journal of Child Psychology and Psychiatry*, 25(2), 315–18. ▶ page 147

Sandell, M.A. and Breslin, P.A.S. (2006). Variability in a taste-receptor gene determines whether we taste toxins in food. *Current Biology*, 16(18), R792–R794. ▶ page 91

Sargent, J.D. and Hanewinkel, R. (2009). Comparing the effects of entertainment media and tobacco marketing on youth smoking in Germany. *Addiction*, 104, 815–23. ▶ page 247

Sarita, E.P., Janakiramaiah, N. and Gangadhar, B.N. (1998). Efficacy of combined ECT after two weeks of neuroleptics in schizophrenia: a double-blind controlled study. *National Institute of Mental Health and Neurosciences Journal*, 16, 243–51. ▶ page 171

Sassin, J.F., Parker, D.C., Mace, J.W., Gotlin, R.W., Johnson, L.C. and Rossman, L.G. (1969). Human growth hormone release: relation to slow-wave sleep and sleep-waking cycles. *Science*, 165(3892), 513–15. ▶ page 20

Savage-Rumbaugh, E.S., Shanker, S.G. and Taylor, T.J. (1998). *Ape Language and the Human Mind*. New York: Oxford University Press. ▶ page 149

Savard, J., Laroche, L., Simard, S., Ivers, H. and Morin, C.M. (2003). Chronic insomnia and immune functioning. *Psychosomatic Medicine*, 65(2), 211–21. ▶ page 25

Scahill, L., Riddle, M.A., McSwiggin-Hardin, M., Ort, S.I., King, R.A., Goodman, W.K., Cicchetti, D. and Leckman, J.F. (1997). Children's Yale-Brown Obsessive Compulsive Scake: reliability and validity. *Journal of the American Academy of Child and Adolescent Psychiatry*, 36(6), 844–52. ▶ page 206

Scerbo, A.S. and Raine, A. (1993). Neurotransmitters and antisocial behavior: a meta-analysis. Cited in A. Raine (ed.) *The Psychopathology of Crime: Criminal Behavior as a Clinical Disorder*. San Diego: Academic Press, 86–92. ▶ page 72

Scharrer E., Kim, D.D., Lin, K.-M. and Liu, Z. (2006). Working hard or hardly working? Gender, humor, and the performance of domestic chores in television commercials. *Mass Communication and Society*, 9, 215–38. ▶ page 229

Scheff, T. (1974). The labelling theory of mental illness. *American Sociological Review*, 39, 444–52. ▶ page 169

Scheff, T. (1999). *Being Mentally Ill: A Sociological Theory* (3rd edn). Chicago: Aldine de Gruyter. ▶ page 168

Schembri, C. and Evans, L. (2008). Adverse relationship processes: the attempts of women with bulimia nervosa symptoms to fit the perceived ideal of intimate partners. *European Eating Disorders Review*, 16(1), 59–66. ▶ page 97

Schiappa, E., Allen, M. and Gregg, P.B. (2007). Parasocial relationships and television: a meta-analysis of effects. In R.W. Preiss, B.M. Gayle, N. Burrell, M. Allen and J. Bryant (eds) *Mass-media Effects Research: Advances Through Meta-analysis*. Hillsdale, NJ: Lawrence Erlbaum. ▶ page 230

Schindler, K.M., Richter, M.A., Kennedy, J.L., Pato, M.T. and Pato, C.N. (2002). Association between homozygosity at the COMT gene locus and obsessive compulsive disorder. *American Journal of Medical Genetics (Neuropsychiatric Genetics)*, 96(6), 721–4. ▶ page 209

Schlegel, A. and Barry III, H. (1986). The cultural consequences of female contribution to subsistence. *American Anthropologist*, 88, 142–50. ▶ page 119

Schnur, P. (2008). Predictable peckers. *Observer – Association for Psychological science, 21(11)*. See http://www.psychologicalscience.org/observer/getArticle.cfm?id=2431 (accessed January 2009). ▶ page 263

Schub, M.H. (2006). A critique of the parapsychological random number generator meta-analyses of Radin and Nelson. *Journal of Scientific Exploration*, 20, 402–19. ▶ page 259

Schwartz, G.E.R., Russek, L.G.S., Nelson, L.A. and Barentsen, C. (2001). Accuracy and replicability of anomalous after-death communication across highly skilled mediums. *Journal of the Society for Psychical Research*, 65(862), 1–25. ▶ page 266

Schwartz, J.M., Stoessel, P.W., Baxter, L.R. Jr., Martin, K.M. and Phelps, M.E. (1996). Systematic changes in cerebral glucose metabolic rate after successful behaviour modification treatment of obsessive compulsive disorder. *Archives of General Psychiatry*, 53, 109–13. ▶ pages 209, 213

Schweinhart, L.J., Barnes, H.V. and Weikart, D.P. (1993). *Significant Benefits: The High-Scope Perry Preschool Study through age 27*. Ypsilanti, MI: High Scope Press. ▶ page 140

Schwerin, H.S. and Newell, H.H. (1981). *Persuasion in Marketing*. New York: Wiley. ▶ page 226

Scott A.I.F. (2004). *The ECT handbook (2nd edn): the Third Report of the Royal College of Psychiatrists' Special Committee on ECT*. London: Royal College of Psychiatrists ECT Review Group. ▶ page 185

Seckel, A. and Klarke, A. (1997). See http://psylux.psych.tu-dresden.de/i1/kaw/diverses%20Material/www.illusionworks.com/html/ames_room.html (accessed June 2012). ▶ page 35

Seepersad, S., Choi, M. and Shin, N. (2008). How does culture influence the degree of romantic loneliness and closeness? *The Journal of Psychology*, 142(2), 209–16. ▶ page 60

Segall, M.H., Campbell, D.T. and Herskovits, M.J. (1963). Cultural differences in the perception of geometric illusions. *Science*, 139, 769–71. ▶ pages 33, 38

Seligman, M.E.P. (1970). On the generality of the laws of learning. *Psychological Review*, 77, 406–18. ▶ pages 91, 129, 194

Seligman, M.E.P. (1975). *Helplessness: On Depression, Development, and Death*. San Francisco, CA: W.H. Freeman. ▶ pages 182, 183

Selman, R. (1976). Social cognitive understanding. In T. Lickona (ed.) *Moral Development and Behavior*. New York: Holt, Rinehart and Winston. ▶ page 156

Selman, R. (1980). *The Growth of Interpersonal Understanding*. New York: Academic Press. ▶ page 156

Selman, R. (2003). Teaching social awareness: an interview with Larsen Professor Robert Selman by A. Bucuvalas. See http://www.gse.harvard.edu/news/features/selman02012003.html (accessed November 2008). ▶ page 157

Selmi, P.M., Klein, M.H. and Greist, J.H. (1990). Computer-administered CBT for depression. *American Journal of Psychiatry*, 147, 51–6. ▶ page 187

Sergent, J., Ohta, S. and MacDonald, B. (1992). Functional neuroanatomy of face and object processing: a positron emission tomography study. *Brain*, 115(1), 15–36. ▶ page 41

Shackelford, T.K., Buss, D.M. and Peters, J. (2000). Wife killing: risk to women as a function of age. *Violence and Victims*, 15, 273–82. ▶ page 76

Shackelford, T.K., Goetz, A.T., Buss, D.M., Euler, H.A. and Hoier, S. (2005). When we hurt the ones we love: predicting violence against women from men's mate retention. *Personal Relationships*, 12, 447–63. ▶ page 77

Shah, K.R., Eisen, S.A. and Xian, H. (2005). Genetic studies of pathological gambling: a review of methodology and analyses of data from the Vietnam twin registry. *Journal of Gambling Studies*, 21, 179–203. ▶ page 238

Shah, R. and Waller, G. (2000). Parental style and vulnerability to depression: the role of core beliefs. *The Journal of Nervous and Mental Disease*, 188, 19–25. ▶ page 183

Shapiro, C.M., Bortz, R., Mitchell, D., Bartel, P. and Jooste, P. (1981). Slow-wave sleep: a recovery period after exercise. *Science*, 214, 1253–4. ▶ page 21

Shaver, P., Hazan, C. and Bradshaw, D. (1988). Love as attachment: the integration of three behavioral systems. In R.J. Sternberg and M.L. Barnes (eds) *The Psychology of Love*. New Haven, CT: Yale University Press. ▶ page 58

Shaver, P.R., Furman, W. and Buhrmester, D. (1985). Transition to college: network changes, social skills, and loneliness. In S. Duck and D. Perlman (eds) *Understanding Personal Relationships: An Interdisciplinary Approach*. London: Sage, 193–219. ▶ page 52

Shaw, R.P. and Wong, Y. (1989). *Genetic Seeds of Warfare*. Cambridge, MA: Unwin Hyman. ▶ page 78

Sheldon, K.M., Abad, N. and Hinsch, C. (2011). A two-process view of Facebook use and relatedness need-satisfaction: disconnectedness drives use and connectedness rewards it. *Journal of Personality and Social Psychology*, 100, 766–75. ▶ page 49

Shields, N.M. and Hanneke, C.R. (1983). Battered wives' reactions to marital rape. In D. Finkelhor, R.J. Gelles, G.T. Hotaling and M.A. Strauss (eds) *The Dark Side of Families: Current Family Violence Research*. Beverly Hills: Sage. ▶ page 76

Shin, C., Kim, J., Lee, S., Ahn, Y. and Joo, S. (2003). Sleep habits, excessive daytime sleepiness and school performance in high school students. *Psychiatry and Clinical Neuroscience*, 57(4), 451–3. ▶ page 19

Shiraishi, H., Suzuki, A., Fukasawa, T., Aoshima, T., Ujiie, Y. and Ishii, G. (2006). Monoamine oxidase A gene promoter polymorphism affects novelty seeking and reward dependence in healthy study participants. *Psychiatric Genetics*, 16, 55–8. ▶ page 231

Shopland, J.C. and Gregory, R.L. (1964). The effect of touch on a visually ambiguous three-dimensional figure. *Quarterly Journal of Experimental Psychology*, 16(1), 66–70. ▶ page 33

Shroff H. and Thompson J.K. (2006). Peer influences, body image dissatisfaction, eating dysfunction and self-esteem in adolescent girls. *Journal of Health Psychology*, 11, 533–51. ▶ page 93

Sieber, J.E. and Stanley, B. (1988). Ethical and professional dimensions of socially sensitive research. *American Psychologist*, 43, 49–55. ▶ page 282

Siegel, J.M. (2003). Why we sleep. *Scientific American*, November, 92–7. ▶ page 20

Siegel, J.M. and Rogawski, M.A. (1988). A function for REM sleep: regulation of noradrenergic receptor sensitivity. *Brain Research Review*, 13, 213–33. ▶ page 20

Siegel, J.M., Nienhuis, R., Gulyani, S., Ouyang, S., Wu, M.F., Mignot, E., Switzer, R.C., McMurry, G. and Cornford, M. (1999). Neuronal degeneration in canine narcolepsy. *Journal of Neuroscience*, 19(1), 248–57. ▶ page 27

Siever, M.D. (1994). Sexual orientation and gender as factors in socioculturally acquired vulnerability to body dissatisfaction and eating disorders. *Journal of Consulting and Clinical Psychology*, 62, 252–60. ▶ page 85

Siffre, M. (1975). Six months alone in a cave. *National Geographic*, March, 426–35. ▶ page 10

Signorelli, N. and Bacue, A. (1999). Recognition and respect: a content analysis of prime-time television characters across three decades. *Sex Roles*, 40, 527–44. ▶ page 117

Simons, A.D., Gordon, J.S., Monroe, S.M., and Thase, M.E. (1995). Toward an integration of psychologic, social, and biologic factors in depression: effects on outcome and course of cognitive therapy. *Journal of Consulting and Clinical Psychology*, 63, 369–77. ▶ page 187

Simpson, J., Collins, W.A., Tran, S. and Haydon, K. (2007). Attachment and the experience and expression of emotion in romantic relationships: a developmental perspective. *Journal of Personality and Social Psychology*, 92(2), 355–67. ▶ page 59

Simpson, J.A., Gangestad, S.W. and Lerma, M. (1990). Perception of physical attractiveness: mechanisms involved in the maintenance of romantic relationships. *Journal of Personality and Social Psychology*, 59, 1192–201. ▶ page 52

Sinclair-de-Zwart, H. (1969). Developmental psycholinguistics. In D. Elkind and J. Flavell (eds) *Studies in Cognitive Development*. Oxford: Oxford University Press. ▶ page 149

Sindelar, J., Elbel, B. and Petry, N.M. (2007). What do we get for our money? Cost-effectiveness of adding contingency management. *Addiction*, 102(2), 309–16. ▶ page 250

Singer, P. (1990). *Animal Liberation* (2nd edn). New York: Avon Books. ▶ page 283

Singh, D. (1994). Is thin really beautiful and good? Relationship between waist-to-hip ratio (WHR) and female attractiveness. *Personality and Individual Differences*, 16, 123–32. ▶ page 98

Singh, R. and Tan, L.S.C. (1992). Attitudes and attraction: a test of the similarity-attraction and dissimilarity-repulsion hypotheses. *British Journal of Social Psychology*, 31, 227–38. ▶ page 49

Sistrunk, F. and McDavid, J.W. (1971). Sex variable in conforming behaviour, *Journal of Personality and Social Psychology* 8, 200–7. ▶ page 113

Skinner, B.F. (1947). Superstition in the pigeon. *Journal of Experimental Psychology*, 38, 168–72. ▶ pages 262, 263

Skyre, I., Onstad, S., Torgersen, S. and Kringlen, E. (1991). High interrater reliability for the structured clinical interview for DSM-III-R. Axis I (SCID-I). *Acta Psychiatrica Scandinavica*, 84, 167–73. ▶ page 192

Slaby, R.G., and Frey, K.S. (1975). Development of gender constancy and selective attention to same-sex models. *Child Development*, 46, 849–56. ▶ page 113

Slack, G. (2007). Source of human empathy found in brain. *New Scientist*, 12 November, 2629. ▶ page 159

Slater, A. and Lewis, M. (2002). *Introduction to Infant Development*. Oxford: Oxford University Press. ▶ page 154

Slater, A., Field, T.M. and Hernandez-Reif, M. (2002). The development of the sense. In A. Slater and M. Lewis (ed.) *Introduction to Infant Development*. Oxford: Oxford University Press. ▶ page 37

Slater, A., Mattock, A. and Brown, E. (1990). Size constancy at birth: newborn infants' responses to retinal and real size. *Journal of Experimental Psychology*, 49, 314–22. ▶ page 36

Slater, M.D., Kelly, K.J., Lawrence, F.R., Stanley, L.R. and Comello, M.L.G. (2011). Assessing media campaigns linking marijuana non-use with autonomy and aspirations: 'Be under your own influence' and ONDCP's 'Above the influence'. *Prevention Science*, 12(1), 12–22. ▶ page 248

Slavin, R.E. (1991). *Educational Psychology: Theory into Practice* (3rd edn). Englewoord Cliffs, NJ: Prentice-Hall. ▶ page 151

Smith, C. and Lloyd, B. (1978). Maternal behaviour and perceived sex of infant: revisited. *Child Development*, 49, 1263–5. ▶ page 116

Smith, K.A., Fairburn, C.G. and Cowen, P.J. (1999). Symptomatic relapse in bulimia nervosa following acute tryptophan depletion. *Archives of General Psychiatry*, 56, 171–6. ▶ page 99

Smith, P.K. and Pellegrini, A. (2008). Learning through play. See http://www.child-encyclopedia.com/documents/Smith-PellegriniANGxp.pdf (accessed June 2012). ▶ page 157

Smith, R. (1999). Opening up BMJ peer review. *British Medical Journal*, 318, 4–5. ▶ page 272

Snarey, J.R. (1985). Cross-cultural universality of social-moral development: a critical review of Kohlbergian research. *Psychological Bulletin*, 97, 202–32. ▶ page 153

Snarey, J.R. and Keljo, K. (1991). In a gemeinschaft voice: the cross-cultural expansion of moral development theory. In W.M. Kurtines and J.L. Gewitz (eds) *Handbook of Moral Behaviour and Development* (vol. 1). Hillsdale, NJ: Lawrence Erlbaum. ▶ page 153

Snyder, M. and DeBono, K. (1985). Appeals to image and claims about quality: understanding the psychology of advertising. *Journal of Personality and Social Psychology*, 49, 586–97. ▶ page 228

Soetens, B., Braet, C., Dejonckheere, P. and Roets, A. (2006). When suppression backfires: the ironic effects of suppressing eating-related thoughts. *Journal of Health Psychology*, 11(5), 655–8. ▶ page 87

Solfvin, J., Leskowitz, E. and Benor, D.J. (2005). Questions concerning the scientific credibility of wound-healing studies authored by Daniel P. Wirth. See http://www.wholistichealingresearch.com/WirthQ.html (accessed January 2009). ▶ page 266

Solomon, C.M. (1993). HR is solving shiftwork problems. *Personal Journal*, 72(8), 36–48. ▶ page 17

Solyom, L., Beck, P., Solyom, C. and Hugel, R. (1974). Some etiological factors in phobic neurosis. *Journal of the Canadian Psychiatric Association*, 19, 69–78. ▶ page 194

Sommerville, J.A., Woodward, A.L. and Needham, A. (2005). Action experience alters 3-month-old infants' perception of others' actions. *Cognition*, 96, B1–11. ▶ page 157

Sood, S. and Rogers, E.M. (2000). Dimensions of parasocial interaction by letter-writers to a popular entertainment-education soap opera in India. *Journal of Broadcasting and Electronic Media*, 44, 386–414. ▶ page 231

Soomro, G.M., Altman, D.G., Rajagopal, S., Oakley-Browne, M. (2008). Selective serotonin re-uptake inhibitors (SSRIs) versus placebo for obsessive compulsive disorder (OCD). *Cochrane Database of Systematic Reviews*, 1. See http://summaries.cochrane.org/CD001765/selective-serotonin-re-uptake-inhibitors-ssris-versus-placebo-for-obsessive-compulsive-disorder-ocd (accessed June 2012). ▶ page 213

Soundy, T.J., Lucas, A.R., Suman, V.J. and Melton III, L.J. (1995). Bulimia nervosa in Rochester, Minnesota from 1980 to 1990. *Psychological Medicine*, 25, 1065–71. ▶ page 99

Speakman, J.R., Djafarian, K., Stewart, J. and Jackson, D.M. (2007). Assortative mating for obesity. *American Journal of Clinical Nutrition*, 86(2), 316–23. ▶ page 49

Spearman, C. (1927). *The Abilities of Man, their Nature, and Measurement*. London: Macmillan Publishing. ▶ page 124

Spielman, A.J. and Glovinsky, P.B. (1991). The varied nature of insomnia. In P.J. Hauri (ed.) *Case Studies in Insomnia*. New York: Plenum Medical Book Co. ▶ page 25

Spivey, C.B. and Prentice-Dunn, S. (1990). Assessing the directionality of deindividuated behavior: effects of deindividuation, modeling, and private self-consciousness on aggressive and prosocial responses. *Basic and Applied Social Psychology*, 11, 387–403. ▶ page 69

SPR (2012). Making sense of psi. See http://www.spr.ac.uk/main/civicrm/event/info?reset=1&id=35 (accessed April 2012). ▶ page 256

Sprafkin, J.N., Liebert, R.M. and Poulos, R.W. (1975). Effects of a prosocial televised example on children's helping. *Journal of Experimental Child Psychology, 20*, 119–26. ▶ page 220

Springer, K.W., Sheridan, J., Kuo, D. and Carnes, M. (2007). Long-term physical and mental health consequences of childhood physical abuse: results from a large population-based sample of men and women. *Child Abuse and Neglect, 31*, 517–30. ▶ page 58

Staddon, J.E.R. and Simmelhag, V.L. (1971). The 'superstition' experiment: a re-examination of its implications for the principles of adaptive behavior. *Psychological Review, 78*, 3–43. ▶ page 263

Stafford, L. and Canary, D.J. (2006). Equity and interdependence as predictors of relational maintenance strategies. *Journal of Family Communication, 6(4)*, 227–54. ▶ page 50

Stanford, C.B. (1999). *The Hunting Apes: Meat-eating and the Origins of Human Behavior*. Princeton: Princeton University Press. ▶ pages 91, 107, 136

Stanford Medical Center (2012). *See* http://med. stanford.edu/school/Psychiatry/narcolepsy/faq1.html (accessed June 2012). ▶ page 26

Stangor, C. and Ruble, D.N. (1989). Differential influences of gender schemata and gender constancy on children's information processing and behavior. *Social Cognition, 7*, 353–72. ▶ page 115

Stanhope, N. and Cohen, G. (1993). Retrieval of proper names: testing the models. *British Journal of Psychology, 84*, 51–65. ▶ page 41

Stankov, L. (1988). Attentional resources and intelligence: a disappearing link. *Personality and Individual Differences, 10*, 957–68. ▶ page 125

Stanley, B.G., Kyrkouli, S.E., Lampert, S. and Leibowitz, S.F. (1986). Neuropeptide Y chronically injected into the hypothalamus: a powerful neurochemical inducer of hyperphagia and obesity. *Peptides, 7*, 1189–92. ▶ page 88

Staub, E. (1999). The roots of evil: social conditions, culture, personality and basic human needs. *Personality and Social Psychology Review, 3(3)*, 179–92. ▶ page 70

Stead, L.F., Perera, R. and Lancaster, T. (2006). Telephone counselling for smoking cessation. *Cochrane Database of Systematic Reviews (3)*. ▶ page 250

Steele, C.M. and Josephs, R.A. (1990). Alcohol myopia: its prized and dangerous effects. *American Psychologist, 45*, 921–33. ▶ page 249

Stehberg, J., Levy, D. and Zangen, A. (2009). Impairment of aversive memory reconsolidation by localised intracranial electrical stimulation. *European Journal of Neuroscience* (published online 5 February). ▶ page 199

Steil, J. and Weltman, K. (1991). Marital inequality: the importance of resources, personal attributes, and social norms on career valuing and domestic influence. *Sex Roles, 24(3/4)*, 161–79. ▶ page 51

Steinberger, K. and Schuch, B. (2002). Classification of obsessive compulsive disorder in childhood and adolescence. *Acta Psychiatrica Scandinavica, 106(2)*, 97–102. ▶ page 207

Steiner, H., Smith, C., Rosenkranz, R.T. and Litt, I. (1991). The early care and feeding of anorexics. *Child Psychiatry and Human Development, 21(3)*, 163–7. ▶ page 93

Steketee, G. and Frost, R. (2003). Compulsive hoarding: current status of the research. *Clinical Psychology Review, 23*, 905–27. ▶ page 215

Stephens, R., Atkins, J. and Kingston, A. (2009). Swearing as a response to pain. *Neuroreport, 20(12)*, 1056–60. ▶ page 294

Stern, R. (1995). *Mastering Phobias: Cases, Causes and Cures*. London: Penguin. ▶ page 194

Sternberg, R.J. (1985). *Beyond IQ: A Triarchic Theory of Human Intelligence*. New York: Cambridge University Press. ▶ page 127

Sternberg, R.J. (1988). *The Triarchic Mind: A New Theory of Human Intelligence*. New York: Viking. ▶ page 126

Sternberg, R.J. (ed.) (2004). *International Handbook of Intelligence*. New York: Cambridge University Press. ▶ page 127

Sternberg, R.J. and Grigorenko, E.L. (2002). Just because we 'know' it's true doesn't mean it's really true: a case study in Kenya. *Psychological Science Agenda, 15(2)*, 8–11. ▶ page 127

Sternberg, R.J., Grigorenko, E.L., Ferrari, M. and Clinkenbeard, P. (1999). The triarchic model applied to gifted identification, instruction, and assessment. In N. Colangelo and S.G. Assouline (eds) *Talent Development III: Proceedings from the 1995 Henry B. and Jocelyn Wallace National Research Symposium on Talent Development*. Scottsdale, AZ: Gifted Psychology Press, 71–80. ▶ page 127

Stevens, A. and Price, J. (2000). *Evolutionary Psychiatry: A New Beginning* (2nd edn). London: Routledge. ▶ page 167

Stevens, P. (1998). Remote psychokinesis. *Journal of Parapsychology, 14*, 68–79. ▶ page 258

Stevens, R.G. (2006). Artificial lighting in the industrialized world: circadian disruption and breast cancer. *Cancer Causes Control, 17*, 501–7. ▶ page 15

Stickgold, R. (2005). Sleep-dependent memory consolidation. *Nature, 437*, 1272–8. ▶ page 20

Stoller, R.J. (1975). *Sex and Gender. Vol. 2: The Transsexual Experiment*. London: Hogarth. ▶ page 110

Stone, V.E. (2007). An evolutionary perspective on domain specificity in social intelligence. In E. Harmon-Jones and P. Winkielman (eds) *Social Neuroscience: Integrating Biological and Psychological Explanations of Social Behaviour*. London: The Guilford Press. ▶ page 158

Storch, E.A., Kaufman, D.A., Bagner, D., Merlo, L.J., Shapira, N.A., Geffken, G.R., Murphy, T.K. and Goodman, W.K. (2007). Florida Obsessive compulsive Inventory: development, reliability and validity. *Journal of Clinical Psychology, I63(9)*, 851–9. ▶ page 207

Storms, M.D. and Nisbett, R.E. (1970). Insomnia and the attribution process. *Journal of Personality and Social Psychology, 16*, 319–28. ▶ page 25

Story, M., French, S.A., Resnick, M.D. and Blum, R.W. (1995). Ethnic/racial and socioeconomic differences in dieting behaviors and body image perceptions in adolescents. *International Journal of Eating Disorders, 18*, 173–9. ▶ page 85

Strickland, P.L., Deakin, J.F.W. and Percival, C. (2002). The bio-social origins of depression in the community: interactions between social adversity, cortisol and serotonin neurotransmission. *British Journal of Psychiatry, 180*, 168–73. ▶ page 181

Striegel-Moore, R.H., Schreiber, G.B., Pike, K.M., Wilfley, D.E. and Rodin, J. (1995). Drive for thinness in black and white pre-adolescent girls. *International Journal of Eating Disorders, 18*, 59–69. ▶ page 85

Strober, M., Freeman, R., Lampert, C., Diamond, J., Treplinsky, C. and DeAntonio, M. (2006). Are there gender differences in core symptoms, temperament and short-term prospective outcome in anorexia nervosa? *International Journal of Eating Disorders, 39*, 570–5. ▶ page 92

Sue, D., Sue, D. and Sue, S. (1994). *Understanding Abnormal Behaviour* (4th edn). Boston: Houghton Mifflin. ▶ page 197

Sugihara, Y. and Katsurada, E. (2002). Gender role development in Japanese culture: diminishing gender role differences in a contemporary society. *Sex Roles, 47(9–10)*, 443–52. ▶ page 119

Sukel, K. (2007). Basal ganglia contribute to learning, but also certain disorders. *See* http://www.dana.org/news/brainwork/detail.aspx?id=6028 (accessed March 2009). ▶ page 208

Sulkunen, P. (2007). Images of addiction: representations of addictions in films. *Addiction Research and Theory, 15(6)*, 543–59. ▶ page 246

Suomi, S.J. and Harlow, H.F. (1978). Early experience and social development in rhesus monkeys. In M.E. Lamb (ed.) *Sociopersonality Development*. New York: Holt, Rinehart and Winston. ▶ page 59

Surbey, M.K. (1987). Anorexia nervosa, amenorrhea, and adaptation. *Ethology and Sociobiology, 8*, 47–61. ▶ page 94

Surgeon General's report on youth violence (2001). *Youth Violence: A Report of the Surgeon General*. United States, Public Health Service: Office of the Surgeon General. ▶ page 75

Sykes, G.M. (1958). *The Society of Captives: A Study of a Maximum Security Prison*. Princeton: Princeton University Press. ▶ page 70

Sylva, K. (1987). Plowden: history and prospect. *Oxford Review of Education, 13(1)*, 3–12. ▶ page 151

Sylvain, C., Ladouceur, R. and Boisvert, J.M. (1997). Cognitive and behavioural treatment of pathological gambling: a controlled study. *Journal of Consulting and Clinical Psychology, 65*, 727–32. ▶ page 251

Symons, D. (1979). *The Evolution of Human Sexuality*. New York: Oxford. ▶ pages 56, 99

Sypeck, M.F., Gray, J.J., Etu, S.F., Ahrens, A.H., Mosimann, J.E. and Wiseman, C.V. (2006). Cultural representations of thinness in women, redux: *Playboy* magazine's depiction of beauty from 1979 to 1999. *Body Image, 3(3)*, 229–35. ▶ page 98

Szasz, T. (1978). *The Myth of Psychotherapy*. Oxford: Oxford University Press. ▶ page 199

Szechtman, H, Sulis, W. and Eilam, D. (1998). Quinpirole induces compulsive checking behavior in rats: a potential animal model of obsessive compulsive disorder (OCD). *Behavioural Neuroscience, 112(6)*, 1475–85. ▶ page 208

Taillieu, T. and Brownridge, D.A. (2010). Prevalence, patterns, and risk factors for experiencing intimate partner violence during pregnancy: a review of the literature and directions for future research. *Aggression and Violent Behavior, 15(1)*, 14–35. ▶ page 77

Takao, M., Takahashi, S. and Kitamura, M. (2009). Addictive personality and problematic mobile phone use. *CyberPsychology & Behavior, 12(5)*, 501–7. ▶ page 244

Takahashi, H., Matsuura, M., Yahata, N., Koeda, M., Suhara, T. and Okubo, Y. (2006). Men and women show distinct brain activations during imagery of sexual and emotional infidelity. *Neuroimage, 32*, 1299–307. ▶ page 77

Tang, Y.P., Shimizu, E., Dube, G.R., Rampon, C., Kerchner, G.A., Zhuo, M., Liu, G. and Tsien, J.Z. (1999). Genetic enhancement of learning and memory in mice. *Nature, 401(6748)*, 25–7. ▶ page 139

Tart, C.T. (1968). A psychophysiological study of out-of-body experiences in a gifted subject. *Journal of the American Society for Psychical Research, 62*, 3–27. ▶ page 268

Tashiro, T. and Frazier, P. (2003). 'I'll never be in a relationship like that again.' Personal growth following romantic relationship break-ups. *Personal Relationships, 10*, 113–28. ▶ page 53

Tate, J.C., Stanton, A.L., Green, S.B., Schmitz, J.M, Le, T. and Marshall, B. (1994). Experimental analysis of the role of expectancy in nicotine withdrawal. *Psychology of Addictive Behaviors, 8*, 169–78. ▶ page 240

Taylor, S.E., Klein, L.C., Lewis, B.P., Grunewald, T.L., Gurung, R.A.R. and Updegraff, J.A. (2000). Biobehavioral responses to stress in females: tend-and-befriend, not fight-or-flight. *Psychological Review, 107(3)*, 411–29. ▶ page 106

Teeson, M., Degenhardt, L. and Hall, W. (2002). *Addictions*. New York: Taylor & Francis.

Tennes, K. and Kreye, M. (1985). Children's adrenocortical responses to classroom activities and tests in elementary school. *Psychosomatic Medicine, 47*, 451–60. ▶ page 72

Thalbourne, M.A. (1998). Transliminality: further correlates and a short measure. *Journal of the Society for Psychical Research, 92*, 402–19. ▶ page 261

Thalbourne, M.A. and Delin, P.S. (1993). A new instrument for measuring the sheep-goat variable: its psychometric properties and factor structure. *Journal of the Society for Psychical Research*, 59, 172–86. ▶ page 261

Tharyan, P. and Adams, C.E. (2005). Electroconvulsive therapy for schizophrenia. *The Cochrane Database of Systematic Reviews*, Issue 2. ▶ page 170

The Daily Telegraph (2008). Mobile phone addiction: clinic treats children. 13 June. *See* http://www.telegraph.co.uk/news/worldnews/2121298/Mobile-phone-addiction-Clinic-treats-children.html (accessed April 2011). ▶ page 244

Thewissen, R., Ven Der Meijden, V.A.F., Havermans, R.C., Van Den Hout, M.A. and Jansen, A. (2008). From the office to the pub: the role of smoking-relevant contexts and cue-elicited urge to smoke, *European Addiction Research*, 14(4), 198–205. ▶ page 243

Thibaut, J.W. and Kelley, H.H. (1959). *The Social Psychology of Groups*. New York: Wiley. ▶ page 50

Thompson, P. (1980). Margaret Thatcher: a new illusion. *Perception*, 9(4), 483–4. ▶ page 41

Thompson, S.K. (1975). Gender labels and early sex-role development. *Child Development*, 46, 336–421. ▶ page 113

Thorgeirsson, T.E., Geller, F., Sulem, P., Rafnar, T., Wiste, A., Magnusson, K.P. et al. (2008) A variant associated with nicotine dependence, lung cancer, and peripheral arterial disease. *Nature*, 452, 638–42. ▶ page 124

Thorpe, I. (2003). Anthropology, archaeology, and the origin of warfare. *World Archaeology*, 35, 145–65. ▶ page 78

Thurstone, L.L. (1938). *Primary Mental Abilities*. Chicago: University of Chicago Press. ▶ page 124

Tienari, P., Wynne, L.C. and Moring, J. (1994). The Finnish adoptive family study of schizophrenia: implications for family research. *British Journal of Psychiatry*, 163(23), 20–6. ▶ page 166

Tienari, P., Wynne, L.C., Moring, J., Laksy, K., Nieminen, P. and Sorri, A. (2000). Finnish adoptive family study: sample selection and adoptee DSM-III-R diagnoses. *Acta Psychiatrica Scandinavica*, 101, 433–43. ▶ page 166

Tiihonen, J., Kuikka, J., Bergstrom, K., Lepola, U., Koponen, H. and Leinonen, E. (1997). Dopamine re-uptake site densities in patients with social phobia. *American Journal of Psychiatry*, 154, 239–42. ▶ page 195

Tilley, A.J. and Wilkinson, R.T. (1982). Sleep performance and shift workers. *Human Factors*, 24, 629–41. ▶ page 16

Tobacyk, J. and Milford, G. (1983). Belief in paranormal phenomena: assessment instrument development and implications for personality functioning. *Journal of Personality and Social Psychology*, 44, 1029–37. ▶ page 261

Topa, G. and Moriano, J.A. (2010). Theory of planned behavior and smoking: meta-analysis and SEM model. *Substance Abuse and Rehabilitation*, 2010(1), 23–33. ▶ page 249

Torgersen, S. (1983). Genetic factors in anxiety disorders. *Archives of General Psychiatry*, 40, 1085–9. ▶ page 194

Torrey, E.F. (1987). Prevalence studies in schizophrenia. *British Journal of Psychiatry*, 150, 598–608. ▶ page 167

Tracy, J.A., Ghose, S.S., Stecher, T., McFall, R.M. and Steinmetz, J.E. (1999). Classical conditioning in a nonclinical obsessive compulsive population. *Psychological Science*, 10, 9–13. ▶ page 211

Trivers, R.L. (1972). Parental investment and sexual selection. In B. Campbell (ed.) *Sexual Selection and the Descent of Man 1871–1971*. Chicago: Aldine Publishing, 136–79. ▶ page 56

Tsao, J. (1996). Compensatory media use: an exploration of two paradigms. *Communication Studies*, 47, 89–109. ▶ page 231

Turkheimer, E., Haley, A., Waldron, M., Onofrio, B., and Gottesman, I. (2003). Socioeconomic status modifies the heritability of IQ in young children. *Psychological Science*, 14(6), 624–8. ▶ page 139

Turnbull, C. (1963). *The Forest People*. London: Reprint Society. ▶ page 38

Turner, E.H., Matthews, A.M., Linardatos, E., Tell, R.A. and Rosenthal, R. (2008). Selective publication of antidepressant trials and its influence on apparent efficacy. *New England Journal of Medicine*, 358(3), 252–60. ▶ page 185

Turner, S.M., Beidel, D.C. and Jacob, R.G. (1994). Social phobia: a comparison of behavior therapy and atenolol. *Journal of Consulting and Clinical Psychology*, 62(2), 350–8. ▶ page 199

Tynjälä, J., Kanna, L. and Välimaa, R. (1993). How young Europeans sleep. *Health Education Research*, 8(1), 69–80. ▶ page 19

Tzedakis, P.C., Hughen, K.A., Cacho, I. and Harvat, K. (2007). Placing late Neanderthals in a climatic context. *Nature*, 449, 206–8. ▶ page 107

Uhl, G.R., Liu, Q.R., Drgon, T., Johnson, C., Walther, D., Rose, J.E., David, S.P., Niaura, R. and Lerman, C. (2008). Molecular genetics of successful smoking cessation: convergent genome-wide association study results. *Archives of General Psychiatry*, 65(6), 683–93. ▶ page 208

Valkenburg, P.M., Krcmer, M., Peeters, A.L. and Marseille, N.M. (1999). Developing a scale to assess three kinds of television mediation: 'instructive mediation', 'restrictive mediation' and 'social co-viewing'. *Journal of Broadcasting and Electronic Media*, 43, 52–66. ▶ page 221

Valladares, E., Peña, R., Persson, L.A. and Högberg, U. (2005). Violence against pregnant women: prevalence and characteristics. A population-based study in Nicaragua. *BJOG: An International Journal of Obstetrics & Gynaecology*, 112, 1243–8. ▶ page 77

Vamos, M. (2010). Organ transplantation and magical thinking. *Australian and New Zealand Journal of Psychiatry*, 44, 883–7. ▶ page 263

van Cauter, E. and Plat, L. (1996). Physiology of growth hormone secretion during sleep. *Journal of Pediatrics*, 128(Pt 2), S32–S37. ▶ page 20

van Cauter, E., Leproult, R. and Plat, L. (2000). Age-related changes in slow wave sleep and REM sleep and relationship with growth hormone and cortisol levels in healthy men. *JAMA*, 284, 861–8. ▶ pages 19, 20

Van den Heuvel, H., Tellegen, G. and Koomen, W. (1992). Cultural differences in the use of psychological and social characteristics in children's self-understanding. *European Journal of Social Psychology*, 22, 353–62. ▶ page 155

van der Kolk, B.A. and Fisler, R. (1994). Childhood abuse and neglect and loss of self-regulation. *Bulletin of Menninger Clinic*, 58, 145–68. ▶ page 58

Van der Linden, M., Brédart, S. and Schweich, M. (1995). Developmental disturbance of access to biographical information and people's names: a single-case study. *Journal of the International Neuropsychological Society*, 1, 589–95. ▶ page 43

Van Leeuwen, M.S. (1978). A cross-cultural examination of psychological differentiation in males and females. *International Journal of Psychology*, 15, 87–122. ▶ page 119

van Lommel, P., van Wees, R., Meyers, V. and Elfferich, I. (2001). Near-death experience in survivors of cardiac arrest: a prospective study in the Netherlands. *The Lancet*, 358, 2039–45. ▶ page 269

van Os, J., Fahy, T.A. and Bebbington, P. (1994). The influence of life events on the subsequent course of psychotic illness: a prospective follow-up of the Camberwell Collaborative Psychosis Study. *Psychological Medicine*, 24(2), 503–13. ▶ page 169

van Weel-Baumgarten, E.M., van den Bosch, W.J. and van den Hoogen, H.J. (2006). The validity of the diagnosis of depression in general practice: is using criteria for diagnosis as a routine the answer? *British Journal of General Practice*, 50, 284–7. ▶ page 179

Vannacci, A., Ravaldi, C., Giannini, L., Rotella, C.M., Masini, E., Faravelli, C. and Ricca, V. (2006). Increased nitric oxide production in eating disorders. *Neuroscience Letters*, 399, 230–3. ▶ page 98

Vasey, M.W. and Dadds, M.R. (2001). *The Developmental Psychopathology of Anxiety*. New York: Oxford University Press. ▶ page 193

Vaughn, C. and Leff, J. (1976). The influence of family and social factors on the course of psychiatric illness: a comparison of schizophrenic and depressed neurotic patients. *British Journal of Psychiatry*, 129, 125–37. ▶ page 171

Verschueren, K. and Marcoen, A. (1999). Representation of self and socioemotional competence in kindergartners: differential and combined effects of attachment to mother and to father. *Child Development*, 70, 183–201. ▶ page 155

Verschueren, K., Buyck, P. and Marcoen, A. (2001). Self-representations and socioemotional competence in young children: a three-year longitudinal study. *Developmental Psychology*, 37, 126–34. ▶ page 155

Vidrine, J.I., Simmons, V.N. and Brandon, T.H. (2007). Construction of smoking-relevant risk perceptions among college students: the influence of need for cognition and message content. *Journal of Applied Social Psychology*, 37(1), 91–114. ▶ page 226

Vink, J.M., Willemsen, G. and Boomsma, D.I. (2005). Heritability of smoking initiation and nicotine dependence. *Behavior Genetics*, 35(4), 397–406. ▶ page 238

Virkkunen, M. (1985). Urinary free cortisol secretion in habitually violent offenders. *Acta Psychiatrica Scandinavica*, 72, 40–4. ▶ page 72

Vogel, G. (1960). Studies in psychophysiology of dreams (III). The dream of narcolepsy. *Archives of General Psychiatry*, 3, 421–8. ▶ page 27

Voracek, M. and Haubner, T. (2008). Twin-singleton differences in intelligence: a meta-analysis. *Psychological Reports*, 102(3), 951–62. ▶ page 139

Vreugdenhil, H.J.I., Slijper, F.M.E., Mukder, P.G.H. and Weisglas-Kuperus, N. (2002). Effects of perinatal exposure to PCBs and dioxins on play behaviour in Dutch children at school age. *Environmental Health Perspectives*, 110(10), A593–A598. ▶ page 111

Vygotsky, L.S. (orig. 1934 reprinted 1962). *Thought and Language*. Cambridge, MA: MIT Press. ▶ page 148

Vygotsky, L.S. (1987). The development of scientific concepts in childhood. In R.W. Rieber and A.S. Carton (eds) *The Collected Works of L.S. Vygotsky* (vol. 1). New York: Plenum Press. ▶ page 150

Wahlsten, D. (1997). The malleability of intelligence is not constrained by heritability. In B. Devlin, S.E. Fienberg and K. Roeder (eds) *Intelligence, Genes and Success: Scientists Respond to the Bell Curve*. New York: Springer, 71–87. ▶ page 141

Walker, L.J., deVries, B. and Trevethan, S.D. (1987). Moral stages and moral orientations in real-life and hypothetical dilemmas. *Child Development*, 58, 842–58. ▶ page 153

Walkerdine, V. (1984). *The Mastery of Reason: Cognitive Development and the Mastery of Reason*. London and New York: Routledge. ▶ page 151

Waller, G., Ohanian, V., Meyer, C. and Osman, S. (2000). Cognitive content among bulimic women: the role of core beliefs. *International Journal of Eating Disorders*, 28(2), 235–41. ▶ page 97

Walsh, B.T., Wilson, G.T. and Loeb, K.L. (1997). Medication and psychotherapy in the treatment of bulimia nervosa. *American Journal of Psychiatry*, 154, 523–31. ▶ page 99

Walsh, B.T., Wilson, G.T., Loeb, K.L., Devlin, M.J., Pike, K.M., Roose, S.P., Fleiss, J. and Waternaux, C. (2000). Medication and psychotherapy in the treatment of bulimia nervosa. *American Journal Psychiatry*, 154, 523–31. ▶ page 99

Walster, E., Walster, G.W. and Berscheid, E. (1978). *Equity: Theory and Research.* Boston: Allyn & Bacon. ▶ page 50

Walters, G.D. (1992). A meta-analysis of the gene-crime relationship. *Criminology, 30,* 595–613. ▶ page 75

Walther, J.B. (1996). Computer-mediated communication: impersonal, interpersonal, and hyperpersonal interaction. *Communication Research, 23(1),* 3–43. ▶ page 225

Wang, G.J., Volkow, N.D., Logan, J., Pappas, N.R., Wong, C.T. and Zhu, W. (2001). Brain dopamine and obesity. *Lancet, 357,* 354–7. ▶ page 95

Wardle, J. and Beales, S. (1988). Control and loss of control over eating: an experimental investigation. *Journal of Abnormal Psychology, 97(1),* 35–40. ▶ page 86

Warshaw, P.R. and Davis, F.D. (1985). Disentangling behavioral intention and behavioral expectation. *Journal of Experimental Social Psychology, 21,* 213–28. ▶ page 249

Watson, J.B. and Rayner, R. (1920). Conditioned emotional reactions. *Journal of Experimental Psychology, 3,* 1–14. ▶ page 196

Watson, N.F., Goldberg, J., Arguelles, L. and Buchwald, D. (2006). Genetic and environmental influences on insomnia, daytime sleepiness, and obesity in twins. *Sleep, 29,* 645–9.▶ page 25

Watson, R.I. Jr. (1973). Investigation into deindividuation using a cross-cultural survey technique. *Journal of Personality and Social Psychology, 25,* 342–5. ▶ page 69

Waylen, A., Leary, S.D., Ness, A.R., Tanski, S.E. and Sargent, J.D. (2011). Cross sectional association between smoking depictions in films and adolescent tobacco use nested in a British cohort study. *Thorax, 66,* 856–61. ▶ page 246

Waynforth, D. and Dunbar R.I.M. (1995). Conditional mate choice strategies in humans: evidence from 'lonely hearts' advertisements. *Behaviour, 132,* 755–79. ▶ page 107

Webb, T.L., Joseph, J., Yardley, L. and Michie, S. (2010). Using the Internet to promote health behavior change: a systematic review and meta-analysis of the impact of theoretical basis, use of behavior change techniques, and mode of delivery on efficacy. *Journal of Medical Internet Research, 12(1).* See www.ncbi.nlm.nih.gov/pmc/articles/PMC2836773/ (accessed April 2011). ▶ page 248

Webb, W.B. (1982). Sleep and biological rhythms. In W.B. Webb (ed.) *Biological Rhythms, Sleep and Performance.* Chichester: Wiley. ▶ page 22

Weber, N.S., Cowan, D.N., Millikan, A.M. and Niebuhr, D.W. (2009). Psychiatric and general medical conditions comorbid with schizophrenia in the National Hospital Discharge Survey. *Psychiatric Services, 60(8),* 1059–67. ▶ page 165

Wegner, D.M. (1994). Ironic processes of mental control. *Psychological Review, 101,* 34–52. ▶ page 86

Wegner, D.M., Schneider, D.J., Carter, S.R. and White, T.L. (1987). Paradoxical effects of thought suppression. *Journal of Personality and Social Psychology, 53,* 5–13. ▶ page 86

Wegner, K.E., Smyth, J.M., Crosby, R.D., Wittrock, D., Wonderlich, S.A. and Mitchell, J.E. (2002). An evaluation of the relationship between mood and binge-eating in the natural environment using ecological momentary assessment. *International Journal of Eating Disorders, 32,* 352–61. ▶ page 84

Weinberger, D.R. and Harrison, P. (2011). *Schizophrenia.* 3rd edn. Hoboken, NJ: Wiley-Blackwell. ▶ page 263

Weintraub, D., Koester, J. Potenza, M.N., Siderowf, A.D., Stacy, M.A., Voon, V., Whetteckey, J., Wunderlich, G.R. and Teeson, A.E. (2010). Impulse control disorders in Parkinson Disease: a cross-sectional study of 3090 patients. *Archives of Neurology, 67(5),* 589–95. ▶ page 245

Welch, J.M., Lu, J., Rodriguiz, R.M., Trotta, N.C., Ding, J.-D., Feliciano, C., Chen, M., Adams, J.P., Luo, J.,

Dudek, S.M., Weinberg, R.J., Calakos, N., Wetsel, W.C. and Feng, G. (2007). Cortico-striatal synaptic defects and OCD-like behaviours in Sapap3-mutant mice. *Nature, 448,* 894–900. ▶ page 209

Wellman, H.M. and Woolley, J.D. (1990). From simple desires to ordinary beliefs: the early development of everyday psychology. *Cognition, 35,* 245–75. ▶ pages 152, 156

Wender, P.H., Kety, S.S. and Rosenthal, D. (1986). Psychiatric disorders in the biological and adoptive families of adopted individuals with affective disorders. *Archives of General Psychiatry, 43(10),* 923–9. ▶ page 180

Wendland, J.R., Moya, P.R., Kruse, M.R., Ren-Patterson, R.F., Jensen, C.L., Timpano, K.R. and Murphy, D.L. (2008). A novel, putative gain-of-function haplotype at SLC6A4 associates with obsessive compulsive disorder. *Human Molecular Genetics, 17,* 717–23. ▶ page 209

Westen, D., Burton, L. and Kowalski, R. (2006). *Psychology* (Australian and New Zealand edition). Milton, QLD: Wiley. ▶ page 131

Whaley, A.L. (2001). Cultural mistrust and clinical diagnosis of paranoid schizophrenia in African-American patients. *Journal of Psychopathology and Behavioral Assessment, 23,* 93–100. ▶ page 165

Wheeler, H.A., Adams, G.R. and Keating, L. (2001). Binge-eating as a means for evading identity issues: the association between an avoidance identity style and bulimic behaviour. *Identity: An International Journal of Theory and Research, 1(2),* 161–78. ▶ page 96

White, G.L., Fishbein, S. and Rutstein, J. (1981). Passionate love and the misattribution of arousal. *Journal of Personality and Social Psychology, 41,* 56–62. ▶ page 290

White, K.M., Robinson, N.G., Young, R., Anderson, P.J., Hyde, M.K., Greenbank, S., Rolfe, T., Keane, J., Vardon, P. and Baskerville, D. (2008). Testing an extended theory of planned behaviour to predict young people's sun safety in a high-risk area. *British Journal of Health Psychology, 13(3),* 435–48. ▶ page 248

Whiten, A. and Byrne, R.W. (1988). Tactical deception in primates. *Behavioural and Brain Sciences, 11,* 233–73. ▶ pages 134, 136

Whiting, J.W.M., Child, I.L. and Lambert, W.W. (1966). *Field Guide for a Study of Socialization.* New York: Wiley. ▶ page 197

Whitson, J.A. and Galinsky, A.D. (2008). Lacking control increases illusory pattern perception. *Science, 322,* 115–17. ▶ pages 261, 262

Wickens, J.R. (2000). Dopamine regulation of synaptic plasticity in the neostriatum: a cellular model of reinforcement, In R.M. Miller and J.R. Wickens (eds) *Brain Dynamics and the Striatal Complex.* New York: Gordon and Breach, 141–50. ▶ page 88

Wicker, B., Keysers, C., Plailly, J., Royet, J.P., Gallese, V. and Rizzolatti, G. (2003). Both of us disgusted in my insula: the common neural basis of seeing and feeling disgust. *Neuron, 40,* 655–64. ▶ page 159

Wilhelm, S., Steketee, G., Reilly-Harrington, N.A., Deckersbach, T., Buhlmann, U. and Baer, L. (2005). Effectiveness of cognitive therapy for obsessive compulsive disorder: an open trial. *Journal of Cognitive Psychotherapy, 19,* 173–9. ▶ page 215

Williams, E., Francis, L.T. and Robbins, M. (2007). Personality and paranormal belief: a study among adolescents. *Pastoral Psychology, 56(9),* 9–14. ▶ page 264

Williams, H.L., Lubin, A. and Goodnow, J.J. (1959). Impaired performance with acute sleep loss. *Psychological Monographs, 73(14, whole no. 484).* ▶ page 21

Williams, J.E. and Best, D.L. (1990a). *Measuring Sex Stereotypes: A Thirty Nation Study* (2nd edn). London: Sage. ▶ page 118

Williams, J.E. and Best, D.L. (1990b). *Sex and Psyche: Gender and Self-viewed Cross-culturally.* Newbury Park, CA: Sage. ▶ page 119

Williams, J.H.G., Whiten, A., Suddendorf, T. and Perrett, D.I. (2001). Imitation, mirror neurons and autism. *Neuroscience and Biobehavioral Reviews, 25(4),* 287–95. ▶ page 159

Williams, M., Turkheimer, E., Schmidt, K.M. and Oltmanns, T.F. (2005). Ethnic identification biases responses to the Padua Inventory for Obsessive compulsive disorder. *Assessment, 12(2),* 174–85. ▶ page 207

Williams, T.M. (1985). Implications of a natural experiment in the developed world for research on television in the developing world. Special issue: television in the developing world. *Journal of Cross-cultural Psychology, 16(3),* 263–87. ▶ page 116

Williams, W.M., Blythe, T., White, N., Li, J., Gardner, H. and Sternberg, R.J. (2002). Practical intelligence for school: developing metacognitive sources of achievement in adolescence. *Developmental Review, 22,* 162–210. ▶ page 127

Willoughby, K. Bowen, R., Lee, E. and Pathy, P. (2005). Season of birth in early onset anorexia nervosa in an equatorial region. *International Journal of Eating Disorders, 37,* 61–4. ▶ page 94

Wilson, D. (2010). Institutional Aggression. *Psychology Review, 15(4),* 2–4. ▶ page 71

Wilson, D.S. (1975). A theory of group selection. *Proceedings of the National Academy of Science, 72,* 143–6. ▶ page 78

Wilson, K. and French, C.C. (2006). The relationship between susceptibility and false memories, dissociativity, and paranormal belief and experience. *Personality and Individual Differences, 41,* 1493–1502. ▶ page 265

Wilson, R.W. and Kolander, C.A. (2003). *Drug Abuse Prevention: A School and Community Partnership* (2nd edn). Sudbury, MA: Jones and Bartlett Publishing. ▶ page 248

Wimmer, H. and Perner, J. (1983). Beliefs about beliefs: representation and constraining function of wrong beliefs in young children's understanding of deception. *Cognition, 13,* 103–28. ▶ page 155

Winter, W.C. (2008), quoted in American Academy of Sleep Medicine (2008). Major League baseball teams with greater circadian advantage are more likely to succeed. *Science Daily* (10 June). See http://www.sciencedaily.com/releases/2008/06/080610072050.htm (accessed May 2009). ▶ page 16

Wirth, D.P. (1990). The effect of non-contact therapeutic touch on the healing rate of full thickness dermal wounds. *Subtle Energies, 1,* 1–20. ▶ page 266

Wirth, D.P., Cram, J.R. and Chang, R.J. (1997). Multisite surface electromyography and complementary healing intervention: a comparative analysis. *Journal of Alternative Complementary Medicine, 3(4),* 355–64. ▶ page 267

Wiseman, R. and Greening, E. (2005). 'Its still bending': verbal suggestion and alleged psychokinetic metal bending. *British Journal of Psychology, 96(1),* 115–27. ▶ page 258

Wiseman, R. and O'Keeffe, C. (2001). Accuracy and replicability of anomalous after-death communication across highly skilled mediums: a critique. *The Paranormal Review, 19,* 3–6. ▶ page 266

Wiseman, R. and Watt, C. (2004). Measuring superstitious belief: why lucky charms matter. *Personality and Individual Differences, 37,* 1533–41. ▶ pages 261, 265

Wiseman, R. and Watt, C. (2006). Belief in psychic ability and the misattribution hypothesis: a qualitative review. *British Journal of Psychology, 97,* 323–38. ▶ page 261

Wiseman, R., Greening, E. and Smith, M. (2003). Belief in the paranormal and suggestion in the séance room. *British Journal of Psychology, 94(3),* 285–97. ▶ page 264

Wolfgang, M.E. and Ferracuti, E. (1967). *The Subculture of Violence: Towards an*

Integrated Theory in Criminology. London: Tavistock Publications. ▶ page 67

Wolfradt, U. (1997). Dissociative experiences, trait anxiety and paranormal beliefs. *Personality and Individual Differences, 23*, 15–19. ▶ page 265

Wolfson, A.R. and Carskadon, M.A. (2005). A survey of factors influencing high-school start times. *NASSP Bulletin, 89(642)*, 47–66. ▶ page 19

Wolpe, J. (1958). *Psychotherapy by Reciprocal Inhibition*. Stanford, CA: Stanford University Press. ▶ page 200

Wood, D.J. and Middleton, D.J. (1975). A study of assisted problem-solving. *British Journal of Psychology, 66*, 181–91. ▶ page 151

Woodard, E.H. (1999). *The 1999 State of Children's Television Report: Programming for Children over Broadcast and Cable Television*. The Annenberg Public Policy Center of the University of Pennsylvania. ▶ page 221

Woodside, D.B. and Kennedy, S.H. (1995). Gender differences in eating disorders. In M.V. Seeman (ed.) *Gender and Psychopathology*. Washington: American Psychiatric Press, 253–68. ▶ page 99

Woody, G.E. and Crits-Christoph, P. (2007). Individual therapy for substance abuse disorders. In G.O. Gabbard (ed.) *Gabbard's Treatments of Psychiatric Disorders* (4th edn). Arlington, VA: American Psychiatric Publishing. ▶ page 251

Woody, S.R., Steketee, G. and Chambless, D.L. (1995). Reliability and validity of the Yale-Brown Obsessive Compulsive Scale. *Behaviour Research and Therapy, 33(5)*, 607–11. ▶ page 206

Wooffitt, R. (2007). Communication and laboratory experience in parapsychology experiments: demand characteristics and the social organization of interaction. *British Journal of Social Psychology, 46(3)*, 477–98. ▶ page 258

Wraga, M., Creem, S.H. and Proffitt, D.R. (2000). Perception-action dissociations of a walkable Müller-Lyer configuration. *Psychological Science, 11*, 239–43. ▶ page 35

Wrangham, R.W. (1975). *The Behavioral Ecology of Chimpanzees in Gombe National Park, Tanzania*. PhD thesis, University of Cambridge. ▶ page 137

Wright, K.P., Hull, J.T. and Czeisler, C.A. (2002). Relationship between alertness, performance, and body temperature in humans. *American Journal of Physiology, 283*, 1370–7. ▶ page 11

Wu, T.X., Li, Y.P., Liu, G.J., Bian, Z., Li, J., Zhang, J., Xie, L., NI, J. (2006). *Investigation of authenticity of 'claimed' randomized controlled trials (RCTs) and quality assessment of RCT reports published in China*. Presented at the XIV Cochrane Colloquium, Dublin, Ireland, 23-10-2006

Xian, H., Scherrer, J.F., Madden, P.A., Lyons, M.J., Tsuang, M., True, W.R. and Eisen, S.A. (2003). The heritability of failed smoking cessation and nicotine withdrawal in twins who smoked and attempted to quit. *Nicotine and Tobacco Research, 5*, 245–54. ▶ page 238

Xiaohe, X. and Whyte, M.K. (1990). Love matches and arranged marriages: a Chinese replication. *Journal of Marriage and the Family, 52(3)*, 709–22. ▶ page 61

Yamamiya, Y., Cash, T.F., Melnyk, S.E., Posavac, H.D. and Posavac, S.S. (2005). Women's exposure to thin-and-beautiful media images: body image effects of media-ideal internalization and impact-reduction interventions. *Body Image, 2*, 74–80. ▶ page 93

Yang, K., Guan, H. Arany, E., Hill, D.J. and Cao, X. (2008). Neuropeptide Y is produced in visceral adipose tissue and promotes proliferation of adipocyte precursor cells via the Y1 receptor. *FASEB (Federation of American Societies for Experimental Biology), 22(7)*, 2452–64. ▶ page 89

Yellowlees, P., Burrage, J., Banks, J. and Dennison, A. (2002). *The Development of a Virtual Visualisation Environment to Model the Hallucinations and Mental Phenomena of Psychosis*. The Royal Australian and New Zealand College of Psychiatrists (RANZCP) Symposium on eHealth, May. ▶ page 169

Yerkes, R.M. (ed.) (1921). Psychological examining in the United States Army. *Memoirs of the National Academy of Sciences, 15*, 1–890. ▶ page 125

Yonas, A., Farr, M. and O'Connor, A. (2001). Seven-month-old but not five-month-old infants extract depth from cast shadows. *Journal of Vision, 1(3)*, 389a. ▶ page 36

Yorulmaz, O., Inozu, M. and Gültepe, B. (2011). The role of magical thinking in Obsessive-Compulsive Disorder symptoms and cognitions in an analogue sample. *Journal of Behaviour Therapy and experimental Psychiatry, 42(2)*, 198–203. ▶ page 263

Yoshida, H. (1972). The determinants of interpersonal attraction. *Memoirs of The Faculty of Education, Toyama University, 20*, 63–82. ▶ page 49

Young, A.W., Hay, D.C. and Ellis, A.W. (1985). The faces that launched a thousand slips: everyday difficulties and errors in recognising people. *British Journal of Psychology, 76*, 495–523. ▶ page 41

Young, A.W., McWeeny, K.H., Hay, D.C. and Ellis, A.W. (1986). Naming and categorisation latencies for faces and written names. *Journal of Experimental Psychology, 38A*, 297–318. ▶ page 41

Young, E. (2008). Sleep tight. *New Scientist*, 15 March, 30–4. ▶ pages 21, 22

Young, K.A., Berry, M.L., Mahaffey, C.L., Saionz, J.R., Hawes, N.L., Chang, B., Zheng, Q.Y., Smith, R.S., Bronson, R.T., Nelson, R.J. and Simpson, E.M. (2002). Fierce: a new mouse deletion of Nr2e1; violent behaviour and ocular abnormalities are background-dependent. *Behavioural Brain Research, 132(2)*, 145–58. ▶ page 75

Zadra, A., Pilon, M. and Montplaisir, J. (2008). Polysomnographic diagnosis of sleepwalking: effects of sleep deprivation. *Annals of Neurology, 63(4)*, 513–19. ▶ page 27

Zajonc, R.B. (1968). Attitudinal effects of mere exposure. *Journal of Personality and Social Psychology (Monograph), 9*, 1–29. ▶ page 292

Zald, D.H. and Pardo, J.V. (1997). Emotion, olfaction, and the human amygdala: amygdala activation during aversive olfactory stimulation. *Proceedings of the National Academy of Sciences of the United States of America, 94*, 4119–24. ▶ page 89

Zammit, G.K., Weiner, J., Damato, N., Sillup, G.P. and McMillan, C.A. (1999). Quality of life in people with insomnia. *Sleep, 22(suppl 2)*, S379–S385. ▶ page 25

Zanarini, M.C., Skodol, A.E., Bender, D., Dolan, R., Sanislow, C., Schaefer, E., Morey, L.C., Grilo, C.M., Shea, M.T., McGlashan, T.H. and Gunderson, J.G. (2000). The collaborative longitudinal personality disorders study: reliability of axis I and II diagnoses. *Journal of Personality Disorders, 14*, 291–9. ▶ page 179

Zepelin, H. and Rechtschaffen, A. (1974). Mammalian sleep, longevity and energy metabolism. *Brain, Behaviour and Evolution, 10*, 425–70. ▶ page 23

Zhang, X., Gainetdinov, R.R. Martin Beaulieu, J.-M., Sotnikova, T.D., Burch, L.H., Williams, R.B., Schwartz, D.A., Ranga, K., Krishnan, R. and Caron, M.G. (2005). Loss-of-function mutation in tryptophan hydroxylase-2 identified in unipolar major depression, *Neuron, 45*, 11–6. ▶ page 181

Zhang, Y., Proenca, R., Maffei, M., Barone, M. and Friedman, J.M. (1994). Positional cloning of the mouse obese gene and its human homologue. *Nature, 372*, 425–32. ▶ page 88

Zhou, J.-N., Hofman, M.A., Gooren, L.J. and Swaab, D.F. (1995). A sex difference in the human brain and its relation to transsexuality. *Nature, 378*, 68–70. ▶ page 110

Zimbardo, P. (2007). *The Lucifer Effect: Understanding how Good People Turn Evil*. New York: Random House. ▶ page 69

Zimbardo, P.G. (1969). The human choice: individuation, reason, and order vs. deindividuation, impulse and chaos. In W.J. Arnold and D. Levine (eds) *Nebraska Symposium on Motivation*. Nebraska: University of Nebraska Press, 237–307. ▶ page 68

Zimmerman, F., Christakis, D.A. and Meltzoff, A.N. (2007). Television and DVD/video-viewing in children younger than 2 years. *Archives of Pediatric and Adolescent Medicine, 161(5)*, 473–9. ▶ page 221

Zimmerman, M., Galione, J.N., Chelminski, I., McGlinchey, J.B., Young, D., Dalrymple, K., Ruggero, C.J. and Francione-Witt, C. (2010). A simpler definition of major depressive disorder. *Psychological Medicine, 40(3)*, 451–7. ▶ page 179

Zohar, J. and Judge, R. (1996). OCD paroxetine study investigators: paroxetine versus clomipramine in the treatment of obsessive compulsive disorder. *British Journal of Psychiatry, 169*, 468–74. ▶ page 213

Zosuls, K.M., Ruble, D.N., Tamis-LeMonda, C.S., Shrout, P.E., Bornstein, M.H. and Greulich, F.K. (2009). The acquisition of gender labels in infancy: implications for sex-typed play. *Developmental Psychology, 45(3)*, 688–701. ▶ page 114

Zucker, K.J., Bradley, S.J. and Lowry Sullivan, C.B. (1996). Traits of separation anxiety in boys with gender identity disorder. *Journal of the American Academy of Child and Adolescent Psychiatry, 35(6)*, 791–8. ▶ page 111

Zuckerman, M. (1979). *Sensation-seeking: Beyond the Optimal Level of Arousal*. Hillsdale, NJ: Lawrence Erlbaum. ▶ page 238

Zuckerman, M. (1983). Sensation seeking and sports. *Journal of Personality and Individual Differences, 4*, 285–93. ▶ page 244

GLOSSARY/INDEX

This is both an index and a glossary. Entries with definitions are **emboldened**.

generalisability of research 15, 39, 105

generalised anxiety disorder An anxiety disorder that involves excessive worry about anything and everything. 191, 192, 194, 195

genetic engineering The deliberate manipulation of the genes of an unborn child, with the intent of making them 'better' in some way, e.g. less aggressive. 75, 139

genetic factors
  addictive behaviour 238, 239
  aggression 74–5
  biological rhythms 15
  body weight 87
  depression 180, 181
  eating behaviour 99
  gender development 104–5
  intelligence 138–41, 276
  OCD 208, 209
  phobic disorders 194, 195
  schizophrenia 166, 167
  sleep disorders 25, 27
  taste 90
  see also determinism;
    diathesis-stress model

genocide 70, 71

ghrelin A hormone produced by the stomach cells, and thought to increase feelings of hunger. 89, 98

Gibson, James 34–5

GID *see* gender identity disorder

glutamate The most common excitatory neurotransmitter in the brain which is thought to be involved in learning and memory. Excessive amounts, caused by brain injury or illness, cause neuronal damage and cell death. 268

gossip 230, 231

Gregory, Richard 32–3, 35

grounded theory A technique used when analysing qualitative data. It is an 'emergent' research process in which theoretical explanations emerge during the course of the investigation. 299

group behaviour 68–71, 78–9

growth hormone A hormone that stimulates growth and cell reproduction. 10, 12, 19, 20

H

habituation method A method of testing infants' perceptual abilities by exposing them to a certain stimulus until they get used to it (i.e. habituate) and show less interest when later shown the same stimulus because it is no longer novel. 37

hallucinations 164

Halverson, Charles 114–15

harm To cause physical or mental injury. In the context of psychological research, harm to participants could include lowered self-esteem or embarrassment. 282

harm-avoidance strategies, in OCD 208

health
  addictive behaviour 238–51
  media influences 226, 227, 246, 247
  psychic healing 266–7

heredity The process by which traits are passed from parents to their offspring, usually referring to genetic inheritance. 166, 167

heritability The ratio between (a) genetic variability of the particular trait and (b) total variability in the whole population. 238

heuristic A strategy used to solve a problem or work something out. It can be a set of rules, an educated guess or just common sense. 261

hibernation theory A variation of the evolutionary theory of sleep, that suggests that sleep serves a similar adaptive purpose to hibernation 22

HLA *see* human leukocyte antigen

holistic process Perceiving the whole display rather than the individual features and/ or the relations between them. 42, 43

homeostasis The tendency of an organism to maintain an internal equilibrium by adjusting physiological processes, e.g. hunger or thirst. 88–9

homicide
  evolutionary theory 76–9
  genocide 72, 73
  lynch mobs 68
  violent criminals 75
  warfare 80, 81
  wife-killing 76, 77

homosexual men 85
  bulimia 97, 99

hopelessness 182, 183

horizon ratio The proportion of an object that is above the horizon divided by the proportion below. Two objects of the same size on a flat surface will have the same horizon ratio. 34, 35

hormones Chemical substances that circulate in the blood and only affect target organs. They are produced in large quantities but disappear very quickly. Their effects are slow in comparison to the nervous system, but very powerful.
  aggression 72, 73
  biological rhythms 10, 12
  eating behaviour 89, 98
  gender development 104
  gender differences 108
  gender dysphoria 110, 111
  menstrual cycle 12, 13

Hovland, Carl 226

Hovland-Yale Model 226

human leukocyte antigen (HLA) 26, 27

hyperphagia In the context of eating behaviour, a refusal or inability to stop eating, arising out of damage to the ventromedial hypothalamus. 88

hypocretin A neurotransmitter that regulates sleep, appetite and energy conservation. 26, 27

hypothalamic-pituitary-adrenal axis A bodily response to chronic (long-term) stress. The hypothalamus stimulates the pituitary gland to secrete adrenocorticotropic hormone (ACTH) which in turn stimulates the adrenal glands to produce cortisol. 180

hypothalamus A part of the brain that functions to regulate body temperature, metabolic processes such as eating, and other autonomic activities including emotional responses. 14, 88–9

hypothesis A precise and testable statement about the assumed relationship between variables.
  perception 32–3, 41
  scientific method 279, 284, 285, 287

hypothetico-deductive model Scientific inquiry in which a hypothesis is put forward in a form that can potentially be falsified by a test on observable data. Such a test either falsifies the hypothesis and thus the theory, or corroborates the theory. 274

hypothetico-deductive reasoning An approach to problem-solving where a person starts with many possible hypotheses and eliminates erroneous ones through testing, thus arriving at the correct solution. 146

I

ICD (International Classification of Disease and Related Health Problems) The classification scheme produced by the World Health Organisation for both physical and mental disorders. 164, 165, 178, 179, 192, 207

idealistic thinking Thinking in terms of abstract principles such as love, liberty and justice. 146

idiographic approach An approach to research that focuses more on the individual case as a means of understanding behaviour rather than a way of formulating general laws of behaviour (the nomothetic approach). 275

IGF2R 138, 139

illusions, perception 32–5

imitation 66–7, 114, 115, 222

immune system 20, 26, 27

importation model 70, 71

imposed etic A technique or theory developed in one culture and then used to study the behaviour of people in a different culture with different norms, values, experiences, etc. 39, 119

impulsiveness 92

in vivo desensitisation Using principles of systematic desensitisation where a patient has direct experience of the hierarchy of situations from least to most fearful (as distinct from covert desensitisation). 200

independent groups design An experimental design where participants are allocated to two (or more) groups representing different experimental conditions. Allocation is usually done using random techniques. 290–3

independent variable (IV) An event that is directly manipulated by an experimenter in order to test its effect on another variable – the dependent variable (DV). 38, 131, 274, 278

indirect theory of perception 32–3, 35

indirect theory (bottom-up) of perception 37

individualist culture A culture that values independence rather than reliance on others, in contrast to many non-Western cultures that could be described as collectivist. 60, 61, 149
  learning 151

inductive reasoning A form of reasoning from the particular to the general, e.g. developing a theory on the basis of a series of research studies. 274

inequality in relationships 50–1

infants
  breastfeeding 139
  face recognition 40
  media influences 221
  perception 36–7

M

Machiavellian intelligence The ability to intentionally deceive another individual. It requires a Theory of Mind in order to comprehend what the other knows or doesn't know. 134, 135, 136, 137, 157

magical thinking 262–3

magnetic resonance imaging (MRI) Produces a three-dimensional image of the static brain which is very precise. A magnetic field causes the atoms of the brain to change their alignment when the magnet is on and emit various radio signals when the magnet is turned off. A detector reads the signals and uses them to map the structure of the brain. 136

major depressive disorder (MDD) Also known as 'major depression,' 'clinical depression,' or 'unipolar disorder,' MDD is a condition characterised by a long-lasting depressed mood or marked loss of interest or pleasure in all or nearly all activities. 178, 179, 181

Mann-Whitney U test An inferential test of difference for independent groups design. 285, 290–3, 296

MAOI *see* monoamine oxidase inhibitor

mark test *see* mirror test

Martin, Carol 114–15

matched pairs design An experimental design where pairs of participants are matched in terms of key variables such as age and IQ. One member of each pair is placed in the experimental group and the other member in the control group. 278, 292

mate choice 54–5, 56, 106, 107, 108, 109

mate retention 76–7

maternal investment 56–7

mating strategies 54–7

maturation The process of ripening. In psychological terms it means a change that is due to innate factors rather than learning. 146, 147, 148, 149, 150, 152, 154, 157

MDD *see* major depressive disorder

mean The arithmetic average of a group of scores, taking the values of all the data into account. 284, 287, 293, 296

measure of central tendency A descriptive statistic that provides information about a 'typical' number for a data set. 284, 296

measure of dispersion A descriptive statistic that provides information about how spread out a set of scores are. 284

meat eating evolution 90, 91, 107, 136–7

media influences 220–33
  addictive behaviour 246, 247
  antisocial behaviour 222–3, 224–5
  attitudes and decisions 226–9
  body image 92, 93, 98
  celebrities 228, 229, 230–3
  gender development 113, 116, 117
  prosocial behaviour 220–1

median The middle value in a set of scores when they are placed in rank order. 284, 296

medication
  addictive behaviour 250, 251
  antidepressants 184, 185, 186, 187
  antipsychotics 170, 171
  chronopharmacology 11
  OCD 212, 213

phobic disorders 198–9
schizophrenia 170, 171

mediums, psychic 266–7

melatonin A hormone that induces sleep, mainly produced in the pineal gland.
  circadian rhythms 10, 14, 15
  seasonal affective disorder 12
  therapy 17, 19

memory, sleep and 20

menstrual cycle 12, 13, 55

mental disorders *see* psychopathology

mental module The assumption within evolutionary psychology that the human mind comprises a number of innate 'structures' that have evolved because they had adaptive functions for our ancestors. 208

mental representation 66

mentalistic Relating to mental phenomena. 157

mere exposure effect 292–5

meta-analysis
  paranormal studies 259, 264

meta-analysis A researcher looks at the findings from a number of different studies in order to reach a general conclusion about a particular hypothesis.
  aggression 69, 72, 74, 75
  depression 183, 185, 187
  gender 87
  intelligence and learning 131, 138, 139, 140
  media psychology 221, 222, 224, 228, 230
  relationships 59
  schizophrenia 166, 171, 172, 173

metabolic rate 22, 23

methadone 250, 251

MI *see* multiple intelligences

microsleep Small periods of sleep during the day which possibly enable some physiological recovery to take place. The individual may not be aware they have been asleep. 21

mirror neuron (MN) A neuron that responds to actions performed by oneself as well as when the same actions are performed by others. 158–9

mirror test An investigative technique used to assess self-awareness by, for example, putting red colour on an individual's nose and showing them their image in a mirror. The individual demonstrates self-awareness if they touch their nose. 134, 135, 154, 155

misinterpretation of intrusive thoughts (MIT) 210

MKO *see* more knowledgeable other

MN *see* mirror neuron

mode The most frequently occurring score in a data set. 284, 294

modelling The process of imitating another's behaviour, which involves cognitive representations of the modelled activities as well as abstractions of the underlying rules of the modelled behaviours. 116, 117

modulated light exposure (MLE) 17

Money, John 105, 108

monkeys All primates that are not prosimians (lemurs and tarsiers) or apes (e.g. gorillas, orangutans) are monkeys. 134, 135, 137

monoamine oxidase inhibitor (MAOI) Creates higher levels of neurotransmitters of the monamine group such as serotonin, noradrenaline and dopamine. 20, 74

monoamines *see* dopamine; serotonin

monogamous species Having only one sexual partner at any one time. 72

monozygotic (MZ) twins Identical twins formed from one fertilised egg (or zygote). 74, 138, 166, 167, 180

monthly cycles 12

mood
  affect 178
  eating behaviour 85, 99, 884
  seasonal affective disorder 12, 13
  see also depression

mood disorder A mental disorder in which disturbance of mood is the central feature. 178

moral understanding 152–3

more knowledgeable other (MKO) A term used by Vygotsky to refer to 'experts' – people with more knowledge who assist the learning process. 150

motion parallax As we move, objects that are closer to us move farther across our field of vision than more distant objects, providing information about depth. 36

motion perception 35, 36

motivation 150

motor cortex The part of the brain cortex responsible for generating the neural impulses controlling execution of movement, located in the frontal lobe of the brain. 158, 159

MRI *see* magnetic resonance imaging

Müller-Lyer illusion Illusion created by fins at the end of a line such that one line looks longer (fins pointing out) than the other (fins pointing in). 32, 33, 38

multiple intelligences (MI) theory 126

mundane realism The extent to which the experimental events in a controlled setting are similar to events in the 'real' world. 49

murder *see* homicide

MZ *see* monozygotic

N

narcolepsy A disorder in which individuals experience sudden and uncontrollable attacks of sleep lasting seconds or minutes at irregular and unexpected times. 26, 27

nativist The view that development is determined by innate factors, that most abilities simply need fine tuning but do not depend on experience for their development. 147

natural experiment A research method in which the experimenter cannot manipulate the independent variable directly, but where it varies naturally, and the effect on a dependent variable can be observed. 39, 278

natural selection The major process that explains evolution whereby inherited traits that enhance an animal's reproductive success are passed on to the next generation and thus 'selected,' whereas animals without such traits are less successful at reproduction and their traits are not selected. 136, 194, 262

naturalistic observation A research method carried out in a naturalistic setting, in which the investigator does not interfere in any way, but merely observes the behaviour(s) in question (likely to involve the use of structured observations). 278

nature Those aspects of behaviour that are innate and inherited. Nature does not simply refer to abilities present at birth but to any ability determined by genes, including those that appear through maturation. 107, 108
  aggression 74
  child development 147, 149, 157, 158
  gender development 104, 105, 107, 108
  intelligence 138
  perception 36, 37, 38, 39, 40–3
nature *versus* nurture
  aggression 74
  child development 147
  gender development 104–19
  intelligence 138–41
  perception 35
NC *see* need for cognition
NDEa *see* near-death experience
Neanderthals 106, 107
near-death experience (NDE) Mystical or other experiences reported by people who have nearly died or who have had some other stressful or traumatic episode. 268–9
need for cognition (NC) A personality variable describing people who enjoy tasks that involve high cognitive effort, such as analysing arguments and brain-teasers. 226, 227
needs in relationships 49–51
negative correlation Describes a correlation where, as one co-variable increases, the other decreases. 286, 287, 296
negative reinforcement Increases the probability that a behaviour will be repeated because it leads to escape from an unpleasant situation. 130, 131
negative/positive symptoms, schizophrenia 164
Neisser's cycle model 35
neocortex The neocortex or 'new' cortex is the six-layered covering of the brain. About 95% of the cerebral cortex is neocortex so that gradually the terms have come to mean the same. The 'old' cortex or 'archicortex' is mainly the limbic system and basal ganglia. 135, 137
neophilia Love of novelty and new things. 230, 231
neophobia Fear of new things, such as unusual or novel foods. 90
neural mechanisms
  eating behaviour 88–9
  OCD 208, 209
  schizophrenia 166, 167
  social cognition 158–9
neurochemical Substances that are involved in the activity of the brain and nervous system. 184, 238
neuropeptide Y (NPY) A neurotransmitter believed to be important in the control of appetite and eating behaviour, especially in response to leptin. 88, 89
neuroscientists Scientists who specialise in the study of the brain and the nervous system. 141
neuroticism 264, 265
neurotransmitters Chemical substances, such as serotonin or dopamine, which play an important part in the workings of the nervous system by transmitting nerve impulses across a synapse.
  addictive behaviour. 238, 239
  aggression 72–3

depression 180, 181, 184
  eating behaviour 88, 94, 95, 98, 99
  narcolepsy 26
  OCD 208, 209, 210, 212
  REM sleep 20
  romantic love 49
  schizophrenia 166, 168, 169, 170
neutral stimulus, classical conditioning 128–9, 131
nicotine addiction 240–51
night terrors A parasomnia related to sleep walking, where nightmares occur during slow wave sleep. It may not be possible to wake a person suffering from night terrors. *see* parasomnias
nitric oxide (NO) 98, 99
nominal data A level of measurement where data are in separate categories. 288, 296
nomothetic approach An approach to research that focuses more on general laws of behaviour than on the individual, possibly unique, case (the idiographic approach). 275
non-clinical population Not relating to a pathological condition or disorder. 211
non-directional hypothesis Predicts that there will be a difference between two conditions or two groups of participants, without stating the direction of the difference. 279, 285, 288, 289
non-rapid eye movement (NREM) sleep Non-rapid eye movement sleep, which includes slow wave sleep. 10, 11, 12, 21, 22–3
noradrenaline A neurotransmitter found mainly in areas of the brain that are involved in governing autonomic nervous system activity, e.g. blood pressure or heart rate. 180, 181, 184
norms 69, 220, 221
NPY *see* neuropeptide Y
null hypothesis An assumption that there is no relationship (difference or association) in the population from which a sample is taken with respect to the variables being studied. 284, 285, 287, 288, 289, 290, 291, 293
nurture Those aspects of behaviour that are acquired through experience, i.e. learned from interactions with the physical and social environment.
  child development. 147, 157
    aggression 74
    gender development 104, 105, 107, 108
    intelligence 138
    perception 36, 37, 38, 39, 40–3

O

OBE *see* out-of-body experience
obedience to authority 70, 71
obesity 86, 87
obesssions 210, 211, 214
object permanence A child's understanding that objects that are no longer visible nevertheless continue to exist. 146, 147
object recognition 32–3, 34–5
objectivity in science 274, 275
observational learning 220, 222
  see also social learning theory
observational studies 278, 280

observational techniques The application of systematic methods of observation in an observational study, experiment or other study. 278, 280
observed value The value of a test statistic calculated for a particular data set. 285, 286, 287, 288, 289, 291, 293
observer bias The tendency for observations to be influenced by expectations or prejudices. 278, 280
obsessions 207
obsessive compulsive disorder (OCD) An anxiety disorder where anxiety arises from both obsessions (persistent thoughts) and compulsions (means of controlling the obsessional thoughts). 206–15
Occam's razor The principle that simpler explanations are preferable, if everything else is equal. 256
occlusion Objects that are closer block out (or occlude) objects that are more distant, providing information about depth. 36, 37, 38
OCD *see* obsessive compulsive disorder
oestrogen The primary female hormone, though also present in males in small amounts. Regulates the menstrual cycle and female development in puberty. 12, 286
older adults 18, 19, 99
  sleep and 24
olfactory processing 88, 89
one-tailed test Form of test used with a directional hypothesis. 285, 287, 288, 291, 293
online shopping 226, 227
open questions Questions that invite respondents to provide their own answers rather than to select an answer that has been provided. Tend to produce qualitative data. 278
operant conditioning Learning that occurs when we are reinforced for doing something, which increases the probability that the behaviour in question will be repeated in the future. Conversely, if we are punished for behaving in a certain way, there is a decrease in the probability that the behaviour will recur. 130–3
  addictive behaviour 242, 243
  OCD 210, 211
  perception studies 36
  phobias 196, 197
  relationship formation 66–7
  relationship forming 48
operationalised Providing variables in a form that can be easily tested. 278, 279
operations
  cognitive 124–5, 146
  surgical 198, 199, 212, 213
opportunity sample A sample of participants produced by selecting people who are most easily available at the time of the study. 281
optic array In Gibson's direct theory of perception, the richness of information available in the environment. 34, 35
optic flow In Gibson's direct theory of perception, the term used to describe how information appears to flow past a moving observer while the point to which they are moving stays still. 34
optical illusions 32–5

REM sleep Rapid eye movement sleep, during which the body is paralysed except for the eyes. REM sleep is often equated with dreaming, though dreams also occur in NREM sleep. 12, 13, 18–19, 20–1, 23

repeated measures design An experimental design where each participant takes part in every condition under test. 290, 292–5

replication If a finding from a research study is true (valid) then it should be possible to obtain the same finding if the study is repeated. This confirms the validity of the finding. 274, 280

representative sample A sample selected so that it accurately stands for or represents the population being studied. 281

repressed A form of ego defence whereby anxiety-provoking material is kept out of conscious awareness as a means of coping. 196, 197

reproduction suppression hypothesis 94, 95

reproductive behaviour
  animal conditioning 132, 133
  evolution 49, 54–9, 61
  parental investment 56–7
  see also romantic relationships; sexual behaviour

reproductive fitness A measure of the success of an individual in passing on their genes to the next generation and beyond. 132, 136

research
  data analysis 284–99
  design 294–5
  methods 223, 225, 274–81
  reporting 276–7
  statistical fallacies 140

researcher bias 37, 258, 259, 260, 275

resistance training 243

resonance In Gibson's direct theory of perception, the ability of an organism to automatically pick up sensory information from the environment. 34

response prevention 214, 215

restoration theory 21–2

restraint theory 86, 87

retinal disparity The difference in the images received by the retina in the right and left eye. 36

retinal image The image formed on the retina, a region of the eye containing photosensitive cells (rods and cones) which record light energy. 32, 33, 35, 36, 37

retinal size The true size of an object as recorded on the retina, as opposed to the perceived size when factors such as distance are taken into account. 36, 38

rewards 48–51, 66–7

right to withdraw The right of participants to refuse to continue with participation in a study if they are uncomfortable in any way, and to refuse permission for the researcher to use any data produced before they withdrew. 282

role models 243

role-taking 156, 157, 159

Rollie and Duck model 52–3

romantic relationships 48–55
  adolescents 59, 60–1
  arousal 290
  breakdown 52–3

bulimia nervosa 96, 97
  childhood/adolescent influences 59
  cultural differences 49, 51, 60–2
  formation 48–51
  maintenance 52–3

S

SAD *see* seasonal affective disorder

safe sex campaigns 227, 249

Sally Anne Test A test used to assess an individual's understanding of false beliefs and Theory of Mind. 155, 156

sampling The process of taking a sample intended to be a representative selection of a target population. 75, 281

satisfaction in relationships 48, 50

savants 126

scaffolding An approach to instruction that aims to support a learner only when absolutely necessary i.e. to provide a support framework (scaffold) to assist the learning process. 148, 150, 151

scattergrams A graphical representation of the relationship (i.e. the correlation) between two sets of scores, each dot representing one pair of data. 284, 296

schema A cluster of related facts based on previous experiences, and used to generate future expectations. 114, 115, 146

schizophrenia A mental disorder in which an individual has lost touch with reality and may experience symptoms such as delusions, hallucinations, grossly disorganised behaviour and flattened emotions. 164–74

schizotypy 264

scientific fraud 266, 267, 276

scientific method 274–81

SCN *see* suprachiasmatic nucleus

séances 267

season of birth 94, 95

seasonal affective disorder (SAD) depression associated with seasonal changes, usually due to the onset of winter and increased darkness. Some people experience a more manic phase in summer, and others experience the reverse – depression in summer. 12, 13

secondary reinforcers Learned phenomena, such as the fact that a hot cooker can burn, as distinct from primary reinforcers. 130

selective breeding programmes A technique whereby animals (or humans) are mated to produce offspring with particular characteristics. 75

selective pressure In evolutionary theory, demands made by the environment resulting in one set of genes being favoured over another. This is the mechanism of natural selection. 23

selective serotonin re-uptake inhibitors (SSRIs) Commonly prescribed drugs for treating depression. They work by selectively preventing the re-uptake of serotonin from the synaptic gap, thus leaving more serotonin available at the synapse to excite surrounding neurons.
  depression 181, 184, 185, 186, 187
  eating behaviour 95, 99
  gambling addiction 250, 251
  OCD 212, 213

phobic disorders 198, 199

self-actualisation 265

self-awareness 154–5

self-control 220

self-efficacy The belief that we can perform competently in a given situation. 66, 246, 248

self-esteem The feelings that a person has about their self-concept.
  addictive behaviour 244, 245
  celebrity attraction 230, 232
  development 154–5
  gender differences 116, 117

self-inflicted harm *see* suicide

self-medication 240, 241

self-recognition 134, 135, 154, 155

self-report method Any research method where participants are asked to report their own attitudes, abilities and/or feelings, such as a questionnaire, interview or psychological test. 92, 278, 281

self-report techniques 249

Selman, R. 156, 157

semiotic mediation Vygotsky's concept that knowledge is constructed (mediated) by the acquisition of symbols such as language and mathematical concepts. 148

semi-structured interview An interview that combines both structured and unstructured interviews. The interviewer has some pre-established questions but also develops questions in response to the answers given. 299

sensation seeking 145, 244

sensorimotor The co-ordination of sensory and motor experiences, such as hand-eye coordination. 146, 147

separation anxiety The distress shown by an infant when separated from his/her caregiver. 197

serotonin A neurotransmitter found in the central nervous system and implicated in many different behaviours and physiological processes, including aggression, eating behaviour, sleep and depression.
  aggression 72–3, 74
  depression 180, 181, 184, 185
  eating behaviour 94, 95, 98, 99
  OCD 208, 210, 212, 213
  phobic disorders 194
  REM sleep 20
  seasonal affective disorder 12

SES *see* socioeconomic status

sex A biological fact, as opposed to gender 104, 106

sex differences *see* gender differences

sexual behaviour
  infidelity 53, 55, 57, 76–7
  mating strategies 54–7
  romantic relationships 54–5
  safe sex campaigns 227, 249

sexual competition hypothesis 98, 99

sexual jealousy 56, 76–7

sexual selection A key part of Darwin's theory explaining how evolution is driven by competition for mates, and the development of characteristics that ensure reproductive success. 54–7, 98, 136, 230, 231

shape constancy 36, 38

shift lag A physiological condition caused by desynchronisation of the body clock as a consequence of working shifts at different times of day and night. 16–17

side effects of therapy 171, 185

Siffre, Michel 10, 11

significance analysis 284

significance level The level of probability (*p*) at which it has been agreed to reject the null hypothesis. 284, 285

significant A statistical term indicating that a set of research findings is sufficiently strong for us to accept the research hypothesis under test. 284, 285, 286, 296, 299

similarity in relationships 48–50

simple conditioning 132

simulation theory (ST) The view that we take another person's perspective (i.e. Theory of Mind) by simulating or experiencing what they are experiencing. 159

size constancy 36, 38

Skinner box experiments 130–1

sleep 18–29
  deprivation 21

sleep walking (somnambulism) A parasomnia that occurs during slow wave sleep and entails a range of activities normally associated with wakefulness (such as eating, getting dressed or walking about); the person has no conscious knowledge of what they are doing. 24, 26–7

slow wave sleep (SWS) Stages 3 and 4 of NREM sleep when brain waves have low frequency and high amplitude. This stage of deep sleep is associated with bodily growth and repair, such as the production of growth hormones. 12, 18, 19, 20, 23

SLT *see* social learning theory

smoking addiction 238–51
  intervention 250, 251

social behaviour 134, 135, 136, 137

social class *see* socioeconomic status

social cognition The study of how cognition (i.e. thinking, beliefs, perception) influences social behaviour. 156–7
  gender 114–15

social constructionism An approach to studying and explaining human behaviour in terms of its social context rather than any objective reality. If behaviour is separated from social context then its true meaning is lost. 109

social context
  addictive behaviour 244, 245
  cognitive development 148–51
  depression 182, 183
  gender development 114–19
  scientific progress 277

social cues, biological rhythms 14, 17

social desirability bias A tendency for respondents to answer questions in a way that they think will present them in a better light. 77, 278, 279

social dominance orientation (SDO) 71

social exchange theory 50–1

social identity theory 244, 245

social information (gossip) 230, 231

social learning theory (SLT) The basic assumption of this theory is that people learn through observing the behaviour of models, mentally rehearsing the behaviours they display, then later imitating them in similar situations.
  addictive behaviour 242, 243, 244, 245

aggression 66–7
  eating behaviour 84, 85
  gender development 113, 116–17
  media influences 220
  phobias 196, 197

social networking sites 224, 225
  addiction 245

social phobia A phobia of situations in the population. involving other people, such as speaking in public or being part of a social group. 192, 193

social role theory, gender 108, 109

social skills 52–3

social skills training (SST) 157

socially sensitive research Any research that might have direct social consequences. 282

social-psychological explanations
  aggression 66–9
  celebrity attraction 230, 231

sociocultural factors
  anorexia nervosa 92, 93
  depression 182, 183
  phobias 197

socioeconomic/socioeconomic status (SES) A measure of an individual's or family's social and economic position, based on income, education, and occupation.
  eating behaviour. 84, 85
  gender roles 119
  intelligence 139, 140, 141
  smoking 244, 245

somnambulism *see* sleep walking

spatial intelligence 126

spatial perception 32–5

Spearman, Charles 124, 125

Spearman's rho An inferential test of correlation. 285, 286–9, 296

specific abilities (s) Specific factors that contribute to a person's intelligence score, as opposed to general intelligence. 124, 126

specific phobia A phobia of specific activities or objects, such as bathing or spiders. 192, 196, 197, 201

split-half method A method of assessing internal reliability by comparing two halves of, for example, a psychological test to see if they produce the same score. 280

sports 78–9, 105

SSRIs *see* selective serotonin re-uptake inhibitors

SST *see* social skills training

ST *see* simulation theory

stages of development 146–7, 150, 152, 154–7, 156

stalking 232–3

standard deviation A measure of dispersion that shows the amount of variation in a set of scores. It assesses the spread of data around the mean. 284, 294

statistics 140, 284, 285–92, 296–9

status 76, 77

stereotyping 114–17, 118, 220
  gender 114–15

stimulus discrimination 243

stimulus generalisation 128–9

stratified sample Groups of participants selected according to their frequency in the population. Within each strata individuals are selected using random sampling. 281

stress *see* **diathesis-stress model**

structural encoding 40

structured questionnaire/interview Any interview in which the questions are decided in advance. 278

sub-clinical An illness that is not clinically manifest, i.e. a person may have the illness but it is not identifiable/diagnosable. 84, 85

suicide
  baiting crowd 69
  celebrity imitation 233
  depression 178, 184, 185, 186
  schizophrenia 165

sun addiction 248

superstition 262–3, 265

suprachiasmatic nucleus (SCN) A tiny cluster of nerve cells in the hypothalamus of each hemisphere that acts as the main endogenous pacemaker. 14, 15

surgery 198, 199, 212, 213

surveys A self-report method for collecting data, such as an interview or questionnaire. 77

SWS *see* slow wave sleep

symbolic mode Learning or thinking using abstract symbols. 146

symbolic thinking skills 146

sympathetic nervous system The part of the autonomic nervous system that is associated with physiological arousal and 'fight or flight' responses. 290

sympathomedullary response The 'fight or flight' response to threat where the sympathetic nervous system is aroused leading to activation of the adrenal medulla and production of adrenaline. 198

synapse A small gap separating neurons. It consists of the presynaptic membrane (which discharges neurotransmitters), the postsynaptic membrane (containing receptor sites for neurotransmitters) and a synaptic gap between the two. 166

systematic desensitisation (SD) A process by which a patient is gradually exposed to (or imagines) a threatening situation under relaxed conditions until the anxiety reaction is extinguished. 200, 201
  OCD 214

systematic sample A method of obtaining a representative sample by selecting every fifth or tenth person. This can be a random sample if the first person is selected using a random method and then every fifth or tenth person is selected. 281

systematising The ability to analyse and explore systems, and extract underlying rules that govern the behaviour of a system. 106, 107

T

tardive dyskinesia 171

target population The group of people that the researcher is interested in and from which a sample is drawn. The group of people about whom generalisations can be made. 281
  see also population

taste aversion 90, 91, 129

teeth grinding (bruxism) 24

telencephalon A large area of the brain including the cerebrum and related parts of the hypothalamus. 135

telephones
  phone psychotherapy 187

phone-use addiction 244

smoking Quitline services 250, 251

television 220–3, 228–9

temperature 14

core body 10, 11

test statistic The numerical value that is calculated for any inferential test. 285

testosterone Testosterone is a hormone produced mainly by the testes in males, but it also occurs in females. It is associated with the development of secondary sexual characteristics in males (e.g. body hair), but has also been implicated in aggression and dominance behaviours. 72, 73, 104, 108

test–retest method A method used to check external reliability. The same test or interview is given to the same participants on two occasions to see if the same results are obtained. 164, 165, 179, 192, 280

texture gradient Objects that are closer to the viewer appear more widely spaced, providing a cue to depth or distance. 34, 36, 38, 39

thalamus A structure lying under the cortex (subcortical) that has been described as the great relay station of the brain because most sensory information first goes to the thalamus, where it is processed and sent on to the cerebral cortex. 198, 208

Thatcher effect An illusion where it is difficult to detect local feature changes when viewing a face upside down. 41, 42

thematic analysis A technique used when analysing qualitative data. Themes or concepts are identified before starting a piece of research, then responses from an interview or questionnaire are organised according to these themes. 298, 299

theory A collection of general principles used to explain specific observations and facts. 274

Theory of Mind (ToM) An individual's understanding that other people have separate mental states and that they see the world from a different point of view from their own. 154, 155, 156, 158

autism 107

Theory of Mind Module (ToMM) 155

theory of planned behaviour (TPB) 248, 249

theory of reasoned action (TRA) 248, 249

'Theory' theory A theory of human development that proposes a middle ground between pure innateness, on the one hand, and the role of experience, on the other. 159

therapeutic touch (TT) 266, 267

thought catching 186

Thurstone, L. L. 125

time sampling An observational technique in which the observer records behaviours in a given time frame, e.g. noting what a target individual is doing every 30 seconds. 278, 281

time-to-contact 35

TMS see transcranial magnetic stimulation

tolerance The progressive reduction of the effect of a drug due to its continued use. 238

ToM see Theory of Mind

ToMM see Theory of Mind Module

tool use 136

top-down Processing that starts from an overview of a system, such as using previous experience and context to enrich sensory input, as opposed to bottom-up processing. 32–3, 35, 37, 296

Tourette's syndrome 209, 211

TPB see theory of planned behaviour

TRA see theory of reasoned action

transcranial magnetic stimulation (TMS) A technique used to trigger brain activity in specific target areas using an electric current to create a magnetic field. 198, 212, 213, 268

treatment outcome studies 173

see also biological therapies; psychological therapies

triangulation Comparing two or more views of the same thing. 298

triarchic theory 126–7

tryptophan An essential amino acid found in the diet, particularly in milk, cheese, fish, nuts and chocolate. Tryptophan is a precursor of the neurotransmitter serotonin, and melatonin, a hormone related to sleep. 99

TT see therapeutic touch

twin studies

addictive behaviour 238

aggression 74–5

depression 180

fraud 276

intelligence 138, 139

OCD 208

phobic disorders 194, 195

problems 139

schizophrenia 166, 167

two-tailed test Form of test used with a non-directional hypothesis. 285, 287, 288, 289, 291, 293

Type 1 error Rejecting a null hypothesis that is true. This is more likely to happen if significance level is too high (lenient e.g. 10%). 261, 285

Type 2 error Accepting a null hypothesis that is in fact not true. This is more likely to happen if the significance level is too low (stringent e.g. 1%). 261, 285

U

ultradian rhythm A pattern of behaviour that occurs less often than once a day, such as the human female menstrual cycle. 12–13

unconditioned stimulus (UCS) 128–9, 132

unilateral sleep A sleep adaptation where one hemisphere of the brain is asleep while the other is awake and therefore the animal is always conscious. 23

unstructured interview An interview that starts out with some general aims and possibly some questions, and lets the interviewee's answers guide subsequent questions. 278

uxorocide (wife-killing) 76, 77

V

validity of beliefs

CBT techniques 172

validity Refers to the legitimacy of a study, the extent to which the findings can be applied beyond the research setting as a consequence of the study's internal and/or external validity. 55, 69, 207, 276–7, 280, 298

diagnosis 178, 179

intelligence theories 127

see also reliability issues

ventromedial hypothalamus Part of the hypothalamus, stimulation of which is thought to lead to the termination of eating behaviour. Damage to the ventromedial hypothalamus leads to excessive food intake. 88, 89

vicarious learning 67

vicarious reinforcement Learning not through direct reinforcement of behaviour, but through observing someone else being reinforced for that behaviour. 66

video games 224–5

violence

genetic factors 74–5

groups 68–71, 78–9

schizophrenia 164

television 222–3

video games 224–5

against women 76–7

visual acuity Acuteness or clearness of vision. 36, 37

visual agnosia The brain's inability to recognise objects, including words (alexia) and faces (prosopagnosia). 42–3

visual constancy We continue to see the shape, size, colour, etc. of familiar objects as the same despite changing retinal images due to perspective and/or lighting conditions. 36, 38

voluntary versus non-voluntary relationships 60–2

volunteer bias A form of sampling bias caused by the fact that volunteer participants are usually more highly motivated than randomly selected participants. 281

volunteer sample A sampling technique that relies solely on volunteers to make up the sample. 281

vulnerability

addictive behaviour 244–5

see also diathesis-stress model

Vygotsky, Lev 148–9, 150–1

W, X, Y, Z

wife-killing 76, 77

Wikipedia 277

Wilcoxon T test An inferential test of difference for related measures design. 285, 292–5, 296

Wood, Wendy 108

working memory An area of memory that deals with information that is being worked on, equivalent to short-term memory. It is divided into separate stores representing different modalities. 169

xenophobia A fear and distrust of strangers, although this is now popularly recognised as a fear and distrust of foreigners. 70–1, 78–9

Y-BOCS-10 206–7

Young, Andrew 40–1, 43

zero correlation A correlation where the co-variables are not linked. 296

Zimmerman, Mary Lou 213

zone of proximal development (ZPD) In Vygotsky's theory, the 'region' between a person's current abilities, which they can perform with no assistance, and their potential capabilities, which they can be helped to achieve with the assistance of 'experts'. 148, 149, 150

Complete Companions for AQA A Psychology

The most popular A Level books for AQA A Psychology
written by renowned authors **Mike Cardwell** and **Cara Flanagan**

Available in this series

The Student Books

978 019 912981 2   978 019 912984 3

The AS Visual Companion

978 185 008548 5

The Research Methods Companion

978 019 912962 1

The Mini Companions

978 019 912983 6   978 019 912986 7

The Exam Companions

978 019 912985 0   978 019 912982 9

The Teacher's Companions

978 185 008295 8   978 185 008396 2

The AS Digital Companion

978 185 008394 8

The AS Audio Companion CD-ROM
with printable activity sheets and site licence

978 019 912972 0

Order your copies now

tel 01536 452620
fax 01865 313472

email schools.enquiries.uk@oup.com
web www.oxfordsecondary.co.uk/psychology

OXFORD
UNIVERSITY PRESS